International Directory of

COMPANY
HISTORIES

International Directory of

COMPANY

HISTORIES

VOLUME 81

Editor

Jay P. Pederson

ST. JAMES PRESS

An imprint of Thomson Gale, a part of The Thomson Corporation

Detroit • New York • San Francisco • New Haven, Conn. • Waterville, Maine • London

International Directory of Company Histories, Volume 81

Jay P. Pederson, Editor

Project Editor
Miranda H. Ferrara

Editorial
Virgil Burton, Donna Craft, Louise Gagné,
Peggy Geeseman, Julie Gough, Linda Hall,
Sonya Hill, Keith Jones, Lynn Pearce, Holly
Selden, Justine Ventimiglia

Production Technology Specialist
Mike Weaver

Imaging and Multimedia
Leslie Light, Michael Logusz

Composition and Electronic Prepress
Gary Leach, Evi Seoud

Manufacturing
Rhonda Dover

Product Manager
Jennifer Bernardelli

LIBRARY OF CONGRESS CATALOG NUMBER 89-190943

ISBN-13: 978-1-55862-585-3   ISBN-10: 1-55862-585-2

This title is also available as an e-book
ISBN-13: 978-1-55862-629-4   *ISBN-10: 1-55862-629-8*

BRITISH LIBRARY CATALOGUING IN PUBLICATION DATA

International directory of company histories, Vol. 81
I. Jay P. Pederson
33.87409

Printed in the United States of America
10 9 8 7 6 5 4 3 2 1

Contents

Preface

The St. James Press series *The International Directory of Company Histories* (*IDCH*) is intended for reference use by students, business people, librarians, historians, economists, investors, job candidates, and others who seek to learn more about the historical development of the world's most important companies. To date, *IDCH* has covered over 7,950 companies in 81 volumes.

INCLUSION CRITERIA

Most companies chosen for inclusion in *IDCH* have achieved a minimum of US$25 million in annual sales and are leading influences in their industries or geographical locations. Companies may be publicly held, private, or nonprofit. State-owned companies that are important in their industries and that may operate much like public or private companies also are included. Wholly owned subsidiaries and divisions are profiled if they meet the requirements for inclusion. Entries on companies that have had major changes since they were last profiled may be selected for updating.

The *IDCH* series highlights 10% private and nonprofit companies, and features updated entries on approximately 50 companies per volume.

ENTRY FORMAT

Each entry begins with the company's legal name; the address of its headquarters; its telephone, toll-free, and fax numbers; and its web site. A statement of public, private, state, or parent ownership follows. A company with a legal name in both English and the language of its headquarters country is listed by the English name, with the native-language name in parentheses.

The company's founding or earliest incorporation date, the number of employees, and the most recent available sales figures follow. Sales figures are given in local currencies with equivalents in U.S. dollars. For some private companies, sales figures are estimates and indicated by the abbreviation *est.* The entry lists the exchanges on which the company's stock is traded and its ticker symbol, as well as the company's NAIC codes.

Entries generally contain a *Company Perspectives* box which provides a short summary of the company's mission, goals, and ideals; a *Key Dates* box highlighting milestones in the company's history; lists of *Principal Subsidiaries*, *Principal Divisions*, *Principal Operating Units*, *Principal Competitors*; and articles for *Further Reading*.

American spelling is used throughout *IDCH*, and the word "billion" is used in its U.S. sense of one thousand million.

Users of the *IDCH* series will notice some changes to the look of the series starting with Volume 77. The pages have been redesigned for better clarity and ease of use; the standards for entry content, however, have not changed.

SOURCES

Entries have been compiled from publicly accessible sources both in print and on the Internet such as general and academic periodicals, books, and annual reports, as well as material supplied by the companies themselves.

CUMULATIVE INDEXES

IDCH contains three indexes: the **Index to Companies**, which provides an alphabetical index to companies discussed in the text as well as to companies profiled, the **Index to Industries**, which allows researchers to locate companies by their principal industry, and the **Geographic Index**, which lists companies alphabetically by the country of their headquarters. The indexes are cumulative and specific instructions for using them are found immediately preceding each index.

SUGGESTIONS WELCOME

Comments and suggestions from users of *IDCH* on any aspect of the product as well as suggestions for companies to be included or updated are cordially invited. Please write:

The Editor
International Directory of Company Histories
St. James Press
27500 Drake Rd.
Farmington Hills, Michigan 48331-3535

St. James Press does not endorse any of the companies or products mentioned in this series. Companies appearing in the *International Directory of Company Histories* were selected without reference to their wishes and have in no way endorsed their entries.

Notes on Contributors

M. L. Cohen
Novelist, business writer, and researcher living in Paris.

Jeffrey L. Covell
Seattle-based writer.

Ed Dinger
Writer and editor based in Bronx, New York.

Robert Halasz
Former editor in chief of *World Progress* and *Funk & Wagnalls New Encyclopedia Yearbook*; author, *The U.S. Marines* (Millbrook Press, 1993).

Frederick C. Ingram
Writer based in South Carolina.

Kathleen Peippo
Minneapolis-based writer.

Nelson Rhodes
Editor, writer, and consultant in the Chicago area.

Carrie Rothburd
Writer and editor specializing in corporate profiles, academic texts, and academic journal articles.

David E. Salamie
Part-owner of InfoWorks Development Group, a reference publication development and editorial services company.

Ted Sylvester
Photographer, writer, and editor of the environmental journal *From the Ground Up*.

Mary Tradii Writer based in Denver, Colorado.

Frank Uhle
Ann Arbor-based writer; movie projectionist, disc jockey, and staff member of *Psychotronic Video* magazine.

A. Woodward
Wisconsin-based writer.

List of Abbreviations

¥ Japanese yen
£ United Kingdom pound
$ United States dollar
A.E. Anonimos Eteria (Greece)
A.O. Anonim Ortaklari/Ortakligi (Turkey)
A.S. Anonim Sirketi (Turkey)
A/S Aksjeselskap (Norway)
A/S Aktieselskab (Denmark, Sweden)
AB Aktiebolag (Finland, Sweden)
AB Oy Aktiebolag Osakeyhtiot (Finland)
AED Emirati dirham
AG Aktiengesellschaft (Austria, Germany, Switzerland, Liechtenstein)
ARS Argentine peso
ATS Austrian shilling
AUD Australian dollar
ApS Amparteselskab (Denmark)
Ay Avoinyhtio (Finland)
B.A. Buttengewone Aansprakeiijkheid (The Netherlands)
B.V. Besloten Vennootschap (Belgium, The Netherlands)
BEF Belgian franc
BHD Bahraini dinar
BRL Brazilian real
Bhd. Berhad (Malaysia, Brunei)
C. de R.L. Compania de Responsabilidad Limitada (Spain)
C.A. Compania Anonima (Ecuador, Venezuela)

C.V. Commanditaire Vennootschap (The Netherlands, Belgium)
CAD Canadian dollar
CEO Chief Executive Officer
CFO Chief Financial Officer
CHF Swiss franc
CIO Chief Information Officer
CLP Chilean peso
CNY Chinese yuan
COO Chief Operating Officer
COP Colombian peso
CRL Companhia a Responsabilidao Limitida (Portugal, Spain)
CZK Czech koruna
Co. Company
Corp. Corporation
D&B Dunn & Bradstreet
DEM German deutsche mark
DKK Danish krone
DZD Algerian dinar
EEK Estonian Kroon
EGP Egyptian pound
ESOP Employee Stock Options and Ownership
ESP Spanish peseta
EUR euro
FIM Finnish markka
FRF French franc
G.I.E. Groupement d'Interet Economique (France)
GRD Greek drachma
GmbH Gesellschaft mit beschraenkter Haftung (Austria, Germany, Switzerland)

HKD Hong Kong dollar
HUF Hungarian forint
I/S Interesentselskap (Norway)
I/S Interessentselskab (Denmark)
IDR Indonesian rupiah
IEP Irish pound
ILS new Israeli shekel
INR Indian rupee
IPO Initial Public Offering
ISK Icelandic krona
ITL Italian lira
Inc. Incorporated (United States, Canada)
JMD Jamaican dollar
K/S Kommanditselskab (Denmark)
K/S Kommandittselskap (Norway)
KG Kommanditgesellschaft (Austria, Germany, Switzerland)
KGaA Kommanditgesellschaft auf Aktien (Austria, Germany, Switzerland)
KK Kabushiki Kaisha (Japan)
KPW North Korean won
KRW South Korean won
KWD Kuwaiti dinar
LBO Leveraged Buyout
Lda. Limitada (Spain)
L.L.C. Limited Liability Company (United States)
Ltd. Limited (Various)
Ltda. Limitada (Brazil, Portugal)

Ltee. Limitee (Canada, France)
LUF Luxembourg franc
mbH mit beschraenkter Haftung (Austria, Germany)
MUR Mauritian rupee
MXN Mexican peso
MYR Malaysian ringgit
N.V. Naamloze Vennootschap (Belgium, The Netherlands)
NGN Nigerian naira
NLG Netherlands guilder
NOK Norwegian krone
NZD New Zealand dollar
OAO Otkrytoe Aktsionernoe Obshchestve (Russia)
OMR Omani rial
OOO Obschestvo s Ogranichennoi Otvetstvennostiu (Russia)
Oy Osakeyhtiö (Finland)
PHP Philippine peso
PKR Pakistani rupee
PLC Public Limited Co. (United Kingdom, Ireland)
PLN Polish zloty
PTE Portuguese escudo
Pty. Proprietary (Australia, South Africa, United Kingdom)

QAR Qatari rial
REIT Real Estate Investment Trust
RMB Chinese renminbi
RUB Russian ruble
S.A. Société Anonyme (Belgium, France, Greece, Luxembourg, Switzerland, Arab speaking countries)
S.A. Sociedad Anónima (Latin America, Spain, Mexico)
S.A. Sociedades Anônimas (Brazil, Portugal)
S.A.R.L. Sociedade Anonima de Responsabilidade Limitada (Brazil, Portugal)
S.A.R.L. Société à Responsabilité Limitée (France, Belgium, Luxembourg)
S.A.S. Societá in Accomandita Semplice (Italy)
S.A.S. Societe Anonyme Syrienne (Arab speaking countries)
S.R.L. Sociedad de Responsabilidad Limitada (Spain, Mexico, Latin America)
S.R.L. Società a Responsabilitá Limitata (Italy)

S.R.O. Spolecnost s Rucenim Omezenym (Czechoslovakia
S.p.A. Società per Azioni (Italy)
SAA Societe Anonyme Arabienne
SAR Saudi riyal
SEK Swedish krona
SGD Singapore dollar
Sdn. Bhd. Sendirian Berhad (Malaysia)
Sp. z.o.o. Spólka z ograniczona odpowiedzialnoscia (Poland)
Ste. Societe (France, Belgium, Luxembourg, Switzerland)
THB Thai baht
TND Tunisian dinar
TRL Turkish lira
TWD new Taiwan dollar
VAG Verein der Arbeitgeber (Austria, Germany)
VEB Venezuelan bolivar
VND Vietnamese dong
YK Yugen Kaisha (Japan)
ZAO Zakrytoe Aktsionernoe Obshchestve (Russia)
ZAR South African rand
ZMK Zambian kwacha

Acciona S.A.

Avda de Europa 18
Parque Empresarial La Moraleja
Alcobendas, E-28108 HM 08
Spain
Telephone: +34 91 663 28 50
Fax: +34 91 663 29 29
Web site: http://www.acciona.es

Public Company
Incorporated: 1931 as Entrecanales y Tavora
Employees: 27,015
Sales: EUR 4.85 billion ($6.21 billion) (2005)
Stock Exchanges: Madrid
Ticker Symbol: ANA
NAIC: 236210 Industrial Building Construction; 236220 Commercial and Institutional Building Construction; 237110 Water and Sewer Line and Related Structures Construction; 237310 Highway, Street, and Bridge Construction; 237990 Other Heavy and Civil Engineering Construction; 238110 Poured Concrete Foundation and Structure Contractors; 238210 Electrical Contractors; 312130 Wineries; 333611 Turbine and Turbine Generator Set Unit Manufacturing; 488119 Other Airport Operations; 524210 Insurance Agencies and Brokerages; 531210 Offices of Real Estate Agents and Brokers; 541330 Engineering Services

■ ■ ■

Acciona S.A. has transformed itself from a focused construction and infrastructure group to a diversified company with three primary sectors: Infrastructure, Energy, and Services. Acciona Infraestructuras represents the company's historical base and includes the group's construction and engineering operations, as well as its transport concessions, including toll road operations. This division is also the group's largest division, accounting for more than half of its total revenues, and includes Acciona Real Estate, which oversees the company's portfolio of properties and real estate development operations. Acciona Energy is active in the development, construction, and operation of power generation facilities, with a specific focus on renewable energy sources. These include the operation and maintenance of hydroelectric dams, but especially the development and operation of wind farms. Acciona is one of the world's leading wind farm groups. In the mid-2000s, Acciona has been expanding its wind farm operations on an international scale, bidding for control of Pacific Hydro in Australia in 2005, launching wind farm operations in Slovenia in 2006, and forming a joint venture in Nantong, China, to construct the world's largest wind turbine factory. Acciona Energy represents a small but fast-growing part of the overall group. Between 2004 and 2005, that division nearly doubled its total revenues, to more than EUR 500 million. Acciona Services combines the group's operations in logistics and airport services, concessions (including car parks, hospital facilities, and funeral services), and waste management and other urban and environmental services. This division also includes Acciona Trasmediterránea, the former state-owned ferry services operator. Together, Acciona's operations combined to generate revenues of more than EUR 4.8 billion ($6.2 billion) in 2005. The company is

COMPANY PERSPECTIVES

Mission: To be leaders in the creation, promotion and management of infrastructures, energy and services, contributing to the wellbeing of society and sustainable development.

Vision: The creation of added value for our shareholders and stakeholders, contributing towards economic growth, the wellbeing of society and environmental balance, through the excellent management of our human, technological and financial resources, so as to allow present and future generations to enjoy a better life.

Our Values: Honesty; Leadership; Excellence; Caring for the environment; Social responsibility; Focusing on the long-term; Financial solvency; Client focus; Innovation; Caring for people.

listed on the Madrid Stock Exchange and is led by Chairman Jose Manuel Entrecanales Domecq. The Entrecanales family is also the company's major shareholder.

MERGING A MAJOR IN 1997

Although Acciona was formed only in 1997, through the merger of Entrecanales y Tavora and Cubiertas y MZOV, its operations dated back to the beginning of Spain's modern construction and engineering industry. The oldest part of the group was MZOV, which dated its origins back to 1862. Other members of the group were developed in the early years of the 20th century. Such was the case of Cubiertas, founded as Cubiertas y Tejados in 1916. Those two companies merged in 1978 to form Cubiertas y MZOV.

Cubiertas y MZOV grew strongly through the 1980s, benefiting from the huge boom in construction in Spain as the country emerged from the long years under the Franco dictatorship, and then joined the European Union. Spain quickly became one of the most dynamic economies in Europe, enjoying steady growth through the 1990s. The Spanish government played a prominent role in the development of the country's construction and engineering sector, launching a long series of large-scale infrastructure projects. The company also entered the property development sector during this period, buying up a number of residential property holdings, located in most of Spain's major cities, in 1987.

As spending slowed during the difficult economic period at the beginning of the 1990s, however, the highly fragmented Spanish construction and engineering sector came under increasing pressure. Cubiertas y MZOV responded by embarking on a diversification strategy in the early 1990s, targeting several new sectors, including property development; waste management and water treatment; services, including security, maintenance and cleaning, and documentation and mail services; and gardening.

As part of this effort, Cubiertas y MZOV made a number of acquisitions, including the purchase of a 45 percent stake in Ingeniera Urbana, boosting its waste management and waste services arm, and Rendos S.A. Both companies were acquired in 1990. The company also continued to acquire property, as well as a number of car park concessions. By 1993 the company operated six car parks. In the meantime, Cubiertas y MZOV also had found a majority shareholder, in the form of rival construction and engineering group Entrecanales, which bought into the company at the end of the 1980s. Through the next decade, the two companies began collaborating on a number of joint ventures and investments.

The two companies moved to cement their relationship at the end of 1996, announcing their decision to merge. That merger was carried out at the beginning of 1997, at which point the company took on the name of NECSO Entrecanales Cubiertas S.A. Yet Entrecanales, and the Entrecanales family, were clearly the controlling force behind the newly enlarged company.

Entrecanales had entered the construction market in 1931 under the leadership of patriarch José Entrecanales Ibarra, a road engineer, and partner Manuel Tavora, who founded the company Entrecanales y Tavora. The company's fortunes took off especially following the end of the Spanish Civil War in 1939. Over the next decades, Entrecanales y Tavora emerged as one of Spain's leading infrastructure groups. The company, which became fully controlled by the Entrecanales family after Tavora died in 1940, also became one of the first Spanish construction groups to launch operations on an international scale.

The second generation of the family took over the direction of the business in 1970, through Jose Maria Entrecanales, and led it through a first consolidation wave in the Spanish market. As such, the company emerged as one of several large-scale Spanish construction companies. Entrecanales also participated in a number of high-profile projects in the 1970s and through the end of the century. Projects during this period included the construction of the Ascuncion Bridge in Paraguay, begun in 1976 and completed in 1979. The

1862: MZOV is created.

1916: Cubiertas y Tejados is founded.

1931: José Entrecanales Ibarra and Manuel Tavora form a road building business, Entrecanales y Tavora.

1940: Tavora dies and the Entrecanales family becomes sole owner of the company.

1978: Cubiertas and MZOV merge and form Cubiertas y MZOV.

1989: Entrecanales acquires a stake in Cubiertas y MZOV.

1997: Entrecanales merges with Cubiertas y MZOV, becoming NECSO.

1999: The company restructures operations and becomes Acciona.

2002: Acciona acquires Trasmediterránea, a leading ferry and shipping group in France.

2003: Acciona acquires 50 percent of EHN, becoming the third largest wind farm group in the world.

2004: Acciona acquires full control of EHN.

2006: Acciona forms a joint venture with China Aerospace and Technology Corporation to launch construction of wind generators in China.

company returned to that country in 1983, building the Concepcion Bridge, which was completed in 1986. Back in Spain, the company launched construction of the Tortosa Bridge, in Tarragona, completed in 1988.

Into the 1990s, Entrecanales served as a major partner in the construction of Spain's high-speed train system. As part of that project, the company completed a series of viaducts, including those at Churreteles, Concejo, Cortaceros, Parrilla, Valle, and Vinuela. Entrecanales also increasingly sought business on the international front; in the mid-1990s, for example, the company entered the Asian market, building the Ting Kau Bridge connecting Hong Kong to the Chinese mainland. Begun in 1995, that project was completed by 1998.

NEW ENERGY FOCUS IN THE NEW CENTURY

Into the late 1990s the Spanish construction sector entered a new period of consolidation, with major play-

ers, including Dragados, FCC, and others jockeying for position at the top of the market. The newly created NECSO took its place among the market leaders and launched a new growth period that saw the company's sales nearly double by the middle of the next decade. Soon after, the company changed its name to Acciona S.A.

In preparation for its next growth phase, the company launched a restructuring effort for its more than 100 subsidiaries. As part of that effort, the company also targeted new areas for its expansion. As such, the company's operations were regrouped into three primary divisions. Most of the company's existing operations were placed under the Infrastructure division, led by NECSO, which functioned as the holding company for the construction, engineering, infrastructure, and concessions operations, as well as real estate, urban services, and environmental and energy services. The second division, Logistics and Airport Services, represented the company's new focus on these markets, which included airport handling and management services, but also newly developing distribution and logistics operations. As a starting point for this business, the company acquired Press Cargo in 1999. The company's third division became Telecommunications, and represented the company's investments into the early 2000s in Spain's mobile telephone sector. These included stakes in businesses such as Airtel, Bilbao Editorial, Ecuality, and Radiotrónica-Telson.

The company also targeted further expansion internationally, notably in Poland, which expected to enter the European Union before the middle of the 2000s. The company entered that market in 1999 with the acquisition of a 24 percent share in Mostostal Warszawa. That company was among the leaders of the Polish infrastructure market, and was particularly strong in the construction of bridges. Acciona subsequently raised its stake in that company to 49 percent in 2001. At the same time, Acciona added a stake in Elektrim Finance, a leader in the Polish telecommunications market.

In 2000, Acciona reached an agreement to transfer its stake in Airtel to European cellular phone giant Vodafone. As a result, Airtel became Vodafone Espana, and Acciona became a prominent stakeholder both in that company and its parent. In 2003, Acciona cashed in part of its stake, raising more than EUR 2 billion.

The cash helped fueled the company's ongoing transformation. The company had beefed up its services operations with the 2001 acquisition of a major stake in Inversiones Tecnicas Urbanas S.L., the leading provider of funeral services in Spain. That company then acquired majority stakes in the Spanish and Portuguese operations of Service Corporation International. In 2002, Acciona won its bid to take over Trasmediterránea, Spain's leading ferry boat and shipping transport operator. That acquisition was completed in 2003.

At the same time, Acciona had developed a new target for its expansion, that of renewable energy production. In 2003, the company paid EUR 383 million to acquire a 50 percent stake in Corporacion Energia Hidroelectrica de Navarra (EHN), a major wind farm operator. As part of that deal, Acciona agreed to transfer its own wind farm holdings to EHN, which then became the world's number three wind power generator. Acciona continued to increase its shareholding in EHN, taking full control by 2004.

Jose Manuel Entrecanales Domecq took over direction of the company from his father in 2004. The younger Entrecanales promised to expand the group's renewable energy interests further, as the company adopted a new sustainability platform to underscore its operations. At the same time, Acciona made an effort toward consolidation within the infrastructure sector, acquiring a 15 percent stake in rival Fomento de Construcciones y Contratas (FCC), with a view toward an eventual merger. By mid-decade, however, such a merger appeared unlikely.

Instead, Acciona continued building up its renewable energy holdings. In 2005, the company posted a winning bid for Pacific Hydro, based in Australia, and a leader in that country's renewable energy market. By then, the company had launched construction of a new wind farm in Alberta, Canada, backed by a EUR 41 million investment. In 2005, the company completed two new wind farms in Germany, and another in France. The company's renewable energy competence also extended to include biodiesel and, with the launch of construction of Nevada Solar in 2005, solar thermoelectric energy.

By 2006, Acciona had emerged as a world leader in wind turbine technology. This position was cemented by the launch of a joint venture with China Aerospace and Technology Corporation, owned by the Chinese government, to launch construction of wind generators using Acciona's technology for the Chinese market. The growth of the company's energy operations, as well as its services component, led it to restructure its business again, regrouping its holding under three core divisions.

With more than EUR 4.8 billion ($6.2 billion) in sales, Acciona had become a prominent actor on the international stage.

M. L. Cohen

PRINCIPAL SUBSIDIARIES

Acciona Airport Services, S.A.; Acciona Biocombustibles, S.A.; Acciona Concesiones, S.L.; Acciona Do Brasil, Ltda.; Acciona Energía, S.A.; Acciona Eólica de Galicia, S.A.; Acciona Infraestructuras, S.A.; Acciona Inmobiliaria, S.L.; Acciona Logística, S.A.; Acciona Serv. Hospitalarios, S.L.; Acciona Servicios Concesionales, S.L.; Acciona Servicios Urbanos y MA, S.L.; Acciona Servicios Urbanos, S.A.; Acciona Wind Power, S.A.; Press Cargo, S.A.; Trasmediterránea Cargo, S.A.

PRINCIPAL COMPETITORS

ACS Actividades de Construccion y Servicios S.A.; Mondragon Corporacion Cooperativa; Fomento de Construcciones y Contratas S.A.; Sacyr Vallehermoso S.A.; Ferrovial Agroman S.A.; Obrascon Huarte Lain S.A.; Grupo Isolux-Corsan S.A.; Constructora San Jose S.A.

FURTHER READING

"Acciona Acquires Half of EHN Stake," *Power Engineering International,* September 2003, p. 17.

"Acciona Lines Up Trasmediterranea Ferries," *Lloyd's List,* June 15, 2006.

"Acciona May Consider Further Acquisitions," *Expansion,* August 20, 2002.

Fortson, Danny, "Spanish Construction Merger Builds," *Daily Deal,* April 28, 2004.

Kohler, Alan, "These Crazy Spaniards at Acciona Must Have Got a Whiff That There's Something in the Wind," *The Age,* March 29, 2005.

"Thames to Sell Spanish Arm for £104 Million," *Utility Week,* March 24, 2006.

White, David, and Andrew Taylor, "Spanish Builders to Merge," *Financial Times,* November 8, 1996, p. 24.

Yeh, Andrew, "Acciona in Joint Energy Deal," *Financial Times,* June 28, 2006, p. 13.

Agri Beef Company

1555 Shoreline Drive, Third Floor
Boise, Idaho 83702
U.S.A.
Telephone: (208) 338-2500
Toll Free: (800) 657-6305
Fax: (208) 338-2605
Web site: http://www.agribeef.com

Private Company
Incorporated: 1978
Employees: 1,000
Sales: $212.6 million (2005 est.)
NAIC: 112111 Beef Cattle Ranching and Farming; 112112 Cattle Feedlots; 311611 Animal (Except Poultry) Slaughtering

■ ■ ■

Agri Beef Company functions as a vertically integrated beef producer, which operates a ranch, cattle feedlots, and beef processing and packaging facilities located primarily in the Pacific Northwest. Breeding programs at IL Ranch in northern Nevada supply Agri Beef's feedlots with more than 5,000 calves and 9,000 lambs annually. Also, the company provides feedlot services to cattle producers in the Pacific Northwest at its four facilities in Idaho and Washington. PerforMix Nutritive Systems manufactures a variety of nutritional supplements for healthy animal growth, while state-of-the-art veterinary centers at the feedlots provide animal care. Agri Beef's Washington Beef subsidiary processes and packages beef products for the company and its customers. Agri Beef

offers cattle management services for client cattle companies, handling 40,000 head annually. Services include custom programs to assist ranchers with cattle procurement, feeding, and nutrition; financing, forward contracting, accounting, and inventory management; inspections; trucking; and end-product merchandising. The company manages the National Beef feedlot and processing and packaging operations in southwestern Kansas, and it owns the Supreme Feeders operations in Liberal, Kansas.

Agri Beef sells its own beef products under the Washington Beef brand in the United States and St. Helen's brand for export. The company's premium brand is Double R Ranch, touted for its quality as grain-fed Northwestern cattle. Agri Beef specializes in American Kobe beef and Kurobuta pork, high quality meats with unique marbling and flavor properties which the company markets to upscale restaurants and specialty retail grocers under the Snake River Farms brand.

A BOY'S DREAM

As a child growing up in northern California during the 1950s, Agri Beef founder Bob Rebholtz aspired to be a cowboy. He dreamed of owning and operating a large agricultural enterprise that would be a source of high quality food to a growing world population. Pragmatic from an early age, Rebholtz spent his childhood summers learning about animal health and nutrition, and as a young man, he attended Stanford Business School. He graduated in 1963 and went to work in the cattle industry. By 1968 he felt prepared to venture into a business of his own. That year, he acquired Snake River

COMPANY PERSPECTIVES

From ranch to table, we will be the leading producer of quality branded meat products. Our company family will accomplish this with employees, partners, and communities using integrity, leadership, and innovation.

Cattle Feeders, a small, 4,000-head cattle feedlot in American Falls, Idaho. The location on the fertile Snake River plain provided the feedlot with cost-efficient sources of potato, barely, wheat, and high-moisture corn.

As an independent businessman, Rebholtz found several factors essential to the successful achievement of his dream. These included hiring innovative, capable people and establishing a business culture oriented to Total Quality Management (TQM) in order to insure production of the highest quality beef. Also important was the development of relationships with suppliers so as to obtain high quality supplies for beef production.

By 1975, Rebholtz was ready to expand the business. The company acquired El Oro Cattle Feeders of Moses Lake, Washington. Eventually, Rebholtz joined with a friend and fellow feedlot owner to incorporate a new livestock feeding business in Boise, Idaho, named Agri Beef, Inc. That year, 1978, Rebholtz relocated company headquarters to Boise. With the move to a sizable Idaho community, Agri Beef sought to attract employees in the field of high technology information systems, who would be capable of developing state-of-the-art systems oriented to the beef industry. Rebholtz saw the efficiency created by information management as one of the cornerstones of future growth.

The long-term growth plan for Agri Beef involved vertical integration of all facets of beef production, from ranching and feeding cattle to processing and packaging beef products. As such, diversification into related industries would simplify supply chain management processes and facilitate development of economies of scale. Animal healthcare figured prominently in achieving this goal. In 1981 Agri Beef purchased MWI Veterinary Supply, a distributor of animal drugs and vaccines, pet food, and animal nutritional products to veterinary practices nationwide. PerforMix Nutrition Systems, founded by Rich Rawlings in 1983 and later acquired by Agri Beef, provided nutritional products specifically designed for cattle. In 1988, the company purchased the IL Ranch near Tuscarora, in northern Nevada. With 1.4 million acres of land, the ranch provided ample space for breeding cattle and sheep. At IL Ranch, Agri Beef developed the Western Red breed, a cross of the Red Angus, Red Braham, Gelbvieh, and Hereford breeds of cattle. IL Ranch enhanced the vertical integration of Agri Beef, as it supplied calves for the company's feedlots in preparation for market.

SPECIALIZATION IN KOBE BEEF

Agri Beef took a bold new direction in 1990, when the company began to specialize in Japanese Kobe beef, a particularly high-quality beef renowned for tenderness and buttery taste. Kobe beef obtained its unique qualities from a rich marbling texture. The fat grew inside the muscle rather than outside of the meat in the manner of commodity beef. Hence, the marbling effect enhanced Kobe beef's tenderness and intense flavor. Produced from Wagyu cattle brought from China to Japan in the second century for use as a draft animal, Kobe beef took its name from the Kobe region of Japan, where superior cattle had been bred for hundreds of years.

In order to develop an American version of Kobe beef, Agri Beef cross-bred American Black Angus cows with Japanese Wagyu bulls. Fifteen bulls, flown to the United States from Japan in a jumbo jet, provided the initial stock for the breeding program. Then Rebholtz sought the highest quality Black Angus cows owned by others; once impregnated, he purchased the cows at a premium price. Agri Beef fed the calves a measured ration of barley, wheat, and alfalfa for about 500 days, compared to 120 days for regular domestic cattle. Thus, a combination of genetics and the slow-grow feeding method generated the Kobe beef's rich flavor and subtle texture. Though myth has it that the Japanese fed the cattle beer and barley, massaged them, and brushed their coats with the liquor sake in order to nurture the unique qualities of Kobe beef, Agri Beef contended that the stress-free living of the wide open American West precluded such measures.

Marketed under the Snake River Farms brand name, Agri Beef began to sell Kobe beef in Japan and the United States in 1991. The quality of Kobe beef presented certain problems for marketing in the United States, however. While public concerns about health and cholesterol pushed the beef industry to produce leaner meat, Kobe beef followed a different health philosophy. Though higher in fat content than commonly consumed cuts of beef, Kobe beef was lower in saturated fat and higher in unsaturated fat, the kind of cholesterol desirable for a healthy diet. Kobe beef did not carry the cholesterol problems generally associated with high fat content in beef. Also, Kobe beef did not fit the U.S. Department of Agriculture's grading system, which would rank it all as prime cut. Agri Beef, in fact, developed its own grades: Silver, with marbling as ten to 15 percent of the total cut, placing it on par with prime beef; Black, with 15 to 20 percent marbling; and Gold, the top grade, with more than 25 percent marbling.

ACQUISITIONS, NEW BUSINESS ENHANCE VERTICAL INTEGRATION

Agri Beef expanded to the Midwest in 1995, when the company purchased Supreme Cattle Feeders, a 70,000 head feedlot in Liberal, Kansas. That enterprise served as Agri Beef's entrance into management of National Beef Packing Company. National Beef signed an agreement with Agri Beef in the expectation that new management would improve the long-term value of the company. National Beef, then the fourth largest beef packer in the United States, comprised a joint venture of Farmland Industries, John R. Miller, and entities owned by Ezra K. Zilkha. The joint venture included slaughter and boxed beef plants in Liberal and Dodge City, Kansas. Agri Beef planned a vertical integration at the southwestern Kansas operations. Responsibilities involved breeding and maintaining a supply of feeder cattle all year round as well as the handling of forward contracting, financing, and related risk management practices.

As part of the vertical integration strategy for Kansas, in 2001 PerforMix Nutrition Systems constructed a new plant in western Kansas to produce a liquid suspension supplement for Supreme Feeders and other customers. Rapid increase in usage of liquid supplements, as well as anticipation of future growth in the feedlot and dairy industry, prompted PerforMix to initiate the joint venture with Cattle Empire LLC, and Doll Feed Services, Inc.

Agri Beef expanded its Idaho feedlot operations with the acquisition of Boise Valley Feeders, LLC in 1998. A state-of-the-art facility, Boise Valley Feeders used the most advanced techniques in cattle feedlots, such as a two to five degree slant in calf bunks to encourage moisture and animal waste to drain away from the bunk for healthier living conditions. The 25,000-head facility provided ample space to maintain health and prevent injury of client cattle, and Boise Valley Feeders used small herd pens in order to provide focused attention. Also, Agri Beef renovated 80 percent of the pens at Snake River Cattle Feeders, the original facility in American Falls, Idaho. The feedlot provided 25,000 head of cattle with one foot of bunk space and 250 square feet of roaming space per calf. The company built a state-of-the-art veterinary center for animal healthcare, as well.

In May 2003, Agri Beef announced that it had acquired Washington Beef, located in Toppenish, in south central Washington. The company processed and packed 1,100 head of cattle per day, including custom beef packing. Agri Beef maintained operations and the company name, including the Washington Beef and St. Helen's brands. Agri Beef acquired Washington Beef to enhance its vertical integration of every aspect of beef production, from raising cattle to feeding, and butchering and packaging. The opening of a PerforMix Nutrition plant furthered that intent. Concurrently, Agri Beef expected the merger with Washington Beef to strengthen the Pacific Northwest beef industry as a whole. The combination would sustain competitiveness by strengthening the domestic cattle supply, particularly as it would reduce reliance on cattle imported from Canada. Agri Beef expected mandatory country-of-origin labeling, beginning in 2004, to reduce sales of Canadian beef in the United States. Also, the combination of Washington Beef and Agri Beef competed more effectively with Tyson Fresh Meats, which owned and operated a larger plant in nearby Pasco; hence, it ensured competitive pricing for area beef producers.

Vertical integration of the beef supply chain proved to be an asset to Agri Beef when concerns about mad cow disease reached the beef industry in the United States. Control of the supply chain gave the company control over quality of production and, therefore, the quality of its products. Moreover, the company implemented safety standards on its own, even before mad cow disease hit the United States. When the U.S. Department of Agriculture mandated a food safety program in 1998, it did not require changes in cattle feeding operations. Agri Beef implemented a safety program anyway. Toward that end, Agri Beef exceeded regulatory standards by implementing a dual ISO/HACCP certification of food safety standards, becoming the first cattle feeding operation to be registered by both the International Organization for Standardization (ISO) and Hazard Analysis Critical Control Point (HACCP), in 2003. Being one of the few U.S. cattle companies to be vertically integrated enabled Agri Beef to establish a system of safety and standardization along the supply chain that was "unprecedented" for efficiency and quality, as well as safety. When instances of mad cow disease arose in the American beef industry, Agri Beef confidently issued its Safe Guarantee, in early 2004.

PREMIUM PRODUCTS AT THE FOREFRONT OF MARKETING EFFORTS

When Congress banned the import of Japanese beef in 2001, due to mad cow disease, Japan responded by banning American beef imports. The situation required Agri Beef to develop markets for Kobe beef within the United States. Indeed, the ban on Japanese beef helped to generate sales of American Kobe beef. Agri Beef sold slightly less than three million pounds of Kobe beef in 2002, a 32 percent increase over the previous year. The high quality meat sold at specialty grocers at $5 per pound for hamburger and $40 per pound for tenderloin, compared to beef commonly sold in supermarkets, priced at $2 per pound for hamburger and $11 per pound for tenderloin.

To further develop consumer demand for American Kobe beef in the United States, Agri Beef applied drama to its marketing strategy. In January 2003, Old Homestead Steak House in Manhattan introduced Snake River Farms to diners by offering an attention-getting $41 hamburger, made with 20 ounces of Kobe beef. The outrageous price attracted media attention, and people called the restaurant asking about the $41 hamburger. Old Homestead sold more than 200 in a day, and celebrity attention contributed to the excitement. James Gandolfini, of the popular television series *The Sopranos,* and Mike Piazza, New York Mets baseball star, both enjoyed the Kobe hamburger at Old Homestead. Attention exceeded expectations, and the strategy facilitated an increase in business for both the restaurant and Snake River Farms.

In March 2003 Agri Beef introduced all-natural pork products with qualities similar to that of Kobe beef, called Kurobuta pork. The company applied the slow-grow method of producing premium meat to purebred Berkshire hogs, said to have been discovered in the Berks region of England by Oliver Cromwell's army during the 1700s. Raised on small family farms in Iowa, the Berkshire hogs were fed at 10 percent slower pace than average hog breeds. The experiment succeeded in producing similar results as the Kobe beef: rich marbling and tender, flavorful meat. Kurobuta pork ranked first on 19 of 25 attributes when judged by the National Pork Board.

Kurobuta pork was not as easy to promote as Kobe beef, which had a standing reputation for its unique qualities. Also, Agri Beef encountered the same problem with the pork as it had with Kobe beef, in that the American public had been educated to think of marbling as bad, that it meant the meat contained too much fat. Consequently, with a $10,000 advertising budget, Agri Beef employed the marketing tactics derived from the bestselling book *The Tipping Point,* by Malcolm Gladwell. The first step was to identify the "connectors" who influence many people. As such, Agri Beef contacted well-known chefs and persuaded them to put Kurobuta pork on their menus. High profile chefs who began to cook with Kurobuta Pork included Wolfgang Puck of Los Angeles, Thomas Keller of Bouchon in Las Vega, Eric Ripert of Le Bernardin in New York, and Jay Murray at Grill 23 in Boston. Renowned New Orleans chef Emeril Lagasse raved about Kurobuta pork on his blog. At Jon Mortimer's restaurant in Boise, pork tenderloin became the most popular meal on the menu, accounting for 20 percent of entree sales. Mortimer showcased the meat at a special meal presentation of Idaho foods at the famous James Beard House in New York City.

Marketing for Kobe beef continued as Agri Beef introduced new products for grocers. In October 2003, the company introduced a package of frozen hamburgers, containing two, eight-ounce Kobe beef hamburger patties. A special patented process allowed cooking to retain 50 percent more juice than regular hamburger by providing space within the meat for juices to cook "into" and settle. In June 2005, Agri Beef introduced American Kobe roast beef, referred to as Butterknife Beef, to be sold in delicatessens or for catering buffets.

Restaurant marketing continued to be a mainstay of promoting Kobe beef. Wolfgang Puck prepared Snake River Farms Kobe beef at two 2005 Academy Awards dinners. After Agri Beef's premier breeding bull, Fukusuru, died in 2005, after 13 years of productivity (normal for Wagyu bulls), Rogue Ale of Newport, Oregon, dedicated St. Rogue Red ale to him. The restaurant and brewery placed the story of American Kobe beef on the bottle label, crediting Fukusuru as the first bull to propagate the line of quality American Kobe beef. Washington State University had ranked Fukusuru as the top bull for marbling. In order to retain Fukusuru's exceptional genetic base, Agri Beef preserved 100,000 units of the bull's semen, which was cryogenically frozen.

Congress extended the ban on Japanese beef imports in 2005, further assisting sales growth at Snake River Farms. As the largest producer of American Kobe beef, Agri Beef sold $15 million of Kobe beef products in 2005, which increased 30 percent over 2004 and accounted for 75 percent of total beef product sales.

In 2005 Agri Beef introduced a new brand of beef product designed to meet consumer demand for locally produced foods. The Double R Ranch brand, named for company founder Robert Rebholtz, intended to laud grain-fed beef from the Pacific Northwest as comparable or better in taste and quality as Midwestern corn-fed beef. Products included Double R Ranch Signature beef, sold to restaurants and upscale grocers, and Double R Ranch Premium cuts of beef. Double R Ranch Quick Chef offered convenience with marinated, heat-and-serve beef products, ready to eat in 20 minutes. Agri Beef marketed Double R Ranch products in 13 Western states.

Mary Tradii

PRINCIPAL SUBSIDIARIES

Boise Valley Feeders LLC; El Oro Cattle Feeders; PerforMix High Plains LLC; PerforMix Nutrition Systems; Snake River Cattle Feeders; Supreme Cattle Feeders LLC; Washington Beef LLC.

PRINCIPAL DIVISIONS

AB Foods; Livestock Division.

PRINCIPAL COMPETITORS

Cargil Meat Solutions, Inc.; ConAgra Meats Co.; Tyson Fresh Meats, Inc.

FURTHER READING

"Agri Beef: Cattle Drive," *Baseline*, November 1, 2004.

"American Kobe Beef," *Stagnito's New Products Magazine*, May 2003, p. 18.

Barrett, Jennifer, "These Little Piggies; Forget Bacon Strips. The Company That Brought Kobe Beef to Americans Now Wants You to Try Kurobuta Pork," *Newsweek*, November 14, 2005, p. 36.

"Butterknife Beef," *Grocery Headquarters*, June 2005, p. 78.

"DIET: American Kobe-Style Beef Has Replaced the Real Japanese Thing," *America's Intelligence Wire*, December 30, 2005.

"Kobe Burgers," *Frozen Food Age*, October 2003, p. 16.

Peck, Cliff, "Northwest Entrepreneur," *Beef Magazine*, January 1, 2002, http://beef-mag.com/mag/beef_northwest_entrepreneur /index.html.

"PerforMix to Build Liquid Supplement Plant," *Feedstuffs*, September 11, 2000, p. 27.

"Rawlings to Retire As PerforMix President," *Feedstuffs*, February 23, 2004, p. 6.

Schuff, Sally, "Agri Beef Production System Verified Under Dual ISO/HACCP Certification," *Feedstuffs*, May 10, 2004, p. 1.

Smith, Rod, "Agri Beef, Buys Washington Beef; Forms Beef System," *Feedstuffs*, May 26, 2003, p. 6.

———, "First-of-the-Kind Challenge to Use Cattle ID, Health Status," *Feedstuffs*, September 17, 2001, p. 9.

Squazzo, Jessica, "Calming Fears About Mad Cow: By Providing Solid Evidence, Retailers Can Alleviate Mad Cow Mayhem and Keep Beef Sales Up," *Grocery Headquarters*, February 2004, p. 26.

Theiler, Jay, "Beef: In-store Demos and Beef Promotions Are Ideal Ways Retailers Can Help Consumers with Their Dinner Decisions, Notes Jay Theiler, Vice President Brand Development for Agri Beef Co.," *Grocery Headquarters*, September 2005, p. S30.

Turcsik, Richard, "A Challenge to Midwestern Beef," *Grocery Headquarters*, May 2005, p. 100.

"Would You Pay $14 for a Hamburger? Probably Not. But New York Diners Are Paying Big Bucks for Idaho-Raised Kobe Beef," *Idaho Statesman*, January 5, 2006.

Alès Groupe

99 rue du Faubourg Saint Honoré 75008
Paris,
France
Telephone: +33 (0)1 34 23 50 00
Fax: +33 (0)1 34 23 50 01
Web site: http://www.alesgroupe.com

Public Company
Incorporated: 1969 as Laboratoires Phytosolba
Employees: 745
Sales: EUR 151.9 million ($207.3 million) (2005)
Stock Exchanges: Euronext Paris
Ticker Symbol: 5465; PHY FP; PHY P.PA
NAIC: 325620 Toilet Preparation Manufacturing

■ ■ ■

Alès Groupe is a France-based producer of high-end hair care and skin care products, perfumes, and cosmetics. The company has distinguished itself through its emphasis on the use of plants and other natural substances for its products' active ingredients. The company targets both the professional and consumer markets with brands such as the Phyto line of shampoos and hair care products; Lierac cosmetics, Phytoderm skin care products, Secret Professionel, targeting the professional hairdresser market; high-end hair coloring products through Laboratoires Ducastel and Kydra by Phyto; ethnic hair care products through PhytoSpecific; and Caron perfumes.

Alès has long carried out its own research and development operations at its Paris headquarters and its main production facilities in Bezons, a Paris suburb, and the Ducastel plant in Castelfranc. The company operates sales and marketing subsidiaries in the United States, the United Kingdom, Canada, Poland, Italy, Switzerland, Belgium, Germany, and Spain. The international market represents the largest part of the group's sales, at 55 percent of total revenues of EUR 152 million ($207 million) in 2005. Listed on the Euronext Paris Stock Exchange, Alès Groupe is led by founder, Chairman, and CEO Patrick Alès. The Alès family holds 66.67 percent of the group's stock.

PLANTING THE SEEDS OF SUCCESS IN THE MID-20TH CENTURY

Patrick Alès arrived in Paris in 1946 to study architecture. After an apprenticeship at the Louis Gervais salon on the Champs Elysees, however, Alès decided to pursue a career in hairdressing instead, and by the mid-1960s had become a well-known name in the high-end Parisian market. By 1965, Alès had opened his own salon, on the avenue Franklin Roosevelt. Success enabled Alès to buy a house in the French countryside, in the Haute Provence, a purchase that was to transform his professional life. In the attic of the home, Alès discovered a number of jars filled with dried flowers and herbs left behind by the house's former owner. Alès quickly developed an interest in herbs and plants, and especially in their potential for use as active ingredients in hair care products.

At the time, hair care products, including shampoos, conditioners and colorants, were based almost entirely

COMPANY PERSPECTIVES

Philosophy: Patrick Alès is an enthusiast. Enthusiastic about nature, plants, hair, beauty, fragrances . ... When he speaks about plants, his eyes light up. And, he can speak for hours on end about the subject. When he was 25, he discovered the plant world: leaves, roots and extracts, which were dried or reduced to powder form and kept in old jars. These were left by a healer in the farm attic he had purchased in the Haute Provence region of France. He was immediately captivated! He wanted to know everything about their properties, powers. He was a leading hair care professional and had only one idea in mind: To create plant-based hair treatments, which were uncommon at the time. With the help of his wife and some scientists, he transformed his garage into a workshop, where he developed the first PHYTO 7 creams, which he mixed together using an old bread kneading machine that had been thrown out. Today, as in the past, he continues to work with his family and friends. His children help create the products and his friends and customers test them. A precursor, PHYTOTHER-ATHRIE was created in 1967. It was the first cosmetic brand to use the PHYTO prefix. However, his work has not always been easy—but that didn't matter! Patrick Alès has incredible drive and passion. He believed in his project and was determined to carry it through. In 1969, he founded the PHYTOSOLBA Laboratory. He then developed other brands and companies that were related to plants, nature and beauty. Today, this small company has grown into an international group, which was called the PHYTO-LIERAC Group, and then renamed ALES GROUP. Yet, Patrick Alès, a highly imaginative and extremely hard-working man continues to take his work a step further. There is always a small flower or grass growing near his home or on the other side of the world that catches his eye and makes him want to learn more. As he says: "A simple field is like an immense open book, of which only a few pages have been discovered!"

on often harsh chemicals. Alès began seeking more gentle alternatives in the plant world, and quickly developed his own preparations, which he began using on customers in his salon. In 1967, Alès trademarked the term "Phytotherathrie" to describe the focus of his hair care products. The term was derived from the Latin words "phyto" (plants), "thera" (care), and "trixos" (hair). Among the products developed by Alès, in partnership with his wife Jacquie, were Huile d'Alès, Phytopolleine, Phytodefrisant, Phytomousse S88, Phytoneutre, Phyto-capucine, and Henne Neutre Moussant.

Patrick and Jacquie Alès initially mixed their products by hand at their Provence home. By 1968, Alès had developed the formula for what was to become the company's biggest and longest-running success, Phyto 7. A mixture of seven ingredients, the product soon stimulated demand not only from Alès's often famous clients, but from dermatologists as well. This led Alès to launch a business dedicated to his growing hair care products line, called Laboratoires Phtyosolba, in 1969. Production nonetheless remained on a small scale, based in the Alès family garage, and using an old bread machine as a mixer.

Into the 1970s, the company enjoyed continued growth in demand, and began supplying its products directly to pharmacists, as well as to dieticians and to the health food market, still in its infancy in France. Alès attempted to interest the larger hair care companies in his plant-based products, but found little success. Instead, Alès decided to invest in expanding the company's production. The company moved to new headquarters, on Paris's Faubourg Saint Honoré, launching a training center and building a sales team.

During the first half of the 1970s, as well, Alès turned increasingly to the scientific community, adding an in-house research and development team. Of importance, Alès also sought clinical proof of the effectiveness of the company's products. The first clinical study, on Phytopolleine, was carried out at the Saint-Louis hospital in 1974. Alès's product line built up the support of more than 200 clinical studies over the next decades, including studies conducted by France's prestigious Academy of Sciences and the French National Center for Scientific Research (CNRS).

The Alès company increasingly took on a professional management approach. In 1977, for example, the company founded a new subsidiary, Caster, which took responsibility for the creation and oversight of the group's brands, trademarks, and patents.

By 1978, Alès had found a major partner, when French cosmetics giant L'Oreal acquired a 44 percent stake in the company, as well as the international distribution rights to the growing Phyto product family. The backing of L'Oreal allowed Alès to extend its growing reputation to the international market.

KEY DATES

1967: Successful Parisian hairdresser Patrick Alès develops the first plant-based hair care products under the Phytotherathrie trademark.

1969: Laboratoires Phytosolba is founded to produce plant-based products for a wider market.

1978: L'Oreal acquires a 44 percent stake in Groupe Alès.

1979: Alès acquires Lierac, a producer of plant-based cosmetics.

1989: Alès creates a U.S. sales subsidiary.

1995: Alès is reorganized under holding company Phyto-Lierac, and the Alès family buys back L'Oreal's stake.

1996: The company lists on the Paris Stock Exchange.

1997: Ducastel, a hair coloring specialist, is acquired.

1998: The company enters the perfume industry with the purchase of Caron.

1999: The company changes its name to Alès Groupe.

2004: A Spanish sales subsidiary is added.

2006: The company launches the Phytoprogenium hair care product line.

Alès's products increasingly went further than simple hair care to take the form of health and dietary supplements. In 1974, for example, the company launched its Phytoplage brand of product, providing protection for the hair against the harmful effects of the sun. In 1982, the company launched a veritable dietary supplement, Phytophanere, meant to fortify the hair and nails.

At the same time, the company had begun to diversify elsewhere. In 1979, the company bought Laboratoires Lierac, a company specialized in the production of cosmetics. Lierac had already developed a line of plant-based cosmetics. Under Alès ownership, the company reformulated many of Lierac's products, increasing the proportion of plant-based active ingredients, and reducing the levels of preservatives and other nonnatural additives.

INTERNATIONAL GROWTH IN THE LATE 20TH CENTURY

Through the 1980s, the company continued its quest for new and more powerful active ingredients. This led the company to pick up additional research and development capacity, through the purchase of Laboratoires de Médecine Vegetale in 1983. That business was later transferred to the group's main headquarters site. By 1988, the company had succeeded in developing a new skin care line with an active ingredient based on the skin of grape seeds, launched under the name Lieractiv. In this way, the Lierac name took the forefront of the soon-to-skyrocket high-performance skin care category.

With sales growing strongly, Alès opened a new production facility in Bezon, on the outskirts of Paris, in 1988. The company then transferred the operations of its various product lines, including its research and development activity, to the new plant, while its Faubourg Saint Honore office became refocused as the group's headquarters and main sales office.

The growing renown of the company's products among France's jet set had enabled it to attract an increasingly international clientele. The company began taking steps to bring its products closer to the foreign market in the late 1980s, with the launching of a first international sales subsidiary in the United States in 1989. That subsidiary was joined by a new subsidiary in Germany in 1991. The company also sought to boost its technology, and in 1992, Alès acquired Cosmodex. That company focused on developing de-pigmentation treatments and other dermatological cosmetic products.

Alès began preparations for continued growth in the mid-1990s, restructuring the company's operations under a new holding company, Phyto-Lierac, in 1995. In that year, the Alès family bought back the 44 percent stake in the company held by L'Oreal, and also regained control of its international distribution rights. The share buyback then led to Phyto-Lierac's public offering, with a listing on the Paris Stock Exchange's secondary market in 1996. The Alès family nonetheless retained majority control of the company, with a two-thirds majority into the mid-2000s.

The public offering enabled Phyto-Lierac to step up its international implantation. In 1996, the company established a sales subsidiary in Italy. This was followed by a Brussels office in 1997, which took over responsibility for the Benelux market. One year later, Phyto-Lierac entered the United Kingdom as well. Supporting the company's growing sales was the inauguration of a new warehouse and logistics facility in Cegry-Pontoise, near Paris.

RIDING THE NATURAL WAVE IN THE NEW CENTURY

Phyto-Lierac also had been building up its range of products and brand names. In 1995, the company acquired the exclusive French distribution rights for the British brand Yardley of London. Also in that year, the company launched a new line dedicated to the professional hair care market, called Secret Professionnel. Two years later, Phyto-Lierac extended its range of hair care products with the purchase of Laboratoires Ducastel, a specialist in high-end hair dyes and other technical hair products. The addition of Ducastel enabled the company to launch a new product line, Kydra by Phyto, of hair coloring products for the professional sector, in 1998.

Phyto-Lierac also entered new territory that year with the acquisition of the noted perfume house Caron. That company had been founded in 1904, and had early success with fragrances such as Narcisse Noir (1911), Bellodgia (1927), and the men's fragrance Pour Un Homme (1934). By then, Caron also had released its highly successful Fleurs de Rocaille. Originally unveiled in 1933, that fragrance was relaunched in 1993. Also in 1998, the company introduced a new line, called Phytospecific, focused on the high-end ethnic hair care market in North America.

Phyto-Lierac changed its name back to Alès Groupe in 1999 as it looked forward to further growth in the new century. The following year, the company made its first step into the retail sector, opening a Caron perfume store in New York City. That opening was soon followed by a second store, at the company's Paris headquarters site. Accompanying the new retail effort was the marketing of two new perfumes, L'Anarchiste, for men, and Lady Caron.

In 2001, Alès acquired its Montreal-based distributor, Jean-Louis Renaud Inc., which was then renamed Alès Groupe Canada. The following year, the company announced a major expansion of its Ducastel site, with plans to double capacity of that facility.

Alès maintained steady growth into the mid-2000s. The company added a new distribution subsidiary in Spain in 2004. In that year, the company renamed its Cosmodex product line under the new Phytoderm brand. This was followed by the acquisition of the company's distributor in Poland in 2005. In that year, as well, Alès stepped up its presence in the United States and Canada with the launch of the Lierac brand of skin care products. At the same time, the Alès Groupe prepared the launch of two new anti-aging hair care brands, Phytodensium, launched in November 2005, and Phytoprogenium, which debuted in May 2006. Alès Groupe had succeeded in establishing itself as a respected name in the global high-end personal products market.

M. L. Cohen

PRINCIPAL SUBSIDIARIES

Alès Group Usa Inc.; Alès Groupe Benelux S.A.R.L. (Belgium); Alès Groupe Canada; Alès Groupe Cosmetic Deutschland GmbH (Germany); Alès Groupe Espana S.L. (Spain); Alès Groupe Industrie; Alès Groupe Italia S.p.A. (Italy); Alès Groupe Polska (Poland); Alès Groupe Suisse (Switzerland); Alès Groupe UK Ltd.; Laboratoires Ducastel; Laboratoires Phytoderm; Laboratoires Lierac; Laboratoires Phytosolba; Parfums Caron.

PRINCIPAL COMPETITORS

Nestlé S.A.; Sunstar Inc; Procter & Gamble Company; Unilever; Johnson and Johnson; E. Merck; Ipiranga Comercial Quimica S.A.; Sanofi-Aventis; L'Oreal S.A.; Natura Cosmeticos S.A.; Colgate-Palmolive Co.; Yves Rocher S.A.

FURTHER READING

"Alès Group USA Inc. Acquires Jean Louis Renaud Inc.," *Soap & Cosmetics,* June 2001, p. 11.

"Alès Investment to Double Capacity," *Cosmetics International,* November 10, 2002, p. 7.

Alès, Patrick, *Le Tchô—Demain viendra toujours,* Paris: Cherche Midi, 2004.

Edgar, Michelle, "Phyto: Caring for the Scalp," *WWD,* May 19, 2006, p. 8.

"Grand Opening," *WWD,* November 8, 1996, p. 8.

Kintish, Lisa, "Seeds of Success," *Soap & Cosmetics,* June 1999, p. 48.

Naughton, Julie, "An Ambitious Fall Lineup for Alès," *WWD,* July 30, 1999, p. 10.

Alienware Corporation

14591 Southwest 120th Street
Miami, Florida 33186
U.S.A.
Telephone: (305) 251-9797
Toll Free: (800) 254-3692
Fax: (305) 259-9874
Web site: http://www.alienware.com

Wholly Owned Subsidiary of Dell, Inc.
Incorporated: 1996
Employees: 504
Sales: $172 million (2005 est.)
NAIC: 334111 Electronic Computer Manufacturing;
334310 Audio and Video Equipment Manufacturing

■ ■ ■

Alienware Corporation manufactures high-performance computer systems designed primarily for video gaming enthusiasts. The company sells its computer systems mainly under the brand names "Area-51," "Aurora," "ALX," and "Lightspeed." Systems range in price from $799 to more than $9,000, averaging between $3,000 and $4,000. Alienware sells its products through its web site to customers in North America, Europe, Australia, and New Zealand, and at a company-owned retail store in Miami, Florida. A stand-alone subsidiary of Dell, Inc., Alienware builds its systems by hand using the most advanced computer components available on the market.

ORIGINS

When Alex Aguila and Nelson Gonzalez founded Alienware in 1996, their business strategy bucked conventional wisdom. The same held true ten years later, but the financial success of their company offered a compelling rebuttal to conventional wisdom and all the naysayers who had scoffed at their chances of survival. Aguila and Gonzalez grew up together in the Miami area, sharing a passion for playing video games that served as the inspiration for their entrepreneurial careers. While they were in high school, the pair spent hours taking apart computers and rebuilding them to handle the demands of resource-hungry video games. Gonzalez had a particular fondness for flight-simulation games, and one in particular, "Falcon 3.0," drove him to start his own company. Gonzalez, using a personal computer (PC) with an Intel 386 microprocessor, needed to install a math coprocessor to play the game, an electronic makeover that directly led to the formation of Alienware. "That's the game," Gonzalez reflected in a March 26, 2006 interview with *Business Week Online*, "that pushed me to say to myself, 'There's gotta be people out there who want machines outfitted to play these games.'"

Gonzalez and Aguila formed Alienware in 1996, convinced there was a market for custom-built, high-performance computers. Gonzalez, 30 years old at the time, was employed as an information technology manager at a small post-production company. Aguila, two years Gonzalez's junior, was working as a medical technician. After years of having to upgrade motherboards, microprocessors, and graphics cards, they both envisioned a consumer need for the same kind of PCs they desired. As gamers themselves, they knew their target customer, but others were unconvinced. The PC market in 1996, as it would be ten years later, was regarded as a low-profit-margin business. Major manufacturers vied for market share by churning out computers by the millions, competing as high-volume producers in a market of ever-declining prices. Gonzalez and Aguila, in the months before desktop PCs were given away as incentives for signing up for Internet service, devised an entirely new business model for Alienware, a name chosen because of Gonzalez's interest in UFOs, science fiction, and the television series *The X Files.* They intended to market PCs as luxury items, not commodities, but they quickly butted against the prevailing perception of what would work in the computer market when they approached bankers and attempted to secure capital for their start-up venture. "Everyone told us, 'This is insane,'" Aguila said in a March 2005 interview with *Entrepreneur.* "We got laughed out of every bank in Miami."

Undeterred by the response to their business idea, Gonzalez and Aguila pooled their savings and relied on their credit cards to come up with the $13,000 they used to launch Alienware. The pair used Gonzalez's garage in Hialeah, a city in the Miami metropolitan area, as Alienware's headquarters. Eventually, they hoped to sell 50 computers per month, perhaps as many as 100 per month, but their initial focus was basic. They at least had to recoup the $13,000 and pay off their credit cards, whose spending limits quickly were reached. They relied on friends and acquaintances from Miami's gaming community at first to sustain their modest operations, barely covering expenses during their first months in business. To reach their upper target of selling 100 computers per month, Gonzalez, who served as chief executive officer, and Aguila, who served as president, needed to earn the respect and the business of the hard-core gamers, the typically young males who would become Alienware's lifeblood.

INDUSTRY RECOGNITION IN 1998

Gonzalez and Aguila knew that the most effective way to develop a reputation was to draw praise from the most prominent gaming magazines, which represented the principal source of information for gaming enthusiasts. In 1997, they sent a complete computer system to *Maximum PC,* regarded as one of the harshest critics of computer hardware. The system, featuring cutting-edge hardware in a black tower emblazoned with the caricature of an alien head, earned a positive review. The publicity failed to inundate Gonzalez's garage with requests for custom-built systems, but it lent legitimacy to the Alienware name. The following year, Gonzalez and Aguila sent another system under the "Area 51" brand to *PC Gamer,* calculating how many more days they could survive without a substantial influx of orders. *PC Gamer* gave Alienware's Area 51 system its esteemed Editor's Choice award for 1998. The editor of the magazine, reportedly, did not want to return Alienware's high-powered system.

"Validation from the industry was great," Gonzalez remembered in a September 21, 2000, interview with the *Miami Herald.* Earning the highest praise from one of the industry's most influential publications gave Alienware all the attention it needed to land a wealth of business. The two partners treated the opportunity presented to them wisely, employing a business model that would prove to be more than financially viable. They employed a direct-sales model, borrowing the example set by Dell, Inc., on its way to becoming the largest computer manufacturer in the world. Having eliminated dealing with retailers by adopting a direct-sales approach, the founders next insisted on payment upfront, freeing them from underwriting receivables and depreciating inventory. To sell its high-priced systems, Gonzalez and Aguila relied on Alienware's web site solely, paying assiduous attention to the company's only distribution channel. Customers who purchased an Alienware system received a manual with their name printed on the front cover. Customer support was available seven days a week, 24 hours a day from Alienware employees, not subcontractors. By keeping a tight control over spending, using just-in-time inventory, and attending to the needs of their customers, Gonzalez and Aguila presided over a financially healthy business. The foundation was set to support growth, which followed at an electric pace.

Of the two founders, Gonzalez possessed the greater knowledge about hardware, the building blocks of Alienware's blazingly fast systems. During its first few years in business, the company benefited from important relationships that were established with leading hardware and software manufacturers. Because of its close ties to those defining the technological vanguard of the computer industry, Alienware received favored treatment, often becoming one of the first vendors to try the latest, fastest components developed by the industry's

KEY DATES
∎

1996: Alienware is founded by Nelson Gonzalez and Alex Aguila.

1998: *PC Gamer* selects Alienware's Area 51 system for its "Editor's Choice" award.

2002: Alienware introduces the Area 51m, a notebook computer capable of running graphically intensive software.

2004: Alienware launches its super-premium ALX line.

2006: Alienware is acquired by Dell, Inc.

elite manufacturers. The company's access to state-of-the-art technology translated into exceptional systems that gamers clamored for, strengthening the company's reputation in the market with each technological advancement. The leading-edge components of Alienware's systems were on display in the company's growing roster of products offerings, which were offered in metallic colors (Nova Yellow, Plasma Purple, Saucer Silver, Conspiracy Blue, Cyborg Green, and Martian Red) for the first time in 2000. By 2000, after garnering three consecutive Editor's Choice awards from *PC Gamer,* an average Alienware system featured a 1.1 gigahertz (GHz) processor, a 40 gigabyte (GB) hard drive, 256 megabytes (MB) of memory, and two video cards. The system sold for $3,227. Sales were expected to reach $8.5 million for the year, as Gonzalez and Aguila, initially hoping for a monthly production volume of between 50 and 100 units, presided over a company with 40 employees who were custom-building 400 units per month. Ahead, much growth was anticipated, as the company planned to add notebooks, workstations, and servers to its product mix. Revenues in 2001 reached $28 million.

The first years of the 21st century saw Alienware record explosive growth, quieting any of the remaining skeptics who questioned viability of selling high-priced products in a low-margin, commodity industry. As orders flowed in, the company experimented with opening up other distribution channels, straying from relying exclusively on its web site for the first time. In December 2001, the company signed a contract with the massive retail chain Best Buy Co., Inc. Under the terms of the agreement Best Buy began offering Alienware products, beginning with the Area 51 2.0 GHz and 1.6 GHz systems, but Alienware ended its involvement with the retailer within a year and returned to using its web site and a direct-sales approach. Demonstration systems were

put on a display at a number of retailers, however, including Electronic Boutique outlets across the nation.

Innovations, market diversification, and new brands highlighted Alienware's progress as it headed toward its tenth anniversary. In 2002, the company introduced the first notebook computer capable of running resource-demanding games. The 11-pound Area 51m featured a 2.4 GHz Pentium 4 processor, 512 MB of memory, a 40 GB hard drive, and a 64 MB video card, retailing for approximately $3,000. In 2003, a new line of custom-built workstations debuted for professional customers, followed by the introduction of two new brands in 2004, "ALX" and "Lightspeed." The ALX brand took the company's affinity for high-performance to the extreme, symbolizing the highest standards in performance. ALX systems featured liquid-cooling technology and state-of-the-art hardware, with a fully customized system selling for more than $9,000. At the other end of the price scale, the Lightspeed brand offered gaming configurations for those on a budget.

DELL ACQUISITION IN 2006

Alienware ranked as one of the fastest-growing private companies in the United States by 2005. Revenues reached $112 million in 2004 and leaped to $172 million in 2005, the year the company opened its first retail store in a Miami mall. Fueled by the ever increasing sales of its gaming equipment and new streams of revenue coming from corporate and government sales, the company's growth put Gonzalez and Aguila at a crossroads on the eve of their tenth anniversary. They needed capital to expand, which meant they needed either to take Alienware public to raise the necessary funds or sell the company to a larger rival. The founders opted for the latter in 2006, agreeing to sell their company to the largest computer manufacturer in the world, Dell, Inc.

For Dell, which had revamped its XPS line in 2001 to feature high-powered components, the acquisition of Alienware complemented its foray into the high end of the market. For Gonzalez and Aguila, the deal, which was completed for an undisclosed price, offered access to Dell's distribution system and the benefits of having a deep-pocketed parent company, all without ceding control over their company. The Alienware brand would continue to exist under Dell's ownership, the company's headquarters would remain in place, and Gonzalez and Aguila would continue to lead the company. "I'm very satisfied because we were able to agree that the best way to make this work was to have an autonomous position," Gonzalez said in a March 23, 2006, interview with the *Miami Herald.* "That makes sense for us and our employees." A Dell spokesperson in the same interview confirmed the company's intention to treat Alienware as an independent company, saying, "We certainly don't plan to go in there and really change anything because we recognize that they're successful and why they're still successful."

In the wake of the acquisition, Alienware embarked on its second decade of business, beginning a new era of existence as it tried to remain true to its loyal customer base. One risk of the Dell-Alienware combination was the potential that gaming enthusiasts, who accounted for 80 percent of Alienware's revenues, would be disaffected by the move into the mainstream, but Gonzalez and Aguila remained confident that they would be supplying hard-core gamers with cutting-edge systems for years to come.

Jeffrey L. Covell

PRINCIPAL DIVISIONS

Alienware Technology.

PRINCIPAL COMPETITORS

Voodoo Computers Ltd.; Falcon Northwest Computer Systems, Inc.; Hewlett-Packard Company.

FURTHER READING

Boodhoo, Niala, "Dell Agrees to Buy Alienware," *Miami Herald,* March 23, 2006.

"Can Alienware Keep Its Cool?," *Business Week Online,* March 24, 2006.

"Dell Goes High-End and Hip," *Business Week Online,* March 23, 2006.

Garcia, Beatrice E., "Dade County, Fla., Company Builds Powerful Computer Systems," *Miami Herald,* September 21, 2000.

Hogan, Mike, "The Outer Limits," *Entrepreneur,* March 2005, p. 42.

Mainelli, Tom, "A (Mostly) Mobile Gaming Laptop," *PC World,* September 2002, p. 74.

Martinez, Ani, "Alienware Founders Open Dadeland Mall Kiosk," *Miami Herald,* December 10, 2005.

Miracle, Barbara, "Games People Play," *Florida Trend,* July 2002, p. 74.

Pain, John, "Alienware Racks Up Gamers, and Millions," *America's Intelligence Wire,* March 13, 2006.

———, "Dell to Buy High-End PC Maker Alienware," *America's Intelligence Wire,* March 23, 2006.

Alliance Resource Partners, L.P.

1717 S. Boulder Avenue
Suite 600
Tulsa, Oklahoma 74119
U.S.A.
Telephone: (918) 295-7600
Fax: (918) 295-7358
Web site: http://www.arlp.com

Public Company
Founded: 1973 as MAPCO Coal Inc.
Employees: 2,300
Sales: $838.7 million (2005)
Stock Exchanges: NASDAQ
Ticker Symbol: ARLP
NAIC: 212111 Bituminous Coal and Lignite Surface
   Mining

■ ■ ■

With its headquarters located in Tulsa, Oklahoma, Alliance Resource Partners, L.P. is the coal industry's only publicly traded master limited partnership, its units listed on the NASDAQ. It has greatly benefited from renewed interest in coal as a power-generation fuel, especially in light of rising oil prices. The partnership's operating holding company, Alliance Coal, is the fifth largest producer of coal in the United States, producing more than 20 million tons each year from seven mining complexes in Kentucky, Indiana, Illinois, and Maryland. More than half of Alliance's steam coal is high-sulfur in content, 30 percent is low-sulfur, and about 15 percent is medium-sulfur. The company has significantly more than 500 million tons of coal reserves. Alliance serves industrial customers but mostly eastern U.S. electric utilities, such as the Tennessee Valley Authority, Virginia Power, and Florida's Seminole Power. The company also operates a major coal loading terminal on the Ohio River at Mt. Vernon, Indiana.

ORIGINS DATING TO 1971

Alliance grew out of the coal mines acquired by MAPCO Inc. in 1971. A dozen years earlier, MAPCO had been formed as the Mid-Continent Eastern Pipeline Co. by Skelly Oil Co. with financial backing from Prudential Insurance Company of America. The Tulsa, Oklahoma-based company started out with the idea of delivering propane from Texas to the Northeast, but soon realized there was greater demand for liquefied petroleum gas in the Midwest farm belt and changed course. It took the name MAPCO in 1968 and began expanding into other energy fields, adding an anhydrous ammonia pipeline, the first in the United States and another way to serve the farmers who bought the company's liquefied gas, and eventually becoming involved in refining and marketing. In 1971 MAPCO used 500,000 shares of stock to buy its first coal mine, the underground Dotiki mine in the Illinois Basin section of Kentucky owned by the Webster County Coal Company. This operation, originally opened in 1966, was soon thriving, turning into one of the country's most productive mines. Its success led MAPCO to begin the development of surface mining operations in Martin County, Kentucky, and the formation of MAPCO Coal in 1973. Martin County's Pontiki underground mine commenced operations in 1977. In that same year, MAPCO Coal began operating

COMPANY PERSPECTIVES

Alliance Resource Partners, L.P. (ARLP) is a diversified coal producer and marketer with significant operations in the eastern United States. The company is the coal-producing industry's only publicly traded master limited partnership.

the underground longwall Mettiki mining complex in Garrett County, Maryland. Then, in 1980, another Illinois Basin underground mine, the Pattiki mine, was opened in White County, Kentucky.

Due to environmental concerns, coal fell out of favor as a source of fuel for power generation in the mid-1970s, putting an end to MAPCO Coal's early growth spurt. In the 1980s MAPCO Coal was just a minor part of MAPCO's business, which included refinery sales, home heating oil, and retail gas, diesel, grocery, and fast food sales. Alliance's longtime chief executive, Joseph W. Craft III, was named president of MAPCO Coal in 1986. With a Bachelor of Science degree in accounting and a law degree, both from the University of Kentucky, Craft worked as an attorney for Falcon Coal Corporation and Diamond Shamrock Coal Corporation before joining MAPCO, where he served as general counsel and chief financial officer. Under Craft's leadership, MAPCO Coal began to add assets to position itself when market conditions for coal improved. In early 1989 the Pontiki mine added reserves by purchasing a nearby inactive mine, and MAPCO Coal also acquired another dormant operation in Kentucky, the Scotts Branch mine, folding it into a subsidiary called MC Mining Inc. Later in the year, the company acquired most of the assets of Baltimore, Maryland-based JNO McCall Coal Company, which included four mining complexes producing a total of 5.8 million tons each year and holding reserves of some 56 million tons of steam and metallurgical coal. As a result, MAPCO Coal emerged as one of the largest coal producers in the eastern United States at the end of the 1980s.

IMPACT OF 1990 CLEAN AIR ACT

The 1990 Clean Air Act required coal-fired utilities to cut back on their emissions, creating strong demand for the kind of low-sulfur coal MAPCO Coal mined at its Martiki complex. In 1994 MAPCO Coal launched a major, $30 million expansion of this surface operation, extending the life of the mine by adding a new 56-cubic-yard shovel and five 240-ton trucks, used to es-

sentially level a mountain piecemeal. Such practices were controversial, of course, and in answer MAPCO Coal was already participating in a reclamation program with Morehead State University to turn a strip-mined mountain top into a farm. Although the project won an award in 1991 for Excellence in Surface Mining and Reclamation from the Interior Department, the farm never made money, and in 1994 MAPCO Coal began shopping the property.

By this time, however, the parent company was considering ways to exit the coal business, which was one of the slower growth segments of its business. In 1996 MAPCO Coal's management, led by Craft, formed Alliance Coal L.L.C., and then with the financial backing of Beacon Group Energy Investment Fund L.P. bought a 75 percent interest in MAPCO Coal for $232.5 million. MAPCO Inc. elected to retain a minority interest, in this way sharing in the growth Alliance expected to achieve as an independent company when it was able to chart its own future, backed by a deep-pocketed investor. Beacon Group Energy was a $658 million investment fund focused on the energy sector, affiliated with the private New York investment firm, the Beacon Group. One of the firm's partners, Preston R. Miller, Jr., explained to *Coal Week* the attraction of the MAPCO coal assets: "Today's consolidating coal industry holds tremendous opportunities and synergies that can be gained through combinations of existing coal operations. Combined with the utility industry deregulation movement, now is the right time, and MAPCO Coal has the right people on which to build a strong, solid energy company."

Although Alliance's management said it would pursue an aggressive growth policy, it did not become a significant consolidator. Rather, it grew at a steady pace. Following the buyout, the company reopened the shuttered Scotts Branch mine acquired several years earlier by the MC Mining unit. Next, in January 1998, Alliance paid $7.3 million in cash for Hopkins County Coal, a Kentucky complex in the Illinois Basin that included both underground and surface operations. Alliance also explored the possibility of expanding to the west and actually signed a preliminary agreement to acquire the coal business of the Atlantic Richfield Company, which included mines in Wyoming, Utah, and Colorado. If that deal had been completed, Alliance would have become the second largest coal operator in the United States, but instead the assets were purchased by Arch Coal for more than $1.1 billion. Nevertheless, because of its increased production, Alliance at the end of 1998 became the sixth largest coal producer in the eastern United States, mining more than 15 million tons of coal that year.

KEY DATES

1971: MAPCO Inc. acquires the Dotiki mine.
1973: MAPCO Coal Inc. is formed.
1986: Joseph W. Craft is named president.
1996: MAPCO Coal becomes Alliance Coal in a management buyout.
1999: Alliance is taken public as Alliance Resource Partners, L.P.
2003: A secondary offering is made to finance the purchase of Warrior Coal, L.L.C.

IPO: 1999

In 1999 Alliance became a public company, the only one in the coal industry, when in May of that year Alliance Resource Partners, L.P. was formed as a publicly traded master limited partnership. It subsequently acquired Alliance Coal, and in August made an initial public offering (IPO) of units, priced at $19 each, raising $147.3 million. The units then began trading on the NASDAQ. Alliance put some of those proceeds to use in late 1999 by starting to develop a new underground mining complex located in Gibson County, Indiana. The company's seventh mining operation went into production in November 2000.

Conditions were challenging for Alliance during its first full year as a public company. The year began with a warmer than usual winter and high coal inventories, leading to low coal prices, but by the end of the year California had undergone a severe energy crisis, and coal became part of the debate about a new national energy policy. Moreover, the eastern United States experienced record cold weather at the end of the year, boosting immediate coal sales. In 2000 Alliance recorded coal sales of $347.2 million, a modest increase over the $345.9 million of 1999. Total revenues dipped to $363.5 million in 2000 compared with $365.9 million, due to a loss in transportation revenues, but net income more than doubled, from $7.6 million in 1999 to $15.6 million in 2000.

The balance sheet grew even healthier in 2001 and 2002 as revenues jumped to $446.3 million in 2001 and $517.7 million in 2002. The improvement in earnings was even more dramatic, as Alliance netted $17.1 million in 2001 and $36.3 million in 2002—this accomplished in spite of a poor national economy. (Also of note in 2002, Alliance bought out the interests of Beacon Group Funds.) Alliance benefited from increasing gas prices in the previous two years. Furthermore, the Bush administration eased up on environmental codes, providing power plants with an incentive to burn more coal, and resulting in a surge in coal mining activity. For its part, Alliance began extending the Pattiki mine into a nearby coal reserve area and began digging a new mine shaft at the Dotiki mine.

In February 2003, Alliance made another public offering, selling 2.25 million common units priced at $22.51 each, netting more than $48 million. The money was earmarked to purchase Warrior Coal, L.L.C., as well as to provide working capital and cash for general partnership purposes. Warrior Coal operated the underground Cardinal mine, located in Hopkins County, Kentucky, and in operation since 1985. Warrior produced high-sulfur coal, most of which would be sold to Synfuel Solutions Operating, L.L.C., a maker of a synthetic fuel using coal fins and a binder material. In April 2003 Synfuel moved its production facility to Warrior in order to use the coal produced at Cardinal as a feedstock. For the year 2003, Alliance reported more record results. Revenues increased to $542.7 million and net income to $47.9 million.

Alliance continued to increase coal production in 2004, but in February the company had to contend with a fire at the Dotiki mine, which took almost a month to extinguish. Although no one was injured, the mine was put out of operation for several weeks. Insurance at least paid the company $27 million for lost production and damages. At the end of the year, over the Christmas holiday, another fire occurred at MC Mining's Excel mine, resulting in a several-week shutdown of that operation as well. A more positive development in 2004 for Alliance came in October when the company entered into a pair of coal leases that together added 100 million tons of high-sulfur coal reserves. The Elk Creek reserves were located in Hopkins County, while the Tunnel Ridge reserves were spread between West Virginia and Pennsylvania.

Once again, Alliance posted record results in 2004. Revenues improved to $653.3 million and net income totaled $76.6 million. The company continued to grow in 2005. Through subsidiary Penn Ridge Coal, Alliance added another 25 million tons to its reserves in the Tunnel Ridge area, and demand for coal remained quite high. For the fifth consecutive year Alliance enjoyed record results, as revenues surged to $838.7 million and net income reached $160 million. In 2006 the company added nearly 100 million tons of high sulfur coal reserves in Union County, Kentucky, through the purchase of River View Coal, L.L.C. Strong sales and earnings continued in the first quarter of 2006.

Ed Dinger

PRINCIPAL SUBSIDIARIES

Alliance Resource Operating Partners, L.P.; Excel Mining, L.L.C.; Gibson County Coal, L.L.C.; Hopkins County Coal L.L.C.; MC Mining, L.L.C.; Mettiki Coal, L.L.C.; Mt. Vernon Transfer Terminal, L.L.C.; Pontiki Coal, L.L.C.; Warrior Coal, L.L.C.; Webster County Coal, L.L.C.; White County Coal, L.L.C.

PRINCIPAL COMPETITORS

Arch Coal, Inc.; CONSOL Energy Inc.; Peabody Energy Corporation.

FURTHER READING

"MAPCO Will Sell Major Share of Coal Operations to Beacon," *Coal Week,* January 22, 1996, p. 2.

Monies, Paul, "Alliance Resource Partners Raises Coal Production," *Daily Oklahoman,* November 7, 2004.

"Tulsa-Based Alliance Resource Partners Plots Coal Developments," *Journal Record* (Oklahoma City, Okla.), October 25, 2004.

Tuttle, Ray, "Mapco Sells 75 Percent Stake in Coal," *Tulsa World,* January 16, 1996, p. E1.

"Twists and Turns Part of MAPCO," *Tulsa World,* November 25, 1997, p. E1.

Wiley, Elizabeth Camacho, "Tulsa, Okla.-Based Coal Manufacturer Hopes Cold Forecast Heats Up Sales," *Daily Oklahoman,* November 3, 2002.

Wilmoth, Adam, "Coal Fuels Sales Volume for Tulsa, Okla.-Based Alliance Resource Partners," *Daily Oklahoman,* November 2, 2003.

American Science & Engineering, Inc.

829 Middlesex Turnpike
Billerica, Massachusetts 01821
U.S.A.
Telephone: (978) 262-8700
Toll Free: (800) 225-1608
Fax: (978) 262-8804
Web site: http://www.as-e.com

Public Company
Incorporated: 1958
Employees: 286
Sales: $163.6 million (2006)
Stock Exchanges: NASDAQ
Ticker Symbol: ASEI
NAIC: 334517 Irradiation Apparatus Manufacturing

■ ■ ■

American Science & Engineering, Inc. (AS&E) is a Boston-area company that develops, manufactures, and markets X-ray inspection systems, as well as providing maintenance and training services. The systems are used around the world at border crossings, ports, airports, military bases, and corporate and government mailrooms to help combat terrorism, illegal immigration, and drug and weapon smuggling. AS&E's product lines include ParcelSearch, featuring a small tunnel system used to inspect mail and luggage, as well as larger, open-tunnel systems to screen larger bags and small cargo. The CargoSearch line is used to inspect palletized cargo, air and sea cargo containers, and vehicles. It can also be outfitted with Radioactive Threat Detection technology. The

company's SmartCheck system is used to inspect people for both metal and nonmetal contraband, including drugs, weapons, and explosives. Key to AS&E systems is the company's patented Z Backscatter technology, which detects and highlights items that contain low atomic number elements, so-called "low Z" materials, such as carbon, hydrogen, oxygen, and nitrogen, found in plastic weapons, explosives, and drugs. Z Backscatter also detects "high Z" materials such as metal weapons. As a result, AS&E systems are able to simultaneously screen for both metal and nonmetal materials. A key element of Z Backscatter systems is the company's patented Flying Spot technology, which instead of the fanlike beam of traditional X-ray systems relies on a more narrow, focused beam. Separate detectors can then translate the information on a pair of television monitors, one showing low-Z materials and the other high-Z materials. It also produces photo-like images and emits low amounts of radiation. Major customers for AS&E include the Department of Homeland Security and the military. AS&E is a public company listed on the NASDAQ.

COMPANY'S FOUNDING IN 1958

AS&E was founded in Cambridge, Massachusetts, in 1958 by 36-year-old Dr. Martin Annis, who had earned a Ph.D. from the Massachusetts Institute of Technology seven years earlier. After teaching for four years, he became the head of physical science at Allied Research in Boston, doing Department of Defense contract research on the effects of nuclear explosions. Following a disagreement with management, he struck out on his own. With the help of MIT professor of physics George W. Clark, a friend and former graduate school colleague,

COMPANY PERSPECTIVES

AS&E specializes in detection technologies that can uncover dangerous and elusive threats, including explosives, plastic and metal weapons, and radioactive devices, such as dirty bombs and nuclear WMD. These X-ray systems are deployed worldwide at ports and borders, and military and high-threat facilities.

who served as a consultant as well as an investor, Annis set up a private research firm he called American Science & Engineering. Other initial investors were chemist Carolus M. Cobb, accountant H. S. Richardson, Jr., and Sol Horwitz, general manager of Boston's West End Iron Works. Together they collected $100,000 in funds and set up operations in a three-room office located above a bank in Cambridge, Massachusetts. The company started out with a Department of Defense contract similar to what Annis had done at Allied Research, investigating the effects of a nuclear explosion above the atmosphere. The business had come through the Air Force Cambridge Research Laboratory (AFCRL), which had funded his previous work and had been pleased with his results.

Annis would soon convince Bruno Rossi, an MIT professor of physics who had once taught Annis, to serve as chairman and AS&E chief scientific adviser. Rossi had been one of the scientists involved in the Manhattan Project, which resulted in the world's first nuclear weapon. He was eager to steer the company away from defense contracts and suggested AS&E develop and produce high school physics kits to accompany the curriculum that was being developed at MIT at the time. Rossi himself had written part of the program's textbook. Through his influence, AS&E was able to secure a deal to produce the kits that would be distributed across the country by the McGraw-Hill Book Company. As a result, AS&E moved to larger accommodations.

Rossi would also have another idea for AS&E, one that would have longer term implications for the company and the field of physics in general. While flying home from a conference, Rossi received a major insight about the soft X-ray portion of the spectrum, which he became convinced could provide a window into the universe to reveal things never before known. Because MIT's Cosmic Ray Group was too busy to pursue this new avenue of inquiry, Rossi turned to Annis and convinced him to have AS&E conduct research

on large-area X-ray detectors and pursue ways to focus soft X-rays, thus laying the foundation for X-ray astronomy. Annis was eager to find non-defense-related research projects and agreed to pursue Rossi's idea. He further suggested that the man to implement such an idea was Riccardo Giacconi, an Italian-born physicist.

In 1959, Giacconi joined AS&E and created an X-ray astronomy team. For the next 14 years, Giacconi's team made a succession of pioneering discoveries and developments in the field of X-ray technology. Giacconi left AS&E in 1973

Even without Giacconi, AS&E continued to make key scientific advances. In 1978 it launched the NASA-funded Einstein Observatory, the largest X-ray telescope in the world. A year later the company designed a special X-ray telescope for NASA, used to study the sun and planets. During the 1980s, AS&E was also looking for the commercial success that came from applied research activities. In 1973 the company patented its Flying Spot technology, which was then employed to develop precursors to the company's present-day line of X-ray screening systems. During the 1970s AS&E became involved in electric utility loan management research. The latter resulted in the 1976 introduction of ASEP, a system that allowed utilities to automatically conduct remote meter reading. ASEP would become a major source of revenues for AS&E through the 1980s. The first personnel X-ray inspection system, called MICRO-DOSE, was introduced in 1977. A year later the company received funding from Pfizer Medical Systems to develop a Medical Micro-Dose system.

GOING PUBLIC IN 1975

AS&E also became a public company in 1975 and gained a listing on the American Stock Exchange. Filings with the Securities and Exchange Commission indicate that AS&E was involved in some ventures that did not pan out. In 1970, for example, it acquired Package House, Inc. of Clifton, New Jersey, a business that was discontinued ten years later. In 1975 American Science & Engineering International Inc. was formed, only to be dissolved in 1986. Furthermore, the filings indicate that AS&E sold an Education Division in 1979.

AS&E introduced the MICRO-DOSE X-Ray System Model 130, used to screen carry-on luggage at airports, and the multipurpose Model 122, used to inspect luggage and parcels. Other versions of the system soon followed, the Model 50 to inspect letters and small parcels, and the Model 100 for large parcels and baggage inspection. In 1985 revenues totaled $22.5 million.

In 1986 AS&E unveiled its Z series of X-ray systems using flying spot technology, receiving a good deal of

KEY DATES

1958: The company is founded by Martin Annis.
1959: Dr. Riccardo Giacconi heads the Ex-ray astronomy team.
1973: Giacconi leaves the company.
1975: The company is taken public.
1986: Z Backscatter technology is introduced.
1993: Annis is ousted as CEO and chairman.
2002: Giacconi wins the Nobel Prize.
2005: The company gains a NASDAQ listing.

attention. *Fortune* magazine, for example, profiled the $55,000 Z system, which it said could detect the Glock 17 pistol, mostly constructed of plastic and "the latest terrorist weapon to menace air travelers around the world." Explaining how the new system worked, *Fortune*'s Eleanor Johnson Tracy wrote that as the flying spot "beam strikes the suitcase, separate detectors display different images simultaneously on two television monitors. One screen shows the high-density materials—for example, a radio and a traveling case. The other reveals the plastic handle of a Glock 17 hidden beside the radio."

AS&E continued to conduct aerospace research in the 1980s. In 1983 it won a contract to build an inspection system for the Trident D-5 solid rocket motors, and in 1984 it teamed up with the Harvard Smithsonian Center for Astrophysics to develop a high-resolution X-ray image detector, which NASA would choose as its contribution to the ROSAT, a German X-ray astronomy satellite. However, with reductions in NASA's budget and the end of the Cold War, which resulted in defense department cutbacks, AS&E became increasingly dependent on its commercial X-ray screening products, used to fight smuggling and terrorism. Despite having the Federal Aviation Administration ordering 40 airports to install AS&E systems to screen luggage, AS&E was struggling at the start of the 1990s. In May 1990 the company was forced to implement a number of cost containment measures, including a 10 percent reduction in staff.

AS&E experienced mixed results in the first half of the 1990s. On the one hand, it achieved a number of successes. In 1990 the company unveiled the predecessor to the CargoSearch product line with the "TOSI" X-ray Inspection System, first used by the U.S. government to ensure the Soviet Union was in compliance with the Intermediate-Range Nuclear Forces (INF) Treaty by screen missiles loaded on Russian railcars. A narcotics-

detection system was introduced in 1992 and was purchased by U.S. Customs, and a year later several new products were put on the market, including Cargo-Search, BodySearch, MailSearch, and LobbySearch. Moreover, in 1994 AS&E won a contract from the Advanced Research Projects Agency to develop the MobileSearch systems, which would be used at the Mexico border to detect both narcotics and illegal immigrants. However, this period would also bring financial difficulties, due to a struggling economy, and controversy involving its founder.

OUSTING THE FOUNDER IN 1993

Annis, who had served as president since the beginning added a new title, chief executive officer, in April 1993. The board over which he presided as chairman also was increased in size to seven, and just four months later, in July 1993, that board terminated his employment. According to a Securities and Exchange Commission (SEC) filing, this action was taken "on the basis of information received indicating that [Annis] had been engaging in activities that were incompatible with his status as an officer and employee of the Company." Annis sued the company and its directors, alleging wrongful termination of employment. A trial was held and when it was concluded in April 1995 a jury determined that Annis had materially breached his fiduciary duty to AS&E. As a result, the company was found to be justified in terminating his employment. Annis continued to feud with his former company, however. In addition to unsuccessfully appealing the 1995 decision, he would be accused of passing along trade secrets to AS&E rival EG&G Inc. He also formed a new X-ray technology company, Annistech, and he and AS&E engaged in litigation over the ownership rights of certain technology. This matter was settled in June 1997. AS&E's rights were affirmed and it also gained rights to some ongoing developments by Annis, although it agreed to license back the technology to Annistech.

Replacing Annis at AS&E in September 1993 was Ralph S. Sheridan, who for the past four years had been operating his own Massachusetts consulting and investment firm. A graduate of Ohio State University, he held a bachelor's degree in chemistry and an M.B.A., and had executive experience at Combustion Engineering, Inc. and HEC Energy Corp. He initiated a turnaround strategy that caused pain in the short run. Sales dropped from $19 million in 1993 to $11.2 million in 1994, but rebounded to $17.8 million in 1996 when the company returned to profitability. Sheridan took over a company that was a contract research house and a parcel X-ray company. Under his leadership, AS&E focused exclusively on providing X-ray imaging solutions, mostly catering to government agencies dealing with security, smuggling, and trade crime.

Further restructuring occurred in the second half of the 1990s, as the company increased its focus on dealing with the problems of drugs and weapons smuggling, terrorism, and trade fraud. Sales reached $28.5 million in 1997 and grew steadily over the next few years, due in large measure to overseas sales. In 1998 the company sold its first system to an international customer, located in the Middle East. Domestically, concern over illegal immigration spurred business as well, and the company's new back-scatter technology proved adept at the job. Sales increased to $57.3 million in 1999 and $60.7 million in 2000, as the company's international client base continued to expand, with systems sold in Abu Dhabi, Bahrain, Egypt, and South Africa.

The terrorist attacks on the United States on September 11, 2001, raised the profile of AS&E, as demand for security products increased dramatically. But, according to *Business Week,* "AS&E was left in the dust. The company's sky-high production costs forced it to price products at premiums many customers refused to pay. And AS&E had only one salesperson." Although sales increased to $67.1 million in 2001, AS&E recorded a profit of only $660,000. To make matters worse, at a time when the company should have been thriving, revenues dipped to $65.4 million in 2002 and $62 million in 2003, and the company lost about $12.5 million during that time.

In May 2003 Sheridan, after a decade at the helm, was removed as CEO. With the company on the verge of being sold, a new CEO was hired, Anthony Fabiano, the former president and chief operating officer at Minnesota-based Dispatch Industries, designer of industrial ovens and furnaces. He also served three years as a vice-president at another Minnesota company, aerospace and defense company Alliant TechSystems. He quickly assessed the problem at AS&E, telling *Business Week,* "We had these gee-whiz products and no way to get them into the marketplace." While building up the sales and marketing staff, he also brought in lean manufacturing practices that cut the production time on some systems from three months to as little as three weeks. Costs came down and the company was able to

competitively price its advanced systems. Moreover, AS&E was now better able to market its products more aggressively to target customers: law enforcement and the military. The company's stock was moved from the American Stock Exchange to the NASDAQ, providing greater visibility with investors. Revenues improved to $76.3 million in 2004 and the company turned a profit of more than $1.9 million. The following year, sales increased to $88.3 million and net income to $11.2 million, although $5.4 million of that total was the result of AS&E selling off its High Energy Systems division. Sales almost doubled in 2006 to $163.6 million and net income soared to $29.8 million. Lean and focused, the company appeared to be well positioned to enjoy even stronger growth in the years to come.

Ed Dinger

PRINCIPAL SUBSIDIARIES

AS&E Radiography Inc.

PRINCIPAL COMPETITORS

GE Infrastructure; OSI Systems, Inc.; Smiths Detection.

FURTHER READING

Bray, Hiawatha, "Billerica, Mass., Firm's X-Ray Technology Helps to Counter Terror Threats," *Boston Globe,* June 3, 2004.

Caffrey, Andrew, "Investors Respond to Firm's Breakthroughs," *Boston Globe,* May 17, 2005, p. 1.

Hawn, Carleen, "Yes, We Have No Illegals," *Forbes,* November 29, 1999, p. 144.

Kerber, Ross, "Share Price Doubles for American Science," *Boston Globe,* May 16, 2006.

O'Brien, Dan, "Anthony Fabiano Rights the Ship at American Science & Engineering," *Lowell Sun,* June 6, 2004.

Tracy, Eleanor Johnson, "A New X-Ray Scanner to Hinder Hijackers," *Fortune,* April 28, 1986, p. 146.

Weiner, Eric, "Terror Creates a Need: Better Bomb Detectors," *New York Times,* May 23, 1990, p. D7.

Weintraub, Arlene, "Its X-Ray Vision Uncovers the Naked Truth," *Business Week,* June 5, 2006, p. 58.

AngioDynamics, Inc.

603 Queensbury Avenue
Queensbury, New York 12804
U.S.A.
Telephone: (518) 798-1215
Toll Free: (800) 772-6446
Fax: (518) 798-3625
Web site: http://www.angiodynamics.com

Public Company
Founded: 1988
Employees: 257
Sales: $67.3 million (2005)
Stock Exchanges: NASDAQ
Ticker Symbol: ANGO
NAIC: 423450 Medical, Dental, and Hospital Equipment and Supplies Merchant Wholesalers

■ ■ ■

AngioDynamics, Inc. is a Queensbury, New York-based medical device company that specializes in products used in the treatment of peripheral vascular disease (PVD) and other noncoronary diseases. PVD is a narrowing of blood vessels that restricts blood flow in the arms and sometimes legs, a condition affecting some 11 million Americans. AngioDynamics designs and manufactures a variety of treatment products, including angiographic catheters, hemodialysis catheters, angioplasty catheters, drainage products, endovascular laser procedure products, image guided vascular access products to guide the placement of catheters, and thrombolytic catheter products used to deliver blood-clot dissolving agents. AngioDynamics relies on a direct sales force to market its products in the United States and a network of distributors to sell to more than 30 other countries. Spun off from E-Z-EM in 2004, AngioDynamics is a public company listed on the NASDAQ.

PARENT COMPANY ROOTS DATING TO 1959

AngioDynamics grew out of E-Z-EM, a company cofounded by Howard S. Stern, who would also cofound AngioDynamics. After earning a Bachelor of Chemical Engineering degree in 1953 and a Master of Science in Chemical Engineering in 1954 from the Massachusetts Institute of Technology, Stern served a stint in the U.S. Navy before landing a job as director of marketing at Radiation Applications Inc., a small New York City radiation applications company. At a dinner party in 1959 a conversation with radiologist Dr. Phillip H. Meyers led to the creation of E-Z-EM. Meyers told Stern of a problem he was having in giving barium enemas to patients about to have their lower intestines X-rayed. (Because it was a heavy element, the barium absorbed X-rays and helped to improve the picture definition and highlight possible problems.) The barium was delivered through a rectal tip attached to a bucket filled with barium, but patients often had to contend with contamination problems. Stern offered a simple yet profound solution: Package the barium in a bag, and make the entire enema disposable. Meyers was convinced the idea had merit and the two men teamed up to launch a business to provide disposable barium enemas.

With a 100-pound barrel of barium sulfate, sheets

COMPANY PERSPECTIVES

Innovation is our future ... the future of our industry, our company, our customers, and most importantly our family and friends.

AngioDynamics' primary focus is to offer an innovative and comprehensive product line for the interventional treatment of peripheral vascular disease (PVD) and other non-coronary diseases. We are dedicated to designing, developing, manufacturing and marketing high quality medical device products that meet the needs of today's interventionalists.

of plastic, and his mother's iron, Stern set to work developing prototypes, which he often hung on the shower curtain at home next to hand-washed pantyhose, a sight that caught the notice of guests. The greatest challenge Stern faced was mixing the barium and the water in the bag, but once he realized the two could be mixed in the bag by kneading and any lumps could be eliminated with a filter, he had a rudimentary kit ready in 1960. To make a truly commercial product he turned to an inflatable vinyl toy manufacturer who agreed to supply the custom bags, and a fishing lure manufacturer was contracted to provide the rectal tips. Unable to find a large company to represent the new product, and having lost his job at Radiation Applications, Stern decided to market the product himself. In 1962 he and Meyers each chipped in $1,000 and established E-Z-EM, setting up shop in a small room in a New York City loft where Stern's father ran a garment factory. Stern generally devoted his mornings to production, able to turn out 100 pre-packaged barium enema kits, while he spent the afternoons making sales calls and deliveries. He limited his overnight trips to such towns as Boston, Philadelphia, and Detroit, where he had friends willing to let him sleep on their couch. It was slow going at first, but sales soon began to pick up, and E-Z-EM turned a profit of $62,000 in the first year. Little of that went into Stern's pocket, however. He once told *Forbes* that in the first three years of the company's existence he made about $10,000.

When Stern learned that some radiologists were using barium sulfate in oral examinations, he also began selling the substance without the bags in different flavors. In 1964 he was able to move his operations to a new plant and later in the decade solidified his hold on the market by offering superior service, more than willing to provide radiologists with special orders. The market for

barium sulfate was not significant enough to attract the attention of large medical products companies, allowing E-Z-EM to dominant the niche, but it also limited Stern's growth potential. By the early 1980s the company was doing close to $30 million in annual sales and enjoying a healthy profit. Stern took E-Z-EM public and sought new opportunities in related fields to take advantage of his many contacts with radiologists. The company became involved in Nucleotome, a noninvasive device used to remove damaged spinal cartilage; PercuCut biopsy needles, used by radiologists to mark the location of breast lesions for surgical treatment; and Flexi-Therm, a thermographic system to detect pain and disease.

LAUNCH OF ANGIODYNAMICS IN 1988

Founded in 1988, AngioDynamics was part of this effort to diversify beyond barium sulfate. It began as a research and development division at E-Z-EM to produce medical plastics products for use in the fast-growing field of interventional radiology. Serving as point person was AngioDynamics' cofounder Eamonn P. Hobbs, who had expertise in the field.

Growing up in Springfield, Massachusetts, Hobbs was a top high school student whose high grades and SAT scores earned him full scholarships to schools such as Duke, Massachusetts Institute of Technology (MIT), and Stanford. Because of his dream of becoming an astronaut, however, he opted for the Air Force Academy, which he began attending shortly after high school graduation. He soon learned that he suffered from progressive astigmatism in his right eye, a condition that would prevent him from flying. Hobbs quit the Academy and returned home. Having lost his opportunity for a scholarship, Hobbs enrolled at the University of Lowell, an affordable school that a friend recommended. It was here that Hobbs earned a plastics engineering degree with a biomaterials emphasis. After graduating in 1980 he went to work at Indiana's Cook Incorporated, which produced cardiology and gastroenterology medical devices used by interventional radiologists. He went to work for E-Z-EM in 1985, but left a year later to launch his own company, Hobbs Medical Inc. After selling the business in 1988 he rejoined E-Z-EM to start a new medical plastics venture with Stern.

Hobbs set major goals for the new E-Z-EM division. In a 2005 interview with *Design News*, he said, "I had a five-year plan to be at $100 million." At the time, however, the Food and Drug Administration office began emphasizing its enforcement role in response to problems in the generic drug business. As a result, the approval process took much longer than expected and Hobbs's

KEY DATES

1962: E-Z-EM is founded.
1988: AngioDynamics is founded as the E-Z-EM research and development division.
1991: The first AngioDynamics products are introduced.
1992: A division is incorporated as A.D., Inc., an E-Z-EM subsidiary.
1996: A.D. becomes AngioDynamics, Inc.
2004: AngioDynamics is spun off as a public company.

business plan was trashed. "We had to scramble to make ends meet," he told *Design News.*

The division's first products were introduced under the AngioDynamics name in 1991: the ProInfusion Catheter, a part that created an even distribution of fluid in the company's line of Pulse*Spray Sets. A year later the business was organized as A.D., Inc., a wholly owned E-Z-EM subsidiary. It moved to its own Queensbury, New York facilities and hired the first sales reps. A second product also was put on the market in 1992: the SOFT VU line of Angiographic Catheters, featuring a soft radiopaque tip to reduce the possibility of blood vessel trauma and a high-torque shaft to improve vessel selection.

In 1996 A.D., Inc. changed its name to AngioDynamics, Inc., and Hobbs, who had been serving as vice-president, was named president and chief executive officer, with Stern acting as chairman. In that same year, the company introduced another new product, the Schon Chronic Angiographic Catheter. Several other products followed in the second half of the 1990s. There were three new offerings in 1997: the ANGIOPTIC Angiographic Catheter, featuring a self-dilating radiopaque tip; the OMNIFLUSH Angiographic Catheter, designed to protect against vessel wall injury; and the Pulse*Spray Injector, an automatic delivery system for thrombolytic agents. AngioDynamics released a pair of products in 1998: the Schon Acute Hemodialysis Catheter, kink resistant and featuring large side holes to reduce clotting and improve flow; and the UNI*FUSE Infusion Catheter, which employed the Flow Thru Hub and its self-adjusting occluding wire to minimize kinking and provide even distribution over longer clots. In 1999 AngioDynamics added three more products to its catalog: the ABCESSION General Drainage Catheter, which was able to recover its shape even if twisted or severely

bent; the ANGIOFLUSH III Contrast & Fluids Managements System; and the WORKHORSE PTA Balloon Catheter, used to inflate a peripheral blood vessel to improve blood flow.

AngioDynamics continued to introduce new products in the early 2000s, starting with the Micro Access Sets that provided physicians with a myriad of choices in creating an image-guided vascular access instrument (three different wires, five needle options, and three sheath dilator options). In 2001 the company introduced its Image-Guided Vascular Access Products, as well as the ABCESSION Biliary Drainage Catheter and the ACCU-VU Sizing Angiographic Catheter, which took further advantage of the company's OMNI-Flush technology. New products in 2002 included the highly durable Dura-Flow Chronic Hemodialysis Catheter, which made use of the HYDRO-TIP to allow for excellent flow rates even if the tip was pressed against a vessel wall; the Endovascular Laser Venous System (renamed two years later as VenaCure Laser Vein Treatment), a less painful alternative to surgical and chemical treatments for varicose veins; and the PVA Plus Embolic Therapy. In 2003 AngioDynamics introduced the AQUALiner Hydrophillic Guidewire, specially coated to reduce friction.

2002 EXPANSION PROGRAM

Business was so strong that in 2002 AngioDynamics launched a $3.5 million expansion program that more than doubled the size of the company's 26,000-square-foot facility to 58,000 square feet and led to the hiring of more than 200 employees over the next few years. Stern retired as E-Z-EM's and AngioDynamics' chairman in February 2004. Suffering from brain cancer, he died two years later, in January 2006. A month after Stern's retirement, E-Z-EM announced that it would spin off AngioDynamics in an initial public offering of stock underwritten by Adams Harkness & Hill Inc. of Boston and RBC Capital Markets of Toronto. The proceeds were earmarked to pay back a 1997 $3 million loan from E-Z-EM and provide working capital. The offering was held in May 2004 when 19.6 percent of the company's stock was sold, netting nearly $18 million for AngioDynamics. In October of that year the spinoff was completed when E-Z-EM distributed the remaining 80.4 percent of AngioDynamics stock as a dividend to its investors.

Now independent, AngioDynamics continued to grow at a strong pace. For the fiscal year that ended on May 29, 2004, the company reported sales of more than $49 million, a marked improvement over the $38.4 million of a year before. Net income also increased from $1.2 million to $3.1 million. The following year saw revenues top $60 million and net income exceed $4.5 million. Record sales and earnings continued into 2006 as the company remained committed to investment in research and development, resulting in the steady introduction of new products, such as the May 2006 launch of the MORPHEUS CT PICC Insertion Kit, a peripherally inserted central catheter (PICC) designed to be inserted at a patient's bedside rather than the hospital's interventional radiology suite where the procedure was usually done. To support its growth, AngioDynamics made plans for a secondary offering of stock in mid-2006.

Ed Dinger

PRINCIPAL SUBSIDIARIES

Leocor, Inc.

PRINCIPAL COMPETITORS

Boston Scientific Corporation; Cook Incorporated; Diomed Holdings, Inc.

FURTHER READING

Byrne, John A., "'Rear Admiral,'" *Forbes,* September 13, 1982, p. 74.

———, "Too Much Cash?," *Forbes,* May 21, 1984, p. 168.

Cochran, Thomas N., "The House That Barium Built," *Barron's,* February 22, 1988, p. 15.

Furfaro, Danielle T., "Warren County, N.Y., Medical Supplies Maker Plans to Double Size of Plant," *Times Union* (Albany, N.Y.), March 21, 2002.

Harlin, Kevin, "Parent Firm to Spin Off Queensbury, N.Y., Medical Device Maker AngioDynamics," *Times Union* (Albany, N.Y.), March 9, 2004.

Maloney, Lawrence D., "Time to Take the Leap?" *Design News,* October 24, 2005.

Much, Marilyn, "Medical Gear Maker Considered a Safe Bet," *Investor's Business Daily,* May 27, 2004, p. A06.

"Stern Ready for New Age in Health Care," *Long Island Business News,* February 28, 1994, p. S24.

aQuantive, Inc.

---

821 2nd Avenue, Suite 1800
Seattle, Washington 98104
U.S.A.
Telephone: (206) 816-8700
Fax: (206) 816-8808
Web site: http://www.aquantive.com

Public Company
Incorporated: 1998 as Avenue A, Inc.
Employees: 1,463
Sales: $308.4 million (2005)
Stock Exchanges: NASDAQ
Ticker Symbol: AQNT
NAIC: 541990 All Other Professional, Scientific and
Technical Services

■ ■ ■

aQuantive, Inc. is a digital marketing company focused on helping online advertisers reap the greatest rewards from their marketing efforts. The company divides its business along three business lines: Digital Marketing Services, Digital Marketing Technologies, and Digital Performance Media. Digital Marketing Services comprises Avenue A/Razorfish, an interactive advertising agency involved in web site development, interactive marketing, creative development, and branding, and a London, England–based company, DNA, that also operates as an interactive advertising agency. Through its Digital Marketing Technologies division, aQuantive licenses its proprietary technology, the Atlas Digital Marketing Suite, to enable clients to manage and to

track online marketing campaigns. DRIVEpm and MediaBrokers compose the company's Digital Performance Media division, which is involved in "behavioral targeting," providing advertisers with information about an online user's behavior, geographic location, and demographic profile.

ORIGINS

When the Internet began to experience its first widespread use in the 1990s, there was no shortage of predictions about how the dawn of the digital age would forever change the way the world operated. The birth of electronic commerce, or e-commerce, in particular, promised to transform the business landscape, fundamentally altering the way nearly every industry conducted its activities. For advertising agencies, the emergence of a digital marketplace offered enormous potential for growth, buttressed by tantalizing claims about advertising's reach and effectiveness in a virtual marketplace, but there remained a gulf between the sanguine prognostications and reality. The founders of aQuantive, Scott Lipsky and Michael Galgon, hoped to bridge the gulf, endeavoring to create a company that would enable online advertising to live up to its billing.

Lipsky and Galgon founded aQuantive in 1997, formally incorporating the following year as Avenue A, Inc. While they were setting up operations in Seattle, Washington, they approached several large advertising agencies to determine why certain clients were reluctant to spend money on online advertising. The response revealed two negative perceptions of online advertising as it was just gaining legitimacy in the marketplace.

These days, customers are difficult to identify, hard to reach and challenging to keep. In addition to drawing on the quantitative consumer data we've accumulated over the years, our multi-disciplinary teams immerse themselves in your audience's world to understand their motivations, interests, likes and dislikes. This research helps us develop insights that form the basis of our solution design. We combine attitudinal and behavioral research to generate actionable insights into your most valuable customer segments. This initial feedback is validated further when we bring real customers into the earliest phases of a project to help us analyze, refine and enhance our work. Then we subject our final solution to rigorous usability testing and campaign optimization. The result is an online experience that accurately reflects user behavior, provides relevant content, high ease of use and minimizes abandonment.

There were concerns about determining the value, or pricing structure, of online advertising, and the effectiveness of the advertisements. Online advertisers followed the model set by the television and print-media industries, which set rates according to how many people saw the advertisement. Accordingly, digital advertisers set their rates by the number of people who clicked on an advertisement, or the number of "click-throughs," but the method struck many as an illusory way of assigning value because advertisers had no way of determining what a user did after clicking the advertisement. A similar uncertainty existed in all other major forms of advertising—television, radio, billboards, and print—but a central component of the lure of online advertising was its superior potential to be precise in targeting consumers. Advertising agencies and their clients wanted evidence of online advertising's effectiveness, proof that the industry's highly touted potential could be measured in an accurate way. Lipsky and Galgon, after receiving feedback from the advertising agencies they consulted, made it their goal to develop a quantitative method of assessing online advertising's effectiveness.

Lipsky, in his early 30s when he helped start Avenue A, was credited for developing the innovation that greatly legitimized online advertising. Before starting Avenue A, Lipsky worked for Amazon.com, where he developed software capable of gathering data that enabled the online retailer to determine the tastes and behavior of its customers. His work for Amazon.com relied on the same sort of expertise he would need to give Avenue A its start, but there were complexities he did not have to confront in developing Amazon.com's data-mining system. "We needed to figure out a system that could serve up ads and also track sales by following what people were doing once they clicked on the ad and landed on an advertiser's site," Lipsky explained in a March 2001 interview with *Fast Company.com*. He developed software that used the conventional way advertisements were transmitted to a computer screen, mimicking the "cookies" that served as unique, anonymous identifiers on every computer browser. Lipsky realized that if he placed what he called "action tags" on pertinent areas of a web site—the home page, registration page, and thank-you page—he could track the online movements and behavior of someone who was online. The technology enabled companies, for the first time, to gauge the effectiveness of their advertising, giving them the ability to calculate the precise return on their marketing investments in the digital world.

Avenue A, boasting an industry first, became a going enterprise with its innovative action tags. Lipsky assumed the role of chief technology officer, while Galgon, who spent the years before Avenue A's formation as an officer in the U.S. Navy and as a full-time volunteer for Volunteers In Service To America, served as general manager and president. The company achieved its greatest growth, both financially and in the breadth of its product offerings, during the early 2000s, a period in which a third executive exerted considerable influence over the company. Brian McAndrews was hired as president and chief executive officer in 1999, giving the young company a seasoned executive to guide it through its early stages of development. A graduate of Harvard University and Stanford University, McAndrews spent five years at General Mills before joining broadcaster ABC, Inc. in 1990. McAndrews spent a decade at ABC, holding various executive positions at ABC Sports, ABC Entertainment, and the ABC Television Network. Under McAndrews' guidance, Avenue A completed its initial public offering (IPO) of stock in 2000, gaining access to capital that would help it embark on its first serious acquisition campaign.

EXPANSION IN THE NEW MILLENNIUM

Acquisitions helped the company broaden its capabilities, giving it a spectrum of services that later would be grouped under the aQuantive banner. At first, however, expansion centered on the same type of services marketed

KEY DATES

1997: aQuantive is founded as Avenue A and incorporated the following year.
1999: Brian McAndrews is appointed president and chief executive officer of Avenue A.
2000: The company completes its initial public offering of stock.
2001: The Digital Marketing Technologies division is established.
2003: aQuantive is adopted as the corporate title for Avenue and its sister companies.
2004: SBI.Razorfish is purchased, more than doubling the size of aQuantive.
2005: A U.K.-based interactive agency, DNA, is acquired.

under the Avenue A name. In 1999, the company acquired iballs LLC, a firm that offered Internet media planning and buying services akin to those offered by Avenue A. The acquisition was notable because it marked the first geographic expansion undertaken by the company, giving it an office in New York City (iballs was renamed Avenue A/NYC in 2001). In 2002, the company added an office in Philadelphia by acquiring an interactive advertising agency named Frontier that also offered services similar to Avenue A. By the time the company acquired Frontier, it had already begun to venture into other areas of the online advertising market. In 2001, a new division was formed to license the company's proprietary technology platform, the Atlas Digital Marketing Suite, to traditional and online advertising agencies. The division, named Digital Marketing Technologies (DMT), became one of three pillars supporting aQuantive in the years ahead.

The company's acquisition campaign kicked off in 2003, the same year aQuantive was adopted as the corporate title under which Avenue A and Atlas operated. In December 2003, the company acquired GO TOAST, a search-management technology provider. By using GO TOAST's technology, advertisers received assistance in the bidding process that was part of having a link show up on search engines such as Google. The $12.6 million acquisition, which was grouped with aQuantive's DMT division and officially purchased by Atlas, occurred the same month the company launched ChannelScope, a product that helped retailers assess online advertising's influence on conventional, off-line sales. The product was launched after two Avenue A clients tested it,

producing data, in one instance, that demonstrated online advertising was responsible for a more than 20 percent increase in the client's in-store sales. "We've always believed," McAndrews said in a January 23, 2004, interview with *Investor's Business Daily,* "that online ads [benefit] offline sales, and for the first time we're able to prove there's a benefit." On the heels of purchasing GO TOAST and launching ChannelScope, aQuantive completed another acquisition, paying $4.5 million for NetConversions in February 2004 and incorporating the company into its growing DMT division. NetConversions, founded five years before being purchased by aQuantive, was a Seattle-based company that identified how web sites could be improved to increase customer-conversion rates, a so-called "Web site usability technology provider." The acquisition coincided with the opening of an office in Chicago, Illinois, by Avenue A to serve JCPenney.com.

Activity on the acquisition front picked up pace as 2004 progressed, adding to the breadth and depth of aQuantive's stance in the digital advertising market. A third division was formed in April 2004 that moved the company into what was known as the "behavioral targeting" field. The division, named Digital Performance Media (DPM), consisted of DRIVEpm, which purchased advertising inventory from online publishers and sold it to advertisers looking for specific shopping behavior on the Internet, demographic attributes, and geographic location. "DRIVEpm," a company executive explained in an April 26, 2004, interview with *ADWEEK Online,* "helps eliminate waste through its targeting capabilities, and, in turn, publishers realize fair value for their inventory, advertisers obtain better results, and consumers benefit from a more relevant, quality surfing experience." The DPM division soon was bolstered by the July 2004 acquisition of U.K.-based MediaBrokers, which became the European arm of the division.

2004 ACQUISITION OF SBI.RAZORFISH

As aQuantive developed a third facet to its business, it made the boldest move in its seven-year history, brokering a deal that thoroughly restructured its original line of business. In June 2004, the company announced it was acquiring Salt Lake City, Utah–based SBI.Razorfish, the largest independent interactive agency in the country. With $93 million in revenue in 2003, SBI.Razorfish served clients such as Ford Motor Co. and Kraft Foods. The acquisition, completed one month after it was announced, more than doubled the size of aQuantive, a $160 million deal that combined Avenue A's strengths as a media-buying agency with SBI.Razorfish's strengths in web site marketing and design. "A lot of Avenue A's competitors also do Web-site design," McAndrews said in a July 12, 2004, interview with *ADWEEK*. "It's important for us to have that full range of capabilities offensively but also defensively. I think we have a better shot of retaining clients the more we're doing with them and the more strategic our relationship with them." The acquisition led to a re-branding and restructuring of aQuantive's DMS segment, which became Avenue A/Razorfish, a combination of Avenue A, SBI.Razorfish, and i-Frontier.

In the wake of the transforming acquisition, aQuantive's financial performance confirmed the decision to go ahead with the deal. Analysts praised the complementary nature of the union, which contributed significantly to the company's results for the first quarter of 2005. aQuantive's net income rose 55 percent to $6.4 million and its revenue leaped 187 percent to $65 million, $25.3 million of which was directly attributable to the purchase of SBI.Razorfish. For the year, the company posted $308 million in revenue, nearly twice the total recorded the previous year. More important, aQuantive registered $35.1 million in net income, its third consecutive year of profitability after racking up more than $100 million in losses during its first six years in business.

Looking ahead, the completion of further acquisitions appeared likely as the company sought to strengthen its presence not only in the United States but abroad as well. In December 2005, aQuantive purchased DNA, a U.K.-based interactive advertising and web development agency that was incorporated into its DMS segment. A $9 million-in-sales firm, DNA served clients such as automobile and motorcycle maker BMW, aid agency Oxfam, and wireless carrier O2. The acquisition was completed to improve aQuantive's ability to serve its U.S.-based clients who desired global advertising and marketing campaigns. Fulfilling such a demand presented aQuantive with the opportunity for enormous growth potential in an era in which online advertising was playing an increasingly important role in connecting companies with consumers. "The Web site," McAn-

drews proclaimed in a May 9, 2005, interview with *AD-WEEK*, "is going to replace the 30-second commercial as the expression of a brand."

Jeffrey L. Covell

PRINCIPAL SUBSIDIARIES

Atlas DMT LLC; Avenue A LLC; aQuantive Paymaster, LLC; Drive Performance Media LLC; Atlas Europe Ltd. (U.K.); MediaBrokers Ltd. (U.K.); DNA Consulting Ltd. (U.K.); NetConversions, Inc.; Avenue A/Razorfish Philadelphia LLC; Avenue A/Razorfish Search, LLC; Atlas OnePoint, LLC; aQuantive Australia Pty Ltd.; Avenue A/Razorfish, Inc.

PRINCIPAL COMPETITORS

Digitas Inc.; DoubleClick Inc.; Euro RSCG Worldwide.

FURTHER READING

Judge, Paul C., "Will Online Ads Ever Click?," *Fast Company.com,* March 2001, p. 182.

Mack, Ann M., "Aquantive Enters Behavioral Targeting Space," *ADWEEK Online,* April 26, 2004.

———, "Aquantive Fills Out Agency Offering with Razorfish Buy," *ADWEEK,* July 12, 2004, p. 9.

———, "To aQuantive, Second Time's a Charm," *ADWEEK,* February 16, 2004, p. 10.

Morrissey, Brian, "Aquantive Denies ValueClick Merger Talks," *ADWEEK Online,* May 9, 2006.

———, "Avenue A/Razorfish Combo Pays Off," *ADWEEK,* May 9, 2005, p. 14.

Much, Marilyn, "Aquantive Inc.," *Investor's Business Daily,* January 23, 2004, p. A5.

Peterson, Kim, "Purchase of U.K. Business Grows aQuantive Abroad," *Seattle Times,* December 6, 2005.

Tsuruoka, Doug, "More Firms Finding the Focused Benefits of Paid Search Ads," *Investor's Business Daily,* November 17, 2004, p. A7.

Argon ST, Inc.

12701 Fair Lakes Circle, Suite 800
Fairfax, Virginia 22033
U.S.A.
Telephone: (703) 322-0881
Fax: (703) 322-0885
Web site: http://www.argonst.com

Public Company
Incorporated: 1969 as Daedalus Enterprises, Inc.
Employees: 637
Sales: $271.75 million (2005)
Stock Exchanges: NASDAQ
Ticker Symbol: STST
NAIC: 334111 Electronic Computer Manufacturing;
334511 Search, Detection, Navigation, Guidance,
Aeronautical, and Nautical System and Instrument
Manufacturing; 334519 Other Measuring and
Controlling Device Manufacturing; 541512
Computer Systems Design Services; 54171 Research
and Development in the Physical, Engineering, and
Life Sciences

∎ ∎ ∎

Argon ST, Inc. is a Washington area systems developer
specializing in the intelligence, surveillance, and reconnaissance end of the C4ISR (command, control, communications, computers, intelligence, surveillance, and
reconnaissance) market. The company was created by
the 2004 merger of military tech contractors Argon
Engineering Associates and Sensytech, Inc.

The U.S. Navy typically accounts for roughly 70

percent of revenues or more. Naval products include
torpedo defense systems and radars. Though most of
Argon ST's business is with the U.S. government, some
of the company's systems have been approved for sale to
certain foreign countries, which accounted for 11 percent
of total revenues in 2005. The company has grown
rapidly in the post-September 11, 2001, war on terrorism, forcing it to prepare for competition without the
aid of the federal government's preferential treatment for
small businesses (of fewer than 750 employees).

Although the majority of Argon's systems focus on
radio frequency (RF) wavelengths used in communications and radar, some analyze underwater sounds. Others intercept and process information on computer
networks. The company also makes imaging systems.

MERGER OF ARGON AND
SENSYTECH: 2004

Argon ST, Inc. is the result of the September 2004
merger of Sensytech, Inc. and Argon Engineering Associates, Inc. These two companies had been built
through decades of mergers among high tech military
contractors. Argon's strength in communications signal
intercept and processing systems complemented Sensytech's sensors business.

Argon Engineering had been formed in 1997. The
company's complex signal identification and processing
systems software was made to run with commercial off-
the-shelf (COTS) hardware, a new priority for the
Defense Department. Argon's first and main client was

COMPANY PERSPECTIVES

Our most important goal is to have our systems demonstrate excellence in field operation. Excellence includes more than technical performance, as it is equally important that they be stable, reliable, and operable. Argon ST has made a commitment to establish, document, implement and maintain a quality management system. We continually improve its effectiveness in accordance with the requirements of CMMI and ISO 9001:2000 by adopting a process approach and a set of standard interrelated processes to enhance customer satisfaction by exceeding customer expectations. We have an obligation to supply those men and women who risk their lives to provide security to our country and our families with the best operational capabilities possible. We can accomplish this only through the efforts of an excellent staff and our customers who place confidence in our ability to produce and deliver quality products.

the U.S. Navy. Argon was part of the Lockheed Martin team bidding for a $6 billion Aerial Common Sensors contract.

Argon had been formed by Terry Collins, Tom Murdock, and Vic Sellier, who had worked together at ERA (Engineering Research Associates), which was acquired by E-Systems Corporation and ultimately became a part of Raytheon. Collins would become president and CEO of Argon ST after the 2004 merger with Sensytech.

Sensytech had been built up through a number of mergers over the years. Formerly called Sensys Technologies, it had been formed by the 1998 merger of Daedalus Enterprises, Inc. with S.T. Research.

DAEDALUS ENTERPRISES: 1968–1998

Daedalus Enterprises Inc. was formed in 1968 in Ann Arbor, Michigan. It was incorporated as a Delaware corporation in January 1969. The company's stated aim was to produce "sensitive equipment"; it would become known for airborne imaging systems used for geographic exploration. Mounted on an aircraft, the sensors recorded heat and visible light data, which could be analyzed by computers to produce images of underground fault lines or likely oil fields.

Daedalus made headlines in the late 1970s over the $3 million sale of infrared oil exploration systems to China, which was considered controversial during the height of the Cold War because of its potential military applications. Company President Alan K. Parker told the *New York Times* that the Defense Department was most worried about the system's tape recorders being used to spy on military communications. Though this technology dated back to the 1950s, it was sensitive enough for the United States to ban its sale to the Soviet Union. The equipment sale also involved an array processor, which generated data by gathering and filtering many different signals.

Daedalus Enterprises, Inc. would be the surviving entity in successive mergers including the one that formed Argon ST, Inc. in 2004. However, in that case, Argon Engineering was deemed the acquirer of Sensytech for financial reporting purposes.

Daedalus had annual revenues of nearly $5 million by the end of the 1980s; net earnings were exceptional at almost $1 million. However, by 1991, sales had slipped below $3 million and the company fell into the red due to delays in a major development award. Daedalus continued to accumulate losses into the mid-1990s.

S.T. RESEARCH: 1972–1998

In 1998, Daedalus merged with S.T. Research Corporation to form Sensys Technologies Inc. S.T. Research, formed in 1972, was based in the high tech center of Fairfax County, Virginia. It specialized in communication and radar signals interception and electronic warfare systems.

S.T. Research's revenues were nearly $12 million in 1990. The company landed a major radar signal detection contract in 1991 after the U.S. Navy limited the contest to small businesses. The giant Litton Corp. supported S.T. in the project.

One niche product of the mid-1990s was a "ruggedized," waterproof portable computer. Company CEO Sandy R. Perrino told the *Washington Post* that Virginia's Center for Innovative Technology had been instrumental in its development.

Perrino became chairman of the combined company, Sensys Technologies, after the 1998 Daedalus/S.T. Research merger. In a statement, he said, "The new entity will be capable of supporting platforms anywhere from under the sea to space." At the time, utilities and transportation industries were key markets, in addition to government business. Sensys Technologies was organized into a Systems Group and Communications Group in Newington, Virginia, with an Imaging Group at the old Daedalus Enterprises home of Ann Arbor, Michigan.

KEY DATES

1968: Daedalus Enterprises Inc. is founded.
1972: S.T. Research Corporation is founded.
1990: Signal processing specialist Radix Technologies is formed.
1997: Naval signal intelligence specialist Argon Engineering is formed.
1998: Daedalus Enterprises merges with S.T. Research to form Sensys Technologies Inc.
1999: Sensys Technologies is renamed Sensytech.
2004: Argon ST, Inc. is formed by merger of Sensytech, Inc. and Argon Engineering Associates.
2005: Argon ST buys Radix Technologies.

SENSYTECH: 1998–2004

Sensys Technologies reported revenues of $22 million for the fiscal year ended September 30, 1998. The company became known as Sensytech, Inc. in September 1999.

The war on terrorism following the September 11, 2001 attacks resulted in more business for Sensytech. While revenues fell 28 percent to $16 million in the fiscal year ended September 30, 2001 (net income was $1.2 million), the next year sales doubled to a record $32 million, while net income reached $2.2 million. In early 2002, Sensytech bought the military electronics assets of FEL Corporation (Frequency Engineering Laboratories), which included a number of naval electronic warfare and communications businesses. The buy added an engineering and manufacturing site in Farmingdale, New Jersey. Sensytech was also growing organically, hiring about 50 tech workers toward the end of the year.

The newly acquired factory in New Jersey was relocated to western Pennsylvania early in the 2004 fiscal year. Sensytech then made a couple of strategic acquisitions before its merger with privately owned Argon. It bought Winter Park, Florida's Image Sensors and Systems, Inc. (ISS), which added forward looking infrared (FLIR) and visible spectrum imaging systems. It also bought ST Productions of Smithfield, Pennsylvania, bringing additional production and testing capacity.

THE ARGON-SENSYTECH MERGER

Like the merger of Daedalus with S.T. Research six years earlier, the combination of Argon and Sensytech brought together complementary business lines. "The synergistic value of bringing together Sensytech sensors with Argon software will permit us to be a more fully integrated supplier of system solutions to our markets," said Sensytech Chairman and CEO S. Kent Rockwell.

Employee-owned Argon Engineering had been about twice as large as Sensytech, which had revenues of $53 million in 2003. Argon had 350 employees to Sensytech's 220. Investors applauded the combination, making the new Argon ST stock one of the top performers in the C4ISR category, which was a $19 billion market in the United States by this time, according to Frost & Sullivan.

Argon ST was primarily involved in intelligence, surveillance, and reconnaissance aspects. The company's CFO, Donald Fultz, told the *Wall Street Transcript* that its competition was mainly from large aerospace companies. Though Argon was on track to outgrow the preferential treatment the federal government accorded to small businesses on certain contracts, Argon ST's relatively small size made it more flexible and responsive than defense industry giants. The company was itself a prime contractor on some programs.

The company was still considering potential acquisitions but was selective, said Fultz. With organic growth running around 40 percent, Argon's immediate challenge was hiring enough skilled employees.

ACQUISITION OF RADIX TECHNOLOGIES: 2005

For the fiscal year ended September 30, 2005, Argon ST reported revenues of $271.8 million, more than double the previous year's figure. Net income also more than doubled, to $21.8 million. The company had a $271 million backlog.

Argon ST acquired signal processing specialist Radix Technologies of Mountain View, California, in October 2005. Radix, established in December 1990, was a pioneer in advanced signal processing for reconnaissance and navigation. The deal cost Argon $10.9 million plus performance-based incentives worth up to $1.5 million.

Frederick C. Ingram

PRINCIPAL SUBSIDIARIES

Radix Technologies, Inc.; Sensytech Financial Services, Inc.

PRINCIPAL DIVISIONS

Active Systems; Imaging Sensors and Systems; Imaging Services; PRO Design Solutions; Radix Technologies.

PRINCIPAL COMPETITORS

The Boeing Company; BAE Systems, Inc.; Lockheed Martin Corporation; Northrop Grumman Corporation; Raytheon Company.

FURTHER READING

"Argon Engineering to Acquire Sensytech," *Defense Daily,* June 8, 2004.

Browne, Malcolm W., "Equipment for China Designed to Analyze a Variety of Signals," *New York Times,* June 9, 1978, p. A5.

Chandrasekaran, Rajiv, "Tying Research to the Bottom Line; After an Abrupt Make-Over, the Center for Innovative Technology Has Become a Catalyst," *Washington Post,* April 14, 1997, p. F12.

"Company Interview: Donald Fultz, Argon ST, Inc.," *Wall Street Transcript,* April 2005.

Gwertzman, Bernard, "U.S. Rejects a Bid to Sell China Device with Possible Military Use," *New York Times,* May 9, 1978, p. 3.

Higgins, Marguerite, "Fairfax Tech Firm Exhibits Fast Start," *Washington Times,* February 22, 2005, p. C8.

———, "Sensytech's Slip Seen As Short Term," *Washington Times,* February 17, 2004, p. C9.

Isaac, David, "Deal Has Military Supplier on the Offensive," *Investor's Business Daily,* June 15, 2004, p. A8.

———, "Maker of High-Tech Defense Gear Uses Buyout to Cover Its Flanks," *Investor's Business Daily,* February 18, 2005, p. A7.

Knight, Jerry, "Merger Led to Big Stock-Price Gains at Argon ST," *Washington Post,* January 3, 2005, p. E3.

Koklanaris, Maria, "S.T. Research Beats Odds on Navy Contract," *Washington Post,* March 18, 1991, p. F6.

"Techworking: A Weekly Conversation with a Local Technology Employer," *Newsbytes News Network,* October 28, 2002.

Weinraub, Bernard, "U.S., in Reversal, Will Sell China Equipment Withheld from Soviet," *New York Times,* June 9, 1978, p. A1.

Your ideas become reality®

Armstrong Holdings, Inc.

2500 Columbia Avenue
Lancaster, Pennsylvania 17603-4117
U.S.A.
Telephone: (717) 397-0611
Fax: (717) 446-8061
Web site: http://www.armstrong.com

Public Company
Founded: 1860
Incorporated: 1891 as Armstrong, Brother & Company, Inc.
Employees: 14,600
Sales: $3.56 billion (2005)
Stock Exchanges: Over the Counter (OTC)
Ticker Symbol: ACKHQ
NAIC: 314110 Carpet and Rug Mills; 321918 Other Millwork (Including Flooring); 326192 Resilient Floor Covering Manufacturing; 327121 Brick and Structural Clay Tile Manufacturing; 327122 Ceramic Wall and Floor Tile Manufacturing; 337110 Wood Kitchen Cabinet and Countertop Manufacturing; 551112 Offices of Other Holding Companies

■ ■ ■

Armstrong Holdings, Inc. is a holding company for Armstrong World Industries, Inc., a leading international manufacturer and marketer of floors, ceilings, and cabinets. The company's flooring lines include vinyl sheet, vinyl tile, linoleum, and wood products for both the residential and commercial markets. In ceilings, Armstrong produces acoustical ceilings and suspension systems for commercial, institutional, and residential applications. The cabinet lines, strictly for the residential market, include kitchen and bath cabinets made of wood, veneer, plywood, particleboard, and fiberboard. Based in Lancaster, Pennsylvania, its home since 1929, Armstrong operates 41 manufacturing facilities in 12 countries, and about 30 percent of its revenues are generated outside North America. In December 2000 Armstrong World Industries began a long stint operating under Chapter 11 bankruptcy protection after facing mounting litigation from personal injury claims stemming from asbestos-containing floors and insulation.

ORIGINATING AS CORK-CUTTING SHOP

In 1860 Thomas Morton Armstrong, a 24-year-old son of Scottish-Irish immigrants from Londonderry, Ireland, used $300 of savings from his job as a shipping clerk to buy a small cork-cutting shop in Pittsburgh. The firm was originally named for his partner in the venture, John O. Glass, but Glass's interest was purchased by Armstrong's brother in 1864 and the company's name was changed to Armstrong, Brother & Company.

Armstrong's original business was cutting cork stoppers, first by hand then after 1862 by machine, from the bark of cork trees, which grow in Portugal, Spain, and northern Africa. During the Civil War, 1861 to 1865, the company made bottle stoppers for the Union Army and was singled out for official praise for fulfilling its contracts at the agreed prices with top-grade corks. This good publicity enabled Armstrong to land a large

COMPANY PERSPECTIVES

Our business strategy focuses on product innovation, product quality and customer service. In our businesses, these factors are the primary determinants of market share gain or loss. Our objective is to ensure that anyone buying a floor or ceiling can find an Armstrong product that meets his or her needs. Our cabinet strategy is more focused—on stock cabinets in select geographic markets. In these segments, we have the same objectives: high quality, good customer service and products that meet our customers' needs. Our markets are very competitive, which limits our pricing flexibility. This requires that we increase our productivity each year—both in our plants and in our administration of the businesses.

contract with a New York drug firm after the war, beginning the move toward national distribution of its products. In 1864 Thomas Armstrong pioneered the concept of brand-name recognition in his industry by stamping "Armstrong" on each cork and offering a written guarantee of quality with each sale.

Originally cork was purchased from American importers, but in 1878 Armstrong made arrangements to purchase, process, and ship corkwood and corks direct from Spain, thus beginning the foreign operations that eventually would make the company the largest cork processor in Spain. By the 1890s Armstrong was the world's largest cork company, employing more than 750 people, most of whom Thomas Armstrong knew by name. In 1891 the company incorporated as Armstrong, Brother & Company, Inc. and, in 1893, purchased the Lancaster Cork Works, beginning its long involvement with the Pennsylvania Dutch area. During the 1890s Armstrong expanded its cork product line to include insulation, corkboard, gaskets, and flexible coverings for machinery. In addition, foreign markets were expanded with sales offices opening in Montreal and Toronto in 1895. In that year the corporate name was changed to Armstrong Cork Company. Thomas Armstrong died in 1908 and was succeeded as president by his son, Charles Dickey Armstrong.

EXPANDING INTO LINOLEUM FLOOR COVERING IN EARLY 20TH CENTURY

Searching for new cork-based products, the company decided to add linoleum floor covering to its line and,

in 1908, the first Armstrong linoleum was produced in a new plant in Lancaster. Invented in England in 1863 by Frederick Walton, linoleum was basically a mixture of cork flour, mineral fillers, and linseed oil, which was pressed under high temperature onto burlap backing and colored with pigments. The linoleum line was the beginning of the company's involvement with floor products, which by the early 2000s, in a variety of modern forms, provided more than half of its sales volume.

Under Charles Armstrong's leadership the firm expanded its product lines with cork insulating board and other insulating materials, packaging closures, and gaskets, as well as linoleum and related flooring materials, becoming in the process a much more consumer-oriented company than before. He also continued his father's policy of responsibility toward his employees by initiating benefits that were rare, if not unprecedented, early in this century. In 1909 he established free dental service for employees. Other pioneering examples of corporate responsibility followed: extra pay for overtime in 1913, shop committees to communicate with management in 1919, paid vacations in 1924, and group life insurance in 1931. Armstrong was one of the first U.S. companies to provide such fringe benefits as pensions and group medical insurance. Thus Charles Armstrong's presidency expressed the company's philosophy that employees should be provided for voluntarily by industry rather than by means of government compulsion.

Charles Armstrong became chairman of the board in 1928 and the next year John J. Evans succeeded him as president. In 1934 the vice-president, Henning Webb Prentis, Jr., who was to have a great impact on the company's development, became the next president of Armstrong.

MARKETING INNOVATIONS BOOSTING SALES

Prentis had joined the firm in 1907 when, as a 23-year-old with an M.A. in economics, he took a job with Armstrong's insulation division in Pittsburgh in order to gain some practical experience before beginning a teaching career. It was a significant hiring decision. Prentis became interested in the possibilities of advertising and public relations. He wrote the first promotional literature on cork products to be published by Armstrong, including selling aids for retailers and booklets on home decoration for consumers. In 1911 he became head of the tiny advertising department and persuaded management to support a three-year, $50,000 advertising campaign. In 1917 he arranged for the company's first national advertisement in the mass media, to appear in

KEY DATES:

1860: Thomas Morton Armstrong buys a small cork-cutting shop in Pittsburgh.

1891: Company is incorporated as Armstrong, Brother & Company, Inc.

1893: Lancaster Cork Works, in the Pennsylvania Dutch area, is acquired.

1895: Company is renamed Armstrong Cork Company.

1908: Armstrong begins producing linoleum at a new plant in Lancaster.

1929: Headquarters are moved from Pittsburgh to Lancaster.
Cork is largely replaced by chemicals and synthetics as the basis of the company's products.

1980: Company changes its name to Armstrong World Industries, Inc.

1990: Armstrong fends off a takeover attempt by the Belzberg family.

1995: Company divests the last of its cork operations.

1998: German firm DLW AG and Dallas-based Triangle Pacific Corporation are acquired.

2000: Armstrong Holdings, Inc. is set up as a holding company for Armstrong World Industries; facing mounting asbestos-related lawsuits, Armstrong World Industries files for Chapter 11 bankruptcy protection.

2002: Company records a pretax charge of $2.5 billion to cover asbestos personal-injury claims.

the September 1917 issue of the *Saturday Evening Post.* He pioneered his industry's recruitment of college graduates as salesmen and, with Charles Armstrong's support, helped develop the strenuous training programs that enormously strengthened company management. He improved distribution practices by initiating price lists with discounts based on quantities purchased, and insisted on the establishment of close, friendly relations with wholesalers and retailers.

Thanks largely to Prentis's marketing innovations, Armstrong grew substantially during the 1920s, reaching nearly $48 million in sales by 1929, when the company moved its headquarters from Pittsburgh to Lancaster, Pennsylvania. When the Great Depression cut sales in

half and produced large losses by 1934, Prentis was appointed president to improve the company's situation. He diversified by purchasing rubber- and asphalt-tile factories, and in 1938 acquired two glass companies, Whitall Tatum and Hart Glass Manufacturing.

The company's personnel policies helped to maintain morale and loyalty during those hard times. One example was the research employee who was laid off because of the Great Depression but continued to come to work without pay and, eventually rehired, made significant contributions to the development of a new flooring process. With Armstrong's debt-free balance sheet, Prentis's efforts were successful. By 1935 dividends on the common stock were restored and in 1936 Armstrong had its most profitable year to that point, a stunning achievement at a time when the country was still in the grip of the Great Depression. By 1937 the common stock had climbed from a low of $3.25 in 1932 to a price of approximately $65.

In addition to improving Armstrong's profitability, Prentis became much more of a public figure than his predecessors. He spoke frequently on behalf of conservative business philosophies in opposition to the New Deal policies of the Roosevelt administration. He served as director of the United States Chamber of Commerce and as president of the National Association of Manufacturers. When World War II began, Prentis organized Armstrong's conversion to war production, including the establishment of a munitions division. In 1942 and 1943 he served as deputy director of the War Production Board for the Philadelphia region, becoming an employee of the government administration he had so frequently criticized.

POSTWAR EMPHASIS ON PRODUCT INNOVATION

After the war, Armstrong prepared to meet the tremendous demand for building materials for new houses. Two more asphalt-tile plants, a fiberboard plant, and a bottle-closure plant were built. In addition the company expanded its industrial-adhesives business and added the production of glass bottles to its packaging division. By 1950 annual sales had climbed to $163 million, and earnings were at record levels. In that year Prentis became chairman of the board and was succeeded as president by Clifford J. Backstrand.

Backstrand's goal was to use the growth to date to increase profits. He emphasized not only marketing but also research, realizing that product innovation was essential for successful competition in the postwar period. He completed the building industry's biggest research-and-development center. To help sell products in the home-remodeling market, in 1953 Armstrong built in Lancaster an "idea house" filled with Armstrong products, to be used as a showcase for dealers and customers. Creativity within the company was encouraged by giving special recognition and awards to employees who came up with ideas for new products and new processes. During the 1950s cork was largely replaced by chemicals and synthetics as the basis of the company's products. By 1960 building materials accounted for 60 percent of sales, and industrial specialties and packaging were each 20 percent of sales. Backstrand improved the company's accounting methods for measuring the profitability of various operations, establishing the concept of return on capital employed as a gauge of achievement. In 1962 Backstrand became chairman and Maurice J. Warnock was appointed president.

By the early 1960s Armstrong had extensive foreign operations, manufacturing textile-mill supplies in India and flooring in plants in Canada, Britain, and West Germany, as well as continuing to process cork in Spain. Warnock attempted to reduce the company's strong dependency on the housing and construction markets by entering the consumer products field with a liquid wax plus detergent that cleaned and polished floors at once. Successful at first, this move to enter the supermarket-oriented consumer market eventually failed to justify its invested capital and was discontinued. Otherwise, Warnock's tenure as president was successful with new efficiencies in organization, improvement in flooring products, and continued growth in sales to $460 million by 1967. In 1966 and 1967 Armstrong entered the carpet business with the purchase of Brinton Carpets and E. & B. Carpet Mills. By the end of the 1960s, over one-third of Armstrong's sales came from products developed by the company within the previous decade. Armstrong invariably promoted from within and, in accordance with this policy, Warnock was succeeded in 1968 by a flooring executive who had spent his entire adult life with the company, James H. Binns.

ADDITION OF FURNITURE

Binns's tenure as president from 1968 to 1978 brought significant changes in the makeup and direction of the company, based on his belief that Armstrong's future lay mainly in the interior-furnishings market, which was entering a boom period. In 1968 Armstrong acquired the furniture manufacturer Thomasville Furniture Industries and the furniture wholesaler Knapp & Tubbs, although the latter company was sold in 1972. In 1969 Binns sold the line of cleansers, waxes, and polishes to Chemway Corporation and the extensive packaging operations to Kerr Glass Manufacturing Company. The

insulation-contracting business was sold to its former employees. Altogether Binns sold off businesses with about $125 million in annual sales, about one-fourth of sales volume. By the early 1970s about 90 percent of sales were concentrated in building products and home furnishings, and about 10 percent in industrial products such as gaskets and textile-mill supplies. This ratio continued into the 1990s.

In 1978 Binns became chairman of the board, and Harry A. Jensen served as president and CEO until his retirement in 1983. Through the 1970s and much of the 1980s Armstrong continued to grow in the same directions. The production of linoleum was discontinued in 1974, but the company continued to develop new types of resilient flooring, among which Solarian no-wax flooring became a well-known brand name. In 1980 the corporate name was changed to Armstrong World Industries, Inc. to reflect its growing international operations and the fact that it was no longer based on the cork business. Sales generally trended upward with some annual fluctuations due to changes in the building cycle, reaching $1 billion in 1977 and $2 billion in 1987. Earnings followed the same pattern with net income increasing from $66 million in 1979 to $187 million in 1989.

ADDITION OF CERAMIC TILE, DIVESTMENT OF CARPET

Between 1983 and 1988, Joseph L. Jones served as president and chairman. His successor, William W. Adams, oversaw a series of significant events in the late 1980s. In 1988 Armstrong entered the ceramic-tile business by acquiring American Olean Tile Company from National Gypsum Company for $330 million, adding about $200 million to 1989 sales. In December 1989 Armstrong completed the sale of its carpet division, abandoning that business which was not producing an adequate return on investment, thus reducing annual sales by about $300 million. In addition, in 1989 the company sold Applied Color Systems, a small digital color-processing-control business.

In July 1989 Armstrong learned that the Belzberg family of Canada had acquired 9.85 percent of its stock and had announced the intention of gaining control of the company and selling its furniture and industrial products divisions. The Belzberg's stock ownership increased in 1990 to 11.7 percent. In April 1990, Senate Bill 1310 of the Pennsylvania legislature, the strongest antitakeover bill passed by any state, with support from Armstrong, became law. The bill provided for seizure of short-term profits in a failed takeover, limited voting rights of hostile shareholders, and guaranteed severance pay to employees who lost jobs because of a corporate takeover. A few days after passage of the law, the Belzbergs lost a proxy attempt at the company's annual meeting, seating only one of four candidates for directors on the board. At the end of the next month, the Belzbergs sold their Armstrong stock at a loss of about $18 million. In June 1990 Armstrong and the Belzberg affiliates resolved the remaining issues between them by withdrawing lawsuits and countersuits against each other.

ROCKY TIMES IN THE 1990S

The early and mid-1990s saw the company continue to be involved in litigation relating to personal-injury suits and other claims based on asbestos-containing insulation products, a business that was sold by Armstrong in 1969. The claims were being paid by insurance income under the Wellington Agreement on asbestos-related claims. In 1988 Armstrong and 20 other companies replaced the Wellington Asbestos Claims Facility with the Center for Claims Resolution, which continued in operation through the mid-1990s. Other cases were brought by public school districts, private property owners, and others, including a lawsuit filed with the U.S. Supreme Court by 29 states. By 1994 Armstrong had recorded $198 million in liability and defense costs on its balance sheet, and estimated that it might be responsible for $245 million in additional liability by 2004.

Overall, this period was fairly rocky for Armstrong, punctuated with restructuring charges and divestments on the one hand and awards for quality and record sales on the other. In 1992 the company posted $165.5 million in restructuring charges, mainly to close four major manufacturing plants, two in the United States, and one each in Canada and Belgium. Another $89.3 million restructuring charge was incurred the following year in relation to the elimination of hundreds of jobs. In fact, Armstrong's workforce became increasingly streamlined as the 1990s went on, with more than 6,300 fewer people employed in 1996 as in 1990. In the midst of these changes came a change in management as well, as George A. Lorch took over Adams's duties as president and CEO in September 1993 and then became chairman as well in April 1994 when Adams retired.

Momentous events proved to transform Armstrong during 1995. Although of only small financial consequence, the company's sale of its champagne cork business in Spain was important symbolically as it marked Armstrong's exit from its original business. More important was the divestment of the company's furniture business, which was struggling as a result of a long recession in the furniture market. In December Armstrong sold Thomasville Furniture to the maker of Broyhill and Lane furniture, INTERCO International Inc., for $331.2 million. Another struggling Armstrong busi-

ness—its ceramic tile operations, which was beset with low-cost competitors in Spain and Italy—was also divested later that same month. In a deal with Dal-Tile International Inc., Armstrong traded $27.6 million and American Olean Tile for about a one-third stake in Dal-Tile. Also in 1995, Armstrong entered the European metal ceilings business through the acquisition of the U.K.-based Cape PLC. Finally, in October the company's Building Products Operations, after twice being named a finalist earlier in the decade, was awarded the prestigious Malcolm Baldrige National Quality Award, an honor that highlighted Armstrong's continued commitment to making quality products.

By 1996, then, Armstrong World Industries was involved in fewer core businesses than it had been for decades but held a leading position in nearly all of them. In the building area, the company specialized in floor coverings, ceilings, and adhesives, while its industrial products were led by insulation and gasketing materials. When its numbers were adjusted to reflect only these ongoing businesses, Armstrong posted record net sales of $2.16 billion in 1996, while net earnings hit $155.9 million, an increase of 26 percent over the previous year.

Following its 1995 divestments, Armstrong concentrated on bolstering its core operations, through joint ventures, alliances, and acquisitions. It also increasingly looked outside its home country for growth opportunities. In 1996 the company completed a joint venture ceiling plant in Shanghai and entered into joint ventures in Europe for the manufacture of soft-fiber and metal ceilings. Armstrong that same year formed an alliance with the Austria-based F. Egger Co. for the manufacture of laminate flooring, a new product category for the Armstrong flooring line. In 1997 the company entered into a battle with Sommer Allibert S.A. concerning which company would take over Domco Inc., a Quebec-based maker of flooring products. Armstrong's bid eventually failed, however, after a lengthy battle.

The deal-making continued in the late 1990s. In 1998 Armstrong sold its stake in the loss-making Dal-Tile after unsuccessfully attempting to gain control of the firm. This ended Armstrong's ten-year foray into the ceramic tile sector. Armstrong also completed two large acquisitions in 1998. The firm significantly bolstered its European operations by purchasing DLW AG for about $275 million plus the assumption of $74 million in debt. Based in Bietigheim-Bissingen, Germany, DLW was the leading flooring manufacturer in Germany and the third largest flooring company in Europe and had revenues of $669 million in 1997. DLW's flooring lines included carpet products, returning Armstrong to the carpet business. Back in the United States, Armstrong snapped up the world's leading producer of hardwood floors, Triangle Pacific Corporation, a Dallas firm whose annual sales totaled $653 million. Triangle produced wood floors under several brands, including Bruce, Hartco, and Robbins, and it derived 28 percent of its revenues from the sale of kitchen and bathroom cabinets, marking a new product line for Armstrong. The price tag for Triangle was a hefty $777 million plus $260 million in assumed debt.

Needing to cut costs, Armstrong late in 1998 announced a workforce reduction of 12 percent, or about 750 jobs worldwide. Restructuring and other charges sent the company into a net loss of $9.3 million for the year. The asbestos-related litigation continued to take its toll as well. Late in 1999 Armstrong took a $335.4 million charge to boost its reserves for pending and future asbestos personal-injury claims. It managed to eke out a profit of $14.3 million that year, but also announced a program to divest itself of noncore assets. Toward that end, Armstrong sold its textile product operations in 1999 and the following year its insulation products division and its installation products group, the latter of which focused on adhesives for installing floors. Armstrong also acquired GEMA Holdings AG, a maker of metal ceilings based in Switzerland, in 2000. To facilitate the completion of both divestments and acquisitions, Armstrong set up a holding company called Armstrong Holdings, Inc. in May 2000. Armstrong Holdings became the publicly traded parent company of Armstrong World Industries, the main operating subsidiary. In August 2000 Lorch retired from his position as chairman and CEO. Named as his successor was Michael D. Lockhart, who had served as chairman and CEO of General Signal Corporation, an industrial controls company acquired by SPX Corporation in October 1998.

OPERATING UNDER CHAPTER 11 BANKRUPTCY

With the company facing mounting asbestos-related lawsuits—nearly 200,000, the payouts from which were projected to total as high as $1.4 billion—and its stock pummeled by the uncertainty surrounding its financial condition, Lockhart made the difficult decision of directing the Armstrong World Industries unit to file for Chapter 11 bankruptcy protection in December 2000. The filing provided Armstrong with considerable breathing room. Pending litigation was immediately frozen, and the company was automatically relieved of its obligation to pay creditors.

While attempting to come up with a resolution of the asbestos litigation, Armstrong continued operating under Chapter 11 protection. The weak economy hurt results in 2001, when sales slid 3.5 percent to $3.14 billion, although the net income of $92.8 million was the firm's best showing since 1997. In 2002 Armstrong unveiled a plan for emerging from bankruptcy that called for all current and future asbestos personal-injury claims to be channeled to a newly formed trust, initially funded by the company; nearly all of Armstrong's stock was slated to go to asbestos claimants and the firm's unsecured creditors, its bondholders, bank lenders, and suppliers. To cover the additional liability anticipated by this plan, Armstrong recorded a pretax charge of $2.5 billion in the fourth quarter of 2002, leading to the largest loss in the firm's 140-plus-year history, $2.14 billion.

Armstrong initially hoped to emerge from bankruptcy in the summer of 2003, but various delays ensued and the company was forced to amend its plan of reorganization several times. A further setback occurred in February 2005 when a federal judge ruled the plan illegal because it envisioned giving current stockholders a kind of option, known as warrants, to buy new Armstrong shares. This ruling was a victory for Armstrong's unsecured creditors, who had opposed the plan, hoping that a better deal might emerge through various asbestos bills that were being considered by the U.S. Congress. The bills called for the creation of a federal trust to pay the asbestos-related claims of the more than 50 corporations that had been pushed into bankruptcy by asbestos lawsuits.

In the meantime, Armstrong posted its third consecutive annual net loss in 2004 as it took a $153 million charge to write down the value of its struggling European resilient flooring business. The company returned to the black in 2005, spurred by strong results from its ceilings and wood flooring operations and by efficiency gains won through a series of cost-cutting initiatives launched over the previous few years. Net profits totaled $112.1 million on revenues of $3.56 billion.

Despite the rosier results, Armstrong's emergence from bankruptcy remained up in the air. The company in early 2006 submitted yet another modification of its reorganization plan, this one dropping the warrants ruled illegal. The unsecured creditors remained in opposition, however, contending that Armstrong was overstating its potential asbestos liabilities and thereby setting aside too much for asbestos claimants at the expense of the creditors' portion of the bankruptcy-plan payouts. The creditors continued to hold out hope for Congressional action, but the passage of a bill during the 2006 election year was far from certain.

Bernard A. Block
Updated, David E. Salamie

PRINCIPAL SUBSIDIARIES

Armstrong World Industries, Inc.; Armstrong Wood Products, Inc.; Armstrong Hardwood Flooring Company; Armstrong DLW AG (Germany); Tapijtfabriek H. Desseaux N.V. (Netherlands); Armstrong Metalldecken Holdings AG (Switzerland).

PRINCIPAL OPERATING UNITS

Armstrong Floor Products; Armstrong Building Products; Armstrong Cabinet Products.

PRINCIPAL COMPETITORS

Congoleum Corporation; Tarkett Aktiengesellschaft; Pergo AB; Shaw Industries, Inc.; Mohawk Industries, Inc.; Forbo Holding SA; Interface, Inc.; Mannington Mills, Inc.; Wilsonart International, Inc.; Gerflor Group; Chicago Metallic Corporation; USG Corporation; Celotex Limited; Knauf Gips KG; Odenwald Faserplattenwerk GmbH; Rockfon A/S; Masco Corporation; American Woodmark Corporation; Fortune Brands, Inc.

FURTHER READING

Armstrong: A Historical Summary, Lancaster, Pa.: Armstrong World Industries, Inc., 1997.

Bomberger, Paul, "Armstrong Betting Heavily on Latest Acquisitions," *Lancaster (Pa.) Intelligencer Journal,* September 14, 1999, p. B8.

———, "Armstrong to Sell Money-Losing Ceramic Tile Stake," *Lancaster (Pa.) Intelligencer Journal,* February 28, 1998, p. A1.

Carlino, Maria, "Armstrong World Industries Inc.," *Journal of Commerce and Commercial,* March 1, 1996, p. 5A.

Coleman, Lisa, "All Dressed Up," *Forbes,* February 3, 1992, p. 108.

Coletti, Richard J., "Armstrong: Calling the Belzberg Bluff," *Financial World,* September 19, 1989, p. 16.

Franklin, Barbara Hackman, "Caught in a Sea Change: Armstrong World Industries vs. the Belzbergs; An Anatomy of an End-of-an-Era Takeover Battle," *Directors and Boards,* Fall 1990, p. 39.

Glater, Jonathan D., "For Armstrong, Bankruptcy Is Lesser of Two Evils," *New York Times,* December 20, 2000, p. C4.

Henkoff, Ronald, "Floored? You *Can* Come Back," *Fortune,* February 21, 1994, pp. 95–96.

Hida, Hilton, "Armstrong World Agrees to Acquire DLW of Germany," *Wall Street Journal,* June 8, 1998, p. B11G.

Jaffe, Thomas, "The Belzbergs, Again," *Forbes,* September 4, 1989, p. 316.

Kim, Queena Sook, "Armstrong Holdings Unit Files Under Chapter 11," *Wall Street Journal,* December 7, 2000, p. A4.

Mehler, William A., Jr., *Let the Buyer Have Faith: The Story of Armstrong,* Lancaster, Pa.: Armstrong World Industries, Inc., 1987, 228 p.

Mekeel, Tim, "Armstrong Bankrupt," *Lancaster (Pa.) New Era,* December 6, 2000, p. A1.

———, "Armstrong Cuts Out Shareholders," *Lancaster (Pa.) New Era,* February 7, 2006, p. A1.

———, "A New Armstrong: Year into Bankruptcy, Evolving Firm Scores Small Victories," *Lancaster (Pa.) New Era,* November 29, 2001, p. A1.

———, "One-Time Charge Leads to Record Armstrong Loss," *Lancaster (Pa.) New Era,* March 19, 2003.

———, "Ruling Leaves Armstrong Still 'Paralyzed,'" *Lancaster (Pa.) New Era,* February 28, 2005, p. B1.

Meyer, Cheryl, "Armstrong Unveils Plan to Purchase German Flooring Firm," *Lancaster (Pa.) Intelligencer Journal,* June 6, 1998, p. B5.

Nomani, Asra Q., "Armstrong World Plans to Acquire Triangle Pacific," *Wall Street Journal,* June 15, 1998, p. A10.

Sparks, Debra, "Armstrong: Weak Legs," *Financial World,* October 25, 1994, p. 20.

Sraeel, Holly A., "Product Testing Begins at Home: Armstrong World Industries, Inc. Uses Its Own Interior Products to Define Space," *Buildings,* July 1988, p. 42.

Weston, Rusty, "Painful Re-engineering Leads to Baldrige Award for Quality," *PC Week,* November 6, 1995, pp. 1, 143.

Wickens, Barbara, "A Fight for Control," *Maclean's,* May 14, 1990, p. 48.

Zweig, Phillip, "Armstrong: Not Just a Takeover Play," *Financial World,* April 5, 1988, p. 21.

Baugur Group hf

Tungoetu 6
Reykjavik, 101
Iceland
Telephone: (+354) 530 7800
Fax: (+354) 530 7801
Web site: http://www.baugur.is

Private Company
Incorporated: 1989 as Bonus
Employees: 62,000
Sales: $16.14 billion (2005)
NAIC: 422330 Women's, Children's, and Infants' Clothing and Accessories Wholesalers; 445110 Supermarkets and Other Grocery (Except Convenience) Stores; 448120 Women's Clothing Stores; 448150 Clothing Accessories Stores; 523999 Miscellaneous Financial Investment Activities; 551112 Offices of Other Holding Companies

∎∎∎

Tiny Iceland's Baugur Group hf has grown into one of Northern Europe's leading retail and investment companies. Baugur operates the Hagar retail group, which includes Iceland's retail leader Hagkaup as well as discount pioneer Bonus and convenience store chain 10-11. Through Hagar, Baugur also operates stores under the Debenhams, Topshop, Utilif, Zara, Adfong, and Hysing names in Iceland, Sweden, and Denmark. The Hagar group operates more than 80 retail stores. Other Icelandic and Scandinavian operations include building materials leader Husasmidjan in Iceland; the Smaralind

shopping mall; the Faroe Islands–based SMS supermarket chain; and, in Denmark, department store group Magasin du Nord and electronics store chain Merlin. Baugur also owns a number of investment and real estate subsidiaries in Iceland, Sweden, and Denmark.

Since the early 2000s, however, Baugur has targeted further expansion in Northern Europe, and especially into the buoyant retail sector in the United Kingdom. Into the mid-2000s, Baugur has built an impressive list of a number of leading British retailers, including Oasis, Coast, Karen Millen and Whistles (grouped within subsidiary Mosaic Fashions Ltd., held at 42 percent by Baugur); MK One; Jane Norman; famed toy shop Hamleys; The Shoe Group; Iceland, a frozen food specialist; Goldsmiths, the second largest jewelry retailer in the United Kingdom; Julian Graves, a luxury foods retailer; and tea and coffee specialist Whittard of Chelsea, among others. In June 2006, Baugur has also been negotiating the possible takeover of the House of Fraser retail group. Baugur's international expansion is largely the work of company President and CEO Jon Asgeir Johannesson, who formed the company with father Johannes Jonsson in 1989. Baugur is a private company controlled by the founding family.

DISCOUNT PIONEER IN ICELAND IN 1989

Johannes Jonsson and son Jon Asgeir Johannesson joined together to open a single store in 1989 and quickly revolutionized Iceland's economic landscape. The elder Jonsson's father had been a grocer, and Jonsson himself had spent much of his career as an executive overseeing

COMPANY PERSPECTIVES

Baugur Group's main policy is to focus on investments in the retail, service and real estate sectors, in Iceland and northern Europe. The company seeks out shares in companies that have a strong market position yet also have the potential for further growth. Baugur Group looks primarily to companies whose operations have thus far been a success and are run by a strong team of managers who are interested in cooperating with the company. This arrangement leads to effective collaboration, in which we provide our managers with unconditional support while demanding excellent performance in return.

the supermarket operation of farmers' cooperative Southern Slaughterhouse Association. Jonsson often traveled to Germany and Denmark, meeting with food exporters, and becoming acquainted with the new discount supermarket concepts introduced in those countries in the late 1970s and 1980s. Jonsson recognized an opportunity to import the discount grocery format to Iceland, where food prices were traditionally high.

Jonsson waited for his son to graduate from business school, which Johannesson did in 1989 when he was just 20 years old. Yet by then, Johannesson had already built up years of experience, starting as a boy when he worked as a stock clerk for his father. At the age of 14, Johannesson sold popcorn, and at 16, traveled to Germany with his father. There, Johannesson bought 20 mechanical rides, which he set up in front of the cooperative's supermarket chain. The rides helped support Johannesson during his studies.

In 1989, Jonsson and Johannesson each put up $4,500 to open their first discount store, named Bonus, in an industrial zone outside of Reykjavik. The father-son team sought out means to drive down costs, in order to cut prices on the goods they sold. For example, rather than invest in costly refrigerators and freezers, and the electricity to run them, the pair converted one room of the two-room store into a cold room. They also invested in bar-code technology, a first in Iceland, which represented significant cost savings. As Jonsson told *Institutional Investor:* "That's the key to our success. Bar codes allowed us to enter income and costs automatically into our books. That basically meant we could run the store with a minimum of manpower."

With just three employees, including Jonsson and Johannesson, the store sold products at discounts of 25 percent or more. The appearance of the discount store in economically troubled Iceland, which still depended almost entirely on its fishing industry at the time, played an important part in revolutionizing not merely the country's retail sector, but its economy altogether. Until then, the island country, with a population of just 250,000 people, had been dominated by just a few prominent families. The appearance, and rapid success of Bonus, signaled the start of a new entrepreneurial era in the country, and a number of Icelandic groups broke free of the country's borders and emerged on the international scene.

The company looked for other means of controlling costs. For one, the Bonus stores only accepted cash from its customers, eliminating the store's credit card fees. The availability of ready cash flow also allowed the company to pay cash on delivery to its suppliers and demand further price reductions. Importantly, the company also broke the domination of the country's two main shipping companies, which each were aligned with the country's two major political parties. Instead of following a party line, Bonus installed a bidding system, shifting the balance of power from importers to distributors. In this way, the company was able to undercut the country's existing supermarkets, which remained politically aligned with the shipping companies. The willingness to buck the political system was, however, to have consequences for the family in the future.

For the first part of the 1990s, in the meantime, Jonsson and Johannesson expanded the Bonus format into a network of stores. By 1992, the company had already opened some six stores, covering much of the country. Yet Bonus faced a new threat in that year, when the country's leading supermarket group, Hagkaup, announced its intention to develop its own discount supermarket format. Jonsson and Johannesson reacted quickly, and surprisingly, offering to sell a 50 percent interest in their company to Hagkaup. The supermarket group agreed. Nonetheless, under terms of the merger, Jonsson and Johannesson retained control of the discount operations, and eventually took control of Hagkaup itself.

In 1993, the two companies formed a combined purchasing subsidiary, named Baugur, ancient Icelandic for "ring of strength." With control of a significant part of the country's retail sector—Hagkaup alone accounted for more than 30 percent of all grocery sales—Baugur was able to negotiate still lower prices from its suppliers.

While Jonsson became the company's public face, Johannesson worked behind the scenes to expand the

KEY DATES

1989: Johannes Jonsson and son Jon Johannesson open Iceland's first discount grocery store, Bonus, outside of Reykjavik.

1992: Bonus agrees to merge with supermarket group Hagkaup, with Jonsson and Johannesson remaining in control of discount stores.

1994: Company launches joint venture to open grocery stores in Faroe Islands.

1998: Jonsson and Johannesson acquire full control of Hagkaup/Bonus group, which they rename Baugur and list on the Iceland stock exchange; company acquires 10-11 convenience store chain.

1999: Baugur acquires Utilif sporting goods stores; company acquires Scandinavian concession for Arcadia (U.K.) stores, opening Miss Selfridge and Top Shop stores in Sweden and Iceland.

2000: Baugur establishes Bonus Dollar in the United States and acquires bankrupt company Bill's Dollar Store in the Southeast.

2001: Company begins acquiring stake in Arcadia, but is forced to withdraw from takeover offer amid fraud allegations.

2002: Baugur acquires stake in Big Food Group, owner of the Iceland retail chain in the United Kingdom.

2003: Baugur acquires stake in House of Fraser and Mothercare; company acquires Hamleys toy store in London and Oasis and Julian Graves, also in the United Kingdom.

2004: Company acquires full control of Big Food and Denmark's Magasin du Nord.

2005: Company acquires Jane Norman in the United Kingdom, Illum in Denmark, a stake in investment group FL Group, and U.K. jewelry retailer Mappin & Web.

2006: Baugur acquires Whittard of Chelsea in the United Kingdom.

company into a true retail empire. In 1994, the company traveled to the Faroe Islands, where it formed a joint venture, SMS, with the islands' major retail group, Rumfatalagerinn. SMS became that market's dominant supermarket group, with two supermarkets and six Bonus stores.

Back in Iceland, however, Bonus ran into a new setback, when the government enacted new antitrust legislation in 1975. In large part, the new laws were drawn up in order to halt the supermarket company's growing dominance of the country's retail sector. As Johannesson told the *Financial Times:* "I do have to spend a lot of time in political circles persuading people that a big company in a small market is not necessarily controlling."

Nonetheless, by the end of the 1990s, the Jonsson/Johannesson family's control of the retail sector had reached its limits. In 1998, after the death of the founder of Hagkaup, Jonsson and Johannesson raised the funds to buy out their partner, acquiring full control of the company and its subsidiaries, including luxury department store format Nykaup, among others. The parent company was then renamed Baugur and listed on the Iceland stock exchange. Soon after, Baugur acquired another Icelandic retailer, Voruveltan, which operated the country's largest chain of convenience stores under the 10-11 name. Also in 1998, Jonsson stepped down from the company, placing Johannesson as group president and CEO.

Unable to continue its foods retailing expansion, Baugur turned toward other sectors. In 1999, for example, the company acquired the sporting goods chain Utilif. Baugur later expanded that format with two additional stores, at the Smaralind mall in 2001 and in the Kringlan shopping mall in 2004. Baugur later added a number of other retail operations, including the Husasmidjan building materials and hardware retail chain, the leader in its sector.

INTERNATIONAL RETAIL POWERHOUSE IN THE NEW CENTURY

At the turn of the century, however, Baugur's domestic growth appeared clearly at the end of the line. The company set its sights on international expansion. Baugur at first targeted the United States, setting up a U.S. branch of its Bonus operations, called Bonus Dollar stores, in 2001. The company then bought bankrupt chain Bill's Dollar Stores, based in Florida, with some 470 stores in the Southeast. Baugur set out to turn the discount store chain around, and initially appeared to have some success, posting a profit by September 2002. Baugur also attempted to introduce new formats under the Bonus name. Yet by 2003, the company's effort appeared in vain, as the Bonus Dollar operation once again headed toward bankruptcy. In that year, Baugur decided to exit the U.S. market and instead focus its attention on its northern European expansion.

Unlike its attempt to enter the United States, Baugur's European expansion had been swift and sure. The company interest turned especially to the U.K. market. In 1999, Baugur acquired the Scandinavian franchise rights for the retail formats of the Arcadia group. Baugur chose to develop Arcadia's youth-oriented retail stores, and especially Top Shop and Miss Selfridge, opening the first stores in Sweden to great success.

By October 2000, Baugur began building a stake in Arcadia itself, acquiring some 20 percent of the British retail giant. Baugur then launched a full-scale acquisition offer for Arcadia. Yet after Johannesson and other members of Baugur management, including his sister, were accused of fraud, the company was forced to pull back from the takeover. The company sold its Arcadia stake for a £55 million profit, however.

By 2002, the company was back in acquisition mode, this time acquiring a major stake in the Big Food Group, the operator of the Iceland frozen food store chain in the United Kingdom. By 2003, the company had acquired shareholdings in a number of other major British retail groups, including House of Fraser and Mothercare. In 2003, Baugur also began buying up a number of retailers outright, including Hamleys, the famed British toy shop chain, and taking controlling stakes in fashion retailer Oasis and luxury foods retailer Julian Graves. In 2004, the company bought discount fashion group MK One, and completed the buyout of Big Food. In that year, also, the company entered Denmark, buying up the Magasin du Nord department store group. These purchases were followed by the acquisition of U.K. fashion retailer Jane Norman, and Danish department store Illum in 2005.

Back at home, Baugur continued to face pressure from the Icelandic government, which had launched a long-running fraud investigation against Johannesson and Jonsson, as well as other members of its management. Faced with a hostile takeover offer from Mundur, the company decided to buy back its shares and delist its stock. Meanwhile, the political pressure on the company continued to build as it expanded its holdings into the media sector, buying up a stake in Frett ehf, a leading publisher, as well as the Northern Lights Group. Baugur also stirred political ire when it bought a 21 percent stake in Icelandair. Into the mid-2000s, Baugur expanded its range of investments into the real estate and property development sectors, and into mobile telephones, acquiring the license to operate the Vodafone service in Iceland.

The political pressure on the company finally came to a head in late 2005, when the Icelandic government brought charges of 40 counts of fraud against Johannesson and other executives at Baugur. The accusations of fraud cast a pall over the group's expansion efforts; the company was forced to withdraw from what would have been its largest acquisition to date, the takeover of the Somerfields supermarket group in the United Kingdom. In the end, however, the judge handling the fraud case threw out all charges against Johannesson and the others.

With his name cleared, Johannesson was able to return his full attention to continuing Baugur's international expansion. By the end of 2005, Baugur had added a major stake in investment firm FL Group, and expanded into the British jewelry sector with the purchase of luxury retailer Mappin & Webb. The company also joined a consortium in the purchase of leading Danish electronics retailer Merlin that year. At the beginning of 2006, the company acquired another leading U.K. retail name, Whittard of Chelsea, a specialist in coffee and tea. With an ever growing, and increasingly diverse, portfolio of businesses, Baugur had clearly established itself as one of northern Europe's most dynamic holding companies.

M. L. Cohen

PRINCIPAL SUBSIDIARIES

A/S Th. Wessel & Vett, Magasin du Nord (Denmark); Atlas Ejendomme A/S (Denmark); Booker (U.K.); Coast and Whistles (U.K.); Dagsbrun; FL Group; Goldsmiths (U.K.); Hagar hf.; Hamleys (U.K.); Husasmidjan hf; Iceland (U.K.); Illum (Denmark); Jane Norman (U.K.); Julian Graves (U.K.); Karen Millen (U.K.); Keops A/S (Denmark); LxB II (U.K.); Mappin & Webb (U.K.); Merlin A/S (Denmark); MK One (U.K.); Mosaic Fashions Ltd. (U.K.); Oasis (U.K.); Stodir; The Shoe Studio Group (U.K.); Whittard of Chelsea (U.K.); Woodward (U.K.).

PRINCIPAL COMPETITORS

Abercrombie & Fitch Co.; Arcadia Group plc; Benetton Group S.p.A.; Debenhams Plc; Diesel SpA; Esprit Holdings Limited; Guess?, Inc.; H&M Hennes & Mauritz AB; Harrods Holdings; Hot Topic, Inc.; James Beattie Plc; Marks and Spencer Plc; N Brown Group Plc; New Look Group plc; NEXT plc; Otto Versand Gmbh & Co; The Gap, Inc.

FURTHER READING

"Baugur Back in Bidding?" *Grocer*, September 10, 2005, p. 8.

"Baugur Back on the Prowl for Another Acquisition," *Daily Mail*, January 21, 2006, p. 109.

"Baugur in Talks with House of Fraser," *Investors Chronicle*, June 2, 2006.

"Baugur's Norman Invasion," *Daily Mail,* July 21, 2005, p. 68.

"Baugur's U.K. Expansion Halted As Boss Faces 40 Court Charges," *Independent on Sunday,* August 14, 2005, p. 9.

Buckley, Sophy, "Hero or Bully?" *Financial Times,* November 20, 2004, p. 3.

————, "Johannesson's High Street Ambitions," *Financial Times,* August 26, 2003, p. 20.

————, "A Viking Raider and His Treasure Chest," *Financial Times,* September 18, 2004, p. 2.

Butler, Sarah, "Company That Has Spread Its Tentacles Far and Wide," *Times,* December 18, 2004, p. 59.

"Cleared," *Grocer,* March 18, 2006, p. 18.

Gumble, Peter, "The Trail Goes Cold," *Time International,* July 18, 2005, p. 10.

Hall, James, "Baugur Digs in for a Long Winter," *Sunday Telegraph,* July 3, 2005.

Lanchner, David, "Iceland's Hottest Company," *Institutional Investor International Edition,* March 2002, p. 23.

"Small Country, Big Ambitions," *Economist,* February 19, 2005, p. 61.

Tricks, Henry, "North Exposure," *Financial Times,* July 8, 2005, p. 17.

BioWare Corporation

200, 4445 Calgary Trail
Edmonton, Alberta T6H 5R7
Canada
Telephone: (780) 430-0164
Fax: (780) 439-6347
Web site: http://www.bioware.com

Private Company
Founded: 1995
Employees: 260
Sales: CAD 16 million (2004 est.)
NAIC: 541512 Computer Systems Design Services

■ ■ ■

BioWare Corporation, established by three men linked by medical school and a love for video games, is widely recognized as resurrecting the role-playing game (RPG). Specializing in computer and console video games, BioWare has produced a series of hits, including the first *Star Wars* based RPG. A merger with Pandemic Studios in 2005 afforded the company greater leverage in the game industry.

NOT YOUR TYPICAL CAREER PATH: LATE 20TH-CENTURY BEGINNINGS

Greg Zeschuk, Ray Muzyka, and Augustine Yip, medical students at the University of Alberta, played video games to relieve stress and relax. The three went on to meld their medical knowledge with their computer savvy, developing patient simulation software. Their small operation, BioWare, took off in another direction when publisher Interplay advanced funding to develop a game demo.

Shattered Chain was released in 1996. BioWare resigned with Interplay and spent three years developing *Baldur's Gate* for the Irvine, California, company. Zeschuk and Muzyka headed up the company as co-CEOs and practiced medicine on a part-time basis. Yip's chose the path of a full-time doctor.

The lack of great electronic role-playing games (RPG) created room for BioWare to fulfill the unsatisfied need of pen and paper players. "What started in 1996 and finished in December 1998 was an RPG that has come to be regarded by many critics as the best *Dungeons and Dragons* computer game ever made. *Baldur's Gate* was one of the rare games that pleased both the hardcore perfectionist and the casual gamer. The game impressed fans and critics with its attention to detail and massive scope," *Radar.com* observed. The company produced $1.5 million in revenue during 1998, driven by the December release of *Baldur's Gate*.

BioWare's home base of Edmonton, meanwhile, had been gaining recognition of its own, as a significant high-tech knowledge-based city. The number of Albertans working in high-tech businesses had climbed 36 percent from 1996 to 1998; BioWare was among the fastest growing businesses in the province.

In March 1999, BioWare captured a prestigious *Computer Gaming World* Premier award for *Baldur's Gate*. Following its release, the game quickly climbed to the top of the sales charts worldwide and was lauded by the industry for its software engine. *Baldur's Gate* contained five CDs with more than 100 hours of play, 10,000 pre-rendered game screens, and nearly 500,000 lines of code, according to *Canadian Business.*

"What's really amazing is that this is BioWare's first role-playing game and they've built a robust and solid engine," Johnny Wilson, *Computer Gaming World* editorial director, told the magazine. "They have a chance to write their own ticket. The acceptance of the engine and this game means it will be easier for them to get the games they want to do."

While developing a *Baldur's Gate* sequel and a console game, the company explored branching out into feature films and animated television shows. BioWare had produced animation for local television as well as limited logo and commercial work, according to an April 1999 *National Post* article. Yet, other opportunities came knocking.

SHOOTING FOR THE STARS: 2000–2004

BioWare received an offer from LucasArts Entertainment Co. in 2000 to create a new computer and video game based on *Star Wars.* The first role-playing *Star Wars* game would be set 4,000 years prior to the *Star Wars* films and feature the conflict between the Jedi and the Sith, with LucasArts handling marketing and distribution.

"What it does is further legitimize us as a developer and what we consider to be a highly talented studio that can compete on the world stage. And it's great we're doing it out of Edmonton," Zeschuk told the *Vancouver Sun.*

The success of *Baldur's Gate* helped BioWare land the deal, according to the *Sun*'s Charles Mandel. Muzyka and Zeschuk, while both *Star Wars* fans, had demonstrated with *Baldur's Gate* the company's ability to successfully carry out an existing story line.

According to trade group figures from *thestar.com*, computer and video game sales in the United States reached $6 billion in 2000. Interactive Digital Software Association predicted total U.S. video game software sales to reach $10 billion by 2004, assuming double-digit growth. BioWare's own growth kept pace; it was employing more than 100 by early 2001. To manage the increase in size, the company divided into specialized departments of designers, programmers, and producers, with the latter directing game development.

In June 2002, BioWare struck gold, again, with the *Dungeons and Dragons* template. *Neverwinter Nights,* which restored the power of the dungeon master, offered a tool set allowing gamers to create their own maps and characters in addition to playing the preprogrammed games.

BioWare previously incorporated many of *Dungeons and Dragons'* rules in *Baldur's Gate,* which allowed up to six players. As many as 64 players could participate in a *Neverwinter* game. In contrast, massive multiplayer games, such as *Diablo II* by Blizzard Entertainment or *Asheron's Call* by Microsoft, hosted thousands of players.

The success of game developers was linked to hardware makers. Nintendo's Game Cube, Microsoft's Xbox, and Sony's PlayStation 2 were the heavy hitters, seeking dominance in the industry. Ubi Soft Entertainment Inc., among the largest game producers worldwide, had the resources to create games for each platform. Smaller companies had no such luxury. If the console they were tied to failed in the market small developers could suffer a crippling, if not fatal, blow.

"You want to pick the winner," Zeschuk told *Macleans.* "You don't want to put all this money into a big *Star Wars* game and not be doing it on the right platform."

Risks aside, the industry proved to be one more lucrative than a Canadian medical practice. Video games offered the enticement of high margins and online subscription sales created an ongoing revenue stream, according to *Canadian Business.* The industry had stepped in to challenge films and music for a cut of consumers' entertainment expenditures. Moreover, the three media had intertwined, with performers licensing music for games and games extending movie plots.

Canada's economic fortune also had become linked to the industry. The country was home not only to BioWare and other independents, but to the largest video game studio in the world, Electronics Arts Canada (EA). Strong computer and multimedia education created a wealth of talent, drawing big entertainment business players.

BioWare's own talent was shown with *Star Wars: Knights of the Old Republic.* The title earned best video game honors for 2003 from more than 40 world publications. The company also took home three Academy of Interactive Arts and Science awards, according to the *National Post.*

```
╔══════════════════════════════════════════╗
║                KEY DATES                   ║
╠══════════════════════════════════════════╣
```

1995: The company is founded by medical doctors to create educational software.
1996: The company's first game, Shattered Steel, is released for personal computers (PC).
1998: Baldur's Gate revives the role-playing game (RPG) genre.
2002: Neverwinter Nights offers a player tool set.
2003: The Star Wars game tops the charts.
2005: The company merges with Pandemic Studios by way of private equity firm Elevation Partners.

BioWare also earned honors as a corporate employer. The co-CEOs placed high value on both a quality product and quality workplace. The company's low turnover rate was a rarity in an industry in which artists and programmers chased after the most lucrative offerings.

BioWare's success fueled takeover rumors during 2004. The cofounders maintained that they were interested in retaining control of the company, the *Vancouver Sun* reported. Many a small game developer had sold out to a publisher or hardware maker in order to climb to a new level or keep pace with the rapidly changing technology. Late in the year BioWare opened an online store, giving consumers a chance to buy digital and physical BioWare products and creating a new source of revenue.

UP A LEVEL: 2005 AND BEYOND

BioWare joined forces with Pandemic Studios L.L.C. by way of Elevation Partners, in 2005. The $300 million deal brought the Edmonton- and Los Angeles-based studios under a new holding company, BioWare/ Pandemic Studios. Combined, the two studios had sold about 27 million games over the past decade.

"We've been an independent operator for close to 11 years now, and we've enjoyed it," Zeschuk said in a *Globe and Mail* October 2005 report. "But when Elevation approached us, it really hit home; we maintain our independence to a degree, but we get to be part of a larger, stronger company."

Elevation Partners included former President and COO of Electronic Arts John Riccitiello; former Apple Computer Inc. CEO Fred Anderson; Silicon Valley investor Roger McNamee; and Bono, lead singer for U2.

The private equity firm had raised about $1.9 billion to invest in media and entertainment companies; the acquisition of controlling interest in BioWare and Pandemic marked its first deal.

BioWare had grown by more than 650 percent over the past half decade, climbing to more than CAD 16 million in annual sales. Pandemic's 2004 sales exceeded $150 million. Riccitiello took the helm as the new CEO of BioWare/Pandemic Studios, but the studios retained a significant level of autonomy. BioWare's joint-CEOs, Zeschuk and Muzyka, remained major shareholders and would continue to manage the company. The pair also would serve as corporate vice-presidents and directors at BioWare/Pandemic Studios.

Founded in 1998, Pandemic's titles included *Mercenaries, Star Wars: Battlefront II,* and *Destroy All Humans!* The studio's action-adventure games complemented BioWare's emphasis on role-playing. BioWare brought its investment in technology and online distribution to the new mix.

Combined, the studios could shoulder a greater level of financial risk related to game development, promising a larger share of the take from sales. The new funding allowed for greater participation on the marketing end of the business.

Talk of a Pixar-like public offering was also in the air. The move, if successful, would be a first for a video game developer. However, as the *New York Times* noted, Wall Street was far more accustomed to funding media conglomerates than individual studios.

During 2005, BioWare/Pandemic Studios produced four of the top ten titles, three of them original games. The two studios, with nearly 500 employees, planned to continue to produce titles independently and work in tandem to create new gaming vistas.

In that light, BioWare announced the formation of a new studio, in March 2006: BioWare Austin had begun developing a new massive multiplayer online game. The company also continued to develop new game engines and license that technology. As for the fans of BioWare games, the company's online community approached three million registered users.

Kathleen Peippo

PRINCIPAL COMPETITORS

Activision; Electronic Arts; SEGA.

FURTHER READING

"A Bio of BioWare," *radar.com*, April 10, 2001.

Evans, Peter, "No Longer Just a Game: 300 Studios, 5,000 Employees and Growing," *National Post,* May 21, 2005.

Guth, Robert A., "Videogame Makers to Join Up in a Private-Equity Maneuver," *Wall Street Journal,* November 3, 2005, p. B4.

Hawaleshka, Danylo, "Gaming Knights," *macleans.ca,* June 11, 2001.

Mandel, Charles, "Game Company Strikes a Deal with Entertainment Giant," *Vancouver Sun,* July 27, 2000, p. E5.

———, "These Doctors Are In," *Canadian Business,* March 26, 1999, pp. 79+.

Marck, Paul, "Computer Games Firm Heads to Hollywood," *National Post,* April 6, 1999, p. C4.

McKeen, Scott, "Edmonton a Hot New Computer Games Centre Player," *Vancouver Sun,* May 15, 1999, p. 1B.

Monk, Katherine, "Canadian Game Makers Lead," *Vancouver Sun,* May 15, 2004, p. H5.

Potkewitz, Hilary, "U2 Singer Investing in Video Games Through Private Equity Partners," *Los Angeles Business Journal,* November 14, 2005, p. 18.

Richtel, Matt, "Ex-Insider Is Out to Shake Up Video Games," *New York Times,* December 16, 2005, p. C6.

Ross, Rachel, "Not Playing Around," *thestar.com,* April 9, 2001.

Saltzman, Marc, "The Ex-Doctors Are In," *National Post,* March 24, 2004, p. AL4.

Sapieha, Chad, "BioWare Gets into the Game with Elevation," *globeandmail.com,* October 11, 2005.

Shulgan, Christopher, and Melanie Collison, "Ray Muzyka and Greg Zeschuk," *Time Canada,* July 22, 2002.

Wahl, Andrew, "We Got Game," *Canadian Business,* November 23, 2003.

Block Communications, Inc.

541 N. Superior Street
Toledo, Ohio 43660
U.S.A.
Telephone: (419) 724-6448
Fax: (419) 724-6080
Web site: http://www.blockcommunications.com

Private Company
Incorporated: 1900 as Paul Block, Inc.
Employees: 3,000
Sales: $438.4 million (2004)
NAIC: 511110 Newspaper Publishers; 513120 Television Broadcasting Stations; 513310 Wired Telecommunications Carriers; 234920 Power and Communication Transmission Line Construction

∎∎∎

Block Communications, Inc. is a regional media conglomerate. Its principal properties include two venerable newspapers, the *Toledo Blade* and the *Pittsburgh Post-Gazette*. It also owns several broadcast television stations: WLIO, in Lima, Ohio; WDRB, in Louisville, Kentucky; WFTE, also in Louisville; KTRV, covering the Boise, Idaho area; and WAND, in Decatur, Illinois. Block also operates a phone, internet, and cable television company, Buckeye Cable Systems, and a business telephone services company, Buckeye Telesystems. In addition, Block Communications runs a home security service company and a construction company, Metro Fiber & Cable Construction. The company was founded by one of the 20th century's great newspapermen, Paul

Block. Block Communications continues in the hands of Block family members.

PAUL BLOCK'S EARLY YEARS

Paul Block was born in 1875 in the city of Koenigsburg, a north German city then the capital of the Duchy of Prussia. His Jewish family had fled poverty and persecution in Russia a few years before Paul was born, and in 1885 the family moved again, seeking better circumstances in the United States. The Blocks settled in Elmira, New York, an upstate town with a large Jewish community and thriving local businesses and cultural institutions. Block's father had been a salesman or peddler in the Old Country, and arriving in Elmira, he began work in the only trade he could manage without any capital: ragpicker or junkman. Paul Block, fourth of five surviving children, went to work at the age of ten. His first job was with the *Elmira Sunday Telegram*, beginning an involvement with newspapers that lasted the rest of his life.

The *Elmira Sunday Telegram* was at that time one of the leading East Coast newspapers, with a circulation only rivaled by the New York City papers. It was sold all over the Northeast, and was even exported to London. Its founder and editor, Harry S. Brooks, was responsible for the quality of the *Sunday Telegram*, which considered itself a highly ethical family newspaper, dedicated to local reporting. Paul Block began work at the *Sunday Telegram* as a messenger boy. Very early on he distinguished himself from the crowd of young boys working for the paper. He was known as fast on his bike, and he also had an unusually good memory as well as a charming manner. Block was given the job of escorting the paper's mascot, a St. Bernard dog called Colonel. The paper used photographs of the diminutive Paul Block and the gigantic dog as a promotion. Block not only fed and cared for Colonel, but he exhibited him throughout Elmira and in other towns such as Corning and Syracuse. Young Block even took Colonel to New York City, where he and the dog were put up in the Waldorf Hotel and took questions from the press in the glittering lobby.

Block continued to attend school while working for the paper. He learned every aspect of putting the *Elmira Sunday Telegram* together, setting type, writing stories, and then at the age of 16 becoming an advertising solicitor. Advertising became Block's real forte. He was a natural salesman, with considerable people skills as well as memory and mathematical acumen, so he easily convinced Elmira businesses to place their advertisements with the *Sunday Telegram*. As with practically every newspaper that he was associated with ever after, the *Sunday Telegram*'s advertising volume increased dramatically once Block was on the scene.

By the time Block was 20 and had graduated from high school, he realized that he could make a good living as an advertising solicitor, but only if he relocated to a larger market. In 1895 he moved to New York City and began working as a so-called publisher's special representative for The Richardson Company. The Richardson Company functioned as an advertising broker for newspapers trying to attract national advertising accounts. Newspapers in Ohio or Colorado, for example, needed to carry advertisements for such nationally distributed brands as Quaker Oats or Wrigley's Gum, in addition to advertisements from local businesses. If they used a special representative in New York, where all the major advertising agencies were clustered, it was much easier than approaching each national brand separately. Block's job was to negotiate between newspapers and advertisers. He became such an expert at marketing that his newspaper customers deferred to him on matters including the timing of ad campaigns and what exactly

they should advertise. Though it was not exactly in his job description, Block sometimes even wrote ad copy himself.

LAUNCHING PAUL BLOCK, INC. IN 1900

In 1900, Block decided to go into business for himself. He opened the offices of Paul Block, Inc. on the Upper West Side of Manhattan and carried on as a special representative. Many of his clients from Richardson moved their accounts to the new company out of loyalty to Block. He continued to perform magnificently as a salesman, and in 1903, publishing trade journal *Editor & Publisher* did a feature on him, referring to him as one of the nation's premier newspapermen. Block was still in his 20s, financially successful but not yet really wealthy, and his association with newspapers was still completely tied to advertising sales. In 1906 he became director of advertising for the *Illustrated Sunday Magazine* and a year later took the same title at the *Pictorial Review*. Under Block's guidance, these became two of the leading magazines of the day.

Block married Dina Wallach in 1907, and from this date through the end of the 1920s, his career was so hectic and varied that it is difficult to put in order. Paul Block, Inc. continued to do well in the advertising soliciting business, and Block had several trusted associates who worked diligently for the company for many years. While this business thrived and expanded, Block built up the two magazines he served as director of advertising for. The *Illustrated Sunday Magazine* was something like today's *Parade* magazine, a Sunday supplement that was inserted in newspapers all across the country. There had been a few forerunners to this style of publication, but the *Illustrated Sunday Magazine* was the first with an entirely independent editorial staff, so that it was not the local product of any particular paper. It is not known who started the magazine before Block took over, but already by 1907, when it was about a year old, it had a circulation of nearly two million customers. Advertising revenue was thought to be more than $500,000 annually, and it was taken up by most of the leading papers in the nation, including the *Boston Herald*, the *Washington Post*, the *Detroit Free Press*, the *Minneapolis Tribune*, and the *Memphis Commercial Appeal* as well as scores of smaller and lesser-known newspapers of the day. The *Illustrated Sunday Magazine* was known for high-quality fiction by Jack London and mystery writer Mary Roberts Rinehart, travel tales, celebrity features, and glossy four-color illustrations by the country's most prominent artists.

At the same time that Block was bringing in loads of national advertising to the *Illustrated Sunday Magazine*,

KEY DATES

1900: Paul Block Inc. is launched.
1916: Block buys first newspaper.
1926: Block buys *Toledo Blade.*
1927: Company acquires *Pittsburgh Post-Gazette.*
1941: Paul Block dies; advertising firm is sold and media holdings pass to sons William and Paul, Jr.
1972: Company moves into television market with purchase of WLIO-TV.
1992: *Post-Gazette* buys and closes *Pittsburgh Press.*
2006: Company hints its newspaper properties might be sold.

he also built up *Pictorial Review,* a women's magazine founded in 1899. *Pictorial Review* was owned and published by an Elmira businessman, William Ahnelt, who started the publication as an offshoot of his dress pattern business. It lagged behind seven other fashion and pattern-magazines when Block came on board, but it gradually increased its circulation to become the number one women's magazine, as well as one of the most profitable magazines of any sort in the United States. Block's role at *Pictorial Review* was complex. The magazine's founder had left editorial decisions to others, and Block's job was ostensibly only with the advertising end. Block did things such as entice Samuel Goldwyn, the Hollywood movie producer, to write a column for the magazine, and Block authorized huge payments to secure the serialization of the novel *The Age of Innocence,* by Edith Wharton. Block endeavored to keep the magazine up-to-date, unique, and attractive, and his reach extended far beyond what might be assumed as an advertising director's role.

STARTING TO PUBLISH NEWSPAPERS IN 1916

Any one of Paul Block's three jobs might have been enough to keep a person busy, but Block found more to do. He began buying newspapers and installing himself as publisher, where he had control of the editorial content as well as the business end. He bought the *Newark Star-Eagle* in 1916. In 1917 he bought the *Detroit Journal,* which he sold in 1922. In 1921 he acquired a controlling interest in the *Memphis News-Scimitar.* He sold the Memphis paper in 1926. In 1921 Block acquired the *Duluth Herald,* of Duluth, Minnesota. Later he bought a second Duluth paper, the *Duluth News-Tribune.* In 1926 he acquired the *Toledo*

Blade, and the next year he bought the *Pittsburgh Post-Gazette.* Amazingly, Paul Block worked hands-on with all these newspapers, even ones he did not hang onto for very long. Unlike the modus operandi at other chain newspapers, he did not attempt to make the papers he owned similar to each other, for example using the same type style. Each one was a separate entity, and Block brought his expertise to bear in unique ways. He traveled between his newspapers frequently, eventually in his own private luxury railway car.

By the 1920s the son of a ragpicker had become a spectacularly wealthy man, and Block was friends with many of the top names in New York society, including New York's mayor "Gentleman Jimmy" Walker, Florenz Ziegfeld of the Ziegfeld Follies, and the financier Bernard Baruch. Block was close to President Coolidge and to Herbert Hoover. His later relationship with President Roosevelt was also close, but not necessarily characterized as friendship, as they were at odds politically. Block was also a close friend, perhaps the only friend, of newspaperman William Randolph Hearst. Block was named executor of Hearst's will, and the two had complicated and often secret business dealings. Hearst's takeover of a newspaper was often met with dismay, as his papers were known for "yellow" journalism, including exaggeration and fabrication. In several instances, Block seemed to have bought a paper with Hearst's money and run it as a Block paper. While Block had ostensibly owned the *Pittsburgh Post-Gazette* since 1927, ten years later he bought it from Hearst for approximately $2.5 million, meaning he bought out his silent partner.

STRUGGLING IN THE DEPRESSION

Block's businesses did well under his stewardship, providing him with enough wealth to outfit a gigantic country estate in Connecticut, where he moved in 1929. The stock market crash of October 1929 and the ensuing Great Depression brought great difficulty to Block's empire. Block continued to believe the Depression would be short-lived. He was a staunch supporter of Herbert Hoover and vehemently against Roosevelt's New Deal. In 1932 his newspaper the *Brooklyn Standard,* which he had bought in 1928, was near bankruptcy, and he sold it. Advertising revenue at all his papers fell as industries cut back on spending and unemployment rose. Block could do nothing but shed the unprofitable papers. By the middle of the Depression, in 1936, Block owned only the *Toledo Blade,* the *Pittsburgh Post-Gazette,* the *Newark Star-Eagle,* and two Milwaukee papers which again were presumably really Hearst's properties. In 1939 Block regretfully sold the *Newark Star-Eagle.*

Though Block was ill and probably depressed with worry over his financial difficulties, he traveled to Europe in the 1930s and met with world leaders, including Italy's Benito Mussolini. Block continued to invest in the *Pittsburgh Post-Gazette,* spending $1.5 million on new facilities in 1937. Though the business could ill afford it, Block thought he had to keep the paper up-to-date or fall prey to competitors. The *Post-Gazette* won journalism's highest award, the Pulitzer Prize, in 1937 for a story Block had set his reporters on, exposing Supreme Court Justice Hugo Black as a member of the Ku Klux Klan. Block died in 1941.

CHANGES AFTER WORLD WAR II

When Block died, his newspaper empire was split between his two sons. The elder son, Paul, Jr., was involved in war work through World War II, while William served in Asia until 1946. After the war, Paul took over the *Toledo Blade* while William went to Pittsburgh and ran the *Post-Gazette.* The advertising company, Paul Block and Associates, was sold to its employees in 1946. The remaining media properties were combined in a holding company called Paul Block, Inc. The Block brothers had evidently learned much from their father, and they were each quite dedicated to their cities and papers. Both made changes to ensure their papers were more politically neutral than they had been in their father's day. Both the Pittsburgh and Toledo markets were quite competitive. The *Post-Gazette* bought a rival paper, the formerly Hearst-owned *Sun-Telegraph,* in 1960. This still left a formidable competitor, the *Pittsburgh Press.* The *Post-Gazette* signed a joint operating agreement with the *Pittsburgh Press* in 1962, which combined the two paper's business ends but maintained separate reporters and editors. This agreement lasted 30 years.

Paul Block, Inc. expanded its media holdings in the 1960s and 1970s. It bought several small newspapers, the *Register,* of Red Bank, New Jersey, in 1965 and the *Daily News* of Port Clinton, Ohio, the next year. In 1967 it acquired the *Peninsula Herald,* of Monterey, California. These smaller papers were sold off by the mid-1980s, except for the *Peninsula Herald.* The company began investing in television in the 1960s as well, and these holdings lasted longer. In Toledo, the company went in with a local cable company to form a new entity, Buckeye Cablevision, in 1965, at the dawn of the cable television era. By the mid-1970s, Block had acquired all the stock in Buckeye and was sole owner. Buckeye was one of the top 20 cable television systems in the United States by the mid-1980s. In 1972, Block acquired its first network television station, WLIO-TV in Lima, Ohio. The company bought another television

station, WDRB, in Louisville, Kentucky, in 1984, and the next year bought a Boise, Idaho station, KTRV.

In Pittsburgh, the *Post-Gazette* and William Block were influential in supporting public works in the city, such as the mass transit system, the airport, and area schools and colleges. William Block was also a patron of the arts, involved with the Pittsburgh Symphony and collecting works by local artists. Likewise, the *Blade* was a big backer of the Toledo Industrial Development Council, which helped revitalize Toledo's port, among other projects. The *Blade* was a strong proponent of downtown development, though civic policy often went the other way. Paul Block, Jr., died in 1987, and his two sons, John and Allan Block, carried on. The other members of the holding company, then called Blade Communications, were their uncle, William Block, and his son, William Block, Jr.

POST-GAZETTE PURCHASE OF *PRESS* IN 1992

A significant change came to the *Post-Gazette* in 1992, when it and the *Pittsburgh Press* suffered a crippling strike. Under the joint operating agreement the two papers had entered in 1962, they used the same presses and the same distribution system. The papers were delivered by drivers represented by the powerful Teamsters union, and the union struck to protest a plan that would have reduced some 200 distribution jobs. The strike dragged on for eight months, until finally the *Press* decided it could not win, and it offered itself up for sale. *Post-Gazette* parent company Blade Communications opted to buy the *Press* in a deal worth $100 million in cash and stock. In addition, Blade traded the *Press*'s owner, newspaper chain E.W. Scripps, its Monterey, California, paper, the *Peninsula Herald.* The new owner then ceased publication of the *Pittsburgh Press,* folding it into the *Post-Gazette.* The paper went back on sale in January 1993, now the reigning paper in the Pittsburgh market. In a highly competitive market, the *Post-Gazette* had finally ended up as the last one standing.

FAMILY BUSINESS BECOMING MORE BUSINESSLIKE

William Block, Sr., was chairman of his family's media holding company until 2001, when he stepped down at the age of 86. That year, his son William Block, Jr., became chairman of what was then called Block Communications, Inc. Paul, Jr.'s son John R. Block became vice-chairman, and his twin brother Allan Block ran the company's television divisions and was managing director of the parent company. William Block, Sr., died in

2005. Allan Block became chairman of Block Communications when William Block, Jr., retired.

As a private company, Block Communications was never required to make its financial records public, but in the early 2000s, news of financial worries at the company began to leak out. The company had invested heavily in facilities, including upgrading its television properties to digital format, and the newspapers had long been known for the generosity of their compensation to their employees. By 2002, Block Communications carried heavy debt, both from its investments in its plants and its obligations to retired employees. Though portions of the company, particularly the telecommunications divisions, had steeply climbing revenue in the early 2000s, the newspapers were less profitable, described by Allan Block in an interview with the *Toledo Business Journal* (December 1, 2002) as performing "substantially below industry standards." Block continued to explain that the poor performance of the newspapers was "something we must address if we are to continue in the newspaper business."

Allan Block made it known that the newspapers needed to be run as businesses, that is, they had to make money. The company let go some non-union personnel, including in 2006 a cartoonist who had been with the *Post-Gazette* for 30 years. The *Blade* had made a splash in 2004, winning a Pulitzer Prize for a series of stories about a Special Forces unit that had committed atrocities during the Vietnam War and gone unreproved for nearly 30 years. The paper was clearly committed to top-drawer journalism. Yet in 2006, Block Communications closed the Washington bureau that had served both the *Blade* and the *Post-Gazette*. Contracts with the ten unions that served the *Blade* and the *Post-Gazette* were scheduled to expire in 2006. The parent company emphasized that it needed to cut costs, particularly labor costs. Block Communications announced that it would consider selling the newspapers if it was unable to bring costs down. This seemed a clear indication that big changes were coming for Block Communications as the third and fourth generations of the Block family took control.

A. Woodward

PRINCIPAL SUBSIDIARIES

Toledo Blade Co.; Pittsburgh Post-Gazette; Buckeye Telesystem Inc.; Metro Fiber & Cable Construction; CPS; WLIO-TV; WDRB-TV; KTRV-TV; WFTE-TV; WAND-TV (66%).

PRINCIPAL COMPETITORS

Advance Publications, Inc.; Gannett Co., Inc.; Knight-Ridder, Inc.

FURTHER READING

"Bill Block," *Pittsburgh Post-Gazette,* June 21, 2005, p. B6.

"Blade Parent Facing Financial Pressures," *Toledo Business Journal,* August 1, 2002, p. 18.

"Block Party," *Pittsburgh Post-Gazette,* October 2, 2000, p. B1.

Brady, Frank, *The Publisher: Paul Block: A Life of Friendship, Power and Politics,* New York: University Press of America, 2001.

Enda, Jodi, "Blocked Out," *American Journalism Review,* April/May 2006, pp. 10–11.

Guy, Pat, "Post-Gazette Back in Circulation," *USA Today,* January 19, 1993, p. 4B.

Harrison, John M., *The Blade of Toledo: The First 150 Years,* Toledo: Toledo Blade Co., 1985.

"An Interview with Block Communications Management," *Toledo Business Journal,* December 1, 2002, p. 14.

McGoughand, Michael, and James O'Toole, "Longtime Publisher of Post-Gazette Dies," *Pittsburgh Post-Gazette,* June 21, 2005, p. A1.

Napsha, Joe, "P-G Fires Cartoonist, Bureau Chief," *Tribune Review* (Greensburg, Pa.), February 4, 2006.

"P-G, Toledo Blade Might Go Up for Sale," *Tribune Review* (Greensburg, Pa.), February 18, 2006.

Santo, Jamie, "Chairman of Block Newspapers Retires," *Editor & Publisher,* December 17, 2001, p. 8.

Thomas, Clarke, "PG Marks 75 Years Since Birth," *Pittsburgh Post-Gazette,* August 4, 2002, p. B1.

C&K Market, Inc.

---

615 Fifth Street
Brookings, Oregon 97415
U.S.A.
Telephone: (541) 469-3113
Fax: (541) 469-6717
Web site: http://www.ckmarket.com

Private Company
Incorporated: 1967
Employees: 1,700
Sales: $361.4 million (2005)
NAIC: 445110 Supermarkets and Other Grocery (Except Convenience) Stores

■ ■ ■

C&K Market, Inc. operates about 55 supermarkets in small to mid-sized rural communities with populations of fewer than 10,000 in southern Oregon and northern California, mostly under the name Ray's Food Place. Some stores are called Price Less Foods and Shop Smart. The chain's competitive strategy is to operate quality grocery stores in niche, underserved markets. Stores are fully equipped with grocery, meat, dairy, produce, and health and beauty aid departments and offer multiple brands at varying price points.

1956–1989: SMALL COMMUNITY MARKET BECOMING A REGIONAL CHAIN

Raymond (Ray) L. Nidiffer came to Brookings, Oregon, from Utah in 1957 and bought a one-half share in the town's local grocery store, the Collins and Kimberly Market. Nidiffer, who replaced Kimberly, jointly operated the 3,200-square-foot store with Collins at its original location until 1963. They then moved the business to a 10,000-square-foot building close by in Brookings. In 1967, the business incorporated as C&K Market, Inc.

In 1969, Nidiffer bought out Collins, who retired. When Nidiffer took over the business, Brookings had the reputation of being a fairly insular community, run by a few families and people. Although Nidiffer was a relative newcomer, the business took off under his leadership. He built up the company's administrative and operations staff and began steadily to acquire other stores in small communities throughout southern Oregon.

Most of the stores that the C&K Market leased or operated had been owned by individuals who were retiring. The company also became a member of United Grocers, a retailer-owned wholesaler, which supplied Sentry stores, and ran most of them under the Ray's Sentry Markets banner.

Nidiffer considered each new acquisition in terms of its size, age, volume of sales, and location, concentrating mostly on small supermarkets in rural locations. The strategy proved a wise one, and, by 1988, C&K had become the 62nd largest private company in Oregon, still closely held and managed. C&K's senior management met in Brookings, Oregon, every Monday, and Nidiffer, an amateur pilot, frequently visited his 23 stores in his Beechcraft Baron twin-engine plane.

```
┌─────────────────────────────────────────────┐
│                                               │
│              KEY DATES                        │
│             ━━━━━ ■ ━━━━━                      │
│                                               │
│  1957:  Raymond Nidiffer buys a half share    │
│         in Collins and Kimberly Market.       │
│  1967:  The business incorporates as C&K      │
│         Market.                               │
│  1969:  Nidiffer becomes the sole owner of    │
│         the company.                          │
│  1994:  The company introduces its own        │
│         private label program.                │
│  1997:  Doug Nidiffer takes over leadership   │
│         of C&K when Ray Nidiffer retires.     │
│  2004:  C&K boosts its number of              │
│         supermarket outlets to 55.            │
│                                               │
└─────────────────────────────────────────────┘
```

1990–1995: INCREASED COMPETITION FROM LARGER COMPETITORS

By 1990, C&K had more than 20 stores and was generating revenues of $144 million. Nonetheless, it was feeling the pinch from its larger supermarket and "big box" competitors. To solve the problem, Nidiffer put a dedicated general manager in each of the chain's stores. The managers went through extensive training to learn about promotional programs and "schematics" to develop the ideal product mix for their location. As a result of this training, C&K eliminated some 2,000 to 9,000 store-keeping units (SKUs).

By 1993, with 27 Ray's Sentry Markets, the rapidly expanding C&K no longer had to advertise for employees, and, in fact, had a waiting list of applicants, unusual for most businesses of its sort. Nidiffer's method of attracting and motivating people was to offer a combination of tangible and intangible rewards designed to recognize and reward employees' for their worth. Although the stores were not unionized, employees' pay was comparable to that of most union shops, and benefits were also good, including a profit sharing plan, a 401K plan, life insurance, and health insurance with vision and dental coverage.

In addition, the company had "an open-door policy" on grievances. "From box boy and girl on up," Nidiffer noted in a 1993 *Progressive Grocer* article, "we work hard to keep employees happy." He went on to claim that "we work them hard too. We don't want them unless they are happy and work hard. If they do a lot of humping, they can be store managers by the time they're 21. ... We get employees locally, but all the top people come from other stores."

By 1994, C&K had 31 stores ranging from Veneta, Oregon, a small town near Eugene, south to Davis, California. In total, they did a volume of $150 million in sales. Twenty-six of the stores operated under the banner Ray's Food Place. Of the other five, one was a Ray's Sentry, and four were Ray's Shop Smart Warehouse stores. The stores varied in size from 5,800 to 46,000 square feet, although the C&K prototype floor plan was mostly in the 40,000-square-foot range.

During the early to mid-1990s, C&K Market became a regional force in the supermarket industry, part of a trend of developing regional chains around the country. It dropped its Sentry affiliation because it had become large enough that it no longer needed to be a part of a marketing group and also because it wanted to distance itself from Sentry's high-price image, though it continued to be a part of the United Grocers group. As C&K grew, it faced increasing competition from other chains, some of them much larger, such as Lucky in California and Safeway, Albertson's, and Fred Meyer in Oregon.

1995–2006: BUILDING BIGGER STORES AND REMODELING

As part of its expansion, C&K began building bigger stores and putting more of an emphasis on cultivating its low-price image. It also mapped out its expansion into other parts of Oregon and into new areas in northern California. According to Nidiffer in a February 1995 *Progressive Grocer* article, there was "a lot of opportunity in northern California." As for Oregon, the chain wanted "to go further north, into Salem."

In 1994, C&K purchased the largest grocery store in Sisters, Oregon. At 31,000 square feet, the Pioneer Sentry was the primary market in a small town and became C&K's easternmost store. C&K also opened three new stores in California in the mid- to late 1990s in Eureka, McKinleyville, and Clearlake, all upwards of 40,000 square feet in area.

In addition, it began upgrading its Shop Smart basic warehouse stores, putting tile on floors and including better product assortments. In one remodel in 1995, it doubled the size of a Shop Smart, added a bakery and deli and a video department, and began to offer more non-food items.

Other C&K stores, too, received remodels. As part of C&K's longtime emphasis on offering perishables as a strategy for differentiating itself from its competition, it began to devote more space in its markets to produce and full-service meat departments and added service delis and bakeries with small seating areas. It also enlarged the size of the health and beauty care departments in stores by as much as 55 percent, both increasing the variety of items and making these departments more visible. Some remodels added service departments that included ATM machines, fax transmission, photocopying, film developing, audio book rentals, money order sales, and Western Union. As part of its increased product mix, C&K also introduced its own private label program of Ray's brand for dairy products, bread, and eggs.

Sales increased by about 20 percent in C&K's 40,000- to 50,000-square-foot stores as a result of re-merchandising in the 1990s. By 1997, the year in which Doug Nidiffer took over leadership of C&K from his father, the chain embarked on the last phase of its promotional program with an increased focus on seasonal merchandising.

According to Daniel Van Zant, the chain's director of general merchandise, in a 1997 *Progressive Grocer* article, the focus "really improved the overall image of the store at these key times of the year." Before, the stores "just didn't have the variety ... to satisfy customers and keep them from shopping our competitors." Once the stores began to put together a regular series of promotions to sell seasonal items, there was an almost immediate increase in seasonal sales of 200 percent. In response, some stores more than doubled the space allocated to seasonal items.

The following year, *Oregon Business* ranked C&K as the 32nd largest privately owned company in the state. The company then operated 18 stores in southwestern Oregon and another 18 in northern California. It employed more than 1,500 workers, 800 of them in Oregon. In 2000, C&K ranked 25th among Oregon's privately owned companies, and in 2002, the parent company of Ray's Food Place, Shop Smart, and Price-Less Foods was number 20.

Although a year later, it had dropped to number 21, the company still opted to follow its strategy of locating stores on the perimeter of population centers to avoid head-to-head competition with larger chains, including Wal-Mart and Costco. "When we went to Davis in 1994, the idea was to fill in down I-5 and into the central part of California. But the big boxes got so aggressive in that area that it hasn't happened. ... You get into metropolitan areas where there are bigger stores and there's serious competition," Doug Nidiffer explained in a 2003 *Mail Tribune* article. "We find smaller towns on the edge of big markets work the best. We ... don't have the economies of scale the 'big boxes' do."

By 2003, C&K, with 50 stores including seven in the Rogue Valley, turned its focus on Jackson County. It purchased Rick's Thriftway in Eagle Point in 2003, and

Shop N Kart in White City and the Jacksonville Market in Jacksonville in 2004. Initial plans called for doubling the White City store in size, but, as was also the case at the Jacksonville location, it was "a neighborhood type of market, quite a bit smaller than most." Growth had to come through efficiency, stacking cans tighter and moving product through faster.

Between 1990 and 2005, more than half of C&K's stores had been remodeled. The family-owned chain also entered its largest market yet with its largest store, a 55,000-square-foot supermarket that it purchased in Eugene, Oregon. The new Ray's had a somewhat more upscale product line, with an emphasis on natural foods, a wide selection of produce, a large meat department, bakery, deli, and an in-store pharmacy, coffee shop, and video outlet. In an effort to reflect the architecture of the community, the building incorporated a brick-and-glass design heavy on natural light and solar features. C&K also bought three stores from the Market of Choice grocery chain in 2004, bringing its total number of stores to 55.

In 2006, Ray's Food Place in Bend took part in a pilot project with the Oregon Liquor Control Commission to locate liquor stores in supermarkets. The pilot proved successful. "We had some pretty lofty expectations for the concept," Nidiffer announced in a 2006 *Knight/Ridder Tribune News* article, "And it has exceeded it." With its experienced management team, dominant position in its markets, and strong local brand image and loyal customer base, C&K Market seemed likely to exceed other expectations as well.

Carrie Rothburd

PRINCIPAL COMPETITORS

Albertson's, Inc.; Safeway Inc.; SUPERVALU Inc.; Wal-Mart Stores, Inc.; Costco Wholesale Corporation.

FURTHER READING

"Back to Basics," *Progressive Grocer*, October 1, 1997.

Chiang, Chuck, "Oregon Panel Grants Permanent Status to Liquor Store Located in Supermarket," *Knight /Ridder Tribune News Service*, April 24, 2006.

"One of Brookings' 'Big Fish' Hooked on a Smaller Pond," *Oregonian*, November 21, 1988, p. C10.

Stiles, Greg, "Jacksonville, Oregon Community Grocery Store to Become Part of Chain," *Mail Tribune*, April 28, 2004.

———, "Parent of Oregon Supermarket Company to Purchase Eagle Point Store," *Mail Tribune*, April 9, 2003.

Weinstein, Steve, "Poised for Growth," *Progressive Grocer*, February 1995, p. 85.

The Charles Schwab Corporation

———■———

101 Montgomery Street
San Francisco, California 94104
U.S.A.
Telephone: (415) 627-7000
Toll Free: (800) 435-4000
Fax: (415) 636-5970
Web site: http://www.schwab.com

Public Company
Incorporated: 1974 as Charles Schwab & Co., Inc.
Employees: 14,000
Total Assets: $47.35 billion (2005)
Stock Exchanges: NASDAQ
Ticker Symbol: SCHW
NAIC: 523110 Investment Banking and Securities Dealing; 523120 Securities Brokerage; 523920 Portfolio Management; and 523930 Investment Advice

■ ■ ■

The Charles Schwab Corporation ranks among the nation's largest financial services firms. Explosive growth within the stock market during the 1990s has helped operating subsidiary Charles Schwab & Co., Inc. become the largest discount stock broker in the United States and the largest provider of online brokerage services. A pioneer in the area of no-transaction fee mutual funds, the company has also earned standing as one of the three largest managers of mutual funds, alongside Fidelity and Vanguard. Despite its reputation as a major player in the industry, Charles Schwab has been forced in the 2000s to scale back, rethink its strategy, and rethink it again.

PIONEER DISCOUNT BROKER

Charles Schwab, the company's founder, had received an M.B.A. degree from Stanford University and had been working for a small California investment adviser when, in 1971, he founded his own company, First Commander Corp. He and two partners created a stock mutual fund that soon had $20 million in assets. They ran into trouble with securities regulators, however, when it was learned that they had failed to register the fund. This error temporarily forced Schwab out of business, but he soon reopened a small money-management firm, Charles Schwab & Co., Inc., in San Francisco, which he incorporated in 1974.

On May 1, 1975, the U.S. Congress deregulated the stock brokerage industry by taking away the power of the New York Stock Exchange to determine the commission rates charged by its members. This opened the door to discount brokers, who took orders to buy and sell securities, but did not offer advice or do research the way larger, established brokers such as Merrill Lynch did. This presented an opportunity to win individual investors well enough versed in the stock market not to need the advice offered by established brokers. Schwab quickly took advantage of deregulation, opening a small San Francisco brokerage, financed primarily with borrowed money, and buying a seat on the New York Stock Exchange.

The new discount brokers, whose commissions might be only 30 percent of the rates before deregulation, were scorned by the old-line brokerages. During his first few years as a discount broker, Schwab had to contend with bad publicity generated by the older firms, some of whom threatened to break their leases if landlords allowed Schwab to rent offices in the same building.

Schwab fought back by buying newspaper ads featuring his photograph and asking customers to contact him personally, helping to build the firm's credibility. Possibly the most important early decision made by Schwab was to open branch offices around the United States. He reasoned that even investors not needing advice would prefer doing business through a local office instead of a toll-free telephone number. The move won customers and helped differentiate Schwab from the large number of discount firms appearing after deregulation.

Over the next few years Schwab did several things to pull away from the pack. The company offered innovative new services including the ability to place orders 24 hours a day. It bought advanced computer systems to deal quickly with huge volumes of orders and continued its heavy advertising, seeking to project an upscale image. Top executives were given expensive foreign cars, and an interior design staff was commissioned to help showcase certain new branches. Some industry analysts maintain that with these measures Schwab helped bring discount brokering into the mainstream of financial institutions.

PURCHASE BY BANKAMERICA: 1983

The firm's rapid expansion was costly, however. Partly as a result of high operating costs and partly because sales were dependent on the sentiments of small investors, profits were erratic. Schwab sometimes turned to employees and larger customers to raise money for further expansion. By 1980 Schwab was by far the largest discounter in the country. That year, to fund further growth, Schwab decided to take the company public. The offering was called off, however, when some problems caused by the attempted conversion to a new computer system proved an embarrassment to the company. Raising sufficient capital in private became more difficult, partly because of the erratic earnings.

Finally, in 1983, Schwab arranged for San Francisco's BankAmerica Corporation to acquire the company for $55 million in BankAmerica stock. BankAmerica also agreed to supply Schwab with capital. The bank loaned Schwab $50 million over the next three years, but Schwab remained one of the most highly leveraged brokerages.

The sale to BankAmerica may have provided needed capital, but it also fettered the company with banking regulations. Schwab wanted to offer new, proprietary lines of investments including Charles Schwab mutual funds. However, federal law at the time forbid banks and their subsidiaries from underwriting such securities. Although Schwab initially sought to challenge the law, as its wording contained some ambiguities, BankAmerica did not want to irritate banking regulators. Tensions between Schwab and its parent were further exacerbated when BankAmerica's stock price began falling, making Schwab's stake in the corporation worth less.

Schwab introduced the Mutual Fund Marketplace in 1984 with an initial investment of $5 million. The Marketplace allowed customers to invest in 250 separate mutual funds and switch between them using Schwab as the bookkeeper. All of a customer's mutual fund accounts were put on a single monthly statement. The company's profile was further raised in 1984 when Schwab's book *How to Be Your Own Stockbroker* was published. In it Schwab presented himself as a populist fighting against Wall Street stockbrokers in the name of the average investor. He contended that there is an inherent conflict of interest when a firm owns stock in inventory, writes favorable research recommendations on those stocks, and has commissioned salespeople sell those stocks to the public. At the same time, Schwab's company was moving into elegant new headquarters in downtown San Francisco.

In 1985 Schwab had 90 branches and 1.2 million customers, generating $202 million in revenue. Though it was far larger than its leading discount competitors, it was small compared with the largest retail brokerages, which had over 300 branches. The firm was growing in other ways, however. It offered personal computer software, called the Equalizer, that allowed investors to place orders via computer as well as to call up stock information and obtain research reports.

BUYBACK AND PUBLIC OFFERING IN 1987

In 1987 Charles Schwab and a group of investors bought the company back from BankAmerica for $280 million. Seven weeks later, he announced plans to take the company public. The buyback had resulted in a debt of

KEY DATES

1971: Charles Schwab and partners form short-lived stock mutual fund.
1975: End of fixed rate commissions opens door for discount brokers.
1980: Public offering is sidetracked by technology problems.
1983: Bank of America buys firm.
1987: Management buyback, followed by public offering, creates new holding company.
1992: Company finds instant success with Mutual Fund OneSource.
1997: Company ranks as top online broker in the United States.
2000: Merger with U.S. Trust is completed.
2002: Company begins building affluent client base.
2004: Company works to regain traditional customers.
2005: Charles Schwab Corporation posts record numbers.

$200 million, and the initial public offering (IPO) was partly designed to eliminate some of this debt. It was also intended to raise money for further expansion. Schwab wanted to increase the number of branches to 120, including offices in Europe. The September 1987 IPO created a new holding company, The Charles Schwab Corporation, with Charles Schwab & Co., Inc. as its principal operating subsidiary.

The discount brokerage business had grown intensely competitive. Discounters handled a significant amount of retail equity trades by 1987, but hundreds of firms had entered the field, including banks, savings and loans, and mutual fund companies. Since Schwab was clearly the player to beat in discounting, competitors' advertisements specifically offered rates lower than Schwab's. Nevertheless, at this time Schwab had 1.6 million customers, about five times as many as its nearest competitor, Quick & Reilly Group. In 1987 the firm had sales of $465 million and profits of $26 million, twice the industry's average profit margin. To achieve this success, Schwab was spending about $15 million a year on advertising.

Schwab was already doing well with its expanded product line. Mutual Fund Marketplace had attracted $1.07 billion in client assets by year-end 1986. The company was also offering Individual Retirement Accounts, certificates of deposit, money-market accounts,

and Schwab One cash-management accounts. Despite these successes, Schwab was badly hurt by the stock market crash of October 1987. By mid-1988, trading volume had fallen to about 10,400 trades a day, a 40 percent drop from the months before the crash. Schwab cut costs to maintain profitability, reducing managerial salaries anywhere from 5 to 20 percent and laying off employees. Charles Schwab cut his own pay by 20 percent for six months and put branch expansion plans on hold. The firm also raised its trading commission by 10 percent, so that it needed only 8,000 trades a day to break even, down from 12,000 trades. Even with the cost-cutting, the firm's 1988 earnings plummeted 70 percent to $7.4 million on sales of $392 million.

RAPID EXPANSION

By 1989 Schwab was expanding again. The company bought Chicago-based Rose & Co. for $34 million from Chase Manhattan; as the fifth largest discount broker in the United States, Rose & Co. brought Schwab 200,000 new customers at a cost of about $70 each. With the purchase, Schwab controlled about 40 percent of the discount market, though discounters made only 8 percent of all retail commissions. Over the long run, Schwab realized its best strategy was to win customers from the full-service brokers. To help create more independent stock investors, it pioneered a service called TeleBroker that let customers place stock orders and get price quotes from any touchtone telephone 24 hours a day. It also released a new version of the Equalizer. The software had already sold 30,000 copies at $169 each since its introduction.

Individual investors returned to the stock market in 1989, and the firm's income surged to $553 million, with profits of $18.9 million. Income was further helped by an increase in client assets, from $16.8 billion in 1987 to $25 billion in early 1990. Commissions accounted for 70 percent of revenue, down from 85 percent in 1987.

Throughout the 1980s, Schwab updated its Mutual Fund Marketplace to allow customers to switch their investments from fund to fund by telephone. Customers paid a commission ranging from .6 percent to .08 percent, with a minimum fee of $29. Analysts were generally positive, pointing out that the amount of interest lost from having a check in the mail would pay for most of the service's commission fees. In 1991 Schwab entered a new and lucrative market with the acquisition of Mayer & Schweitzer, an over-the-counter stock market maker.

Meanwhile, Schwab was opening branch offices at a furious pace—17 in 1992 alone—and doubling the amount of money it spent on advertising. Schwab's aggressive stance helped raise its share of the discount market to 46 percent as the company attracted more than 40,000 new accounts a month. In 1992 Schwab acquired its first corporate jet, spending $12 million on a model with enough fuel capacity to reach London, where it was opening its first European branch. These additional costs helped drag down third-quarter earnings in 1992 when stock trading temporarily tapered off. The dip was a reminder that the company was still highly dependent on commissions and caused its stock to drop 20 percent.

Schwab cut advertising by 20 percent and took other steps to slow cost increases. The company converted a greater share of new branch offices into bare-bones operations with only one broker. Schwab already paid its 2,500 brokers less than other discounters, an average of $31,000 a year, compared with $50,000 at Fidelity Brokerage Services and $36,000 at Quick & Reilly.

INTRODUCTION OF ONESOURCE LEADING TO EXPLOSIVE GROWTH

The firm also continued searching for ways to become less dependent on commissions. The introduction in July 1992 of the Mutual Fund OneSource, a program allowing investors to trade mutual funds (more than 200 in all) from eight outside fund companies, without paying any transaction fees, attracted more than $500 million in assets within two months and over $4 billion by July 1993; it was thus the most successful first-year pilot of any new service in Schwab's history. The fund companies paid Schwab a small percentage fee, typically 0.25 to 0.35 percent, of the fund assets held in Schwab accounts.

During 1992 Schwab customers opened 560,000 new accounts at its 175 branch offices, while assets in customer accounts grew 38 percent to $65.6 billion. Revenue soared to $909 million, with record profits of $81 million. As a result of these successes, Schwab opened 20 more branch offices in 1993, opened an office in London (its first in Europe), and introduced several proprietary mutual funds, including Schwab International Index Fund and Schwab Small-Cap Index Fund.

As the 1990s continued, the OneSource program became wildly successful. By 1997 investors could choose among more than 1,400 mutual funds and had poured $80 billion into the funds through the program. OneSource, aided by the long bull market, helped Schwab grow at an amazing rate in the 1990s. From 1992 through 1997, revenues increased at a 25 percent

compounded annual rate, while customer assets increased 40 percent per year, from $65.6 billion to $353.7 billion. Also fueling this growth was the emergence of Internet trading as Schwab rapidly gained the number one position among online brokerage services. By May 1997 the firm claimed 700,000 of the 1.5 million active, online brokerage accounts in the United States. It also moved into the top five among all U.S. brokerages.

Schwab's explosive growth, which saw customer accounts increase from two million in 1992 to 4.8 million in 1997, was accompanied by several technological snafus, prompting some company clients to conclude that Schwab was growing too fast. For instance, in the summer of 1997 two computer-related outages temporarily left thousands of Schwab clients without access to their accounts. In addition, some clients were mistakenly sent the statements of other clients. Schwab officials contended that these were isolated incidents and not indicative of out-of-control growth.

The company also had to contend with the aging of the baby boom generation, the members of which were somewhat belatedly planning for retirement. Schwab set up a retirement plan services unit offering 401(k) and other retirement plans. Aging investors also tended to want more advice before deciding where to put their money. In response, Schwab bolstered its ability to deliver investment advice to clients, developing written investment kits; providing access to a wide range of research reports, earnings forecasts, and news stories on its web site; and offering the opportunity to meet in person with representatives at company branches. Another new and highly sought-after service added by Schwab in 1997 was access to initial public offerings at the offering price. The firm entered into alliances with Credit Suisse First Boston Corporation, J.P. Morgan & Co., and Hambrecht & Quist Group to gain access to IPOs led by these companies.

On January 1, 1998, David S. Pottruck became president and co-CEO of Charles Schwab Corporation, with Charles Schwab remaining chairman and sharing the co-CEO title. This unusual arrangement seemed to indicate that Pottruck, age 49 at the time, was in line to succeed the 60-year-old Schwab, though the company founder had made no retirement plans. Just a month or so earlier, Timothy F. McCarthy was named president and chief operating officer of Charles Schwab & Co., giving him day-to-day responsibility for the management of the brokerage unit, with Pottruck controlling overall administration, finance, technology, and corporate strategy.

It was this new management team that would have to contend with what would likely be an increasingly volatile stock market in the early 21st century. Also, the shift to more trading on the Internet, where fees were lower, was cutting into Schwab's bread-and-butter commissions. It was reported in September 1998 that the company, which already offered services in Hong Kong and the United Kingdom, was considering entering the Japanese market, among other international expansion possibilities.

A VOLATILE NEW MILLENNIUM

The new century started out with a bang. Schwab put down $3 billion for the 149-year-old U.S. Trust Corp. The wealth advisory company, looking toward the retirement of insiders, had been positioning itself for change. Schwab, meanwhile, wanted to expand its services to investors with very high net worth. When the Gramm-Leach-Bliley Act which allowed financial institutions crossover businesses passed in 1999, the way was eased for a merger between the pair.

A bust followed the bang, however. Schwab soon was reeling from a dramatic drop-off in online trading precipitated by the tech stock collapse and deepened by the September 11, 2001 terrorist attacks and the Enron bankruptcy in December.

To avoid layoffs, Schwab eliminated bonuses, cut executive pay, promoted unpaid sabbaticals and days off, and encouraged part-time or job-share positions, *Fortune* recounted. Yet those and other efforts failed to stem the tide of pink slips to come. During 2001, daily average trades dropped by roughly a third. Yearly revenue fell 25 percent to $4.35 billion and net income was off by 72 percent to $199 million.

Seeking to regain some ground, in May 2002, the firm established Schwab Private Client to serve individuals with more than $500,000 to invest. Concurrently, they began promoting a new in-house computer-based stock grading system. "It's a systematic approach with nothing but objectivity, not influenced by corporate relationships, investment banking, or any of the above," Pottruck told *Business Week*. Meanwhile, households with less than $50,000 to invest were being asked to pay more for Schwab services.

While Schwab had a strong track record bringing new ventures into the financial market, some of its endeavors had of late been less successful. In 1999, Schwab led a consortium to establish Epoch Partners Inc. to underwrite tech IPOs, but it stalled with the tech stock meltdown and Schwab sold its stake in the venture in 2001 to Goldman Sachs. Two other endeavors, wireless-trading service PocketBroker and online-service CyberTrader, had yet to find their stride.

The merger with U.S. Trust (UST) had not yet lived up to expectations, due, in part, to the market downturn. Private banking assets had generally declined, with UST average assets falling more precipitously than its competitors, according to *Institutional Investor*. Another fly in UST's ointment was a $10 million fine for violation of money laundering rules, a judgment handed down after the merger with Schwab. Moreover, a melding of clients between Schwab and UST had yet to manifest itself, as Schwab investment advisers balked at the idea. Late in 2002, Schwab instituted a change of leadership and direction at UST.

Schwab relinquished his position as co-CEO in 2003, leaving Pottruck in charge. Schwab, who controlled 25 percent of the company and continued as chairman, attributed the decision to step down to a current wave of concern regarding corporate governance.

Changes were taking place abroad as well. Charles Schwab Europe, the firm's pound-denominated brokerage in the United Kingdom, was sold to Barclays PLC, *American Banker* reported. The dollar-denominated business continued to offer trades on U.S. exchanges and in U.S. investment products. The company's Canadian brokerage operation had been sold in 2002 and joint ventures in Japan and Australia exited in the final quarter of 2001. The rise, then fall, of the markets prompted Schwab to enter, then exit, online international markets.

In a move to bring in new revenue, the Charles Schwab Bank opened in 2003. The bank planned to focus on mortgages, tapping into the red-hot market. Long-term interest rates were at their lowest levels in more than four decades. Operating primarily online, by phone, and mail, the bank also would offer checking, savings, and certificates of deposit accounts, according to *Long Island Business News*.

During the later half of 2003, Schwab joined the growing list of financial companies targeted for investigation by Eliot Spitzer, New York's attorney general, and the Securities and Exchange Commission (SEC). Schwab faced allegations regarding market timing by a fund family operated by UST and illegal late trading in the Schwab Mutual Fund Marketplace. The tarnishing of its trustworthiness, a trait crucial to the brand, hit Schwab stock harder than other financial operations under investigation. Brokerage stock overall had been climbing as the market recovered.

For much of its history, Schwab had been aided by bull market conditions that drew a broader range of investors into the arena. When the bear market took hold, both revenue and stock price suffered. Revenue of $5.8 billion in 2000 fell to $4.1 billion in 2002. Stock as high as $50.16 per share in April 1999, traded in the $11 per share range in 2003. A quarter of its employees had been axed. Survivors of the cuts lost bonuses, which made up a good deal of compensation, and their 401(k) matches.

In July 2004, the board asked Pottruck to resign. Schwab returned as CEO. The firm's new mission was to win back retail customers and reestablish its discount brokerage status. Some industry watchers expected Schwab to divest noncore, unprofitable businesses such as Schwab Capital Markets, according to *American Banker*. Sale of the upscale U.S. Trust Corp. also was the subject of speculation. Efforts to add multimillionaire clients and sell advisory services to less well-heeled investors produced lackluster results. In addition, while Schwab was moving into new areas, E*Trade Financial Corp. and Ameritrade, offering cheaper trades, eroded Schwab's core market share.

Schwab did sell Schwab Capital Markets in 2004, to USB AG. The firm also settled the SEC's mutual fund late trade investigation by agreeing to pay a $350,000 fine.

In an effort to retain clients and entice new ones Schwab had been cutting fees: seven price cuts in the past 16 months, according to a September 2004 *American Banker* article. The latest cuts included elimination of the annual service fee on accounts of less than $25,000 and the order-handling fee on equity trades.

Cuts in fees, an aggressive nationwide ad campaign, and severance costs at UST ate into 4th quarter earnings in 2005. Another sour note was hit when the New York Stock Exchange fined Schwab $1 million in regard to violations involving disbursement of customer assets. Schwab began trading concurrently on the NYSE and NASDAQ in 2004 and moved solely to the NASDAQ in 2005. On the flip side, trading activity improved at Schwab and UST made gains in new assets. Since May, UST had been headed up by the former CEO of Citigroup's global private bank.

Schwab succeeded in posting record income for the year, at $725 million up from $286 million in 2004. Total client assets reached a new peak, $1.2 trillion. Both net income and earnings per share surpassed previous records set in 2000.

Former Citigroup Global Consumer Group Chair and CEO Marjorie Magner joined the Schwab board of directors in 2006. The addition of Magner, who led one of Citigroup's most profitable business divisions, fueled speculation as to her future role with the company, perhaps that of a successor to the founder.

Scott M. Lewis
Updated, David E. Salamie; Kathleen Peippo

PRINCIPAL SUBSIDIARIES

Charles Schwab & Co., Inc.; U.S. Trust Corporation; Charles Schwab Bank, N.A.; CyberTrader, Inc.

PRINCIPAL COMPETITORS

E*Trade Financial Corporation; FMR Corp.; Merrill Lynch & Co., Inc.; Scottrade, Inc.; TD Ameritrade Holding Corporation.

FURTHER READING

Bianco, Anthony, "Schwab vs. Les Quick," *Business Week*, May 12, 1986.

Blake, Rich, "Breach of Trust: Recasting Itself As a Money Manager, Charles Schwab Is Shaking Up U.S. Trust," *Institutional Investor*, December 2002, pp. 29+.

Cole, Jim, "'Relentless' Fee Cutting, Bigger Profits at Schwab," *American Banker*, September 16, 2005, p. 20.

———, "Schwab Cites Ad, Other Costs in New Guidance," *American Banker*, November 16, 2005, p. 23.

Ferguson, Tim W., "Do It Yourself: Charles Schwab Has Ridden the Bull Market to a Splendid Present, but Its Future Is in Boomer Retirements," *Forbes*, April 22, 1996, p. 70.

Heins, John, "After Cost Cuts, What?" *Forbes*, May 1, 1989.

———, "How Now, Chuck Schwab?" *Forbes*, June 15, 1987.

Kador, John, "Schwab Makes His Move: The Inside Story on How Charles Schwab and His Board Finally Agreed It Was Time for the Fatigued Founder to Step Aside," *Chief Executive* (U.S.), March 2003, p. 56.

Laderman, Jeffrey M., "Remaking Schwab," *Business Week*, May 25, 1998, pp. 122–24, 127–29.

Lee, Louise, and Emily Thornton, "Schwab vs. Wall Street," *Business Week*, June 3, 2002, p. 64.

Lee, Louise, Emily Thornton, and Justin Hibbard, "Restore the Core," *Business Week*, August 2, 2004, p.72.

McGeehan, Patrick, "Charles Schwab's Pottruck Will Share Title of CEO with Company's Founder," *Wall Street Journal*, December 2, 1997, p. B5.

———, "Schwab's Offer of Rivals' Research Meets a Quick End," *Wall Street Journal*, January 19, 1998, pp. C1, C19.

McGough, Robert, "Schwab's Swelling Girth Holds Sway in the Fund Field," *Wall Street Journal*, November 9, 1993, pp. C1, C21.

Mitchell, Russell, "The Schwab Revolution," *Business Week*, December 19, 1994, pp. 88–91, 94–95, 98.

Morris, Betsy, "When Bad Things Happen to Good Companies: Schwab Was the Brokerage Built on Integrity and Fair Play," *Fortune*, December 8, 2003, p. 78.

Oliver, Suzanne L., "One-Stop Shopping," *Forbes*, November 11, 1991.

Pare, Terence P., "How Schwab Wins Investors," *Fortune*, June 1, 1992, p. 52.

Raghavan, Anita, "Schwab's Series of Misfires Puts Firm on the Defensive," *Wall Street Journal,* February 24, 1998, pp. C1, C27.

Raghavan, Anita, and Patrick McGeehan, "Schwab Again Plans to Offer Stock Research," *Wall Street Journal,* July 8, 1998, pp. C1, C15.

Ring, Niamh, "'Brain Drain' or a Facelift at Schwab," *American Banker,* October 1, 2004, p. 1.

———, "'Everything on the Table' with Schwab Back As CEO," *American Banker,* July 21, 2004, p. 1.

———, "Probe Knocking Schwab's Stock for a Loop," *American Banker,* November 18, 2003, p. 8.

———, "Schwab Blames War Jitters for Latest Cuts," *American Banker,* March 14, 2003, p. 8.

———, "Schwab Separates Chairman, CEO," *American Banker,* February 3, 2003, p. 20.

———, "Schwab Settles SEC Probe," *American Banker,* September 15, 2004, p. 18.

Schifrin, Matthew, "Cyber-Schwab: As Retail Brokerage Moves On-line, Charles Schwab Has Grabbed Nearly Half the Market," *Forbes,* May 5, 1997, p. 42.

"Schwab Expands into Banking Biz," *Long Island Business News,* May 2, 2003, pp. 9B+.

Shao, Maria, "Suddenly the Envy of the Street Is Schwab?" *Business Week,* March 19, 1990.

Siconolfi, Michael, "Schwab's Profit Stumbles amid Rise in Expenses Coupled with Less Trading," *Wall Street Journal,* September 29, 1992.

Sommar, Jessica, "Magner Joining Schwab Sparks Succession Talk," *Wall Street Letter,* February 6, 2006, pp. 1+.

CheckFree Corporation

4411 E. Jones Bridge Road
Norcross, Georgia 30092
U.S.A.
Telephone: (678) 375-3000
Fax: (678) 375-1477
Web site: http://www.checkfreecorp.com

Public Company
Incorporated: 1981
Employees: 3,050
Sales: $775.8 million (2005)
Stock Exchanges: NASDAQ
Ticker Symbol: CKFR
NAIC: 541519 Other Computer Related Services

■ ■ ■

CheckFree Corporation is a NASDAQ-listed company based in Norcross, Georgia, that provides a wide range of financial electronic commerce services and products to consumers through financial management software, banks, brokerage firms, and web sites. CheckFree divides its business between three divisions: Electronic Commerce, Investment Services, and Software.

The Electronic Commerce Division offers electronic billing, payment, and electronic funds transfer services to both consumers and businesses. Some 2,000 Internet sites rely on the company's electronic billing and payment technology. CheckFree also offers a walk-in bill payment system to accommodate consumers who prefer to pay bills in person, and subsidiary PhoneCharge Inc. allows billers to accept payments by way of the telephone.

CheckFree's Investment Services Division offers portfolio management services to brokers, money managers, and investment advisers. The main product of this unit is CheckFree APL, a real-time portfolio management system used by 80 percent of the top-50 brokers in the United States and virtually all of the leading money managers. Finally, CheckFree's Software Division licenses, installs, and maintains bank payment, operational risk management/reconciliation, financial messaging/corporate actions, compliance, and electronic billing software solutions. CheckFree maintains offices in more than a dozen U.S. cities, as well as international offices in countries such as Luxembourg, the United Kingdom, and Australia.

FOUNDING THE COMPANY IN 1981

CheckFree was founded in 1981 by Chairman and CEO Peter J. Kight. Raised in Columbus, Ohio, Kight studied philosophy at California State University, but his real interest, as he readily admitted, was finding a major that required little memorization and gave him the best chance to remain eligible for the school's track and field team to continue to participate in his specialty, the decathlon. When he injured his hamstring in his senior year and was unable to compete in 1977 he simply dropped out of school. To remain involved in the sport, he organized a track meet, which led him to rent a Bakersfield, California auditorium for a weightlifting and bodybuilding competition. There he met the publisher of *Muscle Digest*, who immediately hired Kight as the magazine's editor-in-chief. Over the next two years Kight grew *Muscle Digest*, along the way making the acquaintance of Arnold Schwarzenegger before the legendary bodybuilder made his transition to movies and politics. Kight's next stop was Texas, where he was hired as general manager of a small health club chain that was contending with new state laws that tried to rein in some of the industry's notorious sales practices. Knowing that a large number of people joining a health club would fail to keep up a commitment to exercise, owners tried to get customers to pay for a year's membership upfront, meaning in essence that they had to be signed up every year. It was Kight's desire to find an alternative to this practice that led to the creation of CheckFree.

Instead of charging a $250 lump sum annual payment, Kight wanted to charge customers $75 upfront and a $12-a-month automatic payment. To avoid the problem of billing he made an arrangement with a local bank so that a new member gave the club a voided check, delivered to the bank, which automatically made a transfer of money from the customers' checking account to the health club. In this way, after six months the club became profitable at the beginning of each month. Rather than fueling his excitement about the health club business, however, his success led him to quit, sensing there was a far greater opportunity in developing automatic payment systems for businesses other than health clubs.

In 1981 Kight returned to Columbus to pursue his new dream. With just $700 to his name, he moved into his grandmother's basement where he could live, and eat, for free. Unable to afford a computer needed for his endeavor, Kight worked out a barter arrangement with an apartment manager: In exchange for use of the manager's IBM 5120 at night (from 6 p.m. until 8:00 the next morning), he put the man's tenants on an automated payment schedule. To do his programming, Kight hired a man who took on moonlighting assignments and together they developed an automated

clearinghouse (ACH) program. After about seven months they had a working system.

BREAKTHROUGH IN 1984

Kight convinced Columbus-based Banc One Corp. to originate ACH payments and host transactions, provided that he met security requirements, did all the data entry, and found someone who actually wanted the service. Not surprisingly, Kight's first customers were apartment complexes and health clubs. It was slow going at first, with Kight the only employee for two years until he was able to afford a part-time clerk. Looking to expand, in 1983 and 1984 he sought out venture capital firms, none of which saw the merit in an ACH business. By his count he was rejected more than 30 times. Kight also hit the road in the hope of landing larger accounts. According to the *Wall Street Journal,* "He stayed at the worst, cheapest hotels, the kinds of places that gave 2-nights-for-1 coupons. A low point occurred in a ratty New York hotel, where plaster crumbled onto his head as he showered. He tried to shampoo his hair holding a towel over his head, as plaster collected around his feet." Kight's devotion to his business also cost him his new marriage after a year, but he persevered until a Columbus attorney made a suggestion that provided a breakthrough. He suggested Kight talk to life insurance companies, which were familiar with similar backoffice operations. In short order, Kight lined up four Columbus life insurers to invest $3 million in CheckFree. Moreover, in 1984 Columbus Internet service provider CompuServe Incorporated agreed to offer the CheckFree system to its subscribers. The $3 million seed money and the CompuServe contract allowed Kight to develop a consumer personal computer-based business.

One major problem at this point was that banks and billers had been reluctant to participate in an electronic funds transfer system. In fact, some major billers refused to accept electronic payments, forcing CheckFree to cut and send paper checks on behalf of consumers who had given the company permission to pay their bills. When an automatic payment system was offered directly to consumers, who were empowered by personal computers, the advantages became apparent to all. Once consumers demonstrated their interest, the banks and the billers changed their minds. To further persuade reluctant billers, Kight inflicted what he called "paper pain," sending in all of his customers' checks in massive batches at one time. To get around banks that would not participate, CheckFree in 1988 began offering an electronic payment service to consumers who took advantage of the Federal Reserve's automatic clearinghouse network. Although the product (which cost a one-time $25 charge and a $9-a-month service fee

1981: The company is founded by Peter J. Kight.
1984: Funding of $3 million is obtained from life insurance companies.
1995: The company goes public.
1996: Servantis Systems is acquired.
1997: Intuit Services Corporation is acquired.
2000: TransPoint L.L.C. is acquired.
2006: PhoneCharge Inc. is acquired.

for the first 20 transactions) allowed users to pay any creditor electronically, customers did not have the ability to check account balances or transfer money from one account to the other.

CheckFree experienced a steady rise in revenues in the early 1990s, growing from $22.2 million in 1992 to nearly $50 million in 1995. However, the company also had to contend with an infusion of competition. According to *Business Week* in a 2006 profile, "Major banks and software companies jumped into the bill-paying game, including a consortium comprised of Microsoft, Citicorp, and First Data. 'They all thought they could create a technological shortcut,' says Kight, 'but there is [none]. They underestimated how hard the details of the business are.'" To protect its position in the marketplace, CheckFree sued National Payment Clearinghouse, a subsidiary of personal finance software publisher Intuit Inc., claiming an infringement of patented technology that linked PCs to electronic methods of bill paying. Intuit had been a CheckFree customer until 1993 when it acquired National Payment, which had by then been renamed Intuit Services Corp. (ISC). The two parties went on to settle the matter and in January 1997 CheckFree acquired ISC in a $199 million deal that gave Intuit a 23 percent stake in CheckFree.

By this point, CheckFree was becoming increasingly more involved in developing a system to make safe financial transactions over the Internet and had become a public company, having made an initial public offering of stock in September 1995. CheckFree took advantage of Wall Street's rising interest in Internet-related businesses to net more than $50 million for corporate purposes while allowing stockholders, including Kight, to cash in on some of their investment in the company. The proceeds and stock were then put to use in making three key acquisitions that fleshed out the business.

In February 1996 CheckFree spent $165.1 million in cash and stock for Servantis Systems, Inc., a Norcross, Georgia-based company that was a leader, and

competitor, in electronic commerce and financial applications software. Subsequently, CheckFree moved its corporate offices from Columbus, Ohio, to Norcross. Next, in May 1996, CheckFree completed the acquisition of Security APL for $53.3 million in stock. The New Jersey-based company was a leading provider of portfolio management and software services for institutional investment managers. The third major acquisition of the mid-1990s was the ISC purchase. The key product introduction during this period was CheckFree E-Bill, the first available complete electronic billing and payment solution.

With the integration of its acquisitions, CheckFree grew revenues from $51 million in fiscal 1996 to $176.5 million in fiscal 1997 and $233.9 million a year later. Although the company was not yet turning a profit, it had plenty of working capital and was establishing itself in an industry that with the inevitable rise of e-commerce held great promise. At the start of fiscal 1998, only four of the hundreds of financial institutions that offered CheckFree services made those services available over the Internet. By the end of the year 30 more would be added, a number that would continue to grow exponentially. CheckFree closed the 1990s by implementing the Genesis technology platform that had been created to integrate the different data centers it had acquired from Servantis, Security APL, and ISC. Not only did Genesis better serve the electronic billing and payment processing needs of CheckFree's two million customers, its engineering architecture could accommodate the business of 30 million households, making CheckFree a clear leader at a time when electronic bill paying was expected to become commonplace in the new century.

ACQUISITION OF BLUE GILL TECHNOLOGIES IN 2000

CheckFree began the 2000s with another important acquisition, the $239.9 million stock purchase of Blue-Gill Technologies, an international software developer of electronic bill payment solutions. As a result, CheckFree became the only company able to offer a complete, single-source electronic billing solution. Later in the year CheckFree solidified its position in the marketplace by acquiring a key competitor, TransPoint L.L.C., the business launched by Microsoft, First Data, and Citibank. The price tag was a hefty $1.4 billion in stock, but an amount that management believed was warranted. Many billers had been reluctant to chose between market leader CheckFree, or TransPoint, backed by a corporate heavyweight, and simply remained on the sidelines. Once TransPoint was acquired, however, an increasing number of corporate billers signed up for e-billing services. Also an important development in 2000 was an agreement with Bank of America for CheckFree to assume its electronic billing and payment operations. Moreover, CheckFree renewed multiyear contracts with four top U.S. banks: Bank of America, BankOne, Chase Manhattan, and Wells Fargo.

Consumer demand for electronic bill paying did not grow as quickly as expected, creating some disgruntled investors. The price of CheckFree stock, which topped $125 per share at the time of the TransPoint acquisition announcement in February 2000, dipped below $30 a year later. The company also had to contend with a sputtering economy. To placate Wall Street it moved to cut costs and took other steps to improve the balance sheet in fiscal 2001 and 2002 while maintaining its market-leading position. Sales increased to $490.5 million in fiscal 2002, then reached $551.6 million in fiscal 2003 as the company's net loss fell from $441 million to $52.2 million. Moreover, the number of electronic transactions the company completed rose at a strong pace, increasing from 169 million in 2000 to 316 million in 2002 and 434 million in 2003. It appeared that online bill paying was finally becoming a mainstream occurrence, due in large measure to major banks eliminating their monthly online bill payment fees and providing incentives for customers to go "paperless."

In the first quarter of 2004 CheckFree reported its first profit after 18 straight quarters of losing money. The company also took a major step in expanding its international business, establishing a joint venture with BACS, Ltd. to provide electronic bill paying services in the United Kingdom. CheckFree added further to its U.K. business through the May 2005 acquisition of Accurate Software, which was folded into CheckFree's Software Division. For the full year in 2004, CheckFree recorded revenues of $606.5 million and net income of $10.5 million. In 2005, revenues soared to $757.8 million and net income increased to $46.8 million. Business proved to be even stronger in the early quarters of 2006, as CheckFree appeared to have finally turned the corner and taken advantage of its hard-fought position

in the marketplace. Far from content, Kight continued to look for ways to expand the reach of the company. In early 2006 the company paid $100 million to acquire PhoneCharge Inc. to add pay-by-phone capabilities it had previously lacked, which along with walk-in bill-pay services CheckFree hoped to serve the 20 percent of the nation's population that lacked bank accounts. On the other end of the scale, Kight also was interested in providing the back-office infrastructure service needed by Wall Street firms to create customized portfolios for individual investors. After 25 years in business, CheckFree was in many ways just beginning to realize its vast potential.

Ed Dinger

PRINCIPAL DIVISIONS

Electronic Commerce; Investment Services; Software.

PRINCIPAL COMPETITORS

Mastercard Incorporated; Metavante Corporation; Online Resources Corporation.

FURTHER READING

Foust, Dean, "Peter Kight: Chucking the Checkbook," *Business Week,* February 6, 2005, p. 22.

Fung, Amanda, "A Vision of Utility Inspires CheckFree's Kight," *American Banker,* September 21, 2001, p. 18A.

Graham, Jed, "CheckFree Still Waiting to Cash in on E-Payment," *Investor's Business Daily,* April 16, 2001, p. A09.

Hansell, Saul, "CheckFree Sues Rival Over Use of Technology," *New York Times,* January 18, 1995, p. D7.

"Peter Kight's Excellent Adventure," *Business Week Online,* January 30, 2006.

Thomas, Paulette, "A Lesson from ... CheckFree's Pete Kight," *Wall Street Journal,* September 28, 1998, p. 4.

Walker, Tom, "CheckFree Foresees No Check on Growth," *Atlanta Journal-Constitution,* February 10, 2004, p. D1.

Cimarex Energy Co.

1700 Lincoln Street
Suite 1800
Denver, Colorado 80203
U.S.A.
Telephone: (303) 295-3995
Fax: (303) 295-3494
Web site: http://www.cimarex.com

Public Company
Incorporated: 2002
Employees: 689
Sales: $1.1 billion (2005)
Stock Exchanges: New York
Ticker Symbol: XEC
NAIC: 211111 Crude Petroleum and Natural Gas
Extraction

∎ ∎ ∎

Based in Denver, Colorado, Cimarex Energy Co. is an independent oil and gas exploration production company listed on the New York Stock Exchange. The company believes in growth by the drill bit, eschewing the practice of hedging (making a future contract at a set price in order to minimize possible financial loss) to reap the full rewards of its efforts. Cimarex generally avoided growth through acquisition, albeit the $2.1 billion stock purchase of Magnum Hunter Resources in 2005 proved a major exception, in effect doubling the company's size. Rather than hedging, Cimarex achieves balance by drilling in lower-risk areas, the Mid-Continent (Oklahoma, the Texas Panhandle, and southwest Kansas),

and to a lesser extent the Permian Basin region of west Texas and southeast New Mexico, with higher-risk properties in the Gulf of Mexico and the Gulf Coast areas of Texas, south Louisiana, and Mississippi. In addition, Cimarex is involved in projects in California, Michigan, and North Dakota. The company's proved reserves at the end of 2005 totaled 1.4 trillion cubic feet equivalent, of which nearly three-quarters was natural gas.

DEEPEST ROOTS REACHING TO 1920

Cimarex was formed in 2002 when the exploration and production assets of Tulsa-based Helmerich & Payne, Inc. (H&P) were spun off and merged with Denver-based Key Production Company, Inc. Founded in 1920, the H&P operation was by far the older of the two. The men behind the H&P name were Walter Helmerich and William Payne. A member of the U.S. fledgling air force in World War I, Helmerich planned to become a barnstorming stunt pilot, only to have his two partners killed before they had a chance to perform. Instead, Chicago-born Helmerich took a job in the oil industry, in which his father-in-law, Charles F. Colcord, had been a major force in Oklahoma. After he and his brother-in-law struck oil in a Colcord property in Kansas, Helmerich permanently gave up the dangers of stunt flying for the uncertainties of the oil business. He junked his airplanes to raise enough money to buy a drilling rig, and in 1920 teamed up with a Colcord oil scout named William Payne. Unlike Helmerich, who dropped out of college, Payne held a degree from Oklahoma A&M, where he studied bacteriology and chemistry, and did graduate work in microbiology at Massachusetts A&M and Amherst.

The Helmerich and Payne partnership struggled for six years before enjoying their first strike in Braman, Oklahoma. Now established, the company was incorporated, with Payne overseeing the drilling activities and Helmerich handling the administrative responsibilities. Payne split from H&P in 1936 and went on to enjoy success with the Big Chief Drilling Company in Oklahoma City. Helmerich kept Payne's name but almost lost the company to bankruptcy during the final years of the Depression. With World War II came renewed success, and the company thrived for several years after the war, spurred in large part by the United States' growing love affair with the automobile and the need for increasing amounts of gasoline. Growth was curtailed, however, when the oil industry hit one of its periodic slumps in the early 1950s.

In need of a fresh start, H&P turned to a new generation of leadership in 1954 when Helmerich's son, Walter Helmerich III, joined the company as an executive vice-president. A graduate of Harvard Business School, he installed an increased level of professionalism, bringing in a new management team as well as the company's first drilling engineers, who would introduce technology that dramatically increased well production. By the end of the decade, the company went public and in 1960 the younger Helmerich assumed the presidency.

To meet the challenge of another downturn in the oil industry, H&P in the 1960s began to diversify, becoming involved in areas such as the manufacture of products and chemicals used by oil and pipeline companies, the laying of telephone cables, and even real estate. Nevertheless, H&P remained very much an oil and gas company, although much of its business came from contract drilling. With a spike in oil prices caused by the oil embargo of the early 1970s, H&P expanded overseas, drilling wells for both itself and others in Venezuela, Columbia, Ecuador, Peru, Belize, Guatemala, and Bolivia. By the start of the 1980s, H&P had more than 50 drilling rigs in operation.

The 1980s proved to be a brutal period for the oil and gas industry, as about four out of five companies went bankrupt. Unlike its rivals, however, H&P had outside business interests that had acted more conservatively during the boom years of the previous decade. As a result, H&P experienced a serious erosion in revenues during the 1980s but remained profitable. In fact, H&P was the world's only drilling company to turn a profit in 1989. Because it was in solid shape financially and could land long-term drilling contracts with the major oil companies, H&P was able in the early 1990s to add new rigs and compete for even larger contracts.

SPINOFF, MERGER: 2002

The company continued its own exploration activities during the 1990s, but despite enjoying success in both drilling and exploration, boasting the latest in drilling technology, and possessing no long-term debt, the company did not feel it had the respect of investors that it deserved. The company, now headed by a third generation of the Helmerich family, Hans Helmerich, believed the price of its stock was too low. In November 2000 H&P announced that it planned to spin off its production division in order to create a pure-play contract land drilling company that analysts could better evaluate. The investment banking firm of Petrie Parkman & Co. was retained to help find a suitable partner with which to merge the operation. The process took more than a year, during which time a number of candidates were evaluated. Finally, in February 2002, H&P agreed to spin off and merge its production division with Key Production Company, represented by Merrill Lynch. Key was selected, according to the *Oil Daily*, "because of its staff, organizational strength, and the complementary nature of their E&P portfolios, especially in the Midcontinent." They were also a good cultural fit, due in large measure to Key's chairman and chief executive, Francis H. "Mick" Merelli.

Key grew out of Apache Oil Corporation, founded in 1954 in Minneapolis, although it found success drilling in Oklahoma. The company was also an early practitioner of limited partnership investment vehicles, which it would not only apply to oil and gas endeavors but also to commercial real estate. Apache diversified into a number of directions, and in 1971 formed Apache Exploration Company to focus on the oil and gas business. A decade later Apache formed Apache Petroleum Company (APC), the United States' first master limited partnership, which consolidated the interests in more than 30 Apache programs. APC units were traded on the New York Stock Exchange, providing liquidity for investors.

The 1980s was a time of major changes for Apache, as the heyday of limited partnerships, which had for

KEY DATES

1920: Helmerich & Payne, Inc. is founded.
1988: Key Production Company is formed by Apache Corporation.
1993: Key Production is spun off.
2002: Helmerich & Payne's production division merges with Key to form Cimarex Energy Co.
2005: Magnum Hunter Resources, Inc. is acquired.

many years been the company's bread and butter, came to an end. The Tax Reform Act of 1986 eliminated the tax breaks that had made the partnerships so attractive to investors. As they fled, Apache, which like the rest of the industry had to contend with stubbornly low prices, was forced to restructure its approach to the oil and gas business. In 1988 APC investors were given the option either to exchange their units for shares in Apache Corporation, the manager of APC, or in a newly created corporation called Key Production Company, which would become a pure exploration and production company.

For the first four years, Key had no employees and was operated under a management contract. It was mostly in the business of liquidating assets, paying dividends to stockholders, buying back its stock on the open market, and paying off nearly $35 million in debt. By this time, the fees it generated for Apache were so small that it was no longer worth keeping and in 1992 Apache began taking steps to spin off the business. Key would launch active exploration of its undeveloped acreage, which included 23,614 net acres in the Rocky Mountains and 30,284 acres in Oklahoma, Texas, and Louisiana. In preparation of spinning off Key, a move completed in 1993, Mick Merelli, Apache's president and chief operating officer, quit to become Key's president, CEO, and chairman.

A 1959 graduate of the Colorado School of Mines with a degree in petroleum engineering, Merelli started out as a field engineer in Casper, Wyoming, for a company that would become part of Tulsa-based Terra Resources, Inc. Merelli climbed the ranks of Terra, becoming vice-president in 1976 and president and CEO three years later, a position he held until 1988 when he was named president and chief operating officer at Apache, bringing with him a wealth of technical knowledge and managerial experience.

After Key gained its independence, Merelli built up the business over the course of the next decade. He proved adept at growth through the drill bit, pursuing a "base hit" approach to exploration, preferring modest but more predictable successes, and then maximizing the returns by not engaging in the practice of hedging. Nevertheless, Merelli was willing to expand externally when opportunities arose, completing acquisitions in 1994 and 1998, and mergers in 1996 and 2000. As a result of his steady hand, Key was able to achieve growth even during a period of difficult conditions for the oil and gas industry in 1998 and 1999. All told, Key tripled its production from 1992 to 2001, while its market capitalization increased from $25 million to $240 million.

Merelli became interested in merging with H&P because of Key's inability to replace reserves in 2001 due to some mistakes made in the company's Gulf Coast drilling program. He recognized that H&P was a good fit in terms of culture and because their property portfolios complemented one another, especially in the Midcontinent region. Because both companies had enjoyed success in western Oklahoma, the former Cimarron Territory, the executives of the two companies wanted to name the new company Cimarron Exploration. The name was already taken, however, leading to the coining of Cimarex Energy Co., which was formed as a wholly owned H&P subsidiary in February 2002. Over the next several months the parties completed a "spin-merge" maneuver, more formally known as a Morris Trust structure. In July the H&P assets were transferred to the new entity, which then acquired Key on September 30, and on that same day the company was spun off from H&P, with its stock distributed to H&P shareholders on a tax-free basis.

Merelli took over as president, CEO, and chairman of Cimarex, and the rest of the senior management team was split between Key and H&P executives. Given that about 80 percent of the company's reserves were in natural gas, Cimarex became a gas-oriented company. In its first full year in operation, Cimarex invested more than $160 million on exploration and development activities and spent another $2 million on several small acquisitions. Merelli continued to follow his "base hit" approach to drilling, leading to a success rate of more than 80 percent, and as he had done with Key he avoided hedging. With a rise in energy prices during this time, Cimarex was thus able to reap the full reward of its labors. Revenues grew rapidly, from $209.6 million in 2002 to $454.2 million in 2003 and $675 million in 2004. Net income kept pace, increasing from $40 million in 2002 to $94.6 million in 2003 and $153.6 million in 2004.

Cimarex achieved its success with virtually no debt.

The company was able to take advantage of a strong balance sheet to complete a major acquisition in 2005, the $2.1 billion purchase of Texas-based Magnum Hunter Resources, which included the assumption of $645 million in debt. The deal tripled Cimarex's reserves and doubled its production. Cimarex also picked up some unwanted hedging contracts from Magnum Hunter, but they were due to expire in 2005 and 2006.

With the Magnum Hunter properties in the fold, Cimarex experienced a surge in revenues to more than $1.1 billion in 2005, and net income more than doubled to $328.3 million. Continued success followed in the first quarter of 2006 when the company enjoyed an 89 percent success rate with new wells, and revenues more than doubled the amount generated in the same period the previous year. With energy prices remaining high, Cimarex was poised to experience ongoing success. In addition, Merelli, despite approaching 70 years of age, showed no inclination to turn over the reins any time soon. "I don't play golf," he told the *Denver Post.* "This is what I like to do. I don't have any plans for retirement."

Ed Dinger

PRINCIPAL SUBSIDIARIES

Key Production Company, Inc.; Magnum Hunter Resources, Inc.

PRINCIPAL COMPETITORS

Anadarko Petroleum Corporation; BP PLC; Royal Dutch Shell PLC.

FURTHER READING

Blumenthal, Karen, "Two Oil and Gas Limited Partnerships Plan to Change to Traditional Structure," *Wall Street Journal,* August 16, 1988.

"Cimarex Energy Co.," *Oil & Gas Investor,* August 2005, p. 35.

Darbonne, Nissa, "A Nearly Debt-Free Independence," *Oil & Gas Investor,* April 2002, p. 11.

Draper, Heather, "Little Oil Company Tries Harder," *Rocky Mountain News,* August 10, 2001, p. 6B.

Locke, Tom, "CEO Looks to Build Cimarex Before Thinking of Retirement," *Wall Street Journal,* December 18, 2002, p. B3A.

Maxwell, Taryn, "Doubling Down," *Oil & Gas Investor,* April 2005, p. 57.

Raabe, Steve, "Cimarex Builds Stature by Merger," *Denver Post,* January 27, 2005, p. C01.

Reeves, Amy, "Low Debt, No Hedging Are Keys to This Firm," *Investor's Business Daily,* December 27, 2000, p. A8.

Robinson, Rick, "Tulsa, Okla.-Based Helmerich & Payne to 'Spin-Merge' Oil, Gas Division," *Daily Oklahoman,* February 26, 2002.

Spencer, Starr, "Helmerich & Payne to Spin Off E&P Unit, Then Combine It with Key," *Platt's Oilgram News,* February 26, 2002, p. 1.

CITIZEN

Citizen Watch Co., Ltd.

6-1-12, Tanashi-cho
Nishi Tokyo-shi
Tokyo, 188-8511
Japan
Telephone: (+81-42) 466-1231
Fax: (+81-42) 466-1280
Web site: http://www.citizen.co.jp

Public Company
Founded: 1918 as Shokosha Water Research Institute
Incorporated: 1930
Employees: 17,987
Sales: ¥335.94 billion ($2.86 billion) (2006)
Stock Exchanges: Tokyo
Ticker Symbol: 7762
NAIC: 334518 Watch, Clock, and Part Manufacturing; 334119 Other Computer Peripheral Equipment Manufacturing; 334220 Radio and Television Broadcasting and Wireless Communications Equipment Manufacturing; 334419 Other Electronic Component Manufacturing; 334510 Electromedical and Electrotherapeutic Apparatus Manufacturing; 334518 Other Measuring and Controlling Device Manufacturing; 333999 All Other Miscellaneous General Purpose Machinery Manufacturing; 339115 Ophthalmic Goods Manufacturing; 339911 Jewelry (Except Costume) Manufacturing

■ ■ ■

Citizen Watch Co., Ltd. is one the world's largest watchmakers. Although still best known for its watches,

the company has since the mid-1960s diversified its product lines, expanding into clocks, jewelry, and eyeglass frames; electronic devices such as chip LEDs, liquid crystal displays, quartz oscillators, and electronic viewfinders; electronic products such as printers, disk drives, electronic thermometers, and calculators; and industrial machinery, including automatic computer-controlled lathes, robots, general-purpose machine tools, and measuring instruments. About 37 percent of Citizen's net sales are derived from watches, watch parts, and clocks, 33 percent from electronic devices, 7 percent from electronic products, 11 percent from industrial machinery, and the remaining from other products, which include jewelry, eyewear, jigs, and tools. Citizen generates 58 percent of its revenues outside of Japan.

ROOTS IN RESEARCH INSTITUTE IN 1918

Citizen began in Tokyo in 1918 as a horological research center, the Shokosha Watch Research Institute. In 1924 the institute manufactured its first pocket watch. Six years later, the group organized itself as a corporation, Citizen Watch Co., Ltd., to facilitate marketing of its products, under President Yosaburo Nakajima. The new company owed its name to Tokyo Mayor Shinpei Gotoh, who named Shokosha's first timepieces Citizen watches, so that they would, in his words, be "close to the hearts of people everywhere." In addition to watches, Citizen produced precision instruments used in their manufacture. In 1936 the company built the factory in the Tanashi area of Tokyo that remains its main production facility.

Also in 1936, Citizen began selling watches in

Southeast Asia and the South Pacific; China also became a destination for exports. The company's international horizons remained limited to other Asian countries until well after World War II. In fact, Citizen's export business dried up after the outbreak of hostilities with the United States, as the Japanese economy geared itself to meet military needs. In 1941 the company began producing machine tools, a business it retained.

After Japan's defeat by the Allied powers in 1945, Japanese industry lay in ruins, and Citizen, along with the rest of the nation, faced the task of rebuilding. That year, Shinji Nakajima took over company leadership as president. In March 1946, less than a year later, Eiinchi Yamada assumed the post. In 1949 Citizen established a subsidiary, Citizen Trading Co., Ltd., to handle domestic marketing. This move allowed the parent company to focus on manufacturing, research, and development. In 1953 Citizen entered into a joint venture with Rhythm Watch Co., Ltd., another Japanese timepiece manufacturer, to sell the latter's clocks.

The export market began to revive in the 1950s. In 1958 Citizen resumed exporting watches to China, and, two years later, it started selling its machine tools there. In 1960 the company entered the all-important American market by providing Bulova Watch with parts for watches to be assembled and sold in the United States. In 1962, Citizen resumed exporting watches to Southeast Asia, and, in 1965, opened a sales office in West Germany to export watches to Europe.

The timepiece industry in postwar Japan was all but monopolized by four companies: K. Hattori & Company, which produced the Seiko and Pulsar brands among others; Citizen; Ricoh; and Orient. In 1965 Hattori and Citizen by themselves accounted for more than 80 percent of Japanese watch production. Citizen also gained prominence in Japan for several technical advancements: developing Japan's first shock-resistant watch in 1956; marketing the nation's first wristwatch with an alarm in 1958 and also introducing the first Japanese water-resistant watch. Citizen also made a significant public relations gesture in donating 850 synchronized clocks for use in the Olympic Village at the 1964 Summer Olympics in Tokyo.

DIVERSIFYING AND EXPANDING OVERSEAS, 1960–1979

The Japanese timepiece industry hit a slump in the early 1960s, as increased competition, slack domestic demand, and rising production and personnel costs all squeezed profit margins. Ricoh and Orient gradually lost their status as watchmakers of consequence, leaving Citizen and Hattori in competition with each other. Diversification was one strategy for continued survival. In 1967 Citizen entered the gem and jewelry business, establishing a subsidiary, Citizen Jewelry, for that purpose. Citizen Jewelry later was merged into Citizen Trading Co., Ltd. Citizen also placed more emphasis on developing its line of business machines, which was launched in late 1964. The company established a precision machinery division in 1971 to manufacture such industrial equipment as precision lathes.

Another logical solution to the problem of sluggish domestic demand was to expand overseas business. In the 1960s Japanese watchmakers were not the kings of the export trade that they would become 20 years later. In 1967 Switzerland, known for its high-priced luxury watches, ranked first in the world in watch production; the Soviet Union, which produced cheap, generally inferior movements for sale in developing countries, ranked second; and Japan ranked third. It was not until the next year that Citizen established its first overseas subsidiary, a joint venture called Citizen de Mexico S.A. de C.V., which sold and later manufactured Citizen timepieces in Mexico. This was the first time that a Japanese watchmaker founded a joint venture for making and selling watches in a foreign country. In 1970 the company set up a subsidiary in Hong Kong, Sunciti Manufacturers Ltd., to produce cases and dial plates for mechanical watches. This venture was wholly owned by Citizen and its subsidiaries. Also in that year, Citizen and Bulova formed a joint venture, Bulova-Citizen, to produce tuning-fork watches for sale in Japan. Bulova held a majority stake in the new company, making it the first foreign-owned watch manufacturer that the Japanese government had allowed to take root in its own soil.

Citizen continued to diversify and pursue the export trade in the early 1970s. In 1972 the company entered the eyewear business as import and sales agency for Christian Dior frames. The company also entered the leisure-time business that year by converting its Yodobashi factory into a bowling alley and founding another subsidiary, Citizen Kohatsu Co., Ltd., to run it. Citizen Kohatsu also became involved in running skating rinks and tennis facilities. In 1973 Citizen founded another foreign subsidiary, Citizen Latinamerica Corp. The next year, Citizen established Citizen Uhrenfabrik G.m.b.H. to assemble watches in West Germany, and

KEY DATES

1918: Shokosha Watch Research Institute is founded in Tokyo.
1924: Institute manufactures its first pocket watch.
1930: Group organizes itself as a corporation, Citizen Watch Co., Ltd.
1936: Citizen builds its Tanashi factory.
1960: Company enters the U.S. market.
1964: Line of business machines is launched.
1965: Export of watches to Europe begins.
1971: Precision machinery division is established.
1975: U.S. sales subsidiary is established; the Citizen brand is introduced into the U.S. market.
1986: Citizen becomes the world's largest watchmaker.
1992: German machine tool maker Boley G.m.b.H. is acquired.
1996: Eco-Drive watches debut.
1999: Arch-rival Seiko Corporation surpasses Citizen as the world leader in watch movements.

the year after that it established Hanmi Citizen Precision Industry (later known as Citizen Precision of Korea Co., Ltd.) to manufacture watch casings in South Korea. By 1978 overseas production accounted for one-fourth of the company's total output of watches.

Nevertheless, Citizen continued second to Hattori in the 1970s, accounting for roughly 30 percent of Japanese watch production in a two-company industry. The American market was the ripest plum to be picked in the export trade; Citizen could not hope to match, much less surpass, its rival as long as its presence in the United States was only indirect, limited to parts that Bulova assembled and sold under its own name. Hattori's Seiko brand was achieving name recognition in the United States, but Citizen had none. In 1975 the company established a U.S. sales subsidiary, Citizen Watch Company of America, Inc., in Los Angeles; its headquarters later moved to New York City and then to Lyndhurst, New Jersey. Citizen sharply curtailed its parts shipments to Bulova and began selling in the United States under its own name.

American sales started out small, accounting for only 10 percent of Citizen's total sales in 1977. The company made significant inroads in the U.S. midpriced market with its quartz analog and multifunction digital watches, positioning itself for a run at overtaking Hattori. Citizen's success was a major part of the overall success of the Japanese timepiece industry; Japan became the world's second largest watchmaking nation by 1980, boasting a 21 percent share of the world market and shaving Switzerland's lead to a mere ½ percent. Swiss watchmakers refused to acknowledge the growing importance of electronic technology and failed to profit from it until late in the game. Citizen seemed to be on its way to carving out a comfortable niche within the U.S. market.

CONTENDING WITH LOW-PRICED WATCH COMPETITION

The digital watch boom that started in the mid-1970s changed the scene in the next decade. At first, the scenario seemed propitious for Citizen and Hattori. Although American semiconductor companies were the first to develop digital watch technology, they proved less than adept at exploiting it. By 1980, one-third of all watches sold in the United States were digital, but Fairchild Camera–Instrument, Intel, Litronix, and Motorola all had been driven out of the watch business. Texas Instruments was reeling from marketing problems. National Semiconductor was consolidating a modest stake, and venerable Timex found itself unable to get the hang of making digitals.

New players were entering the game to take advantage of this implosion. The old guard of the Far East found itself challenged by an energetic young Japanese rival, Casio Computer, and low-cost manufacturers based in Hong Kong and South Korea. All of these companies prospered by concentrating on the low-priced end of the market, producing a stream of simple, inexpensive, digital watches. These cheaper products proved popular enough to erode Citizen's and Hattori's market shares.

Citizen countered by launching its own line of low-priced digitals, called Vega, but ultimately decided to concentrate on taking the midpriced market away from Hattori. Leadership of Citizen passed to Rokuya Yamazaki, who became president in 1981. In the 1980s Seiko became the best-selling watch brand in the United States, with Citizen ranked number two; in fact, they ranked first and second, respectively, in the world in timepiece sales and production. Yet the threat to market share from the makers of low-priced watches still had to be fended off. The Japanese electronics firm Sharp joined Casio in this business. In an effort to cope with the situation, the traditional rivals joined forces to cut manufacturing costs through economies of scale. In 1985 Citizen and Hattori Seiko Co., Ltd. (the name K. Hattori & Company had assumed in 1983) entered into an agreement to supply each other with parts. Citizen would provide Seiko with hands and special driving devices and receive, in return, quartz oscillators, button batteries, springs, and other mechanical parts.

DIVERSIFYING FURTHER

Citizen also responded to the threat by further diversification. The company decided that non-timepiece products should eventually account for half of total sales, compared with 32 percent in 1985. Citizen expanded its information-equipment group, the descendant of its office-machine business; in 1984, it began exporting its printers and disc drives to the United States. In 1986, the year that Citizen surpassed Seiko in volume to become the world's largest watchmaker, the company introduced a new color liquid-crystal-display television that would spearhead its increased involvement in consumer electronics. The company also strengthened its machine tool and precision instrument businesses. In 1986 it joined with the U.S. manufacturer Perkin-Elmer to form Perkin-Elmer Citizen, a venture to produce and assemble analyzers and semiconductor processing devices in Japan. In 1987 Citizen established Citizen Systems, a research facility for developing new information equipment technology, in Los Angeles, and Citizen Manufacturing (UK) to manufacture printers in Great Britain. That same year, Michio Nakajima succeeded to the presidency.

Nakajima recognized that growth in the mature timepiece market was limited, and he immediately began to pursue diversification, especially in the fast-growing computer and computer-component markets. Citizen quickly became a respected supplier of laptop-computer components and floppy disc drives. Citizen also moved into the production of laptop computers themselves; this began in 1990 when the company started building the LTE notebook computer for Compaq Computer Corporation. In 1994 a similar arrangement began with Digital Equipment Corporation. The company continued to produce printers as well, including the portable PN 60 model, which debuted in November 1994 as the world's smallest, lightest printer.

Other diversification moves also took place in the late 1980s and early 1990s. In the area of electronic equipment, Citizen became much more active in the burgeoning area of electronic healthcare equipment, a sector it had entered in 1983 with the debut of an electronic thermometer. In 1991 the company launched its first digital blood pressure monitor, soon to be followed by antibacterial electric toothbrushes, pedometers, and bathroom scales. Citizen's industrial machinery operations launched the CRS/CRR series of precision industrial robots in October 1991. The company further bolstered its precision industrial sector through the 1992 acquisition of German machine tool maker Boley G.m.b.H. By the mid-1990s, Citizen had diversified enough that watch sales comprised only 45 percent of overall sales, a significant reduction from the two-thirds level of the mid-1980s.

Meanwhile, however, Citizen suffered from the difficult economic conditions of the early 1990s, which led to declines in both net sales and net income in the 1992, 1993, and 1994 fiscal years. In response the company moved aggressively to cut costs and improve productivity, mainly by shifting more manufacturing overseas, particularly to Hong Kong and China. In August 1994 Citizen Watch (China) Co., Ltd. was established to manufacture and sell watches, and by early 1997 nearly all of Citizen's watch case supplies were manufactured in either southern China or in Hong Kong. By 1996 Citizen had managed to cut production costs on its watch movements by almost 50 percent over the preceding five years.

LAUNCH OF ECO-DRIVE WATCHES

At the same time that it was cutting watch production costs, Citizen also sought to grab a larger share of the premium watch sector. May 1995 saw the debut of The Citizen line of limited-edition watch models, which were accurate to within five seconds a year, were water resistant to ten atmospheres, and came with a free ten-year after-sales service and lifetime repair warranty. In April 1996 Citizen launched its Eco-Drive watches, which featured a battery rechargeable from a brief exposure to light and never needing replacement. This new line proved extremely popular. Citizen also developed the world's first radio-controlled watch, which was able to pick up a low-frequency time signal broadcast by a Japanese government signal service to constantly reset itself to the correct time.

Improved economic conditions in the United States and strong sales in Southeast Asia helped Citizen recover somewhat during fiscal 1996, when profits increased 30 percent over the previous year. Ironically, after all the moves to diversify over the preceding decades, it was Citizen's watch segment that led the way in this resurgence.

Hiroshi Hakuta was appointed president in June 1997, becoming the first to attain that post from the non-watch side of Citizen's operations and the first with a background in engineering. The new leader had to contend with a particularly tough economic climate, not only the ongoing weakness in Japan but also the broader Asian economic crisis. Compounding the situation in fiscal 1999 was an oversupply of watch movements and a sharp appreciation in the yen during the second half of the year, resulting in a steep decline in profits for the year. The company concentrated much of its efforts on reducing manufacturing costs during this period, but did so without shifting any production of its watch movements outside of Japan. Citizen reorganized and integrated its network of domestic plants and unified the plants' materials purchasing and parts design. It also continued to roll out dozens of new models of its very successful Eco-Drive line. In the meantime, Seiko Corporation (as Hattori Seiko had been known since 1990) jumped past Citizen as the world's largest producer of watch movements in 1999.

RESTRUCTURING

In the early 2000s Citizen faced a new challenge as sales of watches flattened, particularly in Japan, because of the proliferation of cellular phones and other portable electronics devices, which typically had built-in clocks, making watches less of a necessity. Demand for Citizen watches in North America, however, remained robust as the Eco-Drive models were particularly well received and were generating one-third of North American revenues by 2000. By this time, watch operations were responsible for less than 40 percent of global revenues as the company's diversification drive continued. In 2000 Citizen was bolstered by strong sales of crystal oscillators, LCD modules, and chip-based LEDs for PCs and portable electronics.

In 2001 Citizen's performance weakened thanks to economic downturns in Japan and North America and the slumping information technology industry. Citizen responded with an aggressive restructuring program, launched in October 2001, that included a workforce reduction of 2,000, or about 20 percent, as part of a broader cost-cutting program. Restructuring charges of ¥7.7 billion ($58 million) coupled with ¥6 billion ($45.2 million) in appraisal losses on company shareholdings contributed to a net loss for fiscal 2002 of ¥12.6 billion ($94.7 million), its first in 46 years.

Makoto Umehara, appointed president in June 2002, led Citizen Watch through a period of further restructuring. Between 2002 and 2005 the company implemented numerous changes to its network of subsidiaries and affiliates involved in manufacturing, distribution, and sales, both at home and abroad. For example, Citizen Trading was made into a wholly owned subsidiary in 2002, and then this sales unit was merged into the parent company in October 2004 in order to integrate the watch manufacturing and sales operations. In late 2005 Citizen sought to further improve the efficiency of its group operations by purchasing full control

of three subsidiaries that had been listed on the Jasdaq stock exchange: Citizen Electronics Co., Ltd., a manufacturer of electronic devices; Miyota Co., Ltd., which was involved in watch assembly and making quartz oscillators and electronic viewfinders; and Cimeo Precision Co., Ltd., producer of crystal quartz elements, watch parts, magnets, and magnetic head cores.

As these and other reforms were carried out, Citizen Watch enjoyed three consecutive years of improving profits from fiscal 2003 through fiscal 2005. Sales declined in both fiscal 2005 and 2006, however, and net income fell 8.1 percent in the latter year because of a slump in the firm's electronic device business. Watch sales, by contrast, were improving thanks to several strategies: further developing the Eco-Drive lines; rolling out radio-controlled watches to the European, American, and Chinese markets; and adopting a multibrand approach encompassing the flagship Citizen mark in the midpriced segment and the Vagary brand for low-priced watches. The Vagary brand had been purchased from an Italian manufacturer in the 1990s. Citizen was also fighting back against the cell phone onslaught by adding features to its watches that might provide an incentive for people to wear them. For instance, in June 2006 Citizen announced that it had developed a wristwatch with an integrated Bluetooth interface able to wireless communicate with a cell phone and indicate when a call was being received, by vibrating, lighting up, and displaying the party's name and number. Through such new products, Citizen hoped to stay on the technological cutting edge and retain its place as one of the world's watch leaders, while continuing to augment its position in electronic devices and products.

Douglas Sun
Updated, David E. Salamie

PRINCIPAL SUBSIDIARIES

Citizen Tohoku Co., Ltd.; Citizen Saitama Co., Ltd.; Citizen Heiwa Watch Co., Ltd.; Citizen Electronics Co., Ltd.; Citizen Fine Tech Co., Ltd.; Citizen Miyota Co., Ltd.; Citizen Seimitsu Co., Ltd.; Citizen Seimitsu Kagoshima Co., Ltd.; Citizen Electronics Funehiki Co., Ltd.; Sayama Precision Co., Ltd.; Citizen Yubari Co., Ltd.; Japan CBM Corporation; Citizen T.I.C. Co., Ltd.; Citizen Electronics Co., Ltd.; Citizen Fine Tech Co., Ltd.; Citizen Displays Co., Ltd.; Citizen Electronics Funehiki Co., Ltd.; Citizen Heiwa Watch Co., Ltd.; Citizen Systems Japan Co., Ltd.; Citizen Machinery Co., Ltd.; Citizen Mechatronics Co., Ltd.; Citizen Plaza Co., Ltd.; Silver Denken Co., Ltd.; Tokyo Bijutsu Co., Ltd.; Citizen Jewelry Co., Ltd.; Citizen Watches Australia Pty. Ltd.; C-E (Suzhou) Ltd. (China); Sunciti Manufacters Ltd.

(Hong Kong/China); Astar Precision Co., Ltd. (Hong Kong/China); Farbest Industries Ltd. (Hong Kong/China); Goodrington Co., Ltd. (Hong Kong/China); Citizen Watches (H.K.) Ltd. (Hong Kong/China); First Come Electronics Ltd. (Hong Kong/China); Most Crown Industries Ltd. (Hong Kong/China); C-E (Hong Kong) Ltd.; Crown Young Industries Ltd. (Hong Kong/China); Citizen Precision of Korea Co., Ltd.; C-E (Singapore) Pte. Ltd.; Royal Time Citi Co., Ltd. (Thailand); Citizen Watch Company of America, Inc. (U.S.A.); Citizen Systems America Corporation (U.S.A.); Citizen de Mexico, S.A. de C.V.; Citizen Latinamerica Corp. (Panama); Citizen Watch Europe G.m.b.H. (Germany); Citizen Systems Europe GmbH (Germany); Citizen Machinery & Boley GmbH (Germany); Citizen Watch Italy S.p.A.; Citizen Watch España S.A. (Spain); Citizen Watch United Kingdom, Ltd.

PRINCIPAL COMPETITORS

The Swatch Group Ltd.; Casio Computer Co., Ltd.; Seiko Corporation; Timex Corporation; Fossil, Inc.; Bulova Corporation; Montres Rolex S.A.; Movado Group, Inc.

FURTHER READING

Büogler, Daniel, "Japanese Watch Sector Improves," *Financial Times,* November 13, 1996, p. 28.

"Citizen, Seiko Watch to Strengthen Sales Efforts Abroad," *Nikkei Report,* August 9, 2005.

"Citizen Watch to Expand Low-End Watch Lineup," *Nikkei Report,* September 15, 2005.

"Companies in Footlight: Citizen Watch Co., Ltd.," *Oriental Economist,* February 1978.

"Corporations in the News: Citizen Watch Co.," *Japan Economic Journal,* July 5, 1986.

Dawkins, William, "Falling Sales Take Toll on Japanese Watchmaker," *Financial Times,* May 13, 1994, p. 26.

———, "Hard Times for Japan's Two Biggest Watchmakers," *Financial Times,* November 9, 1994, p. 33.

Isaka, Satoshi, "China's Time Has Come for Watchmaker: Southern Chinese Plants Dominate Production in Citizen's Strategy," *Nikkei Weekly,* May 19, 1997, p. 21.

Neff, Robert, "Citizen Adjusts Its Mainspring," *Business Week,* August 27, 1990, p. 80.

Patton, Robert, "Sidestepping Obsolescence," *Industry Week,* November 3, 1997, pp. 44–46.

"Timepieces Industry," *Oriental Economist,* April 1965.

The Clorox Company

1221 Broadway
Oakland, California 94612-1888
U.S.A.
Telephone: (510) 271-7000
Fax: (510) 832-1463
E-mail: info@clorox.com
Web site: http://www.clorox.com

Public Company
Incorporated: 1913 as The Electro-Alkaline Company
Employees: 7,600
Sales: $4.39 billion (2005)
Stock Exchanges: New York
Ticker Symbol: CLX
NAIC: 311421 Fruit and Vegetable Canning; 311941 Mayonnaise, Dressing, and Other Prepared Sauce Manufacturing; 325191 Gum and Wood Chemical Manufacturing; 325611 Soap and Other Detergent Manufacturing; 325612 Polish and Other Sanitation Good Manufacturing; 325613 Surface Active Agent Manufacturing; 325998 All Other Miscellaneous Chemical Product and Preparation Manufacturing; 326111 Unsupported Plastics Bag Manufacturing; 326199 All Other Plastics Product Manufacturing; 327910 Abrasive Product Manufacturing; 332913 Plumbing Fixture Fitting and Trim Manufacturing; 332999 All Other Miscellaneous Fabricated Metal Product Manufacturing

∎ ∎ ∎

Although best known for the household bleach that bears the firm's name, The Clorox Company is a diversified international manufacturer and marketer of a variety of consumer products ranging from household cleaners to salad dressings and from plastic bags to cat litter. In addition to Clorox bleach (the number one bleach brand in the world), the company's consumer brands include Formula 409, Pine-Sol, Tilex, and S.O.S. household cleaning products; Liquid-Plumr drain openers; Armor All and STP auto-care products; Glad plastic bags, wraps, and containers; Fresh Step and Scoop Away cat litter; Kingsford charcoal briquettes; Hidden Valley and K C Masterpiece dressings and sauces; and Brita water filtration products. Clorox also makes professional cleaning products for the institutional, janitorial, and foodservice markets. About 19 percent of Clorox's sales are derived outside the United States through marketing channels in more than 120 countries. The company maintains manufacturing facilities in 22 countries and three research and development centers in Pleasanton, California; Willowbrook, Illinois; and Buenos Aires, Argentina.

ONE-PRODUCT, INDEPENDENT COMPANY, 1913–1957

Clorox was founded on May 3, 1913, as The Electro-Alkaline Company by five Oakland, California-area businessmen—Edward Hughes, Charles Husband, William Hussey, Rufus Myers, and Archibald Taft, only one of whom had any knowledge of chemistry. Their objective was to convert brine from ocean water into sodium hypochlorite bleach using an electrolytic process considered to be technologically advanced for its time. Each partner invested $100 in the new venture, and in August 1913 they purchased a plant site. The company's

The Clorox Company

The Clorox Company

COMPANY PERSPECTIVES

Clorox begins and ends with the consumer. Our mission is to understand and satisfy consumers in order to build brands that make people's lives easier, healthier and better.

first product, Clorox liquid bleach, was packaged in five-gallon returnable containers and delivered by horse-drawn wagon to local breweries, dairies, and laundries for cleaning and disinfecting their facilities. Labels for the new product identified it as being "made by electricity." The name *Clorox* was an amalgamation of portions of the names of two of the product's key ingredients: *chlorine* and *sodium hydroxide*.

An initial stock issue of 750 shares at $100 each provided $75,000 in start-up capital. The company struggled through its early years and often depended upon personal loans from its directors to pay expenses.

In 1916 a less concentrated liquid bleach product—5¼ percent sodium hypochlorite instead of 21 percent—for household use was developed and sold in amber glass pint bottles. William C. R. Murray, the company's general manager, came up with the idea of producing and promoting household bleach. Murray's wife, Annie, gave away samples of the formula to customers of the family's Oakland-based grocery store. Its value as a laundry aid, stain remover, deodorant, and disinfectant was also promoted by door-to-door salespeople who demonstrated how a solution of Clorox bleach and water could whiten an ink-stained piece of fabric. Orders were collected on the spot and then given to local grocers who purchased the necessary inventory from the company to fulfill them. Small and local at the time, Clorox was not affected by World War I.

In the 1920s Clorox's manufacturing plant could produce about 2,000 cases, or 48,000 bottles of bleach per day. Assembly line workers filled bottles by hand using hoses attached to overhead tanks. After being filled, the bottles were sealed with rubber stoppers and labeled, also by hand. The company was reincorporated twice in the 1920s—as Clorox Chemical Corporation, in 1922, and as Clorox Chemical Co., in 1928—and in the latter year the firm went public with a listing on the San Francisco Exchange.

As demand for Clorox household bleach grew, the company expanded its manufacturing and distribution capabilities nationwide. By the early 1930s Clorox had become the best-selling liquid bleach in the country.

The company was known by its amber glass bleach bottle, which continued to be used with minor adaptations in size and design until the early 1960s, when Clorox became the first bleach manufacturer to use plastic containers.

In 1929 Murray became president of Clorox Chemical. He served in that capacity until his sudden death in 1941, just prior to the United States' entry into World War II and was succeeded by William J. Roth. In contrast to Murray's relatively uneventful tenure, Roth immediately had to deal with the impact of the country's wartime involvement on the company. Because of the decreased availability of chlorine, the U.S. government permitted bleach manufacturers to reduce the concentration of sodium hypochlorite in their products. Roth, however, opted to decrease production rather than change the quality of Clorox bleach and jeopardize customer satisfaction. He also terminated a number of contracts for chlorine that had been negotiated before the war because those agreements paid suppliers too little for a substance in such short supply. Although these decisions were costly at the time, the company retained the respect of the industry and customer loyalty once the war was over.

SUBSIDIARY OF PROCTER & GAMBLE, 1957–1968

By the mid-1950s Clorox, still a one-product company, held the largest share of the domestic market for household bleach, thanks in part to the dozen new U.S. plants built between 1938 and 1956. The Procter & Gamble Company, a successful manufacturer of consumer products, viewed Clorox bleach as a compatible addition to its existing line of laundry products, and acquired the company in August 1957.

Procter & Gamble changed the firm's name to The Clorox Company. Within three months of the purchase, however, the Federal Trade Commission challenged the Clorox acquisition on the grounds that it might lessen competition or tend to create a monopoly in household liquid bleaches, a violation of the Clayton Act. Even though Procter & Gamble allowed Clorox to handle its own affairs, in 1967 the U.S. Supreme Court upheld the commission's order that Procter & Gamble divest itself of the Clorox operation. By 1969 Clorox had been spun off as a public company, with a listing on the New York Stock Exchange, and was once again independent.

DIVERSIFIED FOLLOWING THE REGAINING OF INDEPENDENCE IN 1969

Clorox's new president, former Procter & Gamble executive Robert B. Shetterly, and his top management

INTERNATIONAL DIRECTORY OF COMPANY HISTORIES, VOLUME 81

KEY DATES:

1913: Five Oakland, California-area businessmen found The Electro-Alkaline Company, which soon begins producing Clorox liquid bleach.

1916: Company starts selling a less-concentrated, household version of the product.

1922: Firm is reincorporated as Clorox Chemical Corporation.

1928: Company reincorporates as Clorox Chemical Co. and goes public.

1957: The Procter & Gamble Company (P&G) acquires Clorox, renaming it The Clorox Company.

1969: Clorox regains its independence after P&G is forced to divest it for antitrust reasons; company completes first acquisition, Liquid-Plumr, and introduces first new product, Clorox 2.

1974: Through an alliance with Henkel KGaA, the German firm gains a minority shareholding in Clorox.

1990: The Pine-Sol and Combat brands are acquired.

1996: Armor All Products Corporation is acquired.

1999: Clorox acquires First Brands Corporation, maker of Glad plastic bags and wraps.

2002: Clorox and P&G form joint venture involving the Glad business.

2004: Clorox's relationship with Henkel is ended.

team faced a more competitive marketing environment in which enzyme laundry products were rapidly encroaching on Clorox's core business. Realizing that diversification beyond bleach was essential to the company's survival, Clorox management implemented a three-pronged strategic plan aimed at the acquisition and internal development of a line of nonfood grocery products, the acquisition of a food specialty business, and the development of a line of institutional food and cleaning products. They drew up a list of potential targets for acquisition, many of which were purchased within the year, including Jiffee Chemical Corporation, the manufacturer of Liquid-Plumr drain opener; Shelco, which manufactured Jifoam aerosol oven cleaner; and the 409 division of Harrell International, which produced Formula 409 spray cleaners. Also in 1969 the company introduced Clorox 2, its first entry in the dry, nonchlorine segment of the bleach market.

In 1971 Clorox purchased McFadden Industries, makers of Litter Green cat litter. Clorox had first tested McFadden's product in the market with an option to acquire the entire company if the product proved successful. Clorox also acquired Grocery Store Products Company, which manufactured such specialty food products as B&B mushrooms, Kitchen Bouquet gravy thickener, and Cream of Rice cereal. A year later Clorox added a line of salad dressings and party dips to this operation by buying Hidden Valley Ranch Food Products. Sales of the company's chlorine bleach rebounded in the first years of the decade as concerns arose over the health and environmental effects of enzyme and phosphate detergents.

In 1972 Clorox met the third objective of its strategic plan with the acquisitions of Martin-Brower Corporation, a manufacturer and supplier of disposable packaging and paper goods for the foodservice industry, and Nesbitt Food Products, a manufacturer and distributor of soft drink concentrates. Joining the fold the following year was Kingsford Corporation, a leading manufacturer of charcoal briquettes.

The company soon encountered a series of setbacks, however. Just after the Kingsford acquisition, a cool and wet summer depressed sales of charcoal and the recreational products manufactured by other parts of the Kingsford operation. Clorox's introduction of a new product, Mr. Mushroom, coincided unexpectedly with a nationwide botulism scare, which adversely affected Mr. Mushroom and the company's B&B brand. Mushroom production at its newly acquired Country Kitchen Foods subsidiary in England decreased significantly due to a virus in the fertilizer used. Sales of Clorox's cleaning products also fell because of consumers' fears of recession.

Although these problems led to a temporary halt in further acquisitions, the company successfully negotiated an agreement in 1974 with Henkel KGaA, a German producer of consumer and industrial food and cleaning products. Clorox gained access to Henkel's research-and-development capabilities and acquired manufacturing and marketing rights to Henkel-developed products in the United States, Canada, and Puerto Rico. Henkel in turn became a minority shareholder in Clorox. In 1975 a civil antitrust suit brought against both Clorox and Procter & Gamble by Purex Corporation, a competitor in the bleach market, came to trial. The suit sought over $520 million in damages, which Purex claimed had resulted from Procter & Gamble's acquisition of Clorox in the late 1950s. Purex admitted defeat in 1982, when the Supreme Court refused to hear the case. Both a federal court and federal appeals court had ruled that Purex had failed to prove that either company had caused it to suffer any loss of business.

Shetterly retired as chief executive officer in 1980 and was succeeded by Calvin Hatch, another former Procter & Gamble executive. Under Shetterly's leadership, the company had diversified beyond bleach into a number of other areas; however, most of these new ventures never became profitable. Conceding that Shetterly's growth plan had failed, Clorox sold its Martin-Brower subsidiary at a loss in 1979 to the U.K.-based Dalgety PLC, and Country Kitchen Foods, its British mushroom canning operation, to H.J. Heinz Company, Ltd., the U.K. subsidiary of the U.S. company. These divestitures gave Clorox plenty of capital to use in its search for niches in the consumer packaged-goods market in which the company could develop its own products and capture a dominant share.

Clorox devoted a significant amount of money and corporate support to research and development. Until the company was able to come up with a breakthrough product of its own, however, it continued to rely upon outside acquisitions to diversify its business and fill its new-product pipeline. Some of the acquisitions made under Hatch's leadership, such as the 1979 purchase of the Emil Villa chain of barbecue restaurants, paralleled Shetterly's mistakes in fueling growth but not profits, while other products gained through earlier acquisitions, such as Cream of Rice cereal, fell short of the company's goals and were eventually sold. Efforts to generate and rapidly build a base of international business were also stymied by solidly entrenched competition.

In 1981 the company acquired Comerco, a Tacoma, Washington-based producer of stains and wood preservatives marketed under the Olympic brand name to hardware and home-improvement stores. Two years later, the company purchased Lucite house paints from E.I. du Pont de Nemours & Company. Clorox attempted to model these acquisitions after its successful Kingsford charcoal operation, using marketing techniques and heavy advertising to produce premium-priced, brand-name products. The subsidiary formed to manage these businesses was never effectively able to integrate the operations of these two product lines nor to attain the company's sales expectations, however. It was sold to PPG Industries, Inc. in 1989 at a loss of $20 million.

Over the years, Clorox had retained leadership of the laundry-bleach market despite numerous attempts by competitors to chip away at its share with other brand-name, private-label, and generic products. In 1982 Clorox faced its toughest challenge when Procter & Gamble decided to launch its own bleach product called Vibrant in a test market. Clorox quickly responded by introducing a new bleach with a similar formula called Wave. Although Vibrant never made it out of the test-market stage due to manufacturing problems, this

competitive advance against Clorox set the stage for future attempts by each company to invade the markets for products long dominated by the other.

In 1986 Calvin Hatch retired as chairman, a post he had held since 1982, and was succeeded by President and CEO Charles R. Weaver. Jack W. Collins, the company's executive vice-president and chief operating officer, was promoted to Weaver's former positions. Beginning in 1987, the company diversified into another new business area by purchasing a number of bottled-water companies, including the Deer Park Spring Water Company and Deep Rock Water Company, followed by the Aqua Pure Water Company and Emerald Coast Water Company in 1988.

After several years of uneasy coexistence after the Vibrant incident, the battle between Clorox and Procter & Gamble for dominance of the consumer marketplace erupted. In 1988 the company introduced its Clorox Super Detergent brand of laundry soap powder in four western states and was quickly attacked by Procter & Gamble's new Tide With Bleach brand. Procter & Gamble also began the market test of a new brand of liquid bleach targeted at Clorox customers, a move intended to warn Clorox against entering the laundry detergent market. By mid-1989 Procter & Gamble had withdrawn its bleach product because of disappointing sales. Clorox kept its detergent on the market but continued to face an uphill battle against the entrenched brands. The fact that consumer preferences were slowly moving away from powders toward liquid detergents added to the company's marketing problems. In an attempt to inject new life into its consumer products business, the company acquired the Pine-Sol cleaner and Combat insecticide lines of American Cyanamid Company in 1990 for $465 million, a price generally considered to be too high. That same year, Robert A. Bolingbroke became president, succeeding the retiring Collins.

After spending more than $225 million over three years developing and marketing its detergent, and having thereupon achieved only a 3 percent market share, Clorox in May 1991 abandoned this aggressive but misguided venture. The company took a $125 million pretax charge, largely to exit the detergent business, a charge that cut net earnings to $52.7 million for fiscal 1991, a 65.7 percent drop from the $153.6 million of the previous year. Clorox's entrée into detergent was doubly damaging since Procter & Gamble's counterpunch, Tide With Bleach, also cut into sales of Clorox bleach, with Clorox 2 particularly hard hit, its sales falling 10 percent in fiscal 1991 alone. In addition to exiting the detergent business, Clorox around the same time pulled the plug on other ill-advised products it was testing, including a bar soap called Satine and Hidden Valley Ranch microwavable frozen entrees.

COMPANY TURNAROUND

In the aftermath of the company's largely self-inflicted difficulties, Weaver retired in mid-1992. His selection for a successor, Bolingbroke, was rejected by the company board, who instead chose Craig Sullivan to be the new chairman and CEO. Bolingbroke soon resigned; Sullivan, a 21-year Clorox veteran who had been a group vice-president, eventually assumed the position of president as well; and the position of COO was eliminated in order to flatten the management structure.

Under Sullivan's leadership and with the help of a surging economy in the United States, Clorox achieved a remarkable turnaround during the mid-1990s. The largely single-digit year-on-year increases in net sales of the early 1990s gave way to 11.8 and 14.2 percent increases in fiscal 1996 and 1997, respectively, with net sales hitting a record $2.53 billion in 1997. Net earnings were on the rise as well, with another 1997 record of $249.4 million. Cleaning up and bolstering the company's product portfolio and expanding internationally fueled the resurgence.

Soon after becoming chairman, Sullivan ordered a comprehensive financial and strategic review of the company's entire line of products. The study identified three businesses—the Prince Castle restaurant equipment subsidiary, Deer Park bottled water, and the Moore's and Domani frozen food businesses—that accounted for 10 percent of company sales, 24 percent of its workforce, but none of its profits; these businesses also did not mesh well with the rest of Clorox's portfolio. All three were soon divested: Prince Castle was sold in June 1993; the following month, the bottled water business was sold; and in September 1993 Clorox sold Moore's and Domani to Ore-Ida Foods, a division of H.J. Heinz Company. The bottled water and frozen food businesses were sold for a combined $159.3 million.

The company's portfolio was subsequently shored up through a series of acquisitions and a renewed commitment to new product development. Clorox's strong balance sheet, with relatively low long-term debt and plenty of cash, placed it in perfect position to grow through acquisitions. In January 1994 the company acquired the S.O.S. brand of cleaning products from Miles Inc. for $116.5 million. Building on a joint venture it had been involved in since 1988, Clorox in fiscal 1995 purchased Canada-based Brita International Holdings, Inc., a manufacturer and marketer of Brita water filtration systems. In late 1995 the company extended its presence in the bug-killing business by

purchasing the Black Flag line of insecticides from London's Reckitt & Colman Plc. Clorox then added Lestoil heavy-duty cleaner to its portfolio in mid-1996 in a deal with Procter & Gamble. In December 1996 the company spent $360.1 million to acquire Armor All Products Corporation and its leading line of automotive cleaning products. Armor All became a wholly owned subsidiary of Clorox.

Meanwhile, notable new product successes included Floral Fresh Clorox, introduced in October 1995, and Lemon Fresh Pine-Sol, which debuted in February 1995 and was formulated after a survey discovered that many consumers did not like the smell of pine. During fiscal 1997 Formula 409 carpet cleaner was introduced, while the flagship Formula 409 all-purpose cleaner was reformulated to kill bacteria. The Clorox 2 color-safe bleach brand was revitalized in 1996 and 1997 through the relaunch of Clorox 2 liquid bleach as a concentrate and with the debut of Floral Fresh dry and liquid formulas.

In the long run, Sullivan's emphasis on international growth was perhaps the most important aspect of his multi-pronged revitalization program. During the early 1990s, Clorox derived only 4 percent of its net sales outside the United States. Sullivan created an international team to tackle overseas markets and set an ambitious goal of deriving a full 20 percent of sales from these markets by 2000. By 1997 Clorox was well on its way to meeting this goal as international sales reached 14 percent. Much of this growth was fueled through acquisitions, particularly in Latin America, where the company was able to quickly gain half of the bleach markets in Argentina and Colombia and 90 percent of the bleach market in Chile. Overall, Clorox spent $1 billion acquiring 26 companies from fiscal 1993 through fiscal 1997; 23 of these were non-U.S. companies, primarily Latin American.

Of course, not everything went smoothly in the mid-1990s. In September 1997 the company recalled and stopped production of QuickSilver, an automotive wheel-cleaning product gained via the Armor All acquisition, after it was blamed for the death of a Canadian child.

ACCOMPLISHMENTS AND CHALLENGES ENTERING THE NEW CENTURY

Clorox's acquisition spree culminated in January 1999 with the purchase of First Brands Corporation for approximately $2 billion in stock and assumed debt, the largest acquisition in the company's history. Based in Danbury, Connecticut, First Brands was best known for its Glad plastic wraps and trash bags. The firm also produced STP automotive additives and Fresh Step, Scoop Away, and Jonny Cat cat litters.

Buying First Brands had an immediate impact on Clorox's top line as revenues jumped from $2.74 billion in fiscal 1998 to just over $4 billion the following year. Yet Clorox acquired First Brands at an inauspicious time. Plastic costs were rising, and the company was in the midst of a heavy advertising and promotional campaign for a new line of GladWare plastic containers. At the same time, Glad's market share was on the decline because of intense competition, particularly with the entrance of cheaper, no-name brands into the category. Over the next few years, Clorox struggled to integrate the First Brands products into its portfolio, and both its revenues and profits stagnated; the price of its stock fell to less than half of its peak in fiscal 1999. Some observers laid part of the blame on the decision to fire a large portion of First Brands' managers shortly after the takeover.

In addition to its difficulties with the First Brands acquisition, Clorox also suffered in the early 2000s from the general economic downturn and from failed product introductions, such as its FreshCare home dry-cleaning kit, which debuted in March 2000 and was pulled off the market in the fall of 2001. An initial success but another ultimate failure was the Clorox ReadyMop mopping system, an all-in-one wet mop with disposable cleaning pads that debuted in early 2002. To improve profitability, Clorox cut costs through layoffs and plant closings. The firm also tightened its focus on core brands, divesting peripheral ones, including Jonny Cat litter and Black Flag insecticide, both off-loaded in 2003.

Sullivan's period at the helm ended when he retired and was replaced as CEO by Gerald E. Johnston in July 2003 and as chairman by Robert W. Matschullat in January 2004. Johnston had spent ten years at Procter & Gamble before joining Clorox in 1981 and working his way up to president and COO by 1999. Under Johnston, Clorox began adopting a higher public profile than it did under the publicity-shy Sullivan, and the new leader also placed great emphasis on investing in research and development and technology to produce innovative new products.

The R&D focus paid dividends almost immediately with the introduction in the fall of 2003 of Glad Press 'n Seal sealable plastic wrap, which became a big hit with consumers. Ironically, this was the first product deriving from a joint venture that Clorox had formed in November 2002 with its one-time parent and longtime rival, Procter & Gamble. The venture, centering on the Glad business, aimed to combine the power of the Glad brand with Procter & Gamble's superior manufacturing prowess, particularly some new plastic technologies it had developed. The Cincinnati company gained an initial 10 percent stake in the Glad business but increased its interest to 20 percent in late 2004 by investing an additional $133 million. Using patented technology from Procter & Gamble, the Press 'n Seal product was touted as sticking better to container surfaces than regular plastic wraps, while also not sticking to itself as readily as the older versions tended to do. A second hit product coming out of the Glad joint venture was Glad ForceFlex trash bags, which debuted in 2004. These bags were embossed with a unique diamond-shaped quilted pattern that allowed the plastic to stretch and thereby be less likely to tear under pressure from sharp or heavy objects.

These two Glad products were part of Johnston's drive to develop "game-changers," products that would enable Clorox to dominate certain categories. Most of these heavily-and-creatively-promoted new products, including Clorox disinfecting wipes, Armor All wipes, and the Clorox ToiletWand, were successes. Another innovative new product that found a ready market was the Clorox Bleach Pen, a penlike tool that made it easier for a user to control the application of bleach and that was able to remove stains on a variety of surfaces. The drive to develop new products pushed sales up to $4.39 billion by fiscal 2005, while ongoing cost-containment efforts propelled the profit margin above 12 percent, a vast improvement over the 7.9 percent figure for 2002.

Another significant development during this period occurred in November 2004 when Clorox's relationship with Henkel came to an end. Linked since 1974, the two companies had developed certain technologies together but had never actually jointly produced any commercial products. Henkel elected to divest its 29 percent stake in Clorox in order to help finance its acquisition of Dial Corporation. Clorox gained back the stock by transferring to Henkel $2.1 billion in cash; its insecticides business, including the Combat brand; the Soft Scrub cleaner business; and its 20 percent stake in a joint venture with Henkel focusing on consumer products in Spain and Portugal.

Late in 2005, with soaring energy prices driving up the costs of raw materials, transportation, and utilities, Clorox announced plans to raise prices on 40 percent of its products. Clorox continued to roll out new products and back them and existing products with creative advertising campaigns, but Johnston, the architect of Clorox's turnaround, suffered a heart attack in March 2006, went on leave, and then retired two months later to focus on recovering. Matschullat was named interim chairman and CEO, while the company conducted a search for a successor.

Sandy Schusteff
Updated, David E. Salamie

PRINCIPAL SUBSIDIARIES

A & M Products Manufacturing Company; The Armor All/STP Products Company; Brita Canada Corporation; Brita Manufacturing Company; The Brita Products Company; Clorox Africa Pty. Ltd. (South Africa); Clorox Argentina S.A.; Clorox Australia Pty. Ltd.; Clorox do Brasil Ltda. (Brazil); Clorox Car Care Limited (U.K.); Clorox de Centro America, S.A. (Costa Rica); Clorox Chile S.A.; Clorox China (Guangzhou) Ltd.; Clorox de Colombia S.A.; Clorox Commercial Company; The Clorox Company of Canada Ltd.; The Clorox Company of Puerto Rico; Clorox Diamond Production Company; Clorox Dominicana, C. por A. (Dominican Republic); Clorox Eastern Europe LLC (Russia); The Clorox Far East Company Limited (Hong Kong); Clorox Germany GmbH; Clorox Hong Kong Limited; The Clorox International Company; Clorox International Philippines, Inc.; Clorox Mexicana S. de R.L. de C.V. (Mexico); Clorox de Mexico, S.A. de C.V.; Clorox Netherlands B.V.; Clorox New Zealand Limited; Clorox de Panama S.A.; Clorox Peru S.A.; The Clorox Outdoor Products Company; The Clorox Pet Products Company; Clorox Professional Products Company; The Clorox Sales Company; Clorox Services Company; Clorox Servicios Corporativos S. de R.L. de C.V. (Mexico); Clorox Switzerland S.a.r.l.; Clorox Uruguay S.A.; Corporacion Clorox de Venezuela, S.A.; Electroquimicas Unidas S.A.I.C. (Chile); Evolution Sociedad S.A. (Uruguay); Fabricante de Productos Plasticos, S.A. de C.V. (Mexico); First Brands do Brasil Ltda. (Brazil); First Brands Corporation; First Brands Mexicana, S.A. de C.V. (Mexico); Forest Technology Corporation; Glad Manufacturing Company; The Glad Products Company; The Household Cleaning Products Company of Egypt Ltd.; The HV Food Products Company; HV Manufacturing Company; Invermark S.A. (Argentina); Kaflex S.A. (Argentina); Kingsford Manufacturing Company; The Kingsford Products Company; National Cleaning Products Company Limited (Saudi Arabia); Petroplus Produtos Automotivos S.A. (Brazil); Petroplus Sul Comercio Exterior S.A. (Brazil); Polysak, Inc.; Quimica Industrial S. A. (Chile); STP do Brasil Ltda. (Brazil); STP Products Manufacturing Company; Traisen S.A. (Uruguay); United Cleaning Products Manufacturing Company Limited (Yemen); Yuhan-Clorox Co., Ltd. (Korea).

PRINCIPAL COMPETITORS

The Procter & Gamble Company; S.C. Johnson & Son, Inc.; Reckitt Benckiser plc; Colgate-Palmolive Company; Unilever; The Dial Corporation; Pactiv Corporation.

FURTHER READING

About the Company on Its Diamond Anniversary, Oakland, Calif.: The Clorox Company, [1988].

Anders, George, and Tara Parker-Pope, "Clorox, Still Growing, to Buy First Brands," *Wall Street Journal*, October 20, 1998, p. A3.

Bagamery, Anne, "Laundryman," *Forbes*, July 15, 1985, p. 120.

Baron, Michael, "Clorox CEO Retires, Citing Health," *Wall Street Journal*, May 4, 2006, p. B7.

Barrett, Amy, "Clorox: Washed Up?," *Financial World*, February 4, 1992, pp. 17–18.

Barron, Kelly, "Holding the Bag: Clorox Tries to Clean Up a Fumbled Acquisition," *Forbes*, July 23, 2001, p. 90.

Bole, Kristen, "Southern Lights: South America Brightens Outlook for Clorox," *San Francisco Business Times*, June 14, 1996, p. 3.

Byrne, Harlan S., "Clorox Co.," *Barron's*, December 3, 1990, p. 47.

Calandra, Thom, "In the Hot Seat," *Forbes*, October 12, 1992, p. 126.

Calvey, Mark, "Clorox CEO Seeks 'Bite-Sized' Buys," *San Francisco Business Times*, September 23, 2003, p. 1.

———, "Clorox Pulls Some Pizzazz Out of the Old Bleach Box," *San Francisco Business Times*, April 16, 2004, p. 4.

———, "Troubled Clorox Sharpens Its Ax," *San Francisco Business Times*, December 7, 2001, p. 1.

Campanella, Frank W., "Still the Leader: Clorox Remains No. 1, but It Thrives on Other Household Products," *Barron's*, March 25, 1985, pp. 57+.

Carlsen, Clifford, "Clorox Co. Positioned for Large Acquisition," *San Francisco Business Times*, November 20, 1992, p. 2A.

"Clorox: An R&D Game Plan Is Brightening Its Profit Picture," *Business Week*, April 23, 1984, p. 113.

"Clorox: Picking Up the Pieces of a Diversification That Failed," *Business Week*, March 3, 1980, pp. 42+.

David, Gregory E., "New, Improved ...," *Financial World*, February 15, 1994, pp. 36–37.

Greene, Joan, "Operations at Clorox Take on Brighter Hue," *Barron's*, October 13, 1975, pp. 61+.

Guzman, Doris de, "Clorox Swap Fortifies Henkel's U.S. Consumer Biz," *Chemical Market Reporter*, October 18, 2004, p. 20.

Hamilton, Joan O'C., "Brighter Days at Clorox," *Business Week*, June 16, 1997, pp. 62, 65.

Harvilicz, Helena, "Clorox Has a Good Year but Is Still Digesting First Brands," *Chemical Market Reporter*, August 23, 1999, p. 10.

Hof, Robert D., "A Washout for Clorox?," *Business Week,* July 9, 1990, p. 32.

Jaffe, Thomas, "No Soap," *Forbes,* August 13, 1984, p. 122.

Johnson, Bradley, "Clorox's Identity Crisis," *Advertising Age,* May 6, 1991, pp. 1, 54.

———, "What Sullivan Faces As New Clorox CEO," *Advertising Age,* June 1, 1992, p. 48.

Lappen, Alyssa A., "Battling for a Bleachhead," *Forbes,* November 28, 1988, p. 138.

Levine, Jonathan B., "Clorox Makes a Daring Move in the Laundry Room," *Business Week,* May 2, 1988, p. 36.

Neff, Jack, "Clorox Finds Running with Lions Effective," *Advertising Age,* March 13, 2006, p. 12.

———, "Clorox Seeks Successor for Johnston," *Advertising Age,* May 8, 2006, p. 8.

———, "New Products Pump Clorox Growth," *Advertising Age,* June 16, 1997, p. 22.

Rhine, Jon, "Clorox Aims to Clean Up at P&G's Expense," *San Francisco Business Times,* March 3, 2000, p. 3.

Rosenberg, Alex, "Clorox Picks President As New CEO," *Oakland (Calif.) Tribune,* June 20, 2003.

Shao, Maria, "A Bright Idea That Clorox Wishes It Never Had," *Business Week,* June 24, 1991, pp. 118–19.

Shetterly, Robert B., *Renaissance of the Clorox Company,* New York: Newcomen Society in North America, 1973, 16 p.

Shisgall, Oscar, *Eyes on Tomorrow: The Evolution of Procter & Gamble,* Chicago: J.G. Ferguson Publishing, 1981, 295 p.

"Still No. 1: Clorox Seems to Be Successfully Fending Off Stiff Competition," *Barron's,* August 2, 1982, pp. 38+.

Commercial Vehicle
Group, Inc.

6530 W. Campus Way
New Albany, Ohio 43054
U.S.A.
Telephone: (614) 289-5360
Fax: (614) 289-5367
Web site: http://www.cvgrp.com

Public Company
Incorporated: 2000 as Bostrom Holding, Inc.
Employees: 2,500
Sales: $754.5 million (2005)
Stock Exchanges: NASDAQ
Ticker Symbol: CVGI
NAIC: 336339 All Other Motor Vehicle Parts Manufacturing

■ ■ ■

Commercial Vehicle Group, Inc. (CVG) is a New Albany, Ohio-based global company that supplies the heavy truck, construction, agriculture, and marine industries with products through three primary divisions. The CVG Interior Systems Division includes subsidiaries National Seating, Trim Systems, and Cabarrus Plastics. National manufactures seat systems for heavy trucks, buses, and construction and agricultural vehicles; Trim Systems makes interior trim products for heavy trucks; and Cabarrus produces plastic components for vehicles as well as other industries. The CVG Electrical/Mechanical Division includes Sprague Devices, maker of wiper blade products and systems; MWC (Monora Wire), which manufactures electrical wire harnesses,

power distribution systems, and panel assemblies; Prutsman Mirrors, producer of rearview and other mirrors and mounting supplies; and Roadwatch Safety Systems, provider of instrumentation that tracks air and road temperatures. CVG Structures Division, through Mayflower Vehicle Systems, manufactures complete commercial truck cabs. In addition, CVG sells aftermarket parts provided by its three main divisions through the OE Service/After Market Division, and does business internationally through the CVG Europe and Asia Division, which also includes U.K.-based KAB Seating, producing truck seating systems for the European market. CVG has been a NASDAQ-listed public company since 2004.

ORIGINS DATING TO 1983

The creation of CVG was funded by Canadian investment firm Onex Corporation, founded in Toronto in 1983 by Gerald Schwartz. A Winnipeg native and graduate of the University of Manitoba, Schwartz enrolled in the Harvard Business School, earning an M.B.A. in 1970. For the next several years he worked in investment banking, first in Europe and later on Wall Street, where he learned the art of the deal from corporate raiders Henry Kravis and Jerome Kohlberg. In the late 1970s he returned to Winnipeg to team up with attorney Israel Asper to found CanWest Capital Corporation. After a number of successful acquisitions, the two men fell out, leading to Schwartz moving to Toronto and launching Onex, relying on the same financial backer he had cultivated at CanWest.

Onex was structured as a holding company for a

COMPANY PERSPECTIVES

We take pride in building products the same way that we've built our company; with strength, precision and focused direction.

---

wide range of acquisitions, generally targeting undervalued companies. Schwartz proved creative at financing the deals, relying mostly on debt, but he also restructured the companies and often sold off parts to help offset the purchase price. In some cases, he simply flipped the company, quickly reselling it at a profit.

Around 1987 Schwartz began focusing most of his attention on opportunities in the United States. As part of this strategy, in 1989 he forged an alliance with Hidden Creek Industries, a Minneapolis buyout firm founded by S. A. (Tony) Johnson and Scott D. Rued after Johnson had been dismissed as chief operating officer of Pentair Inc., a Minnesota manufacturer. Prior to that, Johnson, an engineer with an M.B.A. from Stanford, had served as president and chief executive officer of Onan Corp., another Minnesota company, which manufactured electrical generating equipment. Onex owned 80 percent of Hidden Creek and Johnson the remaining 20 percent. Hidden Creek was formed to make acquisitions in the supply industry for automotive and commercial vehicle original equipment manufacturers (OEMs), who were looking to do business with fewer parts manufacturers. Onex hoped to acquire suppliers in order to gain size, achieve economies of scale, and fill that need for larger vendors. Some of the assets accumulated would one day form the core of CVG.

The first acquisition, completed in 1990 by Onex in conjunction with Hidden Creek, was Strasburg, Virginia-based Automotive Industries Inc., the North American auto parts operation of Tate & Lyle PLC. It provided molded plastic auto parts to North American auto manufacturing plants. Later in the year, Dura Automotive was formed to acquire two automotive parts suppliers from Wickes Manufacturing Company of Santa Monica, California: Dura Automotive Hardware and Mechanical Components, makers of parking brakes and other products. Dura became the largest supplier of parking brake systems in the industry, and the Hidden Creek partnership added to the business with the 1994 purchase of Orscheln Company. In 1993 Tower Automotive was acquired, providing structural metal stamping and other assemblies for OEMs. The Tower unit was then bolstered with further acquisitions over

the next two years: Edgewood Toll and Manufacturing, Kalamazoo Stamping and Die, and Trylon Corporation.

ACQUIRING TRIM SYSTEMS IN 1997

The Hidden Creek partnership made its first foray into the OEM heavy truck market in 1997 with the acquisition of Trim Systems Inc., a Minneapolis maker of cloth, vinyl, and carpeted surfaces for truck interiors. It was placed under a company called Heavy Duty Holdings Co., with Onex owning a 41 percent interest at first. A year later Tempress Inc., maker of plastic parts for heavy-duty trucks, was added to the fold. Next, in March 2000 Onex acquired Commercial Vehicle Systems, a manufacturer of wiper, mirror, and control systems for medium-duty and heavy-duty trucks. Later in the year Bostrom PLC was acquired as well. Bostrom, based in the United Kingdom, owned National Seating Corporation, which manufactured truck seating units for the U.S. market, and KAB Seating, providing similar products in the United Kingdom and Europe.

A downturn in the U.K. truck market in 1999 had hurt Bostrom, leading to the sale to Onex. Similar conditions arose in the United States in the beginning of the new century, as declining economic conditions, as usual, were first to hit the trucking industry. Moreover, OEMs had overproduced in the late 1990s, so that when demand for new vehicles tailed off as trucking companies postponed capital improvements, the OEMs had a backlog of vehicles to sell before new parts would be needed. As a result, the companies acquired by Onex, with and without Hidden Creek, were adversely impacted. A number of changes were made in answer to this situation, including cost reduction and the implementation of lean manufacturing practices. Business picked up in the second and third quarters of 2002, and in 2003 there was a demand for new equipment to replace fleets that had been allowed to age. Moreover, demand for trucking services increased, as it became more of an economical alternative than rail.

In March 2003 CVG began to take shape when Bostrom Holding, Inc., formed in 2000 to acquire Bostrom PLC, acquired Commercial Vehicle Systems. Then, in May 2004, Bostrom Holding changed its name to Commercial Vehicle Group, Inc. and acquired Trim Systems. Other brands that were part of the company's portfolio included Sprague Devices and RoadWatch.

Serving as chairman of CVG was Hidden Creek's Scott Rued, and taking over as CEO was Mervin Dunn, who came to the company through Trim Systems, for which he was hired as president in 1999. Holder of a Master of Science degree in Operations from Eastern

KEY DATES

1989: Onex Corporation and Hidden Creek Industries forge a partnership to buy industry sector companies.
1999: Trim Systems Inc. is acquired.
2000: Commercial Vehicle Systems and Bostrom PLC are acquired.
2003: The Onex companies merge to form Commercial Vehicle Group.
2004: The company is taken public.
2005: Mayflower Vehicle Systems is acquired.

and manufacturing processes. CVG's production system is modeled after Toyota. It stresses constant improvement through the involvement of all employees in the manufacturing process." The company also looked to be the number one or number two manufacturer in the markets it chose to serve, and by expanding the number of market-leading truck interior products it had to offer, it built synergies, increasing its chances of selling more products to the same customer.

MAYFLOWER ACQUISITION IN 2005

CVG's first acquisition after becoming a public company came in February 2005 when it paid $107.5 million for Mayflower Vehicle Systems North America Commercial Vehicle Operations, part of the London bus manufacturer that had collapsed the year before. Based in Farmington Hills, Michigan, the Mayflower operation added a number of new products to the mix at CVG, including cab frames, sleeper boxes, and structural components, serving truck manufacturers such as International, Volvo/Mack, and Freightliner. In addition to its Farmington Hills facility, Mayflower operated plants in Detroit; Norwalk and Shadyside, Ohio; and Kings Mountain, North Carolina. The acquisition also brought with it Mayflower's seasoned management team.

In June 2005 CVG spent another $55 million to acquire Naperville, Illinois-based Monona Wire Corp. (MWC), a deal that added both new products and new markets. MWC manufactured electronic wire harnesses and panel assemblies for construction and specialty vehicles. CVG now had access to a new set of customers, including Caterpillar North America, Oshkosh Truck, and John Deere. CVG was already selling heavy plastic molded pieces to the lift truck industry, but now had a greater opportunity to sell some of its other products, such as seats, to this sector. In addition, MWC did business in the agricultural sector, in which CVG had virtually no penetration in the United States. Another plus was a major plant in Mexico that MWC operated. CVG had no facilities in Mexico, but could take advantage of MWC's world-class factory to produce cut-and-sew products and possibly mirrors, wipers, and other items. MWC also brought with it electronic engineering talent that CVG hoped to leverage in the development of products that relied on electronic controls, such as seats, mirrors, and wipers. Moreover, MWC did all of its business in North America, and CVG could use its global resources to sell MWC products in Europe and China.

CVG completed a smaller acquisition in August 2005, paying $12.1 million for Concord, North Carolina-based Cabarrus Plastics, Inc., maker of plastic

Kentucky University, Dunn had a great deal of managerial experience in the truck industry. He worked in the engineering and quality departments of heavy-lift truck manufacturer Hyster Corporation from 1980 to 1985, and joined Johnson Controls Automotive Group, an automotive trim manufacturer, from 1985 to 1988. He then spent the next decade at automotive parts maker Arvin Industries, and from 1998 until the time he joined Trim Systems he served as CEO of a heavy metal stamping company, Bliss Technologies.

About a week after CVG was formed, the company announced plans to make an initial public offering (IPO) of stock. The IPO, completed in August 2006, was lead managed by Credit Suisse First Boston and co-managed by Robert W. Baird & Co. Incorporated, Lehman Brothers Inc., and RBS Capital Markets Corporation. A total of $180 million was raised, of which $54 million was received by Onex, which reduced its stake to 24 percent. In addition, Onex received another $27 million from CVG to repay a debt. CVG also earmarked its share of the proceeds for use in making acquisitions and for product development. In July 2005 Onex would sell its remaining interest in CVG.

At the end of its first year as an independent company, CVG recorded sales of $380.5 million and net income of $17.5 million. It employed 1,850 people at plants in Indiana, North Carolina, Texas, and Virginia. CVG had loftier ambitions, however, and wasted little time in working toward achieving them. The company launched an expansion effort that was intended to provide some diversity in the very cyclical truck supply business by adding product niches as well as expanding its geographic reach. The company's acquisition strategy was simple, according to *Investor's Business Daily:* "It buys companies in high growth segments, then tries to make them more efficient by applying its quality control

molded parts mostly for recreational vehicles, a deal that expanded CVG's hard plastics business. As a result of continued growth of existing operations and the three acquisitions completed in 2006, CVG almost doubled its revenues in 2005 to $755 million, and net income nearly tripled to $49.4 million. Moreover, the price of CVG stock soared, up more than 50 percent since the company's IPO, and the company placed number 76 on *Business Week*'s top 100 list of Hot Growth Companies. CVG continued to grow at a strong pace in 2006, as first quarter sales were up more than 50 percent over the previous year. To more effectively run the business, CVG was divided into its three primary divisions: CVG Interior Systems Division, CVG Electrical/Mechanical Division, and CVG Structures Division.

Ed Dinger

PRINCIPAL DIVISIONS

CVG Interior Systems Division; CVG Electrical/Mechanical Division; CVG Structures Division.

PRINCIPAL COMPETITORS

Accuride Corporation; Tomkins plc; Valeo.

FURTHER READING

Eaton, Dan, "Commercial Vehicle Group Goes on the Road to Growth," *Columbus Business First,* July 25, 2005.

Matthews, Tom, "New Albany Truck Parts Maker Acquires Commercial-Vehicle Operation," *Columbus Dispatch,* February 9, 2005.

McLaughlin, Mark, "Rising Demand Puts Supplier of Truck Parts in the Fast Lane," *Investor's Business Daily,* July 14, 2005, p. A07.

"Onex Subsidiary, Commercial Vehicle Group, Prices $160 Million IPO," *Canadian Corporate News,* August 6, 2004.

Peterson, Susan E., "Dura Automotive Shifts into High Gear with IPO," *Star Tribune* (Minneapolis, Minn.), August 16, 1996, p. 1D.

Silverman, Suzann D., and Jennifer A. Cinguina, "A Joint Effort; Building Blocks," *International Business,* August 1994, p. 68.

Stammen, Ken, "New Albany, Ohio-Based Truck Parts Maker Plans Public Stock Offering," *Columbus Dispatch* (Columbus, Ohio), May 27, 2004.

Corporación Geo, S.A. de C.V.

———————————— ■ ————————————

Margaritas 433
Mexico City, D.F. 01050
Mexico
Telephone: (52) (55) 5480-5000
Toll Free: (866) 360-9002
Fax: (52) (55) 5554-6064
Web site: http://www.casasgeo.com

Public Company
Founded: 1973
Employees: 8,761
Sales: MXN 10.09 billion ($951.26 million) (2005)
Stock Exchanges: Mexico City OTC Madrid
Ticker Symbols: GEOB; CVGFY; XGEO
NAIC: 233210 Single Family Housing Construction

■ ■ ■

Corporación Geo, S.A. de C.V. is a holding company that, through its subsidiaries, functions as the largest homebuilder in Mexico, in terms of annual revenue and houses built. A vertically integrated enterprise, it is involved in all aspects of design, development, construction, marketing, commercialization, and delivery of housing in Mexico. With operations in 19 states, it is also the most geographically diversified homebuilder in Mexico, and, under the "Casas Geo" trademark, is the firm in its field most recognized by the public.

CORPORACIÓN GEO TO 1994

The company was founded in Mexico City in 1973 by Luis Orvañanos Lascurain, an architect by training. Until 1983, it functioned as a general contractor, erecting houses, office buildings, and industrial buildings as well as remodeling and adding to existing structures. It was a contractor for Infonavit and Fovi, the Spanish language acronyms of federal agencies that subsidized low-income homes. It was involved in every sphere of this work, including land acquisition, securing the necessary permits and licensing, and installing infrastructure improvements, as well as the design and construction of the houses.

Geo extended its reach to central Mexico in 1981, northern Mexico in 1985, and Guadalajara in 1986. Between 1983 and 1987 it determined to concentrate its focus on large-scale homebuilding. In the latter year the enterprise introduced "La Morada," a modular system of construction that enabled it to maximize a number of two-level townhouses in a determined area. With this accomplished, the company initiated also the industrialization of its production processes. (A second "La Morada" was developed in 1996 in conjunction with Harvard University.)

Beginning in 1989, Geo decided to specialize in low-income housing. Infonavit was restructured in 1992 in order to function as a mortgage provider to qualified workers, leaving housing development and related activities to the private sector. Companies such as Geo assumed the risk of finding the buyers and delivering houses to their satisfaction. The actual funds were not in doubt, since Infonavit held 5 percent of private-sector employees' salaries. These sums, accumulated in individual accounts, could be used for deposits, and Infonavit granted a guaranteed credit for the rest of the purchase price. Geo initiated its first development of

---

COMPANY PERSPECTIVES

Mission: To further integrated and innovative housing developments that guarantee our leadership, in terms of quality and profit, and that generate benefits for our shareholders, clients, collaborators, and society.

---

more than 1,000 homes in 1992.

The following year it began work on a development of 5,000 homes. By 1994, when the company went public, it was the largest builder of low-income housing in Mexico. It was also the first housing company in Mexico to be listed on the nation's stock exchange.

In a 1995 article published in *Forbes,* Christopher Palmeri described Orvañanos as "a kind of Mexican William Levitt, the man who built Levittowns." For about $14,000, Geo's customers were delivered a two-story, 750-square-foot cement townhouse with a living room and small open kitchen below and two bedrooms and a bathroom upstairs. These homes were designed so that an extra room could be easily added to each level. By this time the average weight (and therefore cost) of the houses had been reduced by designing common walls and making the Spanish colonial style tiled roofs of styrofoam, reinforced with steel and cement. American writers called these Lego-like dwellings, but Orvañanos told Palmeri, "When you've just gotten married and you're living with your grandparents, these places are like the Palace of Versailles." Geo sold 8,174 homes in 1994.

Geo's townhouses did not stand in isolation. They were grouped into 460-unit communities with playgrounds, schools, and shared gardens. Given the large number of Mexicans who make their living outside the formal economy, these communities were not strictly residential in nature. Some housewives converted their homes to hair salons or pharmacies; others sold candy to schoolchildren from the windows. Young men in horse drawn wagons trolled the streets, charging money to pick up garbage.

EXPANDING HOMEBUILDER: 1994–2004

Geo's initial public offering of stock came at a propitious time, since before 1994 had ended the Mexican peso had been devalued, the stock market had virtually collapsed, and it would be years before a company could again raise money by selling shares to the public. The

funds Geo had collected went for land acquisition and development, and in 1995 the company secured another $50 million in a private placement organized on Wall Street. Despite the recession that followed the economic crisis of 1994, Geo built more houses, raised more revenue, and earned a larger operating profit the following year. Houses built and revenue collected (in real terms, discounting inflation) continued to grow each remaining year in the decade. In 1996 the company built the first of nine "macrocenters," or sales offices. These centers allowed prospective clients to observe the quality of Geo's homes and different prototypes of homes suitable to their needs and particular tastes. By early 1997 Geo had projects under development in 13 Mexican states, and two large complexes in Mexico City, one of them containing 3,400 units. That year the company made its third equity placement—three times oversubscribed—and issued five-year notes.

Some of that money was earmarked for projects Geo was conducting outside Mexico for the first time. The company founded Geosal S.A. in Chile and began building 500 subsidized homes in Santiago, the capital, in collaboration with a local partner, Constructora Salfa S.A. By mid-1999, 4,400 homes had been erected. In the United States, Geo teamed with Beazer Homes USA Inc. to build low-income homes in El Paso, Texas, an endeavor that, as in Mexico, involved taking advantage of public housing subsidies. Geo was also considering establishing subsidiaries in Argentina and Brazil.

Within Mexico, the company acquired Fabricaciones Civiles e Industriales de la Laguna, S.A. de C.V. in 1998, with the purpose of opening up new markets in the northern part of the country. This company was the leading builder of low-income housing in the states of Coahuila, Durango, and Zacatecas. In 1998 Geo began work in the state of Mexico on Santa Elena, its first community of more than 5,000 homes. The following year it broke ground on Santa Bárbara. Also located in the state of Mexico, this development was slated to contain more than 12,000 houses.

The two-bedroom El Paso houses built by the Geo Beazer, L.P. joint venture were considerably larger than Geo's Mexican ones, 1,200 square feet on average and with many more amenities, including central heating and air conditioning. They were freestanding rather than townhouses and had fenced-in yards. The price was $39,000, compared to about $15,000 for the Mexican homes. Geo's point man in the venture complained to *Latin Trade* in 1999, however, that the permit process was proving much more onerous than in Mexico. The following year Geo announced that it was taking an

KEY DATES

1973: Luis Orvañanos Lascurain founds the company in Mexico City.

1984: The company introduces a system of modular construction.

1994: Geo makes its initial public offering of stock.

1997: Geo has projects under development in 13 Mexican states.

2001: The company restructures its finances to counter declines in revenue and homes built.

2003: Resurgent Geo has completed five complexes of more than 3,000 or more homes.

2005: Geo sells a record 37,343 houses.

extraordinary loss of an estimated $3.3 million and shutting down the operation. Geo Beazer was liquidated in 2002.

By this time Geo's thoughts had turned from ambitious expansion projects to servicing the $240 million in debt accumulated in its mostly vain attempts to grow its business outside Mexico. Because of an economic slowdown and cuts in housing subsidies, the number of homes built by the company and its revenues (in real terms) had fallen in 2001. Geo replenished its cash flow by negotiating stretched out payment terms with its suppliers, thereby enabling it to retire more short-term debt. It also laid off personnel and "renewed" its ranks of middle managers.

Geo's remedial efforts proved so successful that the Mexican business magazine *Expansión* proclaimed 2003 "the year of Geo" when the year was only a few weeks old. It also noted such positive factors as the federal government's determination to make housing construction a priority, the traditional growth of real estate development during times of economic stagnation, and lower interest rates. By this time Geo had completed five complexes of 3,000 or more houses. The largest of these had no less than 11,285 houses. The company was not only the largest "affordable" (that is, low-income) housing developer in Mexico but in all the Americas, as measured by homes sold. During the summer of 2003 Geo announced that it was establishing a joint venture with Prudential Real Estate Investors, the real estate investment advisory business of Prudential Financial Inc. As its first act, the joint venture bought parcels of land in Mexico City and Acapulco. By early 2005, this partnership had invested $175 million to develop more than 80,000 housing units in 42 projects covering 25

cities in 14 states. A second stage was then announced, with $280 million to invest.

A major objective of the company was to build and sell more unsubsidized homes for Mexico's middle and upper classes. By the end of 2002, Geo was the national leader in this segment. In 2004, Geo constructed 3,323 homes of this type, at prices ranging from $33,000 to $500,000. G-Homes, the company's luxury brand introduced that year, was oriented toward homes with prices in excess of $100,000. Sales of these dwellings required efforts that Geo had not made before: more individual touches to the homes and greater participation of the client in design. Some of these homes were apartments rather than houses.

Making possible exploitation of this market had been lower interest rates, enabling many prospective buyers too affluent to qualify for government aid to obtain mortgage credit for the first time. By the end of 2004 the fall in interest rates had enabled Infonavit and private lenders to sell about $400 million in mortgage-based securities. In addition, a new government agency, SHP by its Spanish acronym, established in 2001, was directing federal funds to commercial banks and Sofoles (specialized lenders) for housing development. Qualifiers for SHP-backed loans could be earning as much as $75,000 a year. The booming housing market enabled Geo's shares to triple in value during 2003 and double in price in 2004. In 2005, Geo became the first Mexican homebuilder to introduce its shares for trading in euros when it entered Latibex, the Latin American market of the Madrid stock exchange.

GEO IN 2005–06

Geo, in 2005, sold a record 37,343 houses, generating revenues of MXN 10.09 billion ($951.26 million). This brought the number of homes that the company had constructed since its inception to about 260,000. Geo's net profit for 2005 came to MXN 1.14 billion ($107.48 million) and its net debt at the end of the year to MXN 883 million ($83 million). However, the total debt rose to MXN 3.67 billion ($346 million), an increase of 37 percent. The company was unusual, in Mexico, in not being dominated by members of a founding family. A controlling group of executives held 22 percent of the shares; U.S. institutional investors held 56 percent; and European institutional investors, 13 percent. Orvañanos was still director general and chairman of the board; Miguel Gómez-Mont Urueta had been executive vice-president for over a decade and was described in English-language publications as chief executive officer.

As a vertically organized holding company, Geo was, through its subsidiaries, engaged in housing design, development, construction, and marketing. Its principal activities in real estate development included land acquisition, obtaining required permits and licenses, installing infrastructure improvements; designing, constructing, and marketing housing developments; and assisting home buyers in obtaining mortgage loans. The company was also acting as a contractor for certain Mexican state government agencies, providing construction activities similar to its development activities. The Casas Geo brand trademark was the most recognized in the Mexican housing industry.

Geo received an award in 2006 from the Mexican Center for Philanthropy as a socially responsible company. The honor was based on such considerations as community ties, quality of life, care and preservation of the environment, and business ethics. The company spent about $3 million during 2005 on social programs that benefited a total of 88,848 persons. Investment in the environment came to almost $6 million more. During its years in business Geo had contributed 200 schools of basic education, 50 health clinics, and more than 20 water treatment plants.

Robert Halasz

PRINCIPAL SUBSIDIARIES

Crelam, S.A. de C.V.; Evitam, S.A. de C.V. (93 percent); Geo Edificaciones, S.A. de C.V.; Geo Hogares Ideales, S.A. de C.V.; Geo Importex, S.A. de C.V.; Inmobiliaria Anson, S.A. de C.V.; Inmobiliaria Camar, S.A. de C.V.; Inmobiliaria Jumais, S.A. de C.V.; Lotes y Fraccionamientos, S.A. de C.V.; Obras y Proyectos Coma, S.A. de C.V.; Promotora Turística Playa Vela S.A. de C.V.

PRINCIPAL COMPETITORS

Consorcio Ara, S.A. de C.V.; Consorcio Hogar, S.A. de C.V.; Desarrolladora Homex, S.A. de C.V.; Urbi Desarrollos Urbanos, S.A. de C.V.

FURTHER READING

Anderson, Bárbara, "El protagonista del *boom* del año," *Expansión,* February 19–March 5, 2003, pp. 66–70.

Celis, Dario, "El casado...casa quiere," *Siempre!,* October 9, 1997, p. 43.

Dombey, Daniel, "Mexican Developer in $67m Share Issue," *Financial Times,* June 20, 1997, p. 25.

Libaw, Oliver, "Affordable Housing: Bridging the Gap," *Business Mexico,* May 1997, pp. 26–28, 30.

Lichtblau, Julia, "Mexican, U.S. Firms Teaming Up to Sell Homes to the Poor in Texas," *Wall Street Journal,* December 10, 1997, p. A19.

"Mexico's Homebuilder Extraordinaire Is the Home of Innovation," *Euromoney,* October 2005, pp. SS4.

Moore, Leslie, "Lego for Adults," *LatinFinance,* September 1988, p. 60.

Morón, Roberto, "G de glamor," *Expansión,* June 22–July 6, 2005, pp. 147–49.

Palmeri, Christopher, "We Have a Mission," *Forbes,* November 20, 1995, pp. 96, 98.

Poole, Claire, "Mi Casa es tu Casa," *Latin Trade,* July 1999, p. 36.

Watson, Andrew, "Windfall of Government Credits Makes This Sector Quite Salacious," *Business Mexico,* December 2002–January 2003, p. 40.

Council on International
Educational Exchange Inc.

7 Custom House Street, Floor 3
Portland, Maine 04101
U.S.A.
Telephone: (207) 553-7600
Toll Free: (800) 407-8839
Fax: (207) 553-7699
Web site: http://www.ciee.org

Nonprofit Company
Incorporated: 1947 as Council on Student Travel
Employees: 450
Operating Revenues: $70.5 million (2005 est.)
NAIC: 611710 Educational Support Services

■ ■ ■

Council on International Educational Exchange Inc. (CIEE) is a nonprofit educational and cultural exchange organization that oversees study abroad programs, teaching programs, and volunteer-run projects on an international basis. The CIEE is involved in approximately 60 study abroad programs and 800 volunteer projects in 30 countries, providing services for individuals, communities, educational institutions, and employers.

ORIGINS

Following World War II, there were numerous efforts to bridge the cultural and political divides separating nations. After six years of hostility and atrocity, the need to achieve a greater sense of international understanding became paramount, spawning the formation of organizations and institutions chartered to promote peaceful coexistence and mutual respect in a world devastated by conflict. Student exchange programs were perceived as one way to improve international relations and to cultivate cultural awareness at the same time, but, according to consensus, educational organizations and other groups devoted to promoting student and teacher travel would need help coordinating their efforts. The CIEE became the entity that accepted such a role, offering itself as an association of organizations committed to promoting harmony among nations by promoting student and teacher travel.

Immediately following the war, securing transportation for overseas travel stood as the greatest impediment to developing exchange programs. Numerous educational agencies interested in sending exchange students abroad to conferences, work camps, and study seminars began petitioning the U.S. Department of State for the use of military troop transports for the summer of 1947. The Department of State obliged, asking the Maritime Commission to supply two C-4 vessels to be used for sending U.S. students on exchange programs to Europe. The United States Lines and Moore-McCormick Line were asked to serve as general agents for the vessels, marking the beginning of what became known as the "Student Ship Project," the primary focus of the CIEE for decades.

The CIEE was formed in May 1947, beginning as the Council on Student Travel (CST). Initially, the CST lacked a permanent office and staff, but it played a significant role in fostering student travel from the start, assigning work to committees such as the American Prince Service Committee, the International Institute of Education and the Experiment in International Living

COMPANY PERSPECTIVES

Since 1947, the Council on International Educational Exchange, known as CIEE and formerly, Council, has been in pursuit of its mission, "to help people gain understanding, acquire knowledge, and develop skills for living in a globally interdependent and culturally diverse world." Our services to young people studying and teaching abroad are more important than ever. As we look ahead, we reaffirm our commitment to the principles and values that guide this mission statement.

to arrange transportation for students who wanted to study abroad. The CST was quick to point out during its first months of existence that it was not a travel agency; travel arrangements were made with travel agent associate members such as American Abroad, Brownell Travel Bureau, Transmarine Tours, and American Express. Instead, it described itself as a nonprofit association interested solely in encouraging and facilitating educational travel abroad, endeavoring to create young "ambassadors" versed in different cultures whose experiences would improve international relations. The CST accepted 32 organizations and institutions during its first year, drawing its membership from U.S. nonprofit educational and cultural agencies that sponsored groups of students traveling to Europe for educational purposes. During its first three years of overseeing the Student Ship Project, the CST coordinated transportation and developed orientation programs for 10,000 U.S. and foreign students, teachers, research workers, and others in the educational and religious fields. The transportation of the 10,000 individuals, which was restricted to the summer months of 1947, 1948, and 1949, was handled by C-4 vessels and several Dutch ships placed in service through joint effort between the Dutch government and the Holland-America Line.

During its first decades of operation, the CST was best known as the organization behind the Student Ship Project. Specifically, the organization earned recognition for its orientation programs conducted during transAtlantic passages, ten-day programs that included lectures and discussions on social, economic, political, and cultural issues related to destination countries. The CST's orientation programs became more comprehensive as the 1950s progressed, evolving into a fundamental aspect of the organization's effort to create ambassadors to Western European countries. Thanks largely to the hugely popular orientation programs, the CST established itself as a

recognized facilitator of international student travel, and its influence quickly grew despite losing access to military vessels. The outbreak of the Korean War prompted the State Department to take back the government's troop ships, forcing the CST to begin chartering vessels in 1951. Traffic to Europe exploded in the years to follow, involving more than 7,000 transAtlantic passages by the mid-1950s, when the CST oversaw the transport of 50,000 U.S. students and 45,000 foreign students annually.

The CST did not wait long before broadening its scope, taking the momentum built up by the popularity of the Student Ship Project to evolve into a more comprehensive facilitator of student travel. In 1952, one year after establishing an office in Paris, it sponsored its first conference on student travel, holding a forum for administrators, educators, and teachers that helped build a network of educational institutions. The conference became an annual event, giving the student travel community an opportunity to discuss policies and the future direction of sponsoring travel abroad. Significantly, conference attendees began looking into booking air transportation and encouraging travel to Africa, Asia, and South America by the mid-1950s. One of the most impressive accomplishments of the CST during the 1950s was an exchange between U.S. students and students living in the Soviet Union. The program, begun in 1958, testified to the influence and the tenacity of the CST and its membership, which totaled 70 organizations and institutions by the end of the decade.

FROM THE CST TO THE CIEE

After firmly establishing itself as a nonprofit organization of note through its association with the Student Ship Project, the CST pressed ahead during the 1960s. The organization had to keep pace with the changing times and the changing needs of its members, a dynamic it responded to by engineering its own evolution. The decade witnessed the end of one era and the beginning of another: The CST began booking transportation programs by air in 1960 and the last student ship sailed in 1969. For an entity whose identity was drawn from its ten-day orientation programs, the switch from sea to air forced a sweeping change in focus. The CST moved away from its specialty in transportation and orientation programs and adopted a more academic approach during the mid-1960s. This profound shift in direction prompted a name change in 1967, when the Council on International Educational Exchange became the new name of the CST. Newly christened, the organization was set to serve the more demanding needs of its 162 primarily college and university members by the end of the decade.

KEY DATES

1947: Council on Student Travel (CST) is formed.

1960: The organization begins booking transportation programs by air.

1967: CST changes its name to Council on International Educational Exchange (CIEE), a symbolic change reflecting a more academically oriented focus.

1979: Jack Egle is appointed chief executive officer and president.

1997: CIEE celebrates its 50th anniversary.

2006: CIEE boasts nearly 250 member institutions.

Under the CIEE banner, the organization struggled to adapt to its new role. Primarily to blame were difficulties related to the flight program, including problems associated with landing rights and escalating fuel costs. Switching from sea to air led to a severe drain of the organization's financial resources, putting the CIEE on the brink of bankruptcy when one of its most influential leaders, Jack Egle, was appointed president and chief executive officer in 1979. Egle joined the organization in 1951, when the CST opened its Paris office. Egle was a doctoral candidate at the University of Paris at the time and he was hired to lend cohesion to the newly formed office, quickly proving to be an indispensable member of the team. Soon, he was appointed European director of the organization, a post he would hold until 1979, when he was selected to replace John Bowman, who had served as the CIEE's chief executive officer for 27 years. Bowman left an impressive legacy, having made the organization the principal association in the country for the promotion and the development of study abroad programs, but the end of his lengthy tenure left Egle with formidable challenges to overcome. Egle inherited profound financial problems, which he addressed by greatly reducing the organization's charter flight program and by turning to alternate flights on scheduled service. He also sought to lessen the load carried by the CIEE, first sparking the interest then soliciting the support of government, business, and finance groups. At the same time, he stressed the importance of developing cooperative arrangements, greatly expanding the use of consortia that would become a pillar supporting the CIEE as it progressed from the 20th century to the 21st century.

Egle registered rousing success in revamping the CIEE, giving the organization the operational stance that enabled it to fulfill its mission and to do so in an economically viable manner. The CIEE, relying heavily on the use of consortia, expanded its activities and programs in southeast Asia, Latin America, Africa, and the Caribbean during the 1980s. The highlights of Egle's era of management, which stretched to 1994, included the globalization of the organization's membership, the establishment of a database that tracked student travel, work, and study patterns, and the reorganization of the CIEE's transportation activities into a separate company. By the time Egle ended his 43-year-long career at the CIEE, the organization boasted approximately 250 members.

THE CIEE IN THE NEW MILLENNIUM

As the CIEE closed out its first half-century of existence, the organization held sway as the largest, nongovernmental, international education entity in the United States. The CIEE's activities, which spanned the globe after robust expansion during the 1980s and 1990s, were organized along four lines: international study programs, training opportunities, work and travel in the United States, and high school programs. The organization's international study programs offered 40 subject areas in 30 countries for college students. For faculty and administrators, the CIEE held international faculty development seminars, a program introduced in 1990 that offered lectures, site visits, and discussions. The CIEE's annual conference, begun in 1952, also was grouped within the organization's international study offerings, giving international educators an opportunity to share teaching methods and plot the future course of study abroad programs. Within its training category, the CIEE acted as the legal sponsor for the U.S. Department of State, offered internship programs for U.S. businesses, and developed programs for U.S. students and graduates to teach abroad. The CIEE also offered programs for foreign students, the purview of the organization's "Work & Travel USA" category. Seasonal work in the United States was offered for international students as well as programs to help U.S. employers hire international students. For high school age students, the CIEE offered study abroad programs for U.S. students and facilitated exchange programs involving host families in the United States and abroad.

Jeffrey L. Covell

PRINCIPAL SUBSIDIARIES

Council on Student Travel.

PRINCIPAL COMPETITORS

International Studies Abroad; Center for International Studies; Institute for the International Education of Students.

FURTHER READING

CIEE: *A Guide to Institutional Self-Study and Evaluation of Educational Programs Abroad*, New York: Council on Student Travel, 1965.

CIEE: *The Power of Educational Exchange. Essays in Honor of Jack Egle*, New York: Council on International Educational Exchange, 1994.

Council on Student Travel, Program Development Department, *Report of 1958 U.S.-U.S.S.R. Summer Exchange Project*.

Mikhailova, Ludmila, *A History of CIEE: Council on International Exchange 1947–1994*, New York: Council on International Educational Exchange, 2002.

Cyprus Airways Public Limited

21 Alkeou Street
P.O. Box 21903
Nicosia, CY-2404 Engomi
Cyprus
Telephone: (+357) 22 661800
Fax: (+357) 22 663167
Web site: http://www.cyprusairways.com

Public Company
Incorporated: 1947
Employees: 1,700
Sales: CYP 201.15 million (2005)
Stock Exchanges: Cyprus
Ticker Symbol: CAR
NAIC: 481111 Scheduled Passenger Air Transportation; 481112 Scheduled Freight Air Transportation; 481211 Nonscheduled Chartered Passenger Air Transportation; 488119 Other Airport Operations

■■■

Cyprus Airways Public Limited is the flag carrier of the Mediterranean island nation of Cyprus. It is publicly traded, though the government owns a majority holding. Its route network stretches from Europe to the Persian Gulf. More than 1.5 million passengers a year fly Cyprus Airways to three dozen destinations in the Mediterranean, Middle East, and Europe. The airline has a fleet of about ten Airbus aircraft. The group includes Eurocypria Airlines Ltd., a charter carrier that specializes in bringing European tourists to Cyprus. Ancillary ventures include a Sabre-affiliated computer reservation system business and duty-free shops.

ORIGINS

Cyprus Airways was formed September 24, 1947. British European Airways held a 44.9 percent stake in the new airline, while the government of Cyprus, then a colony of Great Britain, owned 22.45 percent of shares. Some private investors held the remaining 32.65 percent, according to company literature. Air services were launched on October 6, 1947, according to *A History of the World's Airlines,* with British European Airways (BEA) operating the aircraft for the first several months. At the time, BEA was also establishing new airlines on the British-controlled islands of Gibraltar and Malta.

According to the company, the new airline's original equipment consisted of three Douglas C-47s. This type was an Allied military transport that had launched many civil carriers after World War II. The planes, which carried 21 passengers each, flew on a route network centered in Nicosia that soon included Rome, London (via Athens), Beirut, Athens, Cairo, Alexandria, Istanbul, and Haifa. By the end of the decade, another three C-47s had been added and the list of destinations included Kuwait, Bahrain, Baghdad, Lydda, and Khartoum (via Haifa).

In 1952, BEA took over service to London with an Airspeed Ambassador, which featured a pressurized cabin that allowed nonstop routing. The next year, BEA allocated one of its new Vickers Viscounts to a London-Rome-Athens-Nicosia run. According to the company, this was the world's first regular turboprop service.

COMPANY PERSPECTIVES

Culture that draws on Europe, the Middle East, and 9,000 years of history, traditional Cypriot hospitality, Mediterranean spirit, modern business practices and uncompromised customer commitment, are only some of the ingredients that make up an airline, which is proud for its achievements.

INDEPENDENT IN 1960

The government of newly independent Cyprus became the majority shareholder in 1960 with a 53.2 percent holding, while BEA's stake was reduced to 22.7 percent and private individuals held the rest. Thereafter, Cypriot nationals began to be hired and trained for the flight crews, which had previously been made up of British expatriates from BEA.

Cyprus Airways still relied on the U.K. airline for aircraft. BEA began introducing Comet 4B jets on all routes in 1961 via a joint aircraft pool arrangement that included Greece's Olympic Airways. In 1965, Cyprus began leasing its own Viscounts from BEA for regional routes. Around this time, a winged mountain goat was adopted for the airline's logo.

The Comet and Viscount aircraft were replaced with Trident jets in the early 1970s. Cyprus also leased a BAC 1-11. The faster planes allowed more European trade centers (Frankfurt, Manchester, Brussels, and Paris) to be added to the timetable.

1974 TURK INVASION

Cyprus Airways was forced to improvise after Turkey invaded northern Cyprus in July 1974. The military action destroyed one Trident airline and damaged another one, while the remaining planes were interned after the United Nations took over Nicosia Airport. Within seven months Cyprus had set up an interim airstrip on the island's southern coast. The airline leased Viscount turboprops to fly a stripped down route network to a few key cities in the region: Beirut, Tel Aviv, and Athens via Heraklion, with connections to London on British Airways. Cyprus Airways leased a pair of DC-9 jets in August 1975 to resume its own flights to London (via Salonika). The acquisition of a DC-8 several months later allowed for non-stop service. Cyprus also added flights to Saudi Arabia at this time. The company was soon able to order a pair of new BAC 1-11s.

The DC-8 was involved in an international incident in February 1978. After a group of terrorists took hostages at a conference on the island, the Cypriot government acquiesced to their demand for an escape aircraft, which was manned by volunteers, reported *Aviation Week & Space Technology*. It returned to Cyprus after being denied landing permission elsewhere. An Egyptian journalist had been killed in the hostage taking, and Egypt sent commandos to attack the plane on the ground. While no more hostages were killed, 15 Egyptian troops died in the ensuing battle with the Cypriot soldiers in charge of guarding the airport. It was a disastrous episode in Egypt-Cyprus relations.

The airline ordered still more different aircraft types in the late 1970s; these replaced some earlier aircraft coming off lease. By 1981, Cyprus's fleet included four Boeing 707s and three BAC 1-11s. The route network again extended from Manchester, England, to Baghdad. A change in ownership structure had taken place, with British Airways selling all but 5 percent of the shares it had inherited from BEA to the Cypriot government. Private investors owned the remainder (24.14 percent).

FIRST WIDEBODIES IN 1984

Cyprus made a transition to Airbus aircraft over the course of the decade. Its first A310 widebodies arrived in 1984, followed by A320s in 1989. The order for the eight A320s was worth more than $250 million.

Profits reached record levels in the mid-1980s as the airline added service from new U.K. cities (Cardiff, Newcastle, and Glasgow). Income of CYP 4.8 million ($8 million) in 1983, a record, would be tripled three years later. By this time, the airline was carrying 740,000 passengers a year.

Upgrading the new facilities at Larnaca continued to be a priority as officials sought to develop it into a kind of regional hub through alliances with global carriers. With liberalization of aviation markets sweeping across Europe, it was already clear that the somewhat overstaffed legacy of the state-controlled company would have to operate on a more commercial basis in the future, said chairman Kikis Lazarides. One goal was to reduce dependence on U.K. traffic. Cargo was one growing source of income. By 1989, revenues were CYP 69.7 million ($160.3 million) a year.

A NEW LOOK IN 1991

British Airways divested the last of its shares in 1991, leaving the government with an 80.46 percent stake and private investors, the remainder. The airline was flying high, introducing a livery and uniforms as the Airbuses

KEY DATES

1947: Cyprus Airways is founded with assistance of British European Airlines (BEA).
1960: Government of newly independent Cyprus becomes majority shareholder.
1984: First widebody aircraft increase capacity in booming U.K. market.
1991: British Airways divests last of shares inherited from BEA.
1992: Eurocypria charter airline is launched.
2003: A difficult year in liberalizing market prompts restructuring negotiations.
2004: Cyprus joins the European Union.

plied new routes to Berlin and Helsinki. Cyprus Airways had also joined the SABRE international computer reservations system and set up a tour operation in the United Kingdom.

In 1992 the group established Eurocypria Airlines Ltd. to fly European tourists to Cyprus on a charter basis. It was expanding into ancillary services as well, taking over duty-free operations at Larnaca and Pafos airports.

Cyprus added many new cooperation agreements with other airlines as it developed its international reach by linking Europe and the Middle East. Its partners included KLM and Saudia. By the mid-1990s, more than one million passengers were flying Cyprus Airways every year; another 4,000 chose the charter operation Eurocypria. The airline's market share approached 40 percent. After a rough couple of years, the company posted a CYP 13 million profit in 1994 thanks to cost-cutting and marketing efforts.

Unfortunately, the success was short-lived and the group posted losses in 1996 and 1997 before returning to profitability in 1998. By 1999, revenues were up to CYP 128.8 million; profits were slipping as the carrier dealt with increasing fuel costs and unfavorable exchange rates against the British pound. Cyprus got its first U.S. codeshare partner in 1999 via a link with Northwest Airlines. It joined the Wings global airline alliance led by Northwest and KLM.

A CHALLENGING NEW MILLENNIUM

Cyprus Airways began the new millennium with 1,600 to 2,000 employees (who were represented by five strong

unions) and an economical, standardized fleet of a dozen Airbus aircraft. Its route network included 32 destinations.

The airline introduced restyled livery as it embarked on an ambitious fleet renewal program. Airbus A319s, smaller than its other planes, were added in 2002. The next year, new Airbus A330 aircraft began to replace older A310s on long-haul routes. A fleet of four Boeing 737s was chosen for the Eurocypria charter subsidiary, however.

In 2002, the Cyprus government lowered its ownership stake to 69.62 percent. By this time, the airline was carrying six million passengers a year. As Britain's *Financial Times* noted, more than 100 airlines were then flying to the attractive tourist destination of Cyprus.

At the same time, it was dealing with a weak global economy, the effects of the September 11, 2001 terrorist attacks on the United States and the war in Iraq on the aviation and tourism industries, and rising fuel costs. Nevertheless, the group was able to remain profitable in 2001 and 2002, thanks to an increase in passenger traffic and help from the duty-free stores.

EU MEMBERSHIP IN 2004

In preparation for the country's entry into the European Union in May 2004, Cyprus was gradually opening up its skies to foreign competitors. The state airline was hit with some loss of income on its lucrative U.K. routes, but was sheltered from competition from budget airlines since the Cyprus-London route was too long for the traditional low cost carrier business model, said an executive in *Air Transport Intelligence*. EU membership was expected to boost the airline's cargo business, another official told *Lloyd's List*.

The airline posted a loss of almost CYP 21 million ($43 million) in 2003. This prompted another round of restructuring. Cyprair Tours was closed in November 2004. Two of the airline's 12 planes were taken from service and the 1,800-strong workforce was slated to be cut by 20 percent.

Cyprus Airways had started a small Greek associate called Hellas Jet S.A. in June 2003, in time for the 2004 Olympic Games in Athens. It was 51 percent owned by local interests. Its purpose was to compete as a low-cost carrier on routes between Athens and London, Paris and Brussels. Hellas also flew charter flights to Turkey (Istanbul), which did not recognize the Republic of Cyprus and would not allow Cypriot aircraft to enter its airspace (an inconvenience that reportedly cost Cyprus Airways CYP 1 million a year). The Greek-registered Hellas planes, chartered by a Greek businessman on behalf of tour operators in Cyprus, were allowed in, however.

Cyprus Airways revenues slipped 1.9 percent to CYP 201 million in 2005, though the pre-tax loss was narrowed to CYP 25 million from CYP 41 million. Negotiations over the airline's restructuring continued into 2006. Management was seeking a CYP 55 million (EUR 95 million) loan from the government, while proposing to sell the Eurocypria charter operation to the state.

Frederick C. Ingram

PRINCIPAL SUBSIDIARIES

Cyprus Airways (Duty Free Shops) Ltd.; Eurocypria Airlines Ltd.; Hellas Jet S.A. (Greece; 49%); Zenon National Distribution Centre Ltd.

PRINCIPAL COMPETITORS

Aegean Airlines S.A.; British Airways plc; British Midlands Airways Ltd.; Olympic Airways S.A.

FURTHER READING

"Airline Makes $13 Million Net Profits," *Moneyclips,* February 6, 1995.

Balakrishnan, Ayalur, "Cyprus Airways Starts Major Marketing Drive in Saudi Arabia," *Moneyclips,* February 15, 1993.

Crisp, Andrea, "Cyprus Airways Seeks Turnaround Aid," *Airline Business,* May 1, 2006.

"Cyprus Aircraft Commandeering Could Accelerate Security Rules," *Aviation Week & Space Technology,* February 27, 1978, p. 27.

"Cyprus Airways Expects Air Cargo Profits to Take Off As EU Membership Takes Hold," *Lloyd's List,* September 15, 2004, p. 19.

"Cyprus Airways to Boost Mid-East Operations," *Moneyclips,* June 6, 1992.

Davies, R. E. G., *A History of the World's Airlines,* London: Oxford University Press, 1967.

Donne, Michael, "Cyprus Doubles Airbus Order," *Financial Times* (London), July 15, 1987, p. 5.

Dunn, Graham, "Cyprus Airways Unaffected by Budget Carrier Impact," *Air Transport Intelligence,* May 22, 2004.

Endres, Gunter, "Unions Back Cyprus Airways Survival Plan," *Airline Business,* February 1, 2005, p. 20.

"Greek Cypriot Associate Airline Starts Flights to Turkey," *BBC Monitoring International Reports,* May 12, 2005.

Hope, Kerin, "State Carrier Lines Up for Take-Off to Part-Privatisation," *Financial Times* (London), July 3, 2000, p. 3.

———, "Taxiing to Build a Niche in Greece," *Financial Times* (London), October 9, 2002, p. 5.

Kennedy, Tony, "Northwest Forges Alliance with Cyprus Airways," *Star Tribune* (Minneapolis), September 15, 1999, p. 3D.

Moores, Victoria, "Cyprus Airways Secures Shareholder Backing for Overhaul," *Air Transport Intelligence,* November 30, 2004.

Morrow, David, "Cyprus Airways Reviews Fleet Plans," *Air Transport Intelligence,* October 5, 2001.

"New Boss at Cyprus Airline," *Moneyclips,* September 20, 1993.

"No Access to Turkish Airspace Costly for Cyprus Airways," *World News Connection,* November 1, 2002.

"Open Skies Policy Alarms National Carrier," *Lloyd's List,* September 17, 2002, p. 18.

"The Sky Is the Limit in Cypress; Airlines Prepare for a Boom in the Run-Up to EU Entry," *Travel Weekly,* March 8, 2004, p. 49.

Turner, Aimee, "Cyprus Outlines Recovery Plan for National Carrier," *Air Transport Intelligence,* August 3, 2004.

Digitas Inc.

33 Arch Street
Boston, Massachusetts 02100
U.S.A.
Telephone: (617) 369-8000
Fax: (617) 369-8111
Web site: http://www.digitasinc.com

Public Company
Founded: 1980 as Eastern Exclusives
Employees: 1,500
Sales: $565.5 million (2005)
Stock Exchanges: NASDAQ
Ticker Symbol: DTAS
NAIC: 541611 Administrative Management and General Management

∎∎∎

Digitas Inc. is a Boston-based corporate parent of three global direct and interactive marketing companies. Digitas LLC, the flagship unit, has been a leading direct marketing firm since the 1980s, establishing itself by serving a select number of large corporate customers such as AT&T and American Express, and then increasingly turning its attention to the use of the Internet in the late 1990s. In addition to its Boston office, the subsidiary maintains operations in Chicago, Detroit, and New York. Modem Media has been involved in interactive marketing since 1987. It offers a wide range of services, including interactive and integrated marketing strategies; digital and direct marketing, research, and media buying. Modem Media maintains offices in Atlanta, San Francisco, London, and Norwalk, Connecticut. Finally, Philadelphia, Pennsylvania–based Medical Broadcasting, LLC is devoted to the healthcare industry, offering marketing services to pharmaceutical and other healthcare companies. Digitas is a public company listed on the NASDAQ.

FORMATION IN COLLEGE DORM ROOM: 1980

Digitas was founded by Michael E. Bronner in 1980 while he was a premed student at Boston University as a way to meet tuition payments. Working out of his dormitory room, Bronner launched the University Coupon Book, to market pizza and other goods that appealed to the college demographic. He talked local businesses into offering discount coupons, which he printed as a book and distributed free in student mailboxes. The effort proved so successful that Bronner formed a company called Eastern Exclusives to take his idea to other schools. He then branched out beyond the college market, creating a quarterly coupon book called The City, which targeted Boston office workers. All thoughts of medical school would be forgotten in 1981 when Bronner was able to persuade giant American Express to let him create a coupon book with its name on it, providing discounts on Boston restaurants and for other services, mailed to area cardmembers. Again, Bronner was successful, his relationship with American Express expanded, and his coupon book evolved into the highly successful Membership Rewards program.

The one-man operation turned into a regular direct marketing agency in Boston in the 1980s, focusing on a

COMPANY PERSPECTIVES

DIGITAS INC. is the parent of three leading direct and digital marketing companies: Digitas, Medical Broadcasting Company, and Modem Media. Digitas Inc. companies help blue-chip global brands develop, engage and profit from their customers through digital, direct and indirect relationships.

limited number of large clients. AT&T would soon join American Express on the roster. Bronner added a partner in 1987 when he was joined by Mike Slosberg, the two brought together by a headhunter. Slosberg had a more traditional advertising background, learning the business at one of New York's most venerable agencies, Young & Rubicam, where he was best known as the creator of the "Excedrin Headache" campaign. He later left to become the chief operating officer of another large firm, Wunderman, Ricotta & Kline. A year before joining Eastern Exclusives, Slosberg became involved in direct advertising, named the president of the direct marketing division at the Bozell agency. He became executive creative director for Eastern Exclusives. In 1989 the company changed its name to Bronner Slosberg Associates Inc. One of those associates was Steve Humphrey, a 29-year veteran of the advertising industry, who was named president in 1989. He played a key role in expanding the company and improving its account management and support services. In honor of his important contribution the agency changed its name again in 1991, becoming Bronner Slosberg Humphrey.

INTERACTIVE UNIT LAUNCHED: 1995

Now a well-established direct marketing specialist, Bronner Slosberg was in the vanguard of the advertising industry in exploring the possibilities of the new digital economy. In 1995 it formed the Strategic Interactive Group to provide new interactive services for its current customers. Several employees were recruited from within the shop to launch SIG, and as the Internet gained in popularity, the unit became increasingly important at Bronner Slosberg. Initially, SIG was a separate corporate entity, sharing common ownership with Bronner Slosberg.

As SIG ascended in importance, the top ranks of the agency also began to experience a significant shakeup. In early 1997 Humphrey retired and fresh blood was introduced in the form of 35-year-old David Kenny,

named vice-chairman in January 1997. Nine months later he succeeded Bronner as the company's chief executive officer. A Harvard Business School graduate, Kenny came to Bronner Slosberg from the consulting firm of Bain & Company, where he was a senior partner. He assumed day-to-day control of the third-largest direct marketing agency in the United States, generating more than $100 million in revenues in 1997. Bronner stayed on as chairman, while the 59-year-old Slosberg became chief creative officer, a new title if not a new job. Humphrey's old title would eventually fall to Kathy Biro, a major player in the growth of SIG, which began to overshadow the traditional direct marketing business.

The agency was clearly in a state of flux in the final years of the 1990s. It had experienced rapid expansion, growing from 80 employees in 1992 to 850 in early 1998 after new offices were opened in the New York and San Francisco markets. The 70-person New York operation was established to primarily service American Express and included a promotions and event sponsorship group. According to *Advertising Age,* it was also "an experiment to see if the agency's culture and capabilities [could] be replicated." The 50-person San Francisco office, on the other hand, operated as the Sansome Group, a separate customer relationship management agency, serving major clients Charles Schwab and LA Cellular.

The advertising industry was also in a state of flux as marketing went global and small independent shops, in order to survive and gain an international presence and resources, sold out to massive multinational operations. Bronner Slosberg's accounts needed to be global and according to press reports were pushing the agency to add global reach. This could only be accomplished by acquiring operations country by country or by joining forces with one of the large companies. Bronner Slosberg was actively courted but did not find the right suitor. Instead, in October 1998 management announced plans to form a holding company to operate three businesses: Bronner Slosberg Humphrey, SIG, and Sansome Group. While the plan was carried out, the company sold a 20 percent stake to the San Francisco investment firm of Hellman & Friedman for an estimated $60 million to $80 million. Then, in January 1999 the firm and some other investors gained a majority stake, paying Michael Bronner and his family trust approximately $123 million.

In April 1999 Bronner Slosberg changed its name to Bronnercom, a reflection of the increasing importance of the Internet to the company. Several months later it was reported that Bronnercom was preparing to go public, a move supposedly pushed by Hellman & Friedman. By the end of the year filings were made with the Securities and Exchange Commission for an initial

KEY DATES

1980: Company is founded by Michael E. Bronner as Eastern Exclusives.
1989: Name is changed to Bronner Slosberg Associates.
1991: Name is changed to Bronner Slosberg Humphrey.
1995: Strategic Interactive Group is formed.
1999: Holding company organization is adopted.
2000: Company goes public as Digitas Inc.
2004: Modem Media, Inc. is acquired.
2006: Medical Broadcasting, LLC, is acquired.

public offering of stock, valued around $200 million, under a new corporate name: Digitas Inc. The money was earmarked to pay down debt, fund possible acquisitions, and to be used for general corporate purposes. To prepare for the offering, Digitas made some changes in the top ranks of management, bringing in Michael Goss, former chief financial officer of Playtex Products, a seasoned executive with experience at major public companies, to serve as CFO at Bronnercom. In addition, Robert Galford, former managing director of Counsel to Management, was hired as the head of worldwide human resources. At the same time, Slosberg announced plans to retire by the end of 2000, and Michael Bronner, now 40, was also beginning to ease out of the picture. He took the title of chairman emeritus, and the burden of running the company rested squarely on the shoulders of Kenny, who became CEO and chairman. In 2000 Bronner turned his attention to a new venture, launching UPromise, an e-commerce company that helped families pay for college education by taking advantage of tax-deferred college funds supplemented by rebates from participating companies. He also founded a related nonprofit corporation: UPromise Education Foundation.

IPO: 2000

With Morgan Stanley Dean Witter & Co. acting as lead manager, Bronnercom sold 9.3 million shares at $24 per share on March 14, 2000. When the company's stock, which was priced about $5 higher than expected, began trading on the NASDAQ, it quickly soared to $40. In 2000 total revenues increased by more than 50 percent to a record $414.7 million, and the company opened offices in Chicago, Brussels, and Hong Kong. Nevertheless, it had to contend with a rapidly declining stock price, falling to the neighborhood of $5, due primarily

to the general meltdown of the dotcom sector. Digitas attempted to rebuild Wall Street's confidence by shuffling its management team and bringing in new people. Goss, hired just one year earlier to placate the Street, was cut free, and Biro, who had played a key role in transforming Digitas from a direct marketer to an interactive agency in the late 1990s, gave up the presidency and resigned as a director. Both executives denied they were ousted, however. Goss said that he would have stayed but had left to become the CFO and managing director at Bain Capital. Biro, who took a reduced role at the company, planned to teach, and maintained that the executive changes were in fact a way to build management depth. Her replacement as president was chief operating officer Michael Ward, expected to work closely with Kenny in shaping the future at Digitas.

However, no executive shuffle could help Digitas withstand the confluence of events that took place in 2001 that adversely impacted the company. The global economy soured, leading to contractions in the capital markets. Without ready funding available, companies cut back on their investments in both technology and marketing. Matters grew even worse with the events of September 11, 2001, as the terrorist attacks on U.S. soil crippled the airline and travel industries, and had a ripple effect on the U.S. and global economy. In April 2001 Digitas cut the pay of its 70 highest-paid executives by 5 percent, matched by the layoff of 65 people, or 3 percent of the staff. Total revenues fell off over the next two years, to $335.3 million in 2001 and $321 million in 2002. Digitas held on better than many companies during this difficult period, however. In 2002 it signed half-a-dozen new clients, including Celebrity Cruises, Grainger, Network Solutions, OnStar, Royal Bank of Scotland, and Six Continents.

The economy picked up in 2003, as did the demand for Digitas's services. Although revenues only experienced modest growth, 3 percent to $209.5 million, the company posted its first net profit since going public, nearly $17 million. Digitas continued to rebound in 2004, as total revenues increased 20 percent to $382 million and net income totaled $31 million. Digitas was also able to fund external expansion. In October 2004 it completed the $168.8 million stock purchase of Modem Media, Inc. Based in Norwalk, Connecticut, Modem was an Internet marketing consultancy founded in 1987 that offered interactive marketing strategies; media research, planning, and buying; and digital and direct marketing services. It maintained offices in both San Francisco and London. Major clients included IBM, Home Depot, Kraft, AOL, Philips Electronics, and Sprint. Not only did Digitas add creative talent in the Modem deal, it gained flexibility, having a second agency to handle any potential conflict between clients. In the long-term, as a result, Digitas would be able to sign more clients and free itself from an over-reliance on a handful of customers, a situation that had been a concern for some investors, because as much as 70 percent of revenues came from 10 clients.

Digitas continued to enjoy strong growth in 2005. Total revenues increased to $565.5 million and net income approached $41 million. The company expanded in 2006 by acquiring Medical Broadcasting, LLC for $22.4 million in cash and $8 million in stock, adding a third brand to the Digitas stable and helping the company in its strategy of targeting the healthcare industry. Launched in 1990, the Philadelphia-based Medical Broadcasting offered digital marketing services for a number of major healthcare organizations, including eight of the ten largest pharmaceutical companies in the world. In all likelihood Digitas would continue to seek out additional acquisitions in an effort to further expand what it had to offer and the types of clients it served.

Ed Dinger

PRINCIPAL SUBSIDIARIES

Digitas LLC; Bronner Slosberg Humphrey Inc.; Sonsome Inc.; Modem Media, Inc.; Medical Broadcasting Company.

PRINCIPAL COMPETITORS

AGENCY.COM Ltd.; aQuantive, Inc.; Euro RSCG 4D.

FURTHER READING

Gianatasio, David, "Bronner Remodels to Spur Growth," *Adweek New England Edition,* October 5, 1998, p. 3.

————, "Bronner Shuffles Deck," *Adweek,* February 9, 1998, p. 6.

————, "David's Goliath," *Adweek,* January 24, 2000, p. 61.

————, "Digitas IPO Off to Good Start," *Adweek,* March 20, 2000, p. 6.

————, "Digitas: New Hires Before IPO," *Adweek,* January 10, 2000, p. 3.

————, "Investors Buy into Bronner," *Adweek,* December 14, 1998, p. 2.

————, "This Rebranding of Bronner," *Adweek,* April 19, 1999, p. 2.

Johnson, Quendrith, "Mike Slosberg: The Art of Persuasion," *Boston Business Journal,* February 11, 1991, p. 12.

Krol, Carol, "Direct Marketing Star Bronner Draws Attention of Dealmakers," *Advertising Age,* June 15, 1998, p. 1.

Lee, Richard, "Digital, Direct Marketer Buys Norwalk, Conn.–Based Consultancy's Operations," *Greenwich Times* (Greenwich, Connecticut), October 21, 2004.

Taylor, Catharine P., "Digitas: After a Few Sour Years, Digitas Finds the Sweet Spot," *Adweek,* February 23, 2004, p. 20.

Diodes Incorporated

—■—

3050 East Hillcrest Drive
Westlake Village, California 91362
U.S.A.
Telephone: (805) 446-4800
Fax: (805) 446-4850
Web site: http://www.diodes.com

Public Company
Incorporated: 1959
Employees: 1,621
Sales: $214.7 million (2005)
Stock Exchanges: NASDAQ
Ticker Symbol: DIOD
NAIC: 334413 Semiconductor and Related Device
    Manufacturing

■ ■ ■

Diodes Incorporated manufactures discrete and analog semiconductors, offering a line of more than 4,000 products to manufacturers of electronic devices and electronic components. The company sells its products directly to 150 customers and serves more than 10,000 additional customers through distributors. Diodes' customers include Bose Corporation, Motorola, Inc., Samsung Electronics Co., and Logitech, Inc. Manufacturing, aside from a wafer fabrication facility located in suburban Kansas City, Missouri, is conducted overseas. Diodes operates two production plants in Shanghai, China, and maintains marketing and logistical facilities in Taipei, Taiwan; Shanghai and Shenzhen, China; and Hong Kong. The company's discrete

semiconductors, which provide electronic signal amplification and switching functions, are used in a wide variety of computer and consumer electronic devices, including flat-panel computer displays, notebook computers, digital cameras, MP3 players, television set-top boxes, and mobile telephone handsets. Diodes generates 67 percent of its revenue in Asia, 30 percent in North America, and less than 3 percent in Europe.

ORIGINS

In terms of stature, Diodes lived two different lives during its first half-century of existence. The company spent decades operating as a small, little-known firm before a change in strategy and in management propelled it toward national prominence, creating a profoundly more ambitious enterprise that bore little resemblance to the company that emerged as the 1960s began. Diodes was incorporated in 1959 as a regional, semiconductor-trading company. For the next 30 years, the company operated in relative obscurity, known only within the business community surrounding its headquarters in Westlake Village, California, in suburban Los Angeles. Annual revenues inched upward as the decades passed, but Diodes barely eclipsed the $10 million mark by the time the 1990s arrived, living off only a fraction of the business that would later support the company.

The transforming event in Diodes' history occurred in 1990. That year, Silitek Corporation, a Taiwanese manufacturer of semiconductor rectifiers and other electronic components, took a 46 percent stake in Diodes, gaining majority control over the small, Westlake Village firm. "That was the turnaround of the

COMPANY PERSPECTIVES

As Diodes continues to introduce higher margin, differentiated products, the company is also exploring opportunities to leverage its flexible manufacturing base and proven sales and marketing capabilities. In identifying that customer requirements should drive product development and the factory floor, the company provides superior customer and product service, as well as greater design flexibility and specialized configurations. In order to increase market share, Diodes is working to move these specialized products into high volume applications. The company is also exploring expanding its product offering into adjacent technologies, such as analog and mixed signal, to increase revenue and profitability.

company," a Diodes executive recalled in a March 28, 1994 interview with the *Los Angeles Business Journal.* "They changed the management and the philosophy," the executive said, adding that Diodes had been managed "too casually" before the arrival of Taiwanese management. Silitek transferred control of Diodes to one of its Taiwanese subsidiaries, Lite-On Power Semiconductor Corporation, in 1991, and spearheaded fundamental changes in the way Diodes operated. With new management in place, Diodes began to record its first period of energetic financial growth, drawing new business from an expanded line of products, an emphasis on customer service, and increased inventory. Between 1991 and 1993, revenues nearly doubled, jumping from $14.7 million to $26.4 million. Profits recorded a more impressive leap, increasing from $265,000 to $1.5 million during the two-year period. Further financial gains would be realized from the sweeping restructuring program, but the greatest benefits were achieved from the company's increased activities on the manufacturing front. In 1990, Diodes manufactured only 10 percent of the products it sold, a percentage that would grow substantially as the company shed its anonymity in the semiconductor industry and became one of its rising stars in the early 21st century.

Manufacturing capacity was built up in 1996, centered in mainland China and focused on one specific area, a type of semiconductor that became synonymous with Diodes' activities from the 1990s forward. The company threw all it energies into manufacturing discrete semiconductors, a tiny electronic component that *Investor's Business Daily,* in its May 19, 2004 issue,

referred to as the "chip equivalent of widgets." Discretes, unlike more complex semiconductors such as integrated circuits, performed a single function: regulating the flow of electric current in one direction. A slew of products relied on discretes to control power usage, including videocassette recorders, radios, lighting, toys—virtually any type of electronic device—and discretes, in turn, were produced in hundreds of different versions, varying according to voltage, current, power handling capability, and switching speed. For Diodes, choosing to focus on the production of discretes put the company in a commodity-like business, giving its management far different goals to pursue than those chased by the higher profile members of the semiconductor industry, integrated circuit makers. The integrated circuit market was characterized by rapid changes in technology, both in terms of production techniques and in the applications for the chips, which pit manufacturers in a race to put ever greater circuitry into ever smaller packages. Discrete manufacturers, in contrast, operated in a market largely devoid of rapid technological change. Success depended on the ability of a company to manufacture large numbers of inexpensive components while keeping overhead costs at a minimum.

As Diodes pressed forward in its new role as a manufacturer of discretes, the company succeeded in meeting the criteria of success in its market. Its financial growth, after decades of anemia, reflected an enterprise at last hitting its stride. By 1995, sales reached $61 million, a total drawn from the company's marketing office in Westlake Village and an engineering, manufacturing, purchasing, and sales facility in Taipei, Taiwan, the base of its subsidiary, Diodes Incorporated Taiwan Company, Ltd. In 1996, the company announced an agreement with newly created subsidiary Lite-On, FabTech, Inc. to secure a supply of silicon wafers, the building blocks of semiconductors. The agreement was notable not only because it strengthened Diodes' ability to manufacture discretes but also because the affiliation with FabTech led to a second turning point in the company's development. Making the foray into manufacturing lifted the company's fortunes during the 1990s and gave it a recognizable face in the semiconductor industry, but its greatest financial growth occurred after management leveraged the manufacturing foundation established during the 1990s to pursue a more ambitious growth strategy in the first years of the 21st century. By relying nearly exclusively on the sales of discretes, Diodes increased its revenue to $79 million by the end of the 1990s, a total from which it gleaned $5.5 million in profit. During the ensuing years, a change in strategy produced a far more impressive revenue-to-profit ratio, making the Westlake Village enterprise one of the most lauded companies in the nation.

KEY DATES

1959: Diodes is incorporated.
1990: Silitek Corporation, based in Taiwan, acquires a 46 percent interest in Diodes.
1991: Silitek transfers control of Diodes to one of its subsidiaries, Lite-On Power Semiconductor Corp.
1996: Manufacturing operations are established in mainland China.
2000: Diodes acquires FabTech, a wafer fabrication facility in suburban Kansas City, Missouri.
2005: Keh-Shew Lu is appointed president and chief executive officer.

A NEW STRATEGY FOR THE 21ST CENTURY

As Diodes entered the 21st century, it suffered along with the rest of the semiconductor industry from a severe downturn in the technology sector. To its credit, the company made a bold move toward repositioning itself in the market during the industry-wide crisis, taking its first step as the decade began. In December 2000, the company acquired FabTech, obtaining a foundry in Lee's Summit, Missouri, that made five-inch silicon wafers. FabTech, which operated under its own name as a Diodes subsidiary, specialized in making a type of diode called "Schottky," which provided higher system efficiency. The acquisition reflected a new mindset at Diodes' headquarters, one espoused by the company's new president and chief executive officer, C. H. Chen. Chen joined Diodes in March 2000 after spending 21 years at Texas Instruments, where he rose to the post of vice-president of the company's Taiwan operations. With Chen at the helm, Diodes began pursuing a new growth strategy aimed at manufacturing higher profit-margin products, seeking to produce proprietary products for the computer and consumer electronic equipment market. The ongoing proliferation of consumer electronic devices offered enticing opportunities for growth, and Diodes sought to address the needs of the market with multi-functional products to improve the operating efficiency of cellular telephones, iPods, personal digital assistants (PDAs), digital cameras, notebook computers, and the like.

Diodes remained committed to discrete semiconductors as it approached its 50th anniversary, but the years were most notable for the company's foray into adjacent markets. The company began producing analog and mixed-signal products, offerings, coupled with an expanding market for discretes, that fueled rapid financial growth. Engineers at the company's FabTech subsidiary, in one instance of Diodes' push into more complex products, developed a line of transistors that combined diodes and transistors into a smaller space, making them ideal for battery-powered devices such as PDAs. The introduction of new products lifted annual revenues by 8 percent, joining a product portfolio of more than 4,000 different devices, and enabled the company to eclipse the $100 million-in-sales mark for the first time in 2002. From there, revenue shot upward, making Diodes' progress national news in the business press. Between 2002 and 2005, the company's sales total swelled from $115 million to $214 million, but the greatest gains were achieved in earnings. During the same period, net income skyrocketed from $5.8 million to $33.3 million.

NEW LEADERSHIP FOR THE FUTURE

Diodes' impressive financial growth drew accolades from industry observers, thrusting a company that for decades had labored in obscurity into the limelight. In 2004, *Business 2.0* included Diodes on its list of the 100 fastest-growing technology companies in the nation. *Forbes* recognized Diodes as one of the "200 Best Small Companies" in 2004, an honor it bestowed on the company in 2005 as well. Diodes jumped from the 100th position to the 26th position on *Forbes'* list in 2005, an achievement hailed by the company's new chief executive officer and president, Keh-Shew Lu. "To be ranked 26th in *Forbes'* list of the 200 Best Small Companies, and as the only company in the semiconductor industry, is a great honor," Lu said in an October 24, 2005 interview with *Wireless News.* "The dramatic jump from 100th last year confirms that our strategy to differentiate ourselves with innovative technology, customized product focus, and excellent customer service continues to be successful."

Lu's commitment to the strategy developed by his predecessor promised to deliver robust financial growth in the years ahead. Lu was appointed president and chief executive officer in mid-2005, joining the company after a 27-year career at Texas Instruments. During his stay at Texas Instruments—the former employer of Chen, Diodes' senior vice-president of operations, and the company's vice-president of Asian sales—Lu served as president of Asian operations and managed Texas Instruments' global memory business. The post he held before joining Diodes' board of directors in 2001 was as senior vice-president and general manager of Texas Instruments' analog, mixed-signal and logic products, experience that would serve him well in his efforts to lead Diodes into new markets. "I am very excited about what we can accomplish in the future as we continue to move into adjacent technologies that will build on these strengths and enable us to offer higher margin products," he said in a June 1, 2005 interview with the *Ventura County Star*. In the coming years, the evidence of Lu's success would be on display in Diodes' bottom line, as the company expanded its role in the semiconductor industry.

Jeffrey L. Covell

PRINCIPAL SUBSIDIARIES

Diodes Taiwan Company, Limited; Shanghai KaiHong Electronics Company, Limited (China); FabTech Incorporated; Diodes-Hong Kong Limited (Hong Kong); Shanghai KaiHong Technology Company, Limited (China).

PRINCIPAL COMPETITORS

Fairchild Semiconductor International, Inc.; International Rectifier Corporation; Vishay Intertechnology, Inc.

FURTHER READING

Detar, James, "Nothing Too Discrete About Diodes' Plans for Continued Success," *Investor's Business Daily*, November 22, 2004, p. A5.

"Diodes Gets Accolades," *San Fernando Valley Business Journal*, June 21, 2004, p. 11.

"Diodes Incorporated Joins Forbes Magazine's '200 Best Small Companies' List for 2005," *Wireless News*, October 24, 2005.

Hamashige, Hope, "Semiconductor Company Bests All Other Small Cap Stocks in L.A.," *Los Angeles Business Journal*, March 28, 1994, p. S4.

Hopkins, Brent, "Westlake Village, Calif.–Based Semiconductor Maker Diodes Inc. Bounces Back," *Daily News*, August 1, 2002.

Palazzo, Anthony, "Boost in Asia Helps Diodes Firm in Slow Return to Profitability," *Los Angeles Business Journal*, November 18, 2002, p. 48.

Woolley, Scott, "The Control of Light," *Forbes*, October 31, 2005, p. 70.

DP World

P.O. Box 17000
Dubai,
United Arab Emirates
Telephone: +971 04 8811110
Fax: +971 04 8811331
Web site: http://www.dpworld.com

State-Owned Company
Incorporated: 1972 as Dubai Ports Authority
Employees: 4,500
NAIC: 488320 Marine Cargo Handling; 488510 Freight Transportation Arrangement; 493110 General Warehousing and Storage Facilities

∎ ∎ ∎

In just a few years, DP World has lifted itself to the top ranks of the world's port terminal operators. The Dubai-based company, owned by the Dubai government, is the world's second largest operator of port terminals, handling more than 40 million TEUs (20-foot container equivalent units) at the beginning of 2006. DP World is also one of the fastest growing port operators. Acquisitions have enabled DP World, backed by the deep pockets of Dubai's government, to grow quickly in the mid-2000s. In 2005, the company acquired CSX World Terminals from U.S. railroad group CSX. At the end of that year, the company also agreed to pay nearly $6 billion to acquire the port terminal business of Britain's Peninsular & Oriental Steam Navigation Company. That controversial purchase doubled the group's total capacity and added nearly 100 port terminals operations around

the world. DP World also has been expanding organically, launching greenfield terminal construction projects in Turkey, South Korea, and China. The company has targeted the expansion of its total capacity to more than 70 million TEUs by 2010. In addition to its two port terminal operations in Dubai, the company operates terminals in Australia, China, Hong Kong, Romania, Germany, the Dominican Republic, Venezuela, India, Djibouti, and Saudi Arabia. DP World itself was formed from the merger of Dubai Ports Authority and Dubai Ports International in September 2005. Mohammed Sharaf is the company's CEO.

PORT TERMINALS HUB IN THE PERSIAN GULF

While Dubai has existed for centuries, for most of this time the city was no more than a small village. By the beginning of the 20th century, however, the village had developed a position as one of the Persian Gulf's major trade ports. Traditionally, pearling had been the Dubai region's major industry. Yet the crisis in the pearling industry, which, starting in the 1930s, severely crippled the growing city, encouraged the ruling Al Maktoum family to seek to diversify its economy. The Al Maktoums were members of the Bani Yas tribe, which, for the most part, ruled the region that later became the United Arab Emirates.

Plans were made to improve Dubai's harbor in the early 1950s. In 1959, Dubai, then under British control, began dredging and deepening the creek that separated the city. Completed in 1960, the project permitted Dubai to accept large-scale vessels, establishing the city as the major port in the region. During this time, as well, the discovery and development of the vast oil reserves in the Persian Gulf region had transformed the area into a primary center for the world oil industry. Dubai, too, was able to join the ranks of the oil-rich elite, with the discovery of its own exploitable oil reserves. In the meantime, the city's population had more than doubled, as Dubai became the central hub of the booming Persian Gulf region trade market.

The growing demand for port and port terminal accommodations and services led then-Sheikh Rashid bin Saeed Al Maktoum, who had ruled the city since 1958, to begin developing plans for the construction of a new modern deepwater harbor and port facility. Construction on that project, which became known as Port Rashid, was launched in 1967. The initial plans for the project included four berths capable of accommodating the largest oceangoing vessels and oil tankers; however, with the discovery of Dubai's oil reserves, and the rapid expansion of the region as a whole, Al Maktoum took a risk and soon ordered the expansion of the harbor design to 16 berths.

The decision proved prescient: By the early 1970s, all of the ports in the Persian Gulf were overbooked, and, with a lack of deepwater facilities, many of the largest vessels were forced to wait at anchor in open sea for weeks and even months at a time. The opening of the Port Rashid facility immediately allowed Dubai to secure its position as the trading center for the region. By then, the United Kingdom had ceded control of the region and Dubai had joined in the creation of the

United Arab Emirates, and the city's port and trade industries had become important economic motors.

The Port Rashid facility expanded strongly through the end of the decade, with the addition of 20 new berths starting in 1976. The facility also expanded its port services, adding more than 30,000 square meters of container storage space into the middle of the decade. While Port Rashid catered to larger vessels, the Dubai government constructed a second port for smaller dhows and wooden vessels, Port Hamriya. That project was completed in 1975.

By then, the Dubai authorities had begun the development of a still more ambitious port project, the Port Jebel Ali. This facility, to be constructed south of Port Rashid, marked a new phase in Dubai's emergence as a regional trade capital. Completed in 1979, Jebel Ali counted 67 berths and became the world's single largest manmade port. In support of the Jebel Ali port, and in response to the demand for extended facilities, the Dubai government put into place the Jebel Ali Free Trade Zone. That site opened in 1985. Although the free trade zone at first targeted the international trade market, it soon became a major regional manufacturing center as well, attracting companies from around the world. By the late 1990s, the free trade zone counted more than 1,500 companies from 80 countries. Operation of the zone was turned over to a new body, Jafza.

GLOBAL PORT TERMINALS
PLAYER IN THE NEW CENTURY

The Rashid and Jebel Ali ports initially were operated as separate facilities. In 1991, in the midst of the Persian Gulf crisis, however, administration of the two ports was merged under a single entity, the Dubai Ports Authority (DPA). The new entity then became the region's leading port, boasting a throughput of more than one million TEUs (20-foot container equivalent units). The aftermath of the war with Iraq, and the subsequent trade embargo levied against that country, helped raise Dubai's profile still higher in the region. By 1996, the DPA had boosted its throughput to more than two million TEUs, and by the end of the decade, the DPA had cracked the global top ten in throughput volume. In 2001, the DPA, Jafza, and the country's Customs office were merged together under a single administration, Ports, Customs & Free Zone Corporation.

By the end of the 1990s, however, the Dubai government had recognized that, in the face of the country's dwindling oil reserves, it needed to diversify its economy away from its heavy reliance on the oil industry. The government began developing a new economic strategy. As part of that strategy, the

KEY DATES

1967: The Dubai government begins constructing Port Rashid.
1972: Port Rashid is completed.
1975: Port Hamriya, for smaller vessels, is constructed.
1976: Port Rashid is expanded to 35 berths.
1979: The 67-berth Jebel Ali Port, the world's largest single-location port, opens.
1985: The Jebel Ali Free Trade Zone is launched.
1991: Port Rashid and Jebel Ali operations are merged into a single entity, Dubai Ports Authority (DPA).
1999: Dubai Ports International (DPI) is created in order to enter the global ports market; the first foreign concession is acquired, in Jeddah, Saudi Arabia.
2000: The company receives the Djibouti port concession.
2002: The company enters the Indian port terminals market.
2003: The company is awarded the concession for Constantza Port in Romania.
2004: CSX World Terminals is acquired for $1.5 billion.
2005: DPA and DPI merge to form DP World.
2006: The company acquires P&O's port terminals operations but agrees to sell its U.S. ports operations.

international port and port terminals market became one of the government's target industries. In 1999, the government created a new corporation, Dubai Ports International (DPI), which then began investing in foreign port terminals.

DPI's first success came across the Persian Gulf. In 1999, the company joined the Jeddah Islamic Port project, forming a joint venture with a local partner to operate the South Container Terminal there. That terminal grew rapidly in the early 2000s, becoming the first in the kingdom to top throughput of one million TEUs.

DPI's next success came in Djibouti, where it began developing the Djibouti Port in 2000. The company next entered India, where it took over operation of the Vizag port in 2002. Then at the end of 2003, DPI added Romania to its growing list of international operations,

when it was awarded an 18-year lease to operate the Port of Constantza, on the Black Sea. Back at home, meanwhile, DPA's operations also had expanded significantly, topping six million TEUs by the end of 2004. Elsewhere, the company's Jafza subsidiary had expanded its own international operations, with contracts to develop and operate free trade zones in Malaysia and Tangier.

DPI prepared to enter the global terminals big leagues. In December 2004, the company shot into the number six position when it paid $1.15 billion for CSX World Terminals, the port terminals business of CSX Corporation. That purchase gave the company control of terminals in Australia, Venezuela, the Dominican Republic, and, of importance, terminals in Hong Kong and in mainland China.

Into 2005, DPI continued to develop its network. In March of that year, for example, the company acquired a 30-year concession for the development and operation of a container terminal at Fujairah, in the United Arab Emirates. The company followed this contract with a new concession to operate and manage the Aden Container Terminal, as well as the Ma'alla Container Terminal in Yemen.

In September 2005, the Dubai government moved to merge its two port terminals operators into a single unit, called DP World. Former DPI Managing Director Mohammed Sharaf was named CEO of the new company, which also included the merged operations of the Jebel Ali Free Zone Authority and its global wing Jafza International. As part of the merger, DP World shed DPA's former regulatory and administrative functions, which were brought under a newly created entity, Dubai Ports and Jebel Ali Free Zone Authority.

DP World quickly returned to its international expansion. In November 2005, the company announced that it had agreed to pay $105 million to build a greenfield port in Yarimea, Turkey. Construction of the site was expected to begin in 2006, and to be completed by 2008. In that month, as well, the company agreed to spend some $500 million to build a new container terminal in Qindao, China, deepening its footprint in the fast-growing Chinese port market.

DP World soon found itself making headlines. At the end of November, the company won its bid to acquire the port terminal business of U.K.-based Peninsular & Oriental Steam Navigation Company. The deal, worth £3.3 billion ($5.7 billion), catapulted DP World into the global top three, adding P&O's vast port terminal operations, with some 100 sites, including six ports in the United States.

By early 2006, DP World found itself embroiled in a political controversy concerning the wisdom of turning over operation of a number of U.S. ports to foreign ownership, despite the fact the same ports had already been under foreign ownership. In the end, DP World was forced to agree to sell the U.S. ports, despite President George W. Bush's backing of the purchase. Even though DP World CEO Sharaf admitted to being shocked by the controversy, the sale of the U.S. operations was expected to have little effect on the company's overall health. By then, the company's total throughput had topped 40 million TEUs. As it moved forward, DP World announced that it was upgrading its strategic objectives, targeting 70 million TEUs by 2010.

M. L. Cohen

PRINCIPAL SUBSIDIARIES

Jafza International.

PRINCIPAL COMPETITORS

Hutchison Ports International; PSA Corporation; APM Terminals; China Ocean Shipping Group Cos.; Kenya Ports Authority; Tanzania Harbours Authority; Cargill Inc.; SAGA.

FURTHER READING

"CSX Sells Terminals Unit for $1 Billion," *Trains Magazine,* March 2005, p. 15.

D'Amico, Esther, "Dubai Firm Sinks U.S. Ports Deal," *Chemical Week,* March 15, 2006, p. 11.

"DP World Enters Turkey with $105m Investment," *Gulf News,* November 4, 2005.

"DP World to Develop New Container Terminal in Qindao, China," *Emirates,* November 16, 2005.

"DPI Sails into Fujairah," *MEED Middle East Economic Digest,* March 18, 2005, p. 20.

"DPI to Take Over Black Sea Port," *MEED Middle East Economic Digest,* December 12, 2003, p. 22.

"DPI Wins Aden Port Operation," *MEED Middle East Economic Digest,* June 10, 2005, p. 26.

"Dubai Forecasts Trouble-Free Boom," *Lloyd's List,* October 3, 2005.

"Dubai Ports Authority, DPI Terminals Merge," *Business Line,* October 4, 2005.

Galbraith, Sandy, "New Face on Our Waterfront with Dubai Bid," *Australasian Business Intelligence,* January 5, 2006.

Leach, Peter T., and R. G. Edmonson, "Friend or Foe?," *Journal of Commerce,* February 27, 2006, p. 12.

Mongelluzzo, Bill, "Dubai Ports Goes Global," *Journal of Commerce,* December 20, 2004, p. 24.

———, "High-Stakes Game," *Journal of Commerce,* January 10, 2005, p. S38.

Osborne, Alistair, "What Now for the Old Empire Line?," *Daily Telegraph,* November 30, 2005.

"Ports Dispute a 'Shock' to DP World Chief," *Shipping Digest,* April 3, 2006.

Wright, Robin, "DP World Prepares for Big League," *Financial Times,* November 30, 2005, p. 23.

———, "DP World to Invest in China Terminal," *Financial Times,* November 15, 2005, p. 30.

Dril-Quip, Inc.

13550 Hempstead Highway
Houston, Texas 77040
U.S.A.
Telephone: (713) 939-7711
Fax: (713) 939-8063
Web site: http://www.dril-quip.com

Public Company
Founded: 1981
Employees: 1,514
Sales: $340.8 million (2005)
Stock Exchanges: New York
Ticker Symbol: DRQ
NAIC: 333132 Oil and Gas Field Machinery and Equipment Manufacturing; 213112 Support Activities for Oil and Gas Operations

■ ■ ■

Dril-Quip, Inc. is not widely known outside the offshore oil drilling industry. As its name implies, Dril-Quip designs, manufactures, and installs equipment for oil and gas drilling, primarily for offshore rigs in deep, often treacherous waters. Founded in Texas by four partners, Dril-Quip has since evolved into a public company, known worldwide for its technologically advanced equipment and repair services.

IN THE BEGINNING

Dril-Quip, Inc. was founded in 1981 by four businessmen: Larry Reimert, Gary D. Smith, J. Mike Walker, and Gary W. Loveless. Reimert, Smith, and Walker had all worked for a company called Vetco Offshore, Inc., an oil drilling firm, and had years of experience in the oil, gas, and petrochemical field. They, along with Loveless, who worked for Great Western Resources Corporation at the time, decided to pool their knowledge and funds to form Dril-Quip. The new company was created to provide oil and gas industry professionals in the nearby Gulf of Mexico with state-of-the-art equipment and oilfield services. They set up shop on Hempstead Highway near Houston, Texas, with Reinert, Smith, and Walker as co-chairmen and majority owners (at 30 percent each), and Loveless as an outside consultant with a minority stake (10 percent).

The partners divided duties at the new company, with Reimert, who had a bachelor of science in mechanical engineering (BSME) degree from the University of Houston, heading up the finance, engineering, and product development departments; Smith took on sales, service, training of employees, and administration; and Walker, who had a BSME from Texas A&M, ran the factory, taking care of the new firm's manufacturing and supply needs. Loveless continued working outside the company and consulted on an as-needed basis.

In its early years Dril-Quip distinguished itself with technologically advanced products such as its specialty connectors, which formed an air- and watertight seal for use in oil and gas pipes and tubes. Over the next several years a variety of sturdy, easily installed connectors became one of Dril-Quip's claims to fame. In 1982 came the introduction of MS-15 Mudline Suspension System for oil wells, followed by ocean-floor stabilizing template systems in 1984 for deep-sea oil drilling. The

COMPANY PERSPECTIVES

Dril-Quip, Inc. is one of the world's leading manufacturers of precision-engineered offshore drilling and production equipment that is well suited for use in deepwater, harsh environments and severe service applications. The Company designs and manufactures subsea, surface and offshore rig equipment for use by oil and gas companies in offshore areas throughout the world. Dril-Quip also provides installation and reconditioning services as well as rental running tools for use with its products.

company also realized the importance of top notch customer service to back up its increasingly sophisticated equipment and parts. Field personnel were trained in the proper installation, use, and repair of its products and were available for dispatch at a moment's notice to client facilities.

A major step in the company's future was opening a European headquarters in Aberdeen, Scotland, along the North Sea, in 1983. The new location included offices for sales and service, an engineering department, and a manufacturing plant to spearhead international expansion. Three years later Dril-Quip headed southeast from Great Britain, opening another sales and service office in Beverwijk, the Netherlands. The company debuted a new deepwater drilling product line the same year, called the Subsea Wellhead System. The Subsea system consisted of a huge, high capacity metal platform that handled up to 15,000 psi (pounds per square inch) of pressure during the deepwater drilling process. The Subsea product line proved pivotal to North Sea exploration and drilling, and provided a base for the numerous highly advanced Subsea components developed over the next decade. The company also sought another Houston-area manufacturing plant, outgrowing its 15-acre Hempstead Road facility.

EXPANSION AND GOING PUBLIC

The first part of the decade found Dril-Quip rapidly expanding, establishing a new location in Singapore in 1990 as its Asia and Pacific Rim headquarters. The Singapore facility, like its counterpart in Scotland, housed sales and service offices, engineering labs, and a manufacturing plant. Product innovations and outstanding service kept Dril-Quip at the forefront of the oil and gas industry. New product launches included additional wellhead systems and connectors, as well as deepwater

and platform "trees" in 1992 and 1993, which revolutionized marine drilling operations. Dril-Quip's "trees" were submersible hydraulic pump systems for high maintenance drilling rigs. Dril-Quip opened another sales and service office in Europe, in Stavanger, Norway, in 1994.

By the middle to late 1990s Dril-Quip had more orders than it could handle. An extensive backlog was building and the firm needed not only further manpower (though employees numbered over 900 worldwide), but factory space and equipment to fulfill its obligations. Dril-Quip's three factories—the original on Hempstead Highway, a second Houston-area plant located on 218 acres off North Eldridge Road (construction began in 1991), and its European facility in Aberdeen, Scotland—were at capacity as the orders poured in. Business continued to boom in the United Kingdom, with two-thirds of the company's revenues and almost half of its workforce from this oil-rich region.

Dril-Quip's founding partners decided to go public to finance the company's expansion. An initial public offering would not only raise the necessary funds but foster further recognition for the firm. Dril-Quip reincorporated in Delaware in August, then went public in late October 1997. Initial trading took share prices to $40, though stock prices settled at about $37 per share by the end of the year. Revenues for 1997 reached $146.8 million, with net income of $12.9 million. The following year, 1998, revenues leapt to $177.6 million and net income reached $17.4 million. Stock prices fluctuated in 1998 and 1999, from as low as the teens to rise again to $30 by the close of the decade, with revenues for 1999 at $156.4 million.

THE NEW CENTURY

Dril-Quip established a new sales and service office in Macaé, Brazil, in 2000, bringing the company's sales offices outside the United States to six. As the company continued to expand, its stock price went from a low of $19 in December 2000 (with revenues of $163.9 million) to a high of $27.64 in May 2002, only to fall below $20 by December. Revenues for 2001 and 2002 reached $202.9 million and $215.8 million, respectively, while revenues for 2003 and 2004 increased slightly from $219.5 million and $221.6 million, respectively. Though revenues did not climb significantly, Dril-Quip contained costs and steadily increased its presence in the industry with the delivery of its high-tech subsea tree systems.

By 2004 rising gas and oil prices, which in turn led to capital spending by oil producers, spurred the introduction and testing of several new Dril-Quip products for market. Buzz concerning these new

KEY DATES

1981: Dril-Quip is founded in Texas by four partners.
1983: The company forms a European division in Aberdeen, Scotland.
1986: Dril-Quip opens a sales and service office in the Netherlands.
1990: The company establishes a sales, service, and manufacturing facility in Singapore.
1991: A second manufacturing facility near Houston begins construction.
1994: A new office is established in Esbjerg, Denmark.
1997: Dril-Quip reincorporates in Delaware and goes public.
2005: Three new products are introduced to great success.
2006: Dril-Quip celebrates its 25th anniversary.

items—liner hangers, subsea control systems, and subsea manifolds–grew as they were successfully tested in the field. Stock prices, which had stagnated in the high teens and low 20s, began to rally in 2005 to over $56.30 late in the year. Dril-Quip took advantage of its solid stock prices to raise equity in December 2005, selling 1.5 million shares at $52 each for $74 million in net income.

Dril-Quip's equipment, spanning surface, subsea, and offshore, continued to lead the oil, gas, and petrochemical industry in innovation and solid production. New locations for sales offices were scouted as its worldwide manufacturing facilities tried to keep up with the demand. Its Houston-area plants remained Dril-Quip's biggest manufacturing facilities, fulfilling orders for what the company dubbed the Western Hemisphere (North, South, and Central America); its Scotland plant served clients in the Eastern Hemisphere (Europe and Africa); while its Singapore facility represented its growing Asia and Pacific Rim sector (Asia, Australia, the Middle East, and India).

The lion's share of Dril-Quip revenues continued to be its manufacturing division, though its service and repair sector continued to grow in the early and middle 2000s. The company's products, from large (huge drilling platforms and deep-sea templates) to small (specialty connectors including the Quik-Thread, Quik-Stab, Quik-Lok, and Quik-Jay lines), brought in 86 percent of revenues or $291.3 million for 2005; this figure was further broken down into its three divisions: 49 percent for the Western Hemisphere; 39 percent for the Eastern Hemisphere, and 12 percent for the Asia/Pacific region. Dril-Quip's total revenues for 2005 topped $340.8 million, with its services and repair division representing 14 percent of revenues.

In 2006 Dril-Quip celebrated its 25th anniversary and its fortunes continued to swell. The company had dramatically increased its worldwide presence in the last decade, with sales offices in the United States, Australia, Brazil, Denmark, England, France, Holland, Nigeria, and Norway, in addition to its warehousing and manufacturing facilities. Stock prices hovered in the $70s for the first half of the year, after hitting an all-time high of over $90 per share. New product innovations, including its fiber-optic satellite-controlled subsea tree system for large-scale offshore drilling operations, led to an increased backlog of orders and set the tone for what company executives and analysts believed would be a banner year. Dril-Quip's high-tech equipment, such as the very popular subsea trees (22 of which were delivered in 2005 alone), were designed for not only high production but to withstand harsh or severe oceanic conditions. The company's guarantee to provide round-the-clock service, repairs, and reconditioning for all of its equipment and components made Dril-Quip an international leader in the oil and gas industry.

Nelson Rhodes

PRINCIPAL SUBSIDIARIES

DQ Holdings PTY Ltd. (Australia); Dril-Quip Asia Pacific PTE Ltd. (Singapore); Dril-Quip do Brasil Ltda. (Brazil); Dril-Quip (Europe) Ltd.

PRINCIPAL COMPETITORS

Aker Kvaerner ASA; Cooper Cameron Corporation; FMC Technologies, Inc.; Oil States International, Inc.; Vetco International Ltd.

FURTHER READING

Edmonds, Christopher, "Demand for Oil Rigs Shows No Letup," http://www.thestreet.com/_tscs/comment/chrisedmonds /10235721.html, August 21, 2005.

"Industrial Makes Opportunistic Foray," *Corporate Finance Week*, December 26, 2005, p. 4.

Perin, Monica, "Big Backlog Prompts Energy Manufacturer to Go Public," *Houston Business Journal*, August 22, 1997, p. 4A.

Snyder, Robert, "Slug Suppression Technology in the North Sea," *World Oil*, April 2004, p. 19.

Dynamic Materials
Corporation

5405 Spine Road
Boulder, Colorado 80301
U.S.A.
Telephone: (303) 665-5700
Toll Free: (800) 821-2666
Fax: (303) 604-1897
Web site: http://www.dynamicmaterials.com

Public Company
Incorporated: 1971 as Explosive Fabricators Inc.
Employees: 181
Sales: $79.29 million (2005)
Stock Exchanges: NASDAQ
Ticker Symbol: BOOM
NAIC: 332112 Nonferrous Forging; 332313 Plate Work Manufacturing; 332999 All Other Miscellaneous Fabricated Metal Product Manufacturing; 333132 Oil and Gas Field Machinery and Equipment Manufacturing; 336412 Aircraft Engine and Engine Parts Manufacturing

■■■

Dynamic Materials Corporation (DMC) is a global leader in explosive metalworking. It also employs other metalworking processes, such as underwater forming, machining, and rolling. The company started out as a licensee of DuPont's technology to bond layers of dissimilar metals, then later acquired DuPont's explosive cladding operations. These materials are used to make large pressurized chemical holding tanks, autoclaves, heat exchangers, and other equipment used in the petrochemicals industry. The AMK Welding division performs specialized contract welding services for makers of aircraft engines and power generators. A little more than half of DMC's sales came from North America in 2005. In addition to its Colorado headquarters, the company has operations in Pennsylvania, France, and Sweden.

ORIGINS

The phenomenon of microfusion was observed as early as World War I, when bullets were fired into armor plates to join dissimilar metals that were not able to be welded by conventional methods. This also was observed in the remnants of bombed-out bridges in World War II.

E.I. DuPont de Nemours & Co., the chemicals giant, pioneered the practical application of explosive welding and discovered its Detaclad explosion-weld clad process in 1959. In this, a thin layer of explosive powder was ignited to join two layers of different metals by force, not heat. The metal sheets were set up with small gaps between them. The pressure of the explosion swept a layer of oxides and other contaminants from the surface of the plates so that the metals joined at a molecular level.

Denver aerospace firm Martin Marietta licensed the technology, using it to form jet engine parts. In 1965, a group of Colorado investors formed Explosive Fabricators, Inc. (EFI), which acquired Martin Marietta's explosive cladding business.

The main use of cladding was to retain or improve

COMPANY PERSPECTIVES

Explosion-welded cladding technology is a method to weld metals that cannot be welded by conventional processes, such as titanium-steel, aluminum-steel, and aluminum-copper. It can also be used to weld compatible metals, such as stainless steels and nickel alloys to steel. The cladding metals are typically titanium, stainless steel, aluminum, copper alloys, nickel alloys, tantalum, and zirconium. The base metals are typically carbon steel, alloy steel, stainless steel and aluminum. Although the patents for the explosion-welded cladding process have expired, DMC Clad has proprietary knowledge that distinguishes it from its competitors. The entire explosion-welding process involves significant precision in all stages, and any errors can be extremely costly as they result in the discarding of the expensive raw material metals. DMC Clad's technological expertise is a significant advantage in preventing costly waste.

the properties of a high-performance metal, such as titanium, nickel, copper, or stainless steel, while keeping costs down with a cheap base metal such as carbon steel. The result was ideal for making enormous storage tanks for holding chemicals under pressure as well as heat exchangers.

EFI also had the "Dynaform" process, though this would account for only a fraction of revenues. The process involved using underwater shock waves to push a metal sheet onto a die. This resulted in extremely high tolerances due to the even diffusion of force through the water. It was used to produce precision parts for the aerospace industry: Boeing Company became a leading client, and the process was used to make nose cones for the Trident missile.

EFI was incorporated in Colorado on March 5, 1971. The company's headquarters was in Lafayette, with the explosive operations a two-hour drive away in Deer Trail in eastern Arapahoe County. EFI went public in 1976 under the NASDAQ ticker symbol "BOOM." DMC was reincorporated as a Delaware corporation on May 23, 1997.

Sales were $7.5 million in 1980. The company ended the 1980s with record annual revenues of $11 million. EFI landed a major new contract to produce ten-foot engine intake rings for Boeing Company. By this time EFI had about 100 employees. An executive

told *American Metal Market* that the company then had a 70 percent share of the explosive cladding market.

A NEW DYNAMIC IN 1994

EFI hired a new president and chief executive in October 1993: Paul Lange. Lange, a chemical engineer by training, had previously been in charge of a division of Engelhard Corp., a precious metals supplier. EFI was renamed Dynamic Materials Corporation in December 1994. The company had added a 1,500-ton hydraulic metal press capable of producing three million pounds of force. Revenues were up to $19.5 million in 1995, when DMC had 90 employees.

DMC bought its main rival, DuPont's Detaclad operations, for $5 million in July 1996. This business, based in Pennsylvania, had been DMC's only significant U.S. rival, with annual sales of $11.2 million in 1995. The acquisition, which was the company's first ever, made DMC the largest explosive cladding operation in the world. Its sole competition came from firms in France and Japan, and the technical and financial barriers to entry were considerable. Part of the Detaclad operations included an explosive technology for making synthetic industrial diamonds.

Buying out the competition was a shrewd strategic move, raising DMC's share of the domestic market for explosion-clad metals to 95 percent. The company's income was reaching new highs, and its stock price quadrupled within 12 months. In August 1996, DMC announced its largest order to date: a contract to supply a manufacturer of mining autoclaves in Australia.

Under Lange's five years in charge, the company became more market oriented. It also made greater efforts to attract interest in its stock from the investment community. DMC was becoming more vertically integrated while keeping its newly acquired taste for acquisitions. It acquired equipment from its neighbor, Coors, to allow it to perform its own seam welding, a spokesperson told Boulder's *Daily Camera*.

BUILDING THE AEROSPACE SEGMENT IN 1998

DMC built up an aerospace segment in 1998, starting with the January acquisition of El Segundo, California's Spin Forge, L.L.C., which produced housings for missile motors and titanium tanks. Spin Forge had been a division of Dynamic Materials. Paul Lange stepped down in September 1998 and was replaced as CEO by Spin Forge's former vice-president, Joseph P. Allwein.

Two more aerospace companies were acquired in 1998: AMK Welding of Windsor, Connecticut, and

KEY DATES

1959: DuPont discovers the Detaclad explosion-weld clad process.
1965: Explosive Fabricators, Inc. (EFI) is founded.
1971: EFI is incorporated as a Colorado corporation.
1976: EFI goes public on the NASDAQ.
1994: EFI is renamed Dynamic Materials Corporation (DMC).
1996: DMC buys DuPont's Detaclad business.
1997: DMC becomes a Delaware corporation.
1998: AMK Welding, Spin Forge, and Precision Machined Products (PMP) are acquired to make up the Aerospace segment.
1999: The Louisville, Colorado, operations are relocated to the old DuPont site in Dunbar, Pennsylvania.
2000: France's state-owned Groupe SNPE acquires a majority holding in DMC.
2001: Nobelclad Europe and Nitro Metall are acquired.
2003: PMP is sold.
2004: Spin Forge is sold.
2006: SNPE sells off its majority holding in DMC.

Fort Collins, Colorado's Precision Machined Products, Inc. (PMP). The aerospace segment was making up a third of DMC's business, but it was growing quickly and accounted for more than half of gross profits. At the time, the Asian financial crisis was slowing down a number of capital projects that used materials from the company's explosive cladding business.

In 1999, DMC closed its plant in Louisville, Colorado, and moved the operations there to a new facility it was building in Dunbar, Pennsylvania, the site of the old Detaclad facility. The company kept its headquarters in Lafayette, Colorado, however. This left DMC with a single site for explosion weld cladding. Its operations there involved setting off a few tons of explosives inside mountain caves on a daily basis.

In June 1999 DMC announced that it was selling off the explosive cladding business for $17 million in order to focus on the aerospace industry, specifically the defense and satellite segment. The prospective buyer, Ametek Inc., backed out of the sale a few months later, however.

FRENCH CONTROL: 2000–2006

France's state-owned Groupe SNPE (Société Nationale de Poudres et Explosifs S.A.) had begun buying DMC shares in the spring of 1999 and acquired a majority holding in the company in June 2000. SNPE paid $5.8 million to raise its holding from 14.3 percent to 50.8 percent, and loaned another $1.2 million over five years. Groupe SNPE, a large aerospace, defense, and chemicals conglomerate, already owned the largest clad metal operation in France.

SNPE installed its own CEO but retained Allwein in a high-level executive post. Bernard Fontana, head of the U.S. subsidiary SNPE, Inc., also led DMC until Yvon Pierre Cariou, the former CEO of metal fabricator AstroCosmos Metallurgical Inc., was designated DMC's president and CEO in November 2000. The company soon relocated its headquarters from Lafayette, Colorado, to Boulder.

DMC lost $2 million on revenues of $28 million in 2000; this was accompanied by a considerable drop in share price. The petrochemical industry was showing signs of recovery, however, due to rising oil prices, and the company was logging record orders as energy firms renovated their plants with new equipment.

In 2001 DMC acquired Nobelclad Europe S.A. and its subsidiary Nitro Metall Aktiebolag from Nobel Explosifs France. The acquisition, which was financed by $4 million borrowed from SNPE, added operations in Rivesaltes, France, and Likenas, Sweden, with combined annual sales of $11 million.

In contrast to its strategy of several years prior, DMC divested a couple of its aerospace units to focus on the core explosive cladding and explosive forming businesses. The PMP unit in Fort Collins, Colorado, was sold in October 2003; Spin Forge, the California aerospace business, went in September 2004.

By this time, DMC's explosive clad business was truly booming. Sales for 2004 were up 51 percent to $54.2 million, and the stock price rose to levels not seen since the 1980s. According to the *Rocky Mountain News,* furious trading activity by "short sellers" who had bet against the company helped lift shares tenfold between May 2004 and May 2005. The *Denver Business Journal* pronounced DMC Colorado's fastest growing public company.

Growth in the nickel and aluminum industries also was boosting DMC's sales, noted the *Rocky Mountain News.* Explosive clad products were being used more in aluminum smelting and nickel hydrometallurgy projects. DMC commanded a two-thirds share of the world's explosive cladding market; Japan's Asahi-Kasei was its only major competitor. Although North America accounted for more than half of DMC's $79.3 million in sales in 2005, Asia, particularly China, was an important growth market. The company had a profit of $10.4 million in 2005.

SNPE sold off its DMC shares in a public offering in the spring of 2006. One of DMC's longtime independent directors, Dean Allen, was named chairman in the subsequent reorganization of the board of directors.

Frederick C. Ingram

PRINCIPAL SUBSIDIARIES

Nobelclad Europe S.A. (France); Nitro Metall Aktiebolag (Sweden).

PRINCIPAL DIVISIONS

AMK Welding; Explosive Metalworking Group.

PRINCIPAL COMPETITORS

Asahi-Kasei Corporation.

FURTHER READING

Bradley, Hassell, "Explosion Bonding Booms; Company Explores Cutting Edge of Cladding Technology," *American Metal Market,* June 1, 1990, p. 4.

Cantwell, Rebecca, "An Explosive Purchase Deal: Local Metal Bonding Company Buys Major Competitor, Detaclad; 10 New Jobs Expected," *Rocky Mountain News* (Denver), May 30, 1996, p. 4B.

Dowling, Mark, "Explosive Fabricators Benefits from Boeing's Airplane Boom," *Denver Business Journal,* December 14, 1990, p. 8.

———, "Explosive Fabricators Will Get Charge Out of Minnesota Firm's Equity Stake," *Denver Business Journal,* July 23, 1990, p. 5.

Draper, Heather, "Dynamic Materials Rebounding; Cash Infusion, Increase in Demand Help Metals Firm Make Turnaround," *Rocky Mountain News* (Denver), April 20, 2001, p. 6B.

"Explosive Fabricators Raises $1.2M," *American Metal Market,* September 14, 1990, p. 4.

FitzGerald, Patrick, "Dynamic Materials of Lafayette, Colo., Hires New CEO," *Daily Camera* (Boulder), September 3, 1998.

Freeman, Diane, "Exploding Business Growth; Boulder-Based Firm Has Iron-Clad Grip on Worldwide Industry," *Rocky Mountain News* (Denver), September 10, 2005, p. 7C.

Greco, Matthew, "Dynamics Names Jarman," *Investor Relations Business,* December 9, 1996.

Griffin, Greg, "French-Owned Firm Buys Controlling Stake in Colorado's Dynamic Materials Corp.," *Denver Post,* June 16, 2000.

Hudson, Kris, "Dynamic Materials to Close Louisville, Colo., Plant," *Daily Camera* (Boulder), April 23, 1999.

Isaac, David, "An Explosive Market Has Sales Moving Up," *Investor's Business Daily,* March 18, 2005, p. A6.

Lewis, Al, "Dynamic Materials' Stock Explodes," *Rocky Mountain News* (Denver), November 17, 1996, p. 8B.

Miller, Louise Morrison, "Boulder, Colo., Firm Undergoes Stock Boom But Remains Unnoticed," *Daily Camera* (Boulder), January 21, 1997.

Milstead, David, "Dynamic Metals Living Up to Name," *Rocky Mountain News* (Denver), May 24, 2005, p. 4B.

"New Chairman for Dynamic Materials," *Denver Business Journal,* May 22, 2006.

Peacock, Ryan, "Dynamic Materials' Business Is 'Booming,'" *Denver Business Journal,* October 7, 2005.

Richardson, Glen, "Booming Business: The Most Powerful Name in Metal Fabrication Technology Is Becoming Equally As Powerful at Fabricating Revenue," *Denver Business,* August 1990, pp. 30+.

Romero, Christine L., "Lafayette, Colo.-Based Dynamic Materials Sells Metal Bonding Division," *Daily Camera* (Boulder), June 24, 1999.

Sheeler, Jim, "Colorado-Based Explosive Fabricators Blows Up Metal for Profit," *Knight Ridder/Tribune Business News,* September 6, 1994.

Stokes, Jeanie, "Firm Now Controls Dynamic Materials; Groupe SNPE Ups Stake in U.S. Clad-Metal Maker," *Rocky Mountain News* (Denver), June 16, 2000, p. 3B.

EFJ, Inc.

1440 Corporate Drive
Irving, Texas 75038
U.S.A.
Telephone: (972) 819-0700
Fax: (972) 819-0639
Web site: http://www.efji.com

Public Company
Incorporated: 1923 as E.F. Johnson Company
Employees: 272
Sales: $94.62 million (2005)
Stock Exchanges: NASDAQ
Ticker Symbol: EFJI
NAIC: 334220 Radio and Television Broadcasting and
    Wireless Communications Equipment Manufac-
    turing

■ ■ ■

EFJ, Inc., provides secure communications technology to
the law enforcement, public safety, and defense communities as well as commercial users. The company's
two main operating subsidiaries are built around different technologies. E.F. Johnson Company, a pioneer of
two-way radios, focuses on digital systems or private
wireless communications and accounted for more than
two-thirds of 2005 revenues. Transcrypt International,
Inc. supplies secure analog solutions for customers in
areas that have not switched to digital radio.

ORIGINS

EFJ, Inc., was called Transcrypt International, Inc., before
2002. Its name was changed to reflect the importance of
its subsidiary, E.F. Johnson Company, which had been
acquired a few years earlier.

E.F. Johnson Company was founded in 1923 by
Edgar F. Johnson and his new bride, Ethel. Johnson had
studied electrical engineering at the University of Minnesota before setting up the company in his hometown,
Waseca, about 75 miles south of Minneapolis.

The business originally involved selling electrical
parts to radio stations via mail order. Demand for
military radios kept Johnson busy through World War
II. The company was a leading producer of amateur and
CB radios after the war, introducing its first "ham" radio,
the Viking, in 1949.

Johnson had more than 2,500 employees during its
mid-1970s heyday. However, a flood of cheap imports
from Japan soon wiped out the company's CB radio
business, resulting in a $19 million loss in 1977 alone.
Company founder Edgar Johnson, who had been named
to the Minnesota Business Hall of Fame, retired as
president and chairman the next year. He died in 1991.

Johnson had already developed a new technology
that would win it long-term users in commercial and
government agencies. Its Logic Trunked Radio (LTR)
combined multiple communications channels on an assigned spectrum of bandwidth. LTR became a leading
industry standard. Johnson eventually also licensed
technology allowing it to produce equipment compatible with the systems of its larger rival, Motorola, Inc.

COMPANY PERSPECTIVES

At EFJ, Inc, we design, develop, market and support private wireless communications, including wireless radios, wireless communications infrastructure and systems, and secured communications encryption technologies for analog wireless radios. We provide our products and services to homeland security, defense, public safety and public service and international markets.

We leverage our software and engineering expertise in radio frequency, or RF, applications to provide first responders such as police, fire and other emergency personnel secure, highly reliable wireless radios and systems. The adoption of new digital products and systems is being accelerated by the FCC mandate for narrowband efficiency as well as the need for interoperable communications and information systems related to homeland security. Customers for our products and systems include federal, state and local governmental entities, domestic commercial users, and international entities.

Johnson had another new line of business as well, supplying the nascent cellular phone business.

CHANGING OWNERSHIP: 1982–1996

Revenues were about $60 million in 1981, and E.F. Johnson was able to post a profit of almost $5 million. Western Union Corp. acquired Johnson in 1982 in a $132 million stock swap. However, it was sold off three years later to Diversified Energies Inc. (DEI) for $26 million plus $35 million in assumed debts.

By the mid-1980s, Johnson had revenues approaching $100 million a year and more than 1,100 employees. In 1986, it relocated its headquarters from Waseca to Minneapolis, home of its new corporate parent, DEI.

In December 1990, Johnson's parent DEI merged with Arkansas utility company Arkla Inc. By this time, Johnson had bought a controlling interest in AmeriCom Corp., an Atlanta manufacturer of network switching systems.

Cheap foreign imports had the same affect on the company's cell phone business as they had on the CB radio business earlier. There were layoffs as Johnson began sourcing components and then complete radios in Asia.

Arkla was selling off its non-core businesses and in August 1992 E.F. Johnson was acquired for $40 million by the newly formed EFJ Acquisition Corp. It was led by two New York investors, Bill Weksel and Bob Davies. Weksel was well versed in industrial management in the computer industry, noted *Industrial Communications*, while Davies had experience financing mergers and acquisitions for Bell Atlantic Corp. By this time, Johnson was hiring again, buoyed by a new line of digital radios for public safety and private security users. Other clients included taxi companies and large petrochemical refineries.

The company celebrated its newfound independence by revamping its company museum in Waseca in time for its 70th anniversary. It also held an initial public offering in 1993. EFJ saw growth opportunities overseas, particularly in markets that lacked telecommunications infrastructure. The company established a considerable presence in South America. Unfortunately, EFJ was soon in financial trouble again. It posted a loss of $26.5 million on revenues of $79.3 million in 1996.

TRANSCRYPT PURCHASE OF E.F. JOHNSON IN 1997

Transcrypt International bought E.F. Johnson in July 1997 for $12.4 million, mostly in stock, while agreeing to assume debts worth $13 million. Transcrypt produced scrambling and encryption devices for both analog and digital signals. Its customers included law enforcement agencies and the military.

Transcrypt had been formed in the late 1970s to sell products for securing voice communications. It was based in Lincoln, Nebraska, and was founded by John and Yvonne Kuijvenhoven.

In 1991, Transcrypt was acquired by an investment group led by John Connor. He told the Des Moines *Business Record* that he had screened 200 companies before settling on Transcrypt to invest in following his early retirement from Deloitte & Touche.

Transcrypt's revenues were $8 million by 1995 and growing rapidly. The company went public on the NAS-DAQ (ticker symbol: TRII) in January 1997. However, it soon became the subject of class-action lawsuits from stockholders alleging misleading statements on the part of officials. A round of layoffs followed at E.F. Johnson, which had about 550 employees before 138 positions were cut.

Transcrypt restated results for 1994 through 1997, finding that it had prematurely recognized some sales.

KEY DATES

1923: E.F. Johnson Company is formed to sell electrical parts.

1949: Johnson introduces its Viking amateur radio.

1977: Johnson loses $19 million in one year as cheap CB radios from Japan flood U.S. market.

1978: Transcrypt International is founded in Lincoln, Nebraska.

1982: Western Union Corp. acquires publicly traded E.F. Johnson.

1985: Minnesota's Diversified Energies buys E.F. Johnson from Western Union.

1990: Arkansas utility Arkla acquires E.F. Johnson through merger with Diversified Energies.

1992: New York investors buy E.F. Johnson from Arkla.

1993: E.F. Johnson completes initial public offering.

1997: Transcrypt International goes public, acquires E.F. Johnson.

1998: Johnson's LTR-Net is introduced.

2002: Transcrypt International is renamed EFJ, Inc.; headquarters are moved to Washington, D.C.

2004: Two-way radio manufacturing moves from Waseca, Minnesota, to Irving, Texas.

2005: EFJ relocates headquarters from Washington to Irving, Texas.

As restated, the company posted a net loss of $4.1 million in 1996 on revenues of $10.6 million. The next year, the loss rose to $10.9 million while revenues reached $40.4 million.

NETWORKING AFTER 1998

Voice over Internet protocol (VOIP) was revolutionizing the mobile radio business. In 1998, E.F. Johnson introduced its LTR-Net system. This allowed trunked radios in disparate locations to be connected over the web. It was suited for companies communicating with field employees from a home office.

Michael E. Jalbert was named Transcrypt's CEO in 1999. He had been head of Microdyne Corporation before it was acquired by L-3 Communications. Jalbert scaled back the company's Lincoln, Nebraska, manufacturing area by selling the 76,000-square-foot plant for $5.2 million and leasing back part of it. The E.F. Johnson subsidiary was restructured to boost its sales and support activities. A Washington, D.C., office was opened to help land more government contracts.

In 1999 Transcrypt landed a contract to produce equipment for U.K. land mobile radio producer Radiocoms, a unit of Intek. Intek was aiming to dominate the new market for 220 MHz frequency radios in the United States.

POST-9/11 UPGRADE MARKET

New York fire and police departments responding to the September 11, 2001, terrorist attacks on the United States found their efforts hindered by the inability of different radio systems to work with each other. Interoperability of communications equipment became a major public safety priority after September 11.

Emergency communications equipment had been developed by three manufacturers (including E.F. Johnson) with proprietary technologies. The Association of Public Safety Communications Officials International, Inc. (APCO) had in 1995 set forth Project 25, which provided standards for interoperability and narrower, more efficient divisions of bandwidth. Local governments were slow to purchase new equipment due to the cost involved, however. A federal mandate for more narrow divisions of the radio frequency spectrum by 2008 was a compelling prompt to upgrade. The size of the upgrade market was estimated to be worth several billion dollars.

Transcrypt International was renamed EFJ, Inc. (EFJI) in June 2002 to reflect the importance of its radio business (the initials became the new ticker symbol). Corporate headquarters had been relocated from Lincoln, Nebraska, to Washington, D.C., which was home of its CEO. The company also established an engineering office in Irving, Texas, and in 2004, the two-way radio manufacturing operation was moved there from Waseca, Minnesota. Irving became the home of EFJI's headquarters as well in 2005.

Revenues were up to $56.2 million in 2003 and EFJI was profitable, with net income of $4 million. Profits rose to $10 million on revenues of $80.9 million in 2004. The company was much leaner, with about 260 employees. Most of its revenues, and growth prospects, were with the E.F. Johnson subsidiary.

A secondary public offering in September 2005 raised $48 million, mostly from institutional investors. Jalbert told *Investment Dealers' Digest* that EFJI was interested in bringing new technologies involving video and data into the secure communications market. Many emergency services agencies were still using analog technology, he added, providing substantial opportunity for upgrades. *BusinessWeek* ranked EFJI in the top quarter of its "100 Best Small Companies."

Frederick C. Ingram

PRINCIPAL SUBSIDIARIES

E.F. Johnson Company; Transcrypt International, Inc.

PRINCIPAL COMPETITORS

Motorola, Inc.; M/A-Com, Inc.

FURTHER READING

"Arkla Sells Off Johnson to Investor Group; Somrock Out," *Industrial Communications,* August 7, 1992.

Aronovich, Hanna, "Higher Standards," *US Business Review,* September 2005, pp. 86–87.

"Back in Business," *Business Record* (Des Moines), December 23, 1991, p. 6.

Burcum, Jill, "No Waseca Shutdown Planned," *Successful Business,* March 30, 1992, p. 1.

———, "Owners, City Hoping Firm Enters New Era," *Successful Business,* August 31, 1992, p. 1.

"E.F. Johnson," *Going Public: The IPO Reporter,* November 29, 1993.

"E.F. Johnson Agrees to APCO 25 Compliance; Signs Licensing Agreement with Motorola," *Land Mobile Radio News,* October 28, 1994.

"E.F. Johnson Files IPO for 2.95 Mln Shares," *Reuters News,* November 10, 1993.

"EFJ Benefiting from Emergency Comms Focus," *Investment Dealers' Digest,* September 12, 2005.

Fibison, Michael, "EF Johnson Lays Off 40 Workers," *Successful Business,* July 22, 1991, p. 1.

Freeborn, Dan, "Edgar F. Johnson, Who Founded Waseca Radio Firm, Dies at 91," *Star-Tribune* (Minneapolis), February 12, 1991, p. 1B.

"Kuijvenhoven: Nebraska Offers High-Tech a Home," *Omaha World-Herald,* February 12, 1995, p. 3M.

Larson, Virgil, "EFJ Inc. to Close Waseca, Minn., Two-Way Radio Plant," *Omaha World-Herald,* April 16, 2004.

———, "Lincoln, Neb., Radio Security Company Transcrypt International Changes Name," *Omaha World-Herald,* June 24, 2002.

———, "Subsidiaries of Nebraska-Based Radio Systems Maker EFJ Reorganize Management," *Omaha World-Herald,* July 11, 2002.

Leibs, Anthony, "Transcrypt Could Decode Own Sale," *Mergers & Acquisitions Report,* August 9, 1999.

"Lincoln, Neb.–Based Technology Services Firm Reorganizes Radio Unit," *Knight Ridder/Tribune Business News,* February 17, 2000.

"Lincoln, Neb.–Based Transcrypt Installs New Radio Product," *Knight Ridder/Tribune Business News,* October 4, 1998.

Maxon, Terry, "Tech Firm Relocates to Irving," *Dallas Morning News,* March 2, 2005.

Metz, Robert, "Johnson Ready in Radio Field," *New York Times,* Sec. D., March 13, 1981.

Norris, Melinda, "Chairman of Lincoln, Neb.–Based Transcrypt Offers to Step Down," *Knight Ridder/Tribune Business News,* October 28, 1998.

———, "Lincoln, Neb., Radio Builder Plans to Buy Wireless Firm," *Knight Ridder/Tribune Business News,* June 13, 1997.

Peterson, Susan E., "Arkla Inc. Sells E.F. Johnson to New York Investors; EFJ Acquisition to Pay $40 Million for Communications Unit; Operations to Stay in State," *Star-Tribune* (Minneapolis), August 1, 1992, p. 1D.

———, "E.F. Johnson Lays Off 165, Citing Foreign Competition," *Star-Tribune* (Minneapolis), September 14, 1990, p. 1D.

Smith, J. Sharpe, "Two-Way Radio Manufacturer E.F. Johnson on the Block," *Industrial Communications,* March 13, 1992.

Taylor, John, "CEO of Lincoln, Neb.–Based Maker of Scrambling Equipment Resigns," *Knight Ridder/Tribune Business News,* June 8, 1998.

———, "Lincoln, Neb., Scrambling Devices Maker Restates 1996, 1997 Revenues," *Knight Ridder/Tribune Business News,* July 16, 1998.

"Transcrypt Clears Hurdle with Release of Audited Financials," *Communications Today,* July 17, 1998.

"Transcrypt Hit with Painful Nasdaq Decision," *Communications Today,* May 13, 1998.

"Transcrypt in Outsourcing Radio Production Deal with Intek," *Communications Today,* January 8, 1999.

"Western Union Says It Is Mulling the Sale of E.F. Johnson Unit," *Wall Street Journal,* December 5, 1984.

EMI Group plc

27 Wrights Lane
London, W8 5SW
United Kingdom
Telephone: +44 20 7795-7000
Fax: +44 20 7495-1307
Web site: http://www.emigroup.com

Public Company
Founded: 1931 as Electric and Musical Industries
Incorporated: 1996
Employees: 6,312
Sales: £2.08 billion ($3.70 billion) (2006)
Stock Exchanges: London
Ticker Symbol: EMI
NAIC: 512220 Integrated Record Production/
Distribution; 512230 Music Publishers

∎ ∎ ∎

EMI Group plc is the third largest of the world's "big four" music giants, holding a global market share of approximately 13 percent. Demerged from Thorn EMI plc in 1996, after nearly 17 years of the EMI and Thorn "duet," EMI Group now focuses exclusively on music—music recording through its EMI Music division, which generates about 80 percent of total revenues, and music publishing through EMI Music Publishing, which is responsible for the remaining 20 percent. In the recording arena, EMI Music maintains operations in nearly 50 countries worldwide and has licensees in an additional 20. Its record labels include Angel, Astralwerks, Blue Note, Capitol, Capitol Nashville, EMI, EMI Classics,

EMI CMG, EMI Televisa Music, Mute, Narada, Parlophone, and Virgin. Its 1,300-strong roster of artists includes the Beastie Boys, Coldplay, Gorillaz, Janet Jackson, Norah Jones, Lenny Kravitz, Wynton Marsalis, Moby, Radiohead, the Rolling Stones, KT Tunstall, Keith Urban, Robbie Williams, and Cassandra Wilson. Its recording facilities include two of the most famous in the world: Abbey Road Studios in London and Capitol Studios in Los Angeles.

EMI Music Publishing is the world's largest music publisher, owning the rights to more than one million songs. It derives its revenues from licensing the right to use these songs on CDs; on the radio and in performances; on television programs, and in films, advertisements, and computer games; and in numerous other ways, including cell phone ring tones. Of EMI Group's total revenues, the United Kingdom is responsible for about 17 percent; the rest of Europe, 30 percent; North America, 31 percent; Latin America, 4 percent; and the Asia-Pacific region, 16 percent. Rocked by the digital revolution, as all the music giants have been, EMI Group derives approximately 5 percent of its revenues from digital music.

EARLIEST ROOTS IN THE GRAMOPHONE

Electric and Musical Industries Ltd. (EMI) was formed in 1931 from the merger of The Gramophone Company and Columbia Graphophone Company. The gramophone was invented in 1887 by Emile Berliner. Ten years later, The Gramophone Company was founded in London as both a manufacturer of gramophones and as

COMPANY PERSPECTIVES

EMI Group's strategy is to create shareholder value by developing the best musical content at both our recorded music business, EMI Music, and our music publishing business, EMI Music Publishing, and to exploit fully this valuable content on a global basis through all economically attractive channels.

Our investment in artists and repertoire (A&R) is fundamental to our ability to create new, exciting music. At the core of our A&R strategy is the identification and development of artists and songwriters with the potential to enjoy long-term commercial success across multiple releases and revenue streams. Focusing on long-term career artists has favourable economics, driving increased sales and profitability. By replicating this process across geographies and musical genres, we have assembled in EMI Music and EMI Music Publishing exceptional portfolios of music content which exhibit strength, breadth and depth.

a recorder of records to play on the gramophone. In 1898 the company made its first recordings and opened branches in Germany, France, Italy, and central Europe. Additional offices were established in Russia in 1900, in India in 1901, in Japan in 1902, and in China in 1903. The Gramophone Company had its first major artist when opera singer Enrico Caruso recorded ten songs for the company in 1902.

The increasing popularity of recorded music was evidenced by the ownership of a gramophone by one-third of British households by 1913. As a result of World War I, The Gramophone Company lost its Russian and German operations (the latter continues to exist in the late 2000s in the form of the classical music label Deutsche Grammophon, now owned by Universal Music Group). By 1930 the company's roster of artists included Italian conductor Arturo Toscanini, German opera conductor Wilhelm Furtwängler, English composer Sir Edward Elgar, and English conductor Sir Thomas Beecham. In 1931, the year EMI was formed, the recording studios at Abbey Road were opened and EMI demonstrated stereophonic recordings for the first time.

During the 1940s the company's artist lineup expanded to include Austrian conductor Herbert von Karajan and German conductor Otto Klemperer. The company in this decade also appointed its first A&R

(artists and repertoire) managers to develop popular music talent in the United Kingdom; George Martin, who later signed the Beatles, was among these appointees. In 1952 EMI added Maria Callas to its artistic roster.

Over the years EMI organized a line of sophisticated electronic systems, an outgrowth of its gramophone manufacturing origins, which included early British radar equipment and the BBC's first television system. Meanwhile, the company enlarged its position in the music recording and publishing industries through the 1955 acquisition of Los Angeles-based Capitol Records, one of the leading record companies in the United States, with a roster that included Nat "King" Cole, Frank Sinatra, Peggy Lee, and Gene Vincent. Additional global moves were made when EMI entered the Mexican market in 1957 and with the establishment of joint venture Toshiba-EMI Ltd., a Japanese record company formed in partnership with Toshiba.

BRINGING BEATLES ON BOARD

During the 1960s EMI's recording division experienced tremendous growth, largely on the strength of sales of records by the Beatles, who were signed by Martin in 1962, the same year their first single, "Love Me Do," was released. That same year Capitol Records released the first Beach Boys album, *Surfin' Safari.* The success of EMI in the 1960s was most evident in the British singles charts for 1964, which had eight different EMI artists hold the number one position for 41 weeks of the year. In 1966 the company released its first prerecorded cassettes. The following year EMI signed Pink Floyd. Queen was added to the roster in 1972.

By the late 1960s profits from the EMI recording division surpassed those of the electronics division and enabled EMI to purchase the entertainment organization of Sir Lew Grade and the cinema business of the Associated British Picture Corporation. As a result, EMI had become one of the largest motion picture entertainment concerns in the world by 1970. Adopting its longtime acronym, the company changed its name to EMI Ltd. in 1971.

The late 1960s and early 1970s saw EMI expand in the areas of music publishing and music retailing. In 1966 the company began to expand its HMV music store operation. The first HMV shop had been opened in 1921 on Oxford Street, London, by composer Sir Edward Elgar. By 1970 there were 15 HMVs; six years later there were 35 and HMV had become one of the leading music retailers in the United Kingdom. The music publishing operation was bolstered through a series of acquisitions. EMI purchased Keith Prowse

KEY DATES:

1897: The Gramophone Company is founded in London.
1902: Company gains first major artist, Enrico Caruso.
1921: First HMV shop is opened in London by Sir Edward Elgar.
1931: Gramophone Co. merges with Columbia Graphophone Company to form Electric and Musical Industries Ltd. (EMI).
1955: EMI acquires Los Angeles-based Capitol Records.
1962: EMI signs the Beatles and releases their first single, "Love Me Do."
1971: Company is renamed EMI Ltd.
1973: EMI Music Publishing is formed.
1979: EMI is bought by Thorn Electrical Industries Ltd., forming Thorn EMI plc.
1989: EMI Music Publishing acquires SBK Entertainment World, Inc.
1992: Virgin Music Group Ltd. is acquired.
1996: The EMI music business is demerged from Thorn EMI as EMI Group plc.
1998: EMI effectively exits from retailing by placing its HMV and Dillons chains into the joint venture HMV Media Group.
2000: European regulators block plan to create joint venture with Time Warner's Warner Music Group.
2002: Major restructuring is launched.
2006: Warner Music Group Corp. rejects a $4.2 billion takeover offer from EMI.

Music Publishing and Central Songs in 1969, Affiliated Music Publishing in 1973, and the Screen Gems and Colgens music publishing companies in 1976, both of which were bought from Columbia Pictures Industries. In 1973 EMI had organized its music publishing operations within a newly formed EMI Music Publishing Ltd. subsidiary.

In the early 1970s, however, EMI was also burdened by heavy losses from its Capitol Records operation and a poorly planned investment in an Italian television manufacturer called Voxson. The most significant non-music development for EMI during this period was the introduction of a revolutionary new computed tomographic X-ray scanning device in 1972. The fact that EMI had developed this scanner, with no previous experience in X-ray equipment, caused many to seriously reconsider the company's prospects.

Profitable sales of the scanner in the United States were drastically reduced after the Carter administration restricted government aid to hospitals. In addition, EMI failed to anticipate a strong reaction from its competitors. General Electric Company subsequently introduced a similar but faster model that effectively removed EMI from the market.

By 1977 serious problems with the medical electronics division caused management to be broken up into three divisions, each responsible for its own profitability. At one point EMI even appeared willing to dispense with its recovering music operations. Instead, EMI's path led to its being taken over in 1979.

CREATION OF THORN EMI

The financially ailing EMI became a takeover target for lighting and equipment rental giant Thorn Electrical Industries Ltd. Thorn had been established in 1928 as the Electrical Lamp Service Company by Jules Thorn, who remained at the helm until he retired in 1979, not coincidentally prior to the takeover of EMI (Thorn's domineering personality had squelched a proposed merger between the two firms a few years earlier).

Institutional investors, who held a three quarters voting majority in Thorn, expressed concern that a merger of the two companies would be problematic because Thorn and EMI were very different companies. In the event of a merger, Thorn would have to let EMI management run itself, at least for a few years, because it knew so little about EMI's businesses. Another cause for concern was that EMI's new management team, led by the very capable Lord Delfont, had to prove itself under difficult circumstances.

At the end of October 1979 EMI rejected a £145 million bid by Thorn. The offer was resubmitted the following week for £165 million and accepted. The new company's name was changed to Thorn EMI plc on March 3, 1980.

RESTRUCTURING OF THORN EMI

The various divisions within the old Thorn and EMI organizations continued to operate independently of each other and, to some extent, of the central management group. Management reimplemented a planning model developed by the Boston Consulting Group that provided for the development of new enterprises by channeling funds from profitable operations. This had the effect of starving the successful enterprises within the company of funds needed to maintain competitive product lines. Just as the model failed in the early 1970s, it was failing again a decade later. Thorn EMI was less like a successful operating company and more like a weak investment portfolio.

In an attempt to raise money and reduce losses during 1980 and 1981, the company sold its medical electronics business, its hotels and restaurant division, and parts of the leisure and entertainment division. Later in the 1980s, additional Thorn and EMI businesses were sold, including EMI's entertainment operations. By the late 1980s, under the leadership of CEO Colin Southgate, Thorn EMI had returned to the basic industries upon which Thorn and EMI had been separately built: music, lighting, rental and retail, and technology (including computer software and defense electronics). All told, during the 1980s Thorn EMI divested more than 50 noncore operations, bringing in more than $700 million.

GROWTH IN THE FINAL DECADES OF THE 20TH CENTURY

Although EMI's music operations had been neglected somewhat during the restructuring of Thorn EMI, they became the beneficiary, as much of the cash generated by the asset sales was poured into acquisitions and expansions. In 1986 HMV became a separate division of Thorn EMI and an international expansion of the chain began. In 1990 alone, HMV outlets appeared for the first time in Australia, Japan, Hong Kong, and the United States. By 1996 there were more than 300 stores worldwide in eight countries, including Canada, Germany, and Ireland. In 1995 a U.K. bookstore chain called Dillons was acquired and added to the HMV division.

EMI Music Publishing was bolstered through the 1989 acquisition of SBK Entertainment World, Inc. for £165 million ($337 million). SBK was the onetime publishing unit of CBS Records, which consisted of a 250,000-song catalog, including "Singing in the Rain" and "You've Lost that Lovin' Feeling." This addition made EMI Music Publishing the top music publishing operation in the world; its catalog included more than 850,000 songs by late 1992. EMI's music recording unit, meanwhile, acquired several prominent labels. In 1990, 50 percent of Chrysalis Records was purchased, with the other half acquired two years later. Chrysalis brought such acts as Huey Lewis & The News, Billy Idol, and Sinead O'Connor to the EMI fold. The blockbuster acquisition, however, was that of Virgin Music Group Ltd., bought for £510 million ($957 million) in 1992, a deal that included both record labels and publishing catalogs. The addition of Virgin, whose

artists included the Rolling Stones, Phil Collins, and Janet Jackson, cemented EMI's position as one of the music industry's giants, alongside Time Warner, Sony, PolyGram, MCA (which later became Seagram's Universal Music Group), and Bertelsmann. Also acquired in 1992 was Sparrow Records, the largest Christian music label in the United States, which later became the centerpiece of the EMI Christian Music Group (later renamed EMI CMG). Added in 1994 was Intercord, a leading independent record company in Germany. During the early 1990s EMI garnered blockbuster sales in the United States from the star of its Liberty label, country singer Garth Brooks (who later recorded for EMI's Capitol Nashville label). Virgin signed Janet Jackson to an exclusive, $60 million contract in 1996, the same year that the Beatles' *Anthology* albums posted large sales.

In 1994 EMI entered into the music television arena through joint ventures in Germany, where the VIVA and later the VIVA2 channels were launched, and in Asia, where Channel V was introduced. All of these stations devoted much of their airtime to domestic artists, whereas MTV, even in Germany, for example, tended to showcase English-language acts. The VIVA stations were co-owned by EMI, Bertelsmann, Time Warner, Philips (owner of PolyGram), and Sony. Channel V was 50 percent owned by News Corporation, with EMI, Time Warner, Sony, and Bertelsmann each holding a 12.5 percent stake.

1996 DEMERGER OF THORN EMI

Thorn EMI itself, meanwhile, was continuing to be transformed in the 1990s. Thorn's rental operations became the company's most important nonmusic unit and had been beefed up in 1987 through the £371 million acquisition of Rent-A-Center, a rent-to-own outfit based in the United States. In 1993 Thorn EMI sold its lighting division, the business upon which it had been founded. Over the course of several years and several transactions, the company's defense businesses had been divested by 1996. Thus Thorn EMI in mid-1996 had just two divisions, music and rental, both world leaders. They had little in common, however, leading to the long-anticipated August 29, 1996, demerger of Thorn and EMI, out of which emerged EMI Group plc and Thorn plc, both initially headed by Southgate as chairman. EMI Group included all of Thorn EMI's music-related operations: music recording, publishing, and retailing and the investments in the music channels. It also included the Dillons bookstores, which continued as part of the HMV Division. Several noncore businesses—Central Research Laboratories, Thorn Secure Science International, Thorn Transit Systems

International, and a holding in Thorn Security—which EMI retained after the demerger, were divested less than a year later.

Rumors that the newly independent EMI would be taken over by one of the industry's other giants persisted for some time following the demerger, but had subsided somewhat by late 1996. In October 1996 the debut album by the prefabricated Spice Girls posted huge sales; more than 17.5 million copies had been sold in the 12 months following its October 1996 release. EMI's immediate concern was the need to turn around its flagging North American music operations, which had managed to capture a mere 8 percent of the $12.5 billion U.S. market in 1996. In May 1997 North American management was shaken up, with Ken Berry, who was already president and chief executive of EMI Records Group International and chairman and chief executive of Virgin Music Group Worldwide, taking over. Berry became the worldwide president of the newly formed EMI Recorded Music unit, which comprised all three of these operations. At the same time, a restructuring of the U.S. operations, including the closing of the head offices of EMI-Capitol in New York, led EMI to record a charge of £117.2 million ($192.8 million) in fiscal 1997. Aiming to bolster these U.S. operations were a string of fiscal 1997 acquisitions: 50 percent of rap label Priority Records (including the rapper Ice Cube), 49 percent of New York-based alternative label Matador Records, and all of Forefront Communications, the largest independent Christian music label in the United States, headlined by million-selling artist dc Talk. Later in 1997, EMI Music Publishing, already owner of the rights to more than one million songs, added a catalog of 15,000 songs from the Motown era—including "I Heard It through the Grapevine" and "My Girl"—in a deal with Berry Gordy, founder of Motown Records, worth up to £232 million ($382 million).

EMI enjoyed a string of successful releases in the late 1990s: The Spice Girls' *Spiceworld* album, released in November 1997, went on to sell more than 13 million copies. Sales figures for two Garth Brooks titles released in 1997 and 1998 reached seven million and six million, respectively. Utada Hikaru's *First Love,* released in 1999, became the best-selling album in Japanese history. In addition, Robbie Williams, formerly with the U.K. boy band Take That and signed by EMI in 1996, had established himself by the end of the decade as the top-selling solo artist in the United Kingdom and had gained a strong international following as well, though not in the United States. In 1998 EMI also acquired full control of Priority Records and narrowed its focus still further by transferring its HMV and Dillons chains into a joint venture called HMV Media Group (EMI's 43 percent stake in HMV was reduced to a token holding

of 14.5 percent in 2002 when HMV went public as HMV Group plc). The exit from retailing was accompanied by a 1999 bolstering of EMI Music Publishing through the acquisition of Windswept Pacific Entertainment Co. for $200 million. Windswept, based in Los Angeles, held the rights to 40,000 songs, mainly from the 1950s and 1960s, including such old favorites as "Louie Louie," "Why Do Fools Fall in Love?" and "The Twist."

Alongside these positive developments, however, was a great deal of management turmoil and speculation about the company's future. Southgate had remained firmly in charge of the company but began putting together a succession plan designating James G. Fifield, the president and CEO of EMI Music, as the next CEO of EMI Group. Southgate's intention to remain chairman precipitated a power struggle as Fifield wanted to run the company without any Southgate interference. In early 1998 EMI's board, showing its loyalty to the chairman, rejected the plan to make Fifield CEO, and he soon left the company armed with a hefty severance package. Just one month later, in May 1998, Seagram approached EMI about a merger, but talks collapsed when Southgate demanded a price the Canadian firm deemed too high. Seagram quickly moved on, reaching a deal to acquire PolyGram, which was subsequently merged into Seagram's Universal Music Group, thereby reducing the world's music giants to a "big five." The turmoil at EMI continued later in 1998 when Southgate raised eyebrows by making a serious bid for PolyGram's film division, which Seagram had placed on the block. Southgate abruptly pulled out of the bidding at the last minute. Finally, in July 1999, Eric Nicoli succeeded Southgate as EMI chairman. Recruited from his position as chief executive of cookie-maker United Biscuits (Holdings) plc, Nicoli was a surprising appointment and one that prompted much speculation that the last of the big independent music companies was being readied for a sale.

DEALS GONE AWRY, RESTRUCTURINGS, NEW ARTISTS

The sale scenario quickly became quite real. In September 1999 EMI entered into negotiations with Time Warner that led to a January 2000 agreement. The plan called for EMI's music operations and Time Warner's Warner Music Group to be merged into a joint venture that would comprise the number two music power in the world. European Commission regulators, however, were concerned about further consolidation in the music industry and effectively blocked the deal later in 2000. Complicating the situation with regulators was Time Warner's simultaneous pursuit of a merger with

America Online, Inc., which was ultimately approved, resulting in AOL Time Warner Inc. Nicoli next attempted to engineer a merger with Bertelsmann's BMG Entertainment unit, but this deal also collapsed because of European regulatory resistance.

In the wake of these failed deals, EMI had to face a worsening industry environment as a solo act. Music sales were falling partly because of the increasing popularity of online file-sharing services, such as Napster, and partly because the music companies had thus far failed to develop their own successful paid online services. EMI continued to be hampered by its weak position in the United States, the world's largest music market, where the company's market share of around 10 percent was the lowest of music's global big five. Making matters worse at EMI was a deal Berry signed with pop diva Mariah Carey in early 2001, a multi-album pact valued at more than $80 million. *Glitter,* the first Carey album released by Virgin under this deal, initially flopped commercially (at least in comparison to Carey's previous albums), selling little more than 500,000 copies in the first few months after its September 2001 release.

Berry left the company late in 2001. His replacement as head of EMI Recorded Music was Alain Levy, a Frenchman who had headed PolyGram prior to its purchase by Seagram. Levy was charged with turning around the troubled music recording operations. One of his first moves was to buy Carey out of her disastrous contract, although it took $28 million to do so. Levy also reorganized EMI's labels around two global brands, Capitol and Virgin, deemphasizing the EMI label. In March 2002 Levy launched a sweeping restructuring involving 1,800 job cuts, or 19 percent of the workforce, the combining of the back-office operations of Capitol and Virgin, and the jettisoning of one-quarter of what Levy considered a "bloated" artist roster of 1,600. Most of the roughly 400 unceremoniously cut were unknowns. Restructuring charges and charges related to the Carey debacle contributed to a pretax loss of £152.8 million for the fiscal year ending in March 2002.

Shifting from EMI's past tendency to sign existing stars generally past their prime, Levy aimed to find new, young artists and develop them into world superstars tied to EMI for years to come. Two 2002 releases marked the first fruit of this new strategy. Coldplay's second release, *A Rush of Blood to the Head,* was a multimillion seller for Capitol, while Blue Note scored a huge hit with *Come Away with Me,* jazz-pop chanteuse Norah Jones's debut album, which sold more than 17 million copies, was the world's best-selling album of 2003, and garnered eight Grammy Awards. During 2002, EMI also acquired Mute Records, a leading European independent record company whose roster included Moby, Depeche Mode, and Nick Cave and the Bad Seeds. In addition to parting with most of its HMV stake when that firm went public, EMI in 2002 exited from the music television channel sector by selling its 15.3 percent stake in VIVA Media to AOL Time Warner. Late in 2002 EMI and the other four global music company giants, along with the three largest music retailers, agreed to pay a collective $143.1 million to settle a CD price-fixing lawsuit brought by the states of New York and Florida.

A merger was back on the agenda in late 2003, when the newly named Time Warner Inc. placed Warner Music Group on the block. EMI offered to acquire Warner Music for approximately $1 billion in cash and a 20 percent stake in the combined company. Time Warner elected instead to accept a $2.6 billion offer from a group led by Edgar Bronfman, Jr., the former Seagram chief. Concerns about gaining antitrust approval played a role in the decision as regulators were already wrestling with a proposal from Sony and Bertelsmann to combine their music operations into a joint venture. The resulting Sony BMG Music Entertainment, created in 2004 after regulators proffered their provisional approval, jumped into second place in the industry, behind Universal Music Group.

Despite yet another failed merger, EMI had reason for optimism. Levy's focus on developing new artists continued to pay dividends. Multimillion sellers in 2003 and 2004 included Jones's second offering and the first two releases of Joss Stone. With sales of six million, Robbie Williams's *Greatest Hits* was number six worldwide in 2004. Not resting on its laurels, EMI launched another restructuring in the spring of 2004. This one involved 1,500 job cuts and a further culling of underperforming artists from the roster, a 20 percent cut. In addition to merging several niche labels and some marketing departments, EMI also outsourced its CD and DVD manufacturing operations in North America and Europe. Later in 2004 the company sold its Australian CD manufacturing unit. Restructuring charges sent EMI into another pretax loss, of £52.8 million, for fiscal 2004.

EMI returned to the black the following year and then posted even stronger results in fiscal 2006, when pretax profits jumped nearly 20 percent, to £118.1 million ($210.2 million). The company was buoyed by three albums selling more than five million units each: Gorillaz's *Demon Days,* Williams's *Intensive Care,* and Coldplay's *X&Y,* the latter the world's top seller during the 2005 calendar year at more than eight million copies. It finally appeared that the digital wave could be a benefit to EMI rather than a curse as the company saw its digital music sales increase 139 percent for the year to £112.1

million ($199.5 million), or 5.4 percent of total revenues. Late in 2005 EMI completed its exit from CD and DVD manufacturing by selling the Japanese plant owned by the Toshiba-EMI venture.

Under the leadership of Nicoli and Levy, EMI appeared to be proving that the company could not only survive but also thrive as an independent company. The U.S. market remained a weak area, however, and Nicoli elected to make another run at the now-dubbed Warner Music Group Corp. However, in May 2006 Warner's board of directors unanimously rejected EMI's $4.2 billion takeover offer. Many analysts still considered a merger of the two firms as inevitable because a combined EMI-Warner would rank closer in scale to the two giants of the global industry, Universal Music and Sony BMG.

Updated, David E. Salamie

PRINCIPAL SUBSIDIARIES

Capitol-EMI Music, Inc. (U.S.A.); Capitol Records, Inc. (U.S.A.); Chrysalis Records Ltd.; EMI Music Germany GmbH & Co. KG; EMI Entertainment World, Inc. (U.S.A.); EMI Music Australia Pty. Ltd.; EMI Music France S.A.; EMI Music Italy S.p.A.; EMI Music Publishing Ltd.; EMI Records Ltd.; Jobete Music Co., Inc. (U.S.A.); Priority Records, LLC (U.S.A.); Toshiba-EMI Ltd. (Japan; 55%); Virgin Records America, Inc. (U.S.A.); Virgin Records Ltd.; EMI Group Finance plc; EMI Group Finance (Jersey) Ltd.; EMI Group Holdings (UK) Ltd.; EMI Group International Holdings Ltd.; EMI Group North America Holdings, Inc. (U.S.A.); EMI Group North America, Inc. (U.S.A.); EMI Group Worldwide Ltd.; Virgin Music Group Ltd.

PRINCIPAL DIVISIONS

EMI Music; EMI Music Publishing.

PRINCIPAL COMPETITORS

Universal Music Group; Sony BMG Music Entertainment; Warner Music Group Corp.

FURTHER READING

Blackhurst, Chris, "The MT Interview: Eric Nicoli," *Management Today*, June 2004, pp. 62–67.

Boehm, Erich, "EMI Becoming Takeover That Never Was," *Variety*, December 23, 1996, pp. 29, 30.

Buckingham, Lisa, "EMI Faces the Music," *Management Today*, March 2000, pp. 66+.

Burt, Tim, and Jonathan Loades-Carter, "EMI to Pull Plug on Jobs and Artists," *Financial Times*, April 1, 2004, p. 19.

Clark-Meads, Jeff, "EMI Upbeat on Global Biz," *Billboard*, March 8, 1997, p. 1.

Clark-Meads, Jeff, Adam White, and Don Jeffrey, "Thorn EMI Demerger Proceeding Smoothly," *Billboard*, August 31, 1996, pp. 1, 127.

"Crunch Time at EMI," *Economist*, March 13, 1999, p. 80.

"Duet for One: Thorn EMI," *Economist*, November 27, 1993, p. 71.

Foster, Anna, "Leading Light at Thorn," *Management Today*, August 1988, p. 46.

Foster, Geoffrey, "Three over Thirty," *Management Today*, May 1996, pp. 64–66.

Fuhrman, Peter, "Here Comes House Music," *Forbes*, December 21, 1992, pp. 44–46.

Goldsmith, Charles, "EMI's Decision to Tap Outsider Nicoli to Be Its Next Chairman Raises Concerns," *Wall Street Journal*, March 9, 1999, p. B7.

Goldsmith, Charles, Ethan Smith, and Martin Peers, "In Music World, EMI Is Belle of Merger Ball," *Wall Street Journal*, September 22, 2003, p. B1.

Goldsmith, Charles, and Jennifer Ordonez, "Levy Jolts EMI; Can He Reform Music Industry?," *Wall Street Journal*, September 6, 2002, p. B1.

Goldsmith, Charles, William Boston, and Martin Peers, "EMI-Bertelsmann Unit End Merger Talks," *Wall Street Journal*, May 2, 2001, p. A25.

"Gone Again," *Economist*, May 5, 2001, pp. 55–56.

Gubernick, Lisa, "Don't Worry, He's Happy," *Forbes*, April 17, 1989, p. 154.

Harding, James, "EMI Set to Make 1,000 Job Cuts in Sweeping Overhaul," *Financial Times*, March 15, 2001.

Iliot, Terry, "EMI Faces Thorny Dilemma," *Variety*, September 14, 1992, p. 32.

Kapner, Suzanne, and Laura M. Holson, "EMI to Revamp and Cut Its Work Force 20%," *New York Times*, March 21, 2002, p. C8.

Martland, Peter, *Since Records Began: EMI, the First 100 Years*, Portland, Oreg.: Amadeus Press, 1997, 359 p.

Midgley, Dominic, "Thorn EMI's Fissile Future," *Management Today*, August 1994, pp. 24–28.

Oppelaar, Justin, and Erich Boehm, "EMI Faces the Music: Giant Brit Diskery to Cut 1,800 Jobs in Restructuring," *Variety*, March 21, 2002, pp. 1, 18.

Ordonez, Jennifer, "Twice Jilted, EMI Faces the Music Alone," *Wall Street Journal*, June 6, 2001, p. B2.

Pandit, S. A., *From Making to Music: The History of Thorn EMI*, London: Hodder and Stoughton, 1996, 270 p.

Peers, Martin, and Charles Goldsmith, "Time Warner, EMI Plan Music Merger," *Wall Street Journal*, January 24, 2000, p. A3.

Peers, Martin, Charles Goldsmith, and Philip Shishkin, "Regulators Sink EMI-Time Warner Deal," *Wall Street Journal*, October 6, 2000, p. A3.

Rawsthorn, Alice, "EMI Adds a Little Spice," *Financial Times*, November 23, 1996, p. WFT5.

———, "EMI Cuts Costs in N. America," *Financial Times,* May 28, 1997, p. 21.

———, "In Tune to a Little More Spicy Music," *Financial Times,* May 28, 1997, p. 23.

———, "Motown Founder Sells Hits for Up to $382M," *Financial Times,* July 2, 1997, p. 28.

———, "Thorn and EMI Prepare to Dance to Different Tunes," *Financial Times,* July 22, 1996, p. 23.

Rawsthorn, Alice, and Jeremy Grant, "EMI Eyes Asian Market with Vietnam Tie-Up," *Financial Times,* May 29, 1997, p. 8.

Reilly, Patrick M., "EMI Has Chosen Ken Berry to Run Its North American Music Operations," *Wall Street Journal,* May 27, 1997, p. B11A.

———, "EMI, Hogtied, Finds Out You Don't Mess with Garth," *Wall Street Journal,* November 5, 1997, pp. B1, B12.

———, "Nancy Berry to Run Virgin Records, while Quartararo Is Expected to Leave," *Wall Street Journal,* September 22, 1997, p. B14.

Rifkin, Glenn, "EMI: Technology Brings the Music Giant a Whole New Spin," *Forbes ASAP,* February 27, 1995, pp. 32, 35–36, 38.

Rose, Frank, "Help! They Need Somebody," *Fortune,* May 24, 1999, pp. 213–14, 216, 220.

Rosenbluth, Jean, "Thorn-EMI Buys 50% of Chrysalis," *Variety,* March 29, 1989, pp. 57, 58.

Smith, Ethan, and Aaron O. Patrick, "Warner Rejects EMI Bid, but Case May Not Be Closed," *Wall Street Journal,* May 4, 2006, p. B2.

Solomons, Mark, "EMI Stresses Its Consistency After Management Shift," *Billboard,* May 2, 1998, pp. 1, 86.

"Spice Girl," *Forbes,* November 17, 1997, p. 14.

Timmons, Heather, "EMI to Cut Artist Roster and Close Two CD Plants," *New York Times,* April 1, 2004, p. W1.

———, "Merger of Rivals Throws Up New Hurdle for EMI Chief," *New York Times,* November 10, 2003, p. C12.

Viscusi, Gregory, and Cecile Daurat, "Jilted Again, EMI's Nicoli Left Running Only Pure Play," *Los Angeles Business Journal,* December 1, 2003, p. 14.

White, Adam, "EMI's U.S. Dealings Under the Microscope," *Billboard,* August 2, 1997, p. 59.

The Emirates Group

Airline Centre
P.O. Box 686
Dubai,
United Arab Emirates
Telephone: (+971-4) 214-4444
Fax: (+971-4) 295-2001
Web site: http://www.emirates.com

State-Owned Company
Incorporated: 1985
Employees: 7,067
Sales: AED 24.3 billion ($6.6 billion) (2006)
NAIC: 481111 Scheduled Passenger Air Transportation; 481112 Scheduled Freight Air Transportation; 488119 Other Airport Operations; 488999 All Other Support Activities for Transportation; 721110 Hotels (Except Casino Hotels) and Motels

■ ■ ■

The Emirates Group is composed of Emirates Airlines, airport services provider Dnata (the Dubai National Air Transport Association), other transportation-related activities, and a hotel group. Owned by the government of Dubai, Emirates has flourished under the sheikdom's "wide open skies" policy, which has brought more than 100 foreign airlines to Dubai's efficient airport, the busiest in the Middle East.

The airline, simply known as Emirates, is renowned for luxurious in-flight service as well as consistently profitable growth. It is unique among long-haul airlines in its resistance to joining a global alliance such as the Star Alliance or Oneworld. Emirates does, however, participate in code-sharing arrangements with several carriers and has a minority holding in Sri Lankan Airlines.

ORIGINS

Dubai, established as a fishing village at the southern end of the Arabian Gulf, has grown to become one of the leading trade centers of the Middle East, fueled at first by pearls, then petroleum. The Beni Yas tribe assumed control of the town around 1830. The Maktoum family led the tribe throughout the 19th and 20th centuries. Dubai became one of seven sheikdoms in the United Arab Emirates, which was formed in 1970.

As the British pulled out of Dubai in the late 1950s, Sheikh Saeed Al Maktoum decreed an open seas, open skies, and open trade policy, to develop the country into a regional crossroads for trade and tourism. He also required all government agencies to make a profit. The country was aiming to eliminate its dependence on its finite oil reserves within 50 years.

The Dubai National Air Transport Association (Dnata) was formed in 1959. By the mid-1980s, Dnata had grown to 2,500 employees. In addition to providing support services at Dubai Airport, the company served as sales agent for 26 airlines. Dubai had been used as a stopover on routes between Europe and the Far East since the days of Imperial Airways (precursor to British Airways), which landed its flying boats there en route to Australia. Its open skies policies kept its airport among the busiest in the region.

Gulf Air began to cut back its service to Dubai in

the mid-1980s. As a result, Emirates Airlines was conceived in March 1985 with backing from Dubai's royal family, whose Dubai Air Wing provided two of the airline's first aircraft, used Boeing 727s. (An Airbus A300 and Boeing 737 were two others.) Because of Dubai's unique political structure, wrote Douglas Nelms in *Air Transport World,* Emirates could be described as both government-owned and privately held, though most considered it state-owned. It was required to operate independent of government subsidies, however, apart from $10 million in start-up capital.

Maurice Flanagan was named managing director of the new airline. Formerly of the Royal Air Force, British Airways, and Gulf Air, Flanagan had been seconded to Dnata in 1978 on a two-year assignment as assistant general sales manager. Chairman was Sheikh Ahmed bin Saeed Al Maktoum, nephew of the ruler of Dubai. Only 27 years old in 1985, he had graduated from the University of Colorado just four years earlier (his degree was in political science and economics). Sheik Ahmed also became chairman of Dubai Civil Aviation and Dnata itself. Although he lacked any direct experience in the airline industry, Sheikh Ahmed embraced his new role, learning to fly a variety of aircraft along the way. As Lisa Coleman duly noted in *Chief Executive,* he was indeed experienced in one area that would be the new airline's defining trait: luxury. From the beginning, Emirates boasted a tradition of providing the best creature comforts available at 40,000 feet.

FIRST FLIGHT IN 1985

The first flight, Dubai to Karachi on October 25, 1985, was a Pakistani connection in more ways than one. Emirates had leased the aircraft, an Airbus 300, from Pakistan International Airlines. Bombay and Delhi were the other two earliest destinations. From the beginning, Emirates flights carried both passengers and cargo.

Emirates was profitable within nine months. During its first year, it carried 260,000 passengers and 10,000 tons of freight. Gulf Air, part owned by the much wealthier neighboring emirate Abu Dhabi, had previ-

ously dominated air traffic in the region. Gulf Air's profits fell more than 30 percent during the first year of its new rival's operations, however, prompting it to drop its privatization plans. The next year, Gulf Air posted a loss.

In its second year, Emirates also posted a loss, before setting out on decades of profitable growth. One reason for the success of Emirates was its aggressive marketing. Another was the high level of in-flight service in its new Airbus aircraft, which it outfitted with generously spaced seating.

In 1986, Colombo, Dhaka, Amman, and Cairo were added to the route network. Emirates launched daily nonstop service to London (Gatwick) on July 6, 1987, with two new Airbus A310s. This complemented the overnight flights British Caledonian was sending to and from Dubai. Other destinations added in 1987 were Frankfurt via Istanbul, and Male (Maldive Islands). Emirates lacked a regional feeder network since most of its neighboring countries were shareholders in rival Gulf Air.

This impressive early growth came as the region was experiencing a business downturn, with the Gulf War a contributing factor, as well as the subsequent layoff of expatriate workers—both bad news for the air travel industry. In its second year, competitors accused Emirates of starting a price war. The airline countered that its lower fares were stimulating traffic, not stealing it from its rivals. By the end of 1987, Emirates was serving 11 destinations.

Emirates Sky Cargo, which operated as a separate entity, carried 25,000 tons of freight in 1989. In the early 1990s, a number of Asian firms began using Dubai as a warehousing center for European deliveries. Emirates expanded its route network into the Far East in 1990, serving Bangkok, Manila, and Singapore. Hong Kong was added in 1991. Emirates added Paris, Rome, Zurich, and Jakarta in the summer of 1992.

About the same time as it was extending its reach into Asia, Emirates was courting long-haul business travelers. Calling itself "the finest in the sky," the airline toned down its Arabic identity for a more "corporate" feel, positioning itself as a competitor to global carriers such as British Airways and Singapore Airlines.

Emirates was one of the world's fastest-growing airlines. Revenues increased by about $100 million a year, approaching $500 million in 1993. It carried 68,000 tons of cargo and 1.6 million passengers that year. The Gulf War, ironically, had benefited Emirates by keeping other airlines out of the area. Emirates was the only airline to continue flying in the last ten days of the war, although it had to cover increased insurance

KEY DATES

1959: Dubai National Air Transport Association (Dnata) is formed.
1985: Dubai forms its own airline: Emirates.
1997: New training and maintenance centers open.
1998: Emirates buys a 40 percent stake in Air Lanka.
2001: About six million people fly Emirates; fleet includes 36 aircraft.
2003: Emirates announces $19 billion Airbus/ Boeing order.
2004: Service to the United States is launched via New York.
2005: Emirates orders $10 billion worth of new Boeings.

premiums and higher fuel costs (flying around the war zone added an extra ten hours to flights).

A partnership agreement with US Airways entered in the fall of 1993 allowed Emirates to offer around-the-world service. It had previously inked cooperation agreements with Cyprus Airways.

By 1994, 60 international airlines were flying to Dubai. Emirates was connecting 32 destinations with its 15 aircraft. It was the sixth largest of eight Middle East carriers. Despite its small size, the airline had accumulated numerous awards by lavishing attention and money on passengers and cargo customers. It was the first airline to install personal video systems in all seats, for example. Flight attendants celebrated special occasions with in-flight cakes and Polaroid cameras. Passengers flying first class were served six-course meals on Royal Doulton china.

Emirates took in $643.4 million in the fiscal year ending March 30, 1994. Income increased more than eightfold, to $24.4 million. The young airline had 4,000 employees and carried two million passengers a year between 34 destinations with a fleet of 18 Airbus aircraft.

Seven state-of-the-art Boeing 777s worth $1 billion were ordered in 1992 to satisfy long-range ambitions. They began to arrive in the spring of 1996. One of the planes was used on a new service to Australia (Melbourne) via Singapore. Emirates placed a large order with Airbus later in the year. In spite of the large capital expenditures, the Dubai government had laid out only $50 million since the airline's inception.

A total of 92 air carriers were serving Dubai in the mid-1990s. Emirates was able to flourish, however, in spite of restricted markets abroad and intense competition at home. The Dubai government had been promoting the country as an escape from European winters with great success, much to the benefit of Emirates. (Dubai's summertime weather was grueling, with Fahrenheit temperatures and relative humidity readings in the 100s.) Abroad, its route network was expanding in the Pacific and Africa.

TRAINING AND MAINTENANCE CENTERS OPENING IN 1997

In 1997, Emirates was flying a dedicated freighter to Amsterdam, a point not on its network of passenger routes, in cooperation with KLM Royal Dutch Airlines. It carried about three million passengers during the year. The growing cargo business accounted for 16 percent of the airline's revenues.

Emirates opened a unique, $65 million training center in January 1997. It was built in the shape of an airplane. The airline was then able to provide advanced simulator training for its crew members, who represented 50 different nationalities, and flight and maintenance personnel from around the world. In the fall of 1997, a new air-conditioned maintenance center allowed the group (which consisted of Emirates Airlines and Dnata) to solicit third-party contracts in that capacity as well.

A record group profit of AED 371 million was achieved in 1997. Emirates executives planned a slowdown in the airline's growth in the late 1990s to stabilize its expansive route network.

In May 1998, Emirates paid the Sri Lankan government $70 million for a 40 percent stake in Air Lanka. Emirates received almost full management rights as the Sri Lankan flag carrier was in debt and operating at a loss and had needed new capital to upgrade its fleet.

A new, lighthearted advertising campaign launched in January 1999 enjoined travelers to "Be good to yourself. Fly Emirates." One ad aired in Britain featured a business class passenger calling his dog with the on-board phone.

Emirates signed on in May 2000 as the first launch customer for the Airbus A380, designed to be the largest passenger aircraft ever built. Emirates justified purchasing the 481- to 656-passenger super jumbo to maximize its use of scarce takeoff and landing slots at crowded airports including London's Heathrow. The airline planned to order up to a dozen of the planes, with the first to be delivered in 2006.

Toward the end of 2000, Emirates was planning to start ultra-long-haul service to the East Coast and West

Coast of the United States as well as nonstop flights to Australia and Argentina. Traffic continued to grow at an impressive clip (20 percent) in 1999, and Emirates executives planned to sustain that.

DUBAI BECOMING A GLOBAL AVIATION CENTER AFTER 2000

Nearly six million passengers flew Emirates in 2000. The airline also carried 335,000 tons of cargo. It had a fleet of about three dozen aircraft. Revenues were AED 6.9 billion. Overall, the group had more than 14,500 employees, about 8,700 of them at the airline and 5,700 at Dnata.

Because it was not yet heavily involved in North Atlantic traffic, Emirates was minimally affected by the aftermath of the September 11, 2001, terrorist attacks on the United States, an official told *Air Transport World.* Service to the United States debuted in June 2004 with a 14-hour nonstop flight to New York. The opening of additional routes to the United States would be delayed by high fuel costs.

Compared to its larger neighbor, Abu Dhabi, Dubai itself produced relatively little oil. Emirates emphasized that it received neither support from oil revenues nor discounts on fuel. The airline's sophisticated hedging operation was not enough to shield Emirates from runaway fuel prices in 2006. Nevertheless, the group was able to post net income of $762 million (AED 2.5 billion) on revenues of $6.6 billion (AED 24.5 billion), both records. Emirates continued to grow 20 percent or more a year, as it had done since it was founded.

Emirates announced a colossal order for 71 new Boeing and Airbus aircraft in June 2003. Valued at $19 billion, it was called the world's largest aircraft order to date. The group's ambition was displayed again in a $10 billion (AED 36 billion) order for 42 new Boeing 777s placed in 2005. In April 2006, the airline had 92 aircraft, with another 123 on order. By 2012 it expected to have grown its fleet to 150 planes. The airline was aiming to increase its 50 percent share of flights going through Dubai to 70 percent by 2010. These moves would make Emirates one of the very largest long-haul airlines in the world.

Emirates took the high road following a controversial episode involving another Dubai-owned transportation business, reported the *New York Times.* DP World acquired a half dozen U.S. ports but was obliged to sell them after U.S. politicians raised "security concerns." As a fellow state-owned company, the airline could have extracted royal revenge by diverting billions of dollars worth of aircraft orders from Boeing to its European rival Airbus. Instead, Emirates chose to ignore

the issue in favor of increasing ties with the United States. Plans for a nonstop service to California were in the works.

The latest generation of ultra-long-range aircraft made it possible to connect most destinations in the world via a stop in Dubai. However, as an analyst told the *New York Times,* these planes made it possible for others to compete with nonstop service to the same points.

Dubai itself, already served by more than 100 airlines, continued to attract new competitors such as Virgin Atlantic. The country's economy was growing even faster than that of China, and Dubai was transitioning from a regional hub into a major world commercial center.

Emirates Group's ambitions were not confined to the skies. It was also preparing to develop a global hotel chain. It planned to open a lavish 70-story, $270 million hotel on the Dubai coast in 2007. Another property was being developed in the Blue Mountains of Australia.

Frederick C. Ingram

PRINCIPAL DIVISIONS

Emirates Airlines; Destination and Leisure Management; Dubai National Air Transport Association (Dnata); Galileo Emirates; Mercator; Transguard.

PRINCIPAL COMPETITORS

Gulf Air Company GSC; British Airways Plc; Air France-KLM S.A.; Deutsche Lufthansa AG; Qatar Airways Group.

FURTHER READING

"Air Lanka Finds a Friend in Emirates," *Airfinance Journal,* May 1998, p. 12.

"Airline Competition in the Gulf: The Strength of Emirates," *MidEast Markets,* September 28, 1987.

Allen, Robin, "Dubai: Paradox Wrapped in a Conundrum," *Financial Times,* December 13, 2000, p. 2.

"Cargo Key for Emirates," *Aviation Week & Space Technology,* May 19, 1997, p. 48.

Coleman, Lisa, "Ahmed bin Saeed Al Maktoum," *Chief Executive,* March 1995, p. 29.

"Dermot Mannion," *Airfinance Journal,* December 1999, p. 44.

"Desert Storms," *Airfinance Journal,* September 1996, pp. 38–41.

Done, Kevin, "Airbus Wins First Order for A3XX Super Jumbo," *Financial Times,* May 1, 2000, p. 1.

"Dubai: The Gulf's Gateway to the World," *Asian Business,* July 1991, p. 59.

"Emirates Embarks on Global Hotel Chain," *Business Traveller Middle East,* May–June 2005, p. 6.

"Emirates Plays the Finance Game," *Airfinance Journal,* September 1996, pp. 40–41.

"Emirates Taking Quality to New Heights with Luxury Hotels & Resorts Division," *Middle East,* March 7, 2006.

"Emirates Tries 'Humorous' Ad Campaign," *Marketing Week,* January 21, 1999, p. 8.

Flottau, Jens, "Emirates Updates Its Fleet Planning," *Aviation Week & Space Technology,* November 20, 2000, p. 47.

Fox, Harriot Lane, "Emirates Tries Corporate Ploy," *Marketing,* November 25, 1993, p. 15.

Gostelow, Mary, "Can Emirates Fill the Gulf?," *Director,* July 1987, pp. 69–72.

Hill, Leonard, "Emirates' Success Is No Mirage: On a Growth Roll from Day One, the Dubai-Based Airline Forges On, Undaunted by Global Gloom," *Air Transport World,* January 1, 2002, p. 46.

Kingsley-Jones, Max, and Andrew Doyle, "Emirates Is Looking at Airbus Replacements," *Flight International,* July 3, 1996.

Lennane, Alexandra, "Opportunity Knocks," *Airfinance Journal,* May 1999, pp. 39–41.

Michaels, Daniel, "Flying Sheik: From Tiny Dubai, an Airline with Global Ambition Takes Off," *Wall Street Journal,* January 11, 2005, p. A1.

Michaud, Paul, "Letter from Dubai," *Marketing,* February 10, 1994, p. 7.

Nelms, Douglas W., "Emirates' Open-Trade Routes," *Air Transport World,* February 1998, pp. 83–87.

———, "Genii from the Desert," *Air Transport World,* March 1994, p. 95.

O'Toole, Kevin, "Emirates' Pilot," *Flight International,* March 26, 1997.

Phelan, Paul, "Growing Ambitions," *Flight International,* December 11, 1996.

"Profit for Dubai-Based Airline," *MidEast Markets,* October 27, 1986.

Shane, Bob, "Emirates: An Oasis of Hospitality and Excellence," *Airliners,* January/February 2001, pp. 43–47.

Shifrin, Carole A., "Dubai Training Center Extends Emirates' Reach," *Aviation Week & Space Technology,* May 19, 1997, p. 44.

———, "Emirates Slows Rate of Expansion," *Aviation Week & Space Technology,* May 19, 1997, p. 42.

———, "State-of-Art Maintenance Center Readied for Emirates Group," *Aviation Week & Space Technology,* May 19, 1997, p. 46.

Timmons, Heather, "After Dubai Uproar, Emirates Air Holds No Grudges," *New York Times,* March 29, 2006, p. C1.

Empire Resources, Inc.

———— ■ ————

1 Parker Plaza
Fort Lee, New Jersey 07024
U.S.A.
Telephone: (201) 944-2200
Fax: (201) 944-2226
Web site: http://www.empireresources.com

Public Company
Incorporated: 1990 as Integrated Technology USA, Inc.
Employees: 30
Sales: $358.5 million (2005)
Stock Exchanges: American
Ticker Symbol: ERS
NAIC: 331315 Aluminum Sheet, Plate, and Foil
    Manufacturing

■ ■ ■

Empire Resources, Inc. is a Fort Lee, New Jersey-based company that distributes value-added, semi-finished aluminum products to more than 200 customers in the United States and Canada, and to a lesser degree in Australia, New Zealand, and Europe. The vast majority of sales, almost 84 percent, come from U.S. customers. The company offers aluminum sheet/coil, used in transportation, construction, and foodservice applications; plate, used in the construction of cars, trucks, and ships; the heartier and more aesthetically pleasing tread-plate, its crosshatch design commonly seen on truck running boards; everyday aluminum foil, intended for use in the packaging industry as well as in the home; aluminum circles, used by the lighting industry to make lamps as well as the food industry to fashion pots and pans; and profiles/extrusions, used for a multitude of structural purposes by a variety of industries, including construction, furniture, and electronics. Empire maintains a lean operation, employing around 30 people.

The company purchases its products from sources around the world, although more than half comes from South Africa's Hulett Aluminum Ltd. Rather than spend money to warehouse stock, Empire places orders with its suppliers only after it has itself received an order from a customer. What Empire primarily provides is customer service: helping customers to select the right product; taking care of foreign-exchange transactions; arranging for products to be warehoused until they are needed on a just-in-time basis; arranging for additional finishing or metal processing; and keeping customers abreast of the latest products and market trends. Although a public company listed on the American Stock Exchange, Empire is 54 percent owned by its founder Nathan S. Kahn, who serves as the chief executive, and his wife, Sandra R. Kahn, the company's chief financial officer.

CORPORATE LINEAGE DATING TO 1990

Empire chooses to trace its corporate heritage through a company it acquired in 1999 to gain public company status: Integrated Technology USA, Inc., which was incorporated in Delaware in August 1990. The company's president, chief executive officer, and chairman was Alan P. Haber, who ran a chain of restaurants and started an import/export company for stationery and entertainment products before becoming CEO of

---

COMPANY PERSPECTIVES

Empire Resources, Inc. is a distributor of value added semi-finished aluminum products. We currently serve over 200 customers in diverse industries including transportation, automotive, housing, appliances and packaging.

---

an Israeli subsidiary of Intafile International, a computer and research and development company. Integrated was launched to design, develop, and market products for new computer-related markets. Although it maintained a small U.S. headquarters in Teaneck, New Jersey, the bulk of the company, which at its height employed about 20, consisted of engineers working in Israel. They developed a wireless printing device for laptop computers, but the field they were most interested in exploring was Internet telephony. Integrated hoped to combine the functions of the computer keyboard and telephone to tidy up the modern desk while providing some other capabilities. The resulting product, the CompuPhone 2000, integrated a single-line telephone in a keyboard without the need for a modem, internal card, or serial port connection. A headset plugged into the keyboard, which provided standard phone features such as volume control, flash, mute, and redial, and included a built-in ringer. The system also came with software that allowed users to place calls from an electronic address book and maintained a permanent log of all incoming and outgoing calls. This last function was also part of the product's pitch to telemarketing firms, as well as the system's compatibility with PBX or Centrex phone systems.

A more advanced product, somewhat visionary for the time, was the CompuNet 2000 system, which allowed users not only to place conventional phone calls but also to use the Internet to talk at no charge, other than the subscription paid to an Internet service provider. The party on the other end required compatible software, however, and the quality was poor.

In a way Integrated anticipated the VoIP (Voice over IP) industry that would take shape in the 2000s, but the excitement over having a telephone jack in their keyboard never materialized with consumers, despite Haber's 1995 claim that in a matter of a few years conventional phones would be swept aside by devices such as CompuPhone 2000 and CompuNet 2000. Nevertheless, he was able to generate enough of a buzz to take the company public in 1996 and complete a successful initial public offering (IPO) of stock in October of that year, netting $15.4 million. Sales totaled $804,000 in 1995 when CompuPhone 2000 came on the market and grew to $1.22 million in 1996 after the introduction of CompuNet 2000, but reality quickly set in. In a few months after the IPO, demand for the products failed to take shape and in the first six months of 1997 sales dropped 83 percent, from $600,000 to just $100,000. Shareholders quickly realized that the market for the company's products was unlikely to materialize and took steps to make sure that Integrated did not burn through the more than $10 million that remained from the IPO in a vain attempt to build the business.

INTEGRATED TECHNOLOGY CEASING OPERATIONS IN 1997

In November 1997 the company announced that it would liquidate inventory and cease operations by the end of the year. On the way to its demise, Integrated had laid off its employees and Haber became the last to go, resigning to "pursue other interests." A New York private investor and director of the company, William Spier, took over as interim chief executive and led an effort to find an acquisition partner, perhaps a well established private company that wanted to go public.

Another Integrated director, and chief financial officer until the company discontinued operations, was Simon M. Kahn, brother of Nathan Kahn, who could use a shell company to take his business public. Both were familiar with the metals industry, as their father was involved in the steel importing business through New York City-based Empire Steel Trading Company, which also handled aluminum. Nathan Kahn earned a master's of business administration from Harvard Business School and dreamed of running his own business. "I liked the entrepreneurial life," he told the *Record* of Hackensack, New Jersey, in a rare interview, conducted in 2005. "I wanted to create something." From his father's business he knew about the quality of international aluminum and had the contacts to form his own aluminum importing business, along with his wife Sandra, in lower Manhattan in 1984. It was called Empire Resources. For funding, Kahn turned to a woman banker. According to the *Record*, "Somewhat to his surprise, the banker gave him a $5 million line of credit. 'She had more confidence in me than I had in myself,' said Kahn." Nevertheless, it proved to be a wise investment.

Kahn and his wife steadily grew the business, successfully competing against giant corporations including Alcoa Inc. and Alcan Inc. The difference was Empire's superior customer service. To maintain that edge the Kahns made sure the employees were well treated. "In fact," reported the *Record*, "keeping workers happy was

KEY DATES

1984: Empire Resources, Inc., is founded.
1990: Integrated Technology USA, Inc., is formed.
1996: Empire Resources Pacific Ltd. is formed.
1999: Empire and Integrated are merged.
2004: A used aluminum extrusion press is acquired.

behind the company's move to Fort Lee from Lower Manhattan more than a decade ago. Most of the workers lived in New Jersey and were sick of the commute. The Kahns live in New York City and do a reverse commute; because the office is close to the George Washington Bridge, it's not a difficult trip." The couple also had to find a way to work together, given that Sandra, a certified public accountant, served as the company's chief financial officer. "We generally defer to each other in our areas of expertise," her husband explained.

Empire expanded beyond the North American market in 1996 when it established subsidiary Empire Resources Pacific Ltd. in Australia to sell aluminum products in that country as well as New Zealand. By the end of the 1990s, Empire was doing about $100 million in annual sales, and despite the availability of instant communications, Nathan Kahn continued to maintain customer relations the way he had since the beginning, by hitting the road a few times a month to meet with customers. It allowed him to get a feel for what the customer needed. He told the *Record:* "Sometimes when you're walking out of a plant, you see things that they don't even see. And it's respectful. It shows them that you care enough to get out of your chair and visit."

COMPLETING A REVERSE MERGER IN 1999

In February 1999 Empire signed an agreement to merge with Integrated Technology USA, a "reverse acquisition" completed in September of that year. In essence, Empire exchanged its stock for Integrated's $10 million investment and assumed its American Stock Exchange listing. Three days later Integrated changed its name to Empire Resources Inc. The Kahns maintained their roles as CEO and CFO, and William Spier became non-executive chairman of the board and a director.

Despite having to replace a supplier, Empire completed its first year as a public company by recording $107.1 million in revenues in 1999, a 6 percent increase over 1998's totals. In addition, the company's

net income of $2.5 million represented the 15th straight year of profitability for the company. The United States still provided the lion's share of sales, some 75 percent, followed by Canada with 15 percent and Australia and New Zealand contributing the remaining 10 percent.

Empire continued to enjoy steady growth with the start of the new century. It benefited from a supplier launching full-scale production at a new plant, allowing Empire to expand its customer base and increase sales 54 percent to $165 million. The company did not, however, post the level of earnings it had targeted, due to a slowing economy. In order to make sales, Empire in some cases had to accept less than desirable margins. A deteriorating economy would prove to be even more of a factor in 2001, when demand fell, as did prices, and Empire saw revenues slip to $143.2 million. Nevertheless, the company posted its 17th consecutive profitable year, netting $1.3 million. A factor in achieving those earnings was the opening of a new, cost-effective Baltimore distribution facility in 2001.

Business rebounded in 2002 for Empire, as sales increased 10.8 percent to $158.7 million. The company also expanded on a value-added sales program, resulting in higher margins and improved profits. In addition, the company was benefiting from a move to streamline its shipping operations by adopting a "just in time" approach to delivery. For the year, earnings almost doubled to $2.4 million. Because it was able to obtain more products from suppliers, Empire was able to enjoy an even stronger year in 2003, recording sales of $184.4 million and net income of more than $3.5 million. The company's main supplier, Hulett Aluminum Ltd. of South Africa, came under fire during the year, however. Hulett was accused of dumping 6000 series aluminum alloy rolled plates in the U.S. market through Empire, its exclusive distributor in the market, at a price significantly lower than in its home market. An investigation was launched by the U.S. International Trade Commission, during which time Hulett was allowed to continue to ship plates into the United States, but Empire was concerned with the long-term impact should Hulett run afoul of U.S. regulators. Those fears were allayed in November 2004, however, when the U.S. International Trade Commission ruled that the imports did not materially injure the U.S. aluminum industry.

Sales increased 15 percent to $212.5 million in 2004 and net income increased to $4.8 million. Empire benefited from a steady supply of product as well as price increases. It also took steps in the fall of the year to add another revenue stream by acquiring a used aluminum extrusion press. The plan was to modernize the equipment and have it installed in the company's newest warehouse/distribution facility in Baltimore. The extrusion production, once the press became operational, was expected to be marketed to Empire's current customers. In addition, the operation had the potential to build on Empire's value-added strategy, as other capabilities could be added to process and finishing aluminum, and as a result the company could further improve its sales and profitability.

Generally avoiding publicity, Empire achieved results that caught the notice of investors, and in 2004 the price of its stock began to inch upward after years of neglect. That attention would only grow after Empire increased revenues 69 percent to $358.5 million in 2005, and net income topped $9.5 million. In 2006, as a result, *Business Week* ranked Empire number 32 on its list of Hot Growth companies.

Ed Dinger

PRINCIPAL SUBSIDIARIES

Empire Resources Pacific Ltd.; Empire Resources Extrusions L.L.C.

PRINCIPAL COMPETITORS

Alcan Inc.; Alcoa Inc., Ryerson, Inc.

FURTHER READING

"Integrated Technology USA Joins AMEX," *Record* (Bergen County, N.J.), October 3, 1996, p. B3.

Lavelle, Louis, "High-Tech Firm Shutting Down in Teaneck," *Record* (Bergen County, N.J.) November 7, 1997, p. B1.

Lynn, Kathleen, "Heavily into Metal," *Record* (Hackensack, N.J.), December 25, 2005.

———, "N.J. Microcap Companies' Stocks Soar," *Record* (Hacksensack, N.J.), January 7, 2005.

Encore Wire Corporation

1410 Millwood Road
McKinney, Texas 75069
U.S.A.
Telephone: (972) 562-9473
Toll Free: (800) 962-9473
Fax: (972) 562-4744
Web site: http://www.encorewire.com

Public Company
Incorporated: 1989
Employees: 643
Sales: $758.1 million (2005)
Stock Exchanges: NASDAQ
Ticker Symbol: WIRE
NAIC: 331422 Copper Wire (Except Mechanical) Drawing

■ ■ ■

Located 35 miles north of Dallas in McKinney, Texas, Encore Wire Corporation manufactures NM cable, used for the interior wiring in residential construction, and THHN cable, used in commercial and industrial buildings. The company also has begun offering armored cable, industrial wiring with an aluminum jacket. Although a relatively young company, Encore boasts a seasoned management team, which has assembled the most modern production facilities in the industry. The McKinney operation is vertically integrated, with manufacturing, copper rod production, copper recycling, warehousing, and distribution facilities located on the same site. In this way, Encore is better able to control costs and achieve an order fill rate that is virtually 100 percent. As a result of its dependability, Encore has steadily increased its market share. In 15 years sales have grown from $11 million to more than $750 million.

The company is regarded as an innovator in its field, highly praised for the introduction of color-coded cabling that allows contractors and inspectors to quickly, and safely, determine if a project's cabling is done properly. Although Encore does some direct marketing, its products are mostly sold through a network of more than 30 manufacturer's representatives located across the United States. The company is content to serve the domestic market and is adamant about not straying from the far-from-glamorous field of residential and commercial wiring. "We are conservative, and we stick to our business," Chief Financial Officer Frank J. Bilban once told the *Dallas Morning News*. "We are not going to get into orange juice or ladies' high-heeled shoes."

COFOUNDER'S INVOLVEMENT WITH WIRE SINCE WORLD WAR II

Encore was founded by Vincent A. Rego and his longtime right-hand man, Donald M. Spurgin. Born in 1924, Rego became involved in the wire industry after serving in the military during World War II. In 1953 he became the plant manager for Narragansett Wire Co. when it opened in Plano, Texas, and a year later he began his association with Spurgin. Narragansett was struggling by the start of the 1960s and in 1961 Rego put together a group of investors to acquire the plant. When some of the backers pulled out suddenly, the deal almost had to be scrapped, but Rego was able to convince the Dallas venture capital firm Capital Southwest to provide a loan to make up for the shortfall. The company chose the name Capital Wire and Cable, which Rego and Spurgin took public in 1964. Four years later Stamford, Connecticut-based U.S. Industries, Inc., acquired Capital and the two men managed it as a U.S. Industries division until 1974 when Spurgin left to become chief executive officer of another U.S. Industries' division, Hamilton Industries. Then, in 1978, Rego created a new company called Capital Wire and bought the U.S. Industries cable division for $19 million in another leveraged buyout.

Spurgin rejoined Rego in 1979 and once again they were running a cabling company together. They had hoped to quickly take the new Capital Wire public, but the stock offering had to be put on hold after the company posted a $300,000 loss in 1981, the first loss since the days of Narragansett Wire, and the consequence of Rego straying from his conservative principles. He dabbled in the metal futures market (copper serving as the key raw material in cabling) and got burned, losing $3.5 million on the investment. A year later the board of directors adopted a resolution banning futures trading, but Rego had already learned his lesson about sticking to the basics, one that he would apply later when launching Encore. Capital was finally taken public in April 1986, raising $16 million, and soon it became the object of several unsolicited buyout inquiries. In December 1987 Rego hired Dallas-based investment firm Eppler, Guerin & Turner Inc., which had handled Capital's initial public offering (IPO) of stock, to help sort out the interest. Capital was ultimately sold to the Penn Central Corporation in August 1988.

INCORPORATING IN 1989

Although at retirement age, Rego had no intention of giving up the work he loved. Instead he soon was making plans for an "encore." He lined up investors and in April 1989 he and Spurgin formed Encore Wire Corporation to become involved in the residential wire and cable business. Initially Rego served as chairman and Spurgin became president and chief executive officer.

They bought a former mobile home plant on a 12-acre tract in northeast McKinney and set up their operation with just eight employees, spending the first several months in acquiring equipment and installing and testing it. The company shipped its first NM cable (nonmetallic sheath cable for interior wiring) and UF cable (underground feeder cable) in February 1990, and by the end of the year total sales reached $11 million. In the company's first full year in operation, 1991, sales increased to $31 million. This strong debut took place despite a recession and a housing market that in 1991 was lower than it had been in a generation. Because it was a new operation, Encore was able to install new state-of-the art equipment, while its competitors continued to rely on equipment that had been in use since the 1950s and 1960s. In addition, the company optimized the plant layout to cut down on production time. Hence, Encore had higher production levels, providing a pricing edge. The company also was able to run a lean operation, with the low overhead resulting in fatter profit margins.

Encore was ready to expand and tap the public equity market for the funds needed to fuel its growth. The company filed for an IPO in May 1992 and later in the year about 1.5 million shares (of which 300,000 were owned by existing shareholders) were sold at $9 per share. Not only did the IPO, managed by A.G. Edwards & Sons Inc., raise money that was used to retire bank debt and buy new manufacturing equipment, it also gave management the ability to use stock options to retain and motivate employees. Stock options became available to staff members at all levels. Moreover, the company implemented an incentive pay system, so that about 60 percent of an employee's salary was a base and the rest was determined in terms of productivity and quality—this on top of stock options that extended to all ranks of the company.

In 1992 Encore added to its original 68,000-square-foot facility by building a 38,000-square-foot expansion. More room would soon be needed as the company moved into the commercial wire sector. Encore had already established a strong relationship with its customers because of a near perfect order fill rate, with the ability to reliably deliver a completed order within five days coast to coast. Many of these customers also wanted Encore to supply them with commercial wire as well, and the company accommodated them in 1994. To produce THHN cable, the company added another 231,200-square-foot facility to its McKinney complex.

Sales reached $123 million in 1994 and increased to $151 million in 1995, but in that year Encore also posted a loss, due primarily to the financial problems encountered by competitor Triangle Wire & Cable.

KEY DATES

1989: The company is founded.
1990: The first residential wire is shipped.
1992: An initial public offering of stock is made.
1994: Commercial wire is added.
1999: Color-coded wire is first sold.
2006: The founder retires.

INTRODUCING COLOR WIRE IN 1999

Copper prices began to stabilize by 2000 and Encore was able to increase sales to $284 million in 2000 after dipping as low as $230 million in 1999. The economy began to stall but Encore maintained sales above $280 million over the next two years because of the introduction of color coded wire. The innovation grew out of a Columbus, Ohio, meeting in the mid-1990s that Rego and executive Dan Jones attended with electrical inspectors, maintenance engineers, and electrical contractors. They heard complaints from some of the attendees about the expense in terms of money and time to have electricians identifying cables by wrapping different colored tape around them. To make matters worse, the tape could be ripped off when cable was pulled through piping or dried out over time, making inspections and repair another time-consuming proposition. Moreover, people were known to handle a hot wire that was not marked and were killed. In response to this concern, Encore began developing colored feeder cable, and once the company showed it to safety engineers it was an immediate hit. The product was introduced for the commercial market in 1999 and became available for the residential market in December 2001. Inspectors then suggested that Encore apply the color cable idea to its nonmetallic cable, and that was added as well. Encore's color-coded wire was so well received by contractors that in 2002 trade publication *EC&M/CEE News* named it the product of the year. It not only served to further distinguish Encore from its competition, the new product line allowed it to attract new customers despite poor economic conditions. Encore also was able to continue to add to its production capabilities during this period. In 2001 it completed a 192,000-square-foot plant expansion.

When it was unable to fill its customers' orders, the top three wire companies launched a price war to capture those customers. Distracted by its entry into the commercial wiring sector, Encore failed to keep its prices in line with the competition and lost some customers. Encore shifted its strategy somewhat, placing even more emphasis on customer service, and its exceptional order fulfillment rate, as a way to distinguish itself. The strategy worked, the company returned to profitability, and sales continued to climb.

In 1996 Spurgin retired, but Rego made it clear that he had no intention of following his friend's lead, instead adding the CEO position to his duties. Despite his 72 years, Rego continued to work seven days a week and was known to come in on holidays. In fact, on the verge of his 80th birthday in 2004, he told the *Dallas Morning News,* "Why would I leave this? I'm not going to retire—never—not until they bury me. Hey, I'm still a baby."

Encore's revenues topped the $250 million mark in 1997, but the company's steady growth rate was interrupted for the next five years due to a dip in copper prices that resulted in an industry-wide loss of pricing discipline that adversely impacted revenues and earnings. Nevertheless, Encore continued to expand its operations in order to position itself for a return of better business conditions. In 1997 a 259,200-square-foot distribution center opened, followed a year later by a 50,000-square-foot copper rod mill facility. The company was now able to produce copper sheets to be converted into copper rods that could be fashioned into wire. The facility also was able to reprocess copper scrap produced by Encore and others. As a result, Encore would be able to lower the cost of its copper raw materials and gain a competitive advantage. Also in 1998 Encore constructed a 5,000-foot railroad spur expansion and a 1,000-foot conveyor expansion. Further vertical integration of the business occurred in 1999 when Encore added a 12,400-square-foot plastic mill to produce its own sheathing.

With copper prices stabilized, Encore experienced a surge in sales in 2002 to $385 million, accompanied by $6 million in net income. A year later sales soared even higher, to $603 million, as Encore controlled about 25 percent of the copper wire market, a 7 percent increase in just two years. Moreover, earnings in 2003 increased 141 percent over the prior year to $14.4 million. The trend continued in 2005 when Encore posted revenues of $758 million and net income of more than $50 million.

In the meantime, the company continued to invest money in building up its McKinney complex on the more than 55,000 acres of surrounding land it had purchased since 1998. In 2004 the company added 162,000 square feet to its distribution center as well as another 5,000-foot railroad spur. While Encore was not about to stray too far from its area of expertise, in 2006 it added 150,000 square feet of manufacturing space to accommodate the production of armored cable, industrial wiring using an aluminum jacket, which would also be made available in different colors. It was another case of listening to customers, who were urging Encore to provide this product as well. With an apparent opening in the market—and a demand for all of its products needed in the multiyear rebuilding of the Gulf Coast following the 2005 devastation of the Gulf Coast area—Encore was well positioned to enjoy strong success for an extended period of time. It would do so with less input from its founder, however. In May 2006 Rego suffered from a stroke and was named chairman emeritus as he recovered. He opted not to stand for re-election to the board of directors at the annual stockholders' meeting held that same month. He was replaced as CEO by Daniel L. Jones, who had been groomed for the role by Rego for several years.

Ed Dinger

PRINCIPAL SUBSIDIARIES

EWC Aviation Corporation; EWC GP Corporation; EWC LP Corporation; Encore Wire Limited.

PRINCIPAL COMPETITORS

General Cable Corporation; Southwire Company; Superior Essex Inc.

FURTHER READING

Lucy, Jim, "Encore's Color-Coded Cable," *EC&M,* July 1, 2002.

Quinn, Steve, "Dallas-Area Wire Manufacturer Thrives Despite Shaky Economy," *Dallas Morning News,* July 21, 2002.

————, "79-Year-Old Founder Pours Energy into McKinney, Texas, Copper-Wire Firm," *Dallas Morning News,* February 28, 2004.

Schmeiser, Lisa, "Wire Manufacturer Keeps Making the Right Connections," *Investor's Business Daily,* March 9, 2006, p. A07.

Weil, Jonathan, "After Plant Expansion, Encore Wire Could Unreel Further Stock Gains," *Wall Street Journal,* January 7, 1998, p. T2.

EPCOR Utilities Inc.

10065 Jasper Avenue
Edmonton, Alberta T5J 3B1
Canada
Telephone: (780) 412-3414
Fax: (708) 412-3096
Web site: http://www.epcor.ca

Government-Owned Company
Incorporated: 1996
Employees: 2,600
Operating Revenues: $2.96 billion (2005)
NAIC: 221122 Electric Power Distribution

■ ■ ■

EPCOR Utilities Inc., a top Canadian provider of energy and energy-related services and products, is owned by the city of Edmonton. The operation serves three regions: Alberta; Ontario and the U.S. Northeast; and British Columbia and the U.S. Pacific Northwest. For the bulk of its history, EPCOR operated as a unit of the Canadian government. However, in the mid-1990s, coinciding with the trend toward electrical utility deregulation, EPCOR switched to a corporate structure. Guided by an independent board of directors, the entity has been lauded for its governance model as well as for its dependable operation.

EDMONTON'S INFRASTRUCTURE TAKING SHAPE: 1891 THROUGH THE 20TH CENTURY

EPCOR Utilities Inc. got its start in 1891. A group of entrepreneurs was granted a ten-year permit to build the Edmonton Electric Lighting and Power Company on the banks of the North Saskatchewan River. In 1902, ownership shifted to the municipality and another public utility began to take shape: a water distribution system. A water treatment plant followed a year later.

The infrastructure of the city continued to grow over the next few decades. The city, for example, saw its first traffic light, located at Jasper Avenue and 101 Street, in 1933, and downtown electric lines went underground in 1947. Pollution concerns forced the city to switch from coal-fired to gas boilers in 1955, an EPCOR company history recalled.

As the city grew during the 1960s so did demand for electrical power. Edmonton needed more capacity. Electrical distribution and power plant operations combined in 1970 to form Edmonton Power. A new generation station was commissioned that year and expanded over the decade.

Growth continued into the 1980s. The first Genesee unit began operating at full load in July 1989 and within a few years was Edmonton Power's top producer of electricity. A second Genesee unit commenced commercial operation in early 1994.

Meanwhile, change was in the air for the industry at large and for Edmonton Power. In 1993, David Richard Foy was persuaded by the chair of Edmonton Power to leave his position as president and CEO of Phillips Cables Limited in Toronto and direct the transformation of the company. A climate of deregulation opened the door for the utility to leave its bureaucratic structure behind for one driven by competition and innovation.

COMPANY PERSPECTIVES

We create enduring customer relationships and enrich the quality of life for the people, businesses, and communities we serve by providing competitively priced, safe, reliable, and environmentally responsible water and power.

Edmonton Power, operating in the Alberta market; Aqualta, water supplier to the provincial capital region; and Eltec, a commercial electrical service operation, combined in 1996 to form EPCOR Utilities Inc. The merger was the first of its kind for Canada. A subsidiary of the city of Edmonton, EPCOR was overseen by an independent board of directors.

In 1995, the utility returned $90 million in dividends, revenue taxes, and service charges to the city, according to *Commerce News*. Revenues for the year totaled $462 million. The company posted record earnings for the year and ranked among Canada's most profitable companies. Between 1994 and 1995, net income climbed 26 percent from $74 million to $94 million.

A well-managed as well as profitable company, its rates were among the lowest in North America. Foy was set on turning EPCOR, with combined assets of $2.3 billion and sales approaching $1 billion, into a world class utility. Later in the decade, a new leader, Don Lowry, a longtime telecommunications executive, would arrive to advance the cause.

RESPONDING TO CHANGING MARKETS: 2000–2004

At the dawn of the 21st century, concern over global warming had begun to escalate as the world increasingly took note of events ranging from melting glaciers and increased numbers of catastrophic storms. The Kyoto agreement, which challenged the industrialized world to cut greenhouse emissions, spawned carbon credits trading among power generators. In 2000, EPCOR bought 50,000 tons of carbon credits—typically selling for $1 to $3 per tonne—from Fortum. The company owned a Finnish power plant that converted peat to biomass, according to the *Ottawa Citizen*. The plant, fueled with shrubs and crop harvest residue, qualified for carbon credits, which could be sold on the worldwide market. Once in EPCOR's hands the credits could be banked and used if Canadian emissions limits were exceeded. Carbon credit deals thus far had been "small and experimental," Arthur Max reported. Critics of the practice contended that countries, the United States in particular, would use the practice to evade costly expenditures to cut emissions by their own plants.

On the opposite end of the spectrum, in 2001, EPCOR entered into its largest expansion deal outside Alberta, buying Ontario-based Union Energy and Westcoast Capital from Westcoast Energy Inc. EPCOR paid $160.7 million, a figure considered pricey by some industry watchers, and assumed about $16 million in debt. Union Energy rented water heaters and dealt in heating, ventilation, and air conditioning products and services. Westcoast Capital provided customer financing for Union Energy products. EPCOR saw the purchase as a point of entry into Ontario's retail electricity and natural gas business. Union Energy's customer base included the important Toronto market, crucial to the capture of a hoped for 20 percent of the province's energy business.

"This is a very important strategic move for EPCOR," Brian Vaasjo, president of the energy division told the *Globe and Mail*. "EPCOR is on a very aggressive growth strategy, and we aim to be one of the top three providers of energy and energy-related products in Canada."

EPCOR appeared to be balancing aggressive moves with a more moderated philosophy on the other end of the continent. When electricity market prices crash, power plant projects tend to stall. Nonetheless EPCOR, by avoiding speculative building, working with partners, and seeking out long-term contracts for its power, continued to expand even during down times. The strategy limited growth year over year but created greater stability. "In a commodity business you can't build for the top end," EPCOR President Don Lowry told the *Seattle Post–Intelligencer*.

Consequently, in 2002, in the midst of a slump in the Pacific Northwest market, EPCOR brought a new natural gas-fired generating unit on line. The Frederickson Power Facility, located near Tacoma, Washington, was centrally located: near gas pipelines providing fuel source, the regional transmission grid, and Canadian and California markets. The region's consumption was expected to rebound and grow rapidly over the next two decades.

Yet the challenging energy environment of the times took its toll on EPCOR's total revenue. It fell to $2.7 billion in 2002, down one billion from 2001. Net income dropped from $226.9 million to $184.4 million. Although the company's water, generation and distribution, and transmission remained strong, energy services and power development sectors of the integrated company slipped. Lower electricity prices in Alberta

KEY DATES

1891: Edmonton Electric Lighting and Power Company is founded.

1902: The company becomes the first municipally owned electric utility in Canada.

1903: Edmonton Water and Light Company constructs the first water treatment plant.

1933: Edmonton's first traffic light is installed.

1947: Downtown electric lines are put underground.

1955: Edmonton switches from coal-fired boilers to gas.

1970: Electrical distribution and power plant departments combine to form Edmonton Power.

1989: The first Genesee unit begins operating at full load.

1995: The company is placed under the direction of an independent board of directors.

1996: EPCOR Utilities Inc. is formed.

2003: The company exits the retail business.

2005: EPCOR Power L.P. begins trading on the Toronto Stock Exchange.

reduced energy sales revenue and capital spending on projects such as the Frederick plant and Genesee Phase 3 (G3) elevated capital costs.

In January 2003, EPCOR divested 50 percent of its interest in G3 to TransAlta Corp., gaining $157 million in consideration for construction costs incurred. Through a joint venture agreement, TransAlta would fund half the remaining capital costs for the project. Growth oriented during the first few years of the decade, EPCOR planned to slow the pace during 2003 and "concentrate more on integrating investments, stabilizing operations, conserving capital, and improving operating efficiencies," according to an April 2003 *Canada NewsWire* release.

Consumer resistance to signing fixed contracts for basic electric and gas service prompted EPCOR to withdraw from the retail natural gas and electricity business. In addition, Alberta's deregulation policy, which EPCOR found prohibitive to expansion, contributed to the decision. Generally speaking, the North American electrical generation market had begun to reverse its course regarding deregulation as citizens protested price spikes. EPCOR planned to concentrate on its commercial, industrial, and wholesale markets and power generation, according to the *Ottawa Citizen* in

August 2003. The company would continue to serve its regulated power customers.

A TIGHTER STRATEGY FOR 2005

In early 2005, EPCOR tightened its focus: "Building a strategy that defined us as one company with two lines of business, concentrated in three geographic regions." In that light the company proceeded to strengthen its core power and water businesses.

In September 2005, EPCOR acquired all of Trans-Canada's interest in TransCanada Power L.P. for $529 million. Following the deal, the operation was renamed EPCOR Power L.P. and began trading on the Toronto Stock Exchange. The company ranked as the largest publicly traded entity headquartered in Edmonton.

The limited partnership owned 11 power generation facilities with a total capacity of 744 megawatts. "We saw the partnership as a great fit for EPCOR," Brian Vaasjo, executive vice-president of EPCOR, told *U.S. Business Review.* "It fits with our practice of developing or acquiring generation assets whose output was substantially contracted."

Other projects underway included the development of the Britannia Mine water treatment plant. The long abandoned copper mine, which continued to leach contaminants into the surrounding environment, was a major source of heavy metal pollution in North America. The year also was marked by an increasing presence in renewable energy sources via Ontario's Kingbridge I and II wind power projects.

Meanwhile, the Genesee 3 coal-fired power plant began commercial operation in March. The joint venture between EPCOR and TransAlta was the first of its kind for Canada. The supercritical pressure boiler in the facility incorporated "the best available, economically viable technology that is both environmentally friendly and highly efficient," Vaasjo explained. *Power Engineering Magazine* called it one of the year's top coal-fired power projects worldwide.

The Genesee 3 project, when proposed in 2000, faced a stringent regulatory climate. No coal-fired plants had been approved in the province for two decades. Moreover, the company had not built a comparably sized project for more than ten years. Representing half the company's 2005 generation capacity, the three Genesee units dated back to 1960s coal lease acquisitions.

Chairman Hugh J. Bolton, in the 2005 annual report, looking back at the company's progress, cited three critical decisions made in the 1990s: separating professional management from city government; uniting the power and water operations under a single company and brand; and affirming future ownership by the city of Edmonton.

The city continued to benefit from the structure set in place a decade earlier. From 1995 through 2005, Edmonton received about $1.27 billion in dividend payments, taxes, and franchise fees. In 1996 the shareholder dividend was $62 million; the dividend was set at $125 million for 2006.

Kathleen Peippo

PRINCIPAL SUBSIDIARIES

EPCOR Water Services Inc.; EPCOR Distribution Inc.; EPCOR Energy Inc.; EPCOR Energy Alberta Inc.; EPCOR Merchant and Capital L.P.; EPCOR Generation Inc.; EPCOR Power Development Corporation; EPCOR Preferred Equity Inc.; EPCOR Power L.P.

PRINCIPAL COMPETITORS

Centrica North America; ENMAX; TransAlta Utilities Corporation.

FURTHER READING

Cotter, John, "Alberta's Energy Deregulation Policy Suffers Critical Blow," *Ottawa Citizen,* August 30, 2003. p. D3.

Max, Arthur, "Global Warming Spawns Trading of Pollution Credits: Traders Turn Clean Air into a Commodity to Be Swapped on International Exchange," *Ottawa Citizen,* November 15, 2000, p. E8.

Parkinson, David, and Wendy Stueck, "EPCOR Utilities Snaps Up Westcoast Energy Units," *Globe and Mail,* October 23, 2001, p. B2.

Tiflis, Fernie Grace, "A Focus on Canada: With More Than 100 Years of Experience, EPCOR Utilities Inc. Is One of Canada's Top Providers of Energy-Related and Water Services," *U.S. Business Review,* December 2005, pp. 50+.

Virgin, Bill, "EPCOR Sees Opportunity Where Others Back Away," *Seattle Post–Intelligencer,* October 12, 2002, p. C1.

Ziegler, Gretchen, "In Profile: EPCOR's David R. Foy," *Commerce News,* September 1, 1996, p. 11.

Ethiopian Airlines

PO Box 1755
Addis Ababa,
Ethiopia
Telephone: (251-11) 6612222
Fax: (251-11) 6611474
Web site: http://www.flyethiopian.com

State-Owned Company
Incorporated: 1946 as Ethiopian Air Lines Inc.
Employees: 4,500
Sales: $495 million (2005 est.)
NAIC: 481111 Scheduled Passenger Air Transportation; 481112 Scheduled Freight Air Transportation; 481211 Nonscheduled Chartered Passenger Air Transportation; 481212 Nonscheduled Chartered Freight Air Transportation; 48819 Other Support Activities for Air Transportation

∎∎∎

Ethiopian Airlines is "Africa's Link to the World." More than 1.5 million people a year fly the carrier to 22 domestic and 44 international destinations on four continents. The airline claims the largest network of routes within Africa.

Since its launch in 1946, Ethiopian has been a pioneer in African aviation industry. It has maintained an excellent reputation under the various governments that have ruled Ethiopia over the years.

Cargo operations are a vital part of business; Ethiopian also has a wide array of ancillary services such as Africa's leading maintenance and training operations.

The fleet includes more than two dozen airliners, while various small planes, helicopters, and even crop dusters are employed in the side ventures.

FORMATION FOLLOWING WORLD WAR II

Ethiopian Airlines, formerly Ethiopian Air Lines Inc. (EAL), was created by the decree of Emperor Haile Selassie I at the end of 1945. Trans World Airlines (TWA), the U.S. giant that helped form many carriers in developing nations after World War II, was contracted for technical assistance. Though TWA controlled a couple of board seats for a while, the government of Ethiopia owned all of the airline's equity.

Five war surplus DC-3s formerly based in Cairo made up the original fleet. Within a few years, the carrier had about 20 planes. By this time, EAL had begun to turn a consistent profit, making it a contrast to other airlines being run at a loss by developing countries looking for prestige. The company's international business tended to offset losses on domestic services. Internal routes were doing a thriving cargo trade, carrying tribal commodities such as crocodile skins and livestock. Within a few years, the airline would make it feasible to export coffee from the country's otherwise inaccessible growing areas.

The airline's first scheduled flight was to Cairo from Addis Ababa, with a stop in Asmara, Ethiopia, and occurred on April 8, 1946. Weekly flights to Djibouti and Aden were added later. Connecting the country with the

COMPANY PERSPECTIVES

Ethiopian is a business enterprise committed to the basic objective of providing safe, reliable and profitable air transport services for the passenger and cargo as well as other aviation related services. The airline renews its pledge to further develop its total network with continued emphasis on interconnecting Africa and linking it with the rest of the world. Ethiopian is committed to the provision of quality service to its customers. In order to ensure this, the airline will strive to maintain a highly trained, motivated and dedicated workforce and enhance its internal capacity in various fields.

outside world was more of a priority than developing an internal route network, though a route between Jimma and the capital was added.

In 1947, the airline acquired more aircraft from the U.S. government and introduced colorful new color livery for the planes. By the end of the decade, Ethiopian was flying as far as Bombay and Port Sudan, while new grass airstrips cleared the way for more domestic stops. The new air connections often reduced to hours journeys that once took weeks by mule or days by train through Ethiopia's extreme, mountainous terrain.

The international route network expanded northward from Cairo to Athens and then Frankfurt in the late 1950s. In 1960, a second leg was extended to Monrovia, Liberia, via Khartoum, Sudan; Lagos, Nigeria; and Accra, Ghana. The 19-hour trip was offered on a weekly basis at first. This was considered a milestone in African aviation as it was the continent's first east-west connection since the days of Imperial Airways. Before then, passengers would fly to different countries in Africa via hubs in Europe.

Three new Douglas DC-6 airliners and three Convair 240s were acquired. However, the DC-3 fleet would remain in service for decades. The company had begun operating a small fleet of helicopters in 1957.

Revenues were $8.5 million in 1959, according to a profile of the carrier in *Aviation Week.* EAL then had about 900 employees, most of them locals; 19 of its 40 fixed-wing pilots were from Ethiopia.

FIRST JETS IN 1963

Ethiopian began flying jets, starting an Addis Ababa-Nairobi service with Boeing 720s in January 1963. Ac-

cording to *Aviation Week,* this was necessary to keep the airline from being overshadowed on international routes by other jet-flying competitors. (Most of its rivals were associated with the state airlines of the European colonial powers.) The new jets were financed by a $12 million loan from the Export-Import Bank.

The New Boeing 720s required an extra-long runway in order to operate from the thin air at the capital's 8,500 feet elevation, so Ethiopian moved its operations from the Lideta airfield to the new $8.5 million Bole International Airport.

The company was renamed Ethiopian Airlines in 1965 as its ownership structure changed from corporation to share company. It continued in its role as a leader in the continent's aviation industry. Schools for pilots and mechanics were established at the Bole Airport to train personnel from Africa and the Middle East. The fast-growing airline ended the decade with more than 2,000 employees.

Pioneering long range, thinly traveled routes to unique city pairs was an enduring part of Ethiopian's methodology, noted *Air Transport World.* In 1975, EAL introduced the first direct service to China (Beijing) from Africa. While such moves were risky, they attracted few competitors and generally became profitable within a few years.

1974 REVOLUTION

Some changes at the airline followed after Mengistu Haile Mariam came to power in a socialist revolution in 1974. According to a later profile in the *New York Times,* the quality of service plummeted as staffing became bloated. By the end of the 1970s, the airline had nearly 3,400 employees. Naturally, it was soon losing money.

Captain Mohammed Ahmed, a longtime veteran of the company, was designated chief operating officer in 1980 and tasked with implementing a turnaround. He cut the staff by more than 10 percent while running EAL on a strictly commercial basis.

While Ethiopia's new government was sympathetic to the Soviet Union, EAL continued to choose Western-made aircraft. The fleet was replenished with purchases of Boeing 727s in 1979 and wide-body Boeing 767s in 1984.

Interest payments on the new planes, unfavorable exchange rates, and a slowdown in business from the drought conspired to wipe out the company's restored operating profits in the mid-1980s, Capt. Mohammed explained to the *New York Times.* EAL continued to have a stellar reputation for maintenance and training. It also had an impeccable credit rating. By the end of the

KEY DATES

1946: Ethiopian Airlines begins operations with flights to Cairo.

1957: Network stretches north to Hamburg, Germany.

1960: Ethiopian develops Africa's first scheduled services connecting east and west.

1961: Revenues surpass $10 million.

1963: First jets arrive.

1974: Country undergoes Socialist revolution, which affects the company.

1975: TWA management contract ends; EAL introduces first direct flights between Africa and China.

1991: Marxist dictatorship is overthrown in a coup.

1998: First services to the United States are launched.

2003: Construction begins on new cargo terminal and maintenance hangar.

decade, Britain's *Financial Times* was calling it the most profitable airline in Africa. It posted net income of $24 million on revenues of about $240 million in the 1988/89 fiscal year.

1991 COUP

In 1991 a coup toppled Mengistu's reigning Marxist dictatorship; EAL temporarily relocated its planes to Nairobi as the fighting approached the capital. One of its aircraft, though, was damaged by shrapnel in the breakaway province of Eritrea. In spite of the disruption and chaos, and a downturn in the global aviation industry, and the elimination of tourism due to the war, EAL managed to post a profit. A manager told *Aviation Week & Space Technology* that cargo operations, which supplied more than one-third of revenues, were keeping the airline in the black. Interestingly, the airline formed a crop duster unit in 1993.

50TH ANNIVERSARY IN 1996

The government installed a new management team led by Ahmed Kellow, an Ethiopian native who had taught finance at the University of Wales, in 1994. At the time of Ethiopian's 50th anniversary in 1996, the route network extended as far as Beijing, London, Johannesburg, and the Ivory Coast. Yet another CEO was named in 1997, longtime EAL veteran Ato Bisrat Nigatu.

In July 1998, EAL launched its first services to the United States, which was home to about half a million Ethiopian expatriates. The airline continued to order new aircraft, adding the latest model B737s for mid-length routes.

War once again disrupted plans after a border dispute led to fighting between Ethiopia and Eritrea in May 1998. EAL again relocated its main operations to Nairobi for most of the two-year conflict. This resulted in an enormous increase in fuel costs due to rerouting international flights out of Eritrean airspace. Even with these challenges, Ethiopian was increasing its frequencies and adding new routes. Its financial losses in the late 1990s were minimal.

EAL continued to thrive even in the global aviation downturn which followed the September 11, 2001 terrorist attacks on the United States. The company posted a net profit of $4.5 million on revenues of $278 million (ETB 2.4 billion) in 2000. After the fall of Air Afrique in 2002, no one rivaled Ethiopian in terms of covering the continent of Africa, noted *Air Transport World.*

In 2003, the airline changed its livery for the first time in 56 years. Construction was beginning on a new cargo terminal and a new maintenance hangar. EAL named Ato Gima Waka its latest CEO in 2004 following the retirement of Ato Bisrat Nigatu. In the same year, the airline's Scandinavian gateway, a vital source of tourism traffic, was relocated from Copenhagen to Stockholm. A second China destination was added, the southern trade center of Guangzhou. It had income of $43.4 million on revenues of $495 million in 2005. While expanding its reach overseas, the airline was beginning to face competition from new low-cost carriers on some of its African routes.

"Dedication brought us this far and passion will take us even further" was the company's 60th anniversary slogan. A loyal Boeing customer, Ethiopian began operating its first Airbus, an A330, on a leased basis in 2006. Ethiopian was a launch customer for the Boeing 787 Dreamliner, however, which was due to be delivered beginning in 2008.

Frederick C. Ingram

PRINCIPAL COMPETITORS

British Airways plc; Deutsche Lufthansa AG; Kenya Airways Limited.

FURTHER READING

Cook, Robert H., "Ethiopian Carrier Faces Jet Competition," *Aviation Week & Space Technology,* January 21, 1963, pp. 45+.

Davies, R. E. G., *A History of the World's Airlines,* London: Oxford University Press, 1967.

Duru, Nnamdi, "Ethiopian Airlines Is Africa's First Carrier," *This Day* (Nigeria), July 15, 2005.

"Ethiopia Dreams of an Air Empire," *Business Week,* January 12, 1963, pp. 106–8.

Farrell, Robert E., "Ethiopian Airlines Forges African Link," *Aviation Week,* December 12, 1960, pp. 32–37.

Geiger, Theodore, *TWA's Services to Ethiopia,* Washington, D.C.: National Planning Association, 1959.

Hagos, Gion, "Ethiopian Airlines Survives Two Difficult Years," *Panafrican News Agency (PANA) Daily Newswire,* August 5, 2000.

Lott, Steven, "Ethiopian Leases A330 to Start Libreville Flight," *Aviation Daily,* June 21, 2006, p. 5.

May, Clifford D., "Ethiopia's Capitalist Airline," *New York Times,* August 19, 1985, p. D6.

Ozanne, Julian, "Flying in the Face of Marxist Dogma," *Financial Times* (London), June 22, 1989, p. 36.

Parrish, Wayne W., "Ethiopian Airlines: Envy of Black Africa," *American Aviation,* January 20, 1979, pp. 44–47.

Richburg, Keith, "Flying High Over a Troubled Country; Against All Odds, Ethiopia's State Airline Prospers," *Washington Post,* March 15, 1992, p. H1.

Schaefer, Charles, "Ethiopian Renews Fleet in African Leadership Bid," *Aviation Week & Space Technology,* September 28, 1992, p. 33.

"Survival of Cargo Operations Essential to Carrier's Future," *Aviation Week & Space Technology,* September 28, 1992, p. 39.

Vandyk, Anthony, "An African Success Story," *Air Transport World,* February 1, 1992, p. 110.

———, "Ethiopian Covers the Continent: In Terms of Network, Ethiopia's National Carrier Can Claim to Be the Leading Member of Africa's Air Transport Industry," *Air Transport World,* May 1, 2002, p. 62.

———, "Where Others Fear to Fly," *Air Transport World,* March 1, 1996, p. 90.

Woolsey, James P., "Ethiopian Plays Major Role in Economy," *Aviation Week & Space Technology,* July 26, 1971, pp. 26–28.

———, "Ethiopian Pushing for African Leadership," *Aviation Week & Space Technology,* August 9, 1971, pp. 30–31.

Fleetwood Enterprises,
Inc.

3125 Myers Street
Riverside, California 92503-5527
U.S.A.
Telephone: (951) 351-3500
Fax: (951) 351-3312
Web site: http://www.fleetwood.com

Public Company
Incorporated: 1950 as Coach Specialties Company
Employees: 11,500
Sales: $2.43 billion (2006)
Stock Exchanges: New York
Ticker Symbol: FLE
NAIC: 321992 Prefabricated Wood Building Manufacturing; 336213 Motor Home Manufacturing; 336214 Travel Trailer and Camper Manufacturing

∎∎∎

Fleetwood Enterprises, Inc., is one of the nation's largest makers of both recreational vehicles (including motor homes, travel trailers, and folding trailers) and manufactured housing. The company's line of motor homes are sold under various brands, including Jamboree, Tioga, Terra, Fiesta, Flair, Storm, Bounder, Southwind, Pace Arrow, Expedition, Discovery, Providence, Excursion, Revolution, American Tradition, American Eagle, and American Heritage. Fleetwood's travel trailers are marketed under the names Pioneer, Mallard, Wilderness, Prowler, Terry, Gearbox, Pegasus, Orbit, Pride, and Triumph. The company's folding trailer

division, which leads that sector of the market, manufactures products under the Fleetwood name. As a whole, Fleetwood recreational vehicles (RVs) span the full range of the market, with their retail prices ranging from a few thousand dollars to more than $200,000; they are marketed through a network of approximately 1,300 independent dealers in 49 states and Canada. The company maintains more than a dozen plants in the United States and Ontario to handle its RV production. Manufactured housing is sold under the corporate name, Fleetwood, and is produced at 22 plants throughout the United States. Fleetwood housing is distributed through a network of more than 1,300 dealers in 46 states. Other company operations include two fiberglass manufacturing companies.

FROM WINDOW BLINDS TO
MOBILE HOMES

Fleetwood was founded by John C. Crean in a greenhouse in southern California in 1950. Under the name Coach Specialties Company, he and his wife manufactured and sold a new and improved line of window blinds for travel trailers. At the same time, Crean built a travel trailer for his own use. One of his window blind customers, a trailer dealer, was so impressed by the trailer's construction that a deal was struck for Crean to assemble trailer units with materials supplied to him by the dealer. Production was to be in quantities large enough to make sure the dealer could keep pace with his seasonal orders. Around 1953 Crean changed the name of his company to Fleetwood Trailer Company, adopting the name from the Cadillac automobile line of General Motors Corporation (and leading to a lengthy

COMPANY PERSPECTIVES

Fleetwood will lead the Recreational Vehicle and Manufactured Housing industries in providing quality products, with a passion for customer-driven innovation. We will emphasize training, embrace diversity and provide growth opportunities for our associates and our dealers. We will lead our industries in the application of appropriate technologies. We will operate at the highest levels of ethics and compliance with a focus on exemplary corporate governance. We will deliver value to our shareholders through consistent, positive operating results and industry-leading earnings.

dispute with the automaker, eventually resolved). Soon thereafter, however, Crean shifted his focus from trailers to mobile homes. Mobile homes, currently referred to as manufactured housing, provided a more stable market for growth because of increasing demand for inexpensive housing in southern California. By 1954 the company had outgrown its greenhouse to become a thriving enterprise with three production plants.

The growth of the manufactured home market was caused by the product's moderate price. The cost of a quality manufactured home runs about one-third that of an onsite constructed home, in each case excluding land. Offsite production eliminates the use of many different contractors, construction is not affected by weather, and less time is required for construction because every component arrives at the assembly point ready to use. Manufactured homes are trucked in sections to the homesite, where they are assembled in a matter of days, instead of the normal onsite construction times that can stretch into weeks and months.

EXPANDING INTO RVS

In 1957 the company changed its name and reincorporated as Fleetwood Enterprises, Inc. Having shifted headquarters from Compton to Paramount to Anaheim during its early years, the firm found more lasting roots in Riverside, California, in 1962. During the 1950s the manufactured housing industry had split into two distinct markets. Fleetwood had its feet firmly planted in the mobile home market, and because of its healthy growth had accumulated a large cash surplus. The other market, the recreational vehicle (RV) market, Crean saw offered good opportunities. In 1964 Fleet-

wood acquired Terry Coach Industries, Inc., and Terry Coach Manufacturing, Inc., of El Monte, California. This was a time when an ever increasing number of U.S. outdoor enthusiasts wanted to travel. The company's line of travel trailers included sleeping, eating, and bathroom facilities. As the size and weight of these units grew, Fleetwood designed and built a line of fifth-wheel travel trailers, a model that is exclusively built to be towed by larger pickup trucks. As sales grew and the market expanded, the company continued to open new production plants to meet increasing sales. In 1965 Fleetwood became a public company. Its first public financial statement showed annual sales of $18.5 million.

As the RV market boomed, Fleetwood continued to diversify with the 1969 acquisition of Selgran, a motor home manufacturer based in Brea, California. Fleetwood subsequently rebranded this line under the Pace Arrow name. The acquisition was a logical extension of the company's travel trailer business. Motor homes are similar to travel trailers in construction and use. The interior looks the same as a travel trailer except that the motor home provides an area for the driver. The entire unit is constructed on a purchased truck chassis. The product line offers two types, both of which are self-contained. Type A motor homes are full-size units, with sleeping room for four to eight people and typically equipped with air conditioning, onboard power generators, and stereo systems. Type C units are smaller, built on cutaway van chassis, and usually accommodate fewer people. At a time when inexpensive gasoline and the U.S. public's wanderlust fueled the RV market, Fleetwood was marketing a diverse product line, the prices of which accommodated a wide range of buyers' budgets. The company rounded out its product line with the acquisition, for cash, of Avion Coach Corporation in 1976. Based in Benton Harbor, Michigan, Avion augmented the company's line of trailers with its expensive, luxury class models. In 1977 the company incorporated in the state of Delaware, keeping the same name.

The 1970s was a period of rapid growth and expansion for Fleetwood. As the decade ended, the revolution in Iran, skyrocketing gasoline costs, and the buying public's fear of a recession, along with rising interest rates, created an across-the-board slump in sales. Two-thirds of Fleetwood's product line were vehicles that were intended for use on U.S. highways. Gasoline shortages, which in some states resulted in day-to-day rationing, along with the spiraling costs of fuel, shook the RV market to its foundations. Many manufacturers were forced out of business as RV retailers began closing their doors and defaulting on their bank-financed inventories. The ensuing recession brought with it escalating interest

KEY DATES

1950: John C. Crean forms Coach Specialties Company, which makes window blinds for travel trailers.

1953: Crean begins making travel trailers, changes company name to Fleetwood Trailer Company, but then switches focus to manufactured housing.

1957: Company is reincorporated as Fleetwood Enterprises, Inc.

1962: Headquarters are established in Riverside, California.

1964: Fleetwood reenters the recreational vehicle (RV) market by acquiring Terry Coach Industries, Inc., and Terry Coach Manufacturing, Inc.

1965: Company goes public.

1969: Fleetwood enters the motor home market through acquisition of Selgran, which is renamed Pace Arrow.

1989: Company acquires the Coleman Company's folding trailer business.

1998: Following dispute over the company's move into mobile-home retailing, Crean retires from the company.

2001: Company weathers first of several consecutive years in the red.

2005: Elden L. Smith, the new CEO, takes Fleetwood out of mobile-home retailing.

rates, making mortgages for all types of housing and for financing RVs prohibitive. The company, for the first time since the early 1950s, found itself in a situation calling for drastic cutbacks in production and staffing.

ENCOUNTERING VARIOUS TROUBLES

The year 1980 was difficult for Fleetwood. It was forced to close nine of its production plants. The cutbacks closed three travel trailer plants, three motor home facilities, and three manufactured housing plants. Fleetwood had to consider massive worker layoffs.

Fleetwood was forced to take a close look at its entire structure during these hard times. It developed a tightly focused management policy, employing regionalized management within its housing group, which permitted the company to react more quickly to market trends. Housing design and development was spread to five areas: West Coast, central, Southeast, mid-Atlantic, and Florida. Each plant facility began operation as a separate profit center with day-to-day decisions made locally. Fleetwood slowly rode out the recession, and in 1982 Fleetwood's motor home division was projecting sales of 40,000 units in 1983.

The rapid growth and expansion Fleetwood had experienced in the 1980s had not been without legal and regulatory problems. The company is subject to provisions of the Housing and Community Development Act of 1974. These provisions, which are regulated by the U.S. Department of Housing and Urban Development (HUD), resulted in an action by the department against Fleetwood in 1985 claiming potential safety defects in 4,000 mobile homes made by the company during the years 1981 through 1984. Fleetwood was ordered to notify the owners of the mobile homes in question about possible defects in the units' walls, floors, and beams. The problems did prompt HUD to initiate an investigation into engineering techniques used by other mobile home manufacturers.

The four-year-old dispute came to a head in February 1988, resulting in a U.S. Justice Department complaint filed against Fleetwood in Wilmington, Delaware, seeking civil penalties in excess of $20 million. The complaint alleged the existence of certain standards violations in manufactured homes produced by several of Fleetwood's subsidiaries. On February 9, 1989, Fleetwood entered into a settlement agreement with HUD and the Justice Department. The settlement resulted in the dismissal of government charges against Fleetwood in exchange for a settlement payment.

Fleetwood, along with other companies in the manufactured housing industry, was the target of a class-action suit filed in Delaware in 1985. The complaint alleged that veterans who had purchased mobile homes had paid excessive prices and finance charges as a result of illegal rebates that were falsely certified to the Veterans Administration by the manufacturers. In 1990 the court certified a class of plaintiffs consisting of certain veterans who purchased mobile homes from Fleetwood dating back as far as April 1981. Two of the company's subsidiaries pleaded guilty to six counts of filing false certifications in 1987, resulting in approximately $650,000 in fines and civil settlements.

Fleetwood Credit Corporation (FCC) was established in 1986. The finance company's objective was to become the major source of both wholesale and retail financing of Fleetwood's RV products on a nationwide basis. Using $25 million of its own funds, the company hired Robert B. Baker, former head of Nissan Motor Acceptance Corporation, to head the project. FCC began operations by servicing just 12 Orange County, California, dealers. By the early 1990s the company had lending operations in southern and northern California, Oregon, Indiana, Massachusetts, Georgia, New Jersey, and Texas. Fleetwood Credit showed a net income of $2.9 million in 1990, a 56 percent increase over the previous year.

In 1989 Fleetwood acquired the Coleman Company's folding trailer business. The Coleman product line ranged in retail price from $2,000 to $10,000, and in 1989 it accounted for more than 30 percent of the folding trailer market. With the acquisition of this line, Fleetwood had products for most consumers' budgets. The company also introduced new lower-priced trailer models in response to changing market conditions. That year, revenues surpassed the $1 billion mark for the first time.

UPS AND DOWNS

The 1990s were an up-and-down period for Fleetwood as its results were affected by the economic downturn early in the decade, the mid-1990s recovery, and increasing competition in the later years of the decade. Following the difficult years of 1990 and 1991, revenues and operating income increased each year, although the growth rate for both slowed considerably by fiscal 1996 and 1997, as competitors began to eat away at Fleetwood's market share positions.

Fleetwood began the decade optimistic about the future, as evidenced by its 1990 $6.3 million purchase of a 75-acre parcel in southern California that it planned to develop as a site-built housing tract. This would have been the company's first foray into nonmanufactured housing, but after several years of preliminary work on the project, it decided in 1996 not to pursue the project. By that time the land was worth only $2.8 million, thanks to the collapse of the California real estate market.

Another attempt at expansion failed as well, when the company looked for growth outside the maturing U.S. motor home market. In September 1992 Fleetwood acquired an 80 percent interest in Niesmann & Bischoff, a Koblenz, Germany-based manufacturer of luxury-priced ($150,000 to $300,000) motor homes under the brands Clou Liner and Clou Trend. Continued weakness in the German economy, however, led to slow sales following the purchase, even after Fleetwood introduced lower-priced models. In May 1996 Fleetwood gave up on its European adventure, selling its stake in Niesmann & Bischoff and taking a $28 million charge for fiscal 1996 in the process.

May 1996 also saw another divestment, and a further focusing in on core operations, through the sale of Fleetwood Credit to Associates First Capital Corporation for $156.6 million, resulting in an after-tax gain of $33.9 million for fiscal 1997. In conjunction with the sale, Fleetwood and Associates First Capital signed a long-term operating agreement that assured financing continuity.

These divestments came at a time when Fleetwood needed to devote more attention to its domestic manufactured housing and RV units, both of which were losing ground to aggressive competitors. The company's share of the manufactured housing market reached a peak of 21.6 percent in 1994, then declined to 20.1 percent in 1995 and to 18.5 percent in 1996. On the rise was Auburn Hills, Michigan-based Champion Enterprises, Inc., which had grown rapidly in the mid-1990s through acquisitions, was undercutting Fleetwood's prices, and had attained 16.5 percent of the market by 1996. In the RV sector, Fleetwood's share of the motor home market, the most lucrative RV niche, fell from 34 percent in 1992 to 27.5 percent in 1996. Winnebago Industries, Inc., remained a fairly distant second at 16.7 percent, but Winnebago and other competitors had gained edges over Fleetwood by introducing popular space-increasing slideouts to their motor homes well before Fleetwood added them in fiscal 1996.

Like many an industry leader, Fleetwood had seemed to take its longstanding top positions for granted. The company began in 1996 and 1997 to become more customer-focused, for example by realigning its manufactured housing operations into three autonomous regional units, which brought decision-making closer to the customer level. Fiscal 1997 saw the establishment of 49 Fleetwood Home Centers, which were retail centers selling only Fleetwood homes and designed to offer improved customer service. In October 1997 the company entered into a joint venture (49 percent owned by Fleetwood) with Bloomfield Hills, Michigan-based Pulte Corporation to form Expression Homes Inc., a venture intended to establish a nationwide network of retail centers where manufactured homes would be sold and home financing and insurance would be offered. It intended to grow through acquisitions, including the purchase of some of Fleetwood's independent agents. Fleetwood saw Expression Homes as a way that its homes could be marketed in a more consistent and cohesive way.

PUSH INTO RETAILING, YEARS OF RED INK

The late 1990s were boom years for Fleetwood as the strong economy buoyed sales of both RVs and manufactured housing. Revenues climbed steadily, reaching $3.71 billion by the fiscal year ending in April 2000. Behind the scenes, however, trouble was brewing. Fleetwood's arch-rival on the manufactured housing side, Champion, had aggressively moved into retailing, by early 1998 acquiring dealers that had previously been responsible for one-quarter of Fleetwood's business. A group of executives at Fleetwood led by Glenn F. Kummer, the firm's president and chief operating officer since 1982, pushed for a major expansion into mobile-home retailing, but Crean disagreed, arguing that such a move would backfire by angering the firm's remaining independent distributors. Crean in February 1998 elected to accept a buyout of his remaining 14 percent stake in the company for $177 million and retired from the company. Kummer was named chairman and CEO, while Nelson W. Potter was promoted to president and COO.

The new leaders immediately embarked on an acquisition spree, spending some $350 million in the late 1990s acquiring manufactured housing retailers. The largest deal was the purchase of Houston-based HomeUSA, Inc., in 1998 for approximately $162 million. At the time, HomeUSA was the nation's largest independent mobile-home retailer, with annual revenues in excess of $200 million and more than 100 sales centers in Alabama, Colorado, Kentucky, Mississippi, Oklahoma, Tennessee, Texas, and Washington. Fleetwood also bought out Pulte's stake in Expression Homes. By early 2000 the company had nearly 250 retail locations.

One price of this expansion was a greatly increased debt load. The acquisitions and the buyout of Crean's stock caused debt and preferred stock obligations to skyrocket from $55 million to $367 million. At the same time, sales of manufactured housing were collapsing following a late 1990s overexpansion, and the RV industry, which had enjoyed its best year in two decades in 1999, went into a decline in 2000 as the economy began to weaken. For Fleetwood, the combination of these factors spelled red ink. In August 2000 the company reported its first quarterly net loss in 20 years, and it began aggressively restructuring. During fiscal 2001, two motor home plants and ten manufactured housing plants were shut down, and 73 of the retail centers were either sold or closed. The workforce was reduced from 20,700 to 14,000. Revenues fell 33 percent, to just $2.53 billion, while restructuring charges pushed the net loss for the year to $284 million.

As Fleetwood's losses continued, the company board responded in February 2002 by ousting both Kummer, then serving as chairman, and Potter, who had been promoted to president and CEO. Hired on as CEO in August of that year was Edward R. Caudill, who had been an executive with PACCAR Inc., a manufacturer of heavy- and medium-duty trucks. Caudill appeared to make progress on a turnaround over the next two years. While continuing to suffer from the ongoing slump in the mobile-home market, Fleetwood was buoyed by an improvement in its RV operations, particularly with the introduction of such new products as the Revolution and Excursion diesel-powered motor homes. At this time, gas prices were on the rise, sparking a rise in popularity in diesel RVs, which were quieter, more fuel efficient, and able to haul more weight than gasoline-powered models. However, a $54.7 million loss in the third quarter of fiscal 2005 prompted the board of directors to conclude that new leadership was once again needed. Caudill was ousted in March 2005 and replaced by Elden L. Smith, who had retired from Fleetwood in 1997 after nearly 30 years at the company, having served as head of the RV division from 1972 until his retirement.

Smith returned Fleetwood to its core manufacturing operations. By August 2005 he had sold substantially all of the firm's manufactured housing retail operations and its entire loan portfolio to affiliates of Clayton Homes, Inc. Operationally, surging gas prices were hurting the sales of RVs, but Fleetwood received a boost by filling large orders from the Federal Emergency Management Agency (FEMA) for travel trailers and mobile homes designated as temporary housing for Gulf Coast residents displaced by Hurricanes Katrina and Rita. The FEMA orders totaled $129 million in the third quarter of fiscal 2006, enabling Fleetwood to eke out a small net profit that quarter. Although still headed for its sixth consecutive year in the red, Fleetwood under Smith's leadership finally appeared positioned to end its prolonged slump.

William R. Grossman
Updated, David E. Salamie

PRINCIPAL SUBSIDIARIES

Fleetwood Homes of Arizona, Inc.; Fleetwood Homes of California, Inc.; Fleetwood Homes of Florida, Inc.; Fleetwood Homes of Georgia, Inc.; Fleetwood Homes of Idaho, Inc.; Fleetwood Homes of Indiana, Inc.; Fleetwood Homes of Kentucky, Inc.; Fleetwood Homes of North Carolina, Inc.; Fleetwood Homes of Oregon, Inc.; Fleetwood Homes of Pennsylvania, Inc.; Fleetwood Homes of Tennessee, Inc.; Fleetwood Homes of Texas, LP; Fleetwood Homes of Virginia, Inc.; Fleetwood Homes of Washington, Inc.; Fleetwood Motor Homes of California, Inc.; Fleetwood Motor Homes of Indiana, Inc.; Fleetwood Motor Homes of Pennsylvania, Inc.; Fleetwood Travel Trailers of California, Inc.; Fleetwood Travel Trailers of Indiana, Inc.; Fleetwood Travel Trailers of Kentucky, Inc.; Fleetwood Travel Trailers of Maryland, Inc.; Fleetwood Travel Trailers of Ohio, Inc.; Fleetwood Travel Trailers of Oregon, Inc.; Fleetwood Travel Trailers of Texas, Inc.; Fleetwood Canada Ltd.; Fleetwood Folding Trailers, Inc.; Gold Shield, Inc.; Gold Shield of Indiana, Inc.; Continental Lumber Products, Inc.; Fleetwood Housing International, Inc.; Fleetwood International, Inc.; Fleetwood Vacation Club, Inc.; Gibralter Insurance Company, Ltd. (Bermuda).

PRINCIPAL COMPETITORS

Thor Industries, Inc.; Forest River Inc.; Jayco, Inc.; Coachman Industries, Inc.; Winnebago Industries, Inc.; Monarch Coach Corporation; Clayton Homes, Inc.; Champion Enterprises, Inc.

FURTHER READING

Ashley, Bob, "Smith: Fleetwood Poised to Rebound in Wake of Katrina, Management Reorganization," *RV Business,* October 2005, pp. 7+.

Brammer, Rhonda, "Built to Last," *Barron's,* April 17, 2000, pp. 28, 30, 32.

Clifford, Mark, "Business As Usual," *Forbes,* November 18, 1985, p. 62.

Crean, John, with Jim Washburn, *The Wheel and I: My Life Driving Fleetwood Enterprises to the Top,* Newport Beach, Calif.: J.C. Crean, 2000, 436 p.

Crider, Jeff, "Fleetwood Founder, CEO Retiring After 48 Years," *Riverside (Calif.) Press-Enterprise,* January 14, 1998, p. C1.

———, "Follow the Leader: Fleetwood Is Still the Dominant Company in the Manufactured Housing and RV Industries, but Competitors Have Been Gaining," *Riverside (Calif.) Press-Enterprise,* June 8, 1997, p. G1.

Flint, Jerry, "John Crean's Recipe for Success," *Forbes,* October 25, 1993, pp. 200, 204.

"A Glimpse of Fleetwood Enterprises, Inc.," Fleetwood Enterprises corporate typescript, 1987.

Goldenberg, Sherman, "Fleetwood Stresses '92 Economy, New Quality Program," *RV Business,* October 7, 1991, pp. 1, 11.

Granelli, James S., "Fleetwood, Pulte to Form Alliance," *Los Angeles Times,* October 9, 1997, pp. D2, D6.

———, "Fleetwood's Elden Smith: The View from the Top," *RV Business,* November 1993, pp. 32–33.

McCarthy, Tom, "Fleetwood Plans More European Acquisitions, Class C Production," *RV Business,* November 1992, pp. 11, 12.

Palmeri, Christopher, "Fleetwood: Not a Happy Camper Company," *Business Week,* October 9, 2000, pp. 88, 90.

Paris, Ellen, "Keeping Its Powder Dry," *Forbes,* October 11, 1982, p. 130.

Reingold, Jennifer, "Fleetwood Enterprises: Movin' on Up," *Financial World,* October 26, 1993, p. 22.

Rescigno, Richard, "Revved Up for Recovery: Recreational-Vehicle Makers Seem Ready to Roll Again," *Barron's,* June 17, 1991, pp. 14–15, 37–39.

Shikes, Jonathan, "Fleetwood Enterprises: Retired Officer Takes Wheel at RV Maker," *Riverside (Calif.) Press-Enterprise,* May 17, 2005, p. E1.

Wadley, Jared O., "No Fleeting Fancy: As It Celebrates Its 50th Year, Fleetwood Enterprises Is at a Critical Juncture," *Riverside (Calif.) Press-Enterprise,* June 4, 2000, p. A1.

———, "Two Top Officers Leave Fleetwood," *Riverside (Calif.) Press-Enterprise,* February 12, 2002, p. A1.

Witherall, Graham, "Just a Speed Bump?," *Los Angeles Times,* August 24, 1997, p. D1.

Gildan Activewear, Inc.

725 Montée de Liesse
Montreal, Quebec H4T 1P5
Canada
Telephone: (514) 735-2023
Toll Free: (800) 668-8337
Fax: (514) 735-6810
Web site: http://www.gildan.com

Public Company
Incorporated: 1984 as Textiles Gildan, Inc.
Employees: 12,000
Sales: $653.9 million (2005)
Stock Exchanges: New York Toronto
Ticker Symbols: GIL
NAIC: 422310 Piece Goods, Notions, and Other Dry
    Goods Wholesalers; 315223 Men's & Boys' Cut
    and Sew Shirt (Except Work Shirt) Manufacturing;
    315224 Men's & Boys' Cut and Sew Trouser, Slack,
    and Jean Manufacturing

■ ■ ■

Millions of fashionistas wear Gildan Activewear but probably do not know it. Gildan Activewear, Inc., is a quiet giant in the retail industry, its products sold by the dozen, wholesale, to companies who put their own logos and designs on them. Gildan's "blank" cotton shirts, primarily T-shirts, as well as fleece items, henleys, and polos, are a staple of the worldwide casualwear industry. Rivals Fruit of the Loom (owned by Berkshire Hathaway) and Hanes (owned by Sara Lee Corp.) once held sway in the market, but Gildan overtook them to become the largest T-shirt manufacturer on the continent. Gildan was founded by Greg and Glen Chamandy. Elder brother Greg left the company in 2004 to pursue other interests while Glenn Chamandy continues to run the firm as president and chief executive.

A NEW BEGINNING

The immediate precursor to Gildan Activewear, Textiles Gildan, Inc., was formed in 1984 by brothers H. Greg and Glenn Chamandy. Textiles Gildan was a refashioning of the Chamandy family business, originally founded by the boys' grandfather Joseph decades before as a manufacturer of children's casualwear. With the advent of NAFTA (North American Free Trade Agreement), however, the young Chamandys reoriented the family business, doing away with middlemen and concentrating on two stalwarts of the garment trade: plain T-shirts and sweatshirts. Cost was of paramount importance so the brothers outsourced sewing to Central American factories and kept the quality-control end of the business—knitting, dyeing, and finishing—at their home base in Montreal. Most of the former company's equipment was sold to make way for high-tech knitting and dyeing machinery. Garments were sold wholesale, beginning in 1992, in mass quantities and shipped to North American clients via UPS.

In the early 1990s Textiles Gildan had gained a reputation for high-quality, low-cost pullovers and slowly chipped away at the market share of such U.S. undergarment manufacturers as Kentucky-based Fruit of the Loom (FTL) and North Carolina's Hanes. Textiles Gildan's first full year of production in 1994 brought in

COMPANY PERSPECTIVES

Gildan is a vertically-integrated marketer and manufacturer of premium quality branded basic apparel. The Company manufactures premium quality basic T-shirts, sport shirts, and sweatshirts for sale in the wholesale imprinted sportswear market of the U.S., Canadian, European, and other international markets. The Company sells its products as blanks, which are ultimately decorated by screenprinters with designs and logos for sale to consumers. Gildan has announced plans to sell its products into the mass-market retail channel, in addition to the screenprint market. In conjunction with this strategy, Gildan is expanding its product-line to include underwear and athletic socks.

sales of over $32 million. The following year, the company was renamed Gildan Activewear, Inc., and expanded its product line to include golf-styled collar shirts in several colors. Fruit of the Loom and Hanes, both losing market share, cut prices and fought back against the Canadian upstart with major advertising campaigns.

As the decade came to a close Gildan had become a force to be reckoned with; the company had reached sales of just over $144 million for 1998 and controlled 10 percent of the market, a healthy slice in an industry notorious for slight profit margins and frequent flameouts. The firm had added new products to its clothing line, including henleys and tank tops, and also invested in environmentally friendly dyeing and bleaching systems. New machinery and chemicals went into use, earning Gildan the respect of environmental groups in both Canada and the United States.

The Chamandy brothers, with Greg as chairman and chief executive and Glenn as president and chief operating officer, took Gildan public on the Toronto Stock Exchange (under the ticker symbol GIL) in June 1998, in preparation for entering the New York Stock Exchange (NYSE) the following year. In 1999, as Gildan achieved inclusion at the NYSE and geared up for international expansion, rival garment manufacturer Fruit of the Loom faced bankruptcy, as did several other sportswear and T-shirt firms. Oneita Industries, based in South Carolina, filed for bankruptcy protection in 1998 and shuttered its doors for good in 1999 after 125 years of operation, while two Virginia-based T-shirt and fleece manufacturers, Tultex Corporation and Pluma, Inc., filed for bankruptcy in 1999 around the same time as

Fruit of the Loom. Gildan, however, had wrested market share away from all of them for about 15 percent of the cotton T-shirt market. Sales soared accordingly to $223.9 million for 1999 (ending in October), with net earnings of $32.8 million.

THE NEW MILLENNIUM: 2000–2002

As the new century got underway, Gildan continued to experience record growth due to its tight cost controls and vertically integrated structure. Sewing, previously outsourced, was now completed in company facilities, as was all knitting, dyeing, cutting, and finishing. Up until 2000 Gildan had sold its products only in Canada and the United States, but the Chamandys decided it was time to expand outside North America. The company also debuted a web site for clients, gildanfinder.com, to easily view products, as it established a network of more than 20 distributors in Western Europe. Product-wise, a new 50-50 T-shirt (50 percent traditional cotton, 50 percent polyester) was selling exceptionally well and additional 50-50 products were in the works. At the close of the fiscal year sales topped $312.4 million, net earnings reached $56.3 million, and Gildan Activewear was ranked the United States' second-largest cotton T-shirt wholesaler behind Hanes.

As Gildan began shipping products to Europe and announced a partnership with a Japanese corporation to sell its casualwear in Asia, struggling Fruit of the Loom filed a lawsuit claiming corporate espionage. Fruit of the Loom alleged a former employee, who was hired at Gildan, engaged in "unfair competition" through trade secrets and "stolen" FTL documents. Though Gildan did possess at least one document, sent by an FTL employee to Gildan's executive vice-president, David Cherry (a former FTL employee), most deemed the information less than valuable. Regardless of the legal skirmish, Gildan's first quarter (ending in January) results were phenomenal, with sales quadrupling the previous fiscal year's figure. Stock prices responded as well, climbing 27 cents per share, up from 6 cents per share for the same period in 2000. Year-end sales rose to $329.1 million for 2001, as market share had risen to almost a third of the cotton T-shirt and pullover market to tie Gildan with market leader Hanes. Gildan had also been helped by the effects of 2000's Trade Enhancement Act, which eliminated duty charges on goods from its Caribbean Basin and Central American facilities, similar to the benefits of NAFTA for Mexico.

In 2002 Gildan continued its upward swing and even attempted a takeover of ailing rival Fruit of the Loom. In the end, FTL was acquired by Omaha-based Berkshire Hathaway, Inc., run by legendary stock-picker

KEY DATES

1984: Textiles Gildan, Inc., is founded by the Chamandy brothers.
1995: The company is renamed Gildan Activewear.
1998: Gildan begins trading on the Toronto Stock Exchange.
1999: Gildan begins trading on the New York Stock Exchange.
2001: The company begins selling outside North America.
2004: Cofounder Greg Chamandy leaves the company to pursue other business interests.
2005: Gildan begins selling its own branded shirts.
2006: Gildan buys Kentucky Derby Hosiery Company and starts selling socks.

Warren Buffett. While the takeover and FTL lawsuit (settled quietly in October 2001 without disclosure) did affect Gildan's bottom line, it was not significantly damaging. Year-end figures for fiscal 2001 climbed to $382.3 million with net earnings of over $66.7 million. Increased capacity had helped spur sales; the company enjoyed new manufacturing and distribution plants in North Carolina and an expanding presence in Honduras and Mexico.

LEADING THE INDUSTRY, 2003 AND BEYOND

In early 2003 Gildan opened a newly acquired manufacturing plant with state-of-the-art machinery in its home base of Montreal. The company reportedly spent some $20 million to buy and refurbish the 180,000-square-foot Henri-Bourassa facility, which created 150 new jobs. CEO Greg Chamandy commented to *Wearables Business* (April 2003), "The inauguration of this plant reflects our continued commitment to our business strategy of vertical integration [and] to continue to fulfill our business goal of being the global low-cost producer of apparel for the North American activewear market."

Near the end of 2003 Gildan acquired part-ownership of a yarn spinning plant in Cedartown, Georgia. By this time Gildan operated seven sewing facilities, with three in Honduras, two in Mexico, and one each in Nicaragua and Haiti; two dyeing and finishing facilities in Quebec; three yarn spinning facilities (two in Canada, the one in Georgia); three distribution centers (one in Quebec, two in North Carolina); a cut-

ting plant in New York; and a high-tech integrated textile plant—Gildan's largest at 291,500 square feet—for knitting, dyeing, cutting, and finishing in Rio Nance, Honduras. For fiscal 2003 sales had skyrocketed to $431.2 million and net earnings reached $81.5 million.

At the start of the new fiscal year, in November, Gildan began offering its products in Australia and planned additional Caribbean manufacturing facilities, buying an 18 million-square-foot land tract in the Dominican Republic. In addition, the company's European expansion gained momentum with a total of 37 distributors in 19 countries by January 2004. In mid-2004 Gildan reached an important milestone as the first manufacturer in the wholesale imprinted activewear industry to obtain "Oeko-Tex Standard 100" certification bestowed by Germany's International Textile Research Centre at the Hohenstein Institute and Austria's Textile Research Institute. Gildan was immensely proud of the eco-designation and the company's commitment to environmental awareness.

In August 2004 cofounder Greg Chamandy left Gildan and sold his stake in the company to pursue other business ventures. Younger brother Glenn took the helm of the booming company, which had shipped 27 million dozen T-shirts in 2004, a figure Chamandy believed would more than double within five years. Sales for 2004 reached $533.4 million and net earnings hit $60.3 million, with Gildan topping both Fruit of the Loom and Hanes as North America's largest T-shirt manufacturer. Share prices went from a low on the NYSE of $13.83 per share in October 2004 to a high of $39.13 in September the following year.

In 2005 Gildan, famous for its cost-cutting, was at it again. The company closed two of its Canadian yarn-spinning plants, transferring production to its North Carolina facilities, and took a leap of faith by beginning to sell its own branded activewear, following the lead of competitors Fruit of the Loom and Hanes. Another segue came in early 2006 with the purchase of the Hopkinsville-based Kentucky Derby Hosiery Company for $45 million. Hosiery production was slated to begin in Gildan's high-tech Honduran manufacturing plants; however, the destruction of its sewing facility in San Marcos, Nicaragua, complicated matters. The Nicaraguan plant burned to the ground in June 2006 and most of its operations were sent to nearby Gildan plants or outsourced. Despite the loss of the plant, Gildan continued to soar, besting its own outlook as well as that of industry pundits.

Gildan Activewear, darling of the stock markets, continued to shine in 2006. The little Canadian firm not only came and conquered, but showed American rivals that famous name advertising was not nearly as effective as vertical integration and cost control. Gildan shares traded in the upper $40s for much of 2006; analysts believed prices would top $50 before the end of the year with sales projected to reach at least $700 million, after hitting $653.9 million for 2005.

Nelson Rhodes

PRINCIPAL SUBSIDIARIES

Gildan Activewear SRL; Gildan Activewear Properties (BVI) Inc.; Gildan Activewear San José, S.A.; Gildan Activewear San Miguel, S.A.; Gildan Activewear San Antonio, S.A.; Gildan Activewear Villanueva, S.A.; Gildan Activewear (Clercine), S.A.; Gildan Activewear (San Marcos), S.A.; Gildan Activewear (Rivas), S.A.; Gildan Activewear Castaños, S. de R.L. de C.V.; Gildan Activewear Mexico, S.A. de C.V.; Gildan Activewear Malone, Inc.; Gildan Activewear Honduras Textiles Company, S.A.; Gildan Activewear (UK) Limited; Gildan Choloma Textiles, S.A.; Gildan Honduras Hosiery Factory, S.A.; Gildan Activewear (Eden) Inc.; Gildan Activewear (US Holdings) Inc.; Gildan Activewear Dominican Republic Textile Company Inc.; Gildan Activewear Properties (Dominican Republic) Inc.

PRINCIPAL COMPETITORS

Fruit of the Loom; Hanes Companies, Inc.; Jockey International, Inc.; Russell Corporation; VF Corporation.

FURTHER READING

Burrows, Dan, "Growth in Sales, Cost Reductions Raise Gildan Net," *WWD*, August 11, 2003, p. 17.

Clark, Evan, "Gildan Net Surges in the Fourth Quarter," *WWD*, December 29, 2000, p. 12.

Copple, Brandon, "A Stretch," *Forbes*, May 14, 2001, p. 53.

"Cotton Tee Maker Raises Forecast," *Toronto Star*, June 21, 2006, p. E05.

Dunn, Brian, "Gildan CEO Upbeat on Growth of Company," *WWD*, February 10, 2003, p. 19.

———, "Gildan to Begin Branding Own Apparel," *WWD*, September 29, 2005, p. 31.

———, "Gildan to Expand in Europe," *WWD*, February 12, 2001, p. 27.

———, "Underwear and Socks Cash Cows for Gildan," *WWD*, February 6, 2006, p. 50.

"Gildan Activewear," *Investor's Business Daily*, August 16, 2000, p. A12.

"Gildan Activewear Buys Rival," *Daily Deal*, June 28, 2002.

"Gildan Activewear CEO Seeks Opportunities to Sell T-Shirts in China," *Toronto Star*, December 3, 2004, p. F04.

"Gildan Posts Record Profit, Cofounder Leaves Company," *Toronto Star*, August 5, 2004, p. C04.

Kirby, Jason, "From S to XXXL," *Canadian Business*, December 25, 2000, p. 100.

Linecker, Adelia Cellini, "Gildan Activewear," *Investor's Business Daily*, September 9, 2002, p. A11.

Manor, Robert, "Fruit of the Loom Worker Admits to Sharing Trade Secrets with Competitor," *Chicago Tribune/Knight Ridder Tribune News Service*, April 8, 2001.

McCormack, Scott, "Stick to Your Knitting," *Forbes*, December 28, 1998, p. 82.

Much, Marilyn, "T-Shirt Maker H. Greg Chamandy," *Investor's Business Daily*, May 2, 2001, p. A03.

"Oneita Industries Closes Its Doors After 125 Years in Business," *The Press*, June 1999, p. 10.

"Pluma Ceases Operations," *Wearables Business*, October 1999, p. 8.

Ryan, Thomas J., "Gildan's 71.9-Percent Sales Jump Sets Record First Period Net," *WWD*, February 14, 2000, p. 25.

Tucker, Ross, "Gildan Net Rises 20.1 Percent, H. Greg Chamandy Exits Firm," *WWD*, August 6, 2004, p. 13.

Uhland, Vicki, and Jeff Rundles, "Retooling the T-Shirt," *Wearables Business*, April 2000, p. 51.

"Undergarment Maker Files Suit," *Long Island Business News*, April 13, 2002, p. 6B.

Young, Vicki M., "Tultex Closes Virginia Manufacturing Facility," *Daily News Record*, January 12, 2000, p. 32.

GPS Industries, Inc.

5500 152nd Street, Suite 214
Surrey, British Columbia V3S 5J9
Canada
Telephone: (604) 576-7442
Toll Free: (888) 667-3477
Fax: (604) 576-7460
Web site: http://www.gpsindustries.com

Public Company
Incorporated: 1995 as Diversified Marketing Services, Inc.
Employees: 41
Sales: $5.81 million (2005)
Stock Exchanges: NASDAQ OTC BB
Ticker Symbol: GPSN
NAIC: 511210 Software Publishers

■ ■ ■

GPS Industries, Inc. develops and markets Global Positioning Satellite (GPS) and Wi-Fi wireless multimedia products, selling its products to golf facilities worldwide. The technology is incorporated into the company's Inforemer suite of devices, which provides detailed course maps, distance measurements, food and beverage ordering capabilities, and a wealth of other features available via a cart-mounted or handheld liquid crystal display (LCD) screen. For golf course managers, the Inforemer system helps improve the efficiency of operations by tracking each player's location and identifying pace-of-play problems. GPS Industries sells its products on a worldwide basis through distribution agreements with third-party vendors. The typical deployment of a wireless network and central computer system with management software costs between $100,000 and $250,000, requiring a monthly leasing fee of between $1,500 and $5,000.

ORIGINS

A pioneer in the commercial application of GPS technology, GPS Industries owes its existence to research conducted under the aegis of the U.S. Department of Defense. The use of satellite navigation systems began with the Transit system in 1965, which was comprised of six satellites that were used to provide navigational aid to submarines carrying Polaris nuclear missiles. By analyzing radio signals transmitted by the satellites, which circled the earth continuously in polar orbits, a submarine could determine its location within 10 to 15 minutes. The deployment of the Transit system marked a major breakthrough in navigation science, but military officials soon demanded greater accuracy. GPS, a concept hatched during a brainstorming session at the Pentagon over the Labor Day weekend in 1973, became the solution. Scientists at the meeting determined that the deployment of 24 satellites, each orbiting the earth every 12 hours in a particular formation, would ensure that every point on earth always would be in radio contact with at least four satellites. The discovery led to the first launch of a Navstar satellite in 1978. In 1993, the system reached 24-satellite capability, offering pinpoint accuracy for every location on earth.

GPS Industries was founded not long after the Navstar system became fully operational, becoming one of the early adopters of GPS technology for non-military uses. Technically, the company traces its origins to a Nevada corporation named Diversified Marketing Services, Inc., but the only vestige of the company's relationship with Diversified Marketing is its incorporation date of December 1995. Diversified Marketing was formed for entirely different purposes than to develop GPS-based products for the commercial market. The company was created to develop third-party motor vehicle title and registration offices in California and neighboring states, but, as a development-stage company, it never fulfilled its original mission. In 1999, a reverse merger turned Diversified Marketing into a completely different company with a new name. Diversified Marketing acquired a Canadian corporation named Inforetech Golf Technology 2000 Inc., which had been formed one year earlier by Robert C. Silzer, Sr. Following the reverse merger, Silzer took control of the combined company, which changed its name to Inforetech Wireless Technology, Inc., the direct predecessor to GPS Industries.

Silzer intended to develop the first portable device to incorporate GPS technology for the golf market, a use presumably not envisioned by the developers of Navstar but one Silzer believed would find a receptive audience among the more than 50 million golfers worldwide. Described as a seasoned businessman with numerous entrepreneurial successes to his credit, Silzer was preparing to enter a nascent and promising market as he plotted his course from Inforetech's Vancouver, British Columbia, headquarters. To the south, a handful of companies were developing GPS-based golf management systems, each vying to take the lead in the market. U.S. competitors included Newport Beach, California-based ProShot Golf, Inc.; Sarasota, Florida-based Par-View, Inc.; Dallas, Texas-based PinMark Corporation; Charlestown, Massachusetts-based Player Systems Corporation; Chandler, Arizona-based ProLink, Inc.; and UpLink Corp. based in Austin, Texas. Each of the companies had been formed between 1994 and 1998, offering or in the process of offering GPS-based golf

devices that were mounted on a golf cart. Although Silzer would not shy away from cart-mounted systems, he was endeavoring to make Inforetech the first company to market a portable GPS-based golf handset.

In the months following the reverse merger that gave birth to Inforetech, the company operated as a development-stage company. Hopes for entry into the golf market were pinned to the Inforemer 2000, a system designed to collect data from GPS satellites and transfer the data between a central computer and a number of peripheral components, including a base station, a repeater, mobile handsets, and carrying cradles. Silzer planned to install the Inforemer 2000 in three or four North American golf courses by the fall of 2000, using the installations to fine tune and balance the various components of the system before commencing commercial distribution at the end of 2000. A fine-tuned, market-ready Inforemer 2000 promised to serve as a valuable tool for both golfers and the operators of golf courses. For the players, the company's handheld devices were capable of providing a wealth of pertinent information via an LCD screen, including instant drive measurements from the tee, distance measurements to the flagstick, hazards, and landmarks, and a layout of each hole from maps created from digitized, image-enhanced aerial photographs. Equipped with a fully portable Inforemer 2000, a golfer could enjoy a level of familiarity with a particular course similar to that of a course regular. For golf course operators, the Inforemer 2000 offered numerous benefits, perhaps none more important than the ability of GPS technology to address pace-of-play issues. A major concern of golf course managers, pace-of-play directly influenced the revenue and profit potential of a golf property, reducing both financial figures if one or more slow foursomes created a bottleneck. Golf course managers traditionally relied on course marshals to keep players moving at an appropriate pace, but it was not always immediately apparent where a bottleneck existed. The Inforemer 2000 pinpointed the problem, offering far greater control over pace-of-play, giving course operators the exact location of each golfer.

Although Inforetech was not the first company to apply GPS technology to the golf market, it became recognized as the leader of the industry during the first years of the 21st century. A crucial step towards market dominance was taken in mid-January 2001, when the company chose the most expedient route towards gaining a lead over its competitors. Inforetech bought one of its rivals, acquiring ProShot Golf, Inc. Founded in 1995, ProShot spent $25 million on research and development, engineering, manufacturing, and testing to develop its GPS-based distance and information system, the ProShot Golf System, which had been installed at more

KEY DATES

1995: Diversified Marketing Services, Inc., is incorporated.

1999: Inforetech Golf Technology 2000 Inc., formed the previous year, merges with Diversified Marketing Services, creating Inforetech Wireless Technology, Inc.

2001: Inforetech unveils the Informer 2000, the first GPS handset for the golf market.

2002: Inforetech signs an endorsement agreement with golfer Greg Norman.

2003: Inforetech changes its name to GPS Industries, Inc.

2006: "Inforezone" is introduced, enabling golf courses to become Wireless Internet Service Providers.

than 145 golf courses worldwide at the time of the company's acquisition. The company formed two strategic alliances to aid in the development and to enhance the features of its system, forging its first partnership with Trimble Navigation, the leading GPS hardware company, and Toro Company, the authority in turf care products and irrigation. The company also completed an acquisition itself, purchasing PinMark Corp. in 1999. With PinMark's expertise, ProShot was able to improve its graphics capabilities and provide a platform for color graphics, technology that Inforetech inherited by purchasing ProShot. ProShot, once under Inforetech's control, became a subsidiary named Proshot Golf Network, joining the Silzer-led organization just before it celebrated the first major milestone in its development.

COMMERCIAL DISTRIBUTION BEGINNING IN 2001

At the end of January, two weeks after acquiring ProShot, Inforetech unveiled its flagship product. The Inforetech 2000 made its debut at the PGA (Professional Golfers' Association) Merchandise Trade Show in Orlando, Florida. Attendees were introduced to the advent of a new age, one offering golfers high-resolution screens that provided a full course overview, topography of each green, distance measurements to the pin, green side bunkers, and water hazards. Club owners and course managers focused on the back-end system powering the Informer 2000, which allowed them to monitor course traffic, to communicate instantly with each player, and

to use the handset as a platform for establishing an on-course, e-commerce side to their business. Golfers equipped with one of Inforetech's handheld or cart-mounted devices could order food and beverages, purchase merchandise from the club's shop, or receive advertisements. Orders soon followed, including an agreement for six installations at golf courses in Iowa, Colorado, Nevada, and California, each signed to five-year leases guaranteeing $1.2 million in revenue during the duration of the lease. No longer a development-stage company, Inforetech was beginning to flourish commercially, enjoying a promising start to a decade that would see the advancement of technology add substantially to the capabilities of GPS-based devices on the golf course.

"After years of development and thousands of test rounds, we have finally got the technology to work exactly as it's supposed to," Silzer declared in a September 9, 2002, interview with *Internet Wire*. As the company made the transition from installing its systems on an experimental basis to deploying them commercially, it forged an important partnership to aid in the promotion of its technology. In mid-2002, Inforetech signed an endorsement agreement with Greg Norman, a World Golf Hall of Fame member and winner of 86 international titles. The company paid for the exclusive rights to use Norman's name, voice, and likeness to promote its family of GPS-based products. With a golfing celebrity at its side (Norman also took a seat on the company's board of directors), Inforetech began courting golfers and course managers in earnest, promoting its technology not only to the more than 18,000 golf courses in North America but to the more than 37,000 golf courses worldwide. In the fall of 2002, the company began trading on the Berlin-Bremen Stock Exchange, a move taken to support its advances in Europe. "Having an additional public market and an operating presence in Europe are key steps in our establishing an active international GPS-based golf device business," Silzer explained in an October 4, 2002, interview with *PrimeZone Media Network*.

INTERNATIONAL EXPANSION BUOYING HOPES FOR THE FUTURE

As Silzer sought to spread his company's presence throughout the world, he decided to do so under a different corporate banner. Inforetech changed its name to GPS Industries, Inc., in September 2003 to reflect its broader market focus and the additional market opportunities available to it. "Our company is unique in that we have a core technology which can be leveraged to deliver a wide range of business-critical, location-based applications to many vertical markets," Silzer said in an October 3, 2003, interview with the *America's Intelligence Wire*. The company was recording encouraging progress in expanding into new markets, becoming a truly global company. In mid-2003, the company signed a distribution agreement with Asian GPS Golf Ltd. that provided entry into mainland China, Hong Kong, and Macau, paving the way for installations at a minimum of 32 courses by 2008. In 2004, the company established a presence in Australia with installations at two of the country's leading golf courses, Brookwater and Noosa Springs, which led to a distribution agreement with GPS Golf Vision before the end of the year for sales in Australia, New Zealand, and the North and South Pacific Islands. In 2005, GPS Industries completed installations in France for the first time, establishing a presence in continental Europe's second largest golf market through a distributor named GEPSCO.

Against the backdrop of the company's global expansion, an arguably more profound type of expansion was taking place. Beginning in 2003, the company incorporated its devices into a Wi-Fi network that covered an entire golf course, clubhouse, and resort environs. The melding of the company's GPS-based technology with Wi-Fi created the broader market focus that, in part, inspired the adoption of a new corporate title. "Our core was this GPS product," a company executive explained in a January 27, 2005, interview with *Wireless Business Forecast*, "but what happened is that the infrastructure we put in the golf course has opened up new possibilities." Residential communities, sports venues, and other locations offered settings suitable for the company's technology, creating a wealth of business opportunities for the future.

For the company's mainstay golf market, the expansion of capabilities found expression in "Inforezone," introduced by GPS Industries in early 2006. Inforezone enabled any golf course operator to become a Wireless Internet Service Provider, or WISP, offering golf courses the ability to generate revenue from access fees to their own Wi-Fi "hotspot." GPS Industries' comprehensive Inforezone program included network design and deployment, Web-site hosting, network monitoring, access rate plans, technical support, and payment processing, representing an evolutionary step from the type of services offered at the beginning of the decade. In the years ahead, as GPS Industries strove to maintain its market lead, technological advancements promised to increase the company's importance to golf course operators. Exploiting such opportunity and turning it into consistent profits became the company's primary

focus, as Silzer endeavored to remain on the technological vanguard during his company's second decade of business.

Jeffrey L. Covell

PRINCIPAL SUBSIDIARIES

Inforetech Golf Technology 2000 Inc.

PRINCIPAL COMPETITORS

UpLink Corporation; ProLink/Parview, LLC; Player Systems Corporation.

FURTHER READING

"Completes Acquisition of ProShot Golf to Become the Leader in GPS Golf," *Market News Publishing*, May 21, 2001.

"From Cool Gadget to Wireless Windfall," *Wireless Business Forecast*, January 27, 2005.

"Golfer Greg Norman Signs Endorsement Agreement with Inforetech," *Wireless News*, May 7, 2002.

"GPS Industries Announces Turn-Key Wireless Internet Service Provider Program," *Internet Wire*, April 19, 2006.

"GPS Industries Gets N.A. Global Positioning Patents for Next-Generation Golf Course Apps.," *Wireless News*, November 29, 2004.

"GPS Industries Lands Two French Golf Resorts," *Wireless News*, February 16, 2005.

"Handheld GPS Display Unit for Golfers Gaining Momentum in Media," *Internet Wire*, September 9, 2002.

"Inforetech CEO Outlines Progress As Company Enters Peak Golf Season," *Internet Wire*, May 29, 2003.

"Inforetech Wireless and Asian GPS Golf Reach Significant $6.1 Million Distribution Agreement," *Internet Wire*, May 27, 2003.

"Inforetech Wireless Makes Professional Debut," *Internet Wire*, April 30, 2003.

"Inforetech Wireless Technology Inc.," *Market News Publishing*, July 10, 2001.

"Inforetech Wireless Technology Inc. Begins Trading on the Berlin Stock Exchange," *PrimeZone Media Network*, October 4, 2002.

"Inforetech's Informer 2000 on Par to Change the Way Golfers Navigate on Courses," *Market News Publishing*, June 8, 2001.

"Introduces First Portable Global Positioning System Golf Handset to the World," *Market News Publishing*, June 8, 2001.

"Wireless Channel: GPS Industries Extends Reach into Australia and New Zealand," *Wireless News*, September 30, 2004.

Helix Energy Solutions Group, Inc.

---

400 N. Sam Houston Parkway East
Suite 400
Houston, Texas 77060-3500
U.S.A.
Telephone: (281) 618-0400
Fax: (281) 618-0501
Web site: http://www.helixesg.com

Public Company
Founded: 1965 as California Divers, Inc.
Employees: 1,800
Sales: $799.5 million (2005)
Stock Exchanges: NASDAQ
Ticker Symbol: HELX
NAIC: 213112 Support Activities for Oil and Gas Operations

■ ■ ■

Helix Energy Solutions Group, Inc., is a Houston-based marine energy services company that also is involved in oil and gas production. Although the company mostly operates in the Gulf of Mexico, it also maintains offices in Europe and Southeast Asia. Helix, formerly known as Cal Dive International, has its roots in underwater construction and repair work for offshore drilling units. It provides a host of marine contracting services, including deepwater work, as deep as 10,000 feet below the surface. Using a fleet of 33 vessels, 29 remotely operated vehicles, and trencher systems, Helix helps in construction, supports drilling and well completion, helps companies spur well production, and assists in the decommissioning of deepwater projects. The company also is involved in oil and gas production through subsidiary Energy Resource Technology, Inc., which leases mature properties in the Gulf of Mexico and uses Helix's vessels and expertise to squeeze out remaining, hard-to-reach reserves of oil and gas. This combination of contracting and production keep the assets of Helix utilized as much as possible, while providing a measure of diversity. During cycles of high demand, vessels are contracted out, and during slack periods the fleet turns its attention to company production projects. Helix is a public company listed on the NASDAQ.

POST-WORLD WAR II ROOTS

Helix was founded in southern California, very much a part of the convergence between offshore oil production and the ragtag diving industry. After World War II offshore oil production emerged in the waters of southern California around Santa Barbara, at first from piers and gradually moving away from the shore. Wells were drilled from man-made islands, then barges, and finally from jack-up rigs. In the late 1950s, as production companies moved to exploit oilfields in deeper water using floating barges (the shore quickly dropped off to 250 feet below the surface), they needed divers to replace broken or worn-out drill bits. In northern California a diving industry, started by Japanese divers, had already been established to gather abalone, a gourmet mollusk. From the ranks of abalone divers came the founders of Cal Dive: Lad Handelman, along with his brother Gene, Bob Ratcliffe, and Kevin Lengyel. At first, they were on the outside looking in with envy at a close-knit group of Santa Barbara divers, Associate Divers, who in the late

1950s controlled all drilling work below 200 feet. Unionized, they were able to make as much as $100,000 a year, an amount that proved tempting to men scrambling to make a living in the dangerous world of abalone diving.

Lad Handelman's first venture was General Offshore Divers Inc., which made its mark by pioneering mixed gas diving. Commercial diving to that point relied on tanks of regular air, which only allowed divers to remain in deep water for short periods of time due to the effects of increased air pressure and nitrogen narcosis. General Offshore refined the U.S. Navy's concept of mixing oxygen and helium to develop a new oxy-helium mix that permitted extended time on the bottom while allowing divers to remain clearheaded. As a result, a project that might require 40 dives could be completed in just ten, an advantage that established General Offshore as a player to be reckoned with in the California diving industry. In the meantime, the top Associate divers struck out on their own, forming more diving businesses, and other companies also were formed to take advantage of the oil companies' need for divers.

In the early 1960s many of the diving companies were snapped up by large corporations. General Offshore was acquired in 1964 by Union Carbide and renamed Ocean Systems. Lad Handelman and his three comrades proved too individualistic for corporate ownership and soon quit and returned to the abalone patch. The money to be made in offshore oil lured them back, however, and in 1965 the four men chipped in $5,000 apiece to form California Divers, Inc. Handelman served as president and salesman but more than a year would pass before the ragtag company won its first contract from Humble Oil. Prior to that an opportunity arose in Canada, leading to Handelman forming Can Dive with a construction diver in Vancouver.

Cal Dive was getting its share of work in California in the late 1960s when the state's oil industry was rocked by a much-publicized oil spill that led in 1969 to a halt in drilling activities. Cal Dive's existence was in jeopardy and it entertained an acquisition offer from a large company, Santa Fe International, whose resources would allow Cal Dive to compete in other markets around the world. Fearful of revisiting their experience with Union Carbide, Handelman and his partners elected instead to raise venture capital and combine Cal Dive and Can Dive into a new company called Oceaneering International.

Oceaneering became the dominant force in its field in 1971 when it acquired Divcon, the global leader in diving activities at the time and five times larger than Oceaneering. Divcon had been losing money and its corporate parent, Intentional Utilities Inc., was looking to divest the subsidiary. Oceaneering beat out the next largest diving company, Comex, to acquire Divcon, a classic case of the minnow swallowing the whale, and became the industry giant.

FORMATION OF CAL DIVE INTERNATIONAL IN 1980

While Oceaneering was operating on a world stage, the Cal Dive unit switched its focus from California's shuttered offshore oilfields to Houston, Texas, where it could work in the Gulf of Mexico, the offshore fields of which were experiencing a boom period. Several years later Cal Dive again broke free from corporate ownership. In the late 1970s there was another major oil price collapse, leading the venture capitalists that controlled Oceaneering to attempt to sell the business, a move that Handelman and his associates very much opposed. As a result, he took the Cal Dive unit independent, in 1980 forming Cal Dive International, Inc., an oil services contracting company that specialized in underwater installations, repair, and maintenance services. In addition to its Gulf of Mexico operations, Cal Dive maintained offices on the West Coast as well as Singapore.

With Handelman serving as chief executive and chairman, Cal Dive was generating annual revenues in the $10 million range, but it lacked the financial resources to grow and in 1983 the company was purchased for $6.9 million by Diversified Energies, Inc. (DEI), a Minneapolis-based utility company that in the early 1980s became involved in oil and gas exploration joint ventures and decided to enter the services field. With DEI's backing, Cal Dive branched out beyond human divers to include saturation diving ships. In 1983 the company designed and converted its first vessel, named the *Cal Diver I,* put into service in the Gulf of Mexico in 1984. Two years later the company began offering turnkey contracting in the Gulf, a fixed price to provide customers with a range of subsea construction work. By this time, however, the oil and gas industry was in the throes of a major slump, one that would put a host of companies out of business. To make matters worse for Cal Dive, Handelman broke his neck in 1985

KEY DATES

1965: The company is founded as California Divers, Inc.

1969: Cal Dive is merged with Can Dive to form Oceaneering International.

1980: The company breaks away from Oceaneering as Cal Dive International.

1983: Diversified Energies, Inc. acquires the company.

1990: Management leads a buyout effort.

1992: Energy Resource Technology is formed as a production arm.

1997: Cal Dive is taken public.

2006: The name is changed to Helix Energy Solutions Group.

while snow skiing. Although he would continue to head Cal Dive until 1990, his attention was turning to other endeavors. In Santa Barbara he founded a support organization for people left in wheelchairs following spinal injuries. After he retired from Cal Dive Handelman moved back to Santa Barbara where he cofounded the Marine Mammal Consulting Group to help offshore industries comply with environmental regulations.

In the mid-1980s Cal Dive was forced to retrench, closing its West Coast and Singapore offices, and cutting headcount in half throughout the company. Cal Dive continued to lose money until the beginning of 1989. It would go independent once again, as its new management team, led by Gerald G. Reuhl, bought Cal Dive in 1990 with the financial backing of Connecticut investment banking firm First Reserve Corp. Reuhl joined the company as a diver in 1975 and when Cal Dive broke away from Oceaneering in 1980, he held a series of management positions with both the domestic and international divisions. In 1986 he was put in charge of the Domestic Diving Division, and two years later replaced Handelman as CEO. He became chairman and CEO, and a 19 percent owner, of Cal Dive. His chief lieutenant and chief operating officer was Owen E. Kratz, who had worked as a diver in the North Sea and as a supervisor for a number of international diving companies, and for a spell ran his own marine construction business before joining Cal Dive in 1984.

On its own once again, Cal Dive in the early 1990s was mostly involved in intervention work, making sure well bores were kept free of debris, and as an abandonment contractor, helping companies to shut down

offshore wells by capping them and dismantling the rigs. "During this time, we started noticing that we were shutting-in a lot of reserves," Kratz told *Offshore* in a 2006 interview. Recognizing an opportunity, in 1992 Cal Dive formed Energy Resource Technology to gain interest in mature shallow-water fields. "Through this new venture," Kratz explained, "we used our inherent abandonment liability as currency to acquire our first field." This was the start of the present-day Helix business model, using the company's fleet in the open market during high-peak periods of demand and during down cycles using these assets on the company's own properties. This approach mitigated some of the industry's cyclicality, evened out earnings, and, in short, hedged risk.

As developers moved to deeper waters in the Gulf, Cal Dive followed suit in 1995 by acquiring its first dynamic positioning (DP) vessel, the *Witch Queen,* which was permanently deployed in the Gulf. This was followed in 1996 by the acquisition of the DP semi-submersible, the *Uncle John,* and the *Balmoral Sea,* DP diving support vessel that Cal Dive had been leasing for the past two years. Rather than using anchors, these vessels employed computer-controlled thrusters to maintain their position.

PUBLIC OFFERING IN 1997

Cal Dive was enjoying strong growth and to maintain its momentum the company filed for an initial public offering (IPO) of stock to raise money to pay down debt and expand the services it offered. Underwriting the offering were Schroder Wertheim & Co., Raymond James & Associates, and Simmons & Co. International (headed by Matt Simmons, responsible for raising the money for Handelman to make Oceaneering a reality in 1969). The IPO was completed in July 1997, allowing First Reserve to cash in on some of its investment while netting $39.4 million for Cal Dive. Some of that money was put to use acquiring more deepwater vessels and allowing Energy Resource Technology to acquire additional interest in offshore blocks in the Gulf of Mexico. The company also forged alliances with other offshore service and equipment providers to flesh out its ability to serve customers throughout the life of a field.

Three months prior to the IPO, Kratz succeeded Reuhl as CEO, and in May 1998 he became chairman as well. Kratz took over a company that was enjoying strong growth. Revenues increased from $37.5 million in 1995 to $109.4 million in 1997. During that same period natural and oil production revenues grew from $4.8 million to $16.5 million, and net income jumped from $2.7 million in 1995 to $14.5 million in 1997. Although Cal Dive was able in 1998 to grow revenues to $151.9 million and net income to $24.1 million, by the end of the year it had to contend with another recession in the oil and gas industry. Despite challenging conditions, Cal Dive once again delivered record revenues, $160.1 million, in 1999, although net income fell off to $16.9 million due in large measure to competitive market conditions brought on by the industry slump. The company's business model, combining contracting with development, was now paying dividends. In 2000, as commodity prices rebounded but the demand for contracting services had not yet followed, Cal Dive was able to focus more attention on its production business to drive revenues to more than $181 million and net income to $23.3 million. Contracting competitors, on the other hand, reacted to the situation by cutting their rates to ensure their vessels were in use, and all of them posted losses for the year. Cal Dive's flexibility also helped it to negotiate 2001, a year that began with high commodity prices and every available rig deployed in the Gulf of Mexico but ended with plummeting gas prices and a third of the rigs suddenly out of service. For the year, Cal Dive cracked the $200 million mark in revenues, posting $227.1 million, as well as increasing net income to $28.9 million.

Cal Dive added to its capabilities in 2002 by launching the *Q4000,* the world's first vessel capable of performing intervention and construction work in water as deep as 10,000 feet. It was part of an aggressive capital spending program begun three years earlier that invested $450 million in deepwater assets and another $300 million to add oil and gas properties. The company also grew externally during this period. In 2001 it spent $11.5 million to add the assets of Professional Divers of New Orleans, Inc., which included three utility vessels. Then, in January 2002, Cal Dive bought an 85 percent stake in Canyon Offshore, Inc. for $52.8 million in cash, plus $4.3 million in stock and the assumption of $5 million in debt.

Houston-based Canyon owned 18 remotely operated vehicles used to work on offshore construction projects in depths too great for divers. It also operated another six ROVs owned by other companies. Given that Cal Dive had only three ROVs, two of which worked with the *Uncle John* and *Q4000,* the Canyon assets were a great addition to Cal Dive as it made an increasing commitment to deepwater operations. The two companies had been working together since 1997 when Cal Dive became Canyon's first customer. In July 2002, Cal Dive completed another important acquisition, paying $68.6 million for the Subsea Well Operations Business Unit of CSO Ltd., which did contracting work in the North Sea. The deal brought with it the *Seawell,* a 368-foot support vessel for diving, ROVs, and well operations.

Sales topped $300 million in 2002 and approached $400 million in 2003, while net income grew to $32.8 million in 2003. As oil prices increased, business was even better for Cal Dive in 2004 when sales reached $543.4 million and net income grew to $80 million. The company also benefited from repair work made necessary by Hurricane Ivan, a task that continued into 2005 when the company would take on even more inspection and repair work resulting from Hurricanes Rita and Katrina. At the same time, Cal Dive was pursuing its own development program, spurred by the $200 million buyout of 19 Gulf shelf fields from Murphy Oil in June 2005 and four smaller acquisitions earlier in the year. Altogether they more than doubled the company's oil and gas reserves. Also in November 2005 Cal Dive spent $32.7 million in cash and notes to acquire a Scottish reservoir and well technology service company called Helix Energy Limited. For the year 2005 Cal Dive posted revenues of $799.5 million and net income of $152.6 million.

Cal Dive looked to become even more aggressive on the production side in 2006, early in the year reaching an agreement to acquire Dallas-based Remington Oil and Gas Corp. for $1.4 billion, a deal that would immediately double Cal Dive's oil and gas production. Remington offered even greater future potential, possessing 3-D seismic data covering 4,000 blocks in the Gulf of Mexico. To reflect an increased emphasis on production, Cal Dive changed its name in March 2006, drawing on the name of its new Scottish subsidiary to become Helix Energy Solutions Group, Inc. The company also announced a plan to spin off its Gulf of Mexico shelf marine contracting business into a new company that retained the Cal Dive name. A minority stake in the business was expected to be sold in an IPO later in the year.

Ed Dinger

PRINCIPAL SUBSIDIARIES

Energy Resource Technology, Inc.; Canyon Offshore, Inc.; Well Ops Inc.

PRINCIPAL COMPETITORS

Acergy S.A.; Oceaneering International, Inc.; Subsea 7, Inc.

FURTHER READING

"Cal Dive to Transform into Helix Energy," *Upstream,* March 3, 2006, p. 36.

Elliott, Alan R., "Oil Services Firm Is Having Deep Thoughts," *Investor's Business Daily,* May 28, 2004, p. A05.

———, "Undersea Repair Firm Profits in the Abyss," *Investor's Business Daily,* October 19, 2005, p. A07.

Gonzalez, Angel, "Cal Dive to Buy Remington Oil for $1.36 Billion in Cash, Stock," *Wall Street Journal,* January 24, 2006, p. B2.

Handelman, Lad, "Where Did the Major Diving Companies of Today Originate?," *UnderWater Magazine,* May/June 2000.

Paganie, David, "Evolution of the Next Generation, Integrated Energy Company," *Offshore,* May 1, 2006, p. 56.

Taylor, Gary, "Cal Dive to Spin Off Shelf Contracting Unit," *Platts Oilgram News,* March 2, 2006, p. 2.

High Tech Computer Corporation

23 Hsin Hua Road
Taoyuan 330
Taipei,
Taiwan
Telephone: +886 03 375 3252
Fax: +886 03 375 3251
Web site: http://www.htc.com.tw

Public Company
Incorporated: 1997
Employees: 4,664
Sales: TWD 72.45 billion ($2.23 billion) (2005)
Stock Exchanges: Taiwan
Ticker Symbol: 2498
NAIC: 334210 Telephone Apparatus Manufacturing; 334220 Radio and Television Broadcasting and Wireless Communications Equipment Manufacturing

■ ■ ■

High Tech Computer Corporation (HTC) is the hidden force behind most of the world's Windows Mobile-based clamshell "smartphones" and personal digital assistants (PDAs). The Taiwan-based company operates primarily as an original design manufacturer (ODM) but also as an original equipment manufacturer (OEM) for many of the world's largest telecommunications companies, including Orange, NTT DoCoMo, AT&T Wireless, and T-Mobile, among others. HTC also produces smartphones and PDAs under its own brand, Qtek, to limited markets. In June 2006, however, the company announced its acquisition of Dopod, a major manufacturer and distributor of HTC-based smartphones and PDAs in the Asian region, a move that placed HTC in direct competition with many of its customers.

Founded only in 1997, HTC grew quickly through its close partnership with Microsoft Corporation, helping the software giant impose its operating system on an initially reluctant mobile telecommunications sector. HTC operates manufacturing subsidiaries in mainland China, and sales support subsidiaries in the United States and the United Kingdom, for its North American and European operations, respectively. HTC is led by founder and Chairman Cher Wang, who is also behind chip maker Via Technologies and is the daughter of Y. C. Wang, Taiwan's wealthiest person. Peter Chou serves as the group's president, and H. T. Cho is company CEO. The company is listed on the Taiwan Stock Exchange and produced revenues of TWD 72 billion ($2.23 billion) in 2005.

SMARTPHONE START IN 1997

High Tech Corporation was founded in 1997 to develop a new generation of personal digital assistants and so-called "smartphones," which combined mobile telephone technology with miniaturized computer and other functions. The development of the smartphones became an important step in what many technology market observers viewed as an inevitable drive toward the convergence of various technologies—ranging from telecommunications to music to video and photography to a variety of computer applications—into single, all-

COMPANY PERSPECTIVES

Mission Statement: "Our mission is to become the leading supplier of mobile information and communication devices by providing value-added design, world-class manufacturing, and logistic and service capabilities," Peter Chou, President HTC Corporation, said. He continued, "HTC is working hard to establish a high volume manufacturing facility, and it is focusing on wireless capability, strengthening its R & D team, and developing a software team capable of creating world-class consumer and business applications that will enhance the value of our hardware. It is investing in growing engineering capability in GSM, GPRS and CDMA wireless technologies, investing in sophisticated wireless equipment for both manufacturing and engineering, and investing in protocol software and technology licensing."

encompassing, handheld units. As company founder Cher Wang told *China Daily:* "We started HTC with the vision of offering end-users an easy to use product. We have never believed consumers want to have to carry separate laptops, mobile phones and digital cameras."

HTC was not Wang's first venture into the technology sector. Wang was the daughter of Y. C. Wang, head of Taiwan's largest corporation, Formosa, and recognized as Taiwan's wealthiest person. The Wang family had entered the technology sector during the late 1970s, through Formosa Plastic's semiconductor division, headed by Winston Wang, and through First International Computer, established by Charlene Wang and her husband in 1979. The fourth of five children born to Y. C. Wang's second marriage, Cher Wang started out by working for older sister Charlene at First International Computer. Wang then joined with husband Wenchi Chen to found chip maker Via Technologies in 1992. After the Wang family acquired struggling computer manufacturer Everex Systems, based in the United States, in 1993, Cher Wang was placed in charge of the company, and led its turnaround by mid-decade. Despite the wealth of her family, however, Wang was determined to build her career on her own. As she told *China Daily:* "In my career, I have never got a cent from my father."

By the mid-1990s, Wang had become one of the first to recognize the potential for converging technologies. The proliferation of new handheld technologies, especially mobile telephones and PDAs, as well as the rising popularity of portable computers, had given people, especially professionals, a lot to carry. Wang recognized the need for a new generation of handheld device that could combine most, if not all, of the functionality of the various technologies. This led Wang and Wenchi Chen to found a new company, based around a team of engineers from Digital Equipment, a major customer of First International Computer from when Wang worked there. HTC's research and development team gradually increased to a team of more than 1,000 engineers by the mid-2000s.

HTC at first focused on the laptop computer market, specifically on the newly emerging Pocket PC format. This effort brought the company into its first contact with Microsoft, as HTC received its Windows CE OEM certification at the end of 1997. The company set out to develop the first Pocket PC models for the OEM market and by the end of the decade, its models had captured the industry's attention. In 1998, for example, the company was a finalist in *Byte Magazine*'s Best of CeBIT awards. By the following year, the company had captured the first prize from *PC Week Magazine*'s Best of Comdex Spring awards. Supporting the group's development through this early phase was its early initial public offering, in 1998. The company also became the first in the industry to produce a Pocket PC with a full-color screen.

Yet the company's first years were difficult ones. Within two years, the company was facing mounting losses, and its products failed to capture consumer attention. As Wang told *Business Week:* "The market just wasn't ready for a PDA phone that behaved like a minicomputer." At the same time, the company's products were beset with technical problems, both in their design and operating software. In order to survive, Wang was forced to pump millions of her own money into the company, notably in stepping up the group's engineering and design capacity.

HTC's breakthrough came in 2000, when it was awarded the contract to develop and manufacture a new breed of still smaller handheld computer, known as the personal digital assistant (PDA), for Compaq Corporation. The Ipaq, as the new device was called, became an instant sensation. The success of the Ipaq was a lasting one, too, as the company continued to develop new models through the middle of the decade. Of importance, the Ipaq featured an expandable design, with slots for both the CompaqFlash Expansion Pack and a PC Card Expansion Pack, pointing the way to the future convergence of the computing and telecommunications markets.

KEY DATES

1997: The company is founded.
2000: HTC is awarded the contract to develop and manufacture a PDA, the Ipaq, for Compaq Corporation.
2001: HTC reaches an agreement with Microsoft Corporation to develop a new generation of mobile telephones.
2002: HTC releases its first commercially available smartphone and its first wireless Pocket PC.
2004: HTC's revenues near $1 billion; IA Style is acquired.
2005: HTC becomes the first to release a smartphone based on the new Windows Mobile 5.0 operating system; company sales top $2.2 billion.
2006: HTC agrees to acquire Dopod.

As Peter Chou pointed out in a company press release in 2000: "We are at the beginning of a 2nd wireless revolution; one that will see wireless and Internet integration as the most important technology of this decade."

KEEPING THE LEAD IN THE NEW CENTURY

HTC set out to play the role of leader for the new market. In 2001, the company reached a new agreement with Microsoft to develop a new generation of mobile telephones based on the extension of Microsoft's latest handheld operating system, Windows CE 3.0. By March of that year, the company had debuted its first fully functional prototype of the new "smartphone." The fact that Microsoft CEO Steve Ballmer himself made the demonstration helped dramatically raise HTC's profile among the global telecommunications industry. In support of the new product line, HTC reached a processor supply agreement with Texas Instruments in May 2001.

By 2002, HTC had released its first commercially available smartphone, which was picked up by fast-growing British telecoms group Orange, later part of France Telecom. In that year as well, HTC launched its first wireless Pocket PC. The company quickly signed up new customers, including Germany's T-Mobile, the Philippines Smart Communications, and the United States' AT&T Wireless, which added smartphones in 2003. The successful launch of the new technology also transformed HTC's revenue picture. Whereas the group's

Ipaq sales had dominated its turnover, accounting for some 85 percent of total company sales in 2001, HTC had successfully reduced its reliance on that single device, back to just one-third of sales, by 2003.

By 2003, HTC faced a growing number of new entrants in the smartphone market, including competing Windows versions, and the rival operating system, Symbian, used by Nokia and Motorola, among others. In response, HTC moved to lower its cost by shifting parts of its production to mainland China, incorporating a subsidiary in Suzhou in 2003. The company also focused on new product development, driving its smartphones toward still smaller, sleeker designs. The company also counted its focus on the handheld market as part of its strength against the newly emerging competitors, which entered the smartphone market with a background in personal computers (PCs). A far different sector, the PC market demanded high volumes, with little need for product innovation. The smartphone market, on the other hand, was especially driven by research and development capable of extending functionality.

HTC's sales rose quickly, as more and more of the world's major telecommunications providers adopted the company's smartphones. By the end of 2004, HTC's revenues had neared $1 billion. In that year, the company boosted its software development wing with the acquisition of IA Style, a noted developer of software applications for the Windows Mobile operating system. Following the acquisition, IA Style, which had previously operated in the retail sector, shifted its operations entirely to supporting HTC's own product development. In the meantime, HTC had begun expanding its global operations, launching a subsidiary in the United States in 2003, and a subsidiary in the United Kingdom in 2005. In this way, the company positioned itself closer to its major customers, which included European giants such as O2, Orange, Vodaphone, T-Mobile, and Telefonica. Also in 2005, HTC became the first to release a smartphone based on the new Windows Mobile 5.0 operating system. By the end of that year, the company's sales had doubled, topping $2.2 billion.

In 2006, HTC moved to boost its operations in the Asian markets as well, announcing its agreement to acquire Dopod in June of that year. Dopod was then a major player in the Asian regions with sales of its own HTC-based smartphones. The acquisition raised eyebrows, particularly among HTC's customers, as the addition of Dopod operations placed HTC in direct competition with the company's own customers. The move signaled the company's possible interest in moving out of the shadows in order to achieve recognition as the world leader in smartphone technology.

M. L. Cohen

PRINCIPAL SUBSIDIARIES

Exedea Inc.; H.T.C. (B.V.I.) Corporation; High Tech Computer Corporation (Suzhou) (China); HTC EUROPE Co., Ltd. (U.K.); HTC USA Inc.; HTEK.

PRINCIPAL COMPETITORS

Siemens AG; Sony Corporation; Thomson Multimedia Inc.; Fujitsu Ltd.; AT&T Inc.; Nokia Corporation; Motorola Inc.; Mitsubishi Electric Corporation; Cisco Systems Inc.; BellSouth Corporation; Louis Dreyfus S.A.S.; Tyco Electronics Corporation.

FURTHER READING

Dano, Mike, "HTC Finds Niche in High-End Devices," *RCR Wireless News,* September 12, 2005, p. 3.

Dean, Jason, "Smart Call," *Far Eastern Economic Review,* September 3, 2004.

Einhorn, Bruce, "The Hottest Tech Outfit You Never Heard Of," *Business Week,* April 24, 2006, p. 42.

————, "Meet the Latest Tech All-Star from Taiwan," *Business Week,* March 24, 2003, p. 76D.

"HTC Opens European Branch to Better Serve Customers," *Taiwan Economic News,* December 5, 2005.

"HTC to Acquire Dopod with USD150mn," *Alestron,* June 7, 2006.

Kovac, Matt, "Priestess of the PDA," *Business Week,* July 11, 2005, p. 64.

Li Weitao, "Inspired Vision," *China Daily,* December 19, 2005, p. 5.

Weidenbaum, Murray, and Samuel Hughes, "Asia's Bamboo Network," *Fixing America's Schools,* September/October 1996.

Yeung, Frederick, "Taiwan Smart-Phone Supplier Eyes HK Listing," *South China Morning Post,* June 6, 2006.

Icelandic Group hf

———■———

Borgartun 27
Reykjavik,
Iceland
Telephone: +354 560 7800
Fax: +354 562 1252
Web site: http://www.icelandic.is

Public Company
Incorporated: 1942 as Sölumi'stö' hra'frystihúsanna
   (Icelandic Freezing Plants Corporation)
Employees: 3,300
Sales: EUR 1.2 billion ($1.52 billion) (2005)
Stock Exchanges: Iceland
Ticker Symbol: IG
NAIC: 311712 Fresh and Frozen Seafood Processing;
   311711 Seafood Canning; 424460 Fish and Seafood
   Merchant Wholesalers; 551112 Offices of Other
   Holding Companies

■ ■ ■

Icelandic Group hf is the holding company for an
internationally operating group of companies focused on
the seafood market. Icelandic's companies, which operate for the most part as independent units, are engaged
in the production, processing, and distribution of seafood
products. The largest part of the group's operations are
in the frozen seafood segment, and Icelandic is a major
supplier of frozen fish to the international private-label
and third-party channels. Retail sales represent 39
percent of the group's turnover, and the foodservice
industry adds 38 percent. Industrial and related sales
add the remaining 23 percent to the group's revenues.
The bulk of Icelandic's fish production is in whitefish,
although the company also produces shellfish, shrimp,
and mollusks.

Since the early 2000s Icelandic also has engaged a
strategy targeting the development of production and
distribution operations in the fast-growing fresh and
chilled seafood segments, as consumers increasingly seek
out easy-to-prepare and ready-to-eat foods. As such, the
group has completed a number of acquisitions, including Pickenpack Hussman und Hahn in Germany, and
Seachill and the seafood division of Cavaghan & Gray
in 2005. Also that year, Icelandic Group completed a
merger with fellow Icelander Blue Ice Group, a leading
seafood supplier to the Asian markets. Icelandic Group
has procurement subsidiaries in Iceland, Norway, The
Netherlands, South Korea, and, since 2006, in China.
The company owns production and processing operations in Iceland, the United States, the United Kingdom,
and Germany, and sales and marketing subsidiaries in
Germany, France, Spain, the United Kingdom, the
United States, and Japan. In 2005, the company posted
revenues of EUR 1.2 billion ($1.5 billion). Fresh and
chilled fish represent 25 percent of those sales, while
processed fish has reached 33 percent of sales. Icelandic
Group is listed on the Iceland Stock Exchange.

POSTWAR FROZEN FISH PRODUCER

With an abundance of fish in the oceans around Iceland,
the fishing industry became the country's largest in the
first half of the 20th century. Long ruled by the Danish

crown, Iceland established itself as an independent country in the 1920s. As such, the development of the country's industrial and commercial base became of prime importance for its economy. The fishing industry was to provide the motor for the country's emergence as an independent state, and by the end of the 1930s, Iceland had established itself as an important exporter of fish and fish products.

Into the first years of World War II, Iceland's fishing exports relied on traditional salt curing or pickling preservation techniques. During the war, however, during which time the island country was used as a base first for British and then for American armed forces, the country was introduced to new freezing technologies being developed for the food industries. The possibility of freezing fish, which left the flavor of fish comparatively unaltered, presented a new opportunity for the young country.

In 1942, a group of Icelandic fish producers and processors joined together to form a mutually owned company, called Sölumi'stö' hra'frystihúsanna (Icelandic Freezing Plants Corporation). Icelandic's initial mission was to act as a sales representative for its members, which operated their own freezing plants, developing new markets and customers for the country's frozen fish production. Icelandic also was charged with the procurement of supplies and equipment needed for its members' freezing operations, as well as with developing and improving freezing technologies and frozen fish products. The company operated on a cooperative basis, guaranteeing the purchase of its members' production.

Icelandic quickly began putting in place an international sales network, starting with the United States in 1945. The company opened a sales agency in New York that year, and later developed its own fish processing facilities in that country. The United States represented the most prominent market for frozen fish at the time. For one, frozen food technologies had been developed in the United States, and the country already had a strong infrastructure in place for frozen food transportation, storage, and handling. For another, the country had pioneered the supermarket format, which prominently featured frozen food sections. In turn, the U.S. consumer market had the highest penetration of home freezers in the world; indeed, in many countries, home freezers remained a novelty until well into the 1960s. In the United States, Icelandic quickly became an important brand name in the frozen fish sector. This was reinforced with the launch of production operations in the United States, with the opening of a new processing plant in 1954.

INTERNATIONAL EXPANSION THROUGH THE LATE 20TH CENTURY

Despite its early focus on the United States, the company also sought to build a sales network in Europe. In 1946, Icelandic opened its first European sales office. The United Kingdom represented a close and important market for the company as well, and by 1955, Icelandic had established its first operations in that country. At first, Icelandic focused on the restaurant sector, setting up its own network of fish and chip shops in that country. By 1958, the company also had begun to process fish products locally, with the opening of a plant in Gravesend. This facility enabled the group to enter the retail channel.

Icelandic continued to develop its U.S. operations, launching a production unit in Nanticote, Maryland, through subsidiary Coldwater Seafood Corporation. In

KEY DATES

1942: Sölumi'stö' hra'frystihúsanna (Icelandic Freezing Plants Corporation) is founded as a mutual company representing the frozen fish production of a number of Icelandic fishing companies.

1945: Icelandic opens its first foreign sales office in the United States.

1955: The company enters the United Kingdom, at first as operator of a chain of fish and chips shops.

1967: A second frozen fish processing plant opens in the United States.

1981: A sales subsidiary is established in Germany.

1982: The company builds a frozen fish processing plant in Grimsby, England.

1988: The company enters the French market with a sales subsidiary, which also develops sales in the Spanish market.

1989: The company opens a sales subsidiary in Tokyo.

1996: A dedicated subsidiary is launched in Spain; the company re-incorporates as a limited liability company.

1998: The company goes public on the Iceland Stock Exchange as Icelandic Group.

2002: Icelandic launches a new strategy for expansion in the fresh and chilled fish categories, and acquires a chilled processing factory in England.

2003: The company acquires Ocean to Ocean and Neptune Fisheries in the United States, and Barogel in France.

2004: The company acquires the Seachill and Cavaghan & Gray fishing operations in the United Kingdom and Comigro Geneco in France and forms a Chinese subsidiary.

2005: The company merges with Blue Ice Group; the company acquires Dalian Three Star in China, Fiskval in Iceland, and Pickenpack H&H in Germany.

2006: The company acquires Saltur A/S in Denmark, adding saltfish operations.

1968 Coldwater moved to a new larger processing plant in Cambridge, Maryland. That plant produced frozen fish sticks, by then already becoming a staple food among American youth. The strong sales of that product led the company to expand the Cambridge plant again in 1973.

Icelandic began extending its network of European operations in the 1980s. In 1981, for example, the company opened a sales and marketing subsidiary in Hamburg, Germany. Two years later, the company's U.K. operations refocused around a new production plant in Grimsby, under the Coldwater Seafood banner. These operations replaced the company's earlier involvement in the fish and chips business.

The company next moved into France in 1988, opening a sales office there. The French sales team also was initially responsible for developing sales and distribution in Spain. The company's strong success in Spain, however, later led Icelandic to form a dedicated subsidiary for that market, which began operations in 1996. By then, Icelandic had expanded its sales even farther abroad, setting up a subsidiary in Tokyo, Japan, in 1989. That subsidiary targeted not only the Japanese market, but the wider Asian markets, focusing on a select range of fish types, including Greenland halibut, redfish, and capelin.

In another expansion move, the company merged its U.K. operations with another Grimsby-based company, Faroe Seafood, in 1995. The merged operation, which continued under the Coldwater name, gave Icelandic three production plants for supplying the U.K. market. Coldwater's operations especially targeted the country's retail sector as a frozen fish supplier for third-party labels. In 1998, the company's U.K. operations were regrouped under a new subsidiary, Icelandic UK.

Icelandic underwent its own transformation in 1996. In that year, the company reincorporated as a limited liability company, shedding its mutual status. The change in structure led to the company's listing on the Iceland Stock Exchange in 1998, under the name Icelandic Group. The listing enabled the company's original fish processing owners to sell off their holdings. With a broader shareholder base, Icelandic discontinued the former purchasing obligations it had maintained during its status as a cooperative company.

Following its public listing, Icelandic initially looked to its domestic rivals for its next growth phase. In 1998, the company launched merger negotiations with rival Iceland Seafood. By 1999, however, the two sides had been unable to reach an agreement, and the proposed merger was abandoned.

NEW STRATEGY FOR THE NEW CENTURY

Instead, Icelandic developed a new strategy in line with trends in the consumer markets toward easier-to-prepare and ready-to-eat fresh and chilled food products. Icelandic launched a drive to build up its own fresh and chilled fish capacity.

Acquisitions formed the major part of this effort, starting with the purchase of a chilled fish processing factory in Redditch, England, in 2002. The following year, the company boosted its U.S. presence, acquiring Ocean to Ocean (OTO), a leading importer and distributor of shrimp—the largest chilled seafood category in the United States—and other shellfish products. Soon after, Icelandic bought Norfolk, Virginia-based Neptune Fisheries, which also specialized in shrimp and shellfish imports. While OTO's focus was, in large part, on the retail market, Neptune targeted primarily the foodservice sector.

Meanwhile, Icelandic had expanded its position in the European shrimp and shellfish market as well, buying up Marseilles-based Barogel in 2003. The following year, the company reinforced its French operations, buying counterpart Comigro Geneco, a Paris-based company that operated in the whitefish market, handling a different set of species from Icelandic.

In the United Kingdom, the company continued to build up its presence in Grimsby, acquiring Seachill and the fish operations of Cavaghan & Gray in 2004. The Cavaghan & Gray acquisition gave the company new facilities in Aberdeen, as well as in Grimsby.

Also in 2004, Icelandic, which had focused most of its growth efforts on the European and U.S. markets, targeted a wider presence in the Asian region. In support of this goal, the company launched a subsidiary in China in that year. The biggest boost for the group's new Asian strategy, however, came in 2005 when the company reached an agreement to merge with Iceland-based Blue Ice Group. Blue Ice had been especially active in the Asian markets, and had succeeded in establishing itself as one of that region's leading fish suppliers. The newly merged group retained the Icelandic name for its operations.

Icelandic then expanded its Asian region presence in November 2005 with the purchase of 97 percent of Dalian Three Star Ltd. in China. Also in that month, the company boosted its European fresh fish operations, acquiring Fiskval, based in Iceland. By the end of that year, the company had successfully boosted the share of fresh and chilled fish to 25 percent of its total sales.

Icelandic maintained its growth by acquisition strategy into 2006. The company ended 2005 with the purchase of Germany's Pickenpack Hussman & Hahn Seafood, the largest producer of frozen fish in that market. Following that acquisition, the company closed down its Hamburg office, in February 2006. By April of

that year, Icelandic had spotted a new acquisition opportunity, that of Saltur A/S in Denmark. That purchase gave the company control of two saltfish processing facilities, a new product category for the company. Icelandic Group expected to maintain its strong growth through the end of the decade.

M. L. Cohen

PRINCIPAL SUBSIDIARIES

B.I. Shipping Inc. (South Korea); Coldwater Seafood (UK) Ltd.; Dalian Three Star Seafood Co. Ltd. (China); Danberg ehf.; Darybprom DPR (Russia); Ecomsa S.A. (Spain); Fiskval ehf.; Gadus B.V. (The Netherlands); ic Asia Inc. (South Korea); ic China Trading Co. Ltd.; ic France (S.A.S.); ic Germany GmbH; ic Group UK Ltd.; ic Iberica S.A. (Spain); ic Japan K.K.; ic Norway A.S.; ic Services ehf.; ic UK Ltd.; ic USA Inc.; IFP Trading Ltd. (U.K.); Marinus ehf.; OTO L.L.C. (U.S.A.); Samband of (U.S.A.); Seachill Ltd. (U.K.); Sjóvík ehf. (Blue-Ice); Unifish ehf. a.v.

PRINCIPAL COMPETITORS

Alpesca S.A; Primlaks Nigeria Ltd.; Antarktika Fishing Co.; Hanwa Company Ltd.; Orkla ASA; Mukorob Fishing Proprietary Ltd.; Aker ASA; Maruha Corporation; China Resources Enterprise Ltd.; Nichirei Corporation.

FURTHER READING

"Blue Ice Group, Iceland Seafood Merge to Maximize Markets," *Quick Frozen Foods International,* April 2005, p. 57.

"Fresh Catch: Icelandic USA Inc. Says Its Industry-Leading Seafood Products Bring the Freshness of the Coast of Iceland to Customers Around the World," *Food and Drink,* March-April 2005, p. 148.

"Icelandic Group Aims for Tilapia Farming and Processing in China," *Fishupdate.com,* May 12, 2006.

"Icelandic Group hf Completes Acquisition of Pickenpack Hussmann & Hahn," *Nordic Business Report,* February 1, 2006.

"Icelandic Group on Way to Recovery," *Fishupdate.com,* May 23, 2006.

"Icelandic Group PLC Completes Two Acquisitions," *Nordic Business Report,* November 30, 2005.

"Merger of Icelandic Group PLC and Blue Chip Ice Group Cleared by Board of Directors," *Frozen Food Digest,* July 2005, p. 21.

"Northern Sells Off Cavaghan & Gray Unit; Seafood Business Seen Better on Its Own," *Quick Frozen Foods International,* January 2005, p. 51.

Illinois Tool Works Inc.

3600 West Lake Avenue
Glenview, Illinois 60026-1215
U.S.A.
Telephone: (847) 724-7500
Fax: (847) 657-4261
Web site: http://www.itw.com

Public Company
Founded: 1912
Incorporated: 1915
Employees: 50,000
Sales: $12.92 billion (2005)
Stock Exchanges: New York Chicago
Ticker Symbol: ITW
NAIC: 325510 Paint and Coating Manufacturing; 325520 Adhesive and Sealant Manufacturing; 325998 All Other Miscellaneous Chemical Product and Preparation Manufacturing; 326112 Unsupported Plastics Packaging Film and Sheet Manufacturing; 326113 Unsupported Plastics Film and Sheet (Except Packaging) Manufacturing; 326199 All Other Plastics Product Manufacturing; 333319 Other Commercial and Service Industry Machinery Manufacturing; 333512 Machine Tool (Metal Cutting Types) Manufacturing; 333991 Power-Driven Handtool Manufacturing; 333992 Welding and Soldering Equipment Manufacturing; 333993 Packaging Machinery Manufacturing; 334519 Other Measuring and Controlling Device Manufacturing; 339943 Marking Device Manufacturing; 339993 Fastener, Button, Needle, and Pin Manufacturing

■ ■ ■

In 1912 four Smith brothers advertised for experienced manufacturing workers to help them set up a new business producing metal-cutting tools to serve expanding midwestern industry. With the backing of their wealthy and influential father, Byron Laflin Smith, the brothers formed what would later be called Illinois Tool Works Inc. The Chicago-based company prospered. Under Smith family management through much of its history—the family still owned about 16 percent of the company in the early 2000s—Illinois Tool Works became known as a company with conservative management and innovative products that made big profits on small items. By the 1990s the company was somewhat changed with management placing a greater emphasis on acquisitions, even if it meant going into debt. ITW, as the company is generally called, operates approximately 700 decentralized businesses in 48 countries that manufacture a wide variety of highly engineered products and specialty systems. Approximately 44 percent of revenues are generated outside the United States.

EARLY HISTORY

In 1857, just 20 years after the city of Chicago was incorporated, Byron Laflin Smith's father set up Merchants' Loan & Trust to help fledgling businesses get off the ground, becoming the first Chicago resident to own a Chicago banking institution. The city's population was approximately trebling each decade as railroads and the Great Lakes made it a transportation and manufacturing center. As the city grew, the cor-

COMPANY PERSPECTIVES

Founded in 1912, ITW's recipe for success has been consistent: value added products and outstanding service win the day with customers. We place a high premium on the development of highly engineered products and systems, most of which are developed in tandem with our customers. And we continue to ensure that our customers receive timely, cost-effective service for the innovative products we provide.

responding real estate boom made rich men richer. The elder Smith took advantage of all these opportunities to make his family one of the wealthiest and most influential in the Midwest.

After graduating from the University of Chicago, Byron Smith went to work for his father at Merchants' Loan & Trust. Working in the family business did not last long, however. When he was 25 years old, Smith struck out on his own, founding the Northern Trust Company in 1879, which was to become one of the city's premier banking institutions.

A successful man in his own right by the early years of the 20th century, Smith saw other opportunities in the growing city. Through his business connections, Smith realized that there was an increasing need for large-scale production of machine tools for the growing transportation and communication industries. These emerging industries needed more parts than small machine shops could provide, and Smith thought he and his sons Solomon, Harold C., Walter, and Bruce were just the men to fill the need.

In 1912 the Smiths placed an advertisement for experienced manufacturing workers. They chose Frank W. England, Paul B. Goddard, Oscar T. Hogg, and Carl G. Olson to help get Illinois Tool Works off the ground, and Harold and Walter Smith managed the new company. Solomon Smith continued to work at Northern Trust—he succeeded his father as president when Byron died two years later—and Bruce went to work in New York.

In 1915, the same year that the company was incorporated, Harold C. Smith became president of Illinois Tool Works, and Walter and Solomon Smith continued to serve on the board of directors. Harold built on the company's initial success in selling tools to manufacturers and soon expanded the company's product line into truck transmissions, pumps, compressors, and automobile steering assemblies. While invest-

ing heavily in modern plants and equipment, Smith insisted on the conservative financial approach that ITW became known for, maintaining cash reserves and eschewing debt. Under Smith, ITW also became known for producing high-quality products. Smith's strategy served the growing company well when World War I broke out; the war years boosted company profits handsomely.

EXPANSION INTO FASTENERS

In 1923 ITW engineered a new product that brought it into a different industry niche. The Shakeproof fastener, the first twisted-tooth lock washer, was to lead ITW into the profitable area of industrial fasteners. Shakeproof became a separate operating division offering a full line of related items, including preassembled washers and screws and thread-cutting screws. Each item in the Shakeproof division's product line sold for an average of less than one cent apiece, but ITW took the leadership position in the industry and its sales volume produced strong profits.

Harold C. Smith died in 1936. He had built ITW into an industry leader in metal-cutting tools, manufacturing components, and industrial fasteners. Smith had been an industry leader as well, serving as director of both the Illinois Manufacturers Association and the National Association of Manufacturers. After Smith's death, his son, Harold Byron Smith, became president of ITW. The oldest of four boys, Harold B. Smith had joined the company in 1931. Harold B. Smith followed his father's successful, conservative management practices, but he introduced some innovations as well. Smith emphasized research and development, encouraging engineers to develop new products, even outside of ITW's traditional product areas. He also decentralized the company, setting up separate divisions to pursue specific markets. This philosophy, followed by Smith's successors, meant forming individual operating units that concentrate only on their own product niche.

Under Harold B. Smith, ITW became known as a problem solver. Its salesforce developed new products to answer customers' specific needs, even when customers had not requested a solution, a practice that led to increased sales.

World War II, like World War I, produced a boom for the company, which by this time manufactured components for almost every type of equipment needed for the war effort. Even the wartime labor shortage could not prevent ITW from increasing its cash reserves.

CONTINUING GROWTH

Smith put some of the company's wartime profit into research and development, leading directly to expansion

```
╔══════════════════════════════════════╗
║                                      ║
║            KEY DATES                 ║
║                ■                     ║
╟──────────────────────────────────────╢

1912:   Byron Laflin Smith and sons form Illinois
        Tool Works to begin producing machine
        tools.
1915:   Company is incorporated.
1923:   Company enters the industrial fastener
        market.
1936:   Harold Byron Smith becomes president of
        ITW and later introduces the firm's
        trademark decentralized structure.
1955:   Fastex, a unit focused on plastic products, is
        formed.
1962:   ITW forms Hi-Cone, specializing in plastic
        drink packaging.
1975:   Company enters adhesives industry through
        purchase of Devcon Corporation.
1986:   Signode Industries, Inc., is acquired.
1999:   Acquisition of Premark International, Inc.
        brings to the fold Hobart, Vulcan, Traulsen,
        and Wittco commercial food equipment and
        Wilsonart decorative laminates.
2003:   Revenues surpass $10 billion, while profits
        surge past $1 billion.
```

in the 1950s. One new and profitable area was plastic and combination metal-plastic fasteners. The company already had extensive expertise in the fastener industry with its Shakeproof division. Successful plastics manufacture and marketing led to the formation of another new operating unit, Fastex, in 1955.

Another area of expansion after the war, based in part on ITW's experience with plastics, was into the production of electrical controls and instruments. ITW's Licon division was formed in 1959 to produce electric switches and electromechanical products. ITW became a leader in miniaturizing these components. Its solid-state switches and preassembled switch panels brought the company into the computer and defense industries in addition to increasing sales in its traditional industrial base.

It was clear by this time that Illinois Tool Works was outgrowing its name; it no longer manufactured just tools. Smith set up a separate Illinois Tools division during the 1950s to concentrate on the original cutting-tool business and the company's initials, ITW, became the more frequently used, although unofficial, name for the business as a whole.

ITW's special expertise in gears led to two other

developments during the 1950s. The company set up the Illinois Tools Division Gear School in 1958 to train engineers, especially those of customer firms, in the intricacies of gearing. ITW's development of the Spiroid right-angle gear led Smith to found the Spiroid operating unit in 1959 to produce specialty gearing for defense and general industries.

INTRODUCTION OF PLASTIC SIX-PACK HOLDERS

A new opportunity emerged from ITW research and development in the early 1960s. Company engineers had been looking for less bulky, lower-cost packaging than the traditional cardboard boxing used for six-packs of beverages. Metal holders cut both the fingers of the customers and, occasionally, the cans they were meant to hold. ITW's increasing familiarity with plastics led to the invention of a flexible plastic collar to hold the cans. This simple patented invention generated substantial savings for beverage makers, from 40 percent to 60 percent according to ITW estimates. It led to the formation of another new operating unit, Hi-Cone, in 1962. In the decades since, plastic drink packaging has virtually replaced cardboard packaging for six-packs. The six-pack holder became one of ITW's most important moneymakers, and earnings from the Hi-Cone division offset fluctuations in profits from the company's products that served heavy industry.

In 1970 Harold B. Smith stepped down from the chairmanship of ITW. By this time ITW was an internationally recognized name. The Smith family's emphasis on decentralized operation meant that many of the company's production facilities were near large overseas customers, often under the control of local subsidiaries in the country where they were located. ITW components supplied heavy industries, the food and beverage industries, and the packaging industries in West Germany, Belgium, Australia, Spain, Italy, France, Great Britain, and New Zealand. The company's performance, however, suffered from the inflation that plagued the economy of the 1970s.

With Harold B. Smith's retirement, the first non-Smith, Silas S. Cathcart, became the chairman of ITW. Smith's son, Harold B. Smith, Jr., served as president and chief operating officer from 1972 through 1981, and Smith family members continued to serve on the board of directors. Under this leadership, the 1970s saw some new developments despite the sluggish economy. Most notable was ITW's entry into the adhesives industry with the 1975 purchase of Devcon Corporation. Devcon was a leader in specialty chemicals and manufactured adhesives and sealants.

ACQUISITIONS AT CENTER STAGE

When John D. Nichols took over as CEO in 1982, he was determined to keep ITW growing by investing more cash into the development of new product lines and in acquisitions, while cutting costs elsewhere to maintain profitability. He kept production costs low, for example, by developing what he termed "focus factories," where a single product was produced in a highly automated setting.

Nichols expanded ITW's industrial tools and systems businesses by purchasing Heartland Components, a maker of customized replacement industrial parts, in 1982; Southern Gage, a manufacturer of industrial gages, and N.A. Woodworth, a maker of tool-holding equipment, in 1984; and Magnaflux, a maker of nondestructive testing equipment and supplies, in 1985. Nichols formed a separate operating unit for automotive controls in 1983, and a division for producing equipment for offshore geophysical exploration, Linac, in 1984.

In 1986 Nichols made another significant acquisition when he purchased closely held Signode Industries, Inc., for $524 million. The Glenview, Illinois, manufacturer of plastic and steel strapping for bundling items, sketch film, and industrial tape fit in well with ITW's own plastics line. Nichols followed company tradition by breaking Signode down into smaller units, and within a year and a half over 20 new products had been developed as a result of the acquisition, which nearly doubled ITW's revenues. Also in 1986, Cathcart retired as chairman, with Nichols replacing him, while retaining the position of CEO.

Under Nichols, ITW acquired 27 companies in related product lines in the 1980s, whereas only three firms had been purchased before Nichols's tenure. These acquisitions meant that company debt reached higher levels than in the past, but these levels were not out of line with other industrial firms. More importantly, revenues surpassed the $2 billion mark for the first time in 1989 and earnings continued to increase steadily, reaching $182.4 million that year.

Acquisitions continued to fuel spectacular growth in the 1990s for ITW, growth that was only partially slowed by the recession of the early years of the decade. The largest of 15 acquisitions in 1990 was that of the $200 million revenue DeVilbiss spray painting equipment business of Eagle Industries Inc., which built on the prior year's purchase of Ransburg Corporation, also a maker of spray painting equipment. In 1993 ITW added the Miller Group Ltd., a maker of arc welding equip-

ment which had $250 million in revenues. As usual, Miller's operations were soon broken apart, with seven separate units emerging.

The years 1995 and 1996 were transitional ones for ITW, as Nichols handpicked a successor and then stepped aside. W. James Farrell, a 30-year ITW veteran who had served as president, moved into the CEO position in September 1995, replacing the retiring Nichols as chairman in May 1996. During his 14 years as CEO, Nichols oversaw an amazing period of growth, from $450 million in revenues in 1981 to $4.18 billion in 1995 when earnings reached $387.6 million. Revenues were growing at a rate of about 20 percent per year, and profits were increasing even faster—40 percent in 1995 alone. Through Nichols's aggressive acquisition program and his commitment to a decentralized organizational structure, ITW boasted of 365 separate operating units by 1996. During his tenure, Nichols also increased the company's presence outside the United States such that by 1996 about 35 percent of revenues were derived overseas, primarily from European operations.

The Farrell-led ITW essentially picked up where Nichols left off. The company made 19 acquisitions in 1996, including Hobart Brothers Company, a maker of welding products, and the Australian-based Azon Limited, a manufacturer of strapping and other industrial products. The possibility that Farrell would be even more aggressive than Nichols was raised in late 1995 when ITW made its first hostile takeover bid in the company's history, a $134 million offer for fastener maker Elco Industries Inc., a venture that failed after ITW was outbid for Elco by Textron Inc.

One hallmark of the Farrell era of leadership was the greater prominence given to an ITW management philosophy known as 80/20. Managers of the numerous company units were encouraged to focus most of their efforts on the 20 percent of their customers who accounted for 80 percent of their business. ITW viewed this approach as a way to spark improvements in numerous areas, including product quality, productivity, market share, and customer satisfaction.

In the meantime, the acquisition pace picked up under Farrell in the late 1990s, as ITW completed 30 deals in 1997, 46 in 1998, and 31 in 1999. The vast majority of these were smaller purchases of companies with annual sales of less than $50 million. However, in November 1999 the company completed the biggest acquisition in its history, a $3.4 billion deal for Premark International, Inc. of Deerfield, Illinois. Premark, one-time parent of the Tupperware food-storage product business, produced commercial food equipment for restaurants, hotels, and hospitals under the Hobart, Vulcan, Traulsen, and Wittco brands and the Wilsonart line of decorative laminates for countertops, furniture, and flooring. These were the two main Premark product lines that ITW sought to add for the long haul, and they represented annual revenues of approximately $2.5 billion. Broken apart into more than two dozen smaller autonomous businesses, they also helped increase the number of ITW units to nearly 600 by the end of 2000. Premark was involved as well in the production of consumer products, including West Bend appliances, Precor fitness equipment, and Florida Tile ceramic tiles. These operations fell outside ITW's traditional industrial focus, and they were earmarked for divestiture in December 2001. Consequently, Precor and West Bend were sold in October 2002, and Florida Tile followed in November 2003.

A NEW CENTURY

The economic downturn of the early 2000s interrupted Illinois Tool Works' consistent pattern of growth. Profits fell in both 2001 and 2002, while revenues dropped 2 percent in 2001 before rebounding slightly the following year. As the economy rebounded, ITW resumed its growth trajectory in 2003 when revenues surpassed the $10 billion mark for the first time, and net income surged past $1 billion, also a record. The pace of acquisitions slowed during this period because ITW management felt that business owners were placing excessively high price tags on their companies considering the state of the economy. After spending some $800 million to complete 45 acquisitions in 2000, ITW completed 29 deals for a total of $556 million in 2001 and then 21 deals for just $188 million and 28 deals for $204 million in 2002 and 2003, respectively.

In 2004 the profit figure of $1.34 billion and the revenue total of $11.73 billion both represented sharp jumps from the preceding year. This stellar year was the last with Farrell at the helm, as the executive stepped down from the CEO spot in August 2005. Succeeding him was 27-year company veteran David Speer, who had been an executive vice-president since 1995. Speer became chairman as well in August 2006 upon Farrell's retirement.

Under Speer's guidance, Illinois Tool Works remained on its acquisition-led growth track. During 2005 the company purchased 22 companies for a net total of more than $625 million. While most of these acquisitions continued to be of companies with annual sales of between $30 million and $50 million, two larger purchases were completed that year. In the spring ITW bought Permatex, Inc., a Hartford, Connecticut-based maker of sealants, adhesives, and other products for the automotive aftermarket and industrial markets with annual sales of $125 million. ITW paid about $240 mil-

lion in the fall for Instron Corporation, a Norwood, Massachusetts, manufacturer of materials and structural testing machinery and software. In February 2006 ITW acquired Alpine Engineered Products, Inc., a manufacturer of metal connectors, design software, and related machinery for the design and assembly of trusses for the residential and commercial construction markets. Based in Pompano Beach, Florida, Alpine had 2005 revenues of $201 million.

The ongoing dealmaking brought the number of ITW business units to around 700 by early 2006. Moving forward, Illinois Tool Works planned to continue its expansion through acquisitions, joint ventures, and organic moves into new markets. Speer aimed to boost the share of overall revenues generated overseas from the 2005 level of 44 percent to 50 percent. The Asia-Pacific region was identified as the area with the greatest growth potential. While about 10 percent of revenues originated in that region in 2005, ITW envisioned boosting that figure to 25 percent by 2009.

Ginger G. Rodriguez
Updated, David E. Salamie

PRINCIPAL SUBSIDIARIES

Acme Packaging Corporation; Alpine Engineered Products, Inc.; The DeVilbiss Company Limited (U.K.); Elga AB (Sweden); Foster Refrigerator (U.K.); Hobart Brothers Company; Hobart Corporation; Instron Corporation; ITW Bailly Comte S.A.S. (France); James Briggs (U.K.); Krafft, S.L. (Spain); Mertiex Technology (Suzhou) Co. Ltd. (China); Miller Electric Mfg. Co.; Novadan AS (Norway); Orgapack GmbH (Switzerland); Permatex, Inc.; Pryda (Malaysia) Sdn Bhd; Resopal G.m.b.H. (Germany); Rocol (U.K.); SPIT S.A.S. (France); Strapex GmbH (Switzerland); Tien Tai Electrode Co., Ltd. (Taiwan; 98.73%); Truswal Systems Corporation; Unipac Corporation (Canada); Wilsonart International, Inc.

PRINCIPAL OPERATING UNITS

DeVilbiss; Fibre Glass-Evercoat; Ispra (Italy); ITW Angleboard; ITW Brands; ITW Buildex; ITW CIP; ITW Deltar; ITW Devcon; ITW Drawform; ITW Fastex; ITW Foils; ITW Gema; ITW Hi-Cone; ITW Tek-Fast; ITW Ramset/Red Head; ITW Shakeproof Assembly Components; ITW Stretch Packaging Systems; ITW TACC; ITW Texwipe; Minigrip/Zip-Pak; Paslode; Signode Packaging Systems; Simco; Valeron Strength Films; Vulcan-Hart; Wynn's.

PRINCIPAL COMPETITORS

General Electric Company; Cooper Industries, Ltd.; Eaton Corporation; The Marmon Group, Inc.; Dover Corporation; Enodis plc.

FURTHER READING

Borden, Jeff, "ITW Tightens Its Belt to Ride Out Recession," *Crain's Chicago Business,* June 3, 1991, pp. 36+.

Byrne, Harlan S., "Illinois Tool Works: It's Still Shopping, but Not for Real Big Deals," *Barron's,* May 1, 1989, pp. 39+.

——, "Illinois Tool Works: Satisfying Customers...and Investors," *Barron's,* November 16, 1992, pp. 51–52.

——, "A New Chapter," *Barron's,* December 11, 1995, p. 18.

——, "A Patent Success," *Barron's,* May 23, 1994, p. 23.

——, "Still a Growth Machine," *Barron's,* November 6, 2000, p. 32.

Conlin, Michelle, "The Most Decentralized Company in the World," *Forbes,* January 11, 1999, p. 142.

Dubashi, Jagannath, "Illinois Tool: Buy This Global Niche Meister on Weakness?," *Financial World,* December 24, 1991, pp. 16–17.

——, "Illinois Tool Works, Really!," *Financial World,* July 26, 1988, pp. 12, 14.

Friedman, Dorian, and Paul Glastris, "Tougher Than Nails: Illinois Tool Works Is a Profit Machine," *U.S. News & World Report,* June 10, 1991, pp. 49–51.

Goff, Lisa, "Recent Acquisitions to Bolster ITW," *Crain's Chicago Business,* May 12, 1986, p. 45.

Henkoff, Ronald, "The Ultimate Nuts & Bolts Co.," *Fortune,* July 16, 1990, pp. 70–73.

Lashinsky, Adam, "Blue Bloods Go for Jugular: Why ITW Has Turned Hostile," *Crain's Chicago Business,* September 11, 1995, pp. 3, 54.

Loeffelholz, Suzanne, "Illinois Tool Works: Waiting for Godot," *Financial World,* April 18, 1989, p. 15.

Murphy, H. Lee, "As ITW Names New No. 2, Firm Goes Shopping Again," *Crain's Chicago Business,* August 30, 2004, p. 12.

——, "ITW's CEO Shows Up Critics with Results of Buying Spree," *Crain's Chicago Business,* May 29, 1989, p. 67.

"No Need for Economies of Scale: Illinois Tool Works Revs Up Innovation by Keeping Its 665 Units Separate and Focused," *Business Week,* October 31, 2005, p. MTL6.

Quintanilla, Carl, "Illinois Tool Sets Accord for Premark," *Wall Street Journal,* September 10, 1999, p. A3.

Stevens, Tim, "Breaking Up Is Profitable to Do," *Industry Week,* June 21, 1999, pp. 28–29, 32, 34.

"Strength in Diversity: Illinois Tool Works Prospers in Many Fields," *Barron's,* September 5, 1983, p. 40.

Tatge, Mark, "Conquer and Divide," *Forbes,* April 16, 2001, p. 80.

"Tooling Along: ITW Records Handsome Gains from Array of New Lines," *Barron's,* October 29, 1984, pp. 58+.

Wolf, Carol (Bloomberg News), "Why ITW Is the Smallest $5 Billion Company in U.S.," *Chicago Sun-Times,* October 10, 1999, p. 53.

Immucor, Inc.

3130 Gateway Drive
P.O. Box 5625
Norcross, Georgia 30091-5625
U.S.A.
Telephone: (770) 441-2051
Toll Free: (800) 829-2553
Fax: (770) 441-3807
Web site: http://www.immucor.com

Public Company
Incorporated: 1982
Employees: 531
Sales: $144.78 million (2005)
Stock Exchanges: NASDAQ
Ticker Symbol: BLUD
NAIC: 325412 Pharmaceutical Preparation Manufacturing; 325413 In-Vitro Diagnostic Substance Manufacturing; 325998 All Other Miscellaneous Chemical Product and Preparation Manufacturing; 339112 Surgical and Medical Instrument Manu- facturing

∎ ∎ ∎

Immucor, Inc., is the market leader in North America and Europe in human blood testing systems and related products. The company introduced automated blood testing in the United States and is one of only two companies in the country offering a complete line of blood banking reagents, chemical substances used to test blood prior to a transfusion. Immucor markets and distributes its products directly, and through its subsidiaries in Canada, Europe, and Japan to hospitals, blood banks, and research laboratories worldwide.

ORIGINS

Since its establishment in 1982, Immucor, Inc., has been in the blood bank reagent and instrument business. The company was founded by Edward Gallup, Ralph Eatz, and Richard Still, executives who had worked together for Biological Corporation of America, a Pennsylvania-based blood reagent company. After growing Biological Corp. from $700,000 to $15 million in annual sales in six years, the group defected to start their own enterprise a year after the company was acquired by Cooper Laboratories. The trio raised over 50 percent of their initial capital, more than $500,000, mostly from direct contributions from 18 employees, and set up Immucor headquarters in an office park in Norcross, Georgia.

In the United States, the Food and Drug Administration (FDA) regulates human blood as a drug and a biological product and the transfusion of blood as the administration of a drug and of a biological product. Initially unlicensed and lacking FDA approval, financing was a major hurdle for the new company but more start-up funds came from a bank loan and from doctors, pathologists, and other industry sources. The FDA approved Immucor's Norcross facility in December 1982 and the company began marketing kits used to determine blood types to hospitals and blood banks. In March 1983, Immucor acquired its "solid phase" technology and patent rights from five researchers at the Community Blood Center of Greater Kansas City. After losing money for several years, in October 1985 Immucor announced an initial public offering and in December began listing

Diagnostics Transfusion became a joint venture partner by paying Immucor $4 million for 10 percent of its capital.

COMPANY PERSPECTIVES

Immucor, Inc. is a global in vitro diagnostics company specializing in the area of pre-transfusion diagnostics. We develop, manufacture, and sell products used by hospital blood banks, clinical laboratories, and blood donor centers to detect and identify certain properties of human blood prior to patient transfusion. We have revolutionized the industry through our dedication to automating manual processes in the blood bank laboratory.

---

on the NASDAQ under the ticker symbol BLUD. Stock sold for $7 per share and the company raised $6.1 million.

The year 1986 was a breakout one for Immucor. When the company's fiscal year ended on May 31, the balance sheet showed a profit for the first time. Earnings were $311,000 on revenues of $6.2 million, up from $4.3 million the previous year. An even bigger milestone was achieved when the FDA granted approval for the company to market a blood test based on its proprietary solid phase technology. Capture-P, marketed to hospitals and blood banks, was designed for blood platelet analysis and radically reduced test time from ten hours to one hour. In September, Immucor received FDA approval to begin marketing an AIDS test kit developed by Cellular Products Inc., a New York-based biotechnology firm.

By 1987, Immucor had established a client base in the United States, Canada, and Europe, and in April announced that it had reached an agreement with Sanko Junyaku Co. for Sanko to distribute Immucor blood-banking products in Japan. The firm continued to offer pioneering products in 1988 with the introduction of Capture-R, a test used to detect foreign antibodies in the red cells of donated blood. The procedure utilized the company's solid phase technology in which blood components are dried on a plastic coated surface before immunological tests are carried out. The technology allowed for manual or automated operation and removed the need to mix blood and chemicals in a test tube, potentially cutting labor time and costs by half.

In October 1989, Immucor took steps to boost its overseas activities, which accounted for about one-fourth of its revenues, by forming a marketing alliance with Diagnostics Transfusion, a French firm. The two companies agreed to market each other's products and

1990–1996: EXPANSIONS AND CONTRACTIONS

After completing an expansion of its Norcross production facilities, in February 1990 Immucor rolled out a second Capture-P test. In June it received FDA approval to market two additional solid phase blood tests, Capture-R Ready-Screen, for the detection of unexpected antibodies to red blood cells, and Capture-R Ready-ID, an antibody identification test. The company continued its strategy to expand European operations and market share when it acquired 100 percent of its German distributor in September 1990, and again in 1991, when they bought their Italian distributor, BCI-Human. In April 1991, the FDA granted Immucor approval to market Capture-CMV, a solid phase blood test for the detection of cytomegalovirus, a herpes virus, marking the company's first application of its proprietary technology to infectious disease testing.

In July 1992, Immucor reached an agreement with Bio-Tek Instruments, Inc. of Burlington, Vermont, to begin joint development of the ABS2000, the company's first blood bank instrument system and the industry's first fully automated "walk-away" blood analyzer. The instrument was designed to use Immucor's proprietary Capture reagent product technology. In July 1993, the company announced that its year-end net income had fallen to $1.83 million compared to $3.04 million in 1992. Due to research and development costs on the ABS2000, and shrinking European profits, the company also declared a hiring and salary freeze. Immucor stock sank to $4.75, its 52-week low, after the announcement.

Immucor added to its troubles with investors in August 1994 when it announced a delay in clinical trials of the ABS2000 in order to modify the system's software to permit the reuse of miniaturized test tubes, causing some stock analysts to lower ratings from Hold to Sell. However, by August 1995, Immucor stock had rebounded to $15.50, a 52-week high, on good year-end financial news and premature anticipation of the start of clinical trials for the company's automated blood-testing machine. The firm finally filed an application with the FDA for clearance of the ABS2000 on March 18, 1996. In June, the Medical Devices Bureau of Canada approved the machine, and Italy's Ministry of Health did likewise in October, the same month Immucor announced the start of U.S. clinical trials for its premier product. The year ended with the acquisition of privately held Dominion Biologicals Limited of Dartmouth, Nova Scotia, which gave Immucor a second FDA licensed

KEY DATES

1982: Immucor, Inc., is founded by Edward Gallup, Ralph Eatz, and Richard Still.

1985: Company raises $6.1 million through public offering.

1986: FDA approves proprietary blood test technology that radically reduces labor time and costs.

1992: Immucor begins development of ABS2000, the industry's first fully automated blood analyzer.

1996: Regulatory agencies in Canada and Japan approve use of ABS2000.

1998: FDA clears use of ABS2000 in the United States; Houston-based Gamma Biologicals is acquired.

2002: Company launches second-generation instrument system, the Galileo, in Europe.

2004: FDA clears Galileo for use in the United States; bribery probe of subsidiary is launched in Italy.

manufacturing facility and additional international distribution capabilities.

1998: AUTOMATION AND ACQUISITIONS

In January 1997, Immucor signed an exclusive distribution agreement to market an HIV-monitoring system, IMAGN 2000, in the United States, Canada, and Europe. In November 1997, the FDA approved an Immucor-developed syphilis screening test called Capture(R)-S. In March 1998, Immucor acquired the North American marketing and distribution rights of the Rosys Plato system, a semi-automated blood grouping instrument, from an English company. On July 6, 1998, Immucor received its long-awaited clearance from the FDA to market the ABS2000 in the United States, making it the first fully automated instrument for the hospital blood bank transfusion laboratory in the country when it was launched in September.

In October 1998, Immucor became the market leader in providing blood reagents and systems in the United States and Canada when it acquired Houston-based Gamma Biologicals, a company with 130 employees and annual revenues of $18 million. Adding Gamma's product line, which included the FDA-approved React Test System for detecting red blood cell antibodies, and its client base in over 50 countries, expanded Immucor's core blood reagent business and strengthened its market position worldwide. The company made another major acquisition in April 1999 when it bought the product lines of Biopool International, Inc.'s BCA blood bank division, making Immucor one of only two major players with a complete line of blood bank reagents in the United States.

In November 2000, a group including Kairos Partners acquired a 7.1 percent interest in Immucor through stock purchases, which it raised to 10 percent in July 2001. Kairos, a healthcare industry investment fund, expressed concerns about Immucor's strategic plans and falling stock prices and in August began a hostile proxy contest by announcing plans to replace part of the company's six-member board with four of its own members at the November annual shareholder meeting. Immucor's board of directors prevailed in the showdown when shareholders voted for the company's six director nominees. Immucor brought 2001 to a close with a flurry of late December product rollouts including its I-TRAC Plus System, the first verification and tracking system utilizing PalmPilot technology designed to prevent errors in the blood transfusion process, and the North American launch of ReACT, a new technology for antibody screening and identification. The year also saw the firm win approval from the Japanese Ministry of Health to market the ABS2000 and its related reagents in Japan.

When fiscal 2002 ended in May, Immucor reported an earnings increase of 235 percent from the previous year. In June 2002, Immucor launched its second-generation instrument system, the Galileo, in Europe. Capable of processing 224 different samples at once, the fully automated high-volume system was designed for large hospitals, clinical reference laboratories, and blood donor centers. In January 2003, Immucor reported record revenues and net income for the previous quarter due to renewals of group contracts and reagent price increases at substantially higher prices. The firm's share price had improved more than 600 percent from mid-October 2001 to a high of $25.91 in mid-January. In March 2003, the company signed a development agreement for the production of human collagen mesh with Inamed Corp. that called for Immucor's subsidiary, Gamma Biologicals, to manufacture the product. Revenues for fiscal 2003 totaled a record $98.3 million and the *Atlanta Journal and Constitution* newspaper recognized Immucor as the second best performing company in Georgia for the year.

2004: CLEARING GALILEO FOR U.S. TAKEOFF

On January 30, 2004, Immucor submitted an application for approval to the FDA for Galileo, its flagship product. With over 100 systems already in place in Europe, Galileo was cleared for use in the United States on April 26, 2004, prompting Immucor's stock price to shoot up 20 percent. In May, Immucor made its first U.S. sale of the revolutionary machine, which was eight times faster than any competing instrument, to Detroit-based Henry Ford Health System. In July, the $160,000 blood-test machine was approved in Canada and Japan.

November 2004 brought bad news from abroad when Immucor announced that its CEO and President, Dr. Gioacchino De Chirico, and the company's Italian subsidiary, were subjects of a criminal investigation in Milan, Italy. Dr. De Chirico, formerly president of the Italian subsidiary, was forced to give up his CEO job as the company conducted an internal investigation. The charges centered on improper payments that companies allegedly made to an Italian physician and hospital administrator in exchange for favorable contract awards.

In December 2004, Immucor took the unusual step of canceling contracts with two of the nation's largest group purchasing organizations in order to raise prices on its blood test equipment. The firm asked for an average 105 percent increase on all covered products and invoked a cancellation clause when Novation and Premier turned down its request. Immucor's largest competitor in the U.S. market, Ortho Clinical Diagnostic Systems, a division of Johnson & Johnson, also canceled its contract with Premier after its September 2004 price hike of 110 percent was rejected.

In June 2005, the company entered into a long-term agreement with Canadian Blood Services for the purchase of five Galileo instruments and the related reagents. Hoping to expand its 2 percent share of the world's third largest transfusion diagnostics market, in July, Immucor entered into a joint venture with its Japanese distributor, Kainos Laboratories Inc., a publicly traded company that developed and distributed diagnostic reagents, pharmaceuticals, and medical instruments. In August, the Securities and Exchange Commission announced that its probe into Immucor's Italian unit had turned into a formal investigation of possible violations of the Foreign Corrupt Practices Act. In November, the company announced plans to shut its Houston plant in 2007 in order to cut costs and fatten gross margins.

In February 2006, the company revealed that a prosecutor in Milan, Italy, had completed an investigation into payments made by several companies to Italian physicians and alleged that the former president of Im-mucor's Italian subsidiary, Dr. De Chirico, participated in a payment of $16,094 to one physician and payments of $47,000 to another to gain favorable hospital procurement contracts. The company announced that Dr. De Chirico planned to present further evidence to the prosecutor and intended to dispute the allegations. By the end of February, the company had received purchase orders for a total of 339 Galileo instruments worldwide: 222 in Europe, 115 in North America, and two in Japan. Of those, 263 Galileo instruments were also generating reagent revenues that averaged around $100,000 annually.

In May 2006, Immucor announced its ninth consecutive quarter of record revenues. It attributed the growth to the renewal of customer contracts at higher prices, the continuing sales of ABS2000 in the United States, sales of the Galileo instrument in Europe, Japan and the U.S., the associated reagent growth associated with these instrument placements, and sales of the company's human collagen product. The company also announced that it planned to launch its third generation blood-testing instrument, the Echo, in the last quarter of 2006. The Echo was based on Galileo technology but was designed to serve an estimated 6,000 small-to-medium hospitals, laboratories and donor centers worldwide. On May 24, 2006, the company reported that potential criminal charges could be filed against the company in an ongoing bribery inquiry in Italy.

Immucor, Inc.'s strategy of building its business through the sale of medical instruments, which generated lucrative long-term contracts for its reagents and related proprietary technology, had propelled it to the top of the industry in both the U.S. and European markets. With a third generation blood-tester in the wings, and a toehold in the Japanese market, the company was positioned at the forefront of a global market that was primed for its cheaper and faster automated technology.

Ted Sylvester

PRINCIPAL SUBSIDIARIES

BCA Acquisition Corp; Immucor Gamma Biologicals Inc; Immucor Sales Inc; Dominion Biologicals Ltd (Canada); Immucor Diagnosticos Medicos Lda (Portugal); Immucor France EURL (France); Immucor Gamma Benelux SPRL (Belgium); Immucor Italia Srl (Italy); Immucor-Kainos Inc. (Japan); Immucor Medizinische Diagnostik GmbH (Germany); Immucor SL (Spain).

PRINCIPAL COMPETITORS

Abaxis, Inc; Hemagen Diagnostics, Inc.; Ortho-Clinical Diagnostics, Inc.; TECHNE Corporation.

FURTHER READING

Bartiromo, Maria, "Immucor—Chmn. & CEO Interview," *CNBC/Dow Jones Business Video,* July 18, 2005.

Benesh, Peter, "Maker of Medical Systems Looks to Bleed the Competition Dry," *Investor's Business Daily,* June 27, 2005.

Berkrot, Bill, "Galileo Sparks Immucor's Stellar Stock Performance," *Reuters News,* January 19, 2005.

"Blood Testing Supply Vendors Drop Out of Contracts, Vow to Hike Prices to Hospitals," *Hospital Materials Management,* January 1, 2005.

"Collaborations; Reagent Maker, Kainos Agree to Form Joint Venture," *Gastroenterology Week,* July 18, 2005.

Geewax, Marilyn, "Immucor's Stock Has Positive Reaction: Blood Reagent Firm Poised for Success," *Atlanta Journal and Constitution,* September 1, 1986.

Griffeth, Bill, "Power Lunch: Immucor—Chairman & CEO—Interview," *CNBC/Dow Jones Business Video,* February 22, 2000.

"Immucor Faces Inquiry in Italy on Alleged Payments for Jobs," *Wall Street Journal Europe,* November 3, 2004.

Jenks, Alan, "Blood-Test Agents Carry Immucor," *Atlanta Business Chronicle,* February 12, 1990.

Kanell, Michael E., "Immucor Product in Tests: Automated Blood Analyzer Expected to Be Key Advance," *Atlanta Journal and Constitution,* October 1, 1996.

Saito-Chung, David, "Blood-Test Gear Firm Soaks Up Thick Profit," *Investor's Business Daily,* May 7, 2003.

Schonbak, Judith. "Immucor: A Serious Contender in the Blood Reagent Industry," *Business Atlanta,* December 1986.

Tessler, Joelle, "Immucor Sets 52-Week High As Investors Await Clinical Trials," *Dow Jones News Service,* August 31, 1995.

Toney, Dorrie, "Norcross-Based Immucor to Purchase Gamma Biologicals," *Atlanta Constitution,* September 22, 1998.

Walker, Tom, "Investors Give Immucor's Stock Infusion of Optimism; Analysts Shrug Off Profit Restatement, Late Annual Report," *Atlanta Journal-Constitution,* September 7, 2005.

Imperial Industries, Inc.

1259 NW 21st Street
Pompano Beach, Florida 33069
U.S.A.
Telephone: (954) 917-7665
Fax: (954) 917-2775
Web site: http://www.imperialindustries.com

Public Company
Incorporated: 1968
Employees: 148
Sales: $72.3 million (2005)
Stock Exchanges: NASDAQ
Ticker Symbol: IPII
NAIC: 327999 All Other Miscellaneous Nonmetallic
   Mineral Product Manufacturing

∎ ∎ ∎

Based in Pompano Beach, Florida, Imperial Industries, Inc. is a NASDAQ-listed company that manufactures and distributes building materials, primarily in Florida and Georgia. Most of Imperial's business is conducted through subsidiaries Premix-Marbletite Manufacturing Co. Inc. and Just-Rite Supply, Inc. Premix is Florida's oldest manufacturer of stucco, plaster, and pool finish products. The company also offers interior products such as WONCOTE, a gypsum-based veneer plaster coating, and the TILE-TITE brand of roofing tile mortar. In addition to a manufacturing facility in Pompano Beach, Premix operates plants in Winter Springs, Florida, and Kennesaw, Georgia.

Just-Rite, which contributes most of Imperial's revenues, is a distributor of Premix products as well as other gypsum, roofing, masonry, millwork, insulation, and related building products manufactured by Germany's Degussa Construction Chemicals. With more than a dozen distribution centers in Florida, Georgia, Alabama, and Mississippi, Just-Rite serves the southeastern United States and the Caribbean. The distribution of Premix products is not limited to Just-Rite, however. They also are sold through a large number of supply companies throughout the Southeast and Caribbean as well as Maryland, Illinois, Nebraska, and North Dakota.

COMPANY FOUNDING IN 1968

The man responsible for the rise of Imperial Industries was Eugene C. Ferri, Jr. A Miami native, Ferri made his mark in the early 1960s as a life insurance salesman for Gulf Life Insurance Co. Leo Brinkley, Jr., a former Gulf Life executive, told *Florida Trend* that Ferri was a fixture on the firm's "Million-Dollar Roundtable." Ambitious and insightful, he recognized that Gulf Life needed to invest the premiums he and his fellow salesmen brought in, and he began acting as an unofficial broker between companies in the market for a loan and Gulf Life. Ferri soon broke away to launch his own insurance agency as well as to set up a financial consultancy to help Miami-area companies with fundraising and the completion of acquisitions. Two of his clients were Premix, a producer of gypsum and stucco products founded in Miami in the 1950s, and Imperial Industries, a holding company founded in the city in 1968. Imperial became involved in the building materials business with the 1969 acquisition of Allied Electric Supply and the addition of Regal

---

COMPANY PERSPECTIVES

Mission: To become the premier manufacturer and distributor of selected building products and achieve consistent levels of profitability sufficient to increase stockholder value.

Wood Products Inc., but it did not limit itself to this sector, as reflected by the 1969 acquisition of Pegasus Luggage. In 1971 Imperial moved into the distribution of building materials through the purchase of Adobe Brick and Supply Co.

At the behest of its owners, Ferri bought into Premix in 1967, and a year later became the company's principal shareholder. Imperial remained a client as Ferri took Premix public. Then, in 1971, he engineered a merger with Imperial, which became the holding company for Premix. When the transaction was completed, Ferri emerged as Imperial's largest shareholder. Moreover, he came away with a financial consulting contract that guaranteed a minimum yearly fee of $50,000. For the next four years he did not take a direct hand in the running of Imperial, which began to build up Adobe by forming a chain of Florida retail outlets under the Adobe Home Centers name. In addition, the company became involved in another venture, establishing Empire Plastics, Inc., in 1973.

Pegasus Luggage was spun off in September 1975 and, a month later, the senior officers at Imperial left in a spinoff of Regal Wood Products, forcing Ferri to step into the breach and take a more active role in running Imperial, while continuing to head an insurance agency and serving as a consultant. He assumed control of Imperial at a trying time for the building materials sector, crippled by the worst construction slump the state had seen for many years. Revenues plummeted, and in 1975 the company posted a $1.8 million loss.

In the second half of the 1970s Ferri rebuilt Imperial by snapping up Florida building supply companies that could be bought at reasonable prices and then taking advantage when construction rebounded. Some of the major acquisitions during this period included C&F Electrical Supply Co. in 1977; Solar Systems of Sun Dance, Inc., a year later; and in 1979 Just-Rite Lumber Co., Inc., and Douglas Lumber Co. The Just-Rite acquisition included a subsidiary, New Steel, Inc., a fabricator and distributor of reinforced steel products, which Imperial would shut down two years later. Also in 1979 Imperial acquired Growers Packing Corp., a Florida

City-based tomato packer and distributor. Imperial returned to profitability in 1977 and two years later sales peaked at $90 million, resulting in a net profit of $3.8 million.

In the early 1980s construction once again slowed, and the company posted a loss in 1981, but this time the Ferri magic failed to work. He tried to cut costs by in part selling off most of the Just-Rite assets and spinning off Solar Systems. Anticipating that construction activity was due to pick up, he expanded his distribution operations at the start of 1983, funded by a $6.6 million stock offering and the assumption of debt. In November 1983 Imperial also acquired Miami's C&R Building Materials, Inc. During the last months of 1983 Imperial was once again making money and Ferri was touting the company's stock on trips across the country. He succeeded in building up excitement about Imperial, leading Wall Street to project profits for Imperial in the $3 million range for 1984, but his hype would only lead to serious disappointment when the company in fact lost $280,000 for the year, this despite record revenues of $112.6 million, almost half of which were provided by Adobe.

Imperial's situation grew worse in 1985. Ferri tried to control costs by closing down operations, but the company lacked the cash flow needed to pay suppliers, who reacted by cutting off Imperial. The operations of Allied Electric Supply and Adobe were devastated, essentially leaving Premix, and to a lesser extent Growers Packing, as the only whole businesses left. Together they generated less than $10 million a year in sales. Not surprisingly, Ferri's stewardship of Imperial came under close scrutiny. He was accused of alienating his managers along the way, curtailing profit sharing while at the same time increasing his own compensation. The purchase of a twin-engine airplane, a helicopter, and five condominiums also raised eyebrows. Moreover, Imperial's board of directors was stocked with Ferri's relatives and friends.

Adobe trimmed the number of locations from 37 to 16 in 1985 but because it was unable to buy supplies it was forced to discontinue operations in 1986. Then, in July 1986, Allied, also hamstrung by a loss of working capital, filed for Chapter 11 bankruptcy protection. In early 1987 Allied discontinued its operations as well and the company's assets were assigned to creditors. In the meantime, Imperial Industries was forced into Chapter 11 bankruptcy protection in September 1986 by its creditors.

FERRI'S DEATH IN 1988

While finding a way to salvage Imperial and his own reputation were extremely important to Ferri, he would

KEY DATES

1968: The company is incorporated.
1971: The company merges with Premix-Marbeltit Manufacturing Co.
1975: Eugene C. Ferri, Jr., becomes chairman.
1986: Imperial is forced into bankruptcy.
1988: Ferri dies; the company emerges from bankruptcy.
2000: Just-Rite Supply, Inc., is formed.
2005: An alliance is formed with Degussa Construction Chemicals.

1992, but the company was profitable, earning $136,000. The company posted losses over the next two years, but grew sales to $11.6 million. An important development for Premix came in 1994 when it secured an exclusive five-year licensing agreement to manufacture and sell a new roof tile mortar product in Florida and foreign countries. In that same year, Acrocrete began selling its products, along with complementary products produced by other companies, directly to end-users from a leased warehouse in Savannah, Georgia. This test program proved so successful that similar operations were opened in Jacksonville, Florida, and Norcross, Georgia, in 1996. More distribution facilities were added in Dallas, Georgia, in 1998, and Gadsden, Alabama, a year later. This last operation was relocated to Rainbow City, Alabama, in 2000.

soon have another more pressing concern: cancer. Only in his early 50s, he died from cancer in March 1988. Long before his passing, however, Ferri had engineered a deal with creditors on a reorganization of Imperial with a pair of options, agreed to in November 1986. The creditors were allowed to shop Premix to potential buyers but Imperial retained the right of first refusal. Two offers were presented, but both were laced with so many conditions that Imperial refused. Imperial's creditors pursued the second option, which called for Imperial to pay $2.5 million in three installments, but the company, lacking adequate cash flow, had difficulty making a final $1.2 million payment due three months after Ferri's death. It was at this point that Ferri's daughter, Lisa Thompson, formed an alliance with Miami attorney S. Daniel Ponce to rescue Imperial. A combination of two secured loans and investments from two investors raised the cash needed to satisfy the creditors.

Imperial emerged from bankruptcy in July 1988 and Ponce was installed as the chairman. With the June 1988 sale of Growers Packing, Imperial was left with little more than $6 million in assets and two subsidiaries, Premix and Adobe, which was down to a single retail outlet. "Right now, the future is our core company, Premix-Marbletite Manufacturing Co.," Howard Ehlers, an Imperial vice-president, told *South Florida Business Journal.* Due to its losses, Imperial had some $12 million in carryforwards that could have some value if the company opted to make acquisitions, but Ehlers made it clear that the company was not thinking that far ahead. "We haven't really had the chance to put together a real solid business plan for the future."

Reduced to penny-stock status, Imperial spent the next decade slowly rebuilding. It added another subsidiary, Acrocrete, formed in 1988 to manufacture exterior stucco products that complemented what Premix had to offer. Revenues totaled just $7.1 million by

FORMATION OF JUST-RITE SUPPLY IN 2000

Business continued to pick up for Imperial in the second half of the 1990s. Revenues topped $15 million in 1997 and reached $22.6 million in 1999. Net income during this period peaked in 1998 at $2 million. The next step in Imperial's long comeback came with the January 2000 formation of Just-Rite Supply, Inc., an Acrocrete subsidiary that took over all of the distribution facilities and was established to acquire other building materials distributors. In January 2000 A&R Supply Inc. was acquired, adding distribution facilities in Foley, Alabama, and Pensacola and Destin, Florida. Then, in March 2000, Imperial acquired Panhandle Drywall Supply Inc., which expanded Just-Rite's operations to Panama City Beach and Tallahassee, Florida. Three more distributions were acquired in Hattiesburg, Mississippi, and Gulfport and Pascagoula, Florida, in May 2000. Just-Rite opened a new distribution outlet in Picayune, Mississippi, in October 2000, which led to the closure of the Hattiesburg operation in February 2001.

Imperial's revenues topped $40 million in 2000, accompanied by net income of $534,000. A stalled economy hurt business over the next two years, as sales dipped to $36.5 million in 2002 and the company lost money in both 2001 and 2002. The company regained its momentum in 2004 when sales improved to $41 million and Imperial returned to profitability, netting $640,000. In 2004 revenues jumped to $55.3 million and net income grew fourfold to nearly $2.5 million. By this time, it was Just-Rite leading the way, accounting for nearly 60 percent of Imperial's revenues. At one time producing most of the sales, Acrocrete accounted for just 18 percent of sales. Premix, on the other hand, contributed 24 percent of sales, but was Imperial's most profitable operation.

In May 2005 Imperial graduated from over-the-counter status when it gained a listing on the NAS-DAQ, in that same month reporting its eighth consecutive profitable quarter. The company's prospects would brighten even further in July 2005 when it forged a deal with Germany's Degussa Construction Chemicals. Acrocrete was sold to Degussa Wall Systems for $1.1 million, and in turn Just-Rite was able to distribute Degussa's concrete and stucco-related products. As a result of this alliance, as well as increased construction caused by heavy hurricane damage in Florida, Imperial saw its revenues surge to $72.3 million and net income improve to $3.4 million in 2005. Ponce described Imperial's achievement to *Investor's Business Daily,* as a "17-year overnight success story." It was very likely that even greater success was to follow as record results continued in 2006.

Ed Dinger

PRINCIPAL SUBSIDIARIES

Premix-Marbletite Manufacturing Co., Inc.; Just-Rite Supply, Inc.

PRINCIPAL COMPETITORS

CRH PLC; Holcim Ltd.; Lafarge North America Inc.

FURTHER READING

Aquino, Jorge, "Imperial Emerges from Chapter 11," *South Florida Business Journal,* July 18, 1988, p. 3.

Elliott, Alan R., "Stormy Weather Equals High Demand for Building Supplies Firm," *Investor's Business Daily,* August 11, 2005, p. A07.

"Imperial Industries' Creditors Force Firm into Chapter 11," *Wall Street Journal,* October 3, 1986, p. 1.

Koenig, John, "Did the King of Imperial Industries Topple His Own Empire?," *Florida Trend,* July 1, 1986, p. 46.

InfoSonics Corporation

5880 Pacific Center Blvd.
San Diego, California 92121
U.S.A.
Telephone: (858) 373-1600
Toll Free: (800) 519-1599
Fax: (858) 373-1505
Web site: http://www.infosonics.com

Public Company
Incorporated: 1994
Employees: 28
Sales: $145.79 million (2005)
Stock Exchanges: AMEX
Ticker Symbol: IFO
NAIC: 423690 Other Electronic Parts and Equipment
 Merchant Wholesalers

■ ■ ■

InfoSonics Corporation is a leading distributor of cellular telephone products in North America. The California-based firm sells handsets and accessories from manufacturers including Samsung, VK Mobile, and i-mate to retailers, regional wireless carriers, and through its web site. More than two-thirds of InfoSonics' business comes from Latin America. Founder and CEO Joseph Ram owns a sizable minority stake in the publicly traded firm.

BEGINNINGS

InfoSonics was founded in 1994 in San Diego, California, by Joseph Ram. Born in Israel, Ram had

served as an army captain and studied business and economics at Tel Aviv University before taking a job with an importer of telecommunications equipment from the United States and the Far East. He was recruited to run the international business of American client Procom Supply, and he worked there from 1989 to 1993 before leaving to found a company of his own.

InfoSonics began operations in February 1994, initially distributing telephone equipment and PBX systems to third parties. With cellular telephone sales exploding, Ram soon decided to shift his focus to this market, and the company began distributing the products of such manufacturers as Samsung, which it added in 1997.

In 1998 the firm hired Abraham Rosler to serve as executive vice-president. He had previously worked for a company that sold cell phone accessories in Latin America, where Ram, who was fluent in Spanish, was seeking to expand. Rosler also took a minority equity stake in the firm. With sales growth averaging roughly 50 percent each year, by 1999 InfoSonics' revenues had risen above $24 million.

The company's business consisted of buying cellular telephone handsets and accessories from manufacturers, programming the phones to customers' specifications, and packing and shipping orders. The firm's rapid growth was due in part to the nature of the market, which included frequent technology upgrades, surging numbers of new users, and customers' tendency to switch phone companies, which typically required a new phone. These factors conspired to make the market highly unpredictable, with Ram telling the *Miami Herald,* "This business is like the weather in Miami. If you don't like it, wait 20 minutes."

A critical component of InfoSonics' ability to keep up with industry trends was a web-based data sharing system in which the company offered information about the market while asking customers to tell what they knew about sales and equipment issues. The web site was also used to track shipments of orders and facilitate transmission of essential documents.

OPENING OF MIAMI WAREHOUSE: 2000

In the fall of 2000 InfoSonics opened a second warehouse in Miami, where it had earlier used a third party to supply its Latin American accounts. The company was distributing phones and accessories to 400 carriers who resold them to customers, as well as to more than 9,000 retail locations around the United States. Its clients were primarily firms that were independently owned and/or regional players that lacked the clout of an AT&T or Sprint. The average order was worth $14,000, and the company made a profit of 4 to 8 percent on the price of a handset and 10 to 15 percent on accessories. Two-thirds of the products it shipped were phones.

In December 2000 InfoSonics acquired a cell phone retailer called Axcess Mobile for the forgiveness of $57,000 in accounts payable. Axcess owned a small number of retail kiosks in San Diego shopping malls. The firm was also considering an initial public offering at this time, but pulled back due to unfavorable market conditions.

In December 2001 InfoSonics signed an agreement with PC-EPhone, Inc., to distribute that company's handheld device, which combined features of cell phones, personal digital assistants (PDAs), and computers. InfoSonics was also an authorized reseller of products from such manufacturers as Samsung, Motorola, Ericsson, LG, and Audiovox at that time.

The firm was continuing to expand dramatically, and revenues jumped from $34.2 million in 2001 to $65.1 million in 2003. Some 97 million cell phones were sold in the United States alone during the latter year, and while many were bought by new users, an estimated 20 percent of subscribers acquired a new phone annually.

INITIAL PUBLIC OFFERING IN 2004

In January 2004 the firm bought a company called InfoSonics de Mexico from executives Ram and Rosler, and also filed the paperwork to make its long-delayed initial public stock offering. In June the company took in $12 million from investors on the American Stock Exchange, using the funds to boost sales and marketing efforts, expand warehouse and office facilities, increase the number of retail wireless service activations, and start a logistics service business. Prior to the sale founder Ram had held a 76 percent stake, but his total would fall to 48 percent after the offering.

In July InfoSonics signed an agreement to distribute the wireless remote video monitoring and data systems products of Cenuco, Inc., and a few months later the company extended its distribution agreement with Samsung and added that firm's products to its Latin American offerings.

In October InfoSonics closed four of its Axcess Mobile mall kiosks and sold the other six to The Mobile Solution Corporation. The retail unit had contributed only about 5 percent of the company's revenues, and had not been consistently profitable.

In November the firm unveiled an online store where customers could buy new phones and accessories, and shortly afterwards it also began distributing VK Mobile cell phones. InfoSonics would be the sole North American distributor for the Korean manufacturer. At this time the company was deriving 70 percent of its revenues from sales of handsets to regional wireless carriers, 25 percent from sales to dealers, and 5 percent from online sales. For 2004 InfoSonics reported sales of $73.4 million.

The company's mission had evolved as the cell phone market grew and it took on a number of challenges unique to the industry. In addition to simply ordering, warehousing, and shipping phones and accessories, InfoSonics also marketed new products to both carriers and consumers; tested for compatibility and secured approval from regional service providers; customized and loaded software onto phones; and performed field services including training, support, and warranty fulfillment. In the United States the company's

KEY DATES

1994: Joseph Ram founds InfoSonics Corporation to distribute telephone products.
1995: Firm shifts focus to wireless equipment.
1997: InfoSonics begins distributing Samsung products.
2000: Miami warehouse is added; Axcess Mobile shopping mall kiosks are acquired.
2004: InfoSonics completes its initial public offering; online store begins operations; company becomes exclusive North American distributor for VK Mobile.
2005: Argentine subsidiary is acquired; annual sales double to $146 million.
2006: i-mate, Alcatel, TCL brands are added; private $14.4 million stock sale is completed.

carrier customers were primarily smaller regional ones such as Alaska Cellular, Cincinnati Bell, and SunCom, but in Latin America they included both second-tier providers and market leaders Telefonica and America Movil.

ACQUISITION OF ARGENTINE SUBSIDIARY: 2005

In January 2005 InfoSonics bought an Argentina-based company that distributed Samsung cell phones and accessories, which would give the firm its largest presence in Latin America to date. The company had locations in the United States, Mexico, Argentina, Guatemala, El Salvador, and Colombia, and it was reportedly also studying the feasibility of opening an office in Chile.

In November the firm's credit line was boosted to $25 million through new lender Wells Fargo, and the following month InfoSonics began selling Samsung phones and accessories online. Consumers who went to the Samsung web site and wished to purchase equipment would be redirected to an InfoSonics-run site.

After the company's third quarter financial report showed unexpectedly high revenue, investors sought out its stock and drove the price up threefold by year's end. For 2005 revenues nearly doubled to $146 million, with a net profit of $2.7 million reported. Latin American sales had grown by 226 percent, and accounted for 69 percent of the company's total revenues, up from just 12 percent in 2004.

In January 2006 InfoSonics sold 1.1 million shares

of common stock to institutional investors for $14.4 million. The company also expanded its distribution of Samsung products to Paraguay and Uruguay and began selling i-mate brand cell phones in North America. In February the firm expanded its exclusive VK Mobile distribution territory to include Canada, giving it full coverage of North America. InfoSonics had succeeded in winning approval of that firm's VK530 phone from a number of carriers.

In March the company requested that its stock cease trading on the Berlin-Bremen Stock Exchange, where it had never been approved for sale. The firm blamed pressure from short sellers for the stock's fall from over $23 per share early in the year to just above $10 in March.

The spring also saw InfoSonics take on Caribbean distribution of Alcatel and TCL brand phones, which were less expensive than the Samsung and VK products it primarily sold. Several new VK models were introduced as well, each of which included an MP3 player and other advanced features.

In April InfoSonics leased a new sales, warehouse, and manufacturing facility in Mexico, which would serve as the company's headquarters in that country. Revenues for the first quarter of 2006 were 125 percent higher than those of a year before, and the firm's stock jumped after the figures were announced, topping $30 by June. The company restated its net earnings for the first quarter early that month, however, and with a stock analyst also downgrading their rating, the price declined by more than 50 percent within a few days. The company subsequently attempted to reassure investors, some of whom had filed lawsuits over the restatement, that the company's business was sound.

In just over a decade InfoSonics Corporation had become one of the leading distributors of cellular telephone handsets and accessories in North America. The company was busily expanding in Latin America, where it earned two-thirds of its revenues, while continuing to supply regional carriers and retailers in the United States. The firm looked forward to ongoing growth in the still young market.

Frank Uhle

PRINCIPAL SUBSIDIARIES

InfoSonics Latin America, Inc.; InfoSonics de Mexico S.A. de C.V.; InfoSonics de Guatemala S.A.; InfoSonics El Salvador S.A. de C.V.; InfoSonics S.A. (Uruguay); Axcess Mobile, LLC.

PRINCIPAL COMPETITORS

Brightpoint Inc.; CellStar Corp.; Brightstar Corp.; SED International Holdings, Inc.; TESSCO Technologies, Inc.

FURTHER READING

Allen, Mike, "Cell Phone Distributor Plans Initial Public Offering," *San Diego Business Journal,* February 16, 2004, p. 15.

———, "Exchange Listing Troubles Tech Firm," *San Diego Business Journal,* March 20, 2006, p. 12.

Balint, Kathryn, "InfoSonics Stock Fall Worries Investors," *San Diego Tribune,* June 15, 2006.

"CEO Interview: Joseph Ram, InfoSonics Corporation," *Wall Street Transcript,* August 22, 2005.

Dano, Mike, "Distributors: Consolidation Will Bring Value Back to the Handset," *RCR Wireless News,* January 3, 2005, p. 3.

"Equipment Market Is Hot, But InfoSonics Is Cool Toward IPO," *CT Wireless,* October 26, 2000.

Gallant, Julie, "Executive Profile: Joseph Ram," *San Diego Business Journal,* April 3, 2006, p. 57.

"InfoSonics Begins Distributing i-mate Cellular Handsets," *Business News Americas,* January 12, 2006.

"InfoSonics Enters Agreement to Distribute Alcatel, TCL Brand Phones," *Business News Americas,* March 14, 2006.

"InfoSonics in Pact with Samsung Electronics Latin America," *Dow Jones News Service,* December 27, 2004.

"InfoSonics Reports US $146mn in 2005 Revenues," *Business News Americas,* March 8, 2006.

"InfoSonics Studies Plan for Chile Subsidiary," *Business News Americas,* November 23, 2005.

"InfoSonics to Offer 1.1 Million Shares in Private Placement," *Reuters News,* January 30, 2006.

"IPO Spotlight: InfoSonics Corp. Prospectus Info," *Dow Jones Corporate Filings Alert,* February 2, 2004.

"Proxy: InfoSonics Corp.," *San Diego Business Journal,* December 19, 2005, p. 29.

Vuocolo, Jonathan, "InfoSonics Stk Down 21%," *Dow Jones News Service,* June 6, 2006.

Wise, Christina, "InfoSonics: Cell Industry's Friend," *Investor's Business Daily,* January 30, 2006, p. B2.

inVentiv Health, Inc.

Vantage Court North
200 Cottontail Lane
Somerset, New Jersey 08873
U.S.A.
Telephone: (973) 748-4666
Toll Free: (800) 416-0555
Fax: (732) 537-4912
Web site: http://www.ventiv.com

Public Company
Founded: 1997
Employees: 4,200
Sales: $556.3 million (2005)
Stock Exchanges: NASDAQ
Ticker Symbol: VTIV
NAIC: 541614 Process, Physical Distribution, and Logistics Consulting Services

■ ■ ■

Somerset, New Jersey-based inVentiv Health, Inc., formerly Ventiv Health, Inc., provides outsourced sales, marketing, and other services to about 175 companies in the United States, Europe, and Asia involved in the pharmaceutical, biotechnology, and life sciences industries, including the world's 20 largest pharmaceutical companies. inVentiv divides its business among three segments. inVentiv Clinical assists clients with the clinical drug development and approval process, providing services such as data management and the recruitment of specialists. inVentiv Communications helps clients to shape and deliver messages, and also offers medical

education and patient compliance programs. inVentiv Commercial helps clients to launch new products and maintain sales of established products. The unit also helps in the staffing of sales forces, the establishment of government compliance programs, and marketing support services such as tele-services, direct mail programs, mail-order pharmacy services, fulfillment, distribution, warehousing, and database management. Spun off from Snyder Communications in 1999, inVentiv is a public company listed on the NASDAQ.

FOUNDER'S LAUNCH OF
BUSINESS CAREER IN 1984

The man behind the founding of inVentiv's parent company, Snyder Communications, was Daniel M. Snyder, who was to become better known as the owner of the National Football League's Washington Redskins. Born in New York in 1964, the son of a writer-journalist, he was an indifferent student. After high school he took business, speech, and drama classes at Montgomery College in Maryland before transferring to the University of Maryland where he continued to take business classes before dropping out to concentrate on a budding entrepreneurial career. In 1984, at the age of 19, he launched a business out of his parents' apartment leasing jets to fly college students to spring break destinations, a venture that according to Snyder's claim made him a millionaire. During the fall he operated Sports Tours, a company that bused students to away football games. Continuing to focus on the college market, Snyder in 1988 formed Collegiate Marketing & Communications to publish a magazine called *Campus USA*. He was able to enlist the financial backing of real estate and publish-

---

COMPANY PERSPECTIVES

inVentiv Health's customized solutions enable pharmaceutical and biotech clients to not only achieve their goals, but to do so with flexibility and cost-effectiveness.

---

ing mogul Mort Zuckerman and his partner Fred Drasner, but the venture proved disastrous. The slick magazine was supposed to provide brand advertisers with a way to reach a highly coveted audience by being distributed on 500 campuses, but too few corporations signed up and the publication soon folded after losing $5 million.

Out of the disaster of *Campus USA* came the seeds of Snyder Communications, however. "Though marketers like Procter & Gamble refused to advertise in his magazine," according to *Forbes,* "they were happy to pay him to get college kids to try Crest. Zuckerman and Drasner put up another $1 million." Snyder formed Snyder Communications to pursue his new college marketing idea. When the sampling idea failed to take off, Snyder began doing direct marketing for Procter & Gamble by transferring their print ads to standardized WallBoard display ads, which he then placed throughout the campus. The next step was to apply this idea to other targeted audiences. "It was a nice niche business," reported *Forbes,* "that Snyder soon expanded into field sales and services for telecommunications companies. He landed a big account from AT&T by marketing long distance service to anyone with a foreign-sounding last name, and hired telemarketers who collectively spoke 23 languages."

By the time Snyder took his company public in 1996, and in the process became the youngest CEO on the New York Stock Exchange, four-fifths of his $83 million in revenues came from two telecommunications customers: AT&T and MCI. Yet within a matter of months of the initial public offering, Snyder Communications changed course, becoming involved in direct marketing and healthcare marketing. The assets of the latter formed a new division called Snyder Healthcare Services, inVentiv's predecessor.

To build up Snyder Healthcare, the company went on an acquisition spree. In January 1997 MMD, Inc., a marketer of pharmaceutical products, was acquired to form a foundation for the division. This was followed in August of that year with the purchase of Halliday Sales, providing similar contract sales capabilities in the United

Kingdom. At the end of the year, Snyder Healthcare beefed up both of these operations with the acquisition of Malvern, Pennsylvania-based Pharmsflex, Inc., for $24.5 million, and Winchester, England-based Rapid Deployment Group Ltd., which in addition to the United Kingdom operated in Hungary. Next, in February 1998, the division paid $71 million for Health Products Research, Inc., and its French affiliate, Healthcare Promotions, L.L.C. A month later another French pharmaceutical marketing company, Paris-based Publimed Promotions S.A., was added.

The division's European presence also was bolstered by the acquisition of another French firm, CLI Pharma S.A. and Germany-based MKM Marketinginstitut GmbH. In August 1998 Snyder Healthcare acquired Greenwich, Connecticut-based Clinical Communications, adding marketing services such as satellite-delivered training services, CD-ROMs, and custom publications for pharmaceutical companies. Snyder Healthcare also enjoyed success signing up major clients in its first two years, including Bristol-Myers Squibb, Eli Lilly, Pfizer, Hoechst Marion Rousell, Abbott Laboratories, Upjohn, and Johnson & Johnson.

By the end of 1998, Snyder Healthcare generated sales of more than $320 million, employing about 2,800 people in the United States and more than 4,500 in the United Kingdom, France, Germany, Ireland, Holland, and Hungary. The success of Snyder Communications had made Dan Snyder a rich man, and in 1999 he decided to use some of that wealth to buy the Washington Redskins, a team whose home games he had attended since childhood with his father, a season ticket holder. Before Snyder began to devote most of his attention to the running of the Redskins, he engineered a spinoff of the Snyder Healthcare division, a move that was expected to increase shareholder value because investors had been uncertain about how to view Snyder Communications, whether as a healthcare firm or an advertising and marketing company. The split was further intended to facilitate the growth of Snyder Healthcare, which was looking to take advantage of pharmaceutical companies increasing their outsourcing of sales and marketing in order to save money and focus on the research and development of new products.

SPINOFF IN 1999

In September 1999, Snyder Communications formed Ventiv Health Inc. and folded in the Snyder Healthcare assets. Stockholders received one share of the new company for every two shares of Snyder Communications they owned. While Dan Snyder initially served as chairman, running Ventiv on a day-to-day basis as CEO was Eran Broshy, who had come on board in June 1999.

1997: The company is founded as a division of Snyder Communications.
1999: The unit is spun off as Ventiv Health Inc.
2002: The European businesses are divested.
2005: InChord Communications is acquired.
2006: The name is changed to inVentiv Health.

Holder of an undergraduate degree in civil engineering from the Massachusetts Institute of Technology, a master's from Stanford University, and an M.B.A. from Harvard University, Broshy had 14 years of experience in the healthcare field while a partner at The Boston Consulting Group, working on a myriad of matters with a wide range of clients, including drug companies, managed care organizations, and academic medical centers. In the two years prior to joining Ventiv, Broshy served as CEO for Coelacanth Corporation, a biotechnology company.

After producing revenues of $344.7 million in 1999 and a net loss of $6.8 million, Ventiv began its first full year as an independent company. It expanded its operations with the launch of two new divisions. The first, Ventiv Integrated Solutions, provided companies, especially those in the early stages of development, with a complete package of outsourced marketing services, including product management, market research and analysis, promotion, and sales execution. The second division, E-Ventiv, grew out of a March 2000 alliance with New York-based RxCentric, Inc., which delivered pharmaceutical information to physicians through the Internet. The formation of E-Ventiv soon followed to leverage the power of the Internet for clients. It was subsequently bolstered by a strategic alliance with HeliosHealth.com, making clients' sales and marketing information available on the company's more than 1,000 interactive kiosks located in the waiting rooms of physicians. For the year, Ventiv experienced a 21 percent increase in sales to $416.7 million in 2000 while recording net earnings of $16.8 million.

The contract sales business of Ventiv experienced a major change in the early 2000s, due in part to Quintiles Transnational Corp., which in 1999 moved beyond the flat-fee arrangements that had been in place to sign a cost-and-profit sharing deal with CV Therapeutics. Ventiv soon followed suit. This new type of incentive-laden contract worked for both the client and sales organization. The latter had to lay out cash that it would not recoup if it failed to perform, but Ventiv and its peers were also in line to achieve greater profits if they succeeded. Another trend that worked in favor of Ventiv was a shift in the pharmaceutical industry away from blockbuster drugs to specialized drugs. Small biotechnology companies that specialized in this area did not have the marketing infrastructure to launch a new product and became natural customers for outsourcers such as Ventiv. By the same token, large pharmaceutical firms, faced with the loss of massive sums of money as patents on blockbuster drugs expired, were eager to find ways to cut costs, and turning to contract sales operations made sense. They could save money, primarily because they did not have to pay the salaries of full-time employees during slack periods.

Ventiv increased revenues to nearly $400 million in 2001 but lost $58.5 million due to charges incurred from restructuring and discontinued operations and to lower operating margins. More restructuring followed in 2002 when Ventiv took steps to focus its business by selling off or exiting unprofitable, noncore businesses. A Connecticut-based medical education unit was sold in May and a month later a similar Georgia-based unit was cast off. The company also began to exit the European market to concentrate on its U.S. businesses. In September 2002 Ventiv Health Germany was divested, despite being profitable, and in October U.K.-based Contract Sales Organization, which had been losing money and offered little in the way of cross-selling opportunities, was sold for a total consideration of $12 million. Ventiv also continued to take steps to better control costs while maximizing its infrastructure to offer customers complimentary service offerings. As a result of these changes, sales in 2002 dipped to $215.4 million, but the company was able to turn a net profit of $7.9 million.

SELLING THE EUROPEAN OPERATIONS IN 2003

Ventiv sold its Hungary-based operation in early 2003 and by September 2003 had completely divested its European businesses. For the year, Ventiv increased sales to $224.5 million. Net income decreased to $5.8 million, the result of $4.1 million in losses from discontinued operations. With the ground prepared, the company was ready to implement an aggressive expansion program. Ventiv completed several acquisitions in 2004, adding a number of new services. New Jersey-based Franklin Group, Inc., was acquired in June, adding pharmaceutical compliance services and patient assistance programs. Next, in September 2004, Ventiv acquired Connecticut-based Smith Hanley Corporation, provider of clinical staffing and recruiting services. This business was then supplemented two months later with the addition of HHI Clinical & Statistical Research Services, L.L.C., a Baltimore, Maryland, company that specialized in statistical analysis and data management services for pharmaceutical companies. Ventiv also grew internally in 2004, adding new service offerings such as Ventiv Recruitment Services, Ventiv Professional Development Group, The Therapeutics Institute (providing clinical education services), and the Total Data Solutions Division, which gathered and managed field sales information. As a result of the expansion effort, sales surged more than 50 percent to $352.2 million in 2004 and net income improved to $31.1 million.

The growth program continued in 2005 when Ventiv paid $13.6 million in cash and stock for Pharmaceutical Resource Solutions L.L.C., a Philadelphia, Pennsylvania-area company that provided compliance management and marketing support services. Later in the year, Ventiv completed the largest acquisition in its history, paying $196.8 million in cash and stock for ImChord Communications, Inc., an Ohio marketing company that was the largest independently owned healthcare communications company, composed of ten specialty-communications companies and a network of agencies in ten markets around the world. In one stroke Ventiv became an industry powerhouse. In addition to the contract sales, staffing, compliance, and other services it had to offer, the company included advertising, branding, and marketing expertise.

Revenues increased to $556.3 million in 2005 and net income rose to $43.9 million, impressive totals that were overshadowed by Ventiv's potential for continued growth. In the first quarter of 2006 Ventiv completed three acquisitions: Adheris, Inc., a leader in patient compliance and persistency programs; Jeffrey Simbrow Associates, Canada's top healthcare marketing and communications agency; and Synergos, Inc., a company

expert in the management of clinical trials.

Because of the company's expanded service offerings, management decided to conduct a re-branding initiative in order to make it clear to the industries it served that it had much more to offer than the contract sales services associated with the Ventiv name. Hence the company announced that it would adopt a new name, inVentiv Health, as well as a new tag line, "Accelerate Your Vision." In addition, the business was reorganized into three business segments: inVentiv Clinical, inVentiv Communications, and inVentiv Commercial.

Ed Dinger

PRINCIPAL COMPETITORS

Access Worldwide Communications, Inc; IMS Health Inc.; Quintiles Transnational Corporation.

FURTHER READING

Behr, Peter, "Spinoff to Split Snyder in Two," *Washington Post,* June 24, 1999, p. E01.

Gandel, Stephen, "Writing New Prescriptions for Drug Sales," *Crain's New York Business,* February 7, 2000, p. 27.

Kroll, Luisa, "Changing the Game Plan," *Forbes,* December 13, 1999, p. 81.

Lau, Gloria, "Sales Contractor Bullish on Medical Trend," *Investor's Business Daily,* February 14, 2001, p. A10.

Pandya, Chhandasi, "Ventiv Happy to Help Out Drug Makers," *Star-Ledger* (Newark, N.J.), December 17, 2004, p. 026.

Warner, Judy, "New Kid on the Block," *Adweek Eastern Edition,* April 20, 1998, p. 12.

Wise, Christina, "Spreading Out the Workload," *Investor's Business Daily,* August 15, 2005, p. B02.

Wolf, Barnet D., "Ventiv Health to Westerville, Ohio, Communications Firm for $185M," *Columbus Dispatch* (Columbus, Ohio), September 8, 2005.

Iogen Corporation

—■—

300 Hunt Club Road East
Ottawa, Ontario K1V 1C1
Canada
Telephone: (613) 733-9830
Fax: (613) 733-0781
Web site: http://www.iogen.ca

Private Company
Incorporated: 1974 as Iotech Corporation
Employees: 180
Sales: $43.7 million (2004 est.)
NAIC: 324199 All Other Petroleum and Coal Manufacturing; 325199 All Other Basic Organic Chemical Manufacturing

■■■

Iogen Corporation is a world leader in the development of cellulose ethanol, a renewable transportation fuel made from agricultural waste such as straw and corn stalks. The Canadian biotechnology company owns the world's only cellulose-to-ethanol demonstration plant and is responsible for the world's first shipment of bio-ethanol for commercial use. Iogen's advanced fiber-digesting enzymes are also used throughout Canada, the United States, South America, Europe, India, Australia, and the Pacific Rim to reduce the use of bleaching chemicals in the pulp and paper industries, to soften denim fabric in blue jeans in the textile industry, and to aid in the processing of animal feed.

EARLY YEARS

From its beginnings in 1974 as Iotech Corporation, founder Patrick Foody's vision of converting low-grade wasted biomass into something useful has been the driving force of the biotechnology company based in the Canadian capital of Ottawa. Prompted by the widespread belief that a worldwide food shortage was looming, the engineer and financier initially devoted his spare time to finding ways to break down natural fiber sources such as surplus wood chips into additives for animal feed, thus increasing the amount of grains available for human consumption. Using money from Techtrol Limited, his successful Montreal engineering firm, Foody and three employees worked out of an industrial warehouse and within a few years developed a process that pressure-cooked the chips with steam until they exploded and turned to mush.

In 1978, with the world fearing a potential oil shortage and scientists scrambling for alternative fuel sources, Foody turned his attention, his money, and Iotech's innovative steam-explosion technology toward the revolutionary idea that forestry and farm waste could be turned into alcohol fuel for cars. At the time, the technology to make ethyl alcohol, known as ethanol, relied on grains such as corn and wheat that could easily be broken down into sugars and fermented by yeast into alcohol. What Foody had in mind was to make ethanol from renewable feedstocks drawn from agriculture residues, the inedible parts of plants that would otherwise be discarded or left in the fields.

For the next several years, Foody directed Iotech's research and development efforts toward discovering a

"Iogen is a results-driven company with a vision: to produce a clean, renewable fuel that can be used in cars today, and to lead the way in the reduction of greenhouse gas emissions worldwide. Our employees are key to our success. Working at Iogen means being part of a dynamic environment, and working with talented, committed people. Iogen provides opportunities to learn, develop, contribute and positively impact the environment and the world. Together, we're building a strong, leading edge technology that will benefit everyone." —Brian Foody, company president

method that would speed up the process of converting cellulose—the fibrous, woody components of corn and wheat plants found in stalks, cobs, and straw—into glucose, or sugar, which could then be distilled into ethanol or used to manufacture industrial products. His collaboration with American university-based and government researchers working on ethanol projects brought Foody into contact with an enzyme-secreting fungus that proved essential to many of the company's future advancements. Foody brought the microbe, called trichoderma, to Ottawa and in 1982 directed his eldest son, Brian, to head a 12-member research team to study the fungus. The Iotech team continued to work with leading American scientists and learned to cultivate the fungus in large fermenters and began to customize its properties.

The year 1983 was a big one for Iotech. The Patrick Foody-led enterprise opened a CAD 7.8 million pilot plant on the edge of the Ottawa airport, partially funded with CAD 2.7 million from the Canadian government. The new facility demonstrated on a small scale how to make ethanol from biomass waste. The patented Iotech steam explosion method initially broke down the fibers, which were then converted to sugar using Iotech-developed enzymes, fermented with yeast and distilled into ethanol. In addition to creating a fuel that could be added to gasoline to power cars, the whole process created a glue byproduct called lignin, an environmentally friendly substitute for coal in electrical generation.

1986: IOGEN EMERGING AS INDUSTRIAL ENZYMES LEADER

In 1986, government and corporate support for ethanol research evaporated as the world's crude oil prices fell

dramatically and oil suddenly appeared plentiful and cheap. Iotech had to cut its staff in half and rethink its strategy to stay in business. The name Iotech had been a play on the words "I-owe-Tech," and referred to the source of the company's start-up and operating funds, Patrick Foody's Montreal firm, Techtrol Limited. Techtrol continued to fund the enterprise but during this transition time the company decided to change its name to Iogen Corporation. The newly named company sought government contracts for industrial applications of its enzyme technology and searched for commercially viable products, briefly experimenting with glues for plywood and non-caloric sweeteners.

As the 1980s came to a close and the threat of global warming began to emerge as a public concern, Iogen announced its intention to build a CAD 30-million demonstration plant that would prove that its so-called bioethanol (ethanol made from biomass, not grains) technology was ready for widespread application. Simultaneously, Iogen continued its research and development of other industrial applications for its enzyme technology. In 1991, the company entered into an agreement with Royal DSM N.V. (formerly Roche Vitamins) for the exclusive manufacture and distribution of animal feed enzymes sold under the brand name Roxazyme G2. In 1994, the company posted its first sales revenues from its first commercial product, an enzyme that helped clarify apple juice.

By the end of 1994, Iogen had again entered into a partnership with the Canadian government. The company's collaboration with the National Research Council of Canada (NRCAN) resulted in the advancement and commercialization of unique enzymes that decreased the need for chlorine in the pulp bleaching process and lowered the amount of environmentally harmful organiochlorine effluent and dioxins from the mills. With the successful introduction of an enzyme designed to soften the denim fabric of blue jeans, Iogen made a name for itself as Canada's only manufacturer of industrial enzymes and quickly established itself as a world leader and supplier of enzymes for commercial purposes. NRCAN and Iogen continued their collaboration and in April 1997 released the world's first pulp bleaching enzymes that used sophisticated protein engineering technology, further reducing the reliance of pulp mills on chlorine as a bleaching agent.

1997: IOGEN'S BIOETHANOL R&D GETTING A BOOST

In November 1997, Iogen and Petro-Canada began a partnership that signaled the beginning of renewed corporate interest in the company's bioethanol technology. The announcement came on the heels of a

KEY DATES

1974: Patrick Foody founds Iotech Corporation to find practical uses for wasted biomass.

1983: Iotech opens pilot bioethanol plant with financial help from Canada's federal government.

1986: Company lays off half its staff and changes its name to Iogen Corporation.

1994: Iogen's breakthrough enzymes find widespread use in pulp and textile industries.

1997: Petro-Canada invests CAD 26 million in Iogen's cellulose-to-ethanol demonstration plant.

1999: Iogen secures CAD 10 million loan for demonstration plant from Canadian government.

2002: Royal Dutch/Shell Group buys minority stake in company for CAD 46 million.

2003: Bioethanol demonstration plant hits economic and production targets.

2004: Iogen delivers world's first shipment of cellulose ethanol for commercial use.

2006: Goldman-Sachs invests CAD 30 million to accelerate Iogen's commercialization efforts.

U.S. Department of Energy report that found ethanol made from corn had an emission level only slightly lower than conventional gasoline but motor fuel produced from converted agricultural and wood wastes reduced carbon dioxide emissions by more than 90 percent. The deal included a CAD 15.8 million commitment from Petro-Canada toward building Iogen's planned industrial-scale ethanol demonstration plant, as well as jointly funded research and development, and a licensing option for Petro-Canada to build full-scale commercial ethanol refineries.

In January 1999, Iogen secured a CAD 10 million loan from Canada's federal government toward its biomass-to-ethanol demonstration plant, which was under construction on company grounds in Ottawa. The funds came in equal parts from Technology Partnerships Canada and Natural Resources Canada's Climate Change Fund. The loan was part of a greater effort by the Canadian government to fulfill 1997 Kyoto Protocol commitments to reduce the country's greenhouse gas emissions from such sources as gasoline-powered cars.

Iogen's troubled efforts to achieve targeted produc-

tion goals received needed help in April 2002 when the government of Canada awarded a CAD 2.7 million three-year grant to the company. Then, in May 2002, Iogen received a dramatic boost when the Royal Dutch/Shell Group, at the time owner of 72 percent of Shell Canada Ltd., invested CAD 46 million for a minority stake in the company. Some hailed the deal as the first major investment into bioethanol from the oil industry. It provided Iogen with a guaranteed customer, a distribution network, and capital toward the goal of developing the world's first commercial-scale, biomass-to-ethanol plant.

2003: WORLD'S FIRST BIOETHANOL FOR COMMERCIAL USE

In January 2003, Iogen's demonstration plant was successfully processing 25 tons of wheat straw per week into fermentable sugar and on track to produce 320,000 liters of ethanol annually. It was the first time enzyme technology was used on such a scale to produce fermentable sugar for ethanol from straw. By April 2003, Iogen's pre-commercial plant had doubled its weekly capacity and was on target to produce 700,000 liters of bioethanol annually. The company's achievement of major technical and economic milestones at its demonstration facility triggered Petro-Canada in December 2003 to renew its opportunity to participate in the launching of Iogen's first Canadian commercial-scale cellulose-to-ethanol plant, a right they secured with their 1997 investment.

After more than 25 years and CAD 110 million of research and development, with help from two major oil companies and the government of Canada, Iogen in April 2004 announced that the world's only cellulose ethanol demonstration scale facility was producing the world's first cellulose ethanol fuel for commercial use at an annual rate of one million liters. With CAD 24.7 million invested, Petro-Canada announced that it would be Iogen's first customer by receiving an initial shipment of 5,000 liters of cellulose ethanol at its Montreal refinery, where it was blended with high-octane gasoline. At the same time, Iogen announced that it was continuing to evaluate locations in four possible countries for its first commercial bioethanol plant: Canada (three prairie provinces); the United States (Idaho, Nebraska); the United Kingdom; and Germany. The facility, which would also include an enzyme and power plant, was projected to cost approximately $250 million and would produce about 50 million gallons annually.

In June 2004, Iogen became the first company to acquire a nonexclusive license to use a strain of yeast developed at Purdue University that increased by about

40 percent the amount of ethanol that could be made from sugars derived from agricultural residues. Using the Purdue-developed yeast, Iogen's process converted about two-thirds of the straw to ethanol, with a yield of almost 300 liters of ethanol per ton of straw. The year also brought further support to Iogen's bioethanol enterprise from the Canadian government as Ontario announced a renewable fuels standard (RFS) that required gasoline in the province to contain 5 percent ethanol by 2007 and 10 percent by 2010. In December 2004, Canada's federal government announced that its vehicle fleet would become the world's first to use cellulose ethanol on an ongoing basis, and that Iogen would supply the fuel for its 900 flex-fuel vehicles that ran on E-85, a blend of 15 percent ethanol and 85 percent gasoline.

2005: ON THE BRINK OF FULL-SCALE COMMERCIALIZATION

In 2005, Iogen scored public relations victories when its bioethanol fuel helped power various vehicles used to shuttle leaders of the world's major industrialized nations when the Group of Eight (G8) met in Scotland in June, and again in November, when the United Nation's 11th Conference of Parties Framework Convention on Climate Change was held in Montreal. Perhaps the most important development for Iogen in 2005 was the summer passage by the U.S. Congress of the U.S. Energy Policy Act, which established grants and loan guarantees for the commercialization of cellulose ethanol technology. The bill also required that gasoline refiners collectively blend four billion gallons of ethanol into their products in 2006 and 7.5 billion gallons by 2012.

The company remained in the news in January 2006, when Volkswagen, Europe's largest car producer, and Royal Dutch/Shell announced at the North American International Auto Show in Detroit that they were exploring a partnership with Iogen to locate the world's first cellulose ethanol plant in Germany. The development from Volkswagen was spurred in part by tough European Union objectives for reducing greenhouse emissions from transportation to comply with the Kyoto Protocol. With the price of crude oil at $70-plus a barrel and oil company profits at record highs, U.S. President George W. Bush in his 2006 State of the Union address said, "America is addicted to oil," and indicated that his 2007 budget would include $150 million for biomass-to-ethanol research and development. The president also specifically claimed that cellulosic ethanol could be cost competitive by 2012 with the potential to replace up to 30 percent of the country's fuel use.

In May 2006, Iogen became the first bioethanol technology company to attract a significant investment from a major Wall Street firm when Goldman Sachs & Co. of New York bought a minority stake for CAD 30 million. In June 2006, Iogen announced that it had negotiated tentative contracts with 320 farmers in Idaho to provide 400,000 tons of barley straw a year if the company decided to build its first bioethanol plant in the state. Construction of the plant could begin in the fall of 2007, but company officials said they needed loan guarantees from the U.S. Department of Energy that would cover investment losses if the project failed. An announcement on the loan guarantees was expected in early October.

After more than 30 years of research and development, Iogen's advanced ethanol-making technology seemed on the verge of commercial success. With environmental, economic, and political forces aligning and deep-pocketed partners such as Petro-Canada, Shell, and Goldman Sachs behind it, Iogen was primed to excel in a world where demand for cellulose ethanol was skyrocketing into a multibillion-gallon, multibillion-dollar industry.

Ted Sylvester

PRINCIPAL COMPETITORS

Abengoa, S.A.; Novozymes A/S; Genencor International, Inc.; Cargill, Incorporated; Codexis, Inc; Ag Processing Inc; Badger State Ethanol, LLC; Archer Daniels Midland Company.

FURTHER READING

Brown, Stuart F., "Biorefinery Breakthrough," *Fortune,* February 6, 2006.

Chipello, Christopher J., "Goldman Takes Stake in Iogen," *Wall Street Journal,* May 1, 2006.

———, "Iogen's Milestone: It's Selling Ethanol Made of Farm Waste," *Wall Street Journal,* April 21, 2004.

"Combating the Greenhouse Effect, a Canadian Industrial Opportunity," *Canada News-Wire,* December 12, 1989.

"First Cellulose-Derived Alcohol Fuel Sold into Fuels Market," *Inside Fuels & Vehicles,* May 6, 2004.

Gantz, Rachel, "Iogen: Despite Cost Issues, Cellulose Production 'Ready to Go'," *Renewable Fuel News,* July 12, 2004.

Hall, Kevin G., "Ethanol Has Promise, But Don't Write Off Gasoline Yet," *Knight Ridder/Tribune Business News,* May 21, 2006.

Jaimet, Kate, "Market Better in U.S., Ethanol Pioneer Says: Iogen Laments Lack of Law Requiring Clean Fuel Additives," *National Post,* March 9, 2002.

Milmo, Sean, "Bush's Biofuel Push Hits Barrier," *Chemistry and Industry,* February 20, 2006.

"Purdue Yeast Makes Ethanol from Agricultural Waste More Effectively," *Ascribe News,* June 28, 2004.

Ripley, Richard, "Ottawa Ethanol Plant Raises Hope for Clearer Skies," *Journal of Business-Spokane,* January 11, 2001.

Ryan, Stephanie, "Successful Commercialization of Biotechnology," *Canadian Chemical News,* April 1, 2000.

Scoffield, Heather, "Iogen Sees Benefit from Kyoto Global Deal to Cut Emissions," *Globe and Mail,* December 18, 1997.

Smith, Darrell, "A Crop of Residue," *Farm Journal,* November 1, 2003.

Spears, Tom, "Biotech Firm Makes Jungle Rot Pay: Fungi from Guam Helps Create Ethanol Fuel from Agricultural Waste," *Hamilton Spectator,* January 6, 1998.

Tam, Pauline, " White Lightning: Ethanol and Iogen: Patrick Foody's 20-Year Ethanol Itch Pays Off," *Ottawa Citizen,* March 18, 1998.

Tuck, Simon, "Goldman Sachs Sees Green in Biofuel Firm; Investment Bank Taking Stake in Iogen, a Leader in Cellulose Ethanol Technology," *Globe and Mail,* May 1, 2006.

——, "Royal Dutch/Shell Taking Minority Stake in Iogen," *Globe and Mail,* May 8, 2002.

——, "VW Looks to Build Ethanol Plant: Biofuel Cuts Carbon Dioxide," *Globe and Mail,* January 9, 2006.

Vaughan, Michael, "Cellulose Ethanol Critical to Canada's Green Future," *Globe and Mail,* August 18, 2005.

Wald, Matthew L., "Both Promise and Problems for New Tigers in Your Tank," *New York Times,* October 26, 2005.

IranAir
───────■───────

Mehrabad International Airport
IranAir Headquarters Building
Tehran,
Iran
Telephone: (+98-21) 665-9003
Fax: (+98-21) 603-1343
Web site: http://www.iranair.com

State-Owned Company
Incorporated: 1944 as Iranian Airways Company
Employees: 9,000
Sales: $407.44 million (2003)
NAIC: 481111 Scheduled Passenger Air Transportation;
481112 Scheduled Freight Air Transportation;
481211 Nonscheduled Chartered Passenger Air
Transportation; 481212 Nonscheduled Chartered
Freight Air Transportation; 488119 Other Airport
Operations; 488190 Other Support Activities for
Air Transportation

■ ■ ■

IranAir is the national airline of Iran. About eight million passengers a year fly the carrier and its Iran Air Tours subsidiary. IranAir's route network includes 21 domestic destinations and three dozen international ones. In addition to the airline, the group includes engineering and maintenance, catering, and airport services operations. One of Iran Air's major challenges has been sourcing aircraft and spares following a U.S. embargo on aircraft sales to the country following the 1979 Islamic Revolution. Nevertheless, it has maintained a fleet of about three dozen American and European aircraft, while its Iran Tours unit operates Russian Tupolev airliners.

RAPID GROWTH AFTER WORLD
WAR II

Iran's civil aviation industry dates back at least to the late 1930s, when Iranian State Airlines, a joint venture between the Iranian government and Britain's Imperial Airlines, operated a route between Tehran and Baghdad using de Havilland Rapide biplanes. However, the airline that would be known as IranAir was launched as a private company in 1944 under the name Iranian Airways Company. It operated its first passenger flight from Tehran to Mashhad in 1946 and was flying as far as Baghdad and Beirut by the end of the year. The fleet was originally made up of U.S.-made Douglas DC-3s, the civil version of the ubiquitous U.S. military transport of World War II that equipped dozens of civil airlines after the war. Trans World Airlines (TWA) provided technical expertise and held a 10 percent interest in Iranair until 1949, notes R. E. G. Davies in *A History of the World's Airlines.*

According to a 1958 profile in *Aviation Week,* there was some intrigue behind the airline's founding, which was credited largely to an Iranian businessman, Reza Afshar. The Soviet Union occupied the northern half of Iran at the close of World War II and was beginning to use some of its wartime lend-lease transport aircraft for commercial purposes in the region. Afshar told *Aviation Week* he bought 19 of these DC-3s directly from the planes' owner, the U.S. government. Later, dismayed with the high fees TWA was charging for support, he bought out other shareholders to become the sole owner.

KEY DATES

1944: Iranian Airways Company is established.

1954: Persian Air Services (also Pars Airways) is launched to fly freight between Iran and Europe.

1961: State-owned Iranian National Airlines Corporation (originally United Iranian Airlines) is formed by merger of Persian Air Services and Iranair.

1965: Airline receives first jets (Boeing 727s).

1979: United States imposes sanctions on sales of aircraft to Iran following Islamic Revolution.

2001: Eight million people fly on IranAir and its Iran Air Tours subsidiary.

2006: IranAir grounds a half dozen planes due to problems getting spares for U.S.-made engines.

In the late 1950s, the fleet had evolved to eight DC-4s, three Convair 240s, and three Vickers Viscount turboprops, recorded *Aviation Week*. Its main emphasis was operating domestic routes. The country spanned vast distances of extreme terrain and had primitive ground transportation. Facilitating trade and tourism with the immediate region was another priority for the airline. The route network extended as far west as Karachi, Pakistan, and Kabul, Afghanistan. The airline was carrying 80,000 passengers a year.

MERGER IN 1961

A separate airline, Persian Air Services (PAS) or Pars Airways, had been launched in 1954 to provide a freight connection with Europe. PAS had technical assistance from the British airline Skyways and later, SABENA of Belgium, according to *A History of the World's Airlines*. Following a government decree to create a state airline, PAS was combined with Iranian Airways in 1961 to create United Iranian Airlines, which was later renamed Iranian National Airlines Corporation. Annual revenues were $5 million at the time and the carrier flew 142,000 passengers. Its staff numbered 700 employees. The emblem chosen for the new state airline represented the Homa bird, a mythical bearer of good fortune. The letters HOMA also formed an acronym of the airline's name in Persian.

Pan American World Airways began providing technical assistance to the growing airline in the mid-1960s. The U.S. government, eager to promote trade

and displace Soviet influence, was providing a $1.5 million low-interest loan to fund its development, noted *Aviation Week & Space Technology* in a feature story on IranAir. In the Iranian year ended March 20, 1967, revenues were $22 million as the airline carried 403,000 passengers. Like airlines throughout the Muslim world, IranAir carried thousands of pilgrims during the annual hajj to Mecca.

The fleet had been updated with a couple of Boeing 727 jets for long-haul international flights. The airline was establishing its own training facility and flight kitchen at Tehran's Mehrabad International Airport. The staff, which numbered 2,000 people, was by then made up mostly of Iranians, although foreigners continued to hold certain technical positions. Though its chief pilot was from Pan Am, the flight crew was no longer dominated by Americans. At the time, the company was led by Lt. Gen. Ali M. Khademi, who had been a pilot with IranAir's predecessors since the 1940s.

According to *American Aviation,* the carrier was more modest in its international expansion than some status-seeking airlines in other developing countries. It was maintaining a 25 percent market share on the heavily traveled Tehran-Beirut route in heavy competition with several world carriers. Such was IranAir's stature that its CEO became head of the International Air Transport Association, and Tehran hosted the group's convention in 1970.

SOARING IN THE JET AGE

By 1972, IranAir was flying nearly 800,000 passengers a year. Staff had grown to 3,800 employees. Iran Air had been consistently profitable since 1962. Its financial strength allowed it to shop for the most advanced aircraft on the market, and in the early 1970s it announced its intention to buy Concorde supersonic transports. It was also looking for wide-body aircraft for high density, short-haul routes and eventually ordered five Boeing 747s.

Revenues were $151.4 million in the year ending March 20, 1975, while earnings were up to $22.4 million. The airline had grown to 5,600 employees in spite of a temporary halt on hiring earlier in the decade, noted *International Management.* IranAir was connecting to KLM's computer reservation system in Amsterdam via a microwave link while its own was being readied.

CHANGES AFTER THE ISLAMIC REVOLUTION

In 1979, militants took over the U.S. embassy in Tehran, detaining hostages there for over a year. The United States then broke off relations with Iran and imposed an embargo upon aircraft sales to the country. There were also changes to IranAir's in-flight service after the Islamic Revolution. Female flight attendants were clad in burqas and alcoholic beverages were banned from the cabins.

IranAir was able to acquire a half dozen European-made Airbus A300s between 1979 and 1982. One of these aircraft was lost in July 1988 when the USS *Vincennes* mistakenly shot it down, killing 290 people. Another would be lost in a wreck.

Iran was at war with Iraq between 1982 and 1988. Although one of IranAir's Airbuses was hijacked and stranded in Baghdad for six years, the airline fared well. It benefited when foreign airlines canceled services to Tehran, observed *Air Transport World.*

IranAir bought its first new aircraft in several years in 1990 when it acquired six Fokker 100s for regional routes. Its fleet was still made up of mostly Boeing aircraft, including eight 747 jumbo jets. It was flying as far as Tokyo and Beijing, though most of its six million passengers a year were on domestic flights. IranAir was also moving significant amounts of cargo and three of its jets were dedicated freighters. The company, which included maintenance, catering, and other support operations, then had about 11,000 employees.

Though Iran's relations with the United States remained strained, IranAir was reaching out to other Western countries, reported *Air Transport World.* On some international flights, it brought back its famed first class service, which had been banned after the Islamic Revolution. The airline's overseas flights were more profitable than its internal services, where money-losing routes were operated at low fares for the benefit of the population. A handful of small private airlines had begun to sprout, providing some domestic competition.

IranAir acquired two more Airbus 300 aircraft in late 1994. Included in the sale were a couple of U.S.-made GE engines, approved in a rare exception to the U.S. embargo. An order for four new A330s followed a few years later; however it was hampered by export restrictions on aircraft with more than 10 percent U.S.-made content.

STILL FLYING AFTER 20 YEARS OF SANCTIONS

All of Iran's civil airlines together carried more than 13 million passengers in 2000, according to *Air Transport World,* IranAir accounted for approximately 9.5 million. The staff numbered 10,000 to 12,000 employees and revenues were around IRR 2 billion. After the retirement of some of the older planes, its fleet included eight Boeing 747s, five Boeing 727s, and four 737s. IranAir

soon acquired a couple of previously owned Airbus A310s. A new subsidiary, Iran Air Tours, was flying leased Russian-made Tupolev Tu-154 aircraft. A bid to buy four Airbus aircraft with Rolls-Royce engines from the United Kingdom fell apart within two years over pressures related to U.S. sanctions.

Air Transport World was given rare access to the airline in the spring of 2001 and reported that IranAir was running smoothly even after more than 20 years of U.S. sanctions. A company spokesperson told the publication that it had been allowed to acquire the original replacement parts that were critical to safety. However, though it still flew to Europe and Asia, Iran had been relatively isolated. An official in the civil aviation ministry said the country hoped to eventually return to its place as an international gateway. By this time, there was also talk of partially privatizing the airline and merging it with a couple of the small, privately owned upstarts.

The issue of U.S.-made equipment availability came to the forefront after the crash of two Russian airliners operated by Iran Air Tours. A couple of the Fokker aircraft had also been lost since 1994. IranAir Chairman Davood Keshavarzian lamented to *Flight International* the high price the company had to pay to get spares for its Boeing aircraft.

IranAir carried about six million passengers in 2001; another two million flew with the Iran Air Tours subsidiary. IranAir experienced a temporary falloff in international traffic in the global aviation slowdown following the September 11, 2001 terrorist attacks on the United States. Yet there were positive developments on the international front. The carrier signed code-sharing agreements with KLM and Austrian Airlines. In 2003, IranAir signed an agreement to connect Iranian travel agents to the Amadeus computer reservation system.

IranAir had been able to acquire a handful of Airbus and Fokker aircraft in the previous several years. Though the airline acquired a couple of used A300s in 2005, it was soon forced to ground a half dozen of its Airbuses with U.S.-made GE engines due to a lack of spares, its chairman told *Flight International.* Plans were underway to buy more Airbus and Tupolev airliners in the used market, though company leaders had expressed a preference for new Boeings in the past. Iranian civil aviation officials expressed optimism in one day resuming flights to the United States, which was home to about a million Iranian expatriates.

Frederick C. Ingram

PRINCIPAL SUBSIDIARIES

Homa Hotel Group; Iran Air Tours.

PRINCIPAL DIVISIONS

Airport Services; Catering; Commercial & Field Operations; Cultural, Entertainment & Sport Complex; Engineering & Maintenance; Flight Operations.

PRINCIPAL COMPETITORS

The Emirates Group; Iran Aseman Airlines; Mahan Air; National Air Company Azerbaijan Airlines.

FURTHER READING

Bramley, Eric, "Iran Air Sketches Bright Future in Black Ink," *American Aviation,* September 1967, pp. 49–52.

Davies, R. E. G., *A History of the World's Airlines,* London: Oxford University Press, 1967.

Dinmore, Guy, "Sanctions Clip Iran Air's Wings; U.S. Restrictions Prevent Tehran's Flag-Carrier Buying New Aircraft," *Financial Times* (London), October 15, 2002, p. 14.

Doty, L. L., "Iranian Line Gains Solid Financial Status," *Aviation Week,* November 24, 1958, pp. 38–39.

Duffy, Paul, "Iran Air to Push Airbus for Deal; 'Inflated' Prices for Spares and Support on Boeing Fleet Puts European Manufacturer in Driving Seat," *Flight International,* November 19, 2002, p. 24.

———, "Looking Out Through Closed Windows," *Air Transport World,* June 1, 2001, p. 153.

"Iran Air Evaluating Wide-Body Jets for Long-Haul Operation," *Aviation Week & Space Technology,* June 11, 1973, p. 32.

"Iran Air to Merge with Two Local Regional Carriers," *Aviation Daily,* March 11, 2002, p. 5.

Iranian Airways, "About IranAir," http://www.iranair.com.

Kaminski-Morrow, David, "Iran Air Taps Amadeus for Distribution Package," *Air Transport Intelligence,* October 8, 2003.

Karimi, Nasser, "Iran Air Says It Hopes to Buy U.S. Planes, But Doesn't Explain How Embargo Can Be Evaded," *Associated Press Newswires,* March 6, 2006.

Lelyveld, Michael S., "Questions Fly Over Sale of GE Jet Engines to Iran," *Journal of Commerce,* January 20, 1995, p. 1A.

"Never Mind the Turbulence," *Middle East Economic Digest,* July 12, 2002, p. 28.

Oates, David, "Iran Air Gets a Rein on Its Expansion," *International Management,* April 1976, pp. 32–36.

"One-on-One with Iran Air's Ahmad Kazemi," *World Airline News,* December 10, 1999.

Parrish, Wayne W., "The Remarkable Record of Iran Air," *Airline Management & Marketing,* February 1970, pp. 48–49.

"Sanctions Force Iran Air to Ground A310 Fleet," *Flight International,* June 13, 2006.

"Tehran Faces Up to Turbulent Times," *MEED Weekly Special Report,* July 16, 2004, p. 33.

"Top Airlines in Africa/Middle East by Operating Revenue, 2003," *Air Transport World,* World Airline Report (annual), July 2004, p. 31.

Vandyk, Anthony, "To Raise a Profile; Iran Air, a One-Class Carrier Since the Islamic Revolution, Is Resurrecting First Class and Aiming to Rebuild Its Once-Excellent Service Tradition," *Air Transport World,* July 1, 1991, p. 119.

Watkins, Harold D., "Major Challenges Face Iranian Effort to Build Carrier," *Aviation Week & Space Technology,* June 26, 1967, pp. 42–52.

J.J. Keller & Associates, Inc.

3003 West Breezewood Lane
Neenah, Wisconsin 54956
U.S.A.
Telephone: (920) 722-2848
Toll Free: (800) 685-2391
Fax: (920) 727-7503
Web site: http://www.jjkeller.com

Private Company
Founded: 1953
Incorporated: 1958
Employees: 1,000
Sales: $150 million (2005 est.)
NAIC: 511130 Book Publishers; 511140 Database and
Directory Publishers

■ ■ ■

J.J. Keller & Associates, Inc., a specialty publisher and service provider with more than 275,000 North American customers, offers safety and regulatory solutions geared to satisfy requirements overseen by government agencies. The company's products and services, numbering more than 5,000, range from technical publications and forms to safety consulting and online training. Among its targeted industries are transportation, construction, utilities, manufacturing, and food processing. The family-owned operation began as a small consulting business serving the transportation industry.

ALL IN THE FAMILY

Born in 1918, John J. "Jack" Keller attended elementary, high school, and business college in his hometown of Appleton, Wisconsin. In 1939, Keller was hired by the Kimberly-Clark Corporation and worked in traffic management. Enlisting in the U.S. Army in October 1942, he served in Europe for the duration of World War II. The decorated master major sergeant was honorably discharged in April 1946, according to *Paper Industry International.*

On the cusp of the 1950s, Keller added to his educational experience, studying at the College of Advanced Traffic and the Interstate Commerce Commission (ICC) Law School. In 1951, he joined Kampo Transit, Inc., as vice-president and general manager. Keller had worked for transportation companies during a time when the trucking industry was usurping the hauling business of railroads. The federal government had begun regulating the burgeoning industry during the mid-1930s. Keller observed a growing state of confusion in the market regarding issues such as tariffs, permits, and routes. In 1953, Keller left his position to establish a consulting firm, along with his wife and cofounder, Ethel. The parents of three young children took out a second mortgage on their home to start the venture. First focusing on Department of Transportation (DOT)-related compliance issues and assistance with warehousing and insurance underwriting services, Keller planned to develop a full line of services and products supporting the day-to-day operations of motor carriers. "It was an unproven opportunity," Jack Keller recalled in a company history. "No prior work was assured or guaranteed. The endeavor was pure supposition." Yet companies bogged down by compliance issues were more than ready to sign on if it would save them both time and money.

Keller did the legwork, clarifying matters for his clients and then filing the information he had collected. Accumulated research led to books, pamphlets, and forms produced both internally and by vendors. During the 1960s, Keller purchased printing equipment from a small publisher in order to do more of the work in-house.

When his sons were still in high school, John Keller talked to them about joining the family business. If they joined, he planned to expand the company, but if not he would continue on a more modest level, Avi Stern recounted in a *Knight-Ridder/Tribune Business News* article. Bob and Jim Keller came aboard, in 1956 and 1958, respectively, and would help move the company to a new level.

A WIDER CIRCLE

J.J. Keller expanded through growth in its safety-publishing niche, entering regulation compliance publishing in 1970. By 1994, the company offered 2,000 regulation compliance associated products and served as a consultant to companies across the country seeking up-to-date information on the DOT, Occupational Safety and Health Administration (OSHA), and Environmental Protection Agency (EPA) rules. J.J. Keller also benefited from a trend toward outsourcing as clients hired out customized printing of their safety and training materials. Ranked among the 100 largest privately held companies in Wisconsin, J.J. Keller produced sales of $90 million in 1993.

In an "unprecedented agreement" with the American Trucking Association (ATA), Keller gained access to all ATA customer lists for safety and regulatory products, Arlen Boardman reported in January 1997. Under the agreement, ATA exited the publications business and Keller paid the association royalties for related increases in business. Keller would add about 50,000 new accounts, 34,000 of them corporate, although some overlap

was expected with its existing list of more than 200,000 customers. Keller had been adding about 3,000 customers per month prior to the deal.

ATA, Keller's largest rival in U.S. DOT and transportation safety markets, planned to concentrate on its core lobbying and policy development activities in Washington, D.C., according to the *Knight-Ridder/Tribune Business News* article. Bob Keller said of the deal: "The alliance is slated to cover a 10-year time frame which will help expand the scope of our industry-leading products and services offerings, grow our customer base and improve our technological capabilities as we enter the new millennium."

The new activity and the likelihood of additional business from ATA meant added jobs. Employment at Keller had already climbed by nearly 10 percent during the previous two-year period. While Jack Keller's sons were in charge of the company's 800 employees, family ties alone were not a guaranteed pathway to a leadership position at Keller.

The company, unlike many others, had built a succession component into its business plan, Stern reported for *Knight-Ridder.* "It isn't something we talk about all the time, but we dust it off once and year and discuss ... issues like personnel evaluation, career pathing, retention and recruitment," President and CEO Robert Keller explained. Key management posts would go to the most appropriate candidate, someone from the inside—general management staff numbered 80—or a qualified person from the outside. Bob Keller's son Adam had been flexing his entrepreneurial muscles in a project separate from the family business. Meanwhile, Adam's brother Rustin created a new Internet service for the business their grandfather founded.

In addition to their business interests, the family had a well-established involvement in charitable giving, dating back to the early days of the company. During the 1990s, they established Keller Foundation, Ltd., and a donor advised fund at the Community Foundation for the Fox Valley region, according to *Paper Industry International.*

PROFITABLE NEW ERA

In 2000, J.J. Keller joined with Advance Online, Incorporated, a web-based safety-training solutions company, to develop a dozen new courses targeted at corporate employees and workers. The U.S. Department of Labor's Bureau of Labor Statistics reported 5.9 million cases of injuries and illness within private industry workplaces in 1998, according to an October *PR Newswire* article. The courses addressed issues such as office ergonomics, hazard communications, and respiratory

```
┌─────────────────────────────────────────────┐
│                                               │
│              KEY DATES                        │
│                 ■                             │
│  ─────────────────────────────────────────   │
│                                               │
│  1953:  J. J. Keller along with his wife,     │
│         Ethel, found a consulting business.   │
│  1956:  Son Robert L. Keller joins company,   │
│         followed by his brother James J.      │
│         Keller two years later.               │
│  1958:  J.J. Keller & Associates is           │
│         incorporated.                         │
│  1983:  Net sales reach more than $10         │
│         million.                              │
│  2003:  Company joins homeland security       │
│         effort.                               │
│                                               │
└─────────────────────────────────────────────┘
```

protection. Content developer for the project, J.J. Keller had worked with the online company earlier in the year to adapt one of its popular video-based courses for the web.

In 2001, J.J. Keller produced revenue in excess of $160 million from its 4,000-plus products and services. The company's offerings ranged from compliance publications and regulatory forms and supplies to software and Internet services to workshops and consulting.

During 2003, the specialty publisher received a request from the Department of Homeland Security and the Transportation Security Administration to assist with an online system to relay pertinent information to the nation's truckers. "This alert system will help industry professionals develop a higher level of awareness," J.J. Keller's Washington, D.C.–based Senior Account Executive Greg Scott explained in a *Knight-Ridder/Tribune Business News* article. "It lets them know what's going on, what to look out for, how to better secure themselves, and how to report suspicious activity, all of which will contribute to a safer, more secure country." The endeavor arose from the 50-year-old company's longstanding relationship with regulatory agencies and its transportation industry expertise.

With 90 percent of growth internal, J.J. Keller projected 2004 sales at about $150 million. Target annual growth rate for sales and profits was 12 to 15 percent. The business operated out of a 500,000-square-foot facility, compared to the 1,000-square-foot office in 1953. Net sales had climbed from about $10.5 million in 1983 to more than $111 million in 2002. Employee count (although the company preferred the word associate) had climbed to about 950.

The Kellers were quick to share credit for the company's success with their associates. All were involved in task forces, work groups, or problem-solving teams, which created a sense of commitment to the organization. Profit-sharing, merit pay increases, and

bonus programs provided additional motivation. Approximately 50 new products were added in 2003; all grew from the creativity of the associates, who made suggestions regarding line extensions or additional products, according to Robert Warde, writing for *Marketplace.*

The company averaged 50 to 60 new products per year, but had 150 planned for 2004. Eleven catalogs a year were produced for its customers involved in areas including transportation, hazardous materials, OSHA and workplace safety, human resources, construction, EPA and hazardous waste, and food safety. Among its newer products was a PC-based simulator for truck drivers who engaged in hazardous conditions, defensive driving, and crash avoidance situations. J.J. Keller put approximately $1.5 million into development, which it expected to recoup in about two years, according to *Marketplace.*

Bob Keller, in the January 2004 *Marketplace* article, highlighted three key family decisions: maintaining private ownership; introducing profit sharing; and establishing two foundations. Upon their deaths his parents' assets were slated to go to the Keller Foundation. The second-generation leaders continued to build on the dual goals of giving back to the community and creating a successful business. Moreover, a third generation had begun taking on greater responsibility in the company and in philanthropy.

Robert Warde wrote: "The brothers have plotted a strong future for the company and the family. For 2004, the company wants to reach an operating profit of $20 million, with a $2.8 million contribution to its profit sharing plan. The goal is also to reach ... an unheard of 62 percent gross profit margin."

Ethel Keller, cofounder and member of the board of directors of J.J. Keller, died at the end of 2004. She and her husband had been honored in 2003 with the Outstanding Philanthropist Award from the Northeastern Wisconsin Chapter of the Association of Fundraising Professionals, according to *Transport Topics.* "Dad said he was a commercial missionary, and he said Mom was a spiritual missionary," COO James Keller recalled of his parents in *Panache.* By the winter of 2006 total charitable contributions by the family and the company had topped $9.5 million.

Kathleen Peippo

FURTHER READING

Bach, Pete, "Vinland, Wis., Publisher Relays Security Updates by E-mail to Trucking Firms," *Knight-Ridder/Tribune Business News,* April 15, 2003.

Boardman, Arlen, "Wisconsin Transportation Safety Publisher Signs Deal with Trucking Group," *Knight-Ridder/Tribune Business News,* January 31, 1997.

Dougherty, Terri, "Different Roads, Same Destination: Two Area Printing Firm CEOs Nominated for State Entrepreneur of the Year Award," *Marketplace Magazine* (Waupaca), July 19, 1994, p. 24.

Hummel, Alex, "The Business of Generosity: Keller Synonymous with Philanthropy," *Panache,* Winter 2006, pp. 37–38.

"John (Jack) Keller: 2001 Inductee—Founder/Leadership/ Service," *Paper Industry International,*

http://www.paperhall.org/inductees/bios/01/keller.html.

"Obituary: Ethel Keller, Co-founder, J.J. Keller & Associates," *Transport Topics,* January 10, 2005, p. 32.

Stern, Avi, "Wisconsin Printer and Publisher Bases Success on Common Sense," *Knight-Ridder/Tribune Business News,* May 5, 1998.

Waggoner, Judy, "Appleton, Wis., Entrepreneur Designs, Builds, Sells Cages," *Knight-Ridder/Tribune Business News,* August 7, 2000.

Warde, Robert, "Profile: J.J. Keller & Associates, Navigating the Waters," *Marketplace* (Appleton, Wis.), January 27, 2004, p. 13.

Land O'Lakes, Inc.

Land O'Lakes, Inc.

——— ■ ———

4001 Lexington Avenue North
Arden Hills, Minnesota 55112-6943
U.S.A.
Telephone: (651) 481-2222
Toll Free: (800) 328-4155
Fax: (651) 481-2022
Web site: http://www.landolakes.com

Cooperative
Incorporated: 1921 as Minnesota Cooperative Creamery Association, Inc.
Employees: 7,500
Sales: $7.56 billion (2005)
NAIC: 112310 Chicken Egg Production; 311111 Dog and Cat Food Manufacturing; 311119 Other Animal Food Manufacturing; 311225 Fats and Oils Refining and Blending; 311512 Creamery Butter Manufacturing; 311513 Cheese Manufacturing; 311514 Dry, Condensed, and Evaporated Dairy Product Manufacturing; 424430 Dairy Product (Except Dried or Canned) Merchant Wholesalers; 424910 Farm Supplies Merchant Wholesalers

■ ■ ■

Land O'Lakes, Inc., is one of the leading agricultural supply and food marketing cooperatives in the United States, providing both its members and the public with food products and production materials. Included in the cooperative are more than 1,150 member associations and approximately 5,150 individual members in all 50 states. Land O'Lakes has also increasingly sought growth opportunities outside the United States, and now does business in more than 50 foreign countries. The cooperative is best known for its butter and other quality dairy products, which are marketed under the flagship Land O'Lakes brand as well as Alpine Lace and regional brands such as New Yorker. The cooperative also has several additional operations: Land O'Lakes Purina Feed LLC manufactures and markets feed for farm and livestock animals, for animals used for recreational purposes (such as horses), and for specialized animals such as laboratory and zoo animals. The cooperative's seed division is involved in developing, producing, and marketing seed for alfalfa, soybeans, corn, and grasses and also markets and distributes seeds produced by other companies, including corn, soybeans, sunflowers, canola, sorghum, and sugar beets. MoArk, LLC, is a producer and marketer of eggs. Land O'Lakes is also involved in a joint venture with CHS Inc. called Agriliance, a manufacturer, marketer, and distributor of fertilizers, micronutrients, herbicides, pesticides, and fungicides.

EARLY HISTORY

On June 7, 1921, 350 farmers from all over Minnesota gathered in St. Paul to vote on the organization of a statewide dairy cooperative. With a unanimous vote, the Minnesota Cooperative Creamery Association, Inc., forerunner to Land O'Lakes, was born.

Unlike investor-owned corporations, cooperatives work for and answer to their member-patrons, who benefit in direct proportion to the amount of business they do each year with the cooperative—how many products they supply, or how many they buy. Because

COMPANY PERSPECTIVES

We are a market- and customer-driven cooperative committed to optimizing the value of our members' dairy, crop, and livestock production.

each member-patron has one vote, cooperatives are democratic enough to have appealed to the independent American farmers who first joined.

Still, as the *St. Paul Pioneer Press* was to write 25 years later, skeptics of farm cooperatives existed everywhere in 1921. "Nobody would ever induce American farmers to work together," they claimed, because a farmer was "too individualistic by nature and too firmly set in his own ways to adapt his operating methods to the machinery of any organization." What they did not count on was the energy and dedication of the men who had the vision behind Land O'Lakes.

Beginning with a meager financial stake of $1,375, $1,000 of it borrowed from the Farm Bureau, the cooperative's directors launched a statewide membership campaign. Their project was given a boost when in 1922, after a long fight, the U.S. Senate passed the Capper-Volstead bill, which legalized the marketing of farm products through cooperative agencies. The first year's returns showed a slender profit.

John Brandt, one of the original 15 directors elected to run the organization, became president of the association in 1923. He believed that by working together, competing creameries could raise their profits *and* offer a better product to their patrons. He urged cooperation among farmers, engineered joint shipments of butter, and proposed a common standard of quality. Most importantly, he and the other directors of the cooperative decided to concentrate on the quality production and aggressive marketing of "sweet cream" butter, butter made from cream before it soured. Although more costly to make and not as familiar to the public, sweet butter tasted better and kept longer.

In February 1924 the cooperative announced a contest to capture the public's attention: its high-quality product needed a catchier name than "Minnesota Cooperative Creamery Butter." First prize was $500 in gold. An overwhelming response brought in over 100,000 entries; the contest was tied between two winners who both thought of "Land O'Lakes." Soon thereafter an Indian maiden appeared on the butter's packaging, completing the familiar image. According to a November 2001 article in *Dairy Field* magazine, the image of an Indian maiden was selected because the Minnesota/Wisconsin region was the legendary home of Hiawatha and Minnehaha.

In April 1924 the cooperative won a contract with the U.S. Navy for 430,000 pounds of the new sweet cream butter and soon met with a growing demand from American housewives for its conveniently packaged quarter-pound sticks. As Land O'Lakes was already becoming a household name, only two years after the contest, the cooperative changed its name to Land O'Lakes Creameries, Inc., in 1926.

SEEKING NEW MARKETS, DIVERSIFYING DURING THE GREAT DEPRESSION

Land O'Lakes first ventured outside of the dairy business two years later, when it organized egg and poultry divisions. This step toward diversification was to prove crucial during the Great Depression, when dairy businesses throughout the nation suffered enormous losses. In 1930 dairy production was the lowest it had been in two decades, and by December 1933 butter prices had declined to 15¢ a pound, the lowest figure for that month in 25 years. Excess production and surplus holdings were making it almost impossible for American farmers to get back their cost of production, and dozens of creameries held meetings to decide whether they should continue operating. Although Land O'Lakes suffered setbacks because of these market forces between 1929 and 1940, highly imaginative management and a willingness to fight economic trends cut the cooperative's losses considerably. In fact, for much of the Depression Land O'Lakes sales actually grew because of two central strategies.

The first of these strategies was to seek new markets for its products. Before the Depression Land O'Lakes had dealt mostly with large store chains and other nationwide distributors. With many of these large accounts retrenching or vanishing altogether in the crunch, Land O'Lakes began to set up smaller sales branches that could sell directly to groceries and other small outlets. Partly as a result of this marketing strategy, and partly because Land O'Lakes Sweet Cream Butter was being advertised nationally for the first time, Land O'Lakes was able to sell a record 100 million pounds of butter in 1930.

The second strategy was to diversify the products the cooperative offered both to its member farmers and to the public. Seeking to spread the risks of operation, Land O'Lakes began an Agricultural Services Division in 1929 to try to reduce member costs for feed, seed, and other farming supplies. In 1934 the cooperative joined

KEY DATES

1921: A group of 350 Minnesota farmers form the Minnesota Cooperative Creamery Association, Inc.

1924: The Land O'Lakes brand is introduced.

1926: Cooperative changes its name to Land O'Lakes Creameries, Inc.

1929: Cooperative begins supplying feed, seed, and other farm supplies to its members.

1934: Land O'Lakes enters the cheese making sector.

1937: First milk drying plant opens.

1946: Land O'Lakes enters the ice cream and fluid milk markets.

1970: Cooperative merges with the Farmers Regional Cooperative and shortens its name to Land O'Lakes, Inc.

1987: Cenex/Land O'Lakes Ag Services joint venture is formed.

1997: Land O'Lakes merges with Atlantic Dairy Cooperative; Alpine Lace Brands, Inc., is acquired.

1998: Merger with Dairyman's Cooperative Creamery Association is completed.

2000: Cenex/Land O'Lakes Agronomy and the agronomy operations of Farmland Industries, Inc. merge to form the joint venture Agriliance; Land O'Lakes and Farmland Industries merge their feed operations into the joint venture Land O'Lakes Farmland Feed LLC; Land O'Lakes sells its Upper Midwest fluid milk operations to Dean Foods Company and the two companies enter into marketing alliance.

2001: Cooperative acquires Purina Mills, Inc., which is folded into Land O'Lakes Farmland Feed.

2004: Land O'Lakes takes full control of Farmland Feed, which is renamed Land O'Lakes Purina Feed LLC.

three large cheese cooperatives in the operation of 95 cheese factories, and in 1937 Land O'Lakes opened its first milk drying plant, completing a decade of experimentation that pioneered the production of dry milk. As early as 1926, several individual creameries had begun producing powder from buttermilk, previously a

waste product. Thus, when World War II called for milk in a form that did not require refrigeration and had a fraction of the bulk, Land O'Lakes was prepared. All of these changes were ultimately successful expansions and contributed to Land O'Lakes' relative prosperity in difficult times.

In 1938 workers at the main plant in Minneapolis went on strike for a wage increase and a closed shop policy. The strike was amicably settled when the closed-shop demand was withdrawn and a new wage agreement was approved, but the company suffered $400,000 in losses that year.

During World War II, Land O'Lakes was required by federal order to set aside 30 percent of its butter for sale to the government. The cooperative also had a quota of dry milk for the war effort, stepping up production from 22 million pounds in 1941 to 119 million pounds in 1945. By the war's end, Land O'Lakes was producing dried milk and dried eggs in 22 different plants, and eventually became the world's largest manufacturer of dry milk products.

In 1946 Land O'Lakes celebrated its Silver Jubilee under the banner "Pioneers for 25 Years." It prepared for a prosperous future by entering the ice cream and fluid milk markets for the first time, and by developing the world's first successful milk replacement, a dry meal for nursing calves. This meal, a substitute for the skim milk calves were usually fed, overcame opposition to the use of skim milk as a dry milk base.

In 1952 John Brandt, known as "Mr. Land O'Lakes," died after serving as president and general manager for nearly 30 years. Frank Stone became general manager, and M. H. Mauritson became president. Later, a restructuring of the management changed these positions to president and chairman of the board.

POSTWAR ACQUISITIONS SPARKING RAPID GROWTH

To develop its ice cream line, Land O'Lakes acquired Bridgeman Creameries, a chain of soda-grills in Minnesota and Wisconsin, and the operator of fluid milk businesses in North Dakota and Minnesota. The cooperative also expanded three turkey processing plants in 1954.

During the 1960s, the cooperative continued to grow at an astonishing rate. It acquired Terrace Park Dairies of Sioux Falls, South Dakota, a full-line dairy, and H. C. Christians Company, a Chicago manufacturer of butter, and merged with Dairy Maid Products Cooperative of Eau Claire, Wisconsin. In addition, management responded to the broadening scope of Land

O'Lakes' interests by making 60 new assignments and by restructuring the cooperative's internal organization. By the decade's end, Land O'Lakes' sales had reached $400 million and assets totaled nearly $100 million, figures double those of 1960.

Another key merger occurred in 1970, as Land O'Lakes was joined by the Farmers Regional Cooperative, also known as Felco. This move increased Land O'Lakes' capacity to produce and market agricultural production goods (such as fertilizers and insecticides) for its member-patrons, and also brought Ralph Hofstad, Felco's president, to Land O'Lakes, where he later served as president. Also in 1970 Land O'Lakes Creameries, Inc., changed its name to simply Land O'Lakes, Inc., to better reflect its diverse business.

Expansion and diversification continued at a rapid rate as the 1970s drew to a close. In 1978 the cooperative entered the red meat business for the first time with the acquisition of Spencer Beef, the country's 17th largest meatpacker, and in 1980 Land O'Lakes began soybean processing in conjunction with Dawson Mills. The cooperative also produced new products such as "But-R-Cups" and Country Morning Blend, a spread made of 40 percent sweet cream butter and 60 percent corn oil margarine, offering more options to American households and foodservice businesses. Introduced to the foodservice market in 1975 after ten years of development, "But-R-Cups" were single servings of butter packaged entirely by machine ensuring portion control and standardized freshness. Country Morning Blend appeared in 1981 and was aimed at consumers who preferred the taste of butter but could not afford it. It was cleverly designed to make a dent in the margarine market while keeping converts from butter, always Land O'Lakes' mainstay, to a minimum.

DIFFICULTIES LEADING TO RETREAT FROM DIVERSIFICATION

In 1981 Land O'Lakes moved into its new corporate offices in Arden Hills, Minnesota, just north of the Twin Cities, with facilities for research, testing, sales, and training.

At the end of fiscal 1982, too much supply, too little demand, escalating production costs, and excessive interest rates on existing debts resulted in losses in excess of $19 million. Land O'Lakes had moved too fast and taken on too much in the 1970s and early 1980s, critics said, pointing to the cooperative's ventures in beef, agronomy, petroleum, and soybeans. A merger with Midland Cooperative that year did eventually bring savings in excess of $4 million, and Land O'Lakes' fiscal health was never seriously threatened.

In 1985 a class-action suit brought against Land O'Lakes by 96 turkey farmers claimed that the cooperative had overcharged the farmers for their participation in a marketing pool in 1980. Land O'Lakes eventually settled out of court for approximately $1.5 million.

In the late 1980s, Land O'Lakes showed a continued willingness to expand, while carefully monitoring its less-established commodities. In January 1987 Land O'Lakes launched an extensive joint venture, Cenex/Land O'Lakes Ag Services, with Cenex Cooperative to market feed, seed, farm chemicals, and petroleum. Later in the year it embarked on a more limited venture with Mid-America Dairymen (taking advantage of the fact that Mid-America's regional offices and Land O'Lakes' corporate headquarters were both located in Arden Hills) to operate dairy plants together. Land O'Lakes also left the petroleum resources business in 1987 and soon thereafter divested turkey and red meat businesses, reflecting a concern that industry overproduction, widely fluctuating market prices, and increasing operating costs would continue to make their operation unprofitable.

EXPANDING MARKET AREA DOMESTICALLY AND INTERNATIONALLY

Land O'Lakes entered the 1990s under new leadership, as John E. ("Jack") Gherty, a 19-year cooperative veteran, was named president in September 1989, replacing Hofstad. The Gherty-led Land O'Lakes of the 1990s, while hampered somewhat by the inefficient ways of many of its conservative, cash-strapped Midwestern farmers, posted steadily rising sales and earnings thanks largely to efforts to extend the cooperative's sales area both in the United States and abroad.

In part to counter the maturing of the U.S. market in such cooperative staples as butter, livestock feed, and fertilizers, Land O'Lakes became much more aggressive overseas in the 1990s. The groundwork for these moves began to be laid in 1981, when Land O'Lakes formed an International Development division. This division worked as a subcontractor on projects that were funded through grants from the U.S. Agency for International Development and international development banks and that aimed to build local farm and food economies. Land O'Lakes' involvement in these efforts helped to build business ties that later evolved into joint ventures, as well as developing new customers for exports in the region. By the mid-1990s Poland was turning into one of the International Development division's real success stories as Land O'Lakes entered into joint ventures to operate a feed milling business and a cheese plant there. Exports to Mexico increased in this period led by the 1996 introduction of the Great Start line of swine starter feeds. In March 1996 a feed mill began operating in Taiwan that was part of a joint venture between Land O'Lakes and a Taiwanese firm. Land O'Lakes celebrated its 75th anniversary in 1996 with record net sales of $3.49 billion and near record net earnings of $118.9 million (second only to the $120.5 million of 1995).

Meanwhile, Land O'Lakes was involved in activities at home that brought it closer to being a truly nationwide cooperative. The cooperative's Pacific Northwest region was bolstered through a joint venture with the Seattle-based Darigold Feed Co. cooperative, which was fully operational in 1993 and served to link the Pacific Northwest feed operations of the two cooperatives, bringing gains from the larger scale of the combined operations. Also in 1993 Land O'Lakes acquired the assets of the Waldron Feed Co., the only commercial feed manufacturer in the Hawaiian Islands. This purchase not only gave Land O'Lakes a U.S. presence that stretched from Michigan to Hawaii but it also brought with it Waldron's exports to the Pacific Rim. In early 1997 Land O'Lakes merged with Southampton, Pennsylvania-based Altantic Dairy Cooperative, which had been one of Land O'Lakes' largest dairy cooperative members and which was owned by 3,600 dairy farmers in the Middle Atlantic region. The merger made Land O'Lakes the third-largest processor of dairy foods in the country (with $2.1 billion in annual processing), enhanced the cooperative's butter supply near to its strongest market area, and extended its membership base into a new region and into seven new states, thereby giving Land O'Lakes a coast-to-coast presence. Later in 1997 Land O'Lakes acquired Alpine Lace Brands, Inc., a Maplewood, New Jersey, marketer of cheeses and meat products to supermarket delicatessens, with the top-selling deli Swiss cheese brand in the United States. Through this $60 million deal, Land O'Lakes boosted its deli market share from 13 to 17 percent.

In 1998 the cooperative bolstered its West Coast operations by merging with Dairyman's Cooperative Creamery Association of Tulare, California. Dairyman's had 240 members and annual revenues of about $800 million. The merger increased Land O'Lakes' annual milk production capacity by 50 percent, from 8 billion pounds to 12 billion pounds. Results for 1998 were severely impacted by a $26 million loss suffered by the cooperative's swine operations as a result of low prices in the hog industry.

DEALMAKING AT THE TURN OF THE MILLENNIUM

A host of deals completed between 1999 and 2002 brought fundamental, across-the-board changes. The Cenex/Land O'Lakes Agronomy joint venture acquired the retail operations of Terra Industries Inc., a producer of crop protection, fertilizer, and seed products based in Sioux City, Iowa. This 1999 deal for approximately $360 million was followed one year later by the merger of Cenex/Land O'Lakes Agronomy and the agronomy operations of Farmland Industries, Inc. to form Agriliance, a joint venture for which Land O'Lakes held a 50 percent interest. Also in 2000 the cooperative and Farmland Industries combined their feed operations into another joint venture, Land O'Lakes Farmland Feed LLC, with Land O'Lakes taking an initial 69 percent stake. In 2001 Land O'Lakes spent about $360 million to acquire Purina Mills, Inc., one of the largest animal feed companies in the country. Purina Mills was folded into Land O'Lakes Farmland Feed, after which Land O'Lakes' stake in the feed business stood at 92 percent. Land O'Lakes bought out Farmland's 8 percent stake in 2004, after which the unit was renamed Land O'Lakes Purina Feed LLC.

On the dairy side, Land O'Lakes in 2000 acquired Madison Dairy Produce Company, operator of the largest butter production facility in the Midwest. The cooperative also acquired a Beatrice Group mozzarella cheese plant in Gustine, California, in 2000, and the following year purchased a Kraft Foods Inc. cheese plant in Melrose, Minnesota, through a joint venture with Dairy Farmers of America, Inc. In the face of increasing consolidation in the milk marketing sector, Land O'Lakes elected to sell its Upper Midwest fluid milk operations to Dean Foods Company in a deal that closed in July 2000. Cooperative members continued to supply raw milk to the five facilities that Dean acquired. Concurrently, Land O'Lakes and Dean entered into a 50-50 joint venture giving Dean the right to market sour cream, half and half, and cream nationwide under the Land O'Lakes brand. In 2002 Land O'Lakes and the new Dean Foods Company (created via Suiza Foods Corporation's 2001 acquisition of the original Dean Foods) replaced this joint venture with an expanded alliance giving Dean the right to use the Land O'Lakes name nationally on a range of value-added fluid milk and cultured dairy products.

Through this string of deals, Land O'Lakes had positioned itself as a business with four strong core operations—dairy foods, feed, seed, and agronomy. Through the year 2005 the cooperative concentrated on paying down a significant portion of the debt it had incurred via some of these deals and also consolidating and integrating merged operations. Seeking to focus further on these core areas, Land O'Lakes divested its troubled swine operations in 2005 and also sold off its 38 percent interest in CF Industries, a fertilizer maker based in Long Grove, Illinois, for $315 million. The sale of the CF stake resulted in a net gain of $70 million, pushing net earnings for the year to a record $129 million. Net sales fell slightly, 1.6 percent, to $7.56 billion.

In October 2005 Gherty retired, having left a lasting mark on Land O'Lakes. Succeeding him as president and CEO was Chris Policinski, who had been executive vice-president and chief operating officer of the dairy foods division. One of Policinski's initial focuses was cost containment, and Land O'Lakes in February 2006 shut down its cheddar cheese plant in Greenwood, Wisconsin, which had operated at a loss the previous year. The new leader also continued his predecessor's strategy of focusing on core areas. The principal troubled operation that remained was the egg production and marketing unit, MoArk, LLC. MoArk had been a joint venture from 1998 until January 2006, when Land O'Lakes acquired full control. Land O'Lakes then sold MoArk's liquid egg processing operations to Golden Oval Eggs, LLC, in June 2006 in a $60 million deal. MoArk, which retained its shell egg business, remained a candidate for divestment as it represented a distraction from Land O'Lakes' much larger and stronger core businesses.

Updated, David E. Salamie

PRINCIPAL SUBSIDIARIES

Land O'Lakes Purina Feed LLC; MoArk, LLC.

PRINCIPAL COMPETITORS

Kraft Foods Inc.; Dean Foods Company; Sargento Foods Inc.; Challenge Dairy Products; Keller's Creamery, LP; Pioneer Hi-Bred International, Inc.; Monsanto Company; Syngenta Seeds, Inc.

FURTHER READING

Apgar, Sally, "Land O'Lakes Dairy Fortunes Turn Sour," *Minneapolis Star Tribune*, November 1, 1993, p. 1D.

Clark, Gerry, "Land O'Opportunity," *Dairy Foods*, September 1999, pp. 17+.

Cook, James, "Dreams of Glory," *Forbes*, September 12, 1983, p. 92.

Egerstrom, Lee, "Execs from Land O'Lakes Gearing Up to Deal with Uncertain Future," *Saint Paul Pioneer Press*, July 25, 1993.

El-Hai, Jack, *Celebrating Tradition, Building the Future: Seventy-Five Years of Land O'Lakes*, Minneapolis: Land O'Lakes, Inc., 1996, 132 p.

Howie, Michael, "Land O'Lakes to Be More Focused," *Feedstuffs*, February 27, 2006, p. 6.

Kimbrell, Wendy, "Land O'Lakes Formula for Success," *Dairy Foods*, December 1989, pp. 44+.

Leidahl, Roy, "Land O'Lakes: Ready to Grow More, but Not Out of Midwest," *Feedstuffs*, November 22, 1982, pp. 1+.

Levy, Melissa, "Churning Up More Business: Acquisitions Are Big Part of Land O'Lakes' Growth Effort," *Minneapolis Star Tribune*, February 23, 1998, p. 1D.

———, "Land O'Lakes Sells Fluid Dairy Unit," *Minneapolis Star Tribune*, June 1, 2000, p. 1D.

Merrill, Ann, "Land O'Lakes Buys Purina Mills Inc.," *Minneapolis Star Tribune*, June 19, 2001, p. 1D.

———, "Land O'Lakes Planning to Acquire Alpine Lace," *Minneapolis Star Tribune*, October 2, 1997, p. 1D.

Ruble, Kenneth D., *Land O'Lakes: Farmers Make It Happen*, Minneapolis: privately printed, 1973, 205 p.

———, *Men to Remember: How 100,000 Neighbors Made History*, Chicago: Lakeside Press, 1947, 318 p.

Smith, Pamela Accetta, "The Face of Success," *Dairy Field*, November 2001, pp. 1, 16–21.

Smith, Rod, "LOL Commits Itself to Be Best Dairy Company in U.S.," *Feedstuffs*, March 11, 1991, pp. 6, 17.

———, "LOL Getting Members Ready for Major Push to Global Size," *Feedstuffs*, March 8, 1993, pp. 6, 27.

———, "LOL Makes Agreement to Sell Swine Business," *Feedstuffs*, February 21, 2005, pp. 1, 3.

———, "LOL Notes 'Exhilarating Year'; Reports Second-Best Earnings," *Feedstuffs*, March 5, 1990, pp. 8, 39.

———, "LOL Positions Cooperative for Business-Driven Farming," *Feedstuffs*, March 3, 1997, pp. 10, 11.

———, "LOL Sets Goal to Be 'Dominant' Dairy, Agricultural Supply Cooperative," *Feedstuffs*, March 5, 1990, p. 8.

———, "LOL to Build Brand Strength with Pure, 'Simple Goodness,'" *Feedstuffs*, March 4, 2002, pp. 6–7.

Stern, William M., "Land O'Low Returns," *Forbes*, August 15, 1994, p. 90.

Landor Associates

1001 Front Street
Klamath House
San Francisco, California 94111
U.S.A.
Telephone: (415) 365-1700
Toll Free: (888) 252-6367
Fax: (415) 365-3190
Web site: http://www.landor.com

Wholly Owned Subsidiary of WPP Group PLC
Incorporated: 1941
Employees: 830
NAIC: 541613 Marketing Consulting Services; 541810
Advertising Agencies

∎∎∎

Landor Associates is a subsidiary of WPP Group PLC, a global marketing and communications concern based in the United Kingdom. The firm offers a range of brand strategy, design, naming, and marketing and research services to help strengthen clients' brand power. The company has helped create and develop some of the world's most recognized brands and corporate identities, including Coca-Cola, Levi's, Cotton Inc., Kellogg's, GE, Fuji Film, Saturn, Miller Lite, Alitalia, 20th Century Fox, Philip Morris, Singapore Airlines, 3M, the World Wildlife Fund, Pacific Telesis, Wells Fargo Bank, Dole Foods, Del Monte, Safeway Stores, and Bank of America. Landor has offices in Europe, Asia, Latin America, and throughout the United States.

1941–1964: A PIONEER IN CREATING RECOGNIZED BRANDS AND CORPORATE IDENTITIES

Walter Landor, a German expatriate, founded Walter Landor & Associates in 1941, working from a makeshift desk in his small Russian Hill, San Francisco, apartment with his wife, Josephine, as his associate. Landor, born in Munich in 1912, was the son of a prominent German architect and had been influenced as a youth by the Bauhaus and Werkbund design movements. Landor's father encouraged him to become an architect, but he found that he had no talent for drafting. After trying his hand at industrial design, he turned to graphic design, and, at 18, he decided to focus his career on designing for the mass audience.

Landor went to London to complete his studies at London University's Goldsmith College School of Art in 1931. At 22, he became a founding partner with Misha Black and Miner Gray of England's first industrial design consultancy, Industrial Design Partnership. A year later, he became the youngest Fellow of the Royal Society of Arts in London, and four years after that, in 1939, he traveled to New York to work on Britain's Pavilion at the World's Fair. During this trip, he visited San Francisco and decided to immigrate and begin a business there. "For me, it was a city that looked out on the whole world, a city built on the cultural traditions of East and West—how could I live anywhere else?," Landor is quoted as saying on the company's web site. Landor & Associates was dedicated to employing design and visual imagery to create recognized brands and corporate identities for clients and their commodity products.

The company's reputation grew rapidly, and as it did, Landor began to use consumer research in developing his packaging designs. According to a 1992 *St. Petersburg Times* article, in the 1940s Landor was known to roam the aisles of supermarkets, startling shoppers by holding up two packages of frozen peas—one designed by his firm, the other by a competitor—and asking, "Which would you buy?" Some competitors thought Landor relied on research too much, but as the forerunner in the field of market research, the company became the first, in 1959, to retain in-house specialists to understand how people interact with products and to use this information in design development.

Landor began to simulate the buying process in order to observe customer reactions to differing visual approaches in its research labs. There, the company experimented with new materials, such as cellophane and metallic foils, and introduced new colors, textures, and shapes to packaging. Landor also did more informal research, coming home with bottles of wine or varieties of packaged food and asking his two young daughters which they liked better. Postwar consumer culture responded to Landor's inventiveness, and the company began to attract clients internationally. In the early 1960s, the company opened offices in Italy.

1964–1989: FROM THE FERRYBOAT *KLAMATH* TO YOUNG & RUBICAM

Then, in 1964, Landor moved his firm's headquarters aboard the ferryboat *Klamath,* which he anchored at San Francisco's Pier 5. Built in 1924, the *Klamath* had been a working ferryboat on San Francisco Bay for 32 years until its retirement in 1956. Landor found the *Klamath* sitting in mudflats at the port of Redwood City, California, and purchased it at a bankruptcy sale for $12,000. After renovations, the company's staff moved on board, a move that drew attention to the company and underscored its reputation for innovation and creativity. The *Klamath* eventually housed the company's Museum of Packaging Antiquities and its supermarket test lab.

In 1974, Landor handed over day-to-day control of the firm to John M. Diefenbach, who became its president and chief executive officer. Landor continued to grow both nationally and internationally under Diefenbach, opening offices in Tokyo, Mexico City, and New York and establishing a solid reputation and presence in Europe. The value of corporate branding gained recognition during the decade of the 1970s, and Landor Associates became respected for setting the industry's standards with its seminal methodology for branding. Back aboard the *Klamath,* Landor's researchers continued to explore the connection between a company's visual and verbal identity and its reputation, directing greater attention to naming, retail interiors, and signage. Some of Landor's major clients of the 1970s included Bank of America, Hewlett-Packard, Cotton, Oscar Mayer & Co., and San Francisco International Airport.

During the 1980s, the business of shaping the way a company presented itself to the world grew rapidly as a boom in mergers and acquisitions yielded hundreds of new corporate entities. Landor created design systems for well-known corporations such as Coca-Cola, Fuji Film, 20th Century Fox, and the World Wildlife Fund. It also launched ImagePower, the first-ever comprehensive survey of international brands, intending to reveal how brands were perceived and how they measured up to their competition. (The survey became a subject of controversy when it revealed consumer disatisfaction with some of the more publicized corporate identity changes engineered by Landor's competitors, Anspach and Lippincott & Margulies.) By the end of the decade, however, the beginnings of a recession severely depressed the corporate identity business; airlines merged, eliminating established clients for Landor, while other former clients tightened their belts and eliminated their corporate identity programs. Another of Landor's specialties, retail shop design, also suffered as the retail industry underwent a downturn.

If clients were no longer investing in their corporate identity, however, large advertising companies were beginning to pay more attention to branding as consumers turned from mainstream media to other areas of communication. As Landor entered the late 1980s, it was still one of the largest firms of its kind, with reported revenues of greater than $50 million, and strong prospects for continued growth. In 1988 the company renamed itself Landor Associates, left the *Klamath* (which remained the firm's corporate symbol), and moved into new offices in an old building on Front Street in San Francisco. The following year, it agreed to be purchased by Young & Rubicam (Y & R), one of the larger international marketing and communications agencies, and became a part of the WPP family of companies. As part of the acquisition, Diefenbach rejoined Y & R as

```
┌─────────────────────────────────────────────┐
│                                               │
│              KEY DATES                        │
│              ──────●──────                     │
│  ─────────────────────────────────────────   │
│  1941: Walter Landor founds Walter Landor & As- │
│        sociates in San Francisco.              │
│  1964: The company moves its headquarters aboard │
│        the *Klamath* ferryboat.                │
│  1974: John M. Diefenbach joins the company as its │
│        president.                              │
│  1988: Landor Associates moves its corporate  │
│        headquarters to Front Street.           │
│  1989: The company is acquired by Young & Rubi- │
│        cam; Donald M. Casey becomes president  │
│        and chief executive officer.            │
│  1991: Edward Vick becomes president and chief │
│        executive officer.                      │
│  1993: Clay Timon becomes president and chief  │
│        executive officer.                      │
│  2000: Landor acquires the Chicago-based strategic │
│        brand consultancy, St. James Associates; │
│        Landor, as a subsidiary of Young & Rubicam, │
│        becomes part of WPP Group PLC.          │
│  2003: Craig Branigan becomes president and chief │
│        executive officer.                      │
│  2004: The company acquires the Australian firm │
│        LKS.                                    │
│                                               │
└─────────────────────────────────────────────┘
```

director of corporate development, relinquishing his role as president and chief executive officer to Donald M. Casey.

1990–2005: RETRENCHMENT AND REPOSITIONING FOR A GLOBAL LEADER

Casey headed Landor for the next two years. Then in 1991, Edward Vick took over, charged with engineering the company's financial turnaround. "We're a small company," Vick, great-grandson of the cofounder of the Richardson-Vicks cough drop company, said in a 1992 *San Francisco Chronicle* article, "but we were operating too much like a big company. We should be entrepreneurial and quicker." To act more in line with its real size, from 1990 through 1992, Landor drastically cut its worldwide workforce by 30 percent to 350 people. The company also closed 5 of its 21 offices as revenues dropped to about $40 million. In a move designed to respond to ongoing trends, such as global expansion and growth in digital branding systems, industry deregulation, and mega-mergers, Landor sought out new approaches to serving clients.

By 1993, when Clay Timon of Saatchi & Saatchi Advertising of Paris became the next president and chief executive of Landor, the changes implemented under Vick had resulted in a marked upswing in new business. By the time Walter Landor died in 1995 at the age of 81, the company again employed more than 300 people in 17 offices worldwide. Throughout the early 1990s, Landor had received several important accolades for his long career in design, including two lifetime achievement awards, one from the Package Design Council International in 1991 and another from the University of San Francisco in 1992. He also was honored by the mayor of San Francisco as one of the city's "creative visionaries" in 1992. In 1994, the Smithsonian Institution's National Museum of American History completed the Walter Landor Collections of Design Records and Packaging, which documented Landor Associates' contributions to 20th-century American design history.

In the early 1990s, Landor Associates also took on a new challenge, branding the Olympic Games with partner EvansGroup Marketing. Beginning with the 1992 Olympics in Atlanta, then in Nagano in 1994, and in Salt Lake City in 1996, Landor contracted to conceive the central theme—including logo, mascot, pictograms, and graphics—for the worldwide competition. In 1997, the firm also undertook its second ImagePower study, interviewing the executives of 500 large, medium, and small companies to evaluate brand and company names on five key attributes, which it called share of mind, share of heart, appropriateness, uniqueness, and momentum.

During the next decade under Timon, the world market shrank dramatically, creating new opportunities for Landor. The firm took the approach that brands had to cater to the global consumer while simultaneously paying attention to consumer segments. The first half of this decade saw Landor regaining its former momentum and growth. It experienced annual revenue growth of 15 percent and an increase from 15 to 51 percent in revenues from its top ten clients. It opened offices around the world, including Hamburg, Dubai, Singapore, and Shanghai, as well as Seattle, Cincinnati, and Chicago. In 2000, Landor acquired the Chicago-based strategic brand consultancy, St. James Associates. St. James had been founded in 1991 to integrate brand strategy with business planning and implementation. In 2002, Landor's client roster continued to read like a who's who of business: FedEx, Morgan Stanley, New York Stock Exchange, Microsoft, BP, Delta Airlines, Olympic Games, Alamo, Cathay Pacific, Procter & Gamble, Frito-Lay, France Telecom, VARIG, and Coors.

A year after Craig Branigan became chief executive in 2003, the company acquired LKS, an Australian branding firm, which, since 1979, had conducted major branding programs for blue chip Australian organizations. With LKS now Landor's Australian office, the firm included offices in 22 cities in 17 countries. Branigan had worked for Y & R for ten years before he became director of Landor's San Francisco office in 1996 and president of Landor Europe in 1998. He was joined by Charlie Wrench as president in 2005. Wrench also had worked for Y & R before joining Landor and occupying several management positions.

Landor closed out 2005 with a 12-month pitch-to-win rate of 77 percent and 15 new projects for clients that included HSBC, Danone UK, Numico, KLM-owned Transavia, and Traidcraft. Despite its commitment to broaden the nature of its work to maintain its competitiveness, the company continued to style its growth under Branigan after Landor's original position. As he expressed his outlook in a 1992 *St. Petersburg Times* article: "If the effort doesn't show, then it's a good design. It must never look designed. And a good design should last."

Carrie Rothburd

PRINCIPAL COMPETITORS

FutureBrand; Interbrand Corporation; Lippincott Mercer; Addison Whitney; Brand Institute; BrandLink Corporation; Envoy Communications Group; Euro RSCG 4D; Mires, Siegel & Gale; Wolff Olins; Corporate Branding.

FURTHER READING

Beckett, Jamie, "New Look for Landor: Corporate ID Firm Has Its Own Identity Crisis," *San Francisco Chronicle,* July 1, 1992, p. B1.

Rubin, Sylvia, "Designing Wizard Makes His Trademarks," *St. Petersburg Times,* August 30, 1992, p. 1I.

Landsbanki Islands hf

Austurstraeti 11
Reykjavik,
Iceland
Telephone: +354 440 4000
Fax: +354 440 4001
Web site: http://www.landsbanki.is

Public Company
Incorporated: 1885
Employees: 1,725
Total Assets: ISK 1.4 trillion ($21.06 billion) (2006)
Stock Exchanges: Iceland
Ticker Symbol: LAIS
NAIC: 522110 Commercial Banking

■ ■ ■

Landsbanki Islands hf (the name means National Bank of Iceland) is that country's oldest and largest commercial bank. Established in 1885, Landsbanki operates 48 branches throughout the island country, including 13 branches in Reykjavik. Landsbanki provides a full range of commercial banking services to the private, corporate, and institutional sectors. Formerly a state-owned bank, and at one time the country's central bank, Landsbanki was privatized in the late 1990s. Since then, the bank has more than tripled its assets, topping ISK 1.4 trillion ($21 billion) in total assets at the beginning of 2006.

Landsbanki is one of the world's fastest growing banks. From its base in tiny Iceland, with a population of less than 300,000, Landsbanki has engaged on an international expansion drive. Since the early 2000s, the

bank has acquired or established operations in the United Kingdom, Luxembourg, France, and Ireland. Subsidiaries include the United Kingdom's Heritable Bank Ltd., a specialist lender based in London; French equities broker Kepler Equities S.A.; Landsbanki Luxembourg S.A.; and, since 2005, 50 percent of Merrion Group, a securities firm based in Ireland. Landsbanki is itself in turn controlled by Samson eignarhaldsfelag ehf, which owns more than 40 percent of the group's stock. Samson is an investment holding vehicle of Iceland's wealthiest family, led by Björgólfur Gudmundssons, who also serves as Landsbanki chairman. Sigurjón Th. Árnason and Halldór J. Kristjánsson share the bank's managing directory and CEO positions. Landsbanki Island is listed on the Iceland Stock Exchange, and since 2005 has been listed on the OMX exchanges in Copenhagen, Stockholm, and Helsinki.

ICELAND'S FIRST BANK: LATE 19TH-CENTURY ORIGINS

Throughout much of its history—the first human settlements date only to the eighth century—Iceland had been dominated politically and financially by the Danish crown. The country remained poor, with a population below 50,000 through the 19th century. An independent Icelandic state began to emerge toward the end of the 1800s, starting in 1874 with the drafting of a constitution under which the country claimed dominion over its domestic affairs. The new Icelandic government soon recognized the importance of developing the country's financial independence as well, and especially the need to stimulate the new country's moribund economy. An important component of the government's economic

Landsbanki is Iceland's oldest full-service commercial bank and has played a leading role in the successful economic progress of Iceland since its inception in 1885. Through its extensive domestic branch system and a wide-ranging network of international correspondent banks, coupled with a broad range of financial products and services, the Bank has positioned itself as Iceland's primary source of general and specialised financial services to individuals, corporate entities and institutions.

policy was the development of an industrial infrastructure, supplementing the country's traditional reliance on fishing and shipping.

In order to provide cash for industrial investments, the government's treasury began issuing Iceland's first bank notes, in the form of treasury notes that could be freely exchanged for Danish *Krøner*. The first treasury notes were then turned over to the newly established Landsbanki Islands, or the National Bank of Iceland, created by an act of legislation in 1885. The bank's origins were quite modest, housed in a bookseller's shop in Reykjavik. The bank was nonetheless a state-owned entity, and was charged with providing loans and other funding to help modernize the country's economy. Landsbanki formally began operations in July 1886.

At the same time, the Icelandic government continued to encourage the further development of the country's banking industry. This led to the creation soon after of the country's first savings bank, Sparisjó'ur Reykjavíkur (Reykjavik Savings Bank). Shortly after, that bank was merged into Landsbanki, allowing the state-owned bank to extend itself as a deposit-taking bank in 1887.

Landsbanki remained Iceland's most prominent bank into the next century; in 1899, the bank established its permanent location at the intersection of Reykjavik's Asuturstraeti and Posthusstraeti. The following year, Landsbanki was granted a mandate from the Icelandic government to launch mortgage lending services. Landsbanki also grew to meet the needs of the island's growing population, establishing its first branch office in Akureyri, in the north, in 1902. This was followed by a second branch in 1904, in Isafjordur. The company opened two more branches in the following decade, in

Eskifjör'ur and Selfoss. Reykjavik's place as Iceland's largest city led the bank to open its first branch office in that city in 1931.

Iceland took the next step toward independence in 1904, when it established its system of Home Rule and named its first prime minister. The country remained closely linked with Denmark, however, as evidenced by the founding of Islandsbanki (Bank of Iceland) that same year. That bank, a privately held entity owned by a consortium of Danish investors, was granted the right to issue gold-backed bank notes. Islandsbanki retained this right exclusively through the end of World War I.

In 1918, Iceland and Denmark signed the Act of Crown Union, establishing Iceland as an independent, sovereign state under the Danish crown. Political pressure then began to build to transfer the new country's note-issuing authority from the now officially foreign-controlled Islandsbanki to Landsbanki. This transition was completed in 1927, when a new act of the Althingi, Iceland's parliament, established Landsbanki as Iceland's central bank, with the sole authority to issue bank notes. Landsbanki issued its first note, a 100 *Krøner* bill, in that year. By 1928, the bank has issued bills for 5, 10, and 50 *Krøner* as well.

PRIVATIZATION IN 1998

Following World War II, the Althingi passed legislation creating a new loan department within the Landsbanki in order to stimulate the country's fishing industry. In this way, Landsbanki helped back the emergence of the country's industrial fishing and fish processing industry, as well as its shipping industry, which dominated the country's economy into the 1990s.

Despite its status as Iceland's central bank, Landsbanki's position as the country's dominant commercial bank created a conflict of interest in terms of the setting of monetary policy. The Iceland government began taking steps to correct this situation in 1957, when Landsbanki was split into its central banking and commercial banking components. The two divisions remained linked, although operating independently, until the creation of Se'labanki Íslands (Central Bank of Iceland) in 1961. The new Central Bank then took over as the sole bank note issuer for the country.

Through the rest of the century, Landsbanki continued to build out its network of branch offices. By the end of the 1990s, the bank operated 46 branches and sub-branches, completing its national coverage. The bank remained the country's leading commercial bank, holding more than half of all savings deposits and mortgages. The company's main rival during this time was another state-owned bank, Búna'arbanki Íslands.

KEY DATES

■

1885: Landsbanki Islands, the first commercial bank in Iceland, is created.

1887: Landsbanki takes over Sparisjó'ur Reykjavíkur (Reykjavik Savings Bank) and adds deposit taking services.

1904: Landsbanki opens its first branch office.

1927: Landsbanki becomes Iceland's central bank and takes over as issuer of bank notes.

1946: Landsbanki establishes a loan division for the fishing industry.

1957: Landsbanki operations are divided into Central Banking and Commercial Banking units.

1961: The Central Banking division is spun off and Landsbanki becomes a purely commercial bank.

1989: Securities operations are established.

1997: Landsbanki reincorporates as a limited liability company.

1998: The Icelandic government places the first block of Landsbanki shares on the Iceland Stock Exchange.

2000: Landsbanki acquires 70 percent of Heritable Bank in England.

2003: Privatization of Landsbanki is completed; operations in Luxembourg are acquired.

2005: Landsbanki acquires Kepler Equities in France; Teather & Greenwood in England; and Merrion in Ireland.

In Reykjavik alone, the bank operated 13 offices. Landsbanki also began preparing for its coming privatization, as Iceland itself prepared to enter the European Monetary Union in the first half of the 1990s. As part of this process, Landsbanki sought to expand its range of banking services. In 1989, for example, the bank launched a new subsidiary, Landsbref hf, which began offering securities investment and other private banking and asset management services.

Iceland's government launched the privatization of its banking sector in September 1997, when legislation by the Althingi directed that both Landsbanki and Búna'arbanki Íslands be re-incorporated as limited liability companies. The new bank corporation, Landsbanki Islands hf, became operational at the beginning of January 1998, with the Icelandic government holding 100 percent of its shares.

By the end of 1998, however, Landsbanki had completed its initial public offering, listing 15 percent of its stock on the Iceland Stock Exchange. The government progressively exited its shareholding in Landsbanki. In 1999, a secondary offering of another 15 percent was placed on the stock exchange; in June 2002, the National Treasury sold its 20 percent share of Landsbanki as well. By October of that year, the Icelandic government had agreed to sell a further 45.8 percent of Landsbanki to Samson eignarhaldsfelag ehf, the investment holding company owned by Iceland's wealthiest family, then led by Björgólfur Gudmundssons and son Björgólfur Thor Björgólfursson. The government sold its remaining 2.5 percent share block in February 2003, completing the bank's privatization.

IMPRESSIVE GROWTH IN THE NEW CENTURY

By then, Landsbanki had launched an ambitious expansion program. The company served as a major motor in the modernization and expansion of Iceland's financial sector, helping to found a number of financial bodies, including VISA's Iceland operation, Grei'slumi'lun hf, and the country's Eurocard service, Kreditkort hf. Landsbanki also joined Búna'arbanki Íslands in the creation of the leasing companies Lysing and SP Finance. At the same time, Landsbanki targeted the insurance sector for expansion, which led it to acquire a 44 percent stake in Vátryggingafélag Íslands hf (VÍS, or Iceland Insurance Company).

The major thrust of the bank's expansion effort, however, quickly turned to the international market. In 2000, Landsbanki acquired a 70 percent stake in the United Kingdom's Heritable Bank held by First Union Bank (later Wachovia) in the United States. The London-based firm, originally founded in Scotland in 1877 before transferring to London in the 1950s, operated as a specialist lender targeting the property development, small- to mid-sized business, and residential mortgage markets. Under Landsbanki, Heritable grew quickly, both through the expansion of its range of services and the acquisition of Key Business Finance in 2005. By then, Landsbanki had taken 100 percent control of Heritable.

Landsbanki also entered the Luxembourg market, acquiring Búna'arbanki International in 2003. The Luxembourg operation, established in 2001 as a private banking and asset management services provider for Icelandic and Scandinavian customers, then changed its name to Landsbanki Luxembourg S.A. That deal came as part of a larger shuffling of assets between Iceland's two leading banks. In 2001, Landsbanki exchanged its shareholding in Lysing for a stake in Búna'arbanki, which then absorbed the leasing operation. Landsbanki in its turn acquired the majority of SP Finance in 2002, which then became its leasing subsidiary.

Landsbanki continued to seek out acquisition opportunities as well. The year 2005 proved to be a transformational one for the company as it completed several significant acquisitions. In February of that year, Landsbanki returned to England to acquire brokerage Teather & Greenwood, in a deal worth nearly £43 million.

In August 2005, the company joined with Straumur Investment Bank to divide up the assets of investment group Buretharas hf. Through that deal, Landsbanki added assets including a stake in D. Carnegie & Co. AB, subsequently sold for ISK 10 billion ($150 million), as well as stakes in Intrum Justitia AB, Carrera Global Investments, and Marel hf.

That acquisition was followed in September 2005 with the acquisition of 81.6 percent of Kepler Equities, based in France, for EUR 76.1 million. That purchase gave the bank access to the European securities market. Landsbanki continued to fill out its European profile that year with the December 2005 acquisition of a 50 percent stake in Merrion Capital Group. Based in Ireland, Merrion operated as a stockbrokerage and asset management firm targeting the high-net-worth bracket. As part of the acquisition agreement, Landsbanki was to acquire the remaining 50 percent of Merrion by 2008.

Landsbanki had achieved impressive growth into the middle of the 2000s, more than tripling its total assets, placing it as number nine among the top ten Nordic market banks. Landsbanki was also one of the world's fastest growing banks—a position Iceland's oldest and largest bank expected to maintain in the years to come.

M. L. Cohen

PRINCIPAL SUBSIDIARIES

Heritable Bank Ltd. (U.K.); Hömlur hf; Kepler Equities S.A. (France; 84%); Landsbanki Holdings (Europe) PLC (Luxembourg); Landsbanki Holdings (UK) PLC; Landsbanki Luxembourg S.A.; Landsbankinn - Fjárfesting hf; Landsbankinn eignarhaldsfélag ehf.; Landsbankinn fasteignafélag ehf.; Landsvaki hf; LI Asset Management (U.K.); LI Investments Ltd. (U.K.); Merrion Capital Group Ltd. (Ireland; 50%); SP–Fjármögnun hf; Stofnlánadeild Samvinnufélaga; Teather & Greenwood Holdings PLC; Ver'bréfun hf.

PRINCIPAL COMPETITORS

Kaupthing Bank hf; Glitnir hf; Nordea Bank AB; Skandinaviska Enskilda Banken; Svenska Handelsbanken; Kommuninvest Ek foereningen; Danske Bank A/S; Danmarks Nationalbank Kobenhavn; Jyske Bank (A/S); Nordea Bank Finland PLC; OP Bank Group; Aktia Saeaestoepankki Oyj.

FURTHER READING

Daley, James, "Landsbanki Buys Teathers for £42.8m," *Independent*, February 2, 2005, p. 37.

"Icelandic Government to Divest Bank Stakes," *Nordic Business Report*, February 14, 2003.

"Icelandics Scramble for Funds," *Euromoney*, April 2006, p. 20.

"Landsbanki Completes the Initial Acquisition in Merrion Capital," *Hugin*, December 21, 2005.

"Landsbanki Has Sold Its Entire Stake in Carnegie and Realises ISK 10 Billion (EUR 110 Million) in Capital Gain," *Hugin*, April 27, 2006.

"Landsbanki Islands Acquires Key Business Finance Corporation Plc," *Nordic Business Report*, April 18, 2005.

"Landsbanki Islands hf to Acquire Kepler Equities SA," *Nordic Business Report*, September 5, 2005.

Lee, Peter, "Landsbanki Islands hf to Establish UK Branch Office," *Nordic Business Report*, January 20, 2005.

"Merger of Buretharas hf. with Straumur Investment Bank Ltd. and Landsbanki Islands hf.," *Hugin*, August 2, 2005.

Pretzlik, Charles, "Landsbanki Targets UK for Its £50m-£100m Acquisition Plans," *Financial Times*, October 30, 2002, p. 26.

Romaniello, Sophie, "Icelandic Finance Market Matures," *International Financial Law Review*, October 2004, p. S41.

Lipman Electronic Engineering Ltd.

———————— ■ ————————

11 Haamal Street, Park Afek
Rosh Ha'Ayin, 48092
Israel
Telephone: (97) 23-902-9730
Fax: (97) 23-902-9731
Web site: http://www.lipman.co.il

Public Company
Incorporated: 1974
Employees: 985
Sales: $235.4 million (2005)
Stock Exchanges: NASDAQ Tel Aviv
Ticker Symbol: LPMA
NAIC: 333313 Office Machinery Manufacturing

■ ■ ■

Lipman Electronic Engineering Ltd. is a developer and seller of electronic payment systems and software, ranking as the fourth largest point-of-sale terminal maker in the world. Lipman Electronic's range products include wireless and landline point-of-sale terminals, personal identification number pads, electronic cash registers, and automated teller machines. These products are used to process credit and debit electronic payments and other electronic transactions related to prepaid, cellular-telephone airtime, lottery ticket purchases, loyalty programs, gift cards, and transportation ticketing. The company's products are sold to distributors, payment processors, and banks and credit-card companies, who sell the equipment and software to end-users—retail businesses such as fast-food chains, furniture stores, and convenience store chains. Lipman Electronic's products are sold under the "NURIT" and "Dione" brand names. The Israeli company's three largest markets are the United States, Turkey, and Latin America, accounting for 25 percent, 16 percent, and 15 percent of total sales, respectively. Lipman Electronic sells its products in approximately 16 countries.

ORIGINS

Rami Lipman and Aharon Lipman gave their company a fixed location, basing it in Rosh Ha'ayin, Israel, but it took nearly a decade before the brothers fixed their sights on the market that would drive their company's growth. Lipman Electronic was incorporated under the laws of the State of Israel in 1974, beginning as a small company producing electronic products for tuning communication receivers and digital radios for the defense industry. The company's expertise in developing advanced electronic products would carry it through for decades to come, but the market that would feed its growth into the 21st century had yet to take shape when the Lipman brothers embarked on their entrepreneurial career. The retail industry, not the defense industry, became the arena where Lipman Electronic's skills were put on display, providing fertile conditions that enabled the company to become one of the largest of its kind in the world.

The turning point in Lipman Electronic's development occurred after the introduction of the electronic transaction systems. Specifically, the development of automated, point-of-sale (POS) systems triggered the reorientation of the company's focus. Introduced in the early 1980s, POS systems represented a crucial step in the long-term shift away from cash and check payments toward electronic payment transactions. Compared to paper-based processes, POS systems improved accuracy, lowered costs, decreased transaction times, and improved settlement procedures, facilitating the gradual movement toward electronic payments. Lipman Electronic responded to the nascent yet promising market by abandoning its work for the defense industry in 1982, when the company began developing, manufacturing, and selling testing systems for public telephone exchanges, cash registers, and, most significantly, POS products, gearing all its equipment for use by the retail industry. The company completed the final step of its transformation in 1989, when it focused its product development efforts exclusively on electronic transaction systems, introducing its products under the "NURIT" brand name.

An early entrant into the electronic transaction market, Lipman Electronic, like its competitors, was forced to wait for the market to mature to realize it greatest goals. As the number of card-based transactions increased, the opportunity for growth increased as well. Further, the maturity of the market created a demand for more sophisticated devices, engendering the creation of personal-identification-number (PIN) pads, electronic cash registers, automated teller machines (ATMs), smart cards, and various other products that enabled consum-

ers and merchants to complete their transactions electronically. Greater reliance on electronic payment methods, in turn, heightened the need for security measures, spawning a wealth of business opportunities, but the emergence of all the areas that would contribute to Lipman Electronic's growth would take years to materialize. Consequently, the company's stature was held in check, confined by the limits of its market. Lipman Electronic eventually would vie for global supremacy, but the company did not begin to record energetic growth until the market it served asked more of the company.

Of the two Lipman brothers, Aharon Lipman took the lead in terms of playing an active role in running the company. A director and president of the company at its inception, Aharon Lipman added the role of chairman once his company shelved its work for the defense department and turned its attention to the retail industry. A decade after assuming the post, Lipman led the company into the public sector, completing an offering of stock in 1993, when Lipman Electronic debuted on the Tel Aviv Stock Exchange. The year also marked the formation of Lipman U.S.A., Inc., a wholly owned subsidiary created to serve North American customers. The formation of the subsidiary provided the company access to what would become its largest market, eclipsing the importance of its efforts in Israel. Lipman sold 60 percent of his most important business in 1997 to an unaffiliated company, but at the decade's end he purchased the stake he had previously sold, giving Lipman Electronic the full benefit of its efforts overseas just as the electronic transaction market was beginning to ask for more of its equipment developers and vendors. Lipman Electronic ended the decade, and its first 25 years in business, with nearly $37 million in revenue. At the company's 30th anniversary, management celebrated reaching a figure more than three times the total recorded in 1999. The period witnessed energetic growth, as the electronic payment industry and the POS terminal market in particular offered opportunities to expand that Lipman Electronic exploited.

RAPID GROWTH ENTERING NEW CENTURY

A number of factors contributed to Lipman Electronic's robust financial growth as it entered the 2000s. Advances in technology and the public's growing use of electronic payment methods spawned new types of products that could be used in a variety of new applications. The advent of smart cards and stored-value cards, for instance, promoted the adoption of POS terminals in taxicabs, lottery systems, and by healthcare and government agencies. The use of more traditional cards, such as

KEY DATES

1974: Lipman Electronic is founded.
1982: After serving the defense industry during its inaugural decade, the company tailors its products for the retail industry.
1989: Lipman Electronic introduces its point-of-sale products under the "NURIT" brand.
1993: The company debuts on the Tel Aviv Stock Exchange.
1995: Wireless POS terminals are incorporated in the company's product line.
2004: Dione PLC is acquired.
2006: VeriFone Holdings announces its acquisition of Lipman Electronic.

terminal markets in upwards of 100 countries. Lipman Electronic followed a more disciplined expansion strategy, choosing markets with high growth potential and tailoring its products and services to the needs of its select markets. By 2003, when the company ranked as the fourth largest POS terminal maker in the world, it operated in 16 countries, collecting the bulk of its revenues from the United States, Turkey, and Spain, which, combined, accounted for more than 75 percent of its total sales.

Known for its skill in the wireless segment and for a focused growth strategy, Lipman Electronic stood poised to take on larger rivals as its 30th anniversary approached. The company's sales total in 2003 reached $117 million, which was substantially less than third place Hypercom's $232 million in sales, but Lipman Electronic pushed forward aggressively to narrow the gap. In 2003, the company formed a joint venture with two other partners, taking a 25 percent stake in the partnership, and began to develop and market prepaid cellular airtime payment systems in Israel. The following year it formed another joint venture partnership, this time taking the lead with an 80 percent interest, and began marketing automated teller machines (ATMs) in Israel. Lipman Electronic began installing ATMs in 2005 and seized 9 percent of the market by early 2006, when the company presided over 139 ATMs in its home country.

ACQUISITION OF DIONE IN 2004

The company's most notable achievements in the months surrounding its 30th anniversary took place outside Israel. In January 2004, the company made its debut on the NASDAQ National Market, selling 2.25 million shares and raising nearly $90 million to fund its expansion. Later in the year, the company put the proceeds to work by completing the acquisition of Dione PLC, a POS terminal vendor based in the United Kingdom. The acquisition, completed in October 2004, provided Lipman Electronics with entry into the United Kingdom, which immediately became the company's fourth largest market, added significant sales in Finland and South Africa, and strengthened its capabilities in the U.S. market, particularly its relationship with multi-lane retailers such as large supermarkets.

Lipman Electronic also recorded growth through internal means during the period, increasing its market share in every country within its operating territory. The company registered its greatest growth in countries such as Brazil, China, India, and Turkey, where conventional landline telecommunications were poor, providing an ideal setting for it wireless POS terminals to garner sales. Additionally, the company was recording robust growth

credit and debit cards, increased as well. According to the *Nilson Report,* card-based payments in the United States—Lipman Electronic's largest market—increased from 19.7 percent of total consumer payment transactions in 1995 to 28.6 percent by 2001. Elsewhere, particularly in developing countries where few electronic transaction systems had been in service during the 1990s, the rate of growth was higher, presenting Lipman Electronic with tantalizing opportunities. Conditions were ideal for the company, but it also benefited from its own actions rather than merely waiting for external forces to move it along. Perhaps the most important decision in the company's history was made years before market conditions became conducive toward fast-paced growth. In 1995, the company incorporated wireless POS terminals into its product line, becoming one of the first major POS manufacturers and vendors to delve into the wireless arena. Lipman Electronic's development of wireless POS terminals put it in a prime position to take advantage of the widespread adoption of wireless devices in the first years of the 21st century, giving the company one of its signature strengths when it ranked as a global leader in the POS terminal market.

As Lipman Electronic entered the 21st century, it found itself in a race chasing the industry's three largest vendors, France-based Ingenico S.A. and two U.S.-based companies, VeriFone Holdings, Inc., and Hypercom Corporation. The industry elite branched into the wireless arena, but they made their moves several years after Lipman Electronic had launched its foray. The company's early lead in the wireless market distinguished it from larger rivals, as did its approach to international expansion. Major competitors were active in many more markets than Lipman Electronic, participating in POS in Latin America, where governments were modernizing their economies by using electronic payments to improve value-added tax and sales tax collections. Latin America accounted for $10 million of Lipman Electronic's volume in 2003. By 2005, the region accounted for $35 million of total sales.

The advances made during the first half of the decade brought Lipman Electronic tantalizingly close to passing its closest rival, Hypercom. In 2005, Hypercom generated $245 million in sales. Lipman Electronic collected $235 million during the year. Just as the race between the two companies tightened, however, it appeared to be over. In April 2006, the industry's second largest competitor, VeriFone, announced it had reached an agreement to acquire Lipman Electronic in a bid to usurp Ingenico and become the largest POS terminal vendor in the world. The $793 million deal, expected to be completed in October 2006, was hailed by VeriFone's chairman and chief executive officer, Douglas Bergeron, who coveted Lipman Electronic's wireless capabilities. "Everywhere they compete, they have the leading share of the wireless installed base," Bergeron said, referring to Lipman Electronic in an April 11, 2006, interview with *American Banker*. VeriFone, with $485 million in sales in 2005, was expected to control 33 percent of the global POS terminal market after acquiring Lipman Electronic, eclipsing the 22 percent share held by Ingenico. For Lipman Electronic, the deal meant an end to more than 30 years of independence, but its legacy of achievement,

particularly in the wireless segment, formed a vital component of what promised to be the largest terminal maker in the world.

Jeffrey L. Covell

PRINCIPAL SUBSIDIARIES

Lipman U.S.A., Inc.; Lipman Elektronik ve Danismanlik Ltd. (Turkey); Dione Ltd. (U.K.); Lipman do Brasil Ltda. (Brazil).

PRINCIPAL COMPETITORS

Hypercom Corporation; Ingenico S.A.; VeriFone Holdings, Inc.

FURTHER READING

Breitkopf, David, "In Brief: Report: VeriFone, Israeli Rival in Talk," *American Banker*, March 29, 2006, p. 10.

——, "VeriFone Vaulting to Top Globally in Lipman Buy," *American Banker*, April 11, 2006, p. 5.

"Lipman Bids for Bigger Share of POS Market," *Cardline*, October 8, 2004, p. 1.

"POS Terminal Vendor Lipman Gets NASDAQ Listing," *Cardline*, January 30, 2004, p. 1.

"VeriFone to Buy Lipman Electronic Engineering for $793 Mln," *America's Intelligence Wire*, April 10, 2006.

Lowe's Companies, Inc.

1000 Lowe's Boulevard
Mooresville, North Carolina 28117-8520
U.S.A.
Telephone: (704) 758-1000
Toll Free: (800) 445-6937
Fax: (704) 757-0611
Web site: http://www.lowes.com

Public Company
Incorporated: 1952 as Lowe's North Wilkesboro Hardware, Inc.
Employees: 185,314
Sales: $43.24 billion (2005)
Stock Exchanges: New York
Ticker Symbol: LOW
NAIC: 444110 Home Centers; 443111 Household Appliance Stores; 444120 Paint and Wallpaper Stores; 444130 Hardware Stores; 444190 Other Building Material Dealers; 444210 Outdoor Power Equipment Stores; 444220 Nursery and Garden Centers

∎ ∎ ∎

Lowe's Companies, Inc., is the second largest home improvement retailer in the United States (trailing The Home Depot, Inc.) holding about 6 percent of the $700 billion home improvement market, and also ranks as the seventh largest U.S. retailer overall. More than 1,250 Lowe's stores in 49 states (the exception being Vermont) serve do-it-yourself customers, so-called do-it-for-me customers using the stores' installation services, and commercial customers, including professional contrac-

tors, electricians, landscapers, painters, and plumbers. Lowe's relies on two prototype stores, a 117,000-square-foot version designed for larger metropolitan markets and a 94,000-square-foot model suitable for small and midsized markets. The average Lowe's carries 40,000 products for home decorating, maintenance, repair, remodeling, and construction. Hundreds of thousands more are available through special orders. Lowe's offers installation services in more than 40 product categories, with the greatest sales coming in flooring, millwork, and kitchen cabinets and countertops. Such services generate approximately 6 percent of the corporation's total revenues.

EARLY HISTORY

In 1921 L. S. Lowe opened a hardware store in the small town of North Wilkesboro, North Carolina, under the name Mr. L. S. Lowe's North Wilkesboro Hardware. Following his death, his son, James Lowe, took over the business. James Lowe and his brother-in-law, Carl Buchan, served in the U.S. Army during World War II, and during this period Lowe's sister and mother ran the business.

When Buchan was wounded and discharged from the army in 1943, he returned to North Wilkesboro to help operate Lowe's hardware business. In 1946 Buchan took a 50 percent interest in the store. Buchan quickly sold out much of the store's inventory. He then reorganized the store, which became a wholesale-style seller of hardware and building supplies.

When Lowe was discharged from the army, he returned to aid Buchan in operating the business. The

COMPANY PERSPECTIVES

Our growth is driven by our clear and well-defined strategy to put customers first and offer innovative home improvement products and services to make their lives easier. Our shelves are stocked with the respected brands that our customers trust, at everyday low prices. We continue to enhance the way we meet our customers' needs through advancements in technology and distribution, with services such as professional installation, and with enhancements to the special order process to improve the shopping experience. All of these efforts are designed to drive profitable growth and create value for our customers and shareholders.

two opened a second store and used profits to buy an automobile dealership and a cattle farm. In 1952 Buchan traded his interests in these two businesses for Lowe's interest in their two stores. Three months later, Buchan opened a third store, in Asheville, North Carolina. Also in 1952 the company was incorporated as Lowe's North Wilkesboro Hardware, Inc. According to company lore, Buchan retained the Lowe's name so he could use the slogan "Lowe's low prices." From 1952 to 1959, Buchan expanded operations, and sales increased from $4.1 million to $27 million. The post-World War II construction boom made the hardware business very profitable. The frenzied demand for supplies meant that sales often were made directly from a freight car on the railway siding that ran by the store. By purchasing stock directly from the manufacturer, Lowe's was able to avoid paying the higher prices set by wholesalers, which meant lower prices for customers. By 1960 Buchan had 15 stores.

RAPID GROWTH

The big push to become a major force in the home-building market came in 1960 when Buchan died and an office of the president was created. The company went public in 1961 and was renamed Lowe's Companies, Inc. Even though the company grew and new locations were added, the layout of the stores remained basically the same: a small retail floor with limited inventory and a lumberyard out back near the railroad tracks. The bulk of Lowe's customers were contractors and construction companies. By the late 1960s, Lowe's had more than 50 stores, and sales figures hovered around the $100 million mark.

About this time, the burgeoning do-it-yourself market was beginning to change the face of the construction industry. The rising cost of buying a home or having one remodeled by a professional led more homeowners to take on construction projects themselves. Home centers were becoming the modern version of the neighborhood hardware store. At the same time, the home building market was experiencing periodic slumps, and Lowe's management began to notice that their sales figures were moving up and down in tandem with housing trends.

In spite of the fluctuations in the housing market, however, Lowe's revenues rose from $170 million in 1971 to more than $900 million by 1979 (when there were more than 200 stores in the chain). This was due in large part to Lowe's financing program that helped local builders get loans, coordinated building plans with the Federal Housing Administration (FHA), and then helped contractors fill out the government forms and trained construction companies to build FHA-approved homes.

TARGETING CONSUMERS

When new home construction virtually came to a standstill in the later part of the 1970s, Lowe's made the decision to target consumers. The management team believed that increasing consumer sales would reduce the company's vulnerability during economic and seasonal downswings. In 1980 housing starts decreased, and Lowe's net income fell 24 percent. While studying the track records of do-it-yourself stores that sold solely to consumers, Lowe's found that these stores were recording strong sales even during the home-building slumps.

Robert Strickland came to Lowe's fresh from the Harvard Business School. Rising steadily through the ranks, Strickland had reached the position of chairman of the board in 1978 and, with newly appointed Lowe's President Leonard Herring, spearheaded the decision to attract consumers in a big way. Using the easily recognizable acronym RSVP (standing for retail sales, volume, and profit), Lowe's embarked on the new marketing strategy. A consultant was hired to remodel the showrooms, and the resulting layout was similar to that of a supermarket. Seasonal items, such as lawn mowers, were placed in the front of the store. The traffic pattern drew customers to the interior decorating section, then moved on to the back of the store where traditional hardware materials were displayed. The theory behind this traffic pattern said that most consumers may come for the basics but, by walking through the other departments, end up purchasing more. The store in Morganton, North Carolina, was the first location remodeled under the RVSP plan.

KEY DATES:

1921: L. S. Lowe opens a hardware store in North Wilkesboro, North Carolina, called Mr. L. S. Lowe's North Wilkesboro Hardware.

1946: Carl Buchan buys 50 percent interest in the store.

1952: Buchan gains full control of the concern, which he incorporates as Lowe's North Wilkesboro Hardware, Inc.

1961: Following Buchan's death the previous year, the new managers take the firm public and rename it Lowe's Companies, Inc.

1982: A shift to targeting do-it-yourselfers helps push revenues past the $1 billion mark.

1989: Transition to large, warehouse-style stores begins.

1997: Company opens first stores in an urban market.

1999: Eagle Hardware & Garden, Inc. is acquired.

2004: Store count surpasses the 1,000 mark.

In another aspect of the redesign, poster-sized photographs depicting Lowe's merchandise as it would look in the consumer's home were used to identify departments rather than lettered signs. Product lines were updated, hours were extended, and advertising was increased. The strategy worked; by 1982 sales had reached $1 billion, and when the figure reached $1.43 billion in 1983, it marked the first time that Lowe's had made more money selling to consumers than to contractors.

One aspect of the RSVP plan that did not work was Wood World, an extension of the retail floor into one long bay of the lumber warehouse. Fire code regulations required the installation of expensive fire walls and doors, and the idea was soon scrapped. Paneling and other wood products were then put out on the sales floor with the rest of the merchandise.

SHIFT TO WAREHOUSE-STYLE STORES

By the late 1980s the retail scene in the United States had once again been transformed, and the era of the "big-box" warehouses had begun. Home Depot, Inc. led the way in the home improvement sector and its aggressive expansion of its 105,000-square-foot home improvement superstores quickly moved the upstart past Lowe's and other competitors into the number one

position. Lowe's, meanwhile, had surpassed the 300-store mark in fiscal 1989 but those stores averaged barely more than 20,000 square feet. The company had opened some larger units in 1988, including a 60,000-square-foot store in Knoxville, Tennessee, a 40,320-square-foot unit in Boone, North Carolina, and a 60,480-square-foot store in North Chattanooga, Tennessee, but none approached the size of a Home Depot. Lowe's also made some adjustments to its product lines as core consumer goods areas—hardware, tools, paint, plumbing, home decor, and stereo equipment—were expanded, while such fringe items as exercise equipment, bicycles, and bath linens that had crept in over the previous decade were phased out.

In 1989 Lowe's began a formal shift from being a chain of small stores to being a chain of large, warehouse-style stores, with the company fully committing itself to this change in 1991. During that year, the company took a $71.3 million restructuring charge in order to accelerate the chain conversion. The charge covered the costs of closing, relocating, and remodeling about half of the company's stores, during the period from 1991 to 1995. Over the course of the four-year restructuring, the size of the new or remodeled stores crept upward from 45,000 square feet to 85,000 to 115,000. The largest size was to be reserved for Lowe's stores built in larger markets, such as Greensboro, North Carolina, while in the smaller markets the company traditionally served Lowe's eventually aimed to build 100,000-square-foot units. All of the larger stores featured huge garden centers, as big as 30,000 square feet in size. Overall, Lowe's aimed to generate more of its sales from consumers, while at the same time continuing to serve contractors. It also continued to sell major appliances and home electronics (including home office equipment, which was added to the mix in 1994), two categories usually absent from Home Depot stores.

From 1991 to 1993, the company concentrated almost exclusively on the restructuring and made only modest expansion moves, gaining toeholds in Maryland, Indiana, and Illinois for the first time. Although the chain added only five stores overall during this period, total square footage increased from 8.02 million in 1991 to 14.17 million in 1993, translating into an increase from 26,000 in average square footage to 45,500. In 1994 and 1995 Lowe's added 54 more stores, bringing the total to 365, and adding the states of Iowa, Michigan, and Oklahoma to its territory. Also in 1995, the company began to aggressively expand in Texas, going from two stores in 1994 to 23 stores in 1996. Lowe's also expanded into the state of New York in 1996 and into Kansas in 1997. Meanwhile, in August 1996 Herring retired and was succeeded as president and CEO by Robert L. Tillman, who had served as chief operating officer. Tillman was named chairman as well in January 1998.

By 1996 there were more than 400 Lowe's stores, averaging more than 75,000 square feet per unit. Sales had nearly tripled since the restructuring was announced in 1991, increasing from $3.1 billion to $8.6 billion. Net earnings reached a record $292.2 million in 1996. With more than 70 percent of its stores now "big boxes," Lowe's began to concentrate more on expanding into new territory in the mid-1990s, aiming to reach the 600-store mark by century-end. During 1997 Lowe's opened 42 more stores. Among these, Lowe's included a test of its first stores in an urban market, Dallas, one in which Home Depot was already entrenched. Despite the competition, the Dallas stores exceeded initial expectations by 20 percent, and from then on, Lowe's began targeting both large metropolitan areas and its more traditional small and medium-sized markets for growth.

GOING COAST TO COAST

To aid its expansion, Lowe's built six new, one-million-square-foot distribution centers located around the country. These centers supported further geographic expansion, including a $1.5 billion plan launched in 1998 to build more than 100 new stores in the western United States. Among the initial markets targeted were Los Angeles, San Diego, Las Vegas, Phoenix, and Tucson, Arizona. Lowe's westward expansion was accelerated through the April 1999 acquisition of Eagle Hardware & Garden, Inc. in a stock swap valued at about $1.34 billion. Eagle, based in Renton, Washington, operated 38 big box home improvement stores in ten western states and had revenues of nearly $1 billion. The Eagle outlets were gradually rebranded under the Lowe's name.

By the end of 1999 the Lowe's store count had reached 550, and its revenues of $15.45 billion made it the 15th largest retailer in the country. In 2000 another 75 stores were added, and the company revamped its web site into a major e-commerce site. Early the following year, Lowe's rolled out its first national television advertising campaign, using the tag line, "Improving Home Improvement," and touting itself as cleaner, better organized, and better lit than the warehouse competition (implying, without naming, Home Depot). The campaign's themes were consistent with Lowe's push to attract female consumers, a strategy that a number of analysts considered a key to the company's success; Lowe's catered to women because company research found that females made the vast majority of home improvement decisions. The drive to create a nationwide chain also continued with the launch of a $1.3 billion, five-year move into the Northeast, where Lowe's aimed to open more than 75 stores ranging from Philadelphia to Maine, with 25 alone in the Boston area. The first New York City store opened in the spring of 2001. Late in 2002 Lowe's announced further plans to open more than 60 stores in the New York metropolitan area and northern New Jersey. In 2003 the company introduced a smaller prototype format measuring 94,000 square feet that was designed for smaller, mainly rural markets. A 116,000-square-foot store continued to be the prototype for larger markets.

During the fiscal year ending in January 2005, Lowe's store count passed the 1,000 mark. At the end of the fiscal year, Tillman stepped down from his position as chairman and CEO, having led the company through an amazing period of growth. Between 1996 and 2004, revenues quadrupled, from $9.06 billion to $36.46 billion, while profits jumped sevenfold, from $310 million to $2.18 billion. Lowe's was the 11th largest retailer in the country. Taking on the daunting task of filling Tillman's shoes was Robert Niblock, who had joined Lowe's in 1993 and served as company president since 2003.

Rather than slowing, growth accelerated under the new leader, as no fewer than 150 new Lowe's opened during fiscal 2005, including the first stores in New Hampshire, the 49th state to join the company ranks. A like number or slightly more units were planned to be added over the next two years, toward an eventual total of between 1,800 and 2,000. At the same time, Lowe's was seeking to spur growth by increasing revenues derived from three areas: special orders, installation services, and commercial customers such as contractors, professional tradespeople, and property management professionals. In June 2005 the company announced plans to move into the Canadian market, aiming to open as many as ten stores in the Toronto area during 2007. Expansion into other international markets was under study. As Lowe's posted another record year in fiscal 2005, profits of $2.77 billion on revenues of $43.24 billion, one possible cloud on the horizon was a cooling of what had been a red-hot housing market, which had the potential to precipitate a concomitant downturn in the home improvement industry.

Mary F. Sworsky
Updated, David E. Salamie

PRINCIPAL SUBSIDIARIES

Lowe's Home Centers, Inc.; Lowe's HIW, Inc.

PRINCIPAL COMPETITORS

The Home Depot, Inc.; Menard, Inc.; True Value Company; Wal-Mart Stores, Inc.; Ace Hardware Corporation; Sears, Roebuck and Co.

FURTHER READING

"Analyst Predicts Two to Dominate Industry," *Chilton's Hardware Age,* May 1995, p. 12.

Auchmutey, Jim, "Warehouses Stack the Deck," *Hardware Age,* March 1981.

Berner, Robert, "Lowe's Cos. to Buy Eagle Hardware in $1 Billion Deal," *Wall Street Journal,* November 23, 1998, p. B15.

"Big-Store Bonanza," *Forbes,* December 20, 1993, pp. 14–15.

Carlo, Andrew M., "Catch Me if You Can: Riding High, Lowe's Executives Challenge Competitors," *Home Channel News,* June 16, 2003, pp. 1, 56–57.

Cochran, Thomas, "Handyman's Special," *Barron's,* June 18, 1980.

Curtis, Carol E., "How Much Sheetrock, Ma'am?," *Forbes,* August 30, 1982, p. 70.

———, "Playing Do-It-Yourself," *Forbes,* May 10, 1982, p. 314.

David, Gregory E., "Stomping Elephant," *Financial World,* September 28, 1993, pp. 40–41.

Dyer, Leigh, "Retiring CEO to Leave with Sun Shining on Lowe's," *Charlotte (N.C.) Observer,* November 16, 2004.

Feder, Barnaby J., "In Hardware War, Cooperation May Mean Survival," *New York Times,* June 11, 1997, pp. D1, D7.

Hartnett, Michael, "Lowe's Plan: Think Big," *Stores,* November 1993, pp. 58–60.

Johnson, Roy S., "Lowe's Borrows the Blueprint," *Fortune,* November 23, 1998, pp. 212, 215, 217, 219.

Korn, Don, "Lowe's Gets Ready to Raise the Roof," *Sales Management,* July 7, 1975.

"Lowe's Steps It Up," *Do-It-Yourself Retailing,* August 1995, p. 259.

"Lowe's to Expand into Canada," *Charlotte (N.C.) Business Journal,* June 6, 2005.

"Lowe's Vision—The Wal-Mart of Home Centers," *Chain Store Age Executive,* May 1989.

"Lowe's Zeroes in on Customers," *Chain Store Age Executive,* August 1979.

Lubove, Seth, "A Chain's Weak Links," *Forbes,* January 21, 1991, p. 76.

Mallory, Maria, "This Do-It-Yourself Store Is Really Doing It," *Business Week,* May 2, 1994, p. 108.

Masters, Greg, "Lowe's Turns the Screws on Urban Competition," *Retail Merchandiser,* March 2004, p. 48.

McCormack, Karyn, "Casualties of War," *Financial World,* May 20, 1997, pp. 45–46, 48, 53.

McIntyre, Deni, *No Place Like Lowe's: 50 Years of Retailing for the American Home,* North Wilkesboro, N.C.: Lowe's, 1996, 160 p.

Nannery, Matt, "Lowe's Promise," *Home Channel News,* April 1, 2003, pp. 24, 26, 46.

Pascual, Aixa M., "Lowe's Is Sprucing Up Its House," *Business Week,* June 3, 2002, pp. 56, 58.

Postman, Lore, "Home Repair Giant Lowe's Shapes Strategy Around Aging Handyman," *Charlotte (N.C.) Observer,* July 26, 1998.

Seccombe, Jane, "Lowe's Sets Fast Pace for Growth," *Winston-Salem (N.C.) Journal,* May 29, 1999, p. D1.

"Strickland Positions Lowe's for Conquest," *Building Supply Home Centers,* March 1993, pp. 48–50.

Sutton, Rodney K., "Lowe's Conversion Ends in Its Rebirth," *Building Supply Home Centers,* June 1994, pp. 36–38, 40, 42.

Williams, Christopher C., "The Lowe's Advantage," *Barron's,* April 24, 2006, pp. 33, 35.

LPA Holding Corporation

130 S. Jefferson
Suite 300
Chicago, Illinois 60661
U.S.A.
Telephone: (312) 798-1200
Toll Free: (888) 568-5115
Fax: (312) 382-1776

Private Company
Founded: 1968 as La Petite Academy, Inc.
Employees: 12,700
Operating Revenues: $404.2 million (2005)
NAIC: 624410 Child Day Care Services; 611110 Elementary and Secondary Schools

■ ■ ■

LPA Holding Corporation, based in Chicago, Illinois, is the parent company of La Petite Academy, Inc., and Montessori Unlimited. La Petite Academy, Inc., founded in Overland Park, Kansas, has been around close to four decades, offering working parents quality, reasonably priced day care services. La Petite Academy offers 590 freestanding locations in most major U.S. cities and also operates 30 onsite centers for a number of *Fortune* 500 companies. The La Petite Academy centers are located in 36 states and Washington, D.C. Montessori Unlimited provides an internationally recognized preschool curriculum at 29 locations in the United States.

SMALL BEGINNINGS: 1968–1988

In the 1960s as American women joined the full-time workforce in record numbers, there was an urgent need for child care. Local entrepreneur Robert Brozman recognized this need and created a company to provide day care services at reasonable prices. After buying seven day care centers in Overland Park, Kansas, near Kansas City, Brozman formed La Petite Academy, Inc., in 1968. At the time of its founding, La Petite Academy had few competitors and operated as a private company, owned by another of Brozman's firms, CenCor Inc.

Over the next decade La Petite Academy expanded its services, offering parents both quality child care as well as some educational instruction. By the end of the 1970s there were La Petite locations throughout the Kansas City metropolitan area and Brozman began opening centers in other midwestern states.

In 1983 La Petite Academy, a wholly owned subsidiary of CenCor, went public under the ticker symbol LPAI (OTC), primarily to raise funds for nationwide expansion. Brozman, as chairman and chief executive, retained a healthy chunk of the company and brought his son Jack into the fold. LPA, as a public entity, made strides in the burgeoning child care industry, branching out from the Midwest into the eastern, southern, and western states. Operating revenues for 1984 reached $66.7 million with net income of $3.7 million; the following year revenues had risen to an impressive $82.7 million with net income of $5.4 million.

In 1986 La Petite Academy began a long-term collaboration with the Gaylord Hotels chain, opening a

---

COMPANY PERSPECTIVES

La Petite Academy is committed to serving children and parents by providing high quality care and education in a professional, effective, and caring manner. We exceed our customers' needs now and in the future by maintaining an environment in which the satisfaction of our people is the key to the satisfaction of our families. Innovation, fairness, teamwork, and excellence are the hallmarks by which we are known.

---

child care center in the Opryland Hotel in Nashville. Called the Gaylord Child Development Center, the on-site facility provided care for the Opryland's many employees, featuring state-of-the-art educational tools, plenty of space, and thousands of toys. The collaboration marked an important milestone for La Petite Academy: its segue into providing onsite care services for large corporate clients. La Petite and Gaylord went on to open several additional onsite facilities, and La Petite did the same for other corporate clients in Florida and Alabama within the year. Revenues for 1986 leapt to $104.6 million and net income rose to $7.5 million.

By the late 1980s competition in child care had grown fierce. La Petite Academy's primary rival was Kinder Care Learning Centers, the nation's largest child care provider. Kinder Care, based in Montgomery, Alabama, had more than 1,000 child care centers and was adding up to 120 new locations per year, while La Petite Academy had 625 and opened between 75 and 90 annually. Other competitors included Children's World Learning Centers, which operated more than 400 centers nationwide, and the newest kid on the block, the Watertown, Massachusetts-based Bright Horizons Family Solutions, Inc., formed in 1986, which was opening new locations at a brisk pace.

La Petite Academy's revenues reached $130.1 million in 1987, with net income of slightly more than $10 million and stock prices topping $17 per share. In 1988 La Petite experienced further ups and downs; the company opened 88 new schools but closed down ten underperforming locations. There were about 665 La Petite Academys and 11 new Montessori-styled school centers nationwide, in 29 states. La Petite had an estimated 70,000 children enrolled in its day care and educational centers, and strived to become the premier preschool and care provider in the United States. Stock prices vacillated during the year from a low of just less than $8 to a high of nearly $20, with revenues climbing to $152.1 million.

PUBLIC TO PRIVATE IN THE FINAL DECADE OF THE 20TH CENTURY

By 1991 there were 750 La Petite Academy and Montessori locations in 33 states and the company had grand plans to conquer the remaining 17 states, despite recessionary stresses on the U.S. economy. Instead, the company came under a cloud of scrutiny after the sudden death of Chairman and founder Robert Brozman in June. It was soon disclosed that the elder Brozman had arranged for more than $22 million in loans supposedly for La Petite Academy and Brozman's other companies, which were instead used by Brozman himself.

Jack Brozman, who had been elevated to chief executive and chairman shortly before his father's death, was forced to sell the senior Brozman's majority interest in LPA to pay off numerous banks and creditors. This fire sale led to a leveraged buyout of La Petite Academy, Inc. for $170 million by Vestar Capital Partners, Inc., a New York-based private investment firm. A minority stake of 15 percent went to Fukutake Publishing Company, Ltd., with whom La Petite Academy had an agreement to market educational materials. Revenues for 1993 increased from 1992's $245 million to $260 million.

After the acquisition of the company, LPA was once again private and Jack Brozman resigned. He was replaced as president and CEO by La Petite's vice-president and chief operating officer, Robert Rodriguez. In 1994 La Petite and Fukutake teamed up to open two day care centers in Tokyo, Japan. By the end of 1994 La Petite had slowed its new openings to less than two dozen per year and focused on raising the profitability of its 800-plus centers and 90,000 enrolled participants.

In mid-1998 La Petite underwent another change in ownership, this time when Chase Capital Partners (later renamed JPMorgan Partners) and investor Robert King bought 81 percent of the company from Vestar for a reported $117.5 million. La Petite Academy, Inc., became a wholly owned subsidiary of the new LPA Holding Corporation, headquartered in Chicago, Illinois. Revenues for 1998 reached $314.9 million, a slight increase over the previous year's $302.8 million. La Petite recorded losses of $1.2 million for 1997 and $13.3 million for 1998. By the end of the decade, La Petite Academy continued to struggle, hoping to reposition itself in the new century. Revenues had fallen to $281.1 million, though losses were trimmed to $800,000 through restructuring, layoffs, and closure of underperforming locations.

KEY DATES

1968: La Petite Academy is formed with the purchase of seven day care centers.

1983: La Petite Academy goes public.

1986: The Gaylord Child Development Center opens in Nashville, Tennessee.

1993: LPA is bought by Vestar Capital Partners of New York City.

1994: The company opens two day care centers in Tokyo, Japan, in a joint venture.

1998: LPA Holdings reorganizes and JPMorgan Partners buys a majority stake.

2002: The company partners with Gaylord Hotels to create La Petite Kids Station.

2003: LPA begins a partnership with the Make-A-Wish Foundation.

REGAINING A SOLID POSITION AT THE DAWN OF THE NEW CENTURY

In the new millennium La Petite Academy set its sights high and looked for innovative ways to attract working parents and boost enrollment. One step in this direction was the appointment of a new president and chief executive, Judith Rogala, in January. One such program was to offer traveling executives short-term or one-time-only enrollment at La Petite Academy centers nationwide, beginning in 2001. Offered at its 740 locations nationwide, the only caveat was available space at the time of placement. Travelers with children enrolled in a La Petite Academy could drop off their children at another location free, reserving a space for their targeted dates in advance.

Despite new programs and strides in educational services, La Petite could not stop the flow of red ink. Revenues were stronger at $384.8 million, but the company still recorded a loss of $6.3 million in 2001, the same year in which it opened a new regional office in Charlotte, North Carolina, as part of its ongoing restructuring. In 2002 Gary Graves, formerly executive vice-president of Boston Market, Inc., was appointed chief operating officer of La Petite. Within months Graves added the responsibilities of president and CEO, serving both La Petite Academy and its parent company, LPA Holding Corporation.

After several years of closing more child care centers than opening new ones, La Petite began to stabilize, due in large part to the guidance and no-nonsense approach of chief executive Graves. Graves also spearheaded an effort to team up with the Make-A-Wish Foundation, raising funds and awareness for the service organization, which granted wishes to terminally ill children. By late 2004, more than a year after its initial partnership, La Petite had raised more than $1 million for the Make-A-Wish Foundation. In a company press release (October 14, 2004), Graves commented, "We are a company dedicated to children, so it is only natural for us to support the Make-A-Wish Foundation, a group that does so much good for deserving kids."

By 2005 La Petite's turnaround was almost complete; not only had revenues continued to climb (up to $404.2 million) but net income was approaching black ink. La Petite provided working parents with a wide range of child care options, including before- and after-school care, and all-day curriculums at its 590 La Petite Academy centers in 36 states and Washington, D.C., 30 day care and learning facilities located within corporate centers, 29 Montessori Unlimited schools in seven states, and 80 private kindergarten learning centers across the country. La Petite served children aged six weeks to 12 years, with programs designed and supported by leading educational companies like Scholastic Inc. and the AIMS Science Program.

The day care competition of the late 2000s found LPA trailing the industry's largest player, Knowledge Learning Corporation, which had acquired Kinder Care in 2005. The Portland, Oregon-based behemoth had more than 2,500 locations worldwide, beating both La Petite Academy and Bright Horizons hands down. Although both Knowledge Learning Corp. and Bright Horizons had expanded outside the United States, international growth certainly was not out of the question for La Petite Academy. After years of struggling, La Petite Academy was again on solid ground and ready to compete for dominance in the child care industry of the 21st century.

Nelson Rhodes

PRINCIPAL SUBSIDIARIES

La Petite Academy, Inc.; Montessori Unlimited.

PRINCIPAL COMPETITORS

Bright Horizons Family Solutions, Inc.; Learning Care Group, Inc.; Knowledge Learning Corporation; Noble Learning Communities.

FURTHER READING

Corder, David R., "La Petite's Road to Private Ownership Points to Big Profits," *Kansas City Business Journal*, June 10,

1994, p. 36.

Gilmore, Casey, and Barry Henderson, "Creditors to Be Made Whole, Almost, in Wake of Buyout Planned for La Petite," *Kansas City Business Journal,* July 23, 1993, p. 4.

Ingrassia, Lawrence, "Day-Care Business Lures Entrepreneurs," *Wall Street Journal,* June 3, 1988, p. 1.

Jaffe, Thomas, "La Petite's Petite Prospects," *Fortune,* September 16, 1991, p. 208.

"La Petite Academy, Inc.," *Kansas City Business Journal,* May 22, 1989, p. 22.

Miller, James P., "CenCor Says Late Chairman, Founder Borrowed $27.2M for Own Use," *Wall Street Journal,* July 2, 1991, p. C14.

Stainburn, Samantha, "No Kidding: School Chain's Finances Much Improved Under Former Corporate Exec," *Crain's Chicago Business,* April 18, 2005, p. 36.

Stretton, Hesba, "La Petite Academy, Inc.," *Fortune,* May 9, 1988, p. 70.

Wiggins, Phillip H., "Market Place: Child Day Care Profits Mount," *New York Times,* March 3, 1997, p. D10.

MEMC Electronic Materials, Inc.

---

501 Pearl Drive
St. Peters, Missouri 63376
U.S.A.
Telephone: (636) 474-5000
Fax: (636) 474-5158
Web site: http://www.memc.com

Public Company
Founded: 1959 as Monsanto Electronics Materials
    Company
Employees: 5,500
Sales: $1.12 billion (2005)
Stock Exchanges: New York
Ticker Symbol: WFR
NAIC: 334413 Semiconductor and Related Device
    Manufacturing

■ ■ ■

MEMC Electronic Materials, Inc., is a St. Peters, Missouri-based producer of silicon wafers for semiconductor device manufacturers, the world's largest public company devoted solely to this market. The wafers range in size from 100 millimeters to 300 millimeters and are found in personal computers, mainframe computers, servers, and storage devices, as well as consumer electronics, automobiles, telecommunications devices, industrial automation and control systems, and aerospace and defense systems. MEMC's primary product is the standard polished wafer, featuring crystalline silicon with ultraflat and ultraclean surfaces, achieved through a chemical-mechanical polishing process pioneered by the company in the early 1960s.

MEMC also produces epitaxial wafers featuring a thin, single crystal silicon layer grown on the polished surface of a silicon wafer substrate and used in advanced semiconductor devices. In addition, MEMC offers other advanced branded wafers: Perfect Silicon, relying on a proprietary defect-free crystal growth process, and Magic Denuded Zone wafers, optimized for device fabrication and employing clusters of oxygen deep below the surface to capture harmful metals. MEMC operates three manufacturing facilities in the United States, and six overseas, in Japan, Malaysia, South Korea, Taiwan, and two plants in Italy. It also maintains 13 sales offices in the United States, Europe, and Southeast Asia. MEMC is listed on the New York Stock Exchange, with about one-third of its shares owned by the Texas Pacific Group.

POST-WORLD WAR II DEVELOPMENTS LEADING TO MEMC

Two years after World War II ended, Bell Laboratories produced the first transistor connected to the surface of semiconductor material. This development led to Texas Instruments launching commercial production of silicon transistors in 1954, and four years later the company produced the first computer chip, or integrated circuit. During this time, the labs of St. Louis-based Monsanto Chemical Company, founded in the beginning of the century to produce the artificial sweetener saccharin, began working in this arena. In 1959 the company announced the launch of a new semiconductor business called the Monsanto Electronic Materials Company, or MEMC, its purpose to produce ultra-pure silicon wafers

COMPANY PERSPECTIVES

MEMC Electronic Materials, Inc. is the world's largest public company solely devoted to the supply of wafers to semiconductor device manufacturers. MEMC has been a pioneer in the design and development of wafer technologies over the past four decades.

for use in the manufacture of transistors and rectifiers. Thirty miles west of its headquarters, Monsanto began building a new plant in St. Charles County, where the atmosphere was supposed to be free of the kind of impurities found in a major city like St. Louis. Before the year was out, MEMC produced its first silicon wafer, 19 millimeters in diameter.

As an early participant in the field, MEMC became a pioneer, some of its innovations remaining industry standard into the next century. In 1962 MEMC introduced the Chemical Mechanical Polishing (CMP) process, creating a flatness standard for the smaller, faster circuits that were coming into use at the time. In that same year, MEMC developed and implemented the Czochralski (CZ) crystal growing process, which removed impurities through the application of a direct electrical current to the silicon in a molten state. MEMC researcher Dr. Horst Kramer was responsible for a major development in silicon materials science when in 1966 he discovered Zero Dislocation silicon crystals.

As the semiconductor industry flourished and the demand for ever smaller and faster computer chips grew, MEMC opened a new plant in Kuala Lumpur, Malaysia, which then put 2.25-inch wafers into commercial production. Although the United States had developed the semiconductor industry, Japanese firms began to dominate the field, and U.S. companies steadily fell by the wayside. A notable exception was MEMC, which continued to be an innovative force in the 1970s and beyond. Its researchers routinely made advances in the areas of wafer flatness, chemical mechanical polishing, and Zero Dislocation crystals. In 1979 MEMC became the first company to find a way to control oxygen content. MEMC also became the first to produce 125mm wafers, in 1975.

MEMC advances continued in the 1980s as the company became the first to commercially produce 150mm wafers in 1981, and through a partnership with IBM became the first to commercially produce 200mm wafers in 1984. Other important developments in the 1980s included the use of the "Flip Tran" cassette in 1981 to ship wafers with dry nitrogen to ensure cleanliness, and a year later the revolutionary development of Epi wafers, designed for use in the microchips that powered contemporary computers. The application of an epataxial layer to the wafer's surface allowed for the execution of advanced applications. MEMC also added to its production capacity in the 1980s, opening a plant in Spartanburg, South Carolina, in 1981, and a plant in Japan in 1983, thus becoming the first non-Japanese wafer manufacturer to operate in Japan.

INDUSTRY DOWNTURN IN 1985

Although MEMC was a survivor among American wafer manufacturers, it was basically operating in a commodities business and had a difficult time competing with Japanese companies on price in a highly cyclical business. IBM, Texas Instruments, and Motorola continued to produce wafers, but these chips were of exacting specification and only intended for internal use and represented a mere percentage of these companies' wafer needs. From 1985 through 1987 MEMC lost money, despite sizable growth in sales, and only an increase in wafer prices in 1988 allowed it to net $11 million on sales of $209 million. This kind of performance was not acceptable for a Monsanto unit, however, and starting in the mid-1980s the parent company began looking to divest the business. MEMC was offered to U.S. companies but there were no takers. The most likely suitors appeared to be Japanese companies, in particular the Nippon Steel subsidiary Nittsetu, which had become involved in silicon wafers.

In April 1989 MEMC was sold to a West German company, Huls AG, a subsidiary of industrial conglomerate VEBA AG, which 18 months earlier had become involved in the wafer business through the acquisition of Dynamit Nobel AG. A U.S. subsidiary, Dynamit Nobel Silicon, founded in 1984, was located in the Research Triangle area of North Carolina. After the MEMC sale received U.S. government approval, Huls consolidated the U.S., European, Japanese, and Malaysian operations of MEMC and Dynamit Nobel's U.S. and Italian silicon wafer business under the corporate structure of Dynamit Nobel, which then changed its name to MEMC Electronic Materials, Inc., a reflection of the brand value of the MEMC name. In addition, the corporate headquarters of Dynamit Noble was moved from Palo Alto, California, to St. Peters, Missouri.

To spur the business of the new MEMC, Huls pledged to add $50 million to the company's capital spending program over the next two to three years. Some of that money was put to use in research and development, as MEMC remained in the vanguard of industry

KEY DATES

1959: Monsanto Electronic Materials Company is formed.
1962: MEMC introduces chemical-mechanical polishing technology.
1970: New plant opens in Kuala Lumpur, Malaysia.
1983: MEMC becomes the first non-Japanese company to open wafer factory in Japan.
1989: The company is sold to Huls AG, merged with Dynamit Nobel.
1995: An initial public offering of stock is made.
2001: Texas Pacific Group acquires control.
2003: The company returns to profitability.

innovations. In 1991 it became the first company to add commercial production of 300mm wafers, and in that same year it developed the first process using granular polysilicon, which provided cost and productivity advantages over the traditional "chunk" polysilicon, especially in the production of 300mm wafers. In 1995 MEMC acquired a granular polysilicon production facility, renamed MEMC Pasadena, Inc. (located in Pasadena, Texas), to provide a ready source for an essential raw material. Also in the early 1990s, MEMC teamed up with other companies in joint ventures, including the Posco Huls Company, created in 1991 by MEMC with Samsung Electronics, LTD, and Pohang Iron & Steel Co. Posco Huls concentrated on manufacturing 200mm wafers for the Korean market. In 1994 MEMC joined forces with China Steel and other companies to create Taisil Electronic Materials, Inc., located in Taiwan to serve that country's semiconductor needs. Then, in 1995, MEMC and Texas Instruments formed MEMC Southwest, Inc., to produce wafers in an existing Texas Instruments plant.

PUBLIC OFFERING IN 1995

MEMC went public in 1995, completing an initial public offering (IPO) of stock in July of that year, raising more than $440 million. VEBA AG retained a majority interest, however. The company had been enjoying a nice run, as did the entire chip industry, as an increasingly digital world appeared to have an insatiable appetite for chips. The semiconductor industry as a whole grew 30 percent a year in the first half of the 1990s. However, the good times came to a sudden end for wafer manufacturers in 1996 when demand fell off just as they had built up massive inventories. According to the *St. Louis Post Dispatch,* "Demand was down in

part because chip manufacturers are continually finding ways to reduce the size of circuits and put more chips on each wafer—say, 400 where once they put 80. The industry calls the process 'line shrinkage.'" Although line shrinkage was good news for consumers, who saw the price of electronic devices drop, it was bad news for wafer manufacturers. For a time, increasing sales of electronic devices offset the effects of line shrinkage, but a financial crisis that hit Asia resulted in a drop in demand for electronic devices. A domino effect ensued, as Japanese wafer manufacturers lowered their prices to prop up demand, and with the yen also falling against the dollar, MEMC was unable to keep pace. Sales reached $1.12 billion in 1996, producing a profit of $101.6 million for MEMC, but a year later sales dipped to $986.7 million and the company recorded a loss of $6.7 million.

Revenues fell off another 23 percent in 1998 to $759 million and the company lost $316.3 million. With its stock price plummeting, the company had no choice but to tighten its belt and initiate cost-cutting measures that included large-scale layoffs and plant closings. Sales continued to dip in 1999, reaching $693.6 million, and MEMC lost another $151.5 million. Conditions improved significantly in 2000 as demand picked up, accompanied by more favorable pricing. Thus sales rebounded to $871.6 million. Still, the company lost $43.4 million, and by the end of the year signs of weakness in demand could be detected. The following year saw the semiconductor industry reach historic lows, dropping off 30 percent, or twice as much as the previous trough in 1985.

Well before this juncture, MEMC's corporate parent indicated that it wanted to sell its nearly 72 percent stake in the business. Then in June 2000 VEBA AG merged with VIAG AG to become E.On AG, which decided to focus on its core business of power generation and to divest other non-utility companies in addition to MEMC. E.On hired Merrill Lynch to help in selling its interest in MEMC but the investment banker found no takers, prompting E.On in 2001 to consider bankruptcy for MEMC, which in July announced it might run out of cash by the end of September. But E.On hung on, and in October of that year sold MEMC for a mere dollar to the investment company Texas Pacific Group to simply get out from under a debt load of more than $1 billion or avoid spending the money needed to close down the business. "But the deal is not so stark as it seems at first blush," reported the *St. Louis Post-Dispatch* at the time. "Texas Pacific Group agreed to revise the purchase price to as much as $150 million—if MEMC substantially improves its financial performance next year. ... Texas Pacific also agreed to extend $150 million in debt financing to MEMC."

One of the first changes Texas Pacific made was to restructure MEMC's debt, a move that had a significant impact in 2002 when MEMC began to stage an impressive comeback. Sales increased to $687.2 million from $618 million the year before, and the company shaved its net loss from $523 million to $22.1 million. In addition to benefiting from cost reductions, MEMC was also quick to take advantage of improved market conditions in 2002 to leverage its reputation for innovation to sell new products. The company's change in fortune was reflected in the rising price of its stock, which the *Wall Street Journal* recognized as one of the ten best-performing technology stocks for the year.

MEMC built upon the momentum established in 2002 to produce even stronger results in 2003. Revenues improved to $781.1 million, 30 percent of which came from the sale of products introduced in the previous three years, and the company returned to profitability, netting $116.6 million. The surge continued in 2004 and 2005, when sales topped $1 billion and then increased to more than $1.1 billion, while net income reached $226.1 million in 2004 and $338.2 million in 2005. Business remained strong in the first quarter of 2006 when MEMC set a number of financial records. It appeared that MEMC had completed a dramatic turnaround in a short period of time, but given the cyclical nature of the semiconductor industry, it remained to be seen how the company would react the next time the market experienced a downturn.

Ed Dinger

PRINCIPAL SUBSIDIARIES

MEMC Electronic Materials France S.A.R.L.; MEMC Electronic Materials, GmbH; MEMC Electronic Materials Sdn. Bhd.; MEMC Electronic Materials, S.p.A.; MEMC Electronic Materials (UK) Ltd.; MEMC Holding B.V.; MEMC International, Inc.; MEMC Japan Ltd.; MEMC Korea Company; MEMC Pasadena, Inc.; MEMC Southwest Inc.; Taisil Electronic Materials Corporation.

PRINCIPAL COMPETITORS

Shin-Etsu Handotai Co. Ltd.; Siltronic AG; Sumitomo Mitsubishi Silicon Corporation.

FURTHER READING

D'Amico, Esther, "MEMC Goes Public, Plans to Buy Albemarle Unit," *Chemical Week,* July 19, 1995, p. 10.

Feder, Barnaby J., "A Wafer Maker's Formula for Success: Equal Parts Sand and Grit," *New York Times,* January 27, 1997, p. D1.

Feldstein, Mary Jo, "CEO Gareeb Turns Around MEMC," *St. Louis Post-Dispatch,* March 4, 2004, p. C1.

Hanford, Desiree J., "MEMC Hopes Silicon-Wafer Price Rise Means Makers' Tough Times Are Over," *Wall Street Journal,* November 29, 2000, p. B11.

Hieb, Dan, "MEMC Stock Hits an All-Time Low," *St. Louis Post-Dispatch,* June 13, 1998, p. 29.

Shinkle, Peter, "Downturn Hits MEMC Electronic Materials Inc.," *St. Louis Post-Dispatch,* July 3, 2001, p. C1.

———, "German Owner Is Considering Bankruptcy for MEMC," *St. Louis Post-Dispatch,* August 9, 2001, p. C1.

———, "MEMC Is Sold to Texas Firm for $1," *St. Louis Post-Dispatch,* October 2, 2001, p. C1.

Winkler, Eric, "Huls Melds Monsanto Unit, Dynamit," *Electronic News,* April 3, 1989, p. 1.

Zipper, Stuart, "Monsanto to Sell Silicon Wafer Firm," *Electronic News,* November 14, 1988, p. 1.

Merz Group

Eckenheimer Landstrasse 100
Frankfurt am Main, D-60318
Germany
Telephone: (+49 069) 15 03 0
Fax: (+49 069) 15 03 200
Web site: http://www.merz.de

Private Company
Incorporated: 1908
Employees: 1,748
Sales: EUR 417.19 million ($501 million) (2005)
NAIC: 325412 Pharmaceutical Preparation Manufacturing; 325620 Toilet Preparation Manufacturing

■ ■ ■

Merz Group is the holding company for Merz Pharma, a developer and producer of pharmaceuticals and beauty products, and Sentator, manufacturer of writing instruments. Pharmaceuticals represent Merz's largest operation, accounting for 54 percent of sales in 2005, which topped EUR 417 million ($501 million). The company's drug development specializes in so-called "ethical" drugs, with a particular focus on Alzheimer's disease. Merz's flagship molecule is Memantine, an active ingredient used to treat moderate-to-severe Alzheimer's dementia symptoms. Memantine is distributed under Merz's own brand name Azura, and licensed to Forest Laboratories and Lundbeck. Merz also produces drugs for the treatment of Parkinson's disease, depression, liver-related brain impairment, lipid metabolism disorders, cervical dystonia, blepharospasm, and others.

Merz Pharma is also a leading producer of topical gels for dermatological treatments, including fungal diseases, hair loss, and wrinkles. The company's Mederma is also a leading treatment for scar prevention and reduction, sold both in prescription and over-the-counter (OTC) form.

Merz Pharma's Consumer Products Division adds another 28 percent to Merz Group's sales, and produces a line of beauty products under the Merz Spezial brand, as well OTC products under the tetesept brand. Included under the Consumer Products division is Merz Dental, which focuses on the dentist and dental professionals, and produces artificial teeth, partial dentures, and other prosthesis and casting materials. This division also produces a hyaluronic acid-based gum care treatment, as well as a range of disinfectant and sterilizing materials, and hand and skin care products for dental care professionals. The company's writing products division, conducted through subsidiary Merz & Krell, produces writing instruments under the Sentator and Roubill brands. This division added 16 percent to group sales in 2005; some 70 percent of Merz & Krell's revenues come through promotional and advertising sales. Germany remains Merz's largest market, at 40 percent of sales, while the rest of Europe contributes nearly 30 percent of sales. The North American market, backed by the strong reception of Memantine, is the company's fastest-growing market, and represented 27 percent of sales in 2005. Merz has kicked off an active international expansion effort in the mid-2000s. In 2005, for example, the company established a new subsidiary in Italy, then entered the United Kingdom in 2006 through the acquisition of Denfleet Pharma. Merz Group is a private company controlled by the founding Merz family.

TOPICAL BEGINNINGS IN 1908

Merz Group was founded by Friedrich Merz, born in 1884, who worked as a pharmacist in Frankfurt during the early years of the 20th century. Merz developed, and patented, a topical skin cream with a water-soluble base that permitted the cream's ingredients to be more readily absorbed by the skin. In order to produce the cream on a larger scale, Merz founded a new company in 1908 and set up a production line in a former cigarette factory on Frankfurt's Eckenheimer Landstrasse.

Merz continued to develop the company's line of topical creams and ointments, as well as other healthy and beauty products, including the company's own vitamin formulations. By the end of World War I, Merz himself had begun to explore other business interests. Indeed, Merz proved to be a prolific inventor with a variety of interests. During his lifetime, Merz received a number of patents, ranging from tire chains to a method for filling tubes, to a number of medicines and creams.

Merz's interests also turned to pens and other writing materials. In 1920, Merz joined with brother Georg and Justus Krell, a machine lathe operator, to found Merz & Krell. That company began producing penholders, celluloid-based fountain pens, and pencils, made from artificial horn. The company's writing products were originally produced under the Melbi brand name. Later, the company adopted the Senator brand name as well. Production at the company was shut down during World War II. Re-launched following the war, Merz & Krell grew into a major supplier of writing instruments to the European market. The company was especially strong in the market for promotional writing materials, and by the end of the century had grown into Europe's leading manufacturer of promotional pens and related items.

Meanwhile, Merz had continued developing its health and beauty aids. The company began testing a new product, a specialty "dragee" (using the French term for a type of candy lozenge), designed as an ingestable skin, hair, and nail treatment. The vitamin formulation, developed by the then 80-year-old Merz himself, was launched under the Merz Spezial brand name in 1964. The company's claims for the dragee cure were boosted by a partnership with Dr. Ernst Dichter, a noted psychoanalyst who had been one of the founders of focus-group market research. Ernst, who employed Freudian theory as a marketing tool, had earlier been hired by Mattel Corporation to assist in the launch of the Barbie doll. With Dichter's assistance, Merz developed a highly successful sales pitch based on the tagline: "Can you eat beauty?"

The Merz Special dragee proved immensely popular with the German consumer market. By the end of the century, the brand had become one of the best known in the country, with a market recognition factor of some 87 percent. During the ensuing decades, Merz continued to conduct research on the formulation, and by the 1990s had succeeded not only in clinically proving the product's effectiveness, but also in identifying the active ingredients contributing to its effect. This led the company to be awarded a patent for the formula in 2004.

SHIFTING TO PHARMACEUTICALS DEVELOPMENT FOR THE NEW CENTURY

For the most part, Merz remained focused on the German market through the 20th century. Nonetheless, the company had achieved some degree of international growth. The Senator pen brand, in particular, became an international success and an important part of the company's expansion into the U.S. market. Merz's presence in the United States was extended to Connecticut when it bought E.E. Dickinson, a manufacturer of witch hazel-based products, in 1985. Into the 1990s, Merz established production facilities in North Carolina.

By then, Merz had already begun a transition into a noted international pharmaceuticals group. The company expanded into Austria in 1991, acquiring a business founded by Dr. Walter Kolassa in 1938 in Cologne, Germany, before transferring to Vienna in 1945. The addition of the Kolassa facilities enabled Merz to develop its in-house research and development operations. The company raised its international profile again in 1992, when it purchased the Swiss medical products distributor Adroka, founded in 1942.

During the 1990s, Merz focused on a number of

KEY DATES

1908: Friedrich Merz invents a water-soluble cream and founds a factory in Frankfurt.

1920: Merz, together with brother Georg Merz and Justus Krell, founds Merz & Krell, which specializes in the production of writing instruments.

1964: Merz launches Merz Spezial Dragees, a vitamin and mineral supplement.

1991: Merz acquires Dr. Kolassa in Austria.

1992: Company acquires medical products distributor Adroka in Switzerland.

1997: Mederma, a scar tissue gel, is approved for sale in the United States.

2003: Akatinol Memantine is approved as a treatment for Alzheimer's disease in the United States and Europe.

2005: Merz launches subsidiary as part of international expansion.

2006: Merz acquires Denfleet Pharma in England.

promising areas, notably the treatment of Alzheimer's disease and other neurological conditions, including Parkinson's disease. Merz also continued to develop its expertise in dermatological treatments. Other areas of interest for the company included depression, hair loss, liver disease, as well as the treatment of scars, and the development of cold remedies and vitamin and mineral preparations.

The company achieved European success with the launch of an anti-scar gel, Contratubex in the late 1980s. In 1997, Merz launched that gel in the United States under the Mederma brand name. Mederma quickly became one of the most prescribed scar treatment compounds. By the end of the decade, Merz had also released Mederma in OTC packaging as well.

Into the early 2000s, however, Merz made a new step in its shift toward the pharmaceuticals market with the launch of a new drug, called Memantine, which received approval as a treatment for Alzheimer's disease in Europe in 2002. That drug, based on Akatinol, had been available in Germany for some decades, yet Merz's discovery of its effectiveness on Alzheimer's symptoms came only during the 1990s.

Merz quickly signed up licensees to produce and distribute the drug, including Forest Labs in the United States, and Lundbeck in the Scandinavian region, Grunenthal elsewhere in Europe, and Daiichi Asubio in Japan. The global success of Memantine encouraged Merz to begin planning its own international growth. The company expanded into new markets, including Uruguay, Mexico, India, Russia, Poland, and Italy. In 2006, the company entered the United Kingdom, acquiring that country's Denfleet Pharma. At the same time, Merz targeted further expansion into such markets as Hungary and Turkey.

By 2006, Merz's pharmaceuticals division represented more than half of the company's total sales, which topped EUR 417 million in 2005. The company had also successfully expanded beyond Germany, which by then accounted for just 40 percent of the group's sales. At the same time, Merz's active research and development effort continued to produce strong results in an increasing array of areas. After nearly a century, Merz remained an important contributor to the world pharmaceuticals market.

M. L. Cohen

PRINCIPAL SUBSIDIARIES

Dr. Kolassa + Merz Beteiligungs-GmbH (Austria); Dr. Kolassa + Merz GmbH (Austria); Dr. Kolassa + Merz med.wiss. Informations-GmbH (Austria); Laboratorios Merz Darier S.A. de C.V. (Mexico); M Pharma de Mexico Servicios S.A. de C.V.; Medra Handelsgesellschaft mbH (Austria); Merz & Krell GmbH & Co. KGaA; Merz Beteiligungs GmbH (Austria); Merz Consumer Care GmbH; Merz Dental GmbH; Merz GmbH & Co. KGaA; Merz Incorporated (U.S.A.); Merz Pharma (Schweiz) AG (Switzerland); Merz Pharma GmbH & Co. KGaA; Merz Pharmaceuticals GmbH; Merz Pharmaceuticals LLC (U.S.A.); Modi-Senator (India) Private Limited; MZ Pharma de Mexico S.A. de C.V.; rou bill benelux B.V. (Netherlands); Senator France, S.A.R.L.; Senator Pen LLC (U.S.A.); Senator Pens Limited (U.K.); Senator Polska, S.p.z.o.o., (Poland); Transpharma Handels AG, Zug (Switzerland).

PRINCIPAL COMPETITORS

Pfizer Inc.; Merck & Co., Inc.; Johnson and Johnson; GlaxoSmithKline; Bayer AG; Novartis Inc.; Roche Holding AG; Celesio AG; AstraZeneca PLC; Eli Lilly and Co.

FURTHER READING

"Chains Give Mederma Sales a Boost," *Chain Drug Review,* February 18, 2002, p. 54.

"Merz Enhances Its Position in Dermatology," *Chain Drug Review,* November 8, 1999, p. 9.

"Merz Eradicates Gaps in the Memory," *Chemical Business NewsBase-Chemische Rundschau,* May 20, 2003.

"Merz Pharmaceuticals LLC," *MMR,* October 17, 2005, p. 59.

"Merz Pharmaceuticals, of Frankfurt, Germany, Began a Cooperation with NascaCell IP GmbH, of Munich, Germany, to Use NascaCell's Aptamers to Improve Validation of Different Targets for Products in Merz's Pipeline," *BioWorld International,* September 1, 2004, p. 5.

Seidlitz, Frank, "Merz to Increase Focus on Pharmaceuticals," *Die Welt,* December 27, 2003.

Subramanian, Nithya, "Merz Pharma to Launch Drug for Alzheimer's Dementia," *Business Line,* December 16, 2004.

Naumes, Inc.

2 West Barnett Street
Medford, Oregon 97501
U.S.A.
Telephone: (541) 779-9951
Fax: (541) 772-3650
Web site: http://www.naumes.com

Private Company
Incorporated: 1946 as Nye & Naumes Packing Co. Inc.
Employees: 700
Sales: $39.7 million (2005)
NAIC: 111331 Apple Orchards; 111339 Other Non-
citrus Fruit Farming; 424480 Fresh Fruit and
Vegetable Merchant Wholesalers; 311411 Frozen
Fruit, Juice, and Vegetable Processing

■ ■ ■

Naumes, Inc., grows and ships a variety of fruit and is
the world's largest grower of Bosc and Bartlett pears.
The company is also the leading independent industrial
fruit juice processor in the United States. Operations
encompass 7,000 acres and cold storage and packing
facilities in California, Oregon, and Washington, which
are also the states where Naumes sells its products.

BECOMING ONE OF THE
LARGEST DOMESTIC FRUIT
GROWERS

In 1946, after completing his military service, William
Joseph "Joe" Naumes returned to Medford and founded
Nye & Naumes Packing Co. Inc. with Stephen Nye.

Naumes had been born in Hood River, Oregon, in 1910,
and graduated from Santa Clara University in 1934.
Naumes's grandfather, Peter Naumes, had earlier begun
a fruit growing, packaging, and shipping operation in
Oregon's Rogue Valley on land once owned by John
Sutter. This land now belonged to Joe Naumes.

The Rogue River Valley is an area in Oregon well
known for its rich fertile soil and its many orchards that
produce some of the finest apples and pears in the United
States. Naumes settled into the agricultural business
with his wife, Frances McCormick. After Naumes and
Nye parted company, Naumes renamed his business
Naumes, Inc. The business remained a closely held family venture, involving Naumes, his wife, and the couples'
three children, Susan, Mary, and Michael. The children
started moving irrigation pipe at age 11, and by the
eighth grade, they were picking, thinning, and smudg-
ing (protecting trees against frost and insects) in the
orchards.

From the 1950s through the 1970s, Naumes, Inc.,
grew, acquiring additional acreage for apples as well as
pears in California and storage facilities in and around
Medford. In 1981, the company moved into Washington
State's Yakima Valley. By the late 1980s, the company
holdings totaled close to 3,000 acres in Oregon,
Washington, and California.

As Naumes grew, so did its reputation as one of the
largest domestic growers of pears. Joe Naumes became
known for his warmth and personal integrity. In 1986,
he received the horticultural society's Centennial Award
for distinguished service to his industry. In 1987, the
Oregon Horticultural Society awarded Naumes the

Hartman Cup for his contributions to horticulture, and Santa Clara University gave him the Ignatian Award in recognition of distinguished service to humanity.

However, unfortunately for Naumes and other domestic growers, the market for apples began to change in the late 1980s. From 1987 to 1989, demand for the fruit crashed as people's fears about the chemical alar, which growers used to make apples look better and store longer, spread. New Zealand growers took advantage of the slackened demand for domestic fruit to begin exporting Granny Smith apples, which became almost immediately popular, into the United States. Apples grown in Asia, too, began to make their way into the American market and onto the American table.

By the early 1990s, growers throughout southern Oregon had responded to these foreign incursions by planting the varieties of apples grown abroad—Gala, Braeburn, Fuji, and more. The year after Joe Naumes's death in 1989, Naumes, which had by then become a major regional fruit growing and processing company, filled its new orchard in Grants Pass with dwarf root stock of foreign origin. The dwarf apple trees' small size allowed for as many as 650 trees per acre. "You used to grow apples so they would come into production in 10 to 15 years' time and keep producing for 70 years," explained the company's horticulturist in a 1994 *Oregonian* article. The Grants Pass orchard came into production in 1994 after only four years.

The company unfortunately suffered bad luck of a different sort during the early 1990s as a series of fires broke out in some of the large and aging packing facilities it owned in Oregon. The first of these fires occurred in 1991, and took the life of a worker trapped in a cold storage facility. In 1993, three fires struck in quick succession, the first destroying the roof of a building. The second, which began two weeks later in Medford, destroyed half a block of a packing and processing plant used for fruit sorting operations. The third fire raged through and demolished another two-story packing facility.

DIVERSIFICATION, NEW MARKETING STRATEGIES, ACREAGE REDUCTIONS

Despite such setbacks, Naumes continued to grow. In 1993, it was named one of three Oregon Family Businesses of the Year for its "innovative leadership, community activities, and integration of family and business." Like other Oregon farmers, it had begun to diversity into value-added products, adding fruit processing to its growing operations, to increase profits and deal with the fact that there was more fruit in the world than stores were buying. In 1992, Naumes bought a processing plant in Marysville, Washington, and began producing concentrates for juices, jams, and jellies. A second purchase of a juice concentrate plant in California soon followed. Also during the 1990s, Naumes began selling pears and apples under a label that certified their environmentally friendly farming practices.

However, by 1998, prices for juice apples were only a third of what they had been the year before as competitors from China undercut American growers. China was at the time the world's leading apple producer and had also begun building apple juice processing plants to handle surplus fruit. Though Naumes had become one of the largest pear growers in the world and the largest independent fruit juice processor in the United States, it idled its juice processing plant in Wapato, Washington.

Naumes also reduced its orchard holdings in Jackson County by 800 acres, leaving the land fallow rather than continuing to invest money in harvesting fruit for which there was no market. "We may go down to 2,000 acres, but I don't expect it'll affect our overall production," Mike Naumes, president and chief executive of Naumes, Inc. announced in a 1998 *Oregonian* article. "Our home is here in the Rogue Valley, and we expect we're going to be survivors. We're trying to be cutting edge. We're not just giving up."

Survival also entailed changes in marketing strategies. In Joe Naumes's day, growers sold to hundreds of fruit wholesalers and brokers, who in turn sold to the retail market. With the rise of the grocery giants, however, Naumes had to sell directly to fewer than eight grocery chains. Marketing was viewed as "the final funnel," according to Mike Naumes, in a 1999 *Oregon Business Journal* article. His company's new infrastructure included a computer system to track fruit shipments and informal alliances with competitors to meet the giants' demands.

The company's survival strategies paid off, although times continued to be rocky. In 1998, Naumes won the award for high-value added products at Oregon's agricultural awards. In 1999, it became the primary sup-

KEY DATES

1946: Joe Naumes founds Nye & Naumes Packing Co. Inc. with Stephen Nye.
1981: The company moves into Washington State's Yakima Valley.
1989: Joe Naumes dies.
1992: Naumes buys a fruit processing plant in Marysville, Washington.
1999: Naumes becomes the primary supplier of produce for Albertson's; company purchases Gilco Apple Corp.'s juice plant in Wenatchee, Washington.
2000: The company starts a joint venture called Fresh Products Northwest with Dovex Fruit Co. of Wenatchee, Washington.
2003: The company ranks 110 on *Oregon Business*'s Top 150 list.

introduced two ounce packages of sliced apples designed for lunch boxes with the beginning of the school year in the fall of 2001. It also made plans to introduce pear slices.

CONTINUED HARD TIMES LEADING TO REPLANTING AND REZONING

Still, foreign fruit imports and the concentration of retail distribution channels conspired to create additional financial woes for southern Oregon pear growers as the decade came to a close. With more than 94 percent of the country's pears produced in Oregon, Washington, and California, pressure from imports narrowed the marketability and depressed the price of Pacific Northwest fruit. Lower wages for workers, lenient land use laws, and foreign government subsidies, as well as the use of pesticides and herbicides banned in the United States, meant that foreign farmers could offer fruit at a price well below what domestic farmers spent to grow it. Imported pears doubled between 1996 and 2001.

At the same time, Chinese apple juice began to be substituted for pear juice, devastating the apple market and nudging pear growers out of the fruit juice market entirely. In 1997, juice producers got about $130 for a ton of fruit juice. In 1998, when Chinese apple juice imports started coming in, the price of a ton of domestic juice went down to $30.

Hard times for Jackson County's pear industry got tougher yet in 2002 as the worst case of fire blight in more than a generation destroyed hundreds of acres of trees. A short heat wave in May followed by cooler, wetter weather had initiated the fire blight, a destructive bacterium that attacks pear and apple trees and is spread primarily by bees, insects, and wind. The disease, which breaks down the cambium, the thin layer between the bark and the wood and causes branch tips to turn brown, can kill a tree within hours.

Naumes, which farmed nearly 2,000 acres of pears, had "a couple of real hotspots of 150 to 200 acres," according to Sue Naumes in a 2002 *Mail Tribune* article.

As a result, despite remaining number 110 on *Oregon Business Magazine*'s Top 150 list, Naumes turned its attention to other means of securing its future in 2003. "The economics have totally gone out of the fruit industry. What we get for our product continues to go down and it doesn't pencil out very well," observed Mike Naumes in a 2003 *Mail Tribune* article. The company further reduced acreage in California and Washington and leveled a thousand acres of pear trees in the Rogue Valley. It replanted some of its historic orchard

plier of produce for Albertson's, the second largest grocery chain in the United States. It also purchased Gilco Apple Corp.'s juice plant in Wenatchee, Washington, completing a string of plants from California to Washington and giving it better access to Canadian markets. That plant, however, shut down temporarily in May 2001. "There just aren't enough juice apples to keep that line running," Mike Naumes announced in the August 2001 *Wenatchee Business Journal,* "We'll have to wait until the next crop of apples comes in."

By 2000, Naumes was diversifying in a new direction. It launched a line of prepackaged, fresh-cut bagged apple slices in a joint venture called Fresh Products Northwest that it undertook with Dovex Fruit Co. of Wenatchee, Washington. The fruit was treated with NatureSeal, a vitamin-mineral coating of Vitamin C and calcium, to keep it from turning brown for up to three weeks in a refrigerator. The "Crunch Pak" product was distributed to wholesalers and retailers in 17 states in the west and Midwest. At first it appeared sales of Crunch Pak would be slow, but, within months, Fresh Products Northwest could barely keep up with demand. The Washington Apple Commission did marketing tests that showed that two out of three people chose sliced apples over carrots when presented side by side. Other reports showed that sales of apples had increased 80 percent with the introduction of the apple slices. Marketed through Sysco Food Services of America, schools, and retailers, Fresh Products Northwest

blocks in Oregon with new, denser stock, and replaced apple trees with cherry trees in California and Washington.

The company also rezoned some of its land for commercial, industrial, and residential use. "We'll continue our juice concentrate operations, but we're moving more and more into real estate and real estate development," Naumes said. The company had closed its Wenatchee concentrate plant by 2003, but continued to operate its other plants in Wapato and Marysville.

Then, suddenly in 2004, pear production exceeded expectations by 10 percent. Naumes, which operated 1,700 acres in three states, had "so many young trees coming on and some of the acreage we really haven't heard from" that it produced two and three times what it had in the past. "Coming off a light year, I was surprised how much tonnage there was and the size was about where we like to see it," celebrated Mike Naumes in a 2004 *Mail Tribune* article.

After the banner Bosc harvest of 2004, there was a 25 to 30 percent drop in production in 2005. However, growers benefited from the higher prices brought by California's leanest green Bartlett crop in 45 years. In 2006, as the market for pears rebounded, Naumes began planting 7,500 pear trees on a 60-acre site in Medford, with another 2,500 to follow. "The key thing is we're trying to maintain an overall economic unit," Mike Naumes reasoned in a 2006 *Knight-Ridder/Tribune News* article. "It's a balancing act."

Naumes began supply agreements with Costco and other major retailers. The company planted Golden Bosc, Star Crimson, and French Butter to extend its growing season into the middle of the fall on 500 acres that from the 1980s to 2004 were a Granny Smith apple orchard. With 2,100 acres in production, Naumes was also increasing its cherry orchards and strived to improve operations overall while keeping its eye on importers. "Retailers don't understand agriculture and don't really care," Laura Naumes, Mike Naumes's wife, asserted in the 2006 *Knight-Ridder* piece. "If imports are cheaper, they can make better margins. Because of global competition, you have to do everything well. ... You have to grow it well, pack it well, and have a good sales team marketing it."

Carrie Rothburd

PRINCIPAL SUBSIDIARIES

Naumes Concentrates Inc.

PRINCIPAL COMPETITORS

Chiquita Brands; Dole Food Company, Inc.; Fresh Del Monte Produce; Auvril Fruit; ConAgra, Inc.; Doves Fruit; Gold Digger Apples; Greenridge Fruit; Holtzinger Fruit; Hudson River Fruit; Jones Produce; Liberty Orchards; Matson Fruit Company; Red Jacket Orchards; Riveridge Produce Marketing; Sierra View Sales; Sun Orchard Fruit Company, Inc.; Sunsweet Growers; Tree Top, Inc.; United Apple Sales.

FURTHER READING

Barnard, Jeff, "New Varieties of Apples Tempt U.S. Growers, Buyers," *Oregonian*, September 11, 1994, K4.

Downhill, Shari, "Pear Market in Northwest U.S. Collapses," *Mail Tribune*, April 27, 2001.

"Naumes, Inc. Squeezed in Effort to Make Juice Locally," *Wenatchee Business Journal*, August 2001, p. B20.

Rae, Jamee, "Ripe for Change," *Oregon Business Journal*, November 1999, p. 33.

Scarbrough, Roy, "Trail of Medford Fire Stretches Back to Thirties," *Oregonian*, October 9, 1993, p. D3.

Stiles, Greg, "Blight Attacks Pear Industry in Jackson County, Oregon," *Mail Tribune*, June 25, 2002.

———, "Medford, Oregon–Area Lunchbox Fruit Company Targets Schools," *Mail Tribune*, September 6, 2001.

———, "Medford, Oregon, Company Moves Away from Fruit Production Toward Real Estate," *Mail Tribune*, January 15, 2003.

———, "Oregon Markets Look Favorably at Pear Harvest," *Knight-Ridder/Tribune News Service*, March 3, 2006.

———, "Oregon Pear Harvest Exceeds Projections by 10 Percent," *Mail Tribune*, October 20, 2004.

NETGEAR, Inc.

———■———

4500 Great American Parkway
Santa Clara, California 95054
U.S.A.
Telephone: (408) 907-8000
Fax: (408) 907-8097
Web site: http://www.netgear.com

Public Company
Incorporated: 1996
Employees: 269
Sales: $449.6 million (2005)
Stock Exchanges: NASDAQ
Ticker Symbol: NTGR
NAIC: 334119 Other Computer Peripheral Equipment
    Manufacturing; 517910 Other Telecommunications

■ ■ ■

NETGEAR, Inc. (Netgear) designs networking products for small businesses and home users, specializing in developing wireless devices that create local area networks known as Wi-Fi, or wireless-fidelity. The company's products enable users to share Internet access, peripherals, files, digital multimedia content, and applications among multiple personal computers. Netgear designs its products by using hardware and software sold by other companies and instructing third-party manufacturers based in Taiwan how to construct the devices. The company sells its products through retailers, distributors, and broadband service providers. Netgear stresses new product introductions as the key to its success, striving to release 12 new products every three months. Wireless products account for more than half of the company's sales. International sales account for 56 percent of the company's annual revenue.

ORIGINS

Netgear owes its existence to Patrick Lo, a proponent of computer networking who sensed a market need and capitalized on his vision. Lo, named Ernst & Young Entrepreneur of the Year in 2006, was not, in the strict definition of the word, an entrepreneur. Instead of going it alone and assuming the financial risk of his venture, he turned to his employer for support, a way of transforming his vision into a business that made his achievements no less impressive. Lo studied electrical engineering at Brown University, leaving the Providence, Rhode Island, school with an undergraduate degree that landed him a job at Hewlett-Packard Company, a leading manufacturer of computers and test equipment. Lo joined Hewlett-Packard in 1983, beginning a 12-year stay at the company that saw him assume various responsibilities, including holding management positions in software sales, technical support, sales support and marketing, and network product management. He left in 1995, bound for Billerica, Massachusetts-based Bay Networks, Inc., where he would convince his new employers to back his bid to launch Netgear.

Around the time Lo switched employers, his family provided the inspiration for the business idea he would present to Bay Networks executives. After dinner in the Lo household, each family member rushed to one of the three computers in the home, racing to claim rights to the single dial-up connection to the Internet. "The

COMPANY PERSPECTIVES

NETGEAR has been a worldwide provider of technologically advanced, branded networking products since 1996. Our mission is to be the preferred customer-driven provider of innovative networking solutions for small businesses and homes.

invention of the browser just made everybody want to connect," Lo recalled in a September 15, 2003 interview with *Investor's Business Daily*. "I thought there must be a better way," he added. Convinced that other households with multiple computers faced the same dilemma, Lo saw a market for networking products that would enable small business owners and consumers to connect multiple computers to a single Internet account. The company he joined, Bay Networks, provided networking equipment to large corporations, competing against the best known networking giant, Cisco Systems, Inc., but Lo's proposal marked a more profound departure from Bay Networks' business than appeared at first blush. It required far smaller, vastly less expensive equipment for a market that did not exist. Further, if the products even sold, the profit margins promised to be far less attractive than the sizable percentages earned by selling sophisticated networking systems to large corporations.

Lo joined Bay Networks in August 1995 and quickly set about convincing management that a foray into what was termed as the Small Office/Home Office (SOHO) market was worth the investment. "We had to pitch everybody in the company that it was a good idea," Lo remembered, referring to his partnership with fellow Bay Networks employee Mark Merrill, in his interview with *Investor's Business Daily*. "We told them we were going to take the technology they were selling to big corporations and make it available cheaply and make it easy to install in home networks. Some people laughed at that, but there were enough people there to share the vision." Lo's power of persuasion led to the formation of Netgear in January 1996, a business that was set up as a wholly owned subsidiary of Bay Networks. Lo explained the reasoning behind Netgear's structuring as a subsidiary rather than as another Bay Networks product line in his interview with *Investor's Business Daily*: "Bay Networks had been busy fighting Cisco. They wanted the 50 percent, 60 percent margins, but the consumer market was going to produce 20 percent, 30 percent margins. We set up as a subsidiary so we could have separate books and be valued accordingly."

PRODUCT LAUNCH IN 1996

One of the earliest references to Netgear in the business press appeared in mid-1996. In its June 3, 1996 issue, *PC Week* noted that Santa Clara, California-based Netgear recently had launched a SOHO product line in Japan. The product line, which was slated for release in the United States and Germany in the summer of 1996, featured ten products: five 10BaseT hubs, two Fast Ethernet hubs, two Fast Ethernet switches, and an ISDN router with a terminal adaptor. At the high end of the price range for the products was one of the Fast Ethernet hubs, which retailed for $1,650.

Netgear helped shape the home networking market when it commenced sales in 1996, but being an industry pioneer did little to earn the company an advantage over rivals. One of the primary concerns from Lo's vantage point in 1996 was whether a market for home networking equipment existed at all. Lo's convictions would be confirmed, particularly after high-speed, broadband Internet connections became more prevalent and wireless technology penetrated the consumer market. As the market developed, however, concerns about demand were replaced with new concerns.

The market for the type of equipment designed by Netgear became a commodity-like business characterized by volume sales and slim profit margins, a market populated not by Fast Ethernet hubs that sold for $1,650 but by devices that retailed for far less. "The sweet spot for consumer products is $99, while for small office products it's $299," Lo said in a December 30, 2004 interview with *Investor's Business Daily*. As the market matured, Lo found himself competing for volume sales against a host of competitors, including the giants of the corporate networking market who jumped into the consumer networking market with massive financial resources at their disposal.

To keep competitors at bay, Lo kept a tight control on inventory and costs and focused on new product introductions to win the business of consumers and small business accounts. Netgear, which in later years introduced a dozen new products every three months, used off-the-shelf hardware and software from companies such as Marvell, Broadcom, and Atheros Communications and contracted with Taiwanese firms to manufacture the products. "They do the grunt work of designing circuit boards," Lo explained in his December 30, 2004 interview with *Investor's Business Daily*. "We do the system integration, make sure the whole thing works, [and] write and define which components to use."

As Netgear grew along with the market it helped to create, control over the company changed hands. In August 1998, Bay Networks sold the company to Nortel Networks Corp., a Canadian firm that ranked as one of

KEY DATES

1996: Netgear is formed as a subsidiary of Bay Networks, Inc.
1998: Nortel Networks acquires Netgear.
2000: After being spun off from Nortel Networks, Netgear prepares for an initial public offering of stock but later cancels the offering.
2003: Netgear completes its initial public offering of stock.
2006: Netgear founder, Patrick Lo, is named Ernst & Young Entrepreneur of the Year; annual revenue nears $500 million.

the largest makers of telecommunication equipment in the world. Netgear, with Lo continuing to serve as its chief executive officer, became a wholly owned subsidiary of Nortel, remaining as such until 2000, when Nortel announced it was spinning off the subsidiary. Netgear, at the time of the spinoff, received $15 million in equity financing from Pequot Capital Management Inc., and began to make plans for an initial public offering (IPO) of stock.

The company by this point sold a full range of networking equipment, offering a product line that Lo hoped would attract investors as well as customers. Netgear sold firewall-equipped network routers designed to snap into place behind dial-up modems. For customers who had high-speed Internet connections, which were becoming increasingly more commonplace, Netgear sold digital subscriber line (DSL) and cable modems, which could be used with the company's hubs and network cards to link multiple computers to the home or office network. Netgear's telephone-line networking products were capable of building 10-megabits-per-second links using existing telephone wiring and jacks. Although the product line was strong, enabling the company to generate $176 million in revenue for the year, the timing of the proposed $130 million IPO could not have been worse. The collapse of the Internet sector dashed Lo's plan for going public, forcing him to withdraw his bid officially in February 2001 and to wait for market conditions to improve.

INITIAL PUBLIC OFFERING OF STOCK IN 2003

When Lo revisited the idea of ushering Netgear through an IPO, his decision created a stir of anticipation not only in the networking community but within the

investment community as well. Lo decided to file with the Securities and Exchange Commission (SEC) for an IPO in April 2003, an occasion of note in the aftermath of the events that forced him to scuttle plans for an IPO in late 2000. During the first four months of 2000, 158 companies converted to public ownership, a figure that dropped to 24 for the January-to-April period in 2002, and fell to four during the four months leading up to Lo's announcement.

Lo's decision to push forward with an IPO in April 2003 was made during the slowest period of IPO activity since 1975, making Netgear's public debut a bellwether of investor reaction as the market recovered from the dotcom debacle at the turn of the century. Netgear offered itself to investors with a wide range of networking gear, both wireless and wired by that point, including routers, switches, hubs, adapters, print servers, and access points, completing its IPO at the end of July for $14 per share. The offering raised $98 million, eliciting bids from 18 underwriters—the same investment bankers who shied away from Netgear's IPO three years earlier—and thrust Lo's company into the public spotlight.

As the company embarked on a new era of existence, it faced a slew of competitors. "Walk into a retailer, or go online to Walmart.com or Amazon.com," *Business Week* noted in its May 12, 2003 issue, "and you will surely find Netgear products, but they in no way enjoy favorable placement among a bunch of other brands, including Belkin, D-Link Systems, Linksys, Microsoft, U.S. Robotics, and more." Exacerbating matters, Cisco had entered the market by purchasing Linksys one month before Lo filed for the IPO, vowing to use its estimated $9.5 billion in cash and short-term investments to make sure Linksys maintained its lead in the consumer market.

As Netgear pressed ahead as a publicly traded company, the battle for market share promised to occupy its attention in the coming years. The company ranked third in the market, trailing industry leader Linksys and runner-up D-Link Systems. Netgear derived more than half its sales from wireless products midway through the decade, benefiting from the popularity of wireless networking, or Wi-Fi, in the consumer market. Financially, the company was hitting its stride, recording encouraging gains in net income and revenue. After years of sustaining substantial losses, the company posted profits for four consecutive years between 2002 and 2005, enjoining an increase from 2002's total of $8.1 million to the $33.6 million recorded in 2005. Revenues shot upward during the period as well, jumping from $237.3 million to $449.6 million. A fiercely competitive battle loomed in the years ahead, particularly from Cisco-backed Linksys. With vast financial resources at its disposal, Cisco-Linksys, L.L.C., could sacrifice profits for the sake of increasing market share, presenting Netgear with a formidable foe as it fought to hold on to its number three market position.

Jeffrey L. Covell

PRINCIPAL SUBSIDIARIES

Netgear International, Inc.; Netgear Holdings, Ltd. (Ireland).

PRINCIPAL COMPETITORS

Cisco-Linksys, L.L.C.; D-Link Corporation; 3Com Corporation; Belkin Corporation.

FURTHER READING

Angell, Mike, "NETGEAR Inc. Santa Clara, California; Wireless Gear Maker Avoids Market Potholes," *Investor's Business Daily,* December 30, 2004, p. A6.

———, "Seeing a Market Where None Existed," *Investor's Business Daily,* September 15, 2003, p. A8.

Barker, Robert, "NETGEAR: A Hot IPO That Leaves Me Cold," *Business Week,* May 12, 2003, p. 109.

"Bay to Launch Low-End LAN Line in United States, Germany," *PC Week,* June 3, 1996, p. 3.

"CRN Interview—Patrick Lo, Netgear," *Computer Reseller News,* September 29, 2003, p. 25.

Lavilla, Stacy, "Bay Networks' Netgear Line Ties in SOHO Users," *PC Week,* July 8, 1996, p. 10.

"Netgear's IPO: The Bankers Came Running," *Investment Dealers' Digest,* September 29, 2003.

"Nortel Networks Spin-Off NETGEAR to Focus on High-Growth Home and Small Business Internet Infrastructure Market," *Cambridge Telecom Report,* March 20, 2000.

"Nortel Spins Off Home-Networking Business," *Newsbytes,* March 15, 2000.

NeuStar, Inc.

46000 Center Oak Plaza
Sterling, Virginia 20166
U.S.A.
Telephone: (571) 434-5400
Fax: (571) 434-5401
Web site: http://www.neustar.com

Public Company
Incorporated: 1998
Employees: 502
Sales: $242.5 million (2005)
Stock Exchanges: New York
Ticker Symbol: NSP
NAIC: 517910 Other Telecommunications

∎∎∎

Listed on the New York Stock Exchange, NeuStar, Inc., provides vital impartial clearinghouse services to the communications and Internet industry. Originally formed to oversee government-mandated local telephone number portability, allowing individuals to keep their numbers when changing service providers, the Sterling, Virginia-based company has since expanded its role to include a range of addressing, interoperability, and infrastructure services. As part of its addressing functions, NeuStar acts as the administrator of the North American Numbering Plan (the three-digit area codes and seven-digit numbers used to route telephone calls), assigns new area codes, allocates telephone numbers, acts as a registry for the Common Short Codes used in text messaging and Wireless Do-Not-Call, provides registry

services for .biz and .us Internet domain names, and provides gateway services for .cn (China) and .tw (Taiwan) Internet domain names. NeuStar facilitates the exchange of data between different communications' networks, and includes number portability as well as other order management and exchange services, such as customer account record exchange, enhanced 911, access service request, and local service request. NeuStar's infrastructure services help communication companies to manage their networks, manage changes, and deal with disaster recovery. NeuStar also helps its customers comply with law enforcement requests in areas such as wire taps. NeuStar is 72 percent owned by investment firm Warburg Pincus L.L.C., but the majority of the voting shares, 59 percent, are held by an irrevocable trust, established to maintain the company's position of impartiality.

TELECOMMUNICATIONS ACT OF 1996 LEADING TO NEUSTAR

As the telecommunications industry moved toward an era of greater competition for local telephone service in the 1990s, a number of state regulatory bodies and communication companies began addressing the key issue of local number portability (LNP), the ability of customers to transfer their phone numbers when they changed carriers. Heading an effort funded by a group of communication companies to find a way to allow different networks to efficiently make the necessary exchange of information was NeuStar's chief technology officer, Mark D. Foster. An experienced hand with a degree in physics and computer science from the California Institute of Technology, Foster was the lead inventor of LNP. In the meantime, the Illinois Commerce Commission (ICC) took the lead in selecting a standard LNP architecture, opting for AT&T/Lucent Technologies' system, which was later adopted by the Federal Communications Commission. LNP then became mandated by the Telecommunications Act of 1996, signed into law by President Clinton in February of that year. Two months later Lockheed Martin Corporation's Communications Industry Service division, for whom Foster worked as a consultant, won ICC's first numbering portability contract, establishing a Number Portability Administration Center (NPAC) in Chicago. Seven other regional limited liability companies and LNP databases were established according to the markets of the six Bell Operating Company regions, plus Canada. The system developed by Communications Industry Service was tested and certified in October 1997, and following a successful trial in Chicago, the Lockheed division was selected to serve as LNP administrator by four of the other regional limited liability companies. Perot Systems was selected by the other three, but because it failed to deliver a workable system on time, Lockheed Martin gained the rest of the business.

The Telecommunications Act of 1996 also mandated that the North American Numbering Plan Administration (NANPA) be administered by a neutral party. NANPA had been created in 1947 by AT&T to ensure that there would be enough phone numbers available as the United States underwent a boom in telecommunications, leading to the three-digit area code and the elimination of letter prefixes that relied on words, such as the title of Glenn Miller's Big Band tune "Pennsylvania 6-5000." Canada and 19 Caribbean countries eventually adopted the plan. After the breakup of AT&T in 1984, NANPA became the responsibility of Bellcore, owned by the seven so-called Baby Bells. With the change in the law in 1996, the Federal Communications Commission wanted NANPA turned over to a company that had no vested interest in telecom decisions. While the FCC established an advisory board to pick a

new administrator, Bellcore changed owners and was no longer saddled with a conflict of interest. Nevertheless, it had to compete against three other companies outside of the telecommunications industry, one of which was aircraft and defense contractor Lockheed and its Communications Industry Services division, which was awarded the business in 1997 by outbidding Center for Communications Management Information and Mitrotek Systems.

SPINOFF IN 1999

Lockheed soon developed a conflict of interest itself, however, when in August 1998 it proposed acquiring Comsat Corporation, a company involved in satellite communications. Mitrotek complained that Lockheed would no longer be impartial, since as a carrier Comsat would be turning to Communications Industry Services for phone numbers. Lockheed decided to divest the business, and in December 1998 the management of Communications Industry Services, headed by Jeffrey E. Ganek, formed a corporation and enlisted the backing of Warburg Pincus to buy the division from Lockheed Martin. Mitrotek continued to complain, noting that Warburg had investments in a number of telecom companies, including MCI WorldCom. The original ownership transfer plan was scrapped in July 1999, replaced by a proposal to form a new company called NeuStar Inc., the name a play on the word "neutral." It would be part owned by Lockheed, Warburg, management, and an irrevocable trust, which would hold a majority of the voting shares. In November 1999 the transfer was approved and completed and NeuStar became the new NANPA, with Ganek taking over as CEO and assuming the chairmanship and Foster becoming chief technology officer.

As NANPA, NeuStar had to contend with a more difficult landscape than had BellCore. In the wake of deregulation in the telecommunications field, there were thousands of companies competing, and NeuStar was responsible for maintaining a central database of telephone numbers and providing interoperability among a plethora of diverse service providers and their systems. There was also an escalating demand for local telephone numbers due to the increase in the amount of fax machines, cell phones, and Internet access lines in the 1990s. The result, according to industry jargon, was "number exhaustion." In the second half of the 1990s more than 100 new area codes were added to address the need, but there was not an endless supply and NeuStar had to husband them for as long as possible in order to prevent a costly upgrade in industry systems for as long as possible. Ultimately, it might become necessary to make the switch to an 11- or 12- digit number-

KEY DATES

1996: NeuStar's predecessor is formed as a Lockheed Martin division.
1999: NeuStar is spun off.
2001: The first Internet registry is launched.
2005: NeuStar is taken public.

ing system, but putting off that day as long as possible was a priority. Another factor causing number exhaustion was the decade-old practice of NANPA assigning phone numbers in lots of 10,000, regardless of need. It led to stockpiling, a situation that grew worse with the entry of so many new companies following deregulation. As part of an effort to develop new lines of business, NeuStar won contracts in more than a dozen states to manage telephone number pooling, a way to conserve numbers and stave off the need for new area codes.

NeuStar began the 2000s with three main business lines: NANPA, telephone number pooling, and local number portability administration. Whereas it may have been NeuStar's original business, local number portability was a growth field as people regularly changed service providers, for which NeuStar received a transaction fee, and wireless carriers moved to local number portability as well. As a result, even as the telecommunications industry suffered a difficult year in 2000, NeuStar continued to grow.

Foster soon realized that the clearinghouse functions NeuStar provided for telecommunications providers, and its technical capabilities, could also be applied to the Internet. In November 2000 NeuStar won a contract to provide registry services for the .biz domain name. The registry was launched in October 2001. Another opportunity the company pursued was to match telephone numbers with Internet addresses in a database, so that Internet services could be accessed from devices using telephone keypads limited to 12 numbers. The technology also had other potential applications including the improvement of VoIP technology that permitted telephone calls to be made over the Internet. In 2000 NeuStar was the first to demonstrate the efficacy of the ENUM protocol established by the Internet Engineering Task Force, a major force in the ongoing effort to engineer the development of the Internet. NeuStar then began long-term public trials of an ENUM system.

In June 2001 NeuStar had landed enough state number pooling contracts, more than 20, that it was awarded the FCC's National Pooling contract. Also in 2001, NeuStar launched its Customer Account Record Exchange (CARE), a clearinghouse that handled the exchange of records between local exchange carriers, as well as interexchange carriers. Service switching could be performed more efficiently and save carriers money.

NeuStar grew revenues to $74.2 million in 2001, and while the company lost $46.4 million it was moving closer to profitability. The company also secured $53 million in new capital from investors, including DB Capital Partners and ABS Capital Partners. In 2002 sales increased to $90.1 million and the net loss decreased to $38.3 million. In that year, NeuStar expanded its Internet business by launching a .us registry as well as the .cn and .tw registry gateways for China and Taiwan.

FIRST PROFIT IN 2003

NeuStar introduced a number of initiatives in 2003. It began offering local service request (LSR) and access service request (ASR) services, as well as adding number portability services to the wireless industry. It also opened a registry for the five-digit Common Short Codes used in text messaging by wireless devices. For the year, sales increased to $111.7 million and the company turned its first profit, nearly $14.5 million.

New service offerings continued in 2004. In February NeuStar launched the first convergence clearinghouse, providing services to help in the coordination between wireline, wireless, and cable company service providers, assisting in areas such as order and provisioning, routing, and billing services. NeuStar also began offering number portability for these communication companies. Later in 2004 Neustar launched an IP (Internet protocol) Traffic Exchange relying on ENUM technology to provide coordination services to companies providing IP-based products. Another major service addition was the introduction of the Identity Services Exchange, a system to use identity information of consumers in a secure way to allow wireline and wireless service providers to offer a host of new services, such as calendar sharing and online gaming. In 2004, NeuStar also began offering number portability services in Taiwan, and added non-English .biz domain names (starting with the German language). For the year, revenues jumped to $165 million and net income improved to $35.6 million.

In February 2005 NeuStar grew externally by acquiring Fiducianet, Inc., a provider of law enforcement compliance and fraud management services for wireline, wireless, and cable service providers. The additional service capabilities bolstered NeuStar as it prepared to go public and provide a payback to its investors. In June 2005 the company completed an initial public offering of stock, selling more than 31 million shares of Class A common stock at $22 per share. Another 20 million shares priced at $32.30 per share were sold in December. Because the shares of both offerings were sold by existing shareholders, NeuStar did not receive any of the proceeds, but it did gain stock that could be used in making acquisitions. The company used some of those shares to acquire Foretec Seminars Inc., a provider of secretarial services to the Internet Engineering Task Force.

NeuStar reported sales of $242.5 million in 2005, a significant increase over the prior year, and net income topped $51 million. The company continued to expand in 2006 on a number of fronts. It opened a registry for six-digit Common Short Codes, supplementing its already successful five-digit code registry, and later in the year added a content rating feature. NeuStar completed a significant acquisition in April 2006, paying more than $61 million for UltraDNS Corp., a leading provider of directory infrastructure services to Internet companies. Although in business for a decade, NeuStar remained little known by the general public, but it was steadily becoming an important player in the global communications industry.

Ed Dinger

PRINCIPAL SUBSIDIARIES

NeuLevel, Inc.

PRINCIPAL COMPETITORS

Boston Communications Group, Inc.; The Internet Corporation for Assigned Names and Numbers; Register. com, Inc.

FURTHER READING

Ganek, Jeffrey, "The Neutral Approach," *Telephony,* February 7, 2000.

Gruman, Galen, "InfoWorld CTO 25: Mark Foster," *InfoWorld,* June 5, 2006, p. 17.

Luxner, Larry, "A New Battlefield: Lockheed Martin Takes Over Contentious Numbering and Area Code System," *Telephony Online,* April 6, 1998.

Marcial, Gene G., "NeuStar Has Everybody's Number," *Business Week,* May 1, 2006, p. 104.

Marsan, Carolyn Duffy, "NeuStar Looks to Play Key Role in .BIZ Domains," *Network World,* June 18, 2001, p. 10.

———, "Q&A: NeuStar CEO Touts DNS, VoIP Plans," *Network World,* May 15, 2006, p. 31.

Romero, Simon, "Now You Need an Area Code Just to Call Your Neighbors," *New York Times,* May 7, 2001, p. A1.

Swibel, Matthew, "On Hold," *Forbes,* July 8, 2002, p. 150.

Pacific Ethanol, Inc.

5711 North West Avenue
Fresno, California 93711
U.S.A.
Telephone: (559) 435-1771
Fax: (559) 435-1478
Web site: http://www.pacificethanol.net

Public Company
Incorporated: 2003
Employees: 12
Sales: $87.6 million (2005)
Stock Exchanges: NASDAQ
Ticker Symbol: PEIX
NAIC: 325998 All Other Miscellaneous Chemical Product and Preparation Manufacturing; 311225 Fats and Oil Refining Blending

■■■

Pacific Ethanol, Inc., markets and distributes ethanol, the first step in the company's goal of becoming the leading ethanol producer and marketer in the western United States. The company is building its first ethanol production plant in Madera County, California, the first of five or more production facilities it intends to build. While construction is underway, Pacific Ethanol earns its living through a subsidiary, Kinergy Marketing, LLC, that operates as a marketer and distributor of ethanol, shipping ethanol made in the Midwest to customers in California, Arizona, Nevada, and Oregon. Pacific Ethanol anticipates opening five ethanol production plants by 2008. By 2010, the company hopes to produce 420 million gallons of ethanol annually.

BACKGROUND OF ETHANOL

Rising gasoline prices, federal and state legislation, and the growth of California's dairy industry all played a part in spurring Pacific Ethanol's formation, but central to the company's birth was the commitment of two individuals, Bill Jones and Neil Koehler. The entrepreneurs, one a Republican and the other a member of the Green Party, held a deep-seated belief in the commercial viability of ethanol. Of the two, Koehler assumed a more active role in the ethanol industry during the two decades leading up to Pacific Ethanol's formation, but Jones took the lead in cobbling together the assets that became Pacific Ethanol, a company poised to confirm the commercial value of ethanol in the early 21st century.

Ethyl alcohol, or ethanol, was enjoying renewed popularity when Jones formed Ethanol Pacific. A clear, colorless fuel extracted from the sugars found in grains and other crops, ethanol was the fuel of choice for lighting devices in the United States in the mid-19th century. Its popularity waned after the federal government levied a liquor tax to raise money for the Civil War, which prompted consumers to turn to less expensive alternatives such as kerosene. Automobile mogul Henry Ford sparked an ethanol revival when he designed the Model T to run on a mixture of gasoline and alcohol, but again federal legislation stifled the use of the fuel. Taxed during the Civil War because it was considered alcohol, ethanol received harsher treatment under Prohibition law, with sales of the fuel banned unless it was mixed with petroleum because of its classification as a liquor. Ethanol was used as a fuel again after the end of Prohibition in 1933, but its use only spiked when oil and other resources were scarce, notably during World War II.

It was ethanol's capability of serving as a total or partial replacement for gasoline that prompted the federal government to encourage its use in the wake of the Arab Oil Embargo of 1973. In response to the petroleum shortage, the U.S. Congress passed the Energy Tax Act of 1978, which exempted the four cents per gallon federal excise tax on gasoline if it was blended with at least 10 percent ethanol. The federal government's support of ethanol production, after a history of restricting the industry's development, sparked interest in the market, including the interest of Jones, who was residing in California at the time. A second-generation farmer and cattle rancher, Jones developed what he called a "destination ethanol" business plan that depended on obtaining corn from the Midwest, extracting ethanol from the corn, and selling a byproduct of the extraction process, wet distillers grain—one of the most nutrient-rich cattle feeds available—to dairy farms in central California. He chose not to execute his business plan, however, convinced that the timing was wrong to launch an ethanol production business in California. "When I looked at this opportunity," Jones reflected in a June 11, 2006, interview with the *Fresno Bee*, "we didn't have the cows out here to consume the byproduct, we didn't have the market [for ethanol], and we didn't have the distribution to move the product."

Shelving his immediate plans for starting an ethanol company, Jones continued working on his farm in Fresno County, but he hoped to one day revisit the idea of a destination ethanol business. During the two decades spanning his original interest in the industry and the formation of Pacific Ethanol, Jones divided his time between farming and cattle ranching and pursuing a political career. He was elected to the California As-

sembly in 1982, where he spent a dozen years, including two years as the body's Republican leader, before being elected as California's Secretary of State in 1994. Jones's political career, which also included failed campaigns for the Governor of California and the U.S. Senate, occupied his time until January 2003, when, as quoted in his interview with the *Fresno Bee*, "it looked...like the timing was very good" to enter the ethanol business. For Neil Koehler, proper timing was never an issue as it related to operating an ethanol business. "All I've done in my professional life is ethanol; it's something I saw out of college, and I've dedicated myself to it ever since," he said in his portion of the *Fresno Bee* interview. While Jones bided his time, Koehler jumped into the fray, cofounding Parallel Products, California's first ethanol production company, in 1984. Koehler sold Parallel Products in 1997, but he continued his involvement in the ethanol industry, founding an ethanol sales and distribution company, Kinergy Marketing, that eventually became Pacific Ethanol's financial backbone.

In the years leading up to the formation of Pacific Ethanol, the prospects for running an ethanol production business brightened considerably. Its use during gasoline shortages, notably during World War II and the early and mid-1970s, created surges in demand, but times of crises were not enough to sustain consistent business for ethanol producers. During the mid-1980s, for instance, crude oil and gasoline prices fell sharply, forcing 45 percent of the nation's ethanol producers to go out of business despite exceptionally low prices for corn and a federal subsidy of 60 cents per gallon.

As the years passed, however, another attribute of ethanol added to the commercial viability of producing the renewable fuel. Carbon monoxide emissions became an issue, and ethanol, as an additive to gasoline, worked as an oxygenate, increasing the amount of oxygen in the gasoline blend and improving its air-quality characteristics. State and federal authorities turned to oxygenated fuels as a way to combat smog, leading to the first use of ethanol for such purposes in 1988.

Legislation in succeeding years, including the passage of the Clean Air Act in 1992, mandated the use of oxygenated fuels in certain areas, but the market for oxygenates quickly was dominated by another smog-fighting gasoline additive, Methyl Tertiary Butyl Ether, or MTBE, derived from natural gas and petroleum. At the turn of the century, however, MTBE began to lose its grip on the market. In 1999, some states began to ban MTBE's use after it was discovered that the additive polluted groundwater and caused cancer in animals, prompting the Environmental Protection Agency (EPA) to recommend a national ban the following year.

As the outlook for MTBE soured, ethanol, includ-

<table>
<tr><td colspan="2">

KEY DATES

■

2003: Pacific Ethanol is founded in January.

2005: Kinergy Marketing LLC is acquired, giving Pacific Ethanol a source of revenue.

2006: Pacific Ethanol sells $145 million of stock, securing some of the money the company will need to construct ethanol production plants.

</td></tr>
</table>

ing a derivative of ethanol, Ethyl Tertiary Butyl Ether (ETBE), stood as the only other commercially viable way to make mandated oxygenated fuel. For Jones, who was waiting for the proper conditions to make a foray into ethanol production, the end of his second term as the Secretary of State of California in January 2003 seemed a perfect time to become an ethanol entrepreneur. MTBE was on the brink of being outlawed and, significantly, the dairy industry in central California, mainly centered in Tulare County, had grown substantially, providing a crucial element in the successful implementation of his destination ethanol business model.

PACIFIC ETHANOL TAKES SHAPE

For help in starting Pacific Ethanol, Jones turned to his son-in-law, Ryan Turner. Raised in Redondo Beach, California, Turner attended Stanford University, played football for the university's team, and, according to his June 11, 2006 interview with the *Fresno Bee,* "married into Fresno" after courting Jones's daughter Wendy. Once a member of the Jones family, Turner began working on the farm, starting out as manager of the tomato harvest before working his way up to general manager of the operation. When Pacific Ethanol was founded in January 2003, Turner assumed the post of chief operating officer and attended California State University's Fresno campus at night to earn his M.B.A. From the start, Jones and Turner set their sights on producing ethanol rather than merely distributing the fuel, seeking to earn the 15 percent to 25 percent profit margins commonly enjoyed by ethanol producers instead of subsisting solely on the 1.5 percent to 3 percent profit margins averaged by ethanol distributors. By late 2003, the pair had taken the first step towards production, acquiring a former Coast Grain plant in Madera County for $5.1 million. "What we're trying to take advantage of," Turner explained in a March 4, 2005 interview with the *Fresno Bee,* "is the intersection of the largest fuel market and the largest feed market in the country."

ACQUISITION OF KINERGY: 2005

Jones and Turner faced two major challenges as they went through the permitting process for the Madera plant. Their company needed capital to complete the construction of the Madera plant and the four other plants they hoped to build. Further, the Madera plant was not expected to be completed until late 2006, which left Pacific Ethanol without a source of revenue to sustain itself for at least three years. Jones and Turner chose to start out distributing ethanol, and the way they jumped into the distribution business was by acquiring Koehler's Kinergy Marketing, LLC. Pacific Ethanol completed the acquisition in March 2005, gaining a thriving business and the expertise of Koehler, who became Pacific Ethanol's president and chief executive officer. Kinergy, aided by federal and state clean air regulations requiring oxygenated fuels, recorded robust growth in the years leading up to its merger with Pacific Ethanol. The company generated $15 million in revenue in 2002, a total that leaped to $87.5 million in 2005. Without Kinergy's revenues for 2005, Pacific Ethanol would have recorded a paltry $15,907 in sales for the year.

The purchase of Kinergy coincided with the resolution of the other pressing issue facing the company's leadership. With ethanol production plants requiring roughly $50 million to build, the company needed a substantial infusion of capital to reach its goal of a total of five facilities. Conversion to public ownership offered the most expedient way to obtain capital, and Pacific Ethanol chose a route that quickened the process of going public. In March 2005, the company acquired a publicly traded, healthcare-services firm named Accessity Corp., completing the deal expressly to acquire a public entity. Accessity's lone operating company, Sentaur, was transferred to Accessity's chief executive officer, leaving Jones, Koehler, and Turner with a public shell that made Pacific Ethanol a public company. "We hoped it would be a little cheaper and little quicker," Koehler explained in a November 2005 interview with *Entrepreneur,* "but in hindsight it was exactly the right move. It made us one of the few pure-play ethanol stocks in the public markets."

As Pacific Ethanol faced the start of its life as an ethanol producer, the conditions to support its growth were ideal. California officially phased out the use of MTBE in January 2004, becoming one of 19 states to ban its use. Ethanol use exploded as a result, jumping from 100 million gallons in 2002 to 950 million gallons by 2005. Further, federal legislation was working in the company's favor, specifically the passage of the Energy Policy Act of 2005, which required nearly doubling the use of ethanol to 7.5 billion gallons by 2012. On the finance front, Pacific Ethanol's conversion to public ownership provided access to the capital it needed to build its portfolio of ethanol plants. In November 2005, Cascade Investment LLC, the investment vehicle owned by Microsoft Corporation's Bill Gates, invested $84 million in Pacific Ethanol. The infusion of cash was followed in May 2006 with a $145 million stock sale to institutional investors, which accelerated plans for constructing a second plant near Boardman, Oregon. As the company pressed forward with its plans to complete all five plants by 2008, the years ahead promised to see the demand for ethanol increase substantially, with Pacific Ethanol holding sway as one of the country's largest producers.

Jeffrey L. Covell

PRINCIPAL SUBSIDIARIES

Kinergy Marketing, LLC; Pacific Ethanol Madera, LLC.

PRINCIPAL COMPETITORS

Ag Processing Inc.; Archer Daniels Midland Company; Melrose Resources PLC.

FURTHER READING

Clough, Bethany, "Ethanol Firm Gets $145m Infusion," *Fresno Bee,* May 27, 2006.

————, "Pacific Ethanol Produces a New Crop of Millionaires," *Fresno Bee,* June 11, 2006.

Jones, Bill, "Renewable Fuels," *Research,* July 2005, p. 62.

Kasler, Dale, "Gates Buys into Fresno Ethanol Company," *Sacramento Bee,* November 16, 2005.

"Pacific Ethanol to Buy California Plant," *Feedstuffs,* August 15, 2005, p. 24.

Quick, Becky, "Pacific Ethanol," *America's Intelligence Wire,* March 28, 2006.

Schultz, E. J., "Pacific Ethanol Gets Boost from Merger with Florida Holding Company," *Fresno Bee,* March 4, 2005.

Worrell, David, "Fueling Growth," *Entrepreneur,* November 2005, p. 73.

Packeteer, Inc.

10201 North De Anza Boulevard
Cupertino, California 95014
U.S.A.
Telephone: (408) 873-4400
Toll Free: (800) 697-2253
Fax: (408) 873-4410
Web site: http://www.packeteer.com

Public Company
Incorporated: 1996
Employees: 304
Sales: $112.9 million (2005)
Stock Exchanges: NASDAQ
Ticker Symbol: PKTR
NAIC: 541512 Computer Systems Design Services; 511210 Software Publishers

■ ■ ■

Packeteer, Inc., is the worldwide leader in improving network performance, controlling 36 percent of the global market for devices that manage bandwidth, control data traffic, and prioritize web site access. The company sells its PacketShaper and related devices to approximately 7,000 customers, a customer base comprised of corporate clientele and Internet service providers. Packeteer sells its products through more than 500 distributors and sales offices worldwide.

ORIGINS

Packeteer was the response of a group of accomplished executives to the growing problem of congestion on the Internet. Although there were a number of principal investors in the venture, Steven J. Campbell figured as the dominant personality, spearheading the effort to develop technology that would help network managers control the use of bandwidth, a vital resource always in declining availability. Campbell earned undergraduate and graduate degrees in electrical engineering from Oregon State University and Santa Clara University, respectively, beginning his career at Intel Corporation in 1972. After a six-year stay at the semiconductor maker, Campbell spent five years at a telecommunications company named Rolm Communications before founding StrataCom, Inc., a network-switching equipment company, in 1986. Network appliance giant Cisco Systems, Inc., purchased StrataCom in 1996, freeing Campbell to pursue his next venture, Packeteer.

Packeteer was formed in January 1996, joining the Internet sector during its early years of development. The company received its seed funding from Campbell and another seasoned executive, Joseph A. Graziano. A certified public accountant, Graziano joined Apple Computer, Inc., in 1981, five years after the computer maker's founding and three years before the company recorded its first commercial success, the Apple Macintosh. During this critical period in Apple Computer's development, Graziano served as the company's chief financial officer, a post he would leave in 1985 to serve in the identical capacity for Sun Microsystems, Inc., before returning to Apple Computer as executive vice-president and chief financial officer between 1989 and 1995. Once the start-up funding was in place by February 1996, the company turned to developing technology to manage a web site's outbound

COMPANY PERSPECTIVES

Packeteer bridges the gap between critical business applications and IP networks with an "intelligent overlay" of key technologies for WAN application optimization. Building on an organization's existing infrastructure, Packeteer's scalable platform ensures optimal delivery and performance of networked applications by consolidating best of breed and field proven technologies. Packeteer delivers the ultimate in application performance and end user experience through the PacketShaper family of scalable appliances. Bridging business-critical activities and IP networks, Packeteer provides unmatched application monitoring, shaping, compression, acceleration and management of application traffic across all WAN links.

and inbound traffic, seeking to eliminate the stop-and-go transmissions and stuck server connections that plagued the Internet. Campbell, who had served as StrataCom's chief executive officer for the company's first six months of operation, assumed the same responsibilities at Packeteer during its first four months of existence before handing the reins of command to Craig W. Elliott. Campbell continued to serve as the company's chairman, a post he would occupy during Packeteer's first decade of business, while Graziano took a seat on Packeteer's board of directors.

Craig Elliott provided the leadership that helped Packeteer evolve from being a start-up without a product on market into a commercially active company, serving as the firm's chief executive officer and president during its first six years in business. Elliott earned an undergraduate degree in animal science from Iowa State University, but chose a career in an entirely different field, starting out as a salesman with Beacon Microcomputers. His big break came in 1984, when he became the top salesperson of the newly introduced Apple Macintosh, an achievement that earned him a new Porsche 944 and dinner with Apple Computer's cofounder, Steve Jobs. Elliott spent the next decade working for Apple Computer, serving in various executive positions related to marketing sales, and product development. When he joined Packeteer as its third employee in April 1996, he vacated his post as the international general manager of Apple Computer's Internet division.

Under Elliott's day-to-day supervision, work on the company's first product progressed at headquarters in Campbell, California, Packeteer's home base until it moved near Apple Computer's headquarters in Cupertino, California. Apple Computer became the first company to test Packeteer's flagship product, "Packet-Shaper," at a trade show in Las Vegas in the fall of 1996, the first round of testing before its commercial release. PacketShaper, a hardware and software device, enabled network managers to create and to enforce policies for assigning Internet and intranet access priorities, performing its tasks as it sat between the Internet access router and the web server. By the end of 1996, Packet-Shaper was being evaluated by Eagle River Interactive, a web site developer, and Concentric Network Corp., an Internet service provider, undergoing its last series of tests before being released on the market. The device began shipping in February 1997, registering particular success in Japan and Europe, a phenomenon anticipated by Elliott and his management team. In an August 11, 1997 interview with *Electronic News (1991),* Elliott explained the appeal of a traffic manager such as Packet-Shaper in international markets. "The need for bandwidth allocation and prioritization has become widespread," he said, "especially with the advent of 'push' applications that are flooding networks everywhere. But in Europe and Asia, where wide-area and Internet connections typically are much slower and much more expensive than in the United States, reducing 'world wide wait' is even more critical."

With a unique product to market, Packeteer set out to establish a lasting place for itself in the technology sector, targeting Internet service providers (ISPs) and corporate customers managing wide-area networks (WANs). The company's market presence would be built on the PacketShaper, which sold for $7,250 during its first year on the market, a device that was well received by industry experts. "They have a very important solution to a very pressing problem—the idea of managing bandwidth in the Internet," an analyst said in the August 11, 1997 issue of *Electronic News (1991).* "Given the desire of both organizations and carriers to try to leverage the Internet for commercial benefit, these sort of products are becoming increasingly important," the analyst continued. "The Internet is a fairly chaotic place to operate and without the sort of technology that allows you to control it, you are unlikely to leverage it to its full extent commercially."

PUBLIC DEBUT IN 1999

Despite the positive reaction from customers and pundits, the successful debut of PacketShaper did not eliminate the financial challenges facing Elliott and his management team. Years of annual losses loomed, making access to fresh supplies of capital a necessity to fund

KEY DATES

1996: Packeteer is incorporated.
1997: The company begins shipping its first product, PacketShaper.
1999: Packeteer completes its initial public offering of stock.
2000: The acquisition of Workfire Technologies speeds Packeteer's entry into the web acceleration market.
2002: Dave Côté is appointed president and chief executive officer.
2005: Sales eclipse the $100 million mark for the first time.

management's research and development and marketing programs. In the fall of 1997, the company secured a second round of financing led by a former StrataCom executive, William Stensrud, giving it an additional $4.5 million for a total of $10 million in funding. For its next infusion of capital, the company turned to Wall Street, completing its initial public offering (IPO) of stock in July 1999. Packeteer sold four million shares at $15 per share in its public debut, earning $54. 8 million to fund development and to help offset mounting losses. Not surprising for a start-up venture, Packeteer's losses exceeded sales during its first years in business. After incurring $1.2 million in losses in 1996 while it developed PacketShaper, the company posted a $5.9 million loss in 1997 on revenues of $1.4 million. The following year, sales increased to $7.2 million, but losses increased as well, swelling to $8.8 million. The pattern would continue as Packeteer entered the 21st century, putting mounting pressure on management to achieve profitability, particularly considering its status as a publicly traded company.

The increasing acceptance of PacketShaper offered encouragement to Elliott and his team that improved financial performance lay ahead. The device, bundled with software marketed as "PacketWise," was finding a receptive audience among corporate clientele and ISPs, winning the business of a diverse collection of businesses that included ExxonMobil, Liz Claiborne, Stanford University, and the U.K. Ministry of Defense, and service providers such as AT&T, Japan Telecom, and WorldCom. Hopes for profits also were buoyed by Packeteer's diversification, a move the company first made in 2000 when it entered the web acceleration market. The company unveiled the "AppCelera Internet Content Accelerator," a networking device for web site operators

that compressed pages and images, accelerating the delivery of web pages by an average of 35 percent to 50 percent for 56 kilobits-per-second Internet connections. The technology for AppCelera, which sold for $10,000, was obtained through Packeteer's acquisition in July 2000 of a Canadian firm named Workfire Technologies, a $90 million deal that increased the company's debt but one that gave it a broader position in the market.

With its sights set on turning a profit, Packeteer entered the 21st century confident that PacketShaper, AppCelera, and its growing roster of hardware and software solutions would become a powerful financial engine. After weathering the collapse of the technology sector during the first years of the decade, the company began to record consistent profits on a quarterly basis, a welcomed sign after it posted a staggering $71 million loss in 2001 on $46.6 million in revenue. The celebratory mood at the company's Cupertino headquarters was dampened, however, when Elliott was forced to resign his position in May 2002 because of a serious medical condition. Campbell and the rest of the board of directors immediately began searching for a replacement, taking several months before they settled on a candidate, Dave Côté. Appointed president and chief executive officer in October 2002, Côté joined Packeteer after spending five years as a marketing executive at Integrated Device Technology, Inc., a semiconductor manufacturer. Before working for Integrated Device, Côté distinguished himself as a marketer at SynOptics, Inc., where his 16-year tenure included the launch of a line of stackable hub products that became a financial mainstay for SynOptics. For Packeteer, which had developed a reputation in some circles for enjoying greater success in developing products than in marketing them, the arrival of a skilled marketer seemed an ideal addition to the company's executive team. Packeteer's need for a marketing guru was not lost on Côté, who referred to the challenge facing him in a June 3, 2003 interview with *Investor's Business Daily:* "It's really to hone our message, to build a consistent story about the value proposition Packeteer provides. What we do is unique, and that's good, but that means you have to educate the market."

FIRST PROFITS IN 2002

The beginning of Côté's tenure coincided with a milestone in Packeteer's history. In 2002, for the first time in its existence, the company posted a profit for a full year, recording $3.7 million in net income on $55 million in revenue. The financial success of 2002 set a precedent, ushering in a period of robust, consistent revenue and net income increases that thrust the company into an overwhelming lead in the WAN optimization market. Shortly after Côté took over day-to-day leadership of the company, it introduced "Packeteer," a device that represented more of a promotional tool than a technological advancement. Packeteer was a scaled-down version of PacketShaper, offering network monitoring only, one of many features included with PacketShaper. The device was part of the company's strategy to lure a customer with a less expensive product that would help educate the customer and, it was hoped, lead to a larger sale. "It all starts with knowing what's on the network," Packeteer's vice-president of worldwide marketing explained in a January 2003 interview with *Business Communications Review*. "If you can't see it, you can't control it, and if you don't understand how things are performing, how bandwidth is being consumed, it's really hard to even go about adding more bandwidth in today's market."

Packeteer's financial growth during the years leading up to its tenth anniversary put the company in a commanding lead in the WAN optimization market. After posting $3.7 million in net income in 2002, the company increased its profits in each of the succeeding years, recording totals of $11 million in 2003, $14.5 million in 2004, and $19.1 million in 2005. Revenues during the period more than doubled, swelling from $55 million to $112 million, which represented a 36 percent share of the global market. Projections for the future of the global WAN optimization market called for annual growth rates of nearly 19 percent until 2009, presenting Packeteer with significant opportunity as it pressed ahead and fought to maintain its lead in a fast-growing market.

Jeffrey L. Covell

PRINCIPAL SUBSIDIARIES

Packeteer Holdings, Inc.; Packeteer International Inc.; Packeteer Caymans (Cayman Islands); Packeteer Y.K. (Japan); Packeteer Asia Pacific Limited (Hong Kong); Packeteer Europe B.V. (Netherlands); Packeteer Technologies (Canada); Packeteer Australia Pty Limited (Australia); Packeteer UK Ltd. (United Kingdom); Packeteer GmbH (Germany); Packeteer SAS (France); Packeteer Aps (Denmark); Packeteer Singapore; Packeteer Korea; Packeteer Iberica (Spain); Packeteer Shanghai (China); Packeteer Beijing (China); Packeteer India; Packeteer Malaysia; Packeteer (Thailand) Ltd.; Packeteer Italy s.r.l.

PRINCIPAL COMPETITORS

Cisco Systems, Inc.; Expand Networks, Inc.; Juniper Networks, Inc.

FURTHER READING

Chapman, Eric, "PacketShaper Clears the Pipe," *PC Week*, September 8, 1997, p. 105.

Haber, Carol, "Big Guns Pour Bucks into Startup," *Electronic News (1991)*, August 11, 1997, p. 10.

Krapf, Eric, "Packeteer: Seek and Ye Shall Shape," *Business Communications Review*, January 2003, p. 64.

"Packeteer Inc.," *Venture Capital Journal*, September 1, 1999.

"Packeteer Puts Squeeze on Web Pages," *IPR Strategic Business Information Database*, September 18, 2000, p. 68.

"Packeteer Sets IPO," *Electronic News (1991)*, May 31, 1999, p. 22.

Reeves, Amy, "Packeteer Inc. Cupertino, California; For Maker of Tech Gear, the Sale's the Thing," *Investor's Business Daily*, June 3, 2003, p. A10.

Pakistan State Oil
Company Ltd.

P.O. Box 3983
PSO House
Khayaban-e-Iqbal, Clifton
Karachi,
Pakistan
Telephone: (+92 021) 920 3866/85
Fax: (+92 021) 920 3721
Web site: http://www.psopk.com

Public Company
Incorporated: 1976
Employees: 1,940
Sales: PKR 254 billion ($4.27 billion) (2005)
Stock Exchanges: Karachi
Ticker Symbol: PSOCL
NAIC: 424710 Petroleum Bulk Stations and Terminals;
324110 Petroleum Refineries; 324191 Petroleum
Lubricating Oil and Grease Manufacturing; 424720
Petroleum and Petroleum Products Merchant
Wholesalers (Except Bulk Stations and Terminals);
486910 Pipeline Transportation of Refined
Petroleum Products; 447110 Gasoline Stations with
Convenience Stores; 447190 Other Gasoline
Stations

∎ ∎ ∎

The Pakistani government's move toward a nationalized
oil sector began in 1974, with the passage of Petroleum
Products (Federal Control) Act. Under the new legislation, the government took control of the two Pakistani
oil companies, Pakistan National and Dawood

Petroleum. Following the takeover, Dawood was renamed
Premier Oil Company. Also in 1974, the government
founded a new agency, the Petroleum Storage Development Corporation (PSDC). That entity was subsequently
renamed Pakistan State Oil (PSO) in 1976.

Following the adoption of the new name, PSO then
took over both Pakistan National and Premier, in what
was then the largest ever merger to take place in Pakistan.
One month later, the government also took over the
operations of Esso in Pakistan, which were placed under
PSO. As such, PSO became the undisputed leader in
the Pakistani market.

Pakistan State Oil Company Limited is that
country's leading oil marketing and distribution
company. Formerly a state-run agency, PSO controls approximately 70 percent of Pakistan's total finished fuel
products market, and as much as 80 percent of the total
furnace oil market, the main fuel oil market in the
country. PSO also controls 60 percent of the country's
diesel fuel market. Despite a nationally operating
network of more than 3,750 PSO-branded filling stations, many of which include convenience stores, PSO's
share of the consumer gasoline and lubricants markets
has dropped to just 40 percent, in large part due to
Shell Pakistan's aggressive expansion of its own retail
network. Shell remained PSO's largest competitor in the
country, with a market share of more than 25 percent.
Other major competitors include Total and refinery
operators Attock and Caltex. PSO itself has engaged in a
strategy of developing vertically integrated operations,
including backing the construction of a new refinery.

COMPANY PERSPECTIVES

We are committed to leadership in the energy market through competitive advantage in providing the highest quality petroleum products and services to our customers.

The company also produces and markets a variety of products under its own brand, including motor oils and lubricants. PSO's sales extend to jet fuels and marine fuels, LPG, CNG, kerosene, and other petrochemicals. The company is also the leading supplier to Pakistan's utility and industrial sectors. Nonetheless, retail sales remain the company's largest revenue-generator, representing some 90 percent of the group's sales. These topped PKR 254 billion ($4.27 billion) in 2005, making PSO Pakistan's largest company and the flagship of the Pakistani government's privatization effort in the early 2000s. The Pakistani government continues to hold more than 25.5 percent of PSO's shares, while a group of institutional investors, primarily banks, control more than 37.5 percent of group stock. PSO has been hailed for its dramatic turnaround, from inefficient government-run organization to a streamlined, modern corporation, a transformation largely credited to the leadership of Managing Director Tariq Kirmani. PSO is listed on the Karachi Stock Exchange.

NATIONAL OIL COMPANY IN 1976

The first oil well in Pakistan appeared as early as 1886, at an oil seepage point in Kundal, in Punjab Province. Other exploration efforts followed through the end of the century; these efforts focused on seepage points, which typically yielded little oil, and only for short periods of time. A notable exception was a series of wells drilled in Khattan in 1885, which yielded some 25,000 barrels of oil over a seven-year period.

A better understanding of petroleum deposits and drilling technologies in the early 20th century led to the striking of the region's first major oil producing wells at Khaur-I, in the Potwar Basin, in 1915. This site also provided the first commercially available supplies of oil to the region. By then, exploration efforts, originally led by British-controlled government agencies, had been taken over by private companies, including Attock Oil, Burmah Oil Company, and others. For the most part,

however, the various exploration efforts failed to produce significant quantities of oil, with the exception of those of Attock Oil.

Pakistan's independence in 1947 prompted the need for the new country to develop its own oil industry and legislation governing the sector. By 1949, the Pakistani government had put into place a first set of regulations for the country's oil industry. These included a number of incentives that helped re-stimulate private sector investment in exploration, as well as oil imports, refining, and marketing. Further impetus to the country's oil market came after Pakistan Petroleum Ltd, a joint-venture between Burmah Oil and the Pakistani government, discovered a vast natural gas deposit in Sui, located in Balochistan, the country's largest province, in 1952. Following that discovery, the country also saw the installation of its first pipeline, connecting the Sui field to Karachi. A number of new players then entered the country. Most of the world's top oil companies set up exploration operations in Pakistan, while others, including Shell and Esso (Standard Oil) also began oil and gas marketing operations.

These sales were based on lucrative imports of refined oil products. Despite the discovery of additional natural gas deposits, developing the country's domestic oil reserves proved more difficult. In the meantime, demand for petroleum products had begun to rise rapidly in the country. If the country's oil needs remained below 0.5 million tons at the time of its independence, by the early 1960s, the country required some 3.5 million tons per year, with demand growing at more than 12 percent per year. The lack of other fuel resources in the country further forced the country to rely on imported oil. In the meantime, the lack of success in locating significant oil deposits—despite success in India, Afghanistan, and elsewhere in the region—had led to a new drop-off in exploration efforts.

The Pakistani government itself entered oil exploration in 1961, forming the Oil and Gas Development Corporation in cooperation with the Soviet Union. The Soviet government also offered to help the country build its own refinery, with the restriction that the country only use imported oil from the Soviet Union. The Pakistani government then approached Shell, Esso, and the other private sector companies operating in the country with a request that they join together in construction of a refinery in Karachi. Rather than allow the Pakistani government to take up the Soviets' offer, which would eliminate their profits from oil imports, the private sector companies agreed to build the refinery. Pakistani Oil Refinery, as the complex was called, was in operation by 1964.

1964: Pakistan National Oil (PNO) is founded as Pakistani-owned oil marketing counterpart to Esso and Shell Pakistan.

1967: Dawood Petroleum begins oil products marketing in Pakistan.

1974: New legislation nationalizes Pakistani retail oil sector; government takes over Dawood (renamed as Premier) and PNO; government forms Petroleum Storage Development Corporation (PSDC).

1976: PSDC is renamed Pakistan State Oil (PSO) and takes over Premier and PNO, then takes over Esso's operations in Pakistan.

1981: PSO begins marketing liquefied natural gas.

1994: Company forms joint venture with Hyundai Corporation to build oil refinery.

2001: PSO begins privatization process, listing shares on the Karachi stock exchange; begins modernization effort.

2005: Pakistani government reduces stake in PSO to 25.5 percent.

With the launch of production at the refinery, the Pakistani government provided the backing for the formation of a Pakistani oil company, Pakistan National Oil Company, founded as a private sector company in 1964. This company then entered the petroleum products marketing sector based on the production at the Karachi refinery. Another Pakistani player soon joined the market, when Dawood Petroleum Company Ltd. was established in 1967.

By then, however, the Pakistani government recognized the vulnerability of the country's oil market in regard to its dependence on foreign, privately held companies. During the war with India in 1965, the foreign oil companies were instructed by their parent companies to shut off oil imports to the country. Pakistani Oil Refinery found itself unable to procure crude oil—only Pakistan National Oil managed to continue to bring in crude oil to the country. In order to end the war, Pakistan signed the Tashkent Treaty with India; it has been suggested that the country had been forced to sign the treaty by the oil companies, which refused to resume imports otherwise.

A new war with India in 1971 gave rise to a new, repressive government led by Zulfikar Ali Bhutto. The new government now firmly established a policy of nationalization of the country's industries. The oil sector became a primary target for nationalization, all the more so because of the Arab Oil Crisis and the sudden skyrocketing of global oil prices.

The Pakistani government's move toward a nationalized oil sector began in 1974, with the passage of the Petroleum Products (Federal Control) Act. Under the new legislation, the government took control of the two Pakistani oil companies, Pakistan National and Dawood Petroleum. Following the takeover, Dawood was renamed as Premier Oil Company. Also in 1974, the government founded a new agency, the Petroleum Storage Development Corporation (PSDC). That entity was subsequently renamed Pakistan State Oil (PSO) in 1976.

Following the adoption of the new name, PSO then took over both Pakistan National and Premier, in what was then the largest ever merger to take place in Pakistan. One month later, the government also took over the operations of Esso in Pakistan, which were placed under PSO. As such, PSO became the undisputed leader in the Pakistani market.

TURNAROUND FOR A NEW CENTURY

Over the next decades, PSO's growth and development was hampered by the long period of political stability that gripped the country through the 1980s. The company's growth was further restricted by Pakistan's weak economy, which remained among the lowest in the world. In the meantime, PSO's status as a government-owned and run agency left it exposed to the same endemic corruption that hampered the government itself. The decision-making process was particularly affected by the company's state-owned status, and as often as not, major corporate decisions were taken for political reasons, rather than as part of a well-defined corporate strategy. As a result, the company's operations continued to be defined as "shabby" by many into the late 1990s, provoking a great deal of consumer discontent.

Nonetheless, PSO's position as the government-owned oil marketing operation enabled it to outpace the other players in the market, notably Shell Pakistan, Caltex, and Attock. Through the 1980s and into the 1990s, the company's control of the Pakistani retail fuel market reached as high as 85 percent. The company also developed a growing, if not altogether modern, retail network, with more than 2,000 pumps in operation at the beginning of the 1990s. The company had also launched sales of liquid natural gas in 1981, becoming the industry leader in that sector, and had also built up a fleet of more than 1,000 railway tankers, more than 2,500 tanker trucks, and total storage capacity of some

350,000 tons. By then, too, PSO's sales had topped PKR 40 million (approximately $700 million). Into the early 1990s, PSO adopted a strategy of vertical integration, and in 1994 launched a joint-venture with Hyundai Corporation to build a new refinery. The company also invested in its own blending plants and production facilities for a line of PSO-branded motor oils and related products.

During the 1990s, however, the Pakistani government launched a series of liberalization and deregulation efforts. PSO's competitors began gearing up for the liberalization of the oil market. In particular, the Pakistani government announced its intention to deregulate oil imports, which had been a PSO monopoly, a move carried out in 2000. As part of the preparation for the new era in the Pakistani oil market, Shell, Caltex, and the other private sector players, including new entrant Total, of France, began upgrading their retail networks. The more modern facilities of its competitors helped win over consumers, and PSO soon saw its market share go into decline.

PSO, in the meantime, became one of the flagships of the Pakistani government's new privatization program. The company was placed on the Karachi Stock Exchange, with a 17 percent free float, and a further 35 percent controlled by banks and other institutional investors. The Pakistani government initially maintained a 54 percent stake in the company. Through the mid-2000s, the government reduced its stake, down to 25.5 percent in 2005, with plans to complete the privatization in the second half of the decade.

During this time, PSO was placed under the management of Tariq Kirmani, brought in from outside the government. With some 30 years of experience in the oil sector, Kirmani led the company on a restructuring effort that transformed the company into a more competitive, modern group. As part of that effort, the company revamped its retail operations, upgrading its facilities and further expanding its network to more than 3,750 stations by 2006. A growing number of the group's retail shops also featured modern convenience stores. PSO also launched a system of pre-paid fuel cards, a public service in a country where cash was often in short supply. The company also inaugurated a fleet of mobile oil change vans, bringing that service to its customers' doorstep.

By the mid-2000s, PSO was being upheld as a case study in the redevelopment of a flagging, state-run company into a high-performance market-oriented competitor. The company had succeeded in containing the erosion of its market share, despite the strong efforts of its multinational competitors. In the meantime, PSO's sales had boomed, topping PKR 250 million ($4.6 billion) by the end of 2005. This placed PSO as Pakistan's leading corporation, and provided a strong platform for growth into the future.

M. L. Cohen

PRINCIPAL DIVISIONS

Audit Department; Aviation Marine; Corporate Planning; Imports; Industrial Consumer; IT Achievement; Lube Sales & Agency; Lubricants; Non Fuel Retail; Operations Department; Power Projects; Product Movement; Product Storage; PSO Cards; Quality Assurance; Retail Departments; Retail News; Security Services.

PRINCIPAL COMPETITORS

Shell Pakistan Limited; Total Parco Pakistan Limited; Attock Oil Company Limited; Caltex Oil Pakistan Limited.

FURTHER READING

Ansari, Jahangir N. W., "Pakistan State Oil Committed to Excellence," *Economic Review,* December 1995, p. 109.

Bokhari, Farhan, "War Clouds Pakistani Sell-off," *Asiamoney,* April 2003, p. S42.

"A New Vision, a New Spirit," *Euromoney,* September 2001, p. 255.

"Pakistan President Pervez Musharraf Has Approved the Privatization of the Country's Largest Oil Distribution Company," *Oil and Gas Journal,* February 4, 2002, p. 7.

"PSO Fulfills Economic Needs of Pakistan," *Economic Review,* October 1991, p. 95.

"Sell Off Plan Aims for $4bn," *MEED Middle East Economic Digest,* September 1, 2000, p. 18.

Zia, Shahid A., "Pakistan State Oil," *Nation,* February 7, 2005.

Pentair, Inc.

5500 Wayzata Boulevard, Suite 800
Golden Valley, Minnesota 55416-1259
U.S.A.
Telephone: (763) 545-1730
Toll Free: (800) 328-9626
Fax: (763) 656-5400
E-mail: pentairinfo@pentair.com
Web site: http://www.pentair.com

Public Company
Incorporated: 1966 as Pentair Industries Incorporated
Employees: 14,700
Sales: $2.95 billion (2005)
Stock Exchanges: New York
Ticker Symbol: PNR
NAIC: 332919 Other Metal Valve and Pipe Fitting Manufacturing; 333319 Other Commercial and Service Industry Machinery Manufacturing; 333991 Pump and Pumping Equipment Manufacturing; 334512 Automatic Environmental Control Manufacturing for Residential, Commercial, and Appliance Use; 334419 Other Electronic Component Manufacturing

■ ■ ■

Pentair, Inc. is a diversified manufacturer that divides its operations into two operating units: the Water Group and the Technical Products Group. The Water Group, which generates nearly three-quarters of the company's revenues, specializes in water pumps and systems, pool and spa equipment and accessories, and water filtration products. It operates 25 manufacturing plants in the United States and another 22 located in 11 other countries. The Technical Products Group produces electrical and electronic enclosures and thermal management products, operating 16 plants in the United States and six other countries. More than 82 percent of Pentair's revenues originate in the United States and Canada, while another 13 percent originates in Europe. After an abortive start as a maker of hot-air balloons, Pentair focused on the paper industry from the late 1960s into the 1980s when a diversification drive brought the firm into several new industries: tools, lubrication equipment, vehicle service equipment, water pumps, and enclosures. After the divestment of the cyclical paper business in 1995, Pentair went on an acquisition spree in the late 1990s and early 2000s that concentrated mainly on building up its water technology operations. The company further narrowed its focus by divesting its lubrication and service equipment businesses in 2001 and its tools operations in 2004.

BALLOONS, THEN CANOES, THEN PAPER

Pentair was founded in July 1966 in Arden Hills, Minnesota, as a five-person partnership with the purpose of manufacturing high-altitude research balloons (hence the name *pent air*). The company founders—three engineers, a foreman, and a salesman—were all former employees of a local branch of Litton Industries. The partners incorporated as Pentair Industries, Inc., in August and completed an initial public offering in January 1967 to sustain their seriously undercapitalized business. Further complicating matters at the time was the lagging market for inflatables. Following the guidance of cofounder and acting manager Murray Harpole, the company decided to purchase a neighboring, virtually bankrupt business for the small sum of $14,500. With some modest engineering applications this new venture, the American Thermo-Vac Company, promised at least one saleable product: vacuum-formed, high-quality canoes. By the fall of that year red-and-white Penta Craft canoes were being successfully manufactured and sold. However, both the canoe and inflatables businesses were fraught with problems; by the end of 1967, the company had few assets, zero profits, and little direction.

As Del Marth later reported, "By June, 1968, before Pentair was two years old, the corporate dream had become a nightmare. The company had no product to speak of, it was nearly out of money, one cofounder had died and three others had abandoned the venture." What sustained the company was Harpole's pledge to commit himself entirely to the business for at least five years and the entry of high-risk investor Ben Westby. Although Westby did not formally join the company until May 1968, he had been in close contact with Harpole for some time and had accompanied the founder on a business trip to Wisconsin, to consider the purchase of then debt-ridden, privately owned Peavey Paper Mills, Inc.

A manufacturer of absorbent tissue paper, Peavey was acquired in June and became Pentair's first wholly owned subsidiary. The deal that Westby and Harpole had arranged was important for two reasons. First was the low cost: $10,000 down, $20,000 due in one year, and an additional 5 percent of after-tax profits for the first five years. Second, and most important, was the paper mill's potential: annual sales of $4 million even in its current state of disrepair and mismanagement. Of course, with this ostensibly one-of-a-kind deal came a

particularly painful and hidden price: Peavey's $1.5 million in debt. Despite this preventable surprise, a lesson in cautious and thorough research, the acquisition was made profitable within three months due primarily to Harpole's management and labor-negotiation skills. The purchase also left Pentair free to divest itself of its first two, nonproducing businesses. Now a viable paper company with substantial assets, Pentair began attracting considerable notice from the investment community and, with both a three-year Procter & Gamble Company contract and a preliminary agreement to acquire a Trinidad paper mill, Pentair closed the year on a high note.

PAPER ACQUISITIONS

In 1969, because of Pentair's new status as an acquisition-oriented, international corporation, company stock soared from $2 per share to $25 and a 3-for-1 split was declared. Before the end of the year, however, operations at the Trinidad paper mill were halted because of social and political unrest in that country. The contract with Procter & Gamble to produce absorbent wadding for use in its disposable Pampers fueled the company's growth for the next few years. Still, Harpole and Westby considered Pentair's position tenuous. Ensuing diversifications into leather goods, meat-rendering, and computer software by and large failed to give the company the stability required for uninterrupted long-term growth. Then came the acquisitions of Niagara of Wisconsin Paper, Miami Paper, and Flambeau Paper Corporations, in 1972, 1974, and 1978, respectively. Initial annual sales for the three totaled some $90 million. Although Pentair had sold Peavey in 1976 because of plant and market limitations, it had established itself as a major supplier of coated groundwood, book grade, and commercial printing papers, producing some 350,000 tons annually.

Pentair signaled its arrival as a major corporation by declaring its first quarterly cash dividend in 1976. Four years earlier the company had sustained a debt-to-equity ratio of greater than 7-to-1, but by 1979, after paying down debt with paper profits, it had more than reversed these numbers and gained some valuable banking partners in the process.

The 1970s were also notable for several management developments, including the departure of Westby in 1974 and the hiring of D. Eugene Nugent, an ITT executive, as vice-president of operations in 1975. Harpole, singularly aware that tenacious and disciplined management had become the key to Pentair's success, handpicked Nugent as his likely successor. Both agreed that maintaining a lean corporate staff, which then numbered only ten despite more than 1,000 employees and widespread operations, would be a continuing goal

KEY DATES:

1966: Pentair is founded as a partnership, led by Murray Harpole and focused on making hot-air balloons.

1968: Company shifts focus to paper industry through purchase of Peavey Paper Mills, Inc.

1972: Niagara of Wisconsin Paper Corporation is acquired.

1981: Diversification drive begins with acquisition of portable power tool maker Porter-Cable Corporation.

1984: Woodworking equipment maker Delta International is acquired.

1986: Pentair purchases McNeil Corporation, maker of lubricating products, automotive service equipment, and water pumps.

1988: Electrical enclosures maker Federal-Hoffman Corporation is acquired.

1994: Schroff, maker of electronics enclosures, is acquired.

1995: Company divests all its paper operations.

1997: Pentair buys out General Signal Pump Group.

1998: Company is restructured into three operating groups: Professional Tools and Equipment; Water and Fluid Technologies; and Electrical and Electronic Enclosures.

1999: Pentair completes two major acquisitions: Essef Corporation and DeVilbiss Air Power Company.

2001: Lincoln Industrial automated lubrication and Century Manufacturing automotive service equipment businesses are divested.

2003: Company acquires Everpure, Inc.

2004: Pentair acquires WICOR Industries for $874.7 million; the Tools Group is sold to Black & Decker Corporation for $775 million.

for the company. (Management actually became proportionally leaner as employee levels continued to rise.) As Jeffrey Trachtenberg stated, reporting on Nugent's management style for *Forbes* in 1984, "Big corporation management stifles risk-taking at the operational level. Pentair's setup is that of a slim holding company running herd over a pack of operating subsidiaries.... It pushes decision-making out where it belongs, among the operating managers."

FOCUS ON DIVERSIFICATION

The "pack" Trachtenberg referred to was the early fruition of a carefully thought out strategy by Harpole and Nugent to diversify into industrial products manufactured primarily for industrial users. As early as 1978 the two had commenced their search for such businesses to offset the capital-intensive and cyclical paper group, which, led by Niagara, nonetheless represented a fairly consistent source of cash flow. According to Harpole, whose *Living the American Dream* recounts the corporation's history, he and Nugent "had to be successful on their first venture because the investment community was skeptical of our ability to expand beyond paper." The initial goal was for a company with annual sales of $25 to $100 million, preferably floundering and consequently available at a bargain price. Unfortunately, the realization of the goal was postponed, largely because of a time-consuming battle against a takeover threat by Steak and Ale founder Peter Wray, an attempt that ended only after Pentair agreed to a $4.5 million settlement in early 1981. By the middle of that year Pentair had researched and considered more than 125 manufacturers before deciding in October to acquire Porter-Cable Corporation (the portable power tools division of Rockwell International Corporation) of Jackson, Tennessee, for $16 million. Another debt-laden but revenue-heavy paper mill acquisition in 1983, as well as the 1984 purchase of Rockwell's woodworking machinery division renamed Delta International Machinery Corp., boosted earnings to $21 million on annual sales of $545 million, vaulting the paper-and-tools company into the *Fortune* 500 rankings. The company had flourished beyond anyone's expectations.

With Nugent established as CEO and Harpole imparting a legacy stretching well beyond his retirement as chairperson in 1986, Pentair fortified itself for years to come with additional forays into industrial products, beginning with the acquisition of McNeil Corporation and its two major divisions: Lincoln, a St. Louis-based maker of lubricating products and automotive service equipment, and F.E. Myers, an Ohio-based producer of water pumps. Lincoln was eventually split into Lincoln Automotive and Lincoln Industrial. The transaction expanded the industrial group considerably, so that it accounted for 32 percent of sales and 43 percent of operating profits. In 1988 Pentair completed one of its largest purchases, that of Federal-Hoffman Corporation (FC Holdings, Inc.), a Minnesota-based manufacturer of sports ammunition as well as metal and composite electrical enclosures. Divided into Federal Cartridge and Hoffman Engineering, FC Holdings commanded $300 million in annual sales, or nearly 40 percent of Pentair's total sales for the previous year. A decade after its stated objective to strengthen through diversification, the company had reduced its dependency on paper sales to just 30 percent while multiplying its total equity tenfold.

Late in 1985, the company announced an ambitious $400 million joint venture between Pentair and Minnesota Power of Duluth to form Lake Superior Paper Industries (LSPI). The venture was to be the company's first sustained "ground-floor-up" business, with the culmination of years of technical expertise, industry-specific knowledge, and financial clout put to the test. LSPI, the newest and most efficient paper mill in North America, began operations in late 1987 and, by March 1988, was producing supercalendered, publication-grade paper (SCA) for a highly competitive U.S. market. The difficulty of the market and the huge capital outlay worried investors from the start. Nevertheless, "while others either wrung their hands or snickered," wrote Alyssa Lappen for *Forbes,* "Nugent pressed ahead with a capital investment project that now claims customers ranging from Sears and J.C. Penney to *Rolling Stone.* Foreign competitors like West Germany's Haindl Papier and Feldmühle have been squeezed, while more customers line up for Pentair's paper every day." In its second year of operations, LSPI was operating at 87 percent of its 245,000-ton-per-year capacity and had positioned itself as the domestic leader of SCA. By the end of 1991, production had risen 93 percent and earnings had increased 58 percent over 1990 levels.

EXIT FROM PAPER, ACQUISITION SPREE

In August 1992 Winslow Buxton, former president of Niagara of Wisconsin, succeeded Nugent as CEO; Buxton was then named chairman as well in January 1993. One of his initial goals, inherited from Nugent, was to acquire another manufacturing company with sales from $200 to $500 million while elevating overall corporate sales to $2 billion by 1996. Sales growth in 1990 of only 1 percent and a fractional sales loss in 1991 made such an acquisition a near imperative, given Pentair's history. It would take until January 1994 for Buxton to find a suitable match. That month Pentair acquired Schroff GmbH from Fried. Krupp AG Hoesch-Krupp, the company's first acquisition in almost seven years. Schroff, a maker of electronics enclosures, fit well alongside the Hoffman electrical enclosures unit.

In September 1994 Pentair announced that it was examining the future of its paper businesses. The cyclical nature of the paper industry proved to be a drag on the company's stock. Pentair could no longer afford to ride the ups and downs of a noncore business (only 10 percent of 1994 operating income came from paper), and management decided to jettison all the paper operations. In April 1995 Pentair sold Cross Pointe Paper

Corporation to Noranda Forest, Inc., for $203.3 million. Two months later came the sale of Niagara of Wisconsin, the 50 percent interest in LSPI, and a 12 percent stake in Superior Recycled Fiber Industries to Consolidated Papers, Inc. for $115.6 million and the assumption of debt.

Freed to concentrate on its industrial manufacturing units, Pentair went on a targeted spending spree, in the process building upon its already strong businesses. The acquisitions also led to a January 1998 restructuring of Pentair units into three operating groups: Professional Tools and Equipment; Water and Fluid Technologies; and Electrical and Electronic Enclosures. The first of these operating groups developed around Lincoln Automotive, Delta International, and Porter-Cable. In November 1995 Biesemeyer Manufacturing Corporation, maker of precision woodworking accessories, was acquired and became a subsidiary of Delta. In June 1996 Pentair added a German manufacturer of portable power tools, Flex Elektrowerkzeuge GmbH, which became part of Porter-Cable. Pentair acquired another manufacturer of vehicle service equipment, Century Manufacturing Company, in November 1996. Subsequently added to Century were P&F Technologies Ltd., a manufacturer of automotive refrigerant recycling systems, in July 1997; and T-Tech Industries, specializing in automotive transmission fluid exchanger systems, in April 1998.

The Water and Fluid Technologies group developed around Lincoln Industrial and F.E. Myers. Pentair paid $130 million for Fleck Controls, Inc. in October 1995, gaining a leading maker of control valves for water systems. Pentair bought reciprocating pump maker Aplex Industries, Inc., in January 1996 and made it a subsidiary of F.E. Myers. In December of that year, Italian water conditioning control equipment manufacturer SIATA S.p.A. was acquired and became part of Fleck Controls. In August 1997 Pentair spent $200 million to acquire General Signal Pump Group, a maker of fluid handling products and systems. This business was subsequently combined with F.E. Myers to form the Pentair Pump Group. Also, in January 1998 Pentair purchased OR-SCO, Inc., producer of precision oil dispensing systems. ORSCO became a wholly owned subsidiary of Lincoln Industrial.

Pentair's Electrical and Electronic Enclosures group centered around Hoffman Enclosures Inc. and Schroff Inc. Growth for this unit mainly came in Europe, where Schroff was the leader in electronic enclosures. Pentair bought Transrack S.A. of France in January 1997 and Walker Dickson Group Limited of Scotland in October 1998. Earlier in 1998 the company had attempted to acquire electronics enclosure maker VERO Group plc of

Southampton, England, but was outbid by Applied Power, Inc., of Butler, Wisconsin.

While building up these three core areas, Pentair also made one other significant divestment of a peripheral business, selling Federal Cartridge to Blount International, Inc., for $112 million in October 1997. Looking to increase profitability, Pentair announced in June 1998 that it had launched an effort to cut costs by $60 million over a two-year period by centralizing its purchasing and streamlining some of its administrative functions. A second cost-cutting effort launched in April 1999 involved job cuts totaling 700, a little less than 7 percent of the total workforce, the consolidation of certain operations, and the outsourcing of some manufacturing. This restructuring, for which Pentair incurred a pretax charge of $38 million, aimed to generate $30 million in annual cost savings by 2001.

After the April 1999 purchase of WEB Tool & Manufacturing Inc., a Chicago-based producer of custom electronic enclosures for computer makers, Pentair ended the 1990s with its two largest acquisitions yet. In August 1999 the company purchased Essef Corporation of Chardon, Ohio, for $310 million in cash and the assumption of approximately $120 million in debt. Essef specialized in swimming pool and spa equipment and water pumps, storage tanks, and filtering equipment. Pentair also bolstered its tools segment through the acquisition of DeVilbiss Air Power Company in September 1999 for about $460 million in cash. Based in Jackson, Tennessee, DeVilbiss was a manufacturer of air compressors, pressure washers, and generators. These latest deals pushed Pentair's revenues for 1999 over $2 billion for the first time, to $2.37 billion. In December 1999 Randall Hogan was promoted to president and chief operating officer. Before joining the company in March 1998 as executive vice-president and president of the enclosures group, Hogan had been an executive at two industrial giants, United Technologies Corporation and General Electric Company.

WATER BUSINESS TO THE FORE

The 2000s got off to a rough start for Pentair as part of the 1999 restructuring went horribly wrong. Managers botched a plan to consolidate the operations of Delta and Porter-Cable and build a new distribution center in Jackson, Tennessee, to handle both lines, leading to a spate of problems, including incorrect orders, late shipments, and a huge inventory buildup. Hogan cleaned house, bringing into Jackson an entirely new management team to straighten out the mess. The operational difficulties in the tools group, which led to a $30 million working capital charge, coupled with $24.8 million in pretax restructuring charges, a $24.7 million loss

from discontinued operations, and the effects of the general economic downturn that began late in the year, resulted in Pentair's net income for 2000 being cut in half, from $103.3 million to $55.9 million. The discontinued operations were the Lincoln Industrial automated lubrication unit and the Century Manufacturing automotive service equipment business, both of which were divested in 2001.

At the beginning of 2001, Buxton retired from his position as CEO, having shepherded the company through an eight-year period in which revenues grew from $800 million to nearly $3 billion, and earnings quadrupled. Hogan became Pentair's fourth CEO and took over the chairmanship as well in April 2002, again succeeding Buxton. Hogan's first year as CEO was a rough one as the weak economy hit the company's enclosures business particularly hard, prompting a restructuring that reduced the unit's capacity by 20 percent and its headcount by 25 percent. A pretax restructuring charge of $40.1 million and a pretax loss of $36.3 million on the sale of the Lincoln and Century businesses were major factors in a further reduction in profits for 2001 to $32.9 million.

A strong turnaround in 2002, when net income jumped to $129.9 million, signaled the beginning of another acquisitions spree, this one focused on Pentair's operations in the water technologies industry, which company officials viewed as a fast-growing and lucrative opportunity. Three small companies were acquired between September 2002 and February 2003: Plymouth Products, Inc., a maker of water filtration products based in Sheboygan, Wisconsin; Letro Products, Inc., a Redding, California, producer of swimming pool accessories; and a Fort Myers, Florida-based manufacturer of swimming pool heat pumps, HydroTemp Manufacturing Co., Inc. Then in December 2003 Pentair spent $215 million for Northbrook, Illinois-based Everpure, Inc., a provider of water filtration products for the foodservice, vending, residential, recreational vehicle, marine, and aviation markets. By this time, revenues for Pentair's water business had reached $1 billion and nearly equaled that of the tools business.

The year 2004 marked another turning point in Pentair's history. In July the company completed its largest acquisition yet, the purchase of WICOR Industries from Milwaukee-based Wisconsin Energy Corporation for $874.7 million. WICOR, which had annual revenues of $750 million, 24 global locations, and 3,500 employees, manufactured water system, filtration, and pool equipment products under the Sta-Rite, SHURflo, and Hypro brands. To help fund this major acquisition, Pentair elected to divest its Tools Group, which was struggling in the face of fierce competition.

The Tools Group was sold to Black & Decker Corporation for $775 million in October 2004.

By 2005 Pentair had created a $2 billion business in the water industry through a dozen acquisitions. The water business accounted for nearly three-quarters of total revenues. Pentair's only other business, its enclosures unit, which was generating more than $800 million in revenues, was far from being neglected despite its much smaller size. In December 2005 Pentair paid APW, Ltd., $140 million for its McLean Thermal Management, Aspen Motion Technologies, and Electronic Solutions businesses. The acquired units specialized in thermal management products for the telecommunications, data communication, medical, and security markets. This broadening of the enclosures unit prompted its adoption of a new name, the Technical Products Group, in early 2006. Going forward, Pentair was likely to continue pursuing both organic and acquisition-based growth and was also seeking to boost its international sales, with Asia and Eastern Europe identified as the best regions for growth. Pentair, which generated less than 20 percent of its sales outside North America in 2005, aimed to boost that percentage to 40 percent by 2009.

Jay P. Pederson
Updated, David E. Salamie

PRINCIPAL SUBSIDIARIES

Aplex Industries, Inc.; Aspen Motion Technologies; Axholme Resources Limited (U.K.); Compool Inc.; Davies Pumps & Co. Limited (New Zealand); Electronic Enclosures, Inc.; EuroPentair GmbH (Germany); Everpure, LLC; Fibredyne, LLC; Fleck Controls, Inc.; Hoffman Enclosures Inc.; Hypro, LLC; McLean Midwest Corporation; National Pool Tile Group, Inc.; Nocchi Pompes Europe S.a.r.l. (France); Onga (NZ) Limited; Onga Pump Shop Pty. Ltd. (Australia); Optima Enclosures Limited (U.K.); Pentair Canada, Inc.; Pentair Electronic Packaging Company; Pentair Enclosures Group, Inc.; Pentair Filtration, Inc.; Pentair France SARL; Pentair Pacific Rim (Water) Limited (Hong Kong); Pentair Pacific Rim, Ltd. (Hong Kong); Pentair Poland; Pentair Pump Group Inc.; Pentair Pumps S.p.A. (Italy); Pentair Qingdao Enclosure Company Ltd. (China); Pentair Taunus Electrometalurgica Ltda (Brazil); Pentair U.K. Ltd.; Pentair UK Group Limited; Pentair Water (Suzhou) Company Ltd. (China); Pentair Water Australia Pty Ltd; Pentair Water Belgium NV; Pentair Water Filtration France SAS; Pentair Water Filtration UK Limited; Pentair Water France SAS; Pentair Water Germany GmbH; Pentair Water Group, Inc.; Pentair Water India Private Limited; Pentair Water Italy S.r.l; Pentair Water New Zealand Limited; Pentair Water Pool and Spa, Inc.; Pentair Water South Africa (Proprietary) Limited; Pentair Water Spain, SL; Pentair Water Taiwan Co., Ltd.; Pentair Water Treatment Company; Pentair Water Treatment India Private Limited; Pentair Water, LLC; Pentair Water-Mexico S. de R.L. de C.V.; Porter-Cable de Mexico S.A. de C.V.; Schroff GmbH (Germany); Schroff Inc.; Seneca Enterprises Co.; SHURflo Limited (U.K.); SHURflo, LLC; Sta-Rite Industries, LLC; Structural Iberica (Spain); Webster Electric Company, LLC; WICOR Canada Company; WICOR Global Corp.; WICOR Industries (Australia) Pty. Ltd.

PRINCIPAL OPERATING UNITS

Water Group; Technical Products Group.

PRINCIPAL COMPETITORS

AstralPool; CUNO Incorporated; Ebara Corporation; EcoWater Systems LLC; Flexcon Industries, Inc.; Flowserve Corporation; Franklin Electric Co., Inc.; GE Water and Process Technologies; The Gorman-Rupp Company; Grundfos A/S; Hayward Industries, Inc.; ITT Industries, Inc.; Jandy Pool Products, Inc.; Pall Corporation; Raypak; Wayne Pumps; Groupe Zodiac; Cooper B-Line, Inc.; Elma Electronic AG; Hammond Manufacturing Company Limited; Knürr AG; Rittal GmbH & Co. KG; Saginaw Control & Engineering; Sanmina-SCI Corporation; Hubbell Incorporated; Pfannenberg Inc.

FURTHER READING

Beal, Dave, "Paperless Pentair Extends Its Reach," *St. Paul Pioneer Press,* February 11, 1996.

Black, Sam, "Pentair Pool Unit Makes Splash," *Minneapolis/St. Paul Business Journal,* July 12, 2002, p. 3.

———, "Pentair's Water Chief Shopping for Growth," *Minneapolis/St. Paul Business Journal,* February 18, 2005.

Calian, Sara, "Pentair, After Switching Businesses, Is Often Ignored, but Finds Some Fans," *Wall Street Journal,* May 17, 1993, p. C6.

Carey, Susan, "Pentair to Acquire Wicor, Expanding Its Water Business," *Wall Street Journal,* February 4, 2004, p. A8.

Carideo, Anthony, "Many Are Expecting a Turnaround in '92," *Minneapolis Star Tribune,* August 26, 1991, p. 1D.

DePass, Dee, "Making a Splash: Recent Water-Technology Acquisitions in Minnesota Have Created a $3 Billion Industry Centered in the State," *Minneapolis Star Tribune,* December 5, 2005, p. 1D.

———, "Pentair to Buy Water Business; Also Will Sell Tools Unit, Its Largest Group," *Minneapolis Star Tribune,* February

4, 2004, p. 1D.

Drickhamer, David, "A Cool Clear Vision," *Industry Week,* September 2004, p. 20.

Fraser, Jill Andresky, "The Five Rules of Debt," *Corporate Finance,* December 10, 1991.

Harpole, Murray J., *Living the American Dream: Pentair, Inc.—The First Twenty-Five Years,* St. Paul, Minn.: St. Thomas Technology Press, 1992, 252 p.

Hoonsbeen, Mark, "Paperless Tiger," *Twin Cities Business Monthly,* April 1996.

Jaffe, Thomas, "Paper Profits," *Forbes,* August 25, 1986, p. 162.

Lappen, Alyssa A., "Gene's Dream," *Forbes,* May 30, 1988, pp. 212+.

Marth, Del, "Friendly Takeovers," *Nation's Business,* May 1986.

Mullins, Robert, "Pentair Aims to Grow Fleck Controls After Acquisition," *Business Journal—Milwaukee,* November 11, 1995, p. 26.

"Paper Losses Mean a Real Income Drop for Pentair," *Minneapolis Star Tribune,* February 5, 1991.

"Pentair Agrees to Buy Anoka Holding Firm," *Minneapolis Star Tribune,* November 15, 1988.

Peterson, Susan E., "Pentair Is Not Done Buying," *Minneapolis Star Tribune,* August 14, 1999, p. 1D.

———, "Pentair on the Prowl: The Conglomerate Has Been Seeking a Major Acquisition for More Than a Year," *Minneapolis Star Tribune,* June 20, 1992.

———, "Pentair President to Succeed Buxton As Company's CEO," *Minneapolis Star Tribune,* November 2, 2000, p. 1D.

———, "Pentair's '91 Revenues Dip, but St. Paul Company Reports a 28.2 Percent Increase in Net Income," *Minneapolis Star Tribune,* January 31, 1992, p. 1D.

———, "Pentair Will Acquire Ohio Company in Deal Worth More Than $400 Million," *Minneapolis Star Tribune,* May 1, 1999, p. 3D.

Siekman, Philip, "Pentair Fixes Its Own Mess," *Fortune* (Industrial Management and Technology section), September 30, 2002, pp. 156C+.

Sikora, Marty, "Pentair's Persistent Demand for Value," *Mergers & Acquisitions,* July/August 1995, p. 48.

Trachtenberg, Jeffrey A., "It's Not Glamorous, but It Works," *Forbes,* May 21, 1984, p. 180.

"Turning Problems into Profits: Pentair's Specialty Is Buying Paper Mills Nobody Wants," *Financial World,* October 15, 1979, pp. 134+.

Werner, Larry, "Pentair Acquires Filtration Firm," *Minneapolis Star Tribune,* November 19, 2003, p. 1D.

Youngblood, Dick, "Pentair Transforms Itself Once More," *Minneapolis Star Tribune,* September 18, 1995, p. 2D.

The Pep Boys—Manny, Moe & Jack

3111 West Allegheny Avenue
Philadelphia, Pennsylvania 19132
U.S.A.
Telephone: (215) 430-9000
Toll Free: (800) 737-2697
Fax: (215) 227-7513
Web site: http://www.pepboys.com

Public Company
Incorporated: 1925 as Pep Auto Supply Co.
Employees: 19,000
Sales: $2.2 billion (2005)
Stock Exchanges: New York
Ticker Symbol: PBY
NAIC: 441310 Automotive Parts and Accessories Stores;
     811111 General Automotive Repair

■ ■ ■

The Pep Boys—Manny, Moe & Jack, operating in the U.S. automotive aftermarket, distinguishes itself from competitors by size and service. The typical Pep Boys supercenter's 18,200 square feet of space allows for an extensive selection of products; 12 service bays accommodate preventive maintenance and repair. Pep Boys, with nearly 600 stores in 36 states and Puerto Rico, caters to all four segments of the automotive aftermarket that it identifies as: "do-it-yourself," "buy-for-resale" (sales to professional mechanics and garages), "do-it-for-me" (the service side), and replacement tires. Advertised as "the three best friends your car ever had," the original Pep Boys launched their first auto parts store just as the automobile was coming of age. Things looked less friendly a half decade into the 21st century when losses prompted the company to consider putting itself up for sale.

LORE-FILLED START

Pep Boys was founded by Emanuel (Manny) Rosenfeld, Maurice (Moe) Strauss, Moe Radavitz, and W. Graham (Jack) Jackson, Philadelphians who met and became friends during their World War I stint in the U.S. Navy. In 1921, less than 15 years after mass production came to the auto industry, the four war buddies put up $200 each to open an auto supplies store in their hometown. Strauss, who had already made two unsuccessful attempts at entrepreneurship, started out as a silent partner, since he was employed at a competing store and was not ready to give up the steady income.

The partners rented a small storefront in Philadelphia, so small that only the shortest of names would fit on its marquee. Corporate folklore tells of a brainstorming session that adopted the "Pep" from Pep Valve Grinding Compound, one of the shop's first product lines. Pep Auto Supply fit neatly above the shop's front door, but there is more to the chain's christening. The tale goes on to tell of a street cop who, upon issuing equipment citations, would recommend that the motorists go to the "boys" at Pep for replacement parts. The three Pep Boys who remained after Moe Radavitz cashed out in the early 1920s tacked their own names on in 1923.

The corporate caricatures that would later become famous throughout the country were commissioned shortly thereafter and drawn by Harry Moskovitch. Manny, a reformed cigar smoker with a Charlie Chaplin mustache, was on the left. Moe, who would be known as "the father of the automotive aftermarket," was in the middle. Jack's grinning caricature made a brief appearance before being replaced with that of Moe's brother, Isaac (Izzy) Strauss, on the right. (The company name stayed the same despite the personnel changes—"Manny, Moe and Izzy" just did not sound right.) As the chain grew, the Pep Boys were rendered in cotton on T-shirts, in ink on match books, and in cement as statues in front of stores. The bizarre but distinctive trademark was later joked about in Johnny Carson's *Tonight Show* monologue, parodied on *Saturday Night Live,* and came to life in Claymation for late 1980s television ads.

In the late 1920s, Manny Rosenfeld brought his brother, Murray, into the business and Izzy Strauss broke away to start his own automotive chain. The sometimes convoluted family ties at Pep Boys remained strong through the 1980s, and the Strauss and Rosenfeld families controlled one-fifth of the chain's stock into the early 1990s.

EXPANDING INTO CALIFORNIA; CONSERVATIVE MANAGEMENT

By 1928, Pep Boys had a dozen stores in the Philadelphia area, and Strauss began to feel the pull of the burgeoning California market. He had lived briefly in the state in the early 1920s, when he became convinced that it was an ideal location for an automotive retail business. In 1932, he sent Murray Rosenfeld, called "perhaps the most astute merchandiser of the Philadelphia group" by *Aftermarket Business* in 1991, out to the West Coast to launch what was commonly known as Pep Boys West. The first two California stores were opened in 1933 in Los Angeles. By that time, the chain had 40 Philadelphia outlets.

Although the founders had planned to operate both segments of the business in concert, the physical distance between them soon forced the division of primary merchandising functions. For example, intense competi-

tion compelled Pep Boys West to expand the size of, and selection at, those stores, whereas East Coast outlets concentrated more on service. Manny Rosenfeld stayed in Philadelphia, his brother Murray ran the Los Angeles operation, and Moe Strauss commuted between the two.

During World War II, automotive production was curtailed while car companies focused on war production, and "Murray the merchandiser" stocked Pep Boys West shelves with nonautomotive products such as work clothes, bicycles, and lawn and garden equipment. The West Coast division also experimented with wholesaling and even exporting.

When the retailer went public in 1946, Manny Rosenfeld was named president and Moe Strauss was elected chairman of the board. For the next three decades, the company grew relatively slowly under what was later interpreted as a preponderance of caution. The company insisted on owning, rather than leasing, its stores, and doggedly avoided debt. Under the direction of Moe Strauss, who assumed the additional responsibilities of president in 1960 after Manny Rosenfeld's death, the chain grew by only two new stores over the 20-year period from 1964 to 1984. The fiscally conservative Strauss occupied both posts until 1973, when he relinquished the title of president to son Benjamin; however, he remained chairman through 1977. He was still a member of the board of directors at his death in 1982, over six decades after he helped found the business.

RAPID GROWTH AND MODERNIZATION UNDER NEW MANAGEMENT

Ben Strauss advanced to chairman and CEO that year, and Morton (Bud) Krause, son-in-law of Moe Strauss, was named president. When Krause took an early retirement in 1984 at the age of 54, Ben Strauss shouldered the responsibilities of all three offices. In 1986, Strauss called on Mitchell Leibovitz to become Pep Boys' first president from outside the founding families. Leibovitz had joined the company at the age of 33 in 1978 as controller and was promoted to chief financial officer within a year. He had worked as a teacher and coach before earning an M.B.A. from Temple University by going to night classes. Leibovitz caught Ben Strauss's attention while employed as a CPA for the accounting firm that audited Pep Boys' books. From 1979 to 1984, Leibovitz was in charge of Pep Boys' eastern operations. He closed down 32 "small and stodgy" stores, then opened 60 stores in the ensuing two years. The East Coast expansion was financed with an offering of $50 million in convertible debentures (bonds that can be converted to stock), a debt Moe Strauss would never have taken on.

KEY DATES

1921: Four World War I buddies open an auto supplies store in Philadelphia called Pep Auto Supply, soon renamed Pep Boys.

1923: Official name of business becomes The Pep Boys—Manny, Moe & Jack.

1933: First two California stores are opened in Los Angeles.

1946: Company goes public.

1986: Mitchell Leibovitz becomes the first company president from outside the founding families; the chain includes 159 stores.

1991: Chain has grown to 337 units in 17 states; sales reach $1 billion.

1993: All the company's technicians and mechanics are placed on commission.

1995: A new parts-only store format, PartsUSA, is launched.

1997: PartsUSA outlets are renamed Pep Boys Express; revenues reach $2 billion.

1998: Company sells 100 of its Express outlets to AutoZone and closes an additional nine.

2006: Following several years of roller-coaster earnings, Pep Boys considers its options.

By 1986, when Leibovitz assumed the presidency, Pep Boys was the second largest chain in the highly fragmented, $100 billion automotive aftermarket industry, after Western Auto Supply Co. Its earnings had increased 18 percent annually from 1982 to 1986, but the new leader had even bigger plans for the retailer. As president, Leibovitz mapped out and executed a five-year plan to consolidate Pep Boys' headquarters and simultaneously expand its geographic reach, in the hopes of its becoming the Home Depot of the retail automotive aftermarket industry. In fact, Leibovitz enjoyed the counsel of Bernie Marcus, the executive who catapulted Home Depot to the upper echelon of the do-it-yourself home repair market. Leibovitz recognized the industry-wide changes that could either launch Pep Boys to the top of the heap or see it acquired by a competitor by the end of the century.

During the 1980s, the traditionally fragmented retail automotive aftermarket industry became more competitive as larger chains began to emerge. Many neighborhood service garages were being transformed into convenience stores with gas stations, and some of the larger chains that had provided limited service, such as

J.C. Penney and Kmart, also started phasing out auto repairs. All the while, cars were growing increasingly complex and difficult for non-pros to fix.

In the face of these market shifts, Leibovitz set out a five-year plan for Pep Boys that encompassed six goals: store expansion, a refined merchandise mix, increased warehousing and distribution capacity, improved promotion of the service operations, modernization of systems support, and consolidation of the headquarters in Philadelphia. From February 1986 to February 1991, Pep Boys invested $477 million in the plan, almost as much as 1986's sales of $486 million.

During that period, the number of Pep Boys stores doubled to 337, the number of states with Pep Boys locations reached 17, and product offerings nearly tripled from 9,000 items to 24,000. Individual locations were expanded into a "superstore" or "warehouse" format, with an average size of 23,000 square feet, and the company launched an "everyday low price" strategy. These larger stores also featured an increased number of service bays, a fairly unique feature in the industry, and services offered were expanded. Unlike many of its competitors, which would only install tires and batteries (if anything), Pep Boys' mechanics would perform practically any automotive service except body work and engine replacement. Pep Boys' new computerized merchandising and inventory control helped stores tailor their offerings to the local market. For example, rural stores might carry more truck parts, whereas urban stores might stock more foreign car parts. Weekends were added to the retailer's schedule, and hours were extended to 9 p.m. on weeknights.

To tout the service bays and increase emphasis on national brands, Leibovitz raised Pep Boys' advertising budget and began to divert funds from traditional, full-page newspaper ads to direct mail, catalogs, and electronic media. He also began phasing the Pep Boys caricature out of advertising and promotional material in an effort to modernize the company's image, even though "the boys" had ranked as one of the automotive aftermarket's five most recognized corporate symbols.

In 1991, as the company concluded its five-year plan and celebrated its 70th anniversary, it also topped $1 billion in annual sales, added eight Sunbelt states to its geographic reach, and more than doubled corporate employment from 5,500 to 14,000. Leibovitz advanced to Pep Boys' chief executive office and the company was added to Standard & Poor's 500 Index in 1990. Although the young leader modestly deflected praise of his transformation of Pep Boys to the management team he had assembled, analysts gave him the lion's share of the credit for modernizing the chain.

Pep Boys is considered a noncyclical business, but its massive expenditures and assumption of debt combined with an early 1990s recession to depress profit growth. Net income declined from $42 million in 1989 to $32 million in 1990, then increased incrementally in 1991 and 1992. Pep Boys was able to begin fueling its continuing expansion and retire debt with cash flow in 1992. The company added 30 stores that year and took advantage of an "early conversion expiration" provision (also known as a "screw clause" to investors) to save $2.3 million in interest on a $75 million convertible debenture.

Pep Boys had long been known for its good working conditions and generous benefits, which helped the company attract and retain some of the industry's best employees for decades. Leibovitz instilled his employees with competitive fervor by staging ritual annihilations of competitors. Whenever competitive pressure from Pep Boys closed down a major rival's store, he added a photo of the closed-down outlet to his collection. Baseball caps bearing the vanquished competitors' corporate logos were incinerated, and Leibovitz videotaped the symbolic destruction for in-house pep rallies.

The year 1993 saw the inauguration of yet another change at Pep Boys that was hailed by *Financial World* as "the final step in transforming the old-fashioned family-owned chain into a nationwide leader." After a year of planning, Leibovitz put all his technicians and mechanics on commission in the hopes of attracting top employees and increasing their productivity. Just three months after he made the shift, consumer fraud inspectors in California, Florida, and New Jersey charged Sears, Roebuck and Co.'s auto service division with systematically overcharging customers for unnecessary repairs. The allegations specifically cited Sears's commission program as the locus of the problem. Although chagrined at the negative publicity surrounding commissioned employees generally, Leibovitz confidently stuck with his plan, which incorporated several safeguards. The cornerstone of Pep Boys' system was an ethics policy that dictated termination of mechanics who made unnecessary repairs. Technicians, who were certified by the Institute for Automotive Service Excellence (ASE), also agreed to have their commission docked if their work had to be redone.

Even with commissions, Pep Boys' service cost 20 to 50 percent less than dealerships and independent garages. Service accounted for 13 percent of the retailer's total revenue in fiscal 1993, and income from that segment was increasing more than 10 percent each year in the early 1990s. Sears's subsequent decision to cut back on auto service undoubtedly sent more business to Pep Boys' service bays.

Leibovitz worked to allay customers' ingrained apprehension about gouging in automotive repairs by offering a toll-free "squeal line" and postpaid comment cards addressed to the CEO. Complaints were categorized and tabulated to detect patterns of misconduct, and regional sales managers followed up each complaint with a personal contact. According to the chief, Pep Boys received about 200 complaints and 200 compliments, out of about five million customers, each month. Commendations were reviewed and read on videotape for the firm's "Customer Corner," a video presentation played back in company break rooms across the country.

Pep Boys emerged from the early 1990s recession with strong earnings and stock performance. Even though comparable store sales only increased 1 percent, profits grew by over 20 percent from 1992 to 1993, to $65.6 million and the share price jumped from less than $20 in early 1992 to over $30 by early 1994. Stock market observers predicted that Pep Boys' stock would increase 20 to 30 percent by the end of 1994. Future expansion was planned for new markets in Chicago, Ohio, Denver, Houston, the San Francisco Bay area, and New England. The chain also planned to increase its grip on existing markets in New York, New Jersey, Baltimore, Washington, D.C., Florida, and its historical strongholds in southern California and Philadelphia.

SHIFTING AWAY FROM DIY MARKET

Pep Boys ended 1994 with 432 stores, 4,166 service bays, and revenues of $1.41 billion. Three years later, following the biggest expansion in company history, there were 711 Pep Boys outlets with 6,208 service bays while revenues surpassed the $2 billion mark for the first time. This expansion included the launching in 1995 of a new parts-only store format (with no service bays and no tires) called PartsUSA. By 1997, there were 109 PartsUSA stores, which were rechristened Pep Boys Express that year in an attempt to leverage the name recognition that the Pep Boys brand had gained in its 75-plus-years of existence. The new format was intended to help the company pursue the "buy-for-resale" segment of the automotive aftermarket, which consisted of sales to professional mechanics and garages, as well as traditional do-it-yourself (DIY) customers. The buy-for-resale segment of the market, along with the "do-it-for-me" segment (services), was increasing in importance at the same time that the DIY sector was plateauing. Fewer people were doing their own auto repair in the mid-to-late 1990s because cars were becoming more and more complex. In pursuit of sales to professionals, Pep Boys began rolling out a system for delivering parts to repair shops in 1996. By the end of 1997, about half of the company's units were offering delivery services. At the same time, Pep Boys was pursuing increased service business by signing agreements with fleet customers, such as maintenance agreements with rental car agencies and deals to recondition used cars and make warranty repairs for used car superstores. In 1997 Pep Boys also began testing a service-only format called Pep Boys Service and Tire Center at a location in Moorestown, New Jersey.

With DIY sales continuing to disappoint, Pep Boys decided in October 1998 to refocus on its supercenter format. The company sold 100 of its Express outlets to arch-rival AutoZone, Inc., for $108 million. Pep Boys also closed an additional nine Express units, leaving just 12 in operation. In connection with this contraction, the company recorded pretax charges of $29.5 million, which reduced 1998 net earnings to $5 million. Pep Boys also slowed down its expansion drive, growing by only 24 units in 1999, and worked to improve the performance of the supercenters by remodeling some of the older units and making other enhancements. At the same time, the rollout of the delivery system continued, culminating by 1999 in 88 percent of the stores participating. Sales for 1999 were flat compared to 1998, but net earnings improved to $29.3 million.

In 2000 Pep Boys continued the expansion of its service operations by launching a new program for buyers or sellers of used cars whereby Pep Boys would inspect a vehicle and, assuming the vehicle passed the inspection, provide a certification vouching for the vehicles' mechanical and operational soundness. Pep Boys initially charged between $89.99 and $229.99 for the service.

CHALLENGING TIMES

Pep Boys recorded losses in excess of $50 million for 2000. In a money-saving response, the company closed 38 stores and two distribution centers, eliminated 1,300 jobs, cut back store hours, and moved to pay down debt. Comparable sales and total sales declined during 2001, a reflection of the cost-cutting measures. Just two new stores were planned for 2002; both located in the Northeast.

Many other aftermarket players had dialed back expansion in the light of the economic downturn intensified by the September 11, 2001 terrorist attacks against the United States. Pep Boys concentrated on improving performance in its 628 existing stores. A marketing campaign featured services and the benefits of one-stop shopping. Restructuring efforts began to pay off with four straight quarters of improved earnings, stronger profit margins, reduced inventory, and a

rebounding stock price, *DSN Retailing Today* reported in January 2002.

Profits generated by the growing do-it-for-me market aided Pep Boys cause: 6,500 service bays brought in about half of total revenue. The service aspect of its business made it unique among auto parts retailers. "Our service offering is a competitive advantage," Chairman, President, and CEO Mitch Leibovitz told *DSN Retailing Today.* "Our challenge is to maximize that advantage." Service sales had climbed from 4 percent to 45 percent of business during Leibovitz's watch.

Already the largest store in its retail niche, Pep Boys under Leibovitz desired category dominance. Yet the number one player, AutoZone, was just as determined to grow market share. Its "Get in the Zone" campaign caught fire with younger consumers. Conversely, Pep Boys' ad campaign was skewed toward cable TV sports programming and focused on tire sales, a sector nailed by the weak economy and a 2000 third quarter Firestone tire recall.

To generate buzz among "tuners" Pep Boys signed up for sponsorship of Hot Import Nights. U.S. sales in the import performance category sped toward $2 billion during 2002, compared to just $295 million a half decade earlier, according to *Forbes.* Promising high gross margins, $120 racing gauges, $50 chrome valve covers, and $350 racing mufflers appeared more prominently on Pep Boys shelves, Elisa Williams reported.

The company's parts business needed a boost, coming off a lackluster fiscal 2001 and suffering from a decade-long downward trend in the do-it-yourself sector. On the other hand, Pep Boys' service sales climbed 25 percent from 1998 to 2001, reaching $418 million.

The challenging economic conditions and flat tire market continued to drag on the Pep Boys well into 2002. To create another revenue stream, the aftermarket retail and service chain moved to license its corporate logo for use on products ranging from apparel and toys to car maintenance books. Absent from TV ads for several years, Manny, Moe and Jack fit well with the retro resurgence. Logoed items had already appeared on eBay.com, and the company self-produced T-shirts, baseball caps, and bobbleheads, according to *License!*

Declining comparable store sales during 2002 led to a change of leadership and tightened control on expenses in 2003. While earnings remained in the black, they were well off the pace set in the late 1990s. Moreover, peer group comp sales had risen in 2002, led by AutoZone's 9 percent increase.

New CEO Lawrence Stevenson, who succeeded Leibovitz after his retirement, acted quickly, shaking up merchandising and marketing, closing underperforming stores, and cutting staff. The former head of Canadian book retailer Chapters foresaw an $11 million savings annually by shuttering 33 stores, primarily in California, and eliminating 700 jobs and 160 corporate positions, according to an August 2003 *DSN Retailing Today* article. The closures would reduce the store count to 596, down from a peak of 711 in 1997. A related $75 million annual sales decline was expected.

Changes continued in 2004, including a new store format, new logo, and new name. Operating as Pep Boys Auto, the company planned to remodel every store by 2008, creating more cohesion in its identity and a better experience for customers, in particular, women. New product categories were added, including scooters and organizational items for home garages. The new store design and product offerings debuted in the San Diego market. Test stores, reconfigured to highlight product areas such as electronics, trucks, or maintenance, produced promising sales gains.

Pep Boys returned to profitability in 2004, after recording more than $30 million in losses during 2003. Same store sales gains bypassed its automotive parts and accessories retail peer group, according to *DSN Retail Today*. But while do-it-yourself parts and accessories sales climbed, service revenue remained flat, and tire sales slipped. The segments produced $1.54 billion, $409 million, and $324 million in revenue, respectively.

The service area, despite a significant personnel overhaul, continued to stagnate. The company posted losses during 2005 and a corresponding drop in shareholder value. Over the past year, Pep Boys shares fell 4 percent, versus a 4 percent gain for AutoZone Inc., a 46 percent gain for Advance Auto Parts Inc., and a 41 percent gain for O'Reilly Automotive Inc., Joseph N. DiStefano reported for the *Philadelphia Inquirer* in February 2006.

Searching for a solution, the board asked long-term financial adviser Goldman, Sachs & Co. "to explore strategic and financial alternatives for the Company." Stevenson continued as CEO, but board member William Leonard took over as chairman. James Mitarotonda, the chairman of Barington Capital Group, a major Pep Boys shareholder, laid blame for the setback at Stevenson's feet and predicted a sale or another restructuring.

The service segment and nontraditional product mix diminished prospects of selling the company to another parts supplier, according to *Mergers & Acquisitions Report*. Neither was the standard fare of the automotive aftermarket.

April Dougal Gasbarre
Updated, David E. Salamie; Kathleen Peippo

PRINCIPAL SUBSIDIARIES

Pep Boys—Manny, Moe & Jack of California; Pep Boys—Manny, Moe & Jack of Delaware, Inc.; Pep Boys—Manny, Moe & Jack of Puerto Rico, Inc.; Colchester Insurance Company; PBY Corporation; Carrus Supply Corporation.

PRINCIPAL COMPETITORS

Advance Auto Parts, Inc.; AutoZone, Inc.; CARQUEST Corporation.

FURTHER READING

Andreoli, Teresa, "Manny, Moe, & Jack Are in the Driver's Seat: Pep Boys Looks to Licensing to Supplement Its Auto Aftermarket/Retail Service in Today's Tough Economic Climate," *License!*, July 2003, p. 22.

Byrne, Harlan S., "Wait 'Til Next Year," *Barron's*, January 5, 1998, p. 48.

Catton, Grant, "Pep Boys Tunes Up for a Sale with Goldman by Its Side," *Mergers & Acquisitions Report*, February 20, 2006.

———, "Will Enough Bidders Drive in to Pep Boys?," *Mergers & Acquisitions Report*, May 1, 2006.

DiStefano, Joseph N., "Troubled Pep Boys Hires an Advisor: Goldman Sachs Could Suggest the Car-Parts Chain Sell or Restructure," *Philadelphia Inquirer*, February 11, 2006.

Groeber, Janet, "Start Your Engines: A Pacesetting Prototype Signals Pep Boys Auto's Move into Aftermarket Fast Lane," *Display & Design Ideas*, October 2004, pp. 40+.

Halverson, Richard, "Auto Chains Shift Gears to Wholesale As DIY Sales Skid," *Discount Store News*, September 4, 1995, p. 51.

———, "Pep Boys Expanding Bays," *Discount Store News*, June 23, 1997, pp. 1, 126.

———, "Pep Boys to Transition Away from DIY Market," *Discount Store News*, June 22, 1998, pp. 3, 62.

Hass, Nancy, "Truths of Commission," *Financial World*, January 19, 1993, pp. 28–29.

Howell, Debbie, "New Pep Boys CEO Initiates Extensive Restructuring Program," *DSN Retailing Today*, August 18, 2003, pp. 5+.

———, "Pep Boys' Turnaround Builds Momentum," *DSN Retailing Today*, May 23, 2005, p. 19.

Hutchinson, Katherine, "Pep Boys Puts Expansion on Hold While It Ratchets Up On-Site Service," *DSN Retailing Today*, January 21, 2002, p. 4.

Johnson, Jay L., "Pep Boys on the Fast Track," *Discount Merchandiser*, October 1990, pp. 18–25.

Kharouf, Jim, "Pep Boys Speeding into Area," *Daily Southtown* (Chicago), June 22, 1994, pp. 1–2.

La Monica, Paul R., "Pep Boys: Shifting Gears," *Financial World*, December 5, 1995, p. 24.

Levy, Robert, "Manny, Moe & Jack on the Move," *Dun's Business Month,* July 1986, pp. 28–29.

Lin, Anthony, "Pep Boys Is Revving Up for Its Largest Expansion Drive: Company to Launch Parts-Only Stores and Increase Supercenter Outlets," *Wall Street Journal,* August 10, 1995, p. B4.

Lubove, Seth, "Retail Is Detail," *Forbes,* September 30, 1991, pp. 144, 146.

"Pep Boys: More Than an Industry Leader, an Institution," *Aftermarket Business,* December 1, 1991, pp. 17–39.

"Pep Boys Passes $1 Billion Mark," *Discount Merchandiser,* January 1992, pp. 14–17.

"Pep Boys Tests Service-Only Units," *Discount Store News,* January 26, 1998, pp. 6, 42.

"Pep Boys West, 1933–1983: 50 Years Later, Still Pioneering the Retail Aftermarket," *Home and Auto,* November 15, 1983, pp. 13+.

Rudnitsky, Howard, "Keeping the Family Buggy on the Road," *Forbes,* March 11, 1996, p. 52.

Silverthorne, Sean, "Pep Boys' Mitchell Leibovitz: He Studied Industry Leaders to Recast Auto Parts Store," *Investor's Business Daily,* October 13, 1992, pp. 1–2.

Taylor, Alex, III, "How to Murder the Competition," *Fortune,* February 22, 1993, pp. 87, 90.

Wayne, Leslie, "Pep Boys (Manny, Moe, and Jack) See Their Stock Climb," *New York Times,* April 19, 1994.

Weiss, Gary, "Beware the Turn of the Screw," *Business Week,* June 1, 1992, p. 108.

Werner, Thomas, "Seeking No. 1: Pep Boys Expands Auto-Parts Chain by Big Leaps," *Barron's,* July 6, 1987, pp. 34–35.

Williams, Elisa, "Boyz Under the Hood," *Forbes,* July 8, 2002, p. 54.

Pepperidge Farm,
Incorporated

595 Westport Avenue
Norwalk, Connecticut 06851-4413
U.S.A.
Telephone: (203) 846-7000
Toll Free: (888) 737-7374
Fax: (203) 846-7369
Web site: http://www.pepperidgefarm.com

Wholly Owned Subsidiary of Campbell Soup Company
Founded: 1937
Employees: 5,000
Sales: $1.1 billion (2005 est.)
NAIC: 311412 Frozen Specialty Food Manufacturing;
311812 Commercial Bakeries; 311813 Frozen
Cakes, Pies, and Other Pastries Manufacturing;
311821 Cookie and Cracker Manufacturing

∎ ∎ ∎

Pepperidge Farm, Incorporated, is a leading provider of
premium fresh breads, cookies, crackers, and frozen
foods. The Pepperidge Farm bakery line includes
breakfast breads, English muffins, bagels, Farmhouse
and Natural Whole Grain breads, and an assortment of
rolls; more than 50 varieties of fresh baked breads are
offered in total. The company also produces stuffing and
croutons. The cookie lineup includes the Milano and
Chocolate Chunk varieties, while the cracker portfolio is
headlined by the Goldfish line, a favorite with kids. Pepperidge Farm's frozen food assortment encompasses garlic
toast, French toast, pot pies, cakes, and puff pastries.
Pepperidge Farm was founded in 1937 by Margaret

Rudkin, a Connecticut homemaker and entrepreneur,
and has been wholly owned by Campbell Soup Company
since 1961. The company's products are produced at
eight manufacturing facilities across the United States.
They are distributed in more than 40 countries around
the world.

BEGINNINGS IN MARGARET RUDKIN'S KITCHEN

Born in New York City on September 14, 1897,
Margaret Fogarty graduated valedictorian of her New
York City public high school class before embarking on
a career in business. She spent four years at a local bank
working first as a bookkeeper and then as a teller. In
1919 she took a position with the brokerage firm Mc-
Clure, Jones & Co., where she met Henry Albert Rudkin, one of the company's partners. The two married in
1923 and by decade's end had three sons. In 1926 the
couple bought 125 acres of land near Fairfield, Connecticut, part of which had once been a farm. A
distinguishing feature of the property was a group of
pepperidge trees, an ornamental variety known for its
brilliant scarlet foliage in the fall (the tree is also called
the black tupelo, black gum, and sour gum). The new
owners thereby named the estate Pepperidge Farm.

Margaret Rudkin faced many challenges during the
years of the Great Depression, including dealing with a
serious polo accident that her husband suffered in 1932.
She earned money during this period by selling apples
from the farm's orchard and turkeys they raised. Her
true turn to entrepreneurship arose, however, after her
youngest son, Mark, was diagnosed in 1937 with severe

allergies and asthma that were exacerbated by most commercially processed foods. An allergy specialist recommended a diet of fresh fruits and vegetables and minimally processed foods. Rudkin therefore at the age of 40 ventured to bake her first loaf of bread. She drew on her memories of childhood, when her Irish grandmother taught her to cook, conjuring up her grandmother's recipe for whole wheat bread based on old-fashioned ingredients, including stone-ground whole wheat flour, honey, molasses, natural-sugar syrup, whole milk, cream, and butter. Her first attempt was a miserable failure, something she looked back on humorously in one of the autobiographical sections of *The Margaret Rudkin Pepperidge Farm Cookbook:* "That first loaf should have been sent to the Smithsonian Institution as a sample of bread from the Stone Age, for it was hard as a rock and about one inch high." Through trial and error, Rudkin eventually mastered the use of yeast and the art of breadmaking, producing a loaf that her whole family enjoyed.

The bread also seemed to improve Mark's health, and his doctor was so impressed by a sample Rudkin gave him that he asked her to make bread for him and for his other patients. Armed with a letter of recommendation from this doctor, Rudkin successfully approached other doctors, who passed word of this healthful bread on to their patients. In this fashion, Rudkin developed a sizable mail-order business simply by word of mouth. As demand for the bread from friends and neighbors increased, she soon expanded into distributing loaves to local grocers. Although commercial bread then sold for ten cents a loaf, Rudkin insisted on selling her premium bread, which carried the "Pepperidge Farm" brand, to the grocers for 20 cents, with the bread then retailing for 25 cents. "I reasoned that if the public really wanted a loaf of good, old fashioned bread, they'd be willing to pay for the ingredients that went into it," she later recalled. Her plan worked.

As demand increased, Rudkin hired a young female assistant, Mary Ference, and moved production out of her kitchen—first to her garage and then to an unused outbuilding on the farm, which was converted into a model bakery. In its first three months of operation the business sold $2,500 worth of bread. Through the fall of 1937 Rudkin had continued to produce only whole wheat bread. Knowing that many people still preferred white bread, she began making an old-fashioned all-natural white bread that used only unbleached flour. Around this same time, the Pepperidge Farm business began to have difficulty filling the increasing mail orders from New York City. Rudkin's solution was to expand distribution to New York retailers. Rudkin persuaded Charles and Company, a prestigious specialty food store, to carry her bread, beginning with 24 loaves a day. At first her husband made the deliveries as part of his daily train commute to his Wall Street office, but the use of a trucking company was soon needed as the order reached 1,200 loaves a week. By the end of its first year of operation in September 1938, Margaret Rudkin's bakery was producing 4,000 loaves every week.

EXPANDING INTO A NATIONWIDE BRAND

The high quality and healthfulness of Pepperidge Farm bread, along with its "homemade" image, became known to an ever wider audience following the publication of several enthusiastic newspaper articles as well as a glowing tribute in the December 1939 issue of *Reader's Digest* magazine. This free publicity brought orders pouring in from throughout the United States as well as Canada and several other countries. Under pressure to expand, Rudkin in 1940 moved her operation into an empty service station in nearby Norwalk, Connecticut. During the first year in this rented building, production soared to 50,000 loaves per week, aided by a workforce that had grown to about 50. Annual revenues soon reached $500,000.

Rudkin had planned to stay in this building for only a year before shifting quarters into a newly built modern commercial bakery. However, rationing during World War II led to a cutback in production because Rudkin refused to compromise on quality by making substitutions for top-quality ingredients. Construction of the new plant had to be delayed until after the war's end. Finally, on July 4, 1947, Pepperidge Farm began production at a new $625,000 state-of-the-art plant in Norwalk that Rudkin had designed herself. Initial capacity was 4,000 loaves per hour. Although the company had moved into mass production, Rudkin remained steadfast in her commitment to quality. She continued to use only stone-ground wheat produced at water-powered mills in New England that she helped to restore. The dough was still mixed in small batches and kneaded

KEY DATES

1937: Margaret Rudkin begins making Pepperidge Farm bread, which is initially sold by mail-order and through local grocers.

1940: Production moves to a rented building in Norwalk, Connecticut.

1947: Company opens a new modern bakery in Norwalk.

1955: Production of European-style cookies begins.

1961: Campbell Soup Company acquires Pepperidge Farm.

1962: Pepperidge Farm launches Goldfish crackers.

1966: Margaret Rudkin retires.

1968: Gordon McGovern begins 12-year stint as company president during which time he increases revenues to $300 million.

1984: Richard Shea takes over as Pepperidge Farm president.

1986: American Collection cookie line, later renamed Chocolate Chunk, debuts.

2001: Revenues reach $1 billion.

2003: The original Norwalk bakery is shut down and replaced with a new plant in Bloomfield, Connecticut.

by hand. She further decreed that loaves that were not sold after two days on a store's shelf be returned to the company. As had long been done in home kitchens, Rudkin turned this stale bread into a new product, poultry stuffing. The Pepperidge Farm brand soon extended to dinner rolls and additional varieties of bread as well.

Distribution spread from Maine to Florida and west to the Mississippi. The growing popularity of Pepperidge Farm products led to the opening of a second factory in Downingtown, Pennsylvania, near Philadelphia, in 1949 and a third in Downer's Grove, Illinois, near Chicago, in 1953. The former's capacity was 77,000 loaves per week, while the opening of the latter raised company-wide capacity to one million loaves per week. Adjacent to the Downer's Grove plant the firm built a new mill to stone-grind wheat the old-fashioned way that Rudkin deemed essential to producing quality baked goods. By the end of the 1950s Pepperidge Farm reached nationwide distribution.

This expansion was backed by a move into television advertising. The first ads, which debuted in 1950, featured the founder herself as "Maggie" Rudkin and had a homespun appeal. In 1956 a new campaign was launched featuring a down-home Pepperidge Farm deliveryman named "Titus Moody." This character, who was eventually known simply as "the Old Timer," starred in one of the longest-running TV ad campaigns in history, one that lasted into the early 1990s.

A further broadening of the product line also occurred in the 1950s. On a trip to Belgium, Rudkin discovered a line of premium cookies being produced by Delacre Company. She reached an agreement with the Belgian company to produce and sell the delicate European-style cookies under the Pepperidge Farm banner. A wing was added to the Downingtown factory where a 46-meter-long cookie oven, imported from Belgium, was installed. Production of the Distinctive line of cookies, which initially featured such names as Bordeaux, Geneva, and Brussels, was launched in 1955. This line would later be headed by the popular Milano cookie. Pepperidge Farm also expanded into frozen foods in 1957 through the acquisition of Black Horse Pastry Company of Keene, New Hampshire, maker of frozen puff pastries. A decade later, frozen three-layer cakes were added to the lineup.

SALE TO CAMPBELL SOUP, END OF THE RUDKIN ERA

By 1960 Pepperidge Farm was producing 1.2 million loaves of bread per week and its workforce had reached 1,700. Its more than 50 products were sold through 500 distributors and some 50,000 stores across the country. For the fiscal year ending in April 1960 profits totaled about $1.3 million on revenues of $32 million. The Rudkin family maintained ownership of more than 80 percent of the stock, and Margaret Rudkin continued to handle the production and personnel end of the business, while her husband was responsible for the financial side, as well as marketing, sales, shipping, and other areas, and served as the company chairman. He had gradually retired from his Wall Street job to work full-time at Pepperidge Farm.

In November 1960, however, the Rudkins agreed to sell Pepperidge Farm to Campbell Soup Company as a way of providing their firm with additional financial backing to support further expansion. Campbell bought Pepperidge Farm for about $28.2 million worth of Campbell Soup stock in a deal that closed in January 1961. Margaret Rudkin continued in charge of Pepperidge Farm, Incorporated, which became a wholly owned subsidiary of Campbell, and she also gained a seat on the soup company's board of directors—the first woman to do so. In 1962 her husband retired from the company, Margaret took over the chairmanship, and their son Bill was named president.

Rudkin made one final lasting contribution to the Pepperidge Farm product lineup through another European discovery, this one from Switzerland. There she discovered a unique fish-shaped cheese cracker that Pepperidge Farm launched in 1962 under the name Goldfish. Originally a cocktail cracker, Goldfish later became a favorite kid's snack. Margaret Rudkin retired in September 1966, shortly after her husband's death, having built Pepperidge Farm into a $50 million business. She died of breast cancer on June 1, 1967, at the age of 69.

UPS AND DOWNS

From March 1968 through August 1980, Pepperidge Farm was led by Gordon McGovern, an aggressive marketer who, in a little more than a dozen years, increased the firm's sales from $60 million to $300 million. Under his leadership, Pepperidge Farm pioneered the mass marketing of upscale food products. The company's marketers lured customers into paying premium prices for the company's products by having them placed high on store shelves and emphasizing the products' high quality and all-natural ingredients. New products flowed freely from a seat-of-the-pants approach to new product development. On the advertising side, a nostalgic campaign featuring the tagline "Pepperidge Farm Remembers" ran throughout the 1970s, while the first television advertising for Goldfish crackers debuted in 1977. Finally, distribution was aided and expanded through the opening of a string of new plants. In January 1974 production began at a cookie and frozen food plant in Richmond, Utah. In 1977 two more plants commenced operation: a bakery facility in Aiken, South Carolina, and a cookie facility in Willard, Ohio.

In a side note during this period, Pepperidge Farm in August 1971 was given responsibility for managing Godiva Chocolatier, Inc., which Campbell Soup had acquired in 1966. This arrangement ended in August 1987 when Godiva became an independent Campbell subsidiary.

The McGovern era ended when he was promoted to president and CEO of Campbell Soup. This ushered in a chaotic period in the early 1980s when the Pepperidge Farm presidency changed hands several times and the company suffered through a string of high-profile failed product launches. Three products introduced in the early 1980s all failed miserably in the marketplace: Deli's, a line of pastry-wrapped fruits, vegetables, and meats; Star Wars cookies; and Pepperidge Farm Apple Juice. All three of these products flew in the face of one of the company's founder's key principles:

her emphasis on quality first and foremost. They simply were not up to the standards expected of the Pepperidge Farm brand.

Richard Shea, named president of Pepperidge Farm in June 1984, quickly got the company back on track. He purged hundreds of products from the lineup and improved production efficiency by closing several outdated plants, upgrading the remaining plants, and constructing two new high-tech plants. By the early 1990s Pepperidge Farm had spent $500 million on plant modernization and construction as well as installation of company-wide computerized delivery systems. In August 1987 an $80 million state-of-the-art bakery commenced production in Lakeland, Florida. This was followed by the October 1991 ribbon cutting at a $180 million, 611,000-square-foot facility in Denver, Pennsylvania, designed for both baked goods and cookie production. Through these initiatives, the time required for getting products from the plants to stores was cut in half, improving the freshness of the company's offerings and thereby revitalizing Pepperidge Farm's emphasis on basic quality. The company also scored its first hit new product in years in 1986 with the debut of the American Collection cookie line, which was later renamed Chocolate Chunk. By the time Shea retired from Pepperidge Farm in 1994, sales had reached $600 million.

INTO THE NEW CENTURY

From 1996 to 2002 Pepperidge Farm was led by David L. Albright. Under his watch, the Goldfish brand was successfully repositioned more as a kid's snack item. In 1997 the product was altered for the first time since its 1962 introduction with the addition of a stamped smile, a change backed by the tagline "the snack that smiles back." The product was then extended with the launches of Flavor Blasted Goldfish (1998), Giant Goldfish (2000), Baby Goldfish (2001), and Goldfish Colors (2002). By 2002 sales of the Goldfish brand had doubled to $280 million, and Goldfish had become the number two cracker brand in the United States. Other successful product introductions during this period included frozen pot pies, French toast, and Texas toast. Pepperidge Farm also launched a new umbrella ad campaign in late 1999 featuring the slogan "Never have an ordinary day." In 2001 revenues at Pepperidge Farm exceeded the $1 billion mark for the first time. By this time, bread production had reached 145 million loaves per year, while the company was also producing more than 75 billion Goldfish crackers and more than 500 million Milano cookies annually.

After Albright's departure, Mark A. Sarvary was named Pepperidge Farm president in August 2002. Sarvary, a onetime executive at Nestlé USA, had served as

CEO of retailer J. Crew Group Inc. He oversaw the opening of another new plant in May 2003, a 265,000-square-foot, $72 million facility in Bloomfield, Connecticut, for the production of bread, rolls, stuffing, and croutons. In a historic move, this plant replaced the firm's facility in Norwalk, the one that Margaret Rudkin had designed herself and that had been in operation since 1947. The Norwalk plant closed in July 2003, but Pepperidge Farm kept its headquarters in the building adjacent to the plant. In another historic shift, the company in September 2003 introduced its first new spokesperson in nearly 50 years, an animated character known as "John Dough" who replaced "the Old Timer." In the meantime, Pepperidge Farm scored another hit on the new product front with the July 2003 introduction of five Mini cookie varieties, including Mini Milano, Mini Brussels, and Mini Sausalito.

When Sarvary was promoted to president of Campbell Soup North America in March 2004, Jay Gould succeeded him as president of Pepperidge Farm. Gould had joined the company in December 2002 as chief marketing officer, having previously worked at both General Mills, Inc., and the Coca-Cola Company. Over the next couple of years, Pepperidge Farm continued its tradition of focusing on healthful foods by eliminating trans fats from all of its product lines and by introducing a string of products featuring whole grains, including breads, English muffins, bagels, and Goldfish crackers—the latter clearly harkening back to the founder's original stone-ground whole-wheat-based product. Gould left the company suddenly in January 2006. He was replaced by Pat Callaghan, a Pepperidge Farm veteran who had joined the firm in 1979. Callaghan made an immediate promise to uphold the company's nearly 70-year tradition: "I am committed to maintaining the quality and innovative spirit of Pepperidge Farm's founder, Margaret Rudkin."

David E. Salamie

PRINCIPAL COMPETITORS

Kraft Foods, Inc.; Sara Lee Bakery Group; Kellogg Company; Interstate Bakeries Corporation; Ralcorp Holdings, Inc.; Frito Lay North America; George Weston Limited; Flowers Foods, Inc.

FURTHER READING

Bagnon, Judann, "Slumping Pepperidge Farm Turns Up the Heat on O&M," *Advertising Age,* June 24, 1991, pp. 1, 60.

Bainbridge, John, "Striking a Blow for Grandma," *New Yorker,* May 22, 1948, pp. 38–40+.

Berk, Christina Cheddar, "Pepperidge Farm Plans to Market Whole Grain As Tasty Alternative," *Wall Street Journal,* August 31, 2005, p. B3A.

"Campbell Soup to Buy Pepperidge Farm, Inc., for About $28 Million," *Wall Street Journal,* November 18, 1960, p. 18.

Dougal, April S., "Pepperidge Farm," *Encyclopedia of Consumer Brands,* Vol. 1: *Consumable Products,* edited by Janice Jorgensen, Detroit: St. James Press, 1994, pp. 438–40.

Elliott, Stuart, "Campbell Soup Is Looking Beyond Its Big Agency for Ideas to Pump Up the Sales of Goldfish," *New York Times,* November 24, 2004, p. C5.

"Fame Came from Good Loaf of Bread," *Washington Post,* September 20, 1962, p. C1.

Fernandez, Bob, "Gold (fish) Rush," *Lancaster (Pa.) New Era,* July 6, 1998.

Fleischer, Jo, "Greenfield's Foods Sells Brownie Business to Pepperidge Farm," *Fairfield County (Conn.) Business Journal,* December 5, 1994, p. 8.

Giges, Nancy, "Pepperidge Farm's Fallow Ground," *Advertising Age,* February 21, 1985, pp. 2–3.

Gorton, Laurie, "2002 Wholesale Baker of the Year: Pepperidge Farm," *Baking and Snack,* March 1, 2002.

Hartley, W. B., "Story of Pepperidge Bread: 500,000 Loaves a Week," *Coronet,* August 1953, pp. 61–65.

Hays, Constance L., "Will Goldfish Tactics Help Campbell's Soups?," *New York Times,* October 18, 1998, p. BU4.

Khasru, B. Z., "Pepperidge Farm to Move," *Fairfield County (Conn.) Business Journal,* November 5, 2001, p. 2.

Lahvic, Ray, and Dan Malovany, "Total Freshness and Rapid Response," *Bakery Production and Marketing,* September 24, 1992, pp. 170+.

Lee, Richard, "Pepperidge Farm Removes Trans Fat from Four Product Lines, *Stamford (Conn.) Advocate,* August 19, 2004.

———, "Pepperidge Farm to Unveil New Mascot, Advertising Campaign," *Stamford (Conn.) Advocate,* September 10, 2003.

Machan, Dyan, "Pepperidge Farm's Doughboy," *Forbes,* March 20, 1989, pp. 198+.

Malovany, Dan, "Pepperidge Farm and the Quest for 'What's Next,'" *Snack Food and Wholesale Bakery,* February 2004, pp. 30, 32, 34–37.

"Margaret Rudkin: Champion of the Old-Fashioned," *Time,* March 21, 1960, p. 90.

Mink, Michael, "Serving Up Profit: Margaret Rudkin Followed Her Instincts and Stayed Focused to Build Up Pepperidge Farm," *Investor's Business Daily,* January 6, 2006, p. A3.

Morris, Betsy, "Getting Stirred Up: After a Long Simmer, the Pot Boils Again at Campbell Soup Co.," *Wall Street Journal,* July 16, 1982, pp. 1, 10.

"Mrs. Margaret Rudkin Is Dead; Founder of Pepperidge Farm," *New York Times,* June 2, 1967, p. 41.

"Mrs. Rudkin Revisited," *New Yorker,* November 16, 1963, pp. 42–44.

"Peg Rudkin's Bread," *Newsweek,* September 21, 1942, pp. 68, 70.

"Pepperidge Farm Bread," *Kiplinger Magazine,* October 1947, pp. 43–45.

"Pepperidge Farm Pushes into Meal Biz with Frozen Pot Pies," *Brandweek,* April 5, 1999, p. 14.

"Pepperidge Farm Turns into a Tough Cookie," *Sales and Marketing Management,* January 17, 1983, p. 24.

"Pepperidge Sold to Campbell Soup," *New York Times,* November 18, 1960, p. 43.

Poist, Patricia A., "Fish Farm," *Lancaster (Pa.) New Era,* November 15, 2004.

Ratcliff, J. D., "Bread, de Luxe: Home-Baked Pepperidge Farm Bread," *Reader's Digest,* December 1939, pp. 102–3.

Rudkin, Margaret, *The Margaret Rudkin Pepperidge Farm Cookbook,* New York: Atheneum, 1963, 440 p.

"Rudkin of Pepperidge," *Time,* July 14, 1947, pp. 82, 84.

Salwen, Kevin G., "OSHA Fine Against Pepperidge Farm of $1.4 Million Is Largely Reversed," *Wall Street Journal,* March 29, 1993, p. B4.

Saporito, Bill, "A Smart Cookie at Pepperidge," *Fortune,* December 22, 1986, pp. 67, 70, 74.

Schwadel, Francine, "Revised Recipe: Burned by Mistakes, Campbell Soup Co. Is in Throes of Change," *Wall Street Journal,* August 14, 1985.

Simon, Ellen, "Fish Story: Cracker War Turns Food Giants into Sharks," *Newark (N.J.) Star-Ledger,* January 20, 2000, p. 23.

"Sour Juice and Crumbled Cookies at Pepperidge Farm," *Business Week,* June 4, 1984, pp. 31, 35.

Thompson, Stephanie, "Pepperidge Farm Touts Indulgence in Brand Ads," *Advertising Age,* October 11, 1999, p. 28.

"Through the Mill to Success," *American Home,* April 1951, pp. 64–68.

Pescanova S.A.

Rua de Jose Fernandez Lopez s/n
Chapela-Redondela,
Spain
Telephone: +34 986 81 81 00
Fax: +34 986 81 82 00
Web site: http://www.pescanova.es

Public Company
Incorporated: 1961
Employees: 3,400
Sales: EUR 999.09 million ($1.3 billion) (2005)
Stock Exchanges: Madrid
Ticker Symbol: PES
NAIC: 311712 Fresh and Frozen Seafood Processing;
311111 Dog and Cat Food Manufacturing; 311412
Frozen Specialty Food Manufacturing; 311423
Dried and Dehydrated Food Manufacturing;
311711 Seafood Canning; 311822 Flour Mixes and
Dough Manufacturing from Purchased Flour;
424410 General Line Grocery Merchant Wholesal-
ers; 424460 Fish and Seafood Merchant Wholesal-
ers; 424490 Other Grocery and Related Product
Merchant Wholesalers; 551112 Offices of Other
Holding Companies

■ ■ ■

Pescanova S.A. is one of the world's top fishing
companies. The Spanish company owns the largest
European fleet of fishing vessels, and the second largest
in the world behind the fleet operated by the Chinese
government. Pescanova operates 120 trawler and long-
line vessels through a global network of subsidiaries
operating in most of the world's top fishing markets. In
a number of fishing grounds, including Cuba, Pescanova
has secured exclusive harvesting rights. In this way, Pescanova handles an extremely diversified range of fish
species, from hake, codfish, salmon, and shrimp to
roughy, octopus, and others. The company's fishing and
marketing operations include subsidiaries, and fishing
quotas, in Argentina, Chile, Namibia, Australia, the
United States, and elsewhere. In addition to its large
fishing and on-sea processing fleet, Pescanova has built
up a highly vertically integrated business. In this way,
Pescanova is a leading provider of fresh and frozen fish
and fish products to the three major world markets:
Europe, Japan, and the United States.

The company dominates the Spanish fish and frozen
foods market, with a 65 percent market share, and
remains a leading supplier of fresh and frozen fish, and
other frozen foods, to the European market. The
company's subsidiaries include consumer products
groups, such as Pescafina and Pescafresco, and others,
including Caternova, for the restaurant and catering sector; Cofrio, supplying frozen fish and foods to the
wholesale market; and Riazor, focused on shrimp and
other shellfish and seafood products. Pescanova's
combined sales reached EUR 999 million ($1.3 billion)
in 2005. The company is listed on the Madrid Stock
Exchange and is led by President and Chairman Manuel
Fernandez de Sousa-Faro, son of the company's founder.

FROZEN FISH IDEA IN 1960

Pescanova was founded in 1960 by José Fernandez Lopez, who set out to solve an age-old problem in the

Spanish fishing industry, namely, how to preserve fish caught far away from Spain's ports—in the South Atlantic, for example—so that the fish did not spoil during transport times of as much as three weeks. Traditional preservation techniques included salting fish. Yet Fernandez recognized that the development of refrigeration and freezing technologies offered a new possibility for transporting fish.

By then the Fernandez family had established some degree of prominence in the country. Originally from Sarria, the family had started out as cattle ranchers before branching out into slaughtering and then the distribution of meat products. The Fernandez family, which included siblings Manuel, Concepcion, Antonio, and José, came to prominence during the Spanish Civil War, when the company's location made it a main supplier to the forces led by Francisco Franco.

The family's support for the winning side placed them in a strong position following the war. The Fernandez family quickly began to diversify its business interests. In 1939, for example, the family backed the founding of Zeltia S.A., which grew into a leading

Spanish biotechnology firm. The family's interest in beef also led it to invest in newly developing refrigeration and freezing technologies. Subsequently, the family set up a number of other companies, including Frigolouro, based in Porrino, and Frigsa, based in Lugo. Other operations included the export company Titania, which served the German market during World War II, and Transfesa, which focused on the railroad transportation sector. The developing family fortune also led to investments in the banking sector: The family founded their own bank in Lugo in 1968, and also entered the publishing world through a stake in Editorial Galaxia.

Although his background was in beef, Jose Fernandez recognized that the ocean represented a vast opportunity for food products, if a way could be found to preserve fish caught far from Spain. Having gained more than 20 years of experience in freezing, Fernandez became one of the first in the world to understand the potential for adding on-board flash-freezing and frozen storage capacity. To develop his idea, Fernandez turned to Vigo's Valentín Paz Andrade, who ran a fishing supply business, Industrias Pesqueras.

Fernandez founded his company, Pescanova, in 1960 and began outfitting his first freezer vessel, the *Lemos*. That vessel set sail in 1961, with initial trial runs in the waters off South Africa and Argentina. By November 1961, the *Lemos* had returned with its freezer hold filled with fish supplied by fishermen off the coast of Argentina. By the beginning of 1962, the *Lemos* had completed a run to South Africa, returning with more than 250 tons of hake, a Spanish favorite.

Pescanova immediately set its sights higher. The company acquired its second vessel, a retired cruise ship called the *Habana*, which measured 146 meters in length. Pescanova converted the ship into a giant floating factory, renamed the *Galicia*. That vessel set sail for South Africa in 1964, supported by its own fleet of fishing boats. While the *Galicia* served as a production vessel—including freezing, but also breading and frying facilities—transport back to Spain was provided by a growing fleet of dedicated freezer vessels.

A true innovation in the Spanish food market, Pescanova's frozen fish initially met with a degree of resistance from Spanish consumers. This is because in the early 1960s, frozen foods remained a rarity in the country, all the more so because few consumers, and even fewer stores, were equipped with freezers. At the same time, frozen food, and frozen fish, had earned a reputation for poor quality, because much of the frozen fish then available was actually unsold fresh fish that often had begun to go bad.

ACQUIRING AN INTERNATIONAL SCALE BY THE END OF THE 20TH CENTURY

Pescanova countered this negative reputation through strong advertising efforts. The company also set up its own sales and distribution operations, and even began supplying freezer equipment to grocers so that they could carry the company's products. The effort paid off, and by the early 1970s the company had grown into one of Spain's top 100 companies.

In the meantime, Pescanova had continued to expand its range of operations. In 1964, the company acquired another Vigo-based business, Copiba. That operation gave the company cold storage facilities in Spain, which then served as the basis for the company's expansion into the production of a wide range of processed and frozen foods.

Another major moment in the group's history came in 1968. In that year, Pescanova launched a new vessel, the 100-meter *Gondomar,* then the largest dedicated freezer boat in service. The added vessel allowed the company to claim the title as Europe's leading fishing vessel operator as early as the 1970s.

Fernandez was joined by son Manuel Fernandez de Sousa-Faro by then. In 1975, the younger Fernandez took over as head of the company, a position he maintained into the mid-2000s. Already a major player in the Spanish fish market, Pescanova began to expand into other food areas. In the mid-1980s, the company entered a number of food segments, including frozen vegetables and prepared foods, such as pizzas. Pescanova, through a growing list of subsidiaries and factories, also set up separate operations for supplying the restaurant, catering, and wholesale channels.

Pescanova went public in 1985, listing on the Madrid Stock Exchange, in preparation for a new era in growth. By the end of the 1980s, the company had captured some 25 percent of the Spanish frozen foods market. Spain's entry into the European Common Market presented the group with new opportunities for growth, particularly with the extension of the group's distribution operations into other European countries. The company first entered France, establishing a subsidiary there in 1987. By the end of that year, the company also had created a subsidiary in Portugal, called Frumar. The company next turned to South America, launching Argenova in 1988, based on a single vessel, the *Fuji.* In 1989, Pescanova entered Italy as well.

Yet entry into the ECC also placed the company under newly developing fishing quotas. In response, Pescanova launched an ambitious acquisition strategy, acquiring companies, and their fishing quotas, in new markets. The company began acquiring a number of foreign companies, such as Skeleton Coast Trawling Pty. in Namibia (a major region for hake) and Pesquerias Belnova in Uruguay. Other additions including operations in Ireland (Eiranova Fisheries), Australia (Austral Fisheries), South Africa (Novagroup), Scotland, Mozambique, and elsewhere. By the end of 1994, the company directly controlled 11 subsidiaries in nine countries and, through some 30 joint ventures, held interests in more than 17 countries. Pescanova's international operations represented some 40 percent of the group's total sales, which topped $400 million into the middle of the decade.

GLOBAL LEADER IN THE NEW CENTURY

Pescanova entered the North American market in 1997, setting up subsidiary Pescanova Inc. that year. The following year, Pescanova raised its profile again when it shifted its shares to the Madrid exchange's main board. By the end of the decade, the company's sales had topped EUR 500 million.

In 2000, however, Pescanova confirmed its position as leader through the acquisition of a majority stake in struggling compatriot Pescafina. By 2002, the company had completed the acquisition of Pescafina, boosting its sales by nearly EUR 300 million. The Pescafina addition not only added an important brand name, it also raised Pescanova's percentage of the Spanish frozen fish and foods market to more than 65 percent. The addition of Pescafina also expanded the company's fleet past 120 vessels, giving it the largest fishing fleet in Europe and the second largest in the world, trailing only the Chinese government. In a further extension, the company acquired Spanish trawler group Pesquera Vasco Gallega, a purchase that enabled the company to boost its fishing quotas in Argentina.

Although Pescanova maintained its interest in developing its fishing operations, the company also had launched an investment into fish farming; the company expected its farmed fish to account for as much as 50 percent of turnover through the end of the decade. In 2002, the company moved to expand its fish farming operations, establishing a new base in Namibia. These operations complemented the company's Spanish farm base, with five facilities in operation by 2006.

By the end of 2005, Pescanova had quite nearly broken the EUR 1 billion mark, posting sales of more than EUR 999 million ($1.3 billion). The company continued its active expansion strategy. In 2006, for example, the company added new operations in Mozambique, buying up that country's Companhia de

Pesca do Oceano Índico (COPOIC). Also that year, the company received approval to establish a number of new sea bass farms in Portugal, while also announcing plans to open a turbot facility in Norway. Pescanova expected to maintain its position at the top of the global fishing industry into the new century.

M. L. Cohen

PRINCIPAL SUBSIDIARIES

Argenova, S.A. (Argentina); Bajamar Séptima, S.A.; Eiranova Fisheries Ltd. (Ireland); Frigodís, S.A.; Frinova, S.A.; Insuiña, S.L.; Nave de Argo, S.L.; Newfishing Australia Pty.; Nova Austral (Chile); Novapesca Trading, S.L.; Pesca Chile, S.A.; Pescafina, S.A.; Pescafresca, S.A.; Pescamar, Ltd. (Mozambique); Pescanova France, S.A.; Pescanova Inc. (U.S.A.); Pescanova Italia S.R.L.; Pescanova Portugal Ltda.; Pesquera V. Gallega, S.A.; Pesquerías Belnova, S.A. (Uruguay).

PRINCIPAL COMPETITORS

Unilever; SIF Group hf; Icelandic Group hf; Marine Harvest N.V.; Thai Union Frozen Products Company; Young's Bluecrest Seafood Holdings Ltd.; Trident Seafoods L.L.C.; Red Chamber Co.; Royal Greenland; Pacific Seafood Inc.

FURTHER READING

"Buy the Ships, Get the Quotas: Pescanova Argentine Gambit," *Quick Frozen Foods International,* April 2002, p. 50.

Cherry, Drew, "Pescanova: Spain's Billion-Dollar Dynamo," *Intrafish,* November 2003, p. 14.

Fiorillo, John, and Drew Cherry, "The World's Top Seafood Companies," *Intrafish,* March 2005, p. 22.

"From Spain to Argentina to Australia, Pescanova's in the International Swim," *Quick Frozen Foods International,* October 1994, p. 68.

"Pescanova Gives Cubans a Shrimp Boat," *Cuba News,* June 2003, p. 12.

"Pescanova Plans Fish Farms for Higher Yields," *Namibia Economist,* April 19, 2002.

"Pescanova to Focus on Added Value," *Foodanddrink.com,* October 11, 2002.

"Spanish Firm Signs Deals to Sell Cuban Shrimp and Lobsters," *Cuba News,* March 2001, p. 12.

"Spanish Shrimp Farm Investment," *Caribbean Update,* June 2002.

PetMed Express, Inc.

1441 SW 29th Avenue
Pompano Beach, Florida 33069
U.S.A.
Telephone: (954) 979-5995
Toll Free: (800) 738-6337
Fax: (954) 971-0544
Web site: http://www.1800petmeds.com

Public Company
Incorporated: 1996
Employees: 180
Sales: $108.4 million (2005)
Stock Exchanges: NASDAQ
Ticker Symbol: PETS
NAIC: 453910 Pet and Pet Supplies Stores; 454111
   Electronic Shipping; 454113 Mail-Order Houses

■ ■ ■

PetMed Express, Inc., the nation's largest pet pharmacy, markets discounted prescription and non-prescription pet medications, health and nutritional supplements, and accessories for dogs, cats, and horses through its catalog and postcards, through customer service representatives at its toll free number, and via the Internet. Prescription medications include name-brand as well as generic heartworm treatments, thyroid and arthritis medications, antibiotics, and other specialty medications. Non-prescription items, which include flea and tick control products, bone and joint care products, vitamins and supplements, and hygiene products, account for 70 percent of sales. The company purchases

its products at wholesale prices and ships directly to customers.

1996–1998: RAPID GROWTH LEADS TO TROUBLE WITH THE VETERINARY COMMUNITY

In December 1996, Dr. Marc Puleo, an anesthesiologist, founded PetMed Express, Inc. It was not originally Puleo's intention to enter the world of pet pharmaceuticals; however, with Americans spending more on companion animals overall, Puleo reasoned they would welcome the convenience and discount of ordering medications and products for their animals online. "I was looking to do mail-order marketing of human medications, but Merck was already heavily into that. So I decided to try mail-order pet medicines and assorted pet accessories," Puleo said in a 1998 *Miami Herald* article.

PetMed Express incorporated in July 1996 and grew rapidly by word of mouth. By 1997, it had sales of $600,000, and in fiscal 1998, the company sold $2.8 million worth of pet drugs and other products at a discount of up to 40 percent off veterinarians' office prices. The company, then headquartered in Fort Lauderdale, employed about 70 people, including two on-staff veterinarians, and had a 76-page catalog. PetMed's first catalogs sold numerous antibiotics, wormers, fungicides, vaccines for dog diseases, such as parvovirus, parainfluenza, hepatitis, and distemper, and for cat illnesses, such as feline leukemia and distemper, as well as leashes, shampoos, and toys.

It was not long, though, before PetMed was in trouble with veterinarians, who did not like the

KEY DATES

1996: Dr. Marc Puleo incorporates PetMed Express, Inc.
1998: The American Veterinary Distributors Association files a complaint against PetMed with the Center for Veterinary Medicine.
1999: The Florida Pharmaceutical Board settles on 56 complaints against PetMed.
2000: The company goes public; Tricon Holdings LLC invests in the company.
2001: Menderes Akdag becomes CEO.

company's methods of doing business. Some criticized the way the company obtained its pharmaceutical merchandise, claiming that it purchased drugs from unethical vets, who ordered more than their practice needed from unethical distributors. Others disliked the way PetMed marketed its services. PetMed, like other mail-order companies, obtained public records—in one case in Florida, rabies vaccination lists—to target pet owners with its direct mail ads. In April 1997, Florida state representative Bob Swindler, a veterinarian himself, put forward a measure to exempt rabies lists from public disclosure; instead, records could be obtained only one at a time.

Swindler and other veterinarians across the state insisted that the measure preserved individual privacy and that PetMed's method of obtaining the lists was unscrupulous. Puleo countered in a 1997 *St. Petersburg Times* article, attributing such criticism of the company to the self-interest of veterinarians who "don't want ... us taking their customers from them." His solution to the conflict was simple: "All they need to do is lower their prices." Veterinarians in private practice typically drew about a quarter of their yearly revenues from the prescriptions they wrote and filled.

The company's methods faced other challenges as well. PetMed was required by law to have a prescription on hand any time it sold a drug to a consumer. However, it was unclear whether the prescription could be faxed or called in to PetMed. According to PetMed, in a 2003 *DVM* article, once contacted by a customer wishing to order from the catalog, "[o]ur process is we fax the veterinarian first, and if we don't hear from them, we call. We also call the client."

PetMed insisted that "[b]y not responding or authorizing the prescription for us, veterinarians are limiting consumers' freedom of choice." Problems ensued

when the company went ahead anyway and filled some of these prescriptions while awaiting authorization. During 1998, as mail-order pet pharmacies as a group came under the scrutiny of the veterinary community, the Florida Pharmacy Board received six complaints against PetMed alleging that the company had issued medications without a prescription from a vet.

The American Veterinary Distributors Association also filed a complaint with the Center for Veterinary Medicine, a division of the U.S. Food and Drug Administration, claiming that PetMed Express was selling prescription drugs without the consent of a veterinarian. At issue here were the company's own scripting veterinarians, who prescribed drugs for animals they had never seen. These professionals were not licensed to prescribe in the state of Florida, which insisted that there be a veterinarian-client relationship before a prescription could be filled.

Following several months of controversy and pending an FDA investigation of its practices, PetMed recognized that it had to rebuild its image with some vets. It began "looking to maintain a peaceful relationship with veterinarians," according to Puleo in a 1998 *DVM* article. "We're looking to provide a service to our customers and the veterinary community. ... [W]e think we can help improve both the veterinary field and actually help increase revenue back to the veterinarian's office." More than dispensing medicines, the company's "new mission is to get pets to the vet." The plan was to encourage customers to visit a vet on a regular basis by offering an additional discount on merchandise purchased after a veterinary office visit and by setting up a veterinary referral network.

1999–2002: NEW LEADERSHIP AND REPEATED SANCTIONS

In August 1999, after several months of discussion, the Florida Pharmacy Board settled with the company on 56 complaints. The Board required that PetMed pay a $30,000 fine for costs incurred during its investigation in addition to $8,000 for the two-year investigation. PetMed had to submit quarterly reports to the Pharmacy Board for the next two years, and Puleo and his pharmacy manager had to take 12 hours of continuing education on pharmacy laws and regulations. More generally, PetMed had to adhere to the Board's plan of action for the company, obey state laws relating to the practice of pharmacy, and agree to semiannual inspections for two years. PetMed did not have to admit to any wrongdoing.

The following year, 2000, the company went public. However, there was trouble again when the EPA issued a "stop sales order" to PetMed and several pet stores to which it had sold veterinary-distributed flea control products. The boxes for the widely used products had been purchased outside of the United States and thus gave their dosages in metric, giving rise to the possibility of overdose. Novartis, maker of the misbranded product, also sued PetMed. PetMed and the EPA settled in 2001, with PetMed Express paying a penalty of $100,000 and agreeing to properly dispose of mislabeled products. In 2002, PetMed reached a confidential settlement on their suit.

In the meantime, significant changes were taking place within the company. In March 2001, Puleo stepped down as executive director, though he stayed on as president; Menderes Akdag, former chief executive and president of Lens Express, replaced him. The company also installed state-of-the-art software to facilitate online ordering. It stopped selling about 5,000 non-drug items to focus on the 600 remaining medicine-related products in its inventory. Finally, it began to take a more aggressive stance toward its detractors.

In 2001, a complaint form appeared on PetMed's web site. The letter was intended for customers whose veterinarian withheld a prescription to PetMed for non-medical reasons or charged a client to write out the prescription. According to the letter, which appeared in an August 2003 issue of *DVM,* "[i]n some instances, we find that veterinarians withhold prescription authorization because they want to sell the medication themselves. This restricts freedom of choice and leads to higher prices for consumers and requires the inconvenience of an additional trip to the veterinarian's office." The company offered to e-mail these complaint forms to the federal Consumer Protection Agency, state veterinary regulatory agencies, and state consumer protection agencies.

Late in 2001, the company was once again embroiled in trouble with the Florida Pharmaceutical Board, which went public to say that the company's pharmaceutical license was in jeopardy because it had failed to heed its first warning. Also at issue were fraud charges for PetMed's failure to announce that a second online pharmacy, Savemax, ran out of its offices. In the end, the Board again levied penalties against PetMed ($30,000 in investigative costs and $40,000 in fines) and mandated unannounced state inspections and a three-year probation. Several employees, including Akdag, were ordered to complete training in pharmacy laws.

Although criticized for being a second slap on the wrist, Florida's 2002 settlement was in some ways a benchmark because it set the stage for other states to take action against PetMed. The Missouri Board of Pharmacy put PetMed on probation in 2001 for violating six state statutes, including a law that required nonresident pharmacies to obtain an in-state license to sell prescription drugs in the state; the Board ruled that it could not use its alternative veterinarian program to fill prescriptions in the state. This probation was eventually extended to 2007. In 2002, Missouri issued a temporary restraining order against PetMed for not heeding its warning. The Alabama Board of Pharmacy put the company on a five-year probation, terminated its alternative vet program in the state, and demanded $8,000 in fines in 2001. Utah denied the company's application to renew its out-of-state mail-order license; although it renewed the license when PetMed objected. The Texas State Board of Pharmacy and State Board of Veterinary Medical Examiners Officials began investigating their own case against PetMed in 2002 and alleged in 2004 that PetMed had sold prescription drugs illegally to Texas consumers.

2003–2006: A HOT GROWTH COMPANY FACES CLASS-ACTION SUITS

By 2003, spending on pets in the United States had reached about $3 billion, and veterinary medicine was expanding to meet demand. Pain medications alone topped $150 million, having increased 275 percent in the preceding six years. A survey by the American Animal Hospital Association found that a majority of pet owners said they would go to great lengths to improve the quality of their pet's life, even for a short period of time. Revenues for PetMed increased 71 percent in 2003 to reach $94 million. This figure represented a ninefold increase in sales in four years and 40 percent of the market for pet medications sold via mail or the Internet. Fifty-five percent of revenues came from repeat customers.

In 2004, *BusinessWeek* named PetMed to its annual list of 100 Hot Growth Companies based on the previous three years' revenues and income. During this period, sales had increased 102.2 percent, profits 173.9 percent, and the company had achieved a 51.5 percent average return on capital. In 2004 alone, sales increased 70 percent. Also in 2004, PetMed reached an agreement with the Hartville Group, Inc., one of the leading pet insurance companies, to allow Hartville to market its Healthy Bark & Purr to PetMed Express customers via the web site.

However, 2004 brought six class-action securities lawsuits against PetMed. Shareholders sued, after the company's share price dropped about a third. PetMed claimed that this drop was due to a decline in new customers after the company bought less television advertising time. The suits claimed that the company had delayed disclosing long time veterinarian dissension that hampered sales growth so that company insiders and executives could cash in shares worth $65 million. In June 2004, Puleo sold off a $10 million stake in the company and Tricon Holdings LLC, which had invested in 2000, followed suit in 2005, bringing its holdings down to 21 percent from 70 percent earlier.

Throughout all of its difficulties, PetMed insisted that it had reformed and was in complete compliance with all state and federal regulations. Akdag voiced optimism about PetMed's future, stating in a 2004 *South Florida Sun-Sentinel* article that it was just a matter of time before consumers turned to discount companies, such as PetMed. The company, which had about a 3 percent share of the $3 billion annual market in pet medicines, and made most of its revenues selling treatments for flea and tick control, heartworm, and bone and joint care, saw its biggest opportunity in the prescription end of its business. Even former detractors seemed willing to lend qualified support to the company. "PetMed got off to a bad start," said Donald Schaefer, executive director of the Florida Veterinary Medical Association, in the *Sun-Sentinel* article. "The good news is that the company has made a legitimate effort to respond to the requirements of the Board of Pharmacy."

Carrie Rothburd

PRINCIPAL SUBSIDIARIES

Southeastern Veterinary Exports Inc.; First Image Marketing Inc.

PRINCIPAL COMPETITORS

Drs. Foster & Smith; KV Vet; PetCareRx; Medical Management International, Inc.; Pet Valu; Petco Animal Supplies, Inc.; PETsMART, Inc.; Wal-Mart Stores, Inc.

FURTHER READING

Aschoff, Susan, "Pet Rx," *St. Petersburg Times,* June 10, 2003, p. 1D.

Baumgardner, Kathy, "Complaints Lodged Against PetMed Express," *DVM,* June 1998, p. 38.

———, "Florida Pharmacy Board, PetMed Express Reach Accord," *DVM,* October 1999, p. 1.

———, "PetMed Express 'Redirecting' Image," *DVM,* September 1998, p. 1.

Cohen, Karen-Janine, "Problems Remain at PetMed Despite 70 Percent Jump in Sales," *South Florida Sun-Sentinel,* August 26, 2004.

Fiala, Jennifer, "Across the Nation: Agencies File Grievances Against PetMed Express," *DVM,* March 2002, p, 26.

———, "Investigation Looms Over PetMed Express," *DVM,* October 2001, p. 1.

———, "PetMed Express Abets Complaints to FTC," *DVM,* August 2001, p. 1.

———, "Practitioners Lash Out Against PetMed Express," *DVM,* August 2003, p 1.

Landis, David, "Young Companies on a Roll," *Kiplinger's Personal Finance,* September 2004, p. 42.

Martinez, Draeger, "Pet Supplies Are in the Mail Thanks to Fort Lauderdale, Florida, Firm," *Miami Herald,* November 25, 1998.

Pou Chen Corporation

2 Fu Kung Rd.
Fu Hsing Hsiang
Changhwa Hsien,
Taiwan
Telephone: +886 04 2769 5147
Fax: +886 04 2768 0577
Web site: http://www.pouchen.com.tw

Public Company
Incorporated: 1969
Employees: 289,250
Sales: TWD 150.8 billion ($3.15 billion) (2005)
Stock Exchanges: Taiwan
Ticker Symbol: 9904
NAIC: 316219 Other Footwear Manufacturing; 316213 Men's Footwear (Except Athletic) Manufacturing; 316214 Women's Footwear (Except Athletic) Manufacturing

■ ■ ■

Pou Chen Corporation is a Taiwan-based holding company representing the world's largest OEM/ODM (original equipment manufacture/original design manufacture) footwear design, manufacturing, and distribution group. While Pou Chen itself concentrates on research and development and design activities for the footwear industry, its main subsidiary, Hong Kong Hang Seng Index-listed Yue Yuen Industrial (Holdings) Ltd., oversees the group's footwear production. Pou Chen and Yue Yuen are the manufacturing force behind nine of the world's top ten sports shoe brands, including Nike, adidas, Asics, Puma, New Balance, and Reebok. The company also produces boots, work boots, and shoes for brands such as Timberland, Rockport, Doc Marten, Clarks, and many others. The company produces nearly 190 million pairs of shoes per year, or apporximately one in every six pairs of shoes sold each year, with almost 290,000 employees working at some 350 production lines in China, Vietnam, and Indonesia, as well as at a small number of production units in its Taiwan home base. The company also operates a smaller production unit, Solar Link, for New Balance in the United States.

In addition to shoe production, Pou Chen has branched out into distribution, establishing a 600-strong retail store network in mainland China, where it sells its customers' shoe brands. The company expects to expand its retail chain to 1,000 stores in the near future. Caught up in scandals involving labor conditions at many of its factories, Pou Chen transferred its production operations to its Yue Yuen unit in the early 2000s. Since then, the company has targeted growth beyond the footwear market, establishing operations for the production of LCD displays and related high-tech products. Both Pou Chen and Yue Yuen are dominated by the founding Tsai family, who launched the company in 1969. Pou Chen is listed on the Taiwan Stock Exchange, and Yue Yuen is listed on the Hong Kong Stock Exchange. Nai Fang Tsai is Pou Chen's chairman of the board. In 2005, the company's sales topped TWD 150 billion ($3.15 billion), roughly four times the size of its nearest competitor, fellow Taiwanese producer Feng Tay Enterprises Co.

FROM RAGS TO SHOES IN 1969

Pou Chen was founded in Changwha (alternatively Chang Hwa), Taiwan, by Tsai Chi Jiu and his three brothers as a manufacturer of footwear for the export market. The Tsais came from a family of fabric weavers; Tsai Chi Jiu himself went to Taichung Normal University, where he studied art design. Tsai then began a career as an art teacher for an elementary school. At night, however, Tsai moonlighted as freelance designer for local shoemakers, both as a colorist and as shoe designer. By 1969, Tsai had decided to found his own footwear companies, and together with his brothers launched Pou Chen Corporation.

Pou Chen initially produced plastic shoes; by 1973, the company also had begun shipping plastic sandals. The booming Taiwanese export market, which was rapidly replacing Japan as a global source of cheaply produced goods, enabled the company to achieve strong growth, and by 1974, the company had bought the Fu Hsing Industrial Estate in Changwha and begun preparations for a new factory complex there. By 1976, the company had launched production of plastic casual shoes, which were complemented a year later by the production of boots. During this period, Pou Chen also began developing its contacts with the international footwear market, and increasingly began to take on OEM (original equipment manufacture) and ODM (original design manufacture) contracts from a number of international footwear brands.

The completion of the Fu Hsing factory in 1978 enabled Pou Chen to begin manufacturing a new type of shoe that was to change its destiny. The late 1970s had seen the appearance of a new generation of sports shoe. More technically oriented than their predecessors, the new sneaker types revolutionized the footwear industry, and launched a number of new brand names, including Nike, Reebok, adidas, Puma, and New Balance, on an international level. Pou Chen launched production of sports shoes in 1978, signing on New Balance as one of its first customers.

Pou Chen's true breakthrough came in 1980, when the company signed a contract with adidas, already one of the world's top athletic shoe brands. The adidas contract not only provided the company with a strong revenue source, it also built the group's reputation among the global footwear industry. In this way, Pou Chen rapidly built up partnerships with many, if not most, of the major athletic shoe brands in the world.

Pou Chen expanded its production capacity, as well as its client list, in 1984, with the acquisition of rival Pou Yun Industrial Company. Two years later, the company completed a new extension of the Fu Hsing site, adding an additional factory complex.

Into the second half of the 1980s, however, Pou Chen found itself struggling to maintain a competitive edge amid the rising worth of the Taiwanese dollar, and the rising wages of its workforce. The first signs of a shift in manufacturing in mainland China had begun to be seen by then; yet Pou Chen was restricted from a direct entry into the mainland market by Taiwanese law.

Instead, in 1988, Tsai Chi Jen, one of Tsai Chi Jiu's brothers, moved to Hong Kong to establish a new company, called Yue Yuen Industrial Holdings. This company provided Pou Chen with a conduit into the mainland Chinese market. Backed by a major manufacturing contract for Reebok, Yue Yuen opened its first manufacturing plant in China, in Zhuhai, in 1988. The company also began production of private-label footwear for the department store market in the United States. Over the next three years, Yue Yuen set up three more factories in China, in Dongguan, Zhuhai, and Zhongshan. This expansion enabled Pou Chen to transfer an increasing proportion of its production from Taiwan to the mainland into the early 1990s.

INTERNATIONAL EXPANSION THROUGH THE END OF THE 20TH CENTURY

Through the 1990s, Pou Chen continued to expand its number of production sites in mainland China. By the mid-2000s, the number of Chinese production lines operated by the company in China neared 160, representing more than half of the company's total production. Many of the company's factories in China were established as joint ventures, arranged through a network of investment companies and shell companies registered in the British Virgin Islands. To this mix, Pou Chen added its own directly controlled manufacturing joint venture after the Taiwanese relaxed the island state's foreign investment rules. This allowed Pou Chen to form a 55-45 joint venture with Yue Yuen, called Pou Yuen Industrial, to begin manufacturing in China in

KEY DATES

1969: Tsai Chi Liu and his three brothers establish Pou Chen, a factory for producing plastic footwear in Taiwan.

1980: The company receives a breakthrough contract to produce sports shoes for adidas.

1988: The Tsai family establishes Yue Yuen Industrial in Hong Kong in order to expand production to mainland China.

1992: Yue Yuen goes public on the Hong Kong Stock Exchange; both Pou Chen and Yue Yuen establish the Pou Yuen Industrial joint venture in China.

1993: The first production plant in Indonesia opens.

1994: Production in Vietnam is launched.

1996: Yue Yuen acquires full control of Pou Yuen.

2002: Pou Chen transfers its production operations to Yue Yuen.

2003: Pou Chen enters the high-technology sector, launching a backlight production joint venture; Yue Yuen enters sportswear production with the purchase of the majority of Pro Kingtex.

2006: Yue Yuen announces plans to build a new footwear factory in Indonesia with a production capacity of 3.5 million pairs per year.

1992. In that year, Yue Yuen was listed on the Hong Kong Stock Exchange.

Pou Yuen Industrial also provided a vehicle for the expansion of Pou Chen's industrial infrastructure beyond the Chinese market. The company targeted Indonesia, by then emerging as a new low-cost production center, establishing its first shoe factory there in 1993. Pou Chen and Yue Yuen next teamed up to enter another new market, Vietnam, in 1994. The company quickly began building up its presence in both countries. By the mid-2000s, Pou Chen's and Yue Yuen's holdings reached 72 production lines and 51 production lines in Vietnam and Indonesia, respectively.

Pou Chen continued to transfer its production outside of Taiwan through the 1990s. By the beginning of the 2000s, the company operated just eight production units in Taiwan, in large part to supply the local footwear market. Pou Chen also had transferred its 55 percent of Pou Yuen Industrial to Yue Yuen, in a share

swap deal that gave Pou Chen majority control of the Hong Kong-based company. Both companies continued to be controlled by the Tsai family.

Also during the 1990s, Pou Chen began constructing a vertically integrated operation. On the one hand, the company entered the production of raw materials and shoe components. This was accomplished through the creation of an array of more than 60 subsidiaries, including a number of joint ventures, such as its 50 percent stake in natural leather producer Prime Asia, and a 45 percent stake in split leather producer Cohen, both based in China. The company also established a technical partnership with Kuraray in Japan for the production of high-quality, polyurethane-based synthetic leather. That company, Megatrade, remained a 100 percent subsidiary of Pou Chen.

At the same time as it built its upstream wing, Pou Chen turned toward the downstream side as well. In 1994, the company, in partnership with Yue Yuen, established its first retail operations in China. The company began building up a network of retail stores and in-store counters in the mainland, and by the mid-2000s had opened some 600 stores. These stores were stocked with the branded shoes Pou Chen manufactured for its customers.

EXPLORING NEW MARKETS IN THE NEW CENTURY

Pou Chen found itself at the center of controversy in the late 1990s, however, as the often appalling working conditions at factories under the company's control sparked a wide-ranging scandal throughout much of the global manufacturing market. The resulting controversy, which centered especially around Nike (estimated to account for as much as 53 percent of Pou Chen's sales), contributed to a slowdown in the market into the early 2000s. In part in response to the growing backlash against Asian-produced goods, Pou Chen made the unusual move of establishing a manufacturing subsidiary in the United States. That company, called Solar Link, was dedicated exclusively to the production (chiefly the assembly) of New Balance shoes for the U.S. market.

The continued controversy surrounding the company's labor practices, as well as the undervaluing of especially Yue Yuen's stock due to the complexity of the two companies' organization, led Pou Chen to launch a streamlining drive in the early 2000s. By 2002, Pou Chen had transferred nearly all of its footwear production units to Yue Yuen, at the same time tightening its control over the Hong Kong-based company. The addition of Pou Chen's nearly 70 production subsidiaries helped boost Yue Yuen's status as well, and in 2003 the company was added to the Hong Kong Stock Exchange's blue chip Hang Seng Index.

Yue Yuen continued to grow into the middle of the decade. In 2003, for example, the company extended its product range to the sportswear sector with the purchase of majority control of Pro Kingtex. The following year, the company acquired a 31 percent stake in sports apparel manufacturer Eagle Nice (International) Holdings. The company increased its shareholding in that company to 45 percent in 2005. By then, Yue Yuen also had entered the manufacture of sports bags, backpacks, and related accessories when it acquired Prosperous Industrial Holdings Ltd. At the end of 2005, Yue Yuen expanded again, this time through a joint venture partnership with Golden Chang Group for the production of work, safety, and casual footwear. Yue Yuen also continued developing its wholesale and retail networks in China, gaining the exclusive distribution rights in that country for brands such as Converse, ASICS, Hush Puppy, and Coleman.

The streamlined Pou Chen, in the meantime, in addition to acting as Yue Yuen's holding company, overseeing functions such as human resources and other administrative services, had refocused itself around the research, development, and design of footwear for its major branded and other customers. Yet Tsai Chi Jiu sought new horizons for Pou Chen. Recognizing that future growth prospects for its footwear operation remained limited (the company by then represented some one in six of every pair of shoes sold in the world) Tsai Chi Jiu sought to diversify the company into the high-technology sector. In 2003, for example, the company formed a joint venture with K-Bridge Electronics in Taiwan to manufacture backlight modules and light guide panels at a production plant in Dongguan, China. The following year, Pou Chen added a new joint venture with Quanta Computer to produce LCD monitors.

Observers were somewhat skeptical of Pou Chen's new high-tech interest, particularly because of the company's relatively late entry into the sector. Nonetheless, the company's diversification remained backed by its role as a powerhouse footwear producer in a market already worth more than $20 billion per year in the middle of the 2000s. Pou Chen, through its majority control of Yue Yuen, continued to reinforce its position in that market. In March 2006, for example, the company announced plans to build a major new factory

in Indonesia, with a production capacity of more than 3.5 million pairs of shoes per year. Pou Chen expected to remain the new century's footwear leader.

M. L. Cohen

PRINCIPAL SUBSIDIARIES

Global Brands Manufacture Ltd.; Yue Yuen Industrial (Holdings) Corporation (Hong Kong); Chiya Vietnam Enterprise (51%); Dah-Chen Shoe Materials Ltd. (Vietnam; 51%); Forearn Company Ltd. (British Virgin Islands); Friendsole Limited (Hong Kong); Fu Tai Company Limited; P.T. Nikomas Gemilang (Indonesia); P.T. Pou Chen Indonesia; P.T. Sukespermata Indonusa (Indonesia); P.T. Variadhana Citraselaras (Indonesia); Pou Chen Vietnam Enterprise Ltd.; Pou Chien Chemical (Holdings) (British Virgin Islands); Pou Chien Chemical Company (Taiwan); Pou Sung Vietnam Industrial; Pou Yuen Industrial (Hong Kong); Pou Yuen International Limited (British Virgin Islands); Pou Yuen Marketing Company (British Virgin Islands); Pou Yuen Vietnam Enterprise Ltd.; Solar Link International Inc. (U.S.A.); Yue Yuen Industrial Limited (Hong Kong).

PRINCIPAL COMPETITORS

Feng Tay Enterprises Co.; Shanghai Leather Corporation; Korindo Group, PT; Hardaya Aneka Shoe Industry, PT; Omzest Business Division; Hyosung Corporation; C and J Clark International Ltd.; Binh Tien Imex Corporation Private Ltd.; Garuda Indawa, PT.

FURTHER READING

"Pou Chen Expands from Footwear Manufacturing into Retailing," *Taiwan Economic News,* November 30, 2005.
"Pou Chen to Tap Global Market for Working Shoes," *Taiwan Economic News,* October 18, 2005.
"Pou Chen Unit to Build Plant in Indonesia," *China Times,* March 19, 2006.
"Pou Chen, World's Biggest Footwear Maker, Predicts Continued Growth," *Taiwan Economic News,* March 21, 2003.
"A Successful Tsai Is an Average Joe," *Taipei Times,* June 10, 2003, p. 10.
"Taiwan's Two Footwear Giants Benefit from Noted Sports Games," *CENS,* June 2, 2006.
Zarocostas, John, "Pou Chen Bulks Up Vietnam Production," *Footwear News,* July 5, 2004, p. 4.

The Pharmaceutical Development Company

POZEN Inc.

▪

1414 Raleigh Road
Suite 400
Chapel Hill, North Carolina 27517
U.S.A.
Telephone: (919) 913-1030
Fax: (919) 913-1039
Web site: http://www.pozen.com

Public Company
Incorporated: 1996
Employees: 38
Sales: $28.6 million (2005)
Stock Exchanges: NASDAQ
Ticker Symbol: POZN
NAIC: 325412 Pharmaceutical Preparation Manufacturing

■ ■ ■

POZEN Inc. (Pozen) is a small, Chapel Hill, North Carolina-based pharmaceutical company that seeks to develop drugs it can license to larger partners to commercialize. The company has been targeting the acute migraine market, which numbers as many as 30 million people in the United States alone, developing pain-treatment drugs using triptans with different delivery technologies. Its primary drug candidate, developed in collaboration with GlaxoSmithKline, is Trexima, which combines a triptan with a nonsteroidal anti-inflammatory drug (NSAID) in an effort to alleviate the pain of migraines while avoiding the gastrointestinal side effects caused by other drugs. In addition to

Trexima, Pozen is developing a migraine drug using lornoxicam, another NSAID. Pozen is also interested in moving beyond the migraine field to develop other drugs where it believes there are unmet needs and opportunity. Pozen is a public company listed on the NASDAQ.

COMPANY FOUNDED IN 1996

Pozen was founded and incorporated in 1996 by Dr. John R. Plachetka, Dr. Peter J. Wise, and Joseph J. Ruvane, Jr. The idea for the company came from Plachetka. After earning an undergraduate degree in Pharmacy from the University of Illinois College of Pharmacy and a Doctor of Pharmacy from the University of Missouri-Kansas City, he spent a decade working at Glaxo Inc. He then became chief executive of a clinical research organization, Clinical Research Foundation-America, from 1990 to 1992, and spent two years as vice-president of development at Texas Biotechnology Corporation before starting Pozen. During his time at Glaxo, Plachetka served as director of cardiovascular clinical research, involved in the development of several drugs, including Imitrex. Introduced in 1991, Imitrex was the first drug in half a century to be formulated to relieve migraine pain. It proved such a bestseller that it engendered a host of competing drugs, all relying on 5HT1 receptor antagonists.

Plachetka wanted to pursue a drug development approach different from what was practiced at large pharmaceutical firms. "We don't say, 'Here's a great molecule. What do we do with it?'" Plachetka told Raleigh, North Carolina's the *News & Observer*. "We look at the marketplace and say, 'There is a hole here.

What can we do that makes sense and fill that gap?'" The immediate gap in the marketplace Plachetka recognized was related to migraines. The 5HT1 drugs targeted only severe headaches, leaving an opportunity to develop a treatment for the millions of people who suffered from milder headaches and could not take 5HT1 drugs.

To help launch Pozen, Plachetka recruited Wise, a former colleague at Glaxo, where he worked from 1979 to 1993 and ultimately became senior vice-president of Medical Operations and chief medical officer. After leaving Glaxo and before joining Plachetka, he served as president and chief operating officer at North Carolina-based Pharmaceutical Product Development, Inc., a major contract research firm. Wise would become Pozen's senior medical affairs adviser and lend a measure of credibility to the start-up company.

Providing even greater legitimacy to Pozen was its third cofounder, 71-year-old Ruvane, a giant in the pharmaceutical industry. He served as chairman and CEO of Glaxo from 1981 to 1989, and during his tenure there pioneered the first co-promotion agreement between two U.S. drug makers. The Glaxo alliance with Hoffmann LaRoche to co-promote a new anti-ulcer drug, Zantac, dramatically increased Glaxo's ability to compete with the much larger SmithKline Beckman. As a result, Zantac became the most successful new drug launch in the United States to that point. After leaving Glaxo, Ruvane became the chairman of Durham, North Carolina-based Sphinx Pharmaceuticals, which in 1994 he sold to Eli Lilly & Co. With Ruvane on board, fledgling Pozen had no difficulty in raising funds. One biotechnology industry expert interviewed by the *News & Observer* commented, "All Joe Ruvane has to do is call his friends and he'll be well financed." In a matter of 90 days the company raised $6.7 million from individual investors. A second round of venture capital financing later raised another $6.8 million.

Part of Plachetka's vision for Pozen was to essentially create a virtual company, one that focused on drug development and farmed out a lot of the work, and could reduce the costs involved and the time it took to get a product to the market. In a 2000 letter to shareholders, Plachetka explained how Pozen benefited from the lessons he and his colleagues had learned over the years: "We concentrate only on the development phase of a drug's life, thus avoiding the high risk and high costs of both discovery research and building a sales and marketing organization." Pozen hoped to commercialize products through partners and make money from upfront and milestone payments, and once the products were in the marketplace it would receive royalties. In addition, Pozen planned to pursue what Plachetka called a license-back model, essentially finding new uses for old drugs. Pozen would acquire the products, finance the development of them through Phase 3 of the Food and Drug Administration (FDA) process, and then give the discovering company a chance to reacquire the reformulated product, with a fresh patent lifespan, and market it.

In the beginning Plachetka identified three drugs, all non-5HT1 drugs without patent protection, that he and his colleagues believed could be used to develop an alternate migraine pain reliever. Although this was Pozen's initial focus, because of its founders' backgrounds and success with other drugs, the company expected to pursue opportunities in five therapeutic areas: antibiotics, cardiovascular, central nervous system, gastrointestinal, and respiratory.

COMMENCEMENT OF FIRST CLINICAL TRIALS IN 1997

In addition to raising money and incorporating, Pozen filed its first patents in 1996. Then in 1997 Plachetka set up operations in an office park in Chapel Hill, North Carolina, and began hiring employees. Also in that first full year of operation, Pozen took initial steps in gaining FDA approval on a drug. In order to do that, it needed to conduct clinical trials to ensure the efficacy and safety of the drug. FDA trials are divided into phases. Phase 1 trials use a small sample of healthy volunteers to determine dosage, document how a drug is metabolized and excreted by the body, and uncover adverse side effects. Additional safety information and preliminary evidence that a drug offers beneficial effects is gathered in Phase 2 trials. If both the benefits and the risks warrant it, the FDA allows Phase 3 trials, in which the drug is tested with much larger samples of subjects over an extended period of time. Both Phase 2 and Phase 3 studies usually involve a "control" group of subjects given an inactive placebo. Only when the FDA is satisfied with the results from the clinical trials does it grant approval and the drug can be sold to the public. In 1997 Pozen completed a Phase 1 study on MT 100, a combination of naproxen sodium and metoclopramide hydrochloride in a sequential release formulation that

```
┌─────────────────────────────────────────────┐
│                                               │
│              KEY DATES                        │
│              ──────■──────                     │
│                                               │
│  1996:  The company is founded.               │
│  1999:  Chairman Joseph J. Ruvane retires.    │
│  2000:  The company is taken public.          │
│  2003:  A marketing agreement is struck with  │
│         GlaxoSmithKline.                       │
│                                               │
└─────────────────────────────────────────────┘
```

was intended as a first-line therapy. It then filed an Investigational New Drug (IND) application with the FDA to further the approval process.

In 1998 the MT 100 Phase 2 study was completed, and Pozen made progress on its two other migraine drugs. MT 300, a highly purified formulation of dihydroergotamine mesylate (DHE) in an injectable form for severe migraine attacks for use at home, finished its Phase 2 trials, and a pilot study was conducted for MT 400, a first-line migraine therapy that combined a triptan with a NSAID in a single tablet. Pozen began Phase 3 trials on MT 100 in 1999, and in that same year the company reached a license-back agreement with Roche Bioscience on a migraine preventative treatment, MT 500, a 5-HT2B that Roche had already shepherded through Phase 1 trials. Also of note in 1999, Ruvane stepped down as chairman in December, replaced by Plachetka. His health failing, Ruvane died of cancer several months later.

IPO IN 2000

In March 2000 Pozen raised another $18 million in venture capital, and in that same month a new chief financial officer was hired, Matthew E. Czajkowski, an experienced investment banker. Two months later Pozen filed with the Securities and Exchange Commission (SEC) to make an initial public offering (IPO) of stock, and Czajkowski became the point person for that effort. With U.S. Bancorp Jaffray acting as lead underwriter, and participation from Prudential Vector Healthcare and Pacific Growth Equities, Pozen completed its offer in October 2000, netting around $68 million before fees. The money was earmarked for drug development, the acquisition of products, and general corporate purposes.

Pozen was making solid progress on gaining FDA approval, resulting in a strong IPO, but in 2001 its plans to submit MT 100 for approval by the end of the year after the completion of Phase 3 trials were short-circuited when the FDA requested further carcinogenicity studies, which forced a delay on the filing. With plenty of cash on hand and conservative management,

Pozen could afford to be patient and it initiated the requested studies on MT 100 in the hope of making a New Drug Application (NDA) submission in the first half of 2003. On other fronts, MT 300 began Phase 3 trials, and the company hoped an NDA submission could be submitted by the end of 2002. MT 400 also began Phase 2 trials in 2001.

MT 100 received good news in 2002 when preliminary results in mice showed it was not carcinogenic. In addition, the MT 300 submission was filed in 2002 as hoped. Pozen received a major boost in June 2003 when it reached an agreement with GlaxoSmithKline on marketing rights to the MT 400 formulation. Pozen received $25 million upfront and was in line for another $55 million in milestone payments, as well as royalties on sales if the drug made the market. Later in the year Pozen struck a deal with Xcel Pharmaceuticals, Inc., to market MT 300. The terms called for a $2 million upfront fee, a further $8 million in milestone payments, and a royalty on sales. During 2003 Pozen filed an NDA for MT 100. In October the FDA sent a not-approvable letter regarding MT 300 on a previously filed NDA, citing that MT 300 failed to achieve statistical significance versus a placebo. Thus Pozen had to return to clinical trials in an effort to prove to the FDA's satisfaction that MT 300 was indeed as effective as the company believed it was.

Czajkowski resigned as CFO in early 2004 for what were described as personal and family reasons. The company continued to seek approval for its first drug in 2004. Early on in the year it submitted the rat study to complete the NDA on MT 100, resulting in a sharp rise in the price of Pozen's stock. That enthusiasm waned by June when the FDA rejected the application, leading to a steep decline in the price of Pozen's stock to less than $5 per share.

In November 2005 Pozen received regulatory approval in the United Kingdom for MT 100, the company's first success with a drug application, and it began seeking out a marketing partner to sell the migraine treatment in the United Kingdom. After experiencing problems with MT 100 and Mt 300 in the United States, Pozen pinned greater hopes on MT 400, which became known by the brand name Trexima. Partner GlaxoSmithKline thought so highly of the drug that it listed it as one the firm's top five key product launches and filings. The NDA for Trexima was filed in August 2005 and there was every expectation that it would gain FDA approval in the second quarter of 2006. Unfortunately for Pozen, in June 2006 it received an approvable letter from the FDA indicating that while Trexima was an effective treatment for migraine headaches, the agency still had safety concerns that needed to be addressed, perhaps requiring new studies. Pozen and GlaxoSmithKline hoped to alleviate these concerns as soon as possible, but after a decade of effort the frustrations of getting a product onto the market continued to mount. Nevertheless, the company had cash on hand, major partners, and a number of other drugs in the pipeline, including some that did not treat migraines. There was still reason to believe that the Pozen model for a new kind of drug development company could ultimately work.

Ed Dinger

PRINCIPAL SUBSIDIARIES

POZEN UK Limited.

PRINCIPAL COMPETITORS

Bristol-Myers Squibb Company; Lannett Company, Inc.; Novartis AG.

FURTHER READING

Krishnan, Anne, "Approval Process Poses Headache for Chapel Hill, N.C.-Based Drug Maker," *Herald-Sun* (Durham, N.C.), June 2, 2004.

———, "Successful Drug Trials Boost Durham, N.C.-Based Pharmaceutical Firm's Stock," *Herald-Sun* (Durham, N.C.), January 29, 2004.

Marcial, Gene G., "Pozen's Trexima: Going to Market with Glaxo," *Business Week,* February 27, 2006, p. 96.

Ranii, David, "Chapel Hill, N.C.-Based Drug Discovery Company Starts IPO Process," *News & Observer* (Raleigh, N.C.), May 2, 2000.

———, "Pozen Attracts Capital," *Herald-Sun* (Durham, N.C.), August 15, 1997, p. C8.

———, "Raleigh, N.C.-Area Biotechnology Company Goes Public," *Herald-Sun* (Durham, N.C.), October 12, 2000.

PPG Industries, Inc.

One PPG Place
Pittsburgh, Pennsylvania 15272-0001
U.S.A.
Telephone: (412) 434-3131
Fax: (412) 434-2448
E-mail: corporateinfo@ppg.com
Web site: http://www.ppg.com

Public Company
Incorporated: 1883 as Pittsburgh Plate Glass Company
Employees: 30,800
Sales: $10.2 billion (2005)
Stock Exchanges: New York Pacific Philadelphia
Ticker Symbol: PPG
NAIC: 325510 Paint and Coating Manufacturing; 325520 Adhesive Manufacturing; 325181 Alkalies and Chlorine Manufacturing; 325188 All Other Basic Inorganic Chemical Manufacturing; 327211 Flat Glass Manufacturing; 327212 Other Pressed and Blown Glass and Glassware Manufacturing

■ ■ ■

PPG Industries, Inc., is a global producer of protective and decorative coatings, adhesives, sealants, flat glass, continuous-strand fiberglass, fabricated glass products, and industrial and specialty chemicals. PPG is a leading supplier of products for the aerospace, automotive, building, chemical processing, electronics, optical, packaging, pharmaceutical, and numerous other industries. The company operates about 100 production facilities in Argentina, Australia, Brazil, Canada, China, France, Germany, India, Ireland, Italy, Malaysia, Mexico, the Netherlands, the Philippines, Singapore, South Korea, Spain, Taiwan, Turkey, the United Kingdom, the United States, and Venezuela; and supports six main research and development facilities, four of which are located in Pennsylvania, with one each in North Carolina and the Netherlands. PPG has grown from the dream of two men into a global corporation that derives more than 35 percent of its revenues from outside the United States.

FOUNDING IN 1883 AS A PLATE GLASS MANUFACTURER

Captain John B. Ford and John Pitcairn created the Pittsburgh Plate Glass Company (PPG) in 1883. The first financially successful U.S. plate glass manufacturer, the company was located in Creighton, Pennsylvania, northeast of Pittsburgh. It moved its headquarters to Pittsburgh in 1895. Prior to the 1880s over a dozen plate glass makers had tried unsuccessfully to compete with their European counterparts. Despite American technical ability, plate glass for America's growing cities continued to be imported from Belgium, England, France, and Germany.

Manufacturing profits on glass were inconsistent partly due to the independents who controlled glass distribution. In 1896 Pitcairn established a commercial department and PPG became its own warehouser and distributor. Because of disagreements with Pitcairn regarding distribution, John Ford's sons sold their PPG interests and formed the Edward Ford Plate Glass Company. During the Great Depression, Ford merged with Libbey-Owens Sheet Glass to form Libbey-Owens-Ford Glass Company, which became Pilkington North America Inc., a subsidiary of Pilkington plc of the United Kingdom.

Pitcairn became president of PPG, and in 1899 he built the Columbia Chemical Company at Barberton, Ohio. This independent company produced soda ash, a major raw material used in making glass. This plant was a forerunner of PPG's chemical group. By the following year PPG was selling 13 million square feet of plate glass a year and had become the nation's most successful plate glass maker.

EXPANDING INTO PAINTS BY EARLY 20TH CENTURY

Pitcairn continued to expand PPG's product line. Because paints and brushes were distributed through the same channels as glass, they were a logical addition to the company. By the end of 1900 PPG had acquired a major interest in Milwaukee, Wisconsin-based Patton Paint Company, the precursor to PPG's coatings and resins operations. In 1902 PPG established operations in Europe, becoming one of the first U.S. manufacturers to do so.

In the early years PPG had manufactured only plate glass. It marketed but did not produce window glass, or sheet glass. In 1907, however, the first window-glass factory was added to company operations, in Mount Vernon, Ohio. In 1915 a second plant was opened in Clarksburg, West Virginia. Pitcairn's strong interest in innovation and diversification led to the opening of the company's first research and development facility in 1910.

The first stage of PPG's development came to an end in 1916 with Pitcairn's death. In 33 years he had led the company through economic panics, foreign competition, and restrictive distribution channels to become the nation's largest plate glass manufacturer. He was also the force behind diversification of the company's product line as well as the development of raw material sources and expansion of marketing outlets for its many products.

In 1919 subsidiaries yielded more than 50 percent of net return for the year. In November 1920 PPG stockholders voted unanimously to fold the company's subsidiaries into the parent company, making them divisions.

BECOMING AUTOMOTIVE SUPPLIER

The 1920s were prosperous for PPG. As steel-cage and concrete-reinforced construction became the standard for building, architects were able to design structures with larger window units, and glass consumption reached record levels in the United States. During this decade, the automobile industry also began using more glass. The switch from the open touring car to the sedan caused an expanded need for glass, and PPG met the demand.

PPG also made several technological innovations during the 1920s. In 1924 the company switched from the batch method of making plate glass to the straight-line conveyor-based ribbon method. With this revolutionary PPG innovation, molten glass from a constantly replenished melting furnace flowed through water-cooled shaping rollers. The glass was then cooled and cut into large plates.

In 1928 PPG first mass-produced sheet glass, using the Pittsburgh Process, which improved quality and sped up production. For the first time PPG became a major supplier of window glass. The Pittsburgh Process, invented by PPG, involves drawing a continuous sheet of molten glass from a tank vertically up a four-story forming-and-cooling line. In 1928 the Creighton Process was developed. An economical process for laminating glass for automobile windshields, PPG introduced Duplate laminated safety glass through a glass-plastic unit.

In 1924 PPG produced its first auto lacquer, which the company marketed in only a limited number of conservative colors. By 1929 PPG supplied "no less than 500 harmonious hues" to 40 automakers. The company had also begun using a long-lasting, fast-drying finish developed by the Ditzler Color Company, a subsidiary acquired in 1928.

Always seeking to diversify, in 1923 PPG began to use limestone screening, a waste product of soda ash, to manufacture Portland cement. During the Great Depression, PPG developed new paint and glass products. In the 1930s the company developed titanium dioxide pigments, which greatly increased the opacity of light colors. It also created fast-drying Wallhide flat

KEY DATES

1883: John B. Ford and John Pitcairn form the Pittsburgh Plate Glass Company (PPG), based in Creighton, Pennsylvania.

1895: Headquarters are moved to Pittsburgh.

1896: Ford's sons sell their interest in PPG, leaving Pitcairn as president.

1899: Pitcairn builds a soda ash plant in Barberton, Ohio, the first PPG chemicals business.

1900: PPG acquires Milwaukee-based Patton Paint Company, the foundation of its coatings operations.

1924: Company revolutionizes plate glass making with the straight-line conveyor-based ribbon method.

1952: PPG enters the fiberglass business.

1968: Company is renamed PPG Industries, Inc.

1985: Heirs of Pitcairn sell their remaining stake in PPG back to the company.

1989: The Olympic and Lucite paint brands are acquired.

1990: PPG and Essilor International SA form Transitions Optical, Inc. joint venture.

1999: Two major acquisitions are completed: PRC-DeSoto International, Inc. and the bulk of Imperial Chemical Industries plc's automotive refinishing and industrial coatings businesses.

2002: PPG takes an after-tax charge of $484 million to cover its part of a $2.7 billion settlement of asbestos-related litigation involving Pittsburgh Corning Corporation.

2005: Revenues surpass $10 billion for the first time.

paint, which made it possible to apply two coats of paint in one day. In 1934 PPG introduced Solex heat-absorbing glass. Also in 1934, it perfected a glass-bending technique that made the production of car windshields easier. In 1938 PPG introduced Herculite tempered glass. Herculite glass was several times stronger and more shatter resistant than ordinary plate glass.

Diversification paid off again for PPG during World War II. In 1940, the year before Japan attacked Pearl Harbor, the glass division had developed Flexseal laminated aircraft glass. During the war, when production of automobiles was temporarily halted and building was curtailed, PPG converted much of its production into materials for military use. Because of the shortage of raw materials during the war, PPG worked hard to develop synthetic resins, which inspired the development of plastics and high-performance paints and industrial coatings.

EXPLOSIVE POSTWAR GROWTH

During the 1950s car production and construction of new homes and glass-and-steel buildings exploded. PPG stepped up production to meet demand, and continued to diversify. Fiberglass had been a laboratory novelty until the 1930s. By 1950, however, it was being used in decorative fabrics and for insulation. In 1952 PPG opened its fiberglass business, making both textiles and reinforcements.

Also during the 1950s, PPG developed lead-free house paints. In 1951 the company created the first latex-based interior paint and three years later brought a latex exterior house paint to the market. PPG was also one of the first companies to produce a no-wax car finish, and its chemical division introduced several new products, including a swimming pool purifier.

In 1955 PPG's sales topped $500 million. The company employed 33,000 people in seven glass plants, three glass-fabricating plants, two specialty plants, two fiberglass plants, 17 coating and resins plants, and five chemical plants. In the early 1960s PPG produced materials for the building, transportation, appliance, container, boating, textile, paper, television, and chemicals industries. In 1963 it became the first U.S. company to manufacture float glass, used in place of plate glass by architects. In the same year, PPG introduced Herculite K, glass three to five times more shatter resistant than ordinary window glass. Herculite K became popular for residential storm- and sliding-door units because of its low cost.

During the early part of the 1960s a heavy capital-investment program moved the company toward $1 billion in sales, a goal it reached in 1968. In the same year, the company changed its name to PPG Industries, Inc., to reflect its size, diversification, and global presence.

During the mid-1960s the company developed a coating process called electrodeposition. Electrodeposition involves submerging positively charged metal parts in a tank containing negatively charged paint particles suspended in water. The opposite charges attract each other, and the metal is coated more uniformly than if it had been sprayed or dipped. In 1969 the chemicals group won the Kirkpatrick Chemical Engineering Achievement Award for developing a process for the simultaneous production of perchloroethylene, widely used in dry-cleaning, and trichloroethylene, a degreaser.

The oil embargo, the increased price of oil, natural gas, and electricity, and the dwindling production of fuels in the United States revived interest in solar energy in the 1970s. PPG was the first major corporation to develop a flat-plate solar collector, a unit first marketed in 1975. PPG also continued to work on high-luster, long-life automotive finishes. It improved its acrylic lacquers and developed acrylic dispersion topcoat finishes with lower solvent emissions during baking, which are less harmful to the environment. In the early 1970s more Americans began to repair and refinish automobiles in order to extend their cars' lifespan. PPG's Ditzler unit developed easy-to-apply primers and topcoats that matched factory-applied coatings in performance and appearance.

During the 1970s tinted, insulated, and reflective plate and float glasses came to be known as "performance" glass, or "environmental" glass, as the energy efficient and attractive glass became the preferred material for curtain walls. In 1973 the last plate glass production line was phased out and was replaced by the float glass production method. Also in 1973, Wallhide Microflo consumer paints were introduced. The Microflo process created air pockets in paint films that helped reflect light more efficiently as well as producing easy-to-apply paint with a smooth, washable surface. In 1975 PPG continued to broaden its color line by introducing a new custom-tinting system for consumer paints called the DesignaColor System.

In 1975 PPG established a fifth division, plastic fabricating, and closed several outmoded plants. The corporation also restructured its marketing organization, disbanding the merchandising division established by John Pitcairn in 1896, and continued to develop high-performance glasses, coatings, and fiberglass products. In 1976 PPG reached $2 billion in sales.

The year 1985 was the end of a chapter in PPG's history as the heirs of Pitcairn sold their remaining stake in PPG back to the company for $530 million. PPG's biomedical systems division was established in 1986 and 1987 with the acquisition of medical-electronics operations from Honeywell Inc., Litton Industries Inc., and Allegheny International Inc. The group produced computer-assisted cardiac recording equipment, patient-monitoring systems, electrocardiogram instruments, defibrillators, and related products for the healthcare industry. In 1989 PPG significantly expanded its standing as a leading producer of architectural finishes (in layperson's terms, house paints) with the acquisition of Olympic stains and paints and Lucite paints from the Clorox Company for $134 million.

The drop in the U.S. auto and construction markets during the late 1980s hurt PPG's sales. Automakers were PPG's largest customers, and fluctuations in that market reduced the company's profits. In 1989 the company's earnings dropped 1 percent, interrupting a six-year upward trend. Nevertheless, Vincent A. Sarni, who became chairman in 1984 and CEO in 1983, felt PPG was making progress toward goals set for the ten-year period from 1985 to 1994. On February 26, 1990, *Barron's* reported that "The company has stayed consistently ahead of a goal to show an average annual return on equity of 18%." Sarni believed that by 1994 PPG would reach targeted annual sales of $8 billion even without acquisitions.

DIFFICULT STRETCH GIVING WAY TO RECOVERY

PPG fell far short of Sarni's ambitious sales goal as growth was derailed by the recession of the early 1990s, which hit the construction and automotive sector particularly hard. Following the peak of $6.02 billion in 1990, revenues actually declined to $5.75 billion by 1993. Nevertheless, PPG did manage to stay profitable throughout the recession, despite the difficult environment.

Sarni was more successful with his aim of expanding PPG globally. About one-quarter of the company's revenues came from outside the United States in 1986, but by the early 1990s the figure had grown to more than one-third. Much of this growth was accomplished through acquisitions. In 1990 the company acquired its partners' interests (the two-thirds not already owned by PPG) in Silenka B.V., a Dutch fiberglass producer, bolstering its already strong position in the European fiberglass market. That same year, PPG also bought Finland's Tamglass Automotive OY, which gave PPG a significant presence in the European replacement glass business, and Etablissements Robert Ouvrie S.A. of France, a maker of surfactants and paper specialty chemicals. In June 1991 PPG acquired the automotive coatings business of ICI Canada.

In September 1993 PPG's board surprised many when, for the first time in company history, it appointed an outsider, Jerry E. Dempsey, as chairman and CEO, to replace the retiring Sarni. The board evidently felt that none of the in-house candidates were quite ready to assume the leadership mantle. Dempsey, an engineer by training, had been president and COO of auto parts maker Borg-Warner Corporation from 1979 to 1984 before heading Chemical Waste Management, Inc. Meanwhile, the company decided in 1993 to sell its Biomedical Systems Division. This noncore operation was completely divested by January 1995. The move left

PPG with its three core segments: coatings and resins, glass, and chemicals.

Under Dempsey's leadership, PPG enjoyed sales growth of 10 and 11.5 percent in 1994 and 1995, respectively. Profits grew even faster, highlighted by a 50 percent increase in 1995. Fueling this revival was Dempsey's emphasis on heightened marketing efforts, with a particular stress on seeking out new niches for PPG that required skillful marketing. For example, by 1995 Dempsey had transformed Transitions Optical, Inc., a troubled joint venture (formed in 1990 with France's Essilor International SA) that made color-changing sunglasses, into a $100 million business growing at a rate of 40 percent per year. Dempsey also sought out new ways to leverage PPG's existing expertise, as for example in the coatings unit's running of entire paint operations in auto plants. During this period, growth was also achieved through acquisitions, including the 1995 purchases of the American Finishes refinish coatings business of Lilly Industries, Inc., and of Matthews Paint Company, a leading manufacturer of paints for outdoor metal signs.

Dempsey retired in late 1997, with PPG on the upswing and his having overseen an orderly leadership succession. In December 1995 Executive Vice-President Raymond W. LeBoeuf, who had joined the company in 1980 as treasurer, became president and chief operating officer. LeBoeuf subsequently succeeded Dempsey as CEO in July 1997 and as chairman in November 1997. LeBoeuf immediately set lofty goals for PPG for the year 2000, aiming for $10 billion in sales (compared to $7.22 billion in 1996) and a doubling of net earnings from the $744 million of 1996.

INTO THE NEW CENTURY ON THE HEELS OF AN ACQUISITION SPREE

LeBoeuf's targets proved too ambitious as PPG's late 1990s performance was undermined by the economic crises that hit certain Asian markets and Brazil and by the start of a deflationary trend in the manufacturing sectors of Europe and the United States. The 2000 results, net income of $610 million on revenues of $8.63 billion, were aided by an acquisition spree that LeBoeuf directed in the late 1990s. One of the aims of the deals was to make the company less dependent on the more cyclical and mature portions of its portfolio, namely the chemical and glass businesses, while bolstering faster-growing operations, such as coatings and optical products. Thus, in 1998, PPG sold its European flat and automotive glass businesses to the Belgium firm Glaverbel S.A. for $266 million, while acquiring Courtaulds plc's packaging coatings and U.S. architectural

coatings businesses in a deal valued at approximately $285 million. Included in the Courtaulds deal was the architectural coatings firm Porter Paints, a paint retailer in the southeastern United States mainly catering to paint contractors. PPG had flirted with exiting from the architectural paint sector, but elected not only to stay in the business but to expand its operations in this area. Architectural paints had great potential for growth, and because it was an area in which PPG dealt more directly with the end customer, executives viewed the firm's presence in the sector as a way to balance out PPG's industrial side.

The acquisitions pace quickened in 1999, when PPG spent more than $1.34 billion on a string of deals, two of them major, both concluded in July. PPG paid $677 million for the bulk of Imperial Chemical Industries plc's automotive refinishing and industrial coatings businesses in Europe, Asia, Latin America, and the United States. It spent another $524 million to take over PRC-DeSoto International, Inc., from the Dutch firm Akzo Nobel N.V. Based in Glendale, California, PRC-DeSoto produced coatings and sealants for aircraft and sealants for architectural insulating glass units. These blockbuster deals were followed by two smaller deals that bulked up PPG's architectural coatings operations: Atlanta-based Wattyl Paint (July 1999) and Houston-based Monarch Paint Co. (February 2000).

PPG largely curtailed its acquisition program in 2000 as concerns grew about an economic slowdown and executives elected to preserve cash, in part to pay down debt. Between 2000 and 2004, long-term debt was cut from $1.81 billion to $1.18 billion, even as working capital jumped from $550 million to $1.83 billion. As its earnings continued to be flat, PPG launched restructurings in both 2001 and 2002 that aimed to cut annual operating expenses by a total of about $150 million. These overhauls involved the layoff of approximately 2,500 workers and the closure of a number of plants.

In 2002 PPG suffered a net loss as a result of an asbestos-related settlement. PPG and Corning Incorporated had been 50-50 partners in Pittsburgh Corning Corporation, which was formed in 1937 and made pipe insulation containing asbestos from 1962 to 1972. Lawsuits against Pittsburgh Corning alleging personal injury from its asbestos-laden products began proliferating in the 1970s, eventually forcing the company to file for Chapter 11 bankruptcy protection in April 2000. PPG, Corning, and the companies' insurance companies announced in May 2002 that they had agreed to pay a total of $2.7 billion to settle all the litigation relating to Pittsburgh Corning. PPG consequently took an after-tax charge of $484 million, which led to a net loss of $69 million for 2002.

Strong results from four businesses—aerospace coatings and sealants, architectural coatings, optical products, and Asian coatings—helped push PPG's revenues past the $10 billion mark for the first time in 2005. Despite an economy on the upswing, profits were under pressure because of surging energy and raw material costs. Midyear, LeBoeuf retired from PPG. During his tenure, he accelerated PPG's shift from a focus on glass and chemicals to paints, coatings, and optical products. By 2005, fully 55 percent of revenues were generated by the coatings operations.

Taking over as chairman and CEO was Charles E. Bunch, who had been president and COO and had joined PPG in 1979 as assistant to the corporate controller. Bunch's biggest immediate concern was the ongoing increases in raw materials expenses, and he began investigating alternative sources to cut costs. While not promising the types of blockbuster deals that his predecessor pulled off, Bunch aimed to pick up the acquisition pace, concentrating on smaller companies with annual revenues of as much as $250 million. PPG completed a string of smaller deals in China, Thailand, and Hong Kong in the later months of 2005 and the first half of 2006 toward meeting Bunch's goal of generating $2 billion in annual sales in Asia within five to seven years. In April 2006 PPG beefed up its optical products side, another key area for growth, by acquiring Parma, Italy-based Intercast Europe, S.p.A., the world's leading maker of nonprescription hard-resin sunglass lenses. Around this same time, PPG agreed to pay $60 million to settle a lawsuit alleging it had conspired with other glass makers to overcharge for flat glass products.

Virginia L. Smiley
Updated, David E. Salamie

PRINCIPAL SUBSIDIARIES

LYNX Services, L.L.C.; PPG Architectural Finishes, Inc.; PPG Auto Glass, LLC (66%); PPG Industries Fiber Glass Products, Inc.; PPG Kansai Automotive Finishes U.S., LLC (60%); PRC-DeSoto International, Inc.; Stan-Mark, Inc.; The CEI Group, Inc. (75%); Transitions Optical, Inc. (51%); PPG Canada, Inc.; Bellaria S.p.A. (Italy); HOBA Lacke und Farben GmbH (Germany); PPG Coatings B.V. (Netherlands); PPG Coatings SA (France; 99.85%); PPG Holding SAS (France); PPG Holdings B.V. (Netherlands); PPG Holdings (U.K.) Limited; PPG Iberica, S.A. (Spain); PPG Industries Chemicals B.V. (Netherlands); PPG Industries Europe (France); PPG Industries Europe Srl (Switzerland); PPG Industries Fiber Glass B.V. (Netherlands); PPG Industries France SAS; PPG Industries Italia S.r.l. (Italy); PPG Industries Kimya Sanayi ve Ticaret Anonim Sirketi (Turkey); PPG Industries Lacke GmbH (Germany); PPG Industries Lackfabrik GmbH (Germany); PPG Industries Netherlands BV; PPG Industries Poland Sp. Zo.o.; PPG Industries (UK) Limited; PPG Ireland International Financial Company Limited; PPG Kansai Automotive Finishes U.K. LLP (60%); PPG Luxembourg Finance S.R.L.; PPG Luxembourg Holdings S.R.L.; PPG Optical Holdings Ireland; PPG Service Sud S.r.l (Italy); PPG-Sipsy SAS (France); Transitions Optical Holdings B.V. (Netherlands; 51%); Transitions Optical Limited (Ireland; 51%); PPG Coatings (Hong Kong) Co., Limited; PPG Coatings (Malaysia) Sdn. Bhd.; PPG Coatings (Thailand) Co., Ltd.; PPG Coatings (Tianjin) Co., Ltd. (China); PPG Industries Australia PTY Limited; PPG Industries New Zealand Limited; PPG Industries (Singapore) Pte., Ltd.; PPG Japan Ltd.; PPG Packaging Coatings (Suzhou) Co., Ltd. (China; 90.4%); PPG Paints Trading (Shanghai) Co., Ltd. (China); PRC-DeSoto Australia Pty Ltd.; Taiwan Chlorine Industries Ltd. (60%); Transitions Optical Philippines, Inc (51%); PPG Industrial do Brasil - Tintas E Vernizes - Ltda. (Brazil); PPG Industries Argentina S.A.; PPG ALESCO Automotive Finishes Mexico, S. de R.L. de C.V. (60%); PPG Industries de Mexico, S.A. de C.V.; EPIC Insurance Co. Ltd. (Bermuda).

PRINCIPAL OPERATING UNITS

Aerospace; Architectural Coatings; Automotive Coatings; Automotive OEM Glass; Automotive Refinish; Automotive Replacement Glass; Chlor-Alkali and Derivatives; Fiber Glass; Fine Chemicals; Industrial Coatings; Insurance and Services; Optical Products; Packaging Coatings; Performance Glazings; Silicas.

PRINCIPAL COMPETITORS

Akzo Nobel N.V.; The Sherwin-Williams Company; BASF Aktiengesellschaft; E. I. du Pont de Nemours and Company; Imperial Chemical Industries plc.

FURTHER READING

Baker, Stephen, "A New Paint Job at PPG," *Business Week*, November 13, 1995, pp. 74, 78.

Berss, Marcia, "Leveraged for Takeoff," *Forbes*, November 22, 1993, pp. 86, 88.

Byrne, Harlan S., "PPG Industries Inc.: It Tops the Goals Set in Its Ambitious 'Blueprint,'" *Barron's*, February 26, 1990, pp. 48–49.

A Concern for the Future: A History of PPG Industries, Inc., Pittsburgh: PPG Industries, 1976.

Curtis, Carol E., "Patience Money in Pittsburgh," *Forbes,* March 11, 1985, p. 40.

Gannon, Joyce, "New PPG Chief Eyes Expansion, Acquisitions," *Pittsburgh Post-Gazette,* April 22, 2005, p. C1.

———, "PPG Net Drops, Company to Lay Off 1,000 Worldwide," *Pittsburgh Post-Gazette,* April 19, 2002, p. C10.

———, "PPG's LeBoeuf to Retire: Bunch Takes Over," *Pittsburgh Post-Gazette,* April 1, 2005, p. B11.

Hunter, David, "Specialities Surge for PPG's Chemicals Group: A Big Push for International Growth," *Chemical Week,* March 2, 1994, p. 26.

Lappen, Alyssa A., "Buying Back the Family Jewels," *Forbes,* September 17, 1990, pp. 101, 104, 108.

Lindeman, Teresa F., "LeBoeuf Unhappy with PPG Showing," *Pittsburgh Post-Gazette,* April 17, 1998, p. E1.

Milmo, Sean, "Akzo Closes in on Courtaulds, Will Sell Fibers Units to PPG," *Chemical Market Reporter,* June 8, 1998, p. 8.

———, "ICI Sells Major Coatings Units to PPG in a Surprise Move," *Chemical Market Reporter,* May 3, 1999, p. 1.

Norton, Erle, "PPG Industries Selects Two Contenders for CEO's Post to Newly Created Office," *Wall Street Journal,* April 6, 1994, p. B9.

———, "PPG Names LeBoeuf, President, Chief of Operations, Positions Heir Apparent," *Wall Street Journal,* December 15, 1995, p. B11.

Paull, Barbara I., "Signature: Vincent A. Sarni," *Managing,* July 1985, p. 19.

"PPG: A 'Maverick' Chairman Tries to Take a B-Performer to the Head of the Class," *Business Week,* November 12, 1984, pp. 128+.

"PPG Industries Reaches $2.7 Billion Groundbreaking Asbestos Settlement," *Chemical Market Reporter,* May 20, 2002, pp. 2, 24.

"PPG's Dictum: Avoid the Dinosaur Route," *Chemical Week,* August 19, 1981, pp. 47+.

"PPG Stays in Acquisition Mode with German Auto Coats Buy," *Chemical Market Reporter,* January 19, 1998, p. 5.

Saporito, Bill, "PPG: Shiny, Not Dull," *Fortune,* July 17, 1989, p. 107.

Scheraga, Dan, "PPG Continues Its Coatings Push by Buying PRC-DeSoto from Akzo," *Chemical Market Reporter,* June 7, 1999, p. 1.

Sheeline, William E., "Managing a Clan Worth $1 Billion," *Fortune,* June 4, 1990, pp. 239, 242, 246.

Storck, William J., "PPG Belies Its Age," *Chemical and Engineering News,* January 26, 1998, pp. 18+.

———, "PPG's New Chairman Looks to Continue Company's Winning Ways," *Chemical and Engineering News,* January 10, 1994, pp. 10–12.

Warren, Susan, "PPG Agrees to Pay $2.7 Billion to Resolve Asbestos Litigation," *Wall Street Journal,* May 15, 2002, p. B4.

Westervelt, Robert, "PPG: Top-Line Growth at Last," *Chemical Week,* June 9, 2004, pp. 20–22, 25.

———, "PPG's Priorities: Pumping Up the Portfolio," *Chemical Week,* February 25, 1998, pp. 27, 30–31.

Programmer's Paradise, Inc.

1157 Shrewsbury Avenue
Shrewsbury, New Jersey 07702-4321
U.S.A.
Telephone: (732) 389-8950
Toll Free: (800) 445-7899
Fax: (732) 389-0010
Web site: http://www.programmersparadise.com

Public Company
Incorporated: 1982 as Voyager Software Corporation
Employees: 116
Sales: $137.7 million (2005)
Stock Exchanges: NASDAQ
Ticker Symbol: PROG
NAIC: 423430 Computer and Computer Peripheral
Equipment and Software Merchant Wholesalers

■ ■ ■

Programmer's Paradise, Inc., is a New Jersey-based
marketer of technical and general business application
software and personal computer (PC) hardware and
components aimed at technology professionals, including web designers, software engineers and development
managers, systems integrators, and technical support
specialists. Represented publishers and manufacturers
include Adobe, Borland, Computer Associates, IBM,
and Quest. Programmer's Paradise markets its wares
through catalogs and web sites tailored to specific audi-
ences, e-mail and direct mail materials, as well as in
industry magazines and at national trade shows. In addition to the Programmer's Paradise division, Program-

mer's Paradise, Inc., operates two other divisions.
Lifeboat Distribution is a wholesaler geared toward helping emerging software publishing companies. The newest division, TechXtend, has been established to provide
solutions and onsite services to IT professionals, focusing on services such as backup, disaster recovery, and
server consolidation. Programmer's Paradise maintains
offices in Shrewsbury, New Jersey; Hauppauge, New
York; and Mississauga, Ontario, Canada. Programmer's
Paradise is a public company listed on the NASDAQ.

COMPANY FOUNDED IN 1982

Programmer's Paradise was incorporated in 1982 as
Voyager Software Corporation and started out as a
wholesaler and reseller of educational software. Backed
by the venture capital firm of Hudson Technologies and
other investors, the company expanded in 1986 when it
acquired Lifeboat Associates, which had been founded a
decade earlier to publish software and act as a wholesale
distributor. In that same year, Voyager launched a business called Programmer's Paradise to market technical
software through catalogs. Voyager also added Science &
Engineering Software, a unit that distributed scientific
and technical engineering software packages. The
company did not perform especially well, generating
revenues of less than $7 million, and in 1988 Hudson
Technologies recruited a new president and chief executive officer, Roger Paradis.

Paradis possessed a broad range of experience. He
graduated from the U.S. Naval Academy in 1957, earning an undergraduate degree in engineering and the

equivalent of a master's degree in physics. He then completed a four-and-one-half-year stint in the Navy, serving aboard a Poseidon nuclear submarine. He then enrolled at Harvard Business School, receiving an M.B.A. in 1974. Paradis went to work for AT&T as the telecommunications giant was becoming more involved in computers, soon becoming one of the youngest division managers in the history of the corporation. He then struck out on his own in 1980 to found a high-technology consulting business, Tetrion Consulting Group, and later in the decade cofounded Skantek Corp., a company that used fiber-optic technology to scan and print engineering drawings. Prior to joining Voyager, Paradis headed the New Jersey venture capital firm of Amerinex Corp. and helped turn around several companies involved in computer software, component, and system fields.

Shortly after Paradis took charge, Voyager acquired a fourth company, Corsoft, a value-added software reseller founded five years earlier that boasted major customers such as AT&T and Bell Labs. It was supposed to be merged with Lifeboat, Programmer's Paradise, and Science & Engineering under the Magellan Software name and compete against Corporate Software and Egghead Discount Software, the leading software resellers in the United States. The Magellan name, however, was already being used by another company and Lotus Development had trademarked it for a desktop search engine program. As a result, Voyager retained its name.

Voyager grew steadily in the early 1990s as a three-division company that focused on the software needs of corporate technology professionals. Lifeboat acted as the distributor, with Corsoft as the corporate reseller and Programmer's Paradise as the mail-order operation. In 1992 Voyager completed a minor acquisition, paying $200,000 for South Mountain Software, Inc. A year later, Voyager entered the European marketplace when it acquired a 67 percent stake in software distributor Lifeboat Associates Italia S.R.L., and over the course of the next several months purchased the remaining shares. Voyager added to its European business in June 1994 by acquiring the German software reseller ISP*D International Software Partners GmbH and a subsidiary, with operations in both Germany and Austria. In that

same year, Voyager launched a catalog operation in the United Kingdom. By the end of 1994 Voyager's revenues topped $70 million, a tenfold increase in just six years, to go with a net profit of more than $1 million.

NAME CHANGE IN 1995

In May 1995 Voyager changed its name to Programmer's Paradise, Inc., and prepared to make an initial public offering (IPO) of stock, which was completed in July of that year when nearly 2.2 million shares of stock were sold at $10 a share. Some of the proceeds were used to establish the first web site for Programmer's Paradise in November 1995. Although the general public had not yet embraced the Internet in mass numbers, the target market for Programmer's Paradise was early adopters of new technology, so that an Internet presence was important in the company's ability to maintain growth. The online catalog was then supplemented in May 1996 with e-commerce capability. A software-downloading option became available in the summer through an agreement with Cybersource, the leading electronic distributor of software, to use its technology on the back end of the web site. A second site, Programmer's SuperShop, was added to the fold in July 1996 after Programmer's Paradise paid $11 million for its chief U.S. catalog competitor, The Software Developer's Company, Inc., known for its catalog *The Programmer's Supershop*. In a related move, the company also launched a new catalog in 1996, *Internet Paradise*, geared toward Internet developers.

While it staked out online space in the mid-1900s, Programmer's Paradise continued to increase its international footprint. In December 1995 it beefed up its U.K. subsidiary with the acquisition of Systematika Ltd., a major technical software reseller in England and publisher of the well established catalog *System Science*. Several weeks later, Programmer's Paradise established ISP*F International Software Partners France S.A., a Paris-based corporate reseller of PC software. Then, in September 1997, Programmer's Paradise acquired Logicsoft Holding B.V. to sell software in Belgium, The Netherlands, and Luxembourg. Earlier in 1997 Programmer's Paradise also expanded into Canada by establishing Programmer's Paradise Canada to produce catalogs specifically tailored for the Canadian market.

Revenues increased at a steady clip in the mid-1900s, reaching $93.3 million in 1995, $127.6 million in 1996, and $176.2 million in 1997. Net income in 1997 totaled nearly $4 million. After ten years at the helm, Paradis resigned in July 1998, a move that the company insisted had nothing to do with quarterly projections that failed to hit the mark. A spokesperson said he was "leaving to pursue other interests," and in a statement Paradis echoed

KEY DATES

1982: The company is founded as Voyager Software Corporation.
1988: Roger Paradis is named CEO.
1995: The company is taken public.
1998: Paradis resigns.
2001: The European operations are sold.

the rationale, maintaining he had "a desire to do some other things that I need some time to do." He also said he would stay on as a consultant to help with what he hoped would be "a seamless and very effective transition" to a new management team. In any event, he was replaced by 61-year-old William H. Willett, who had been on the board for the past year and was named as both CEO and chairman of the board. Willett had three decades worth of marketing and sales experience, including stints at Time Inc. and Avon Products Inc., where he served as president of the catalog division. He came to Programmer's Paradise after serving as the CEO of Colorado Prime, a direct-to-home grocery venture.

A major part of Willett's mandate was to aggressively build up the company's Internet business, and the results of 1998 reflected this emphasis. While sales in general increased 33 percent to $234 million, Internet sales surged almost 500 percent to nearly $3 million. In 1999 that amount increased to around $15 million. As a result of the Internet, catalogs, which were the mainstay of Programmer's Paradise, began to change their function. Although catalog sales continued to grow both domestically and internationally, increasingly the catalogs served as banner advertising for the company's web sites, drawing customers to the web sites where they could order a shrink-wrapped copy of a software package or download it electronically. The web sites also served as a repository for information not available in the catalogs. Because the web sites were so important to the future of the company, Programmer's Paradise stopped having outside firms do the development work. Instead, employees were added to take the work in-house. Ironically, at a time when virtually any stock related to the Internet was a Wall Street darling, Programmer's Paradise, which actually had considerable Internet sales and was profitable, was not viewed as an Internet stock and its share price was little higher than its IPO level. As nettlesome as this neglect may have seemed at the time, Programmer's Paradise also avoided the devastation that would visit the Internet sector when the dot-com bubble burst.

SELLING THE EUROPEAN OPERATIONS IN 2000

Internet sales increased 275 percent in 1999, but overall Programmer's Paradise experienced a modest increase in revenues of just 4 percent to $244 million. The primary culprit was the concern over Year 2000 (Y2K) readiness, prompting many firms to postpone systems changes and the purchase of new software. Of more importance was a drop-off in European sales in 2000, as revenues declined from $163.4 million in 1999 to $127.9 million in 2000. In the meantime, the North American business improved 10 percent, or nearly $8 million, to $88.6 million. Programmer's Paradise, as a result, decided to shed its European operations, selling them to Germany's PC-Ware Information Technologies AG in January 2001 for $12.8 million.

A North America-only business, Programmer's Paradise experienced a negligible increase in revenues to $89.5 million in 2001, due in large measure to a decision to discontinue negotiating Microsoft Select and Enterprise volume licensing agreements for new customers, a business that monopolized too much time for too little profit. This shift in focus resulted in staff cuts and a loss of revenues. More important to the longer-term health of Programmer's Paradise was the troubled U.S. economy, especially in the technology sector. Although Programmer's Paradise may have avoided the difficulties experienced by pure-play Internet companies, it still had to contend with the reluctance of corporate customers to upgrade their information technology during a period of economic uncertainty. The full effects of poor business conditions would be felt in 2002 and 2003, when Programmer's Paradise reported sales of $65.2 million and $65.6 million, respectively. The company was only marginally profitable during this period, earning $28,000 in 2002 and $966,000 in 2003. Softening the blow was the fact that the company had no debt and plenty of cash on hand.

Corporate spending finally picked up in the second half of 2003, leading to an increase in sales for the year to $103.6 million, accompanied by a healthy $6.3 million net profit. Business continued to build in 2005, when Programmer's Paradise recorded sales of $137.6 million. Net income dipped to $2.7 million, but this decline was in fact an accounting matter, resulting from a $4.1 million reversal of a deferred tax valuation allowance.

Major changes were in store for 2006. At the beginning of the year, Willett turned over the CEO position to 34-year-old Simon F. Nynens, while staying on as chairman. A certified public accountant and a graduate of the Advanced Management Program at Harvard Business School, Nynens had been with Programmer's Paradise for eight years, starting with the European operations before becoming chief financial officer in 2002. Then, in May 2006, the company announced that it intended to change its name to Wayside Technology Group, Inc., as part of an effort to pursue distinct market segments. Programmer's Paradise would revert once again to division status and focus on serving the needs of the software development community. Lifeboat would operate as a wholesale division devoted to distributing the products of emerging software publishing companies as well as difficult-to-source hardware lines and accessories. A third division called TechXtend was established to provide information technology organizations with solutions in areas such as business continuity, backup, disaster recovery, and server consolidation. In a press statement, Nynens explained the reason behind the changes: "The re-naming of the company will provide us with greater flexibility to continue to build on our strong brands while we launch new divisions focused on consultative services."

Ed Dinger

PRINCIPAL SUBSIDIARIES

Programmer's Paradise Catalogs, Inc.; Programmer's Paradise.com, Inc.; Programmer's Paradise, (Canada) Inc.; International Software Partners, Inc.; Corsoft, Inc.; Lifeboat Distribution, Inc.

PRINCIPAL DIVISIONS

Programmer's Paradise; Lifeboat Distribution; TechXtend.

PRINCIPAL COMPETITORS

Cyberian Outpost, Inc.; Insight Enterprises, Inc.; PC Mall, Inc.

FURTHER READING

Brown, Lauren, "Four Firms Merge, Form Software Reseller Aiming to Compete at the Top," *PC Week,* July 25, 1988, p. 115.

Cho, Joshua, "Paradise in Canada," *New Canaan,* October 1997, p. 12.

Cotlier, Moira, "Programmer's Bids Adieu to Europe," *Catalog Age,* January 2001, p. 14.

Fazzi, Raymond, "CEO Resigns from New Jersey-Based Technical Software Seller," *Asbury Park Press* (N.J.), July 15, 1998.

Fitzgerald, Beth, "Geeks Get the Goods Via the Middleman," *Star Ledger* (Newark, N.J.), June 7, 1999, p. 63.

———, "Programmers Find Paradise by the Computer Screen's Light," *Star Ledger* (Newark, N.J.), March 18, 1999, p. 33.

Frye, Lori, "Roger Paradis Chmn. and CEO of Programmer's Paradise," *Dow Jones Investor Network,* August 27, 1996.

Oberndorf, Shannon, "Programmer's Paradise," *Catalog Age,* September 1, 1997, p. 57.

Taft, Darryl K., "Programmer's Paradise to Acquire Chief Competitor," *Computer Reseller News,* June 10, 1996, p. 103.

Quality Systems, Inc.

18191 Von Karman Avenue, Suite 450
Irvine, California 92612
U.S.A.
Telephone: (949) 255-2600
Toll Free: (800) 888-7955
Fax: (949) 255-2605
Web site: http://www.qsii.com

Public Company
Incorporated: 1974
Employees: 418
Sales: $119.3 million (2005)
Stock Exchanges: NASDAQ
Ticker Symbol: QSII
NAIC: 511210 Software Publishers

■ ■ ■

Quality Systems, Inc. and its wholly owned subsidiary, NextGen Healthcare Information Systems, Inc., develop and market healthcare information systems that automate aspects of medical and dental practices, networks of practices, ambulatory care centers, community health centers, and medical and dental schools. NextGen focuses on medical practices, marketing electronic medical records and practice management systems for managing patient information, appointments, billing, referral, and insurance claims. The company's QSI division offers practice management software for dental and niche medical practices. Each division operates as a stand-alone company. Quality Systems, Inc., has corporate headquarters in Irvine, California, and other major

facilities in Horsham, Pennsylvania, and Atlanta, Georgia.

1974–1994: PIONEERING THE ELECTRONIC MEDICAL RECORDS FIELD

In 1974, Sheldon Razin founded Quality Systems, Inc. (QSI), placing himself and his company at the forefront of the developing market for electronic medical records. Razin, a graduate of Massachusetts Institute of Technology, had held various technical and managerial positions with Rockwell International prior to founding QSI. As president and board chair of the new company, Razin oversaw the installation of QSI's first system in 1976. In 1979, QSI implemented managed-care features into its systems, anticipating the mainstream introduction of capitalized health plans.

The company tended toward growth, but with some ups and downs. After it went public in 1982, it reached revenues of $11.5 million the following year. In 1987, however, revenues were back down to $9.6 million. They fell further in 1989 to $8.8 million before heading up again, to $9.6 million in 1990 and $13.1 million in 1991. By 1995, the company had more than 450 clients in 45 states as well as in Canada and Saudi Arabia.

1995–1998: BRANCHING OUT INTO DENTAL AND MEDICAL PRACTICE MANAGEMENT SOFTWARE

Also in 1995, QSI partnered with Clinitec International, Inc., of Horsham, Pennsylvania, a company that had been developing and marketing electronic medical records software, or practice management systems, since 1979. The following year, QSI purchased the remainder of Clinitec's shares and absorbed the company into itself as a wholly owned subsidiary.

Clinitec's product, NextGen, permitted scanning, annotation, retrieval, and analysis of medical records in all formats, whether documents, photographs, or x-rays. NextGen's Patient Records System, an electronic medical records system, integrated completely with QSI's Practice Management System. It captured clinical data in custom-built templates that could be accessed through PC workstations or handheld wireless tablets.

By the end of 1996, 5,000 dentists in large group practices were using QSI's office-based practice management systems, whose software applications allowed for patient registration, online appointment scheduling, patient billing, electronic insurance claims processing, managed care, referral tracking, management reporting, and word processing.

At the same time, new competitors were making significant inroads into the electronic practice management market, and demand for QSI's products was weakening. To increase its market share, QSI rolled out QSINET to reach the 80,000 small dental practices in the United States, few of which could afford the thousands of dollars it cost to install a dental management system. QSINET allowed solo dentists to access a practice management system via the Internet. It offered up-to-date information on insurance eligibility and benefits as one of its main advantages.

The following year, 1997, QSI also acquired MicroMed HealthCare Systems Inc. of Atlanta, Georgia, which became its second wholly owned subsidiary. MicroMed provided physician practice management systems via a master patient index and enterprise-wide scheduling. In 1999, QSI combined its subsidiaries into its QSI division.

Both the QSI and NextGen divisions each operated as a stand-alone company. QSI offered practice management software for dental and niche medical practices, while NextGen focused on medical practices, marketing electronic medical records and practice management systems for managing patient information, appointments, billing, referral, and insurance claims. The system itself generated chart notes, produced necessary forms, checked for drug interactions, faxed prescriptions, printed patient education materials, and sent an electronic charge record to billing.

Both NextGen and QSI distinguished themselves in the field of electronic management systems by their products' flexibility. "Our customers have complete control over screen design, logic flow, and all output," explained Patrick Cline, founder and head of Clinitec in a 1998 *Directory of Medical Computer Systems* article. "The user interface seems so simple because it's what the provider's accustomed to using."

1999–2006: STEADY GROWTH IN THE FACE OF GOVERNANCE CONFLICT

The year 1999 was a profitable one for QSI with revenues of $34 million and earnings of close to $600,000, compared to $4.6 million in losses the year before. However, overshadowing the good news was a conflict that erupted between Razin and a group of QSI's investors, led by Ahmed Hussein and Andrew Shapiro, who sought to change control of QSI's board of directors.

Trouble had already begun brewing for the company in the spring of 1997. After QSI's stock price dropped more than 80 percent during the second half of 1996, a group of shareholders filed a class-action lawsuit against QSI for misleading stockholders. In March 1999, a second shareholder lawsuit alleged poor corporate governance. Hussein, an Egyptian investor, who owned 18.5 percent of the company, and Shapiro, president of San Francisco-based Lawndale Capital Management, which controlled 10 percent, accused Razin, who himself owned 25 percent, of deals with large investors to retain control of the board. They pointed to poor growth as a sign of poor management. QSI's single-digit and low double-digit growth was "nothing to brag about," according to Shapiro in a 1999 *Orange County Register* article, when "industry peers [were] chewing up ... market share with 25 percent growth."

Hussein and Shapiro put forth a proposal for consideration by QSI's shareholders during its annual meeting in September 1999. This proposal set guidelines for an independent board of directors and excluded

KEY DATES

1974: Sheldon Razin founds and incorporates QSI.
1982: QSI holds its initial public offering.
1996: The company purchases Clinitec International.
1997: QSI acquires MicroMed HealthCare Systems Inc.
1999: QSI merges MicroMed and Clinitec into a single company.
2000: Razin resigns as head of the company; Patrick Cline becomes interim chief executive officer, replaced by Louis E. Silverman.

Razin from being board chair. In August 1999, Razin instituted virtually all of the corporate governance measures Hussein and Shapiro proposed; he backed down as chief executive officer of the company in April 2000. Patrick Cline of Clinitec, meanwhile, became interim chief executive officer, replaced in 2000 by Louis E. Silverman, who became both president and chief executive officer. Silverman, who held a master of business administration from Harvard Graduate School of Business Administration, came from CorVel, where his leadership strategies had resulted in record revenues.

By 2002, QSI had a client base of about 10,000 physicians, which represented about 6 percent of the market for practices with 50 or more doctors and 3 percent of the market for practices with 10 to 49 doctors. However, practice management had become much more competitive, and, as a result, QSI pushed to get as many systems in place as quickly as possible. "The horse race is an adequate characterization," according to Silverman in a 2002 *Investor's Business Daily* article. Although revenues had grown to $44 million in 2001, with fewer than 10 percent of U.S. medical practices utilizing adequate information technology systems, "[a] lot of our task is to get the word out, let doctors know it exists. Adoption of these systems has been a stumbling block because physicians are resistant to change."

To increase revenues, the company embarked on a three-pronged approach to expansion. Beginning in 2001, it launched an advertising campaign targeting IT-related medical journals. It expanded its sales force by about 30 percent a year. The company also began to collect client testimonials on the benefits of its products. The passage of the Health Insurance Portability and Accountability Act, HIPPA, in 1996 had also proved a welcome boon to QSI in its expansion efforts. While

designed to simplify transactions and protect patients' privacy and the security of information, HIPPA became a burden to medical practices because it dealt with the exchange of clinical and administrative information. Therefore it was difficult for doctors to comply with HIPPA without an electronic system.

By 2003, in part thanks to HIPPA and in part because, as Silverman observed in a 2003 *Investor's Business Daily* article, "[t]he practice management market, or the billing and scheduling software market, [was] a far more established market that [was] nearly fully penetrated," QSI chose to focus on electronic records management as its area of growth.

NextGen had become QSI's main growth driver. In 2002, it introduced NextGen PDA, which let doctors gain access to a patient's medical records, enter lab orders, get results, and write prescriptions via a hand-held personal digital assistant (PDA). In 2003, Next-Gen's sales increased about 21 percent per quarter. With only about 5 to 20 percent of practices having made the switch to electronic records, there was plenty of room for continued growth.

In 2004 QSI made *Forbes* magazine's list of the 200 best small companies at number 32. The following year, it moved up to occupy 11th place. QSI also ranked among the hottest growth companies on *Business Week's* 2004 list. Although Ahmed Hussein again publicly questioned the independence of the QSI board in 2004, calling the compensation packages that members voted for themselves and company executives detrimental to shareholders' interests, company revenues continued to grow, reaching $89 million in 2005 and $119 million in 2006. In fact, the firm had grown in sales and profit every year since 1999, doubling in income between 2004 and 2006.

Carrie Rothburd

PRINCIPAL SUBSIDIARIES

NextGen Healthcare Information Systems, Inc.

PRINCIPAL COMPETITORS

AMICAS, Inc.; Cerner Corporation; IDX Systems Corporation; CareCentric; CPSI; Eclipsys; Emdeon; Epic Healthcare; Global Med; MEDITECH; Misys Healthcare; QuadraMed; QCSI; VantageMed.

FURTHER READING

Cariaga, Vance, "Quality Systems Inc. Irvine, California; Software Maker Kicks Marketing into a Higher Gear,"

Investor's Business Daily, November 18, 2002, p. A7.

"Clinitec: Introducing the Next-Generation EMR Systems," *Directory of Medical Computer Systems,* Spring 1998, p. 34.

Crabtree, Penni, "Power Struggle Overshadows Earnings at Tustin, California–Based Software Firm," *Orange County Register,* June 11, 1999.

————, "Tustin, California–Based Medical Software Maker Faces Shareholder Revolt," *Orange County Register,* April 15, 1999.

Gondo, Nancy, "Quality Systems Inc. Irvine, California; Software Maker Offers a Little Less Color, But a Lot More Efficiency," *Investor's Business Daily,* October 1, 2003, p. A8.

Hindo, Brian, with Christopher Palmeri, "They May Not Sound Hot, but They're Staying on Top," *Business Week,* June 5, 2006, p. 54.

Milbourn, Mary Ann, "Quality Systems Inc. Faces Showdown Vote Over the Membership of Its Board," *Orange County Register,* September 17, 2005.

"Quality Systems Gives Dentists an Internet Option," *Health Data Network News,* December 20, 1996.

"Quality Systems, Inc.; Providing the Total Solution for Your Healthcare Information-Management Systems Needs," *Directory of Medical Computer Systems,* Spring 1998, p. 29.

Reingold, Jennifer, "The Gary Cooper of Governance," *Business Week,* May 29, 2000, p. 232.

Reliance Industries Ltd.

19, Walchand Hirachand Marg
Ballard Estate
Mumbai, 400 038
India
Telephone: +91 (222) 2847000
Fax: +91 (222) 2870072
Web site: http://www.ril.com

Public Company
Incorporated: 1958
Employees: 12,113
Sales: $19.97 billion (2006)
Stock Exchanges: Mumbai
Ticker Symbol: RIL
NAIC: 324110 Petroleum Refineries; 221210 Natural
    Gas Distribution; 313230 Nonwoven Fabric Mills

∎ ∎ ∎

Reliance Industries Ltd. is India's largest private-sector
company, generating revenues of $19.97 billion, or more
than 3 percent of India's total gross domestic product.
Founded as a textiles company, Reliance has successfully
completed a backward integration strategy that has
transformed it into India's largest private-sector petrochemicals company, and number two overall (behind
state-owned India Oil). Reliance's petrochemicals division is fully integrated and includes exploration and
production; refining (the company has built one of the
world's largest and most modern refinery complexes at
Jamnagar in Gujarat); marketing, through a chain of
more than 1,000 service stations; and the production of

petrochemicals, including polymers, polyester, polyester
intermediates, and others. These chemicals are used to
support Reliance's continued textile operations, which
focus particularly on the production of polyester fabrics.
Following the 2004 acquisition of Trevira, the company
has become the world's leading polyester manufacturer,
with production levels topping 25 million meters per
year. The company's textile range includes other fabrics,
such as acrylics, and finished garments.

Reliance Industries represents the continuation of
India's greatest corporate success story since the country's
independence. Founded by Dhirubhai H. Ambani in
1958, Reliance grew to include holdings in energy
production and distribution, telecommunications, and
capital finance. After a public feud between Mukesh D.
Ambani and younger brother Anil, these operations were
split off into a new company controlled by Anil Ambani.
Reliance Industries is listed on the Mumbai Stock
Exchange. Mukesh Ambani is company chairman and
managing director.

RAGS IN 1958

Dhirajlal Hirachand Ambani (Dhirubhai was a
nickname) was born to a lower middle class
schoolteacher's family in Chorwad, an impoverished village in Gujarat in 1932. Instead of becoming a teacher
himself—because the family could not afford to send
him on to university—the young Ambani traveled to
the port city of Aden at the age of 16. There, Ambani
began working as a clerk pumping gas at a service station.
Ambani remained in Aden for nearly ten years, rising to
become Burmah Shell's marketing manager. By then,

COMPANY PERSPECTIVES

Growth through Commitments. We care about: Quality; Research & Development; Health, Safety & Environment; Human Resource Development; Energy Conservation; Corporate Citizenship.

Reliance believes that any business conduct can be ethical only when it rests on the nine core values of Honesty, Integrity, Respect, Fairness, Purposefulness, Trust, Responsibility, Citizenship and Caring.

The essence of these commitments is that each employee conducts the company's business with integrity, in compliance with applicable laws, and in a manner that excludes considerations of personal advantage.

We do not lose sight of these values under any circumstances, regardless of the goals we have to achieve. To us, the means are as important as the ends.

however, Ambani had begun to dream of founding his own business.

Ambani quit Burmah Shell and for a time worked in the insurance field. In the late 1950s, the political situation in Aden had become increasingly unstable. In 1958, therefore, Ambani decided to return to India and start up a new business as an exporter of Indian goods to Aden. Finding housing for his young family in a Mumbai slum, Ambani at first rented office space, or rather a desk, for two hours per day. Initially, Ambani's exports included spices as well as fabrics.

Textiles, starting with textile yarns, which Ambani sold to textile manufacturers, provided Ambani with his strongest sales, and quickly became the company's focus. Ambani also rapidly proved himself adept at negotiating the intricate bureaucracy of the socialist Indian government. In particular, Ambani was able to develop a network of relationships with the country's political leaders, including Prime Minister Indira Gandhi. In this way, Ambani was able to develop a thriving business importing and exporting nylon, rayon, and polyester.

In the mid-1960s, Ambani developed still greater ambitions, becoming determined to enter textile manufacturing. The company set up its first factory in 1966, placing him in competition with his own customers. Success in the new venture came quickly, with the launch of the highly popular Vimal fabric brand. By the end of the decade, Ambani operated four factories. Part of the company's success came from its determination to use only the most modern, highly efficient production equipment. In this way, the company easily outpaced competitors, which relied on equipment often decades old.

Into the early 1970s, however, India's economy remained dominated by a handful of families; between them, and under the auspices of the Indian government, they controlled virtually every industry. This included the textile industry, whose distribution side soon formed an obstacle to the growth of Ambani's fabric sales. In response, Ambani became determined to set up his own distribution arm, which later included not only the sale of raw fabrics, but also the company's own clothing fashions.

PUBLIC OFFERING REVOLUTION IN 1977

The "old boy" network that dominated India's political, industrial, and financial circles also meant that Ambani had to look elsewhere for investment capital to back his growing ambitions. Cut off from funding from the Indian government, Ambani instead took the then-revolutionary step of turning to the stock market. In 1977, Ambani launched Reliance Textile Industries' initial public offering (IPO). The IPO of 2.8 million shares raised $1.8 million, and was considered among the largest in India at the time. By circumventing the traditional reliance on the state for capital investment, Ambani sparked a revolution in India, and was widely credited for setting the stage for the country's emergence as a major regional industrial center.

Ambani's deftness at working the Indian bureaucracy enabled him to take advantage of the country's arcane license system, which also imposed stiff import duties, virtually assuring license-holders of a captive market. In 1981, for example, Ambani received a license to construct a factory in Patalganga to produce polyester filament yarn. Soon after the factory launched production, the Indian government sharply raised import duties on polyester yarn. The Patalganga plant completed its second phase in 1985. The following year, the site added a new polyester staple fiber plant as well.

Into the early 1980s, Ambani was joined by sons Mukesh and Anil. Both had been sent to the United States for their education and, upon their return to India, played a prominent part in implementing Reliance's next phase of growth. Just as the company had moved from the sale of textiles to their manufacture, Reliance became determined to continue its backward integration in order to produce the chemicals from which the textile yarns were made.

The company's new strategy led it to enter the

KEY DATES

1948: Gujarat native Dhirubhai H. Ambani, aged 16, travels to Aden and begins working as a clerk at a service station.

1958: Ambani returns to India and sets up an import-export business, eventually focusing on the textile market, which becomes Reliance Textiles.

1966: Reliance launches textile manufacturing, building its first factory.

1977: Reliance goes public in one of India's first and largest public offerings.

1981: The company begins construction of a polyester filament yarn facility in Patalganga.

1986: After Ambani suffers a stroke, sons Mukesh and Anil take over day-to-day direction of the company; the company launches its first petrochemicals production as part of a vertical integration strategy.

1991: Reliance Refineries Ltd. is established in preparation for further vertical integration.

1993: Reliance Refineries goes public and changes its name to Reliance Petroleum.

1997: Reliance Petroleum launches construction of India's largest oil refinery at Jamnagar.

1999: Reliance wins a bid for 12 exploration blocks auctioned off by the Indian government.

2002: Reliance locates the largest Indian natural gas field in decades; Dhirubhai Ambani dies at age 69; Reliance Petroleum is merged into Reliance Industries.

2004: Reliance discovers a new natural gas field in the Bay of Bengal; the company acquires Germany's Trevira, becoming the world's leading manufacturer of polyester.

2006: Reliance Industries is broken up between the Ambani brothers.

petrochemicals industry, building its first plant for the production of purified terephtalic acid in 1986. In that year, following a stroke that left Dhirubhai Ambani partially paralyzed, the company's day-to-day direction was taken over by brothers Mukesh and Anil. Their father nonetheless remained chairman and the guiding hand of the business's growth until his death in 2002.

The following year, the company added a unit for the production of linear alkyl benzene, followed by the opening of a paraxylene plant in 1988. The company then began developing a new petrochemicals complex at Hazira, which began production of vinyl chloride monomer and polyvinyl chloride. In this way, the company developed market leadership both in polyesters and in polymers. By 1992, the company had launched production of high-density polyethylene at the Hazira complex as well.

INDIAN PETROLEUM GIANT AT THE START OF THE 21ST CENTURY

Reliance's vertical integration strategy naturally led to an interest in extending its operations to petroleum refining, and even to exploration and production. Yet these sectors remained tightly under state control, following the nationalization of the Indian oil industry in 1976 amid the global oil crisis. Although the state-owned oil companies were able to meet domestic demand through the 1980s, by the early 1990s, the country's existing oilfields were showing signs of depletion. At the same time, demand had been rising steadily, yet the oil companies, propped up by state subsidies, were too strapped for cash to invest in further exploration efforts. An initial attempt to liberalize the production and refining sectors failed, however, amid strong union protests.

In the meantime, Reliance made preparations for its move into the petroleum industry. In 1991, the company set up a new subsidiary, Reliance Refineries Private Ltd., clearly signaling its objectives. The subsidiary later changed its name to Reliance Petroleum Limited, and in 1993 launched a public offering, which at that time was India's largest ever IPO. While Reliance affirmed its plans to construct India's largest oil refinery, the company began developing its petroleum products marketing and distribution operations, including a network of some 1,000 service stations.

Reliance continued to pioneer financing channels in India. In 1993, for example, the company became the first Indian company to raise capital on the foreign market, through a Global Depositary Receipt (GDR) issue in Luxembourg. The company completed a second successful GDR issue in 1994. The company used the new capital in part to expand its petrochemicals wing, building the world's largest multi-feed cracker at the Hazira site. The company also added production plants for monoethylene glycol, polyethylene, and purified terephthalic acid. The new units launched production in 1998.

Reliance's opportunity for entry into petroleum refining came in 1997, when the Indian oil industry reached a state of near collapse. Unable to fund further exploration operations, and lacking the capital to expand its existing production, the government was forced to liberalize the sector. In that year, Reliance announced a plan to build one of the world's largest and most modern petroleum refining complexes in Jamnagar, Gujarat, at a cost of some $6 billion. The government agreed to the plan, and granted the company the right to import petroleum directly, rather than going through Indian Oil, which helped Reliance greatly drive down operating costs.

Constructed in record time, the Jamnagar site was commissioned in 1999. The site's production capacity was double that of any other Indian refinery and ranked among the top five in the world. The addition of the new facility also placed Reliance at the top rank of the country's private-sector companies. In 2002, Reliance Petroleum was merged into Reliance Industries, which then became one of the country's top three companies, including state-owned entities.

BREAKING UP IN 2006

Dhirubhai Ambani died in 2002, and the Ambani brothers took over as heads of the company. In that year, the company increased its dominance of the country's petrochemicals sector through its acquisition of main private-sector rival Indian Petrochemicals Corporation. Also in 2002, Reliance launched a diversification effort, targeting the telecommunications sector, especially the fast-growing cellular phone market. Reliance set up its own phone service, Reliance Infocomm, in that year.

Yet the petroleum industry remained the company's major growth focus. In 1999, the Indian government auctioned off 25 blocks for exploration; bids were given in the form of royalty percentage offers. Reliance won 12 of the blocks and promptly set in place its own team of exploration experts, backed by oilfield services from Halliburton and Schlumberger. Reliance's investment quickly paid off with the discovery of natural gas reserves estimated at some 14 trillion cubic feet, the largest natural gas field discovered in India in decades, in the Krishna-Godavari Basin in the Bay of Bengal. In 2004, the company struck again, locating a new gas field in the Bay of Bengal, off the Orissa Coast.

Buoyed by its successful exploration efforts, Reliance unveiled an ambitious expansion program for the second half of the 2000s. The company's plans included a $6 billion extension of the Jamnagar site, doubling it in size and making it the world's largest refinery by 2009. The company also announced that it intended to spend $10 billion on further oil exploration efforts, targeting the international market. In this way, the company hoped to increase its production tenfold by the end of the century. At the other end of the petroleum market, the company launched a $1.5 billion expansion of its Reliance gas station chain, with the goal of 6,000 stations. The company also expanded internationally, becoming the world's leading manufacturer of polyester yarn with the acquisition of Germany's Trevira. In addition, the company boosted its telecommunications wing, acquiring U.K.-based FLAG Telecom, an operator of a 50,000-kilometer underwater fiber-optic cable network.

In the meantime, rising tensions between Mukesh and Anil Ambani came to a head in late 2005, when a long-simmering disagreement over company strategy broke out into an open and highly publicized feud. In the end, a truce was brokered by the brothers' mother, who proposed a breakup of Reliance Industries into two roughly equal components. Mukesh Ambani remained as head of the company's petroleum, petrochemical, and textiles operations, and Anil Ambani regrouped the company's telecommunications, energy, capital finance, and other operations into a new company. The breakup of the company took place in 2006. As a result, Reliance Industries emerged as a focused and highly integrated petroleum and petrochemicals challenger to the global heavyweights.

M. L. Cohen

PRINCIPAL SUBSIDIARIES

Reliance Industrial Investments and Holdings Ltd.; Reliance Infrastructure Limited; Reliance Middle East DMCC (U.A.E.); Reliance Netherlands B.V.; Reliance Petroleum Limited; Reliance Retail Limited; Reliance Strategic Investments Limited; Reliance UK Ltd. (50%); Reliance Ventures Ltd.

PRINCIPAL COMPETITORS

Indian Oil Corporation Ltd.; Hindustan Petroleum Corporation Ltd.; Bharat Petroleum Corporation Ltd.; Indian Petrochemicals Corporation Ltd.; Mangalore Refinery and Petrochemicals Ltd.; Kochi Refineries Ltd.; Chennai Petroleum Corporation Ltd.; Parker Agrochem Exports Ltd.

FURTHER READING

Alperowicz, Natasha, "Reliance Enters Biopharmaceuticals," *Chemical Week*, February 1, 2006, p. 32.

———, "Reliance Industries: Chasing the Energy Majors," *Chemical Week*, May 3, 2006, p. 17.

———, "Reliance on Course to Double in Size," *Chemical Week*, December 18, 1996, p. 39.

Chakravarty, Subrata N., "A Lot of American Companies Are Like Taxis," *Forbes,* September 22, 1986, p. 100.

Elliott, John, "Breaking Up Is Hard to Do: Reliance," *Fortune International,* June 13, 2005, p. 14.

———, "Here Comes the Son," *Fortune International,* November 25, 2002, p. 34.

Helman, Christopher, and Naazneen Karmali, "The Mogul of Mumbai," *Forbes,* May 8, 2006.

"India's Reliance," *Business Week,* June 25, 2001, p. 20.

Mazumdar, Sudip, "Trouble in the Family," *Newsweek International,* December 27, 2004, p. 59.

Pitta, Julie, "Like Father, Like Son," *World Trade,* April 2003, p. 38.

Shah, Jigar, "The Reliance Road to Succession," *Asiamoney,* February 2003, p. SS26.

Tattum, Lyn, "Growth Is Life," *Chemical Week,* September 25, 2002, p. S3.

Reser's Fine Foods, Inc.

15570 Southwest Jenkins Road
Beaverton, Oregon 97075
U.S.A.
Telephone: (503) 643-6431
Toll Free: (800) 333-6431
Fax: (503) 646-9233
Web site: http://www.resers.com

Private Company
Incorporated: 1950 as Mrs. Reser's Salads
Employees: 1,000
Sales: $375 million (2005 est.)
NAIC: 424490 Prepared Foods (Except Frozen), Merchant Wholesalers; 424420 Prepared Foods, Frozen (Except Dairy), Merchant Wholesalers

■ ■ ■

Reser's Fine Foods, Inc., is a leading national manucturer and distributor of refrigerated processed foods, principally prepackaged deli items such as salads, pasta, salsa, and chip dip. Reser's also sells cooked cut potatoes, meat products, dinner entrees, Mexican foods, and desserts. The company runs 12 processing plants, with facilities in Oregon, Utah, Hawaii, Ohio, North Carolina, Washington, Maryland, and Kansas. Founded in Oregon, the company is best known in the West, yet sells all across the United States and into Canada. It sells its products retail through big and small groceries, and also does wholesale business with large clients in the foodservice industry, including restaurant chains. Besides the Reser's brand lines of salads, potatoes, desserts, dips

and spreads, meats, salsa, and deli case goods, the company also manufactures several other distinct brands. These include the Reser's Organic line of organic packaged foods; Baja Café, a line of Mexican entrees, tortillas, and salsa; Main Street Bistro, a line of fully cooked entrees and sides such as meatloaf and mashed potatoes; Potato Express, a line of cooked, ready-to-serve potatoes; Sidari's brand pasta and pasta sauces; and its Stonemill Kitchen brand prepared salads. The company was publicly traded from 1960 to 1986, but has always been in the hands of the founding Reser family.

A HOMEGROWN BUSINESS

Reser's Fine Foods, Inc., began as a small operation called Mrs. Reser's Salads, founded by Mildred and Earl Reser in their farmhouse kitchen in Cornelius, Oregon. The Resers had moved in 1949 to Oregon from Kansas, where Mildred Reser had also operated a salad business. In their new town, however, they worked in a restaurant, Earl as a cook, Mildred as a waitress. In 1950, the couple began Mrs. Reser's Salads as a sideline. Mrs. Reser cooked at home at night, making batches of up to 200 pounds of potato salad, and her husband worked as both salesman and distributor, delivering the product to area groceries and butcher shops. In 1951, the business took a huge step forward when Mildred got up the nerve to ask a local Safeway, a chain grocery, if it would consider stocking her potato salad. To her surprise, Safeway responded that it would like her to make enough potato salad not just for the local store but for all its outlets in Oregon. With this one large account, the success of the young company seemed assured, and the company left the family kitchen and established a commercial space in downtown Cornelius.

The whole Reser family, including son Al and Mildred's aged father, as well as many neighbors and former colleagues from the restaurant, found employment at Mrs. Reser's Salads. The company grew steadily, expanding into adjacent buildings for more production and storage space. Reser's technology was relatively primitive, and salads were made by the batch, with workers sometimes cooking and packing all night long in preparation for Sunday deliveries. The company's truckers also functioned as the sales force, asking around for more outlets for the Reser's line, which grew to four salads as well as gelatin. The trucks were not refrigerated in the early days, so the company relied on dry ice to keep the goods cool. Many independent area groceries took up Reser's salads, as well as area chains such as Chet's Market, Hank's Markets, and Tipton's.

Al Reser had been helping out with the business since he was 12 years old. He studied food science at Oregon State University, and in addition to working long hours at the company, he developed a new product, the company's first chip dip. This was a crucial product, as sales of salads ran high in the summer but slowed down a lot in the cooler months. The chip dip sold well in the winter, and soon accounted for about a third of Reser's sales volume. Then in 1960, Earl Reser started a new business in Seattle, a food brokerage company. Consequently, he sold his stock in Mrs. Reser's Salad to his son. Al Reser became president, moved the company to Beaverton, Oregon, and renamed it, incorporating as Reser's Fine Foods. At that time, the company had three or four refrigerated trucks, and brought in some $300,000 annually.

TAKING THE COMPANY PUBLIC

Al Reser was just out of college when he became president of the family business. Although he was only in his 20s, he had over a decade of experience. He was determined to take risks and think big in order to let the company grow. So very shortly after taking over management, Reser went to New York, found investors, and took the company public. In 1960 Reser's Fine

Foods began trading publicly on the Over-the-Counter (OTC) exchange. With capital in hand, Reser's moved to much larger quarters, finding a 33,000-square-foot space in Beaverton. The company bought its first continuous cooker, meaning production could as much as triple from the old batch method. Though the new plant at first seemed much bigger than the company could use, Reser's soon ran out of space and had to construct additional cooler and freezer facilities.

The company found ways to balance its strong line of potato salads and other deli salads with products that would sell year-round. In 1967, Reser's bought German Boy, a maker of sausage and processed meats. The next year, Reser's began making tortillas. Tortillas were something of a novelty product at the time, and in the Northwest were principally available commercially only frozen or canned. Reser's was the first company to produce tortillas on a large scale in the Northwest, and though the venture at first seemed risky, the tortilla line sold well and the plant was soon at capacity.

The company continued to grow through the 1970s. As its production facilities became too cramped, Reser's bought a 16-acre lot in Beaverton. It built a new plant on the lot, opening a 52,000-square-foot factory in 1978. By that time, the Reser's product line had grown to some ten different kinds of potato salad, a dozen different chip dips, a handful of distinct macaroni salads, and at least 20 gelatin salads. Sales expanded all over the West, into Montana, the Dakotas, Wyoming, and Washington by the late 1970s. The third generation of Resers began joining the company around that time. Eventually all five of Al Reser's children found positions with Reser's Fine Foods.

FIGHTING OFF A TAKEOVER BID

Al Reser took the company public when he became president as a way of raising needed capital. He had been turned down by Oregon banks in his search for credit, but New York investors were interested in small companies with the potential for rapid growth. Much of the stock was owned by Reser family members and by company employees. In the early 1980s, Al Reser received a notice from the Securities and Exchange Commission (SEC) informing him that a Chicago investment firm had acquired 10 percent of Reser's stock. The firm had been moving quietly to buy not only Reser's stock but the stock of some eight to ten similarly sized food companies, with the goal, evidently, of putting together its own food conglomerate. Within the next few years, the Chicago investor had acquired four small food companies, and it gobbled up over 40 percent of Reser's stock.

This was the downside of having taken the company

```
┌─────────────────────────────────────────────┐
│                                               │
│              KEY DATES                        │
│                  ■                            │
│  ───────────────────────────────────────     │
│  1950:  Company is founded in farmhouse       │
│         kitchen as Mrs. Reser's Salads.       │
│  1960:  Son of founders incorporates          │
│         business as Reser's Fine Foods;       │
│         company goes public.                  │
│  1978:  Beaverton factory opens.              │
│  1986:  After fending off hostile takeover    │
│         bid, company is taken private again.  │
│  1991:  Reser's opens plant in Topeka,        │
│         Kansas.                               │
│  2002:  Reser's acquires Made Rite Foods      │
│         and Wilson Foods.                     │
│                                               │
└─────────────────────────────────────────────┘
```

ACQUISITIONS AND NEW PRODUCTS

As sales increased, Reser's plant had trouble keeping pace with production. In 1989, the plant was at capacity for salad, so Reser's bought a California manufacturer, Salad Host. Two years later, Reser's opened a 50,000-square-foot salad production plant in Topeka, Kansas. The company had three plants for its salads, in three states. It also acquired another salad maker in the early 1990s, the Memphis-based Mrs. Weaver's Salads. The Topeka plant did very well, but its busiest season was in the summer, and winter months were slack. Consequently, in the early 1990s, Reser's experimented with selling cut, cooked potatoes in pouches. These were sold in grocery store produce aisles. This was a new concept, though Al Reser had seen something like it in Europe, and it seemed to do well initially. However, Reser's was uncertain whether refrigerated potatoes was just a fad or a long-term trend. Reser's decided to gamble that refrigerated potatoes were here to stay. It expanded the Topeka plant, and growth in the refrigerated potato category took off. By the end of the 1990s, the Topeka plant could not handle all the volume, and Reser's broke ground on another facility, in Pasco, Washington.

The company added a marketing department for the first time in the early 1990s. Through the decade, Reser's reviewed and overhauled its packaging and graphics. The company had grown to include many different brands, either offshoots of Reser's lines or lines taken over from Reser's acquisitions. By the end of the 1990s, the company had a unified look despite the wide variety of products and brands it sold.

Reser's continued to acquire other small food companies. In 1993, it bought two Italian food makers, Bellissima Italia, Inc., of Oregon, and the Cleveland-based Sidari's Italian Foods. That year it also acquired Manor Hill Foods, a company based in Baltimore, Maryland. Both Manor Hill and Sidari's had been owned by a British food conglomerate, Geest Corporation Plc. Reser's also bought a half-interest in a Mexican food plant in Topeka in 1996. Mexican food was a real growth category, and Reser's stepped up its tortilla production. In partnership with the Topeka company La Siesta and an Oregon manufacturer, La Burrita, Reser's modified the manufacturing and marketing of its tortillas, aiming them towards the Hispanic market. Reser's then formed a partnership with another Mexican food manufacturer, Don Pancho, and transferred its tortilla production for the Western states to Don Pancho plants in Oregon and Washington.

By the mid-1990s, Reser's was selling its products across the United States, in Canada, Mexico, and also in some Asian markets. Salsa was its biggest seller, and the

public. With so much stock in its kitty, the investor was close to being able to enact a hostile takeover, perhaps pushing family management out. Reser's stock had been trading for three or four dollars a share when this activity started. Al Reser was determined to hang onto the company, but he had to pay a premium to do so. He set up a right-of-first-refusal agreement with employee stockholders, giving him the right to acquire their stock for a higher price if anyone else offered to buy it. This was an expensive but effective tactic that left the Reser family paying as much as $14 a share for Reser's Fine Foods stock. By 1986, the company had frozen out the Chicago interest, and the family took Reser's private again. The escapade had left Reser's in debt, while the takeover artist had profited handsomely. Nevertheless, maintaining family control was of utmost importance. Al Reser was extremely committed to the company, touring food processing plants and groceries even while on vacation, and always looking for new niche products. Revenue increased by 10 percent or more year after year under his tutelage, and reached $100 million by 1990.

The company became more sophisticated in the 1980s, matching its sales growth with technological innovation and new processes. For example, Reser's had had no in-house quality control until 1981. It had sent samples to a lab to meet quality control requirements, and such procedures as checking inventory were done by eye; if a bag of potatoes looked rotten, it was sent back. When the company hired a research and development director, the company's systems became much more standardized and scientific. Potatoes were not merely eyeballed but tested for percentage of sugar vs. starch, for example. Employee practices were improved, recipes were made consistent, and during the 1980s the company came to exceed industry standards for food safety and quality control.

company made more than 200 different kinds of refrigerated salads. It also sold meats and sausages, desserts, and tortillas. Though it began life as a salad company, by the 2000s Reser's thought of itself more broadly as a refrigerated food company. Still a relatively small player, and with a dedicated management team that had seen the company through many changes, Reser's was able to react quickly to possible market trends and try out new products. Al Reser constantly brought back ideas from his travels, and the company was a frequent innovator. Reser's steadily increased its exposure to the Mexican food market in the 2000s, acquiring part-interest in another Western tortilla maker, Puentes Brothers, in 2002, and also buying that year the Utah firm Wilson Foods Company, a maker of frozen burritos. It bought a refrigerated salad company in North Carolina, Made Rite Foods, in 2002, giving Reser's more access to East Coast markets.

A new development in the mid-2000s was a brand extension called Main Street Bistro. This was a line of fully cooked restaurant-style meals that Reser's positioned in grocery meat departments. A Main Street Bistro meal included a meat dish and a potato side—items that Reser's had long made separately, but now were packaged together. According to the trade journal *Refrigerated & Frozen Foods* (May 2004), the so-called prepared meal category was a hot trend in the 2000s, growing at about 25 percent a year and bringing in a total of approximately $500 million across the category. Reser's had at first been somewhat reluctant to commit to prepared meals, but took the plunge at the beginning of the 2000s; by mid-decade, the company found itself one of the leading players in the niche. Reser's came out with a similar line of prepared meals with a Mexican theme, and marketed these under the brand name Baja Café.

By the mid-2000s, Reser's sales were estimated at around $375 million, and the company hoped its revenue would rise to $500 million over the next few years. The company had grown and consolidated, reaching beyond its Oregon roots with manufacturing plants in the Midwest and East and even in Hawaii. From making potato salad, its product line had grown to include myriad forms of cooked potatoes, fresh salads, prepared meals, tortillas, Mexican and Italian foods and entrees, salsa, dips, and desserts. Sales reached beyond the Western states to penetrate into Canada and Mexico and some overseas markets. The company remained private, with the third generation of Resers in top management positions.

A. Woodward

PRINCIPAL COMPETITORS

Orval Kent Foods Co.; Bob Evans Farms, Inc.; Campbell Soup Company.

FURTHER READING

Garrison, Bob, "Meat and Potatoes," *National Provisioner,* May 2004, pp. 56–60.

Gonzalez, Cristine, "Reser's Rise," *Oregonian,* February 9, 1995, p. M1.

Hill, Jim, "Reser's Fine Foods Bags Bigger Market," *Oregonian,* March 19, 1993, p. D8.

Kadel, Steve, "Beaverton's Al Reser Keeps Eyes Open As Food Business Thrives," *Oregonian,* February 22, 1990.

Major, Meg, "All You Can Eat," *Progressive Grocer,* May 1, 2005, pp. 128–29.

Mitchell, Leslie, "Beaverton, Ore.–Based Reser's Acquires Wilson Foods of Utah," *Salt Lake Tribune,* August 8, 2002.

Riell, Howard, "Fridge Fresh," *Frozen Food Age,* February 2004, p. 60.

Suber, Jim, "Reser's: No Small Potatoes," *Topeka Capital Journal,* November 29, 1994, p. 1.

Resources Connection, Inc.

---

695 Town Center Drive, Suite 600
Costa Mesa, California 92626
U.S.A.
Telephone: (713) 430-6400
Toll Free: (800) 900-1131
Fax: (714) 428-6090
Web site: http://www.resourcesglobal.com

Public Company
Incorporated: 1997 as Resources Connection, LLC
Employees: 3,231
Sales: $633.8 million (2006)
Stock Exchanges: NASDAQ
Ticker Symbol: RECN
NAIC: 541611 Administrative Management and General Management Consulting Services; 541211 Offices of Certified Public Accountants; 561110 Office Administrative Services; 561310 Employment Placement Agencies; 561320 Temporary Help Agencies

∎∎∎

Resources Connection, Inc., provides professionals on a project basis through its operating entity, Resources Global Professionals (RGP). Its specialties are accounting and finance, risk management and internal audit, information technology, human resources, supply chain management, and law. The company was formed in 1996 as a unit of Big Four accounting firm Deloitte & Touche and was spun off three years later to avoid regulatory conflicts. RGP has 65 offices in ten countries.

Among its 1,600 clients are dozens of *Fortune* 100 companies.

ORIGINS

Resources Connection, Inc. began in June 1996 as a division of Deloitte & Touch,e LLP (later Deloitte Touche Tohmatsu). It was led by Donald B. Murray, a partner at Deloitte who had been in charge of Deloitte's large auditing practice in Santa Ana, California. The unit's specialty was having experienced, senior-level financial professionals set up new accounting systems or handle mergers and acquisitions details for corporations on a project basis, at a lower cost than farming out the work to top tier firms. In 1997, the division became Resources Connection LLC, a wholly owned subsidiary of Deloitte & Touche.

Murray originally envisioned most demand for the firm's services among companies going public for the first time or engaged in mergers and acquisitions, noted a later profile in the *Orange County Register.* According to the *Mergers and Acquisitions Report,* Resources Connection did supply personnel for high profile takeovers such as the $10 billion acquisition of Bankers Trust Corp. by Deutsche Bank AG in 1999. However, the firm would also be kept busy during the wave of bankruptcies and downsizing that accompanied the burst of the tech bubble. Company CFO Steve Giusto told the *Wall Street Transcript* that the company averaged a nearly 140 percent annual growth rate in its first four years.

Within a few years Resources Connection was employing 850 people in 27 U.S. offices and was posting revenues of more than $100 million annually. Deloitte decided to spin off the unit to avoid costly regulatory burdens designed to keep auditing and consulting practices separate. Murray told Reuters that the company also believed the unit could grow faster on its own. Resources Connections LLC underwent a $55 million buyout by its 100 managers in April 1999. A new entity, RC Transaction Corp., had been formed five months earlier to acquire the company. Investment bank Evercore Capital Partners L.P. acquired slightly more than half of the outstanding shares. RC Transaction Corp. was renamed Resources Connection, Inc. in August 2000.

PUBLIC AND INTERNATIONAL IN 2000

Resources Connection, Inc. debuted on the NASDAQ in a December 2000 initial public offering (IPO) that raised $78 million. The success of the services-related IPO came in a market that had soured on tech stocks, noted the *Daily Deal*.

By this time, the company was supplying human resources workers as well as those in accounting and finance. It had also formed an information technology division. In 2000, half of its project employees and consultants were CPAs, however.

While there were fewer large mergers after 2000, according to the *Mergers and Acquisitions Report*, Resources Connection continued to benefit from a trend toward outsourcing. Another impetus towards growth would be the increasingly stringent financial reporting regulations that public companies were required to adopt following

a wave of corporate accounting scandals in 2002.

HELP FROM SARBANES-OXLEY

Resources Audit Solutions, LLC (RAS), officially started in June 2002 to help U.S. public companies deal with the new regulatory requirements of the Sarbanes-Oxley Act.

Other large accounting firms had gotten into consulting sidelines of their core audit and tax services, but these would be curtailed after a rash of accounting scandals. They ultimately divested such businesses to avoid perceived conflicts of interest. The Big Four would be its clients, as well as competitors. Other rivals included specialized units of employment agencies and temp services.

Resources Connection had grown purely organically before 2002. It began to make acquisitions in order to stretch its range of offerings and to expand geographically. Resources Connection was building up a practice in the United Kingdom. It acquired Ernst & Young's Executive Search and Selection unit in the spring of 2002. This was followed several months later by the opening of an office in Birmingham.

The RECN of Texas, LP, subsidiary was formed in May 2002. In October 2002, Resources Connection bought a Houston supply chain management services firm called The Procurement Centre, LLC, for $9 million (most of it in cash).

The firm's earnings slipped in the early years of the millennium, but came back strong with a recovering economy in 2003. Revenues rose 63 percent to $328 million in 2003. Much of the growth was from Europe and Asia. Sarbanes-Oxley work accounted for a third of revenues, an analyst told *Investor's Business Daily*. Another called Resources Connection "the biggest and purest play" in the new multibillion-dollar Sarbanes-Oxley compliance industry.

FISCAL 2004 ACQUISITIONS

Resources Connection made its first move into Continental Europe when Executive Temporary Management BV (ETM) of the Netherlands was acquired from Ernst & Young in July 2003. The price was $29.8 million in cash. ETM, based in Maarssen, had been created in 1989. After the acquisition, it was renamed Resources Global Professionals Europe BV (RGPE).

The company also bought a subsidiary of Deloitte Touche Tohmatsu Australia. It paid $1 million for Deloitte Re:sources Pty Ltd. in June 2003, which was also

KEY DATES

1996: Company is formed as a division of Deloitte & Touche LLP.

1997: Company becomes a subsidiary of Deloitte & Touche.

1999: Company is spun off in management buyout.

2000: Company goes public on the NASDAQ, opens first international offices.

2002: Houston supply chain management firm The Procurement Centre is acquired.

2003: Executive Temporary Management of the Netherlands is acquired.

2004: Deloitte Re:sources Pty Ltd. is acquired in Australia.

2005: Operating company is renamed Resources Global Professionals.

renamed. Re:sources had offices in Sydney and Melbourne. A little later, the company announced it had purchased policyIQ, an Internet-based internal controls and risk management tool. This was folded into the Resources Audit Solutions (RAS) subsidiary.

In August 2004 the company paid $4.6 million for an 80 percent holding in Nordic Spring Management Consulting AB of Stockholm, Sweden. Nordic Spring had been established by former principals of Ernst & Young.

EXPANDING AROUND THE WORLD IN 2005

The company was averaging better than 60 percent revenue growth. RAS accounted for nearly 40 percent of revenues in 2005. By this time, its market capitalization had risen from $288 million in the 2000 IPO to more than $800 million.

Some analysts wondered where the company's growth would come if its clients became accustomed to Sarbanes-Oxley requirements and began handling more of the drudgery themselves. Murray told the *Investor's Business Daily* the firm could find work in good times and bad. "We're not selling product," he said. "We just manage change."

In January 2005, the company announced its Resources Connection, LLC operating company would begin doing business as Resources Global Professionals (RGP) to reflect its global scope. A second Canadian office was opened in Alberta in May 2005. The company

was expanding in northern Europe and giving special attention to its growing business in the Pacific Rim and India. Resources Connection had 1,900 clients in 39 countries in 2005. By this time, more than 20 percent of total revenues were coming from outside the United States.

The number of associates working for Resources Connection on an employee or contracting basis had risen from less than 1,200 to more than 2,600 in two years. These were supported by about 600 corporate staffers. Revenues of $537.6 million in 2005 were a colossal leap from the $328.33 million reported in the previous year and the $202.02 million reported in 2003.

In December 2005, RGP opened an office in Beijing, China. In addition to the Western multinational corporations doing business there, there were also more and more local firms adjusting their financial records to international standards in order to raise money from abroad, Murray told the *Financial Times*. He expected revenues from China to match those in the United States within ten years. RGP also had a local Shenzhen-based affiliate and offices in Taiwan and Hong Kong.

Entering another booming national economy, Resources Connection acquired the non-assurance business advisory services practice of Rajeesh Rajeev & Associates of Mumbai, India. It was renamed Resources Global Professionals India Private Limited.

No matter where in the world RGP was operating, one of its main challenges was finding an adequate supply of talent. Its associates typically had a dozen or more years of experience before joining RGP and usually boasted either a C.P.A. or an M.B.A. degree.

Frederick C. Ingram

PRINCIPAL SUBSIDIARIES

Nordic Spring Management Consulting AB (Sweden); RC Holdings I, LLC; RC Holdings II, LLC; RC Management Group, LLC; RCG, LP; RECN of Texas, LP dba Resources Global Professionals LP; Resources Audit Solutions, LLC; Resources Connection Australia Pty Ltd. dba Resources Global Professionals Australia; Resources Connection Holdings BV (Netherlands); Resources Connection, LLC dba Resources Global Professionals, etc.; Resources Connection Taiwan Ltd.; Resources Connection (UK) Ltd.; Resources Global Professionals Europe BV (Netherlands); Resources Global Professionals, Inc. (Canada); Resources Global Professionals India Private Limited; Resources Global Professionals Japan K.K.; Resources Global Professionals Limited (HK) (China).

PRINCIPAL OPERATING UNITS

Accounting and Finance; Risk Management and Internal Audit; Information Technology; Human Resources; Supply Chain Management; Legal.

PRINCIPAL COMPETITORS

Deloitte Touche Tohmatsu; Ernst & Young International; KPMG International; PriceWaterhouseCoopers International Limited; Protiviti Inc.; Jefferson Wells International, Inc.

FURTHER READING

Cecil, Mark, "Resources Connection VP Does Not Feel New M&A Heat," *Mergers and Acquisitions Report,* February 2, 2004.

"CEO/Company Interview: Stephen J. Giusto, Resources Connection, Inc.," *Wall Street Transcript,* March 12, 2001.

"Company Interview: Stephen J. Giusto, Resources Connection, Inc.," *Wall Street Transcript,* March 2002.

Hennessey, Raymond, "Resources Connection Shares Rise After IPO," *Dow Jones News Service,* December 15, 2000.

Johansson, Catrine, "Costa Mesa, Calif., Professional Services Firm Acquires Swedish Consultant," *Orange County Register,* August 31, 2004.

Lau, Justine, "RGP to Open Office in Beijing; US Firm Aims to Tap into Increasing Demand for Professional Services," *Financial Times* (London), September 21, 2005, p. 11.

Mathewson, Judy, "$103.5 Million Goal Attached to IPO Filing; Resources Connection of Costa Mesa Applies to Sell Shares at a Price to Be Announced," *Orange County Register,* September 5, 2000, p. C2.

Milbourn, Mary Ann, "Costa Mesa, Calif., Staffing Firm's Temporary Workers Find Permanency," *Orange County Register,* April 20, 2003.

————, "Costa Mesa, Calif.–Based Staffing Firm to Buy Dutch Ernst & Young Subsidiary," *Orange County Register,* May 22, 2003.

"One Year After Sarbanes-Oxley: How the Industry Is Coping with New Mandates," *EFT Report,* August 6, 2003.

Reckard, E. Scott, and Bonnie Harris, "Resources Connection's IPO Brings in $78 Million; The Costa Mesa Temp-Staffing Outfit Will Repay Debt and Expand in a Mushrooming Market," *Los Angeles Times,* December 16, 2000, p. C2.

"Resources Connection Consultants Moving In," *Birmingham Post* (England), November 19, 2002, p. 25.

Shinkle, Kirk, "The Numbers Add Up for Consulting Firm," *Investor's Business Daily,* June 4, 2004, p. A5.

————, "Rebound in Spending Helps Consulting Firm Back to Growth Mode; After Two Years of Profit Declines, It's Bounced Back Along with Market," *Investor's Business Daily,* September 19, 2003, p. A5.

Smith, Elizabeth, "Deloitte & Touche Unveils Management Buyout of Unit," *Reuters News,* April 8, 1999.

Sreenivas, I. Satya, "Accountants Diversify Services to Stay in the Black," *Silicon Valley/San Jose Business Journal,* May 16, 1997.

"Stock of the Day: Resources Connection—CFO, CNNfn," *CEO Wire,* July 19, 2004.

Walsh, Andrew, "Temp Firm Connects in $78M IPO," *Daily Deal,* December 15, 2000.

ROFIN-SINAR
Technologies Inc.

40984 Concept Drive
Plymouth, Michigan 48170
U.S.A.
Telephone: (734) 455-5400
Fax: (734) 455-2741
Web site: http://www.rofin-sinar.com

Public Company
Incorporated: 1975 as Sinar Laser Systems
Employees: 1,400
Sales: $375.19 million (2005)
Stock Exchanges: NASDAQ Frankfurt
Ticker Symbols: RSTI 902757
NAIC: 333512 Machine Tool (Metal Cutting Types) Manufacturing; 333992 Welding and Soldering Equipment Manufacturing; 339943 Marking Device Manufacturing

■ ■ ■

ROFIN-SINAR Technologies Inc. is a leading producer of industrial lasers. It has sold nearly 40,000 laser sources in its first 30 years and has one of the widest product ranges in the industrial laser industry, making diode, CO_2 solid-state systems. The company was spun off from Siemens AG in 1996.

Rofin-Sinar has operational headquarters in Plymouth, Michigan, and Hamburg, Germany, and manufacturing facilities in Germany, the United States, Japan, the United Kingdom, Spain, Sweden, Singapore, and China and sales and support offices in a number of other countries as well. More than half of revenues came

from Europe in 2005. A third of the company's sales were to the machine tool industry. The semiconductor and electronics (12 percent) and automotive industries (9 percent) were also significant.

ORIGINS

The story of ROFIN-SINAR Technologies Inc. begins with the launch of Sinar Laser Systems (Sinar Lasersysteme) in Hamburg, Germany, in 1975. It was formed by Samuel Simonsson, who would be its first president, and two partners. In the days before widespread industrial use of lasers, the enterprise had trouble finding funding until local venture capitalist Eberhard Lohss bought a holding, according to the *Wall Street Journal.* Within a few years, Sinar bought Rofin of the United Kingdom and adopted the name Rofin-Sinar G.m.b.H.

Simonsson told the *Wall Street Journal* that the company originally sold lasers made by others. Rofin-Sinar produced its first laser in 1982 and by the end of 1986 had sold more than 300 of them to industrial clients, who used them for cutting and welding. Revenues were growing at a 70 percent annual rate and by the mid-1980s, Rofin-Sinar was the world's third largest manufacturer of industrial lasers.

The *Wall Street Journal* held the company up as an example of how Germany was beginning to match the high tech prowess of the United States and Japan. Germany was investing more in laser development, which complemented traditional Teutonic strengths in optics and precision machining, than its overseas rivals. Still, tiny Rofin-Sinar, with sales of roughly $25 million, was less than one-eighth the size of the leading commercial laser manufacturer at the time, California's Spectra-Physics Inc. The total world laser market was valued at $500 million; Rofin-Sinar then competed in a small niche, mainly catering to auto makers. Its custom-installed laser units were priced at $50,000 to $1 million and weighed as much as one ton each.

The company was inventive enough to license one of its early designs to Spectra-Physics for sale in the United States. In its first decade, Rofin-Sinar was focusing its research on making industrial lasers more powerful and more reliable by developing new types of power sources and other components.

ACQUISITION BY SIEMENS IN 1987

Siemens AG, the German electrical and electronics giant, acquired Rofin-Sinar in 1987, seeking access to its laser technology. Under Siemens, Rofin-Sinar invested heavily to become a vertically integrated enterprise while entering new market segments and geographical areas. The company bought its U.S. licensee, the Industrial Laser Division of Spectra Physics Corporation, in 1988. It soon entered the French market by buying Optilas Laser Industriel. The 1989 acquisition of Coherent General Inc.'s Laser-Optronic GmbH brought Rofin-Sinar into the laser marking business. This process used lasers to inscribe nearly indelible code numbers on items such as auto parts and computer chips. Laser-Optronic was renamed the Laser Marking Division in 1992.

Unfortunately, the global recession of the early 1990s hit machine tool manufacturers, Rofin's main customers, hard. By 1992, competition for remaining business was so fierce that laser manufacturers were cutting prices, noted a company financial report. Layoffs and other cost-cutting measures followed, including outsourcing, leasing excess office space, and closing a site in San Jose, California. Rofin-Sinar posted a $20 million

net loss on revenues of $60 million in 1993 but was in the black again within a couple of years. In 1995, the company achieved a $3.2 million profit on revenues of $92.5 million. Rofin-Sinar then had 450 employees. The U.S. and European markets for industrial lasers were showing signs of recovery, but the company was looking to Asia for its strongest growth.

1996 SPINOFF

Rofin-Sinar was spun off from Siemens AG in 1996. The company had sold approximately 4,000 laser sources in its first 20 years. A Delaware corporation, ROFIN-SINAR Technologies Inc. (RSTI), was formed in July 1996 as a holding company for Rofin-Sinar Inc. and Rofin-Sinar Laser GmbH. RSTI went public that October in an offering that raised $70.1 million.

In 1997 Rofin-Sinar bought DILAS Diodenlaser, bringing into the fold a third type of technology, semiconductor diode lasers, in addition to its existing CO_2 and Nd:YAG (Neodymium Yttrium Aluminium Garnet, a solid-state crystal) laser systems. Diode lasers were much smaller, more efficient, and less expensive to buy. (These are the types of lasers found in CD players.) The company made two more purchases in the late 1990s: the assets of Palomar Technologies UK Ltd. (1998), which formed the basis of a new U.K. subsidiary, and RasantAlcotec Beschichtungstechnik GmbH (1999).

According to *Crain's Detroit Business*, U.S. carmakers were exhibiting a renewed interest in lasers as a means to more efficient production. The industry used CO_2 lasers for cutting steel and the lower-powered Nd:YAG lasers for welding.

Rofin-Sinar made 800 lasers in 1999 and by the end of the year counted an installed base of more than 6,000 laser units around the world. The company had added manufacturing plants in the United States, United Kingdom, and Japan. It was enjoying increased sales to the electronics industry during the tech boom, though the effects of the Asian financial crisis would be a drag on earnings.

PURCHASE OF BAASEL LASERTECH: 2000

Another new business was added in 2000 with the $40 million acquisition of Baasel Lasertech Group from Mannesmann Demag Krauss-Maffei AG. This would become the basis of the new Micro unit, whose products were used to perform intricate procedures in the jewelry, dental, medical equipment, and electronics industries. (Baasel also had a significant laser marking business.) This purchase, which was the company's largest to date,

KEY DATES

1975: Sinar Laser Systems (Sinar Lasersysteme) is formed in Hamburg, Germany.
1978: Sinar acquires Rofin of the United Kingdom and becomes ROFIN-SINAR.
1987: Siemens AG buys ROFIN-SINAR.
1988: Company buys U.S.-based Industrial Laser Division of Spectra Physics as well as Optilas Laser Industriel of France.
1989: Laser marking specialist Laser-Optronic GmbH is acquired.
1993: Company restructures following global recession, posts $20 million loss.
1996: ROFIN-SINAR Technologies Inc. is spun off from Siemens and goes public.
1997: DILAS Diodenlaser is acquired, adding diode laser technology.
1998: Assets of Palomar Technologies UK Ltd. are acquired.
1999: RasantAlcotec Beschichtungstechnik GmbH is acquired.
2000: BAASEL Lasertech purchase starts ROFIN-SINAR's Micro business.
2001: Z-Laser S.A. is acquired.
2004: Optoskand, PRC, and Lee Laser are acquired.

brought Rofin-Sinar's total annual revenues from $124 million to about $200 million while diversifying the company's client base.

Baasel's medical laser business was sold to Hamburg's WaveLight Laser Technologie AG in 2001; Rofin-Sinar bought Z-Laser S.A. during the year. In June 2001 Rofin's shares were listed on Germany's Neuer Markt (they continued to trade on the NASDAQ in the United States).

Net income of $15 million in 2003 was three times the previous year's figure. Revenues had risen from $222 million to $258 million.

THREE SIGNIFICANT ACQUISITIONS IN 2004

One of the company's suppliers, Sweden's Optoskand AB, was acquired in February 2004 (actually, Rofin obtained a 90 percent holding), a couple of years after it was spun off from Permanova Lasersystem AB. Optoskand made fiber-optic systems for high-power solid-state lasers (but not the laser sources) and had about two dozen employees and annual sales of $3 million. It had been one of Rofin's suppliers for years.

ROFIN-SINAR acquired two other companies in 2004. One was PRC Laser Corporation, which specialized in providing high-power CO_2 lasers for the machine tool industry. Based in Landing, New Jersey, PRC had grown to employ five dozen people since its founding in 1986.

Lee Laser Inc. of Orlando, Florida, had been acquired by PRC in 1999 and was also acquired by ROFIN-SINAR. Lee had been formed 20 years earlier and focused on low power laser sources (as opposed to complete, installed systems) for marking and micro applications in the semiconductor and electronics industries. Lee and PRC were acquired from Dover Industries Inc. of Elgin, Illinois. The two had combined sales of about $30 million, most of it from outside the United States. Rofin-Sinar CEO Peter Wirth told *Investor's Business Daily* that Lee and PRC were attractive acquisitions targets because they brought Rofin into new markets. In addition, Rofin was looking to reduce its exposure to foreign currencies by buying the two U.S. companies.

The acquisitions of Lee Laser, PRC, and Optoskand were funded by a secondary stock offering that raised $75 million. Rofin-Sinar's share price had doubled between July and December 2004. The company was continuing to shop for acquisition targets, according to Wirth, who stepped down after suffering a stroke in January 2005. He was ultimately replaced by Gunther Braun, the company's chief financial officer since 1996.

STRONG GROWTH IN 2005

North America and Asia provided strong growth for the company in 2005. Sales for the fiscal year ended September 30 rose 16 percent to $375.2 million, while net income was up 17 percent to $38 million. Europe accounted for 54 percent of revenues, and North America, 29 percent. In all, ROFIN-SINAR shipped 3,100 laser sources during the year.

ROFIN-SINAR continued to expect its greatest growth in Asia and set up a subsidiary in Shanghai, China, in 2005. By this time, the total world laser market was estimated to be worth $1.5 billion. According to the company, its only rival of similar scale and product range was another German firm, TRUMPF GmbH + Co. KG.

Frederick C. Ingram

PRINCIPAL SUBSIDIARIES

ROFIN-SINAR, Inc.; ROFIN-SINAR Technologies Europe S.L. (Spain); Lee Laser, Inc.; PRC Laser Corp.

PRINCIPAL OPERATING UNITS
Laser Macro; Laser Micro; Laser Marking.

PRINCIPAL COMPETITORS
TRUMPF GmbH + Co. KG.

FURTHER READING

Bridgeforth, Arthur, Jr., "Light Makes Right: Rofin-Sinar Aims Its Lasers at Manufacturers," *Crain's Detroit Business,* March 10, 1997, p. 17.

Dietderich, Andrew, "Growth, Acquisitions Fuel Laser-Maker Rofin-Sinar's Rise," *Crain's Detroit Business,* February 7, 2005, p. 4.

Kincade, Kathy, "Rofin-Sinar Acquires Swedish Fiberoptics Firm," *Laser Focus World,* April 2004, p. 53.

Much, Marilyn, "Maker of Laser Gear Homes In on More Buys," *Investor's Business Daily,* December 23, 2004, p. A5.

O'Boyle, Thomas F., "German Technology Gains on U.S., Japan—Laser Maker's Success Exemplifies the Progress," *Wall Street Journal,* December 15, 1986.

Reeves, Amy, "Acquisition Puts Focus on Growing Laser Field," *Investor's Business Daily,* July 16, 2001, p. A10.

"Rofin Buys PRC, Lee Laser," *Metalworking Insiders' Report,* September 30, 2004, pp. 1+.

"Rofin-Sinar Acquires Carl Baasel Lasertechnik," *Laser Focus World,* December 2000, p. 55.

"Rofin-Sinar Moves Forward with New CEO," *Optoelectronics Report,* May 15, 2005, p. 3.

Smith, Patricia L., "Size Doesn't Matter," *American Machinist,* July 1998, pp. 78+.

Tate, Pamela, "Rofin-Sinar Closes Buy of Baasel Lasertech for $40 Million Cash," *Dow Jones News Service,* May 11, 2000.

Vasilash, Gary S., "A New Look at Lasers at Rofin-Sinar," *Production,* September 1, 1994, p. 46.

Royal Bank of Canada

200 Bay Street
Toronto, Ontario M5J 2J5
Canada
Telephone: (416) 974-5151
Toll Free: (800) 769-2599
Fax: (416) 955-7800
Web site: http://www.rbc.com

Public Company
Incorporated: 1869 as the Merchants' Bank of Halifax
Employees: 59,429
Total Assets: CAD 502.89 billion ($448.89 billion) (2006)
Stock Exchanges: Toronto New York Swiss
Ticker Symbol: RY
NAIC: 551111 Offices of Bank Holding Companies; 522110 Commercial Banking; 522293 International Trade Financing; 523110 Investment Banking and Securities Dealing; 523120 Securities Brokerage; 523920 Portfolio Management; 523930 Investment Advice; 524113 Direct Life Insurance Carriers; 524114 Direct Health and Medical Insurance Carriers; 524126 Direct Property and Casualty Insurance Carriers; 524130 Reinsurance Carriers; 525910 Open-End Investment Funds; 525920 Trusts, Estates, and Agency Accounts

∎∎∎

Royal Bank of Canada is Canada's largest financial institution. Operating under the umbrella brand name of RBC Financial Group, the bank maintains more than 1,100 branches and nearly 4,000 automated banking machines in Canada, where it is among the leaders in consumer loans, home mortgages, personal deposits, business loans, money management, and mutual funds. Royal Bank also owns RBC Dominion Securities (also called RBC Capital Markets), Canada's biggest full-service investment dealer, and RBC Action Direct, the nation's second largest self-directed brokerage service. RBC Insurance is one of the ten largest providers of life insurance in Canada and also specializes in health, home, auto, and travel insurance. In the early 21st century, RBC made an aggressive, acquisition-led move into the U.S. market, where it provides retail banking, insurance, full-service brokerage, and corporate and investment banking services through such units as RBC Centura Bank, RBC Builder Finance, RBC Insurance, RBC Dain Rauscher, and RBC Capital Markets. Based in North Carolina, RBC Centura Bank offers personal, business, and commercial banking services in the southeastern United States. RBC also maintains a large Caribbean retail banking network. In Europe, South America, the Middle East, the Asia-Pacific region, and Australia, Royal Bank offers private banking services and provides business customers a variety of services, including corporate and investment banking, trade finance, correspondent banking, and treasury services.

FOUNDING AS MERCHANTS BANK IN NOVA SCOTIA IN 1864

Founded in 1864 by a group of eight businessmen in Halifax, Nova Scotia, the Merchants' Bank, as it was then called, began with CAD 200,000 in capital to support local commerce. The bank's establishment coincided

COMPANY PERSPECTIVES

In the face of dramatic changes and challenges, Royal Bank has maintained the entrepreneurial spirit of its Halifax founders, with dedicated people working together to create client and shareholder value. In the social arena, employees continue to participate in their communities and speak responsibly on issues that impact North Americans and reflect the financial services industry's concern for providing clients with the best possible services.

with a sharp increase in the area's commercial activity, a result of the American Civil War—Halifax was a thriving center for blockade runners crossing the U.S. border. The bank made a successful start under these conditions, and was incorporated five years later as the Merchants' Bank of Halifax. Thomas C. Kinnear, one of the original founders, was its first president.

During the next few years, the bank expanded conservatively, opening branches in several more maritime towns. Then from 1873 to the end of the decade, a business depression hit Nova Scotia's shipbuilding industry hard and kept the bank's growth slow.

When the business environment rebounded for a short time in the early 1880s, the bank resumed its growth plan, and in 1882 opened its first branch outside Canada, in Hamilton, Bermuda, before it had even expanded as far as Ontario domestically. Although this branch closed in 1889, the bank remained committed to international operations, opening several branches in Latin America before it was well established in western Canada.

By 1896, Merchants' Bank's assets totaled CAD 10 million. The gold rush in the early 1890s in southern British Columbia gave it the impetus to open agencies there in 1897 and 1898, especially because, with the completion of the Canadian Pacific Railway in 1885, the area seemed ripe for development.

In 1899 two more branches were established in New York and Havana. The bank took a conservative approach in developing its Cuban business and made only a handful of initial loans. As confidence in Cuba's future grew, particularly with the formation of the Republic of Cuba in 1902 and the continuing growth of the sugar industry, the bank gradually expanded, opening several branches around the country. (This business upswing

came to a temporary halt when the sugar market suffered its first collapse, in 1920.)

In an effort to distinguish the bank from two other institutions with similar names, the bank was renamed The Royal Bank of Canada in 1901. For the next hundred years, the bank was often referred to simply as "the Royal."

RELOCATED HEADQUARTERS TO MONTREAL IN 1907

The dawn of a new century heralded a period of growth and prosperity in Canada, especially in the area between Winnipeg and the Rocky Mountains. The bank grew too, opening more branches and acquiring several smaller institutions. With this growth, the bank decided in 1907 to relocate from Halifax to Montreal, where the general manager was based. The move reflected Montreal's growing importance as a financial center and the relative decline of maritime commerce.

By the following year, Royal Bank had 109 branches and CAD 50 million in assets. This strong base provided the foundation for the bank's acquisition, in 1910, of the 54-year-old Union Bank of Halifax. Subsequent acquisitions of the Traders Bank of Canada and the Bank of British Honduras in 1912 more than doubled the number of operating branches and doubled its asset base by the end of the next year.

At the start of World War I, the Canadian real estate market had collapsed and very little capital was flowing into the country from abroad. In this uncertain atmosphere, the bank could not even promise staff who had enlisted reinstatement upon their return. Soon, however, business expanded sharply as wartime industry geared up, and the bank was forced to break with tradition and hire women.

Although the war put pressure on the Royal's day-to-day operations, the bank continued to grow, buying the Quebec Bank in 1917, the Northern Crown Bank in 1918, and two other banks in British Guiana and Nassau. By the end of the war, the Royal was the second largest bank in Canada, with 540 branches, assets of more than CAD 422 million, and a new foreign trade department to handle its growing international presence.

The Royal Bank weathered the period of economic collapse that followed the end of World War I and, by 1925, had resumed its quest for expansion with the purchase of the Bank of Central and South America and the Union Bank of Canada. The Union Bank was the Royal Bank's largest takeover yet, and strengthened its presence in the three prairie provinces.

The bank's solid structure and leading position in

KEY DATES

1864: Eight businessmen in Halifax, Nova Scotia, form the Merchants' Bank.
1869: Bank is incorporated as Merchants' Bank of Halifax.
1901: Bank is renamed The Royal Bank of Canada.
1907: Headquarters are shifted to Montreal.
1910: Union Bank of Halifax is acquired.
1912: The Royal acquires the Traders Bank of Canada.
1917: The Quebec Bank is purchased.
1918: Royal Bank acquires the Northern Crown Bank.
1925: Union Bank of Canada is acquired.
1941: The Royal becomes Canada's largest bank by assets.
1988: Royal Bank acquires majority interest in Dominion Securities.
1990: Bank shortens its name to Royal Bank of Canada.
1993: Voyageur Travel Insurance Ltd. and Royal Trust are acquired.
1996: Company acquires Westbury Canadian Life Insurance Company.
1997: RBC Dominion Securities acquires Richardson Greenshields Limited.
1998: Royal Bank's proposed merger with Bank of Montreal is blocked by the Canadian government.
2000: The insurance subsidiaries of Liberty Corporation are acquired.
2001: Bank completes three major U.S. acquisitions: Centura Banks, Inc., Dain Rauscher Corporation, and Tucker Anthony Sutro Corporation; new global brand strategy is launched using RBC Financial Group as a "master brand name."

the banking industry helped it survive the stock market crash relatively well, but it was not totally immune. Asset and profit levels fell, branches were closed, staff were laid off, and expenditures and the salaries of remaining employees were cut. Yet, whereas banks in the United States were closing in record numbers, not one Canadian chartered bank failed during this time.

By 1939, total assets were more than CAD 1 billion, for the second time in ten years, and the bank was ready to take advantage of the opportunities World War II offered. In cooperation with other banking institutions, the Royal actively participated in war measures, and it was instrumental in operating a ration coupon system for food and gasoline. Basically the war meant increased government expenditures for the war effort. The bank's domestic business flourished, though internationally its European branches were constrained under German occupation. During the war, specifically in 1941, the Royal gained its longstanding position as Canada's largest bank based on assets, surpassing Bank of Montreal.

After World War II, the Royal led the way in developing the country's oil, gas, and resource exploration industries by providing banking services in remote locations. It opened an oil and gas department in Calgary in 1951, and also established banking services in cities along the British Columbian route of a massive project undertaken by the Aluminum Company of Canada. The bank continued its international expansion with the establishment of the Royal Bank of Canada Trust Company in New York in 1951 as well.

When Fidel Castro came to power in Cuba in 1959, the Cuban banking system was nationalized. The Royal Bank of Canada and the Bank of Nova Scotia were, alone among banks, permitted to operate independently, but the losses they incurred as nationalized businesses transferred their banking to the nationalized system were too heavy, and Royal Bank sold its Cuban assets to the Banco Nacional de Cuba in December 1960.

OFFERING NEW SERVICES

In 1962, almost 100 years after its founding, The Royal Bank of Canada adopted a new emblem to replace its original coat of arms. The emblem's design incorporated a lion, a crown, and a globe to symbolize the bank's position as a leading force in international banking. That same year, the bank's offices moved into a new, 42-story skyscraper later known as Place Ville-Marie. The building's construction set in motion a large-scale urban development plan that turned midtown Montreal into a vital commercial district.

At the same time, the bank sharpened its focus on consumer-oriented financial services by entering the market with a product called TermPlan, a package of credit and insurance benefits. Six years later, in partnership with three other banks, the bank introduced Chargex, a credit card that allowed holders to make purchases within a specified credit limit and obtain cash advances through any of four participating institutions.

The 1967 revision of the Bank Act sparked vigorous competition among Canada's chartered banks, which had long operated under a morass of special restrictions. In removing many of these constraints, the act permitted banks to vie for loans, deposits, and conventional mortgages on an equal basis with other lending and borrowing institutions. By 1967 Royal Bank had written more than half of the residential mortgage loans provided by all of the chartered banks combined.

In the early 1970s, Royal Bank joined forces with five other banks to form Orion, a London-based merchant banking organization designed to enter the financial services market. Although Canadian law prohibited banks from entering this market domestically, Orion competed successfully in placing international bond issues and securities. Orion became a wholly owned subsidiary of the Royal Bank in 1981, enabling the bank to diversify its operations up to the limits imposed by Canada's banking laws and position itself for the possibility of international banking deregulation.

In 1979 Rowland Frazee, who had been with the bank for 40 years, was appointed chief executive officer. He replaced W. Earle McLaughlin, who became chairman after a popular 18-year reign as CEO.

CONTINUING DIVERSIFICATION

By 1981, Royal Bank was the fourth largest bank in North America, with assets of CAD 53 billion. Although one-third of that total was attributed to its international activities, the bank had lost its early advantage in many foreign markets to other institutions. One of Frazee's first orders of business was to strengthen the bank's influence in the United States. He poured new capital into the Royal Bank and Trust Company in New York and increased its staff. A second Frazee priority was the development of a Global Energy Group, based in Calgary, to provide technical consultation as well as capital for energy-related projects on an international basis. To manage its newly aggressive stance, the bank reorganized into four groups, two responsible for Canadian retail and commercial business, and two to handle corporate banking and international operations.

In 1986 Allan Taylor became chairman and CEO of Royal Bank. Taylor's rise from junior clerk at the age of 16 to chairman 37 years later was a remarkable one. His appointment as chairman replaced the bank's traditional conservatism with a more entrepreneurial approach to the challenges the bank faced.

One of the first challenges Taylor met was the relaxation of rules governing the ownership of brokerage firms by banks. The Royal began negotiations with Wood Gundy, a leading Canadian brokerage firm, in the spring of 1987, some months before the law actually changed. That deal fell through, but the Royal went on to acquire

Dominion Securities (later renamed RBC Dominion Securities), the largest investment house in Canada, and one with a history dating back to 1901. An agreement on the purchase was struck just after the stock market crash in October 1987. Although it was one of the last of Canada's big banks to enter the brokerage market, by waiting, the Royal got the best deal of all, saving a significant amount over pre-crash prices. When the deal closed in March 1988, Royal Bank owned a 67 percent stake in Dominion Securities; full ownership was obtained by 1996. In the meantime, the bank shortened its name to Royal Bank of Canada in 1990.

FOCUSING ON FEE-BASED BUSINESSES

Royal Bank was the second largest bank in North America by 1991 and was seeking to defend its strong position, and further raise its profile in the United States, by acquiring a U.S. retail bank. However, the bank was unable to find a suitable prospect at the right price. In 1991, however, RBC Dominion Securities was given permission to participate in stock underwriting by the U.S. Federal Reserve. Still, problems in the domestic economy in 1991 and 1992, which led the bank to set aside CAD 1.29 billion for loan losses in the fourth quarter of 1992, forced a retreat from Royal Bank's ambitious U.S. plans. Concentrating more on augmenting its Canadian operations, the bank in 1991 acquired McNeil Mantha Inc., a Quebec-based investment dealer, for CAD 22 million.

As the 1990s progressed, Royal Bank concentrated on achieving revenue growth through a focus on fee-based businesses. Much of this was growth achieved through additional acquisitions, mainly domestic. The bank moved quickly in response to a June 1992 change in Canadian law that allowed banks to own 100 percent of insurance companies and to offer travel insurance with the early 1993 acquisition of Voyageur Travel Insurance Ltd., the largest provider of travel insurance in Canada. Also acquired in 1993 was Royal Trustco for CAD 1.3 billion, a deal that increased Royal Bank's assets by about CAD 1.1 billion, or 10 percent. Royal Trustco was Canada's largest money manager, including the handling of a large family of mutual funds, and had a strong position in global private banking.

In late 1994, John Cleghorn, a 20-year Royal Bank veteran who had been president and chief operating officer, replaced Taylor as chairman and CEO. Under Cleghorn, the bank continued to acquire fee-based businesses. In 1995 RBC Dominion Securities bolstered its investment banking operation through the acquisition of Kidder Peabody's equity derivatives team. During 1996 and early 1997 Royal Bank made four additional significant acquisitions. In January 1996 Westbury Canadian Life Insurance Company, based in Hamilton, Ontario, was purchased, bringing with it CAD 90 million in annual premiums. In August of that same year, Royal Bank bought the CAD 47-billion-in-assets institutional and pension custody business of Toronto-Dominion Bank and Trust, then in February 1997 acquired Bank of Nova Scotia's institutional and pension custody business and its CAD 120 billion in assets under administration. These deals moved Royal Bank into the top ten worldwide among securities-custody service businesses. Meanwhile, in November 1996 RBC Dominion Securities added to its already strong portfolio the operations of Richardson Greenshields Limited, acquired for CAD 480 million. Richardson Greenshields was a Canadian full-service investment dealer with CAD 16 billion in private client assets.

The strong North American economy of the mid-1990s helped Royal Bank post record 1996 net income of CAD 1.43 billion, a huge increase over the CAD 107 million of 1992 and an indication that the bank's strategy of concentrating on increasing its fee-based businesses through the careful yet aggressive pursuit of acquisitions and alliances was paying dividends. Total assets by this time had reached nearly CAD 218 billion ($163 billion). In late 1995 Royal Bank was listed on the New York Stock Exchange in a move intended as prelude to an anticipated acquisition of a U.S. money-management business. In the meantime, the bank attempted in mid-1997 to acquire London Insurance Group Inc., the fifth largest life insurer in Canada, but its CAD 2.4 billion ($1.74 billion) offer was topped by Great-West Lifeco Inc.'s offer of CAD 2.9 billion ($2.09 billion). Soon after this failure, Royal Bank entered into an agreement with HB Group Insurance Management Ltd. whereby the two companies would share technology, systems, and expertise to help Royal Bank establish and grow a property and casualty insurance business.

In January 1998, shortly after reporting fiscal 1997 profits of CAD 1.68 billion, a record for a Canadian bank, Royal Bank made a stunning announcement. The bank had reached an agreement with Bank of Montreal on what promised to be the largest merger in Canadian history and one creating the second largest bank in North America with CAD 435 billion ($312 billion) in assets. Then in April a second shock wave hit the Canadian financial services industry: two more of the "Big Six" Canadian banks, the Toronto-Dominion Bank and the Canadian Imperial Bank of Commerce, revealed plans for their own merger. In December 1998, however, Finance Minister Paul Martin rejected both of the blockbuster deals. Ignoring the banks' insistence that they needed to merge in order to compete in the increasingly globalized financial services market, Martin concluded that from the standpoint of Canadians the mergers would create two banks with too much power and would severely reduce competition.

After setting another profit record in fiscal 1998, CAD 1.82 billion, Royal Bank saw its profits fall slightly the following year as revenue increases failed to keep pace with rising expenses. The bank launched a plan to shave CAD 400 million off its annual expenses in part by cutting up to 6,000 jobs from the payroll by the end of 2001, mainly through attrition but also via a retirement program and layoffs. On the acquisition front, in the meantime, Royal Bank remained stymied in its quest to secure a U.S. wealth management company, but in 1999 did complete the CAD 156 million acquisition of Connor Clark Ltd., a Toronto-based high-end money manager.

BIG SOUTH-OF-THE-BORDER PUSH

Royal Bank had made some small moves into the U.S. market in the late 1990s, such as the 1998 purchase of Atlanta-based Security First Network Bank, the world's first Internet bank. It was in the early 2000s, though, that Royal Bank made a concerted push south of the border via a string of acquisitions. In April 2000 Prism Financial Corporation, a Chicago mortgage broker, was acquired for $115 million. Prism operated 159 retail branches in 25 states. Royal Bank next took a big step into the U.S. insurance industry by acquiring the insurance subsidiaries of Liberty Corporation of Greenville, South Carolina, for $580 million. Through this November 2000 deal, the bank took over Liberty Life Insurance Company and its 625 sales agents and Liberty Insurance Services Corporation, an administrator of third-party life and health insurance and a provider of underwriting, billing, and claims processing services. Also in 2000 Royal Bank's RT Capital Management pension fund unit agreed to pay a fine of CAD 3 million ($2 million) to the Ontario Securities Commission to settle charges of stock manipulation. The unit had admitted artificially inflating the price of 26 stocks in 1998 and 1999 leading not only to the fine but also to the resignation of several top officials at the unit and its sale to UBS AG in 2001.

During 2001 Royal Bank completed three major acquisitions that substantially broadened its presence in the U.S. market. Royal entered U.S. retail banking through the $2.2 billion purchase of Centura Banks, Inc., a midsized regional based in Rocky Mount, North Carolina. Centura had assets of $11.5 billion and operations in North Carolina, South Carolina, and Virginia and ranked as the 14th largest bank in the southeastern United States. The other two big deals of 2001 finally provided Royal Bank with its long-sought toehold in the U.S. wealth-management market. The bank spent $1.23 billion early in the year for Dain Rauscher Corporation, a regional, midsized brokerage firm based in Minneapolis that generated approximately $930 million in revenue in 1999. Later in 2001 Royal Bank paid nearly $600 million for Tucker Anthony Sutro Corporation, another regional brokerage house, this one based in Boston. Tucker Anthony fit nicely alongside Dain Rauscher given that the former's 80 offices were concentrated on the U.S. East and West Coasts, while the latter's 108 offices were in the Midwest, Southwest, and Pacific Northwest.

In August 2001, in the midst of this acquisition spree, Cleghorn retired. At this time, with corporate governance reform much in the air, Royal Bank elected to split Cleghorn's duties. Guy Saint-Pierre was named chairman, while Gordon M. Nixon was promoted to president and CEO. Nixon had previously headed RBC Dominion Securities. One of Nixon's first initiatives was to oversee the implementation in late 2001 of a new global brand strategy designed to forge a common identity for Royal's ever expanding operations. While keeping Royal Bank of Canada as its legal name, the bank began operating under the umbrella banner of RBC Financial Group. A new logo was unveiled that incorporated this new brand name, and the RBC prefix was added to the name of each business unit and operating subsidiary. For instance, the retail banking operations in Canada became known as RBC Royal Bank, and the U.S. retail bank unit was renamed RBC Centura Banks. The two recently acquired U.S. brokerage houses were merged as RBC Dain Rauscher.

Over the next few years, RBC made several smaller, fill-in type acquisitions, while staying away from any big deals. Results at the U.S. operations were disappointing, and the bank worked to revamp some of its acquired operations and jettisoned a couple of the more troubled ones, including Liberty Insurance Services and RBC Mortgage Company, its U.S. mortgage unit. During the fourth quarter of fiscal 2004 RBC recorded charges of CAD 322 million to write down the value of the mortgage unit and to eliminate nearly 1,700 jobs from the RBC head office. Nixon also shook up the senior management team, bringing Barbara G. Stymiest on board as chief operating officer in November 2004. Stymiest was lured away from the Toronto Stock Exchange, where she had served as president and CEO.

Fiscal 2005 brought more special charges. RBC set aside CAD 591 million to cover potential legal costs associated with several lawsuits alleging that the bank had helped Enron Corporation manipulate its financial statements. Property insurance claims from damage caused by Hurricanes Katrina, Rita, and Wilma amounted to another CAD 203 million. Despite these special items, RBC managed a fiscal 2005 profit of CAD 3.39 billion ($2.87 billion), another record for a Canadian bank and a 21 percent increase over the previous year. The performance of RBC's U.S. and international personal and business operations were much improved, with profits surging from just CAD 22 million to CAD 345 million. In January 2006 RBC and Belgian banking giant Dexia NV/SA merged their administrative services arms that provided various custodial services for institutional investors. The resulting RBC Dexia Investor Services ranked as one of the world's top ten global custodians with assets under custody of about $2 trillion.

Royal Bank of Canada, over its 140-plus-year history, had grown from a modest regional bank into a major domestic and international force, with total assets of more than half a trillion Canadian dollars. With its U.S. business improving, RBC in March 2006 announced plans to expand RBC Centura Banks by opening a dozen new branches in 2006 and then upping this figure to between 15 and 20 annually starting in 2008. RBC was also in the process of expanding its Canadian investment banking and brokerage division, RBC Dominion Securities, which was achieving particularly strong profitability in fiscal 2006.

Updated, David E. Salamie

PRINCIPAL SUBSIDIARIES

Royal Bank Mortgage Corporation; Royal Trust Corporation of Canada; The Royal Trust Company; Royal Mutual Funds Inc.; RBC Capital Trust; RBC Technology Ventures Inc.; RBC Capital Partners Limited; RBC Dominion Securities Limited; Royal Bank Holding Inc.; RBC Insurance Holdings Inc.; Royal Bank Action Direct Inc.; RBC Asset Management Inc.; RBC Holdings (U.S.A.) Inc.; RBC Dain Rauscher Corp. (U.S.A.); RBC Capital Markets Corporation (U.S.A.); RBC Mortgage Company (U.S.A.); RBC Insurance Holding (USA) Inc.; Liberty Life Insurance Company (U.S.A.); Royal Bank of Canada (Asia) Limited (Singapore); RBC Centura Banks, Inc.; RBC Finance B.V. (Netherlands); RBC Investment Management (Asia) Limited (China).

PRINCIPAL OPERATING UNITS

RBC Canadian Personal and Business (consisting of RBC Royal Bank, RBC Investments, RBC Dominion Securities, RBC Insurance, and RBC Liberty Insurance); RBC U.S. and International Personal and Business (consisting of RBC Centura, RBC Dain Rauscher, RBC

Builder Finance, Royal Bank of Canada Global Private Banking, and RBC Royal Bank of Canada); RBC Capital Markets.

PRINCIPAL COMPETITORS

The Toronto-Dominion Bank; The Bank of Nova Scotia; Bank of Montreal; Canadian Imperial Bank of Commerce; National Bank of Canada.

FURTHER READING

Baragar, Geoff, "Reflections of a Royal Banker," *Canadian Business Review,* Summer 1987, p. 8.

Blackwell, Richard, "Royal Bank Buys U.S. Broker," *Globe and Mail,* September 29, 2000, p. B1.

———, "Royal Bank Slashes Jobs Despite Hefty Profit," *Globe and Mail,* November 20, 1999, p. A1.

Boraks, David, "RBC Embraces Its Plan B," *American Banker,* December 8, 2004, p. 1.

Cherney, Elena, "Royal Bank of Canada Agrees to Acquire Dain Rauscher," *Wall Street Journal,* September 29, 2000, p. B4.

D'Arcy, Jenish, "The Royal Throne," *Maclean's,* March 19, 2001, pp. 32+.

Darroch, James L., *Canadian Banks and Global Competitiveness,* Montreal: McGill-Queen's University Press, 1994, 334 p.

Donlon, J. P., and Joseph L. McCarthy, "Southern Strategy," *Chief Executive* (U.S.), October 1992, pp. 38+.

Gibson, Paul, "The Royal What?," *Forbes,* January 19, 1981, p. 36.

Graham, George, "RBC to Spend C$500m on Consumer Banking," *Financial Times,* November 21, 1996, p. 36.

Greenberg, Larry M., "Royal Bank to Buy Back Shares amid Reduced Need for Capital," *Wall Street Journal,* September 13, 1996, p. B4.

———, "Shareholders' Revolt, the Canadian Way: Bash Bank Bosses," *Wall Street Journal,* January 16, 1997, p. B9.

Hartley, Tom, "Disappointing Free Trade Leads to Royal Bank's Exit," *Business First of Buffalo,* November 9, 1992, p. 3.

Howlett, Karen, "RBC Takes Charge on Rabobank Settlement," *Globe and Mail,* February 17, 2004, p. B1.

———, "Royal Bank's Head Retiring," *Globe and Mail,* February 24, 2001, p. B1.

———, "Royal Buys U.S. Bank Centura," *Globe and Mail,* January 27, 2001, p. B1.

———, "Royal Makes Big U.S. Insurance Acquisition," *Globe and Mail,* June 20, 2000, p. B1.

Ince, Clifford H., *The Royal Bank of Canada: A Chronology, 1864–1969,* Montreal: Royal Bank of Canada, 1970, 152 p.

Koenig, Peter, "Royal Flush—Or a Bank in Turmoil?," *Euromoney,* November 1987, p. 50.

"Looking for Elbow Room," *Banker,* June 1986, pp. 61+.

Maley, Dianne, "Building the Bank of Future," *Canadian Banker,* January/February 1996, pp. 21–25.

McDowell, Duncan, *Quick to the Frontier: Canada's Royal Bank,* Toronto: McClelland and Stewart, 1993, 478 p.

Newman, Peter C., "Allan Taylor's Deal of the Century," *Maclean's,* April 5, 1993, p. 44.

Noble, Kimberley, "Bitterness on Bay Street: Ottawa Hands the Banks a Resounding Defeat," *Maclean's,* December 28, 1998, pp. 70–73.

———, "How the Banks Blew It," *Maclean's,* December 7, 1998, pp. 26–30.

Partridge, John, "RBC Nails New Bank Profit Record," *Globe and Mail,* December 1, 2005, p. B1.

———, "Royal Bank Gets a Makeover," *Globe and Mail,* August 21, 2001, p. B1.

———, "Royal Bank Grabs U.S. Broker," *Globe and Mail,* August 2, 2001, p. B1.

Partridge, John, and Susanne Craig, "Banks Drop $40-Billion Bombshell," *Globe and Mail,* January 24, 1998, p. A1.

Pitts, Gordon, "The RBC Dynasty Continues," *Globe and Mail,* January 30, 2006, p. B1.

Reguly, Eric, "Decision on RBC's U.S. Assets Puts Nixon's Career on the Line," *Globe and Mail,* May 25, 2004, p. B1.

Reguly, Eric, Andrew Willis, and Sinclair Stewart, "Is RBC in Full U.S. Retreat?," *Globe and Mail,* September 11, 2004, p. B5.

Sanford, Jeff, "A Royal Return," *Canadian Business,* April 25, 2006, pp. 42+.

Simon, Bernard, "Each to His Own," *Banker,* August 1994, pp. 46–48.

Stewart, Sinclair, "RBC Sets Up $2.3-Trillion Asset Merger," *Globe and Mail,* June 10, 2005, p. B3.

———, "RBC's U.S. Mortgage Unit Sold for About $108-Million," *Globe and Mail,* May 28, 2005, p. B4.

———, "RBC to Push Harder into U.S.," *Globe and Mail,* May 31, 2003, p. B1.

Waldie, Paul, "RBC Sets Enron Lawsuits Reserve," *Globe and Mail,* October 19, 2005, p. B1.

———, "RBC to Speed Expansion of Operations in the U.S.," *Globe and Mail,* March 30, 2006, p. B5.

Willoughby, Jack, "Southern Exposure," *Financial World,* June 11, 1991, pp. 40–43.

RPC Group PLC

Lakeside House
Higham Ferrers,
United Kingdom
Telephone: +44 01933 410064
Fax: +44 01933 410083
Web site: http://www.rpc-group.com

Public Company
Incorporated: 1983
Employees: 6,229
Sales: £513.28 million ($892.5 million) (2005)
Stock Exchanges: London
Ticker Symbol: RPC
NAIC: 326160 Plastics Bottle Manufacturing; 326122
   Plastics Pipe and Pipe Fitting Manufacturing

■ ■ ■

RPC Group PLC claims the position as the leading manufacturer of rigid plastic packaging products in Europe, with sales of £513 million ($892 million). Yet the group's operations represent a share of roughly 3 percent of the total market, suggesting vast potential for future expansion. RPC is the only major European plastics packaging group with production capacity in all three primary plastics conversion processes: blow molding, injection molding, and thermofolding. The company's operations are grouped under several "clusters," including UK Injection-moulding, Tedeco Gizeh Cups, Bebo, Bramlage, and Cobelplast. Acquisitions have formed a primary part of the company's growth, which was formed as an independent operation

following a management buyout in 1991. As such, the group has acquired operations in 12 countries in Europe, and boasts nearly 50 production facilities. In 2006, the company also opened its first manufacturing plant in the United States.

The company's production spans the entire range of packaging markets, including food packaging; buckets, pails, pots, tubs, and lids; vending and drinking cups, bottles, jars, and caps; margarine packaging; coffee packaging systems; and personal care and beauty products. RPC's growth has been driven since the late 1980s by Ron Marsh. The company is listed on the London Stock Exchange.

RIGID PLASTIC PACKAGING SPECIALIST IN 1991

The origins of RPC Group traced back to Denmark's Superfos, which established a plastic packaging production unit in Oakham, England, in 1973. Founded in 1892, Superfos had grown into a highly diversified conglomerate by then, and had entered the plastic packaging market only in 1964. Through the 1970s, Superfos built the Oakham site into one of the United Kingdom's major plastic packaging producers. The U.K. subsidiary initially specialized in the production of plastic buckets, and quickly dominated that product sector. In the 1970s, the Oakham plant also developed a new plastic paint can, called the Paintainer, which became a long-lasting success, not only for Superfos, but for the later RPC Group as well.

In 1983, Superfos sold the Oakham plant to Reed International, which at the time was still involved in the

COMPANY PERSPECTIVES

RPC Group is Europe's leading manufacturer of rigid plastic packaging and is unique in that it is able to offer products made by all three conversion processes, blow moulding, injection moulding and thermoforming. It has 47 operations in 12 different countries and employs over 6,500 people. RPC services a comprehensive range of customers—from the largest European manufacturers of consumer products to the smallest national businesses. It has particularly strong positions in the beauty and personal care sector, the vending and drinking cup market, the margarine industry, and in multi-layer sheet and packs for oxygen sensitive food products. Our objectives are to further strengthen RPC's position in these and other sectors of the European market and to optimise our production, thereby generating a satisfactory return for our shareholders and the best possible security for our employees, suppliers and customers.

paper and packaging markets. Reed invested strongly in the Oakham plant, launching mass production of the Paintainer. Under Reed, the Oakham unit expanded its production facilities as well, building a plant in Corby in 1986, then acquiring two more plants, in Raunds and Rushden, from Smith's Containers. That purchase gave the company a number of new packaging markets, such as for chemicals, fruit juices, and food oils. Two years later, the company built a new factory in Blackburn as an extension of the Oakham plant's production.

By then, Reed had undergone a major diversification effort, which lasted through the 1970s and much of the 1980s. Publishing formed a major part of Reed's operations, and the purchase of Octopus Publishing in 1987 had encouraged Reed to refocus itself as a publishing group. As such, Reed began selling off its noncore operations, including its do-it-yourself (DIY) and paints businesses in 1987.

Reed's paper and packaging division was the next to go. In 1988, that division was spun off as a new company, Reedpack, in a management buyout. The following year, Reedpack was restructured into more of a holding company format serving as central hub for the company's business units. These included Reedpack's rigid plastic production operation, based at the Oakham, Blackburn, Raunds, Rushden, and Corby plants. Ron Marsh, who had already led the rigid plastics busi-

ness under Reed, was appointed CEO of that business unit, Reedpack Containers, in 1989. The following year, Reedpack Containers was expanded with the acquisition of blow molding production machinery from rival Rockware Plastics. The acquisition of this unit not only strengthened Reedpack's production capacity in the high-barrier bottles, it also narrowed the number of competitors with rival blow molding technology to just one.

Reedpack's independence did not last long. In 1990, the company agreed to be acquired by Swedish paper and packaging group Svenska Cellulosa. Following that purchase, Svenska Cellulosa sold off the Reedpack Containers unit, including its five U.K. production sites, in a new management buyout led by Ron Marsh. The newly independent company, formed in 1991, took on the name of RPC Containers Ltd.

ACQUIRING SCALE FOR THE APPROACH OF THE 21ST CENTURY

RPC immediately embarked on an expansion course driven by acquisition. The first of these came with the purchase of the Swindon-based injection molding capacity of CarnaudMetalbox in 1991. That purchase boosted RPC's paintainer production capacity, while also providing it with facilities for producing custom-molded food packaging and containers.

The company's next purchase came in 1993, when it bought Bunzl PLC's blow molding production unit. This purchase boosted RPC's production of household chemicals and toiletries packaging systems. Setting its sights on further growth, RPC moved to raise capital, listing its shares on the London Stock Exchange in that year. At the same time, the company adopted a new name, RPC Group PLC.

RPC's focus remained on the U.K. plastics packaging market into the middle of the decade. In 1994, the company added to its leading position there with the acquisition of McKechnie PLC's plastic packaging operations. That purchase, which cost RPC £6 million, brought it three new factories in Market, Rasen, and Halstead.

Into the late 1990s, RPC recognized the potential for developing itself into an internationally operating packaging provider. In this way, the company would be able to serve its increasingly multinationally operating customer base. RPC took a major step into transforming itself into the European rigid plastics packaging leader in 1997, when it paid £63 million to acquire Continental Plastics Europe. A unit of can maker Schmalbach Lubeca (later acquired by Ball Industries), Continental Plastics

KEY DATES

1973: Superfos establishes a plastic bucket production facility in Oakham, England.

1983: The Oakham site is sold to Reed International.

1985: The Corby factory is opened.

1986: The company acquires Smith's Containers and its two factories in Raunds and Rushden.

1987: The company buys a factory in Blackburn.

1988: Reed spins off the packaging operations as Reedpack.

1989: Ron Marsh becomes CEO of the RPC Containers rigid plastic packaging unit of Reedpack.

1990: Svenska Cellulosa acquires Reedback.

1991: RPC Containers is spun off in a management buyout led by Ron Marsh.

1993: A public offering is made on the London Stock Exchange and the company changes its name to RPC Group.

1994: McKechnie's U.K. packaging operations are acquired.

1997: RPC becomes the European leader through the acquisition of Continental Plastics Europe and its 13 European production sites.

1998: RPC acquires Bunzl Group's Stag Plastics in Bristol, two thermoforming plants from AEP Industries in The Netherlands, and Gizeh, based in Germany.

1999: RPC acquires Able Industries' blow molding assets and three Cressdale factories in the United Kingdom.

2000: TWP and Wiko are acquired.

2004: RPC acquires four factories from Rexam and seven factories from Nampak; the company launches the Tassimo capsule coffee system in partnership with Kraft and Braun in France.

2006: A factory is built in the United States in support of the Tassimo launch.

three plastics conversion processes. With sales nearing £250 million following the Continental acquisitions, RPC became the leading rigid plastics packaging group in Europe.

RPC maintained its growth momentum through the end of the decade. In 1998, the company made three new acquisitions, starting with Stag Plastics, based in Bristol, a part of the Bunzl Group. The company acquired two thermoforming sites in The Netherlands from AEP Industries Inc. that year as well, paying $4 million. The company then combined those operations, which specialized in the production of trays and food containers, into its Bebo business in Germany and Poland. Next, RPC paid £16.5 million to acquire the disposable plastic products operations from Gizeh, adding factories in France and Poland, and a distribution business in Germany.

At the close of the decade, RPC continued to add to its operations, buying up an Italian sheet plastic business from Montonate in 1999 for £7.9 million. A larger acquisition came in April of that year, with the purchase of Able Industries PET stretch-blow molding machinery and other assets for £4 million. At the end of that year, the company rescued the three British factories of bankrupt Cressdale Ltd.

EUROPEAN LEADER IN THE NEW CENTURY

Already the largest European rigid plastics packaging producer in terms of sales, RPC nonetheless controlled less than 3 percent of the highly fragmented European market. RPC set out to lead the consolidation of the industry, launching a new series of acquisitions into the new decade. The first of these came with the £6 million purchase of TWP Packaging Twente, a manufacturer of tubs and trays based in The Netherlands with operations in Poland as well. The company next bought Germany's Wiko, including its three German sites. The Wiko acquisition also gave the company a sales office in the United States.

RPC returned to Poland in 2001, buying a thermoforming facility in Kruszwica from Autobar. Whereas the group experienced strong growth through most of its operations, its factory in Oevel, Belgium, had proven to be a money-loser, and in June 2001 the company closed that site.

That closure remained an anomaly for the company, however, as its sales built rapidly into the middle of the decade; by 2006, the company had doubled its turnover. Acquisitions remained a key element in this growth, and included the 2004 purchases of four factories from Rexam in the United Kingdom, France, Belgium, and

brought 13 factories located throughout the European continent, including Germany, Belgium, The Netherlands, Spain, Poland, Hungary, and South Wales, as well as the Bebo brand. The purchase also enabled RPC to expand its production capacity into the third major plastics packaging segment, thermoforming. As such, RPC became the sole European producer using all

the Czech Republic, and another seven factories from Nampak in the United Kingdom, The Netherlands, Belgium, and France. Yet RPC also had invested in its organic growth, building new factories in the United Kingdom in 2002 and in Romania in 2003.

With sales of more than £500 million ($820 million), RPC turned its attention to a wider international expansion. The company had teamed up Braun and Kraft to develop the Tassimo capsule-based coffee system, launched in France in 2004. A rival to the Nespresso system, Tassimo featured capsules developed by RPC. In support of the launch of Tassimo in the United States, RPC built its first factory in that country, in Morgantown, Pennsylvania, which also took over the operations of the company's existing U.S. sales unit. RPC expected to play a role not only in the consolidation of the European plastics packaging sector, but in the increasingly global market as well.

M. L. Cohen

PRINCIPAL SUBSIDIARIES

RPC Bebo CR S.R.O. (Czech Republic); RPC Bebo Nederland B.V. (Netherlands); RPC Bebo Plastik GmbH (Germany); RPC Bebo Polska Sp. z.o.o.; RPC Bramlage-Wiko USA Inc.; RPC Cobelplast Montonate S.R.L. (Italy); RPC Cobelplast N.V. (Belgium); RPC Containers Limited; RPC Envases S.A. (Spain); RPC Formatec GmbH (Germany); RPC Packaging Holdings B.V. (Netherlands); RPC Packaging Holdings Limited; RPC Packaging Holdings US Inc.; RPC Tedeco-Gizeh (UK) Limited; RPC Tedeco-Gizeh GmbH (Germany); RPC Tedeco-Gizeh Kft (Hungary); RPC Tedeco-Gizeh Polska Sp. z.o.o.; RPC Tedeco-Gizeh Romania S.R.L.; RPC Tedeco-Gizeh S.A.S. (France); RPC Tedeco-Gizeh Troyes SASU (France); TW Packaging Polska Sp. z.o.o.

PRINCIPAL COMPETITORS

Rexam Beverage Packaging AB; The Savola Group; Mitsubishi Plastics Inc.; Groupe Sidel; Graham Packaging Holdings Co.; Daetwyler Holding Inc.; Ball Packaging Europe; Crown European Holdings Inc.; Itera Group; Hilfort Plastics Proprietary Ltd.; Superfos A/S.

FURTHER READING

Hebblethwaite, Erika, "£62.7m Deal to Make RPC Euro Leader," *Packaging Week,* January 2, 1997, p. 3.

Higgs, Richard, "RPC Group Nixes Plan to Buy Cressdale Unit," *Plastics News,* December 6, 1999, p. 63.

———, "RPC to Shut Belgium Plant, Cut 150 Jobs," *Plastics News,* June 25, 2001, p. 10.

Kaleido, Leanie, "RPC's Decade of Profitability," *Packaging Magazine,* June 29, 2000, p. 12.

Murphy, Mary, "Contracted to Expansion," *Packaging Magazine,* March 26, 1998, p. 46.

"RPC Group Nabs Blowmolder," *Modern Plastics,* December 2004, p. 8.

"RPC Group PLC Launches Its First US Plant," *Plastics News,* May 29, 2006, p. 24.

"RPC Keeps on Growing," *Printing World,* December 11, 2003, p. 14.

"RPC's Cool Deal Strengthens Its European Spread," *Packaging Today International,* April 2004, p. 5.

"RPC Tightens European Grip with £15.6m Spend," *Packaging Magazine,* July 16, 1998, p. 11.

Santos

Santos Ltd.

∎

Level 29 Santos House
91 King William Street
Adelaide,
Australia
Telephone: +61 08 8218 5111
Fax: +61 08 8218 5274
Web site: http://www.santos.com.au

Public Company
Incorporated: 1954 as South Australia Northern Territory Oil Search
Employees: 1,534
Sales: AUD 2.46 billion ($1.88 billion) (2005)
Stock Exchanges: Australia
Ticker Symbol: STO
NAIC: 211111 Crude Petroleum and Natural Gas Extraction; 211112 Natural Gas Liquid Extraction; 486110 Pipeline Transportation of Crude Oil

∎ ∎ ∎

Santos Ltd. is one of Australia's leading and fastest-growing oil and gas exploration and production companies. The Adelaide-based company operates throughout most of Australia, with extensive exploration licenses, and a major share in the Cooper Basin oil fields in central Australia. In the 2000s, Santos launched an ambitious international expansion program, adding operations and shareholdings in markets including the United States (where the company owns Tipperary Corp. and Esenjay Corp.), Indonesia, Egypt, Papua New Guinea, and Kyrgyzstan.

The company's holdings include the Australia Timor-Leste Joint Petroleum Development Area; offshore gas fields in the Carnarvon Basin in Western Australia; the Oyong and Maleo projects in East Java, as well as the Casino offshore field in Victoria. Santos is one of Australia's leading natural gas producers and suppliers, serving all major markets in Australia. The company also supplies oil and other petroleum- and gas-based liquids to the national and international market, and is a leading supplier of ethane to Sydney. The company's total production in 2005 topped 56 mmboe (million barrels of oil equivalent). Santos is listed on the Australian Stock Exchange and is led by Chairman Stephen Gerlach and Managing Director John Ellice-Flint. In 2005, the company's revenues neared AUD 2.5 billion ($1.9 billion).

POST-WORLD WAR II AUSTRALIAN EXPLORATION EFFORT

Australia launched a national effort to develop its own oil reserves in the years immediately following World War II. Oil exploration first began in 1946 and continued into the next decade. The discovery of oil deposits at Rough Range, near Exemouth in Western Australia in 1953 sparked a wave of enthusiasm throughout Australia. The prospect of reducing the country's reliance on imported fuel, as well as the huge potential for profit, encouraged a number of major oil players, including Esso and BHP, to enter the Australian oil market in that decade. Yet there was also a homegrown effort to develop a national oil industry.

South Australia had been the subject of some

COMPANY PERSPECTIVES

VISION: Santos has a vision that by the end of the decade it will become the leading energy company in South East Asia with a share price that continues to grow and a reputation for sustainability in its operations. Santos' vision of future success is to be a safe, low cost, fast-moving explorer and producer and an agile niche player with a well developed ability to manage relationships with employees, partners and other stakeholders.

As the Company grows, it will provide a working environment that encourages innovation across the business and where employees are engaged in something which is tangibly more than just a job.

controversy over its potential for profitable oil deposits. Indeed, the Australian government's official position held against the possibility of oil reserves in the region. Nonetheless, a number of others considered it to be the area of the country with the most potential for oil deposits.

Among them was Robert Bristow, who, joined by friend John Bonython, had begun researching the region in the early 1950s. In 1954, Bristow applied for one of the oil exploration licenses (OEL) being awarded by the Australian government. Bristow was originally granted the OEL 7, an area that encompassed more than 312,000 square kilometers. By the end of the year, Bristow and Bonython had acquired the adjoining OEL 6, which included the northeast tip of the region, and added almost 200,000 square kilometers more. Both OELs were transferred to a new company set up by Bristow and Bonython in 1954, called South Australian Northern Territory Oil Search, or Santos for short. Bonython was then named chairman of the new company.

Santos went public in February 1955 as it launched its oil exploration operations. The company at first explored the area north of Port Augusta, and drilled its first 24 holes in the Wilkatana region that same year. While those holes did not reveal any oil, the operation received a great deal of publicity and sparked the interest of Premier Thomas Playford IV. Through Playford's influence, the Australian government reversed its stance on the South Australian oil exploration effort, which brought over noted American petroleum geologist Dr. A. I. Levorsen to assist the company. Levorsen encouraged Santos to drill still further to the northeast.

Levorsen also recognized that Santos lacked the resources, both financially and in terms of experience, to carry out exploration operations in an area roughly the size of the state of Texas. Levorsen, therefore, helped Santos arrange a partnership with Dallas, Texas' Delhi-Taylor Oil Corporation (later known as Delhi International).

With Delhi's backing, Santos at first began drilling at Oodnadatta in 1957. By the following year, however, Santos had begun putting into place the infrastructure to drill at Innamincka. In 1959, Santos completed its first deep well there. This and additional wells drilled at the site were unable to locate commercially viable quantities of oil. Nonetheless, the drilling efforts revealed encouraging geological evidence for the existence of strong oil and gas deposits in the region. As a result, the region attracted a new wave of investment interest, not only for its potential oil and gas reserves, but also for its important mineral deposits. Santos also benefited from the interest in the region, when French Petroleum Company, a subsidiary of France's Total, invested some AUD 800,000 in the company, becoming one of its major shareholders.

Into the early 1960s, the Delhi-Santos exploration efforts had begun to focus on the Cooper Basin. This focus paid off in 1963, when the company discovered a major natural gas deposit at the second well drilled at Gidgealpa. That deposit became the company's first commercially viable well, with a flow rate of 3.2 million cubic feet per day.

Delhi and Santos continued to explore the Cooper Basin and, by 1965, the partners had discovered a new major natural gas deposit, at Moomba. By 1966, the company had begun to exploit the Moomba reserve. Combined with the natural gas available at Gidgealpa, Santos was not capable of meeting the demand for all of South Australia. The company then signed a supply contract with the South Australian Gas Company, owned by the state government, and launched construction of a pipeline to connect the Cooper Basin with Adelaide. The pipeline, nearly 800 kilometers long, was completed in 1969. By then, the company also had begun construction on its own gas processing plant at the Moomba site.

BUILDING GAS RESERVES IN THE LATE 20TH CENTURY

Santos's continuing exploration operations brought it to Tirrawarra in 1970. There the company not only discovered gas reserves of some 7.8 million cubic meters per day, but also its first petroleum deposit, flowing at 650 barrels per day. Santos also picked up new customers into the early 1970s, adding the Electricity Trust of South Australia in 1969, then signing a contract to sup-

KEY DATES

1954: Robert Bristow and John Bonython lead in the formation of South Australia Northern Territory Oil Search (Santos) oil and gas exploration company.

1963: Santos makes its first major gas discovery at Gidgealpa, in Cooper Basin.

1970: Gas and oil deposits are discovered at Tirrawarra.

1977: The company discovers Strzelecki 3, the first significant discovery of oil in Ergomanga Basin, with a production of more than 2,400 barrels per day.

1989: Santos acquires Peko Oil, a company with holdings in the Timor Sea, as well as in the United Kingdom and United States.

2002: Esenjay Corporation in the United States is acquired.

2005: The company acquires Tipperary Corporation in the United States, a company with significant holdings in Queensland, Australia.

2006: Santos adopts a new strategy of becoming the leading southeast Asian energy company.

ply the Australian Gas Light Company in New South Wales in 1971. In support of that contract, the company built a new pipeline connecting its sites to New South Wales. That pipeline was completed in 1976.

By then, the company had made another major new gas discovery, in the Ergomanga Basin north of Cooper Basin. Then, in 1977, Santos and partners drilled a new well in the Ergomanga Basin at Poolowanna, in the Simpson Desert, producing the first oil in that area. That well was quickly followed by Strzelecki 3, the first significant discovery of oil in Ergomanga, with a production of more than 2,400 barrels per day.

Santos and Delhi agreed to a breakup of their partnership in 1979, with Delhi taking over exploration operations in the Cooper Basin, while Santos became responsible for the production and further development of the area's gas and oil fields. At the same time, Santos joined another partnership, the Cooper Basin Liquids Project, which called for the construction of an AUD 1.5 billion condensate production facility, pipeline, and port facility. Launched in 1981, initial shipments of condensates began in early 1983, followed by crude oil that same year; by 1985, the facility also had begun shipments of LPG as well.

Santos also began looking beyond the South Australia region. In 1984, the company acquired two other companies, Reef Oil, and Alliance Oil Development. The latter had been active in the Otway Basin region, at Australia's southern tip. By then, too, Santos had completed a new pipeline, the Jackson-Moonie pipeline, giving it access to the port of Brisbane. The pipeline enabled Santos to begin its first export shipments, of LPG to Japan, in 1984.

Other acquisitions followed through the 1980s. These included a majority stake in Vamgas, which had been active in the Cooper Basin region since the 1960s. The company also acquired a majority of Latec Investments, active in the Amadeus Basin in the Northern Territory, as well as the holdings of Total and Western Mining Corporation in the Cooper Bay and Ergomanga Basin areas in 1987. That same year, Santos's importance in the Australian petroleum market was underscored when the company was placed in charge of the production and development of Queensland oil and gas market.

By the end of the decade, Santos had begun taking its first step into the international market. In 1988, the company bought Peko Oil, a company with holdings in the Timor Sea, as well as in the United Kingdom and United States. That acquisition also brought Santos its first offshore operations. A second purchase, of holdings of Elf Aquitaine Exploration Australia, further boosted Santos's presence both in the Timor Sea and in the Bonaparte Basin region. By 1989, the company had made a new major oil field discovery, at Talbot 1 in the Timor Sea. That site boasted a production of 4,900 barrels per day. At the same time, the company launched production at the Challis field in the Timor Sea.

By the end of the decade, Santos had made a new gas field discovery, at Elevala in Papua New Guinea. In that same year, Santos brought its first offshore facility online, at Talisman Oil Field in the Carnarvon Basin near the coast of Western Australia.

INTERNATIONAL FOCUS FOR THE NEW CENTURY

Santos maintained an active acquisition strategy through the 1990s as it solidified its position as a leader in the Australian petroleum and gas sectors. The company extended its reach into Queensland with the completion of a new raw gas pipeline between Moomba and Ballera in 1992. The following year, the company acquired the production assets of the Australian Gas Light Company, which included fields in Surat Basin, the Timor Gap, and elsewhere. In 1996, Santos added two more companies, Parket and Parsley Australasia, and MIM Petroleum, adding exploration and production operations in Surat Basin, Cooper, and Ergomanga, and offshore sites in Papua New Guinea, Indonesia, and Western Australia. By 1999, the company had added operations in Victoria, with the purchase of shares of a site in Otway Basin and an offshore site in Gippsland Basin. In that year, the company also bought a 25 percent stake in a gas field in Papua New Guinea.

Through this period, the company also continued its organic growth. In 1993, the company became the major backer of the discovery effort behind the Stag 1 oil field in Carnarvon Basin. The following year, the company added two new oil field discoveries, at Elang and Kakatua in the Timor Sea. In 1995, the company boosted its gas and condensate holdings with the discovery of the Undan field in the Timor Gap.

As the new century approached, Santos adopted a new strategy of building itself into one of the leading energy groups in the southeast Asian region. As part of this strategy, the company sought not only to solidify its position in Australia, but to expand its operations more deeply into the international markets.

The company launched this new effort in 2000 with the purchase of Shell Australia's Carnarvon Basin assets. This acquisition was followed with the purchase of a 40 percent stake in the Evans Shoal gas field in 2001. The following year, the company gained a significant presence in the United States when it purchased Esenjay Exploration, formerly known as Frontier Natural Gas Corp. At the end of 2005, the company's U.S. operations grew again with the acquisition of Tipperary Corporation, which, in addition to exploration operations in Colorado and Nebraska, also brought Santos strong operations in the Queensland, Australia coalseam and gas markets.

By then, Santos also had stepped up its exploration activities in Indonesia and, since 2004, had launched exploration operations in the Gulf of Suez in Egypt as well. In continued extensions of the company's business, Santos entered the Kyrgyzstan exploration market in 2005, then bought into Premier Oil's offshore exploration holdings in Vietnam in early 2006. Santos appeared well on its way to achieving its goal of becoming a southeast Asian energy leader for the new century.

M. L. Cohen

PRINCIPAL SUBSIDIARIES

Alliance Petroleum Australia Pty Ltd.; Basin Oil Pty. Ltd.; Coveyork Pty. Ltd.; Farmout Drillers Pty. Ltd.; Kipper GS Pty. Ltd.; Santos Asia Pacific Pty. Ltd.; Santos International Holdings Pty. Ltd.; Santos Americas and Europe Corporation (U.S.A.); Santos USA Corporation; Santos International Operations Pty. Ltd.; Bonaparte Gas & Oil Pty. Limited; Tipperary Corporation (U.S.A.); TMOC Exploration Proprietary Limited.

PRINCIPAL COMPETITORS

BHP Billiton Group; Shell Australia Ltd.; ExxonMobil Australia Proprietary Ltd.; BP Australia Group Proprietary Ltd.; Wesfarmers Ltd.; Origin Energy Ltd.; The Australian Gas Light Co.; Woodside Petroleum Ltd.; ENERGEX Ltd.; Siemens Ltd.; Alinta Ltd.; BOC Ltd.; Clough Ltd.; Auscom Holdings Proprietary Ltd.; Integrated Group Ltd.

FURTHER READING

Antosh, Nelson, "Australian Firm Will Buy Esenjay; Santos Offer Is $80 Million," *Houston Chronicle,* March 19, 2002, p. 2.

"Australia-Based Santos Ltd. Has Completed the Acquisition of Tipperary Corp., Denver," *Oil and Gas Investor,* December 2005, p. 90.

Maksoud, Judy, "Santos Expands in Southeast Asia," *Offshore,* July 2005, p. 12.

——, "Southeast Asia on an Exploration Binge," *Offshore,* May 2004, p. 26.

Moon, Ted, "Casino Subsea Field Onstream Early," *Offshore,* March 2006, p. 19.

O'Neil, B., "History of Petroleum Exploration and Development," in E. M. Alexander and J. Hibburt (eds.), *The Petroleum Geology of South Australia, Vol. 2: Ergomanga Basin,* Adelaide: Department of Mines and Energy, 1996.

"Santos," *Euroweek,* October 19, 2001, p. 19.

"Santos Expands Indonesian Holdings," *Oil and Gas Journal,* December 22, 1997, p. 27.

"Santos Ltd. Is Expanding Its Oil and Gas Exploration Acreage in the Sorrell Basin, Offshore Tasmania with the Award of a Gas Block," *Offshore,* September 2005, p. 10.

Snow, Nick, "Australia's Santos Gains Additional US Assets," *Oil and Gas Investor,* May 2002, p. 79.

Shiseido Company, Limited

7-5-5, Ginza
Chuo-ku
Tokyo, 104-0061
Japan
Telephone: (+81-3) 3572-5111
Fax: (+81-3) 3289-1235
Web site: http://www.shiseido.co.jp/e

Public Company
Founded: 1872 as Shiseido Pharmacy
Incorporated: 1927
Employees: 25,781
Sales: ¥670.96 billion ($5.71 billion) (2006)
Stock Exchanges: Tokyo Over the Counter (OTC)
Ticker Symbol: SSDOY (ADRs)
NAIC: 325620 Toilet Preparation Manufacturing;
446120 Cosmetics, Beauty Supplies, and Perfume
Stores; 812112 Beauty Salons

■ ■ ■

Shiseido Company, Limited is the leading cosmetics company in Japan and the fourth-largest in the world. At home and in more than 60 countries abroad, Shiseido (pronounced "she-say-doe") offers a variety of makeup, skin-care, hair-care, body-care, sun-care, and fragrance products. In Japan and selected foreign countries, the company markets additional products, including toiletries, health and beauty foodstuffs, pharmaceuticals, and fine chemicals. In addition to the flagship Shiseido brand, the company markets products under a number of other brands, including Aqua Label, Bénéfique, d'ici là, Elixir Superieur, Integrate, IPSA, Maquillage, Tsubaki, and Uno. Shiseido has built a network of some 25,000 franchised cosmetics retail outlets in Japan, both stand-alone and within department stores and supermarkets; additional retails outlets are located overseas, particularly in China. Going beyond company-controlled outlets, Shiseido products are distributed through approximately 83,000 stores in Japan and about 39,000 overseas. The company also runs various salons, upscale boutiques, and restaurants. Of Shiseido's sales, about 79 percent come from its cosmetics division; about 9 percent from its toiletries division, which is comprised of soaps, hair-care products, mass-market cosmetics, and fine toiletries; and the remaining 11 percent from a catch-all "others" division which includes beauty salon products, health and beauty foods, pharmaceuticals, fashion goods, and fine chemicals. Increasingly global in its emphasis, Shiseido now derives nearly 30 percent of its sales from outside of Japan. The company's various products are manufactured at eight plants in Japan and a dozen abroad.

BEGINNINGS AS WESTERN-STYLE PHARMACY

In 1872 Yushin Fukuhara, former head pharmacist for the Japanese Admiralty, opened the Shiseido Pharmacy on the Ginza in Tokyo, a bold stroke that created Japan's first Western-style pharmacy. The characters in the store's name and the store's philosophy were derived from classic Asian philosophy. Shiseido's name implies "richness of life," which, according to Confucian thought, can be reached only through harmony of mind, body, and soul. The small store, in a populous shopping area, attracted

Shiseido commenced operations as Japan's first Western-style pharmacy in Tokyo's Ginza district in 1872. The name Shiseido derives from a Chinese expression meaning "praise the virtues of the great Earth, which nurtures new life and brings forth new values." In line with this expression, our founding spirit of "serving our customers and contributing to society by integrating all things on Earth to create new value," lives on in our corporate mission of "identifying new, richer sources of value to create beauty in daily lives and culture." This policy has led to high-value-added products and services in the cosmetics and other businesses promoting people's beauty and well-being.

purchasers of traditional remedies as well as curiosity-seekers interested in the novelty of Western imports; personalized service and high-quality products won their loyalty. In the 1880s Shiseido began to manufacture medicines, and in 1888 the company introduced a new product to Japan: toothpaste. Shiseido began selling cosmetic products that were processed by the standards used for medicines in 1897. The first such product was Eudermine skin lotion.

During the late 19th century, Japan was transformed by changes that had swept the country since the lowering of the two-centuries-old international trade barriers in the mid-1850s: some women still wore traditional white rice powder, hair lacquer, and stylized brows; others wore the lip salve, rouge, and skin-tone powder worn by Western women.

Traditional Japanese cosmetics and medicinal remedies came from herbs, other plants, and minerals that were ground and processed according to recipes that had been part of the Japanese culture since being introduced from China in the sixth and seventh centuries. Similar ingredients and processes were used to produce both lip balm and lipstick. The pharmacist was the purveyor of both.

In Japan, cosmetics for men had their heyday in the courtly and elegant latter part of the first millennium A.D. During the 19th century men still wore theatrical makeup—only males were permitted stage careers—but during the period, many Kabuki performers were poisoned by the lead in their makeup. In order to prevent future tragedies, the Japanese government established

strict product and marketing regulations which were so elaborate, frustrating, and time-consuming that few foreign companies tackled the Japanese market. The regulations also hurt domestic companies, however. In the two years it took to license a product, many products lost their timeliness, and thus their appeal.

EMPHASIS ON COSMETICS IN THE EARLY 20TH CENTURY

Japanese shipping was impeded in both the late 19th and early 20th century, due first to the Sino-Japanese War of 1894 to 1895, then to the Russo-Japanese War of 1904 to 1905. Because of the difficulty in obtaining imports, by 1915 Shiseido's cosmetics replaced foreign products in popularity, to the point that the company began to shift its emphasis away from pharmaceuticals and to concentrate almost exclusively on the manufacture of cosmetics. In addition, in 1902 the company opened Japan's first soda fountain. The sale of foods remained a modest but profitable venture.

Shinzo Fukuhara, the son of Yushin Fukuhara, led Shiseido during this period and became Shiseido's first president in 1927. Shinzo Fukuhara had spent five years studying pharmacology at Columbia University in New York City, and had visited France for one year. In France, he made important ties with artists whose ideas influenced the development of Shiseido's marketing, advertising, and packaging. Shiseido's marketing director, Noboru Matsumoto, had also studied in the United States, at New York University.

Tokyo's growth helped the family business grow and prosper, even through World War I, when production and delivery of the company's products were adversely affected by wartime restrictions. It was after the war, in 1923, remembered in Japan as the year of the great Kanto Earthquake, that Shiseido took a daring step that would eventually expand its business far beyond the city and make it a national concern. At Matsumoto's urging, the company opened a series of retail outlets for Shiseido products in a franchise operation, in principle not unlike the franchise concept Ray Kroc of McDonald's Corporation introduced in the United States some 30 years later.

Shiseido had built its business as a family-run operation, paying special attention to the needs of its customers in Tokyo and the surrounding area. Repeat business resulted both from product excellence and personalized service. Special needs were recorded along with transactional details so that reminders could be tailored to each customer and timed to catch orders for replenishment. The franchised shops were to replicate the Tokyo store, with stock variations responding to lo-

KEY DATES

1872: Yushin Fukuhara opens the Shiseido Pharmacy in Tokyo, Japan's first Western-style pharmacy.

1888: Shiseido introduces toothpaste to Japan.

1897: Company begins selling high-quality cosmetics, its first such product being Eudermine, a skin lotion.

1923: Shiseido starts opening a string of franchised retail outlets.

1927: Company is incorporated as Shiseido Company, Limited, with stock listed on the Tokyo Stock Exchange.

1957: International expansion begins.

1981: Shiseido begins marketing cosmetics in China.

1988: Company acquires Zotos International, Inc., the leading U.S. supplier of professional hair and salon products.

1996: Helene Curtis's North American professional hair-care line is acquired.

2001: Shiseido suffers its first net loss in 55 years.

2003: Plans to build a retail network in China comprised of approximately 5,000 stores are launched.

2004: Company initiates its first early-retirement program, paring the workforce by more than 1,300.

2005: "Megabrand" strategy is launched with the introduction of the Maquillage and Uno brands.

cal tastes and needs. The idea caught on because most franchisees, like the founding family, were willing to work long hours to earn customer loyalty.

In addition to over-the-counter retail sales, franchise owner-operators began conducting a mail-order business in 1937. They called it the Camellia Club, referring to the art nouveau-inspired flower logo designed by Matsumoto that Shiseido began using in 1915. The 25,000 franchise stores continued to do a steady large-volume business, with club members reaching about 9.6 million by the late 1980s. By then, the stores issued credit cards to members and kept in touch through a monthly magazine featuring fashion and beauty pointers.

The company's size ballooned quickly, outgrowing its status as a limited partnership. Reorganized as a corporation in 1927, Shiseido was listed on the Tokyo Stock Exchange. Neither the depression nor the following years of Japanese military buildup and war did much to flatten the company's growth curve.

By the 1940s Shiseido had become a trendsetter in the cosmetics industry. Even the bombing and devastation of many manufacturing sites during World War II did not result in the company's destruction. With the economic policies introduced by General Douglas MacArthur during the postwar years, Shiseido reorganized, and in 1949 the company was again listed on the Tokyo Stock Exchange.

Regaining its position as the country's cosmetics leader in the early 1950s, a position not seriously tested until the 1970s when foreign companies began to challenge Shiseido in earnest, Shiseido opened thousands of additional outlets, prospering with the franchisees as the economy's upsurge produced newly affluent customers. In 1952 the company set up a wholesale network for sales of soap, toothpaste, and sundries. The following year the Shiseido Institute of Beauty Technology was opened.

OVERSEAS EXPANSION BEGINNING IN 1957

In 1957 Shiseido began international operations when it initiated manufacturing and sales operations in Southeast Asia. In 1960 the company began marketing in Hawaii. International operations boomed in the 1960s, as subsidiaries were established in Hawaii, New York, and Milan. Others opened during the following two decades in Singapore, New Zealand, Bangkok, Australia, France, West Germany, and the United Kingdom. In 1965 Shiseido began marketing products that were formulated especially for export markets.

During the early 1970s Shiseido introduced its broad product line in the United States, but the expected sales volume failed to materialize. About ten years later, Yoshio Ohno, at that time director of overseas operations, took a different, more successful approach: Shiseido offered an exclusive product line to each of several top-flight fashion retailers, including Bloomingdale's in New York and Bullock's in Los Angeles. By the mid-1980s these lines were earning $75 million annually and growing by 40 percent each year. This strategy succeeded not only in the United States, but in other countries as well.

REVAMPING OF PRODUCT LINES

During the 1970s interest in the company's broad product line as a whole began to wane, and Shiseido began to consider new organizational and marketing directions. Many owner-operators who had worked diligently for decades to maintain a loyal customer following were nearing retirement and seemed out of touch with the interests and tastes of the new generation of consumers. To young consumers, the stores lacked the freshness and excitement that earlier generations had found in them. Shiseido refurbished the stores, and new marketing analysis and techniques were applied.

Serge Lutens, a French "international image creator," joined Shiseido in 1980. The following year, the company began marketing cosmetics in China. Segmentation of the broad product line into five age groups for marketing purposes was instituted in 1982, with encouraging results. Other ideas that succeeded as part of this new approach were product diversification and retail diversification among the company's stores. Rather than making each store an outlet for all product lines, stores were organized into subspecialties targeted at specific markets. Some became convenience stores, carrying household products as well as cosmetics. Others carried youth-oriented fashions. High-end beauty consultation services and exclusive product lines, similar to those in the high-fashion centers overseas, were other specialties. Still other stores carried cosmetics and fitness aids for men and women. In spite of this diversification, Shiseido had no intention of departing from its major role in the cosmetics industry; Shiseido stores carried other products primarily to attract customers for the company's beauty aids.

Despite Shiseido's size, the company did not abandon its founder's practice of associating beauty aids with health. For example, products in the Elixir skincare product line contained an ingredient to protect sunbathers from ultraviolet rays. The company carefully researched all market segments, targeting them with certain products. For the rapidly growing older group, Shiseido introduced Medicated Flowline Active, used to prevent hair loss, promote its regeneration, and aid in circulation of the blood. Cle de Peau Program Care was designed to prevent skin from aging and to help it recover a youthful look. A chain of sports clubs and restaurants and a line of health foods also promoted physical fitness. In 1986 Shiseido acquired Carita S.A., a French beauty salon and beautician school chain, and in 1987 Shiseido opened another beauty salon, Alexandre Zouari, in Paris. The company acquired Zotos International, Inc., the leading U.S. supplier of professional hair and salon products in 1988, and Davlyn Industries, Inc., a U.S. maker of cosmetics, the following year.

Some product lines were discarded despite brisk sales. Environmental concerns caused Shiseido to phase out products such as aerosol spray cans and nonbiodegradable diapers. New products and product lines continued to spur additional business. Research and development had been important to Shiseido's operations since its earliest days, and during the 1980s pharmaceuticals, as well as cosmetics, were being developed and tested in the company's domestic and overseas research centers. In 1988 pharmaceuticals reentered the Shiseido product family with the introduction of a line of over-the-counter drugs. Shiseido introduced its first prescription drug in 1993 with Opelead, used in cataract surgery and cornea transplants.

During the late 1980s Shiseido entered a three-year reorganization under the direction of President and CEO Yoshiharu Fukuhara, a grandson of Shiseido's founder and nephew of Shinzo Fukuhara. This restructuring strengthened the company's sales network and reaffirmed its long-held leadership position in the field. At the same time, Shiseido also bolstered its research and development operations by opening new research facilities in France in 1988, and in the United States in 1989.

GLOBAL EXPANSION

During the early and mid-1990s, Shiseido stepped up its efforts to become a global power in cosmetics. In part this was a response to price deregulation in Japan, which began in 1991. With the company losing its traditional control over the pricing of its products at the retail level, revenues and profits inevitably began to fall. The effect of deregulation was compounded by the simultaneous rise in Japan of the type of discount chains that were prevalent in the United States. As the decade continued, Japanese trade barriers to imported cosmetics began to fall, and Shiseido faced serious competition at home for the first time in its history.

In response to these threats to its home market, Shiseido, which had traditionally targeted the high end of the cosmetics market, made a conscious effort to develop more lower-priced products. The company also divided its domestic cosmetics business into two units: cosmetics, which handled consultation-oriented products, and "cosmenity," which handled self-selected products. The two sectors were differentiated further in April 1996 when the marketing operations of the two units were completely separated.

It was in the overseas market, however, that Shiseido was making serious waves, building and acquiring factories, expanding into new markets, and growing through joint ventures and acquisitions. In 1990 the company established Beaut;aae Prestige International S.A. in Paris to develop and market fragrances. The following year, production of perfumes and skin-care products began at the company's first European factory, located in Gien, France. After some tentative moves in China in the early 1980s, Shiseido became more serious about this rapidly growing market in the 1990s. In 1991 a joint venture called Shiseido Liyuan Cosmetics was set up with Beijing Liyuan Co. to develop, produce, and market premium cosmetics. Two years later production began at a new factory in Beijing, which led in 1994 to the debut of the highly successful, high-end, Aupres line of cosmetics, developed exclusively for the Chinese market. By mid-1997, Shiseido products were available in 130 stores in 32 Chinese cities. By the same time, company products were marketed in more than 50 countries worldwide, with the addition of Lebanon in 1995; Brazil, Cyprus, Israel, and Turkey in 1996; and the Czech Republic, Hungary, Croatia, and Vietnam in 1997. With sales in Asia and Europe increasing, Shiseido moved to increase its capacity by starting construction on a second plant in Taiwan in May 1997, and by reaching an agreement in June 1997 to develop a new production site in France's Loire region, which began operations a couple of years later.

On the other side of the Pacific Ocean, meanwhile, Shiseido was just as busy. In November 1996 the company bought the North American Hair Salon Division of Helene Curtis Inc. from Unilever United States, Inc., thereby adding the Helene Curtis professional salon hair-care lines to those of Zotos. Helene Curtis Japan Inc. was added in early 1997. Manufacturing capacity in North America was a concern, and in March 1997 Shiseido bought its fourth U.S. factory, a New Jersey facility that it converted into one of the largest cosmetic plants in the world.

This heightened activity outside of Japan was intended to help the company reach the ambitious goals set by management in 1996. As part of a "Global No. 1" five-year plan, Shiseido aimed by 2001 to increase net sales from foreign operations to ¥120 billion, from ¥64.5 billion in fiscal 1997. The company also wanted overseas sales, which had grown from only 8 percent of total revenues in fiscal 1997 to 13.4 percent in fiscal 1998, to 25 percent by 2001.

A year filled with noteworthy events, 1997 was also Shiseido's 125th anniversary, and the company marked the occasion by introducing Eudermine, its original product, to markets outside of Japan (1997 happened to also be the centenary of Eudermine's debut). In June 1997 Yoshiharu Fukuhara took over as chairman, while Akira Gemma, a Shiseido veteran with nearly 40 years of experience at the firm, succeeded Fukuhara as president and CEO.

Under Gemma, Shiseido continued its global expansion. The company's marketing reach extended to

Kuwait, Russia, Poland, Iceland, and Finland by the end of the 1990s. In 1998 Shiseido opened its first freestanding retail unit in the United States, an outlet called 5S that was located in New York City's SoHo district. The new 5S brand, positioned as a mid-market line, was designed specifically for the U.S. market and encompassed aromatherapeutic fragrances as well as cosmetics. Also in 1998, Shiseido further bolstered its U.S. professional hair-care lines with the acquisition of the hair-salon business of Lamaur Corporation. In the increasingly important Chinese market, the company introduced a new mid-market brand, Za (pronounced zee-eh). The following year, Shiseido began selling a line of Hello Kitty soap, shampoo, and baby powder through a license agreement with Sanrio Company, Ltd., the firm that owned the very popular brand. Also in 1999, the company introduced its cié de peau Beauté line of cosmetics into international markets as a top-of-the-line brand.

SEEKING A LASTING RECOVERY

Adding to its portfolio of brands, Shiseido in 2000 purchased majority control of Laboratories Decléor S.A., the leading aromatherapy cosmetics manufacturer in France, and also purchased the Sea Breeze line of hair-care and body-care products from Bristol-Myers Squibb Company. Sea Breeze had been launched in the United States in 1906. Other overseas brands acquired in 2000 included the professional makeup brand Nars and the male grooming line Zihr. That same year, Shiseido entered into a joint venture with the U.S. firm Intimate Brands, Inc. (later known as Limited Brands, Inc.) to develop a new upscale beauty and skin-care brand. In 2002 this venture began opening up aura science shops, the first of which opened in Columbus, Ohio. The stores were later shut down, however, although the aura science brand was integrated into Limited Brands' Victoria's Secret and Bath & Body Works stores.

Largely because of the prolonged Japanese economic slump, during which time consumption of personal goods fell off dramatically and competition intensified, Shiseido suffered four straight years of declining sales, between fiscal years 1998 and 2001. In fiscal 2001 the company reported its first net loss in 55 years, a ¥45.09 billion ($372.3 million) shortfall stemming from a ¥69.07 billion ($570.3 million) writeoff of a shortage in retirement and pension obligations. Soon after reporting these dismal results, Gemma was named chairman and was replaced as president and CEO by Morio Ikeda. The new leader's first year was a rough one thanks to the continuation of the slump in domestic consumption as well as costs incurred because of new regulations requiring Japanese cosmetic makers to list all ingredients on product labels. Sales declined slightly, dropping for the fifth consecutive year, while Shiseido incurred another net loss, this one totaling ¥22.77 billion ($177.5 million). On a positive note, overseas sales surged 25 percent and now comprised 22 percent of total sales, up from the 18 percent level of the previous year. In the meantime, brand expansion continued with the late 2001 acquisition of the U.S. brand Joico by the Zotos International subsidiary, and the launch in 2002 of the FITIT mid-market cosmetics brand.

Shiseido returned to the black in fiscal 2003 as a result of inventory reductions, aggressive cutting of operating expenses in Japan in part by drastically cutting its array of cosmetic brands, and the introduction of a point-of-sale system to its extensive network of domestic retail outlets in order to better track and manage sales and inventories. The firm was aided by growing overseas sales in Asia, particularly in China, where Shiseido had established itself as the leading prestige cosmetic brand and enjoyed a 25 percent jump in sales for the year. In September 2003 the company announced plans to create a cosmetics store network in China similar to the one it had built at home. Shiseido aimed to manage a chain of approximately 5,000 stores, mainly located in coastal cities, by 2008 and to boost annual sales in China from about ¥20 billion to ¥100 billion.

In 2004 Shiseido continued to overhaul its domestic operations. In March the company announced plans to close two domestic manufacturing facilities, located in Kyoto and Tokyo, by 2006. In December 2004 Shiseido launched its first-ever early-retirement program, leading more than 1,300 employees to leave the company by March 2005. The retirement program resulted in a special loss of ¥30.99 billion ($295.1 million) for fiscal 2005 as well as a return to red ink, a net loss of ¥8.86 billion ($84.3 million).

In mid-2005 Ikeda moved up to the chairmanship, while Shinzo Maeda was promoted from general manager of corporate planning to president and CEO. In addition to continuing to oversee the push into China and further restructuring efforts centered on improving profitability, Maeda was charged with implementing a new "megabrand" strategy aimed at shoring up Shiseido's position at home. Through this initiative, Shiseido sought to further streamline its once-bloated brand lineup by creating big brands that could capture the number one position in Japan in each category. The Maquillage brand, which took its name from the French word for makeup, was launched in August 2005 as a blending of two former makeup brands, Piéds Nus and Proudia. The men's brand Uno was reintroduced that same month, followed by the debuts of the skin-care brand Aqua Label, which was aimed at the self-selection market centered on drugstores, in February 2006, and the hair-care brand Tsubaki, in March 2006. All of these soon ranked as the top brand in their respective categories. Scheduled for launch later in 2006 were Elixir Superieur, a new low-end to mid-range skin-care line, and Integrate, a new makeup line.

While this aggressive rollout continued, Maeda also had to contend with a newly enlarged domestic competitor as Kao Corporation secured for itself the number two position in Japanese cosmetics by acquiring the cosmetics arm of Kanebo, Ltd. in early 2006. This deal promised to create further competition in China as well because Kao immediately announced aggressive plans for that burgeoning market. Thanks to its restructuring efforts and megabrand strategy, Shiseido appeared better positioned to deal with this new challenge.

Betty T. Moore
Updated, David E. Salamie

PRINCIPAL SUBSIDIARIES

Hanatsubaki Factory Co., Ltd.; Shiseido Sales Co., Ltd.; Shiseido FITIT Co., Ltd.; Shiseido International Inc.; d'ici là Co., Ltd.; IPSA Co., Ltd.; AYURA Laboratories Inc.; Ettusais Co., Ltd.; KINARI Inc.; Fullcast Co., Ltd.; Shiseido Beautech Co., Ltd.; Beauty Technology Co., Ltd.; ETWAS Co., Ltd.; Orbit, Inc.; AXE Co., Ltd.; Beauté Prestige International Co., Ltd.; InterAct Co., Ltd.; Tai Shi Trading Co., Ltd.; Mieux Products Co., Ltd.; FT Shiseido Co., Ltd.; Amenity Goods Co., Ltd.; Shiseido Irica Technology Inc.; Shiseido Professional Co., Ltd.; Shiseido Beauty Salon Co., Ltd.; Shiseido Pharmaceutical Co., Ltd.; Shiseido Beauty Foods Co., Ltd.; The Ginza Co., Ltd.; Shiseido Parlour Co., Ltd.; Shiseido Kaihatsu Co., Ltd.; Shiseido Logistics Co., Ltd.; Shiseido Information Network Co., Ltd.; Shiseido Astech Co., Ltd.; Shiseido Lease Co., Ltd.; Shiseido Investment Co., Ltd.; Shiseido America, Inc. (U.S.A.); Davlyn Industries, Inc. (U.S.A.); Shiseido International Corporation (U.S.A.); Shiseido Cosmetics (America) Ltd. (U.S.A.); Shiseido of Hawaii, Inc. (U.S.A.); Shiseido Travel Retail America Inc. (U.S.A.); Shiseido (Canada) Inc.; Shiseido do Brasil Ltda. (Brazil); Beauté Prestige International, Inc. (U.S.A.); Nars Cosmetics, Inc. (U.S.A.); Zirh International Corporation (U.S.A.); Decléor U.S.A., Inc.; Zotos International, Inc. (U.S.A.); Piidea Canada, Ltd.; Shiseido International France S.A.S.; Laboratories Decléor S.A. (France); Shiseido International Europe S.A. (France); Shiseido Europe S.A.S. (France); Shiseido Deutschland GmbH (Germany); Shiseido Cosmetici (Italia) S.p.A. (Italy); Shiseido France S.A.; Shiseido España S.A. (Spain);

Shiseido United Kingdom Co., Ltd.; Beauté Prestige International S.A. (France); Beauté Prestige International GmbH (Germany); Beauté Prestige International S.A.U. (Spain); Beauté Prestige International S.p.A. (Italy); Beauté Prestige International SPRL (Belgium); Beauté Prestige International GmbH (Austria); Beauté Prestige International B.V. (Netherlands); Beauté Prestige International Ltd. (U.K.); Noms de Code S.A.S. (France); Decléor UK Ltd.; Carita S.A. (France); Carita International S.A. (France); Carita UK Ltd.; Les Salons du Palais Royal Shiseido S.A. (France); FIPAL S.A. (France); 331 International S.A.S. (France); SMB S.A.S. (France); Joico Holding B.V. (Netherlands); Joico Laboratories Europe B.V. (Netherlands); Shiseido Liyuan Cosmetics Co., Ltd. (China); Shanghai Zotos Citic Cosmetics Co., Ltd. (China); Taiwan Shiseido Co., Ltd.; Shiseido (N.Z.) Ltd. (New Zealand); Shiseido China Co., Ltd.; Shiseido China Research Center Co., Ltd.; Beijing Huazhiyou Cosmetics Sales Center (China); Shiseido Dah Chong Hong Cosmetics Ltd. (China); Shiseido Dah Chong Hong Cosmetics (Guangzhou) Ltd. (China); FLELIS International Inc. (Taiwan); Shiseido Korea Co., Ltd.; Shiseido Thailand Co., Ltd.; SAHA Asia-Pacific Co., Ltd. (Thailand); Shiseido (Australia) Pty., Ltd.; Shiseido Singapore Co., (Pte.) Ltd.; Shiseido Malaysia Sdn. Bhd.; Shiseido Philippines, Inc.; Shiseido Travel Retail Asia Pacific Pte. Ltd. (Singapore); Beauté Prestige International Pte. Ltd. (Singapore); Shiseido Professional (Thailand) Co., Ltd.

PRINCIPAL COMPETITORS

Kao Corporation; L'Oréal SA; The Procter & Gamble Company; Unilever; The Estée Lauder Companies Inc.; Kose Corporation.

FURTHER READING

Anai, Ikuo, "Shiseido Aims to Be World's Top 'Beauty Creator,'" *Daily Yomiuri* (Tokyo), January 1, 1998.

Azuma, Naoto, "Shiseido Gives Cosmetics Business a Makeover," *Daily Yomiuri* (Tokyo), October 10, 2005.

Born, Pete, "Shiseido Builds a Market from the Ground Up," *WWD*, May 26, 2006, p. 19.

———, "Shiseido Celebrates 125th with Eudermine," *WWD*, July 11, 1997, p. 13.

———, "Shiseido's Vision for Global Expansion," *WWD*, April 26, 1996, p. 6.

Borrus, Amy, "Will Shiseido's Make-Over Leave It Less Glamorous?," *Business Week*, November 2, 1987, p. 82.

Chang, Leslie, "Shiseido Targets China with 200 New Stores," *Asian Wall Street Journal*, March 24, 2004, p. A2.

Cody, Jennifer, "Shiseido Strives for a Whole New Look," *Wall Street Journal*, May 27, 1994, p. A5.

do Rosario, Louise, "Cleaned and Preened," *Far Eastern Economic Review*, April 1, 1993, pp. 68–69.

———, "Make Up and Mend," *Far Eastern Economic Review*, December 19, 1991, pp. 70–71.

"Fragrance Helps You Live Longer," *Economist*, October 23, 1993, p. 86.

Fuyuno, Ichiko, "Shiseido's Make-Over," *Far Eastern Economic Review*, May 22, 2003, p. 40.

Hutton, Bethan, "Acquisitions Behind Surge at Shiseido," *Financial Times*, November 12, 1997, p. 17.

Ishibashi, Asako, "Shiseido Builds Foundation As Asia's Cosmetics Leader," *Nikkei Weekly*, July 8, 2002.

"Japan's Shiseido Plans New Cosmetics Line for the U.S. Market," *Wall Street Journal*, May 23, 1997, p. A11.

Kilburn, David, "Shiseido Blooms Anew: Fukuhara Expands the Vision of Japanese Giant," *Advertising Age*, October 3, 1988, p. 12.

Ono, Yumiko, "Japan's Shiseido, Intent on Shopping, Finds Little to Buy," *Wall Street Journal*, September 16, 1999, p. A24.

———, "Japan's Shiseido Studies Moves in U.S. Market," *Wall Street Journal*, April 19, 1996, p. B7.

Prasso, Sheridan, "Battle for the Face of China," *Fortune*, December 12, 2005, pp. 156+.

Rahman, Bayan, "Shiseido Looks Better with Its Return to Black," *Financial Times*, January 7, 2003, p. 27.

Schultz, Jennifer, "Facing Up to Change," *Far Eastern Economic Review*, August 16, 2001, p. 42.

Shirouzu, Norihiko, "Deregulation Jolts Shiseido's Foundation: Cosmetics Firm Looks to U.S. As Home Rivalries Grow," *Wall Street Journal*, June 14, 1996, p. A10.

"Shiseido Aims to Become Global No. 1 in Worldwide Cosmetics," *Cosmetics International*, November 25, 1996, p. 10.

"Shiseido Is Seeking to Acquire Its Fourth Factory in the U.S.," *Wall Street Journal*, December 2, 1996, p. B12.

"Shiseido's New Face in the U.S.," *Business Week*, May 11, 1981, pp. 100+.

Slavin, Barbara, "Saving Face," *Forbes*, December 31, 1984, p. 138.

Tanner, Andrew, "Is Beauty More Than Skin-Deep?" *Forbes*, December 16, 1985, p. 148.

Thornton, Emily, Dexter Roberts, and Mia Trinephi, "Shiseido Is Giving Itself a Whole New Look," *Business Week*, June 2, 1997, p. 20.

"The Two Faces of Shiseido," *Economist*, July 10, 1999, p. 57.

"Wrinkled," *Economist*, November 4, 1995, p. 69.

SkillSoft Public Limited Company

Belfield Office Park
Clonskeagh, Dublin 4
Ireland
Telephone: (35) 31-218-1000
Fax: (35) 31-283-0379
Web site: http://www.skillsoft.com

Public Company
Incorporated: 1989
Employees: 1,140
Sales: $215.6 million (2006)
Stock Exchanges: NASDAQ
Ticker Symbol: SKIL
NAIC: 511210 Software Publishers

■ ■ ■

SkillSoft Public Limited Company lays claim to being the largest e-learning company in the world. SkillSoft serves corporate clientele, offering Internet-based educational and instructional courses. The company offers thousands of software titles that cover a variety of topics, including leadership, customer interaction, human resources, finance, and information technology. SkillSoft serves more than 2,800 customers, marketing its products and services in more than 45 countries.

ORIGINS

SkillSoft's development into the largest e-learning company in the world involved a number of business combinations undertaken by two principal businesses, SmartForce PLC and SkillSoft Corporation. The older of the two companies was SmartForce, a company formed in Ireland in 1989 under the name CBT Group PLC. Based in Dublin, CBT Group evolved into its area of expertise, starting its business life pursuing a more broadly defined objective than developing educational tools for corporate clientele. The company was formed to serve as a holding company for investment purposes, and for the first two years of its existence it acquired stakes in a number of companies involved in various industries. A turning point in its development occurred in September 1991, when the foundation for what eventually became known as SkillSoft first took shape.

The earliest antecedents of SkillSoft's business in the 21st century originated within SmartForce, the successor to CBT Group. In September 1991, CBT Group established an Irish subsidiary named CBT Systems Limited and an English subsidiary named CBT Systems U.K. Limited to develop interactive, information-technology (IT) education and training software. A presence in the United States had been established a year earlier, forming what became known as CBT Systems USA, Ltd. At the time the Irish and English subsidiaries were formed, CBT Group sold or dissolved all its interests unrelated to IT education and training software. From September 1991 forward, as CBT Group developed into SmartForce and SmartForce developed into SkillSoft, all revenues and operating expenses were attributable to interactive, IT education and training software.

When CBT focused its efforts on IT education and training, the global market represented $11.8 billion worth of business. The volume of business would triple during the next dozen years, providing fertile conditions

COMPANY PERSPECTIVES

Our products and services are designed to link learning strategy to business strategy and to maximize human capital investments. With a comprehensive learning solution, comprised of high-quality learning resources and flexible technology approaches, we help our customers achieve sustainable and measurable business results. These solutions are designed to support all levels of the organization and can easily be adapted to meet strategic business initiatives, on-demand information needs and individual job roles.

to support the company's development into the largest of its kind in the world. To extend its geographic reach, broaden its capabilities, and add to the 44 titles of instructional software it marketed in 1992, CBT made a series of moves during the 1990s. In 1994, the company established, via an acquisition, CBT Systems Africa (Proprietary) Ltd., forming a direct sales presence in southern Africa. In November 1995, the company acquired a developer of interactive educational software named Personal Training Systems, and in May 1996 it acquired a German educational software company, CLS Consult, and its exclusive distributor in Canada, New Technology Training Ltd. The acquisitions provided a meaningful boost to CBT Group's stature, but they paled in strategic significance to a partnership forged at the end of 1996. In December, the company concluded negotiations with Street Technologies, Inc., a developer of technology that allowed the "streaming" of multimedia and other large data files, thereby permitting real-time delivery of the files over local- and wide-area networks, corporate intranets, and the Internet. Under the terms of the agreement, both companies began working together to deploy CBT Group's software over corporate intranets and the Internet, the focus of SkillSoft's endeavors in the 21st century.

The first phase of expansion led to substantial gains in CBT Group's stature. After five years of focusing exclusively on the IT spending of its corporate clientele, the company had increased the size of its library, expanding from 44 software titles to 328 software titles that offered 1,250 hours of education and training. Revenues during the period swelled from less than $10 million to $66.3 million, as CBT Group, which boasted 1,250 corporate customers by the end of 1996, enjoyed robust growth by gaining the business of corporate

luminaries such as AT&T, Compaq Computer, Wells Fargo & Co., and Sprint Corp.

Supported by a solid business foundation midway through the decade, the company's pace of growth quickened during the late 1990s as it more than doubled the size of its customer base and more than quadrupled the number of products it offered. By the end of the decade, the company offered more than 1,300 software titles to more than 2,500 customers. Revenues shot upward as a result, nearly reaching $200 million in 1999. CBT Group changed its name as it exited the decade, adopting SmartForce Public Limited Company as its corporate title, which led to a re-branding of its educational and training software to "SmartCourses." Under their new name, the software titles began to address topics outside the IT field for the first time, widening their scope to include subject matters such as management skills and interpersonal skills.

INDUSTRY CONSOLIDATION

SmartForce entered the 21st century having recorded energetic growth during its first decade in the e-learning sector. The jump from less than $10 million in annual sales to nearly $200 million in annual sales was particularly impressive given the highly fragmented nature of the industry. The largest 15 vendors in the IT training and education market accounted for only 20 percent of worldwide sales, with no company controlling more than 3 percent of the market. Because of the growth the company achieved during the 1990s, it could entertain playing an aggressive role as the industry consolidated, something that would happen during the first years of the new century. The largest companies in the business looked to take advantage of industry conditions, seeking to acquire smaller companies in a bid to gain a dominant position in a market largely up for grabs. It became a case of either acquire or be acquired for IT training and education companies, and Smart-Force, enjoying a volume of nearly $200 million, stood poised to figure as one of the consolidators in an industry whose ranks promised to be thinned by mergers and acquisitions.

As SmartForce prepared for a period of consolidation within its industry, it strove to become a more comprehensive competitor. Led by Greg Priest, who was named president and chief executive officer in December 1998, the company increased its commitment to developing a diversified product line. Throughout the 1990s, the company's focus was to "chase IT training dollars," according to Priest in a July 19, 2001 interview with *Investor's Business Daily,* but he began emphasizing a more diversified approach as consolidation within the industry began to take place. Priest marshaled his forces

KEY DATES

1989: SmartForce PLC is formed as CBT Group PLC.
1991: CBT Group focuses its efforts on developing information technology (IT) education and training software.
1996: CBT Group forges an agreement with Street Technologies, Inc. to develop online educational software.
1998: SkillSoft Corp. is formed.
1999: CBT Group changes its name to SmartForce PLC.
2002: SmartForce PLC and SkillSoft Corp. merge, creating SkillSoft PLC.
2006: Sales reach $215 million.

to develop Internet-based training solutions that corporate clientele could use to improve sales tactics, facilitate new product introduction, and train employees about sexual harassment policies, among a variety of other topics. "We now sell to a much wider range in the enterprise," Priest said in his interview with *Investor's Business Daily*.

Equipped with a more diversified product portfolio, SmartForce began searching for acquisition candidates, intent on taking the lead in an industry set to consolidate. The company made its first move in 2002, announcing in January that it had reached an agreement to acquire Lexington, Massachusetts–based Centra Software Inc., a developer of e-learning software designed to help businesses with product development, employee training, and customer sales. The agreement for the $248 million, all-stock deal promised to give SmartForce a significant boost to its stature, but within months the merger was canceled. When financial results were announced for the first quarter of 2002, the figures failed to meet the expectations of Wall Street. Analysts had expected SmartForce to post a profit of five cents per share and revenues of $66 million. SmartForce announced it expected to lose between 26 and 27 cents per share and to post revenues of around $43 million. Centra fell short of expectations as well, blaming a decrease in corporate spending for its failure to meet Wall Street guidance. "They both missed their numbers so dramatically," said an analyst quoted in the April 3, 2002 issue of the *Daily Deal*. "They need to get their own ships in order before they can undertake a merger like this." When the termination of the merger was an-

nounced, SmartForce's stock declined 32 percent in one day, delivering a stinging blow to a company intending to make a bold move forward. In the wake of the scuttled merger, SmartForce and Centra opted for a scaled-back version of their union, striking an agreement that called for the companies to co-market each other's products and for SmartForce to re-sell Centra's knowledge-delivery and management software.

MERGER OF SMARTFORCE AND SKILLSOFT: 2002

Priest did not wait long after the disappointment of the Centra deal to strike again. In June 2002, the company announced it had reached an agreement to acquire SkillSoft Corp., a Nashua, New Hampshire–based e-learning company. SkillSoft had been formed four years earlier by Chuck Moran, who used $20 million in venture capital to start the company. Moran took SkillSoft Public in January 2000 and raised $40 million from the initial public offering (IPO) of stock. An additional $88 million was raised in a secondary offering in July 2001, adding to the funds at Moran's disposal to build SkillSoft into a leading competitor in the e-learning sector. By the time the merger with SmartForce was announced, SkillSoft had developed a strong reputation as a developer of programs used to hone management skills, striking Priest as an ideal business combination for his company. Under the terms of the proposed merger, Priest was to become chairman and chief strategy officer of the combined company and Moran was to assume the duties of president and chief executive officer, with SmartForce shareholders slated to own 58 percent of the company and SkillSoft shareholders to own 42 percent of the stock. Technically, the transaction was structured as a merger of SkillSoft into a newly formed subsidiary of SmartForce.

The merger was completed in September 2002 in a stock deal valued at more than $500 million. With corporate headquarters in Dublin and North American headquarters in Nashua, the company stood as the largest e-learning company in the world, offering more than 5,000 courses and 2,500 digitized books in 15 languages. The company operated under the SkillSoft name following the merger, legally changing its name to SkillSoft Public Limited Company in November 2002.

Although the merger created a formidable force in the e-learning industry, it also ignited considerable controversy. In November 2002, SkillSoft announced it would delay filing its third quarter financial results and it would have to restate SmartForce's earnings for at least three years. At issue was the manner in which SmartForce recognized its revenue, specifically the booking of revenue from software re-sellers before the company received payment. The problem prompted the Securities and Exchange Commission (SEC) to launch an investigation into the matter in February 2003, beginning a period of scrutiny that would drag on for several years. The investigation cast a cloud of uncertainty over the company—the SEC's Boston office recommended civil action against the company in mid-2005, according to the July 12, 2005 edition of the *Telegraph.* Presuming the conclusion of the investigation did not harm SkillSoft in the long term, the company could look forward to a promising future. In a consolidating industry, SkillSoft took an early lead, establishing itself as a dominant force in the growing e-learning industry. In the years ahead, further bold moves would be required to keep the company ahead of the pack, as it endeavored to increase its share of a fragmented market.

Jeffrey L. Covell

PRINCIPAL SUBSIDIARIES

SkillSoft Corporation; SkillSoft Ireland Ltd.; SkillSoft UK Limited (U.K.); SkillSoft Asia Pacific Pty Ltd. (Australia); Books24x7.com, Inc.; SkillSoft Finance Limited (Cayman Islands); CBT Technology Limited (Ireland); SkillSoft Canada Limited; SmartForce Business Skills Ltd. (Ireland); SmartCertify Direct, Inc.; SkillSoft Deutschland GmbH (Germany); SkillSoft New Zealand Ltd.; SkillSoft France SARL; SmartForce Benelux B.V. (Netherlands); SkillSoft Asia Pacific PTE Ltd. (Singapore).

PRINCIPAL COMPETITORS

Canterbury Consulting Group, Inc.; Global Knowledge Training LLC; The Thomson Corporation.

FURTHER READING

Kennedy, Eileen, "Nashua, N.H.–Based Software Firm Able to Keep Listing on Nasdaq," *Telegraph,* January 23, 2003.

———, "Online Business-Course Developer Skill Soft Goes from Profit to Loss," *Telegraph,* April 3, 2004.

———, "SEC Investigates Nashua, N.H.–Based Online Business Course Taker," *Telegraph,* July 12, 2005.

———, "SEC Probes Nashua, N.H., Educational-Software Firm's Financial Statements," *Telegraph,* January 21, 2003.

Leighton, Brad, "Web-Based Business Course Developer with Nashua, N.H., Headquarters Posts Loss," *Telegraph,* January 21, 2003.

"Software Integrates with Learning Management Systems," *Product News Network,* March 4, 2005.

Spiller, Karen, "Internet-Based Training Software Firm SkillSoft PLC to Lay Off 133 Employees," *Telegraph,* December 1, 2004.

———, "Nashua, N.H.–Based Online Course Provider Makes Profit Despite Settlement," *Telegraph,* September 2, 2004.

———, "Nashua, N.H.–Based Teaching Software Maker Adds Disability Upgrades," *Telegraph,* October 30, 2003.

Sonic Solutions, Inc.

———— ■ ————

101 Rowland Way
Novato, California 94945
U.S.A.
Telephone: (415) 893-8000
Fax: (415) 893-8008
Web site: http://www.sonic.com

Public Company
Incorporated: 1986
Employees: 637
Sales: $148.68 million (2005)
Stock Exchanges: NASDAQ
Ticker Symbol: SNIC
NAIC: 511210 Software Publishers

■ ■ ■

Sonic Solutions, Inc., is the world's leading maker of software for creating CDs and DVDs. The company's professional line includes Scenarist, which is used to master the bulk of DVDs released worldwide; and AuthorScript, a CD and DVD-burning program that is licensed to firms including Microsoft, America Online, and Yahoo. Sonic Solutions' consumer software includes such popular titles as Easy Media Creator, MyDVD, PhotoSuite, and RecordNow, which are sold under the Roxio brand name.

EARLY YEARS

Sonic Solutions was founded in San Francisco in 1986 by Robert Doris, James "Andy" Moorer, and Mary Sauer to use digital technology to remove hiss, clicks, and other imperfections from analog recordings. The three had worked for *Star Wars* director George Lucas's computer audio firm Droid Works, with the Harvard-educated Doris serving as its president. He would also head the new firm.

In mid-1987 the company's NoNoise system was unveiled, and it quickly proved a sensation in professional audio circles. The software program, which ran on a modified Apple Macintosh computer, analyzed a digital copy of an analog recording in two ways. The first compared an example of steady noise such as tape hiss or amplifier hum with the rest of a recording and then removed the audible frequencies of the offending sound throughout. The second removed clicks and other unwanted transient noises and then replaced each with sound synthesized from the digital information immediately before and afterward.

Sonic Solutions charged $103 per minute for cleaning up stereo sound, or about $6,000 for an hour-long compact disc. Processing an hour of music took as much as ten hours' time depending on the complexity of the work being done. One of the young firm's first assignments was a live recording by rock band The Doors in which some 12 minutes of lead singer Jim Morrison's vocals had been marred by static noise bursts due to a faulty microphone cable. Sonic Solutions was able to remove the noise and make the previously unusable material releasable. Other early restoration jobs included a 1930s recording of Ravel's "Bolero" conducted by the composer, and vintage albums by Louis Armstrong, Liberace, Barbra Streisand, and the Grateful Dead. Most reviewers praised the system, which was a major step up from older, less precise methods that used filters to eliminate certain frequencies or a razor blade to slice out a millisecond of sound where an unwanted click occurred. Application of NoNoise required a skilled technician, however, and over-use could remove some of the original sound or make vintage recordings lose their natural warmth.

In 1988 the company introduced the Desktop Audio system, which enabled users to perform digital mixing, equalization, and mastering of a compact disc (CD). The Macintosh-based system was priced at $44,100, with NoNoise software costing an additional $60,000. Two years later it was expanded with the addition of the CD Maker compact disc recording device, which had been developed by Sony Corp. and Start Lab. It could create a unique "burned" CD that would play on any standard deck or could be used as a master disc for replication. Users included radio stations and theater companies that needed to play back unique bits of digital audio repeatedly. In 1992 the less expensive SonicStation audio processing workstation was introduced at a more affordable price of $4,995.

For the fiscal year ended in March 1993 Sonic Solutions had revenues of $9.43 million and a profit of $1.21 million. In the fall of that year the company announced it would begin integrating Sony's higher-definition Super Bit Mapping CD audio technology into its products. The firm's equipment was being used by most major record companies, studios such as London's famed Abbey Road, and organizations such as the British Broadcasting Corporation.

1994: INITIAL PUBLIC OFFERING, INTRODUCTION OF MEDIANET

In early 1994 Sonic Solutions made an initial public stock offering on NASDAQ, selling 1.9 million shares at $9.50 each, of which about a third came from existing shareholders. The firm also introduced a new product called MediaNet, which was a high-speed local area computer network that could store and transmit digital files via fiber-optic cables. It was targeted at recording studios and companies that worked with computer graphics or digital video files, and could serve up to 64 users with overall bandwidth of one gigabyte of data per second from both Macintosh and UNIX-based computers. MediaNet was also compatible with the products of other firms including Cisco Systems, Silicon Graphics, and Sun Microsystems.

Sonic Solutions' software was being incorporated into such products as Digidesign's popular Pro Tools recording studio system and editing gear from Avid Technology. The company was continually upgrading its offerings, and by the fall had added more enhancements to the NoNoise and MediaNet systems, including a new 500-disc CD jukebox and database system option for the latter, as well as several entry-level models that retailed for as low as $2,995. The firm was also beginning to get its feet wet in the realm of digital video, and in 1994 introduced the SonicCinema MPEG Video-CD PreMastering System, which provided the ability to record video on compact discs in a format that had recently been announced by Sony, Philips, JVC, and others.

During 1994 the company introduced a new sound processing card, the Ultra-Sonic Processor (USP), but there were serious problems with both its design and manufacturing. Other projects were put on hold as Sonic Solutions tried to appease a host of dissatisfied customers, causing earnings to drop. The firm subsequently improved its internal procedures for getting products from design to manufacturing and added more oversight.

In 1995 the company introduced the Multitrack USP Sonic System, an audio editing and mixing device that could handle up to 64 channels of input and output. The firm's audio workstations continued to be popular, with more than half of the 300 songs nominated for Grammy Awards in 1995 mastered on Sonic Solutions equipment. Its products were also finding uses in other areas, with the tape of a telephone call made to 911 operators by O. J. Simpson's wife enhanced for prosecutors using the NoNoise program.

DVD CREATOR, HIGH-DENSITY AUDIO DEBUT IN 1996

The firm was working hard to develop products for digital video applications, and in mid-1996 introduced the industry's first integrated digital video disc (DVD) pre-mastering system, DVD Creator. Standards had recently been set for the DVD format, with the first players due to ship in late 1996, and the company helped

<table>
<tr><td colspan="2">KEY DATES
■</td></tr>
<tr><td>1986:</td><td>Sonic Solutions is founded in San Francisco, California.</td></tr>
<tr><td>1987:</td><td>NoNoise system debuts.</td></tr>
<tr><td>1994:</td><td>Company holds initial public stock offering; MediaNet is introduced.</td></tr>
<tr><td>1996:</td><td>First DVD-authoring product is developed.</td></tr>
<tr><td>1999:</td><td>Consumer-grade disc-burning program DVDit! debuts.</td></tr>
<tr><td>2002:</td><td>Company purchases Veritas Software desktop and mobile division.</td></tr>
<tr><td>2004:</td><td>Acquisitions of InterActual, Roxio boost size of firm.</td></tr>
<tr><td>2006:</td><td>New high-definition DVD-authoring system is introduced.</td></tr>
</table>

form an alliance of content providers and production firms to streamline the process of bringing DVD titles to consumers.

Sonic Solutions also upgraded its audio line in 1996 with the SonicStudio High-Density workstation, which could handle the new 96kHz sampling rate and 24-bit data samples. This data-intensive audio format was expected to form the basis of the next generation of digital audio on higher-capacity DVD discs. A group of interested companies were engaged to test and promote the new equipment, and Sonic Solutions partnered with Sony to use that firm's Direct Stream Digital audio format in its system.

Despite such initiatives, audio workstation sales were falling off significantly, and revenues for the fiscal year ending in March dropped from $20.2 million a year earlier to $13.9 million. With the firm pouring resources into developing new DVD mastering systems, it also recorded a loss of $3.6 million. One positive note during the year was an Emmy Award won in the fall by the NoNoise program for its contribution to television sound quality.

In January 1997 Sonic Solutions received $5.1 million in new financing from Hambrecht & Quist, but losses grew to $5.2 million for the March-ended fiscal year as its engineers continued to focus on digital video products, for which there were few sales as yet. In September the firm introduced the industry's first integrated DVD-authoring system, the Sonic DVD Creator Workstation, priced at $99,999, while the Macintosh-based authoring software, DVD Producer, was available separately for $24,999.

At the start of 1998 Sonic Solutions secured $7 million in new equity-based funding, and during the year the firm announced new products including Sonic DVD Vobulator (for creators of multimedia DVD-ROM discs, priced at $7,999), and Sonic DesktopDVD for business users ($39,999). Shipment of some products was delayed while the company addressed problems that had begun cropping up with DVD Creator, however.

INTRODUCTION OF CONSUMER-FRIENDLY DVDIT! SOFTWARE: 1999

By whis time, computers were increasingly being produced with built-in DVD drives, while home DVD players were dropping in price from initial levels of more than $1,000. In August 1999 Sonic Solutions introduced the $499 DVDit! software program which allowed home users to create DVDs on computers with DVD-burning drives. It was soon bundled with products from such firms as Avid, Media 100, and NEC, and variations including a professional edition were subsequently added. Also during 1999, the firm secured an additional $12 million in equity-based funding.

As sales of DVDit! started taking off, a web site was launched to sell the product while Broadfield Distributing began wholesaling it via a network of 3,000-plus retailers. By February 2000 more than 10,000 copies had been sold.

New products added during 2000 included eDVD, which enabled DVD Creator users to add links to World Wide Web content; Streaming DVD, which allowed corporations and educators to stream video over the Internet; DVD Fusion, for corporate video makers and artists; and MyDVD, a more consumer-friendly, lower-cost version of DVDit! In 2001 Royal Philips Electronics began bundling the latter with its new DVD recorder and Dell, NEC, and Hewlett-Packard loaded it onto their computers.

In late 2001 and early 2002 Microsoft, Adobe Systems, and Sony licensed the firm's new AuthorScript DVD-authoring software for their products, and in November of the latter year Sonic Solutions bought Veritas Software Corporation's desktop and mobile division for $9.2 million. The company soon began selling Veritas's RecordNow CD and DVD-ROM burning software and data backup programs.

In early 2003 Sonic Solutions reached an agreement with America Online (AOL), which would use AuthorScript in its MusicNet download service. For 2003, ended in March, revenues leapt from the $19.1 million reported in 2002 to $32.7 million, with net income in the black for the first time in several years. By

August, total sales of the MyDVD and DVDit! programs had topped six million. The firm had an estimated 85 percent share of the market for such products, while its professional DVD-authoring software had been used to prepare some 80 percent of the commercial DVD titles released worldwide.

During 2003 the company also introduced Sonic PrimeTime for Windows XP Media Center, began licensing AuthorScript for set-top DVD recorders, and opened a new development facility in Shanghai, China. The firm completed several additional stock offerings during the year as its share price continued to rise.

In February 2004 Sonic Solutions announced plans to sell up to $80 million worth of stock and warrants in additional periodic offerings. That same month saw the acquisition of InterActual, which made Internet-linking DVD software for computers and home entertainment equipment. More than half of the 160-plus million computers expected to be sold in 2004 were likely to have a CD or DVD burner, or both, and Sonic Solutions was working to boost its original equipment manufacturer (OEM) agreements with computer makers such as Dell. Sales jumped again during the latest fiscal year to $56.9 million, with a net profit of $11.1 million recorded.

ACQUISITION OF ROXIO

In December 2004 Sonic Solutions purchased the consumer software division of rival Roxio, Inc., which would henceforth become known as Napster as it focused on a music download service. Roxio/Napster would receive $70 million in cash and $10 million worth of stock. The software unit, which had annual sales of approximately $80 million, produced popular products including Toast, Easy Media Creator, VideoWave, Photo-Suite, and Easy DVD Copy. Some were similar to Sonic Solutions offerings, but Roxio had a greater presence in retail stores, with Sonic's sales generated more from online vendors. The firm's Desktop Products unit was soon merged into Roxio and renamed the Roxio division, with other units also merged and/or restructured. The company's other divisions consisted of a professional products group and an advanced technology group.

December also saw an office opened in Burbank, California, to serve the needs of the successful InterActual subsidiary's customers. Sonic Solutions had product development offices in Toronto, Shanghai, and Germany, in addition to several locations in California, and numerous sales offices internationally.

In the spring of 2005 the company released new software packages that combined popular Sonic Solu-tions and Roxio programs such as MyDVD, Record-Now, Easy Media Creator, and Easy DVD Copy. They would be marketed under the Roxio name, which was more familiar at retail. More than 10,000 stores carried the line.

In early 2005 the company introduced new software that could burn dual-layer DVDs, which had nearly double the data storage capacity of standard ones, and announced plans for a product that would let users burn DVDs legally downloaded from the Internet. In May the AuthorScript disc-burning program was licensed by Yahoo for its music download service, with other deals having been made with Kodak, Microsoft, TiVo, and Iomega. Sonic Solutions was also busy developing upgraded versions of its products or creating new ones, and the fall saw new versions of the Roxio Easy Media Creator suite, Toast, and iPod-friendly video program Popcorn released to strong sales.

In September 2005 the firm appointed Dave Habiger, who had begun serving as president several months earlier, to the position of CEO. Cofounder Bob Doris would take the title of non-executive chairman of the board.

In the spring of 2006 the new CineVision encoding workstation and Scenarist 4 were released. The latter was an authoring program for high-definition DVDs, which were expected to come to market during the year. An alliance of interested parties including Sony, Samsung, and Pioneer was formed to advise the firm on further developments to the software, which could handle both the Blu-Ray and HD-DVD formats that had been proposed. Avid Technology also signed an agreement to use Sonic HD software in its Avid DVD product, while a consumer-grade Roxio HD authoring product began shipping with Blu-Ray recorders from Pioneer, Sony, and Fujitsu. In other business areas, the firm was working with digital photography company Lucidiom to supply it with photo-DVD burning software for photo kiosks, and Sonic Solutions' advanced technology group was developing products for the medical imaging and automotive entertainment sectors.

In June 2006 the company launched Roxio Labs Web, which allowed users to try new software applications from Sonic Solutions or outside vendors and offer suggestions for improvements. For the fiscal year ended in March, the company reported record sales of $148.7 million and net income of $19.3 million.

In 20 years Sonic Solutions, Inc., had established itself as the leading producer of software for digital audio and video creators. With the technology constantly evolving, and new formats such as Blu-Ray and HD-DVD periodically entering the marketplace, continued growth appeared certain.

Frank Uhle

PRINCIPAL SUBSIDIARIES

InterActual Technologies, Inc.; Sonic IP, Inc.; Sonic Solutions International, Inc.; MGI Software Corp. (Canada); Live Picture S.A.R.L. (France); OLI V R Corporation Ltd. (Israel); Sonic Solutions Japan, KK; Sonic Software (Shanghai) Co., Ltd. (China); Roxio UK, Ltd.

PRINCIPAL COMPETITORS

Adobe Systems, Inc.; Apple Computer, Inc.; ArcSoft, Inc.; Avid Technology, Inc.; BHA Corp.; CyberLink Corp.; InterVideo Inc.; MedioStream, Inc.; Nero AG; NewTech Infosystems, Inc.

FURTHER READING

"Clay Leighton Interview," *Wall Street Transcript*, January 24, 2005.

Fisher, Lawrence M., "Removing the Static from Old Recordings," *New York Times*, December 21, 1988.

Gillen, Marilyn A., "Pact with Sony Is Sonic's Solution for Workstation," *Billboard*, October 23, 1993, p. 52.

Nathans, Stephen F., "Sonic Acquires Roxio Software," *Emedia*, October 1, 2004, p. 7.

Rama, Michelle, "Sonic Solutions Shares Rise After America Online Pact," *Dow Jones Business News*, February 26, 2003.

Seavy, Mark, "Sonic Solutions Readying Software for DVD Download Services," *Warren's Consumer Electronics Daily*, August 18, 2005.

———, "Sonic Solutions to Integrate Roxio Brand by Fall," *Warren's Consumer Electronics Daily*, January 5, 2005.

"Sonic Solutions," *Going Public—The IPO Reporter*, January 3, 1994.

"Sonic Solutions Shares Gain amid Cost-Cutting, New-Product Optimism," *Dow Jones Online News*, February 19, 1998.

"Sonic's New DVD Producer," *One to One*, October 1, 1997, p. 5.

"Sony and Sonic to Collaborate on DSD," *PSN Europe*, October 1, 1996, p. 15.

Verna, Paul, "Warner, Sonic Solutions Get Early Start on DVD Audio," *Billboard*, September 5, 1998, p. 87.

Sunrise Senior Living, Inc.

7902 Westpark Drive
McLean, Virginia 97501
U.S.A.
Telephone: (703) 273-7500
Toll Free: (888) 434-4648
Fax: (703) 744-1601
Web site: http://www.sunriseseniorliving.com

Public Company
Incorporated: 1994
Employees: 40,288
Operating Revenues: $1.8 billion (2005)
Stock Exchanges: New York
Ticker Symbol: SRZ
NAIC: 623311 Continuing Care Retirement Communities; 623213 Homes for the Elderly; 623990 Other Residential Care Facilities; 624110 Child and Youth Services; 624120 Services for the Elderly and Persons with Disabilities

■ ■ ■

Sunrise Senior Living, Inc., operates more than 420 assisted living communities with a resident capacity of more than 52,000 throughout the United States, Canada, Germany, and the United Kingdom. It has an interest in about half of these facilities and manages the other half for third parties. The company's communities offer a range of services, including at-home assisted living, independent living, community assisted living, Alzheimer's care, and nursing and rehabilitative care. Communities, which are built to resemble Victorian mansions, operate under the Sunrise, Brighton Gardens, or The Fountains banners.

1981–1993: SUNRISE'S FORMATIVE YEARS

In 1981, Paul and Terry Klaassen sold their home, borrowed money from friends, and bought and moved into an old nursing home in Fairfax, Virginia. Their goal was to create an "assisted living facility," an alternative to the conventional nursing home that provided care and services in a warm, homelike setting. "Assisted living," a term the Klaassens are credited with coining, is a concept of care based on the principles of preserving dignity, encouraging independence and freedom of choice, protecting privacy, personalizing services, nurturing the spirit, and involving family and friends.

This concept was formed as a result of the couple's prior personal experiences with family members needing long-term care. Terry, as a teenager, had provided in-home care for her terminally ill mother after her family eliminated its only alternative: long-term care in an impersonal, institutional setting. Paul's grandmothers both lived in senior residential homes, called *verzorginstehuizen,* in his native Holland.

The Klaassens' original facility opened in Oakton, Virginia, with the Klaassens in residence from 1981 to 1982. They cared for their first 25 residents personally, including bathing and cooking for them. They were in their late 20s at the time. That first year set the basis for the company's corporate culture. "We learned a lot about the services that assisted living needs to provide and how important the family [is] in the whole process,"

Paul explained in a 2003 *Multifamily Executive* article.

As their business grew to include more facilities and more employees, the Klaassens placed an emphasis on incorporating elements from the Dutch senior care system and their own experience, striving to make resident satisfaction the center of all efforts. "Terry and I visit all of our communities and make sure the values we started with are institutionalized deep into the company and that as we grow, we don't lose them," Paul Klaassen confided in the 2003 *Multifamily Executive* article.

In 1985, Sunrise Assisted Living opened two new Sunrise communities—Sunrise of Leesburg and Sunrise of Warrenton, both in Virginia—and the Klaassens debuted the first Sunrise training program for its employees to ensure that they understood and practiced the hallmarks of assisted living. The program later developed into Sunrise University, which provided team members with a career track within the organization and an active, organization-wide mentoring program.

In 1988, the first Sunrise prototype home opened in Arlington, Virginia. The building was designed in consultation with a professor of architecture and gerontology at the University of Southern California, and modeled after a Victorian mansion; it won the company's first of many awards for architecture and interior design. This and later Sunrise homes were a dramatic departure from the typical nursing facility in every aspect; instead of fluorescent lights, long corridors, or institutional designs, there were porches, lots of common areas, cut flowers and tablecloths, a concierge, and service to rival a hotel's. Drawing on northern European models, the Sunrise prototype incorporated the symbolic design elements of a grand staircase as "a metaphor for a mansion," Paul Klaassen explained in a 1996 *Washingtonian* article. "You couldn't walk into a mansion without seeing a beautiful staircase. Many of our

residents are proud that they're able to take the stairs, that they have the opportunity to choose between the stairs and the elevator."

1994–2005: REDEFINING SUNRISE AS AN INTERNATIONAL, PUBLICLY OWNED MANAGEMENT COMPANY

In 1994, Sunrise incorporated with 30 successful senior communities. As more families embraced the concept of assisted living, it broadened its model of care to create environments with special features for seniors with special needs. Reminiscence Neighborhoods, built around Sunrise's Reminiscence Program for the memory impaired, debuted in 1995. Sunrise's Bradford Concept incorporated assistive devices and design elements to maximize mobility and independence for seniors with low vision.

Sunrise earned $34 million in revenues in 1994 and faced a major decision about the company's future course. The executive staff wanted to expand further and needed capital, $10 million for each new facility, to do so. In June 1996, the company followed in the steps of other assisted-living providers, and made its initial public offering on the NASDAQ. Its revenues for that year were $47 million.

Revenues continued to rise steadily throughout the second half of the 1990s, paralleling Sunrise's growth in homes. In 1997, the company brought in $89 million. In 1998, that number increased to $170 million. The following year, Sunrise's sales were at $255 million. As the company grew, the Sunrise management team followed a strict, yet simple formula: Develop in areas with a high number of 45- to 64-year-old adult children; avoid Texas and Florida where this demographic was low; and plan construction three to four years in advance to avoid "not-in-my-backyard" (NIMBY) issues. "It only takes one or two neighbors to oppose something," Klaassen explained in 2003 *Multifamily Executive* article. "NIMBYism, when combined with a willingness to spend legal dollars, can stall a project," which often required rezoning for a multifamily residence.

The company opened its first residence in the United Kingdom outside of London in 1999. It also began to sell off properties selectively that year, deciding that it was more profitable to partner with others and to manage their facilities for them. Although Sunrise's stock stumbled by 40 percent in response to the sale of its first facility, the move was timely. The mid- to late 1990s had seen an industry-wide surge in the construction of senior housing, as providers rushed in to fill a perceived need. Development, however, over-anticipated demand

KEY DATES

1981: The Klaassens open their first facility in Oakton, Virginia.

1988: Sunrise builds its first signature community in Arlington, Virginia.

1996: The company holds its initial public offering on NASDAQ.

1999: Sunrise builds its first community in the United Kingdom.

2000: Thomas B. Newell becomes president of Sunrise; the company opens its first community in Canada.

2001: Sunrise stock moves to the New York Stock Exchange.

2003: Sunrise acquires Marriott Senior Living Services; the company changes its name to Sunrise Senior Living.

2005: Sunrise builds its first community in Germany.

since the bulk of the baby boomers were not due to turn 60 until the years 2015 to 2020. It thus peaked in 1999, then dropped dramatically in 2000 and continued to drop. By the new century, there was a surplus of senior housing units and the years 2000 to 2002 represented a difficult stretch for the assisted living industry.

By contrast, while other assisted living providers floundered during the industry slump, Sunrise continued to grow. In 2000, Thomas Newell assumed the role of president of Sunrise, and the company introduced at-home assisted living. This new care alternative served seniors still capable of living on their own but needing some assistance with the activities of daily living. (The company had first introduced a home-care practice in 1985, but dissolved it in 1988 to focus all of its attention on assisted living.) Also in 2000, a year in which Sunrise earned $345 million in revenues, the company opened its first facility in Canada.

From 1995 through 2002, Sunrise opened 25 new communities a year. In the year 2001, with close to 200 communities and $428 million in revenues, it was named a "Great Place to Work" by *Washington Magazine. Forbes* magazine named it 141st of the 200 Best Small Companies in 2002.

Sunrise was prepared for its next big move, which it took in 2003. It acquired Marriott Senior Living Services, adding more than 120 communities to its total

to reach 400 communities that housed more than 30,000 residents. The Marriott properties added more independent living and skilled nursing services to Sunrise's portfolio. Also in 2003, it acquired EdenCare, further broadening its care options. The company changed its name in 2003 to Sunrise Senior Living Inc. in order to reflect the full range of its short- and long-term elder care services.

With the addition of Marriott, revenues for the year jumped to close to $1.2 billion from $506 million in 2002, and Sunrise became the largest operator in the senior living market with a mere 2.4 percent of the entire senior housing market. The acquisition also marked another big step for the company, part of the shift it had begun in 1998 from owning and managing facilities to just managing them. Although there were signs of stabilization in the assisted living industry beginning in 2003, Sunrise began selling the majority ownership interest in all its properties. From here on out, all new developments were with partners that owned the majority of the real estate for its communities.

In 2005, Sunrise furthered its identity as a management services company when it signed a deal with The Fountains Continuum of Care Inc. to add 19 properties to its management portfolio; it obtained a minority interest in 18 of them. It also opened its first facility in Germany in the suburbs of Hamburg, and began plans to increase its U.K. presence from six to nine facilities. Back home, it joined with MetLife to develop ten assisted living communities in the Southeast, Southwest, and Midwest. Greystone Communities, a wholly owned subsidiary that Sunrise acquired in 2005, developed an additional three communities to be managed for not-for-profit third parties.

2006: CONTINUING DIVERSIFICATION AND EXPANSION

Development continued in 2006, bringing the total number of Sunrise communities in the United States, Canada, Germany, and the United Kingdom to 423. During the first quarter alone, Sunrise opened four new communities in the United States, three in the United Kingdom, and one in Germany and assumed management of an additional three.

Also in 2006, Sunrise developed its first senior condominium project, allowing for equity ownership within a service-enriched environment that included large community areas, dining options, and a health spa with indoor pool, exercise room, and massage and treatment room.

The company also introduced a new publication, *Sunrise* magazine, in 2006, targeting women between the ages of 45 and 64, the vast majority of caregivers, who were likely to be balancing family, work, and the needs of aging parents. In addition to articles on inspirational topics, health, nutrition, and happy homes, the magazine offered expert advice on relationships, legal planning, and long-term finances.

Occupancy rates for senior housing of all sorts were on the rise by the mid-2000s. Community care residences averaged close to 94 percent occupancy in late 2005 as compared with 88.5 percent in 2002, while independent living facilities went from 87.5 percent occupancy to 90.5 percent. Assisted living facilities increased to 90.3 percent occupancy from 85.5 percent in 2001, and skilled nursing jumped to 89.7 percent from 83.5 percent in 2001. Investors were once again looking for a return in senior housing options and the cost of occupancy was on the rise.

Sunrise, the assisted living industry's largest player, continued to look for more expansion and diversification options in 2005 and 2006. According to Klaassen, in a 2005 *Nursing Homes* article, "You need to think what the next [trend] is going to be, how to make … existing products just five percent better every year." While it was difficult to say where diversification would take assisted living communities in the future, in the years leading up to the sunset of the baby boomers, the industry and Sunrise were guaranteed to grow.

Carrie Rothburd

PRINCIPAL SUBSIDIARIES

Karrington Operating Company, Inc.; LandCal Investments SL, Inc.; Legacy Healthcare Management, LLC; Martha Child Interiors, Inc.; Sunrise Development, Inc.

PRINCIPAL COMPETITORS

Beverly Enterprises, Inc.; Manor Care, Inc.; Mariner; Emeritus; Extendicare Health Services, Inc.; NeighborCare, Inc.; Sun Healthcare Group Inc.

FURTHER READING

Bilyeu, Susan, "Your Place or Theirs?: Facility-Based Providers Are Bringing the Nursing Home," *Contemporary Long Term Care,* March 2002, p. 18.

Brady, Angela, and Anya Martin, "Assisted Living Providers Look to Diversification for New Revenue Streams," *Nursing Homes,* January 2005, p. 52.

Guyton, Kate, "Just Like Home: Designers Use Touches Like Bistros, Grand Staircases, and Vegetable Gardens to Make Assisted-Living Facilities Feel Like Home," *Washingtonian,* October 1996, p. 163.

Shaver, Les, "Managed Care: Sunrise's Growth Spurt Leads to Changes—Including a Move Away from Ownership," *Multifamily Executive,* May 15, 2003.

Thomas Crosbie Holdings Limited

97 South Mall
Cork,
Ireland
Telephone: (353) (0) 21 427 2214
Fax: (343) (0) 21 427 4234
Web site: http://www.tch.ie

Private Company
Incorporated: 1841
Employees: 700
Sales: EUR 84.25 million (2004)
NAIC: 51111 Newspaper Publishers; 515112 Radio Stations; 51611 Internet Publishing and Broadcasting

■ ■ ■

Thomas Crosbie Holdings Limited (TCH) is one of Ireland's leading newspaper groups. Based in Cork, it publishes a number of regional and national titles. TCH also has investments in radio and Internet ventures. The group's flagship, the *Irish Examiner,* claims the title of Ireland's oldest daily newspaper; it was launched in 1841 as the *Cork Examiner.* The Crosbie family, which owns TCH, first became involved with the *Examiner* a year after it was formed. Thomas Crosbie and generations of his descendants have served as editor of the *Examiner* as well as head of the holding company. The family ultimately placed day-to-day management of the business in the hands of outsiders, however.

BEGINNINGS IN CORK: 1841

The story of the *Irish Examiner* and the rest of the Thomas Crosbie empire begins in the 19th century, when John Francis Maguire began publishing a thrice-weekly evening newspaper called the *Cork Examiner.* The first issue was dated August 30, 1841. It became a morning paper, printed six days a week, in 1858.

At the time of the *Examiner*'s launch, local news was said to be dominated by the *Cork Constitution,* which catered to Anglo-Irish landowners. The new paper set out to be the voice of the common people. Maguire later represented local districts in the House of Commons.

While the *Examiner* was initially focused on the local community, its location near one of the first ports of call for transatlantic ships gave it an advantage over European papers in gaining eagerly sought news from abroad. After the arrival of the telegraph, the *Examiner* set up a branch in London.

The paper's location gave it a unique perspective on one major historical event. An *Examiner* photographer, Tom Barker, was the last to take pictures on the deck of the *Titanic* before its final voyage in 1912.

Thomas Crosbie became the paper's owner after the death of John F. Maguire in 1872. He had started working for the *Examiner* in 1842 at the age of 15 and had progressed up the ranks to editor.

Thomas Crosbie died in 1899, leaving business to his son George. By this time, the firm was known as Thomas Crosbie and Co. Limited. Like his father, George Crosbie was also involved in public office, serving as a Fine Gael senator in the 1930s.

COMPANY PERSPECTIVES

Characterised by innovation, creativity and exceptional service levels, TCH offers advertisers unique communication solutions across our growing portfolio of media brands. Recognising the dynamic nature of the media landscape we are absolutely committed to developing our own brands as well as those brands which we serve. While recognising fully that each of our media brands is unique in terms of the audience they serve we believe strongly that there are greater synergies to be explored to the benefit of our clients. Put simply, through ensuring that we have a detailed understanding of our clients brand, marketing and communication strategies we can, when appropriate, bring these synergies to bear in a very positive way.

By the mid-1990s, Thomas Crosbie Holdings Limited (TCH) had grown larger than Ireland's other family-owned provincial newspapers. In 1994, TCH's Examiner Publications unit had revenues of IEP 20 million. The holding company also had interests in property, forestry, and other investments. A buying spree to follow would cement its role as the largest media group based outside Dublin.

LAUNCH OF BUYING SPREE: 1995

The company had a new low-cost union agreement that helped keep the group afloat during a few perilous years for the industry, while allowing margins sufficient to finance a major acquisitions spree. Before the mid-1990s, TCH's publishing empire was limited to the *Cork Examiner, Evening Echo,* and the *Waterford News & Star.* The group would acquire 17 new provincial titles from 1995 to 2005. These publications had typically been run by the same family for generations.

Western People, a weekly newspaper in County Mayo, was acquired in 1995. It had been in the hands of the Devere family for roughly 90 years. The group had a circulation of 24,000 and, with its contract printing business, annual revenues of IEP 2 million. The business also had some radio holdings. A year later, the new subsidiary acquired the *Sligo Weekender,* a small, free paper.

The *Cork Examiner* was renamed simply the *Examiner* in 1996. TCH was by this time handling the printing for England's *London Times* in Ireland. During the year, TCH acquired 15 percent of a new youth-oriented FM station, Radio Ireland, with the aim of cross-selling print and radio ads. The company was also part of a group applying for a London radio license. However, it pulled out of the Radio Ireland group within a few months.

In the late 1990s, regional newspapers were reaping record margins. This fueled continued acquisition activity not just from TCH but from its rivals in Ireland and the United Kingdom. Kingdom Newspapers Ltd. and Kingdom Publications Ltd., publishers of Kerry's *Kingdom* newspaper, were bought by TCH in 1999.

Around this time, Anthony Dinan became TCH's managing director. He had joined the company in 1980; his family had been involved with the firm for four generations, noted *Business & Finance.* Dinan was acquiring minority holdings in the provincial papers TCH was buying. These stakes were all sold to TCH in 2005, reported the *Irish Times.*

NEW NAME IN 2000

Revenues were £37.8 million (EUR 48 million) in 2000, producing pre-tax income of a little less than £5 million (EUR 6.4 million). The *Examiner* was renamed the *Irish Examiner* in 2000. It had a reported circulation of about 55,000 to 60,000. Two weekly papers, the *Down Democrat* and its sister publication the *Newry Democrat,* were bought for £500,000 in 2000. This was TCH's first deal in Northern Ireland.

The next year, 2001, TCH acquired the aptly named Provincial Newspapers, which published the *Nationalist & Leinster Times,* the *Kildare Nationalist,* and the *Laois Nationalist.* Also during the year, Alan Crosbie traded his position at Examiner Publications for the chairmanship of the holding company TCH. He had drawn on his experience to write a book about passing down a family business through the generations.

TCH was an investor in RedFM, a Cork area radio station launched in January 2002 for a younger audience. It also had shares in North West Radio and MidWest Radio.

TCH acquired the *Sunday Business Post* from Trinity Mirror in April 2002. The price for the Dublin-based paper was EUR 10 million. The *Business Post* was TCH's 12th publication. It had been launched in 1989 and acquired by Times Mirror in 1997.

In 2003, TCH acquired the *Irish Post* from Jefferson Smurfit for £1.7 million (EUR 2.5 million). The company's first acquisition in Britain, the *Post* was a publication for Irish expatriates and had a circulation of about 31,000. It was established in 1970.

The early decades of the new millennium were dif-

KEY DATES

1841: The *Cork Examiner* is launched.
1872: Editor Thomas Crosbie becomes the *Examiner*'s owner after the death of founder John F. Maguire.
1892: Crosbie launches the *Evening Echo*.
1896: Crosbie launches the *Weekly Examiner*.
1899: Thomas Crosbie dies, leaving business to his son George.
1976: Linotype presses are replaced with offset lithography, allowing color printing.
1995: Thomas Crosbie Holdings, or TCH, acquires controlling interest in *Western People* group of County Mayo.
1996: The *Cork Examiner* is renamed the *Examiner*; *Sligo Weekender* is acquired.
1999: Recruit Ireland web site debuts; *Kerry's Kingdom* is acquired.
2000: The *Examiner* is renamed the *Irish Examiner*; *Down Democrat* and *Newry Democrat* are acquired.
2002: TCH acquires *Sunday Business Post*.
2003: TCH acquires the *Irish Post* in Great Britain.
2004: TCH acquires *Rosecommon Herald*.
2005: Headquarters are relocated from Cork's downtown to docklands.
2006: TCH acquires Wexford's *Echo*; printing operations are outsourced to new plant.

ficult financially. However, after losing EUR 857,594 in 2002, the group posted pre-tax income of EUR 6.2 million in 2003 on revenues of EUR 76 million, up EUR 10 million from the previous year. In 2004, sales reached EUR 84 million as pre-tax profit rose nearly 50 percent to EUR 10 million. Most of this increase was from the sale of the *Cork Examiner*'s headquarters building.

BIG CHANGES IN 2004

In 2004, TCH announced it was closing down its own printing operations after 153 years. A new company, Webprint Concepts Ltd., was being created to print TCH's papers at a new plant in nearby Mahon. It was also farming out ad sales on its web sites, which included topic-specific portals such as motornet.ie and pages associated with its newspapers.

In March 2004, TCH acquired the *Rosecommon Herald*, a Boyle paper dating back to 1859. It had previ-

ously been owned by the Nerney family. The *Herald* had estimated sales of EUR 2 million a year.

After more than a decade of consolidation among provincial newspapers in Ireland, TCH bought the last remaining independent in 2006 when it acquired the Echo Newspaper Group. This included the *Wexford Echo* and papers in Enniscorthy, New Ross, and Gorey with a combined circulation of more than 22,000.

It had been founded in 1902 and had previously been owned by Eamonn and Norman Buttle. The Echo Group acquisition lifted TCH's total circulation to nearly 80,000.

Another major change was the sale of TCH's offices in downtown Cork, its home for about 165 years, to a real estate developer. About 280 employees were being relocated from Academy Street to Cork's docklands in 2006. TCH was a partner in Cork 2005: European Capital of Culture. The company helped its hometown celebrate via some of its publications and online ventures.

Frederick C. Ingram

PRINCIPAL SUBSIDIARIES

Examiner Publications (Cork) Ltd.; Mid West Radio (15%); Red FM (36%); TCH Recruit Ireland Limited.

PRINCIPAL OPERATING UNITS

Irish Examiner; Sunday Business Post; Evening Echo; Western People; Kildare Nationalist; Laois Nationalist; Waterford News & Star; The Kingdom; Sligo Weekender; Newry Democrat; Down Democrat; Irish Post; Roscommon Herald; The Echo; The Gorey Echo; Wexford Echo; New Ross Echo; RecruitIreland.com; Motornet.ie; TCM.

PRINCIPAL COMPETITORS

Alpha Newspapers; Associated Newspapers Ltd.; Celtic Media Group Limited; Independent News & Media Plc.

FURTHER READING

"Alan Crosbie Appointed to Family Business Centre," *Irish Examiner*, June 20, 2006.

Brennan, Ciaran, "Thomas Crosbie Holdings Buys Sunday Business Post," *Irish Times*, April 24, 2002, p. 17.

"Business Squalls Ahead As Captain Alan Quits Examiner Bridge," *Irish Independent*, February 10, 2001.

Creaton, Siobhan, "Crosbie Holdings Takes Over Sligo Free Newspaper," *Irish Times*, September 28, 1996, p. 14.

Crosbie, Alan, *Don't Leave It to the Children: Starting, Building and Sustaining a Family Business,* Cork: Marino Books, 2002.

"Examiner Group Buys Wexford's Echo," *Business World,* February 9, 2006.

"'Examiner' Owner Initiates High Court Case," *Irish Times,* June 4, 1999, p. 51.

Flood, Linda, "Evening Echo Moves to Exploit an 'Unlimited' Growth Potential," *Sunday Business Post,* October 28, 2001.

Foley, Michael, "London Radio Licence Sought," *Irish Times,* June 13, 1996, p. 8.

———, "Newspaper to Benefit from Radio Connection," *Irish Times,* February 10, 1996, p. 16.

"'Irish Examiner' Moving to New Location in Cork," *Irish Times,* November 19, 2004, p. 6.

"Journalist's Libel Action Against Irish Newspaper Fails," *Times* (London), March 11, 1933.

"Journalist's Libel Action Against Irish Newspapers," *Times* (London), March 10, 1933.

Keane, Conor, "Mahon Print Plant Gears-Up for Production," *Irish Examiner,* January 10, 2006.

McCaughren, Samantha, "Local Newspaper Group Sold for 20m," *Europe Intelligence Wire,* February 9, 2006.

McGrath, Brendan, "Regional Newspapers Now Takeover Targets," *Irish Times,* June 24, 2000, p. 19.

McGurk, Helen, "Purchase Is Boost for Weekly Papers," *Belfast News Letter,* November 4, 2000, p. 15.

O'Driscoll, Des, ed., *Irish Examiner: 100 Years of News,* Dublin: Gill & Macmillan, 2005.

O'Halloran, Barry, "Some Industry Observers Are Already Speculating About How Thomas Crosbie Holdings...," *Business and Finance,* May 2, 2002, p. 14.

O'Kane, Paul, "Press the Point: Thomas Crosbie Holdings Has Turned into a Major Player in the Irish Media with Its Purchase Last Week of the 'Sunday Business Post,'" *Sunday Tribune* (Ireland), April 28, 2002, p. 4.

———, "Thomas Crosbie Takes Major Interest in the Western People," *Irish Times,* September 2, 1995, p. 23.

O'Keefe, Barry, "Examiner Leaves Radio Ireland," *Irish Times,* January 10, 1997.

O'Kelly-Brown, John, "Examiner Boss Gives Up Helm," *Irish Times,* February 16, 2001, p. 65.

O'Mahoney, Catherine, "TCH Sees 20 Potential Targets in Regional Papers," *Sunday Business Post,* March 28, 2004.

Oliver, Emmet, "Examiner and TV3 to Seek Dublin Radio License," *Irish Times,* September 8, 2003, p. 16.

———, "'Irish Examiner' Publisher Buys 'Irish Post' in UK for £1.7m," *Irish Times,* April 12, 2003, p. 17.

———, "'Rosecommon Herald' Bought Out by TCH Group," *Irish Times,* March 24, 2004, p. 19.

———, "TCH Managing Director Sells Shareholding to Subsidiaries," *Irish Times,* September 27, 2005, p. 22.

———, "Thomas Crosbie Group Printing to Be Outsourced," *Irish Times,* June 1, 2004, p. 19.

———, "Thomas Crosbie to Outsource Its Web Ad Space," *Irish Times,* June 15, 2004, p. 15.

"Profits Slip at Publisher of Examiner," *Irish Independent,* December 18, 2003.

"Recruitment Website Is to Keep Employers in Touch," *Sunday Business Post,* October 24, 1999.

Riegel, Ralph, "Crosbie-Family Dosh for Dinan," *Sunday Independent,* October 2, 2005.

———, "Empires Do Not Come Cheap, As the Crosbies Are Finding Out," *Sunday Independent,* March 28, 2004.

———, "'Examiner' Sheds 80 Jobs As Printing Operation Is Outsourced," *Irish Independent,* June 1, 2004.

"Takeover Fever," *Business & Finance Magazine,* February 23, 2006.

"Thomas Crosbie Holdings Announces Official Partnership with Cork 2005," *Irish Examiner,* November 5, 2004.

Wall, Vincent, "Examiner's Dublin HQ to Generate EUR 2m Windfall for TCH," *Business and Finance,* August 15, 2002, p. 5.

———, "Looking at the Post," *Business and Finance,* August 15, 2002, p. 18.

"Webprint and TCH Sign Printing Deal," *Irish Examiner,* July 5, 2005.

TomTom N.V.

Rembrandtplein 35
Amsterdam, 1017 CT
Netherlands
Telephone: (+31) (20) 850 0800
Fax: (+31) (20) 850 1099
Web site: http://www.tomtom.com

Public Company
Incorporated: 1991 as Palmtop Software
Employees: 435
Sales: EUR 720.03 million (2005)
Stock Exchanges: Euronext Amsterdam
Ticker Symbol: TOM2
NAIC: 334111 Electronic Computer Manufacturing; 334511 Search, Detection, Navigation, Guidance, Aeronautical, and Nautical System and Instrument Manufacturing; 511210 Software Publishers

■ ■ ■

TomTom N.V. is Europe's leading producer of integrated personal navigation equipment. It is also a developer of software for handheld computers and smart phones. TomTom started out making software for PDAs before progressing to navigation-related applications. Phenomenal success followed the introduction of TomTom's self-contained, easy-to-use personal navigation devices. After years of triple-digit growth, the company was expecting to ship nearly four million integrated devices a year in 2006. However, competition was intensifying with the entry of giant consumer electronic firms into the market. Based in Amsterdam, TomTom has been strongest in Europe; it maintains offices in Germany, the United Kingdom, the United States (Massachusetts), and Taiwan.

PALMTOP ORIGINS

TomTom N.V. was formed in 1991 as Palmtop Software. Its founders were Peter-Frans Pauwels and Pieter Geelen, fresh graduates of Amsterdam University. As the name suggests, the company began by making software for handheld computers. It was most closely associated with the Psion brand, and developed most of the leading programs for the Psion Series 3. One of Psion Plc's executives, Corrine Vigreux, became Palmtop's third partner in 1994. She was credited with helping to bring Palmtop's software to the global market.

Because they were awkward to use and not very powerful, early generations of handheld computers failed to find a wide audience. The 1996 introduction of Palm, Inc.'s cleverly designed Palm Pilot made them not only popular, but ubiquitous, at least among ambitious young businesspeople. Palmtop Software turned its attentions to the new generation of PDAs (personal digital assistants), including those made with Microsoft's operating system. Palmtop began releasing programs under its own brand in mid-1997.

NAVIGATING THE NEW MILLENNIUM

TomTom launched a mobile listing service in February 2000. Installed on WAP-enabled smart phones and PDAs, it downloaded local maps via the Internet. It was capable of planning the best routes whether the user was driving or walking. Information on points of interest (POIs) such as nearby restaurants was readily available, as was relevant traffic data. Mobile phone manufacturer Telefonaktiebolaget LM Ericsson was an early partner in the TomTom service, while the famous Michelin Red Guide was soon tapped for POI information.

Harold Goddijn, formerly managing director of Psion Computers, became Palmtop's leader and acquired a 25 percent shareholding in 2001. Sales for 2002 were up to nearly EUR 8 million, and the company was profitable, with net income of EUR 1.4 million. There were only about 40 employees at the time.

TomTom Navigator software had made its debut in September 2002. This application allowed Pocket PCs to be used as in-car navigation systems; a GPS receiver and compressed digital maps were supplied with the program. An updated version, TomTom Navigator 2, came out within a few months. TomTom posted sales of EUR 39 million and net profits of EUR 6 million for 2003.

INTRODUCTION OF GO: 2004

TomTom unveiled a portable, self-contained auto navigation unit called GO in the spring of 2004. The simplicity of the GO product found enormous popular acceptance in the market. While many car navigation units required auto manufacturer or dealer installation, GO was shipped ready for use out of the box. Its appeal extended beyond PDA users and tech-minded gadget junkies. The GO launch was followed a few months later by the debut of MOBILE software, which converted the new generation of smart phones into auto navigation units.

Profits and sales both quadrupled in 2004. TomTom had net income of EUR 28 million ($40 million) on revenues of EUR 192 million ($263 million). GO accounted for about 70 percent of sales. The company claimed almost one million customers in 16 countries. Most of its business was in Europe, but it was also quickly building a presence in the United States, with the GO products being carried by CompUSA and major online web sites such as Amazon.com. Circuit City stores were added in 2005. Still, the United States then accounted for just 3 percent of TomTom's total sales.

GO was TomTom's first step into manufacturing consumer electronics devices, as opposed to just software. The company managed the transition by outsourcing non-core functions.

PUBLIC IN 2005

The fast-growing company capitalized on its momentum by completing an initial public offering (IPO) on the Amsterdam Stock Exchange in May 2005. The offering, Amsterdam's largest in five years, raised about EUR 469 million ($587 million). According to *The Deal.com,* TomTom had not previously tapped any venture capital funding. The company was valued at nearly EUR 2 billion after the IPO. The four partners who had owned the company before the IPO continued to hold a majority of shares. (Before going public, the company had been known for a time as Versalis Group BV, but was renamed TomTom Group BV in May 2005. This was merged into TomTom Nederland BV, which was then converted into TomTom NV.)

While TomTom was growing phenomenally, the consumer electronics business it entered was fickle and extremely competitive, warned analysts. Price competition from new rivals was already putting pressure on the company's operating margins. In addition, more new cars were being shipped with GPS units already installed.

TomTom managed to crack into the OEM market. It signed deals to supply navigation units to Opel, Toyota, Lancia, Citroen, Chevrolet, Smart, and Nissan. These for the most part were not factory installed systems, though special products were developed for Toyota and Opel.

TomTom was already lowering its prices to cater to a wider market. A top-of-the-line, full-featured GO navigator could cost almost EUR 900 ($1,070), but the company's budget-oriented ONE series, brought out in October 2005, was priced at just EUR 400 ($475). The ONE would be supplied with a line of economy cars produced by Spanish automaker SEAT, as well as the Spanish version of Ford Motor Co.'s Fiesta. TomTom had also developed a product for motorcycles and scooters called RIDER.

KEY DATES

1991: Palmtop Software is formed to develop software for PDAs.
2000: TomTom navigation software is introduced.
2002: TomTom Navigator software for Pocket PCs is introduced.
2004: GO and MOBILE navigation devices is unveiled.
2005: TomTom goes public; Datafactory AG is acquired.
2006: Scotland's Applied Generics is acquired.

TomTom acquired Datafactory AG in September 2005. Headquartered in Leipzig, Germany, Datafactory produced web-based solutions for tracking vehicle fleets. It had 30 employees and sales of about EUR 5 million ($6 million) a year. Datafactory's logistics-oriented systems were the basis for TomTom's WORK line, introduced in April 2006.

TomTom was developing relationships with mobile phone companies, though this proved more difficult than working with auto manufacturers. The company did sign up to produce the hardware for a new navigator device from MapQuest Inc., a leading mapping software company in the United States.

The company shipped two million units in 2005; by the end of the year it had grown to more than 400 employees. Revenues rose 275 percent to EUR 720 million. Net profit of EUR 143 million was up 411 percent. TomTom was aiming to pass the EUR 1 billion mark in 2006 in spite of supply problems in the second quarter. It was expecting to sell nearly four million navigation devices.

NEW FEATURES, CHALLENGES IN 2006

CEO Harrold Goddijn told AFX News that with up to 30 companies making personal navigation devices, the market was ripe for a shakeout. TomTom was the clear leader in Europe, with a 50 percent or better market share, but in the United States was far behind Garmin Ltd., the well established leader. The business had reportedly already attracted the attention of Dutch consumer giant Royal Philips Electronics NV.

TomTom was facing some legal challenges. Garmin was suing the company for alleged patent infringement. TomTom lost a similar case in the United States to National Products Inc. and was also being sued by San Francisco's Next Innovation LLC.

New products and features were being announced on nearly a monthly basis. A new line of network-based services, called PLUS, was introduced to provide live traffic information and weather news. The ability to locate friends was one of the features TomTom was including in an updated European version of the RIDER product. (A unit of Italy's Piaggio Group SpA began supplying the RIDER with its Norge 1200 GTL model in May 2006.) The GO series was updated with the GO 910, which added a larger screen, more memory, and the ability to read out street names. It could also play mp3 audio files.

Scotland's Applied Generics Ltd. was acquired in early 2006. This added technology for providing real-time road traffic information gained from cell phone networks. Applied Generics had a staff of 18 and annual revenues of about EUR 1 million. TomTom was looking to China and Taiwan as future growth markets. It made navigators that were adaptable to the millions of bicycles there, as well as the increasing number of automobiles.

Frederick C. Ingram

PRINCIPAL SUBSIDIARIES

TomTom International BV; TomTom Sales BV; TomTom Inc. (U.S.A.); TomTom Software Ltd. (U.K.); TomTom Asia Ltd. (Taiwan); Drivetech Inc. (Taiwan); Datafactory AG (Germany); Applied Generics Ltd. (U.K.).

PRINCIPAL COMPETITORS

Garmin Ltd.; Thales Navigation, Inc.

FURTHER READING

"Autonavigatie is geen sciencefiction meer," *De Financieel Economische Tijd,* January 15, 2003, p. 13.

Cordes, Renee, "TomTom Beats IPO Drum," *TheDeal.com,* May 16, 2005.

———, "TomTom Reaps $587M from IPO," *TheDeal.com,* May 31, 2005.

Cuny, Delphine, "Les GPS de TomTom bientôt dans l'indice AEX," *La Tribune* (France), January 31, 2006.

"Dutch TomTom Enters Cooperation with Spanish SEAT," *Dutch News Digest,* January 25, 2006.

"Dutch TomTom Launches New Product," *Dutch News Digest,* October 24, 2005.

"Dutch TomTom Launches New Version of TomTom RIDER," *Dutch News Digest,* May 15, 2006.

"Dutch TomTom Loses 1.2 Bln Euro of Stock Value After Results Publication," *Dutch News Digest,* October 27, 2005.

"Dutch TomTom Not to Be Profitable in USA 2005," *Dutch News Digest,* July 28, 2005.

"Dutch TomTom to Deliver TomTom GO 500 to Nissan France," *Dutch News Digest,* September 12, 2005.

"Dutch TomTom to Sell TomTom GO Product Via U.S. Circuit City," *Dutch News Digest,* May 27, 2005.

"Dutch TomTom to Supply Navigation Tool to Italian Moto Guzzi," *Dutch News Digest,* May 30, 2006.

"Dutch TomTom, U.S. MapQuest Enter Cooperation," *Dutch News Digest,* September 27, 2005.

"Ericsson, Palmtop to Launch Mobile Map Services," *Reuters News,* February 28, 2000.

"Interview: TomTom CEO Says Progress in Mobile Phone Market 'Disappointing'," *AFX International Focus,* May 5, 2006.

Schiffers, Mathijs, "TomTom's Model to Be Tested As Rivals Close In," *Dow Jones International News,* August 18, 2005.

Simons, Stefan, "Dutch TomTom to Offer Around 28 Million Shares in IPO," *Dow Jones International News,* May 13, 2005.

———, "TomTom Loses Lawsuit Against National Products," *Dow Jones International News,* June 22, 2006.

———, "TomTom Needs to Prove It's No One Product Wonder," *Dow Jones International News,* May 24, 2005.

———, "TomTom to Further Drive Down Product Prices," *Dow Jones International News,* May 27, 2005.

Simons, Stefan, and Mathijs Schiffers, "TomTom CEO: To Enter Chinese, Taiwanese Mkts in '06," *Dow Jones International News,* February 14, 2006.

———, "TomTom: Sales of GO Range Constrained During 2Q," *Dow Jones International News,* July 7, 2006.

"TomTom Falls on News of Garmin Patent Lawsuit," *AFX International Focus,* February 10, 2006.

"TomTom Falls on Philips' Move into Personal Navigator Device Sector," *AFX International Focus,* June 20, 2006.

"TomTom Higher in Opening Trade vs 17.50 Eur IPO Price," *AFX International Focus,* May 27, 2005.

"TomTom IPO Price Set at 17.50 Eur/Share, Raising 125 Mln Eur for Company," *AFX International Focus,* May 27, 2005.

"TomTom Raises $740-Million in IPO," *Globe and Mail* (Canada), May 28, 2005, p. B8.

"TomTom to Buy Datafactory AG," *Dow Jones International News,* August 24, 2005.

Tottenham Hotspur PLC

Bill Nicholson Way
748 High Road
Tottenham
London,
United Kingdom
Telephone: +44 020 8365 5000
Fax: +44 020 8365 5005
Web site: http://www.spurs.co.uk

Public Company
Incorporated: 1882
Employees: 239
Sales: £70.6 million ($130.9 million) (2005)
Stock Exchanges: London
Ticker Symbol: TTNM
NAIC: 711211 Sports Teams and Clubs; 448150 Clothing Accessories Stores

■ ■ ■

Tottenham Hotspur PLC is the holding company for the Tottenham Hotspur Football Club. One of the oldest of Britain's Premier League football (soccer) teams, Tottenham Hotspur was also the first club to go public, in 1982. Tottenham routinely ranks among the United Kingdom's top soccer teams, and is one of a handful—alongside Manchester United, Arsenal, and Aston Villa—to enjoy international recognition. Based in northern London, Tottenham Hotspur PLC represents the operations of the football club, as well as its stadium, known as White Hart Lane, and related concessions, including sales of clothing and other memorabilia.

The largest part of the group's turnover, which topped £70 million ($130 million) in 2005, comes from television and other media rights. These represented approximately 36 percent of the group's turnover that year. Gate receipts, including competition cup receipts, added 25 percent to sales; sponsorships, including those of Puma, Thomson, and Carlsberg, added 20 percent to sales; and merchandising generated 7 percent of company turnover. These activities also combined to produce a net operating profit of nearly £13 million, which was supplemented by player trading profits of £5.6 million. That figure was generated in large part through the sale of just four players. Listed on the London Stock Exchange, Tottenham Hotspur PLC is controlled by investment group ENIC, which owns nearly 30 percent of the company, and which also controls sports teams such as Vicenza Calcio, Slavia Prague, AEK Athens, the Glasgow Rangers, and FC Basel. ENIC is in turn controlled by Daniel Levy and backed by Bahamian billionaire Joe Lewis. Levy is Tottenham Hotspur's chairman.

LONDON FOOTBALL ORIGINATOR IN THE LATE 19TH CENTURY

Like many of England's football (soccer) teams, Tottenham Hotspur originated as an amateur football club established by a group of school friends from the local grammar school in Hotspur. Similarly, the football club was originally associated with a more established cricket club, the Hotspur cricket club, reflecting the larger appeal of cricket over the relatively younger sport of

COMPANY PERSPECTIVES

COMPANY PERSPECTIVES

What is the Company's strategy for growth? To continue to strive for success in domestic and European football. Development of the Company's Principal Fixed Assets, being the Academy and the Stadium. Continue to build the Tottenham Hotspur brand both domestically and internationally.

football at the time. Established in 1882, Hotspur FC played its first games in 1883 on what was then known as the Tottenham marshes. In 1884, in order to distinguish themselves from another team playing at the time, London Hotspur, the club adopted the new name of Tottenham Hotspur FC.

Tottenham Hotspur entered its first competition play in 1885, for the London Association Cup. By 1888, the club had moved to a new field in Northumberland Park. The move also allowed the club to begin charging admission that year. By 1895, Tottenham Hotspur was ready to turn professional, and in 1896 the club joined the Southern League. With attendance topping 6,000 per game, and reaching as high as 14,000, the club incorporated as a limited liability company in 1898. The following year, Tottenham Hotspur moved to a new, and subsequently permanent, location on White Hart Lane. The property, attached to the White Hart pub owned by the Charrington brewery, had formerly served as a plant nursery. As such, the grounds provided fertile soil for the laying down of a football pitch.

The period also proved a successful one for the team itself. After winning the Southern League title in 1900, the club went on to win the FA Cup in 1901, becoming the only nonleague team ever to win that title. These wins helped establish Tottenham Hotspur as a name to be recognized within British football, and also established the club as one of the country's top attendance drawers. The company began expanding its stadium, and in the early years of the 20th century the White Hart Lane stadium boasted a total capacity of some 32,000, including seating for 500, and covering for another 12,000. The company's lease restricted further capacity expansion. In 1905, therefore, the company privately sold a series of shares in the club, raising the funds to buy its leasehold. This allowed the club to expand its capacity to 40,000, and then to 50,000 by 1912. By then, the club had joined the Football League, playing its first league games in the Second Division in 1908.

The following year, however, Tottenham Hotspur was promoted to the First Division. Although the club occasionally lapsed back to the Second Division (for example, in 1915, 1928, and 1977), Tottenham Hotspur FC became one of the leading fixtures of British professional football's First Division. Despite the club's ups and downs through the first half of the century, it also succeeded in developing a highly devoted fan base. By the late 1930s, before play was suspended for the duration of World War II, the club attracted as many as 75,000 spectators per game.

In the postwar period, Tottenham Hotspur began to distinguish itself as much for its style of play, particularly with the development of the so-called "push and run" attack. The tactic helped the club win its first First Division League championship in 1951. Two years later, the club began hosting its first night games after installing floodlights at the White Hart Land stadium. These were later upgraded in 1957, and again in 1961.

PUBLIC OFFERING PIONEER IN 1982

The early 1960s marked a new era of success for the club, with a series of championship victories including the Football League championship and the FA Cup win in 1961, making it the first club to complete the so-called "Double" in the 20th century. Other wins followed, including a new FA Cup victory in 1962, the European Cup in 1963, and the FA Cup again in 1967.

The club's winning record continued into the 1970s, with the Football League Cup win in 1971, the UEFA Cup in 1972, and the Football League Cup again in 1973. By the end of the decade, however, Tottenham Hotspur had stumbled again, and found itself relegated to the Second Division by 1977. Although the club managed to return to the First Division the following year, its financial situation had become increasingly unstable. Part of the group's financial difficulties stemmed from the construction of a new West Stand, which began in 1980 and was completed only in 1982.

The financial uncertainty surrounding the West Stand project attracted the interest of local businessman and longtime fan Irving Scholar. At first, Scholar, who had made a fortune as a real estate developer, offered to lend assistance to the club in order to sort out its financial tangles. Rebuffed by the club's directors, however, Scholar quietly began buying up shares in the team, offering highly attractive prices. Before long, Scholar had succeeded in gaining control of the football club.

Scholar's effort was soon joined to that of Paul Bobroff, also a property developer and loyal Spurs fan, who

KEY DATES

1882: A group of students found the Hotspur football club in association with the Hotspur cricket club.

1895: Tottenham Hotspur, as the club is now called, turns professional.

1898: The team incorporates as a limited liability company and moves to White Hart Lane.

1908: The team joins the Football League Second Division.

1951: The team wins the first First Division title.

1982: Irving Scholar and Paul Bobroff acquire control of the company, take it public the following year, and then lead it on a diversification drive.

1991: On the verge of financial collapse, the team is acquired by Alan Sugar, chairman of Amstrad.

2001: Sugar sells control of the team to Daniel Levy-controlled ENIC.

2003: Levy, backed by Joe Lewis, acquires a majority stake in the company directly.

2006: Tottenham Hotspur unveils a new club crest and brand.

had been amassing his own block of shares. Bobroff initially offered to sell his shares to Scholar; by then, however, Scholar had control of the club and declined the offer. Instead, the pair took over as joint heads of the club in 1982. The following year, Scholar and Bobroff listed Tottenham Hotspur on the London Stock Exchange, and the club became the first sports team in the United Kingdom to convert to public company status.

Scholar became chairman of the football club, while Bobroff became chairman of its publicly listed holding company, Tottenham Hotspur PLC. The decision to accept Bobroff as a partner soon came to haunt Scholar and the Tottenham team. Through the 1980s, Bobroff launched an attempt to diversify the company's operations. At first, Bobroff sought to transform Tottenham Hotspur into a leisure-oriented company. By the end of the decade, however, Bobroff's diversification efforts had led the team into areas such as sportswear sales, a fashion company designing women's clothing, as well as ticketing operations.

In the meantime, Tottenham Hotspur FC appeared to be back on the winning track. In 1982, the team won its seventh FA Cup title, then qualified as one of four British teams competing in 1983's UEFA Cup. The following year, the team carried off the UEFA Cup victory. By 1987, the team competed in its eighth FA Cup final, though the team had to wait until 1991 to claim its eighth victory. In that year also, Tottenham Hotspur clinched the European championship as well.

Yet the company's business end was quickly approaching collapse. The diversification effort had proven to be a total disaster. The company had continued adding operations, including a retail travel agency, Spurs Travel, and, in 1987, two companies, Martex and Stumps, the former of which was an import agent to the latter's distribution of women's apparel and sportswear. The company also began developing restaurant and conference facilities at its stadium complex and, late in 1987, entered boxing promotion with the Bruno-Bugner fight of that year.

At the same time, Scholar and Bobroff had lost the favor of the team's fan base. This was especially exacerbated after the company launched plans to rebuild White Hart Lane's East Stand. The plans in particular included replacing the so-called "Shelf" standing area favored by many of the team's fans with executive boxes. Amid protests from the team's fan base, however, the company was forced to back down. In the end, the Shelf remained, although the standing area was replaced with seating in 1994.

By the beginning of the 1990s, the group's diversified operations became too heavy a burden for the company. At the same time, Scholar experienced his own financial difficulties as the British property market collapsed. In order to raise money, Scholar indicated a possible sale of his stake to media tycoon Robert Maxwell. When news of the talks with Maxwell leaked out, the team's financial situation also was exposed.

REBRANDING IN THE NEW CENTURY

In the end, control of the team was acquired by Amstrad Chairman Alan Sugar. While a Spurs supporter, Sugar made it clear that his interest in the club was in running Tottenham Hotspur PLC, leaving the direction of the team itself to then Managing Director, and former Spurs player, Terry Venables. Sugar worked on reducing the club's £20 million debt and selling off a number of the team's top players, including Paul Gascoigne. That deal, the largest for a football player at the time, raised £5.5 million for the company in 2002. Also that year, Tottenham Hotspur became one of the founding members of the new FA Premier League.

Yet the relationship between Sugar and Venables soon soured, and by 1993 Venables had been dismissed in what became a bitter legal battle. With the team struggling to maintain its place in the FA Premier league, the company became embroiled in a new league investigation accusing it of financial misdealings involving illegal loans made to a number of players in the late 1980s. Then the team's new managing director, Ossie Ardiles, went on a buying binge, buying a number of high-priced players, including Germany's Jurgen Klinsmann. Although Klinsmann became a fan favorite, the high ticket purchases, which continued into 1995 with the record signing of Chris Armstrong for £4.5 million, failed to turn the team's fortunes around.

Meanwhile, the company had continued investing in its White Hart Lane premises, rebuilding the North Stand and adding new hospitality sections to the South Stand. While these operations helped boost the stadium's capacity to more than 36,000, it also helped load the company with debt. Adding to the company's debt burden were several more high-priced player signings, including a £6 million deal for Les Ferdinand and, in 2000, an £11 million deal for Sergei Rebrov. These helped push the company into £70 million in debt, more than its total annual revenues. Meanwhile, as the team's division ranking continued to slide, Sugar became the object of personal attacks from the team's fans.

In 2001, Sugar threw in the towel, selling out his stake in the company to leisure investment group ENIC, led by Daniel Levy and backed by Bahamian billionaire Joe Lewis. In 2003, Levy increased his direct control over the club. By then, Tottenham Hotspur had also raised a £75 million loan to pay down the company's debts and launch a new investment program.

That program, which included plans to develop a hotel complex, was part of an overall team rebranding effort. Into the mid-2000s, the team, backed by new British legislation, moved to take tighter control of its trademark. This effort was linked to the increasing popularity of England's football teams on an international level, as clubs such as Manchester United and Arsenal had launched successful brand marketing campaigns. In 2006, the team's rebranding effort included the unveiling of a new club crest. Tottenham Hotspur also lined up a new series of sponsorships, including the signing of an agreement making Carlsberg the team's official beer in 2004. In 2006, the company

signed a new sponsorship deal, for sports equipment from Puma. Tottenham Hotspur, which had seen its revenues jump to £70 million by then, hoped to score fresh victories as a global brand name in the new century.

M. L. Cohen

PRINCIPAL SUBSIDIARIES

Paxton Road Limited; Stardare Limited; Tottenham Hotspur Finance Company Limited; Tottenham Hotspur Football and Athletic Co. Limited; White Hart Lane Stadium Limited.

PRINCIPAL COMPETITORS

The Football Association Ltd.; Manchester United PLC; Chrysalis Group PLC; Arsenal Football Club PLC; Chelsea Village PLC; Arsenal Holdings PLC; Newcastle United PLC; Liverpool FC; Leeds United AFC Ltd; Celtic PLC; The Rangers Football Club PLC; Burnden Leisure PLC; Aston Villa PLC; Manchester City PLC.

FURTHER READING

Bond, David, "New Dawn at Spurs As Sugar's Era Ends," *Evening Standard,* February 28, 2001, p. 81.

"Carlsberg Seals Tottenham Deal," *Marketing,* August 18, 2004, p. 6.

Hering, Ingrid, "Spurs Stands Its Ground, Unlike Its Rival Arsenal," *Managing Intellectual Property,* March 2003, p. 16.

Hughes, Rob, "Spurs' Reprieve May Be Temporary," *Times,* May 13, 1994, p. 42.

"Levy Becomes Tottenham's Primary Shareholder," *Sports Network,* March 10, 2003.

"Navy Blue Rebrands Spurs As Trademark Law Takes Effect," *Design Week,* September 8, 2005, p. 5.

"Puma Signs Tottenham Hotspur Deal," *just-style.com,* February 13, 2006.

"Spurs Agrees £75m Loan to Pay Off Club Debts," *Leisure Report,* December 2002, p. 8.

"Spurs Transfers Shares to AIM," *Leisure Report,* February 2004, p. 8.

"Tottenham Hotspur," *Investors Chronicle,* April 7, 2006.

Veysey, Wayne, "Levy: Give Me Trophies," *Evening Standard,* October 5, 2005, p. 64.

Universal Technical Institute, Inc.

Universal Technical Institute, Inc.

20410 N. 19th Avenue
Suite 200
Phoenix, Arizona 85027
U.S.A.
Telephone: (623) 445-9500
Toll Free: (800) 859-7249
Fax: (623) 445-9501
Web site: http://www.uticorp.com

Public Company
Incorporated: 1965
Employees: 2,300
Sales: $310.8 million (2005)
Stock Exchanges: New York
Ticker Symbol: UTI
NAIC: 611519 Other Technical and Trade Schools

■ ■ ■

Universal Technical Institute, Inc., operates schools in eight states that train students to be automotive, collision, diesel, motorcycle, and marine repair technicians. The firm also runs more than 20 training centers in partnership with such manufacturers as Porsche, Volvo, Mercedes-Benz, Toyota, Ford, Kawasaki, and Harley-Davidson to service their products, and operates the NASCAR Technical Institute in association with the racing organization. The company trains more than 15,000 students annually.

EARLY YEARS

The origins of Universal Technical Institute (UTI) date to 1965, when Robert I. Sweet founded an auto repair training school in Phoenix, Arizona. The small firm began with a single building and an initial class of 11 students. In 1968 the school's offerings were expanded with an automotive and diesel repair program, and the following year air conditioning and heating repair training were added.

In 1980 a division called the Custom Training Group was created to provide onsite instruction for corporate technicians. Three years later a second campus opened in Houston to train students in automotive and diesel technology, and in 1986 a new building was added for the firm's air conditioning technology program. In 1987 a 14,000-square-foot high-tech facility was added in Houston to train mechanics for Chrysler, Dodge, and Plymouth dealerships in southern Texas, and in 1988 UTI opened a school near Chicago in Glendale, Illinois, that offered automotive, diesel, and air conditioning service training.

UTI's programs attracted students who might not attend college, but wanted a higher-paying job than a high school diploma alone could yield. With competition from similar for-profit schools as well as local community colleges that charged much lower tuition, the company budgeted 26 percent of its revenues for recruitment, using print and television advertisements as well as a network of recruiters in 38 states. Unlike similar schools whose recruiters received a commission when they signed a student, UTI had a progressive fee that

COMPANY PERSPECTIVES

We are industry's choice for providing professional technicians for the customers we serve in the automotive, diesel, collision repair, motorcycle and marine industries, and related aftermarkets. We set the standard in professional and technical education, lifelong learning and employment services.

ACQUISITION OF MMI IN 1998

In early 1998 the company was recapitalized with an investment from The Jordan Company and senior management to fund the $26.3 million purchase of Clinton Harley Corporation, which owned the Motorcycle Mechanics Institute and Marine Mechanics Institute (MMI). Founded in 1973, MMI had campuses in Phoenix and Orlando, Florida, and working relationships with manufacturers like Harley-Davidson, Kawasaki, and Yamaha. After the merger, Clinton/MMI President John C. White would take the positions of chief strategic planning officer and board chairman of UTI.

The year 1998 also saw the firm expand to California with a new campus in Rancho Cucamonga. Located in a 72,000-square-foot building, it would employ 60 instructors and support staff, with an initial enrollment of 200 taking a special graduate level Mercedes-Benz technical program. An alliance with Peterson Companies' *Hot Rod Magazine* enabled the company to offer a course in "super street high performance" to all of its 5,300 students, as well. UTI was looking to boost enrollment, and increased its staff of recruiters from 80 to 120. They visited shop and vocational education programs at 8,000 high schools around the United States.

In May 1999 UTI and racing organization NASCAR formed an educational partnership to train technicians in automotive and collision repair, with some students gaining internship opportunities with racing teams. Classes would begin in 2000 at UTI's Houston campus, with a dedicated training facility planned for North Carolina, where more than three-fourths of the NASCAR racing teams were headquartered.

During 1999 UTI also reached agreements to provide specialized training programs for carmakers Porsche, Jaguar, Volkswagen, Ford, and Honda, and added a new collision repair and refinishing technology facility to its Houston campus. DuPont Performance Coatings would supply the latter with equipment, grants, job placement, and curriculum development assistance. For 1999 the company's revenues topped $78 million. UTI employed more than 800.

Demand for mechanics was still far outstripping supply, and the firm's graduates had little or no trouble finding jobs, especially those in its automaker-sponsored programs. An estimated 70,000 new mechanics were needed each year out of a total of 700,000 employed in the United States. Whereas some of the openings were created by retirement, many were due to older workers leaving the field because they could not keep up with the growing complexity of automotive systems.

was paid in full upon graduation. This encouraged recruiters to sign individuals who were less likely to drop out or default on their student loans, though even with such efforts students at the Houston campus had a default rate of more than 30 percent in the late 1980s. Three-fourths of the total received government loans.

In 1990 president and 11-year company veteran Robert Hartman was named CEO. Concerned about developing a strategy for the future, Hartman decided to add a board of directors to help advise him in this area. He recruited a group that included several former CEOs and a corporate psychologist, and with their input and that of his staff the firm boosted enrollment while cutting out some expensive but less effective recruiting programs.

By 1995 some 4,000 students were taking UTI classes each year. Tuition was priced at about $10,000, with the longest course of study lasting 63 weeks. The firm had annual revenues of $34 million.

As automobile manufacturers began adding computers, pollution control devices, airbags, and other complicated new systems to their products, car dealerships found it harder and harder to locate qualified service personnel. In 1996 BMW of North America formed an alliance with UTI to develop the Service Technician Education Program (STEP). The carmaker would train instructors and provide the school with cars to work on, while UTI added a new facility in Phoenix to house the school. Graduates of the six-month extended program, who were chosen from the top 5 percent of UTI trainees, could expect initial wages of $15 to $17 per hour and signing bonuses of up to $4,000. BMW dealerships had previously spent as much as $4,000 training each mechanic, while diverting experienced service personnel from their work. They would pay the car manufacturer $7,500 per technician for their training via UTI.

In October 2000 UTI sold its Glendale Heights, Illinois, training facility to W.P. Carey & Co., which would then lease it back to the firm. It was the second such transaction the company had completed with Carey. New training partnerships formed during the year included Audi, Volvo, and truck maker Navistar International.

In 2001 new buildings were added to UTI's Pennsylvania, Illinois, and Florida campuses, with the latter dedicated to Harley-Davidson and marine technician training. The company also formed an educational partnership with Toyota/Lexus during the year, and dropped a computer-aided drafting program it had been offering.

RECAPITALIZATION IN 2002

In 2002 UTI was recapitalized with an investment of $45.5 million from Charlesbank Capital Partners and Penske Capital Partners, each of which took a sizable minority ownership stake. At the same time the company's debt was refinanced with a new $70 million credit facility.

In May the new NASCAR Technical Institute opened in Mooresville, North Carolina, in a $12 million, 146,000-square-foot facility that would be owned by W.P. Carey & Co. and leased back to the firm. It could train up to 1,800 students per year in 57- and 69-week programs, with scholarships available from a variety of sources, including automaker Dodge.

Also during 2002, the firm expanded its Florida and Phoenix campuses and relocated all air conditioning

repair classes to the latter due to declining enrollment. Annual revenues topped $144 million, and a profit of $9.7 million was recorded. It was UTI's first profitable year since MMI had been acquired.

In 2003 the company announced plans to spend $54.2 million to expand its facilities around the country and hire up to 100 new instructors. The firm subsequently broke ground on a new $21 million, 287,000-square-foot campus in Avondale, Arizona, which would consolidate its Phoenix area teaching operations. The facility would employ 200 and accommodate 3,000 students. UTI's corporate headquarters subsequently moved into a new, larger space in Phoenix. The company had annual enrollment of 10,500 students.

With demand for auto technicians still surging, in August the firm announced that it would completely discontinue air conditioning repair training and sold the program's equipment to crosstown rival Refrigeration School, Inc. The company also partnered with continuing education and online learning institution the University of Phoenix during the year, which would give credit for UTI courses to its students.

In October 2003 the company's board appointed Kimberly McWaters CEO. Hired as a part-time receptionist in 1984, she had risen through the ranks to become president in 2000.

INITIAL PUBLIC OFFERING IN DECEMBER 2003

In December the firm made an initial public offering on the New York Stock Exchange. Some 7.5 million shares were sold, more than half of which came from existing shareholders. The $60.1 million raised by the company was primarily used to pay down long-term debt brought on by the acquisition of the motorcycle and marine training programs in 1998.

In July 2004 UTI opened a new 160,000-square-foot campus near Philadelphia at Exton, Pennsylvania, that could accommodate up to 2,000 students and a staff of 200. The firm was already offering advanced training for automakers nearby. UTI also boosted the capacity of its Florida campus and added automotive repair training there during the year, and began a relocation of its California campus that would nearly double its capacity to 2,000 students. The company subsequently boosted the number of recruiters in the field to 150 to help fill the additional seats.

In September the firm introduced a new part-online learning program called FlexTech and bought a 170,000-square-foot facility near Boston, Massachusetts, for $12.4 million. In November, a 22.5-acre site near Sacramento, California, was leased to serve as a new campus in that state.

In 2005 the company enlarged its Exton, Pennsylvania, campus with a new 41,000-square-foot facility that offered diesel technology training and automotive training, and also expanded its Texas, Illinois, Florida, and Rancho Cucamonga, California, campuses. UTI's Massachusetts campus opened in the summer, and in October 60 students began training at a temporary facility in Sacramento, California, in anticipation of a permanent site opening there the following year. For 2005 the company had revenues of $310.8 million and a net income of $35.8 million. Enrollment topped 16,000.

In early 2006 the company initiated a $30 million stock buyback program just before its share price dropped by more than 20 percent when analysts' earnings predictions were not met. Rising gas prices and other factors were leading to a reduced outlook for car repair jobs, while the company itself had lost momentum due to problems with its advertising agency and a call center, though both were quickly rectified. In May, an agreement was signed with Nissan North America to provide specialized training. Similar agreements had been signed with Federal Express and Kawasaki Motors Corp., though carmaker Jaguar had ended its association with the firm.

More than 40 years after its founding, Universal Technical Institute, Inc., had grown to become a national leader in training auto, motorcycle, and marine mechanics. The firm operated eight regional campuses around the United States, and also had more than 20 agreements with car, cycle, and personal watercraft makers to train technicians for their brands. The company's growth was ongoing as it added new campuses and expanded others.

Frank Uhle

PRINCIPAL SUBSIDIARIES

UTI Holdings, Inc.; Universal Technical Institute of Arizona, Inc.; Universal Technical Institute of Texas, Inc.; U.T.I. of Illinois, Inc.; Universal Technical Institute of California, Inc.; Universal Technical Institute of Pennsylvania, Inc.; Universal Technical Institute of Northern California, Inc.; Universal Technical Institute of North Carolina, Inc.; Universal Technical Institute of Massachusetts, Inc.; Universal Technical Institute of Phoenix, Inc.; Custom Training Group, Inc.; Clinton Education Group, Inc.

PRINCIPAL COMPETITORS

Corinthian Colleges, Inc.; Lincoln Educational Service Corporation.

FURTHER READING

Boyer, Trevor, "Move Is on to Train More Technicians," *Ward's Dealer Business,* December 1, 1999, p. 75.

Conlin, Elizabeth G., "Pieces of Advice," *Inc.,* May 1, 1995, p. 57.

Fahey, Jonathan, "Bumper-to-Bumper Education," *Forbes,* September 6, 2004, p. 77.

Harris, Donna Lawrence, "BMW Wants a Few Good Techs," *Tire Business,* April 28, 1997, p. 6.

Kisiel, Ralph, "Retirements Create Service Technician Shortage," *Automotive News,* August 2, 2004, p. 32.

"NASCAR Tech Institute Should Ease Tech Shortage," *Aftermarket Business,* July 1, 2002, p. 8.

"NASCAR, UTI to Address Shortage of Technicians," *Aftermarket Business,* November 1, 2000, p. S66.

Siegel, James J., "UTI Takes on Recruitment," *Air Conditioning, Heating & Refrigeration News,* June 24, 2002, p. 13.

"UTI Expands Automotive Training," *Techniques,* February 1, 2005, p. 11.

Urbi Desarrollos Urbanos, S.A. de C.V.

Av. Reforma 1401-F
Mexicali, Baja California 21100
Mexico
Telephone: (52) (686) 552-8528
Fax: (52) (686) 553-0281
Web site: http://www.urbi.com.mx

Public Company
Incorporated: 1988
Employees: 3,007
Sales: MXN 8.19 billion ($765 million) (2005)
Stock Exchanges: Mexico City
Ticker Symbol: URBI
NAIC: 321992 Prefabricated Wood Building Manu-
cturing

∎ ∎ ∎

Urbi Desarrollos Urbanos, S.A. de C.V. is Mexico's second largest homebuilder in terms of annual revenue and the largest in terms of market value. Originally operating in the states that border the U.S. Southwest, Urbi is doing an increasing amount of business in the metropolitan areas of Mexico's three largest cities. Like other big Mexican homebuilders, Urbi depends largely on low-income buyers subsidized in one way or another by the federal government, but a growing number of its sales are coming from unsubsidized middle- and upper-class customers.

MASTER PLAN: 1981–99

Cuauhtémoc Pérez Román, the founder of Urbi, did not have the usual background for an entrepreneur. Of Cachanilla Indian ancestry, he was named for the Aztec prince who heroically but vainly led the resistance to Mexico's Spanish conquerors, and was the older son of a journalist who wrote about life in his adopted city of Mexicali and also wrote poetry. (Another son, Netzahual-cóyotl, was named for an earlier Aztec king who was a philosopher and poet.) The entrepreneurial spirit seems rather to have passed to them from their paternal grandfather, who built homes in Mexicali without any knowledge of engineering. While Cuauhtémoc was attending the Hermosillo, Sonora, branch of Monterrey's Technological Institute of Graduate Studies, he founded Urbi with fellow students, including another pair of brothers, Raymundo and Javier García de León. The partners pooled the equivalent of $70,000 to start operations on a handshake basis in November 1981. They thought big, envisaging as their goal that in 20 years they would rival Empresa ICA Sociedad Controlodora, S.A. de C.V., the largest construction firm in Mexico. They signed a document in which, in words that serve as the company mission statement, they pledged "to stimulate, protect and recompense all action and thought that develops the Great Spirit." By that they did not mean religion, but agreement to defend the values of honesty, trust, and conformity between what they said and what they did.

The enterprise, like most housing construction companies in Mexico, was dedicated to building government-subsidized homes. The first undertaking was a two-stage development project: one of 211 houses and

COMPANY PERSPECTIVES

Our promise: To stimulate, protect, and recompense all action and thought that develops the Great Spirit, which consists of: Seeking truth. Trusting in you and others. Seeking well-being. Giving in order to grow. Seeking beauty. Being part of a whole.

one of 204. From the fast food franchises and assembly plants of Mexicali, which lies on the frontier with California, they had learned that repetitive processes should be analyzed in such a way as to simplify each step. The enterprise was divided into a number of areas, such as finance, planning, organizational development, technique, and design, coordinated to function like a Swiss watch and to combine efficiency, aesthetics, and functionality. It was dedicated not just to putting up houses but also to linking housing with education, recreation, and business services, and even to creating a homeowning culture, one not easily translated to poor people in the northern frontier cities of Mexico.

A Spanish colonial style was adopted for both the construction and finish of Urbi's houses. They were designed to permit add-ons when the homeowners had the money to make their dwellings larger. Even though these homes were subsidized, Urbi's founders considered their owners to have the right to live in houses that were dignified and secure. These rights, however, came with certain responsibilities, such as paying the allotment for maintenance and respecting the urban image of the development as a whole.

Urbi formed a close association with Mexico's largest cement company, Cemex, S.A. de C.V., Urbi's "big brother," as some called it within the company, helped develop a formula called Concreto Comfortable, to save homeowners energy. Hewlett-Packard Co. helped the company design Urbinet, a system that allowed Urbi to anticipate changes in the tastes and needs of the housing market. Urbi did not become an official enterprise until 1988. The shares that had been in the names of the partners were redistributed between them in accordance with a system of points that took into account the initial capital contributed by each, the time devoted to the project, and a risk factor that was defined by the team. In this form Cuauhtémoc Pérez Román obtained the largest percentage of the shares.

Like most of the more than 2,000 Mexican firms engaged in housing construction, Urbi was competing for funds allocated by the federal government to subsidize this activity. Urbi's main client became the Institute of the National Fund for Workers' Housing, which in its Spanish form became the acronym Infonavit. Starting in 1972, employers were required to pay 5 percent of their workers' monthly salaries directly to this federal agency, whose mandate was to finance affordable housing for workers, chiefly by loans to homebuilders. Because Infonavit was said to have assigned construction in a preferential and inefficient manner, the agency, as of 1992, was barred from making these contracts. However, it continued to be the essential agency for subsidized housing because it extended mortgages to qualified workers and made loans to construction companies for worker housing. Also important was another federal agency, the Operating and Bank Financing Fund for Housing, known by its Spanish acronym Fovi, whose mission was similar to that of Infonavit but dedicated exclusively to public-sector workers. In 1997 the government announced a new housing credit and subsidy program called Provasi that would provide qualified applicants with direct cash subsidies instead of just offering below-market interest rates, as Infonavit and Fovi.

EXPANDING AND GOING PUBLIC: 1999–2004

Urbi, by 1999, was the second largest company in its field in Mexico and the largest in northern Mexico. It had built more than 50,000 homes and had 43 housing developments underway in 11 cities throughout the country. Furthermore, the company had territorial reserves covering more than 2,500 acres, sufficient in size for the construction of about 55,000 additional units. Because of its success in controlling costs, Urbi had the best gross profit margin in its sector, over 34 percent. Although the vast bulk of its revenue came from subsidized homes, about 5 percent derived from free market houses for middle- and upper-income clients. These homes, built in northern Mexico cities, shared certain similarities with the subsidized ones. They were, for example, in a colonial style, organized in enclosed communities, and prefabricated in such a way that each unit could be finished in two weeks. Cuauhtémoc Pérez Román, the chief executive officer, headed an experienced team that included 60 executives who had been with the company for ten or more years.

One of Urbi's strengths was in the area of post-sale service. It received a government award in 1999 for the effectiveness of its program to respond rapidly and effectively to customer complaints. Peréz Román claimed that 40 percent of the company's sales were coming from the word-of-mouth recommendations of satisfied customers. By 2005, when Urbi, in collaboration with

KEY DATES

1981: Founding of the Urbi enterprise by a group of graduate students.

1988: Urbi Desarrollos Urbanos is formalized as a company.

1999: Urbi has become the second largest home-builder in Mexico.

2004: Urbi makes its initial public offering of stock, raising $183 million.

2005: Urbi's chief executive is named 2004 man of the year by the business magazine *Expansión*.

Seguros Inbursa, S.A. de C.V., began offering a homeowners' insurance policy for clients subsidized by Infonavit, this percentage was said by the company to have climbed to 60 percent.

The government of President Vicente Fox Quesada took office in 2000 with one of its principal goals to stimulate the economy by increased home ownership. His overall goal was to grant two million mortgages during his six-year term. By 2005 the government agencies involved in this activity included the Federal Mortgage Society (SHF, by its Spanish acronym), established in 2001, which directed funds to commercial banks and Sofoles (specialized lenders). Qualifiers for SHF-backed loans could be earning as much as $75,000 a year; on the other hand, they could be very poor and completely outside the formal economy, thereby ineligible for Infonavit loans. These direct efforts to stimulate homebuilding were enhanced by economic policies aimed at reducing interest rates. Through the first four years of Fox's presidency, 1.3 million mortgage loans were made, and the beneficiaries included companies such as Urbi.

Urbi had desired for several years to go public but postponed the effort because of low demand for Mexican equities. In 2004, however, it raised $183 million in an offering that was four times oversubscribed. This offering was made not only on the Bolsa Mexicana de Valores, Mexico's stock exchange, but also in the United States and Europe, in what was the first Mexican initial public offering of stock internationally distributed since 2000. About 60 percent of the stock sold was in the form of American Depositary Receipts on the NAS-DAQ, and another 10 percent was sold outside of North America. The funds were expected to be used to pay down debt and purchase more land on which to build new units. Some of the money was needed to pay off the García de León brothers, who had decided to cash in their one-fifth holding in the enterprise.

By the end of 2004, Urbi's shares had risen more than 50 percent since the initial offering of stock. The Mexican housing market was booming because low rates of interest had allowed Infonavit and private lenders to sell about $400 million in mortgage-backed securities. Urbi ended the year with a gross profit margin greater than any of its competitors, and still almost 34 percent. It also had a greater market value ($1.22 billion) than any of its rivals.

The business magazine *Expansión* named Pérez Román its man of the year. Interviewed in a small book-lined office that aides called his "minibunker," he told Adolfo Ortega that he believed the houses that Urbi was selling, and the small cities where they were located, were the physical spaces that, together with education, most supported Mexico's middle class, which had lived through almost three decades of crises. On a side wall of the room hung a blackboard bearing the words, "Why am I doing all this?" and, below, color graphics and scrawled words comprehensible only to Urbi employees. On his desk was a book by business consultant C. K. Prahalad, arguing that the world's poor actually make up the future of the global economy. Pérez Román was said to practice yoga and meditation daily. When Urbi was preparing to go public, he left some analysts nonplussed by evoking the "Great Spirit" so often that Mexico's biggest bank ordered one of its executives to translate the entrepreneurial philosophy of the company into language that businesspeople could understand.

URBI IN 2005

Urbi recorded sales of MXN 8.19 billion ($765 million) in 2005, one-fifth higher (in real peso terms, thereby discounting inflation) than the previous year and 135 percent (in real terms) higher than in 2000. Its net profit was more than three times as high as in 2000. Its long term debt came to MXN 3.6 billion ($339.4 million) at the end of 2005. Urbi constructed a record 24,865 units in 2005, 14 percent more than in 2004 and 70 percent more than in 2000. However, the kinds of houses it was constructing and selling had been changing during this period. In 1999, almost 97 percent of the homes Urbi built were subsidized. In 2003, only 77 percent were subsidized, and sales of these houses accounted for only 60 percent of Urbi's revenues. Unsubsidized middle- and upper-class homes accounted for the remainder. The average subsidized home sold for about $22,000 in 2005, while Urbi's upper-class homes and its most expensive middle-class homes averaged almost $64,000 in price.

Urbi maintained, at the end of 2005, a land reserve of 2,874 hectares (7,101 acres) in five Mexican states, four of them bordering the United States, and the metropolitan areas of Guadalajara, Mexico City, and Monterrey. These reserves gave the company enough land to build an estimated 155,739 homes. Urbi had constructed more than 178,000 homes since its inception. The company had 58 housing developments in progress in 13 cities.

As a vertically integrated company, Urbi typically began the design and planning of a housing development with a market survey, the main purpose of which was to analyze demand for housing, the target location for the development, and design alternatives for the development and the architecture of the homes. It then obtained the necessary authorizations, approvals, permits and licenses required from government bodies and any private interests. After obtaining commitments from mortgage loan providers, Urbi prepared a work plan and timeline for the installation of infrastructure, connection of utilities, and roadways to the urban grid. A typical affordable entry-level home took approximately two to three months to build, using mainly mass-produced materials delivered to the development and assembled onsite. Approximately 90 percent or more of the construction process was being subcontracted to third parties.

At the end of 2005, Cuahtémoc Pérez Román owned nearly 30 percent of Urbi's shares of common stock. Netzahualcóyotl Pérez Román owned 22.5 percent, and public shareholders had 35.5 percent.

Robert Halasz

PRINCIPAL SUBSIDIARIES

Constructora Metropolitana Urbi, S.A. de C.V.; Cyd Desarrollos Urbanos, S.A. de C.V.; Ingenería y Obras, S.A. de C.V.; Obras y Desarrollos Urbi, S.A. de C.V.; Promoción y Desarrollos Urbi, S.A. de C.V.; Propulsora Mexicana de Parques Industriales, S.A. de C.V.; Tec Diseño e Ingenería, S.A. de C.V.; Urbi Construcciones del Pacífico, S.A. de C.V.

PRINCIPAL COMPETITORS

Consorcio Ara, S.A. de C.V.; Consorcio Hogar, S.A. de C.V.; Corporación Geo, S.A. de C.V.; Desarrolladora Homex, S.A. de C.V.

FURTHER READING

Carstens, Catherine Mansell, "New Lease on Life for Infonavit," *Business Mexico*, April 1992, p. 24.

Galloway, Jennifer, "While the Going's Good," *LatinFinance*, July 2004, p. 35.

"Mexican Homebuilder Raises Equity," *LatinFinance*, June 2004, p. 6.

Ortega, Adolfo, "El hombre de Expansión," *Expansión*, January 19–February 2, 2005, pp. 37–40, 42.

Ruíz, Ramón, "Mortgaging for Growth," *Business Mexico*, March 2005, pp. 18–21, 49.

Ruíz, Yolanda, "Cosecha en el desierto," *Expansión*, November 24–December 8, 1999, pp. 98, 100.

USG Corporation

125 South Franklin Street
Chicago, Illinois 60606-4678
U.S.A.
Telephone: (312) 606-4000
Fax: (312) 606-4093
Web site: http://www.usg.com

Public Company
Founded: 1901 as U.S.G. Company
Incorporated: 1984
Employees: 13,787
Sales: $5.14 billion (2005)
Stock Exchanges: New York Chicago
Ticker Symbol: USG
NAIC: 212399 All Other Nonmetallic Mineral Mining; 327420 Gypsum Product Manufacturing; 332323 Ornamental and Architectural Metal Work Manufacturing; 423330 Roofing, Siding, and Insulation Material Merchant Wholesalers; 423390 Other Construction Material Merchant Wholesalers; 551112 Offices of Other Holding Companies

∎ ∎ ∎

Gypsum products are the principal goods manufactured by USG Corporation, the largest maker of such products in North America. The manufacture of gypsum is a highly competitive and price-sensitive undertaking, with easy entry and exit from the field. As a result of these conditions USG Corporation, or U.S.G. Company, as it was originally incorporated, has exerted substantial influence in the building supplies field because of its market size. With such brand names as Sheetrock, USG ranks as the leading maker of gypsum wallboard in the United States, where it holds approximately one-third of the market, and in eastern Canada and Mexico. Through its L&W Supply Corporation subsidiary, USG is also the leading distributor of gypsum wallboard in the United States; L&W Supply distributes other building products as well. Via other USG subsidiaries, USG holds sway as the world's largest manufacturer of ceiling suspension grid and the second largest producer of ceiling tile (trailing only Armstrong World Industries, Inc.). In June 2006 the company emerged from a five-year period operating under Chapter 11 bankruptcy protection. USG was forced into bankruptcy because of the mounting lawsuits it faced stemming from its manufacture of asbestos-containing joint compounds and plaster from the 1930s to 1977.

GYPSUM PRODUCTION IN THE UNITED STATES

Understanding gypsum production methods is essential to an understanding of USG's corporate character. Gypsum, or hydrous calcium sulphate, is, in pure form, a white mineral commonly called alabaster. Large quantities of gypsum exist throughout North America. One of the first uses for gypsum was as a fertilizer. Gypsum is made suitable for commercial use by a process called calcination, which involves heating the mineral to remove approximately three-quarters of its water. Calcined gypsum, or plaster of Paris, can recrystallize into any shape with the simple addition of water. In the 1890s gypsum manufacturers perfected a method of strengthening plaster by adding a retarder, which controlled the setting time, thus creating a viable competitor to traditional lime plaster. Because gypsum was plentiful, and available at a relatively low price, and because the manufacturing process was so simple, new firms flooded the market and placed constant downward pressure on prices.

In the early years of the 20th century, several key businesses emerged as gypsum-product leaders. The English family of Nebraska; C.G. Root, Emil Durr, S.Q. Fulton, and Charles Pullen of Wisconsin; Waldo Avery and B.W. McCausland of Michigan; and, lastly, the largest manufacturer in the United States, J.B. King of New York, were all important gypsum processors. By 1901 several attempts to organize some of the industry's producers into a corporate combination had failed.

CONSOLIDATION IN 1901

In 1901 35 gypsum companies consolidated into the U.S.G. Company. The participating firms traded their assets for securities and acquired a $200,000 loan. Directors of the new company, which controlled about 50 percent of U.S. gypsum output, chose B. W. McCausland as its first president. The company was based in Chicago.

Between 1901 and 1905 each director remained largely concerned with the success of his own plants. This polarization ended in 1905, when McCausland was replaced as president by Sewell Avery, his partner's son. Avery's tenure as president would extend 35 years, until November 12, 1936. Avery then served as chairman between 1937 and 1951. He and his brother, Waldo Avery, were the company's largest stockholders, controlling about 3.6 percent of the company's stock. During Sewell Avery's presidency, his character permeated the company's culture. Avery was a conservative business-

man who had the last word in virtually all matters. In 1931, when Montgomery Ward & Co. was on the verge of financial collapse, Avery became chairman of the board of that company, a position he held until 1955.

Avery had managed his father's firm, the Alabaster Company, since 1894. When U.S.G. absorbed Alabaster, he became a U.S.G. director and its Buffalo, New York, sales manager. Avery built a strong research division after his promotion to president from his post as Cleveland sales manager. Staffed by engineers and chemists, the new division sought to find new uses for gypsum. In 1909 Avery set out to diversify the company with one of his first acquisitions, the Sackett Plaster Board Company of New York. Augustine Sackett had invented gypsum wallboard and the specialized machinery to make it. This basic wallboard quickly became one of U.S.G.'s major products. Wallboard, a layer of gypsum plaster sandwiched between two pieces of paper, is a convenient building material with strong fireproofing and insulating qualities.

U.S.G., which was reincorporated in 1920 as the United States Gypsum Company (U.S. Gypsum), improved on Sackett's concept and patented a wallboard (later branded Sheetrock) that had paper folded over its edges to seal in plaster residue, which often escaped during the wallboard's installation. In 1927 CertainTeed Products Corporation introduced its own wallboard, which did not have enclosed edges, and challenged U.S. Gypsum for market share. CertainTeed's managers believed that their less expensive version had a good chance of success. The result was a price contest between the two companies, beginning in 1927 and ending in 1929. U.S. Gypsum had a much larger market than CertainTeed. It therefore was able to sell wallboard at a loss only in those markets that CertainTeed also served. In all other markets U.S. Gypsum kept prices up. CertainTeed, however, was forced to sell its product at a loss in all its markets. By 1929 CertainTeed was beaten. The smaller company was licensed to produce U.S. Gypsum's patented wallboard and was forced to sell the product at the price set by U.S. Gypsum. This incident marked the start of U.S. Gypsum's unrivaled leadership in gypsum materials.

WEATHERING THE GREAT DEPRESSION

In 1928 Avery successfully predicted a recession that eventually became the Great Depression. Avery's instinct for predicting business cycles helped U.S. Gypsum get through the Depression without a single year of losses; this situation was quite unusual for a business involved in the cyclical building industry. Avery moved to protect the company, in part by ordering the construction of

KEY DATES

1901: Thirty-five gypsum companies are consolidated into U.S.G. Company based in Chicago.
1905: Sewell Avery begins long stint first as president and then as chairman.
1909: Company enters gypsum wallboard market through acquisition of Sackett Plaster Board Company.
1920: Company is reincorporated as the United States Gypsum Company.
1971: L&W Supply Corporation is created as a building materials distribution subsidiary.
1984: USG Corporation is incorporated.
1985: USG Corporation becomes holding company for U.S. Gypsum and several other subsidiaries.
1986: Company fends off takeover attempt by the Belzberg brothers of Canada.
1988: Another takeover attempt is foiled.
1993: Company reorganizes through a "prepackaged" Chapter 11 bankruptcy plan.
2001: Facing mounting asbestos litigation, USG files for Chapter 11 bankruptcy protection.
2005: An after-tax, asbestos-related charge of $1.9 billion leads to a net loss of $1.44 billion.
2006: With its equity intact, USG emerges from bankruptcy having set up a trust fund to pay all current and future asbestos claimants.

new plants closer to East Coast metropolitan centers. Because gypsum is a high-bulk, relatively low-value commodity, transportation costs typically have a large effect on pricing.

U.S. Gypsum's greatest advantage was size. The company was able to use its size to keep manufacturing and transportation costs down and to compete more effectively. Three specific policies, set by Avery, helped U.S. Gypsum to counter the Depression and maintain its number one position in the industry. According to the February 1936 issue of *Fortune,* diffusion of production facilities allowed U.S. Gypsum to keep transportation costs, and thus total costs down. U.S. Gypsum was also vertically integrated, from mine floor to retailer, and employed highly mechanized techniques when possible. The third element in U.S. Gypsum's success, according to *Fortune,* was a devotion to product diversification. U.S. Gypsum marketed a broad cross section of building

materials. Broken down into individual units these products would have been prohibitively expensive to transport. Combined, however, transportation costs were much more reasonable.

Avery took advantage of the company's strong cash position at the beginning of the Depression to purchase nearly a dozen building material firms weakened by the economic downturn. In 1930 U.S. Gypsum bought into the insulation board business with the purchase of the Greenville Insulating Board Corporation of Greenville, Mississippi. Also in 1930, it bought into the metal-lath business with the purchase of the Youngstown Pressed Steel Company of Warren, Ohio, and the metal-lath division of Northwestern Expanded Metal Company. Avery also made U.S. Gypsum, which had already been in the lime business for 15 years, a leading lime producer in 1930 with the acquisition of lime-producing firms such as the Farnam Cheshire Lime Company. Producers of mineral wool and asphalt roofing acquired in 1933, and asbestos-cement siding acquired in 1937, rounded out the Depression-era acquisitions. It was also during this period that U.S. Gypsum introduced its first acoustical ceiling panel under the Acoustone brand. The company countered the downturn in new construction by exploiting the remodeling and industrial markets. During the Depression, 15 percent of sales were to industrial users. Glassmakers used gypsum as a packing material. Cement producers used it to retard setting, and moviemakers used flaked gypsum as snow.

THE 1940 PRICE-FIXING SUIT

In 1940 a new problem confronted the company's management when the U.S. Justice Department filed suit against U.S. Gypsum and six other wallboard manufacturers, charging them with price fixing. The claim stemmed from U.S. Gypsum's 1929 cross-licensing of its patented wallboard. The agreement set prices at which the wallboard must be sold. In 1950 the U.S. Supreme Court forced U.S. Gypsum and its six licensees, who produced all of the wallboard sold east of the Rocky Mountains, to cease setting prices, and U.S. Gypsum was enjoined from exercising its patent-licensing privilege.

Between 1946 and 1949 U.S. Gypsum invested over $51 million in expansion under the direction of William L. Keady, who had become president in 1942. In 1949, however, Chairman Avery predicted another depression, incorrectly, and began to rein in expansion. Keady resigned as a result of Avery's intervention. Although there was a slight recession in 1949, the company did not step up capital spending again until 1954. In May 1951, when Avery resigned as U.S. Gypsum's chairman and CEO, his replacement, Clarence H. Shaver, inherited a company that had a capitalized value of $61 million and produced more than 75 commodities in 47 mines or factories. Avery's imprint was an extreme conservatism marked by strong centralized control, rigid cost-cutting practices, and few benefits for employees.

EXPANSION IN MID-CENTURY

Toward the end of the 1950s U.S. Gypsum extended its expansion internationally. One of its principal discoveries during the decade was the gypsum deposit in Mexico's San Luis Potosi State. This find, one of the world's largest, was conservatively estimated to contain at least 300 million tons of commercial deposits.

In the 1960s U.S. Gypsum became the first major U.S. corporation to undertake privately funded housing renovation on a large scale. The highly publicized project began in 1964, when U.S. Gypsum purchased six adjoining tenements in the East Harlem section of New York City. U.S. Gypsum paid $9,125 to renovate each unit; the cost of constructing new units averaged $22,500. U.S. Gypsum's president, Graham J. Morgan, saw these projects as an opportunity to get in on the ground floor of a potential $20 billion market. Morgan felt the renovation would open up because of the Federal Housing Administration's willingness to provide financing for such projects. By 1969 the company had completely remodeled 32 buildings in New York, Cleveland, Chicago, and Detroit.

In 1973 U.S. Gypsum settled a class-action civil antitrust suit brought against it by wallboard users and buyers. Settlement of those cases, which alleged price fixing, cost U.S. Gypsum $28 million. This case led to a criminal indictment of U.S. Gypsum and three competitors in 1973. The criminal trial eventually found its way to the U.S. Supreme Court, which ordered a new trial, and in 1980 U.S. Gypsum settled the case, agreeing to pay $2.6 million in taxes on deductions from earlier civil antitrust judgments. Meanwhile, in 1971, U.S. Gypsum expanded into the distribution of wallboard and other building materials through the creation of the L&W Supply Corporation subsidiary.

In October 1984 USG Corporation (USG) was incorporated as a holding company. On January 1, 1985, U.S. Gypsum and eight smaller operating companies became subsidiaries of the new holding company. Chairman and CEO Edward W. Duffy reportedly formed the holding company to protect the bulk of company operations from asbestos litigation against U.S. Gypsum. Asbestos had been a standard additive in wallboard manufacture for decades. U.S. Gypsum had already begun to face property damage suits in 1984 with a $675,000 award to a South Carolina school district.

TAKEOVER BATTLES

In November 1986 the Belzberg brothers of Canada attempted a hostile takeover of USG. USG immediately instituted a plan to buy back 20 percent of its common stock in an effort to fend off the takeover. By December 1986, however, USG had purchased Samuel, William, and Hyman Belzberg's 4.9 percent stake, for $139.6 million. The Belzberg family's profits on the transaction were in excess of $25 million.

In 1987 USG acquired DAP Inc., maker of caulking and sealants, for $127 million. In October of that year a partnership led by Texans Cyril Wagner, Jr., and Jack E. Brown's Desert Partners attempted to gain control of the company. Wagner and Brown's main business venture was a Midland, Texas, oil and gas partnership with secondary real estate operations. They purchased their 9.83 percent stake in USG as USG tried to recover financially from the Belzberg takeover attempt. In April 1988 a federal court refused to block USG's poison-pill antitakeover plan. In May 1988 USG announced a restructuring and recapitalization plan designed to further block the takeover attempt, and by June the plan had succeeded.

The plan was expensive, however, and $2.5 billion in new debt (on top of previous debt of $851 million) left USG in a precarious financial state. Several noncore assets were sold over the next few years to help pay down debt. In October 1988 USG sold its Masonite Corporation subsidiary, purchased in 1984. International Paper Corporation paid $400 million for Masonite. Sold the following year were the Kinkead division (to Kohler Company) and Marlite (to Commercial and Architectural Products Inc.). In September 1991 USG sold DAP to U.K.-based Wassall plc for $90 million.

1993–2000: "PREPACKAGED" BANKRUPTCY, STRONG RECOVERY

These moves proved inadequate, however, as USG's management had not anticipated the depressed state of the housing market in the late 1980s and early 1990s. With revenues declining and the company posting a net loss for 1990, USG defaulted on $40 million in loans in 1991. USG, led by CEO Eugene B. Connolly starting in January 1990, attempted to reorganize outside of bankruptcy court through negotiations with its lenders. Finally, in March 1993 USG was forced to declare Chapter 11 bankruptcy, although it quickly emerged only two months later, following the implementation of a "prepackaged" plan of reorganization. Banks and bondholders ended up owning 97 percent of the common stock of USG in exchange for the elimination of $1.4 billion in debt. The company was also able to reduce its annual interest payments by $200 million.

USG emerged from bankruptcy with a still high debt load of $1.56 billion, and set a goal of reducing that to $650 million within five years. In 1994 the housing market, and USG's future outlook, had improved enough to enable the company to raise $224 million through a stock offering, the proceeds of which were used to pay down debt. Connolly retired in early 1996, replaced as chairman and CEO by William C. Foote. Later that year USG sold its insulation manufacturing operation. The company returned to profitability in 1996, posting net income of $15 million on net sales of $2.59 billion.

The following year was even better, as sales hit $2.87 billion, while net income increased almost tenfold, to $148 million. Improving economic conditions played a big role in USG's turnaround as did heavy capital expenditures that aimed at achieving organic, profitable growth. From the company's emergence out of bankruptcy through year-end 1997, USG had spent $532 million in capital expenditures, including the beginning of construction in mid-1997 of a new $110 million wallboard plant in Bridgeport, Alabama, USG's largest nonacquisition capital investment ever. In April 1997 USG announced that it would build a plant in Gypsum, Ohio, to manufacture gypsum wood fiber panels, which combined gypsum with cellulosic fibers to create strong, impact-resistant panels, under the Fiberock brand. In November of that year USG purchased a 60 percent stake in Zhongbei Building Material Products Company, China's largest ceiling grid company. By the end of 1997 total debt had been reduced to $620 million, marking the achievement of the firm's debt reduction target.

Throughout the 1990s the company continued to be involved in litigation relating to personal injury suits and other claims based on asbestos-containing products, which were sold by USG from the 1930s through 1977. The claims were being paid by insurance income under the 1985 Wellington Agreement on asbestos-related claims. In 1988 USG and 19 other former producers of asbestos-containing products replaced the Wellington Asbestos Claims Facility with the Center for Claims Resolution (CCR), which continued in operation through the late 1990s. A class-action lawsuit resulted in a $1.3 billion agreement with the CCR in 1993, but in June 1997 the U.S. Supreme Court invalidated the settlement, finding that the class was defined improperly. USG estimated in 1997 that it was the defendant in

about 73,000 personal injury cases and that the average settlement would be about $1,600.

USG had itself sued nearly two dozen insurance companies who had refused to cover these claims. By 1997 the company had reached settlements with a number of these insurers, resulting in about $325 million in coverage for the company. USG expected to receive substantial additional payments, between $200 million and $265 million, as the remaining suits reached settlements.

During 1998 USG continued to spend heavily on capital improvement projects and the construction of new plants. In April the company announced it would build a new $112 million wallboard factory in Aliquippa, Pennsylvania. In September USG announced plans to construct two new, state-of-the-art wallboard plants in Plaster City, California, and Rainier, Oregon, for a total cost of $225 million. Replacing older facilities with modern, low-cost plants aided USG's overall productivity. With the economic boom of the mid- to late 1990s making for an exceptionally strong building industry, and with the company's debt load finally eased, USG was in its best financial shape in years. Perhaps most indicative of its recovery was USG's September 1998 announcement that it would pay a quarterly dividend for the first time in a decade, as well as repurchase as many as five million of its common shares.

The robust construction market powered USG to record heights in both 1998 and 1999. In the latter year, a shortage of wallboard drove up prices and helped revenues reach $3.6 billion, an 88 percent increase since the 1993 restructuring. Net earnings quadrupled over the same period, surging to $421 million. The first of USG's new wallboard plants, the Bridgeport facility, opened in May 1999, after which an older plant in Plasterco, Virginia, was shut down. In November a new plant in East Chicago, Indiana, replaced an old one in that same location. Also in 1999, USG became a NASCAR sponsor as part of an aggressive new marketing push.

In 2000, as USG brought more new plants online and shuttered additional outdated facilities, the wallboard industry went into another cyclical downturn as overcapacity in the market sent wallboard prices into a sharp decline. This trend, coupled with ongoing concerns about the asbestos litigation, sent USG shares down 60 percent by late 2000. At this stage, some investors began viewing the stock as a bargain, including legendary value investor Warren Buffett, who in December 2000 bought a 15 percent stake in USG through his investment vehicle, Berkshire Hathaway Inc.

2001–2006: RESTRUCTURING UNDER BANKRUPTCY PROTECTION

Despite Buffett's vote of confidence, USG's position deteriorated in 2001. Early in the year, the company announced that it would take year-end 2000 after-tax charges of $557 million to cover the estimated cost of settling asbestos lawsuits through 2003. This led to a net loss for 2000 of $259 million. In May 2001 the company announced that it would once again stop paying a dividend. As asbestos litigation mounted, USG lobbied the U.S. Congress for a legislative solution that would limit the lawsuits, but when no such outcome seemed likely, the company opted to once again file for Chapter 11 bankruptcy protection. By the time of the filing in June 2001, USG had been named in 250,000 asbestos-related personal-injury cases and had paid out more than $450 million before insurance recoveries. Its annual asbestos-related costs had increased from $30 million in 1997 to more than $160 million in 2000, and the company had expected the 2001 costs to top $275 million.

Unlike the previous brief stint in bankruptcy, this foray proved to be a prolonged one as USG struggled to come up with a plan to resolve its asbestos liabilities while continuing to lobby for legislative action. The company's operations, meantime, prospered. Riding a booming market for housing and commercial construction, USG expanded its production and distribution capabilities. Product shipments reached new highs, and record revenues were recorded in both 2004 and 2005. Sales surged to $5.14 billion in 2005, when gross profits hit an all-time high of $1.1 billion. USG ramped up its marketing efforts that year when it began sponsoring the USG Sheetrock 400, a NASCAR race held at the Chicagoland Speedway.

Because of the stellar financial performance, USG's stock actually rose sharply over the course of the bankruptcy, from less than $4 a share at the time of the filing to around $80 in early 2006. This remarkable, if not unprecedented, recovery of the stock of a company operating under bankruptcy protection impressed Buffett, who told the *Wall Street Journal* in February 2006, "It's the most successful managerial performance in bankruptcy that I've ever seen." In June 2006 USG emerged from bankruptcy via a complex plan through which the shareholders retained their ownership of the company, a highly unusual outcome.

USG set up a trust fund to settle all of its current and future asbestos claims. It made an initial $900 million payment into the fund, and also planned to make two subsequent payments totaling $3.05 billion by mid-2007, unless the U.S. Congress stepped in to create a national trust to handle all asbestos-exposure cases, an occurrence most observers considered unlikely. To raise money for the fund and to help pay its creditors, USG set up a rights issue whereby current stockholders could buy one new share of company stock for each share already owned, at $40 per share, a price well under the then-current trading level. This $1.8 billion rights offering was backed up by Buffett's Berkshire Hathaway, which promised to buy any shares not snapped up by other shareholders. In the fourth quarter of 2005, USG recorded an after-tax charge of $1.9 billion as a provision for asbestos claims, leading to a net loss for the year of $1.44 billion. With its asbestos headache seemingly under control, USG was well positioned to continue its sharp recovery, although a long-expected slowdown in the U.S. housing industry appeared certain to provide new challenges.

John C. Bishop
Updated, David E. Salamie

PRINCIPAL SUBSIDIARIES

United States Gypsum Company; USG Interiors, Inc.; L&W Supply Corporation; CGC Inc. (Canada); USG Mexico S.A. de C.V.

PRINCIPAL OPERATING UNITS

USG International.

PRINCIPAL COMPETITORS

National Gypsum Company; BPB plc; Georgia-Pacific Corporation; Eagle Materials Inc.; Temple-Inland Forest Products Corporation; Lafarge North America Inc.; Pacific Coast Building Products, Inc.; Panel Rey, S.A.; Armstrong World Industries, Inc.; Worthington Industries, Inc.; Chicago Metallic Corporation; Odenwald Faserplattenwerk GmbH; AMF Mineralplatten GmbH Betriebs KG; Gypsum Management and Supply, Inc.; Rinker Materials Corporation; KCG, Inc.; The Strober Organization, Inc.; Allied Building Products Corp.

FURTHER READING

Arndorfer, James B., "For USG's CEO, Bankruptcy Paying Off," *Crain's Chicago Business,* May 12, 2003, p. 1.

———, "USG's Buffett Boom: Investment Guru's Buy Boosts Management," *Crain's Chicago Business,* December 4, 2000, p. 4.

Brat, Ilan, "USG Settles Asbestos Lawsuits, Swings to a $1.78 Billion Loss," *Wall Street Journal,* January 31, 2006, p. B4.

Callahan, Patricia, "USG Takes Charge of $557 Million for Asbestos Costs," *Wall Street Journal,* January 12, 2001, p. B8.

Duff, Christina, "Costly Recapitalization Drives USG Corp. to the Wall," *Wall Street Journal,* June 3, 1992, p. B4.

Fitch, Stephane, "The Gypsum King," *Forbes,* February 5, 2001, pp. 68–70.

Gilbert, Nick, "USG: Now a Value Play," *Financial World,* May 9, 1995, p. 26.

Greising, David, "USG's Remodeling May Mean Gutting the House," *Business Week,* January 21, 1991, pp. 54–55.

Guy, Sandra, "'Affordable' USG Asbestos Plan: Complex Plan Wins Support of Victim Groups," *Chicago Sun-Times,* January 31, 2006, p. 51.

——, "Builders Sold on USG—but Investors Aren't," *Chicago Sun-Times,* October 4, 1999, p. 49.

——, "New Look for USG: Wallboard-Manufacturing Giant Says It's Made the Most of Its Retooling Time," *Chicago Sun-Times,* May 11, 2006, p. 52.

——, "USG Eliminates Dividend," *Chicago Sun-Times,* May 10, 2001, p. 59.

——, "USG Files Bankruptcy," *Chicago Sun-Times,* June 26, 2001, p. 45.

——, "USG Hangs in There: Wallboard Maker Out of Bankruptcy with Clean Slate," *Chicago Sun-Times,* June 21, 2006, p. 67.

"Gyp," *Fortune,* February 1936.

"Home Run? U.S. Gypsum Is Hoping for One, to Cash in on Its Lower Costs," *Barron's,* September 29, 1980, pp. 52+.

Mehlman, William, "USG Positioned for Success in Restructured Housing Arena," *Insiders' Chronicle,* July 21, 1986, pp. 1+.

Miller, James P., "USG Modifies 'Prepackaged' Chapter 11 Plan," *Wall Street Journal,* January 25, 1993, p. A11.

Richardson, Karen, "Years into Filing, USG Is Smiling," *Wall Street Journal,* February 15, 2006, pp. C1, C4.

Saporito, Bill, "The Benefits of Bankruptcy," *Fortune,* July 13, 1993, p. 98.

Taub, Stephen, "The 1980s Legacy Still Stalks USG," *Financial World,* August 21, 1990, p. 11.

"U.S. Gypsum: No Nonsense," *Fortune,* September 1955.

ValleyCrest Companies

24151 Ventura Boulevard
Calabasas, California 91302
U.S.A.
Telephone: (818) 223-8500
Fax: (818) 223-8142
Web site: http://www.valleycrest.com

Private Company
Incorporated: 1949 as Valley Crest Landscape Nurseries
Inc.
Employees: 5,000
Sales: $700 million (2005 est.)
NAIC: 541320 Landscape Architectural Services; 561730
Landscaping Services

■ ■ ■

ValleyCrest Companies is the largest privately owned landscape company in the United States. The company operates through a half-dozen business units that offer a full range of landscape services, including design, development, and maintenance. Prominent projects completed by the company include landscape work for The Getty Center, the Bellagio Hotel and Casino in Las Vegas, and Invesco Field at Mile High Stadium. The company also operates a retail nursery and provides maintenance services to golf courses. ValleyCrest Companies operates 100 branch offices nationwide and through its sole subsidiary, U.S. Lawns, oversees 151 franchises. The company is owned and managed by the Sperber family.

ORIGINS

A landscaping giant, ValleyCrest represented the life's work of Burton S. Sperber, an innovator in his field who demonstrated a steadfast commitment to expanding his business. Sperber's more than half-century of involvement in the landscaping industry began while he was attending North Hollywood High School in southern California's San Fernando Valley. Sperber took a part-time job at a small local nursery named MG Nursery, where he spent his hours after school planting shrubs, seeding and mowing lawns, and transplanting trees. His part-time job turned into the start of an entrepreneurial career when the owner of the nursery died in 1949. The owner's widow offered to sell the business to the 19-year-old Sperber, and Sperber, after gaining the support of his father, agreed, paying $700 for the business and old pickup truck. The father-and-son team rechristened the business "Valley Crest Landscape Nurseries Inc.," confident that postwar economic growth would fuel the expansion of the business. Their expectations were confirmed within a matter of months: "The San Fernando Valley started booming with houses," Sperber recalled in an October 2005 interview with *Calabasas Magazine*. "When I started out, the Valley was predominantly agricultural. As homes and communities were built, fruit-tree groves were replaced by landscaped parks, schools, freeways, and subdivisions."

Valley Crest Landscape Nurseries established itself as something far more than a local nursery during the 1950s. Initially, Sperber attended to the landscaping and tree-moving functions of the business, while his father ran the nursery. Soon after starting out, however, the growth of the business required more than the simple

COMPANY PERSPECTIVES

With more than 50 years of experience, no landscape company in America can claim greater depth of expertise or a more comprehensive track record of effective problem-solving and consistent execution. While the size and scope of our projects has expanded, we have never lost sight of our core values: customer service; continual innovation; flawless execution; attention to detail.

division of labor between two partners. The Sperbers seized the opportunity presented by the energetic development of the San Fernando Valley, securing contracts to landscape the region's schools and along the freeways. The company's operational foundation expanded explosively as a result, giving the Sperbers a growing inventory of the tools of their trade—the tractors, hand tools, and maintenance equipment required for large-scale projects. By the end of the decade, the small nursery had been thoroughly transformed, taking aim at a highly fragmented industry to become one of its leaders. Shortening its name to "Valley Crest Landscape Inc." in 1959, the company was poised for expansion in the coming decade, as it solicited contracts for an ever widening array of jobs, including landscape design, commercial and industrial projects, model home development, and golf course development.

The 1960s witnessed profound growth, both in the scope of the company's operations and in the development of its corporate structure. Any vestige of a small, local nursery was swept away during the decade, as the company began an expansion program that would ultimately see it compete on a national basis, a rarity in the fragmented landscape industry. At the start of the 1960s, Valley Crest Landscape began to adopt a layered corporate structure, adding the business units that gave it a broadly based attack on the landscape market. The company had pioneered the practice of growing trees in boxes, thereby enabling year-round planting, which became the exclusive purview of Valley Crest Tree Company. Formed in 1961 with the help of Burton Sperber's brother, Stuart Sperber, Valley Crest Tree initially was established to supply the landscaping business with trees, but its Sepulveda, California–based operations soon began serving the needs of other companies. Significant geographic expansion also occurred during the decade as the company used a branch system to widen its area of influence. In 1964, Valley Crest Landscape opened an office in Santa Ana to handle the company's business in Orange County. The establishment of a computerized information system occurred the following year, giving the Sperbers and their growing management team the ability to connect offices together as the company pushed beyond the borders of California.

Valley Crest Landscape, becoming bigger with each passing year, possessed the resources to bid for large-scale projects by the 1960s. High-profile landscape projects became the company's forte, and one of the first to be completed occurred during the 1960s. In 1966, Valley Crest Landscape was awarded a multimillion-dollar contract to landscape Rossmoor Leisure World in northern California, one of the largest retirement communities in the United States at the time. Other major projects followed, giving the company the opportunity to hone its skills in designing and building complete gardens featuring ponds, waterfalls, and fence overhangs.

FORMATION OF HOLDING COMPANY: 1969

One result of Valley Crest Landscape's reliance on large-scale projects was that the company itself was forced to evolve to handle the demands of its high-profile clientele. The company became a genuine corporation, taking on the attributes of a modern, sophisticated business. In 1969, the Sperbers aped the corporate trend of the day and formed a holding company, Environmental Industries Inc., which became the new banner under which its various landscape activities were conducted. One year later, Environmental Industries was organized into three divisions, giving the Sperbers the organizational structure capable of taking on large-scale projects. Environmental Care Inc. became the entity dedicated to providing landscape maintenance services. Valley Crest, the heart of Environmental Industries, retained its control over landscape construction activities. Valley Crest Tree, as it had since 1961, focused on providing nursery services. The Sperbers took the newly structured company public to finance expansion, but operating in the public sector did not suit the family and the stock was purchased a decade later to return the company to its status as a private company. "The company was too small and every time the earnings would go up the stock would go down," Burton Sperber lamented in a December 14, 1998 interview with *Forbes.*

The Sperbers settled into their more comfortable role as managers of a private company and led Environmental Industries toward prominence during the last decades of the 20th century. Expansion continued throughout the 1980s, as the company settled into a

---

KEY DATES

1949: Burton Sperber and his father acquire MG Nursery and rename it Valley Crest Landscape Nurseries Inc.

1961: Valley Crest Tree Company is formed as a separate tree-growing operation.

1969: Environmental Industries Inc. is formed as a holding company for the Sperbers' landscape business.

1980: Headquarters are moved to Calabasas, California.

1990: Environmental Golf is formed.

1996: U.S. Lawns is acquired.

2002: ValleyCrest Companies becomes the new name of Environmental Industries Inc.

2006: The company strengthens its design capabilities with the acquisition of HRP LanDesign and Site Works.

---

new headquarters location in Calabasas at the start of the decade, a facility ringed by date palm trees transplanted from the Canary Islands. Its most ambitious projects were taken on during the 1990s, a decade of numerous achievements for the 40-year-old company. In 1990, Environmental Industries formed Environmental Golf to oversee the company's golf construction and maintenance contracts. Through the newly formed business unit, the Sperbers owned, built, managed, and maintained golf courses, eventually building and managing more than 600 golf courses before the family sold its interests in the properties except for one golf course, Glen Annie Golf Course in Santa Barbara, California. The company also entered the franchising business by acquiring U.S. Lawns in 1996. Based in Florida, U.S. Lawns became an Environmental Industries subsidiary offering lawn and landscape franchises on a national basis.

On other fronts, the company was involved in major projects that only a few of its competitors could hope to undertake. For the Atlantis Paradise Island casino in the Bahamas, Environmental Industries uprooted 1,500 coconut palms from Jamaica, transported them by barge to the Bahamas, and planted them on the Atlantis Paradise Island property. The company re-sodded Atlanta's Olympic Stadium after the opening ceremonies of the XXVI Summer Olympic Games, landscaped Steve Wynn's Bellagio hotel in Las Vegas, and developed 400 acres for Walt Disney Co.'s Animal Kingdom theme

park in Orlando, Florida. One of its mostly highly regarded projects of the decade was the development of 130 acres of ground surrounding the Getty Center in Los Angeles. A seven-year, $10 million contract, the project involved the planting of a two-acre azalea garden floating in a reflecting pool, the installation of an elaborate irrigation system, and the planting of several thousand trees. "We do God's work," Stuart Sperber said in a December 14, 1998 interview with *Forbes*. "We really do."

By the end of the 1990s, Environmental Industries could lay claim to being the largest company of its kind in the private sector. Annual revenues reached $425 million as 50th anniversary celebrations were underway, a total drawn from the company's sprawling operations. Environmental Industries boasted nine regional offices and 37 branch offices in seven states. Its nursery operations comprised 1,500 acres in Sylmar, Farmington, and Irvine, California, which produced more than three million trees, roughly 90 percent of which were sold to other companies. Its landscaping maintenance business unit provided services to more than 6,000 indoor and outdoor gardens. The company's financial mainstay was its landscape construction segment, accounting for 70 percent of the overall revenues. "Some people call us a conglomerate," Burton Sperber remarked in a November 3, 1997 interview with the *Los Angeles Business Journal*. "But all of our company's functions are pretty much similar; they tie together to do site beautification work." The only other company in the landscape industry that approached the size and scope of Environmental Industries was LandCare USA, a rival the Sperbers shrugged aside as they led the company into the next century.

VALLEYCREST IN THE 21ST CENTURY

Environmental Industries' progress during the first years of the 21st century was highlighted by acquisitions and a company-wide reorganization. The company approached its growth phase ranking as the largest site development, landscape, and horticultural services contractor in the country. In 2000, Environmental Industries strengthened its presence on the East Coast with the purchase of Oakton, Virginia–based STM Landscape Services, a $12 million-in-sales contractor. The acquisition was hailed by Burton Sperber's son, Richard Sperber, who had risen through the company's ranks to become vice-president and chief operating officer at the time of the acquisition. "With this acquisition," Richard Sperber said in a February 3, 2000 interview with *Daily News*, "we can provide superb competitive advantages to a larger segment of the business community and dramatically expand our reach throughout Virginia, North Carolina, and the greater District of Columbia." (STM Landscape Services, after a name change in 2003, became ValleyCrest Landscape Maintenance.) Next, the company completed a much larger acquisition, purchasing the TruGreen LandCare assets owned by ServiceMaster Company. The acquisition, completed in 2001, gave Environmental Industries landscape construction operations in Texas, Massachusetts, Illinois, Minnesota, Virginia, and Maryland, increasing its payroll to more than 7,000 employees and lifting annual revenues to nearly $600 million.

Pressing ahead, Environmental Industries aimed its sights on the $1 billion mark, a financial goal it would pursue after re-branding its identity in 2002. "The driving force for the re-branding is to simplify the way customers view us and better communicate the scope of the company's services," Burton Sperber announced in an October 1, 2002 company press release. "We want people to instantly recognize ValleyCrest as the nation's leading landscape resource when they see our new red truck fleet and uniformed workforce whether they are on a golf course, at a hotel, around the corporate campus, or in their neighborhood." The only entities within the organization unaffected by the name change were U.S. Lawns and Valley Crest Tree Company. Every other aspect of the Sperbers' business was given the "Valley-Crest" name, starting with the holding company, which changed its name from Environmental Industries to ValleyCrest Companies. Environmental Care, the landscape maintenance division with 60 offices in 17 states, became ValleyCrest Landscape Maintenance. Environmental Golf, which provided maintenance services to more than 50 golf courses, became Valley-Crest Golf Maintenance. Valley Crest, the nation's largest landscape construction company, became ValleyCrest Landscape Development. The company's landscape-design activities were grouped within its ValleyCrest Landscape Architecture business unit.

In the wake of adopting a unified image for the company, the Sperbers continued their acquisition campaign. In 2004, the company acquired Omni Landscape Group and organized its assets within the ValleyCrest Landscape Maintenance business unit. The acquisition, which added $50 million in annual revenue, consisted of operations in Georgia, Pennsylvania, Maryland, Virginia, New York, and New Jersey. In 2006,

the company acquired two landscape architecture companies, HRP LanDesign, based in California, and Site Works, based in Alabama. Richard Sperber, who had previously been promoted to president of Valley-Crest Companies, explained the strategic importance of the acquisitions in a March 1, 2006 company press release. "We believe that, similar to trends in other sectors of the construction market, design-build will play an increasingly important role in the landscape industry in the next several years." As ValleyCrest Companies moved forward, with Richard Sperber expected to inherit the reins of command from his father, it was likely that the nation's largest landscape development company would continue to hold sway well into the future.

Jeffrey L. Covell

PRINCIPAL SUBSIDIARIES

U.S. Lawns.

PRINCIPAL OPERATING UNITS

ValleyCrest Landscape Development; ValleyCrest Landscape Architecture; ValleyCrest Landscape Maintenance; ValleyCrest Golf Course Maintenance; Estate Gardens By ValleyCrest; Valley Crest Tree Company.

PRINCIPAL COMPETITORS

The Davey Tree Expert Company; OneSource Landscape and Golf Services, Inc.; TruGreen LandCare L.L.C.

FURTHER READING

Cohen, Jason Z., "Landscape Firm Gets Mid-Atlantic Foothold," *Daily News,* February 3, 2000, p. B2.

"Dallas Garden Center Sells Landscaping Business to California Company," *Dallas Morning News,* December 6, 2000.

Davis, Joyzelle, "Valley Crest Keeps Clients Getty, Disney in the Green," *Los Angeles Business Journal,* November 3, 1997, p. 37.

Flans, Robyn, "If You Build It, They Will Come," *Calabasas Magazine,* October 2005, p. 118.

"Golden Anniversary for National Giant," *Landscape & Irrigation,* November 1999, p. 28.

Lubove, Seth, "Green Begets Green," *Forbes,* December 14, 1998, p. 142.

Vonage Holdings Corp.

———————————— ■ ————————————

23 Main Street
Holmdel, New Jersey 07733
U.S.A.
Telephone: (732) 528-2600
Fax: (732) 287-9119
Web site: http://www.vonage.com

Public Company
Incorporated: 2001
Employees: 1,355
Sales: $269.2 million (2005)
Stock Exchanges: New York
Ticker Symbol: VG
NAIC: 513390 Other Telecommunications

■ ■ ■

Vonage Holdings Corp. provides broadband telephone services, offering services to residences and small businesses in the United States, Canada, and the United Kingdom. Vonage provides its customers with unlimited local and long-distance calling, using broadband connections and Voice over Internet Protocol technology to carry telephone conversations. Customers pay a flat monthly fee depending on their plan. Vonage's "Basic 500" plan, priced at $14.99, includes 500 minutes anywhere in the United States, Canada, and Puerto Rico. The "Premium Unlimited" plan offers unlimited local and long distance calls in the United States, Canada, Puerto Rico, and to certain European countries for $24.99. Vonage also offers two plans for business customers. The "Small Business Unlimited" plan, priced at $49.99,

offers a dedicated fax line and unlimited local and long distance calls in the United States, Canada, Puerto Rico, and to certain European countries. The "Small Business Basic" plan features a dedicated fax line and 1,500 minutes anywhere in the United States, Canada, and Puerto Rico. Vonage's broadband-based service uses public Internet lines.

ORIGINS

Before launching his assault on the telecommunications industry, Vonage founder Jeffrey A. Citron was forced out of his first profession, ordered never to return. The interdiction of the Securities and Exchange Commission (SEC) ended what had been an enormously successful career for the Staten Island, New York, native who developed an interest in the finance sector while in high school. Citron's interest was piqued by a stock-selection game developed by his economics teacher, which prompted him to apply for a job on Wall Street in the late 1980s right after finishing high school. "I don't have a lot of patience for things," he said in an August 23, 2004 interview with *Time,* referring to his decision to forgo college. "When I see something that I want, I completely go after it." Citron joined Datek Securities as a trader and flourished. By the time he turned 21 in 1992, he had made his first million dollars. He founded Island ECN, a developer of computerized, order-executing systems for stocks, in 1995, and became chief executive officer of Datek Online three years later. By the end of the 1990s, he had amassed a vast personal fortune, but his career on Wall Street quickly ended after the SEC began investigating him for stock manipulation. Citron resigned in 1999 and sold most of

COMPANY PERSPECTIVES

We believe that our strong brand identity and reputation for quality communications services are instrumental to building our customer base. Our core business strategy is to enhance our brand image and the quality of our services in order to attract new customers. As we build on our leading brand and our above-mentioned strengths, we are pursuing the following additional business strategies: develop additional innovative features and products; expand distribution capabilities; continue to improve customer experience; expand into new geographic markets.

his interest in Datek Online for $225 million as the SEC conducted its investigation. The investigation concluded in 2003, when Citron, who admitted to no wrongdoing, paid a $22.5 million fine and was banned permanently from "associating with any broker or dealer," according to SEC documents.

The intervention of federal authorities put Citron at a crossroads in his career, forcing the young executive to begin another career before his 30th birthday. The Wall Street outcast opted to play the role of revolutionary with his next venture, founding Vonage in 2001. Vowing "to change the entire telecommunications landscape," as quoted in the August 23, 2004 issue of *Time,* Citron raised $12 million in private financing to launch Vonage, a company that promised to offer telephone service via high-speed Internet connections. His plan was to exploit Voice over Internet Protocol, or VoIP, a technology that enabled voice transmissions to be digitized, divided into small electronic packets, and routed to their destination over the public Internet. Telephone calls carried by Vonage would travel alongside e-mail messages, digital photos, and countless other packets of data sent and received through the Internet, offering consumers telephone service at a substantially reduced price. For conventional telephone companies, who relied on landlines to provide their service, Citron's concept sidestepped their billions of dollars worth of infrastructure, threatening, as its promoter had promised, to alter the way the telecommunications industry operated.

Designated as an "information service," VoIP was exempted from many of the taxes, fees, and, regulations applicable to conventional telephone companies. Consequently, Citron was able to offer service roughly half as expensive as regular telephone service, touting a flat monthly fee with unlimited long distance in the United States. The savings Citron could offer to potential customers gave him a clear advantage over his vastly larger and wealthier rivals, but there were numerous obstacles to overcome to make Vonage a financial success and a market winner. VoIP depended on high-speed Internet connections, through either a cable modem or a digital subscriber line (DSL). Despite sanguine predictions that foresaw droves of consumers embracing broadband, the market matured slowly, thereby limiting Vonage's potential base. Further, since Vonage relied on the public Internet to route its calls, rather than owning its own network, the company could not totally control the quality of the service it offered. Citron also faced the impending swoop of traditional communications companies into the fray, as well as a host of start-up VoIP ventures. The titans of telephony, industry pundits pointed out, had underestimated the threat posed by cellular-telephone companies, and they were unlikely to commit the same mistake with VoIP. Finally, Citron faced the challenge of creating a financially viable business model. Operating costs threatened to mushroom as he attempted to convince consumers to forsake conventional telephone service for the decidedly more obscure VoIP-based service.

SERVICE BEGINNING IN 2002

Braced for the challenges ahead, Citron launched Vonage's service in March 2002, presiding over the company's commercial debut as its chairman and chief executive officer. He and his technology team scored an early success by developing components capable of carrying telephone calls over public Internet lines. The company's system, consisting of a telephone connected to a modem-like box that, in turn, was connected to a cable modem or DSL line, attracted a fair number of converts to VoIP-based service. By the end of the year, Vonage had signed up nearly 8,000 customers who completed five million calls over the network. The totals represented only a fraction of the figures that major telephone companies boasted—there were, for instance, 112 million traditional telephone lines in existence at the time—but Citron was convinced the numbers would increase exponentially in the coming months.

To spur demand for his VoIP services, Citron turned to marketing and promotional campaigns. He had to educate the public about the legitimacy of VoIP and win their business, an endeavor that would chew through the financial resources at his disposal. He gained another $35 million in financing in 2003, enabling him to launch a $15 million national campaign during the year that consisted of radio and television commercials. The campaign characterized Vonage as leading a grassroots

KEY DATES

2001: Vonage is founded.
2002: Vonage's Internet-based telephone service is launched in March.
2003: Nearly 80,000 Vonage customers complete 107 million calls over the Internet.
2005: Vonage signs its one millionth customer.
2006: The company completes its initial public offering of stock.

movements against the telecommunications establishment, proclaiming, "Down with high phone bills, switch to Vonage." Thanks largely to marketing efforts, the company ended 2003 with more than 85,000 customers, a more than tenfold increase from the previous year's total. Revenues for the year reached $16.9 million, the company's first full year of operation. Vonage was beginning to gain momentum, "jumping from being an obscure little company no one has ever heard of to one that people are writing about and talking about," *AD-WEEK* noted in its October 13, 2003 issue, but the stir created by Citron also was attracting unwanted attention. The major telecommunication companies had noticed the gains made by the Holmdel, New Jersey–based company and they were preparing to offer their response.

Citron faced a critical stage in Vonage's development as he prepared for 2004. He had $20 million set aside for marketing for the year, funds that would be used to support the company's "People Do Stupid Things" campaign, and he would need all the exposure he could afford to prevail against the industry giants ready to enter the VoIP fray. AT&T launched its own web-based telephone service, CallAdvantage, in March 2004. Verizon, branding its service VoiceWing, entered the market in July 2004. Cable behemoths Comcast and Time Warner were poised to launch their own VoIP services by the end of the year. The arrival of the industry's elite onto the scene gave industry observers little hope that Vonage would survive the onslaught. Cable companies such as Comcast and Time Warner could bundle their voice service with video, broadband access, and wireless service, while a company such as AT&T owned its own network, thereby maintaining full control over call quality. Further, each enjoyed vast financial resources, well-established distribution systems, and marketing arms with the ability to crush Vonage. Industry pundits gave Citron little chance of staving off the advances of his rivals. "In the long run," one analyst said in a June 20, 2005 interview with *Business Week,*

"Vonage can't afford to be just about cheap phone calls." Another analyst, in an August 23, 2004 interview with *Time,* offered an equally pessimistic assessment of the company's chances for long-term success. "It's a question of being passed in the far left lane," the analyst said.

Despite consensus that Vonage inevitably would be subsumed by its larger rivals, Citron pressed ahead, confident that his company could withstand the competitive pressure. He raised a total of $145 million in two rounds of financing during 2004 and used the money to add as many new subscribers as possible. Vonage was adding 1,000 new customers a day midway through the year, selling its service through its web site and through a new distribution channel created during the year. Citron forged partnerships with retail companies to sell Vonage's services, reaching his first national agreement with Circuit City Stores. Partnerships with RadioShack, Best Buy, and Amazon.com followed, helping to increase Vonage's subscriber base to nearly 400,000 by the end of the year. In 2005, a year during which $200 million was raised in the company's fifth round of financing, Citron ventured into the wireless arena, hoping that a broader attack on the voice-service market would improve the company's chances of success. He began looking for partnerships to enable Vonage customers to use so-called Wi-Fi "hot spots," the Internet connections available in locations such as coffee shops and hotels, which promised to give Vonage customers service outside their residences or businesses. Wi-Fi telephones were unveiled in 2005.

PUBLIC DEBUT IN 2006

Vonage reached a milestone in 2005 when its subscriber rolls eclipsed one million, but the exponential increase in customers did not translate into financial success. The company generated $269.2 million in revenues during the year and lost nearly as much, posting a $261.3 million deficit. With annual losses mounting, Citron was forced to consider either selling the company to one of his rivals or taking it public to relieve some of the financial strain. Citron reportedly wanted to sell the company, but he could not find a suitor willing to agree to his estimation of Vonage's worth. Consequently, he chose to take the company public, filing with the SEC in February 2006 for an initial public offering (IPO) of stock. That same month, he stepped aside as chief executive officer and assumed the title of "Chief Strategist." Citron's replacement was Mike Snyder, the former president of a security systems firm named ADT who took over day-to-day control of Vonage. In the months leading up to the IPO, the company waived its international calling rates to landlines in France, Ireland,

Italy, and Spain for subscribers signed up to its Premium Unlimited Plan and its Small Business Unlimited Plan.

Vonage completed its IPO in May 2006, but its debut reflected the less than optimistic perception of the company held by parts of the investment community. Vonage shares were priced a $17 per share for the IPO, but the price fell to $14.85 by the end of the day's trading, a 12.7 percent decline that represented the worst first-day performance in two years. There remained many questions to be answered as Vonage sought to put to use the $531 million it raised from the IPO and plotted its course for the future. Internet-based telephone service offered plenty room for growth, with the number of subscribers projected to increase from roughly three million subscribers in 2006 to 27 million by 2009, but it remained to be seen whether Vonage would be able to turn a profit and effectively compete against a host of rivals.

Jeffrey L. Covell

PRINCIPAL SUBSIDIARIES
Vonage America, Inc.

PRINCIPAL COMPETITORS
AT&T Inc.; Time Warner Telecom Inc.; Comcast Corp.; Deltathree, Inc.; Dialpad Communications, Inc.; Net2Phone, Inc.

FURTHER READING
Brand, Constant, "Internet Phone Provider Vonage Shares Drop in NYSE Debut," *America's Intelligence Wire,* May 24, 2006.

Crockett, Roger O., "Vonage: Spending as Fast as It Can," *Business Week,* June 20, 2005, p. 106.

Elstrom, Peter, "Vonage on the Line," *Business Week Online,* May 23, 2006.

Gross, Doug, "Update 12-Vonage Falls 12.7%—Becomes Weakest IPO of 2006," *America's Intelligence Wire,* May 24, 2006.

Hibbard, Justin, "Vonage Is Dialing for Dollars," *Business Week,* May 16, 2005, p. 8.

Nakamoto, Michiyo, "The Internet's Next Big Talking Point," *Financial Times,* September 9, 2005, p. 17.

Odell, Mark, "The Stand-Alone Pioneers," *Financial Times,* September 9, 2005, p. 17.

Reeves, Amy, "Vonage Story Gives Street Something to Talk About," *Investor's Business Daily,* August 30, 2005, p. A6.

Thottam, Jyoti, "The Internet Is Calling," *Time,* August 23, 2004, p. 42.

"Vonage Files for IPO," *InternetWeek,* February 8, 2006.

"Vonage Puts Its Money on the Line," *Business Week Online,* March 11, 2005.

"Vonage Tanks in Market Debut," *InternetWeek,* May 24, 2006.

Zammit, Deanna, "Vonage Starts Rallying Cry for Broadband Phones," *ADWEEK,* October 13, 2003, p. 18.

WebEx Communications, Inc.

—————— ■ ——————

3979 Freedom Circle
Santa Clara, California 95054
U.S.A.
Telephone: (408) 435-7000
Toll Free: (877) 509-3239
Fax: (408) 496-4303
Web site: http://www.webex.com

Public Company
Incorporated: 1995 as Silver Computing
Employees: 2,091
Sales: $308.42 million (2005)
Stock Exchanges: NASDAQ
Ticker Symbol: WEBX
NAIC: 511210 Software Publishers; 518210 Data Processing, Hosting, and Related Services

■ ■ ■

WebEx Communications, Inc. is the world's leading provider of online meeting services. Through its web site, clients can host real-time business meetings, conferences, and training seminars in which multimedia presentations and software programs can be simultaneously viewed and/or controlled by participants. Other WebEx offerings enable users to remotely operate, program, or troubleshoot computers. The company serves more than 23,000 customers that range from small businesses to *Fortune* 500 corporations and the U.S. Department of Defense.

EARLY YEARS

WebEx Communications was founded in California in 1995 by Subrah Iyar and Min Zhu. India-born Iyar had immigrated to the United States in 1982 to seek business opportunities, and worked for Apple Computer and Intel before serving as vice-president and general manager of Quarterdeck Corporation's Internet business division. Zhu had grown up in Communist China and come to the United States on a scholarship to Stanford University, after graduation working for IBM and Price Waterhouse. In 1991 he founded a software company called Future Labs to market a document collaboration software program he had developed. Several years later the firm was purchased by Quarterdeck for $13 million, and Zhu and Iyar went into business together under the name Silver Computing.

At first the company had a hard time making ends meet, and half of its engineering staff was soon hired out to consulting projects to bring in revenue. Although they initially avoided seeking venture capital, Iyar and Zhu later sold stakes to several firms including Baan Investments.

In mid-1997 Silver changed its name to Stellar Computing, and then in December to ActiveTouch. In early 1998 the firm bought the technology assets of Zhu's former company Future Labs from Quarterdeck, and a few months later the ActiveTouch Server and ActiveMeetings software application were introduced. From the company's web site clients could schedule or instantly activate meetings for sales, support, or business purposes. All participants could access information in a variety of formats, with presentation sharing, screen synchronization, form completion, and other features available. ActiveTouch also licensed its software to other firms for incorporation into their products.

In February 1999 the company introduced a variation on ActiveMeetings called WebEx, which was a free service that allowed up to six Internet-connected customers to meet in real time to share presentations, documents, and software applications. Unlike competing products such as Microsoft's NetMeeting, it did not require that all computers have the same software loaded onto them, with users able to share their own programs directly through the WebEx browser. The free service was supported by advertisements, but customers could upgrade for a fee to a commercial-free version that offered more features. To facilitate the online meetings, ActiveTouch provided telephone conference call services as well.

Customized versions of the software were also available, and some companies licensed it for incorporation into their own programs. The first such agreement was reached with Compaq, which integrated it into a customer care product called NetACD. ActiveTouch promoted WebEx with various methods including a Volkswagen Beetle giveaway, and by the fall over 25,000 businesses were using it and more than 100 had paid for enhanced services. In September, ActiveTouch became known as WebEx, Inc.

INITIAL PUBLIC OFFERING IN 2000

In early 2000 the company changed its name to WebEx Communications, Inc., and filed for an initial public stock offering, and in July 3.5 million shares were sold on the NASDAQ. Investors were enthusiastic, and the price jumped from $14 to $58 per share within a month. The firm continued to be led by Chairman and CEO Subrah Iyar and President and Chief Technical Officer Min Zhu.

WebEx soon began shifting toward an all-paid service model and signed 700 new users during the third quarter of the year including 3M, Toyota, and Hewlett-Packard, while AT&T and Global Crossing integrated its programs into their own software products. In August the WebEx Meeting Center was introduced, which allowed users of Windows, Macintosh, and Solaris computers to collaborate across all three platforms. The company also opened a European headquarters in Amsterdam and sales offices in Australia and Hong Kong, while boosting its staff by 67 to 362.

In the fall WebEx formed a new consulting services unit, and Oracle and Logitech integrated its software into their products. For 2000 the company reported revenues of $25.4 million, up from just $2.6 million the year before. Spending for sales and marketing (which included commercials featuring flamboyant entertainer RuPaul) was high, however, and a loss of $52.4 million was reported. The firm's stock-based compensation plan, which helped it attract employees, had cost an additional $28 million. In May 2001 the company sold an additional $21.5 million worth of stock in a private placement.

The U.S. economy was stumbling, and companies began seeking out collaborative software programs such as WebEx's to save them money on business travel. By late summer, the firm's client total had reached 4,000. The terrorist attacks on the United States of September 11 boosted sales even further when air travel plummeted, with many new customers signed during the fall including pharmacy giant CVS and electronics maker Samsung. The firm also began offering its services through France Telecom and BEA Systems.

In late 2001 WebEx's conferencing software was upgraded to offer multiple language interfaces while Hewlett-Packard added the company's Access Anywhere remote computer control system to its handheld and notebook computers. Sales jumped to $81.2 million for the year and losses fell to $27.6 million.

Competition was heating up, however, and in early 2002 both Microsoft and Oracle announced they were planning similar products to those of WebEx. The firm soon upgraded its Meeting Center program with technology called MediaTone, which used the international fiber-optic network WebEx had been building for several years, and added an interactive teaching product called Training Center. In April research firm Frost & Sullivan reported that WebEx had a 57.5 percent share of the conferencing software market.

KEY DATES

1995: Silver Computing is founded by Subrah Iyar and Min Zhu.

1997: Name is changed to Stellar Computing, then to ActiveTouch.

1998: Assets of Zhu's former company Future Labs are acquired; ActiveTouch interactive communications software and server is introduced.

1999: WebEx free meeting-hosting service debuts.

2000: Name is changed to WebEx Communications; company completes initial public offering.

2002: Three Chinese engineering companies are acquired; firm reports first annual profit.

2003: Presenter, Inc. and CyberBazaar are purchased.

2005: Intranets.com is acquired; small-business meeting offerings are added.

EUROPEAN EXPANSION, NEW SERVICES IN 2002

In the summer of 2002 the firm expanded its Amsterdam office, and in the fall added an online customer assistance feature called Support Center. WebEx also signed a two-year contract to provide conferencing services to Boeing Co., unveiled a product to facilitate wireless meetings with the Microsoft Tablet PC, and bought three small Chinese engineering firms from cofounder Min Zhu during the year. Sales reached $140 million and a first-time profit of $16.4 million was recorded.

In early 2003 WebEx launched an $8 million advertising campaign featuring comedian Lily Tomlin and introduced a new Enterprise Edition of its software, which integrated the Meeting Center, Training Center, Support Center, and OnStage products into a single package. In the spring, with *Forbes* magazine naming WebEx the fastest-growing technology company in the United States, the firm's Meeting Center was incorporated into Yahoo's Messenger program and WebEx services were launched in Iyar's homeland of India in conjunction with a company called CyberBazaar. A few months later WebEx acquired the latter for $4 million and renamed it WebEx India.

In July 2003 the company bought Presenter, Inc., a web conference recording software maker, and began offering its products under the name Presentation Studio. In September WebEx used an online focus group of customers to help edit a new ad campaign, and in December the company launched a new service that enabled U.S. government employees to host secure online conferences with a credit card.

Sales for 2004 rose to $189 million, with the firm's profit of $59.8 million due in part to a one-time $21.4 million tax benefit. The firm had more than 1,200 employees working at offices in 11 countries and some 8,850 companies using its services, including such new customers as Ingram Micro and Dow Corning. Despite its international presence, more than 93 percent of sales came from the United States. WebEx's market share had risen to 64 percent, though competition continued to be strong as Microsoft and Cisco Systems acquired key competitors.

In early 2004 the company launched a new multilingual European service with telecommunications firm BT, began working with audio/video conferencing provider VCON, partnered with virtual event manager KRM Information Services, and joined with Modern HighTech to introduce service to Korea. WebEx also announced an alliance with cell phone maker Siemens to bring conferencing services to mobile phones via that firm's OpenScape program, and integrated its software into the online customer service offerings of Salesforce.com.

SMARTTECH DEBUTS IN 2004

In April a new offering called SMARTtech was introduced that allowed computer service personnel to remotely operate and repair software problems, while additional multimedia capabilities were added to the firm's other programs, and an e-commerce module was installed in the latest release of Training Center. In June a new agreement was signed with America Online (AOL) to integrate WebEx offerings into that firm's Instant Messenger program. The company was shifting much of its support work to India and hiring more employees there, while also initiating a $40 million stock buyback program. In the fall of 2004 WebEx introduced Sales Center to support online sales efforts.

In January 2005 the U.S. Department of Defense chose WebEx to supply it with secure web conferencing services as part of a pilot program, and the company launched a new product called MyWebExPC. Derived from the older Access Anywhere program, it allowed users to remotely access another computer's desktop and was geared toward persons who needed to reach their work computer while on the road or at home. It was initially offered for free to compete with a product of Citrix Systems, which had entered the online conferencing arena. In February WebEx filed suit against Citrix, alleging that its rival had committed "cybersquatting" by purchasing ten domain names similar to WebEx's on the day it launched the MyWebExPC service.

Early 2005 saw the company begin offering a new flat rate pricing plan featuring unlimited monthly usage, which helped boost sales. In the summer WebEx introduced a product called Automatic Record Retention, which could record and archive web conferences for companies needing to comply with newly tightened U.S. securities regulations. The firm also launched an online customer support product called Customer Connect in Japan in partnership with NTT Communications, and acquired a small-business online meeting services firm called Intranets.com of Massachusetts for $45 million. The latter was folded into the newly created WebExOne division, which subsequently introduced small-business meeting services MeetMeNow, PCNow, WebOffice Workgroup, and WebOffice Personal. For 2005 the firm recorded revenues of $308.4 million and net income of $52.7 million. WebEx had by now invested more than $150 million in network infrastructure on five continents to give its users what one reviewer called the "Cadillac" of web conferencing services.

In January 2006 a new on-demand information technology service, WebEx Systems Management Services, was added, and in February a new paid instant messaging service, AIM Pro, was launched in collaboration with AOL. March saw an alliance formed with Xerox Corp. to include WebEx in the new DocuShare CPX application, as well as the introduction of WebEx services through Mexican telecommunications firm Avantel. International sales were growing and now comprised 12 percent of revenues, as the company boosted sales and marketing abroad. The firm's customer total topped 23,000 and it was hosting some 50,000 meetings a day.

In just over a decade WebEx Communications, Inc., had grown to control nearly two-thirds of the market for online meeting services against strong competitors including Microsoft and Cisco Systems. The firm's sizable investment in infrastructure and its numerous strategic alliances positioned it strongly for the future, with many international markets still to be tapped.

Frank Uhle

PRINCIPAL SUBSIDIARIES

WebEx Australia Pty. Ltd.; WebEx Asia Ltd. (Hong Kong); WebEx China Ltd.; WebEx Communications B.V. (Netherlands); WebEx Communications Deutschland GmbH (Germany); WebEx Communica-

tions France, SARL; WebEx Communications India Pvt. Ltd.; WebEx Communications Japan K.K.; WebEx Communications U.K., Ltd.; WebEx Worldwide B.V. (Netherlands); WebExOne, Inc.; Intranets K.K. (Japan).

PRINCIPAL COMPETITORS

Adobe Systems, Inc.; Cisco Systems, Inc.; Citrix Systems, Inc.; Genesys Telecommunications Laboratories, Inc.; International Business Machines Corp.; Microsoft Corporation; Netviewer GmbH; NTRglobal; Oracle Corporation; PCVisit Software AG; Saba Software, Inc.; Salesforce.com, Inc.; West Corporation.

FURTHER READING

Auchard, Eric, "WebEx to Buy Intranets.com for $45 Million in Cash," *Reuters News,* August 1, 2005.

Becker, David, "Web Conferencing Market Heats Up," *CNETNews.com,* March 1, 2004.

Breeden, John II, "Is It Live, or WebEx?," *Newsbytes News Network,* July 27, 2005.

Brown, Ken Spencer, "WebEx Vs. Citrix Battle Gains Steam," *Investor's Business Daily,* January 24, 2005, p. A4.

Bryce, Robert, "WebEx Communications," *Interactive Week,* July 10, 2001.

Cooper, Evan, "Conferencing on the Web," *On Wall Street,* November 1, 2004.

Elstein, Aaron, "Big Firms Push Web Conferencing," *Wall Street Journal Online,* December 28, 2001.

"Ernestine Helps WebEx," *Technology Advertising & Branding Report,* January 27, 2003.

Hicks, Matt, "WebEx Slaps Citrix with Cyber-Squatting Suit," *eWeek,* February 3, 2005.

———, "WebEx Ties Web Conferencing with IP Phones," *eWeek,* April 1, 2004.

———, "WebEx Turns Training into Cash," *eWeek,* May 25, 2004.

Hosford, Christopher, "Has WebEx Got a Deal for You!," *Sales & Marketing Management,* May 1, 2006, p. 24.

Lien, Jennifer, "The Capitalist Road to NASDAQ," *Business Times Singapore,* December 3, 2002.

Linecker, Adelia Cellini, "Rival Looms Large at Web Conferencing Firm," *Investor's Business Daily,* September 25, 2003.

Natarajan, Arun, "Real-Time Meetings at Webex.com," *Business Line,* April 8, 1999.

Schaff, William, "Businesses Turn to Web Conferencing," *InformationWeek,* April 19, 2004.

Solheim, Shelley, "WebEx Taps Intranets.com Tools to Reel in SMBs," *eWeek,* October 11, 2005.

Spangler, Todd, "WebEx: 'Cadillac' Tool Is Pricey, Too," *Baseline,* March 6, 2006.

Swett, Clint, "San Jose-Calif.-Based Internet Technology Firm to Expand in Sacramento," *World Reporter,* September 14, 2000.

Varon, Elana, "Subrah Iyar," *CIO,* October 1, 2002.

Veverka, Mark, "Just Starting to Glow: Why WebEx Will Shine," *Barron's,* June 12, 2006, p. 26.

"WebEx Communications, Inc.—History," *Datamonitor Company Profiles,* July 20, 2004.

"WebEx Sells 2M Shares for $21.5M," *Dow Jones News Service,* May 21, 2001.

"WebEx Strikes Deals, Shares Rise Over 10 Percent," *Reuters News,* October 22, 2001.

"WebEx to Acquire India's CyberBazaar," *Reuters News,* December 17, 2003.

Whiting Petroleum Corporation

1700 Broadway, Suite 2300
Denver, Colorado 80290
U.S.A.
Telephone: (303) 837-1661
Fax: (303) 861-4023
Web site: http://www.whiting.com

Public Company
Incorporated: 1983 as Whiting Oil and Gas Corporation
Employees: 309
Sales: Sales: $540.4 million (2005)
Stock Exchanges: New York
Ticker Symbol: WLL
NAIC: 211111 Crude Petroleum and Natural Gas Extraction

■ ■ ■

Whiting Petroleum Corporation is an oil and natural gas company involved in the acquisition, exploration, and production of properties in the Rocky Mountain, Permian Basin, Gulf Coast, Michigan, and Mid-Continent regions of the United States. The company has proved reserves of 199.2 million barrels of oil (MMBbl) and 386.4 billion cubic feet of natural gas (Bcf) for total proved reserves of 236.6 million barrels of oil equivalent (MMBOE), a figure calculated by converting natural gas volumes to equivalent oil barrels; six thousand cubic feet of natural gas is equal to one barrel of oil. On a daily basis, Whiting Petroleum produces 40,700 barrels of oil equivalent. Of the company's five operating regions, the Permian Basin

stands as the most important area, accounting for slightly more than half of its total proved reserves. Known for its aggressive stance on the acquisition front, Whiting Petroleum more than quintupled its revenue volume and its reserves between 2001 and 2005.

ORIGINS

During its first quarter-century of business, Whiting Oil and Gas rose from a start-up in the oil and gas industry into a prominent member of the community. The company, originally named Whiting Oil and Gas Corporation, was formed by two industry veterans, J. B. "Bert" Ladd and Kenneth R. Whiting, who remained, serving under various capacities, with Whiting Petroleum through its silver anniversary year. The company operated both as an independent exploration and production firm and as a subsidiary of a larger corporation, displaying a penchant for acquiring properties while pursuing its own agenda and adhering to the direction of a parent company.

From the start, Whiting Oil and Gas gained legitimacy in the industry through the reputations of its founders. Both were seasoned executives well versed in the nuances of the business, having established themselves as adept managers well before founding Whiting Oil and Gas in 1980. Of the two, Ladd was the more experienced, beginning his career in the oil and gas industry after earning an undergraduate degree in petroleum engineering from the University of Kansas in 1949. After college, Ladd joined The Texas Co., a company that became better known as Texaco Inc. He spent nearly a decade at The Texas Co., leaving in 1957

COMPANY PERSPECTIVES

Whiting's growth strategy is focused on increasing reserves and production per share through producing property acquisitions, exploitation and exploration. Whiting strives to increase reserves and daily production through complementary acquisitions, efficiently exploiting our undeveloped oil and natural gas reserves and drilling a number of exploratory wells in our core regions.

to join Consolidated Oil & Gas, where he served as vice-president of operations. After his stay at Consolidated Oil, Ladd formed his own company in 1968, a company named Ladd Petroleum Corporation that at one point counted Kenneth Whiting as its executive vice-president. Whiting, who earned an undergraduate degree in business from the University of Colorado and a law degree from the University of Denver, joined Webb Resources, Inc., after leaving Ladd Petroleum, serving as the company's president from 1978 to 1979, ending his stay at Webb Resources the same year Ladd retired as president and chairman of Ladd Petroleum.

Ladd and Whiting based their entrepreneurial creation in Colorado, where Whiting Oil and Gas would remain despite being acquired later by another corporation. "We've always seen ourselves as a Colorado-based company," a company executive said in a December 9, 2003 interview with the *Rocky Mountain News*. The company began operating with less than $3 million in assets, a total that would grow exponentially as the years passed. Whiting Oil and Gas's ability to expand its asset base was increased substantially once the company converted to public ownership, a step the company took in 1983. The year Whiting Oil and Gas completed its initial public offering (IPO) also marked the arrival of an executive who would lead the company 20 years later. James J. Volker, who attended the same schools as Whiting attended (the University of Denver and the University of Colorado) joined Whiting Oil and Gas in August 1983 as the company's vice-president of corporate development.

ACQUISITION BY ALLIANT
ENERGY: 1992

On its own as a public company, Whiting Oil and Gas spent the remainder of the 1980s building up its assets, fashioning itself into a company coveted by others. After nearly a decade operating in the public arena, the

company drew the attention of a Madison, Wisconsin-based utility named Alliant Energy Corp. Alliant, an energy services provider involved in both regulated and non-regulated businesses, acquired Whiting Oil and Gas in 1992. Whiting Oil and Gas, with $30 million in assets at the time of its acquisition, became an indirect, wholly owned subsidiary of Alliant once the deal was completed, but it retained its key personnel and its affiliation with the state of Colorado. Volker became a contract consultant for Whiting Oil and Gas after the Alliant acquisition. Whiting traded his posts as president and chief executive officer for a seat on the company's board of directors, where he sat alongside Ladd.

Whiting Oil and Gas entered a new era of existence once within the Alliant fold. Although the company remained active on the acquisition front, its retreat from the public market reduced its visibility in the oil and gas industry, engendering a quiet period in its history. As it was later revealed, Whiting Oil and Gas's efforts to expand ratcheted up during the company's 20th anniversary, an event, perhaps not coincidentally, that also marked the appointment of Volker to a managerial position. Vice-president of corporate development during Whiting Oil and Gas's first decade of business and a contract consultant following the Alliant merger, Volker was given the titles of executive vice-president and chief operating officer in August 2000. The year became the starting point of an expansion campaign that would be revealed after Alliant's management made an important decision in late 2002. In November, the company announced it intended to divest all of its non-regulated subsidiaries to focus its efforts on its core, regulated utility business. Executives at headquarters in Madison mulled over different ways to monetize their investment in Whiting Oil and Gas, whittling their options down to three choices: sell the company's assets, either in whole or in parts; sell the company to another company; or take it public. Management chose the last option, setting the stage for the company's return to independence and the public sector.

WHITING PETROLEUM SPINOFF:
2003

As the company prepared to embark on its new era of freedom, Volker was promoted to president and chief executive officer in January 2002. Under Volker's command, Whiting Oil and Gas assumed an aggressive posture towards acquisitions, but the company already was feverishly acquiring oil and gas properties before Volker's promotion. Between 2000 and 2002, Whiting Oil and Gas completed 41 separate acquisitions, adding 369.6 billion cubic feet equivalent (Bcfe). The acquisitions doubled the company's reserves, bolstering its asset

KEY DATES

1980:   Whiting Petroleum is founded as Whiting Oil and Gas Corporation.
1983:   The company completes its initial public offering of stock.
1992:   Alliant Energy acquires Whiting Oil and Gas.
2003:   Whiting Petroleum Corporation is spun off as a separate, publicly traded company.
2004:   Whiting Petroleum acquires Equity Oil Co.
2005:   Whiting Petroleum pays roughly $800 million for oil and gas properties owned by Celero Energy LP.

base spread across Michigan, the Rockies, the Gulf Coast, the Permian Basin in western Texas, and the Mid-Continent region. In the coming years, as it set out on its own for the second time in its history, Whiting Oil and Gas would add properties to its existing geographic base and venture into new territories, recording enviable financial growth as it did so.

In the months following Alliant's decision to shed its non-regulated assets, anticipation of the spinoff of Whiting Oil and Gas and its implications for the company's future grew both at headquarters in Denver and within the industry. Industry analysts predicted a more expansion-minded company, and Volker's management team in Denver was ready to fulfill such expectations. "It will make Whiting more independent," one pundit said in a November 18, 2003 interview with the *Denver Post.* "By going out and being independent of Alliant, it will free Whiting to do things that might not have been available to them as a subsidiary." To complete the spinoff, Whiting Petroleum Corporation was formed as holding company for Whiting Oil and Gas, one of the final steps taken as Volker eyed what he hoped would be a $240 million IPO. The IPO was completed in November 2003, raising $230 million in an offering that set the subsidiary free from its parent. Volker, armed with capital and expressing a desire to acquire, wasted little time before pressing ahead with his company's expansion program.

Whiting Petroleum's board of directors, which included Ladd and Whiting, believed Volker to be the ideal executive to lead the company forward after its separation from Alliant. Volker was appointed to the additional post of chairman in January 2004, giving him the three most powerful positions in the company, and he quickly responded by adding to Whiting Petroleum's

reserves by brokering an important deal. In February 2004, less than 90 days after becoming a public company, Whiting Petroleum announced the acquisition of Equity Oil Co. for approximately $72 million. An independent oil and gas exploration and production company for more than 80 years, Equity owned properties in California, Colorado, North Dakota, and Wyoming. The acquisition set the tone for what was to follow. "We're not done," Volker declared in a February 9, 2004 interview with *Corporate Financing Week.* "It's a good first step for us. We will be doing other things," he promised. The acquisition of Equity, which was completed in July 2004, was part of Volker's broader strategy for growth. In the same interview, he related his intention to "acquire good properties, exploit the underdeveloped reserves of those properties, and explore—meaning take higher risks and look for a bigger rate of return than you get from acquisitions."

Volker made good on his promise of further acquisitions in the months leading up to Whiting Petroleum's 25th anniversary. In the wake of the Equity deal, the company completed a series of acquisitions, concentrating its efforts on adding to its oil reserves. There were notable exceptions, however, including the purchase of fields in Colorado, Wyoming, Louisiana, and Texas in August 2004 for $63.5 million that contained primarily natural gas reserves. In March 2005, the company completed the purchase of additional natural gas properties, paying $65 million for five producing fields in the Green River Basin of Wyoming, but more than 80 percent of the reserves added in 2004 and 2005 bolstered the company's oil holdings. By far the largest of the acquisitions completed during the two-year period was a deal brokered with Midland, Texas–based Celero Energy LP in July 2005. The acquisition was completed in two stages for a total of roughly $800 million, the largest deal in Whiting Petroleum's history. The first part of the transaction to close was the Postle Field in Oklahoma, a property comprising five producing fields stretched across more than 25,000 acres. The Postle Field part of the Celero Energy purchase closed in August 2005, two months before the North Ward Estes Field officially became part of Whiting Petroleum's portfolio. The largest asset owned by the company, the North Ward Estes Field covered 58,000 acres containing six fields with 636 producing wells.

As Volker plotted Whiting Petroleum's future course, further acquisitions appeared likely. Within two years of its separation from Alliant, the company acquired 206.3 MMBOE, paying nearly $1.5 billion for the enormous increase to its reserves. The outlay delivered robust financial growth, as annual revenues nearly doubled. Perhaps most important, Volker and his management team achieved such growth without sacrificing profitability. Net income during the two-year period swelled from $70 million to $121.9 million. The glowing financial results, recorded at a time of record-setting profits in the oil and gas industry, confirmed the value of the company's acquisition strategy, providing Volker with all the encouragement he needed to continue expanding in the years ahead.

Jeffrey L. Covell

PRINCIPAL SUBSIDIARIES

Whiting Oil and Gas Corporation; Equity Oil Company; Whiting Programs, Inc.

PRINCIPAL COMPETITORS

Anadarko Petroleum Corporation; Black Hills Corporation; Cabot Oil & Gas Corporation.

FURTHER READING

"At OGIS for the First Time, Whiting Petroleum Already Had Experience Talking to Investors," *Oil and Gas Investor,* June 2004, p. SSS21.

"E&P Outfit on the Prowl for Buys," *Corporate Financing Week,* December 13, 2004, p. 3.

Kelley, Joanne, "Whiting Hoists Its Own Flag," *Rocky Mountain News,* December 9, 2003, p. 5B.

Mehring, James, "Whiting Petroleum Buys Delta Texas-Louisiana Fields, Plus Four in Colorado-Wyoming," *America's Intelligence Wire,* August 23, 2004.

"New Kid on the Block Whiting Ties Up Biggest Deal to Date," *Oil Daily,* September 3, 2004.

"Newly Public Oil Co. Looks for More Acquisitions," *Corporate Financing Week,* February 9, 2004, p. 9.

Oberbeck, Steven, "Salt Lake City-Based Equity Oil to Be Acquired by Denver's Whiting Petroleum," *Salt Lake City Tribune,* February 3, 2004.

Raabe, Steve, "Denver-Based Alliant Spinoff Whiting Petroleum Eyes Initial Public Offering," *Denver Post,* November 18, 2003.

———, "Denver-Based Energy Firm to Expand Holdings with Texas Purchase," *Denver Post,* July 28, 2005.

Sullivan, John A., "Whiting Petroleum Continues Property Buying Spree into 2005," *Natural Gas Week,* January 24, 2005, p. 5.

Toal, Brian A., "A New Face on the Street," *Oil and Gas Investor,* March 2004, p. 51.

Wetuski, Jodi, "Newly Public Whiting to Buy Equity Oil for Stock," *Oil and Gas Investor,* March 2004, p. 104.

"Whiting Petroleum Corp., Denver, Has Entered Two Purchase Agreements with Midland, Texas–Based Celero Energy LP," *Oil and Gas Investor,* September 2005, p. 106.

WIREMOLD

L7 legrand®

The Wiremold Company

60 Woodlawn Street
West Hartford, Connecticut 06110-2326
U.S.A.
Telephone: (860) 233-6251
Fax: (860) 232-2062
Web site: http://www.wiremold.com

Wholly Owned Subsidiary of Legrand Holding SA
Founded: 1900 as The Richmondt Electric Wire Conduit
    Company
Employees: 900
Sales: $470 million (2005 est.)
NAIC: 335932 Noncurrent-Carrying Wiring Device
    Manufacturing; 335931 Current-Carrying Wiring
    Device Manufacturing; 335999 All Other Miscel-
    laneous Electrical Equipment and Component
    Manufacturing

■ ■ ■

The Wiremold Company is one of the leading producers of wiring and cable management products for both
the residential housing and commercial building markets.
The tens of thousands of products the firm produces
include raceway, in-floor, overhead, open space, and
furniture management systems, and Wiremold also
makes power and data quality products such as surge
protectors. Wholly owned by the French electrical
equipment maker Legrand since 2000, Wiremold came
to prominence after Art Byrne was brought onboard as
CEO in 1991. Byrne introduced "lean" business practices
and just-in-time management techniques based on *kai-*

zen, the Japanese system of continuous improvement.
Byrne's initiatives were so successful—for example,
increasing sales from $100 million to more than $450
million in less than ten years—that Wiremold became a
widely discussed model for a new way of conducting
business.

EARLY 20TH-CENTURY ORIGINS

Prior to its acquisition by Legrand, Wiremold spent a
century under the ownership and control of the Murphy
family. D. Hayes Murphy was the driving force behind
the company's founding. The firstborn son of an Irish
immigrant, Murphy was interested in going into the
manufacturing business after graduating from college in
1900. His father, Daniel E. Murphy, a very successful
Milwaukee-based insurance agent for the Northwestern
Mutual Life Insurance Company, had him investigate a
Milwaukee manufacturer called Richmondt Electric Wire
Conduit Company.

The firm was headed by C. D. Richmondt and was
one of a growing number of companies attempting to
meet the burgeoning demand for conduit for the still
nascent electricity industry. Richmondt's firm specialized
in a unique rigid conduit for household wiring,
essentially zinc-coated water pipe lined on the inside
with enamel to protect the wiring. D. H. Murphy was
impressed by the business's potential but not by Richmondt's management of it, for the firm was nearly
insolvent and lacked the production capacity to meet
the large orders Richmondt had secured. Late in 1900
then, Daniel Murphy bought the firm from Richmondt
for $10,000. Although the father was named the

company's president and the son, secretary, it was D. H. Murphy who was charged with running the business.

In an attempt to fulfill Richmondt's overly ambitious orders, D. Hayes Murphy moved the company in November 1901 to Waukegan, Illinois, where he had found a larger factory. He also changed the name of the firm to The American Interior Conduit Company. Pressure from competitors, however, forced Murphy into a 1902 merger with Pittsburgh-based Safety Armorite Conduit Company, the nation's largest conduit maker. The Garland family, owners of Safety Armorite, controlled American Interior Conduit, which began operating as the Waukegan branch of Safety Armorite. In 1904, the Waukegan operations were moved to Safety Armorite's West Pittsburgh facilities to be closer to the pipe supply. That same year, American Interior Conduit began producing loom conduit, a type of flexible, nonmetallic tubing made from cotton impregnated with resin. Marketed under the Wireduct brand, the loom product was a great success for Murphy's operation.

The Garland family, meanwhile, had purchased another conduit company, the American Conduit Manufacturing Company, which they continued to run separately. Murphy, aiming to once again control his own company, viewed this firm as his vehicle for doing so, and he eventually, in 1909, angled his way into the company presidency. Aiding his ambitions was his success in securing some stock in Safety Armorite when

that firm began consolidating its subsidiary companies, including American Interior Conduit, in 1906. When the Garlands and Safety Armorite ran into serious financial difficulties in 1911, Murphy persuaded the Garlands to essentially trade American Conduit Manufacturing for his Safety Armorite stock. At age 34, Murphy was the owner and president of his own company.

INTRODUCTION OF WIREMOLD RACEWAY

Based in New Kensington, Pennsylvania, American Conduit produced a variety of products, including rigid conduit and loom. By 1914 it had distributors in 33 states and two territories, was selling directly to contractors in 13 other states, and included among its customers major shipbuilders and large manufacturers such as the American Locomotive Company and the Pullman Company. That year, Murphy invested in a new factory, while he was also experimenting with various ways to reward his employees. In 1916 he introduced a successful profit-sharing plan at a time when few businesses offered such a benefit.

During this period, American households had the opportunity to purchase increasing numbers of electric products, including table lamps, portable fans, clothes irons, and carpet sweepers. Most homes, however, had a decided lack of electrical outlets into which these devices could be plugged. American Conduit came up with a solution: Wiremold raceway. Most existing forms of conduit were designed to carry electric wiring through the walls of buildings. By contrast, the Wiremold product was a lightweight, molded metal conduit designed to be installed on walls and ceilings and along baseboards, making it ideal for retrofitting homes with inadequate wiring. Ease of installation was one of its main selling points, as the wiring could easily be fed through the raceway, and various fittings, such as outlet boxes and receptacle bases, were offered as part of the Wiremold line and meshed smoothly with raceway itself. Wiremold was also much less expensive than earlier, unsuccessfully introduced metal moldings for wiring.

The Wiremold 500 series (the number referred to the product's wiring capacity) was introduced in June 1916 at the annual convention of the National Electrical Contractors Association, where the attendees expressed much interest in the new product. Its full rollout was held up, however, when a competitor secured an injunction that delayed the all important approval of the product by Underwriters Laboratory. Wiremold was eventually approved, and in early 1918 a revised version of the National Electrical Code was distributed to that effect.

KEY DATES

1900: Daniel E. Murphy buys Milwaukee-based Richmondt Electric Wire Conduit Company; his son D. Hayes Murphy is charged with running the firm.

1901: D. H. Murphy moves the firm to Waukegan, Illinois, and renames it The American Interior Conduit Company.

1902: Murphy's firm merges with Pittsburgh-based Safety Armorite Conduit Company, controlled by the Garland family.

1904: American Interior Conduit's operations are moved to West Pittsburgh.

1906: Safety Armorite begins consolidating its subsidiary companies, including American Interior Conduit.

1909: Murphy gains the presidency of a separate Garland family firm, American Conduit Manufacturing Company.

1911: Murphy purchases American Conduit from the Garland family.

1916: Company introduces the Wiremold 500 series raceway.

1919: The firm's rigid conduit business is sold to General Electric Company; American Conduit relocates to Hartford, Connecticut.

1920: Company is renamed The American Wiremold Company.

1926: Company is renamed The Wiremold Company.

1929: Wiremold moves to West Hartford, Connecticut.

1942: Production of flexible air duct begins.

1947: The Plugmold line debuts.

1955: Murphy's son John is named Wiremold president.

1979: Warren Packard becomes the first president and CEO from outside the Murphy family.

1981: Wiremold enters the do-it-yourself consumer market with a line of plastic raceway.

1988: Divestment of the flexible duct business is completed.

1991: New CEO Art Byrne launches an ambitious program of quality and process improvement using the *kaizen* approach.

2000: In a $770 million deal, Legrand SA of France acquires Wiremold.

Unfortunately, American Conduit's rigid conduit business simultaneously encountered a host of troubles, including pipe supply difficulties in part due to World War I shortages, a $40,000 inventory discrepancy, and $30,000 worth of unfulfilled orders. Murphy was forced to hold off on further production of Wiremold while straightening out the rigid conduit mess. Once he restored the solvency of this sector of his business, he sold the rigid conduit operations to General Electric Company for $1 million. This 1919 deal enabled American Conduit to focus its resources on its Wiremold raceway and loom products. Murphy used some of the proceeds to relocate his business to Hartford, Connecticut, where he set up operations at the former Franklin Lamp Works, a five-story brick building that spanned more than a city block. A driving force behind the move was Murphy's desire to escape the pollution of industrial Pittsburgh and to settle in a location where he could indulge his passion for sailing.

After the move to Hartford, Murphy overhauled American Conduit's marketing and distribution arrangements—a successful endeavor, perhaps too successful. A huge increase in orders for loom overtaxed the new factory, leading to the shipment in the fall of 1919 of a huge batch of defective loom valued at more than $80,000. To maintain his customers' loyalty, Murphy offered to make up for this mistake by replacing the bad loom with a new delivery of twice as much loom as had been originally ordered.

It took the company several years to make up for these losses. In the meantime, Murphy staked the firm's future on Wiremold raceway. This shift in emphasis was enshrined in 1920 when Murphy renamed the company The American Wiremold Company; a further refinement came six years later when the word *American* was dropped from the name. Through tenacious marketing efforts, both consumers and contractors were increasingly catching on to the Wiremold product, which finally began showing a profit in 1923. New Wiremold lines were introduced, including the 700 series in 1921 and the 1000 series in 1928, both offering slight increases in wiring capacity. The company's growth during the 1920s paralleled that of the electricity industry. Wiremold benefited from the electrification of the United States as the number of electrified homes jumped during the decade from less than 25 percent to 65 percent. Wiremold ended the decade by shifting to a newly built facility at 60 Woodlawn Street in West Hartford. The 39,300-square-foot building was sited conveniently adjacent to a rail line.

PLUGGING AWAY DURING THE GREAT DEPRESSION

The crash of the stock market, which occurred shortly after Wiremold's latest relocation, ushered in the lean years of the Great Depression. Murphy vowed not to lay off any employees unless he had no other choice. He kept his promise, though the dropoff in demand led the managers to resort at times to make-work. Murphy later remarked, "When there was nothing else, we washed windows. We had the cleanest windows in town."

Murphy mitigated the effects of the Depression through such innovations as the "school-on-a-truck" program. These trucks traveled throughout the West Coast and the South during the early 1930s equipped with samples of all the company's product lines, its salesmen educating electrical contractors about Wiremold's new generation of products. New product development was not curtailed despite the difficult times, and in 1932 Wiremold 1100 raceway debuted, accommodating multiple plug receptacles. Debuting a year later was the fifth Wiremold raceway, the 200, which was designed for low-density wiring. Next, Wiremold introduced the 1500 overfloor raceway in 1936. A flat raceway designed to minimize obstruction, the 1500 carried wiring from walls across floors to installations in the center of rooms, such as desks or equipment tables. The 2100 raceway was introduced in 1937.

After the worst years of the Depression had passed, Murphy confidently expanded Wiremold's facilities. In 1935 the first half of a second unit at the West Hartford headquarters was completed, as was a new two-story office building. Two years later the second half of the second unit was completed. Following the introduction of fluorescent lighting in 1938, Wiremold created a lighting division the next year to attempt to meet some of the burgeoning demand for the popular new product. Also in 1939, the company's workforce unionized under the International Brotherhood of Electrical Workers. Wiremold had always enjoyed good relations with its workers, who had in fact never asked to join a union. However, having a unionized workforce had become necessary because Wiremold had encountered strong

resistance to its products in trade union strongholds, such as New York City. The 1930s ended with another new Wiremold product, the 3000 raceway. This perimeter product was the firm's first two-piece raceway (comprised of a base and a cover) and was designed to fit in aesthetically with baseboard.

During World War II, Wiremold contributed to the war effort in many ways. In addition to providing loom for a variety of military wiring needs, the firm reconfigured some of its loom machines to produce more than 1.6 million yards of webbing, which the U.S. Army used for parachute harnesses and other strapping applications. Among the other products Wiremold produced during the war were various engine parts, Navy rocket shipping containers, shell shipping containers, and glider parts.

In 1942 the company also established an air duct division, which had the ability to produce long lengths of flexible air duct. This division originally made flexible ducts that the Army Air Corps wanted to use to preheat aircraft engines in the Arctic. Wiremold, however, stayed in the duct business after the war's end, despite its lack of synergy with the core conduit operations. This proved to be a wise move as the company quickly shifted into producing heater and defroster duct for the automobile market, becoming the dominant producer of these auto parts.

BOOMING POSTWAR YEARS

The immediate postwar years, in addition to the new air duct revenue stream, also brought a building boom that drove demand for Wiremold's core products. The Plugmold line, launched in 1947 with the 1900 model, proved quite popular for both retrofit and new construction applications. The 1900 was a perimeter product featuring built-in outlets along its length. The Plugmold 2000, introduced to the market in 1952, was a multi-outlet raceway system offering a higher capacity than the 1900. In 1956 Wiremold debuted the Plugmold 2200, which had a wider raceway and was designed to take the place of wooden baseboard. These products aimed to meet the needs of the American consumer, whose appetite for electrical gadgets seemed to be ever growing.

D. H. Murphy ended his long reign as president of Wiremold in 1955, when his son John was named to succeed him. The founder remained involved in the business as chairman of the board until the mid-1960s, and he passed away in 1973. When John Murphy took over the presidency, he was already a longtime Wiremold veteran, having joined the firm in 1934. He worked closely with his brother Robert, who joined Wiremold in 1936 and was named executive vice-president in 1955.

Throughout the remainder of the 1950s and into the 1960s, Wiremold prospered thanks to the postwar housing boom and automobile craze. Sales of Plugmold products remained extremely strong, and the duct business diversified into other automobile products, such as air conditioning ducts and air intakes for carburetors. By the end of the 1950s Wiremold was the world's leading maker of automobile air-duct products. The company also continued to produce loom, a business on the decline but nonetheless still turning a profit. Ever prudent, the Murphy brothers initiated a streamlining and clean-up effort in 1959 that freed up enough additional operating space to stave off any further infrastructure expansion for a few more years. As the company continued to grow, however, the need to expand production and make it more efficient led to the construction in 1965 of a new 57,000-square-foot factory addition, Building 4, which increased the manufacturing space by approximately 40 percent. A further expansion in 1967 added more plant space as well as a new administration building.

The mid-1960s also saw Wiremold introduce its first lines of multichannel raceways: the 6000, debuting in 1964, and the 4000, in 1966. These products were designed more for commercial buildings, for cases in which two or more raceway runs would have previously been needed. The new raceways could hold two or more electrical lines, for instance, in a shop needing electrical outlets that could handle more than one type of voltage, or could carry both power and communications wiring, such as in an office equipped with a computer network. The proliferation of advanced telecommunications and computers in offices, coupled with the move toward open floor plans, led to Wiremold's introduction of Tele-Power Poles in 1969. Power and communications wiring could be fed from dropped ceiling grids through these poles down to the desks and cubicles on the office floor.

END OF FAMILY MANAGEMENT

As Wiremold grew, but remained a family company, John and Robert Murphy began to see the wisdom of bringing some outsiders onboard to build a management team for the future. In 1973 they hired Warren Packard as company treasurer. Packard, who had been a partner at the Hartford office of the accounting firm Coopers & Lybrand, was named executive vice-president and a member of the board of directors in 1977. At that same time, John Murphy was named chairman and CEO, while Robert Murphy became president and COO. In 1975, meanwhile, Wiremold celebrated its 75th anniversary and also acquired the Chan-L-Wire overhead lighting system from the Rucker Company of Oakland,

California. Chan-L-Wire was a track lighting system particularly suited for large retail establishments and industrial factories.

In May 1979 Packard was named president and CEO, becoming the first person outside the Murphy family to hold these positions. John Murphy remained chairman, while his brother Robert was named vice-chairman. Over the next few years, Packard led the company through several significant changes. Later in 1979, Wiremold gained its first manufacturing operation outside the United States by acquiring the electrical division of Conduits-Amherst Ltd. of Mississauga, Ontario. The acquired unit was renamed Wiremold Canada, Inc. Also in 1979, Packard made the difficult decision to divest the longstanding loom business, as demand for loom was on a significant decline. The unit was sold to Frank D. Saylor & Sons, Inc., of Birmingham, Michigan. In 1981 Wiremold successfully entered the do-it-yourself (DIY) consumer market with a line of plastic raceway. Plastic products soon became the fastest-growing segment of Wiremold's business, in both the DIY and commercial markets. Revenues for 1981 set an all-time record, exceeding $50 million. Wiremold in 1982 also expanded into the flat conductor cable market with a new line of flat cable designed for installation of power under carpet tiles.

Two other significant events marked the Packard era. Wiremold's flexible duct division (the former air duct division) was not as strong a force as it had been in the immediate postwar era, thanks in part to the emergence of competitors and to the more unpredictable nature of the auto industry. The unit was thus earmarked for divestment in 1986, and its operations were sold by 1988. Proceeds from this divestiture were used to expand into the growing field of power and data quality products, such as surge protectors. Two companies in this field were soon acquired: Philadelphia-based Brooks Electronics Inc., in 1988, and Chicago-based Shape Electronics Inc., in 1990.

TURNAROUND UNDER ART BYRNE'S IMPLEMENTATION OF *KAIZEN*

Although one of the leaders in its field, Wiremold by the mid-1980s had become a victim of its own success. Weighed down by antiquated manufacturing and inventory systems, the company became incapable of moving quickly. It was taking too long to get new products to market, deliveries were lagging, customer service was declining, and overall growth was falling off. Under Packard's watch, Wiremold launched several initiatives aimed at righting the ship, including a first stab at implementing a Japanese style just-in-time production system, but these all failed for various reasons. Packard himself realized the company needed a new leader to make the sort of fundamental changes which would spark a turnaround. He thus announced in early 1991 that he planned to retire and then led the search for his replacement. Late in the year Art Byrne was hired on as the new CEO.

Byrne came onboard with several years of experience as a group executive with the Danaher Corporation, where he had successfully used the Japanese system of continuous improvement known as *kaizen.* At Wiremold, he first reduced the workforce, offering early retirement packages to unionized workers and implementing a modest layoff of salaried employees. He then replaced the traditional hierarchical management system with a team model. The team structure provided the framework for his implementation of both *kaizen,* in which small groups participate in problem-solving sessions, and just-in-time manufacturing. Within a few years the manufacturing process had shown a steady stream of improvements, and both defects and inventory were dramatically reduced. Productivity improved by 20 percent in each of the first three years after Byrne joined the company. Between 1991 and 1995, inventory levels were reduced by more than 75 percent. The time to develop new products was reduced from three years to less than six months. Sales, wages, and profits were all growing at a substantially greater pace, with revenues doubling from $100 million to $200 million between 1991 and 1995. As a result of the lean techniques that Byrne had championed, Wiremold became a model to be emulated, its turnaround story told in the books *Lean Thinking* (1996) and *Better Thinking, Better Results* (2003).

The productivity gains and inventory reductions freed up cash which Byrne invested in a string of acquisitions that bolstered and broadened Wiremold's product lines. Among the firms acquired in 1993 were Perma Power Electronics Inc., a producer of super suppressors, line conditioners, and uninterruptible power supplies, and Walker Electrical Products, maker of in-floor and overhead systems for distributing power, lighting, and communications. The 1995 purchase of Raceway Components, Inc., enhanced the Walker line with the leading brand of poke-thru systems, which provided invisible wire and cable management for open-space areas. The *kaizen* approach also aided new product development efforts. One of the splashier introductions came late in the 1990s when Access 5000 decorator raceway debuted. This nonmetallic multichannel raceway came in a selection of finishes, including real wood veneers, thus offering a combination of architectural trim and cable and wire management in one package. By 1999 the acquisitions and new products had helped revenues double yet again, to approximately $400 million.

ACQUISITION BY LEGRAND IN 2000

The rejuvenated Wiremold caught the attention of French electrical equipment maker Legrand SA, which acquired the still privately held company in July 2000 for $770 million in cash and assumed debt. This deal ended 100 years of control by the Murphy family. Wiremold became one of Legrand's key North American companies and began working cooperatively with a sister Legrand company, Ortronics, Inc., based in New London, Connecticut, on a line of integrated data/communications connectivity products. When Byrne retired in 2002, Mike Gambino, the CEO of another sister company, Syracuse, New York-based Pass & Seymour, was named president of Wiremold. Gambino had more than 25 years of experience in the electrical industry. Wiremold continued to crank out innovative new products, such as the Designer Series 4000 steel raceway, which hit the market in September 2005. This perimeter raceway offered the option of configuring receptacles and data jacks in a downward position, provided higher cable capacity than previous models, and was also available prewired.

David E. Salamie

PRINCIPAL SUBSIDIARIES

Wiremold Canada, Inc.; Wiremold International Sales Corporation.

PRINCIPAL COMPETITORS

Graybar Electric Company, Inc.; Cooper Industries, Ltd.; WESCO International, Inc.; Anixter International Inc.; Hubbell Incorporated; Consolidated Electrical Distributors, Inc.; Eaton Corporation.

FURTHER READING

Csir, Floyd J., "Conn. Company to Buy Butler Manufacturing," *Parkersburg (W.Va.) News,* November 6, 1993.

Emiliani, Bob, *Better Thinking, Better Results: Using the Power of Lean As a Total Business Solution,* Kensington, Conn.: Center for Lean Business Management, 2003, 305 p.

Fiume, Orest J., "Lean at Wiremold: Beyond Manufacturing, Putting People Front and Center," *Journal of Organizational Excellence,* Summer 2004, pp. 23–32.

Haar, Dan, "Wiremold Following New Path: Company Leads by Its Example," *Hartford (Conn.) Courant,* August 12, 1995, p. F1.

————, "Wiremold Selling Itself to Grow: French Buyer Will Make Company a Global Player," *Hartford (Conn.) Courant,* July 18, 2000, p. E1.

"A Paragon of Lean Success: Breaking the Mold at Wiremold," *Manufacturing News,* January 31, 2002, pp. 1, 5–12.

Remez, Mike, "Japanese Philosophy Working at Wiremold in West Hartford," *Hartford (Conn.) Courant,* June 16, 1993, p. C1.

Schut, Jan H., "Why Are These Men Smiling?," *Plastics Technology,* January 1999.

Smith, Jim H., *The Wiremold Company: A Century of Solutions,* Lyme, Conn.: Greenwich Publishing Group, 2000, 160 p.

Tillier, Alan, and Katie Anderson, "High-Voltage Deal for Low-Voltage Leader," *Daily Deal,* July 17, 2000.

Votapka, Timothy, "Wiremold Adding Power with Perma Acquisition," *Electronic Buyers' News,* August 2, 1993, p. 22.

Womack, James P., and Daniel T. Jones, *Lean Thinking: Banish Waste and Create Wealth in Your Corporation,* New York: Simon and Schuster, 1996, 350 p.

Young's Bluecrest Seafood
Holdings Ltd.

Ross House
Wickham Road
Grimsby,
United Kingdom
Telephone: +44 01472 242242
Fax: +44 01472 585158
Web site: http://www.youngsbluecrest.co.uk

Wholly Owned Subsidiary of CapVest
Founded: 1805
Employees: 3,272
Sales: £1 billion ($1.6 billion) (2006 est.)
NAIC: 311712 Fresh and Frozen Seafood Processing;
424460 Fish and Seafood Merchant Wholesalers

■ ■ ■

Young's Bluecrest Seafood Holdings Ltd. is the leading producer and distributor of frozen, fresh, and chilled seafood in the United Kingdom. The largest part of the group's sales come through its flagship Young's brand, which features a range of frozen and chilled fish, shrimp, and shellfish, for both the retail and foodservice channels. Other brand names in the Young's Bluecrest family include Ross, focused on the retail frozen segment; Bluecrest, which produces chilled and frozen fish for the retail and foodservice channels; King Frost, dedicated to the foodservice market; Marr, which produces frozen fish for the foodservice channel; Scotpak, producing chilled seafood products for the retail market; and Macrae, a Scotland-based producer of frozen and chilled fish for the retail market.

In addition, Young's Bluecrest operates a specialists foodservice subsidiary, Young's Bluecrest Foodservice, focused specifically on the restaurant and catering industry. Another company subsidiary, Polarfrost Seafoods, specializes in fish frozen at sea. Young's Bluecrest dates its origins back to the early 19th century; the company in its present state was formed through the merger of Young's and Bluecrest in 1999. The company has been owned by investment group CapVest since 2002. In January 2006, CapVest acquired the northern European operations of the Findus brand. The addition of the Findus operations to Young's Bluecrest is expected to boost the company's revenues past £1 billion. In June of that year, the company became a frontrunner for the acquisition of Unilever's frozen foods business, including flagship brands Bird's Eye and the remaining Findus operations. If completed, Young's Bluecrest's revenues will more than double, establishing the company among the world's leading seafoods specialists. Young's Bluecrest is led by Chairman M. Parker and Managing Director Wynne Griffiths.

EARLY 19TH-CENTURY ORIGINS

Young's Bluecrest was formed in 1999 through the merger of two of the United Kingdom's leading seafoods groups. The oldest member of the new company was Young's, which traced its origins to the beginning of the 19th century. The Young family had originally been a fishing family, based in Greenwich on the River Thames since the mid-1700s. Selling the fish was an occupation left to others, such as Elizabeth Martha, who began selling on the Greenwich quays in 1805 when she was 14 years old. In 1811, Martha married William

COMPANY PERSPECTIVES

Young's is the U.K.'s leading specialist fish brand. With 200 years' experience, the brand's reputation for fish expertise provides reassurance to seafood consumers.

We aim to make using fish easy for consumers and offer superb product quality, whether frozen or chilled. With access to fish species from around the world, Young's provides a wide range of products, from traditional favourites such as Prawns and Scampi to Chip Shop Battered Fish, Ocean Pie and Seafood Meals.

Timothy Young, and the pair decided to combine the fishing and selling businesses for the first time, setting up a small shop in town. The business prospered, and later moved downriver to Leigh-on-Sea.

By the end of the 19th century, the family business, under William Joseph Young, had emerged as a prominent fish merchanting and wholesaling company, operating its own fleet of "bawleys," small fishing boats, especially for whitebait and shrimp fishing, used by fishermen in the River Thames region near Kent and Essex. Whitebait, which referred to a variety of small, often young fish, generally battered and eaten whole, was then one of the most popular seafoods in England. Its popularity extended to the country's gentry, and by the late 1880s, Young's had built up a strong business catering to the London market. In 1890, the company moved its headquarters to London, a move that permitted the company to begin supplying the city's catering market. A particular boost to the company came with the organization of the Whitebait Dinners, which were held to celebrate the conclusion of parliamentary sessions. The company's London business also developed strongly after 1895 when the railroad connecting Leigh-on-Sea to London enabled the company's morning catch to arrive in the city before lunchtime.

Through the 1920s, Young's expanded its operations, becoming one of the first in England to begin importing salmon. The fish variety quickly gained in popularity, topping one million pounds by the end of the decade, and ten million pounds by the end of the 1930s. In the meantime, Young's had begun investing in its distribution wing, acquiring its first motorized delivery vehicles in 1923. In 1928, the company opened a new sales office in London, on Royal Mint Street.

That era also marked the debut of the company's most successful product, potted shrimp.

The next generation of the Young family—brothers Gordon, Stanley, Douglas, and Malcolm—joined the family business in the 1920s and took over as heads of the operation in the late 1930s. In 1938, the company expanded its range of operations again, setting up a new subsidiary, W. Young & Son (Wholesale Fish Merchants) Ltd., for its increasingly important wholesaling business. The company added another subsidiary following World War II, W. Young & Son (Grimsby) Ltd., which added dockside purchasing and processing operations in northern England. Grimsby later emerged as the United Kingdom's (and for a time, the world's) busiest fishing port. Also following the war, the company set up an operation dedicated to its potted shrimp business. Interrupted during the war, production of potted shrimp had picked up strongly as rationing was lifted. By the 1950s, the company operated five production facilities for its potted shrimp production.

POSTWAR SHIFT TO FREEZING

The arrival of freezing technologies in the United Kingdom, and the spread of home freezers in the country in the 1950s, provided a new boost for Young's. The company redeveloped the packaging for its potted shrimp, and began developing new frozen products, launching its first frozen foods production in 1946. A highly successful new product launch followed in 1949, with the introduction of packaged frozen shrimp scampi. The company added frozen peeled prawns and, later, King's Prawns and Queen's Prawns. In the meantime, the company's early investment in freezing technology enabled it to claim a leading position in the country's frozen fish sector.

Douglas Young took up the company's chairmanship in 1959. That year, however, marked the end of Young's independence, after the company was purchased by the larger Ross Group. Ross had been active in England's fishing industry since 1920, when it was established as a small family-owned fish merchanting company in Grimsby. By the outbreak of World War II, the company operated branches in Leeds, Leicester, and Fleetwood as well. Ross also had diversified into trawling, starting with a small fleet of four vessels in the 1930s; by the mid-1960s, the company's fleet grew to 65 trawlers. During the 1950s, Ross had made its first inroads into the fish processing industry, and later into food processing in general. The company also acquired its own shipyard, which began building the company's trawlers. By the early 1960s, Ross's holdings included poultry, frozen and fresh foods, including fish, as well as its fish trawling, merchanting, and other operations. Yet

KEY DATES

1750: The Young family begins whitebait fishing in the River Thames area.

1805: Elizabeth Martha begins selling fish quayside in Greenwich.

1811: Martha marries William Young and they set up their first fish shop.

1890: The Youngs move the business to London.

1938: A wholesale subsidiary, W. Young & Son (Wholesale Fish Merchants) Ltd., is established.

1959: Ross Group acquires Young's.

1969: Imperial Tobacco acquires Ross Group, regrouped as Ross Young, and launches expansion of Young's operations.

1975: Frank Flear founds Bluecrest in Grimsby.

1985: Bluecrest is acquired by Fitch Lovell.

1986: Hanson PLC acquires Imperial Tobacco.

1988: Hanson sells Ross Young to United Biscuit and Rossfish to Booker PLC.

1990: Fitch Lovell sells Bluecrest to Booker.

1999: LGV acquires Young's and Bluecrest, which are merged as Young's Bluecrest.

2002: Capvest backs the management-led buyout of Young's Bluecrest.

2003: Young's Bluecrest acquires Albert Fisher chilled seafood and Marr Group.

2004: Young's Bluecrest acquires Macrae Food Group.

2006: Young's Bluecrest acquires the Findus U.K. operations; the company enters negotiations to acquire Bird's Eye and Findus Europe from Unilever.

the company's trawling operations, which by then represented just 5 percent of group sales, had become perennial money-losers. As part of Ross, Young's maintained its own operations, and especially its nationally known brand name. Douglas Young, and later other members of the Young family, remained in charge of the company's direction as well.

Ross's and Young's frozen foods operations grew strongly through the 1960s. A period of railroad cutbacks forced the companies to develop a new distribution system, and through the 1960s both Ross and Young's set up a network of distribution depots, as well as completing the acquisition of a number of wholesalers throughout the country. By the mid-1960s, the group's share of the United Kingdom's frozen food sector topped 5 percent in the retail channel, and as much as 13 percent in the catering market. By the end of that decade, Young's itself was recognized as the leader in the U.K. frozen fish sector.

The continued losses of Ross Group's trawling operations, however, continued to plague the company through the decade. In 1969, Ross Group agreed to be acquired by Imperial Tobacco, which had launched its own diversification into the foods sector. As part of that acquisition, Ross's trawling business was spun off into British United Trawlers, and Ross was renamed Imperial Foods. Both the Ross and Young's names survived as independently operating divisions of the new U.K. foods heavyweight. Imperial Tobacco itself became a division of the newly renamed Imperial Group.

As part of Imperial, Young's expanded onto a national level. With Imperial Group's deep pockets, Young's was able to invest in expanding its production capacity. The company also developed a new centralized distribution system, which enabled it to expand to a truly national scale. By the middle of the 1970s, Young's sales had more than doubled since the company had become part of Imperial Group, topping £23 million in sales in 1974. The company by then operated 18 factories for its frozen fish and frozen shellfish products.

EUROPEAN LEADERSHIP FOR THE NEW CENTURY

By the mid-1980s, however, Imperial's diversification efforts appeared to have run out of steam. The company was criticized for having created a "patchwork" of companies. By the middle of the decade, Imperial was swept up in the era of hostile takeovers, becoming the object of interest for a number of companies, including United Biscuits PLC.

United Biscuits failed to win its bid for Imperial Group, which was instead acquired in a hostile takeover by fast-growing U.K. conglomerate Hanson PLC. Hanson's interests, however, were strictly for Imperial's tobacco holdings. As such, Hanson began selling off Imperial's other holdings. Ross Young's turn came in 1988, when the division was broken up and Ross Foods, including Young's, was sold to United Biscuits. As part of United Biscuits, the frozen seafoods operation was placed under the direction of Wynne Griffiths, who had led the integration of this division following the Hanson takeover. Into the early 1990s, Griffiths redeveloped Young's as a standalone division.

This set the stage for the next phase in Young's ownership. In the mid-1990s, United Biscuits launched its own restructuring effort, streamlining its product mix. Young's turn came in 1999, when the company was sold to a management buyout, led by Griffiths and backed by Legal & General Ventures (LGV), which had also acquired another leading U.K. seafood group, Bluecrest.

Bluecrest was founded in 1975 by Frank Flear and quickly became an important player in the Grimsby fish market. The company was subsequently acquired by Fitch Lovell in 1985, and under its new ownership tacked on a number of further acquisitions through the 1980s. In 1990, Fitch Lovell sold Bluecrest to Booker PLC, which also had acquired the Rossfish division from Hanson Group. The two companies were merged together as Bluecrest, forming Booker's Fish Division.

The newly created Young's Bluecrest was the clear leader in the U.K. frozen fish sector, having surpassed longtime rivals Bird's Eye, owned by Unilever, and Findus, owned by EQT Scandinavia in the United Kingdom. (Unilever owned the Findus brand elsewhere in Europe.) Griffiths remained as head of the enlarged Young's Bluecrest, which also reunited the company with the Ross brand.

In 2000, Young's Bluecrest set out a major relaunch of the Young's branded products family, which played the role of company flagship and top revenue generator. The company, which by then boasted a turnover of more than £320 million, also launched an investment drive to boost its production capacity. Young's also began preparing an ambitious expansion strategy, designed to drive the consolidation of the still fragmented British fish sector.

LGV, however, declined to back this expansion, and instead, in 2002, the investment firm sold Young's Bluecrest in a new management buyout, again led by Griffiths, but this time backed by CapVest. Young's soon made good on its expansion objectives, making its first acquisition, of the chilled seafood division of Albert Fisher, based in Newcastle, in June 2003. This purchase was followed by the acquisition of the Pinegain Group, and its Marr Foods division in October 2003. That company operated three factories in the United Kingdom and added its range of salmon, smoked fish, and tuna, as well as the Marr brand name, to the Young's lineup. Young next turned to Scotland, where it bought a 34 percent stake in Macrae Food Group, the largest dedicated producer of ready-to-eat seafood in Scotland. That purchase was completed in September 2004.

Young's also invested in boosting its own capacity, spending some £15 million to expand its Humber-based operation in 2004. In 2005, the company launched the refurbishing and expansion of its Grimsby-based Humberstone facility, which had formerly housed the Findus operation in that city. In 2006, the company also launched a £10 million expansion of its Macrae plant in Edinburgh.

By then, Young's had completed the next phase of its expansion, when it acquired the U.K.-based Findus seafoods operations from EQT Scandinavia, a purchase completed in January 2006. The addition of Findus boosted Young's total sales to an estimated £1 billion ($1.7 billion). Young's then set its sights on still further growth. By June 2006, the company had been acknowledged as the front runner for the acquisition of the frozen seafoods operations of consumer products giant Unilever, a purchase that included not only the Bird's Eye brand family, but the European Findus operations. If completed, Young's Bluecrest was expected to double its annual sales, and become one of the top seafood specialists in Europe.

M. L. Cohen

PRINCIPAL SUBSIDIARIES

Macrae Food Group; Polarfrost Seafoods Ltd.; Young's Bluecrest Foodservice.

PRINCIPAL COMPETITORS

Alpesca S.A.; Orkla ASA; Aker ASA; Maruha Corporation; Unilever Deutschland GmbH; Icelandic Group hf; Perkins Foods Holdings Ltd.; Green Isle Food Group Ltd.

FURTHER READING

"The Businessman with Young's at Heart," *Yorkshire Post,* January 11, 2005.

"Capvest Acquires Young's," *Acquisitions Monthly,* April 2002, p. 73.

"Capvest Considers Unified Young's, Birds Eye, Findus," *Grocer,* May 13, 2006, p. 6.

Davies, Kit, "Young's Warns of Rising Fish Prices," *Grocer,* March 4, 2006, p. 67.

"Experiment with Fish, Says Young's," *Grocer,* March 11, 2006, p. 57.

McDonagh, Vince, "Merged Company Ploughs Money into Improvements," *Frozen & Chilled Foods,* April 2000, p. 2.

———, "Young's Brand Breaks Through £200 Million Barrier," *Frozen & Chilled Foods,* September-October 2005, p. 9.

———, "Young's Moves Fish Operation from Hull to Scotland," *Frozen & Chilled Foods,* November-December 2005, p. 13.

———, "Young's Serves Up 15m Humber Expansion Plan," *Fish & Chips and Fast Food,* May 2004, p. 4.

McLelland, Fiona, "Young's Could Be Up for Sale," *Grocer,* January 25, 2005, p. 5.

Merrell, Caroline, "Suitors Line Up for £1bn Unilever Business," *The Times,* June 12, 2006, p. 32.

"Young's Bluecrest Expanding Macrae Plant in Edinburgh," *QFFI's Global Seafood Magazine,* January 2006, p. 45.

"Young's Bluecrest Merger Creates Strongest Seafood Company in the UK," *Frozen & Chilled Foods,* August 1999, p. 2.

Index to Companies

AHSC Holdings Corp. *see* Alco Health Services Corporation.
Ahtna AGA Security, Inc., **14** 541
AI Automotive, **24** 204
AIC *see* Allied Import Company.
AICA, **16** 421; **43** 308
AICPA *see* The American Institute of Certified Public Accountants.
Aid Auto, **18** 144
Aida Corporation, **11** 504
AIG *see* American International Group, Inc.
AIG Global Real Estate Investment Corp., **54** 225
AIG Latin America Equity Partners, Ltda., **74** 48
AIG/Lincoln International L.L.C., **54** 225
Aigner *see* Etienne Aigner AG.
Aiken Stores, Inc., **14** 92
Aikenhead's Home Improvement Warehouse, **18** 240; **26** 306
AIL Technologies, **46** 160
AIM Create Co., Ltd. *see* Marui Co., Ltd.
AIM Management Group Inc., **65** 43–45
AIMCO *see* Apartment Investment and Management Company.
Ainsworth Gaming Technologies, **54** 15
Ainsworth National, **14** 528
AIP *see* American Industrial Properties; Amorim Investimentos e Participaço.
Air & Water Technologies Corporation, **6** 441–42 *see also* Aqua Alliance Inc.
Air Berlin GmbH & Co. Luftverkehrs KG, **71** 15–17
Air BP, **7** 141
Air By Pleasant, **62** 276
Air Canada, **6** 60–62; **23** 9–12 (upd.); **59** 17–22 (upd.)
Air China, **46** 9–11
Air Compak, **12** 182
Air de Cologne, **27** 474
Air Express International Corporation, **13** 19–20
Air France *see* Groupe Air France; Societe Air France.
Air Global International, **55** 30
Air-India Limited, **6** 63–64; **27** 24–26 (upd.)
Air Inter *see* Groupe Air France.
Air Inuit, **56** 38–39
Air Jamaica Limited, **54** 3–6
Air La Carte Inc., **13** 48
Air Lanka Catering Services Ltd. *see* Thai Airways International.
Air Liberté, **6** 208
Air Liquide *see* L'Air Liquide SA.
Air London International, **36** 190
Air Mauritius Ltd., **63** 17–19
Air Methods Corporation, **53** 26–29
Air Midwest, Inc. *see* Mesa Air Group, Inc.
Air New Zealand Limited, **14** 10–12; **38** 24–27 (upd.)
Air NorTerra Inc., **56** 39
Air Pacific Ltd., **70** 7–9
Air Products and Chemicals, Inc., **I** 297–99; **10** 31–33 (upd.); **74** 6–9 (upd.)

Air Pub S.à.r.l., **64** 359
Air Russia, **24** 400
Air Sahara Limited, **65** 14–16
Air Sea Broker AG, **47** 286–87
Air Southwest Co. *see* Southwest Airlines Co.
Air Taser, Inc. *see* Taser International, Inc.
Air Transport International LLC, **58** 43
Air Wisconsin Airlines Corporation, **55** 10–12
Airborne Freight Corporation, **6** 345–47; **34** 15–18 (upd.)
Airbus Industrie *see* G.I.E. Airbus Industrie.
AirCal, **I** 91
Airco, **25** 81–82; **26** 94
Aircraft Modular Products, **30** 73
Aircraft Turbine Center, Inc., **28** 3
Airex Corporation, **16** 337
AirFoyle Ltd., **53** 50
Airgas, Inc., **54** 7–10
Airguard Industries, Inc., **17** 104, 106; **61** 66
AirLib *see* Société d'Exploitation AOM.
Airline Interiors Inc., **41** 368–69
Airlines of Britain Holdings, **34** 398; **38** 105–06
Airlink Pty Ltd *see* Qantas Airways Ltd.
Airmark Plastics Corp., **18** 497–98
Airopak Corporation *see* PVC Container Corporation.
Airpax Electronics, Inc., **13** 398
Airport Leather Concessions LLC, **58** 369
Airrest S.A., **64** 359
Airshop Ltd., **25** 246
Airstream *see* Thor Industries, Inc.
AirTouch Communications, **11** 10–12 *see also* Vodafone Group PLC.
Airtours Plc, **27** 27–29, 90, 92
AirTran Holdings, Inc., **22** 21–23
AirWair Ltd., **23** 399, 401–02
AirWays Corporation *see* AirTran Holdings, Inc.
Aisin Seiki Co., Ltd., **III** 415–16; **48** 3–5 (upd.)
AIT Worldwide, **47** 286–87
Aitchison & Colegrave *see* Bradford & Bingley PLC.
Aitken, Inc., **26** 433
AITS *see* American International Travel Service.
Aiuruoca, **25** 85
Aiwa Co., Ltd., **30** 18–20
Ajax Iron Works, **II** 16
Ajax Repair & Supply, **58** 75
Ajinomoto Co., Inc., **II** 463–64; **28** 9–11 (upd.)
AJS Auto Parts Inc., **15** 246
AK Steel Holding Corporation, **19** 8–9; **41** 3–6 (upd.)
Akamai Technologies, Inc., **71** 18–21
Akane Securities Co. Ltd., **II** 443
AKAY Flavours & Aromatics Ltd., **70** 56
Akbank TAS, **79** 18–21
Akemi, **17** 310; **24** 160
Aker RGI, **32** 99
AKG Acoustics GmbH, **62** 3–6
AKH Co. Inc., **20** 63

Akin, Gump, Strauss, Hauer & Feld, L.L.P., **33** 23–25
Akorn, Inc., **32** 22–24
Akro-Mills Inc., **19** 277–78
Akron Brass Manufacturing Co., **9** 419
Akron Extruders Inc., **53** 230
Akroyd & Smithers, **14** 419
Aktia Sparbank Abp, **69** 177, 179
Aktiebolaget Electrolux, **22** 24–28 (upd.) *see also* Electrolux A.B.
Aktiebolaget SKF, **III** 622–25; **38** 28–33 (upd.)
Aktieselskabet Dampskibsselskabet Svendborg, **57** 3, 5
Akzo Nobel N.V., **13** 21–23; **41** 7–10 (upd.)
Al-Amin Co. For Securities & Investment Funds *see* Dallah Albaraka Group.
Al Copeland Enterprises, Inc., **7** 26–28; **32** 13–15
Al-Tawfeek Co. For Investment Funds Ltd. *see* Dallah Albaraka Group.
Alaadin Middle East-Ersan, **IV** 564
Alabama Bancorp., **17** 152
Alabama Farmers Cooperative, Inc., **63** 20–22
Alabama Gas Corporation, **21** 207–08
Alabama National BanCorporation, **75** 21–23
Alabama Power Company, **38** 445, 447–48
Alabama Shipyards Inc., **21** 39–40
Aladdin Industries, **16** 487
Aladdin Mills Inc., **19** 276; **63** 300
Alagasco, **21** 207–08
Alagroup, **45** 337
Alain Afflelou SA, **53** 30–32
Alain Manoukian *see* Groupe Alain Manoukian.
Alamac Knit Fabrics, Inc., **16** 533–34; **21** 192
Alamito Company, **6** 590
Alamo Engine Company, **8** 514
Alamo Group Inc., **32** 25–28
Alamo Rent A Car, Inc., **6** 348–50; **24** 9–12 (upd.)
Alamo Water Refiners, Inc. *see* The Marmon Group, Inc.
Alania, **24** 88
ALANTEC Corporation, **25** 162
ALARIS Medical Systems, Inc., **65** 17–20
Alarm Device Manufacturing Company, **9** 413–15
Alaron Inc., **16** 357
Alascom, Inc. *see* AT&T Corporation.
Alaska Air Group, Inc., **6** 65–67; **29** 11–14 (upd.)
Alaska Commercial Company, **12** 363
Alaska Junk Co., **19** 380
Alaska Native Wireless LLC, **60** 264
Alaska Railroad Corporation, **60** 6–9
Alaska Steel Co., **19** 381
Alatas Mammoet, **26** 279
Alba Foods, **27** 197; **43** 218
Alba-Waldensian, Inc., **30** 21–23
Albany Cheese, **23** 219

Albany International Corporation, 8
  12–14; 51 11–14 (upd.)
Albany Molecular Research, Inc., 77
  9–12
Albaugh Inc., **62** 19
Albemarle Corporation, 59 23–25
Alberici Corporation, 76 12–14
Albert E. Reed & Co. Ltd. *see* Reed
  International PLC.
The Albert Fisher Group plc, 41 11–13
Albert Heijn NV, **II** 641–42; **38** 200, 202
Albert Nipon, Inc., **8** 323
Albert Willcox & Co., **14** 278
Albert's Organics, Inc. *see* United Natural
  Foods, Inc.
Alberta Energy Company Ltd., 16
  10–12; 43 3–6 (upd.)
Alberta Gas Trunk Line Company, Ltd. *see*
  Nova Corporation of Alberta.
Alberto-Culver Company, 8 15–17; 36
  23–27 (upd.)
Albertson's, Inc., II 601–03; **7 19–22**
  (upd.); 30 24–28 (upd.); 65 21–26
  (upd.)
Albion Industries, Inc., **16** 357
Albright & Wilson Ltd., **12** 351; **16** 461;
  38 378, 380; **50** 282; **59** 25
Albuquerque Gas & Electric Company *see*
  Public Service Company of New
  Mexico.
Albuquerque Gas, Electric Light and
  Power Company, **6** 561–62
Alcan Aluminium Limited, IV 9–13; **31**
  7–12 (upd.)
Alcan Inc., **60** 338
Alcatel S.A., 9 9–11; **36 28–31 (upd.)**
Alchem Capital Corp., **8** 141, 143
Alchem Plastics *see* Spartech Corporation.
Alco Capital Group, Inc., **27** 288
Alco Health Services Corporation, III
  9–10 *see also* AmeriSource Health
  Corporation.
Alco Office Products Inc., **24** 362
Alco Standard Corporation, I 412–13
ALCO Trade Show Services, **26** 102
Alcoa Inc., 56 7–11 (upd.)
Alcon Laboratories, **10** 46, 48; **30** 30–31
Alden Merrell Corporation, **23** 169
Alderwoods Group, Inc., 68 11–15
  (upd.)
Aldi Group, 13 24–26
Aldila Inc., 46 12–14
Aldine Press, **10** 34
Aldiscon, **37** 232
Aldus Corporation, 10 34–36
Alenia, **7** 9, 11
Alert Centre Inc., **32** 373
Alert Management Systems Inc., **12** 380
Alès Groupe, 81 10–13
Alessio Tubi, **IV** 228
Alestra, **19** 12
Alex & Ivy, **10** 166–68
Alex Lee Inc., 18 6–9; 44 10–14 (upd.)
Alexander & Alexander Services Inc., 10
  37–39
Alexander & Baldwin, Inc., 10 40–42;
  40 14–19 (upd.)
Alexander and Lord, **13** 482

Alexander Hamilton Life Insurance Co.,
  II 420; **29** 256
Alexander Howden Group, **10** 38–39
Alexander-Schroder Lumber Company, **18**
  514
Alexander Smith, Inc., **19** 275
Alexander's, Inc., 45 14–16
Alexandria Petroleum Co., **51** 113
Alexis Lichine, **III** 43
Alfa Corporation, 60 10–12
Alfa-Laval AB, III 417–21; **64 13–18**
  (upd.)
Alfa Romeo, 13 27–29; 36 32–35 (upd.)
Alfa, S.A. de C.V., 19 10–12
Alfa Trading Company, **23** 358
Alfalfa's Markets, **19** 500–02
alfi Zitzmann, **60** 364
Alfred A. Knopf, Inc., **13** 428, 429; **31**
  376–79
Alfred Bullows & Sons, Ltd., **21** 64
Alfred Dunhill Limited, **19** 369; **27**
  487–89
Alfred Marks Bureau, Ltd. *see* Adia S.A.
Alfred McAlpine plc, **51** 138
Alfred Ritter GmbH & Co. KG, 58 3–7
Alfried Krupp von Bohlen und Halbach
  Foundation, **IV** 89
ALG *see* Arkla, Inc.
Alga, **24** 83
Algamar, S.A., **64** 91
Algemeen Burgerlijk Pensioenfonds, **26**
  421
Algemeen Dagblad BV, **53** 273
Algemene Bank Nederland N.V., II
  183–84
Algerian Saudi Leasing Holding Co. *see*
  Dallah Albaraka Group.
Algo Group Inc., 24 13–15
Algoma Steel Corp., **8** 544–45
Algonquin Gas Transmission Company,
  14 124–26
ALI *see* Aeronautics Leasing, Inc.
Aliança Florestal-Sociedade para o
  Desenvolvimento Agro-Florestal, S.A.,
  60 156
Alicia S.A. *see* Arcor S.A.I.C.
Alico, Inc., 63 23–25
Alidata SpA *see* Alitalia—Linee Aeree
  Italiana, S.P.A.
Alienware Corporation, 81 14–17
Aligro Inc., **II** 664
Alimenta (USA), Inc., **17** 207
Alimentation Couche-Tard Inc., 77
  13–16
Alimentos Indal S.A., **66** 9
Alimondo, **17** 505
Alitalia–Linee Aeree Italiana, S.p.A., 6
  68–69; 29 15–17 (upd.)
Aljazeera Satellite Channel, 79 22–25
Alkor-Oerlikon Plastic GmbH, **7** 141
All American Airways *see* USAir Group,
  Inc.
All American Communications Inc., 20
  3–7
All American Gourmet Co., **12** 178, 199
All American Sports Co., **22** 458–59
All British Escarpment Company LTD,
  25 430

All-Clad Metalcrafters Inc., **34** 493,
  496–97
The All England Lawn Tennis &
  Croquet Club, 54 11–13
All-Glass Aquarium Co., Inc., **58** 60
All Nippon Airways Co., Ltd., 6 70–71;
  38 34–37 (upd.)
All Seasons Vehicles, Inc. *see* ASV, Inc.
All Woods, Inc., **18** 514
Allami Biztosito, **III** 209; **15** 30
Allcom, **16** 392
Alldays plc, 49 16–19
Allders plc, 37 6–8
Alleanza Assicurazioni S.p.A., 65 27–29
Alleghany Corporation, 10 43–45; 60
  13–16 (upd.)
Allegheny Airlines *see* USAir Group, Inc.;
  US Airways Group, Inc.
Allegheny Beverage Corp., **7** 472–73
Allegheny Energy, Inc., 38 38–41 (upd.)
Allegheny International, Inc., **8** 545; **9**
  484; **22** 3, 436
Allegheny Ludlum Corporation, 8
  18–20
Allegheny Power System, Inc., V
  543–45 *see also* Allegheny Energy, Inc.
Allegheny Steel and Iron Company, **9** 484
Allegheny Steel Distributors, Inc. *see*
  Reliance Steel & Aluminum Company.
Allegiance Life Insurance Company, **22**
  268; **50** 122
Allegis, Inc. *see* United Airlines.
Allegretti & Co., **22** 26
Allen & Co., **12** 496; **13** 366; **25** 270
Allen & Ginter, **12** 108
Allen-Bradley Co., **I** 80; **III** 593; **11**
  429–30; **17** 478; **22** 373; **23** 211
Allen Canning Company, 76 15–17
Allen-Edmonds Shoe Corporation, 61
  20–23
Allen Foods, Inc., 60 17–19
Allen Group Inc. *see* TransPro, Inc.
Allen Organ Company, 33 26–29
Allen-Stuart Equipment Company, **49** 160
Allen Systems Group, Inc., 59 26–28
Allen Tank Ltd., **21** 499
Allen's Convenience Stores, Inc., **17** 170
Allerderm *see* Virbac Corporation.
Allergan, Inc., 10 46–49; 30 29–33
  (upd.); 77 17–24 (upd.)
ALLETE, Inc., **71** 9
Allforms Packaging Corp., **13** 442
Allgemeine Elektricitäts-Gesellschaft *see*
  AEG A.G.
Allgemeine Handelsgesellschaft der
  Verbraucher AG *see* AVA AG.
Allgemeine Schweizerische Uhrenindustrie,
  26 480
Allhabo AB, **53** 85
Allia S.A., **51** 324
Alliance Amusement Company, **10** 319
Alliance Assurance Company, **III** 369–73;
  55 333
Alliance Atlantis Communications Inc.,
  39 11–14
Alliance Capital Management Holding
  L.P., 63 26–28
Alliance de Sud, **53** 301

APS *see* Arizona Public Service Company.
APS Healthcare, **17** 166, 168
APSA, **63** 214
AptarGroup, Inc., 69 38–41
Apura GmbH, **IV** 325
Aqua Alliance Inc., 32 52–54 **(upd.)**
Aqua Cool Pure Bottled Water, **52** 188
Aqua de Oro Venture, **58** 23
Aquafin N.V., **12** 443; **38** 427
Aquarium Supply Co., **12** 230
Aquarius Group *see* Club Mediterranee SA.
Aquarius Platinum Ltd., 63 38–40
Aquatech, **53** 232
Aquila Energy Corp., **6** 593
Aquila, Inc., 50 37–40 **(upd.)**
Aquitaine *see* Société Nationale des Petroles d'Aquitaine.
AR Accessories Group, Inc., 23 20–22
AR-TIK Systems, Inc., **10** 372
ARA *see* Consorcio ARA, S.A. de C.V.
ARA Services, II 607–08 *see also* Aramark.
Arab-Israel Bank Ltd., **60** 50
Arab Japanese Insurance Co., **III** 296
Arab Leasing International Finance, **72** 85
Arab Radio & Television, **72** 85
Arabian American Oil Co. *see* Saudi Arabian Oil Co.
Arabian Gulf Oil Company *see* Natinal Oil Corporation.
Arabian Investment Banking Corp., **15** 94; **26** 53; **47** 361
Aracruz Celulose S.A., 57 45–47
Aral AG, 62 12–15
ARAMARK Corporation, 13 48–50; **41** 21–24 **(upd.)**
Aramco *see* Arabian American Oil Co.; Saudi Arabian Oil Company.
Aramis Inc., **30** 191
Arandell Corporation, 37 16–18
Arapuã *see* Lojas Arapuã S.A.
Aratex Inc., **13** 49
ARBED S.A., IV 24–27; **22** 41–45 **(upd.)**
Arbeitsgemeinschaft der öffentlich-rechtlichen Rundfunkanstalten der Bundesrepublik *see* ARD.
The Arbitron Company, 38 56–61
Arbor Acres, **13** 103
Arbor Drugs Inc., 12 21–23 *see also* CVS Corporation.
Arbor International *see* VeriFone Holdings, Inc.
Arbor Living Centers Inc., **6** 478
Arbor Software Corporation, **76** 188
Arby's Inc., 14 32–34
ARC *see* American Rug Craftsmen.
Arc International, 76 29–31
ARC Materials Corp., **III** 688
ARC Propulsion, **13** 462
ARCA *see* Appliance Recycling Centers of America, Inc.
Arcadia Group plc, 28 27–30 **(upd.)**
Arcadia Partners, **17** 321
Arcadian Corporation, **18** 433; **27** 317–18

Arcadian Marine Service, Inc., **6** 530
Arcadis NV, 26 21–24
Arcata Corporation, **12** 413
Arcata National Corp., **9** 305
Arcelor Gent, 80 9–12
ARCH Air Medical Service, Inc., **53** 29
Arch Chemicals, Inc., 78 17–20
Arch Mineral Corporation, 7 32–34
Arch Petroleum Inc., **39** 331
Arch Wireless, Inc., 39 23–26
Archbold Container Co., **35** 390
Archbold Ladder Co., **12** 433
Archer Daniels Midland Company, I 419–21; **11** 21–23 **(upd.); 32** 55–59 **(upd.); 75** 30–35 **(upd.)**
Archer Management Services Inc., **24** 360
Archibald Candy Corporation, **36** 309; **71** 22
Archie Comics Publications, Inc., 63 41–44
Archipelago RediBook, **48** 226, 228
Archon Corporation, 74 23–26 **(upd.)**
Archstone-Smith Trust, 49 27–30
Archway Cookies, Inc., 29 29–31
ArcLight, LLC, **50** 123
ARCO *see* Atlantic Richfield Company.
ARCO Chemical Company, 10 110–11
ARCO Comfort Products Co., **26** 4
Arco Electronics, **9** 323
Arco Pharmaceuticals, Inc., **31** 346
Arcon Corporation, **26** 287
Arcor S.A.I.C., 66 7–9
Arcorp Properties, **70** 226
Arctco, Inc., 16 31–34
Arctic Alaska Fisheries Corporation, **14** 515; **50** 493–94
Arctic Cat Inc., 40 46–50 **(upd.)**
Arctic Enterprises, **34** 44
Arctic Slope Regional Corporation, 38 62–65
ARD, 41 25–29
Ardal og Sunndal Verk AS, **10** 439
Arden Group, Inc., 29 32–35
Ardent Risk Services, Inc. *see* General Re Corporation.
Ardent Software Inc., **59** 54–55
Argenbright Security Inc. *see* Securicor Plc.
Argentaria Caja Postal y Banco Hipotecario S.A. *see* Banco Bilbao Vizcaya Argentaria S.A.
Argentaurum A.G. *see* Pall Corporation.
Argentine National Bank, **14** 46
Argon Medical, **12** 327
Argon ST, Inc., 81 34–37
Argonaut, **10** 520–22
Argos, **I** 426; **22** 72; **50** 117
Argos Retail Group, **47** 165, 169
Argos Soditic, **43** 147, 149
Argosy Gaming Company, 21 38–41
Argosy Group LP, **27** 197
Argus Corp., **IV** 611
Argus Energy, **7** 538
Argus Motor Company, **16** 7
Arguss Communications, Inc., **57** 120
Argyle Television Inc., **19** 204
Argyll Group PLC, II 609–10 *see also* Safeway PLC.

Aria Communications, Inc. *see* Ascend Communications, Inc.
Ariba, Inc., 57 48–51
Ariel Capital Management, **28** 421
Ariens Company, 48 32–34
Aries Technology, **25** 305
Ariete S.P.A. *see* De'Longhi S.p.A.
Aris Industries, Inc., 16 35–38
Arista Laboratories Inc., **51** 249, 251
Aristech Chemical Corp., **12** 342
Aristocrat Leisure Limited, 54 14–16
Aristokraft Inc. *see* MasterBrand Cabinets, Inc.
The Aristotle Corporation, 62 16–18
Arizona Airways, **22** 219
AriZona Beverages *see* Ferolito, Vultaggio & Sons
Arizona Daily Star, **58** 282
Arizona Edison Co., **6** 545
Arizona Growth Capital, Inc., **18** 513
Arizona One, **24** 455
Arizona Public Service Company, **6** 545–47; **19** 376, 412; **26** 359; **28** 425–26; **54** 290
Arizona Refrigeration Supplies, **14** 297–98
Arjo Wiggins Appleton p.l.c., 34 38–40
Ark Restaurants Corp., 20 25–27
Arkansas Best Corporation, 16 39–41
Arkansas Louisiana Gas Company *see* Arkla, Inc.
Arkia, **23** 184, 186–87
Arkla, Inc., V 550–51
Arla Foods amba, 48 35–38
Arlington Securities plc, **24** 84, 87–89
Arlon, Inc., **28** 42, 45
Armani *see* Giorgio Armani S.p.A.
Armaris, **75** 126
Armaturindistri, **III** 569
Armco Inc., IV 28–30 *see also* AK Steel.
Armement Sapmer Distribution, **60** 149
Armin Corporation *see* Tyco International Ltd.
Armor All Products Corp., 16 42–44
Armor Elevator, **11** 5
Armor Holdings, Inc., 27 49–51
Armour *see* Tommy Armour Golf Co.
Armour & Company, **8** 144; **12** 198; **13** 21, 506; **23** 173; **55** 365
Armour-Dial, **8** 144; **23** 173–74
Armour Food Co., **12** 370; **13** 270
Armstrong Air Conditioning Inc. *see* Lennox International Inc.
Armstrong Holdings, Inc., III 422–24; **22** 46–50 **(upd.); 81** 38–44 **(upd.)**
Armstrong Tire Co., *see* Pirelli & C. S.p.A.
Armtek, **7** 297
Army and Air Force Exchange Service, 39 27–29
Army Cooperative Fire Insurance Company, **10** 541
Army Ordnance, **19** 430
Army Signal Corps Laboratories, **10** 96
Arnold & Porter, 35 42–44
Arnold Clark Automobiles Ltd., 60 39–41
Arnold Communications, **25** 381
Arnold Electric Company, **17** 213

Bangkok Airport Hotel *see* Thai Airways International.
Bangkok Aviation Fuel Services Ltd. *see* Thai Airways International.
Bangladesh Krishi Bank, **31** 220
Bangor and Aroostook Railroad Company, **8** 33
Bangor Mills, **13** 169
Bangor Punta Alegre Sugar Corp., **30** 425
Banister Continental Corp. *see* BFC Construction Corporation.
Bank Austria AG, 23 37–39
Bank Brussels Lambert, II 201–03
Bank Central Asia, **18** 181; **62** 96, 98
Bank du Louvre, **27** 423
Bank für Elektrische Unternehmungen *see* Elektrowatt AG.
Bank Hapoalim B.M., II 204–06; 54 33–37 (upd.)
Bank Hofmann, **21** 146–47
Bank Leumi le-Israel B.M., 60 48–51
Bank of America Corporation, 46 47–54 (upd.)
The Bank of Bishop and Co., Ltd., **11** 114
Bank of Boston Corporation, II 207–09 *see also* FleetBoston Financial Corporation.
Bank of Britain, **14** 46–47
Bank of China, 63 55–57
Bank of Delaware, **25** 542
Bank of East Asia Ltd., 63 58–60
Bank of England, **10** 8, 336; **14** 45–46; **47** 227
Bank of Hawaii Corporation, 73 53–56
Bank of Ireland, 50 73–76
Bank of Italy, **III** 209, 347; **8** 45
The Bank of Jacksonville, **9** 58
Bank of Lee County, **14** 40
Bank of Mexico Ltd., **19** 188
The Bank of Milwaukee, **14** 529
Bank of Mississippi, Inc., 14 40–41
Bank of Montreal, II 210–12; 46 55–58 (upd.)
Bank of Nettleton, **14** 40
Bank of New England Corporation, II 213–15; 9 229
Bank of New Orleans, **11** 106
Bank of New South Wales *see* Westpac Banking Corporation.
Bank of New York Company, Inc., II 216–19; 46 59–63 (upd.)
Bank of North Mississippi, **14** 41
The Bank of Nova Scotia, II 220–23; 59 70–76 (upd.)
Bank of Oklahoma, **22** 4
The Bank of Scotland *see* The Governor and Company of the Bank of Scotland.
Bank of Sherman, **14** 40
Bank of the Ohio Valley, **13** 221
Bank of the Philippine Islands, 58 18–20
Bank of Tokyo-Mitsubishi Ltd., II 224–25; 15 41–43 (upd.)
Bank of Tupelo, **14** 40
Bank of Wales, **10** 336, 338
Bank One Corporation, 36 68–75 (upd.)

Bank-R Systems Inc., **18** 517
BankAmerica Corporation, II 226–28 *see also* Bank of America.
BankAtlantic Bancorp., Inc., **66** 273
BankBoston *see* FleetBoston Financial Corporation.
BankCard America, Inc., **24** 394
Bankers and Shippers Insurance Co., **III** 389
Bankers Corporation, **14** 473
Bankers Life and Casualty Co., **10** 247; **16** 207; **33** 110
Bankers Life Association *see* Principal Mutual Life Insurance Company.
Bankers National Life Insurance Co., **10** 246
Bankers Trust Co., **38** 411
Bankers Trust New York Corporation, II 229–31
Bankhaus August Lenz AG, **65** 230, 232
Banknorth Group, Inc., 55 49–53
Bankruptcy Services LLC, **56** 112
Banksia Wines Ltd., **54** 227, 229
BankWatch, **37** 143, 145
Banner Aerospace, Inc., 14 42–44; 37 29–32 (upd.)
Banner International, **13** 20
Banner Life Insurance Company, **III** 273; **24** 284
Banorte *see* Grupo Financiero Banorte, S.A. de C.V.
Banpais *see* Grupo Financiero Asemex-Banpais S.A.
BanPonce Corporation, **41** 312
Banque Bruxelles Lambert *see* Bank Brussels Lambert.
Banque de Bruxelles *see* Bank Brussels Lambert.
Banque de France, **14** 45–46
Banque de la Société Générale de Belgique *see* Generale Bank.
Banque de Paris et des Pays-Bas, **10** 346; **19** 188–89; **33** 179
Banque Indosuez, **II** 429; **52** 361–62
Banque Internationale de Luxembourg, **42** 111
Banque Lambert *see* Bank Brussels Lambert.
Banque Nationale de Paris S.A., II 232–34 *see also* BNP Paribas Group.
Banque Paribas *see* BNP Paribas Group.
Banque Sanpaolo of France, **50** 410
La Banque Suisse et Française *see* Crédit Commercial de France.
Banque Worms, **27** 514
Banta Corporation, 12 24–26; 32 73–77 (upd.); 79 50–56 (upd.)
Bantam Ball Bearing Company, **13** 522
Bantam Doubleday Dell Publishing Group, **see** Random House Inc.
Banyan Systems Inc., 25 50–52
Banyu Pharmaceutical Co., **11** 290; **34** 283
Baoshan Iron and Steel, **19** 220
Baosteel Group International Trade Corporation *see* Baosteel Group International Trade Corporation.
BAP of New York, Inc., **15** 246

Bar-S Foods Company, 76 39–41
Bar Technologies, Inc., **26** 408
Barastoc Stockfeeds Pty Ltd., **62** 307
Barat *see* Barclays PLC.
Barber Dental Supply Inc., **19** 291
Barberet & Blanc, **I** 677; **49** 350
Barcel, **19** 192
Barclay Furniture Co., **12** 300
Barclay White Inc., **38** 436
Barclays Business Credit, **13** 468
Barclays PLC, II 235–37; 20 57–60 (upd.); 64 46–50 (upd.)
BarclaysAmerican Mortgage Corporation, 11 29–30
Barco Manufacturing Co., **16** 8; **26** 541
Barco NV, 44 42–45
Barcolo Manufacturing, **15** 103; **26** 100
Barden Companies, Inc., 76 42–45
Bardon Group *see* Aggregate Industries plc.
Bareco Products, **15** 352
Barefoot Inc., **23** 428, 431
Bari Shoes, Inc., **22** 213
Barilla G. e R. Fratelli S.p.A., 17 35–37; 50 77–80 (upd.)
Baring Brothers & Co., Ltd., **39** 5
Barings PLC, 14 45–47
Barker & Dobson, **II** 629; **47** 367
Barker and Company, Ltd., **13** 286
Barlow Rand Ltd., I 422–24
Barlow Specialty Advertising, Inc., **26** 341
Barmag AG, 39 39–42
Barneda Carton SA, **41** 326
Barnes & Noble, Inc., 10 135–37; 30 67–71 (upd.); 75 50–55 (upd.)
Barnes Group, Inc., 13 72–74; 69 58–62 (upd.)
Barnett Banks, Inc., 9 58–60
Barnett Brass & Copper Inc., **9** 543
Barnett Inc., 28 50–52
Barney's, Inc., 28 53–55
Barnstead/Thermolyne Corporation, **14** 479–80
Baroid, **19** 467–68
Baron de Ley S.A., 74 27–29
Baron Industries Corporation, **53** 298
Baron Philippe de Rothschild S.A., 39 43–46
Barr *see* AG Barr plc.
Barr & Stroud Ltd., **III** 727
Barr Pharmaceuticals, Inc., 26 29–31; 68 46–49 (upd.)
Barracuda Technologies, **47** 7, 9
Barratt Developments plc, I 556–57; 56 31–33 (upd.)
Barrett Business Services, Inc., 16 48–50
Barricini Foods Inc., **27** 197
Barrick Gold Corporation, 34 62–65
Barris Industries, Inc., **23** 225
Barry Callebaut AG, 29 46–48; 71 46–49 (upd.)
Barry Wright Corporation, **9** 27; **32** 49
Barry's Jewelers *see* Samuels Jewelers Incorporated.
Barsab Investment Trust *see* South African Breweries Ltd.
Barsotti's, Inc. *see* Foster Wheeler Corp.

Bearings, Inc., 13 78–80
Beasley Broadcast Group, Inc., 51 44–46
Beasley Industries, Inc., 19 125–26
Beatrice Company, II 467–69 *see also* TLC Beatrice International Holdings, Inc.
Beatrice Foods, 21 322–24, 507, 545; 25 277–78; 38 169; 43 355
Beatrix Mines Ltd., 62 164
Beaulieu of America, 19 276
Beauté Prestige International S.A. *see* Shiseido Company Limited.
BeautiControl Cosmetics, Inc., 21 49–52
Beauty Biz Inc., 18 230
Beauty Systems Group, Inc., 60 260
Beaver Lake Concrete, Inc. *see* The Monarch Cement Company.
Beazer Homes USA, Inc., 17 38–41
Beazer Plc., 7 209
bebe stores, inc., 31 50–52
BEC Group Inc., 22 35; 60 133
BEC Ventures, 57 124–25
Bechstein, 56 299
Bechtel Group, Inc., I 558–59; 24 64–67 (upd.)
Beck & Gregg Hardware Co., 9 253
Beck's North America, Inc. *see* Brauerei Beck & Co.
Becker Drill, Inc., 19 247
Becker Group of Germany, 26 231
Beckett Papers, 23 48–50
Beckley-Cardy Group *see* School Specialty, Inc.
Beckman Coulter, Inc., 22 74–77
Beckman Instruments, Inc., 14 52–54
BECOL *see* Belize Electric Company Limited.
Becton, Dickinson & Company, I 630–31; 11 34–36 (upd.); 36 84–89 (upd.)
Bed Bath & Beyond Inc., 13 81–83; 41 49–52 (upd.)
Bedcovers, Inc., 19 304
Beddor Companies, 12 25
Bedford Chemical, 8 177
Bedford-Stuyvesant Restoration Corp., II 673
Bee Chemicals, I 372
Bee Discount, 26 476
Bee Gee Shoe Corporation, 10 281
Beech Aircraft Corporation, 8 49–52
Beech Holdings Corp., 9 94
Beech-Nut Nutrition Corporation, 21 53–56; 51 47–51 (upd.)
Beecham Group PLC, I 668; 9 264; 14 53; 16 438
Beechcroft Developments Ltd., 51 173
Beechwood Insurance Agency, Inc., 14 472
Beeck-Feinkost GmbH, 26 59
ZAO BeeOnLine-Portal, 48 419
Beerman Stores, Inc., 10 281
Beers Construction Company, 38 437
Befesa *see* Abengoa S.A.
Behr GmbH & Co. KG, 72 22–25
Behr-Manning Company, 8 396

Behring Diagnostics *see* Dade Behring Holdings Inc.
Behringwerke AG, 14 255; 50 249
BEI Technologies, Inc., 65 74–76
Beiersdorf AG, 29 49–53
Beijing Contact Lens Ltd., 25 56
Beijing Dentsu, 16 168
Beijing-Landauer, Ltd., 51 210
Beijing Liyuan Co., 22 487
Beijing Yanshan Petrochemical Company, 22 263
Beijing ZF North Drive Systems Technical Co. Ltd., 48 450
Beirao, Pinto, Silva and Co. *see* Banco Espírito Santo e Comercial de Lisboa S.A.
Bejam Group PLC *see* The Big Food Group plc.
Bekins Company, 15 48–50
Bel *see* Fromageries Bel.
Bel Air Markets, 14 397; 58 290
Bel Fuse, Inc., 53 59–62
Bel/Kaukauna USA, 76 46–48
Belco Oil & Gas Corp., 40 63–65
Belcom Holding AG, 53 323, 325
Belden CDT Inc., 19 43–45; 76 49–52 (upd.)
Beldis, 23 219
Beldoch Industries Corp., 17 137–38
Belgacom, 6 302–04
Belgian Rapid Access to Information Network Services, 6 304
Belglas, 16 420; 43 307
Belgo Group plc, 31 41
Belize Electric Company Limited, 47 137
Belk, Inc., V 12–13; 19 46–48 (upd.); 72 26–29 (upd.)
Bell and Howell Company, 9 61–64; 29 54–58 (upd.)
Bell Aerospace, 24 442
Bell Aircraft Company, 11 267; 13 267
Bell Atlantic Corporation, V 272–74; 25 58–62 (upd.) *see also* Verizon Communications.
Bell Canada Enterprises Inc. *see* BCE, Inc.
Bell Canada International, Inc., 6 305–08
Bell Communications Research *see* Telcordia Technologies, Inc.
Bell Fibre Products, 12 377
Bell Helicopter Textron Inc., 46 64–67
Bell Helmets Inc., 22 458
Bell Industries, Inc., 47 40–43
Bell Laboratories *see* AT&T Bell Laboratories, Inc.
Bell Microproducts Inc., 69 63–65
Bell Mountain Partnership, Ltd., 15 26
Bell-Northern Research, Ltd. *see* BCE Inc.
Bell Pharmacal Labs, 12 387
Bell Resources, III 729; 10 170; 27 473
Bell Sports Corporation, 16 51–53; 44 51–54 (upd.)
Bell System, 7 99, 333; 11 500; 16 392–93
Bell Telephone Manufacturing, II 13
Bellcore *see* Telcordia Technologies, Inc.
Belle Alkali Co., 7 308
Belleek Pottery Ltd., 71 50–53

Bellofram Corp., 14 43
BellSouth Corporation, V 276–78; 29 59–62 (upd.)
Bellway Plc, 45 37–39
Belmin Systems, 14 36
Belmont Savings and Loan, 10 339
Belo Corporation *see* A.H. Belo Corporation
Beloit Corporation, 14 55–57
Beloit Tool Company *see* Regal-Beloit Corporation.
Beloit Woodlands, 10 380
Belron International Ltd., 76 53–56
Bemis Company, Inc., 8 53–55
Ben & Jerry's Homemade, Inc., 10 146–48; 35 58–62 (upd.); 80 22–28 (upd.)
Ben Bridge Jeweler, Inc., 60 52–54
Ben E. Keith Company, 76 57–59
Ben Franklin Retail Stores, Inc. *see* FoxMeyer Health Corporation.
Ben Franklin Savings & Trust, 10 117
Ben Hill Griffin, III 53
Ben Myerson Candy Co., Inc., 26 468
Ben Venue Laboratories Inc., 16 439; 39 73
Benair Freight International Limited *see* Gulf Agency Company
Benchmark Capital, 49 50–52
Benchmark Electronics, Inc., 40 66–69
Benchmark Tape Systems Ltd, 62 293
Benckiser Group, 37 269
Benckiser N.V. *see* Reckitt Benckiser plc.
Benderson Development Company, 69 120
Bendick's of Mayfair *see* August Storck KG.
Bendix Corporation, I 141–43
Beneficial Corporation, 8 56–58
Beneficial Finance Company, 27 428–29
Beneficial Standard Life, 10 247
Benefit Consultants, Inc., 16 145
Benefits Technologies, Inc., 52 382
Benelli Arms S.p.A., 39 151
Benesse Corporation, 76 60–62
Bénéteau SA, 55 54–56
Benetton Group S.p.A., 10 149–52; 67 47–51 (upd.)
Benfield Greig Group plc, 53 63–65
Benguet Corporation, 58 21–24
Benihana, Inc., 18 56–59; 76 63–66 (upd.)
Benjamin Moore and Co., 13 84–87; 38 95–99 (upd.)
Benjamin Sheridan Corporation, 62 82
Benlee, Inc., 51 237
Benlox Holdings PLC, 16 465
Benn Bros. plc, IV 687
Bennett Industries, Inc., 17 371–73
Bennett's Smokehouse and Saloon, 19 122; 29 201
Bennigan's, 7 336; 12 373; 19 286; 25 181
Benpres Holdings, 56 214
BenQ Corporation, 67 52–54
Bensdorp, 29 47
Benson & Hedges, Ltd. *see* Gallaher Limited.

Big B, Inc., **17** 45–47
Big Bear Stores Co., **13** 94–96
Big D Construction Corporation, **42** 432
Big Dog Holdings, Inc., **45** 40–42
Big Entertainment, Inc., **58** 164
Big 5 Sporting Goods Corporation, **55** 57–59
Big Flower Press Holdings, Inc., **21** 60–62
Big Fluke Wine Co. *see* Click Wine Group.
The Big Food Group plc, **68** 50–53 (upd.)
Big Foot Cattle Co., **14** 537
Big Guns, Inc., **51** 229
Big Horn Mining Co., **8** 423
Big Idea Productions, Inc., **49** 56–59
Big Lots, Inc., **50** 98–101
Big M, **8** 409–10
Big O Tires, Inc., **20** 61–63
Big Rivers Electric Corporation, **11** 37–39
Big Sky Resort *see* Boyne USA Resorts.
Big Sky Western Bank, **35** 197, 199
Big V Supermarkets, Inc., **25** 66–68
Big Y Foods, Inc., **53** 66–68
BigBen Interactive S.A., **72** 33–35
BigBurger Ltda., **74** 48
Bigelow-Sanford, Inc., **31** 199
BII *see* Banana Importers of Ireland.
Bike Athletics, **23** 449
BIL *see* Brierley Investments.
Bilfinger & Berger AG, **I** 560–61; **55** 60–63 (upd.)
Bill & Melinda Gates Foundation, **41** 53–55
Bill Acceptance Corporation Ltd., **48** 427
Bill Barrett Corporation, **71** 54–56
Bill Blass Ltd., **32** 78–80
Bill France Racing, **19** 222
Bill's Casino, **9** 426
Billabong International Ltd., **44** 55–58
Billboard Publications, Inc., **7** 15
Billing Concepts, Inc., **26** 35–38; **72** 36–39 (upd.)
Billiton International, **IV** 532; **22** 237
BillPoint Inc., **58** 266
Bilsom, **40** 96–97
Bilt-Rite Chase-Pitkin, Inc., **41** 416
Biltwell Company, **8** 249
Bimar Foods Inc., **19** 192
Bimbo Bakeries USA, **29** 341
Bimbo, S.A., **36** 162, 164
Bin Zayed Group, **55** 54, 56
Binderline Development, Inc., **22** 175
Bindley Western Industries, Inc., **9** 67–69
The Bing Group, **60** 55–58
Bingham Dana LLP, **43** 68–71
Binghamton Container Company, **8** 102
Bingo Express Co., Ltd., **64** 290
Bingo King *see* Stuart Entertainment Inc.
Binks Sames Corporation, **21** 63–66
Binney & Smith Inc., **25** 69–72
Binnie & Partners, **22** 89
Binter Canarias *see* Iberia.
Bio Balance Corporation *see* New York Health Care, Inc.

Bio-Clinic, **11** 486–87
Bio-Dental Technologies Corporation, **46** 466
Bio-Dynamics, Inc., **10** 105, 107; **37** 111
Bio Foods Inc. *see* Balance Bar Company.
Bio Synthetics, Inc., **21** 386
Biodevelopment Laboratories, Inc., **35** 47
Biogemma, **74** 139
Biogen Idec Inc., **14** 58–60; **36** 90–93 (upd.); **71** 57–59 (upd.)
Bioindustrias, **19** 475
bioKinetics, **64** 18
Biokyowa, **III** 43; **48** 250
Biomedical Reference Laboratories of North Carolina, **11** 424
Biomega Corp., **18** 422
bioMérieux S.A., **75** 69–71
Biomet, Inc., **10** 156–58
Bionaire, Inc., **19** 360
BioScience Communications, **62** 115
Bioscot, Ltd., **63** 351
Biosite Incorporated, **73** 60–62
Biovail Corporation, **47** 54–56
BioWare Corporation, **81** 50–53
Biralo Pty Ltd., **48** 427
Bird & Sons, **22** 14
Bird Corporation, **19** 56–58
Birdair, Inc., **35** 99–100
Birds Eye Foods, Inc., **69** 66–72 (upd.)
Birdsall, Inc., **6** 529, 531
Bireley's, **22** 515
Birkbeck, **10** 6
Birkenstock Footprint Sandals, Inc., **12** 33–35; **42** 37–40 (upd.)
Birmingham & Midland Bank *see* Midland Bank plc.
Birmingham Slag Company, **7** 572–73, 575
Birmingham Steel Corporation, **13** 97–98; **40** 70–73 (upd.) *see also* Nucor Corporation
Birra Moretti, **25** 281–82
Birra Peroni S.p.A., **59** 357
Birse Group PLC, **77** 54–58
Birthdays Ltd., **70** 20–22
Biscayne Bank *see* Banco Espírito Santo e Comercial de Lisboa S.A.
Biscayne Federal Savings and Loan Association, **11** 481
Bishop & Co. Savings Bank, **11** 114
Bishop National Bank of Hawaii, **11** 114
BISSELL, Inc., **9** 70–72; **30** 75–78 (upd.)
Bisset Gold Mining Company, **63** 182–83
The BISYS Group, Inc., **73** 63–65
Bit LLC, **59** 303
Bit Software, Inc., **12** 62
Bitco Corporation, **58** 258
Bits & Pieces, **26** 439
Bitumen & Oil Refineries (Australia) Ltd. *see* Boral Limited.
Bituminous Casualty Corporation, **58** 258–59
Bivac International, **55** 79
BIW *see* Bath Iron Works.
BIZ Enterprises, **23** 390
Bizarro e Milho, Lda., **64** 91
BizBuyer.com, **39** 25

Bizimgaz Ticaret Ve Sanayi A.S., **55** 346
Bizmark, **13** 176
BizMart, **6** 244–45; **8** 404–05
BJ Services Company, **25** 73–75
BJ's Pizza & Grill, **44** 85
BJ's Restaurant & Brewhouse, **44** 85
BJ's Wholesale Club, **12** 221; **13** 547–49; **33** 198
BJK&E *see* Bozell Worldwide Inc.
BK Tag, **28** 157
BK Vision AG, **52** 357
BL Systems *see* AT&T Istel Ltd.
BL Universal PLC, **47** 168
The Black & Decker Corporation, **III** 435–37; **20** 64–68 (upd.); **67** 65–70 (upd.)
Black & Veatch LLP, **22** 87–90
Black Box Corporation, **20** 69–71
Black Clawson Company, **24** 478
Black Diamond Equipment, Ltd., **62** 34–37
Black Entertainment Television *see* BET Holdings, Inc.
Black Hawk Broadcasting Group, **10** 29; **38** 17
Black Hills Corporation, **20** 72–74
Black Pearl Software, Inc., **39** 396
BlackBerry *see* Research in Motion Ltd.
Blackfoot Telecommunications Group, **60** 59–62
Blackhawk Holdings, Inc. *see* PW Eagle Inc.
Blackhorse Agencies, **II** 309; **47** 227
BlackRock, Inc., **79** 66–69
Blacks Leisure Group plc, **39** 58–60
Blackstone Dredging Partners LP, **69** 197
The Blackstone Group, L.P., **II** 434, 444; **IV** 718; **11** 177, 179; **13** 170; **17** 238, 443; **22** 404, 416; **26** 408; **37** 309, 311; **61** 208; **69** 101, 103; **75** 378
Blackstone Hotel Acquisition Co., **24** 195
Blackwater USA, **76** 70–73
Blackwell Publishing (Holdings) Ltd., **78** 34–37
Blaine Construction Company *see* The Yates Companies, Inc.
Blair Corporation, **25** 76–78; **31** 53–55
Blakeman's Floor Care Parts & Equipment *see* Tacony Corporation.
Blandburgh Ltd., **63** 77
Blanes, S.A. de C.V., **34** 197
BLC Insurance Co., **III** 330
BLD Europe, **16** 168
Blendax, **III** 53; **8** 434; **26** 384
Blessings Corp., **14** 550; **19** 59–61
Blimpie International, Inc., **15** 55–57; **49** 60–64 (upd.)
Bliss Manufacturing Co., **17** 234–35
Blitz-Weinhart Brewing, **18** 71–72; **50** 112, 114
Blizzard Entertainment, **78** 38–42
Bloch & Guggenheimer, Inc., **40** 51–52
Block Communications, Inc., **81** 54–58
Block Drug Company, Inc., **8** 62–64; **27** 67–70 (upd.)
Block Financial Corporation, **17** 265; **29** 227
Block Management, **29** 226

The British Petroleum Company plc, **IV** 378–80; **7** 56–59 (upd.); **21** 80–84 (upd.) *see also* BP p.l.c.

British Printing and Communications Corp., **IV** 623–24, 642; **7** 312; **12** 224

British Railways Board, V 421–24

British Satellite Broadcasting, **10** 170

British Shoe Corporation *see* Sears plc.

British Sky Broadcasting Group plc, 20 79–81; **60** 66–69 (upd.)

British Steel plc, IV 41–43; **19** 62–65 (upd.)

British Sugar plc, **13** 53; **41** 30, 32–33

British Telecommunications plc, V 279–82; **15** 66–70 (upd.) *see also* BT Group plc.

British Thermoplastics and Rubber *see* BTR plc.

British Timken Ltd., **8** 530

British Trimmings Ltd., **29** 133

British Twin Disc Ltd., **21** 504

The British United Provident Association Limited, 79 81–84

British Vita plc, 9 92–93; **33** 77–79 (upd.)

British World Airlines Ltd., 18 78–80

Britoil, **IV** 380; **21** 82

Britt Airways, **I** 118

Britt Lumber Co., Inc., **8** 348

Brittania Sportswear, **16** 509

Britvic Soft Drinks Limited *see* Britannia Soft Drinks Ltd. (Britvic)

BritWill Healthcare Corp., **25** 504

BRK Brands, Inc., **28** 134

BRK Electronics, **9** 414

Bro-Well, **17** 56

Broad, Inc., **11** 482

Broad River Power Company, **6** 575

Broadband Networks Inc., **36** 352

Broadbandtalentneet.com, **44** 164

Broadbase Software, Inc., **51** 181

Broadcast Music Inc., 23 74–77

Broadcast Technology Systems, Inc., **13** 398

Broadcaster Press, **36** 341

Broadcom Corporation, 34 76–79

Broadcom Eireann Research, **7** 510

Broadcort Capital Corp., **13** 342

Broadgate Property Holdings Limited, **54** 40

The Broadmoor Hotel, 30 82–85

BroadVision Inc., **18** 543; **38** 432; **76** 370

Broadway & Seymour Inc., **17** 264; **18** 112

Broadway.com, **58** 167

Broadway-Hale Stores, Inc., **12** 356

Broadway Stores, Inc., **31** 193

Broadwing Corporation, 70 29–32

Brobeck, Phleger & Harrison, LLP, 31 74–76

Brock Candy Company *see* Brach and Brock Confections, Inc.

Brock Hotel Corp., **13** 472–73; **31** 94

Brock Residence Inn, **9** 426

Brockhaus *see* Bibliographisches Institut & F.A. Brockhaus AG.

Brockway Glass Co., **15** 128

Brockway Standard Holdings Corporation *see* BWAY Corporation.

Broder Bros. Co., 38 107–09

Broderbund Software, Inc., 13 113–16; **29** 74–78 (upd.)

Les broderies Lesage, **49** 83

Brok SA, **54** 315, 317

Broken Hill Proprietary Company Ltd., IV 44–47; **22** 103–08 (upd.) *see also* BHP Billiton.

Bronson Laboratories, Inc., **34** 460

Bronson Pharmaceuticals, **24** 257

Brooke Bond, **32** 475

Brooke Group Ltd., 15 71–73 *see also* Vector Group Ltd.

Brooke Partners L.P., **11** 275

Brookfield Athletic Shoe Company, **17** 244

Brookfield International Inc., **35** 388

Brookfield Properties Inc., **67** 72

Brooklyn Union Gas, 6 455–57

Brooks Brothers Inc., 22 109–12

Brooks Fashion, **29** 164

Brooks Fiber Communications, **41** 289–90

Brooks Fiber Properties, Inc., **27** 301, 307

Brooks, Harvey & Company, Inc., **16** 376

Brooks Shoe Manufacturing Co., **16** 546

Brooks Sports Inc., 32 98–101

Brookshire Grocery Company, 16 63–66; **74** 50–53 (upd.)

Brookstone, Inc., 18 81–83

Brother Industries, Ltd., 14 75–76

Brother International, **23** 212

Brothers Foods, **18** 7

Brothers Gourmet Coffees, Inc., 20 82–85

Brotherton Chemicals, **29** 113

Brotherton Speciality Products Ltd., **68** 81

Broughton Foods Co., 17 55–57

Brown & Bigelow, **27** 193

Brown & Brown, Inc., 41 63–66

Brown & Haley, 23 78–80

Brown & Root, Inc., 13 117–19 *see also* Kellogg Brown & Root Inc.

Brown & Sharpe Manufacturing Co., 23 81–84

Brown and Williamson Tobacco Corporation, 14 77–79; **33** 80–83 (upd.)

Brown Boveri *see* BBC Brown Boveri.

Brown Brothers Harriman & Co., 45 64–67

Brown Cow West Corporation, **55** 360

Brown-Forman Corporation, I 225–27; **10** 179–82 (upd.); **38** 110–14 (upd.)

Brown Group, Inc., V 351–53; **20** 86–89 (upd.) *see also* Brown Shoe Company, Inc.

Brown Institute, **45** 87

Brown Jordan International Inc., 74 54–57 (upd.)

Brown Printing Company, 26 43–45

Brown-Service Insurance Company, **9** 507

Brown Shipbuilding Company *see* Brown & Root, Inc.

Brown, Shipley & Co., Limited, **45** 65

Brown Shoe Company, Inc., 68 65–69 (upd.)

Browning-Ferris Industries, Inc., V 749–53; **20** 90–93 (upd.)

Browning International, **58** 147

Browning Manufacturing, **II** 19

Browning Telephone Corp., **14** 258

Broyhill Furniture Industries, Inc., 10 183–85

BRS Ltd. *see* Ecel plc.

Bruce Foods Corporation, 39 67–69

Bruce Power LP, **49** 65, 67

Bruce's Furniture Stores, **14** 235

Bruckmann, Rosser, Sherill & Co., **27** 247; **40** 51 *see also* Lazy Days RV Center, Inc.

Bruegger's Corporation, 63 79–82

Brugman, **27** 502

Brummer Seal Company, **14** 64

Bruno's Supermarkets, Inc., 7 60–62; **26** 46–48 (upd.); **68** 70–73 (upd.)

Brunswick Corporation, III 442–44; **22** 113–17 (upd.); **77** 68–75 (upd.)

Brunswick Mining, **64** 297

The Brush Electric Light Company, **11** 387; **25** 44

Brush Electrical Machines, **III** 507–09

Brush Engineered Materials Inc., 67 77–79

Brush Moore Newspaper, Inc., **8** 527

Brush Wellman Inc., 14 80–82

Bruster's Real Ice Cream, Inc., 80 51–54

Bruxeland S.P.R.L., **64** 91

Bryce Brothers, **12** 313

Brylane Inc., **29** 106–07; **64** 232

Bryn Mawr Stereo & Video, **30** 465

Brynwood Partners, **13** 19

BSA *see* The Boy Scouts of America.

BSB, **IV** 653; **7** 392

BSC *see* Birmingham Steel Corporation; British Steel Corporation.

BSH Bosch und Siemens Hausgeräte GmbH, 67 80–84

BSkyB, **IV** 653; **7** 392; **29** 369, 371; **34** 85

BSN Groupe S.A., II 474–75 *see also* Groupe Danone

BSN Medical, **41** 374, 377

BT Group plc, 49 69–74 (upd.)

BTG, Inc., 45 68–70

BTI Services, **9** 59

BTM *see* British Tabulating Machine Company.

BTR Dunlop Holdings, Inc., **21** 432

BTR plc, I 428–30

BTR Siebe plc, 27 79–81 *see also* Invensys PLC.

B2B Initiatives Ltd. *see* O.C. Tanner Co.

Bubbles Salon *see* Ratner Companies.

Bublitz Case Company, **55** 151

Buca, Inc., 38 115–17

Buchanan Electric Steel Company, **8** 114

Buck Consultants, Inc., 55 71–73

Buck Knives Inc., 48 71–74

Buckaroo International *see* Bugle Boy Industries, Inc.

Byron Weston Company, **26** 105

C

C&A, 40 74–77 **(upd.)**
C&A Brenninkmeyer KG, V 23–24
C&D *see* Church & Dwight Co., Inc.
C&E Software, **10** 507
C&G *see* Cheltenham & Gloucester PLC.
C & G Systems, **19** 442
C & H Distributors, Inc., **27** 177
C&J Clark International Ltd., 52 56–59
C&K Aluminio S.A., **74** 11
C&K Market, Inc., 81 59–61
C & O *see* Chesapeake and Ohio Railway.
C&R Clothiers, **17** 313
C&S Bank, **10** 425–26
C&S Co., Ltd., **49** 425, 427
C&S/Sovran Corporation, **10** 425–27; **18** 518; **26** 453; **46** 52
C & S Wholesale Grocers, Inc., 55 80–83
C&W *see* Cable and Wireless plc.
C-COR.net Corp., 38 118–21
C-Cube Microsystems, Inc., 37 50–54
C-Mold *see* Moldflow Corporation.
C.A. Delaney Capital Management Ltd., **32** 437
C.A. La Electricidad de Caracas, **53** 18
C.A. Muer Corporation, **65** 205
C.A.S. Sports Agency Inc., **22** 460, 462
C.A. Swanson & Sons *see* Vlasic Foods International Inc.
C Corp. Inc. *see* Alimentation Couche-Tard Inc.
C.D. Haupt, **IV** 296; **19** 226
C.E. Chappell & Sons, Inc., **16** 61–62; **50** 107
C.E.T. *see* Club Européen du Tourisme.
C.F. Burns and Son, Inc., **21** 154
C.F. Hathaway Company, **12** 522
C.F. Martin & Co., Inc., 42 55–58
C.F. Mueller Co., **12** 332; **47** 234
C.F. Orvis Company *see* The Orvis Company, Inc.
C.G. Conn, **7** 286
C. Hoare & Co., 77 76–79
C.H. Boehringer Sohn, 39 70–73
C.H. Heist Corporation, 24 111–13
C.H. Masland & Sons *see* Masland Corporation.
C.H. Musselman Co., **7** 429
C.H. Robinson Worldwide, Inc., 11 43–44; **40** 78–81 **(upd.)**
C.I. Traders Limited, 61 44–46
C. Itoh & Co., **I** 431–33 *see also* ITOCHU Corporation.
C.J. Lawrence, Morgan Grenfell Inc., **II** 429
C.J. Smith and Sons, **11** 3
C.M. Aikman & Co., **13** 168
C.M. Armstrong, Inc., **14** 17
C.M. Barnes Company, **10** 135
C.M. Life Insurance Company, **53** 213
C.M. Page, **14** 112
C-MAC Industries Inc., **48** 369
C.O.M.B. Company, **18** 131–33
C. Of Eko-Elda A.B.E.E., **64** 177
C/P Utility Services Company, **14** 138

C.P.T. Holding B.V., **56** 152
C.P.U., Inc., **18** 111–12
C.R. Anthony Company, **24** 458
C.R. Bard, Inc., 9 96–98; **65** 81–85 **(upd.)**
C.R. Eggs, Inc., **25** 332
C.R. Meyer and Sons Company, 74 58–60
C-Tec Corp. *see* Commonwealth Telephone Enterprises, Inc.
C.V. Gebroeders Pel, **7** 429
C.W. Acquisitions, **27** 288
C.W. Costello & Associates Inc., **31** 131
C.W. Zumbiel Company, **11** 422
C. Wuppesahl & Co. Assekuranzmakler, **25** 538
CAA *see* Creative Artists Agency LLC.
Cabana (Holdings) Ltd., **44** 318
Cabela's Inc., 26 49–51; **68** 74–77 **(upd.)**
Cable & Wireless HKT, 30 95–98 **(upd.)**
Cable and Wireless plc, V 283–86; **25** 98–102 **(upd.)**
Cable Design Technologies Corporation (CDT) *see* Belden CDT Inc.
Cable London, **25** 497
Cable Management Advertising Control System, **25** 497
Cable News Network, **9** 30; **12** 546
Cable One, Inc., **73** 240
Cabletron Systems, Inc., 10 193–94
Cablevision Electronic Instruments, Inc., 32 105–07
Cablevision Systems Corporation, 7 63–65; **30** 99–103 **(upd.)**
Cablex AG, **58** 337
CABLO Metall-Recycling & Handel GmbH, **62** 253
Cabot, Cabot & Forbes, **22** 100
Cabot Corporation, 8 77–79; **29** 79–82 **(upd.)**
Cabot Medical Corporation, **21** 117, 119
Cabot-Morgan Real Estate Co., **16** 159
Cabot Noble Inc., **18** 503, 507; **50** 457
Cabrera Vulcan Shoe Corp., **22** 213
Cache Incorporated, 30 104–06
CACI International Inc., 21 85–87; **72** 49–53 **(upd.)**
Cacique, **24** 237
Cactus Feeders, Inc., **63** 120
Cadadia, **II** 641–42
Cadbury Schweppes PLC, II 476–78; **49** 75–79 **(upd.)**
CADCAM Technology Inc., **22** 196
Caddell Construction Company, **12** 41
Cademartori, **23** 219
Cadence Design Systems, Inc., 11 45–48; **48** 75–79 **(upd.)**
Cadence Industries Corporation, **10** 401–02
Cadet Uniform Services Ltd., **21** 116
Cadillac Fairview Corporation Ltd., **61** 273, 275
Cadillac Plastic, **8** 347
Cadisys Corporation, **10** 119
Cadmus Communications Corporation, 23 100–03

CAE USA Inc., 48 80–82
Caere Corporation, 20 101–03
Caesar's Entertainment Inc., **62** 179
Caesars World, Inc., 6 199–202
Caf'Casino, **12** 152
Café Express, **47** 443
Caffarel, **27** 105
Caffè Nero Group PLC, 63 87–89
Cagiva Group, **17** 24; **30** 172; **39** 37
Cagle's, Inc., 20 104–07
Cahners Business Information, 43 92–95
Cahners Publishing, **IV** 667; **12** 561; **17** 398; **22** 442
CAI Corp., **12** 79
Cain Chemical *see* Occidental Petroleum Corporation.
Cain Sloan, Inc., **68** 114
Cains Marcelle Potato Chips Inc., **15** 139
Cains Pickles, Inc., **51** 232
Cairncom Pty Limited, **56** 155
Cairo Petroleum Refining Co., **51** 113
Caisse de dépôt et placement du Quebec, **II** 664
Caisse des Dépôts—Développement (C3D), **48** 107
Caisse Nationale de Crédit Agricole, **15** 38–39
Caithness Glass Limited, **38** 402; **69** 301, 303
Cajun Bayou Distributors and Management, Inc., **19** 301
Cajun Electric Power Cooperative, Inc., **21** 470
CAK Universal Credit Corp., **32** 80
CAL *see* China Airlines.
Cal Circuit Abco Inc., **13** 387
CAL Corporation, **21** 199, 201
Cal-Dive International Inc., **25** 104–05
Cal/Ink, **13** 228
Cal-Maine Foods, Inc., 69 76–78
Cal-Van Tools *see* Chemi-Trol Chemical Co.
Cala, **17** 558
Calais Railroad Company, **16** 348
Calavo Growers, Inc., 47 63–66
Calcast Ltd., **63** 304
Calcined Coke Corp., **IV** 402
Calcitherm Group, **24** 144
CalComp Inc., 13 126–29
Calcot Ltd., 33 84–87
Calder Race Course, Inc., **29** 118
Caldera Systems Inc., **38** 416, 420
Caldor Inc., 12 54–56
Caledonian Airways *see* British Caledonian Airways.
Caledonian Bank, **10** 337
Calgary Power Company *see* TransAlta Utilities Corporation.
Calgene, Inc., **29** 330; **41** 155
Calgon Carbon Corporation, 73 76–79
Calgon Vestal Laboratories, **37** 44
Calgon Water Management, **15** 154; **40** 176
Cali Realty *see* Mack-Cali Realty Corporation.

Canrad-Hanovia, **27** 57
Canstar Sports Inc., 16 79–81
Canteen Corp., **II** 679–80; **13** 321
Cantel Medical Corporation, 80 55–58
Canterbury Park Holding Corporation, 42 62–65
Canterra Energy Ltd., **47** 180
Cantine Giorgio Lungarotti S.R.L., 67 88–90
Canton Railway Corp., **IV** 718; **38** 320
Cantor Fitzgerald Securities Corporation, **10** 276–78
CanWest Global Communications Corporation, 35 67–703
Canyon Cafes, **31** 41
Canyon Offshore, Inc. *see* Helix Energy Solutions Group, Inc.
Cap Gemini Ernst & Young, 37 59–61
Cap Rock Energy Corporation, 46 78–81
Capacity of Texas, Inc., **33** 105–06
CAPCO *see* Central Area Power Coordination Group; Custom Academic Publishing Company.
Capco Energy, Inc., **33** 296
Capcom Co., **7** 396
Cape and Vineyard Electric Co., **14** 124–25
Cape Cod-Cricket Lane, Inc., **8** 289
Cape Cod Potato Chip Company, Inc., **41** 233
Cape PLC, **22** 49
Capel Incorporated, 45 84–86
Capezio/Ballet Makers Inc., 62 57–59
Capita Group PLC, 69 79–81
AB Capital & Investment Corporation, **6** 108; **23** 381
Capital Advisors, Inc., **22** 4
Capital Bank N.A., **16** 162
Capital Cities/ABC Inc., II 129–31 *see also* ABC, Inc.
Capital Concrete Pipe Company, **14** 250
Capital Controls Co., Inc. *see* Severn Trent PLC.
Capital Distributing Co., **21** 37
Capital Factors, Inc., **54** 387
Capital-Gazette Communications, Inc., **12** 302
Capital Grille, **19** 342
Capital Group, **26** 187
Capital Holding Corporation, III 216–19 *see also* Providian Financial Corporation.
Capital Life Insurance Company, **11** 482–83
Capital Management Services *see* CB Commercial Real Estate Services Group, Inc.
Capital One Financial Corporation, 52 60–63
Capital Radio plc, 35 71–73
Capital Senior Living Corporation, 75 80–82
Capital Trust Corp., **17** 498
Capitalia S.p.A., 65 86–89
Capitol-EMI, **11** 557
Capitol Film + TV International, **IV** 591
Capitol Films, **25** 270

Capitol Pack, Inc., **13** 350
Capitol Printing Ink Company, **13** 227–28
Capitol Publishing, **13** 560
Capitol Transamerica Corporation, **60** 16
Capseals, Ltd., **8** 476
Capstar, **62** 119
CapStar Hotel Company, 21 91–93
Capstone Pharmacy of Delaware, Inc., **64** 27
Capstone Turbine Corporation, 75 83–85
Captain D's, LLC, 59 104–06
Car-lac Electronic Industrial Sales Inc., **9** 420
Car Toys, Inc., 67 91–93
Car-X, **10** 415
Caraco Pharmaceutical Laboratories Inc., **57** 345–46
Caradco, Inc., **45** 216
Caradon plc, 20 108–12 **(upd.)** *see also* Novar plc.
Carando Foods, **7** 174–75
Carat Group *see* Aegis Group plc.
Caratti Sports, Ltd., **26** 184
Caraustar Industries, Inc., 19 76–78; **44** 63–67 **(upd.)**
Caravali, **13** 493–94
Caravelle Foods, **21** 500
The Carbide/Graphite Group, Inc., 40 82–84
Carbo PLC, 67 94–96 **(upd.)**
Carbocol, **IV** 417
Carboline Co., **8** 455
CarboMedics, **11** 458–60
Carbon Research Laboratories, **9** 517
Carbone Lorraine S.A., 33 88–90
La Carbonique, **23** 217, 219
Carborundum Company, 15 80–82 *see also* Carbo PLC.
Cardàpio, **29** 444
Cardell Corporation, **54** 239
Cardem Insurance Co., **III** 767; **22** 546
Cardiac Pacemakers, Inc., **11** 90; **11** 458; **22** 361
Cardinal Distributors Ltd., **II** 663
Cardinal Freight Carriers, Inc., **42** 365
Cardinal Health, Inc., 18 96–98; **50** 120–23 **(upd.)**
Cardinal Holdings Corporation, **65** 334
Cardo AB, 53 83–85
Cardon-Phonocraft Company, **18** 492
Care Advantage, Inc., **25** 383
Care Group, **22** 276
Career Education Corporation, 45 87–89
Career Horizons Inc., **49** 265
CareerCom Corp., **25** 253
CareerStaff Unlimited Inc., **25** 455
Caremark Rx, Inc., 10 198–200; **54** 42–45 **(upd.)**
Carenes, SA, **12** 377
CareScience, Inc. *see* Quovadx Inc.
CareTel, Inc., **53** 209
CareUnit, Inc., **15** 123
CareWise, Inc., **36** 365, 367–68

Carey Diversified LLC *see* W.P. Carey & Co. LLC.
Carey International, Inc., 26 60–63
Carey-McFall Corp. *see* Springs Industries, Inc.
Carey Straw Mill, **12** 376
S.A. CARFUEL, **12** 152
Cargill, Incorporated, II 616–18; **13** 136–38 **(upd.);** **40** 85–90 **(upd.)**
Cargill Trust Co., **13** 467
Cargo Express, **16** 198
Cargo Furniture, **31** 436
Cargolux Airlines International S.A., 49 80–82
CARGOSUR *see* Iberia.
Cargotec Corporation, **76** 225, 228
Carhartt, Inc., 30 110–12; **77** 88–92 **(upd.)**
Caribiner International, Inc., 24 94–97
Caribou Coffee Company, Inc., 28 62–65
Carintusa Inc., **8** 271
Carisam International Corp., **29** 511
Caritas Internationalis, 72 57–59
Carl Allers Etablissement A/S, 72 60–62
Carl Ed. Meyer GmbH, **48** 119
Carl I. Brown and Company, **48** 178
Carl Karcher Enterprises, Inc., **19** 435; **46** 94
Carl Marks & Co., **11** 260–61
Carl-Zeiss-Stiftung, III 445–47; **34** 92–97 **(upd.)**
Carl's Jr. *see* CKE Restaurants, Inc.
Carl's Superstores, **9** 452
Carlin Foods Corporation, **62** 50
Carlin Gold Mining Company, **7** 386–87
Carling O'Keefe Ltd., **I** 229, 254, 269, 438–39; **7** 183; **12** 337; **26** 305
Carlisa S.A. *see* Arcor S.A.I.C.
Carlisle Companies Incorporated, 8 80–82
Carlisle Memory Products, **14** 535
Carlon, **13** 304–06
Carlova, Inc., **21** 54
Carlsberg A/S, 9 99–101; **29** 83–85 **(upd.)**
Carlson Companies, Inc., 6 363–66; **22** 125–29 **(upd.)**
Carlson Restaurants Worldwide, 69 82–85
Carlson Wagonlit Travel, 55 89–92
Carlton and United Breweries Ltd., I 228–29 *see also* Foster's Group Limited
Carlton Cards Retail, Inc., **39** 87; **59** 34–35
Carlton Communications plc, 15 83–85; **50** 124–27 **(upd.)**
Carlton Foods Corporation, **57** 56–57
Carlton Investments L.P., **22** 514
Carlyle & Co. Jewelers *see* Finlay Enterprises, Inc.
The Carlyle Group, **11** 364; **14** 43; **16** 47; **21** 97; **30** 472; **43** 60; **49** 444; **73** 47; **76** 315
Carlyle Management Group, **63** 226
Carma Laboratories, Inc., 60 80–82
CarMax, Inc., 55 93–95
Carmeda AB, **10** 439

Europoligrafico SpA, **41** 326
Europspace Technische Entwicklungen, **51** 17
Euroquipment Ltd, **72** 221
Eurosar S.A., **25** 455
Eurotech BV, **25** 101
Eurotec S.A.S., **72** 332
Eurotechnique, **III** 678; **16** 122
Eurotel Praha, spol. s.r.o., **64** 73
Eurotunnel Group, **13** 206–08; **37** 134–38 (upd.)
Eurovida, **III** 348
Euthenics Systems Corp. *see* Michael Baker Corporation.
Euvia Media AG & Co., **54** 295, 297
EVA Airways Corporation, **51** 121–23
Evac International Ltd, **51** 324
Evaluation Associates, LLC *see* Milliman USA.
Evans & Sutherland Computer Corporation, **19** 145–49; **78** 98–103 (upd.)
Evans Drumhead Company, **48** 232
Evans, Inc., **30** 192–94
Evans Products Co., **13** 249–50, 550
Evans Rents, **26** 101
Evansville Brewing Company *see* Pittsburgh Brewing Company.
Evansville Paint & Varnish Co. *see* Red Spot Paint & Varnish Co.
Evansville Veneer and Lumber Co., **12** 296
Evelyn Wood, Inc., **7** 165, 168
Evence Coppée, **III** 704–05
Evenflo Companies, Inc., **19** 144; **54** 73
Ever Ready Ltd., **7** 209; **9** 179–80; **30** 231
Everan Capital Corp., **15** 257
Evercore Capital Partners, **59** 383
Everdream Corporation, **59** 12
Everest & Jennings, **11** 200
Everett Pulp & Paper Company, **17** 440
Everex Systems, Inc., **16** 194–96
Everfresh Beverages Inc., **26** 326
Evergenius, **13** 210
Evergreen Air Cargo Service Co., **51** 123
Evergreen Healthcare, Inc., **14** 210
Evergreen International Aviation, Inc., **53** 130–33
Evergreen Marine Corporation (Taiwan) Ltd., **13** 209–11; **50** 183–89 (upd.)
Evergreen Media Corporation, **24** 106
Evergreen Resources, Inc., **11** 28
Everlast Worldwide Inc., **47** 126–29
Everlaurel, **13** 210
Everready Battery Co., **13** 433; **39** 338
Everyday Learning Corporation, **22** 519, 522
Everything for the Office, **22** 154
Everything Yogurt, **25** 180
Everything's A Dollar Inc. (EAD), **13** 541–43
EVI, Inc., **39** 416
Evinrude Outboard Motor Company, **27** 75
Evity, Inc., **55** 67
EWTN *see* Eternal Word Television Network, Inc.

Ex-Lax Inc., **15** 138–39
Exabyte Corporation, **12** 161–63; **40** 178–81 (upd.)
Exactis.com Inc., **49** 423
ExamOne World Wide, **48** 256
Exar Corp., **14** 182–84
Exatec A/S, **10** 113; **50** 43
Exbud, **38** 437
Excaliber, **6** 205
EXCEL Communications Inc., **18** 164–67
Excel Corporation, **11** 92–93; **13** 138, 351; **54** 168
Excel Industries Inc., **53** 55
Excel Mining Systems, Inc., **13** 98
Excel Technology, Inc., **65** 139–42
Excelsior Life Insurance Co., **21** 14
Excelsior Printing Company, **26** 105
Excerpta Medica International *see* Reed Elsevier
Excite, Inc. *see* At Home Corporation.
Exco International, **10** 277
Execu-Fit Health Programs, **11** 379
Executive Aircraft Services, **27** 21
Executive Airlines, Inc., **28** 22
Executive Fund Life Insurance Company, **27** 47
Executive Gallery, Inc., **12** 264
Executive Income Life Insurance Co., **10** 246
Executive Jet, Inc., **36** 189–91
Executive Life Insurance Co., **III** 253–55; **11** 483
Executive Money Management, **57** 269
Executive Risk Inc., **37** 86
Executive Systems, Inc., **11** 18
Executone Information Systems, Inc., **13** 212–14; **15** 195
ExecuTrain *see* International Data Group, Inc.
Executrans, Inc., **21** 96
Exel Ltd., **13** 150
Exel plc, **51** 124–30 (upd.)
Exelon Corporation, **48** 156–63 (upd.); **49** 65
Exeter & Hampton Electric Company, **37** 406
Exide Electronics Group, Inc., **20** 213–15
Exmark Manufacturing Company, Inc., **26** 494
Exp@nets, **37** 280, 283
Expand SA, **48** 164–66
Expedia, Inc., **58** 117–21
Expeditors International of Washington Inc., **17** 163–65; **78** 104–08 (upd.)
Experian Information Solutions Inc., **45** 152–55
Experian Ltd., **47** 165, 168–69
Explorer Motor Home Corp., **16** 296
Export & Domestic Can Co., **15** 127
Express Airlines, Inc., **28** 266
Express Baggage Reclaim Services Limited, **27** 21
Express Gifts Ltd., **60** 122
Express Newspapers plc, **IV** 687; **28** 503
Express Rent-a-Tire, Ltd., **20** 113

Express Scripts Inc., **17** 166–68; **44** 173–76 (upd.)
Expression Homes, **22** 205, 207
ExpressJet Holdings Inc., **52** 89, 93
Exsa, **55** 188
ExSample Media BV, **53** 362
Extel Financial Ltd., **IV** 687
Extended Stay America, Inc., **41** 156–58
Extendicare Health Services, Inc., **6** 181–83
Extron International Inc., **16** 538; **43** 33
EXX Inc., **65** 143–45
Exxon Mobil Corporation, **IV** 426–30; **7** 169–73 (upd.); **32** 175–82 (upd.); **67** 175–86 (upd.)
Eyckeler & Malt AG, **59** 4–5
Eye Care Centers of America, Inc., **69** 158–60
Eye Masters Ltd., **23** 329; **76** 243
Eyefinity *see* Vision Service Plan Inc.
Eyeful Home Co., **III** 758
Eyes Multimedia Productions Inc., **51** 286–87
EZ Direkt Marketing GmbH *see* Manutan International S.A.
EZ Paintr Corporation, **9** 374
Ezaki Glico Company Ltd., **72** 123–25
EZCORP Inc., **43** 159–61
EZPor Corporation, **12** 377

F

F. & F. Koenigkramer Company, **10** 272
F&G International Insurance, **III** 397
F & J Meat Packers, Inc., **22** 548–49
F & M Distributors, **12** 132
F&N Foods Ltd., **54** 116–17
F & R Builders, Inc., **11** 257
F&W Publications, Inc., **71** 154–56
F.A. Computer Technologies, Inc., **12** 60
F.A.O. Schwarz *see* FAO Schwarz
F.B. McFarren, Ltd., **21** 499–500
F.C. Internazionale Milano SpA, **44** 387
The F. Dohmen Co., **77** 142–45
F.E. Compton Company, **7** 167
F. Egger Co., **22** 49
F.H. Tomkins Buckle Company Ltd., **11** 525
F. Hoffmann-La Roche & Co. A.G., **I** 642–44; **50** 190–93 (upd.)
F.K.I. Babcock, **III** 466
F. Kanematsu & Co., Ltd. *see* Kanematsu Corporation.
F. Korbel & Bros. Inc., **68** 144–46
F.N. Herstal *see* Groupe Herstal S.A.
F.W. Means & Company, **11** 337
F.W. Sickles Company, **10** 319
F.W. Witt & Co. *see* Newly Weds foods, Inc.
F.W. Woolworth & Co. Ltd. *see* Kingfisher plc.
F.W. Woolworth Co. *see* Woolworth Corporation.
F.X. Matt Brewing Co., **18** 72; **50** 114
F.X. Schmid Vereinigte Münchener Spielkartenfabriken GmbH & Co. KG, **64** 325
Fab-Asia, Inc., **22** 354–55
Fab Industries, Inc., **27** 142–44

Freeman Chemical Corporation, **61** 111–12

Freeman, Spogli & Co., **17** 366; **18** 90; **32** 12, 15; **35** 276; **36** 358–59; **47** 142–43; **57** 11, 242

Freemans *see* Sears plc.

FreeMark Communications, **38** 269

Freeport-McMoRan Copper & Gold, Inc., IV 81–84; **7** 185–89 (upd.); **57** 145–50 (upd.)

Freeport Power, **38** 448

Freeze.com LLC, 77 156–59

Freezer Queen Foods, Inc., **21** 509

Freezer Shirt Corporation, **8** 406

Freight Car Services, Inc., **23** 306

Freight Outlet, **17** 297

Freixenet S.A., 71 162–64

Frejlack Ice Cream Co., **II** 646; **7** 317

Fremont Canning Company, **7** 196

Fremont Group, **21** 97

Fremont Investors, **30** 268

Fremont Partners, **24** 265

Fremont Savings Bank, **9** 474–75

French Connection Group plc, 41 167–69

French Fragrances, Inc., 22 213–15 *see also* Elizabeth Arden, Inc.

French Kier, **I** 568

French Quarter Coffee Co., **27** 480–81

Frequency Electronics, Inc., 61 103–05

Frequency Sources Inc., **9** 324

Fresenius AG, 56 138–42

Fresh America Corporation, 20 226–28

Fresh Choice, Inc., 20 229–32

Fresh Enterprises, Inc., 66 125–27

Fresh Fields, **19** 501

Fresh Foods, Inc., 29 201–03

Fresh Start Bakeries, **26** 58

Freshbake Foods Group PLC, **II** 481; **7** 68; **25** 518; **26** 57

Freshlike, **76** 17

Fretter, Inc., 10 304–06

Freudenberg & Co., 41 170–73

Friction Products Co., **59** 222

Frictiontech Inc., **11** 84

Friday's Front Row Sports Grill, **22** 128

Friden, Inc., **30** 418; **53** 237

Fried, Frank, Harris, Shriver & Jacobson, 35 183–86

Fried. Krupp GmbH, IV 85–89 *see also* Thyssen Krupp AG.

Friede Goldman Halter, **61** 43

Friedman, Billings, Ramsey Group, Inc., 53 134–37

Friedman's Inc., 29 204–06

Friedrich Grohe AG & Co. KG, 53 138–41

Friendly Hotels PLC, **14** 107

Friendly Ice Cream Corporation, 30 208–10; **72** 141–44 (upd.)

Friesland Coberco Dairy Foods Holding N.V., 59 194–96

Frigidaire Home Products, 22 216–18

Frigoscandia AB, **57** 300

Frimont S.p.A, **68** 136

Frisby P.M.C. Incorporated, **16** 475

Frisch's Restaurants, Inc., 35 187–89

Frisdranken Industries Winters B.V., **22** 515

Frisk Int. Nv, **72** 272

Frito-Lay North America, 32 205–10; **73** 151–58 (upd.)

Fritz Companies, Inc., 12 180–82

Fritz Gegauf AG *see* Bernina Holding AG.

Fritz Schömer, **75** 56–57

Fritz W. Glitsch and Sons, Inc. *see* Glitsch International, Inc.

Frolich Intercon International, **57** 174

Fromagerie d'Illoud *see* Bongrain SA.

Fromageries Bel, 23 217–19; **25** 83–84

Fromarsac, **25** 84

Frome Broken Hill Co., **IV** 59

Front Range Pipeline LLC, **60** 88

Frontec, **13** 132

Frontenac Co., **24** 45

Frontier Airlines, Inc., 22 219–21

Frontier Communications, **32** 216, 218

Frontier Corp., 16 221–23

Frontier Electronics, **19** 311

Frontier Expeditors, Inc., **12** 363

Frontier Pacific Insurance Company, **21** 263

Frontier Vision Partners L.P., **52** 9

FrontLine Capital Group, **47** 330–31

Frontline Ltd., 45 163–65

Frontstep Inc., **55** 258

Frosch Touristik, **27** 29

Frost & Sullivan, Inc., 53 142–44

Frost National Bank *see* Cullen/Frost Bankers, Inc.

Frozen Food Express Industries, Inc., 20 233–35

Fru-Con Holding Corporation, **I** 561; **55** 62

Fruehauf Corp., I 169–70

Fruit of the Loom, Inc., 8 200–02; **25** 164–67 (upd.)

The Frustum Group Inc., **45** 280

Fruth Pharmacy, Inc., 66 128–30

Fry's Electronics, Inc., 68 168–70

Fry's Food Stores, **12** 112

Frye Copy Systems, **6** 599

Frymaster Corporation, 27 159–62

FSA Corporation, **25** 349

FSI International, Inc., 17 192–94 *see also* FlightSafety International, Inc.

FSP *see* Frank Schaffer Publications.

FT Freeport Indonesia, **57** 145

FTD *see* Florists Transworld Delivery, Inc.

FTI Consulting, Inc., 77 160–63

FTP Software, Inc., 20 236–38

Fubu, 29 207–09

Fuddruckers, **27** 480–82

Fuel Pipeline Transportation Ltd. *see* Thai Airways International.

Fuel Resources Development Co., **6** 558–59

Fuel Resources Inc., **6** 457

FuelCell Energy, Inc., 75 150–53

FuelMaker Corporation, **6** 569

Fuji Bank, Ltd., II 291–93

Fuji Electric Co., Ltd., II 22–23; **48** 180–82 (upd.)

Fuji Gen-Gakki, **16** 202; **43** 171

Fuji Heavy Industries, **I** 207; **9** 294; **12** 400; **13** 499–501; **23** 290; **36** 240, 243; **64** 151

Fuji Kaolin Co. *see* English China Clays Ltd.

Fuji Photo Film Co., Ltd., III 486–89; **18** 183–87 (upd.); **79** 177–84 (upd.)

Fuji Seito, **I** 511

Fuji Television, **7** 249; **9** 29

Fuji Xerox. *see* Xerox Corporation.

Fujian Hualong Carburetor, **13** 555

Fujisawa Pharmaceutical Company, Ltd., I 635–36; **58** 132–34 (upd.)

Fujitsu-ICL Systems Inc., 11 150–51

Fujitsu Limited, III 139–41; **16** 224–27 (upd.); **40** 145–50 (upd.)

Fujitsu Takamisawa, **28** 131

Fukuoka Mitsukoshi Ltd., **56** 242

Fukuoka Paper Co., Ltd., **IV** 285

Fukutake Publishing Co., Ltd., **13** 91, 93

Ful-O-Pep, **10** 250

Fulbright & Jaworski L.L.P., 47 138–41

Fulcrum Communications, **10** 19

The Fulfillment Corporation of America, **21** 37

Fulham Brothers, **13** 244

Fullbright & Jaworski, **28** 48

Fuller Company *see* FLSmidth and Co. A/S.

Fuller Smith & Turner P.L.C., 38 193–95

Fulton Bank, **14** 40

Fulton Manufacturing Co., **11** 535

Fulton Performance Products, Inc., **11** 535

Funai Electric Company Ltd., 62 148–50

Funco, Inc., 20 239–41 *see also* GameStop Corp.

Fund American Companies *see* White Mountains Insurance Group, Ltd.

Fundimensions, **16** 337

Funk & Wagnalls, **22** 441

Funnel Cake Factory, **24** 241

Funtastic Limited, **52** 193

Fuqua Enterprises, Inc., 17 195–98

Fuqua Industries Inc., I 445–47

Furnishings International Inc., **20** 359, 363; **39** 267

Furniture Brands International, Inc., 39 170–75 (upd.)

The Furniture Center, Inc., **14** 236

Furon Company, 28 149–51

Furr's Restaurant Group, Inc., 53 145–48

Furr's Supermarkets, Inc., 28 152–54

Furst Group, **17** 106

Furukawa Electric Co., Ltd., III 490–92

Futronix Corporation, **17** 276

Future Diagnostics, Inc., **25** 384

Future Graphics, **18** 387

Future Now, Inc., 12 183–85

Future Shop Ltd., 62 151–53

FutureCare, **50** 123

Futurestep, Inc., **34** 247, 249

Fuyo Group, **72** 249

FWD Corporation, **7** 513

FX Coughlin Inc., **51** 130

Geriatrics Inc., **13** 49

Gericom AG, **47** 152–54

Gerling-Konzern Versicherungs-Beteiligungs-Aktiengesellschaft, **51** 139–43

Germaine Monteil Cosmetiques Corp., **I** 426

German American Bancorp, **41** 178–80

German-American Car Company *see* GATX.

The German Society *see* The Legal Aid Society.

Germania Fluggesellschaft mbH, **76** 132

GERPI, **51** 16

Gerrard Group, **61** 270, 272

Gerresheimer Glas AG, **43** 186–89

Gerrity Oil & Gas Corporation, **11** 28; **24** 379–80

Gerry Weber International AG, **63** 169–72

GESA *see* General Europea S.A.

Gesbancaya, **II** 196

Geschmay Group, **51** 14

Gesellschaft für musikalische Aufführungs-und mechanische Vervielfältigungsrechte *see* GEMA.

Gesellschaft für Tierernährung, **74** 117

GET Manufacturing Inc., **36** 300

Getchell Gold Corporation, **61** 292

Getronics NV, **39** 176–78

Getty Images, Inc., **31** 216–18

Getty Oil Co., **6** 457; **8** 526; **11** 27; **17** 501; **18** 488; **27** 216; **47** 436 *see also* ChevronTexaco.

Getz Corp., **IV** 137

Gevaert *see* Agfa Gevaert Group N.V.

Gevity HR, Inc., **63** 173–77

Geyser Peak Winery, **58** 196

GFI Informatique SA, **49** 165–68

GfK Aktiengesellschaft, **49** 169–72

GFL Mining Services Ltd., **62** 164

GFS *see* Gordon Food Service Inc.

GFS Realty Inc., **II** 633

GGT Group, **44** 198

GHI, **28** 155, 157

Ghirardelli Chocolate Company, **30** 218–20

GI Communications, **10** 321

GI Export Corp. *see* Johnston Industries, Inc.

GIAG, **16** 122

Gianni Versace SpA, **22** 238–40

Giant Bicycle Inc., **19** 384

Giant Cement Holding, Inc., **23** 224–26

Giant Eagle, Inc., **12** 390–91; **13** 237

Giant Food Inc., **II** 633–35; **22** 241–44 (upd.)

Giant Industries, Inc., **19** 175–77; **61** 114–18 (upd.)

Giant Resources, **III** 729

Giant Stores, Inc., **7** 113; **25** 124

Giant TC, Inc. *see* Campo Electronics, Appliances & Computers, Inc.

Giant Tire & Rubber Company, **8** 126

Giant-Vac Manufacturing Inc., **64** 355

Giant Video Corporation, **29** 503

Giant Wholesale, **II** 625

GIB Group, **V** 63–66; **26** 158–62 (upd.)

Gibbons, Green, van Amerongen Ltd., **II** 605; **9** 94; **12** 28; **19** 360

Gibbs and Dandy plc, **74** 119–21

Gibbs Construction, **25** 404

GIBCO Corp., **17** 287, 289

Gibraltar Casualty Co., **III** 340

Gibraltar Steel Corporation, **37** 164–67

Gibson, Dunn & Crutcher LLP, **36** 249–52

Gibson Energy Ltd. *see* Hunting plc

Gibson Greetings, Inc., **12** 207–10

Gibson Guitar Corp., **16** 237–40

Gibson McDonald Furniture Co., **14** 236

GIC *see* The Goodyear Tire & Rubber Company.

Giddings & Lewis, Inc., **10** 328–30

GiFi S.A., **74** 122–24

Giftmaster Inc., **26** 439–40

Gil-Wel Manufacturing Company, **17** 440

Gilbane, Inc., **34** 191–93

Gilbert & John Greenall Limited, **21** 246

Gilbert Lane Personnel, Inc., **9** 326

Gildan Activewear, Inc., **81** 165–68

Gildemeister AG, **79** 193–97

Gildon Metal Enterprises, **7** 96

Gilead Sciences, Inc., **54** 129–31

Gilkey Bros. *see* Puget Sound Tug and Barge Company.

Gill Interprovincial Lines, **27** 473

Gillett Holdings, Inc., **7** 199–201

The Gillette Company, **III** 27–30; **20** 249–53 (upd.); **68** 171–76 (upd.)

Gilliam Furniture Inc., **12** 475

Gilliam Manufacturing Co., **8** 530

Gilliam S.A., **61** 104

Gilman & Ciocia, Inc., **72** 148–50

Gilman Paper Co., **37** 178

Gilmore Steel Corporation *see* Oregon Steel Mills, Inc.

Gilroy Foods, **27** 299

Gimbel Brothers, Inc. *see* Saks Holdings, Inc.

Gimbel's Department Store, **I** 426–27; **8** 59; **22** 72; **50** 117–18

Gimelli Productions AG, **73** 332

Gindick Productions, **6** 28

Gingiss Group, **60** 5

Ginn & Co., **IV** 672; **19** 405

Ginnie Mae *see* Government National Mortgage Association.

Gino's East, **21** 362

Ginsber Beer Group, **15** 47; **38** 77

Giorgio Armani S.p.A., **45** 180–83

Giorgio Beverly Hills, Inc., **26** 384

Giraud Restaurant System Co. Ltd. *see* Odakyu Electric Railway Co., Ltd.

Girbaud, **17** 513; **31** 261

Girl Scouts of the USA, **35** 193–96

Giro Sport Designs International Inc., **16** 53; **44** 53–54

GiroCredit Bank, **69** 156

Girod, **19** 50

Girsa S.A., **23** 170

Girvin, Inc., **16** 297

Gist-Brocades Co., **III** 53; **26** 384

Git-n-Go Corporation, **60** 160

The Gitano Group, Inc., **8** 219–21

La Giulia Ind. S.P.A., **72** 272

GIV *see* Granite Industries of Vermont, Inc.

Givaudan SA, **43** 190–93

GIW Industries Inc., **62** 217

GJM International Ltd., **25** 121–22

GK Technologies Incorporated, **10** 547

GKH Partners, **29** 295

GKN plc, **III** 493–96; **38** 208–13 (upd.)

Glaces Thiriet S.A., **76** 164–66

Glitsch International, Inc., **76** 153, 155

Glacier Bancorp, Inc., **35** 197–200

Glacier Park, Inc. *see* Viad Corp.

Glacier Water Services, Inc., **47** 155–58

Glamar Group plc, **14** 224

Glamis Gold, Ltd., **54** 132–35

Glamor Shops, Inc., **14** 93

Glanbia plc, **59** 204–07, 364

Glass Glover Plc, **52** 419

Glasstite, Inc., **33** 360–61

GlasTec, **II** 420

Glastron *see* Genmar Holdings, Inc.

Glatfelter Wood Pulp Company, **8** 413

Glaverbel Group, **80** 130–33

Glaxo Holdings plc, **I** 639–41; **9** 263–65 (upd.)

GlaxoSmithKline plc, **46** 201–08 (upd.)

Gleason Corporation, **24** 184–87

Glemby Co. Inc., **70** 262

Glen & Co., **I** 453

Glen Alden Corp., **15** 247

Glen Dimplex, **78** 123–27

Glen-Gery Corporation, **14** 249

Glencairn Ltd., **25** 418

Glencore International AG, **52** 71, 73; **73** 391–92

The Glenlyte Group, **29** 469

Glenlyte Thomas Group LLC, **29** 466

Glenmoor Partners, **70** 34–35

Glenn Advertising Agency, **25** 90

Glenn Pleass Holdings Pty. Ltd., **21** 339

GLF-Eastern States Association, **7** 17

Glico *see* Ezaki Glico Company Ltd.

The Glidden Company, **8** 222–24

Glimcher Co., **26** 262

Glitsch International, Inc. *see* Foster Wheeler Corp.

Global Access, **31** 469

Global Apparel Sourcing Ltd., **22** 223

Global Berry Farms LLC, **62** 154–56

Global BMC (Mauritius) Holdings Ltd., **62** 55

Global Card Holdings Inc., **68** 45

Global Communications of New York, Inc., **45** 261

Global Crossing Ltd., **32** 216–19

Global Engineering Company, **9** 266

Global Health Care Partners, **42** 68

Global Hyatt Corporation, **75** 159–63 (upd.)

Global Imaging Systems, Inc., **73** 163–65

Global Industries, Ltd., **37** 168–72

Global Information Solutions, **34** 257

Global Interactive Communications Corporation, **28** 242

Global Marine Inc., **9** 266–67

Global Motorsport Group, Inc. *see* Custom Chrome, Inc.

Groupe Partouche SA, **48** 196–99
Groupe Pechiney, **33** 89
Groupe Pinault-Printemps-Redoute, **19** 306, 309; **21** 224, 226
Groupe Poliet, **66** 363–64
Groupe Poron, **35** 206
Groupe Promodès S.A., **19** 326–28
Groupe Rallye, **39** 183–85
Groupe Rothschild, **22** 365
Groupe Rougier SA, **21** 438–40
Groupe Roussin, **34** 13
Groupe Salvat, **IV** 619
Groupe SEB, **35** 201–03
Groupe Sidel S.A., **21** 252–55
Groupe Soufflet SA, **55** 176–78
Groupe Tetra Laval, **53** 327
Groupe Victoire, **III** 394
Groupe Vidéotron Ltée., **20** 271–73
Groupe Yves Saint Laurent, **23** 236–39
Groupe Zannier S.A., **35** 204–07
Groupement d'Achat AVP SAS, **58** 221
Groupement des Mousquetaires *see* ITM Entreprises SA.
Groupement Français pour l'Investissement Immobilier, **42** 153
Groupement Laitier du Perche, **19** 50
Groupement pour le Financement de la Construction *see* Gecina SA.
GroupMAC *see* Encompass Services Corporation.
Groux Beverage Corporation, **11** 451
Grove Manufacturing Co., **9** 393
Grove Worldwide, Inc., **59** 274, 278
Grow Biz International, Inc., **18** 207–10 *see also* Winmark Corporation.
Grow Group Inc., **12** 217–19
Growing Healthy Inc., **27** 197; **43** 218
Growth International, Inc., **17** 371
Groz-Beckert Group, **68** 184–86
GRS Inns Ltd *see* Punch Taverns plc.
Grubb & Ellis Company, **21** 256–58
Gruma, S.A. de C.V., **31** 234–36
Grumman Corp., **I** 61–63; **11** 164–67 **(upd.)**
Grundig AG, **27** 189–92
Gruner + Jahr AG & Co., **7** 245; **22** 442; **23** 85
Gruntal & Co., L.L.C., **20** 274–76
Gruntal Financial Corp., **III** 264
Grupo Acerero del Norte, S.A. de C.V., **22** 286; **42** 6
Grupo Aeropuerto del Sureste, S.A. de C.V., **48** 200–02
Grupo Antarctica Paulista *see* Companhia de Bebidas das Américas.
Grupo Banco Bilbao Vizcaya Argentaria S.A., **54** 147
Grupo Bimbo, S.A. de C.V., **31** 236
Grupo Bufete *see* Bufete Industrial, S.A. de C.V.
Grupo Cabal S.A., **23** 166
Grupo Campi, S.A. de C.V., **39** 230
Grupo Carso, S.A. de C.V., **21** 259–61
Grupo Casa Saba, S.A. de C.V., **39** 186–89
Grupo Clarín S.A., **67** 200–03
Grupo Corvi S.A. de C.V., **7** 115; **25** 126
Grupo Cruzcampo S.A., **34** 202

Grupo Cuervo, S.A. de C.V., **31** 91–92
Grupo Cydsa, S.A. de C.V., **39** 190–93
Grupo de Ingenieria Ecologica, **16** 260
Grupo Dina *see* Consorcio G Grupo Dina, S.A. de C.V.
Grupo Dragados SA, **55** 179–82
Grupo DST, **41** 405–06
Grupo Editorial Random House Mondadori S.L., **54** 22
Grupo Elektra, S.A. de C.V., **39** 194–97
Grupo Empresarial Angeles, **50** 373
Grupo Eroski, **64** 167–70
Grupo Ferrovial, S.A., **40** 217–19
Grupo Financiero Asemex-Banpais S.A., **51** 150
Grupo Financiero Banamex S.A., **54** 143–46
Grupo Financiero Banorte, S.A. de C.V., **51** 149–51
Grupo Financiero BBVA Bancomer S.A., **54** 147–50
Grupo Financiero Galicia S.A., **63** 178–81
Grupo Financiero Inbursa, **21** 259
Grupo Financiero Inverlat, S.A., **39** 188; **59** 74
Grupo Financiero Serfin, S.A., **19** 188–90
Grupo Gigante, S.A. de C.V., **34** 197–99
Grupo Hecali, S.A., **39** 196
Grupo Herdez, S.A. de C.V., **35** 208–10
Grupo Hermes, **24** 359
Grupo ICA, **52** 394
Grupo IMSA, S.A. de C.V., **44** 193–96
Grupo Industrial Alfa, S.A. de C.V. *see* Alfa, S.A. de C.V.
Grupo Industrial Atenquique, S.A. de C.V., **37** 176
Grupo Industrial Bimbo, **19** 191–93
Grupo Industrial Durango, S.A. de C.V., **37** 176–78
Grupo Industrial Maseca S.A. de C.V. (Gimsa) *see* Gruma, S.A. de C.V.
Grupo Industrial Saltillo, S.A. de C.V., **54** 151–54
Grupo Irsa, **23** 171
Grupo Leche Pascual S.A., **59** 212–14
Grupo Lladró S.A., **52** 147–49
Grupo Marsans, **69** 9, 11–12
Grupo Martins, **59** 361
Grupo Mexico, S.A. de C.V., **40** 220–23
Grupo Modelo, S.A. de C.V., **29** 218–20
Grupo Nacional Provincial, **22** 285
Grupo Pipsamex S.A., **37** 178
Grupo Portucel Soporcel, **60** 154–56
Grupo Posadas, S.A. de C.V., **57** 168–70
Grupo Protexa, **16** 210
Grupo Pulsar *see* Pulsar Internacional S.A.
Grupo Quan, **19** 192–93
Grupo Salinas, **39** 196
Grupo Sanborns S.A. de C.V., **35** 118
Grupo Servia, S.A. de C.V., **50** 209
Grupo TACA, **38** 218–20
Grupo Televisa, S.A., **18** 211–14; **54** 155–58 **(upd.)**
Grupo TMM, S.A. de C.V., **50** 208–11
Grupo Transportación Ferroviaria Mexicana, S.A. de C.V., **47** 162–64

Grupo Tribasa, **34** 82
Grupo Tudor, **IV** 471
Grupo Xtra, **39** 186, 188
Gruppo Banco di Napoli, **50** 410
Gruppo Buffetti S.p.A., **47** 345–46
Gruppo Coin S.p.A., **41** 185–87
Gruppo Editoriale L'Espresso S.p.A., **54** 19–21
Gruppo GFT, **22** 123
Gruppo IRI, **V** 325–27
Gryphon Development, **24** 237
Gryphon Holdings, Inc., **21** 262–64
GS Financial Services L.P., **51** 148
GSD&M Advertising, **44** 197–200
GSG&T, Inc. *see* Gulf States Utilities Company.
GSG Holdings Ltd., **39** 87
GSI *see* Geophysical Service, Inc.
GSI Acquisition Co. L.P., **17** 488
GSI Commerce, Inc., **67** 204–06
GSR, Inc., **17** 338
GSU *see* Gulf States Utilities Company.
GT Bicycles, **26** 183–85
GT Global Inc. *see* AMVESCAP PLC.
GT Interactive Software, **31** 237–41 *see also* Infogrames Entertainment S.A.
GTE Corporation, **V** 294–98; **15** 192–97 **(upd.)** *see also* British Columbia Telephone Company; Verizon Communications.
GTE Northwest Inc., **37** 124–26
GTECH Holdings, Inc., **27** 381
GTI Corporation, **29** 461–62
GTM-Entrepose, **23** 332
GTM Group, **43** 450, 452; **54** 392
GTO *see* Global Transport Organization.
GTS Duratek, Inc., **13** 367–68
GTSI *see* Government Technology Services Inc.
GTSI Corp., **57** 171–73
GU Markets, **55** 83
Guangzhou Kurabo Chemicals Co. Ltd., **61** 229
Guangzhou M. C. Packaging, **10** 130
Guangzhou Pearl River Piano Group Ltd., **49** 177–79
Guangzhou Railway Corporation, **52** 43
Guarantee Life Cos., **69** 368
Guarantee Reserve Life Insurance Company, **59** 246
Guaranty Bank & Trust Company, **13** 440
Guaranty Federal Bank, F.S.B., **31** 441
Guaranty Federal Savings & Loan Assoc., **IV** 343
Guaranty Properties Ltd., **11** 258
Guaranty Savings and Loan, **10** 339
Guaranty Trust Co. *see* J.P. Morgan & Co. Incorporated.
Guardforce Limited, **45** 378
Guardian Bank, **13** 468
Guardian Federal Savings and Loan Association, **10** 91
Guardian Financial Services, **11** 168–70; **64** 171–74 **(upd.)**
Guardian Media Group plc, **53** 152–55
Guardian Mortgage Company, **8** 460

Hachette S.A., **IV** 617–19 *see also* Matra-Hachette S.A.

Haci Omer Sabanci Holdings A.S., 55 186–89 *see also* Akbank TAS

Hacker-Pschorr Brau, **35** 331

Hackman Oyj Adp, 44 212–15

Hadco Corporation, 24 201–03

Hadron, Inc. *see* Analex Corporation.

Haemocell, **11** 476

Haemonetics Corporation, 20 277–79

Haftpflichtverband der Deutschen Industrie Versicherung auf Gegenseitigkeit V.a.G. *see* HDI (Haftpflichtverband der Deutschen Industrie Versicherung auf Gegenseitigkeit V.a.G.).

Hagemeyer N.V., 39 201–04

Hagemeyer North America, **63** 289

Haggar Corporation, 19 194–96; 78 137–41 (upd.)

Haggen Inc., 38 221–23

Hägglunds Vehicle AB, **47** 7, 9

Hahn Automotive Warehouse, Inc., 24 204–06

Hahn Department Stores *see* Allied Stores Corp.

Hahn, Inc., **17** 9

Haier Group Corporation, 65 167–70

Haile Mines, Inc., **12** 253

The Hain Celestial Group, Inc., 27 196–98; 43 217–20 (upd.)

Hair Cuttery *see* Ratner Companies.

Hake Group, Inc. *see* Matrix Service Company.

Hakone Tozan Railway Co., Ltd., **68** 281

Hakuhodo, Inc., 6 29–31; 42 172–75 (upd.)

Hakunetsusha & Company, **12** 483

HAL Inc., **9** 271–73 *see also* Hawaiian Airlines, Inc.

Hale and Dorr, **31** 75

Hale-Halsell Company, 60 157–60

Haleko Hanseatisches Lebensmittel Kontor GmbH, **29** 500

Halewood, **21** 246

Half Price Books, Records, Magazines Inc., 37 179–82

Halfords Ltd., **24** 75

Halkin Holdings plc, **49** 338–39

Hall Bros. Co. *see* Hallmark Cards, Inc.

Hall, Kinion & Associates, Inc., 52 150–52

Hall Laboratories, Inc., **45** 209

Hall-Mark Electronics, **23** 490

La Halle aux Chaussures, **17** 210

Haller, Raymond & Brown, Inc., **II** 10

Hallhuber GmbH, **63** 361, 363

Halliburton Company, III 497–500; 25 188–92 (upd.); 55 190–95 (upd.)

Hallmark Cards, Inc., IV 620–21; 16 255–57 (upd.); 40 228–32 (upd.)

Hallmark Chemical Corp., **8** 386

Hallmark Holdings, Inc., **51** 190

Hallmark Investment Corp., **21** 92

Hallmark Residential Group, Inc., **45** 221

Halo Lighting, **30** 266

Haloid Company *see* Xerox Corporation.

Halsam Company, **25** 380

Halstead Industries, **26** 4; **52** 258

Halter Marine, **22** 276

Hambrecht & Quist Group, **10** 463, 504; **26** 66; **27** 447; **31** 349

Hambro American Bank & Trust Co., **11** 109

Hambro Countrywide Security, **32** 374

Hambros Bank, **16** 14; **27** 474; **43** 7

Hamburg-Amerikanische-Packetfahrt-Actien-Gesellschaft *see* Hapag-Lloyd AG.

Hamburgische Electricitaets-Werke AG, **57** 395, 397

Hamelin Group, Inc. *see* Spartech Corporation.

Hamer Hammer Service, Inc., **11** 523

Hamersley Holdings, **IV** 59–61

Hamil Textiles Ltd. *see* Algo Group Inc.

Hamilton Beach/Proctor-Silex Inc., 17 213–15

Hamilton Group Limited, **15** 478

Hamilton Industries, Inc., **25** 261

Hamilton/Hall-Mark, **19** 313

Hamilton National Bank, **13** 465

Hamilton Oil Corp., **IV** 47; **22** 107

Hamilton Standard, **9** 417

Hamilton Sundstrand, **76** 319

Hamish Hamilton, **IV** 659; **8** 526

Hammacher Schlemmer & Company Inc., 21 268–70; 72 160–62 (upd.)

Hammarplast, **13** 493

Hammermill Paper Co., **23** 48–49

Hammers Plastic Recycling, **6** 441

Hammerson plc, IV 696–98; 40 233–35 (upd.)

Hammery Furniture Company, **14** 302–03

Hammes Co., **38** 482

Hamming-Whitman Publishing Co., **13** 559

Hampton Affiliates, Inc., 77 175–79

Hampton Industries, Inc., 20 280–82

Hampton Inns, **9** 425–26

Hampton Roads Food, Inc., **25** 389

Hamworthy Engineering Ltd., **31** 367, 369

Han Comm Inc., **62** 174

Han-Fa Electrification Co. Ltd., **76** 139

Hancock Fabrics, Inc., 18 222–24

Hancock Holding Company, 15 207–09

Hancock Jaffe Laboratories, **11** 460

Hancock Park Associates *see* Leslie's Poolmart, Inc.

Hancock Textile Co., Inc., **27** 291

Handleman Company, 15 210–12

Handspring Inc., 49 183–86

Handy & Harman, 23 249–52

Handy Andy Home Improvement Centers, Inc., **16** 210; **26** 160–61

Hanes Corp., **8** 202, 288; **25** 166

Hanes Holding Company, **11** 256; **48** 267

Hang Chong, **18** 114

Hang Seng Bank Ltd., 60 161–63

Hanger Orthopedic Group, Inc., 41 192–95

Haniel & Cie. GmbH, **27** 175

Hanjin Group *see* Korean Ail Lines Co. Ltd.

Hanjin Shipping Co., Ltd., 50 217–21

Hankook Tyre Manufacturing Company, **V** 255–56; **19** 508

Hankuk Glass Industry Co., **III** 715

Hankyu Corporation, V 454–56; 23 253–56 (upd.)

Hankyu Department Stores, Inc., V 70–71; 62 168–71 (upd.)

Hanley Brick, **14** 250

Hanmi Financial Corporation, 66 169–71

Hanna Andersson Corp., 49 187–90

Hanna-Barbera Cartoons Inc., 23 257–59; 387

Hanna Mining Co., **8** 346–47

Hanna Ore Mining Company, **12** 352

Hannaford Bros. Co., 12 220–22

Hannen Brauerei GmbH, **9** 100

Hannifin Corporation *see* Parker Hannifin Corporation.

HANNOVER International AG für Industrieversicherungen, **53** 162

Hannover Papier, **49** 353

Hanover Bank *see* Manufacturers Hanover Corporation.

Hanover Compressor Company, 59 215–17

Hanover Direct, Inc., 36 262–65

Hanover Foods Corporation, 35 211–14

Hanover House, Inc., **24** 154

Hanover Insurance Company, **63** 29

Hansa Linie, **26** 279–80

Hansen Natural Corporation, 31 242–45; 76 171–74 (upd.)

Hansgrohe AG, 56 149–52

Hansol Paper Co., **63** 315–16

Hanson Building Materials America Inc., 60 164–66

Hanson Industries, **44** 257

Hanson PLC, III 501–03; 7 207–10 (upd.); 30 228–32 (upd.)

Hansvedt Industries Inc., **25** 195

Hanwha Group, 62 172–75

Hapag-Lloyd AG, 6 397–99

Happy Air Exchangers Ltd., **21** 499

Happy Kids Inc., 30 233–35

Haralambos Beverage Corporation, **11** 451

Harbert Corporation, 14 222–23

HARBIN Samick Corp., **56** 300

Harbison-Walker Refractories Company, 24 207–09

Harbor Group, **41** 262–63

Harborlite Corporation, **10** 45; **60** 16

Harbour Group, **24** 16

Harco, Inc., **37** 31

Harcourt Brace and Co., 12 223–26

Harcourt Brace Jovanovich, Inc., IV 622–24

Harcourt General, Inc., 20 283–87 (upd.)

Harcros Investment Trust Ltd. *see* Harrisons & Crosfield PLC.

Hard E Beverage Co., **75** 166

Hard Rock Cafe International, Inc., 12 227–29; 32 241–45 (upd.)

Henkel KGaA, III 31–34; 34 205–10
  (upd.)
Henkel Manco Inc., 22 257–59
Henkell & Söhnlein Sektkellereien KG,
  51 102, 105
Henley Drilling Company, 9 364
The Henley Group, Inc., III 511–12
Henlys Group plc, 35 63, 65
Hennes & Mauritz AB, 29 232–34
Hennessy Company, 19 272
Henney Motor Company, 12 159
Henningsen Foods, Inc., 57 202, 204
Henredon Furniture Industries, III 571;
  11 534; 20 362; 39 266
Henri Bendel Inc., 17 203–04
Henry Boot plc, 76 175–77
Henry Broderick, Inc., 21 96
Henry Denny & Sons, 27 259
Henry Gordy International, Inc. see EXX
  Inc.
Henry Holt & Co., IV 622–23; 13 105;
  27 223; 35 451
Henry I. Siegel Co., 20 136
Henry J. Kaiser Company, Ltd., 28 200
Henry J. Tully Corporation, 13 531
The Henry Jones Co-op Ltd., 7 577
Henry Jones Foods, 7 182; 11 212
Henry L. Doherty & Company, 12 542
Henry Lee Company, 16 451, 453
Henry, Leonard & Thomas Inc., 9 533
Henry Meadows, Ltd., 13 286
Henry Modell & Company Inc., 32
  263–65
Henry Pratt Company, 7 30–31
Henry S. Miller Companies, 21 257
Henry Schein, Inc., 31 254–56; 70
  116–19 (upd.)
Henry Willis & Co. see Willis Corroon
  Group Plc.
Hensel Phelps Construction Company,
  72 174–77
Hensley & Company, 64 178–80
HEPCO see Hokkaido Electric Power
  Company Inc.
Hepworth plc, 44 438
Her Majesty's Stationery Office, 7
  215–18
Heraclio Fournier S.A., 62 383–84
Heraeus Holding GmbH, IV 98–100;
  54 159–63 (upd.)
Heraeus Surgical, Inc., 67 228
Herald Publishing Company, 12 150
Heralds of Liberty, 9 506
Herbalife International, Inc., 17
  226–29; 41 203–06 (upd.)
Herbert Clough Inc., 24 176
Herbert W. Davis & Co., III 344
Herby's Foods, 36 163
Herco Technology, IV 680
Hercules Inc., I 343–45; 22 260–63
  (upd.); 66 184–88 (upd.)
Hercules Offshore Drilling, 28 347–48
Hereford Paper and Allied Products Ltd.,
  14 430
Herff Jones, 25 254
Heritage Bankcorp, 9 482
Heritage Federal Savings and Loan
  Association of Huntington, 10 92

Heritage House of America Inc. see
  Humana Inc.
Heritage Media Group, 25 418
Heritage Springfield, 14 245
Heritage 21 Construction, 60 56
Herley Industries, Inc., 33 187–89
Herman Goelitz, Inc., 28 186–88 see also
  Jelly Belly Candy Company.
Herman Miller, Inc., 8 255–57; 77
  180–86 (upd.)
Herman's World of Sports, II 628–29; 15
  470; 16 457; 43 385
Hermann Pfauter Group, 24 186
Hermès International S.A., 14 238–40;
  34 211–14 (upd.)
Hermosillo, 51 389
Héroux-Devtek Inc., 69 205–07
Herrburger Brooks P.L.C., 12 297
Herrick, Waddell & Reed see Waddell &
  Reed, Inc.
Herring-Hall-Marvin Safe Co. of
  Hamilton, Ohio, 7 145
Herschend Family Entertainment
  Corporation, 73 173–76
Hershey Foods Corporation, II 510–12;
  15 219–22 (upd.); 51 156–60 (upd.)
F.N. Herstal see Groupe Herstal S.A.
Hertel AG, 13 297
Hertie Waren- und Kaufhaus GmbH, V
  72–74
Herts Pharmaceuticals, 17 450; 41
  375–76
The Hertz Corporation, 9 283–85; 33
  190–93 (upd.)
Hertz-Penske Leasing see Penske
  Corporation.
Hervillier, 27 188
Heska Corporation, 39 213–16
Hespeler Hockey Inc., 22 204
Hess see Amerada Hess Corporation.
Hess Department Stores Inc., 16 61–62;
  19 323–24; 41 343; 50 107
Hesse Newman & Co. AG, 72 21
Hesston Corporation, 13 17; 22 380
Hetteen Hoist & Derrick see Polaris
  Industries Inc.
Heublein Inc., I 259–61
Heuer see TAG Heuer International SA.
Heuga Holdings B.V., 8 271
Hewden Stuart PLC see Finning
  International Inc.
Hewitt & Tuttle, 17 355–56
Hewitt Associates, Inc., 77 187–90
Hewlett-Packard Company, III 142–43;
  6 237–39 (upd.); 28 189–92 (upd.);
  50 222–30 (upd.)
Hexal AG, 69 208–10
Hexagon AB, 78 154–57
Hexalon, 26 420
Hexcel Corporation, 28 193–95
Heyer-Schulte, 26 286
Heytesbury Party Ltd., 34 422
HFC see Household Finance Corporation.
HFS Inc., 21 97; 22 54, 56; 53 275
HG Hawker Engineering Co. Ltd. see
  Hawker Siddeley Group PLC.
HGCC see Hysol Grafil Composite
  Components Co.

HH Finch Ltd., 38 501
HI see Houston Industries Incorporated.
Hi-Bred Corn Company, 9 410
Hi-Flier, Inc. see EXX Inc.
Hi-Lo Automotive, Inc., 26 348–49
Hi Tech Consignments, 18 208
Hi-Tek Polymers, Inc., 8 554
Hibbett Sporting Goods, Inc., 26
  189–91; 70 120–23 (upd.)
Hibbing Taconite Company, 62 74
Hibernia Corporation, 37 187–90
Hichens Harrison Ltd see Sanlam Ltd.
Hickman Coward & Wattles, 24 444
Hickory Farms, Inc., 17 230–32
Hickory Specialties, Inc., 63 69, 71
Hickorycraft, III 571; 20 362
Hicks & Greist, 6 40
Hicks, Muse, Tate & Furst, Inc., 24 106;
  30 220; 36 423; 55 202
Hicksgas Gifford, Inc., 6 529
Hickson International PLC see Arch
  Chemicals Inc.
Hickson Kerley see Tessenderlo Group.
Hidden Creek Industries, Inc., 16 397; 24
  498
HiFi Buys, 30 465
Higgs International Ltd., 51 130
High Falls Brewing Company LLC, 74
  144–47
High Integrity Systems, 51 16
High Retail System Co. see Takashimaya
  Co., Limited.
High River Limited Partnership, 73 259
High Tech Computer Corporation, 81
  178–81
Highgate Hotels, Inc., 21 93
Highland Distillers Ltd., 60 355
Highland Gold Ltd., 63 182, 184
Highland Superstores, 9 65–66; 10 9–10,
  304–05, 468; 23 51–52
Highland Telephone Company, 6 334
Highlander Publications, 38 307–08
Highmark Inc., 27 208–11
Highsmith Inc., 60 167–70
Highteam Public Relations Co. Ltd., 60
  143
Highveld Steel and Vanadium
  Corporation Limited, 59 224–27
Hilb, Rogal & Hobbs Company, 77
  191–94
Hilbun Poultry, 10 250
Hildebrandt International, 29 235–38
Hilex Poly Co., Inc., 8 477
Hill & Knowlton Inc. see WPP Group
  PLC.
Hill Engineering see Comtech
  Tellecommunications Corp.
Hill 50 Ltd., 63 182, 184
Hill-Rom Company see Hillenbrand
  Industries, Inc.
Hill's Pet Nutrition, Inc., 27 212–14
Hillard Oil and Gas Company, Inc., 11
  523
Hillards, PLC, II 678
Hillenbrand Industries, Inc., 10
  349–51; 75 188–92 (upd.)
Hiller Aircraft Company, 9 205; 48 167
Hiller Group, 14 286

AB Ingredients, **II** 466

Ingredients Technology Corp., **9** 154

Ingres Corporation, **9** 36–37; **25** 87

Ingwerson and Co., **II** 356

INH *see* Instituto Nacional de Hidrocarboros.

Inha Works Ltd., **33** 164

INI *see* Instituto Nacional de Industria.

Initial Electronics, **64** 198

Initial Security, 64 196–98

Initial Towel Supply *see* Rentokil Initial Plc.

Inktomi Corporation, 45 200–04

Inland Container Corporation, 8 267–69

Inland Motors Corporation, **18** 291

Inland Paperboard and Packaging, Inc., **31** 438

Inland Pollution Control, **9** 110

Inland Steel Industries, Inc., IV 113–16; 19 216–20 (upd.)

Inland Valley, **23** 321

Inmac, Inc., **16** 373

Inmobiliaria e Inversiones Aconcagua S.A., **71** 143

Inmos Ltd., **11** 307; **29** 323

Inmotel Inversiones, **71** 338

InnCOGEN Limited, **35** 480

The Inner-Tec Group, **64** 198

InnerCity Foods Joint Venture Company, **16** 97

Inno-BM, **26** 158, 161

Inno-France *see* Societe des Grandes Entreprises de Distribution, Inno-France.

Innova International Corporation, **26** 333

Innovacom, **25** 96

Innovation, **26** 158

Innovative Marketing Systems *see* Bloomberg L.P.

Innovative Pork Concepts, **7** 82

Innovative Products & Peripherals Corporation, **14** 379

Innovative Software Inc., **10** 362

Innovative Sports Systems, Inc., **15** 396

Innovative Valve Technologies Inc., **33** 167

Innovex Ltd. *see* Quintiles Transnational Corporation.

Inovoject do Brasil Ltda., **72** 108

Inpaco, **16** 340

Inpacsa, **19** 226

Inprise/Borland Corporation, **33** 115; **76** 123–24

Input/Output, Inc., 73 184–87

INS *see* International News Service.

Insa, **55** 189

Insalaco Markets Inc., **13** 394

Inserra Supermarkets, 25 234–36

Insight Enterprises, Inc., 18 259–61

Insight Marques SARL IMS SA, **48** 224

Insignia Financial Group, Inc. *see* CB Richard Ellis Group, Inc.

Insilco Corporation, 16 281–83

Insley Manufacturing Co., **8** 545

Inso Corporation, 26 215–19

Inspiration Resources Corporation, **12** 260; **13** 502–03

Inspirations PLC, **22** 129

Insta-Care Holdings Inc., **16** 59

Insta-Care Pharmacy Services, **9** 186

Instant Auto Insurance, **33** 3, 5

Instant Interiors Corporation, **26** 102

Instapak Corporation, **14** 429

Instinet Corporation, 34 225–27

Institute de Development Industriel, **19** 87

Institute for Professional Development, **24** 40

Institute for Scientific Information, **8** 525, 528

Institution Food House *see* Alex Lee Inc.

Institutional Financing Services, **23** 491

Instituto Bancario San Paolo di Torino, **50** 407

Instituto Nacional de Industria, I 459–61

Instromet International, **22** 65

Instrument Systems Corp. *see* Griffon Corporation.

Instrumentarium Corp., **13** 328; **25** 82; **71** 349

Instrumentation Laboratory Inc., **III** 511–12; **22** 75

Instrumentation Scientifique de Laboratoire, S.A., **15** 404; **50** 394

Insul 8 Corporation, **76** 139

Insurance Auto Auctions, Inc., 23 285–87

Insurance Company of North America *see* CIGNA Corporation.

Insurance Company of the Southeast, Ltd., **56** 165

Insurance Partners L.P., **15** 257

InsurMark, **72** 149

InSync Communications, **42** 425

Intabex Holdings Worldwide, S.A., **27** 126

Intalco Aluminum Corp., **12** 254

Intamin, **17** 443

Intarsia Corp., **38** 187

Intat Precision Inc., **48** 5

Integra-A Hotel and Restaurant Company, **13** 473

Integral Corporation, **14** 381; **23** 446; **33** 331

Integrated Business Information Services, **13** 5

Integrated Computer Systems *see* Learning Tree International Inc.

Integrated Defense Technologies, Inc., 54 178–80

Integrated Genetics, **8** 210; **13** 239; **38** 204, 206

Integrated Health Services, Inc., **11** 282

Integrated Medical Systems Inc., **12** 333; **47** 236

Integrated Resources, Inc., **11** 483; **16** 54; **19** 393

Integrated Silicon Solutions, Inc., **18** 20; **43** 17; **47** 384

Integrated Software Systems Corporation, **11** 469

Integrated Systems Engineering, Inc., **51** 382

Integrated Systems Operations *see* Xerox Corporation.

Integrated Systems Solutions Corp., **9** 284; **11** 395; **17** 264

Integrated Telecom Technologies, **14** 417

Integris Europe, **49** 382, 384

Integrity Inc., 44 241–43

Integrity Life Insurance, **III** 249

Intel Corporation, II 44–46; 10 365–67 (upd.); 36 284–88 (upd.); 75 196–201 (upd.)

Intelcom Support Services, Inc., **14** 334

Intelicom Solutions Corp., **6** 229

Intelig, **57** 67, 69

IntelliCorp, Inc., 45 205–07

Intelligent Electronics, Inc., 6 243–45

Intelligent Interactions Corp., **49** 421

Intelligent Software Ltd., **26** 275

Intelligraphics Inc., **33** 44

Intellimetrics Instrument Corporation, **16** 93

Intellisys, **48** 257

Inter American Aviation, Inc. *see* SkyWest, Inc.

Inter-American Satellite Television Network, **7** 391

Inter-City Gas Ltd., **19** 159

Inter-City Products Corporation, **52** 399

Inter-City Wholesale Electric Inc., **15** 385

Inter-Comm Telephone, Inc., **8** 310

Inter-Continental Hotels and Resorts, **38** 77

Inter-Europa Bank in Hungary, **50** 410

Inter-Island Airways, Ltd., **22** 251; **24** 20

Inter-Island Steam Navigation Co. *see* Hawaiian Airlines.

Inter Island Telephone *see* Pacific Telecom, Inc.

Inter Link Foods PLC, 61 132–34

Inter-Ocean Corporation, **16** 103; **44** 90

Inter Parfums Inc., 35 235–38

Inter-Regional Financial Group, Inc., 15 231–33 *see also* Dain Rauscher Corporation.

Inter Techniek, **16** 421

Inter-Urban, Inc., **74** 370

Interactive Computer Design, Inc., **23** 489, 491

InterActive Corporation, **71** 136–37

Interactive Media CCSP AG, **61** 350

Interactive Search Holding *see* Ask Jeeves, Inc.

Interactive Systems, **7** 500

InterAd Holdings Ltd., **49** 422

Interamericana de Talleras SA de CV, **10** 415

Interbake Foods, **II** 631

InterBold, **7** 146; **11** 151

Interbrand Corporation, 70 131–33

Interbrás, **IV** 503

Interbrew S.A., 17 256–58; 50 274–79 (upd.)

Interceramic *see* Internacional de Ceramica, S.A. de C.V.

Interchemical Corp., **13** 460

Intercity Food Services, Inc., **II** 663

Interco Incorporated, III 528–31 *see also* Furniture Brands International, Inc.

International Silver Company, **12** 472; **14** 482–83

International SMC Ltd., **60** 278

International Specialty Products, Inc., **22** 225, 228–29

International Speedway Corporation, 19 221–23; 74 157–60 (upd.)

International Stores, **I** 427

International Supply Consortium, **13** 79

International Talent Group, **25** 281

International Talent Management, Inc. *see* Motown Records Company L.P.

International Telcell Group, **7** 336

International Telecommunications Satellite Organization, **46** 328

International Telephone & Telegraph Corporation, I 462–64; 11 196–99 (upd.)

International Television Corporation Entertainment Group, **23** 391

International Thomson Organisation Ltd. *see* The Thomson Corporation.

International Thomson Organization Ltd., **23** 92

International Total Services, Inc., 37 215–18

The International Tourist Corporation, **68** 281

International Transmission Company *see* ITC Holdings Corp.

International Utilities Corp., **6** 444

International Well Control *see* Boots & Coots International Well Control, Inc.

International Wind Systems, **6** 581

International Wine & Spirits Ltd., **9** 533

International Wire Works Corp., **8** 13

International Wireless Inc., **21** 261

Internationale Nederlanden Group, **24** 88

Internet Shopping Network, **26** 441

Interocean Management Corp., **9** 509–11

Interpac Belgium *see* Belgacom.

Interpretive Data Systems Inc. *see* IDX Systems Corporation.

Interprovincial Pipe Line Ltd. *see* Enbridge Inc.

The Interpublic Group of Companies, Inc., I 16–18; 22 294–97 (upd.); 75 202–05 (upd.)

Interra Financial *see* Dain Rauscher Corporation.

InterRedec, Inc., **17** 196

Interscience, **17** 271

Interscope Communications, Inc., **23** 389, 391; **27** 121

Interscope Music Group, 31 267–69

Intersec, Inc., **27** 21

Interstate & Ocean Transport, **6** 577

Interstate Assurance Company, **59** 246–47

Interstate Bakeries Corporation, 12 274–76; 38 249–52 (upd.)

Interstate Brick Company, **6** 568–69

Interstate Electric Manufacturing Company *see* McGraw Electric Company.

Interstate Finance Corp., **11** 16

Interstate Financial Corporation, **9** 475

Interstate Hotels & Resorts Inc., 58 192–94

Interstate Iron and Steel Company *see* Republic Engineered Steels, Inc.

Interstate Logos, Inc. *see* Lamar Advertising Company.

Interstate Paint Distributors, Inc., **13** 367

Interstate Power Company, **6** 555, 605; **18** 404

Interstate Properties Inc., **45** 15–16

Interstate Public Service Company, **6** 555

Interstate Supply Company *see* McGraw Electric Company.

Interstate United Corporation, **II** 679; **13** 435

InterTAN, Inc. *see* Circuit City Stories, Inc.

Intertec Design, Inc., **34** 371–72

Intertec Publishing Corp., **22** 441

Intertechnique SA, **36** 530

Interturbine Holland, **19** 150

Intertype Corp., **II** 37

Intervideo TV Productions-A.B., **II** 640

Intervision Express, **24** 510

InterVU Inc. *see* Akamai Technologies, Inc.

InterWest Partners, **16** 418

Intimate Brands, Inc., 24 237–39

InTouch Systems, Inc., **43** 118

Intrac Handelsgesellschaft mbH, **7** 142

Intraco Corp., **56** 157–58

Intrado Inc., 63 202–04

The Intrawest Corporation, 15 234–36

Intrepa L.L.C. *see* Manhattan Associates, Inc.

Intrepid Corporation, **16** 493

Intrigue Technologies, Inc., **69** 245

IntroGene B.V., **13** 241

Intuit Inc., 14 262–64; 33 208–11 (upd.); 73 188–92 (upd.)

Intuitive Surgical, Inc., 79 217–20

Invacare Corporation, 11 200–02; 47 193–98 (upd.)

Invenex Laboratories, **17** 287

inVentiv Health, Inc., 81 205–08

Invensys PLC, 50 286–90 (upd.)

Invento Products Corporation, **21** 269

Invep S.p.A., **10** 150

Inverfal S.A., **69** 312

Inverness Medical Innovations, Inc., 63 205–07

Inverness Medical Technology, Inc., **45** 210

Inversale, **9** 92

Inversiones Financieras del Sud S.A., **63** 120–21

Inversiones Freire Ltda., **71** 139, 141

Inversiones y Desarrollo Los Andes S.A., **69** 142

INVESCO PLC *see* AMVESCAP PLC.

Invesgen S.A., **26** 129

Investcorp SA, 57 179–82

Investimentos Itaú S.A., **19** 33

Investindustrial LP, **76** 326

Investor AB, 63 208–11

Investors Bank and Trust Company, **18** 152

Investors Diversified Services, Inc., **II** 398; **8** 348–49; **10** 43–45, 59, 62; **21** 305; **25** 248; **38** 42

Investors Management Corp., **10** 331

Investors Overseas Services, **10** 368–69

InvestorsBancorp, **53** 222, 224

Investrónica S.A., **26** 129

Invista Capital Management, **III** 330

Invitrogen Corporation, 52 182–84

Invivo Corporation, 52 185–87

The Invus Group, Ltd., **33** 449

Iogen Corporation, 81 209–13

Iomega Corporation, 21 294–97

IONA Technologies plc, 43 238–41

Ionia S.A., **64** 379

Ionics, Incorporated, 52 188–90

Ionpure Technologies Corporation *see* Eastern Enterprises.

Iowa Beef Packers, **21** 287

Iowa Beef Processors, **II** 516–17; **13** 351

Iowa Mold Tooling Co., Inc., **16** 475

Iowa Public Service Company, **6** 524–25

IP Services, Inc., **IV** 597

IP Timberlands Ltd., **IV** 288

IP&L *see* Illinois Power & Light Corporation.

IP Vista, **74** 143

Ipalco Enterprises, Inc., 6 508–09

IPC *see* International Publishing Corp.

IPC Communications, Inc., **15** 196

IPC Magazines Limited, 7 244–47

IPD *see* International Periodical Distributors.

IPEC Holdings Ltd., **27** 474–75

Iphotonics Inc., **48** 369

Ipiranga S.A., 67 216–18

Ipko-Amcor, **14** 225

IPL Energy Inc. *see* Enbridge Inc.

IPM *see* International Pharmacy Management, Inc.

IPS Praha a.s., **38** 437

IPS Publishing, **39** 341–42

Ipsen International Inc., 72 192–95

IPSOA Editore, **14** 555

Ipsos SA, 48 221–24

Ipswich Bancshares Inc., **55** 52

iQuantic Buck, **55** 73

IQUE, Inc., **21** 194

IranAir, 81 214–17

Irby-Gilliland Company, **9** 127

Irdeto, **31** 330

Irex Corporation, **59** 382–83

IRI *see* Instituto per la Ricostruzione Industriale.

Irideon, Inc., **35** 435

Iridian Asset Management LLC, **52** 172

Iris Associates, Inc., **25** 299, 301

Irish Agricultural Wholesale Society Ltd. *see* IAWS Group plc.

Irish Air *see* Aer Lingus Group plc.

Irish Life & Permanent Plc, 59 245–47

Irish Life Assurance Company, **16** 14; **43** 7

Irkut Corporation, 68 202–04

Iron and Steel Industrial Corporation, **59** 224

Iron and Steel Press Company, **27** 360

Iron City Brewing Company *see* Pittsburgh Brewing Company.

Iron Cliffs Mining Company, **13** 156

Iron Mountain Forge, **13** 319

J. Horner's, **48** 415

J.I.C. Group Limited, **61** 233

J.I. Case Company, 10 377–81 *see also* CNH Global N.V.

J.J. Farmer Clothing Inc., **51** 320–21

J.J. Keller & Associates, Inc., 81 218–21

J.J. Kenney Company, Inc., **51** 244

The J. Jill Group, Inc., 35 239–41

J.K. Armsby Co., **7** 130–31

J.K. Starley and Company Ltd, **7** 458

J.L. Clark, Inc. *see* Clarcor Inc.

J.L. French Automotive Castings, Inc. *see* Onex Corporation.

J.L. Hammett Company, 72 196–99

J.L. Hudson Company *see* Target Corporation.

J.L. Shiely Co. *see* English China Clays Ltd.

J.L. Wright Company, **25** 379

J. Levin & Co., Inc., **13** 367

J.M. Brunswick & Brothers, **III** 442

J.M. Douglas & Company Limited, **14** 141

J.M. Huber Corporation, **40** 68

J.M. Kohler Sons Company, **7** 269

The J.M. Smucker Company, 11 210–12

J.M. Tull Metals Co., Inc., **IV** 116; **15** 250; **19** 219

J.M. Voith AG, 33 222–25

J. Mandelbaum & Sons, **19** 510

J-Mar Associates, **31** 435–36

J.P. Heilwell Industries, **II** 420

J.P. Morgan Chase & Co., II 329–32; **30** 261–65 (upd.); **38** 253–59 (upd.)

J.P. Stevens Inc., **8** 234; **12** 404; **16** 533–35; **17** 75; **19** 420; **27** 468–69; **28** 218; **62** 283

J.R. Brown & Sharpe *see* Brown & Sharpe Manufacturing Co.

J.R. Simplot Company, 16 287–89; **60 179–82** (upd.)

J Sainsbury plc, II 657–59; **13** 282–84 (upd.); **38** 260–65 (upd.)

J. Sears & Company *see* Sears plc.

J. Spiegel and Company *see* Spiegel, Inc.

J.U. Dickson Sawmill Inc. *see* Dickson Forest Products, Inc.

J.W. Bateson, **8** 87

J.W. Charles Financial Services Inc., **25** 542

J.W. Childs Associates, L.P., **46** 220; **64** 119

J.W. Childs Equity Partners LP, **40** 274

J.W. Foster and Sons, Inc. *see* Reebok International Ltd.

J.W. Spear, **25** 314

J.W. Wassall Ltd. *see* Wassall PLC.

J. Walter Thompson Co. *see* JWT Group Inc.

J. Weingarten Inc., **7** 203; **28** 163

J. Wiss & Sons Co., **II** 16

J.Z. Sales Corp., **16** 36

J. Zinmeister Co., **II** 682

Jabil Circuit, Inc., 36 298–301

Jacintoport Corporation, **7** 281

Jack Daniel Distillery, **10** 180

Jack Daniel's *see* Brown-Forman Corporation.

Jack Eckerd Corp., **16** 160; **19** 467

Jack Frain Enterprises, **16** 471

Jack Henry and Associates, Inc., 17 262–65

Jack Houston Exploration Company, **7** 345

Jack in the Box, Inc. *see* Foodmaster, Inc.

Jack Schwartz Shoes, Inc., 18 266–68

Jackpot Enterprises Inc., 21 298–300

Jackson & Perkins *see* Bear Creek Corporation.

Jackson Cushion Spring Co., **13** 397

Jackson Furniture of Danville, LLC, **48** 246

Jackson Hewitt, Inc., 48 234–36

Jackson Ice Cream Co., **12** 112

Jackson Mercantile Co. *see* Jitney-Jungle Stores of America, Inc.

Jackson National Life Insurance Company, 8 276–77

Jackson Purchase Electric Cooperative Corporation, **11** 37

Jaco Electronics, Inc., 30 255–57

Jacob Holm & Sons A/S, **22** 263

Jacob Leinenkugel Brewing Company, 28 209–11

Jacobs Brake Manufacturing Company, **7** 116–17

Jacobs Engineering Group Inc., 6 148–50; 26 220–23 (upd.)

Jacobs Suchard (AG), **II** 520–22 *see also* Kraft Jacobs Suchard AG.

Jacobson Stores Inc., 21 301–03

Jacoby & Meyers, **20** 435

Jacor Communications, Inc., 23 292–95

Jacques Borel International, **II** 641; **10** 12; **49** 126

Jacques Chocolaterie S.A., **53** 315

Jacuzzi Brands Inc., 23 296–98; **76 204–07** (upd.)

Jade Accessories, **14** 224

Jade KK, **25** 349

Jadepoint, **18** 79–80

JAFCO Co. Ltd., 79 221–24

Jafra Cosmetics, **15** 475, 477

Jagenberg AG, **9** 445–46; **14** 57

Jaguar Cars, Ltd., 13 285–87

JAI Parabolic Spring Ltd., **III** 582

JAIX Leasing Company, **23** 306

JAKKS Pacific, Inc., 52 191–94

JAL *see* Japan Air Lines.

Jalate Inc., 25 245–47

Jaluzot & Cie *see* Pinault-Printemps-Redoute S.A.

Jamaica Water Supply Company *see* JWP Inc.

Jamar Company, **64** 30, 32

Jamba Juice Company, 47 199–202

James Avery Craftsman, Inc., 76 208–10

James Beattie plc, 43 242–44

James Burn/American, Inc., **17** 458

James C. Heintz Company, **19** 278

James Ericson, **III** 324

James Felt Realty, Inc., **21** 257

James Fison and Sons *see* Fisons plc.

James G. Fast Company *see* Angelica Corporation.

James Galt & Co. Ltd., **60** 124

James Hardie Industries N.V., 56 174–76

James Heekin and Company, **13** 254

James Industries, Inc., **61** 298

James McNaughton Ltd., **IV** 325

James Publishing Group, **17** 272

James R. Osgood & Company, **10** 356

James River Corporation of Virginia, IV 289–91 *see also* Fort James Corporation.

James Talcott, Inc., **11** 260–61

James Wellbeloved, **39** 354, 356

James Wholesale Company, **18** 7

Jamestown Insurance Co. Ltd., **55** 20

Jamestown Publishers, **22** 522

Jamesway Corporation, **13** 261; **23** 177

Jamie Scott, Inc., **27** 348

Jamieson & Co., **22** 428

Jan Bell Marketing Inc. *see* Mayor's Jewelers, Inc.

Janata Bank, **31** 219

Janco Overseas Limited, **59** 261

Jane Jones Enterprises, **16** 422; **43** 309

Jane's Information Group, **8** 525

Janesville Electric, **6** 604

Janin, S.A., **36** 163

Janna Systems Inc., **38** 433

Janssen Pharmaceutica N.V., 80 164–67

Janson Publications, **22** 522

JanSport, Inc., 70 134–36

N.V. Janssen M&L, **17** 147

JANT Pty. Ltd., **IV** 285

Jantzen Inc. *see* VF Corporation.

Janus Capital Group Inc., 57 192–94

Japan Advertising Ltd., **16** 166

Japan Airlines Company, Ltd., I 104–06; 32 288–92 (upd.)

Japan Brewery *see* Kirin Brewery Company, Limited.

Japan Broadcasting Corporation, 7 248–50

Japan Creative Tours Co., **I** 106

Japan Elanco Company, Ltd., **17** 437

Japan Energy Corporation, **13** 202; **14** 206, 208; **59** 375

Japan Food Corporation, **14** 288

Japan Leasing Corporation, 8 278–80

Japan Medico, **25** 431

Japan Photo Holding Norge AS, **76** 85, 87

Japan Pulp and Paper Company Limited, IV 292–93

Japan Rifex Co., Ltd., **64** 261

Japan Telecom, **7** 118; **13** 482

Japan Telegraphic Communication Company (Nihon Denpo-Tsushin Sha), **16** 166

Japan Tobacco Inc., V 403–04; 46 257–60 (upd.)

Japan Trustee Services Bank Ltd., **53** 322

Japan Try Co., **III** 758

Japan Vilene Company Ltd., **41** 170–72

Japan Xanpak Corporation *see* JSP Corporation.

Kawai Musical Instruments
  Manufacturing Co.,Ltd., 78 189–92
Kawamata, 11 350
Kawasaki Denki Seizo, II 22
Kawasaki Heavy Industries, Ltd., III
  538–40; 63 220–23 (upd.)
Kawasaki Kisen Kaisha, Ltd., V 457–60;
  56 177–81 (upd.)
Kawasaki Steel Corporation, IV 124–25
Kawecki Berylco Industries, 8 78
Kawsmouth Electric Light Company *see*
  Kansas City Power & Light Company.
Kay-Bee Toy Stores, 15 252–53 *see also*
  KB Toys.
Kay Home Products, 17 372
Kay Jewelers Inc., 61 327
Kaydon Corporation, 18 274–76
Kaye, Scholer, Fierman, Hays & Handler,
  47 436
Kayex, 9 251
Kaynar Manufacturing Company, 8 366
Kayser Aluminum & Chemicals, 8 229
Kayser Roth Corp., 8 288; 22 122
Kaytee Products Incorporated, 58 60
KB Home, 45 218–22 (upd.)
AO KB Impuls, 48 419
KB Investment Co., Ltd., 58 208
KB Toys, 35 253–55 (upd.)
KBLCOM Incorporated, V 644
KC *see* Kenneth Cole Productions, Inc.
KC Holdings, Inc., 11 229–30
KCI Konecranes International, 27 269
KCK Tissue S.A., 73 205
KCPL *see* Kansas City Power & Light
  Company.
KCS Industries, 12 25–26
KCSI *see* Kansas City Southern Industries,
  Inc.
KCSR *see* Kansas City Southern Railway.
KD Acquisition Corporation, 34 103–04;
  76 239
KD Manitou, Inc. *see* Manitou BF S.A.
KDI Corporation, 56 16–17
KDT Industries, Inc., 9 20
Keane, Inc., 56 182–86
Keck's *see* Decorator Industries Inc.
The Keds Corp., 37 377, 379
Keebler Foods Company, 36 311–13
Keegan Management Co., 27 274
Keene Packaging Co., 28 43
KEG Productions Ltd., IV 640; 26 272
Keil Chemical Company, 8 178
Keio Teito Electric Railway Company, V
  461–62
The Keith Companies Inc., 54 181–84
Keithley Instruments Inc., 16 299–301
Kelco, 34 281
Kelda Group plc, 45 223–26
Keliher Hardware Company, 57 8
Kelkoo S.A. *see* Yahoo! Inc.
Keller Builders, 43 400
Keller-Dorian Graveurs, S.A., 17 458
Kelley & Partners, Ltd., 14 130
Kelley Drye & Warren LLP, 40 280–83
Kellock, 10 336
Kellogg Brown & Root, Inc., 62
  201–05 (upd.)

Kellogg Company, II 523–26; 13
  291–94 (upd.); 50 291–96 (upd.)
Kellwood Company, 8 287–89
Kelly & Cohen, 10 468
Kelly-Moore Paint Company, Inc., 56
  187–89
Kelly Nason, Inc., 13 203
Kelly Services, Inc., 6 35–37; 26
  237–40 (upd.)
The Kelly-Springfield Tire Company, 8
  290–92
Kelsey-Hayes Group of Companies, 7
  258–60; 27 249–52 (upd.)
Kelso & Co., 12 436; 19 455; 21 490;
  33 92; 63 237; 71 145–46
Kelty Pack, Inc., 10 215
Kelvinator Inc., 17 487
Kelvinator of India, Ltd., 59 417
KemaNobel, 9 380–81; 13 22
Kemet Corp., 14 281–83
Kemi Oy, IV 316
Kemira Oyj, 70 143–46
Kemper Corporation, III 269–71; 15
  254–58 (upd.)
Kemper Financial Services, 26 234
Kemper Snowboards, 22 460
Kencraft, Inc., 71 22–23
Kendall International, Inc., 11 219–21
Kendall-Jackson Winery, Ltd., 28
  221–23
Kenetech Corporation, 11 222–24
Kenhar Corporation *see* Cascade
  Corporation.
Kenmore Air Harbor Inc., 65 191–93
Kennametal, Inc., 13 295–97; 68
  212–16 (upd.)
Kennecott Corporation, 7 261–64; 27
  253–57 (upd.) *see also* Rio Tinto PLC.
Kennedy Automatic Products Co., 16 8
Kennedy-Wilson, Inc., 60 183–85
Kenner Parker Toys, Inc., 9 156; 12 168;
  14 266; 16 337; 25 488–89
Kenneth Cole Productions, Inc., 25
  256–58
Kenneth O. Lester, Inc., 21 508
Kenny Rogers' Roasters, 22 464; 29 342,
  344
Kenroy International, Inc., 13 274
Kensey Nash Corporation, 71 185–87
Kensington Associates L.L.C., 60 146
Kent Electronics Corporation, 17
  273–76
Kentrox Industries, 30 7
Kentucky Electric Steel, Inc., 31 286–88
Kentucky Fried Chicken *see* KFC
  Corporation.
Kentucky Institution for the Education of
  the Blind *see* American Printing House
  for the Blind.
Kentucky Utilities Company, 6 513–15
Kenwood Corporation, 31 289–91
Kenwood Silver Company, Inc., 31 352
Kenwood Winery, 68 146
Kenyon & Eckhardt Advertising Agency,
  25 89–91
Kenyon Corp., 18 276
Kenzo, 25 122
Keo Cutters, Inc., III 569; 20 360

Keolis SA, 51 191–93
Kepco *see* Korea Electric Power
  Corporation; Kyushu Electric Power
  Company Inc.
Keppel Corporation Ltd., 73 201–03
Keramik Holding AG Laufen, 51
  194–96
Kerasotes ShowPlace Theaters LLC, 80
  179–83
Kern County Land Co., 10 379
Kernite SA, 8 386
Kernkraftwerke Lippe-Ems, V 747
Kerr Concrete Pipe Company, 14 250
Kerr Corporation, 14 481
Kerr Drug Stores, 32 170
Kerr Group Inc., 24 263–65
Kerr-McGee Corporation, IV 445–47;
  22 301–04 (upd.); 68 217–21 (upd.)
Kerry Group plc, 27 258–60
Kerry Properties Limited, 22 305–08
Kerzner International Limited, 69
  222–24 (upd.)
Keski-Suomen Tukkukauppa Oy, 8 293
Kesko Ltd (Kesko Oy), 8 293–94; 27
  261–63 (upd.)
Kessler Rehabilitation Corporation *see*
  Select Medical Corporation.
Ketchikan Paper Company, 31 316
Ketchum Communications Inc., 6
  38–40
Kettle Chip Company (Australia), 26 58
Kettle Foods Inc., 48 240–42
Kettle Restaurants, Inc., 29 149
Kewaunee Scientific Corporation, 25
  259–62
Kewpie Kabushiki Kaisha, 57 202–05
Key Computer Laboratories, Inc., 14 15
Key Industries, Inc., 26 342
Key Pharmaceuticals, Inc., 11 207; 41
  419
Key Production Company, Inc. *see*
  Cimarex Energy Co.
Key Safety Systems, Inc., 63 224–26
Key Tronic Corporation, 14 284–86
KeyCorp, 8 295–97
Keyes Fibre Company, 9 303–05
KeyLabs, 65 34–35
Keypage *see* Rural Cellular Corporation.
Keypoint Technology Corporation *see*
  ViewSonic Corporation.
KeySpan Energy Co., 27 264–66
Keystone Consolidated Industries, Inc., 19
  467
Keystone Foods Corporation, 10 443
Keystone Frozen Foods, 17 536
Keystone Health Plan West, Inc., 27 211
Keystone Insurance and Investment Co.,
  12 564
Keystone International, Inc., 11 225–27
Keystone Life Insurance Co., III 389; 33
  419
Keystone Paint and Varnish, 8 553
Keystone Portland Cement Co., 23 225
Keystone Savings and Loan, II 420
Keystone Tube Inc., 25 8
Keytronics, 18 541
KFC Corporation, 7 265–68; 21
  313–17 (upd.)

Leeann Chin, Inc., **30** 285–88

Leeds & Northrup Company, **28** 484; **63** 401

Lees Carpets, **17** 76

Leewards Creative Crafts Inc., **17** 322

Leeway International Company Ltd., **68** 69

Lefrak Organization Inc., 26 260–62

Legacy Homes Ltd., **26** 290

Legacy Hotels Real Estate Investment Trust, **69** 163

Legal & General Group plc, III 272–73; **24** 283–85 (upd.)

The Legal Aid Society, 48 261–64

Legal Technologies, Inc., **15** 378

Legault and Masse, II 664

Legent Corporation, 10 394–96

Legetøjsfabrikken LEGO Billund A/S *see* Lego A/S.

Legg Mason, Inc., 33 259–62

Leggett & Platt, Inc., 11 254–56; **48** 265–68 (upd.)

Leggett Stores Inc., **19** 48

Lego A/S, 13 310–13; **40** 287–91 (upd.)

Legrand SA, 21 348–50

Lehigh Acquisition Corp., **34** 286

Lehigh Portland Cement Company, 23 325–27

Lehman Brothers, **14** 145; **22** 445; **25** 301; **38** 411; **48** 59

Lehman Merchant Bank Partners, **19** 324

Lehmer Company *see* Centel Corporation.

Lehser Communications, Inc., **15** 265

Leica Camera AG, 35 266–69

Leica Microsystems Holdings GmbH, 35 270–73

Leigh-Mardon Security Group, **30** 44

Leighton Holdings Ltd., **19** 402

Leinenkugel Brewing Company *see* Jacob Leinenkugel Brewing Company.

Leiner Health Products Inc., 34 250–52

The Leisure Company, **34** 22

Leisure Concepts, Inc., **59** 187–89

Leisure System Inc., **12** 359

Leitch Technology Corporation *see* Harris Corporation

Leitz *see* Esselte Worldwide.

LeMaster Litho Supply, **13** 228

Lemmerz Holding GmbH, **27** 202, 204

Lemmon Co., **54** 363

Lempereur, **13** 297

Lend Lease Corporation Limited, IV 707–09; **17** 283–86 (upd.); **52** 218–23 (upd.)

Lender's Bagel, **32** 69

Lending Textiles, **29** 132

Lenel Systems International Inc., **24** 510

Lennar Corporation, 11 257–59

Lennon's, II 628

Lennox Industries, Inc., **22** 6

Lennox International Inc., 8 320–22; **28** 232–36 (upd.)

Lenoir Furniture Corporation, **10** 183

Lenovo Group Ltd., 80 209–12

Lenox, Inc., 12 312–13

Lens, Inc., **30** 267–68

LensCrafters Inc., 23 328–30; **76** 242–45 (upd.)

Lentheric, **I** 426

L'Entreprise Jean Lefebvre, 23 331–33

Leo Burnett Company, Inc., I 22–24; **20** 336–39 (upd.)

Leo d'Or Trading Co. Ltd., **56** 242

The Leo Group, **32** 140; **40** 140

Leon Burnett Company, Inc., **76** 254

Léon Gaumont et Cie *see* Gaumont SA.

Leonard Bernstein Music Publishing Company, **23** 391

Leonard Development Group, **10** 508

Leonard Green & Partners LP, **12** 477–78; **24** 173

Leonard Machinery Corp., **16** 124

Leonard Parker Company, **26** 196

Leonard Silver, **14** 482

Leonardi Manufacturing, **48** 70

Leonardo Editore, IV 587

Leprino Foods Company, 28 237–39

Lerner Plastics, **9** 323

Lernout and Hauspie, **51** 202

Leroux S.A.S., 65 212–14

Leroy Merlin SA, 54 219–21

Les Abeilles International SA, **60** 149

Les Boutiques San Francisco, Inc., 62 228–30

Les broderies Lesage, **49** 83

Les Echos *see* Groupe Les Echos.

Les Grands Magasins Au Bon Marché: Etablissements Vaxelaire-Claes, **26** 159–60

Les Industries Ling, **13** 443

Les Papeteries du Limousin, **19** 227

Les Schwab Tire Centers, 50 314–16

Lesaffre et Compagnie, **52** 305

Lesco Inc., 19 248–50

The Leslie Fay Company, Inc., 8 323–25; **39** 255–58 (upd.)

Leslie Paper, IV 288

Leslie's Poolmart, Inc., 18 302–04

Lesser-Goldman, II 18

Lester Ink and Coatings Company, **13** 228

Lester of Minnesota, Inc., **62** 55

Lestrem Group, IV 296; **19** 226

Létang et Rémy, **44** 205

Lettuce Entertain You Enterprises, **38** 103

Leucadia National Corporation, 11 260–62; **71** 196–200 (upd.)

Leumi & Company Investment Bankers Ltd., **60** 50

Leuna-Werke AG, **7** 142

Leupold & Stevens, Inc., 52 224–26

Level Five Research, Inc., **22** 292

Level 13 Entertainment, Inc., **58** 124

Level 3 Communications, Inc., 67 233–35

Levenger Company, 63 242–45

Lever Brothers Company, 9 317–19 *see also* Unilever.

Leverage Group, **51** 99

Levernz Shoe Co., **61** 22

Levi Strauss & Co., V 362–65; **16** 324–28 (upd.)

Leviathan Gas Pipeline Company, **21** 171

Levin Furniture *see* Sam Levin Inc.

Levine, Huntley, Vick & Beaver, **6** 28

Leviton Manufacturing Co., Inc., **54** 372

Levitt Corp., **21** 471

Levitt Industries, **17** 331

Levitt Investment Company, **26** 102

Levitz Furniture Inc., 15 280–82

Levolor Hardware Group, **53** 37

Levtex Hotel Ventures, **21** 363

Levy *see* Chas. Levy Company LLC.

Levy Home Entertainment, LLC, **60** 83, 85

Levy Restaurants L.P., 26 263–65

Lew Liberbaum & Co., **27** 197

The Lewin Group, Inc., **21** 425

Lewis and Marks, **16** 27; **50** 32

Lewis Batting Company, **11** 219

Lewis Galoob Toys Inc., 16 329–31

Lewis Group Ltd., **58** 54–55

Lewis Homes, **45** 221

Lewis Refrigeration Company, **21** 500

Lex Electronics, **10** 113; **50** 42

Lex Service plc, **19** 312; **50** 42

Lexecon, Inc., **26** 187

Lexington Furniture Industries, III 571; **20** 362

Lexington Ice Company, **6** 514

Lexington Utilities Company, **6** 514; **11** 237

LEXIS-NEXIS Group, 33 263–67

Lexitron, II 87

Lexmark International, Inc., 18 305–07; **79** 237–42 (upd.)

Leybold GmbH, IV 71; **48** 30

Leyland Motor Corporation, **7** 459

LF International, Inc., **59** 259

LFC Financial, **10** 339

LFC Holdings Corp. *see* Levitz Furniture Inc.

LFE Corp., **7** 297

LG&E Energy Corporation, 6 516–18; **51** 214–17 (upd.)

LG Chemical Ltd., **26** 425

LG Electronics Inc., **13** 572, 575; **43** 428

LG Group, **18** 124; **34** 514, 517–18

LG Semiconductor, **56** 173

LGT Asset Management *see* AMVESCAP PLC.

Lhomme S.A., **8** 477

Li & Fung Limited, 59 258–61

Liaison Agency, **31** 216–17

Lianozovo Dairy, **48** 438

Libbey Inc., 49 251–54

Libbey-Owens-Ford Company, III 640–42, 714–15, 731; **7** 292; **16** 7–9; **22** 434; **23** 83; **26** 353; **31** 355

Libeltex, **9** 92

Liber, **14** 556

Liberty Bank of Buffalo, **9** 229

Liberty Brokerage Investment Company, **10** 278

Liberty Can and Sign Company, **17** 105–06

The Liberty Corporation, 22 312–14

Liberty Gauge Company, **17** 213

Liberty Hardware Manufacturing Corporation, **20** 363

Liberty Life, IV 97

Liberty Livewire Corporation, 42 224–27

Liberty Media Corporation, 50 317–19

Little Leather Library, **13** 105
Little, Royal, **8** 545; **13** 63
Little Switzerland, Inc., 60 202–04
Little Tikes Company, 13 317–19; **62**
231–34 (upd.)
Littlewoods Financial Services, **30** 494
Littlewoods plc, V 117–19; **42** 228–32
(upd.)
Litton Industries Inc., I 484–86; **11**
263–65 (upd.) *see also* Avondale
Industries.
Litwin Engineers & Constructors, **8** 546
LIVE Entertainment Inc., 20 347–49
Live Nation, Inc., 80 217–22 (upd.)
LiveAquaria.com., **62** 108
Liverpool Daily Post & Echo Ltd., **49**
405
Liverpool Mexico S.A., **16** 216
Living Arts, Inc., **41** 174
Living Centers of America, **13** 49
Living Videotext, **10** 508
LivingWell Inc., **12** 326
Liz Claiborne, Inc., 8 329–31; **25**
291–94 (upd.)
LKQ Corporation, 71 201–03
Lledo Collectibles Ltd., **60** 372
LLJ Distributing Company *see* Spartan
Stores Inc.
Lloyd Aereo de Bolivia, **6** 97
Lloyd Creative Staffing, **27** 21
Lloyd George Management, **18** 152
Lloyd Instruments, Ltd., **29** 460–61
Lloyd Italico, **III** 351
Lloyd Thompson Group plc, **20** 313
Lloyd Triestino company, **50** 187
Lloyd-Truax Ltd., **21** 499
Lloyd's, III 278–81; **22** 315–19 (upd.);
74 172–76 (upd.)
Lloyd's Electronics, **14** 118
Lloyds Chemists plc, **27** 177
Lloyds Life Assurance, **III** 351
Lloyds TSB Group plc, II 306–09; **47**
224–29 (upd.)
LLP Group plc, **58** 189
LM Ericsson *see* Telefonaktiebolaget LM
Ericsson.
LMC Metals, **19** 380
LME *see* Telefonaktiebolaget LM Ericsson.
LNM Group, **30** 252
Lo-Cost, **II** 609
Lo-Vaca Gathering Co., **7** 553
Loblaw Companies Limited, 43 268–72
see also George Weston Limited.
Local Data, Inc., **10** 97
Lockhart Corporation, **12** 564
Lockheed Martin Corporation, I 64–66;
11 266–69 (upd.); **15** 283–86 (upd.)
Locksmith Publishing Corp., **56** 75
Lockwood Banc Group, Inc., **11** 306
Lockwood Greene Engineers, Inc., **17** 377
Lockwood National Bank, **25** 114
Lockwood Technology, Inc., **19** 179
Loctite Corporation, 8 332–34; **30**
289–91 (upd.)
Lodding Engineering, **7** 521
Lodestar Group, **10** 19
Lodge Plus, Ltd., **25** 430

**LodgeNet Entertainment Corporation,
28** 240–42
The Lodging Group, **12** 297; **48** 245
Loehmann's, Inc., 24 297–99
The Loewen Group, Inc., 16 342–44;
40 292–95 (upd.) *see also* Alderwoods
Group Inc.
Loewenstein Furniture Group, Inc., **21**
531–33
Loews Cineplex Entertainment Corp., **37**
64
Loews Corporation, I 487–88; **12**
316–18 (upd.); **36** 324–28 (upd.)
LOF Plastics, Inc. *see* Libbey-Owens-Ford.
Loffland Brothers Company, **9** 364
Logan's Roadhouse, Inc., 29 290–92
Loganair Ltd., 68 235–37
Logic Modeling, **11** 491
Logica plc, 14 317–19; **37** 230–33
(upd.)
Logicon Inc., 20 350–52
Logility, **25** 20, 22
Logistics.com, Inc. *see* Manhattan
Associates, Inc.
Logistics Data Systems, **13** 4
Logistics Industries Corporation, **39** 77
Logistics Management Systems, Inc., **8** 33
Logitech International S.A., 28 243–45;
69 242–45 (upd.)
LOGIX Benelux, **74** 143
Logo Athletic, Inc., **35** 363
Logo 7, Inc., **13** 533
Logon, Inc., **14** 377
Lohja Corporation, **61** 295
LoJack Corporation, 48 269–73
Lojas Americanas S.A., 77 240–43
Lojas Arapuã S.A., 22 320–22; **61**
175–78 (upd.)
Loma Linda Foods, **14** 557–58
Lomak Petroleum, Inc., **24** 380
Lomas & Nettleton Financial
Corporation, **III** 249; **11** 122
London & Hull, **III** 211
London & Midland Bank *see* Midland
Bank plc.
London & Overseas Freighters plc *see*
Frontline Ltd.
London & Rhodesia Mining & Land
Company *see* Lonrho Plc.
London and Scottish Marine Oil, **11** 98
London & Western Trust, **39** 90
London Assurance Corp., **55** 331
London Brick Co., **14** 249
London Brokers Ltd., **6** 290
London Buses Limited *see* London
Regional Transport.
London Cargo Group, **25** 82
London Central, **28** 155–56
London Drugs Ltd., 46 270–73
London East India Company, **12** 421
London Electricity, **12** 443; **41** 141
London Fog Industries, Inc., 29 293–96
London Insurance Group, **III** 373; **36**
372
London International Group *see* SSL
International plc.
London Precision Machine & Tool, Ltd.,
39 32

London Records, **23** 390
London Regional Transport, 6 406–08
London Rubber Co., **49** 380
London Scottish Bank plc, 70 160–62
London South Partnership, **25** 497
London Stock Exchange Limited, 34
253–56
London Transport, **19** 111
Londontown Manufacturing Company *see*
London Fog Industries, Inc.
Lone Star Brewing Co., **I** 255
Lone Star Funds, **59** 106
Lone Star Industries, **23** 326; **35** 154
**Lone Star Steakhouse & Saloon, Inc.,
51** 227–29
Lone Star Technologies, Inc., **22** 3
Lonely Planet Publications Pty Ltd., 55
253–55
Long Distance Discount Services, Inc., **8**
310; **27** 305
Long Distance/USA, **9** 479
Long Island Bancorp, Inc., 16 345–47
Long Island Cable Communication
Development Company, **7** 63
Long Island College Hospital *see*
Continuum Health Partners, Inc.
Long Island Lighting Company, V
652–54
Long Island Power Authority, **27** 265
**The Long Island Rail Road Company,
68** 238–40
Long John Silver's, 13 320–22; **57**
224–29 (upd.)
Long Lac Mineral Exploration, **9** 282
Long Life Fish Food Products, **12** 230
**Long-Term Credit Bank of Japan, Ltd.,
II** 310–11
Long Valley Power Cooperative, **12** 265
The Longaberger Company, 12 319–21;
44 267–70 (upd.)
Longchamps, Inc., **38** 385; **41** 388
LongHorn Steaks Inc., **19** 341
Longman Group Ltd., **IV** 611, 658
Longs Drug Stores Corporation, V 120;
25 295–97 (upd.)
Longview Fibre Company, 8 335–37; **37**
234–37 (upd.)
Lonmin plc, 66 211–16 (upd.)
Lonrho Plc, 21 351–55 *see also* Lonmin
plc.
Lonza Group Ltd., 73 212–14
Lookers plc, 71 204–06
Loomis Armored Car Service Limited, **45**
378
Loomis Fargo Group, **42** 338
Loomis Products, Inc., **64** 349
Loop One2, **53** 240
Loose Leaf Metals Co., Inc., **10** 314
Lor-Al, Inc., **17** 10
Loral Space & Communications Ltd., 8
338–40; **54** 231–35 (upd.)
Lord & Taylor, **13** 44; **14** 376; **15** 86; **18**
137, 372; **21** 302
L'Oréal, III 46–49; **8** 341–44 (upd.); **46**
274–79 (upd.)
Lorentzen & Wettre AB, **53** 85
Lorillard Industries, **V** 407, 417; **18** 416;
22 73; **29** 195

Marico Acquisition Corporation, **8** 448, 450

Marie Brizard & Roger International S.A., 22 342–44

Marie Callender's Restaurant & Bakery, Inc., 28 257–59

Marina Mortgage Company, **46** 25

Marine Bank and Trust Co., **11** 105

Marine Computer Systems, **6** 242

Marine Harvest, **13** 103; **56** 257

Marine Manufacturing Corporation, **52** 406

Marine Midland Corp., **9** 475–76; **11** 108; **17** 325

Marine Products Corporation, 75 247–49

Marine Transport Lines, Inc., **59** 323

Marine United Inc., **42** 361

Marinela, **19** 192–93

MarineMax, Inc., 30 303–05

Marinette Marine Corporation, **59** 274, 278

Marion Brick, **14** 249

Marion Foods, Inc., **17** 434; **60** 268

Marion Laboratories Inc., I 648–49

Marion Manufacturing, **9** 72

Marion Merrell Dow, Inc., 9 328–29 **(upd.)**

Marionet Corp., **IV** 680–81

Marionnaud Parfumeries SA, 51 233–35

Marisa Christina, Inc., 15 290–92

Maritime Electric Company, Limited, **15** 182; **47** 136–37

Maritz Inc., 38 302–05

Mark Controls Corporation, **30** 157

Mark Cross, Inc., **17** 4–5

Mark Goldston, **8** 305

Mark IV Industries, Inc., 7 296–98; **28** 260–64 **(upd.)**

The Mark Travel Corporation, 80 232–35

Mark Trouser, Inc., **17** 338

Mark's Work Wearhouse Ltd. *see* Canadian Tire Corporation, Limited.

Markborough Properties, **V** 81; **8** 525; **25** 221

Market Development Corporation *see* Spartan Stores Inc.

Market Growth Resources, **23** 480

Market National Bank, **13** 465

Marketing Data Systems, Inc., **18** 24

Marketing Equities International, **26** 136

MarketSpan Corp. *see* KeySpan Energy Co.

Märklin Holding GmbH, 70 163–66

Marks and Spencer p.l.c., V 124–26; **24** 313–17 **(upd.)**

Marks-Baer Inc., **11** 64

Marks Brothers Jewelers, Inc., 24 318–20

Marlene Industries Corp., **16** 36–37

Marley Co., **19** 360

Marley Holdings, L.P., **19** 246

Oy Marli Ab, **56** 103

Marman Products Company, **16** 8

The Marmon Group, Inc., IV 135–38; **16** 354–57 **(upd.); 70** 167–72 **(upd.)**

Marmon-Perry Light Company, **6** 508

Marolf Dakota Farms, Inc., **18** 14–15

Marotte, **21** 438

Marpac Industries Inc. *see* PVC Container Corporation.

Marquam Commercial Brokerage Company, **21** 257

Marquette Electronics, Inc., 13 326–28

Marquis Who's Who, **17** 398

Marr S.p.A., **57** 82–84

Marriner Group, **13** 175

Marriot Inc., **29** 442

Marriot Management Services, **29** 444

Marriott International, Inc., III 102–03; **21** 364–67 **(upd.)**

Mars, Incorporated, 7 299–301; **40** 302–05 **(upd.)**

Marsh & McLennan Companies, Inc., III 282–84; **45** 263–67 **(upd.)**

Marsh Supermarkets, Inc., 17 300–02; **76** 255–58 **(upd.)**

Marshall & Ilsley Corporation, 56 217–20

Marshall Amplification plc, 62 239–42

Marshall Die Casting, **13** 225

Marshall Field's, 63 254–63 *see also* Target Corporation.

Marshall Industries, **19** 311

Marshalls Incorporated, 13 329–31

Marship Tankers (Holdings) Ltd., **52** 329

Marstellar, **13** 204

Marstons, **57** 412–13

The Mart, **9** 120

Martank Shipping Holdings Ltd., **52** 329

Martek Biosciences Corporation, 65 218–20

Marten Transport, **27** 404

Martha Lane Adams, **27** 428

Martha Stewart Living Omnimedia, Inc., 24 321–23; **73** 219–22 **(upd.)**

Martin & Pagenstecher GMBH, **24** 208

Martin-Baker Aircraft Company Limited, 61 195–97

Martin Band Instrument Company, **55** 149, 151

Martin Bros. Tobacco Co., **14** 19

Martin Collet, **19** 50

Martin Dunitz, **44** 416

Martin Franchises, Inc., 80 236–39

Martin Gillet Co., **55** 96, 98

Martin Guitar Company *see* C.F. Martin & Co., Inc.

Martin Hilti Foundation, **53** 167

Martin Industries, Inc., 44 274–77

Martin Marietta Corporation, I 67–69 *see also* Lockheed Martin Corporation.

Martin Mathys, **8** 456

Martin Sorrell, **6** 54

Martin Theaters, **14** 86

Martin-Yale Industries, Inc., **19** 142–44

Martin Zippel Co., **16** 389

Martin's, **12** 221

Martindale-Hubbell, **16** 398

Martini & Rossi SpA, 63 264–66

Martinus Nijhoff, **14** 555; **25** 85

Martz Group, 56 221–23

Marubeni Corporation, I 492–95; **24** 324–27 **(upd.)**

Maruetsu, **17** 124; **41** 114

Maruha Group Inc., 75 250–53 **(upd.)**

Marui Company Ltd., V 127; **62** 243–45 **(upd.)**

Marusa Co. Ltd., **51** 379

Maruti Udyog Ltd., **59** 393, 395–97

Maruzen Co., Limited, 18 322–24

Maruzen Oil Co., Ltd., **53** 114

Marva Maid Dairy *see* Maryland & Virginia Milk Producers Cooperative Association, Inc.

Marvel Entertainment, Inc., 10 400–02; **78** 212–19 **(upd.)**

Marvin H. Sugarman Productions Inc., **20** 48

Marvin Lumber & Cedar Company, 22 345–47

Marwick, Mitchell & Company, **10** 385

Marx, **12** 494

Mary Ann Co. Ltd., **V** 89

Mary Ann Restivo, Inc., **8** 323

Mary Ellen's, Inc., **11** 211

Mary Kathleen Uranium, **IV** 59–60

Mary Kay Corporation, 9 330–32; **30** 306–09 **(upd.)**

Maryland & Virginia Milk Producers Cooperative Association, Inc., 80 240–43

Maryland Cup Company, **8** 197

Maryland Medical Laboratory Inc., **26** 391

Maryland National Corp., **11** 287

Maryland National Mortgage Corporation, **11** 121; **48** 177

Maryland Square, Inc., **68** 69

Marzotto S.p.A., 20 356–58; **67** 246–49 **(upd.)**

Masayoshi Son, **13** 481–82

Maschinenfabrik Augsburg-Nürnberg *see* M.A.N.

Masco Corporation, III 568–71; **20** 359–63 **(upd.); 39** 263–68 **(upd.)**

Masco Optical, **13** 165

Mase Westpac Limited, **11** 418

Maserati *see* Officine Alfieri Maserati S.p.A.

Maserati Footwear, Inc., **68** 69

Mashantucket Pequot Gaming Enterprise Inc., 35 282–85

MASkargo Ltd. *see* Maladian Airlines System Bhd.

Masland Corporation, 17 303–05

Mason Best Co., **IV** 343

Masonite International Corporation, 63 267–69

Mass Rapid Transit Corp., **19** 111

Massachusetts Capital Resources Corp., **III** 314

Massachusetts Electric Company, **51** 265

Massachusetts Mutual Life Insurance Company, III 285–87; **53** 210–13 **(upd.)**

Massachusetts Technology Development Corporation, **18** 570

Massachusetts's General Electric Company, **32** 267

Massey Energy Company, 57 236–38

MasTec, Inc., 55 259–63 **(upd.)**

Master Builders, **I** 673

Monterey Homes Corporation *see* Meritage Corporation.

Monterey Mfg. Co., **12** 439

Monterey Pasta Company, 58 240–43

Monterey's Acquisition Corp., **41** 270

Monterey's Tex-Mex Cafes, **13** 473

Monterrey, Compania de Seguros sobre la Vida *see* Seguros Monterrey.

Monterrey Group, **19** 10–11, 189

Montgomery Elevator Company *see* KONE Corporation.

Montgomery Ward & Co., Incorporated, V 145–48; **20** 374–79 **(upd.)**

Montiel Corporation, **17** 321

Montinex, **24** 270

Montreal Engineering Company, **6** 585

Montreal Mining Co., **17** 357

Montres Rolex S.A., 13 353–55; **34** 292–95 **(upd.)**

Montrose Capital, **36** 358

Montrose Chemical Company, **9** 118, 119

Montupet S.A., 63 302–04

Monumental Corp., **III** 179

Moody's Corporation, 65 242–44

Moody's Investors Service,

Moog Inc., 13 356–58

Moog Music, Inc., 75 261–64

Mooney Aerospace Group Ltd., 52 252–55

Mooney Chemicals, Inc. *see* OM Group, Inc.

Moonlight Mushrooms, Inc. *see* Sylvan, Inc.

Moonstone Mountaineering, Inc., **29** 181

Moore and McCormack Co. Inc., **19** 40

Moore Corporation Limited, IV 644–46

Moore Gardner & Associates, **22** 88

The Moore Group Ltd., **20** 363

Moore-Handley, Inc., 39 290–92

Moore McCormack Resources Inc., **14** 455

Moore Medical Corp., 17 331–33

Moquin Breuil *see* Smoby International SA.

Moran Group Inc., **II** 682

Moran Health Care Group Ltd., **25** 455

Moran Towing Corporation, Inc., 15 301–03

Morana, Inc., **9** 290

More Group plc *see* JCDecaux S.A

Moretti-Harrah Marble Co. *see* English China Clays Ltd.

Morgan & Banks Limited, **30** 460

Morgan Construction Company, **8** 448

Morgan Edwards, **II** 609

Morgan Engineering Co., **8** 545

Morgan Grampian Group, **IV** 687

Morgan Grenfell Group PLC, II 427–29 *see also* Deutsche Bank AG.

The Morgan Group, Inc., 46 300–02

Morgan Guaranty Trust Company *see* J.P. Morgan & Co. Incorporated.

Morgan, Lewis & Bockius LLP, 29 332–34

Morgan, Lewis, Githens & Ahn, Inc., **6** 410

Morgan Schiff & Co., **29** 205

Morgan Stanley Dean Witter & Company, II 430–32; **16** 374–78 **(upd.); 33** 311–14 **(upd.)**

Morgans Hotel Group Company, 80 256–59

Moria Informatique, **6** 229

Morinaga & Co. Ltd., 61 222–25

Morino Associates, **10** 394

Mormac Marine Group, **15** 302

Morning Star Technologies Inc., **24** 49

Morning Sun, Inc., **23** 66

Morningstar Inc., 68 259–62

Morningstar Storage Centers LLC, **52** 311

Morris Air, **24** 455; **71** 346

Morris Communications Corporation, 36 339–42

Morris Motors, **7** 459

Morris Travel Services L.L.C., 26 308–11

Morrison & Co. Ltd., **52** 221

Morrison & Foerster LLP, 78 220–23

Morrison Homes, Inc., **51** 138

Morrison Knudsen Corporation, 7 355–58; **28** 286–90 **(upd.)** *see also* The Washington Companies.

Morrison Machine Products Inc., **25** 193

Morrison Restaurants Inc., 11 323–25

Morse Equalizing Spring Company, **14** 63

Morse Industrial, **14** 64

Morse Shoe Inc., 13 359–61

Morse's Ltd., **70** 161

Mortgage Associates, **9** 229

Mortgage Guaranty Insurance Corp. *see* MGIC Investment Corp.

Mortgage Resources, Inc., **10** 91

MortgageRamp Inc. *see* OfficeTiger, LLC.

Morton Foods, Inc., **27** 258

Morton International, Inc., 9 358–59 **(upd.); 80** 260–64 **(upd.)**

Morton Thiokol Inc., I 370–72 *see also* Thiokol Corporation.

Morton's Restaurant Group, Inc., 30 329–31

Mos Magnetics, **18** 140

MOS Technology, **7** 95

Mosby-Year Book, Inc., **IV** 678; **17** 486

Moscow Bank for Reconstruction & Development, **73** 303–04

Moseley, Hallgarten, Estabrook, and Weeden, **III** 389

Mosher Steel Company, **7** 540

Mosinee Paper Corporation, 15 304–06 *see also* Wausau-Mosinee Paper Corporation.

Moskatel's, Inc., **17** 321

Moss Bros Group plc, 51 252–54

Moss-Rouse Company, **15** 412

Mossgas, **IV** 93

Mossimo, Inc., 27 328–30

Mostek Corp., **11** 307–08; **13** 191; **20** 175; **29** 323

Mostjet Ltd. *see* British World Airlines Ltd.

Móstoles Industrial S.A., **26** 129

Mostra Importaciones S.A., **34** 38, 40

Motel 6, 13 362–64; **56** 248–51 **(upd.)** *see also* Accor SA

Mother Karen's, **10** 216

Mothercare plc, 17 334–36; **78** 224–27 **(upd.)**

Mothers Against Drunk Driving (MADD), 51 255–58

Mothers Work, Inc., 18 350–52

Motif Inc., **22** 288

Motion Designs, **11** 486

Motion Factory, Inc., **38** 72

Motion Picture Association of America, **37** 353–54

Motion Picture Corporation of America, **25** 326, 329

Motiva Enterprises LLC, **41** 359, 395

MotivePower *see* Wabtec Corporation.

The Motley Fool, Inc., 40 329–31

Moto Photo, Inc., 45 282–84

Moto S.p.A., **57** 84

Moto-Truc Co., **13** 385

Motor Cargo Industries, Inc., 35 296–99

Motor Club of America Insurance Company, **44** 354

Motor Coaches Industries International Inc., **36** 132

Motor Parts Industries, Inc., **9** 363

Motor Wheel Corporation, **20** 261; **27** 202–04

Motorcar Parts & Accessories, Inc., 47 253–55

Motoren-und-Turbinen-Union, **I** 151; **9** 418; **15** 142; **34** 128, 131, 133

Motorola, Inc., II 60–62; **11** 326–29 **(upd.); 34** 296–302 **(upd.)**

Motorsports International Corporation, **74** 157

Motospecs *see* Repco Corporation Ltd.

Motown Records Company L.P., 26 312–14

Mott's Inc., 57 250–53

Moulinex S.A., 22 362–65

Mound Metalcraft *see* Tonka Corporation.

Mount *see also* Mt.

Mount Hood Credit Life Insurance Agency, **14** 529

Mount Isa Mines, **IV** 61

Mount Vernon Group, **8** 14

Mount Washington Hotel *see* MWH Preservation Limited Partnership.

Mountain Fuel Supply Company *see* Questar Corporation.

Mountain High Casino *see* Ameristar Casinos, Inc.

Mountain Pass Canning Co., **7** 429

Mountain Safety Research, **18** 445–46

Mountain States Mortgage Centers, Inc., 29 335–37

Mountain States Power Company *see* PacifiCorp.

Mountain States Wholesale, **II** 602; **30** 25

Mountain Valley Indemnity Co., **44** 356

Mountain West Bank, **35** 197

Mountleigh PLC, **16** 465

Mouvement des Caisses Desjardins, 48 288–91

Movado Group, Inc., 28 291–94

Mövenpick Holdings, **63** 328

Movie Gallery, Inc., 31 339–41

Movie Star Inc., 17 337–39

Myrurgia S.A., **60** 246

N

N.A. Woodworth, **III** 519; **22** 282

N. Boynton & Co., **16** 534

N.C. Cameron & Sons, Ltd., **11** 95

N.C. Monroe Construction Company, **14** 112

N.E.M., **23** 228

N.E. Restaurant Co. Inc. *see* Bertucci's Corpration.

N.F. Smith & Associates LP, 70 199–202

N.H. Geotech *see* New Holland N.V.

N.L. Industries, **19** 212

N M Electronics, **II** 44

N M Rothschild & Sons Limited, 39 293–95

N. Shure Company, **15** 477

N.V. *see under first word of company name*

N.Y.P. Holdings Inc., **12** 360

Na Pali, S.A. *see* Quiksilver, Inc.

Naamloze Vennootschap tot Exploitatie van het Café Krasnapolsky *see* Grand Hotel Krasnapolsky N.V.

Nabari Kintetsu Gas Company Ltd., **60** 236

Nabisco Brands, Inc., II 542–44 *see also* RJR Nabisco.

Nabisco Foods Group, 7 365–68 (upd.) *see also* Kraft Foods Inc.

Nabisco Holdings Corporation, **25** 181; **42** 408; **44** 342

Nabisco Ltd., **24** 288

Nabors Industries, Inc., 9 363–65

Nacamar Internet Services, **48** 398

NACCO Industries, Inc., 7 369–71; **78** 232–36 (upd.)

Nacional de Drogas, S.A. de C.V., **39** 188

NACO Finance Corp., **33** 398

Naco-Nogales, **51** 389

Nadler Sportswear *see* Donnkenny, Inc.

Naegele Outdoor Advertising Inc., **36** 340

Naf Naf SA, 44 296–98

NAFI Corp. *see* Chris-Craft Industries, Inc.

Nagasakiya Co., Ltd., V 149–51; **69** 259–62 (upd.)

Nagasco, Inc., **18** 366

Nagase & Co., Ltd., 8 376–78; **61** 226–30 (upd.)

Nagase-Landauer, Ltd., **51** 210

Nagel Meat Markets and Packing House, **II** 643

Nagoya Mitsukoshi Ltd., **56** 242

NAI *see* Natural Alternatives International, Inc.; Network Associates, Inc.

NAI Technologies, Inc., **58** 101

Naiman Co., **25** 449

Nairn Linoleum Co., **18** 116

Nakano Vinegar Co. Ltd., **26** 58

Nalco Chemical Corporation, I 373–75; **12** 346–48 (upd.)

Nalge Co., **14** 479–80

NAM *see* Nederlandse Aardolie Maatschappij.

Nam Tai Electronics, Inc., 61 231–34

Name Development Ltd. *see* Marchex, Inc.

Namibia Breweries Ltd., **33** 75

NAMM *see* North American Medical Management Company, Inc.

Namor Productions, **58** 124

Namur Re S.A., **51** 143

Nan Ya Plastics Corp., **14** 197–98; **58** 130

NANA Regional Corporation, **7** 558

Nance Petroleum Corporation, **63** 347

NANCO *see* Provimi

Nancy's Notions *see* Tacony Corporation.

Nanfang South China Motor Corp., **34** 132

Nanotechnologies Inc., **74** 9

Nantucket Allserve, Inc., 22 369–71

Nantucket Corporation, **6** 226

Nantucket Mills *see* Jockey International.

NAPA *see* National Automotive Parts Association.

NAPC *see* North American Philips Corp.

Napocor *see* National Power Corporation.

NAPP Systems, Inc., **11** 253

Napster, Inc., 69 263–66

Narragansett Electric Company, **51** 265

NAS *see* National Audubon Society.

NASA *see* National Aeronautics and Space Administration.

NASCAR *see* National Association for Stock Car Auto Racing.

NASD, 54 242–46 (upd.)

NASDAQ, **37** 132

Nash DeCamp Company, **23** 356–57

Nash Finch Company, 8 379–81; **23** 356–58 (upd.); **65** 249–53 (upd.)

Nashua Corporation, **8** 382–84

The Nashville Network, **11** 153

Nashville Speedway USA, Inc., **43** 139–41

Naspers Ltd., 66 230–32

NASRIN Services LLC, **64** 346

Nassco Holdings Inc., **36** 79

Nastech Pharmaceutical Company Inc., 79 259–62

Nasu Nikon Co., Ltd., **48** 295

Nat Robbins, **37** 269–70

NaTec Ltd. *see* CRSS Inc.

Nathan's Famous, Inc., 29 342–44

The National Academy of Television Arts & Sciences, **55** 3

National Acme Company *see* Acme-Cleveland Corp.

National Advertising Company, **27** 280

National Aeronautics and Space Administration, **11** 201, 408; **12** 489; **37** 364–65

National Air Transport Co., **9** 416; **11** 427

National Allied Publications *see* DC Comics Inc.

National Aluminum Company, **11** 38

National American Corporation, **33** 399

National Amusements Inc., 28 295–97

National Aquarium in Baltimore, Inc., 74 198–200

National Association for Stock Car Auto Racing, 32 342–44

National Association of Securities Dealers, Inc., 10 416–18 *see also* NASD.

National Audubon Society, 26 320–23

National Auto Credit, Inc., 16 379–81

National Automotive Fibers, Inc. *see* Chris-Craft Industries, Inc.

National Automotive Parts Association, **26** 348

National Bancard Corporation, **11** 111–13

National Bancorp of Arizona, **12** 565

National Bank for Cooperatives, **8** 489–90

National Bank of Arizona, **53** 378

National Bank of Commerce, **9** 536; **11** 105–06; **13** 467

National Bank of Commerce Trust & Savings Association, **15** 161

National Bank of Greece, 41 277–79

The National Bank of Jacksonville, **9** 58

National Bank of New Zealand, **II** 308; **19** 155

The National Bank of South Carolina, 76 278–80

National Bank of Washington, **13** 440

National BankAmericard Inc. *see* Visa International.

National Basketball Association, **12** 457

National Beverage Corp., 26 324–26 *see also* Faygo Beverages Inc.

National Binding Company, **8** 382

National BioSystems, **47** 37

National Bridge Company of Canada, Ltd., **8** 544

National Broadcasting Company, Inc., II 151–53; **6** 164–66 (upd.); **28** 298–301 (upd.) *see also* General Electric Company.

National Building Society, **10** 6–7

National Cable & Manufacturing Co., **13** 369

National Cable Television Association, **18** 64

National Can Corp., I 607–08; **13** 255

National Car Rental System, Inc., 10 419–20 *see also* Republic Industries, Inc.

National Carriers Ltd *see* Exel plc.

National Cash Register Company *see* NCR Corporation.

National Cement Co., **35** 419; **70** 343

National Cheerleaders Association, **15** 516–18

National Chemsearch Corp. *see* NCH Corporation.

National Child Care Centers, Inc., **II** 607

National City Bancorporation, **56** 219

National City Bank, **9** 475

National City Corp., 15 313–16

National Coach, **56** 223

National Comics Publications *see* DC Comics Inc.

National Commercial Bank, **11** 108; **12** 422; **13** 476

National Components Industries, Inc., **13** 398

National-Southwire Aluminum Company, **11** 38; **12** 353

National Stamping & Electric Works, **12** 159

National Standard Co., **13** 369–71

National Starch and Chemical Company, **49** 268–70

National Steel and Shipbuilding Company, **7** 356

National Steel Corporation, **12** 352–54 *see also* FoxMeyer Health Corporation.

National Student Marketing Corporation, **10** 385–86

National System Company, **9** 41; **11** 469

National Tea, **II** 631–32

National Technical Laboratories, **14** 52

National TechTeam, Inc., **41** 280–83

National Telecommunications of Austin, **8** 311

National Telephone and Telegraph Corporation *see* British Columbia Telephone Company.

National Telephone Co., **7** 332, 508

National Thoroughbred Racing Association, **58** 244–47

National Trading Manufacturing, Inc., **22** 213

National Transcommunications Ltd. *see* NTL Inc.

National Union Electric Corporation, **12** 159

National Utilities & Industries Corporation, **9** 363

National Westminster Bank PLC, **II** 333–35

National Wine & Spirits, Inc., **49** 271–74

Nationale-Nederlanden N.V., **III** 308–11

Nationar, **9** 174

NationsBank Corporation, **10** 425–27 *see also* Bank of America Corporation

NationsRent, **28** 388

Nationwide Cellular Service, Inc., **27** 305

Nationwide Credit, **11** 112

Nationwide Group, **25** 155

Nationwide Income Tax Service, **9** 326

Nationwide Logistics Corp., **14** 504

Nationwide Mutual Insurance Co., **26** 488

NATIOVIE, **II** 234

Native Plants, **III** 43

NATM Buying Corporation, **10** 9, 468

Natomas Company, **7** 309; **11** 271

Natref *see* National Petroleum Refiners of South Africa.

Natrol, Inc., **49** 275–78

Natronag, **IV** 325

NatSteel Electronics Ltd., **48** 369

NatTeknik, **26** 333

Natudryl Manufacturing Company, **10** 271

Natura Cosméticos S.A., **75** 268–71

Natural Alternatives International, Inc., **49** 279–82

Natural Gas Clearinghouse *see* NGC Corporation.

Natural Gas Corp., **19** 155

Natural Gas Pipeline Company, **6** 530, 543; **7** 344–45

Natural Gas Service of Arizona, **19** 411

Natural Ovens Bakery, Inc., **72** 234–36

Natural Selection Foods, **54** 256–58

Natural Wonders Inc., **14** 342–44

NaturaLife International, **26** 470

Naturalizer *see* Brown Shoe Company, Inc.

The Nature Company, **10** 215–16; **14** 343; **26** 439; **27** 429; **28** 306

The Nature Conservancy, **28** 305–07

Nature's Sunshine Products, Inc., **15** 317–19

Nature's Way Products Inc., **26** 315

Naturin GmbH *see* Viscofan S.A.

Naturipe Berry Growers, **62** 154

Natuzzi Group *see* Industrie Natuzzi S.p.A.

NatWest Bancorp, **38** 393

NatWest Bank *see* National Westminster Bank PLC.

Naugles, **7** 506

Naumes, Inc., **81** 257–60

Nautica Enterprises, Inc., **18** 357–60; **44** 302–06 (upd.)

Nautilus International, Inc., **13** 532; **25** 40; **30** 161

Navaho Freight Line, **16** 41

Navajo LTL, Inc., **57** 277

Navajo Refining Company, **12** 240

Navajo Shippers, Inc., **42** 364

Navan Resources, **38** 231

Navarre Corporation, **24** 348–51

Navigant International, Inc., **47** 263–66

Navigation Mixte, **III** 348

Navire Cargo Gear, **27** 269

Navisant, Inc., **49** 424

Navistar International Corporation, **I** 180–82; **10** 428–30 (upd.) *see also* International Harvester Co.

NAVTEQ Corporation, **69** 272–75

Navy Exchange Service Command, **31** 342–45

Navy Federal Credit Union, **33** 315–17

Naxon Utilities Corp., **19** 359

Naylor, Hutchinson, Vickers & Company *see* Vickers PLC.

NBC *see* National Broadcasting Company, Inc.

NBC Bankshares, Inc., **21** 524

NBC/Computer Services Corporation, **15** 163

NBD Bancorp, Inc., **11** 339–41 *see also* Bank One Corporation.

NBGS International, Inc., **73** 231–33

NBSC Corporation *see* National Bank of South Carolina.

NBTY, Inc., **31** 346–48

NCA Corporation, **9** 36, 57, 171

NCB *see* National City Bank of New York.

NCC Industries, Inc., **59** 267

NCC L.P., **15** 139

NCH Corporation, **8** 385–87

nChip, **38** 187–88

NCL Corporation, **79** 274–77

NCL Holdings *see* Genting Bhd.

NCNB Corporation, **II** 336–37

NCO Group, Inc., **42** 258–60

NCR Corporation, **III** 150–53; **6** 264–68 (upd.); **30** 336–41 (upd.)

NCS *see* Norstan, Inc.

NCS Healthcare Inc., **67** 262

NCTI (Noise Cancellation Technologies Inc.), **19** 483–84

nCube Corp., **14** 15; **22** 293

ND Marston, **III** 593

NDB *see* National Discount Brokers Group, Inc.

NDL *see* Norddeutscher Lloyd.

NE Chemcat Corporation, **72** 118

NEA *see* Newspaper Enterprise Association.

Nearly Me, **25** 313

Neatherlin Homes Inc., **22** 547

Nebraska Bell Company, **14** 311

Nebraska Book Company, Inc., **65** 257–59

Nebraska Cellular Telephone Company, **14** 312

Nebraska Furniture Mart, **III** 214–15; **18** 60–61, 63

Nebraska Light & Power Company, **6** 580

Nebraska Power Company, **25** 89

Nebraska Public Power District, **29** 351–54

NEBS *see* New England Business Services, Inc.

NEC Corporation, **II** 66–68; **21** 388–91 (upd.); **57** 261–67 (upd.)

Neckermann Versand AG *see* Karstadt AG.

Nedcor, **61** 270–71

Nederland Line *see* Stoomvaart Maatschappij Nederland.

Nederlander Organization, **24** 439

Nederlands Talen Institut, **13** 544

Nederlandsche Electriciteits Maatschappij *see* N.E.M.

Nederlandsche Handel Maatschappij, **26** 242

Nederlandsche Heidenmaatschappij *see* Arcadis NV.

Nederlandsche Kunstzijdebariek, **13** 21

N.V. Nederlandse Gasunie, **V** 658–61

Nedlloyd Group *see* Koninklijke Nedlloyd N.V.

NedMark Transportation Services *see* Polar Air Cargo Inc.

Neeco, Inc., **9** 301

Needham Harper Worldwide *see* Omnicom Group Inc.

Needlecraft, **II** 560; **12** 410

Needleworks, Inc., **23** 66

Neenah Foundry Company, **68** 263–66

Neenah Printing, **8** 360

NEES *see* New England Electric System.

Neff Corp., **32** 352–53

Neff GmbH, **67** 81

NEG Micon A/S, **73** 375

Negromex, **23** 171–72

NEI *see* Northern Engineering Industries PLC.

Neico International, Inc., **67** 226

NeighborCare, Inc., **67** 259–63 (upd.)

Neighborhood Restaurants of America, **18** 241

New York City Off-Track Betting
  Corporation, 51 267–70
New York City Transit Authority, 8 75
New York Community Bancorp, Inc., 78
  247–50
New York Daily News, 32 357–60
New York Electric Corporation *see* New
  York State Electric and Gas.
New York Envelope Co., 32 346
New York Evening Enquirer, 10 287
New York Eye and Ear Infirmary *see*
  Continuum Health Partners, Inc.
New York Fabrics and Crafts, 16 197
New York Gas Light Company *see*
  Consolidated Edison Company of New
  York.
New York Health Care, Inc., 72 237–39
New York Life Insurance Company, III
  315–17; 45 291–95 (upd.)
New York Magazine Co., 12 359
New York Marine and Gotham Insurance,
  41 284
New York Philharmonic *see*
  Philharmonic-Symphony Society of
  New York, Inc.
New York Presbyterian Hospital *see*
  NewYork-Presbyterian Hospital.
New York Quotation Company, 9 370
New York Restaurant Group, Inc., 32
  361–63
New York Sports Clubs *see* Town Sports
  International, Inc.
New York State Electric and Gas
  Corporation, 6 534–36
New York Stock Exchange, Inc., 9
  369–72; 39 296–300 (upd.)
New York Telephone Co., 9 321
The New York Times Company, IV
  647–49; 19 283–85 (upd.); 61
  239–43 (upd.)
New York Zoological Society *see* Wildlife
  Conservation Society.
New York's Bankers Trust Co., *see* Bankers
  Trust Co.
New Zealand Aluminum Smelters, *see* Rio
  Tinto.
New Zealand Countrywide Banking
  Corporation, 10 336
Newa Insurance Co. Ltd., 64 280
Neways, Inc., 78 251–54
Newark Electronics Co., 9 420
Newbridge & Gilbert, 56 285
Newco Waste Systems *see* Browning-Ferris
  Industries, Inc.
Newcor, Inc., 40 332–35
Newcrest Mining Ltd., IV 47; 22 107
Newell Rubbermaid Inc., 9 373–76; 52
  261–71 (upd.)
Newfield Exploration Company, 65
  260–62
Newfoundland Brewery, 26 304
Newfoundland Energy, Ltd., 17 121
Newfoundland Light & Power Co. *see*
  Fortis, Inc.
Newfoundland Processing Ltd. *see*
  Newfoundland Energy, Ltd.
Newhall Land and Farming Company,
  14 348–50

Newly Weds Foods, Inc., 74 201–03
Newman's Own, Inc., 37 272–75
Newmark & Lewis Inc., 23 373
Newmont Mining Corporation, 7
  385–88
Newnes, 17 397
NewPage Corporation, 76 270
Newpark Resources, Inc., 63 305–07
Newport Corporation, 71 247–49
Newport News Shipbuilding Inc., 13
  372–75; 38 323–27 (upd.)
News & Observer Publishing Company,
  23 343
News America Publishing Inc., 12
  358–60
News Communications & Media Plc, 35
  242
News Corporation Limited, IV 650–53;
  7 389–93 (upd.); 46 308–13 (upd.)
News Extracts Ltd., 55 289
News International Corp., 20 79
News of the World Organization
  (NOTW), 46 309
News World Communications, 73 356
Newsco NV, 48 347
Newsfoto Publishing Company, 12 472;
  36 469
Newspaper Co-op Couponing, 8 551
Newspaper Enterprise Association, 7
  157–58
Newsquest plc, 32 354–56
Newth-Morris Box Co. *see* Rock-Tenn
  Company.
Newtherm Oil Burners, Ltd., 13 286
Newton Yarn Mills, 19 305
NewYork-Presbyterian Hospital, 59
  309–12
Nexans SA, 54 262–64
Nexar Technologies, Inc., 22 409
NEXCOM *see* Navy Exchange Service
  Command.
Nexen Inc., 79 282–85
NexFlash Technologies, Inc. *see* Winbond
  Electronics Corporation.
Nexity S.A., 66 243–45
Nexstar Broadcasting Group, Inc., 73
  238–41
NeXstar Pharmaceuticals Inc., 54 130
NeXT Incorporated, 34 348
Next Media Ltd., 61 244–47
Next plc, 29 355–57
Nextel Communications, Inc., 10
  431–33; 27 341–45 (upd.)
Nextera Enterprises, Inc., 54 191, 193
NEXTLINK Communications, Inc., 38
  192
NextNet Wireless, Inc. *see* Clearwire, Inc.
Neyveli Lignite Corporation Ltd., 65
  263–65
NFC Castings Inc., 68 265
NFC plc, 6 412–14 *see also* Exel plc.
NFL *see* National Football League Inc.
NFL Films, 75 275–78
NFL Properties, Inc., 22 223
NFO Worldwide, Inc., 24 352–55
NFT Distribution Limited, 61 258,
  260–61
NGC *see* National Grid Company.

NGC Corporation, 18 365–67 *see also*
  Dynegy Inc.
NGI International Precious Metals, Ltd.,
  24 335
NGK Insulators Ltd., 67 264–66
NH Hoteles S.A., 79 286–89
NHB Group Ltd. *see* MasterBrand
  Cabinets, Inc.
NHK *see* Japan Broadcasting Corporation.
NHK Spring Co., Ltd., III 580–82
NI Industries, 20 362
Ni-Med, 50 122
Niagara Corporation, 28 314–16
Niagara First Savings and Loan
  Association, 10 91
Niagara Mohawk Holdings Inc., V
  665–67; 45 296–99 (upd.)
Niagara of Wisconsin, 26 362–63
Nice Day, Inc., II 539
Nice Systems, 11 520
NiceCom Ltd., 11 520
Nichido Fire and Marine Insurance Co.
  see Millea Holdings Inc.
Nichii Co., Ltd., V 154–55
Nichimen Corporation, IV 150–52; 24
  356–59 (upd.)
Nichimo Sekiyu Co. Ltd., IV 555; 16 490
Nichirei Corporation, 70 203–05
Nicholas Turkey Breeding Farms, 13 103
Nichols & Company, 8 561
Nichols Aluminum-Golden, Inc., 62 289
Nichols-Homeshield, 22 14
Nichols plc, 44 315–18
Nichols Research Corporation, 18
  368–70
Nicholson File Co., II 16
Nicholson Graham & Jones, 28 141
Nickelodeon, 25 381
Nickerson Machinery Company Inc., 53
  230
Nicklaus Companies, 45 300–03
Nicolet Instrument Company, 11 513
Nicolon N.V. *see* Royal Ten Cate N.V.
NICOR Inc., 6 529–31
Nidec Corporation, 59 313–16
Nielsen, 10 358
Nielsen Marketing Research *see* A.C.
  Nielsen Company.
Niemann Chemie, 8 464
Niesmann & Bischoff, 22 207
Nieuw Rotterdam, 27 54
NIF Ventures Co. Ltd., 55 118
Nigerian National Petroleum
  Corporation, IV 472–74; 72 240–43
  (upd.)
Nigerian Shipping Operations, 27 473
Nihon Keizai Shimbun, Inc., IV 654–56
Nihon Kohden Corporation, 13 328
Nihon Lumber Land Co., III 758
Nihon Noyaku Co., 64 35
Nihon Styrene Paper Company *see* JSP
  Corporation.
Nihon Sugar, I 511
Nihon Synopsis, 11 491
Nihon Timken K.K., 8 530
Nihon Waters K.K., 43 456
Nihron Yupro Corp. *see* Toto Ltd.
NII *see* National Intergroup, Inc.

Nora Industrier A/S, **18** 395

Norampac Inc., **71** 95

Norand Corporation, **9** 411; **72** 189

Noranda Inc., IV 164–66; **7** 397–99 (upd.); **64** 294–98 (upd.)

Norandex, **16** 204

Norbro Corporation *see* Stuart Entertainment Inc.

Norcal Pottery Products, Inc., **58** 60

Norcal Waste Systems, Inc., **60** 222–24

Norcen Energy Resources, Ltd., **8** 347

Norco Plastics, **8** 553

Norcon, Inc., **7** 558–59

Norcore Plastics, Inc., **33** 361

Nordbanken, **9** 382

Norddeutsche Affinerie AG, **62** 249–53

Norddeutscher-Lloyd *see* Hapag-Lloyd AG.

Nordea AB, **40** 336–39

Nordic Baltic Holding *see* Nordea AB.

Nordica S.r.l., **10** 151; **15** 396–97; **53** 24

NordicTrack, **22** 382–84 *see also* Icon Health & Fitness, Inc.

Nordisk Film A/S, **80** 269–73

Nordson Corporation, **11** 356–58; **48** 296–99 (upd.)

Nordstrom, Inc., V 156–58; **18** 371–74 (upd.); **67** 277–81 (upd.)

Nordwestdeutsche Kraftwerke AG *see* PreussenElektra AG.

Norelco Consumer Products Co., **26** 334–36

Norelec, **27** 138

Norex Leasing, Inc., **16** 397

Norfolk Carolina Telephone Company, **10** 202

Norfolk Shipbuilding & Drydock Corporation, **73** 47

Norfolk Southern Corporation, V 484–86; **29** 358–61 (upd.); **75** 289–93 (upd.)

Norfolk Steel, **13** 97

Norge Co., **18** 173–74; **43** 163–64

Noric Corporation, **39** 332

Norinchukin Bank, II 340–41

Norlin Industries, **16** 238–39; **75** 262

Norm Thompson Outfitters, Inc., **47** 275–77

Norma AS *see* Autoliv, Inc.

Norman BV, **9** 93; **33** 78

Normandy Mining Ltd., **23** 42

Normark Corporation *see* Rapala-Normark Group, Ltd.

Norment Security Group, Inc., **51** 81

Normond/CMS, **7** 117

Norrell Corporation, **25** 356–59

Norris Cylinder Company, **11** 535

Norris Grain Co., **14** 537

Norris Oil Company, **47** 52

Norshield Corp., **51** 81

Norsk Aller A/S, **72** 62

Norsk Helikopter AS *see* Bristow Helicopters Ltd.

Norsk Hydro ASA, **10** 437–40; **35** 315–19 (upd.)

Norsk Rengjorings Selskap a.s., **49** 221

Norske Skog do Brasil Ltda., **73** 205

Norske Skogindustrier ASA, **63** 314–16

Norstan, Inc., **16** 392–94

Norstar Bancorp, **9** 229

Nortek, Inc., **34** 308–12

Nortel Inversora S.A., **63** 375–77

Nortel Networks Corporation, **36** 349–54 (upd.)

Nortex International, **7** 96; **19** 338

North African Petroleum Ltd., IV 455

North American Aviation, **7** 520; **9** 16; **11** 278, 427

North American Carbon, **19** 499

North American Cellular Network, **9** 322

North American Coal Corporation, **7** 369–71

North American Company, **6** 552–53, 601–02

North American Dräger, **13** 328

North American Energy Conservation, Inc., **35** 480

North American InTeleCom, Inc., IV 411

North American Light & Power Company, **12** 541

North American Medical Management Company, Inc., **36** 366

North American Mogul Products Co. *see* Mogul Corp.

North American Nutrition Companies Inc. (NANCO) *see* Provimi

North American Philips Corporation, **19** 393; **21** 520

North American Plastics, Inc., **61** 112

North American Printing Ink Company, **13** 228

North American Rockwell Corp., **10** 173

North American Site Developers, Inc., **69** 197

North American Systems, **14** 230

North American Training Corporation *see* Rollerblade, Inc.

North American Van Lines *see* Allied Worldwide, Inc.

North American Watch Company *see* Movado Group, Inc.

North Atlantic Energy Corporation, **21** 411

North Atlantic Laboratories, Inc., **62** 391

North Atlantic Packing, **13** 243

North Atlantic Trading Company Inc., **65** 266–68

North British Rubber Company, **20** 258

North Broken Hill Peko, IV 61

North Carolina Motor Speedway, Inc., **19** 294

North Carolina National Bank Corporation *see* NCNB Corporation.

North Carolina Natural Gas Corporation, **6** 578

North Carolina Shipbuilding Co., **13** 373

North Central Financial Corp., **9** 475

North Central Utilities, Inc., **18** 405

North East Insurance Company, **44** 356

North Eastern Bricks, **14** 249

The North Face, Inc., **18** 375–77; **78** 258–61 (upd.)

North Fork Bancorporation, Inc., **46** 314–17

North New York Savings Bank, **10** 91

North of Scotland Hydro-Electric Board, **19** 389

North Pacific Group, Inc., **61** 254–57

North Pacific Paper Corp., IV 298

North Ridge Securities Corporation, **72** 149–50

North Sea Ferries, **26** 241, 243

North Sea Oil and Gas, **10** 337

North Shore Gas Company, **6** 543–44

North Shore Land Co., **17** 357

North Star Communications Group Inc., **73** 59

North Star Container, Inc., **59** 290

North Star Egg Case Company, **12** 376

North Star Marketing Cooperative, **7** 338

North Star Mill, **12** 376

North Star Steel Company, **18** 378–81

North Star Transport Inc., **49** 402

North Star Tubes, **54** 391, 393

North Star Universal, Inc., **25** 331, 333

North State Supply Company, **57** 9

North Supply, **27** 364

The North West Company, Inc., **12** 361–63

North-West Telecommunications *see* Pacific Telecom, Inc.

North West Water Group plc, **11** 359–62 *see also* United Utilities PLC.

Northbridge Financial Corp., **57** 137

Northbrook Corporation, **24** 32

Northbrook Holdings, Inc., **22** 495

Northcliffe Newspapers, **19** 118

Northeast Federal Corp., **13** 468

Northeast Petroleum Industries, Inc., **11** 194; **14** 461

Northeast Savings Bank, **12** 31; **13** 467–68

Northeast Utilities, V 668–69; **48** 303–06 (upd.)

Northeastern New York Medical Service, Inc., III 246

Northern Animal Hospital Inc., **58** 355

Northern Arizona Light & Power Co., **6** 545

Northern California Savings, **10** 340

Northern Dairies, **10** 441

Northern Drug Company, **14** 147

Northern Electric Company *see* Northern Telecom Limited.

Northern Energy Resources Company *see* NERCO, Inc.

Northern Engineering Industries Plc *see* Rolls-Royce Group PLC.

Northern Fibre Products Co., I 202

Northern Foods plc, **10** 441–43; **61** 258–62 (upd.)

Northern Illinois Gas Co., **6** 529–31

Northern Indiana Power Company, **6** 556

Northern Indiana Public Service Company, **6** 532–33

Northern Infrastructure Maintenance Company, **39** 238

Northern Leisure, **40** 296–98

Northern Light Electric Company, **18** 402–03

Northern National Bank, **14** 90

Northern Natural Gas Co. *see* Enron Corporation.

One Stop Trade Building Centre Ltd. *see* Gibbs and Dandy plc.
O'Neal, Jones & Feldman Inc., **11** 142
OneBeacon Insurance Group LLC, **48** 431
Oneida Bank & Trust Company, **9** 229
Oneida County Creameries Co., **7** 202
Oneida Gas Company, **9** 554
Oneida Ltd., **7** 406–08; **31** 352–55 (upd.)
ONEOK Inc., **7** 409–12
Onex Corporation, **16** 395–97; **65** 281–85 (upd.)
OneZero Media, Inc., **31** 240
Ong First Pte Ltd., **76** 372, 374
Onion, Inc., **69** 282–84
Onitsuka Co., Ltd., **57** 52
Online Financial Communication Systems, **11** 112
Only One Dollar, Inc. *see* Dollar Tree Stores, Inc.
Onoda Cement Co., Ltd., **III** 717–19 *see also* Taiheiyo Cement Corporation.
Onomichi, **25** 469
OnResponse.com, Inc., **49** 433
Onsale Inc., **31** 177
Onstead Foods, **21** 501
OnTarget Inc., **38** 432
Ontario Hydro Services Company, **6** 541–42; **32** 368–71 (upd.)
Ontario Power Generation, **49** 65, 67
Ontario Teachers' Pension Plan, **61** 273–75
OnTrack Data International, **57** 219
OnTrak Systems Inc., **31** 301
Onyx Acceptance Corporation, **59** 327–29
Onyx Software Corporation, **53** 252–55
O'okiep Copper Company, Ltd., **7** 385–86
Opel AG *see* Adam Opel AG.
Open *see* Groupe Open.
Open Board of Brokers, **9** 369
Open Cellular Systems, Inc., **41** 225–26
Open Market, Inc., **22** 522
Open Text Corporation, **79** 301–05
OpenTV, Inc., **31** 330–31
OPENWAY SAS, **74** 143
Operadora de Bolsa Serfin *see* Grupo Financiero Serfin, S.A.
Operation Smile, Inc., **75** 297–99
Operon Technologies Inc., **39** 335
Opinion Research Corporation, **46** 318–22
Opp and Micolas Mills, **15** 247–48
Oppenheimer *see* Ernest Oppenheimer and Sons.
Oppenheimer & Co., Inc., **17** 137; **21** 235; **22** 405; **25** 450; **61** 50
The Oppenheimer Group, **76** 295–98
Oppenheimer Wolff & Donnelly LLP, **71** 262–64
Opryland USA, **11** 152–53; **25** 403; **36** 229
Opsware Inc., **49** 311–14
Optel S.A., **17** 331; **71** 211
OPTi Computer, **9** 116
Opti-Ray, Inc., **12** 215

Optical Corporation *see* Excel Technology, Inc.
Optical Radiation Corporation, **27** 57
Optilink Corporation, **12** 137
Optima Pharmacy Services, **17** 177
Option Care Inc., **48** 307–10
Optische Werke G. Rodenstock, **44** 319–23
OptiSystems Solutions Ltd., **55** 67
Opto-Electronics Corp., **15** 483
Optus Communications, **25** 102
Optus Vision, **17** 150
Opus Group, **34** 321–23
Oracle Corporation, **6** 272–74; **24** 367–71 (upd.); **67** 282–87 (upd.)
Orange *see* Wanadoo S.A.
Orange and Rockland Utilities, Inc., **45** 116, 120
Orange Glo International, **53** 256–59
Orange Julius of America, **10** 371, 373; **39** 232, 235
Orange Line Bus Company, **6** 604
Orange PLC, **24** 89; **38** 300
Orange Shipbuilding Company, Inc., **58** 70
OraSure Technologies, Inc., **75** 300–03
Orb Books *see* Tom Doherty Associates Inc.
Orb Estates, **54** 366, 368
ORBIS Corporation, **59** 289
Orbis Entertainment Co., **20** 6
Orbis Graphic Arts *see* Anaheim Imaging.
Orbital Engine Corporation Ltd., **17** 24
Orbital Sciences Corporation, **22** 400–03
Orbitz, Inc., **61** 276–78
Orbotech Ltd., **75** 304–06
Orchard Supply Hardware Stores Corporation, **17** 365–67
Orchid Biosciences Inc., **57** 309, 311
Orcofi, **III** 48
OrderTrust LLP, **26** 440
Ore-Ida Foods Inc., **13** 382–83; **78** 279–82 (upd.)
Orebehoved Fanerfabrik, **25** 464
Oregon Ale and Beer Company, **18** 72; **50** 112
Oregon Chai, Inc., **49** 315–17
Oregon Coin Company, **74** 14
Oregon Craft & Floral Supply, **17** 322
Oregon Cutting Systems, **26** 119
Oregon Dental Service Health Plan, Inc., **51** 276–78
Oregon Freeze Dry, Inc., **74** 228–30
Oregon Metallurgical Corporation, **20** 406–08
Oregon Pacific and Eastern Railway, **13** 100
Oregon Steel Mills, Inc., **14** 368–70
O'Reilly Automotive, Inc., **26** 347–49; **78** 283–87 (upd.)
Orenda Aerospace, **48** 274
The Organic and Natural Food Company, **74** 384
Organic Valley (Coulee Region Organic Produce Pool), **53** 260–62
Organización Soriana, S.A. de C.V., **35** 320–22

Organizacion Techint, **66** 293–95
Organon, **63** 141
ORI *see* Old Republic International Corporation.
Orico Life Insurance Co., **48** 328
Oriel Foods, **II** 609
Orient, **21** 122
Orient Express Hotels Inc., **29** 429–30
Orient Leasing *see* Orix Corporation.
Orient Overseas, **18** 254
Oriental Brewery Co., Ltd., **21** 320
Oriental Precision Company, **13** 213
Oriental Trading Corp., **22** 213
Oriental Yeast Co. *see* Nisshin Seifun Group Inc.
Origin Energy Limited *see* Boral Limited.
Origin Systems Inc., **10** 285
Origin Technology, **14** 183
Original Arizona Jean Company *see* J.C. Penney Company, Inc.
Original Cookie Co. *see* Mrs. Fields' Original Cookies, Inc.
Original Musical Instrument Company (O.M.I.), **16** 239
Origins Natural Resources Inc., **30** 190
Orioala, **72** 258
Orion Capital Corporation, **55** 331
Orion Healthcare Ltd., **11** 168
Orion Oyj, **72** 256–59
Orion Personal Insurances Ltd., **11** 168
Orion Pictures Corporation, **6** 167–70
Orit Corp., **8** 219–20
ORIX Corporation, **II** 442–43; **44** 324–26 (upd.)
Orkem, **IV** 560; **21** 205
Orkin Pest Control, **11** 431–32, 434
Orkla A/S, **18** 394–98
Orleans Homebuilders, Inc., **62** 260–62
Orlimar Golf Equipment Co., **45** 76
Orm Bergold Chemie, **8** 464
Ormco Corporation, **14** 481
ÖROP, **IV** 485–86
Orowheat Baking Company, **10** 250
La Oroya, **22** 286
Orrick, Herrington and Sutcliffe LLP, **76** 299–301
ORSCO, Inc., **26** 363
Orszagos Takarekpenztar es Kereskedelmi Bank Rt. (OTP Bank), **78** 288–91
Ortho Diagnostic Systems, Inc., **10** 213; **22** 75
Ortho Pharmaceutical Corporation, **10** 79–80; **30** 59–60
Orthodontic Centers of America, Inc., **35** 323–26
Orthofix International NV, **72** 260–62
Orthopedic Services, Inc., **11** 366
Ortloff Engineers, Ltd., **52** 103–05
Orval Kent Food Company, Inc., **7** 430
Orville Redenbacher/Swiss Miss Foods Co., **17** 241
The Orvis Company, Inc., **28** 336–39
Oryx Energy Company, **7** 413–15
OSA Technologies *see* Avocent Corporation.
Osaka Gas Company, Ltd., **V** 679–81; **60** 233–36 (upd.)

PACE Entertainment Corp., **36** 423–24
Pace Express Pty. Ltd., **13** 20
Pace Foods Ltd. *see* Campbell Soup Company.
Pace Management Service Corp., **21** 91
PACE Membership Warehouse, Inc. *see* Kmart Corporation.
Pace Pharmaceuticals, **16** 439
Pacemaker Plastics, Inc., **7** 296
Pacer International, Inc., 54 274–76
Pacer Technology, 40 347–49
Pacer Tool and Mold, **17** 310
Pacific Advantage, **43** 253
Pacific Air Freight, Incorporated *see* Airborne Freight Corp.
Pacific Air Transport, **9** 416
Pacific and European Telegraph Company, **25** 99
Pacific Bell *see* SBC Communications.
Pacific Car & Foundry Company *see* PACCAR Inc.
Pacific Coast Feather Company, 67 294–96
Pacific Communication Sciences, **11** 57
Pacific Destination Services, **62** 276
Pacific Dunlop Limited, 10 444–46 *see also* Ansell Ltd.
Pacific Electric Light Company, **6** 565; **50** 365
Pacific Enterprises, V 682–84 *see also* Sempra Energy.
Pacific Ethanol, Inc., 81 269–72
Pacific Finance Corp., **9** 536; **13** 529; **26** 486
Pacific Forest Products Ltd., **59** 162
Pacific Fur Company, **25** 220
Pacific Gamble Robinson, **9** 39
Pacific Gas and Electric Company, V 685–87 *see also* PG&E Corporation.
Pacific Glass Corp., **48** 42
Pacific Guardian Life Insurance Co., **III** 289
Pacific Home Furnishings, **14** 436
Pacific Indemnity Corp., **III** 220; **14** 108, 110; **16** 204
Pacific Integrated Healthcare, **53** 7
Pacific Lighting Corp. *see* Sempra Energy.
Pacific Linens, **13** 81–82
Pacific Link Communication, **18** 180
Pacific Lumber Company, **III** 254; **8** 348–50
Pacific Magazines and Printing, **7** 392
Pacific Mail Steamship Company *see* APL Limited.
Pacific Media K.K., **18** 101
Pacific Monolothics Inc., **11** 520
Pacific National Insurance Co. *see* TIG Holdings, Inc.
Pacific Natural Gas Corp., **9** 102
Pacific Northwest Laboratories, **10** 139
Pacific Northwest Pipeline Corporation, **9** 102–104, 540; **12** 144
Pacific Northwest Power Company, **6** 597
Pacific Petroleums Ltd., **9** 102
Pacific Plastics, Inc., **48** 334
Pacific Power & Light Company *see* PacifiCorp.
Pacific Pride Bakeries, **19** 192

Pacific Publications, **72** 283–84
Pacific Recycling Co. Inc., **IV** 296; **19** 226; **23** 225
Pacific Resources Inc., **IV** 47; **22** 107
Pacific Sentinel Gold Corp., **27** 456
Pacific/Southern Wine & Spirits, **48** 392
Pacific Stock Exchange, **48** 226
Pacific Sunwear of California, Inc., 28 343–45; **47** 425
Pacific Telecom, Inc., 6 325–28
Pacific Telesis Group, V 318–20 *see also* SBC Communications.
Pacific Teletronics, Inc., **7** 15
Pacific Towboat *see* Puget Sound Tug and Barge Company.
Pacific Trail Inc., **17** 462; **29** 293, 295–96
Pacific Western Extruded Plastics Company *see* PW Eagle Inc.
Pacific Wine Co., **18** 71; **50** 112
PacifiCare Health Systems, Inc., 11 378–80
PacifiCorp, Inc., V 688–90; **26** 357–60 **(upd.)**
Package Products Company, Inc., **12** 150
Packaged Ice, Inc., **21** 338; **26** 449
Packaging Corporation of America, 12 376–78; **51** 282–85 **(upd.)**
Packard Bell Electronics, Inc., 13 387–89
Packard Motor Co., **8** 74; **9** 17
Packerland Packing Company, **7** 199, 201
Packeteer, Inc., 81 273–76
Pacolet Manufacturing Company, **17** 327
Pact, **50** 175
PacTel *see* Pacific Telesis Group.
Paddock Publications, Inc., 53 263–65
PAFS *see* Pacific Alaska Fuel Services.
Page, Bacon & Co., **12** 533
Page Boy Inc., **9** 320
Page Plus NV *see* Punch International N.V.
PageAhead Software, **15** 492
Pageland Coca-Cola Bottling Works, **10** 222
PageMart Wireless, Inc., **18** 164, 166
PagesJaunes Groupe SA, 79 306–09
Paging Network Inc., 11 381–83
Pagnossin S.p.A., 73 248–50
Pagoda Trading Company, Inc. *see* Brown Shoe Company, Inc.
Paid Prescriptions, **9** 346
Paige Publications, **18** 66
PaineWebber Group Inc., II 444–46; **22** 404–07 **(upd.)**
Painter Carpet Mills, **13** 169
PairGain Technologies, **36** 299
Paisley Products, **32** 255
La Paix, **III** 273
Pak-a-Sak, **II** 661
Pak Mail Centers, **18** 316
Pak Sak Industries, **17** 310; **24** 160
Pakhoed Holding, N.V., **9** 532; **26** 420; **41** 339–40
Pakistan International Airlines Corporation, 46 323–26
Pakistan State Oil Company Ltd., 81 277–80
Pakkasakku Oy, **IV** 471

Paknet, **11** 548
Pakway Container Corporation, **8** 268
PAL *see* Philippine Airlines, Inc.
Palace Station Hotel & Casino *see* Station Casinos Inc.
Paladar, **56** 116
Palais Royal, Inc., **24** 456
Palazzo Feroni Finanziaria SpA, **62** 313
Palco Industries, **19** 440
Pale Ski & Sports GmbH, **22** 461
Palestine Coca-Cola Bottling Co., **13** 163
The Palestine Post Limited, **62** 188
PALIC *see* Pan-American Life Insurance Company.
Pall Corporation, 9 396–98; **72** 263–66 **(upd.)**
Pallas Textiles, **57** 207, 209
Palm Beach Holdings, **9** 157
Palm Harbor Homes, Inc., 39 316–18
Palm, Inc., 36 355–57; **75** 310–14 **(upd.)**
Palm Management Corporation, 71 265–68
Palm Shipping Inc., **25** 468–70
Palmafina, **IV** 498–99
Palmax, **47** 153
Palmer & Cay, Inc., 69 285–87
Palmer Candy Company, 80 277–81
Palmer Communications, **25** 418
Palmer G. Lewis Co., **8** 135
Palmolive Co. *see* Colgate-Palmolive Company.
Palo Alto Brewing, **22** 421
Palo Alto Products International, Inc., **29** 6
Palo Alto Research Center, **10** 510
Paloma Industries Ltd., 71 269–71
Palomar Medical Technologies, Inc., 22 408–10
PAM Group, **27** 462
Pamida Holdings Corporation, 15 341–43
Pampa OTT, **27** 473
The Pampered Chef Ltd., 18 406–08; **78** 292–96 **(upd.)**
Pamplemousse, **14** 225
Pamplin Corp. *see* R.B. Pamplin Corp.
Pan-Alberta Gas Ltd., **16** 11
Pan-American Life Insurance Company, 48 311–13
Pan American World Airways, Inc., I 115–16; **12** 379–81 **(upd.)**
Pan Asia Paper Company Ltd., **63** 314–16
Pan European Publishing Co., **IV** 611
Pan Geo Atlas Corporation, **18** 513
Pan Pacific Fisheries, **24** 114
PanAgora Asset Management Inc., **60** 220
Panalpina World Transport (Holding) Ltd., 47 286–88
Panamerican Beverages, Inc., 47 289–91; **54** 74
PanAmSat Corporation, 46 327–29
Panasonic, **9** 180; **10** 125; **12** 470; **43** 427
Panavia Aircraft GmbH, **24** 84, 86–87
Panavision Inc., 24 372–74
PanCanadian Petroleum Ltd., **27** 217; **45** 80

The Pittston Company, IV 180–82; 19 319–22 (upd.) *see also* The Brink's Company.
Pittway Corporation, 9 413–15; 33 334–37 (upd.)
Pivot Rules, Inc. *see* Bluefly, Inc.
Pivotpoint, Inc., 55 258
Pixar Animation Studios, 34 348–51
Pixel Semiconductor, 11 57
Pixelworks, Inc., 69 298–300
Pizitz, Inc., 19 324
Pizza Dispatch *see* Dominos's Pizza, Inc.
Pizza Hut Inc., 7 434–35; 21 405–07 (upd.)
Pizza Inn, Inc., 46 346–49
PizzaCo, Inc., 7 152
Pizzeria Uno, 25 178
PJ's Coffee, 64 327
PJS Publications, 22 442
PKF International, 78 315–18
Place du Marché S.A., 76 355
Place Two *see* Nordstrom, Inc.
Placer Development Ltd., IV 19
Placer Dome Inc., 20 430–33; 61 289–93 (upd.)
Placid Oil Co., 7 228
Plaid Holdings Corp., 9 157
Plain Jane Dress Company, 8 169
Plains Cotton Cooperative Association, 57 283–86
Plains Dairy, 53 21
Plainwell Paper Co., Inc., 8 103
Planar Systems, Inc., 61 294–97
Planet Hollywood International, Inc., 18 424–26; 41 307–10 (upd.)
Planet Smoothie Franchises LLC, 64 327–28
Planet Waves, 48 232
Plantation Pipe Line Company, 68 290–92
Plante & Moran, LLP, 71 280–83
Planters Company, 24 287
Planters Lifesavers, 14 274–75
Plas-Techs, Inc., 15 35
Plastibec Ltd. *see* Royal Group Technologies Limited.
Plastic Coating Corporation, 8 483
Plastic Containers, Inc., 15 129; 25 512
Plastic Engineered Products Company *see* Ballard Medical Products.
Plastic Parts, Inc., 19 277
Plastic-Plate, Inc., 61 158, 160
Plastics, Inc., 13 41
Plasto Bambola *see* BRIO AB.
Plate Glass Group, 24 450
Plateau Holdings, Inc., 12 260; 13 502
Platinum Entertainment, Inc., 35 341–44
Platinum Holdings, 74 146
PLATINUM Technology, Inc., 14 390–92
Plato Learning, Inc., 44 344–47
Platte River Insurance Company, 60 16
Play by Play Toys & Novelties, Inc., 26 374–76
Play It Again Sam (PIAS), 44 164
Play It Again Sports, 18 207–08
Playboy Enterprises, Inc., 18 427–30

PlayCore, Inc., 27 370–72
Players International, Inc., 22 431–33
Playland, 16 389
Playmates Toys, 23 386–88
Playmaxx, Inc., 55 132
Playmobil *see* geobra Brandstätter GmbH & Co. KG.
Playskool, Inc., 25 379–81
Playtex Products, Inc., 15 357–60
Playworld, 16 389–90
Plaza Coloso S.A. de C.V., 10 189
PLC *see* Prescription Learning Corporation.
Pleasant Company, 27 373–75 *see also* American Girl, Inc.
Pleasant Holidays LLC, 62 274–76
Pleasurama PLC, 12 228; 32 243
Plessey Company, PLC, II 81–82
Plex Co., Ltd., 55 48
Plexco, 7 30–31
Plexus Corporation, 35 345–47; 80 287–91 (upd.)
Plezall Wipers, Inc., 15 502
Plitt Theatres, Inc. *see* Cineplex Odeon Corporation.
PLIVA d.d., 70 223–25
PLLN C.V. Partnership, 72 265
Plough Inc. *see* Schering-Plough.
Plum Associates, 12 270
Plum Creek Timber Company, Inc., 43 304–06
Pluma, Inc., 27 376–78
Plumb Tool, II 16
Plus Development Corporation, 10 458–59
Plus Mark, Inc., 7 24
Plus System Inc., 9 537
Plus-Ultra, II 196
Plus Vita, 36 162
Pluto Technologies International Inc., 38 72
Ply Gem Industries Inc., 12 396–98
Plymouth County Electric Co., 14 124
Plymouth Mills Inc., 23 66
PM Management Incorporated, 74 234
PM Resources, Inc., 74 381
PMC Contract Research AB, 21 425
PMI Corporation *see* Physical Measurements Information
The PMI Group, Inc., 49 331–33
PMP Ltd., 72 282–84
PMR Corporation *see* Psychiatric Solutions, Inc.
PMS Consolidated, 8 347
PMT Services, Inc., 24 393–95
PN Gaya Motor, 56 284
The PNC Financial Services Group Inc., II 342–43; 13 410–12 (upd.); 46 350–53 (upd.)
Pneumo Abex Corp., I 456–58; III 512; 10 553–54; 38 293–94
Pneumo Dynamics Corporation, 8 409
PNL *see* Pacific Northwest Laboratories.
PNM Resources Inc., 51 296–300 (upd.)
PNP *see* Pacific Northwest Power Company.

POAS *see* Türkiye Petrolleri Anonim Ortakliği
POB Polyolefine Burghausen GmbH, IV 487
Pocahontas Foods USA, 31 359, 361
Pochet SA, 55 307–09
Pocket Books, Inc., 10 480; 13 559–60
Poclain Company, 10 380
Poe & Associates, Inc., 41 63–64
Pogo Producing Company, 39 330–32
Pohang Iron and Steel Company Ltd., IV 183–85 *see also* POSCO.
Pohjan Sellu Oy, IV 316
Point Chehalis Packers, 13 244
Polak & Schwarz Essencefabricken, 9 290
Poland Spring Natural Spring Water Co., 31 229
Polar Air Cargo Inc., 60 237–39
Polar Manufacturing Company, 16 32
Polar S.A., 59 418
Polar Star Milling Company, 7 241
Polaris Industries Inc., 12 399–402; 35 348–53 (upd.); 77 330–37 (upd.)
Polaroid Corporation, III 607–09; 7 436–39 (upd.); 28 362–66 (upd.)
Polbeth Packaging Limited, 12 377
Polenghi, 25 84
Policy Management Systems Corporation, 11 394–95
Policy Studies, Inc., 62 277–80
Poliet S.A., 33 338–40
Polioles, S.A. de C.V., 19 10, 12
Politos, S.A. de C.V., 23 171
Polk Audio, Inc., 34 352–54
Pollenex Corp., 19 360
Polo Food Corporation, 10 250
Polo/Ralph Lauren Corporation, 12 403–05; 62 281–85 (upd.)
Polser, 19 49, 51
Polski Koncern Naftowy ORLEN S.A., 77 338–41
Polskie Linie Lotnicze S.A. *see* LOT Polish Airlines.
Poly-Glas Systems, Inc., 21 65
Poly-Hi Corporation, 8 359
Polyblend Corporation, 7 4
Polydesign, 16 421
Polydor B.V., 23 389
Polydor KK, 23 390
Polydress Plastic GmbH, 7 141
Polygon Networks Inc., 41 73
PolyGram N.V., 23 389–92
Polyken Technologies, 11 220
Polymer Technologies Corporation, 26 287
PolyMedica Corporation, 77 342–45
Polyphase Corporation *see* Overhill Corporation.
Polysius AG, IV 89
Pomeroy Computer Resources, Inc., 33 341–44
Pomeroy's, 16 61; 50 107
Pommery et Greno, II 475
Pompes Guinard S.A., 62 217
Ponderosa Steakhouse, 15 361–64
Ponderosa System Inc., 12 199
Pont-à-Mousson S.A., 16 119, 121–22; 21 253

Ralston Purina Company, II 561–63; 13 425–27 (upd.) *see also* Ralcorp Holdings, Inc.

Ramada International Hotels & Resorts, IV 718; 9 426; 11 177; 13 66; 21 366; 25 309; 28 258; 38 320; 52 281

Rambol, 25 84

Rampage Clothing Co., 35 94

Ramparts, Inc., 57 159

Ramsay Youth Services, Inc., 41 322–24

Ranbar Packing, Inc. *see* Western Beef, Inc.

Ranbaxy Laboratories Ltd., 70 247–49

Ranchers Packing Corp. *see* Western Beef, Inc.

Rand Capital Corp., 35 52–53

Rand McNally & Company, 28 378–81; 53 122

Randall's Food Markets, Inc., 40 364–67

Randgold & Exploration, 63 182–83

Random House, Inc., 13 428–30; 31 375–80 (upd.)

Randon Meldkamer, 43 307

Randon S.A. Implementos e Participações, 79 348–52

Randstad Holding n.v., 16 420–22; 43 307–10 (upd.)

Range Resources Corporation, 45 353–55

The Rank Group plc, II 157–59; 14 399–402 (upd.); 64 317–21 (upd.)

Ranks Hovis McDougall Limited, II 564–65; 28 382–85 (upd.)

Ransburg Corporation, 22 282

Ransom and Randolph Company, 10 271

Ransom Industries LP, 55 266

RAO Unified Energy System of Russia, 45 356–60

Rapala-Normark Group, Ltd., 30 368–71

Rapides Bank & Trust Company, 11 107

Rapidforms, Inc., 35 130–31

Rare Hospitality International Inc., 19 340–42

RAS *see* Riunione Adriatica di Sicurtà SpA.

Rascal House, 24 243

Raskas Foods, Inc. *see* Shearer's Foods, Inc.

Rathbone Brothers plc, 70 250–53

Ratin A/S, 49 376

Rational GmbH, 22 354

Ratner Companies, 72 294–96

Ratti Vallensasca, 25 312

Raufast et Fils, 35 205

Rauma-Repola Oy *see* Metso Corporation

Raumtechnik Messebau & Event Marketing GmbH, 60 143

Rauscher Pierce Refsnes, Inc., 15 233

Raven Industries, Inc., 33 359–61

Raven Press, 14 555

Ravenna Metal Products Corp., 12 344

Ravensburger AG, 64 322–26

Ravenseft Properties Ltd. *see* Land Securities PLC.

Ravenswood Aluminum Company, 52 72–73

RAVIcad, 18 20; 43 17

Raving Brands, Inc., 64 327–29

Rawlings Sporting Goods Co., Inc., 24 402–04

Rawls Brothers Co., 13 369

Ray Industries, 22 116

Ray Simon, 24 94

Ray Strauss Unlimited, 22 123

Raychem Corporation, 8 446–47

Raymar Book Corporation, 11 194

Raymond James Financial Inc., 69 308–10

Raymond International Inc., 28 201

Raymond Ltd., 77 351–54

Raymond, Trice & Company, 14 40

Raynet Corporation, 8 447

Rayonese Textile, Inc., 29 140

Rayonier Inc., 24 405–07

Rayovac Corporation, 13 431–34; 39 336–40 (upd.)

Raytech Corporation, 61 306–09

Raytheon Aircraft Holdings Inc., 46 354–57

Raytheon Company, II 85–87; 11 411–14 (upd.); 38 372–77 (upd.)

Razel S.A., 55 62

Razorback Acquisitions, 19 455

Razorfish, Inc., 37 321–24

RB&W Corp., 17 372

RBC Dominion Securities, 25 12

RBS Global Inc. *see* Rexnord Corporation.

RCA Corporation, II 88–90

RCA Global Communications, Inc., 27 304

RCG International, Inc., III 344

RCM Technologies, Inc., 34 371–74

RCN Corporation, 70 254–57

RDMS Direct Marketing BV, 53 362

RDO Equipment Company, 33 362–65

RE/MAX International, Inc., 59 344–46

REA *see* Railway Express Agency.

Rea & Derick, II 605

Rea Construction Company, 17 377

React-Rite, Inc., 8 271

Read-Rite Corp., 10 463–64

The Reader's Digest Association, Inc., IV 663–64; 17 392–95 (upd.); 71 295–99 (upd.)

Reader's Garden Inc., 22 441

Reading Etc., 72 172

Reading International Inc., 70 258–60

Reading Railroad, 9 407

Ready Mixed Concrete, 28 82

Real Color Displays, 53 117

Real Decisions, 21 236

Real Estate Maintenance, 25 15

Real Fresh, 25 85

Real Goods Trading Company, 41 177

Real Madrid C.F., 73 274–76

Real-Share, Inc., 18 542; 76 368

Real Times, Inc., 66 261–65

Real Turismo, S.A. de C.V., 50 373–75

RealCom Communications Corporation, 15 196

Realeum, Inc., 58 11

Reality Group Limited, 47 165, 169

Realty Information Group, Inc. *see* CoStar Group, Inc.

The Really Useful Group, 26 393–95

RealNetworks, Inc., 53 280–82

Realty Development Co. *see* King Kullen Grocery Co., Inc.

Realty Investment Group, 25 127

Realty Parking Properties II L.P., 18 104

Reavis & McGrath, 47 139

Rebekah W. Harkness Foundation, 52 199

Recaro North America Inc., 26 231

Reckitt Benckiser plc, II 566–67; 42 302–06 (upd.)

Reckson Associates Realty Corp., 47 329–31

Record Bar / Licorice Pizza, 9 361

Record Merchandisers *see* Entertainment UK.

Record World Inc., 9 361

Recordati S.p.A., 52 135

Recording for the Blind & Dyslexic, 51 312–14

Recoton Corp., 15 381–83

Recoupe Recycling Technologies, 8 104

Recovery Centers of America, III 88

Recovery Engineering, Inc., 25 392–94

Recreational Equipment, Inc., 18 444–47; 71 300–03 (upd.)

Recticel S.A., 17 182–84

Recubrimientos Interceramic, S.A. de C.V., 53 175

Recycled Paper Greetings, Inc., 21 426–28

RED, 44 164

Red & White, II 682

The Red Adair Company, 37 171

Red Ant Entertainment, 17 14

Red Apple Group, Inc., 23 406–08

Red Ball, Inc., 18 300

Red Brick Systems Inc., 30 246

Red Bull GmbH, 60 252–54

Red Carpet Food Systems, 39 409

Red Chisinau, 51 389

Red-E-Food Systems, Inc. *see* Del Taco, Inc.

Red Food Stores, Inc., 19 327–28

Red Hat, Inc., 45 361–64

Red House Books Ltd., 29 426

Red Kap *see* VF Corporation.

Red L Foods, 13 244

Red Line HealthCare Corporation, 47 236

Red Lion Entertainment, 29 503

Red Lobster Inns of America, 16 156–58

Red Lobster Restaurants, 19 258

Red Oak Consulting, 42 244

Red Owl Stores, Inc., II 670; 18 506; 50 456

Red Pepper Software Co., 59 77

Red River Commodities, Inc. *see* Deli Universal NV.

Red Robin Gourmet Burgers, Inc., 56 294–96

Red Roof Inns, Inc., 18 448–49

Red Rooster, V 35

Red Spot Paint & Varnish Company, 55 319–22

Red Star Express, 14 505

Red Storm, 41 409

Santa Margherita S.p.A. *see* Industrie Zignago Santa Margherita S.p.A.
Santa Rosa Savings and Loan, **10** 339
Santal, **26** 160
Santiago Land Development Corporation, **58** 20
Santone Industries Inc., **16** 327
Santos Ltd., **81** 360–63
Sanus Corp. Health Systems, **III** 317
Sanwa Bank, Ltd., **II** 347–48; **15** 431–33 (upd.)
Sanwa USA Inc., **70** 213
Sanyo Chemical Manufacturing Co., **III** 758
Sanyo Electric Co., Ltd., **II** 91–92; **36** 399–403 (upd.)
Sanyo-Kokusaku Pulp Co., Ltd., **IV** 327–28
Sanyo Semiconductor, **17** 33
Sanyo White Cement Co. Ltd., **60** 301
Sao Paulo Alpargatas S.A., **75** 347–49
SAP AG, **16** 441–44; **43** 358–63 (upd.)
SAPAC *see* Société Parisienne d'Achats en Commun.
Sapeksa, **55** 189
Sapirstein Greeting Card Company *see* American Greetings Corporation.
Sappi Limited, **49** 352–55
Sapporo Breweries Limited, **I** 282–83; **13** 454–56 (upd.); **36** 404–07 (upd.);
SAPRA-Landauer Ltd., **51** 210
Saputo Inc., **59** 363–65
Sara Lee Corporation, **II** 571–73; **15** 434–37 (upd.); **54** 322–27 (upd.)
Saracen's Head Brewery, **21** 245
Saratoga Partners, **24** 436
Sarawak Trading, **14** 448
Sargent & Lundy, **6** 556
SARL, **12** 152
Sarma, **26** 159–61
Sarmag, **26** 161
Sarnoff Corporation, **57** 309–12
Saros Corp., **15** 474; **62** 141
Sarotti GmbH, **53** 315
Sarpe, **IV** 591
Sarriò S.A., **41** 325–26
Sartek Industries Inc., **44** 441
The SAS Group, **34** 396–99 (upd.)
SAS Institute Inc., **10** 476–78; **78** 328–32 (upd.)
Saskatchewan Oil and Gas Corporation, **13** 556–57
Sasol Limited, **IV** 533–35; **47** 340–44 (upd.)
Sasu Ldc Sable, **68** 234
SAT *see* Stockholms Allmänna Telefonaktiebolag.
Satcom Group of Companies, **32** 40
Satellite Business Systems, **21** 14; **23** 135; **27** 304
Satellite Software International, **10** 556
Satellite Television PLC, **23** 135
Satellite Transmission and Reception Specialist Company, **11** 184
Saturn Corporation, **7** 461–64; **21** 449–53 (upd.); **80** 332–38 (upd.)
Saturn Industries, Inc., **23** 489
SATV *see* Satellite Television PLC.

Satyam, **59** 129
Saucona Iron Co., **7** 48
Saucony Inc., **35** 386–89
Sauder Woodworking Co., **12** 433–34; **35** 390–93 (upd.)
Saudi Arabian Airlines, **6** 114–16; **27** 132, 395–98 (upd.)
Saudi Arabian Oil Company, **IV** 536–39; **17** 411–15 (upd.); **50** 412–17 (upd.) *see also* Arabian American Oil Co.
Saudi Arabian Parsons Limited, **8** 416
Saudi Basic Industries Corporation (SABIC), **58** 325–28
Saudia *see* Saudi Arabian Airlines.
Sauer-Danfoss Inc., **61** 320–22
Saul Ewing LLP, **74** 291–94
Saunders, Karp, and Megrue, LP, **26** 190; **28** 258; **70** 121
Sauza, **31** 92
Sav-on Drug, **II** 605; **12** 477
Sav-X, **9** 186
Sava Group, **20** 263
Savacentre Ltd., **II** 658; **13** 284
Savage, **19** 430
Savannah Electric & Power Company, **38** 448
Savannah Foods & Industries, Inc., **7** 465–67
Savannah Gas Company, **6** 448; **23** 29
Save & Prosper Group, **10** 277
Save-A-Lot, **II** 682; **11** 228
Save Mart, **14** 397; **27** 292
Save.com, **37** 409
Savia S.A. de C.V., **29** 435
Savio, **IV** 422
Oy Savo-Karjalan Tukkuliike, **8** 293
Savoy Group, **24** 195
Savoy Industries, **12** 495
Savoy Pictures Entertainment Inc., **25** 214
Sawdust Pencil Company, **29** 372
Sawgrass Asset Management, LLC, **48** 18
Sawhill Tubular Products, **41** 3
Sawtek Inc., **43** 364–66 (upd.)
Sawyer Electrical Manufacturing Company, **11** 4
Sawyer Industries, Inc., **13** 532
Sawyer Research Products, Inc., **14** 81
Saxby, S.A., **13** 385
Saxon Oil, **11** 97
Saxon Petroleum, Inc., **19** 162
Saxonville USA, **61** 254, 256
Sayers & Scovill *see* Accubuilt, Inc.
SB Acquisitions, Inc., **46** 74
SBAR, Inc., **30** 4
Sbarro, Inc., **16** 445–47; **64** 339–42 (upd.)
SBC Communications Inc., **32** 399–403 (upd.)
SBC Transportation, Inc. *see* Schwebel Baking Company.
SBC Warburg, **14** 419–21
SBC Warburg Dillon Read, **52** 355
Sberbank, **62** 314–17
SBI *see* State Bank of India.
SBK Entertainment World, Inc., **22** 194; **24** 485; **26** 187
SBM Group, **71** 178–79

SBS Broadcasting, **61** 58
SBS Technologies, Inc., **25** 405–07
SCA *see* Svenska Cellulosa AB.
SCA Services, Inc., **9** 109
SCAC *see* Société Commercial d'Affrètements et de Combustibles.
Scaldia Paper BV, **15** 229
Scali, McCabe & Sloves, **71** 158
Scan Screen, **IV** 600
SCANA Corporation, **6** 574–76; **56** 305–08 (upd.)
Scanair, **34** 397–98
Scancem, **38** 437
Scandic Hotels AB, **49** 193
Scandinavian Airlines System, **I** 119–20 *see also* The SAS Group.
Scandinavian Broadcasting System SA, **53** 325
ScanDust, **III** 625
Scania-Vabis *see* Saab-Scania AB.
ScanSource, Inc., **29** 413–15; **74** 295–98 (upd.)
Scantron Corporation, **17** 266–68
Scarborough Public Utilities Commission, **9** 461–62
Scaturro Supermarkets, **24** 528
SCB Computer Technology, Inc., **29** 416–18
SCEcorp, **V** 715–17 *see also* Edison International.
Scenic Airlines, Inc., **25** 420, 423
Scenographic Designs, **21** 277
SCG Corporation, **56** 323
Schäfer, **31** 158
Schaper Mfg. Co., **12** 168
Schauman Wood Oy, **IV** 277, 302
Schawk, Inc., **24** 424–26
SCHC, Inc. *see* Shoe Carnival Inc.
Scheels All Sports Inc., **63** 348–50
Scheid Vineyards Inc., **66** 276–78
Schein Pharmaceutical Inc., **13** 77; **56** 375
Schell Brewing *see* August Schell Brewing Company Inc.
Schenker Deutschland AG, **59** 391
Schenker-Rhenus Ag, **6** 424–26
Schenley Industries Inc., **9** 449; **24** 140
Schenley Distilleries Inc., **68** 99
Scherer *see* R.P. Scherer.
Schering A.G., **I** 681–82; **50** 418–22 (upd.)
Schering-Plough Corporation, **I** 683–85; **14** 422–25 (upd.); **49** 356–62 (upd.)
Schiavi Homes, Inc., **14** 138
Schibsted ASA, **31** 401–05
Schick Products, **41** 366
Schick Shaving, **38** 363, 365
Schick-Wilkinson Sword *see* Wilkinson Sword Ltd.
Schieffelin & Somerset Co., **61** 323–25
Schindler Holding AG, **29** 419–22
Schlitz Brewing Co., **I** 255, 268, 270, 291, 600; **10** 100; **12** 338; **18** 500; **23** 403
Schlotzsky's, Inc., **36** 408–10
Schlumberger Limited, **III** 616–18; **17** 416–19 (upd.); **59** 366–71 (upd.)

Sheffield Silver Company, **67** 322–23

Shekou Container Terminal, **16** 481; **38** 345

Shelby Insurance Company, **10** 44–45

Shelby Steel Processing Co., **51** 238

Shelby Williams Industries, Inc., 14 435–37

Shelco, **22** 146

Sheldahl Inc., 23 432–35

Shelf Life Inc. *see* King Kullen Grocery Co., Inc.

Shell *see* Royal Dutch/Shell Group; Shell Oil Company; Shell Transport and Trading Company p.l.c.

Shell Canada Limited, **32** 45

Shell Chemical Corporation, **IV** 531–32, 540; **8** 415; **24** 151

Shell Forestry, **21** 546; **50** 58

Shell France, **12** 153

Shell Oil Company, IV 540–41; **14** 438–40 (upd.); **41** 356–60 (upd.)

Shell Transport and Trading Company p.l.c., IV 530–32 *see also* Royal Dutch Petroleum Company; Royal Dutch/Shell.

Shell Western E & P, **7** 323

Sheller-Globe Corporation, I 201–02

Shells Seafood Restaurants, Inc., 43 370–72

Shelly Brothers, Inc., **15** 65

Shenzhen Namtek Co., Ltd., **61** 232–33

Shepherd Hardware Products Ltd., **16** 357

Shepherd Neame Limited, 30 414–16

Shepherd Plating and Finishing Company, **13** 233

Shepler Equipment Co., **9** 512

Sheraton Corp. of America, **III** 98–99; **11** 198; **13** 362–63; **21** 91

Sherborne Group Inc./NH Holding Inc., **17** 20

Sherbrooke Paper Products Ltd., **17** 281

Sheridan Bakery, **II** 633

Sherr-Gold, **23** 40

Sherritt Gordon Mines, **7** 386–87; **12** 260

The Sherwin-Williams Company, III 744–46; **13** 469–71 (upd.)

Sherwood Brands, Inc., 53 302–04

Sherwood Equity Group Ltd. *see* National Discount Brokers Group, Inc.

Sherwood Medical Group, **I** 624; **10** 70; **50** 538

Sherwood Securities, **66** 308

Shiara Holdings, Inc., **53** 88

Shidler Group *see* First Industrial Realty Trust, Inc.

Shieh Chi Industrial Co., **19** 508

Shields & Co., **9** 118

Shihen Technical Corporation, **60** 272

Shihlin Electric & Engineering Group, **49** 460

Shikoku Electric Power Company, Inc., V 718–20; **60** 269–72 (upd.)

Shiley, Inc., **38** 361

Shillito's, **31** 192

Shimano Inc., 64 347–49

Shimizu Construction Company Ltd., **44** 153

Shin-Nihon Glass Co., **I** 221

Shinko Rayon Ltd. *see* Mitsubishi Rayon Co., Ltd.

Shinko Securities Co. Ltd., **58** 235

Shintech, **11** 159–60

Shinwa Pharmaceutical Co. Ltd., **48** 250

Shionogi & Co., Ltd., III 60–61; **17** 435–37 (upd.)

Ship 'n Shore, **9** 156–57

Shipley Co. Inc., **26** 425

Shipper Group, **16** 344

Shipstad & Johnson's Ice Follies, **25** 313

Shiseido Company, Limited, III 62–64; **22** 485–88 (upd.); **81** 364–70 (upd.)

Shizuoka Itaku Co., Ltd., **64** 261

SHL Systemhouse Inc., **27** 305

Shobiz, Inc., **60** 143

Shochiku Company Ltd., 74 302–04

Shockley Electronics, **20** 174

Shoe Carnival Inc., 14 441–43; **72** 326–29 (upd.)

Shoe Supply, Inc., **22** 213

Shoe-Town Inc., **23** 310

Shoe Works Inc., **18** 415

Shonac Corporation *see* DSW Inc.

Shonco, Inc., **18** 438

Shoney's, Inc., 7 474–76; **23** 436–39 (upd.)

Shop 'n Save Warehouse Foods Inc., **63** 129

Shop At Home Network LLC *see* The E.W. Scripps Company.

SHOP Channel, **64** 185

Shop Rite Foods Inc. *see* Big V Supermarkets, Inc.

ShopKo Stores Inc., 21 457–59; **58** 329–32 (upd.)

Shoppers Drug Mart Corporation, 49 367–70

Shoppers Food Warehouse Corporation, 66 290–92

Shoppers World Stores, Inc. *see* LOT$OFF Corporation.

ShopRite *see* Foodarama Supermarkets, Inc.

Shopwell/Food Emporium, **II** 638; **16** 247, 249

ShopWise.com Inc., **53** 13

Shore Manufacturing, **13** 165

Shorewood Packaging Corporation, 28 419–21

Shorouk Airways, **68** 227

Short Brothers, **24** 85

Shoseido Co., **17** 110

Shotton Paper Co. Ltd., **IV** 350

Showa Aluminum Corporation, **8** 374

Showa Denko, **IV** 61

Showa Marutsutsu Co. Ltd., **8** 477

Showa Products Company, **8** 476

Showa Shell Sekiyu K.K., IV 542–43; **59** 372–75 (upd.)

ShowBiz Pizza Time, Inc., **13** 472–74 *see also* CEC Entertainment, Inc.

Showboat, Inc., 19 400–02

Showcase of Fine Fabrics, **16** 197

Showco, Inc., **35** 436

Showscan Entertainment Inc., **34** 230

Showscan Film Corporation, **28** 206

Showtime Networks, Inc., 78 343–47

Shred-It Canada Corporation, 56 319–21

Shreve and Company, **12** 312

Shreveport Refrigeration, **16** 74

Shriners Hospitals for Children, 69 318–20

Shu Uemura, **III** 43

Shubert Organization Inc., 24 437–39

Shubrooks International Ltd., **11** 65

Shuffle Master Inc., 51 337–40

Shuford Mills, Inc., **14** 430

Shugart Associates, **8** 466; **22** 189

Shulman Transport Enterprises Inc., **27** 473

Shure Inc., 60 273–76

Shurfine International, **60** 302

Shurgard Storage Centers, Inc., 52 309–11

Shuttleworth Brothers Company *see* Mohawk Industries, Inc.

Shuwa Corp., **22** 101; **36** 292

SHV Holdings N.V., 55 344–47

SI Holdings Inc., **10** 481; **29** 425

The Siam Cement Public Company Limited, 56 322–25

Siam Makro, **62** 63

SIAS, **19** 192

SIATA S.p.A., **26** 363

SIB Financial Services, **39** 382

Sibco Universal, S.A., **14** 429

Sibel, **48** 350

Siberian Moloko, **48** 438

Sibneft *see* OAO Siberian Oil Company.

Siboney Shoe Corp., **22** 213

SiCAP AG, **58** 338

SICC *see* Univision Communications Inc.

Sichuan Changhong Electric Co. Ltd., **63** 36

Sichuan Station Wagon Factory, **38** 462

Sick's Brewery, **26** 304

Siclet, **25** 84

Sicma Aero Seat, **36** 529

Sideco Americana S.A., 67 346–48

Sidel *see* Groupe Sidel S.A.

Siderar S.A.I.C., 66 293–95

Siderca S.A.I.C., **41** 405–06

Sidley Austin Brown & Wood, 40 400–03 Sidmar N. V. *see* Arcelor Gent

Sidney Frank Importing Co., Inc., 69 321–23

Siebe plc *see* BTR Siebe plc.

Siebel Group, **13** 544–45

Siebel Marketing Group, **27** 195

Siebel Systems, Inc., 38 430–34

Siebert Financial Corp., 32 423–25

Siegel & Gale, 64 350–52

Siemens AG, II 97–100; **14** 444–47 (upd.); **57** 318–23 (upd.)

Siemens Solar Industries L.P., **44** 182

The Sierra Club, 28 422–24

Sierra Designs, Inc., **10** 215–16

Sierra Health Services, Inc., 15 451–53

Sierra Leone External Telegraph Limited, **25** 100

Sierra Nevada Brewing Company, 70 291–93

SPAO, **39** 184
Spar Aerospace Limited, **32** 435–37
SPAR Handels AG, **35** 398–401
Sparbanken Bank, **18** 543
SPARC International, **7** 499
Spare Change, **10** 282
SpareBank 1 Gruppen, **69** 177, 179
Sparks Computerized Car Care Centers, **25** 445
Sparks-Withington Company *see* Sparton Corporation.
Sparrow Records, **22** 194
Sparta, Inc., **18** 369
Sparta Surgical Corporation, **33** 456
Spartan Communications, **38** 308–09
Spartan Industries, Inc., **45** 15
Spartan Insurance Co., **26** 486
Spartan Motors Inc., **14** 457–59
Spartan Stores Inc., **8** 481–82; **66** 302–05 (upd.)
Spartech Corporation, **19** 413–15; **76** 329–32 (upd.)
Sparton Corporation, **18** 492–95
SPCM, Inc., **14** 477
Spear & Jackson, Inc., **73** 320–23
Spear, Leeds & Kellogg, **66** 306–09
Spec's Music, Inc., **19** 416–18
Special Agent Investigators, Inc., **14** 541
Special Foods, **14** 557
Special Project Films, Inc., **58** 124
Special Zone Limited, **26** 491
Specialist Computer Holdings Ltd., **80** 356–59
Specialized Bicycle Components Inc., **50** 445–48
Specialty Brands Inc., **25** 518
Specialty Coatings Inc., **8** 483–84
Specialty Equipment Companies, Inc., **25** 439–42
Specialty Foods Inc., **29** 29, 31; **74** 202
Specialty Products & Insulation Co., **59** 381–83
Specialty Products Co., **8** 386
Specialty Restaurant Group, LLC, **71** 319
Specialty Retailers, Inc., **24** 456
Spectra-Physics, Inc. *see* Newport Corporation.
Spectra Star, Inc., **18** 521
Spectradyne, **28** 241
Spectral Dynamics Corporation *see* Scientific- Atlanta, Inc.
Spectron MicroSystems, **18** 143
Spectrum Brands *see* United Industries Corporation.
Spectrum Club, **25** 448–50
Spectrum Communications Holdings International Limited, **24** 95
Spectrum Concepts, **10** 394–95
Spectrum Control, Inc., **67** 355–57
Spectrum Data Systems, Inc., **24** 96
Spectrum Dyed Yarns of New York, **8** 559
Spectrum Health Care Services, **13** 48
Spectrum Medical Technologies, Inc., **22** 409
Spectrum Numismatics International, Inc., **60** 146
Spectrum Organic Products, Inc., **68** 346–49

Spectrum Technology Group, Inc., **7** 378; **18** 112
Spectrumedia, **21** 361
Speech Design GmbH, **62** 38–39
Speed-O-Lac Chemical, **8** 553
SpeeDee Oil Change and Tune-Up, **25** 443–47
Speedway Motorsports, Inc., **32** 438–41
Speedway SuperAmerica LLC, **49** 330
Speedy Auto Glass, **30** 501
Speedy Europe, **54** 207
Speedy Muffler King, **10** 415; **24** 337, 339
Speizman Industries, Inc., **44** 396–98
Spelling Entertainment, **14** 460–62; **35** 402–04 (upd.)
Spenard Builders Supply *see* Lanoga Corporation.
Spencer & Spencer Systems, Inc., **18** 112
Spencer Gifts, Inc., **15** 464
Spencer Stuart and Associates, Inc., **14** 463–65
Sperry & Hutchinson Co., **12** 299; **23** 243–44
Sperry Aerospace Group, **6** 283
Sperry Corporation, *see* Unisys Corporation.
Sperry New Holland *see* New Holland N.V.
Sperry Top-Sider, Inc., **37** 377, 379
Spezialpapierfabrik Blankenstein GmbH, **64** 275
Sphere Drake Holdings Ltd., **57** 136
Sphere Inc., **8** 526; **13** 92
Sphere SA, **27** 9
Spherion Corporation, **52** 316–18
Spicecraft Co. *see* Newly Weds Foods, Inc.
Spider Software, Inc., **46** 38
Spie *see* Amec Spie S.A.
Spie Batignolles SA, **13** 206; **24** 79
Spiegel, Inc., **10** 489–91; **27** 427–31 (upd.)
SPIEGEL-Verlag Rudolf Augstein GmbH & Co. KG, **44** 399–402
Spike's Holding, Inc. *see* The Finish Line, Inc.
Spin Master, Ltd., **61** 335–38
SpinCircuit Inc., **38** 188
Spinelli Coffee Co., **51** 385
Spinnaker Exploration Company, **72** 334–36
Spinnaker Industries, Inc., **43** 276
Spinnaker Software Corp., **24** 276
Spirax-Sarco Engineering plc, **59** 384–86
SPIRE Corporation, **14** 477
Spire, Inc., **25** 183
Spirella Company of Great Britain Ltd. *see* Coats plc.
Spirit Airlines, Inc., **31** 419–21
Spirit Cruises, **29** 442–43
Spliethoff, **26** 280
SPN Resources, LLC, **65** 334
Spode *see* The Porcelain and Fine China Companies Ltd.
Spoerle Electronic, **10** 113; **50** 42

Spokane Falls Electric Light and Power Company *see* Edison Electric Illuminating Company.
Spokane Falls Water Power Company, **6** 595
Spokane Natural Gas Company, **6** 597
Spokane Street Railway Company, **6** 595
Spokane Traction Company, **6** 596
Spom Japan, **IV** 600
Spon Press, **44** 416
Spoornet, **6** 435
Sporis, **27** 151
Sporloisirs S.A., **9** 157
Sport Chalet, Inc., **16** 454–56
Sport Developpement SCA, **33** 10
Sport Maska Inc., **70** 126
Sport Supply Group, Inc., **23** 448–50
Sporting Dog Specialties, Inc., **14** 386
Sportland, **26** 160
Sportmagazine NV, **48** 347
Sportmart, Inc., **15** 469–71 *see also* Gart Sports Company.
Sports & Co. *see* Hibbett Sporting Goods, Inc.
Sports & Recreation, Inc., **17** 453–55
The Sports Authority, Inc., **16** 457–59; **43** 385–88 (upd.)
The Sports Club Company, **25** 448–51
Sports Experts Inc., **II** 652
Sports Holdings Corp., **34** 217
Sports Inc., **14** 8; **33** 10
Sports Plus, **44** 192
Sports-Tech Inc., **21** 300
Sports Traders, Inc., **18** 208; **74** 393
Sportservice Corporation, **7** 133–35
The Sportsman's Guide, Inc., **36** 443–46
Sportstown, Inc., **15** 470
Sportsystems Corporation, **7** 133, 135
Spotless Group Limited, **62** 391
Sprague Devices, Inc., **11** 84
Sprague Technologies, **21** 520
Spraysafe, **29** 98
Sprecher & Schub, **9** 10
Spreckels Sugar Company, Inc., **32** 274, 277
Spring Co., **21** 96, 246
Spring Forge Mill, **8** 412
Spring Group plc, **54** 191–93
Spring Grove Services, **45** 139–40
Spring Valley Brewery *see* Kirin Brewery Company, Limited.
Springer Verlag GmbH & Co., **IV** 611, 641
Springfield Bank, **9** 474
Springfield Gas Light Company, **38** 81
Springhouse Corp. *see* Reed Elsevier.
Springmaid International, Inc., **19** 421
Springs Industries, Inc., **V** 378–79; **19** 419–22 (upd.)
Sprint Canada Inc., **44** 49
Sprint Communications Company, L.P., **9** 478–80 *see also* Sprint Corporation; US Sprint Communications.
Sprint Corporation, **46** 373–76 (upd.)
Sprint PCS, **33** 34, 36–37; **38** 433
Sprocket Systems, **50** 320
Sprout Group, **37** 121

Starrett Corporation, 21 471–74
Star's Discount Department Stores, 16 36
Startech Semiconductor Inc., 14 183
StarTek, Inc., 79 392–95
Startel Corp., 15 125
Starter Corp., 12 457–458
Starwood Capital, 29 508
Starwood Hotels & Resorts Worldwide,
Inc., 54 345–48
The Stash Tea Company, 50 449–52
State Auto Financial Corporation, 77
415–19
State Bank of Albany, 9 228
State Bank of India, 63 354–57
State Farm Insurance Companies, 27 30;
29 397; 39 155
State Farm Mutual Automobile
Insurance Company, III 362–64; 51
341–45 (upd.)
State Finance and Thrift Company, 14
529
State Financial Services Corporation, 51
346–48
State Leed, 13 367
State Mutual Life Assurance Company, 63
29
State-o-Maine, 18 357–59
State Savings Bank and Trust Co., 11 180;
42 429
State Street Corporation, 8 491–93; 57
340–44 (upd.)
Staten Island Advance Corp. *see* Advance
Publications Inc.
Staten Island Bancorp, Inc., 39 380–82
Stater Bros. Holdings Inc., 64 364–67
Statex Petroleum, Inc., 19 70
Static, Inc., 14 430
Static Snowboards, Inc., 51 393
Station Casinos Inc., 25 452–54
Stationers Distributing Company, 14 523
Stationers, Inc., 28 74
Statoil ASA, 61 344–48 (upd.)
StatScript Management Services, 26 73
The Staubach Company, 62 338–41
Stauffer Chemical Company, 8 105–07;
21 545
Stauffer Communications, Inc., 36
339–41
Stax Records, 23 32
STC PLC, III 162–64
Stead & Miller, 13 169
Steak & Ale, 7 336; 12 373
The Steak n Shake Company, 41
387–90
Steam Boiler Works, 18 318
Steamboat Ski and Resort Corporation,
28 21
Stearns & Foster, 12 439
Stearns Catalytic World Corp., II 87; 11
413
Stearns Coal & Lumber, 6 514
Stearns, Inc., 43 389–91
Stearns Manufacturing Co., 16 297
Steego Auto Paints, 24 160
Steel Authority of India Ltd., IV
205–07; 66 317–21 (upd.)
Steel Co. of Canada Ltd. *see* Stelco Inc.
Steel Dynamics, Inc., 52 326–28

Steel Technologies Inc., 63 358–60
Steelcase Inc., 7 493–95; 27 432–35
(upd.)
Steely, IV 109
Steen Production Services, Inc., 51 248
Steenfabriek De Ruiterwaard, 14 249
Steenkolen Handelsvereniging NV, 39
176; 50 335
Stefanel SpA, 63 361–63
Stefany, 12 152
Stegbar Pty Ltd., 31 398–400
Steger Furniture Manufacturing Co., 18
493
Steiff *see* Margarete Steiff GmbH.
Steil, Inc., 8 271
Steilman Group *see* Klaus Steilmann
GmbH & Co. KG.
Stein Mart Inc., 19 423–25; 72 337–39
(upd.)
Stein Printing Company, 25 183
Stein Robaire Helm, 22 173
Steinbach Inc., 14 427
Steinbach Stores, Inc., 19 108
Steinberg Incorporated, II 662–65
Steinberger, 16 239
Steiner Corporation (Alsco), 53 308–11
Steinheil Optronik GmbH, 24 87
Steinmüller Verwaltungsgesellschaft *see*
Vereinigte Elektrizitaswerke Westfalen
AG
Steinway & Sons, 16 201; 43 170
Steinway Musical Properties, Inc., 19
426–29
Stelco Inc., IV 208–10; 51 349–52
(upd.)
Stella Bella Corporation, 19 436
Stella D'Oro Company, 7 367
Stellar Systems, Inc., 14 542
Stelmar Shipping Ltd., 52 329–31
Stelux Manufacturing Company, 13 121;
41 71
Stelwire Ltd., 51 352
Stena AB, 25 105; 29 429–30
Stena Line AB, 38 345
Stena-Sealink, 37 137
Stens Corporation, 48 34
Stentor Canadian Network Management,
6 310
Stenval Sud, 19 50
Stepan Company, 30 437–39
The Stephan Company, 60 285–88
Stephen F. Whitman & Son, Inc., 7 429
Stephens Inc., 67 129–30
Stephenson Clarke and Company, 31
368–69
Sterchi Bros. Co., 14 236
Steria SA, 49 382–85
Stericycle, Inc., 33 380–82; 74 316–18
(upd.)
STERIS Corporation, 29 449–52
Sterling Capital Partners, 57 56–57
Sterling Chemicals, Inc., 16 460–63; 78
356–61 (upd.)
Sterling Drug Inc., I 698–700
Sterling Electronics Corp., 18 496–98
Sterling Engineered Products, III 640,
642; 16 9

Sterling European Airlines A/S, 70
300–02
Sterling Forest Corp., III 264
Sterling House Corp., 42 4
Sterling Inc., 61 326–27
Sterling Industries, 13 166
Sterling Manhattan, 7 63
Sterling Organics Ltd., 12 351; 50 282
Sterling Software, Inc., 11 468–70
Sterling Stores Co. Inc., 24 148
Sterling Winthrop, 7 164; 36 174; 49
351
Stern & Stern Textiles, 11 261
Stern Bros. Investment Bank, 19 359
Stern Bros., LLC, 37 224
Stern Publishing, 38 478
Stern's, 9 209
Sternco Industries, 12 230–31
Sterner Lighting, 76 185
STET *see* Società Finanziaria Telefonica
per Azioni.
Stet Hellas, 63 378–79
Steuben Glass *see* Corning Inc.
Stevcoknit Fabrics Company, 8 141–43
Steve's Ice Cream, 16 54–55
Stevedoring Services of America Inc., 28
435–37
Steven Madden, Ltd., 37 371–73
Stevens Linen Associates, Inc., 8 272
Stevens Sound Proofing Co., 7 291
Stevens, Thompson & Runyan, Inc. *see*
CRSS Inc.
Stevens Water Monitoring Systems, 52
226
Stew Leonard's, 56 349–51
Stewart and Richey Construction Co., 51
170
Stewart & Stevenson Services Inc., 11
471–73
Stewart Enterprises, Inc., 20 481–83
Stewart Information Services
Corporation, 78 362–65
Stewart Systems, Inc., 22 352–53
Stewart, Tabori & Chang, 58 155
Stewart's Beverages, 39 383–86
Stewart's Shops Corporation, 80
360–63
Steyr Walzlager, III 625
Stichting Continuiteit AMEV, III 202
Stickley *see* L. and J.G. Stickley, Inc.
Stieber Rollkupplung GmbH, 14 63
Stihl *see* Andreas Stihl AG & Co. KG.
Stilecraft, 24 16
Stillwater Mining Company, 47 380–82
Stilwell Financial Inc. *see* Janus Capital
Group Inc.
Stimson & Valentine, 8 552
Stimson Lumber Company Inc., 78
366–69
Stimsonite Corporation, 49 38
Stinnes AG, 8 494–97; 23 451–54
(upd.); 59 387–92 (upd.)
Stirling Group plc, 62 342–44
STM Systems Corp., 11 485
STMicroelectronics NV, 52 332–35
Stock Clearing Corporation, 9 370
Stock Yards Packing Co., Inc., 37
374–76

Teixeira Duarte, **76** 94

Tejas Gas Co., **41** 359

Tejas Snacks LP, **44** 349

Tejon Ranch Company, 35 417–20

Teklogix International, **45** 346, 348

Tekmunc A/S, **17** 288

Teknekron Infoswitch Corporation, **22** 51

Teknika Electronics Corporation, **43** 459

Tekno Books, **58** 167

Tektronix, Inc., 8 517–21; **78** 385–91 (upd.)

Tel-A-Data Limited, **11** 111

TelAutograph Corporation, **29** 33–34

Telcon *see* Telegraph Construction and Maintenance Company.

Telcordia Technologies, Inc., 59 399–401

Tele-Communications, Inc., II 160–62

Tele Consulte, **14** 555

Tele Danmark *see* TDC A/S.

Télé Luxembourg, **44** 376

Tele Norte Leste Participações S.A., 80 369–72

Tele-Response and Support Services, Inc., **53** 209

Telebook, **25** 19

Telec Centre S.A., **19** 472

TeleCheck Services, **18** 542

TeleCheck Services, Inc., **11** 113

TeleChef, **33** 387, 389

Teleco Oilfield Services Inc., **6** 578; **22** 68

TeleColumbus, **11** 184

Telecom Argentina S.A., 63 375–77

Telecom Australia, 6 341–42

Telecom Canada *see* Stentor Canadian Network Management.

Telecom Corporation of New Zealand Limited, 54 355–58

Telecom Eireann, 7 508–10 *see also* eircom plc.

Telecom Finland, **57** 363

Telecom FL AG, **58** 338

Telecom Italia Mobile S.p.A., 63 378–80

Telecom Italia S.p.A., 43 415–19

Telecom New Zealand, **18** 33

Telecom-900, **59** 303

Telecom One, Inc., **29** 252

Telecom Personal S.A., **63** 376

Telecom*USA, **27** 304

Telecom Ventures, **73** 5

Telecom XXI, **59** 303

TelecomAsia, **62** 63

Telecommunications of Jamaica Ltd., **25** 101

Telecomunicações do Paraná *see* Brasil Telecom Participações S.A.

Telecredit, Inc., **6** 25

Telectronic Pacing Systems, **10** 445

Teledyne Technologies Inc., I 523–25; **10** 520–22 (upd.); **62** 358–62 (upd.)

Teleflora LLC, **19** 12; **21** 259; **28** 138; **37** 337

Telefonaktiebolaget LM Ericsson, V 334–36; **46** 407–11 (upd.)

Telefónica de Argentina S.A., 61 362–64

Telefónica de España, S.A., V 337–40

Telefonica Moviles, **69** 304, 306

Telefónica S.A., 46 412–17 (upd.)

Telefonos de Mexico S.A. de C.V., 14 488–90; **63** 381–84 (upd.)

Téléfrance, **25** 174

telegate AG, **18** 155; **47** 345, 347

Teleglobe Inc., **14** 512

Telegraph Construction and Maintenance Company, **25** 98–100

Telegraphic Service Company, **16** 166

Teleklew Productions, Inc. *see* The Welk Group, Inc.

Telekom Malaysia Bhd, 76 342–44

Telekomunikacja Polska SA, 50 464–68

Telelistas Editors Ltda., **26** 520

TeleMarketing Corporation of Louisiana, **8** 311

Telemarketing Investments, Ltd., **8** 311

Telematics International Inc., **18** 154, 156

Télémécanique, **19** 166

Telemundo Communications Group Inc., **III** 344; **24** 516; **63** 161, 166

Telenet Communications, **18** 32

Telenet Information Services, **47** 37

Telenor ASA, 69 344–46

Teleos Communications Inc., **26** 277

Telepar *see* Brasil Telecom Participaçoes S.A.

Telephone and Data Systems, Inc., 9 494–96

Telephone Company of Ireland, **7** 508

Telephone Exchange Company of Indianapolis, **14** 257

Telephone Management Corporation, **8** 310

Telephone Utilities, Inc. *see* Pacific Telecom, Inc.

Telephone Utilities of Washington *see* Pacific Telecom, Inc.

TelePizza S.A., 33 387–89

Teleport Communications Group *see* AT&T Corporation.

Teleprompter Corp., **7** 222; **10** 210; **18** 355

Telerate Systems Inc., **IV** 603, 670; **10** 276–78; **21** 68; **47** 102–03

Telerent Europe *see* Granada Group PLC.

TeleRep *see* Cox Enterprises, Inc.

TeleRoss LLC, **59** 209–211

Telesat Cable TV, Inc., **23** 293

Telesis Oil and Gas, **6** 478

Telesistema, **18** 212

Telesistema Mexico *see* Grupo Televisa.

TeleSite, U.S.A., Inc., **44** 442

TeleSphere, **8** 310; **60** 62

Telesystems SLW Inc., **10** 524

Teletrade Inc., **60** 146

Telettra S.p.A., **V** 326; **9** 10; **11** 205

Tele2 AB, **26** 331–33

Teletype Corp., **14** 569

Televimex, S.A., **18** 212

Television de Mexico, S.A., **18** 212

Television Española, S.A., 7 511–12

Télévision Française 1, 23 475–77

Television Sales and Marketing Services Ltd., **7** 79–80

Teleway Japan, **7** 118–19; **13** 482

Telex Corporation, **II** 87; **13** 127

TeleZüri AG, **53** 324

Telfin, **V** 339

Telia AB *see* TeliaSonera AB.

Telia Mobitel, **11** 19; **26** 332

TeliaSonera AB, 57 361–65 (upd.)

Telihoras Corporation, **10** 319

Telinq Inc., **10** 19

Telios Pharmaceuticals, Inc., **11** 460; **17** 288

Tellabs, Inc., 11 500–01; **40** 426–29 (upd.)

TELMARK, Inc., **57** 284

Telmex *see* Teléfonos de México S.A. de C.V.

Telpar, Inc., **14** 377

Telport, **14** 260

Telstra Corporation Limited, 50 469–72

Telrad Networks Ltd., **68** 222, 225

Teltrend, Inc., **57** 409

Telvent *see* Telecom Ventures.

Telxon Corporation, 10 523–25

Tembec Inc., 66 322–24

Temerlin McClain, **23** 479; **25** 91

TEMIC TELEFUNKEN, **34** 128, 133, 135

Temp Force, **16** 421–22; **43** 308

Temple, Barker & Sloan/Strategic Planning Associates, **III** 283

Temple Frosted Foods, **25** 278

Temple Inks Company, **13** 227

Temple-Inland Inc., IV 341–43; **31** 438–42 (upd.)

Templeton, **II** 609

TEMPO Enterprises, **II** 162

Tempo-Team, **16** 420; **43** 307

Tempur-Pedic Inc., 54 359–61

Tempus Expeditions, **13** 358

Tempus Group plc, **48** 442

TemTech Ltd., **13** 326

Ten Cate *see* Royal Ten Cate N.V.

Ten Speed Press, **27** 223

Tenacqco Bridge Partnership, **17** 170

Tenaris SA, 63 385–88

Tenby Industries Limited, **21** 350

Tencor Instruments, Inc. *see* KLA-Tencor Corporation.

Tender Loving Care Health Care Services Inc., **64** 39

Tenet Healthcare Corporation, 55 368–71 (upd.)

TenFold Corporation, 35 421–23

Tengelmann Group, 27 459–62

Tengelmann Warenhandelsgesellschaft OHG, **47** 107

Tennant Company, 13 499–501; **33** 390–93 (upd.)

Tenneco Inc., I 526–28; **10** 526–28 (upd.)

Tennessee Book Company, **11** 193

Tennessee Eastman Corporation *see* Eastman Chemical Company.

Tennessee Gas Pipeline Co., **14** 126

Tennessee Gas Transmission Co., **13** 496; **14** 125

Tennessee Insurance Company, **11** 193–94

Tennessee Paper Mills Inc. *see* Rock-Tenn Company.

Tennessee Restaurant Company, **9** 426; **30** 208–9; **72** 141–42

Thomas Nationwide Transport *see* TNT.
Thomas Nationwide Transport Limited *see* TNT Post Group N.V.
Thomas Nelson Inc., 14 498–99; **38** 454–57 (upd.)
Thomas Publishing Company, 26 482–85
Thomas Y. Crowell, **IV** 605
Thomaston Mills, Inc., 27 467–70
Thomasville Furniture Industries, Inc., 12 474–76; **74** 339–42 (upd.)
Thompson and Formby, **16** 44
Thompson Aircraft Tire Corp., **14** 42
Thompson-Hayward Chemical Co., **13** 397
Thompson Medical Company *see* Slim-Fast Nutritional Foods International Inc.
Thompson Nutritional Products, **37** 286
Thompson PBE Inc., **24** 160–61
Thomsen Greenhouses and Garden Center, Incorporated, 65 338–40
Thomson BankWatch Inc., **19** 34
Thomson-Brandt, **II** 13, 116–17; **9** 9
The Thomson Corporation, 8 525–28; **34** 435–40 (upd.); **77** 433–39 (upd.)
Thomson International, **37** 143
Thomson-Jenson Energy Limited, **13** 558
THOMSON multimedia S.A., II 116–17; **42** 377–80 (upd.)
Thomson-Ramo-Woolridge *see* TRW Inc.
Thona Group *see* Hexagon AB
Thonet Industries Inc., **14** 435–36
Thor Industries, Inc., 39 391–94
Thorn Apple Valley, Inc., 7 523–25; **22** 508–11 (upd.)
Thorn EMI plc, I 531–32 *see also* EMI plc; Thorn plc.
Thorn plc, 24 484–87
Thorncraft Inc., **25** 379
Thorndike, Doran, Paine and Lewis, Inc., **14** 530
Thornhill Inc., **64** 217
Thornton Baker *see* Grant Thornton International.
Thornton Stores, **14** 235
Thorntons plc, 46 424–26
Thoroughgood, **II** 658
Thorpe Park, **55** 378
Thorsen Realtors, **21** 96
Thos. & Wm. Molson & Company *see* The Molson Companies Limited.
Thousand Trails, Inc., 33 397–99
Thousands Springs Power Company, **12** 265
THQ, Inc., 39 395–97
Threads for Life, **49** 244
Threadz, **25** 300
Three-Diamond Company *see* Mitsubishi Shokai.
The 3DO Company, 43 426–30
3 Guys, **II** 678, **V** 35
3 Maj, **25** 469
Three Ring Asia Pacific Beer Co., Ltd., **49** 418
Three Rivers Pulp and Paper Company, **17** 281
Three Score, **23** 100

3 Suisses International, **12** 281
3Com Corporation, 11 518–21; **34** 441–45 (upd.) *see also* Palm, Inc.
3D Planet SpA, **41** 409
3dfx Interactive Inc., **54** 269–71
3Dlabs, **57** 78, 80
3i Group PLC, 73 338–40
3M Company, 61 365–70 (upd.)
360 Youth Inc., **55** 15
360networks inc., **46** 268
Threshold Entertainment, **25** 270
Thrift Drug, **V** 92
Thrift Mart, **16** 65
ThriftiCheck Service Corporation, **7** 145
Thriftimart Inc., **12** 153; **16** 452
Thriftway Food Drug, **21** 530
Thriftway Foods, **II** 624; **74** 365
Thrifty Corporation, **25** 413, 415–16; **55** 58
Thrifty PayLess, Inc., 12 477–79
Thrifty Rent-A-Car *see* Dollar Thrifty Automotive Group, Inc.
Throwing Corporation of America, **12** 501
Thrustmaster S.A., **41** 190
Thummel Schutze & Partner, **28** 141
Thunder Bay Press, **34** 3–5
Thüringer Schokoladewerk GmbH, **53** 315
Thurmond Chemicals, Inc., **27** 291
Thurston Motor Lines Inc., **12** 310
Thyssen Krupp AG, IV 221–23; **28** 452–60 (upd.)
Thyssen-Krupp Stahl AG, **26** 83
Thyssengas, **38** 406–07
TI *see* Texas Instruments.
TI Corporation, **10** 44
TI Group plc, 17 480–83
TIAA-CREF *see* Teachers Insurance and Annuity Association-College Retirement Equities Fund.
Tianjin Automobile Industry Group, **21** 164
Tianjin Bohai Brewing Company, **21** 230; **50** 202
Tianjin Paper Net, **62** 350
Tibbett & Britten Group plc, 32 449–52
TIBCO Software Inc., 79 411–14
Tiber Construction Company, **16** 286
Tichenor Media System Inc., **35** 220
Ticketmaster, 13 508–10; **37** 381–84 (upd.); **76** 349–53 (upd.)
Ticketron, **13** 508–09; **24** 438; **37** 381–82
TicketsWest.com, **59** 410, 412
Tichnor & Fields, **10** 356
Ticor Title Insurance Co., **10** 45
Tidel Systems, **II** 661; **32** 416
Tidewater Inc., 11 522–24; **37** 385–88 (upd.)
Tidewater Utilities, Inc., **45** 275, 277
Tidi Wholesale, **13** 150
TIE *see* Transport International Express.
Tien Wah Press (Pte.) Ltd., **IV** 600
Tierco Group, Inc., **27** 382
Tierney & Partners, **23** 480

Tiffany & Co., 14 500–03; **78** 396–401 (upd.)
TIG Holdings, Inc., 26 486–88
Tiger Accessories, **18** 88
Tiger Aspect Productions Ltd., 72 348–50
Tiger International, Inc., **17** 505; **18** 178; **42** 141
Tiger Management Associates, **13** 158, 256
Tiger Oats, **I** 424
TigerDirect, Inc., **52** 342–44
Tigon Corporation, **41** 288
Tiki Corp., **69** 365
Tilcon Capaldi, Inc., **64** 98
Tilcon-Connecticut Inc., 80 373–76
Tilden Interrent, **10** 419
Tile & Coal Company, **14** 248
Tilia Inc., 62 363–65
Tilley Endurables, Inc., 67 364–66
Tillinghast, Nelson & Warren Inc., **32** 459
Tillotson Corp., 15 488–90
TIM *see* Telecom Italia Mobile S.p.A.
Tim Horton's Restaurants *see* TDL Group Ltd.; Wendy's Inc.
Timber Lodge Steakhouse, Inc., 73 341–43
Timber Realization Co., **IV** 305
The Timberland Company, 13 511–14; **54** 375–79 (upd.)
Timberline Software Corporation, 15 491–93
TIMCO *see* Triad International Maintenance Corp.
Time Distribution Services, **13** 179
Time Electronics, **19** 311
Time Industries, **26** 445
Time-Life Books, Inc. *see* AOL Time Warner Inc.
Time Life Music, **44** 242
Time Out Group Ltd., 68 371–73
Time Saver Stores, Inc., **12** 112; **17** 170
Time-Sharing Information, **10** 357
Time Warner Inc., IV 673–76; **7** 526–30 (upd.) *see also* AOL Time Warner Inc.
Timeplex, **9** 32
Times Fiber Communications, Inc., **40** 35–36
The Times Mirror Company, IV 677–78; **17** 484–86 (upd.)
Times Newspapers, **8** 527
Times Publishing Group, **54** 116, 118
Timeshare Resale Brokers Inc. *see* ILX Resorts Incorporated.
TIMET *see* Titanium Metals Corporation.
Timex Corporation, 7 531–33; **25** 479–82 (upd.)
The Timken Company, 8 529–31; **42** 381–85 (upd.)
Timothy Whites, **24** 74
Tioga Gas Plant Inc., **55** 20
Tioxide Group plc, **44** 117, 119
Tip Top Drugstores plc, **24** 269
Tip Top Tailors, **29** 162
TIPC Network *see* Gateway 2000.
Tiphook PLC, **13** 530

Torchmark Corporation, **9** 506–08; **33** 405–08 (upd.)

Torfeaco Industries Limited, **19** 304

The Toro Company, 7 534–36; **26** 492–95 (upd.); **77** 440–45 (upd.)

Toromont Industries, Ltd., 21 499–501

Toronto and Scarborough Electric Railway, **9** 461

The Toronto-Dominion Bank, II 375–77; **49** 395–99 (upd.)

Toronto Electric Light Company, **9** 461

Toronto Maple Leafs *see* Maple Leaf Sports & Entertainment Ltd.

Toronto Raptors *see* Maple Leaf Sports & Entertainment Ltd.

Toronto Sun Publishing Company *see* Sun Media.

Torrent Systems, Inc., **59** 56

The Torrington Company, 13 521–24

Torrington National Bank & Trust Co., **13** 467

Torstar Corporation, 29 470–73 *see also* Harlequin Enterprises Limited.

Toscany Co., **13** 42

Tosco Corporation, 7 537–39

Toshiba Corporation, I 533–35; **12** 483–86 (upd.); **40** 435–40 (upd.)

Toshin Building Co. Ltd., **74** 348

Toshin Kaihatsu Ltd. *see* Takashimaya Co., Limited.

Toshin Paper Co., Ltd., **IV** 285

Tosoh Corporation, 70 327–30

Tostem *see* Toyo Sash Co., Ltd.

Total Audio Visual Services, **24** 95

Total Beverage Corporation, **16** 159, 161

Total Compagnie Française des Pétroles S.A., IV 557–61 *see also* TOTAL S.A.

Total Entertainment Restaurant Corporation, 46 427–29

Total Exploration S.A., **11** 537

Total Filtration Services, Inc., **61** 66

Total Fina Elf S.A., 50 478–86 (upd.)

Total Global Sourcing, Inc., **10** 498

Total Home Entertainment (THE), **39** 240, 242

Total Petroleum Corporation, **21** 500

TOTAL S.A., 24 492–97 (upd.)

Total System Services, Inc., 18 516–18

Totem Resources Corporation, 9 509–11

Totino's Finer Foods, **26** 436

TOTO LTD., III 755–56; **28** 464–66 (upd.)

Tottenham Hotspur PLC, 81 392–95

Touch America Inc., **37** 127; **44** 288

Touch-It Corp., **22** 413

Touche Remnant Holdings Ltd., **II** 356

Touche Ross *see* Deloitte Touche Tohmatsu International.

Touchstone Films *see* The Walt Disney Company.

Toupargel-Agrigel S.A., 76 354–56

Le Touquet's, SA, **48** 197

Tourang Limited, **7** 253

Touristik Union International GmbH. and Company K.G., II 163–65 *see also* Preussag AG.

Tourtime America, **56** 223

TOUSA *see* Technical Olympic USA, Inc.

Toval Japon, **IV** 680

Towa Optical Manufacturing Company, **41** 261–63

Tower Air, Inc., 28 467–69

Tower Automotive, Inc., 24 498–500

Tower Records, **9** 361; **10** 335; **11** 558; **30** 224 *see also* MTS Inc.

Towers, **II** 649

Towers Perrin, 32 458–60

Towle Manufacturing Co., **14** 482–83; **18** 69

Town & Country Corporation, 19 451–53

Town Sports International, Inc., 46 430–33

Towngas *see* Hong Kong and China Gas Company Ltd.

Townsend Hook, **IV** 296, 650, 652; **19** 226

Townsends, Inc., 64 385–87

Toxicol Laboratories, Ltd., **21** 424

The Toxicology Group, LLC *see* NOF Corporation.

Toy Biz, Inc., 18 519–21 *see also* Marvel Entertainment, Inc.

Toy Liquidators, **13** 541–43; **50** 99

Toy Park, **16** 390

Toyad Corp., **7** 296

Toymax International, Inc., 29 474–76

Toyo Ink Manufacturing, **26** 213

Toyo Kogyo, **II** 361

Toyo Microsystems Corporation, **11** 464

Toyo Pulp Co., **IV** 322

Toyo Rayon *see* Toray Industries, Inc.

Toyo Sash Co., Ltd., III 757–58

Toyo Seikan Kaisha Ltd., I 615–16

Toyo Soda Manufacturing Co *see* Tosoh Corporation.

Toyo Tire & Rubber Co., **V** 255–56; **9** 248

Toyo Toki Co., Ltd. *see* Toto.

Toyo Trust and Banking Co., **17** 349

Toyoda Automatic Loom Works, Ltd., III 636–39

Toyota Industrial Equipment, **27** 294, 296

Toyota Motor Corporation, I 203–05; **11** 528–31 (upd.); **38** 458–62 (upd.)

Toyota Tsusho America, Inc., **13** 371

Toys 'R Us, Inc., V 203–06; **18** 522–25 (upd.); **57** 370–75 (upd.)

TP Transportation, **39** 377

TPA *see* Aloha Airlines Incorporated.

TPCR Corporation *see* The Price Company.

TPG N.V., 64 388–91 (upd.)

TPS SNC, **76** 274

Trac Inc., **44** 355

Trace International Holdings, Inc., **17** 182–83; **26** 502

Tracinda Corporation, **25** 329–30

Tracker Marine *see* Bass Pro Shops, Inc.

Tracker Services, Inc., **9** 110

Traco International N.V., **8** 250; **32** 249

Tracor Inc., 17 490–92

Tractebel S.A., 20 491–93 *see also* Suez Lyonnaise des Eaux.

Tractor Supply Company, 57 376–78

Tradax, **II** 617; **13** 137

Trade Development Bank, **11** 415–17

Trade Secret Development Corp. *see* Regis Corporation.

Trade Source International, **44** 132

Trade Waste Incineration, Inc., **9** 109

Trade-Winds Environmental Restoration, Inc., **62** 389

Trademark Metals Recycling LLC, **76** 130

Trader Classified Media N.V., 57 379–82

Trader Joe's Company, 13 525–27; **50** 487–90 (upd.)

Trader Media Group, **53** 152

Trader Publications, Inc., **IV** 597

Trader Publishing Company, **12** 302

Traders Group Ltd., **11** 258

Trading Cove Associates *see* Kerzner International Limited.

Trading Post Group Pty Ltd., **57** 381

The Trading Service, **10** 278

Tradition Financial Services *see* Viel & Cie.

Traex Corporation, **8** 359

Trafalgar House Investments Ltd., **IV** 259, 711; **20** 313; **23** 161; **24** 88; **36** 322

Trafalgar House PLC, **47** 178

TrafficLeader *see* Marchex, Inc.

Traffix, Inc., 61 374–76

Trafford Park Printers, **53** 152

Trafiroad NV, **39** 239

Trailer Bridge, Inc., 41 397–99

Trailways Lines, Inc., **I** 450; **9** 425; **32** 230

Trak Auto Corporation, **16** 159–62

TRAK Communications Inc., **44** 420

TRAK Microwave Corporation, **18** 497, 513

Trammell Crow Company, 8 532–34; **57** 383–87 (upd.)

Trane, 78 402–05

Trans-Canada Air Lines *see* Air Canada.

Trans Colorado, **11** 299

Trans-Continental Leaf Tobacco Company, (TCLTC), **13** 491

Trans Continental Records, **52** 430

Trans Freight Lines, **27** 473–74

Trans International Airlines, **41** 402

Trans Louisiana Gas Company, **43** 56–57

Trans-Lux Corporation, 51 380–83

Trans-Mex, Inc. S.A. de C.V., **42** 365

Trans-Natal Coal Corp., **IV** 93

Trans Ocean Products, **8** 510

Trans-Pacific Airlines *see* Aloha Airlines Incorporated.

Trans-Resources Inc., **13** 299

Trans Tech Electric Inc. *see* Quanta Services, Inc.

Trans Thai-Malaysia, **56** 290

Trans Union Corp., **IV** 137; **6** 25; **28** 119

Trans Western Publishing, **25** 496

Trans World Airlines, Inc., I 125–27; **12** 487–90 (upd.); **35** 424–29 (upd.)

Trans-World Corp., **19** 456; **47** 231

Trans World Entertainment Corporation, 24 501–03; **68** 374–77 (upd.)

Ugly Duckling Corporation, 22 524–27
see also DriveTime Automotive Group
Inc.

Uhlmans Inc., **24** 458

UI International, **6** 444

UIB *see* United Independent Broadcasters,
Inc.

UICI, 33 418–21

Uinta Co., **6** 568

Uintah National Corp., **11** 260

UIS Co., **13** 554–55; **15** 324

Uitgeversmaatschappij Elsevier *see* Reed
Elsevier.

Uitzendbureau Amstelveen *see* Randstad
Holding n.v.

UJB Financial Corp., **14** 473

UKF *see* Unie van Kunstmestfabrieken.

Ukrop's Super Market's, Inc., 39
402–04

UL *see* Underwriters Laboratories, Inc.

Ullrich Copper, Inc. *see* Foster Wheeler
Corp.

Ullstein Langen Müller, **IV** 591

ULN *see* Union Laitière Normande.

Ulstein Holding ASA, **27** 494

Ulster Television PLC, 71 366–68

Ultimate Electronics, Inc., 18 532–34;
69 356–59 **(upd.)**

Ultimate Leisure Group PLC, 75
383–85

Ultra Mart, **16** 250

Ultra Pac, Inc., 24 512–14

Ultra Petroleum Corporation, 71
369–71

UltraCam *see* Ultrak Inc.

UltraCare Products, **18** 148

Ultrak Inc., 24 508–11

Ultralar, **13** 544

Ultralife Batteries, Inc., 58 345–48

Ultramar Diamond Shamrock
Corporation, IV 565–68; **31** 453–57
(upd.)

Ultrametl Mfg. Co., **17** 234

ULVAC, Inc., 80 388–91

Umacs of Canada Inc., **9** 513

Umberto's of New Hyde Park Pizzeria, **16**
447

Umbro Holdings Ltd. *see* Stone
Manufacturing Company.

UMC *see* United Microelectronics Corp.

UMG *see* Universal Music Group.

UMI Company, **29** 58

NV Umicore SA, 47 411–13

Umpqua River Navigation Company, **13**
100

Unadulterated Food Products, Inc., **11**
449

UNAT, **III** 197–98

Unbrako Socket Screw Company Ltd., **30**
429

Uncas-Merchants National Bank, **13** 467

UNCF *see* United Negro College Fund,
Inc.

Uncle Ben's Inc., 22 528–30

Under Armour Performance Apparel, 61
381–83

Underwood, **24** 269

Underwriter for the Professions Insurance
Company, **55** 128

Underwriters Laboratories, Inc., 30
467–70

Underwriters Reinsurance Co., **10** 45

Unefon, S.A., **39** 194, 196

UNELCO *see* Union Electrica de Canarias
S.A.

Unelec, Inc., **13** 398

UNG *see* United National Group, Ltd.

Ungaro SA, **62** 313

Uni-Cast *see* Sturm, Ruger & Company,
Inc.

Uni Europe, **III** 211

Uni-Marts, Inc., 17 499–502

Uni-President Group, **49** 460

Unibail SA, 40 444–46

Unibanco Holdings S.A., 73 350–53

Unibank, **40** 336; **50** 149–50

Unic *see* GIB Group.

Unica Corporation, 77 450–54

Unicapital, Inc., **15** 281

Unicare Health Facilities, **6** 182; **25** 525

Unicco Security Services, **27** 22

Unice, **56** 335

UNICEF *see* United Nations International
Children's Emergency Fund
(UNICEF).

Unicel *see* Rural Cellular Corporation.

Unicer, **9** 100

Unichem, **25** 73

Unichema International, **13** 228

Unicom Corporation, 29 486–90 **(upd.)**
see also Exelon Corporation.

Unicon Producing Co., **10** 191

Unicoolait, **19** 51

UNICOR *see* Federal Prison Industries,
Inc.

Unicord Company, **24** 115; **64** 60

UniCorp, **8** 228

UniCredito Italiano, **50** 410

Uniden, **14** 117

Unidrive, **47** 280

UniDynamics Corporation, **8** 135

Uniface Holding B.V., **10** 245; **30** 142

Unifi, Inc., 12 501–03; **62** 372–76
(upd.)

Unified Energy System of Russia *see* RAO
Unified Energy System of Russia.

Unified Western Grocers, **31** 25

UniFirst Corporation, 21 505–07

Uniflex Corporation, **53** 236

Uniforce Services Inc., **40** 119

Unigate PLC, II 586–87; **28** 488–91
(upd.) *see also* Uniq Plc.

Unigesco Inc., **II** 653

Uniglory, **13** 211

Unigro *see* Laurus N.V.

Unigroup, **15** 50

UniHealth America, **11** 378–79

Unijoh Sdn, Bhd, **47** 255

Unik S.A., **23** 170–171

Unilab Corp., **26** 391

Unilever PLC/Unilever N.V., II 588–91;
7 542–45 **(upd.); 32** 472–78 **(upd.)**

Unilife Assurance Group, **III** 273

UniLife Insurance Co., **22** 149

Unilog SA, 42 401–03

Uniloy Milacron Inc., **53** 230

UniMac Companies, **11** 413

Unimetal, **30** 252

Uninsa, **I** 460

Union Aéromaritime de Transport *see*
UTA.

Union Bag–Camp Paper Corp. *see* Union
Camp Corporation.

Union Bank *see* State Street Boston
Corporation.

Union Bank of California, 16 496–98
see also UnionBanCal Corporation.

Union Bank of New York, **9** 229

Union Bank of Scotland, **10** 337

Union Bank of Switzerland, II 378–79
see also UBS AG.

Union Bay Sportswear, **17** 460

Union Biscuits *see* Leroux S.A.S.

Union Camp Corporation, IV 344–46

Union Carbide Corporation, I 399–401;
9 516–20 **(upd.); 74** 358–63 **(upd.)**

Union Cervecera, **9** 100

Union Colliery Company *see* Union
Electric Company.

Union Commerce Corporation, **11** 181

Union Commerciale, **19** 98

Union Corporation *see* Gencor Ltd.

Union des Assurances de Paris, III
391–94

Union des Coopératives Bressor, **25** 85

Union des Cooperatives Laitières *see*
Unicoolait.

Union des Mines, **52** 362

Union des Transports Aériens *see* UTA.

Union Electric Company, V 741–43 *see*
also Ameren Corporation.

Unión Electrica Fenosa *see* Unión Fenosa
S.A.

Union Equity Co-Operative Exchange, **7**
175

Unión Fenosa, S.A., 51 387–90

Union Financiera, **19** 189

Union Financière de France Banque SA,
52 360–62

Union Fork & Hoe Company *see* Acorn
Products, Inc.

Union Gas & Electric Co., **6** 529

l'Union Générale des Pétroles, **IV** 560

Union Hardware, **22** 115

Union Laitière Normande *see* Compagnie
Laitière Européenne.

Union Levantina de Seguros, **III** 179

Union Light, Heat & Power Company *see*
Cincinnati Gas & Electric Company.

Union Minière *see* NV Umicore SA.

Union Mutual Life Insurance Company
see UNUM Corp.

Union National Bank of Wilmington, **25**
540

Union of European Football Association,
27 150

Union of Food Co-ops, **II** 622

Union Oil Co., **9** 266

Union Oil Co. of California *see* Unocal
Corporation.

Union Pacific Corporation, V 529–32;
28 492–500 **(upd.); 79** 435–46 **(upd.)**

Union Pacific Resources Group, **52** 30

ValleyCrest Companies, 81 411–14
(upd.)
Vallourec SA, 54 391–94
Valmet Corporation, III 647–49 see also
Metso Corporation.
Valmont Industries, Inc., 19 469–72
Valois S.A. see AptarGroup, Inc.
Valores Industriales S.A., 19 473–75
The Valspar Corporation, 8 552–54; 32
483–86 (upd.); 77 462–68 (upd.)
Valtek International, Inc., 17 147
Value America, 29 312
Value City Department Stores, Inc., 38
473–75
Value Foods Ltd., 11 239
Value Giant Stores, 12 478
Value House, II 673
Value Investors, III 330
Value Line, Inc., 16 506–08; 73 358–61
(upd.)
Value Merchants Inc., 13 541–43
Value Rent-A-Car, 9 350; 23 354
ValueClick, Inc., 49 432–34
Valueland, 8 482
ValueVision International, Inc., 22
534–36; 27 337
ValuJet, Inc. see AirTran Holdings, Inc.
Valvtron, 11 226
VAMED Gruppe, 56 141
Van Ameringen-Haebler, Inc., 9 290
Van Camp Seafood Company, Inc., 7
556–57 see also Chicken of the Sea
International.
Van Cleef & Arpels Inc., 26 145
Van de Kamp's, Inc., 7 430
Van der Moolen Holding NV, 37 224
Van Dorn Company, 13 190
Van Houtte Inc., 39 409–11
Van Kirk Chocolate, 7 429
Van Kok-Ede, II 642
Van Lanschot NV, 79 456–59
Van Leer Containers Inc., 30 397
Van Leer Holding, Inc., 9 303, 305
Van Leer N.V. see Royal Packaging
Industries Van Leer N.V.; Greif Inc.
Van Mar, Inc., 18 88
Van Nostrand Reinhold, 8 526
Van Ommeren, 41 339–40
Van Sickle, IV 485
Van Waters & Rogers, 8 99; 41 340
Van Wezel, 26 278–79
Van Wijcks Waalsteenfabrieken, 14 249
Van's Aircraft, Inc., 65 349–51
Vanadium Alloys Steel Company
(VASCO), 13 295–96
Vanant Packaging Corporation, 8 359
Vance International Airways, 8 349
Vance Publishing Corporation, 64
398–401
Vanderbilt Mortgage and Finance, 13 154
Vanessa and Biffi, 11 226
The Vanguard Group, Inc., 14 530–32;
34 486–89 (upd.)
Vanguard Health Systems Inc., 70
338–40
Vanguard International Semiconductor
Corp., 47 385
Vanity Fair see VF Corporation.

Vans, Inc., 16 509–11; 47 423–26
(upd.)
Vanstar, 13 176
Vantage Analysis Systems, Inc., 11 490
Vantage Components see Bell
Microproducts Inc.
Vantive Corporation, 33 333; 38 431–32
Varco International, Inc., 42 418–20
Varco-Pruden, Inc., 8 544–46
Vare Corporation, 8 366
Vari-Lite International, Inc., 35 434–36
Varian Associates Inc., 12 504–06
Varian, Inc., 48 407–11 (upd.)
Varibus Corporation see Gulf States
Utilities Company.
Variety Wholesalers, Inc., 73 362–64
Variflex, Inc., 51 391–93
Variform, Inc., 12 397
VARIG S.A. (Viação Aérea
Rio-Grandense), 6 133–35; 29
494–97 (upd.)
Varity Corporation, III 650–52
Varlen Corporation, 16 512–14
Varney Speed Lines see Continental
Airlines, Inc.
Varo, 7 235, 237
Varsity Spirit Corp., 15 516–18
Varta AG, 23 495–99
VASCO Data Security International,
Inc., 79 460–63
Vascoloy-Ramet, 13 295
Vaserie Trevigiane International S.p.A., 73
248–49
VASP (Viação Aérea de Sao Paulo), 31
444–45
Vasset, S.A., 17 362–63
Vast Solutions, 39 24
Vastar Resources, Inc., 24 524–26
Vattenfall AB, 57 395–98
Vaughan Harmon Systems Ltd., 25 204
Vaughan Printers Inc., 23 100
Vaungarde, Inc., 22 175
Vauxhall Motors Limited, 73 365–69
Vax Ltd., 73 331–32
VBB Viag-Bayernwerk-Beteiligungs-
Gesellschaft mbH, IV 232; 50 170
VCA Antech, Inc., 58 353–55
VCH Publishing Group see John Wiley &
Sons, Inc.
VDM Nickel-Technologie AG, IV 89
VEAG, 57 395, 397
Veba A.G., I 542–43; 15 519–21 (upd.)
see also E.On AG.
Vebego International BV, 49 435–37
VECO International, Inc., 7 558–59
Vector Automotive Corporation, 13 61
Vector Casa de Bolsa, 21 413
Vector Gas Ltd., 13 458
Vector Group Ltd., 35 437–40 (upd.)
Vector Video, Inc., 9 74
Vectra Bank Colorado, 53 378
Vectura Holding Company L.L.C., 69
197
Veda International, 54 395–96
Vedelectric, 13 544
Vedior NV, 35 441–43
Veeco Instruments Inc., 32 487–90
Veeder-Root Company, 7 116–17

VeggieTales see Big Idea Productions, Inc.
Veit Companies, 43 440–42
Vel-Tex Chemical, 16 270
Velcarta S.p.A., 17 281
Velcro Industries N.V., 19 476–78; 72
361–64 (upd.)
Velda Farms, Inc., 26 448
VeloBind, Inc., 10 314
Velocity Express Corporation, 49
438–41
Velva-Sheen Manufacturing Co., 23 66
Vemar, 7 558
Venator Group Inc., 35 444–49 (upd.)
see also Foot Locker Inc.
Venbo Comercio de Alimentos Ltda., 74
48
Vencemos, 20 124
Vencor, Inc., 16 515–17
Vendex International N.V., 13 544–46
see also Koninklijke Vendex KBB N.V.
(Royal Vendex KBB N.V.).
Vendôme Luxury Group plc, 27 487–89
Vendors Supply of America, Inc., 7
241–42; 25 241
Venetian Casino Resort, LLC, 47
427–29
Venevision, 54 72–73, 75
Venevision, 24 516, 517
Ventana Medical Systems, Inc., 75
392–94
Ventshade Company, 40 299–300
Ventura, 29 356–57
Venture Out RV, 26 193
Venture Stores Inc., 12 507–09
Ventures Limited, 49 137
Venturi, Inc., 9 72
Veolia Environnement SA, 66 68
Vepco see Virginia Electric and Power
Company.
Vera Imported Parts, 11 84
Verafumos Ltd., 12 109
Veragon Corporation see Drypers
Corporation.
Veratex Group, 13 149–50
Veravision, 24 510
Verbatim Corporation, 14 533–35; 74
371–74 (upd.)
Verbundnetz Gas AG, 38 408
Verd-A-Fay, 13 398
Verdugt, 70 143, 145
Vereinigte Elektrizitäts und Bergwerke
A.G. see VEBA A.G.
Vereinigte Elektrizitätswerke Westfalen
AG, IV V 744–47
Vereinigte Glanzstoff-Fabriken, 13 21
Vereinigte Industrie-Unternehmungen
Aktiengesellschaft see VIAG
Vereinigte Papierwerke Schickedanz AG,
26 384
Vereinigte Stahlwerke AG, 14 327
Verenigde Bedrijven Bredero, 26 280
Verenigde Nederlandse Uitgeverijen see
VNU N.V.
Verenigde Spaarbank Groep see VSB
Groep.
Veri-Best Baking Co., 56 29
Veridian Corporation, 54 395–97
Verifact Inc. (IVI), 46 251

W.A. Whitney Company, 53 353–56
W. Atlee Burpee & Co., 27 505–08
W.B Doner & Co., 56 369–72
W.B. Saunders Co., IV 623–24
W.C. Bradley Co., 69 363–65
W.C.G. Sports Industries Ltd. *see* Canstar
Sports Inc.
W.C. Smith & Company Limited, 14 339
W. Duke Sons & Company, 27 128
W.E. Andrews Co., Inc., 25 182
W.E. Dillon Company, Ltd., 21 499
W.F. Kaiser, 60 364
W.F. Linton Company, 9 373
W.G. Yates & Sons Construction
Company *see* The Yates Companies,
Inc.
W.H. Brady Co., 16 518–21 *see also*
Brady Corporation.
W. H. Braum, Inc., 80 407–10
W.H. Gunlocke Chair Co. *see* Gunlocke
Company.
W.H. Smith & Son (Alacra) Ltd., 15 473
W H Smith Group PLC, V 211–13
W Jordan (Cereals) Ltd., 74 382–84
W.L. Gore & Associates, Inc., 14
538–40; 60 321–24 (upd.)
W.M. Bassett Furniture Co. *see* Bassett
Furniture Industries, Inc.
W.O. Daley & Company, 10 387
W.P. Carey & Co. LLC, 49 446–48
W.R. Bean & Son, 19 335
W.R. Berkley Corporation, 15 525–27;
74 385–88 (upd.)
W.R. Breen Company, 11 486
W.R. Case & Sons Cutlery Company *see*
Zippo Manufacturing Company.
W.R. Grace & Company, I 547–50; 50
522–29 (upd.)
W. Rosenlew, IV 350
W.S. Barstow & Company, 6 575
W.T. Grant Co., 16 487
W.T. Rawleigh, 17 105
W.W. Grainger, Inc., V 214–15; 26
537–39 (upd.); 68 392–95 (upd.)
W.W. Kimball Company, 12 296; 18 44
W.W. Norton & Company, Inc., 28
518–20
Waban Inc., 13 547–49 *see also*
HomeBase, Inc.
Wabash National Corp., 13 550–52
Wabash Valley Power Association, 6 556
Wabtec Corporation, 40 451–54
Wachbrit Insurance Agency, 21 96
Wachovia Bank of Georgia, N.A., 16
521–23
Wachovia Bank of South Carolina,
N.A., 16 524–26
Wachovia Corporation, 12 516–20; 46
442–49 (upd.)
Wachtell, Lipton, Rosen & Katz, 47
435–38
The Wackenhut Corporation, 14
541–43; 63 423–26 (upd.)
Wacker-Chemie GmbH, 35 454–58
Wacker Oil Inc., 11 441
Waco Aircraft Company, 27 98
Wacoal Corp., 25 520–24
Waddell & Reed, Inc., 22 540–43

Wade Smith, 28 27, 30
Wadsworth Inc., 8 526
WaferTech, 18 20; 43 17; 47 385
Waffle House Inc., 14 544–45; 60
325–27 (upd.)
Wagenseller & Durst, 25 249
Waggener Edstrom, 42 424–26
The Wagner & Brown Investment Group,
9 248
Wagner Castings Company, 16 474–75
Wagner Litho Machinery Co., 13 369–70
Wagner Spray Tech, 18 555
Wagonlit Travel, 22 128; 55 90
Wagons-Lits, 27 11; 29 443; 37 250–52
Waha Oil Company *see* Natinal Oil
Corporation.
AB Wahlbecks, 25 464
Waitaki International Biosciences Co., 17
288
Waitrose Ltd. *see* John Lewis Partnership
plc.
Wakefern Food Corporation, 33 434–37
Wako Shoji Co. Ltd. *see* Wacoal Corp.
Wal-Mart de Mexico, S.A. de C.V., 35
459–61 (upd.)
Wal-Mart Stores, Inc., V 216–17; 8
555–57 (upd.); 26 522–26 (upd.); 63
427–32 (upd.)
Walbridge Aldinger Co., 38 480–82
Walbro Corporation, 13 553–55
Walchenseewerk AG, 23 44
Waldbaum, Inc., 19 479–81
Walden Book Company Inc., 17
522–24
Waldorf Corporation, 59 350
Wales & Company, 14 257
Walgreen Co., V 218–20; 20 511–13
(upd.); 65 352–56 (upd.)
Walk Haydel & Associates, Inc., 25 130
Walk Softly, Inc., 25 118
Walker & Lee, 10 340
Walker Dickson Group Limited, 26 363
Walker Digital, 57 296–98
Walker Interactive Systems, 11 78; 25 86
Walker Manufacturing Company, 19
482–84
Walkers Shortbread Ltd., 79 464–67
Walkers Snack Foods Ltd., 70 350–52
Walkins Manufacturing Corp., III 571;
20 362
Walkup's Merchant Express Inc., 27 473
Wall Drug Store, Inc., 40 455–57
Wall Street Deli, Inc., 33 438–41
Wallace & Tiernan Group, 11 361; 52
374
The Wallace Berrie Company *see* Applause
Inc.
Wallace Computer Services, Inc., 36
507–10
Wallace International Silversmiths, 14
482–83
Wallbergs Fabriks A.B., 8 14
Wallin & Nordstrom *see* Nordstrom, Inc.
Wallis *see* Sears plc.
Wallis Arnold Enterprises, Inc., 21 483
Wallis Tractor Company, 21 502
Walnut Capital Partners, 62 46–47
Walrus, Inc., 18 446

Walsin-Lihwa, 13 141
Walsworth Publishing Company, Inc.,
78 445–48
The Walt Disney Company, II 172–74;
6 174–77 (upd.); 30 487–91 (upd.);
63 433–38 (upd.)
Walter Bau, 27 136, 138
Walter E. Heller, 17 324
Walter Herzog GmbH, 16 514
Walter Industries, Inc., III 765–67; 22
544–47 (upd.); 72 368–73 (upd.)
Walter Kidde & Co., 73 208
Walter Wilson, 49 18
Walter Wright Mammoet, 26 280
Walton Manufacturing, 11 486
Walton Monroe Mills, Inc., 8 558–60
Wanadoo S.A., 75 400–02
Wang Global, 39 176–78
Wang Laboratories, Inc., III 168–70; 6
284–87 (upd.)
WAP, 26 420
Waples-Platter Co., II 625
Warbasse-Cogeneration Technologies
Partnership, 35 479
Warburg Pincus, 9 524; 14 42; 24 373;
61 403; 73 138
Warburg USB, 38 291
Warburtons Bakery Cafe, Inc., 18 37
Ward's Communications, 22 441
Wards *see* Circuit City Stores, Inc.
Waremart *see* WinCo Foods.
WARF *see* Wisconsin Alumni Research
Foundation.
Waring and LaRosa, 12 167
The Warnaco Group Inc., 12 521–23;
46 450–54 (upd.) *see also* Authentic
Fitness Corp.
Warner & Swasey Co., 8 545
Warner Communications Inc., II
175–77 *see also* AOL Time Warner Inc.
Warner Cosmetics, III 48; 8 129
Warner Electric, 58 67
Warner-Lambert Co., I 710–12; 10
549–52 (upd.)
Warner Roadshow Film Distributors
Greece SA, 58 359
Warners' Stellian Inc., 67 384–87
Warrantech Corporation, 53 357–59
Warrell Corporation, 68 396–98
Warren Apparel Group Ltd., 39 257
Warren Bancorp Inc., 55 52
Warren Bank, 13 464
Warren Frozen Foods, Inc., 61 174
Warren, Gorham & Lamont, 8 526
Warren Oilfield Services, 9 363
Warren Petroleum, 18 365, 367; 49 121
Warrick Industries, 31 338
Warrington Products Ltd. *see* Canstar
Sports Inc.
Warrior River Coal Company, 7 281
Warwick Chemicals, 13 461
Warwick International Ltd., 13 462
Warwick Valley Telephone Company, 55
382–84
Wasatch Gas Co., 6 568
Wascana Energy Inc., 13 556–58
Washburn Graphics Inc., 23 100
The Washington Companies, 33 442–45

Index to Industries

Automotive

Cummins Engine Company, Inc., I; 12
(upd.); 40 (upd.)
Custom Chrome, Inc., 16
Daihatsu Motor Company, Ltd., 7; 21
(upd.)
Daimler-Benz A.G., I; 15 (upd.)
DaimlerChrysler AG, 34 (upd.); 64 (upd.)
Dana Corporation, I; 10 (upd.)
Danaher Corporation, 77 (upd.)
Deere & Company, 42 (upd.)
Delphi Automotive Systems Corporation,
45
Don Massey Cadillac, Inc., 37
Donaldson Company, Inc., 49 (upd.)
Douglas & Lomason Company, 16
DriveTime Automotive Group Inc., 68
(upd.)
Ducati Motor Holding S.p.A., 30
Eaton Corporation, I; 10 (upd.)
Echlin Inc., I; 11 (upd.)
Edelbrock Corporation, 37
Faurecia S.A., 70
Federal-Mogul Corporation, I; 10 (upd.);
26 (upd.)
Ferrari S.p.A., 13; 36 (upd.)
Fiat SpA, I; 11 (upd.); 50 (upd.)
FinishMaster, Inc., 24
Ford Motor Company, I; 11 (upd.); 36
(upd.); 64 (upd.)
Ford Motor Company, S.A. de C.V., 20
Fruehauf Corporation, I
General Motors Corporation, I; 10 (upd.);
36 (upd.); 64 (upd.)
Gentex Corporation, 26
Genuine Parts Company, 9; 45 (upd.)
GKN plc, 38 (upd.)
Group 1 Automotive, Inc., 52
Harley-Davidson Inc., 7; 25 (upd.)
Hastings Manufacturing Company, 56
Hayes Lemmerz International, Inc., 27
The Hertz Corporation, 33 (upd.)
Hino Motors, Ltd., 7; 21 (upd.)
Holden Ltd., 62
Holley Performance Products Inc., 52
Hometown Auto Retailers, Inc., 44
Honda Motor Company Limited (Honda
Giken Kogyo Kabushiki Kaisha), I; 10
(upd.); 29 (upd.)
Hyundai Group, 56 (upd.)
Insurance Auto Auctions, Inc., 23
Isuzu Motors, Ltd., 9; 23 (upd.); 57
(upd.)
INTERMET Corporation, 77 (upd.)
Jardine Cycle & Carriage Ltd., 73
Kawasaki Heavy Industries, Ltd., 63
(upd.)
Kelsey-Hayes Group of Companies, 7; 27
(upd.)
Key Safety Systems, Inc., 63
Kia Motors Corporation, 12; 29 (upd.)
Kwik-Fit Holdings plc, 54
Lazy Days RV Center, Inc., 69
Lear Corporation, 71 (upd.)
Lear Seating Corporation, 16
Les Schwab Tire Centers, 50
Lithia Motors, Inc., 41
LKQ Corporation, 71
Lookers plc, 71

Lotus Cars Ltd., 14
Lund International Holdings, Inc., 40
Mack Trucks, Inc., I; 22 (upd.); 61 (upd.)
The Major Automotive Companies, Inc.,
45
Marcopolo S.A., 79
Masland Corporation, 17
Mazda Motor Corporation, 9; 23 (upd.);
63 (upd.)
Mel Farr Automotive Group, 20
Metso Corporation, 30 (upd.)
Midas Inc., 10; 56 (upd.)
Mitsubishi Motors Corporation, 9; 23
(upd.); 57 (upd.)
Monaco Coach Corporation, 31
Monro Muffler Brake, Inc., 24
Montupet S.A., 63
National R.V. Holdings, Inc., 32
Navistar International Corporation, I; 10
(upd.)
New Flyer Industries Inc. 78
Nissan Motor Co., Ltd., I; 11 (upd.); 34
(upd.)
O'Reilly Automotive, Inc., 26; 78 (upd.)
Officine Alfieri Maserati S.p.A., 13
Oshkosh Truck Corporation, 7
Paccar Inc., I
PACCAR Inc., 26 (upd.)
Pennzoil-Quaker State Company, IV; 20
(upd.); 50 (upd.)
Penske Corporation, 19 (upd.)
The Pep Boys—Manny, Moe & Jack, 11;
36 (upd.); 81 (upd.)
Perusahaan Otomobil Nasional Bhd., 62
Peugeot S.A., I
Piaggio & C. S.p.A., 20
Pirelli & C. S.p.A., 75 (upd.)
Porsche AG, 13; 31 (upd.)
PSA Peugeot Citroen S.A., 28 (upd.)
R&B, Inc., 51
Randon S.A., 79
Regie Nationale des Usines Renault, I
Renault Argentina S.A., 67
Renault S.A., 26 (upd.); 74 (upd.)
Repco Corporation Ltd., 74
Republic Industries, Inc., 26
The Reynolds and Reynolds Company, 50
Robert Bosch GmbH., I; 16 (upd.); 43
(upd.)
RockShox, Inc., 26
Rockwell Automation, I; 11 (upd.); 43
(upd.)
Rolls-Royce plc, I; 21 (upd.)
Ron Tonkin Chevrolet Company, 55
Rover Group Ltd., 7; 21 (upd.)
Saab Automobile AB, 32 (upd.)
Saab-Scania A.B., I; 11 (upd.)
Safelite Glass Corp., 19
Safety Components International, Inc., 63
Saturn Corporation, 7; 21 (upd.); 80
(upd.)
Sealed Power Corporation, I
Sheller-Globe Corporation, I
Sixt AG, 39
Skoda Auto a.s., 39
Sonic Automotive, Inc., 77
Spartan Motors Inc., 14
SpeeDee Oil Change and Tune-Up, 25

SPX Corporation, 10; 47 (upd.)
Standard Motor Products, Inc., 40
Strattec Security Corporation, 73
Superior Industries International, Inc., 8
Suzuki Motor Corporation, 9; 23 (upd.);
59 (upd.)
Sytner Group plc, 45
Tower Automotive, Inc., 24
Toyota Motor Corporation, I; 11 (upd.);
38 (upd.)
TransPro, Inc., 71
Triumph Motorcycles Ltd., 53
TRW Automotive Holdings Corp., 75
(upd.)
TRW Inc., 14 (upd.)
Ugly Duckling Corporation, 22
United Auto Group, Inc., 26; 68 (upd.)
United Technologies Automotive Inc., 15
Universal Technical Institute, Inc., 81
Valeo, 23; 66 (upd.)
Vauxhall Motors Limited, 73
Volkswagen Aktiengesellschaft, I; 11
(upd.); 32 (upd.)
Walker Manufacturing Company, 19
Winnebago Industries Inc., 7; 27 (upd.)
Woodward Governor Company, 49 (upd.)
ZF Friedrichshafen AG, 48
Ziebart International Corporation, 30; 66
(upd.)

Beverages
A & W Brands, Inc., 25
Adolph Coors Company, I; 13 (upd.); 36
(upd.)
AG Barr plc, 64
Allied Domecq PLC, 29
Allied-Lyons PLC, I
Anchor Brewing Company, 47
Anheuser-Busch Companies, Inc., I; 10
(upd.); 34 (upd.)
Asahi Breweries, Ltd., I; 20 (upd.); 52
(upd.)
Asia Pacific Breweries Limited, 59
August Schell Brewing Company Inc., 59
Bacardi Limited, 18
Baltika Brewery Joint Stock Company, 65
Banfi Products Corp., 36
Baron de Ley S.A., 74
Baron Philippe de Rothschild S.A., 39
Bass PLC, I; 15 (upd.); 38 (upd.)
BBAG Osterreichische
Brau-Beteiligungs-AG, 38
Beringer Blass Wine Estates Ltd., 22; 66
(upd.)
The Bernick Companies, 75
Bols Distilleries NV, 74
The Boston Beer Company, Inc., 18; 50
(upd.)
Brauerei Beck & Co., 9; 33 (upd.)
Britannia Soft Drinks Ltd. (Britvic), 71
Brown-Forman Corporation, I; 10 (upd.);
38 (upd.)
Budweiser Budvar, National Corporation,
59
Cadbury Schweppes PLC, 49 (upd.)
Canandaigua Brands, Inc., 13; 34 (upd.)
Cantine Giorgio Lungarotti S.R.L., 67
Carlsberg A/S, 9; 29 (upd.)

Bio-Technology

Chiron Corporation, 10; 36 (upd.)
Covance Inc., 30
CryoLife, Inc., 46
Cytyc Corporation, 69
Delta and Pine Land Company, 33
Dionex Corporation, 46
Embrex, Inc., 72
Enzo Biochem, Inc., 41
Eurofins Scientific S.A., 70
Gen-Probe Incorporated, 79
Genentech, Inc., 32 (upd.)
Genzyme Corporation, 38 (upd.)
Gilead Sciences, Inc., 54
Howard Hughes Medical Institute, 39
Huntingdon Life Sciences Group plc, 42
IDEXX Laboratories, Inc., 23
ImClone Systems Inc., 58
Immunex Corporation, 14; 50 (upd.)
IMPATH Inc., 45
Incyte Genomics, Inc., 52
Inverness Medical Innovations, Inc., 63
Invitrogen Corporation, 52
The Judge Group, Inc., 51
Life Technologies, Inc., 17
LifeCell Corporation, 77
Lonza Group Ltd., 73
Martek Biosciences Corporation, 65
Medtronic, Inc., 30 (upd.)
Millipore Corporation, 25
Minntech Corporation, 22
Mycogen Corporation, 21
New Brunswick Scientific Co., Inc., 45
Pacific Ethanol, Inc., 81
Qiagen N.V., 39
Quintiles Transnational Corporation, 21
Seminis, Inc., 29
Serologicals Corporation, 63
Sigma-Aldrich Corporation, 36 (upd.)
Starkey Laboratories, Inc., 52
STERIS Corporation, 29
Stratagene Corporation, 70
Tanox, Inc., 77
TECHNE Corporation, 52
TriPath Imaging, Inc., 77
Waters Corporation, 43
Whatman plc, 46
Wisconsin Alumni Research Foundation, 65
Wyeth, 50 (upd.)

Chemicals

A. Schulman, Inc., 8
Aceto Corp., 38
Air Products and Chemicals, Inc., I; 10 (upd.); 74 (upd.)
Airgas, Inc., 54
Akzo Nobel N.V., 13; 41 (upd.)
Albemarle Corporation, 59
AlliedSignal Inc., 22 (upd.)
American Cyanamid, I; 8 (upd.)
American Vanguard Corporation, 47
Arch Chemicals Inc. 78
ARCO Chemical Company, 10
Asahi Denka Kogyo KK, 64
Atanor S.A., 62
Atochem S.A., I
Avantium Technologies BV, 79
Avecia Group PLC, 63

Baker Hughes Incorporated, 22 (upd.); 57 (upd.)
Balchem Corporation, 42
BASF Aktiengesellschaft, I; 18 (upd.); 50 (upd.)
Bayer A.G., I; 13 (upd.); 41 (upd.)
Betz Laboratories, Inc., I; 10 (upd.)
The BFGoodrich Company, 19 (upd.)
BOC Group plc, I; 25 (upd.); 78 (upd.)
Brenntag AG, 8; 23 (upd.)
Burmah Castrol PLC, 30 (upd.)
Cabot Corporation, 8; 29 (upd.)
Calgon Carbon Corporation, 73
Caliper Life Sciences, Inc., 70
Cambrex Corporation, 16
Catalytica Energy Systems, Inc., 44
Celanese Corporation, I
Celanese Mexicana, S.A. de C.V., 54
Chemcentral Corporation, 8
Chemi-Trol Chemical Co., 16
Church & Dwight Co., Inc., 29
Ciba-Geigy Ltd., I; 8 (upd.)
The Clorox Company, III; 22 (upd.); 81 (upd.)
Croda International Plc, 45
Crompton Corporation, 9; 36 (upd.)
Cytec Industries Inc., 27
Degussa-Hüls AG, 32 (upd.)
DeKalb Genetics Corporation, 17
The Dexter Corporation, I; 12 (upd.)
Dionex Corporation, 46
The Dow Chemical Company, I; 8 (upd.); 50 (upd.)
DSM N.V., I; 56 (upd.)
Dynaction S.A., 67
E.I. du Pont de Nemours & Company, I; 8 (upd.); 26 (upd.)
Eastman Chemical Company, 14; 38 (upd.)
Ecolab Inc., I; 13 (upd.); 34 (upd.)
Elementis plc, 40 (upd.)
Engelhard Corporation, 72 (upd.)
English China Clays Ltd., 15 (upd.); 40 (upd.)
Enterprise Rent-A-Car Company, 69 (upd.)
Equistar Chemicals, LP, 71
Ercros S.A., 80
ERLY Industries Inc., 17
Ethyl Corporation, I; 10 (upd.)
Ferro Corporation, 8; 56 (upd.)
Firmenich International S.A., 60
First Mississippi Corporation, 8
Formosa Plastics Corporation, 14; 58 (upd.)
Fort James Corporation, 22 (upd.)
G.A.F., I
The General Chemical Group Inc., 37
Georgia Gulf Corporation, 9; 61 (upd.)
Givaudan SA, 43
Great Lakes Chemical Corporation, I; 14 (upd.)
Guerbet Group, 46
H.B. Fuller Company, 32 (upd.); 75 (upd.)
Hauser, Inc., 46
Hawkins Chemical, Inc., 16
Henkel KGaA, 34 (upd.)

Hercules Inc., I; 22 (upd.); 66 (upd.)
Hoechst A.G., I; 18 (upd.)
Hoechst Celanese Corporation, 13
Huls A.G., I
Huntsman Chemical Corporation, 8
IMC Fertilizer Group, Inc., 8
Imperial Chemical Industries PLC, I; 50 (upd.)
International Flavors & Fragrances Inc., 9; 38 (upd.)
Israel Chemicals Ltd., 55
Kemira Oyj, 70
Koppers Industries, Inc., I; 26 (upd.)
L'Air Liquide SA, I; 47 (upd.)
Lawter International Inc., 14
LeaRonal, Inc., 23
Loctite Corporation, 30 (upd.)
Lonza Group Ltd., 73
Lubrizol Corporation, I; 30 (upd.)
Lyondell Chemical Company, 45 (upd.)
M.A. Hanna Company, 8
MacDermid Incorporated, 32
Mallinckrodt Group Inc., 19
MBC Holding Company, 40
Melamine Chemicals, Inc., 27
Methanex Corporation, 40
Minerals Technologies Inc., 52 (upd.)
Mississippi Chemical Corporation, 39
Mitsubishi Chemical Corporation, I; 56 (upd.)
Mitsui Petrochemical Industries, Ltd., 9
Monsanto Company, I; 9 (upd.); 29 (upd.)
Montedison SpA, I
Morton International Inc., I; 9 (upd.); 80 (upd.)
Nagase & Company, Ltd., 8
Nalco Chemical Corporation, I; 12 (upd.)
National Distillers and Chemical Corporation, I
National Sanitary Supply Co., 16
National Starch and Chemical Company, 49
NCH Corporation, 8
Nisshin Seifun Group Inc., 66 (upd.)
NL Industries, Inc., 10
Nobel Industries AB, 9
NOF Corporation, 72
Norsk Hydro ASA, 35 (upd.)
Novacor Chemicals Ltd., 12
NutraSweet Company, 8
Occidental Petroleum Corporation, 71 (upd.)
Olin Corporation, I; 13 (upd.); 78 (upd.)
OM Group, Inc., 17; 78 (upd.)
OMNOVA Solutions Inc., 59
Penford Corporation, 55
Pennwalt Corporation, I
Perstorp AB, I; 51 (upd.)
Petrolite Corporation, 15
Pfizer Inc., 79 (upd.)
Pioneer Hi-Bred International, Inc., 41 (upd.)
Praxair, Inc., 11
Quantum Chemical Corporation, 8
Reichhold Chemicals, Inc., 10
Renner Herrmann S.A., 79
Rhodia SA, 38

Conglomerates

Containers

Drugs & Pharmaceuticals

Chugai Pharmaceutical Co., Ltd., 50
Ciba-Geigy Ltd., I; 8 (upd.)
D&K Wholesale Drug, Inc., 14
Discovery Partners International, Inc., 58
Dr. Reddy's Laboratories Ltd., 59
Elan Corporation PLC, 63
Eli Lilly and Company, I; 11 (upd.); 47
    (upd.)
Endo Pharmaceuticals Holdings Inc., 71
Eon Labs, Inc., 67
Express Scripts Inc., 44 (upd.)
F. Hoffmann-La Roche Ltd., I; 50 (upd.)
Fisons plc, 9; 23 (upd.)
Forest Laboratories, Inc., 52 (upd.)
FoxMeyer Health Corporation, 16
Fujisawa Pharmaceutical Company Ltd., I
G.D. Searle & Co., I; 12 (upd.); 34
    (upd.)
GEHE AG, 27
Genentech, Inc., I; 8 (upd.); 75 (upd.)
Genetics Institute, Inc., 8
Genzyme Corporation, 13, 77 (upd.)
Glaxo Holdings PLC, I; 9 (upd.)
GlaxoSmithKline plc, 46 (upd.)
Groupe Fournier SA, 44
H. Lundbeck A/S, 44
Hauser, Inc., 46
Heska Corporation, 39
Hexal AG, 69
Hospira, Inc., 71
Huntingdon Life Sciences Group plc, 42
ICN Pharmaceuticals, Inc., 52
Immucor, Inc., 81
IVAX Corporation, 55 (upd.)
Janssen Pharmaceutica N.V., 80
Johnson & Johnson, III; 8 (upd.)
Jones Medical Industries, Inc., 24
The Judge Group, Inc., 51
King Pharmaceuticals, Inc., 54
Kos Pharmaceuticals, Inc., 63
Kyowa Hakko Kogyo Co., Ltd., 48 (upd.)
Laboratoires Arkopharma S.A., 75
Leiner Health Products Inc., 34
Ligand Pharmaceuticals Incorporated, 47
Marion Merrell Dow, Inc., I; 9 (upd.)
Matrixx Initiatives, Inc., 74
McKesson Corporation, 12; 47 (upd.)
Medicis Pharmaceutical Corporation, 59
MedImmune, Inc., 35
Merck & Co., Inc., I; 11 (upd.); 34
    (upd.)
Merz Group, 81
Miles Laboratories, I
Millennium Pharmaceuticals, Inc., 47
Monsanto Company, 29 (upd.), 77 (upd.)
Moore Medical Corp., 17
Murdock Madaus Schwabe, 26
Mylan Laboratories Inc., I; 20 (upd.); 59
    (upd.)
Nastech Pharmaceutical Company Inc., 79
National Patent Development
    Corporation, 13
Natrol, Inc., 49
Natural Alternatives International, Inc., 49
Novartis AG, 39 (upd.)
Noven Pharmaceuticals, Inc., 55
Novo Nordisk A/S, I; 61 (upd.)
Omnicare, Inc., 49

Par Pharmaceutical Companies, Inc., 65
Perrigo Company, 59 (upd.)
Pfizer Inc., I; 9 (upd.); 38 (upd.); 79
    (upd.)
Pharmacia & Upjohn Inc., I; 25 (upd.)
PLIVA d.d., 70
PolyMedica Corporation, 77
POZEN Inc., 81
QLT Inc., 71
The Quigley Corporation, 62
Quintiles Transnational Corporation, 21
R.P. Scherer, I
Ranbaxy Laboratories Ltd., 70
Roberts Pharmaceutical Corporation, 16
Roche Bioscience, 14 (upd.)
Rorer Group, I
Roussel Uclaf, I; 8 (upd.)
Sandoz Ltd., I
Sankyo Company, Ltd., I; 56 (upd.)
The Sanofi-Synthélabo Group, I; 49
    (upd.)
Schering AG, I; 50 (upd.)
Schering-Plough Corporation, I; 14
    (upd.); 49 (upd.)
Sepracor Inc., 45
Serono S.A., 47
Shionogi & Co., Ltd., 17 (upd.)
Sigma-Aldrich Corporation, I; 36 (upd.)
SmithKline Beecham plc, I; 32 (upd.)
Solvay S.A., 61 (upd.)
Squibb Corporation, I
Sterling Drug, Inc., I
Sun Pharmaceutical Industries Ltd., 57
The Sunrider Corporation, 26
Syntex Corporation, I
Takeda Chemical Industries, Ltd., I
Taro Pharmaceutical Industries Ltd., 65
Teva Pharmaceutical Industries Ltd., 22;
    54 (upd.)
The Upjohn Company, I; 8 (upd.)
Virbac Corporation, 74
Vitalink Pharmacy Services, Inc., 15
Warner-Lambert Co., I; 10 (upd.)
Watson Pharmaceuticals Inc., 16; 56
    (upd.)
The Wellcome Foundation Ltd., I
Zila, Inc., 46

Electrical & Electronics
ABB ASEA Brown Boveri Ltd., II; 22
    (upd.)
ABB Ltd., 65 (upd.)
Acer Incorporated, 16; 73 (upd.)
Acuson Corporation, 10; 36 (upd.)
ADC Telecommunications, Inc., 30 (upd.)
Adtran Inc., 22
Advanced Micro Devices, Inc., 30 (upd.)
Advanced Technology Laboratories, Inc., 9
Agere Systems Inc., 61
Agilent Technologies Inc., 38
Agilysys Inc., 76 (upd.)
Aiwa Co., Ltd., 30
AKG Acoustics GmbH, 62
Akzo Nobel N.V., 13; 41 (upd.)
Alienware Corporation, 81
Alliant Techsystems Inc., 30 (upd.); 77
    (upd.)
AlliedSignal Inc., 22 (upd.)

Alpine Electronics, Inc., 13
Alps Electric Co., Ltd., II
Altera Corporation, 18; 43 (upd.)
Altron Incorporated, 20
Amdahl Corporation, 40 (upd.)
American Power Conversion Corporation,
    24; 67 (upd.)
American Technical Ceramics Corp., 67
Amkor Technology, Inc., 69
AMP Incorporated, II; 14 (upd.)
Amphenol Corporation, 40
Amstrad plc, 48 (upd.)
Analog Devices, Inc., 10
Analogic Corporation, 23
Anam Group, 23
Anaren Microwave, Inc., 33
Andrew Corporation, 10; 32 (upd.)
Anritsu Corporation, 68
Apex Digital, Inc., 63
Apple Computer, Inc., 36 (upd.); 77
    (upd.)
Applied Power Inc., 32 (upd.)
Argon ST, Inc., 81
Arrow Electronics, Inc., 10; 50 (upd.)
Ascend Communications, Inc., 24
Astronics Corporation, 35
Atari Corporation, 9; 23 (upd.); 66 (upd.)
ATI Technologies Inc., 79
Atmel Corporation, 17
AU Optronics Corporation, 67
Audiovox Corporation, 34
Ault Incorporated, 34
Autodesk, Inc., 10
Avnet Inc., 9
AVX Corporation, 67
Ballard Power Systems Inc., 73
Bang & Olufsen Holding A/S, 37
Barco NV, 44
Bell Microproducts Inc., 69
Benchmark Electronics, Inc., 40
Bicoastal Corporation, II
Blonder Tongue Laboratories, Inc., 48
BMC Industries, Inc., 59 (upd.)
Bogen Communications International,
    Inc., 62
Bose Corporation, 13; 36 (upd.)
Boston Acoustics, Inc., 22
Bowthorpe plc, 33
Braun GmbH, 51
Broadcom Corporation, 34
Bull S.A., 43 (upd.)
Burr-Brown Corporation, 19
C-COR.net Corp., 38
Cabletron Systems, Inc., 10
Cadence Design Systems, Inc., 48 (upd.)
Cambridge SoundWorks, Inc., 48
Canon Inc., 18 (upd.); 79 (upd.)
Carbone Lorraine S.A., 33
Carl-Zeiss-Stiftung, 34 (upd.)
CASIO Computer Co., Ltd., 16 (upd.);
    40 (upd.)
CDW Computer Centers, Inc., 52 (upd.)
Celestica Inc., 80
Checkpoint Systems, Inc., 39
Chi Mei Optoelectronics Corporation, 75
Chubb, PLC, 50
Chunghwa Picture Tubes, Ltd., 75
Cirrus Logic, Inc., 48 (upd.)

Engineering & Management Services

Entertainment & Leisure

First Choice Holidays PLC, 40
First Team Sports, Inc., 22
Fisher-Price Inc., 32 (upd.)
Florida Gaming Corporation, 47
Focus Features 78
4Kids Entertainment Inc., 59
Fox Entertainment Group, Inc., 43
Fox Family Worldwide, Inc., 24
The GAME Group plc, 80
GameStop Corp., 69 (upd.)
Gaumont SA, 25
Gaylord Entertainment Company, 11; 36 (upd.)
GC Companies, Inc., 25
Geffen Records Inc., 26
Gibson Guitar Corp., 16
Girl Scouts of the USA, 35
Global Outdoors, Inc., 49
GoodTimes Entertainment Ltd., 48
Granada Group PLC, II; 24 (upd.)
Grand Casinos, Inc., 20
The Green Bay Packers, Inc., 32
Grévin & Compagnie SA, 56
Groupe Partouche SA, 48
Grupo Televisa, S.A., 54 (upd.)
Hallmark Cards, Inc., 40 (upd.)
Hanna-Barbera Cartoons Inc., 23
Hard Rock Cafe International, Inc., 32 (upd.)
Harlem Globetrotters International, Inc., 61
Harpo Inc., 28; 66 (upd.)
Harrah's Entertainment, Inc., 16; 43 (upd.)
Harveys Casino Resorts, 27
Hasbros, Inc., 43 (upd.)
Hastings Entertainment, Inc., 29
The Hearst Corporation, 46 (upd.)
The Heat Group, 53
Herschend Family Entertainment Corporation, 73
Hilton Group plc, III; 19 (upd.); 49 (upd.)
HIT Entertainment PLC, 40
HOB Entertainment, Inc., 37
Hollywood Casino Corporation, 21
Hollywood Entertainment Corporation, 25
Hollywood Media Corporation, 58
Hollywood Park, Inc., 20
Home Box Office Inc., 7; 23 (upd.); 76 (upd.)
Horseshoe Gaming Holding Corporation, 62
IMAX Corporation 28; 78 (upd.)
IMG 78
Indianapolis Motor Speedway Corporation, 46
Infinity Broadcasting Corporation, 48 (upd.)
Infogrames Entertainment S.A., 35
Integrity Inc., 44
International Creative Management, Inc., 43
International Family Entertainment Inc., 13
International Game Technology, 41 (upd.)
International Olympic Committee, 44

International Speedway Corporation, 19; 74 (upd.)
Interscope Music Group, 31
The Intrawest Corporation, 15
Irvin Feld & Kenneth Feld Productions, Inc., 15
Isle of Capri Casinos, Inc., 41
iVillage Inc., 46
Iwerks Entertainment, Inc., 34
Jackpot Enterprises Inc., 21
Japan Broadcasting Corporation, 7
Jazz Basketball Investors, Inc., 55
Jazzercise, Inc., 45
Jillian's Entertainment Holdings, Inc., 40
The Jim Henson Company, 23
The Joffrey Ballet of Chicago, 52
Jurys Doyle Hotel Group plc, 64
Juventus F.C. S.p.A, 53
K'Nex Industries, Inc., 52
Kampgrounds of America, Inc. (KOA), 33
Kerasotes ShowPlace Theaters LLC, 80
Kerzner International Limited, 69 (upd.)
King World Productions, Inc., 9; 30 (upd.)
Klasky Csupo Inc. 78
Knott's Berry Farm, 18
Kuoni Travel Holding Ltd., 40
The Kushner-Locke Company, 25
Ladbroke Group PLC, II; 21 (upd.)
Lakes Entertainment, Inc., 51
Landmark Theatre Corporation, 70
Las Vegas Sands, Inc., 50
Lego A/S, 13; 40 (upd.)
Liberty Livewire Corporation, 42
Liberty Media Corporation, 50
Liberty Travel, Inc., 56
Life Time Fitness, Inc., 66
Lifetime Entertainment Services, 51
Lincoln Center for the Performing Arts, Inc., 69
Lionel L.L.C., 16
Lions Gate Entertainment Corporation, 35
LIVE Entertainment Inc., 20
Live Nation, Inc., 80 (upd.)
LodgeNet Entertainment Corporation, 28
Lucasfilm Ltd., 12; 50 (upd.)
Luminar Plc, 40
Manchester United Football Club plc, 30
Mandalay Resort Group, 32 (upd.)
Maple Leaf Sports & Entertainment Ltd., 61
The Marcus Corporation, 21
The Mark Travel Corporation, 80
Märklin Holding GmbH, 70
Martha Stewart Living Omnimedia, Inc., 73 (upd.)
Mashantucket Pequot Gaming Enterprise Inc., 35
MCA Inc., II
McMenamins Pubs and Breweries, 65
Media General, Inc., 7
Mediaset SpA, 50
Mega Bloks, Inc., 61
Metro-Goldwyn-Mayer Inc., 25 (upd.)
Metromedia Companies, 14
Métropole Télévision, 33
Métropole Télévision S.A., 76 (upd.)

Metropolitan Baseball Club Inc., 39
The Metropolitan Museum of Art, 55
Metropolitan Opera Association, Inc., 40
MGM Grand Inc., 17
MGM/UA Communications Company, II
Midway Games, Inc., 25
Mikohn Gaming Corporation, 39
Milan AC, S.p.A., 79
Milwaukee Brewers Baseball Club, 37
Miramax Film Corporation, 64
Mizuno Corporation, 25
Mohegan Tribal Gaming Authority, 37
Moliflor Loisirs, 80
Monarch Casino & Resort, Inc., 65
Motown Records Company L.P., 26
Movie Gallery, Inc., 31
MTR Gaming Group, Inc., 75
Multimedia Games, Inc., 41
Muzak, Inc., 18
National Amusements Inc., 28
National Aquarium in Baltimore, Inc., 74
National Association for Stock Car Auto Racing, 32
National Broadcasting Company, Inc., II; 6 (upd.)
National Football League, 29
National Hockey League, 35
National Public Radio, Inc., 19; 47 (upd.)
National Rifle Association of America, 37
National Thoroughbred Racing Association, 58
Navarre Corporation, 24
Navigant International, Inc., 47
NBGS International, Inc., 73
NCL Corporation, 79
New Line Cinema, Inc., 47
New Orleans Saints LP, 58
New York City Off-Track Betting Corporation, 51
News Corporation Limited, 46 (upd.)
NFL Films, 75
Nicklaus Companies, 45
Nintendo Company, Ltd., 28 (upd.); 67 (upd.)
Nordisk Film A/S, 80
O'Charley's Inc., 19
Orion Pictures Corporation, 6
Outrigger Enterprises, Inc., 67
Paradise Music & Entertainment, Inc., 42
Paramount Pictures Corporation, II
Pathé SA, 29
Paul-Son Gaming Corporation, 66
PDS Gaming Corporation, 44
Peace Arch Entertainment Group Inc., 51
Penn National Gaming, Inc., 33
Philadelphia Eagles, 37
Philharmonic-Symphony Society of New York, Inc. (New York Philharmonic), 69
Pierre & Vacances SA, 48
Pittsburgh Steelers Sports, Inc., 66
Pixar Animation Studios, 34
Platinum Entertainment, Inc., 35
Play by Play Toys & Novelties, Inc., 26
Players International, Inc., 22
Pleasant Holidays LLC, 62
PolyGram N.V., 23
Poof-Slinky, Inc., 61

Financial Services: Banks

Financial Services: Excluding Banks

Food Products

Randall's Food Markets, Inc., 40
Rare Hospitality International Inc., 19
Raving Brands, Inc., 64
Red Robin Gourmet Burgers, Inc., 56
Restaurant Associates Corporation, 66
Restaurants Unlimited, Inc., 13
RFC Franchising LLC, 68
Richfood Holdings, Inc., 7
Richtree Inc., 63
The Riese Organization, 38
Riser Foods, Inc., 9
Roadhouse Grill, Inc., 22
Rock Bottom Restaurants, Inc., 25; 68
  (upd.)
Romacorp, Inc., 58
Roundy's Inc., 58 (upd.)
RTM Restaurant Group, 58
Rubio's Restaurants, Inc., 35
Ruby Tuesday, Inc., 18; 71 (upd.)
Ruth's Chris Steak House, 28
Ryan's Restaurant Group, Inc., 15; 68
  (upd.)
Safeway PLC, II; 24 (upd.); 50 (upd.)
Santa Barbara Restaurant Group, Inc., 37
Sbarro, Inc., 16; 64 (upd.)
Schlotzsky's, Inc., 36
Schultz Sav-O Stores, Inc., 21
Schwan's Sales Enterprises, Inc., 26 (upd.)
Seaway Food Town, Inc., 15
Second Harvest, 29
See's Candies, Inc., 30
Seneca Foods Corporation, 17
Service America Corp., 7
SFI Group plc, 51
Shaw's Supermarkets, Inc., 56
Shells Seafood Restaurants, Inc., 43
Shoney's, Inc., 7; 23 (upd.)
ShowBiz Pizza Time, Inc., 13
Skyline Chili, Inc., 62
Smart & Final, Inc., 16
Smith's Food & Drug Centers, Inc., 8; 57
  (upd.)
Sobeys Inc., 80
Sodexho Alliance SA, 29
Somerfield plc, 47 (upd.)
Sonic Corporation, 14; 37 (upd.)
The Southland Corporation, II; 7 (upd.)
Spaghetti Warehouse, Inc., 25
SPAR Handels AG, 35
Spartan Stores Inc., 8
Starbucks Corporation, 77 (upd.)
Stater Bros. Holdings Inc., 64
The Steak n Shake Company, 41
Steinberg Incorporated, II
Stew Leonard's, 56
The Stop & Shop Supermarket Company,
  II; 68 (upd.)
Subway, 32
Super Food Services, Inc., 15
Supermarkets General Holdings
  Corporation, II
Supervalu Inc., II; 18 (upd.); 50 (upd.)
SWH Corporation, 70
SYSCO Corporation, II; 24 (upd.); 75
  (upd.)
Taco Bell Corporation, 7; 21 (upd.); 74
  (upd.)
Taco Cabana, Inc., 23; 72 (upd.)

Taco John's International, Inc., 15; 63
  (upd.)
TelePizza S.A., 33
Tesco PLC, II
Texas Roadhouse, Inc., 69
Timber Lodge Steakhouse, Inc., 73
Tops Markets LLC, 60
Total Entertainment Restaurant
  Corporation, 46
Toupargel-Agrigel S.A., 76
Trader Joe's Company, 13; 50 (upd.)
Travel Ports of America, Inc., 17
Tree of Life, Inc., 29
Triarc Companies, Inc., 34 (upd.)
Tubby's, Inc., 53
Tully's Coffee Corporation, 51
Tumbleweed, Inc., 33; 80 (upd.)
TW Services, Inc., II
Ukrop's Super Market's, Inc., 39
Unique Casual Restaurants, Inc., 27
United Dairy Farmers, Inc., 74
United Natural Foods, Inc., 32; 76 (upd.)
Uno Restaurant Holdings Corporation,
  18; 70 (upd.)
Uwajimaya, Inc., 60
Vail Resorts, Inc., 43 (upd.)
VICORP Restaurants, Inc., 12; 48 (upd.)
Village Super Market, Inc., 7
The Vons Companies, Incorporated, 7; 28
  (upd.)
W. H. Braum, Inc., 80
Waffle House Inc., 14; 60 (upd.)
Wakefern Food Corporation, 33
Waldbaum, Inc., 19
Wall Street Deli, Inc., 33
Wawa Inc., 17; 78 (upd.)
Wegmans Food Markets, Inc., 9; 41
  (upd.)
Weis Markets, Inc., 15
Wendy's International, Inc., 8; 23 (upd.);
  47 (upd.)
The WesterN SizzliN Corporation, 60
Wetterau Incorporated, II
White Castle System, Inc., 12; 36 (upd.)
White Rose, Inc., 24
Whittard of Chelsea Plc, 61
Whole Foods Market, Inc., 50 (upd.)
Wild Oats Markets, Inc., 19; 41 (upd.)
Winchell's Donut Houses Operating
  Company, L.P., 60
WinCo Foods Inc., 60
Winn-Dixie Stores, Inc., II; 21 (upd.); 59
  (upd.)
Wm. Morrison Supermarkets PLC, 38
Wolfgang Puck Worldwide, Inc., 26, 70
  (upd.)
Worldwide Restaurant Concepts, Inc., 47
Young & Co.'s Brewery, P.L.C., 38
Yucaipa Cos., 17
Yum! Brands Inc., 58
Zingerman's Community of Businesses,
  68

Health & Personal Care Products

Advanced Medical Optics, Inc., 79
Advanced Neuromodulation Systems, Inc.,
  73

Akorn, Inc., 32
ALARIS Medical Systems, Inc., 65
Alberto-Culver Company, 8
Alco Health Services Corporation, III
Alès Groupe, 81
Allergan, Inc., 10; 30 (upd.); 77 (upd.)
American Safety Razor Company, 20
American Stores Company, 22 (upd.)
Amway Corporation, III; 13 (upd.)
AngioDynamics, Inc., 81
ArthroCare Corporation, 73
Atkins Nutritionals, Inc., 58
Aveda Corporation, 24
Avon Products, Inc., III; 19 (upd.); 46
  (upd.)
Bally Total Fitness Holding Corp., 25
Bausch & Lomb Inc., 7; 25 (upd.)
Baxter International Inc., I; 10 (upd.)
BeautiControl Cosmetics, Inc., 21
Becton, Dickinson & Company, I; 11
  (upd.)
Beiersdorf AG, 29
Big B, Inc., 17
Bindley Western Industries, Inc., 9
Biosite Incorporated, 73
Block Drug Company, Inc., 8; 27 (upd.)
The Body Shop International plc, 53
  (upd.)
Boiron S.A., 73
The Boots Company PLC, 24 (upd.)
Boston Scientific Corporation, 77 (upd.)
Bristol-Myers Squibb Company, III; 9
  (upd.)
C.R. Bard Inc., 9
Candela Corporation, 48
Cantel Medical Corporation, 80
Cardinal Health, Inc., 18; 50 (upd.)
Carson, Inc., 31
Carter-Wallace, Inc., 8
Caswell-Massey Co. Ltd., 51
CCA Industries, Inc., 53
Chattem, Inc., 17
Chesebrough-Pond's USA, Inc., 8
Chronimed Inc., 26
Church & Dwight Co., Inc., 68 (upd.)
Cintas Corporation, 51 (upd.)
The Clorox Company, III; 22 (upd.); 81
  (upd.)
CNS, Inc., 20
Colgate-Palmolive Company, III; 14
  (upd.); 35 (upd.)
Combe Inc., 72
Conair Corp., 17
Connetics Corporation, 70
Cordis Corp., 19
Cosmair, Inc., 8
Coty, Inc., 36
Cybex International, Inc., 49
Cytyc Corporation, 69
Dade Behring Holdings Inc., 71
Datascope Corporation, 39
Del Laboratories, Inc., 28
Deltec, Inc., 56
Dentsply International Inc., 10
DEP Corporation, 20
DePuy, Inc., 30
Diagnostic Products Corporation, 73
The Dial Corp., 23 (upd.)

Direct Focus, Inc., 47
Drackett Professional Products, 12
Elizabeth Arden, Inc., 8; 40 (upd.)
Empi, Inc., 26
Enrich International, Inc., 33
The Estée Lauder Companies Inc., 9; 30 (upd.)
Ethicon, Inc., 23
Farouk Systems Inc. 78
Forest Laboratories, Inc., 11
Forever Living Products International Inc., 17
French Fragrances, Inc., 22
Gambro AB, 49
General Nutrition Companies, Inc., 11; 29 (upd.)
Genzyme Corporation, 13; 77 (upd.)
The Gillette Company, III; 20 (upd.)
Groupe Yves Saint Laurent, 23
Guerlain, 23
Guest Supply, Inc., 18
Guidant Corporation, 58
Hanger Orthopedic Group, Inc., 41
Helen of Troy Corporation, 18
Helene Curtis Industries, Inc., 8; 28 (upd.)
Henkel KGaA, III
Henry Schein, Inc., 31; 70 (upd.)
Herbalife International, Inc., 17; 41 (upd.)
Huntleigh Technology PLC, 77
Immucor, Inc., 81
Inamed Corporation, 79
Inter Parfums Inc., 35
Intuitive Surgical, Inc., 79
Invacare Corporation, 11
IVAX Corporation, 11
IVC Industries, Inc., 45
The Jean Coutu Group (PJC) Inc., 46
John Paul Mitchell Systems, 24
Johnson & Johnson, III; 8 (upd.); 36 (upd.); 75 (upd.)
Kanebo, Ltd., 53
Kao Corporation, III; 79 (upd.)
Kendall International, Inc., 11
Kensey Nash Corporation, 71
Kimberly-Clark Corporation, III; 16 (upd.); 43 (upd.)
Kyowa Hakko Kogyo Co., Ltd., III
L'Oréal SA, III; 8 (upd.); 46 (upd.)
Laboratoires de Biologie Végétale Yves Rocher, 35
The Lamaur Corporation, 41
Lever Brothers Company, 9
Lion Corporation, III; 51 (upd.)
Luxottica SpA, 17
Mannatech Inc., 33
Mary Kay Corporation, 9; 30 (upd.)
Maxxim Medical Inc., 12
Medco Containment Services Inc., 9
Medline Industries, Inc., 61
Medtronic, Inc., 8; 67 (upd.)
Melaleuca Inc., 31
The Mentholatum Company Inc., 32
Mentor Corporation, 26
Merck & Co., Inc., I; 11 (upd.); 34 (upd.)
Merit Medical Systems, Inc., 29

Merz Group, 81
Natura Cosméticos S.A., 75
Nature's Sunshine Products, Inc., 15
NBTY, Inc., 31
NeighborCare, Inc., 67 (upd.)
Neutrogena Corporation, 17
New Dana Perfumes Company, 37
Neways Inc. 78
Nikken Global Inc., 32
NutriSystem, Inc., 71
Nutrition for Life International Inc., 22
Ocular Sciences, Inc., 65
OEC Medical Systems, Inc., 27
OraSure Technologies, Inc., 75
Orion Oyj, 72
Patterson Dental Co., 19
Perrigo Company, 12
Pfizer Inc., 79 (upd.)
Physician Sales & Service, Inc., 14
Playtex Products, Inc., 15
PolyMedica Corporation, 77
The Procter & Gamble Company, III; 8 (upd.); 26 (upd.); 67 (upd.)
PZ Cussons plc, 72
Quidel Corporation, 80
Reliv International, Inc., 58
Revlon Inc., III; 17 (upd.)
Roche Biomedical Laboratories, Inc., 11
S.C. Johnson & Son, Inc., III
Safety 1st, Inc., 24
Schering-Plough Corporation, 14 (upd.)
Shaklee Corporation, 39 (upd.)
Shionogi & Co., Ltd., III
Shiseido Company, Limited, III; 22 (upd.); 81 (upd.)
Slim-Fast Nutritional Foods International, Inc., 18
Smith & Nephew plc, 17
SmithKline Beecham PLC, III
Soft Sheen Products, Inc., 31
Sola International Inc., 71
Spacelabs Medical, Inc., 71
STAAR Surgical Company, 57
Straumann Holding AG, 79
Stryker Corporation, 79 (upd.)
Sunrise Medical Inc., 11
Tambrands Inc., 8
Terumo Corporation, 48
Tom's of Maine, Inc., 45
The Tranzonic Companies, 37
Turtle Wax, Inc., 15
Tutogen Medical, Inc., 68
United States Surgical Corporation, 10; 34 (upd.)
USANA, Inc., 29
Utah Medical Products, Inc., 36
Ventana Medical Systems, Inc., 75
VHA Inc., 53
VIASYS Healthcare, Inc., 52
VISX, Incorporated, 30
Vitamin Shoppe Industries, Inc., 60
Water Pik Technologies, Inc., 34
Weider Nutrition International, Inc., 29
Weleda AG 78
Wella AG, III; 48 (upd.)
West Pharmaceutical Services, Inc., 42
Wright Medical Group, Inc., 61
Wyeth, 50 (upd.)

Zila, Inc., 46
Zimmer Holdings, Inc., 45

Health Care Services

Acadian Ambulance & Air Med Services, Inc., 39
Adventist Health, 53
Advocat Inc., 46
Alterra Healthcare Corporation, 42
Amedysis, Inc., 53
The American Cancer Society, 24
American Healthways, Inc., 65
American Lung Association, 48
American Medical Association, 39
American Medical International, Inc., III
American Medical Response, Inc., 39
American Red Cross, 40
AMERIGROUP Corporation, 69
AmeriSource Health Corporation, 37 (upd.)
AmSurg Corporation, 48
Applied Bioscience International, Inc., 10
Assisted Living Concepts, Inc., 43
ATC Healthcare Inc., 64
Beverly Enterprises, Inc., III; 16 (upd.)
Bon Secours Health System, Inc., 24
C.R. Bard, Inc., 65 (upd.)
Capital Senior Living Corporation, 75
Caremark Rx, Inc., 10; 54 (upd.)
Children's Comprehensive Services, Inc., 42
Children's Hospitals and Clinics, Inc., 54
Chronimed Inc., 26
COBE Laboratories, Inc., 13
Columbia/HCA Healthcare Corporation, 15
Community Health Systems, Inc., 71
Community Psychiatric Centers, 15
CompDent Corporation, 22
CompHealth Inc., 25
Comprehensive Care Corporation, 15
Continental Medical Systems, Inc., 10
Continuum Health Partners, Inc., 60
Coventry Health Care, Inc., 59
DaVita Inc., 73
Easter Seals, Inc., 58
Erickson Retirement Communities, 57
Express Scripts Incorporated, 17
Extendicare Health Services, Inc., 6
Eye Care Centers of America, Inc., 69
FHP International Corporation, 6
Fresenius AG, 56
Genesis Health Ventures, Inc., 18
Gentiva Health Services, Inc., 79
GranCare, Inc., 14
Group Health Cooperative, 41
Hazelden Foundation, 28
HCA - The Healthcare Company, 35 (upd.)
Health Care & Retirement Corporation, 22
Health Management Associates, Inc., 56
Health Risk Management, Inc., 24
Health Systems International, Inc., 11
HealthSouth Corporation, 14; 33 (upd.)
Highmark Inc., 27
The Hillhaven Corporation, 14
Hooper Holmes, Inc., 22

Hotels

Information Technology

Legal Services

Manufacturing

Westerbeke Corporation, 60
Western Digital Corp., 25
Wheaton Science Products, 60 (upd.)
Wheeling-Pittsburgh Corporation, 58 (upd.)
Whirlpool Corporation, III; 12 (upd.); 59 (upd.)
White Consolidated Industries Inc., 13
Wilbert, Inc., 56
Wilkinson Sword Ltd., 60
William L. Bonnell Company, Inc., 66
William Zinsser & Company, Inc., 58
Williamson-Dickie Manufacturing Company, 45 (upd.)
Wilson Sporting Goods Company, 24
Wincor Nixdorf Holding GmbH, 69 (upd.)
Windmere Corporation, 16
Winegard Company, 56
WinsLoew Furniture, Inc., 21
The Wiremold Company, 81
WMS Industries, Inc., 15; 53 (upd.)
Wolverine Tube Inc., 23
Wood-Mode, Inc., 23
Woodcraft Industries Inc., 61
Woodward Governor Company, 13; 49 (upd.)
Wright Medical Group, Inc., 61
Württembergische Metallwarenfabrik AG (WMF), 60
Wyant Corporation, 30
Wyman-Gordon Company, 14
Wynn's International, Inc., 33
X-Rite, Inc., 48
Xerox Corporation, 69 (upd.)
Yamaha Corporation, III; 16 (upd.)
The York Group, Inc., 50
York International Corp., 13
Young Innovations, Inc., 44
Zebra Technologies Corporation, 53 (upd.)
Zero Corporation, 17
ZiLOG, Inc., 72 (upd.)
Zindart Ltd., 60
Zippo Manufacturing Company, 18; 71 (upd.)
Zodiac S.A., 36
Zygo Corporation, 42

Materials

AK Steel Holding Corporation, 19
American Biltrite Inc., 16
American Colloid Co., 13
American Standard Inc., III
Ameriwood Industries International Corp., 17
Apasco S.A. de C.V., 51
Apogee Enterprises, Inc., 8
Asahi Glass Company, Limited, III
Asbury Carbons, Inc., 68
Bairnco Corporation, 28
Bayou Steel Corporation, 31
Blessings Corp., 19
Blue Circle Industries PLC, III
Bodycote International PLC, 63
Boral Limited, III
British Vita PLC, 9
Brush Engineered Materials Inc., 67

California Steel Industries, Inc., 67
Callanan Industries, Inc., 60
Cameron & Barkley Company, 28
Carborundum Company, 15
Carl-Zeiss-Stiftung, 34 (upd.)
Carlisle Companies Incorporated, 8
Carter Holt Harvey Ltd., 70
Cemex SA de CV, 20
Century Aluminum Company, 52
CertainTeed Corporation, 35
Chargeurs International, 21 (upd.)
Chemfab Corporation, 35
Cimentos de Portugal SGPS S.A. (Cimpor), 76
Cold Spring Granite Company Inc., 16; 67 (upd.)
Columbia Forest Products Inc. 78
Compagnie de Saint-Gobain S.A., III; 16 (upd.)
Cookson Group plc, III; 44 (upd.)
Corning Incorporated, III
CSR Limited, III
Dal-Tile International Inc., 22
The David J. Joseph Company, 14; 76 (upd.)
The Dexter Corporation, 12 (upd.)
Dyckerhoff AG, 35
Dynamic Materials Corporation, 81
Dyson Group PLC, 71
ECC Group plc, III
Edw. C. Levy Co., 42
84 Lumber Company, 9; 39 (upd.)
ElkCorp, 52
Empire Resources, Inc., 81
English China Clays Ltd., 15 (upd.); 40 (upd.)
Envirodyne Industries, Inc., 17
Feldmuhle Nobel A.G., III
Fibreboard Corporation, 16
Florida Rock Industries, Inc., 46
Foamex International Inc., 17
Formica Corporation, 13
GAF Corporation, 22 (upd.)
The Geon Company, 11
Giant Cement Holding, Inc., 23
Gibraltar Steel Corporation, 37
Granite Rock Company, 26
Groupe Sidel S.A., 21
Harbison-Walker Refractories Company, 24
Harrisons & Crosfield plc, III
Heidelberger Zement AG, 31
Hexcel Corporation, 28
Holderbank Financière Glaris Ltd., III
Holnam Inc., 39 (upd.)
Holt and Bugbee Company, 66
Homasote Company, 72
Howmet Corp., 12
Huttig Building Products, Inc., 73
Ibstock Brick Ltd., 14; 37 (upd.)
Imerys S.A., 40 (upd.)
Imperial Industries, Inc., 81
Internacional de Ceramica, S.A. de C.V., 53
International Shipbreaking Ltd. L.L.C., 67
Joseph T. Ryerson & Son, Inc., 15
Lafarge Coppée S.A., III
Lafarge Corporation, 28

Lehigh Portland Cement Company, 23
Manville Corporation, III; 7 (upd.)
Material Sciences Corporation, 63
Matsushita Electric Works, Ltd., III; 7 (upd.)
McJunkin Corporation, 63
Medusa Corporation, 24
Mitsubishi Materials Corporation, III
Nippon Sheet Glass Company, Limited, III
North Pacific Group, Inc., 61
OmniSource Corporation, 14
Onoda Cement Co., Ltd., III
Otor S.A., 77
Owens-Corning Fiberglass Corporation, III
Pilkington plc, III; 34 (upd.)
Pioneer International Limited, III
PPG Industries, Inc., III; 22 (upd.); 81 (upd.)
Redland plc, III
Rinker Group Ltd., 65
RMC Group p.l.c., III
Rock of Ages Corporation, 37 Rogers Corporation, 80 (upd.)
Royal Group Technologies Limited, 73
The Rugby Group plc, 31
Schuff Steel Company, 26
Sekisui Chemical Co., Ltd., III; 72 (upd.)
Severstal Joint Stock Company, 65
Shaw Industries, 9
The Sherwin-Williams Company, III; 13 (upd.)
The Siam Cement Public Company Limited, 56
SIG plc, 71
Simplex Technologies Inc., 21
Siskin Steel & Supply Company, 70
Solutia Inc., 52
Sommer-Allibert S.A., 19
Southdown, Inc., 14
Spartech Corporation, 19; 76 (upd.)
Ssangyong Cement Industrial Co., Ltd., III; 61 (upd.)
Steel Technologies Inc., 63
Sun Distributors L.P., 12
Symyx Technologies, Inc., 77
Tarmac plc, III, 28 (upd.)
Tilcon-Connecticut Inc., 80
TOTO LTD., III; 28 (upd.)
Toyo Sash Co., Ltd., III
Tuscarora Inc., 29
U.S. Aggregates, Inc., 42
Ube Industries, Ltd., III
United States Steel Corporation, 50 (upd.)
USG Corporation, III; 26 (upd.); 81 (upd.)
Usinas Siderúrgicas de Minas Gerais S.A., 77
Vicat S.A., 70
voestalpine AG, 57 (upd.)
Vulcan Materials Company, 7; 52 (upd.)
Wacker-Chemie GmbH, 35
Walter Industries, Inc., III
Waxman Industries, Inc., 9
Weber et Broutin France, 66
Wienerberger AG, 70
Wolseley plc, 64

Zoltek Companies, Inc., 37

Mining & Metals

A.M. Castle & Co., 25
Aggregate Industries plc, 36
Agnico-Eagle Mines Limited, 71
Aktiebolaget SKF, 38 (upd.)
Alcan Aluminium Limited, IV; 31 (upd.)
Alcoa Inc., 56 (upd.)
Alleghany Corporation, 10
Allegheny Ludlum Corporation, 8
Alliance Resource Partners, L.P., 81
Alrosa Company Ltd., 62
Altos Hornos de México, S.A. de C.V., 42
Aluminum Company of America, IV; 20 (upd.)
AMAX Inc., IV
AMCOL International Corporation, 59 (upd.)
Amsted Industries Incorporated, 7
Anglo American Corporation of South Africa Limited, IV; 16 (upd.)
Anglo American PLC, 50 (upd.)
Aquarius Platinum Ltd., 63
ARBED S.A., IV; 22 (upd.)
Arcelor Gent, 80
Arch Mineral Corporation, 7
Armco Inc., IV
ASARCO Incorporated, IV
Ashanti Goldfields Company Limited, 43
Atchison Casting Corporation, 39
Barrick Gold Corporation, 34
Battle Mountain Gold Company, 23
Benguet Corporation, 58
Bethlehem Steel Corporation, IV; 7 (upd.); 27 (upd.)
BHP Billiton, 67 (upd.)
Birmingham Steel Corporation, 13; 40 (upd.)
Boart Longyear Company, 26
Bodycote International PLC, 63
Boliden AB, 80
Boral Limited, 43 (upd.)
British Coal Corporation, IV
British Steel plc, IV; 19 (upd.)
Broken Hill Proprietary Company Ltd., IV, 22 (upd.)
Brush Engineered Materials Inc., 67
Brush Wellman Inc., 14
Buderus AG, 37
Cameco Corporation, 77
Carpenter Technology Corporation, 13
Chaparral Steel Co., 13
Christensen Boyles Corporation, 26
Cleveland-Cliffs Inc., 13; 62 (upd.)
Coal India Ltd., IV; 44 (upd.)
Cockerill Sambre Group, IV; 26 (upd.)
Coeur d'Alene Mines Corporation, 20
Cold Spring Granite Company Inc., 16; 67 (upd.)
Cominco Ltd., 37
Commercial Metals Company, 15; 42 (upd.)
Companhia Siderúrgica Nacional, 76
Companhia Vale do Rio Doce, IV; 43 (upd.)
CONSOL Energy Inc., 59

Corporacion Nacional del Cobre de Chile, 40
Corus Group plc, 49 (upd.)
CRA Limited, IV
Cyprus Amax Minerals Company, 21
Cyprus Minerals Company, 7
Daido Steel Co., Ltd., IV
De Beers Consolidated Mines Limited/De Beers Centenary AG, IV; 7 (upd.); 28 (upd.)
Degussa Group, IV
Dofasco Inc., IV; 24 (upd.)
Echo Bay Mines Ltd., IV; 38 (upd.)
Engelhard Corporation, IV
Eramet, 73
Falconbridge Limited, 49
Fansteel Inc., 19
Fluor Corporation, 34 (upd.)
Freeport-McMoRan Copper & Gold, Inc., IV; 7 (upd.); 57 (upd.)
Fried. Krupp GmbH, IV
Gencor Ltd., IV; 22 (upd.)
Geneva Steel, 7
Gerdau S.A., 59
Glamis Gold, Ltd., 54
Gold Fields Ltd., IV; 62 (upd.)
Grupo Mexico, S.A. de C.V., 40
Handy & Harman, 23
Hanson Building Materials America Inc., 60
Hanson PLC, 30 (upd.)
Harmony Gold Mining Company Limited, 63
Hecla Mining Company, 20
Hemlo Gold Mines Inc., 9
Heraeus Holding GmbH, IV
Highveld Steel and Vanadium Corporation Limited, 59
Hitachi Metals, Ltd., IV
Hoesch AG, IV
Homestake Mining Company, 12; 38 (upd.)
Horsehead Industries, Inc., 51
The Hudson Bay Mining and Smelting Company, Limited, 12
Hylsamex, S.A. de C.V., 39
IMCO Recycling, Incorporated, 32
Imerys S.A., 40 (upd.)
Imetal S.A., IV
Inco Limited, IV; 45 (upd.)
Industrias Penoles, S.A. de C.V., 22
Inland Steel Industries, Inc., IV; 19 (upd.)
Intermet Corporation, 32
Iscor Limited, 57
Ispat Inland Inc., 30; 40 (upd.)
Johnson Matthey PLC, IV; 16 (upd.)
JSC MMC Norilsk Nickel, 48
Kaiser Aluminum & Chemical Corporation, IV
Kawasaki Heavy Industries, Ltd., 63 (upd.)
Kawasaki Steel Corporation, IV
Kennecott Corporation, 7; 27 (upd.)
Kentucky Electric Steel, Inc., 31
Kerr-McGee Corporation, 22 (upd.)
Kinross Gold Corporation, 36
Klockner-Werke AG, IV
Kobe Steel, Ltd., IV; 19 (upd.)

Koninklijke Nederlandsche Hoogovens en Staalfabrieken NV, IV
Laclede Steel Company, 15
Layne Christensen Company, 19
Lonmin plc, 66 (upd.)
Lonrho Plc, 21
The LTV Corporation, 24 (upd.)
Lukens Inc., 14
Magma Copper Company, 7
The Marmon Group, IV; 16 (upd.)
Massey Energy Company, 57
MAXXAM Inc., 8
Meridian Gold, Incorporated, 47
Metaleurop S.A., 21
Metallgesellschaft AG, IV
Minerals and Metals Trading Corporation of India Ltd., IV
Minerals Technologies Inc., 11; 52 (upd.)
Mitsui Mining & Smelting Co., Ltd., IV
Mitsui Mining Company, Limited, IV
Mueller Industries, Inc., 52 (upd.)
National Steel Corporation, 12
NERCO, Inc., 7
Newmont Mining Corporation, 7
Neyveli Lignite Corporation Ltd., 65
Niagara Corporation, 28
Nichimen Corporation, IV
Nippon Light Metal Company, Ltd., IV
Nippon Steel Corporation, IV; 17 (upd.)
Nisshin Steel Co., Ltd., IV
NKK Corporation, IV; 28 (upd.)
Noranda Inc., IV; 7 (upd.); 64 (upd.)
Norddeutsche Affinerie AG, 62
North Star Steel Company, 18
Nucor Corporation, 7; 21 (upd.); 79 (upd.)
Oglebay Norton Company, 17
Okura & Co., Ltd., IV
Oregon Metallurgical Corporation, 20
Oregon Steel Mills, Inc., 14
Outokumpu Oyj, 38
Park Corp., 22
Peabody Coal Company, 10
Peabody Energy Corporation, 45 (upd.)
Peabody Holding Company, Inc., IV
Pechiney SA, IV; 45 (upd.)
Peter Kiewit Sons' Inc., 8
Phelps Dodge Corporation, IV; 28 (upd.); 75 (upd.)
The Pittston Company, IV; 19 (upd.)
Placer Dome Inc., 20; 61 (upd.)
Pohang Iron and Steel Company Ltd., IV
POSCO, 57 (upd.)
Potash Corporation of Saskatchewan Inc., 18
Quanex Corporation, 13; 62 (upd.)
RAG AG, 35; 60 (upd.)
Reliance Steel & Aluminum Co., 19
Republic Engineered Steels, Inc., 7; 26 (upd.)
Reynolds Metals Company, IV
Rio Tinto PLC, 19 (upd.); 50 (upd.)
RMC Group p.l.c., 34 (upd.)
Roanoke Electric Steel Corporation, 45
Rouge Steel Company, 8
The RTZ Corporation PLC, IV
Ruhrkohle AG, IV
Ryerson Tull, Inc., 40 (upd.)

Petroleum

Publishing & Printing

Real Estate

Fingerhut Companies, Inc., 9; 36 (upd.)
The Finish Line, Inc., 29; 68 (upd.)
Finlay Enterprises, Inc., 16; 76 (upd.)
Finning International Inc., 69
First Cash Financial Services, Inc., 57
Fleming Companies, Inc., 17 (upd.)
Florsheim Shoe Group Inc., 9; 31 (upd.)
FNAC, 21
Follett Corporation, 12
Foot Locker, Inc., 68 (upd.)
Footstar, Incorporated, 24
Fortunoff Fine Jewelry and Silverware
   Inc., 26
The Forzani Group Ltd., 79
Frank's Nursery & Crafts, Inc., 12
Fred Meyer Stores, Inc., V; 20 (upd.); 64
   (upd.)
Fred's, Inc., 23; 62 (upd.)
Frederick Atkins Inc., 16
Frederick's of Hollywood, Inc., 59 (upd.)
Freeze.com LLC, 77
Fretter, Inc., 10
Friedman's Inc., 29
Fruth Pharmacy, Inc., 66
Fry's Electronics, Inc., 68
Funco, Inc., 20
Future Shop Ltd., 62
G.I. Joe's, Inc., 30
Gadzooks, Inc., 18
Gaiam, Inc., 41
Galeries Lafayette S.A., V; 23 (upd.)
Galyan's Trading Company, Inc., 47
GameStop Corp., 69 (upd.)
Gander Mountain, Inc., 20
Gantos, Inc., 17
The Gap, Inc., V; 18 (upd.); 55 (upd.)
Garden Ridge Corporation, 27
Gart Sports Company, 24
GEHE AG, 27
General Binding Corporation, 10
General Host Corporation, 12
Genesco Inc., 17
Genovese Drug Stores, Inc., 18
Genuine Parts Company, 45 (upd.)
Gerald Stevens, Inc., 37
Giant Food Inc., 22 (upd.)
GIB Group, V; 26 (upd.)
Gibbs and Dandy plc, 74
GiFi S.A., 74
Glacier Water Services, Inc., 47
Global Imaging Systems, Inc., 73
The Good Guys, Inc., 10; 30 (upd.)
Goodwill Industries International, Inc., 16
Goody's Family Clothing, Inc., 20; 64
   (upd.)
Gordmans, Inc., 74
Gottschalks, Inc., 18
Grand Piano & Furniture Company, 72
GrandVision S.A., 43
Graybar Electric Company, Inc., 54
The Great Universal Stores plc, V; 19
   (upd.)
Griffin Land & Nurseries, Inc., 43
Grossman's Inc., 13
Groupe Alain Manoukian, 55
Groupe Castorama-Dubois
   Investissements, 23
Groupe DMC (Dollfus Mieg & Cie), 27

Groupe Go Sport S.A., 39
Groupe Lapeyre S.A., 33
Groupe Monnoyeur, 72
Groupe Zannier S.A., 35
Grow Biz International, Inc., 18
Grupo Casa Saba, S.A. de C.V., 39
Grupo Elektra, S.A. de C.V., 39
Grupo Eroski, 64
Grupo Gigante, S.A. de C.V., 34
Gruppo Coin S.p.A., 41
GT Bicycles, 26
GTSI Corp., 57
Gucci Group N.V., 15; 50 (upd.)
Guilbert S.A., 42
Guitar Center, Inc., 29; 68 (upd.)
GUS plc, 47 (upd.)
Gymboree Corporation, 69 (upd.)
Hahn Automotive Warehouse, Inc., 24
Hale-Halsell Company, 60
Half Price Books, Records, Magazines
   Inc., 37
Hallmark Cards, Inc., 40 (upd.)
Hammacher Schlemmer & Company Inc.,
   21; 72 (upd.)
Hancock Fabrics, Inc., 18
Hankyu Department Stores, Inc., V; 62
   (upd.)
Hanna Andersson Corp., 49
Hanover Compressor Company, 59
Hanover Direct, Inc., 36
Harold's Stores, Inc., 22
Harrods Holdings, 47
Harry Winston Inc., 45
Harvey Norman Holdings Ltd., 56
Hasbro, Inc., 43 (upd.)
Haverty Furniture Companies, Inc., 31
Hechinger Company, 12
Heilig-Meyers Company, 14; 40 (upd.)
Helzberg Diamonds, 40
Hennes & Mauritz AB, 29
Henry Modell & Company Inc., 32
Hensley & Company, 64
Hertie Waren- und Kaufhaus GmbH, V
Hibbett Sporting Goods, Inc., 26; 70
   (upd.)
Highsmith Inc., 60
Hills Stores Company, 13
Hines Horticulture, Inc., 49
HMV Group plc, 59
Hobby Lobby Stores Inc., 80
The Hockey Company, 34
Holiday RV Superstores, Incorporated, 26
Holt's Cigar Holdings, Inc., 42
The Home Depot, Inc., V; 18 (upd.)
Home Hardware Stores Ltd., 62
Home Interiors & Gifts, Inc., 55
Home Shopping Network, Inc., V; 25
   (upd.)
HomeBase, Inc., 33 (upd.)
Hot Topic, Inc., 33
House of Fabrics, Inc., 21
House of Fraser PLC, 45
HSN, 64 (upd.)
Hudson's Bay Company, V; 25 (upd.)
Huttig Building Products, Inc., 73
Ihr Platz GmbH + Company KG, 77
IKEA International A/S, V; 26 (upd.)
InaCom Corporation, 13

Indigo Books & Music Inc., 58
Insight Enterprises, Inc., 18
International Airline Support Group, Inc.,
   55
Intimate Brands, Inc., 24
Isetan Company Limited, V; 36 (upd.)
Ito-Yokado Co., Ltd., V; 42 (upd.)
J&R Electronics Inc., 26
J. Baker, Inc., 31
The J. Jill Group, Inc., 35
J.C. Penney Company, Inc., V; 18 (upd.);
   43 (upd.)
J.L. Hammett Company, 72
Jack Schwartz Shoes, Inc., 18
Jacobson Stores Inc., 21
Jalate Inc., 25
James Beattie plc, 43
Jay Jacobs, Inc., 15
Jennifer Convertibles, Inc., 31
Jetro Cash & Carry Enterprises Inc., 38
JG Industries, Inc., 15
JJB Sports plc, 32
Jo-Ann Stores, Inc., 72 (upd.)
John Lewis Partnership plc, V; 42 (upd.)
JUSCO Co., Ltd., V
Just For Feet, Inc., 19
K & B Inc., 12
K & G Men's Center, Inc., 21
K-tel International, Inc., 21
Karstadt Aktiengesellschaft, V; 19 (upd.)
Kash n' Karry Food Stores, Inc., 20
Kasper A.S.L., Ltd., 40
kate spade LLC, 68
Kaufhof Warenhaus AG, V; 23 (upd.)
Kaufring AG, 35
Kay-Bee Toy Stores, 15
Kiabi Europe, 66
Kiehl's Since 1851, Inc., 52
Kingfisher plc, V; 24 (upd.)
Kinney Shoe Corp., 14
Kmart Corporation, V; 18 (upd.); 47
   (upd.)
Knoll Group Inc., 14
Kohl's Corporation, 9; 30 (upd.); 77
   (upd.)
Koninklijke Vendex KBB N.V. (Royal
   Vendex KBB N.V.), 62 (upd.)
Kotobukiya Co., Ltd., V; 56 (upd.)
Krause's Furniture, Inc., 27
Krispy Kreme Doughnuts, Inc., 61 (upd.)
L. and J.G. Stickley, Inc., 50
L. Luria & Son, Inc., 19
L.A. T Sportswear, Inc., 26
L.L. Bean, Inc., 38 (upd.)
La Senza Corporation, 66
La-Z-Boy Incorporated, 14; 50 (upd.)
Lamonts Apparel, Inc., 15
Lands' End, Inc., 9; 29 (upd.)
Lane Bryant, Inc., 64
Lanier Worldwide, Inc., 75
Lanoga Corporation, 62
Laura Ashley Holdings plc, 37 (upd.)
Lazare Kaplan International Inc., 21
Le Chateau Inc., 63
Lechmere Inc., 10
Lechters, Inc., 11; 39 (upd.)
LensCrafters Inc., 23; 76 (upd.)
Leroy Merlin SA, 54

Recreational Equipment, Inc., 18; 71 (upd.)
Reeds Jewelers, Inc., 22
Reliance Steel & Aluminum Company, 70 (upd.)
Rent-A-Center, Inc., 45
Rent-Way, Inc., 33; 75 (upd.)
Restoration Hardware, Inc., 30
Revco D.S., Inc., V
REX Stores Corp., 10
Rhodes Inc., 23
Richton International Corporation, 39
Riklis Family Corp., 9
Rinascente S.p.A., 71
Rite Aid Corporation, V; 19 (upd.); 63 (upd.)
Ritz Camera Centers, 34
Roberds Inc., 19
Rocky Shoes & Boots, Inc., 26
Rogers Communications Inc., 30 (upd.)
RONA, Inc., 73
Ronco Corporation, 15; 80 (upd.)
Rooms To Go Inc., 28
Roots Canada Ltd., 42
Rose's Stores, Inc., 13
Ross Stores, Inc., 17; 43 (upd.)
Roundy's Inc., 14
Rush Enterprises, Inc., 64
Ryoshoku Ltd., 72
S&K Famous Brands, Inc., 23
S.A.C.I. Falabella, 69
Saks Inc., 24; 41 (upd.)
Sally Beauty Company, Inc., 60
Sam Ash Music Corporation, 30
Sam Levin Inc., 80
Sam's Club, 40
Samuels Jewelers Incorporated, 30
Sanborn Hermanos, S.A., 20
SanomaWSOY Corporation, 51
Scheels All Sports Inc., 63
Schmitt Music Company, 40
Schneiderman's Furniture Inc., 28
School Specialty, Inc., 68
Schottenstein Stores Corp., 14
Schultz Sav-O Stores, Inc., 31
The Score Board, Inc., 19
Scotty's, Inc., 22
The Scoular Company, 77
SCP Pool Corporation, 39
Seaman Furniture Company, Inc., 32
Sean John Clothing, Inc., 70
Sears plc, V
Sears Roebuck de México, S.A. de C.V., 20
Sears, Roebuck and Co., V; 18 (upd.); 56 (upd.)
SED International Holdings, Inc., 43
Seibu Department Stores, Ltd., V; 42 (upd.)
Seigle's Home and Building Centers, Inc., 41
The Seiyu, Ltd., V; 36 (upd.)
Selfridges Plc, 34
Service Merchandise Company, Inc., V; 19 (upd.)
7-Eleven, Inc., 32 (upd.)
Seventh Generation, Inc., 73
Shaklee Corporation, 12

The Sharper Image Corporation, 10; 62 (upd.)
Shoe Carnival Inc., 14; 72 (upd.)
ShopKo Stores Inc., 21; 58 (upd.)
Shoppers Drug Mart Corporation, 49
Shoppers Food Warehouse Corporation, 66
SIG plc, 71
Signet Group PLC, 61
SkyMall, Inc., 26
Sleepy's Inc., 32
Smith & Hawken, Ltd., 68
Solo Serve Corporation, 28
Sophus Berendsen A/S, 49
Sound Advice, Inc., 41
Source Interlink Companies, Inc., 75
Southern States Cooperative Incorporated, 36
Spartan Stores Inc., 66 (upd.)
Spec's Music, Inc., 19
Spiegel, Inc., 10; 27 (upd.)
Sport Chalet, Inc., 16
Sport Supply Group, Inc., 23
Sportmart, Inc., 15
Sports & Recreation, Inc., 17
The Sports Authority, Inc., 16; 43 (upd.)
The Sportsman's Guide, Inc., 36
Stage Stores, Inc., 24
Stanhome Inc., 15
Staples, Inc., 10; 55 (upd.)
Starbucks Corporation, 34 (upd.)
Starcraft Corporation, 30
Stefanel SpA, 63
Stein Mart Inc., 19; 72 (upd.)
Stewart's Shops Corporation, 80
Stinnes AG, 8
The Stop & Shop Companies, Inc., 24 (upd.)
Storehouse PLC, 16
Strauss Discount Auto, 56
Stride Rite Corporation, 8
Strouds, Inc., 33
Stuller Settings, Inc., 35
Successories, Inc., 30
Sun Television & Appliances Inc., 10
Sunglass Hut International, Inc., 21; 74 (upd.)
Supreme International Corporation, 27
Swarovski International Holding AG, 40
Syms Corporation, 29; 74 (upd.)
Systemax, Inc., 52
Takashimaya Company, Limited, V; 47 (upd.)
The Talbots, Inc., 11; 31 (upd.)
Target Corporation, 61 (upd.)
Target Stores, 10; 27 (upd.)
Tati SA, 25
Tattered Cover Book Store, 43
Tech Data Corporation, 10; 74 (upd.)
Tengelmann Group, 27
Tesco plc, 24 (upd.); 68 (upd.)
Thomsen Greenhouses and Garden Center, Incorporated, 65
Thrifty PayLess, Inc., 12
Tiffany & Co., 14; 78 (upd.)
The Timberland Company, 54 (upd.)
The TJX Companies, Inc., V; 19 (upd.); 57 (upd.)

Today's Man, Inc., 20
Tokyu Department Store Co., Ltd., V; 32 (upd.)
Too, Inc., 61
Topco Associates LLC, 60
Tops Appliance City, Inc., 17
Total Fina Elf S.A., 50 (upd.)
Toys 'R' Us, Inc., V; 18 (upd.); 57 (upd.)
Tractor Supply Company, 57
Trans World Entertainment Corporation, 68 (upd.)
Travis Boats & Motors, Inc., 37
Travis Perkins plc, 34
Trend-Lines, Inc., 22
True Value Company, 74 (upd.)
TruServ Corporation, 24
Tuesday Morning Corporation, 18; 70 (upd.)
Tupperware Corporation, 28; 78 (upd.)
TVI, Inc., 15
Tweeter Home Entertainment Group, Inc., 30
U.S. Vision, Inc., 66
Ultimate Electronics, Inc., 18; 69 (upd.)
Ultramar Diamond Shamrock Corporation, 31 (upd.)
Uni-Marts, Inc., 17
United Rentals, Inc., 34
The United States Shoe Corporation, V
United Stationers Inc., 14
Universal International, Inc., 25
Uny Co., Ltd., V; 49 (upd.)
Urban Outfitters, Inc., 14; 74 (upd.)
Uwajimaya, Inc., 60
Vallen Corporation, 45
Valley Media Inc., 35
Value City Department Stores, Inc., 38
Value Merchants Inc., 13
ValueVision International, Inc., 22
Vans, Inc., 47 (upd.)
Variety Wholesalers, Inc., 73
Venator Group Inc., 35 (upd.)
Vendex International N.V., 13
Venture Stores Inc., 12
The Vermont Teddy Bear Co., Inc., 36
VF Corporation, 54 (upd.)
Viewpoint International, Inc., 66
Viking Office Products, Inc., 10
Vivarte SA, 54 (upd.)
Volcom, Inc., 77
Von Maur Inc., 64
Vorwerk & Co., 27
W. Atlee Burpee & Co., 27
W.W. Grainger, Inc., V
Waban Inc., 13
Wacoal Corp., 25
Wal-Mart de Mexico, S.A. de C.V., 35 (upd.)
Wal-Mart Stores, Inc., V; 8 (upd.); 26 (upd.); 63 (upd.)
Walden Book Company Inc., 17
Walgreen Co., V; 20 (upd.); 65 (upd.)
Wall Drug Store, Inc., 40
Warners' Stellian Inc., 67
Weiner's Stores, Inc., 33
West Marine, Inc., 17
Western Beef, Inc., 22
The Wet Seal, Inc., 18; 70 (upd.)

Rubber & Tires

Telecommunications

Perry Ellis International, Inc., 41
Phat Fashions LLC, 49
Phoenix Footwear Group, Inc., 70
Pillowtex Corporation, 19; 41 (upd.)
Plains Cotton Cooperative Association, 57
Pluma, Inc., 27
Polo/Ralph Lauren Corporation, 12; 62 (upd.)
Prada Holding B.V., 45
PremiumWear, Inc., 30
Puma AG Rudolf Dassler Sport, 35
Quaker Fabric Corp., 19
Quiksilver, Inc., 18; 79 (upd.)
R.G. Barry Corporation, 17; 44 (upd.)
Raymond Ltd., 77
Recreational Equipment, Inc., 18
Red Wing Shoe Company, Inc., 30 (upd.)
Reebok International Ltd., V; 9 (upd.); 26 (upd.)
Reliance Industries Ltd., 81
Rieter Holding AG, 42
Rocawear Apparel LLC, 77
Rollerblade, Inc., 15
Royal Ten Cate N.V., 68
Russell Corporation, 8; 30 (upd.)
St. John Knits, Inc., 14
Salant Corporation, 51 (upd.)
Salvatore Ferragamo Italia S.p.A., 62
Sao Paulo Alpargatas S.A., 75
Saucony Inc., 35
Schott Brothers, Inc., 67
Shaw Industries, Inc., 40 (upd.)
Shelby Williams Industries, Inc., 14
Skechers U.S.A. Inc., 31
Sophus Berendsen A/S, 49
Springs Industries, Inc., V; 19 (upd.)
Starter Corp., 12
Stefanel SpA, 63
Steiner Corporation (Alsco), 53
Steven Madden, Ltd., 37
Stirling Group plc, 62
Stoddard International plc, 72
Stone Manufacturing Company, 14; 43 (upd.)
The Stride Rite Corporation, 8; 37 (upd.)
Stussy, Inc., 55
Sun Sportswear, Inc., 17
Superior Uniform Group, Inc., 30
Tamfelt Oyj Abp, 62
Tarrant Apparel Group, 62
Teijin Limited, V
Thomaston Mills, Inc., 27
Tilley Endurables, Inc., 67
The Timberland Company, 13; 54 (upd.)
Tommy Hilfiger Corporation, 20; 53 (upd.)
Too, Inc., 61
Toray Industries, Inc., V
True Religion Apparel, Inc., 79
Tultex Corporation, 13
Under Armour Performance Apparel, 61
Unifi, Inc., 12; 62 (upd.)
United Merchants & Manufacturers, Inc., 13
United Retail Group Inc., 33
Unitika Ltd., V
Vans, Inc., 16; 47 (upd.)
Varsity Spirit Corp., 15

VF Corporation, V; 17 (upd.); 54 (upd.)
Vicunha Têxtil S.A. 78
Volcom, Inc., 77
Walton Monroe Mills, Inc., 8
The Warnaco Group Inc., 12; 46 (upd.)
Wellman, Inc., 8; 52 (upd.)
West Point-Pepperell, Inc., 8
WestPoint Stevens Inc., 16
Weyco Group, Incorporated, 32
Williamson-Dickie Manufacturing Company, 14
Wolverine World Wide, Inc., 16; 59 (upd.)
Woolrich Inc., 62

Tobacco

Altadis S.A., 72 (upd.)
American Brands, Inc., V
B.A.T. Industries PLC, 22 (upd.)
British American Tobacco PLC, 50 (upd.)
Brooke Group Ltd., 15
Brown & Williamson Tobacco Corporation, 14; 33 (upd.)
Culbro Corporation, 15
Dibrell Brothers, Incorporated, 12
DIMON Inc., 27
800-JR Cigar, Inc., 27
Gallaher Group Plc, V; 19 (upd.); 49 (upd.)
General Cigar Holdings, Inc., 66 (upd.)
Holt's Cigar Holdings, Inc., 42
House of Prince A/S, 80
Imasco Limited, V
Imperial Tobacco Group PLC, 50
Japan Tobacco Incorporated, V
KT&G Corporation, 62
Nobleza Piccardo SAICF, 64
North Atlantic Trading Company Inc., 65
Philip Morris Companies Inc., V; 18 (upd.)
R.J. Reynolds Tobacco Holdings, Inc., 30 (upd.)
RJR Nabisco Holdings Corp., V
Rothmans UK Holdings Limited, V; 19 (upd.)
Seita, 23
Souza Cruz S.A., 65
Standard Commercial Corporation, 13; 62 (upd.)
Swisher International Group Inc., 23
Tabacalera, S.A., V; 17 (upd.)
Taiwan Tobacco & Liquor Corporation, 75
Universal Corporation, V; 48 (upd.)
UST Inc., 9; 50 (upd.)
Vector Group Ltd., 35 (upd.)

Transport Services

Abertis Infraestructuras, S.A., 65
Aéroports de Paris, 33
Air Express International Corporation, 13
Airborne Freight Corporation, 6; 34 (upd.)
Alamo Rent A Car, Inc., 6; 24 (upd.)
Alaska Railroad Corporation, 60
Alexander & Baldwin, Inc., 10, 40 (upd.)
Allied Worldwide, Inc., 49
AMCOL International Corporation, 59 (upd.)

Amerco, 6
AMERCO, 67 (upd.)
American Classic Voyages Company, 27
American President Companies Ltd., 6
Anderson Trucking Service, Inc., 75
Anschutz Corp., 12
APL Limited, 61 (upd.)
Aqua Alliance Inc., 32 (upd.)
Arriva PLC, 69
Atlas Van Lines, Inc., 14
Attica Enterprises S.A., 64
Avis Group Holdings, Inc., 75 (upd.)
Avis Rent A Car, Inc., 6; 22 (upd.)
BAA plc, 10
Bekins Company, 15
Berliner Verkehrsbetriebe (BVG), 58
Bollinger Shipyards, Inc., 61
Boyd Bros. Transportation Inc., 39
Brambles Industries Limited, 42
The Brink's Company, 58 (upd.)
British Railways Board, V
Broken Hill Proprietary Company Ltd., 22 (upd.)
Buckeye Partners, L.P., 70
Budget Group, Inc., 25
Budget Rent a Car Corporation, 9
Burlington Northern Santa Fe Corporation, V; 27 (upd.)
C.H. Robinson Worldwide, Inc., 40 (upd.)
Canadian National Railway Company, 71 (upd.)
Canadian National Railway System, 6
Canadian Pacific Railway Limited, V; 45 (upd.)
Cannon Express, Inc., 53
Carey International, Inc., 26
Carlson Companies, Inc., 6
Carolina Freight Corporation, 6
Celadon Group Inc., 30
Central Japan Railway Company, 43
Chargeurs, 6
CHC Helicopter Corporation, 67
CHEP Pty. Ltd., 80
Chicago and North Western Holdings Corporation, 6
Christian Salvesen Plc, 45
Coach USA, Inc., 24; 55 (upd.)
Coles Express Inc., 15
Compagnie Générale Maritime et Financière, 6
Consolidated Delivery & Logistics, Inc., 24
Consolidated Freightways Corporation, V; 21 (upd.); 48 (upd.)
Consolidated Rail Corporation, V
CR England, Inc., 63
Crowley Maritime Corporation, 6; 28 (upd.)
CSX Corporation, V; 22 (upd.); 79 (upd.)
Danzas Group, V; 40 (upd.)
Dart Group PLC, 77
Deutsche Bahn AG, V; 46 (upd.)
DHL Worldwide Network S.A./N.V., 6; 24 (upd.); 69 (upd.)
Dollar Thrifty Automotive Group, Inc., 25
Dot Foods, Inc., 69

Utilities

Waste Services

Geographic Index

Grupo Industrial Durango, S.A. de C.V., 37
Grupo Industrial Saltillo, S.A. de C.V., 54
Grupo Mexico, S.A. de C.V., 40
Grupo Modelo, S.A. de C.V., 29
Grupo Posadas, S.A. de C.V., 57
Grupo Televisa, S.A., 18; 54 (upd.)
Grupo TMM, S.A. de C.V., 50
Grupo Transportación Ferroviaria
  Mexicana, S.A. de C.V., 47
Hylsamex, S.A. de C.V., 39
Industrias Bachoco, S.A. de C.V., 39
Industrias Penoles, S.A. de C.V., 22
Internacional de Ceramica, S.A. de C.V., 53
Kimberly-Clark de México, S.A. de C.V., 54
Organización Soriana, S.A. de C.V., 35
Petróleos Mexicanos, IV; 19 (upd.)
Pulsar Internacional S.A., 21
Real Turismo, S.A. de C.V., 50
Sanborn Hermanos, S.A., 20
Sears Roebuck de México, S.A. de C.V., 20
Telefonos de Mexico S.A. de C.V., 14; 63 (upd.)
Tubos de Acero de Mexico, S.A. (TAMSA), 41
TV Azteca, S.A. de C.V., 39
Urbi Desarrollos Urbanos, S.A. de C.V., 81
Valores Industriales S.A., 19
Vitro Corporativo S.A. de C.V., 34
Wal-Mart de Mexico, S.A. de C.V., 35 (upd.)

Nepal
Royal Nepal Airline Corporation, 41

Netherlands
ABN AMRO Holding, N.V., 50
AEGON N.V., III; 50 (upd.)
Akzo Nobel N.V., 13; 41 (upd.)
Algemene Bank Nederland N.V., II
Amsterdam-Rotterdam Bank N.V., II
Arcadis NV, 26
ASML Holding N.V., 50
Avantium Technologies BV 79
Baan Company, 25
Bols Distilleries NV, 74
Buhrmann NV, 41
The Campina Group, The 78
CNH Global N.V., 38 (upd.)
CSM N.V., 65
Deli Universal NV, 66
DSM N.V., I; 56 (upd.)
Elsevier N.V., IV
Endemol Entertainment Holding NV, 46
Equant N.V., 52
European Aeronautic Defence and Space
  Company EADS N.V., 52 (upd.)
Friesland Coberco Dairy Foods Holding N.V., 59
Getronics NV, 39
Granaria Holdings B.V., 66
Grand Hotel Krasnapolsky N.V., 23
Greenpeace International, 74

Gucci Group N.V., 50
Hagemeyer N.V., 39
Head N.V., 55
Heijmans N.V., 66
Heineken N.V., I; 13 (upd.); 34 (upd.)
IHC Caland N.V., 71
Indigo NV, 26
Ispat International N.V., 30
Koninklijke Ahold N.V. (Royal Ahold), II; 16 (upd.)
Koninklijke Luchtvaart Maatschappij, N.V. (KLM Royal Dutch Airlines), I; 28 (upd.)
Koninklijke Nederlandsche Hoogovens en Staalfabrieken NV, IV
Koninklijke Nedlloyd N.V., 6; 26 (upd.)
Koninklijke Philips Electronics N.V., 50 (upd.)
Koninklijke PTT Nederland NV, V
Koninklijke Vendex KBB N.V. (Royal Vendex KBB N.V.), 62 (upd.)
Koninklijke Wessanen nv, II; 54 (upd.)
KPMG International, 10; 33 (upd.)
Laurus N.V., 65
Mammoet Transport B.V., 26
MIH Limited, 31
N.V. AMEV, III
N.V. Holdingmaatschappij De Telegraaf, 23
N.V. Koninklijke Nederlandse
  Vliegtuigenfabriek Fokker, I; 28 (upd.)
N.V. Nederlandse Gasunie, V
Nationale-Nederlanden N.V., III
New Holland N.V., 22
Nutreco Holding N.V., 56
Océ N.V., 24
PCM Uitgevers NV, 53
Philips Electronics N.V., II; 13 (upd.)
PolyGram N.V., 23
Prada Holding B.V., 45
Qiagen N.V., 39
Rabobank Group, 33
Randstad Holding n.v., 16; 43 (upd.)
Rodamco N.V., 26
Royal Dutch/Shell Group, IV; 49 (upd.)
Royal Grolsch NV, 54
Royal KPN N.V., 30
Royal Numico N.V., 37
Royal Packaging Industries Van Leer N.V., 30
Royal Ten Cate N.V., 68
Royal Vopak NV, 41
SHV Holdings N.V., 55
Tennet BV 78
TNT Post Group N.V., V, 27 (upd.); 30 (upd.)
Toolex International N.V., 26
TomTom N.V., 81
TPG N.V., 64 (upd.)
Trader Classified Media N.V., 57
Triple P N.V., 26
Unilever N.V., II; 7 (upd.); 32 (upd.)
United Pan-Europe Communications NV, 47
Van Lanschot NV 79
Vebego International BV, 49
Vedior NV, 35
Velcro Industries N.V., 19

Vendex International N.V., 13
VNU N.V., 27
Wegener NV, 53
Wolters Kluwer NV, 14; 33 (upd.)

Netherlands Antilles
Orthofix International NV, 72
Velcro Industries N.V., 72

New Zealand
Air New Zealand Limited, 14; 38 (upd.)
Carter Holt Harvey Ltd., 70
Fletcher Challenge Ltd., IV; 19 (upd.)
Fonterra Co-Operative Group Ltd., 58
Telecom Corporation of New Zealand Limited, 54
Wattie's Ltd., 7

Nigeria
Nigerian National Petroleum Corporation, IV; 72 (upd.)

Norway
Braathens ASA, 47
Den Norse Stats Oljeselskap AS, IV
Helly Hansen ASA, 25
Jotun A/S, 80
Kvaerner ASA, 36
Norsk Hydro ASA, 10; 35 (upd.)
Norske Skogindustrier ASA, 63
Orkla A/S, 18
Schibsted ASA, 31
Statoil ASA, 61 (upd.)
Stolt Sea Farm Holdings PLC, 54
Telenor ASA, 69

Oman
Petroleum Development Oman LLC, IV

Pakistan
Pakistan International Airlines Corporation, 46
Pakistan State Oil Company Ltd., 81

Panama
Panamerican Beverages, Inc., 47
Willbros Group, Inc., 56

Peru
Southern Peru Copper Corporation, 40

Philippines
Bank of the Philippine Islands, 58
Benguet Corporation, 58
Manila Electric Company (Meralco), 56
Mercury Drug Corporation, 70
Petron Corporation, 58
Philippine Airlines, Inc., 6; 23 (upd.)
San Miguel Corporation, 15; 57 (upd.)

Poland
Agora S.A. Group, 77
LOT Polish Airlines (Polskie Linie Lotnicze S.A.), 33
Polski Koncern Naftowy ORLEN S.A., 77
Telekomunikacja Polska SA, 50

Portugal
Banco Comercial Português, SA, 50

United States

Arch Wireless, Inc., 39
Archer Daniels Midland Company, I; 11
  (upd.); 32 (upd.); 75 (upd.)
Archie Comics Publications, Inc., 63
Archon Corporation, 74 (upd.)
Archstone-Smith Trust, 49
Archway Cookies, Inc., 29
ARCO Chemical Company, 10
Arctco, Inc., 16
Arctic Cat Inc., 40 (upd.)
Arctic Slope Regional Corporation, 38
Arden Group, Inc., 29
Argon ST, Inc., 81
Argosy Gaming Company, 21
Ariba, Inc., 57
Ariens Company, 48
Aris Industries, Inc., 16
The Aristotle Corporation, 62
Ark Restaurants Corp., 20
Arkansas Best Corporation, 16
Arkla, Inc., V
Armco Inc., IV
Armor All Products Corp., 16
Armor Holdings, Inc., 27
Armstrong Holdings, Inc., III; 22 (upd.);
  81 (upd.)
Army and Air Force Exchange Service, 39
Arnold & Porter, 35
ArQule, Inc., 68
Arrow Air Holdings Corporation, 55
Arrow Electronics, Inc., 10; 50 (upd.)
The Art Institute of Chicago, 29
Art Van Furniture, Inc., 28
Artesyn Technologies Inc., 46 (upd.)
ArthroCare Corporation, 73
Arthur D. Little, Inc., 35
Arthur J. Gallagher & Co., 73
Arthur Murray International, Inc., 32
Artisan Entertainment Inc., 32 (upd.)
ArvinMeritor, Inc., 8; 54 (upd.)
Asanté Technologies, Inc., 20
ASARCO Incorporated, IV
Asbury Automotive Group Inc., 60
Asbury Carbons, Inc., 68
ASC, Inc., 55
Ascend Communications, Inc., 24
Ascential Software Corporation, 59
Ashland Inc., 19; 50 (upd.)
Ashland Oil, Inc., IV
Ashley Furniture Industries, Inc., 35
Ashworth, Inc., 26
ASK Group, Inc., 9
Ask Jeeves, Inc., 65
Aspect Telecommunications Corporation,
  22
Aspen Skiing Company, 15
Asplundh Tree Expert Co., 20; 59 (upd.)
Assisted Living Concepts, Inc., 43
Associated Estates Realty Corporation, 25
Associated Grocers, Incorporated, 9; 31
  (upd.)
Associated Milk Producers, Inc., 11; 48
  (upd.)
Associated Natural Gas Corporation, 11
The Associated Press, 13; 31 (upd.); 73
  (upd.)
Association of Junior Leagues
  International Inc., 60

AST Research Inc., 9
Astec Industries, Inc. 79
Astoria Financial Corporation, 44
Astronics Corporation, 35
ASV, Inc., 34; 66 (upd.)
At Home Corporation, 43
AT&T Bell Laboratories, Inc., 13
AT&T Corporation, V; 29 (upd.); 68
  (upd.)
AT&T Wireless Services, Inc., 54 (upd.)
Atari Corporation, 9; 23 (upd.); 66 (upd.)
ATC Healthcare Inc., 64
Atchison Casting Corporation, 39
The Athletics Investment Group, 62
Atkins Nutritionals, Inc., 58
Atlanta Bread Company International,
  Inc., 70
Atlanta Gas Light Company, 6; 23 (upd.)
Atlanta National League Baseball Club,
  Inc., 43
Atlantic American Corporation, 44
Atlantic Coast Airlines Holdings, Inc., 55
Atlantic Energy, Inc., 6
The Atlantic Group, 23
Atlantic Premium Brands, Ltd., 57
Atlantic Richfield Company, IV; 31 (upd.)
Atlantic Southeast Airlines, Inc., 47
Atlas Air, Inc., 39
Atlas Van Lines, Inc., 14
Atmel Corporation, 17
Atmos Energy Corporation, 43
Attachmate Corporation, 56
Atwood Mobil Products, 53
Au Bon Pain Co., Inc., 18
The Auchter Company, The 78
Audible Inc. 79
Audio King Corporation, 24
Audiovox Corporation, 34
August Schell Brewing Company Inc., 59
Ault Incorporated, 34
Auntie Anne's, Inc., 35
Aurora Casket Company, Inc., 56
Aurora Foods Inc., 32
The Austin Company, 8; 72 (upd.)
Austin Powder Company, 76
Authentic Fitness Corporation, 20; 51
  (upd.)
Auto Value Associates, Inc., 25
Autobytel Inc., 47
Autocam Corporation, 51
Autodesk, Inc., 10
Autologic Information International, Inc.,
  20
Automatic Data Processing, Inc., III; 9
  (upd.); 47 (upd.)
AutoNation, Inc., 50
Autotote Corporation, 20
AutoZone, Inc., 9; 31 (upd.)
Avado Brands, Inc., 31
Avalon Correctional Services, Inc., 75
AvalonBay Communities, Inc., 58
Avco Financial Services Inc., 13
Aveda Corporation, 24
Avedis Zildjian Co., 38
Avery Dennison Corporation, IV; 17
  (upd.); 49 (upd.)
Aviall, Inc., 73
Aviation Sales Company, 41

Avid Technology Inc., 38
Avis Group Holdings, Inc., 75 (upd.)
Avis Rent A Car, Inc., 6; 22 (upd.)
Avista Corporation, 69 (upd.)
Avnet Inc., 9
Avocent Corporation, 65
Avon Products, Inc., III; 19 (upd.); 46
  (upd.)
Avondale Industries, 7; 41 (upd.)
AVX Corporation, 67
Awrey Bakeries, Inc., 56
Aydin Corp., 19
Azcon Corporation, 23
Aztar Corporation, 13; 71 (upd.)
B&G Foods, Inc., 40
B. Dalton Bookseller Inc., 25
The B. Manischewitz Company, LLC, 31
B.J. Alan Co., Inc., 67
B/E Aerospace, Inc., 30
Babbage's, Inc., 10
Baby Superstore, Inc., 15
Bachman's Inc., 22
Back Bay Restaurant Group, Inc., 20
Back Yard Burgers, Inc., 45
Bad Boy Worldwide Entertainment
  Group, 58
Badger Meter, Inc., 22
Badger Paper Mills, Inc., 15
BAE Systems Ship Repair, 73
Bailey Nurseries, Inc., 57
Bain & Company, 55
Bairnco Corporation, 28
Baker & Hostetler LLP, 40
Baker & McKenzie, 10; 42 (upd.)
Baker & Taylor Corporation, 16; 43
  (upd.)
Baker and Botts, L.L.P., 28
Baker Hughes Incorporated, III; 22
  (upd.); 57 (upd.)
Balance Bar Company, 32
Balchem Corporation, 42
Baldor Electric Company, 21
Baldwin & Lyons, Inc., 51
Baldwin Piano & Organ Company, 18
Baldwin Technology Company, Inc., 25
Ball Corporation, I; 10; 78 (upd.)
Ball Horticultural Company 78
Ballantyne of Omaha, Inc., 27
Ballard Medical Products, 21
Bally Manufacturing Corporation, III
Bally Total Fitness Holding Corp., 25
Baltek Corporation, 34
Baltimore Aircoil Company, Inc., 66
Baltimore Gas and Electric Company, V;
  25 (upd.)
Baltimore Orioles L.P., 66
The Bama Companies, Inc., 80
Banana Republic Inc., 25
Bandag, Inc., 19
Banfi Products Corp., 36
Bank of America Corporation, 46 (upd.)
Bank of Boston Corporation, II
Bank of Hawaii Corporation, 73
Bank of Mississippi, Inc., 14
Bank of New England Corporation, II
The Bank of New York Company, Inc., II;
  46 (upd.)
Bank One Corporation, 10; 36 (upd.)

Federal Paper Board Company, Inc., 8
Federal Prison Industries, Inc., 34
Federal Signal Corp., 10
Federal-Mogul Corporation, I; 10 (upd.); 26 (upd.)
Federated Department Stores Inc., 9; 31 (upd.)
FedEx Corporation, 18 (upd.); 42 (upd.)
Feed The Children, Inc., 68
FEI Company 79
Feld Entertainment, Inc., 32 (upd.)
Fellowes Manufacturing Company, 28
Fender Musical Instruments Company, 16; 43 (upd.)
Fenwick & West LLP, 34
Ferolito, Vultaggio & Sons, 27
Ferrellgas Partners, L.P., 35
Ferro Corporation, 8; 56 (upd.)
F5 Networks, Inc., 72
FHP International Corporation, 6
FiberMark, Inc., 37
Fibreboard Corporation, 16
Fidelity Investments Inc., II; 14 (upd.)
Fidelity National Financial Inc., 54
Fieldale Farms Corporation, 23
Fieldcrest Cannon, Inc., 9; 31 (upd.)
Fifth Third Bancorp, 13; 31 (upd.)
Figgie International Inc., 7
Fiji Water LLC, 74
FileNet Corporation, 62
Fili Enterprises, Inc., 70
Film Roman, Inc., 58
FINA, Inc., 7
Fingerhut Companies, Inc., 9; 36 (upd.)
The Finish Line, Inc., 29; 68 (upd.)
FinishMaster, Inc., 24
Finlay Enterprises, Inc., 16; 76 (upd.)
Firearms Training Systems, Inc., 27
Fireman's Fund Insurance Company, III
First Albany Companies Inc., 37
First Alert, Inc., 28
The First American Corporation, The 52
First Aviation Services Inc., 49
First Bank System Inc., 12
First Brands Corporation, 8
First Cash Financial Services, Inc., 57
First Chicago Corporation, II
First Commerce Bancshares, Inc., 15
First Commerce Corporation, 11
First Data Corporation, 30 (upd.)
First Empire State Corporation, 11
First Executive Corporation, III
First Fidelity Bank, N.A., New Jersey, 9
First Financial Management Corporation, 11
First Hawaiian, Inc., 11
First Industrial Realty Trust, Inc., 65
First Interstate Bancorp, II
First Mississippi Corporation, 8
First Nationwide Bank, 14
First of America Bank Corporation, 8
First Security Corporation, 11
First Team Sports, Inc., 22
First Tennessee National Corporation, 11; 48 (upd.)
First Union Corporation, 10
First USA, Inc., 11
First Virginia Banks, Inc., 11

The First Years Inc., 46
Firstar Corporation, 11; 33 (upd.)
Fiserv Inc., 11; 33 (upd.)
Fish & Neave, 54
Fisher Companies, Inc., 15
Fisher Controls International, LLC, 13; 61 (upd.)
Fisher Scientific International Inc., 24
Fisher-Price Inc., 12; 32 (upd.)
Fisk Corporation, 72
5 & Diner Franchise Corporation, 72
Flagstar Companies, Inc., 10
Flanders Corporation, 65
Flanigan's Enterprises, Inc., 60
Fleer Corporation, 15
FleetBoston Financial Corporation, 9; 36 (upd.)
Fleetwood Enterprises, Inc., III; 22 (upd.); 81 (upd.)
Fleming Companies, Inc., II; 17 (upd.)
Flexsteel Industries Inc., 15; 41 (upd.)
Flight Options, LLC, 75
FlightSafety International, Inc., 9; 29 (upd.)
Flint Ink Corporation, 13; 41 (upd.)
FLIR Systems, Inc., 69
Florida Crystals Inc., 35
Florida East Coast Industries, Inc., 59
Florida Gaming Corporation, 47
Florida Progress Corporation, V; 23 (upd.)
Florida Public Utilities Company, 69
Florida Rock Industries, Inc., 46
Florida's Natural Growers, 45
Florists' Transworld Delivery, Inc., 28
Florsheim Shoe Group Inc., 9; 31 (upd.)
Flour City International, Inc., 44
Flow International Corporation, 56
Flowers Industries, Inc., 12; 35 (upd.)
Flowserve Corporation, 33; 77 (upd.)
Fluke Corporation, 15
Fluor Corporation, I; 8 (upd.); 34 (upd.)
Flying Boat, Inc. (Chalk's Ocean Airways), 56
Flying J Inc., 19
FMC Corporation, I; 11 (upd.)
FMR Corp., 8; 32 (upd.)
Foamex International Inc., 17
Focus Features 78
Foley & Lardner, 28
Follett Corporation, 12; 39 (upd.)
The Food Emporium, 64
Food For The Poor, Inc., 77
Food Lion LLC, II; 15 (upd.); 66 (upd.)
Foodarama Supermarkets, Inc., 28
FoodBrands America, Inc., 23
Foodmaker, Inc., 14
Foot Locker, Inc., 68 (upd.)
Foote, Cone & Belding Worldwide, I; 66 (upd.)
Footstar, Incorporated, 24
Forbes Inc., 30
The Ford Foundation, 34
Ford Motor Company, I; 11 (upd.); 36 (upd.); 64 (upd.)
FORE Systems, Inc., 25
Forest City Enterprises, Inc., 16; 52 (upd.)
Forest Laboratories, Inc., 11; 52 (upd.)

Forest Oil Corporation, 19
Forever Living Products International Inc., 17
Formica Corporation, 13
Forrester Research, Inc., 54
Forstmann Little & Co., 38
Fort Howard Corporation, 8
Fort James Corporation, 22 (upd.)
Fortune Brands, Inc., 29 (upd.); 68 (upd.)
Fortunoff Fine Jewelry and Silverware Inc., 26
Forward Air Corporation, 75
Fossil, Inc., 17
Foster Poultry Farms, 32
Foster Wheeler Corporation, 6; 23 (upd.)
Foster Wheeler Ltd., 76 (upd.)
FosterGrant, Inc., 60
Foundation Health Corporation, 12
Fountain Powerboats Industries, Inc., 28
4Kids Entertainment Inc., 59
Fourth Financial Corporation, 11
Fox Entertainment Group, Inc., 43
Fox Family Worldwide, Inc., 24
Foxboro Company, 13
FoxMeyer Health Corporation, 16
FPL Group, Inc., V; 49 (upd.)
Frank J. Zamboni & Co., Inc., 34
Frank Russell Company, 46
Frank's Nursery & Crafts, Inc., 12
Frankel & Co., 39
Franklin Covey Company, 11; 37 (upd.)
Franklin Electric Company, Inc., 43
Franklin Electronic Publishers, Inc., 23
The Franklin Mint, 69
Franklin Resources, Inc., 9
Franz Inc., 80
Fred Meyer Stores, Inc., V; 20 (upd.); 64 (upd.)
Fred Usinger Inc., 54
The Fred W. Albrecht Grocery Co., 13
Fred Weber, Inc., 61
Fred's, Inc., 23; 62 (upd.)
Freddie Mac, 54
Frederick Atkins Inc., 16
Frederick's of Hollywood, Inc., 16; 59 (upd.)
Freedom Communications, Inc., 36
Freeport-McMoRan Copper & Gold, Inc., IV; 7 (upd.); 57 (upd.)
Freeze.com LLC, 77
French Fragrances, Inc., 22
Frequency Electronics, Inc., 61
Fresh America Corporation, 20
Fresh Choice, Inc., 20
Fresh Enterprises, Inc., 66
Fresh Foods, Inc., 29
Fretter, Inc., 10
Fried, Frank, Harris, Shriver & Jacobson, 35
Friedman's Inc., 29
Friedman, Billings, Ramsey Group, Inc., 53
Friendly Ice Cream Corporation, 30; 72 (upd.)
Frigidaire Home Products, 22
Frisch's Restaurants, Inc., 35
Frito-Lay North America, 32; 73 (upd.)
Fritz Companies, Inc., 12

Hauser, Inc., 46
Haverty Furniture Companies, Inc., 31
Hawaiian Airlines, Inc., 22 (upd.)
Hawaiian Electric Industries, Inc., 9
Hawk Corporation, 59
Hawkins Chemical, Inc., 16
Haworth Inc., 8; 39 (upd.)
Hayes Corporation, 24
Hayes Lemmerz International, Inc., 27
Hazelden Foundation, 28
HCA - The Healthcare Company, 35 (upd.)
HCI Direct, Inc., 55
HDOS Enterprises, 72
HDR Inc., 48
Headwaters Incorporated, 56
Headway Corporate Resources, Inc., 40
Health Care & Retirement Corporation, 22
Health Communications, Inc., 72
Health Management Associates, Inc., 56
Health O Meter Products Inc., 14
Health Risk Management, Inc., 24
Health Systems International, Inc., 11
HealthExtras, Inc., 75
HealthSouth Corporation, 14; 33 (upd.)
Healthtex, Inc., 17
The Hearst Corporation, IV; 19 (upd.); 46 (upd.)
Heartland Express, Inc., 18
The Heat Group, 53
Hechinger Company, 12
Hecla Mining Company, 20
Heekin Can Inc., 13
Heery International, Inc., 58
HEICO Corporation, 30
Heidrick & Struggles International, Inc., 28
Heilig-Meyers Company, 14; 40 (upd.)
Helen of Troy Corporation, 18
Helene Curtis Industries, Inc., 8; 28 (upd.)
Helix Energy Solutions Group, Inc., 81
Heller, Ehrman, White & McAuliffe, 41
Helmerich & Payne, Inc., 18
Helmsley Enterprises, Inc., 9; 39 (upd.)
Helzberg Diamonds, 40
Henkel Manco Inc., 22
The Henley Group, Inc., III
Henry Modell & Company Inc., 32
Henry Schein, Inc., 31; 70 (upd.)
Hensel Phelps Construction Company, 72
Hensley & Company, 64
Herbalife International, Inc., 17; 41 (upd.)
Hercules Inc., I; 22 (upd.); 66 (upd.)
Herley Industries, Inc., 33
Herman Goelitz, Inc., 28
Herman Miller, Inc., 8; 77 (upd.)
Herschend Family Entertainment Corporation, 73
Hershey Foods Corporation, II; 15 (upd.); 51 (upd.)
The Hertz Corporation, 9; 33 (upd.)
Heska Corporation, 39
Heublein, Inc., I
Hewitt Associates, Inc., 77

Hewlett-Packard Company, III; 6 (upd.); 28 (upd.); 50 (upd.)
Hexcel Corporation, 28
Hibbett Sporting Goods, Inc., 26; 70 (upd.)
Hibernia Corporation, 37
Hickory Farms, Inc., 17
High Falls Brewing Company LLC, 74
Highmark Inc., 27
Highsmith Inc., 60
Hilb, Rogal & Hobbs Company, 77
Hildebrandt International, 29
Hill's Pet Nutrition, Inc., 27
Hillenbrand Industries, Inc., 10; 75 (upd.)
Hillerich & Bradsby Company, Inc., 51
The Hillhaven Corporation, 14
Hills Stores Company, 13
Hilton Hotels Corporation, III; 19 (upd.); 62 (upd.)
Hines Horticulture, Inc., 49
Hispanic Broadcasting Corporation, 35
Hitchiner Manufacturing Co., Inc., 23
HMI Industries, Inc., 17
HNI Corporation, 74 (upd.)
Ho-Chunk Inc., 61
HOB Entertainment, Inc., 37
Hobby Lobby Stores Inc., 80
Hoechst Celanese Corporation, 13
Hoenig Group Inc., 41
Hoffman Corporation 78
Hogan & Hartson L.L.P., 44
HOK Group, Inc., 59
Holberg Industries, Inc., 36
Holiday Inns, Inc., III
Holiday RV Superstores, Incorporated, 26
Holland & Knight LLP, 60
Holland Burgerville USA, 44
Hollander Home Fashions Corp., 67
Holley Performance Products Inc., 52
Hollinger International Inc., 24
Holly Corporation, 12
Hollywood Casino Corporation, 21
Hollywood Entertainment Corporation, 25
Hollywood Media Corporation, 58
Hollywood Park, Inc., 20
Holme Roberts & Owen LLP, 28
Holnam Inc., 8; 39 (upd.)
Holophane Corporation, 19
Holson Burnes Group, Inc., 14
Holt and Bugbee Company, 66
Holt's Cigar Holdings, Inc., 42
Homasote Company, 72
Home Box Office Inc., 7; 23 (upd.); 76 (upd.)
The Home Depot, Inc., V; 18 (upd.)
The Home Insurance Company, III
Home Interiors & Gifts, Inc., 55
Home Products International, Inc., 55
Home Properties of New York, Inc., 42
Home Shopping Network, Inc., V; 25 (upd.)
HomeBase, Inc., 33 (upd.)
Homestake Mining Company, 12; 38 (upd.)
Hometown Auto Retailers, Inc., 44
HomeVestors of America, Inc., 77
HON INDUSTRIES Inc., 13

Honda Motor Company Limited, I; 10 (upd.); 29 (upd.)
Honeywell Inc., II; 12 (upd.); 50 (upd.)
Hooker Furniture Corporation, 80
Hooper Holmes, Inc., 22
Hooters of America, Inc., 18; 69 (upd.)
The Hoover Company, 12; 40 (upd.)
HOP, LLC, 80
Hops Restaurant Bar and Brewery, 46
Horace Mann Educators Corporation, 22
Horizon Organic Holding Corporation, 37
Hormel Foods Corporation, 18 (upd.); 54 (upd.)
Horsehead Industries, Inc., 51
Horseshoe Gaming Holding Corporation, 62
Horton Homes, Inc., 25
Hospira, Inc., 71
Hospital Central Services, Inc., 56
Hospital Corporation of America, III
Hospitality Franchise Systems, Inc., 11
Hospitality Worldwide Services, Inc., 26
Hoss's Steak and Sea House Inc., 68
Host America Corporation 79
Host Marriott Corporation, III
Hot Topic, Inc., 33
Houchens Industries Inc., 51
Houghton Mifflin Company, 10; 36 (upd.)
House of Fabrics, Inc., 21
Household International, Inc., II; 21 (upd.)
Houston Industries Incorporated, V
Hovnanian Enterprises, Inc., 29
Howard Hughes Medical Institute, 39
Howard Johnson International, Inc., 17; 72 (upd.)
Howmet Corp., 12
HSN, 64 (upd.)
Hub Group, Inc., 38
Hubbard Broadcasting Inc., 24; 79 (upd.)
Hubbell Inc., 9; 31 (upd.); 76 (upd.)
Hudson Foods Inc., 13
Hudson River Bancorp, Inc., 41
Huffy Corporation, 7; 30 (upd.)
Hughes Electronics Corporation, 25
Hughes Hubbard & Reed LLP, 44
Hughes Markets, Inc., 22
Hughes Supply, Inc., 14
Hulman & Company, 44
Humana Inc., III; 24 (upd.)
The Humane Society of the United States, 54
Hungarian Telephone and Cable Corp., 75
Hungry Howie's Pizza and Subs, Inc., 25
Hunt Consolidated, Inc., 27 (upd.)
Hunt Manufacturing Company, 12
Hunt Oil Company, 7
Hunt-Wesson, Inc., 17
Hunter Fan Company, 13
Huntington Bancshares Inc., 11
Huntington Learning Centers, Inc., 55
Hunton & Williams, 35
Huntsman Chemical Corporation, 8
Hutchinson Technology Incorporated, 18; 63 (upd.)
Huttig Building Products, Inc., 73